Barnes & Noble

Spanish Dictionary

English-Español
Spanish-Inglés

Arthur Swift Butterfield

S0-BZB-838

Barnes & Noble
BOOKS
NEW YORK

This edition published by Marboro Books Corp.,
a division of Barnes & Noble, Inc.,
by arrangement with Pan Books Ltd.

1992 Barnes & Noble Books

ISBN 0-88029-939-X

Printed and bound in the United States of America

M 9 8 7 6 5 4 3 2

Abbreviations/Abreviaciones

adj adjective, adjetivo
adv adverb, adverbio
aero aeronautics, aeronáutica
agr agriculture, agricultura
anat anatomy, anatomía
arch architecture
arq arquitectura
art article, artículo
astrol astrology, astrología
astron astronomy, astronomía
auto automobile, automóvil
bot botany, botánica
chem chemistry
coll colloquial
com comercio
comm commerce
conj conjunction, conjunción
culin culinario
derog derogatory
econ economics, economía
elec electricity, electricidad
f feminine, femenino
fam familiar, colloquial
ferr ferrocarril
fig figurative, figurativo
foto fotografía
geog geography, geografía
geol geology, geología
gram gramática
gramm grammar
impol impolite

interj interjection, interjección
interrog interrogative, interrogativo
invar invariable
jur jurisprudencia
m masculine, masculino
mar marítimo
mat matemáticas
math mathematics
mec mecánica
mech mechanics
med medicine, medicina
mil military, militar
mot motoring
n noun
naut nautical
phone telephone
phot photography
pl plural
pol politics, política
prep preposition, preposición
pron pronoun, pronombre
psych psychology
quím química
rail railways
rel religion, religión
s sustantivo
sing singular
tech technology, technical
tecn tecnología
v verb, verbo
V vide (see, vea)
zool zoology, zoología

Spanish pronunciation

a cada ['kaða]
e entre ['entre]
i libro ['liβro]
o loco ['loko]
u lunes ['lunes]
j nieve ['njeβe]
b bueno ['bweno]
d desde ['desðe]
f fácil ['faθil]
g grande ['grande]
k poco ['poko]
l salud [sa'luð]

m hombre ['ombre]
n noche ['notʃe]
p lápiz ['lapiθ]
r cerca ['θerka]
rr perro ['perro]
s servir [ser'βir]
t todo ['toðo]
w luego ['lwego]
θ cerveza [θer'βeθa]
β hábil ['aβil]
tʃ muchacho [mu'tʃatʃo]
ð ciudad [θju'ðað]
ʎ calle ['kaʎe]
ɲ señor [se'ɲor]
x ojo, ágil ['oxo], ['axil]

The symbol ' indicates that the following syllable should be stressed.

Pronunciación del inglés

a hat [hat]
e bell [bel]
i big [big]
o dot [dot]
ʌ bun [bʌn]
u book [buk]
ə alone [ə'loun]
a: card [ka:d]
ə: word [wə:d]
i: team [ti:m]
o: torn [to:n]
u: spoon [spu:n]
ai die [dai]
ei ray [rei]
oi toy [toi]
au how [hau]
ou road [roud]
eə lair [leə]
iə fear [fiə]
uə poor [puə]
b back [bak]
d dull [dʌl]
f find [faind]

g gaze [geiz]
h hop [hɒp]
j yell [jel]
k cat [kat]
l life [laif]
m mouse [maus]
n night [nait]
p pick [pik]
r rose [rouz]
s sit [sit]
t toe [tou]
v vest [vest]
w week [wi:k]
z zoo [zu:]
θ think [θiŋk]
ð those [ðouz]
ʃ shoe [ʃu:]
ʒ treasure ['treʒə]
tʃ chalk [tʃo:k]
dʒ jump [dʒʌmp]
ŋ sing [siŋ]

El signo de acentuación ' se coloca directamente delante de la sílaba aguda.
El signo , se coloca delante de la sílaba aguda secundaria.

Guide to the dictionary

The infinitives of all irregular verbs appearing in the headword list are marked with an asterisk. These and examples of Spanish stem-changing verbs, and the tenses in which such changes occur, can be found in the following verb tables. Composite verbs, such as *deshacer* from *hacer*, are also included under the parent verb.

The Spanish alphabet includes three symbols or combinations of letters that are not found in the English alphabet. These are **ch, ll,** and **ñ,** which are treated as individual letters and follow **c, l,** and **n** respectively in the alphabetical order.

The plurals of almost all Spanish nouns are formed regularly by the addition of *s* or *es* to the singular form. Occasional irregular plural forms are shown immediately after the part of speech referring to the headword. Some nouns do not change in the plural and these are marked *invar* (invariable).

Adverbs are regularly formed by adding *-mente* to the feminine (or occasionally masculine) form of the adjective, and are not normally shown unless a different translation is called for.

Guía al diccionario

Los plurales irregulares de los sustantivos se hallen junto al encabezamiento. Las categorías siguientes de los plurales se consideran regulares en inglés:

cat	cats
glass	glasses
fly	flies
half	halves
wife	wives

Los verbos irregulares en la lista de encabezamientos se señalan por medio de un asterisco y se hallen en las tablas de los verbos.

Los adverbios regulares no se indican. Los adverbios ingleses que se forman añadiendo -(al)ly al adjetivo, se consideran regulares. Los adverbios españoles que se forman añadiendo -mente al adjetivo femenino (de vez en cuando masculino), se consideran regulares y no se indican sino exigiendo una traducción diferente.

Spanish verb tables

1. The final consonants preceding the infinitive endings (**-ar**, **-er**, and **-(u)ir**) change, for reasons of euphony, when they occur before certain vowels.

Infinitives	Change	Before
-car	the **c** to **qu**	e
-cer	the **c** to **z**	a or o
-cir	the **c** to **z**	a or o
-gir	the **g** to **j**	a or o
-guir	the **gu** to **g**	a or o
-quir	the **qu** to **c**	a or o
-gar	the **ga** to **gu**	e
-zar	the **z** to **c**	e

2. Verbs adding **z**. There are numerous verbs ending in **-ecer** (*e.g.* **parecer**) and other verbs ending in a vowel + **-cer** (*e.g.* **conocer**). When the ending of these verbs is **a** or **o** (specifically, present indicative 1 *sing*, and present subjunctive, all persons), a **z** is added before the **c** (*e.g.* **parezco**, **conozco**).

3. Verbs in the following tables change the vowels in their stems in certain persons and tenses. The sections below are arranged according to the vowel change involved and are followed by a selection of verbs exemplifying the change. Note that composite verbs (*e.g.* **desplegar**) are conjugated in the same way as their base forms (*e.g.* **plegar**).

   (i) Stem changes **e** to **ie** in present indicative and present subjunctive 1, 2, 3 *sing* and 3 *pl*, and in imperative *sing*.

acertar	aterrar	comenzar	dentar	entender
acrecentar	aventar	concertar	desalentar	entesar
aferrar	calentar	confesar	descender	fregar
apretar	cegar	contender	desempedrar	gobernar
arrendar	cerner	decentar	despernar	hacendar
ascender	cerrar	defender	despertar	heder

helar	merendar	recentar	sembrar	tentar
hender	negar	recomendar	sentar	trascender
herrar	nevar	regar	serrar	trasegar
incensar	pensar	remendar	sosegar	trasverter
invernar	perder	restregar	soterrar	tropezar
manifestar	plegar	reventar	temblar	verter
mentar	quebrar	segar	tender	

(ii) Stem changes o to ue in present indicative and present subjunctive
   1, 2, 3 *sing* and 3 *pl*. and in imperative *sing*.

acordar	colar	jugar	resollar	soñar
acostar	colgar	moler	rodar	torcer
aforar	contar	mostrar	rogar	tostar
almorzar	costar	mover	solar	trocar
apostar	doler	poblar	soldar	tronar
aprobar	encontrar	probar	soler	voler
avergonzar	forzar	recordar	soltar	volcar
azolar	holgar	renovar	sonar	volver

(iii) Stem changes from e to i in present indicative 1, 2, 3 *sing* and 3 *pl*;
   preterite 3 *sing* and *pl*; present, imperfect, and future subjunctives,
   all persons; imperative *sing* and present participle.

colegir	derretir	henchir	regir	seguir
concebir	elegir	medir	rendir	servir
corregir	gemir	pedir	repetir	vestir

(iv) Stem changes e to ie in present indicative and present subjunctive
   1, 2, 3 *sing* and 3 *pl*; imperative *sing*.
   Stem changes e to i in preterite 3 *sing* and *pl*; present subjunctive
   1, 2 *pl*; imperfect and future subjunctives, all persons; present
   participle.

advertir	digerir	hervir	preferir
cernir	divertir	inferir	requerir
convertir	hendir	ingerir	sentir
diferir	herir	mentir	sugerir

4. The verbs shown below change in various ways. In the table, 1 and 3 *sing* are shown under the present indicative and 1 *sing* under the preterite and future.

Infinitive	Present Indicative	Preterite	Future	Past Participle
andar	ando, anda	anduve	andaré	andado
caber	quepo, cabe	cupe	cabré	cabido
caer	caigo, cae	caí	caeré	caido
dar	doy, da	di	daré	dado
decir	digo, dice	dije	diré	dicho
dormir	duermo, duerme	dormí	dormiré	dormido
erguir	yergo, yergue	erguí	erguiré	erguido
errar	yerro, yerra	erré	erraré	errado
estar	estoy, está	estuve	estaré	estado
haber	he, ha	hube	habré	habido
hacer	hago, hace	hice	haré	hecho
huir	huyo, huye	huí	huiré	huido
ir	voy, va	fui	iré	ido
oír	oigo, oye	oí	oiré	oido
oler	huelo, huele	olí	oleré	olido
poder	puedo, puede	pude	podré	podido
poner	pongo, pone	puse	pondré	puesto
querer	quiero, quiere	quise	querré	querido
reducir	reduzco, reduce	reduje	reduciré	reducido
reír	río, ríe	reí	reiré	reido
saber	sé, sabe	supe	sabré	sabido
ser	soy, es	fui	seré	sido
tener	tengo, tiene	tuve	tendré	tenido
traer	traigo, trae	traje	traeré	traído
valer	valgo, vale	valí	valdré	valido
venir	vengo, viene	vine	vendré	venido
ver	veo, ve	vi	veré	visto

Verbos irregulares ingleses

Infinitivo	Pretérito	Participo Pasado	Infinitive	Pretérito	Participo Pasado
abide	abode	abode	**deal**	dealt	dealt
arise	arose	arisen	**dig**	dug	dug
awake	awoke	awoken	**do**	did	done
be	was	been	**draw**	drew	drawn
bear	bore	borne	**dream**	dreamed	dreamed
		or born		*or* dreamt	*or* dreamt
beat	beat	beaten	**drink**	drank	drunk
become	became	become	**drive**	drove	driven
begin	began	begun	**dwell**	dwelt	dwelt
behold	beheld	beheld	**eat**	ate	eaten
bend	bent	bent	**fall**	fell	fallen
bet	bet	bet	**feed**	fed	fed
beware			**feel**	felt	felt
bid	bid	bidden	**fight**	fought	fought
		or bid	**find**	found	found
bind	bound	bound	**flee**	fled	fled
bite	bit	bitten	**fling**	flung	flung
bleed	bled	bled	**fly**	flew	flown
blow	blew	blown	**forbid**	forbade	forbidden
break	broke	broken	**forget**	forgot	forgotten
breed	bred	bred	**forgive**	forgave	forgiven
bring	brought	brought	**forsake**	forsook	forsaken
build	built	built	**freeze**	froze	frozen
burn	burnt	burnt	**get**	got	got
	or burned	*or* burned	**give**	gave	given
burst	burst	burst	**go**	went	gone
buy	bought	bought	**grind**	ground	ground
can	could		**grow**	grew	grown
cast	cast	cast	**hang**	hung	hung
catch	caught	caught		*or* hanged	*or* hanged
choose	chose	chosen	**have**	had	had
cling	clung	clung	**hear**	heard	heard
come	came	come	**hide**	hid	hidden
cost	cost	cost	**hit**	hit	hit
creep	crept	crept	**hold**	held	held
cut	cut	cut	**hurt**	hurt	hurt

Infinitivo	Pretérito	Participo Pasado	Infinitivo	Pretérito	Participo Pasado
keep	kept	kept	say	said	said
kneel	knelt	knelt	see	saw	seen
knit	knitted	knitted	seek	sought	sought
	or knit	or knit	sell	sold	sold
know	knew	known	send	sent	sent
lay	laid	laid	set	set	set
lead	led	led	sew	sewed	sewn
lean	leant	leant			or sewed
	or leaned	or leaned	shake	shook	shaken
leap	leapt	leapt	shear	sheared	sheared
	or leaped	or leaped			or shorn
learn	learnt	learnt	shed	shed	shed
	or learned	or learned	shine	shone	shone
leave	left	left	shoe	shod	shod
lend	lent	lent	shoot	shot	shot
let	let	let	show	showed	shown
lie	lay	lain	shrink	shrank	shrunk
light	lit	lit	shut	shut	shut
	or lighted	or lighted	sing	sang	sung
lose	lost	lost	sink	sank	sunk
make	made	made	sit	sat	sat
may	might		sleep	slept	slept
mean	meant	meant	slide	slid	slid
meet	met	met	sling	slung	slung
mow	mowed	mown	slink	slunk	slunk
must			slit	slit	slit
ought			smell	smelt	smelt
pay	paid	paid		or smelled	or smelled
put	put	put	sow	sowed	sown
quit	quitted	quitted			or sowed
	or quit	or quit	speak	spoke	spoken
read	read	read	speed	sped	sped
rid	rid	rid		or speeded	or speeded
ride	rode	ridden	spell	spelt	spelt
ring	rang	rung		or spelled	or spelled
rise	rose	risen	spend	spent	spent
run	ran	run	spill	spilt	spilt
saw	sawed	sawn		or spilled	or spilled
		or sawed	spin	spun	spun

Infinitivo	Pretérito	Participo Pasado	Infinitivo	Pretérito	Participo Pasado
spit	spat	spat	**swim**	swam	swum
split	split	split	**swing**	swung	swung
spread	spread	spread	**take**	took	taken
spring	sprang	sprung	**teach**	taught	taught
stand	stood	stood	**tear**	tore	torn
steal	stole	stolen	**tell**	told	told
stick	stuck	stuck	**think**	thought	thought
sting	stung	stung	**throw**	threw	thrown
stink	stank	stunk	**thrust**	thrust	thrust
	or stunk		**tread**	trod	trodden
stride	strode	stridden	**wake**	woke	woken
strike	struck	struck	**wear**	wore	worn
string	strung	strung	**weave**	wove	woven
strive	strove	striven	**weep**	wept	wept
swear	swore	sworn	**win**	won	won
sweep	swept	swept	**wind**	wound	wound
swell	swelled	swollen	**wring**	wrung	wrung
	or swelled		**write**	wrote	written

Glossary of menu terms

Americans dining in Spain, Mexico, and the Spanish Caribbean are in for a pleasant surprise, for Spanish cooking is far more diverse than the few dishes that have become part of the American diet would indicate. Neither is it as hot and spicy (**picante**) as the food often served in the Southwest. Food in Spain is tasty but relatively bland; even in Mexico, the "hot" comes mainly from the red and green sauces found on the table.

The Spanish menu lacks the gourmet tradition of France. Dishes tend to be less delicate, heartier and more filling. Menu items not imported are those that are grown locally, hence many ingredients are those that have always been readily available: rice and olive oil, for instance, are used over and over. Caribbean cooking makes frequent use of such fruits as pineapples, bananas and the smaller plaintain, and other, less familiar, tropical fruits. Mexican cooking combines corn, beans, tomatoes (both red and green), and countless varieties of peppers and **chiles** in intriguing combinations.

A first-time visitor to Spanish-speaking countries may find the times for eating more exotic than the food itself. Full breakfasts are seldom found in Spain outside of large hotels catering to tourists. In the Americas, however, a large breakfast is easy to get — often to be eaten about the middle of the morning rather than first thing (coffee or hot chocolate help tide you over). The midday meal, the **comida**, is taken between 1:00 and 3:00 p.m. in Mexico, 2:00 and 4:00 in Spain. Most "business dinners" take place at **comida**. Traditionally, most offices closed for the delightful custom, the **siesta**, although long commuting times have made the break for a nap less common in large cities. The last meal of the day, the **cena**, is much lighter than **comida** and is eaten late in the evening, sometimes very late (any time between 8:00 and midnight with the emphasis on the later hours).

You would have to work hard, however, to go hungry. It often seems that Spanish-speaking societies never stop eating. Snacking is not only common, but the occasion for sampling some of the most representative local foods. Spain has even institutionalized the between-meal snack, the **merienda**, which consists of a variety of hors d'oeuvre eaten with a few **copas** of wine around 6:00 p.m. No visitor should leave Spain without visiting a few taverns for **merienda** and sampling the local specialties, **tapas**. Indeed, it is considered customary to have a light snack whenever one stops for morning coffee or after-work cocktails.

In general, restaurants of comparable quality are less expensive than their U.S. counterparts, especially in Mexico and the Caribbean. Service appears more formal, although it is often acceptable to attract a waiter's attention by hissing, making a kissing sound, or slapping hands, depending on local custom. Better not try it until you see someone else do it first! The economy-minded visitor should be warned that such ordinary extras as soft drinks, coffee, even bread, are sometimes priced out of proportion to the rest of the menu; second cups of coffee are seldom free. On the other hand, one is never rushed to pay the bill and leave; you may linger forever over one drink or coffee. Indeed, getting a waiter to bring the check (**cuenta**) can be a major challenge. You have to ask for it and probably remind the waiter a few times before he produces it. Finally, as a general rule, the more American-looking a restaurant, the higher its prices.

A typical Spanish menu is completely à la carte. The standard headings include **entremeses** and/or **tapas** (appetizers); **sopas** (soups); sometimes **sopas secas** (literally dry soups, usually a pasta or rice course); **carnes** (red meats); **aves** (poultry); **pescados** (fish); **mariscos** (shellfish); **ensaladas** (salads); **legumbres** (vegetables); **postres** (desserts); and **bebidas** (beverages). The people who live in the country you are visiting will probably eat an astonishing number of courses, but you can order from as many or as few categories as you like to make up a meal that suits your tastes and appetite.

An exception to the à la carte menu is the multicourse combination usually available at the midday meal, the **comida**. Called the **menu turístico**, **comida corrida**, or simply **comida**, it offers few choices and (sometimes) smaller portions, but it is a good bargain. Be sure to inform the waiter that you are having the set meal and restrict yourself to the choices offered.

Finally, it is important to remind yourself that although the menu may be in English, the waiter does not always speak English. Spanish and English entrées are usually listed in the same order for this reason.

Basic Terms

a la mexicana Mexican-style: mixed with peppers, tomatoes, onions, and **chiles**

caldo thick stew-like soup with solid ingredients

cilantro fresh coriander; if you don't like the taste, ask for your food **sin** (without) **cilantro**

mole a spicy sauce with many variations, some quite **picante**, others bland; the famous dish is **mole poblano de guajolote**, turkey in dark chocolate-flavored sauce in the style of Puebla

rellenos stuffed, often vegetables with stuffing

salsa sauce; some common ones are **salsa mexicana** (see above), **salsa verde** (made with green tomatoes called **tomatillos**), and **salsa ranchera** (quite hot, used for **huevos rancheros**)

sofrito common base of tomatoes, vegetables, onions, garlic lightly fried in olive oil

tortillas The Mexican tortilla is, with beans and peppers, the basic ingredient in Mexican cooking. A tortilla is a flat pancake made from **masa harina**, a flour made of corn from which the husks and germ have been removed, and water. Tortillas are baked on an ungreased griddle and are used as bread with many meals and combined with other ingredients to make a number of common Mexican menu items:

chalupas small tortillas filled with meat or other toppings, served as hors d'oeuvre

chilaquiles strips of stale tortillas fried, then combined with meat or chicken, sauces, and meats and baked; green chilaquiles feature chicken and green **tomatillo** sauce while red chilaquiles usually have beef and red tomato (**jitomate**) sauce; both topped with cheese

enchiladas tortillas dipped in **chile** sauce, then fried to receive various fillings, e.g. chicken, cheese, and sour cream to make **enchiladas suizas** (Swiss enchiladas)

nachos similar to chalupas

quesadillas small raw tortillas, filled with cheese or other savory fillings, sealed, and baked or fried on a grill

taco ubiquitous Mexican counterpart of the American sandwich; a tortilla is rolled around filling and either eaten as is or fried on a grill; **taco al carbón: a** taco made with meat only

tamales not tortillas, but soft dumplings made by wrapping tortilla dough around various fillings, securing the whole in corn husks, and steaming

tostado taco for which the tortilla is first fried until crisp in deep fat

Entremeses or Tapas (Appetizers)

ceviche a seafood cocktail made of raw fish or shellfish "cooked" by marinating in lime juice and mixed with spices; many different versions exist

chalupas see **tortillas**

cóctel de camarones shrimp cocktail

cóctel de ostiones oyster-like cocktail; shellfish is served out of the shell in cocktail sauce

nachos see **tortillas**

pescado Santo Domingo cold sea bass served as hors d'oeuvre

quesadillas see **tortillas**

Sopas (Soups)

albóndigas very thick soup made with ground beef and rice

caldo de pescado fish soup

caldo Tlalpeño rich clear chicken soup with vegetables and dried **chiles**; very good

gazpacho classic cold soup made of raw tomatoes and other vegetables and oil and vinegar

menudo tripe soup; very hearty and filling

pozole soup made of pork, hominy, and **chiles**; often very hot, always very filling

sopa de ajo popular garlic soup prepared by browning garlic cloves and bread in oil

sopa de cebolla onion soup, often with cheese

sopa de frijol negro black bean soup

sopa de judías coloradas black bean soup with ham and hard-cooked egg

sopa de tortilla delicious soup made with chicken broth, tortilla strips, and many flavorings

Entrées or Platillo Fuerte or Platos Principales (Main Dishes)

Carnes (Red Meats)

albóndigas meat balls, often very **picante**, sometimes served as an appetizer as well

carne asada literally grilled meat, this is almost always filet of beef sliced fair-

ly thin **with** the grain, broiled medium-well, and served with any combination of a number of side dishes; a safe dish to order almost anywhere

cocido popular stew with many variations but usually including meat, chicken, bacon, chick peas, and vegetables

cocido de riñones kidney stew in a sofrito base

cochinillo asado roast suckling pig; no one should go through life without it

cochinillo pibil Yucatecan-style barbecued pork

chiles rellenos stuffed chile poblanos (stuffing is usually ground pork but can be cheese)

chorizo popular red-colored sausage

empanada Galacian hot turnover usually filled with a meat mixture

fabada stew of pork, beans, and spices

guisado stew, usually of meat and other vegetables

hígado liver

jamón en dulce ham preserved in sugar, i.e. sugar-cured ham, served cold

lechón asada another name for roast suckling pig

lengua de res ox tongue

lomo de cerdo loin of pork

olla podrida same as **cocido**

piononos deep-fried plaintain rings with tasty ground-beef filling

pote same as **cocido**

puchero same as **cocido**

puerco en mole verde pork in green mole sauce; also called **pipián verde** sauce (**pipián** means a sauce made with ground nuts or seeds, in this case with green pumpkin seeds, **pepitas**)

riñones kidneys

Aves (Poultry)

arroz con pollo common rice with chicken dish including saffron, peas, and other vegetables and seasonings in endless variations; always a good and safe bet

guisado de pollo chicken stew with potatoes, peas, and wine sauce

mole poblano one of the national dishes of Mexico, traditionally made with turkey, though chicken is often used

pato duck

pechuga de pollo breast of chicken

pollo a la chilindrón chicken sautéed with peppers, tomatoes, and olives

pollo en pipián rojo chicken in a red sauce flavored with sesame seeds; may be referred to as **en pipián colorado** (red **pipián**)

Huevos (Eggs)

huevos a la flamenca fried eggs on a sofrito base

huevos motuleños as they are made in the town of Motul in Yucatán, incorporating chopped ham and peas

huevos rancheros soft fried eggs on tortillas covered with hot sauce (**salsa ranchera**) served with refried beans; guaranteed to wake you up

huevos revueltos a la mexicana eggs scrambled with chopped tomatoes, onions, and **chiles**

pisto manchego mixed vegetables, bits of ham, and eggs, a sort of omelette, easy on the eggs; there are many variations from region to region

tortilla in Spain only, a sturdy omelette containing many combinations of ingredients other than eggs

Pescados y Mariscos (Fish and Shellfish)

adobo de pescado fish casserole with tomatoes

aguacates rellenos literally stuffed avocados; often the stuffing is a seafood salad or a vegetable mixture; sometimes served as an appetizer or first course

asopao Puerto Rican rice stew with seafood

bacalao a la Vizcaína salt cod and tomatoes, of Basque origin

blanco de Pátzcuaro white fish from Lake Pátzcauro in Mexico

calamares en su tinta squid in a sauce made with their ink; much tastier than it sounds

camarones shrimp

huachinango a la Veracruzana red snapper in the style of Veracruz; baked with tomatoes, onions, and chiles

paella famous rice-based casserole usually containing shellfish, chicken, peas, and sometimes sausages; spices include saffron; every chef has his own version, but be prepared to wait because it is always cooked to order

pescado guisado fish stew

zarzuela mixed seafood stew in a sauce of wine and brandy; many variations, almost all delicious

Snacks, Side Dishes, etc.

bocadillo literally sandwich, it is also the standard hard roll, very soft inside; a real staple

bolillo the Mexican standard roll

bombas de camarones deep-fried potato cakes with shrimp in the dough

burritos wheat-flour tortillas rolled around a variety of fillings similar to those used for the corn tortillas; if then fried, usually called **chimichangas**

churros long deep-fried pastry made from a doughnut-like dough and dipped in granulated sugar; served for breakfast in Spain and also for late-night **merienda** with coffee or chocolate in Mexico

frijoles refritos "refried" beans; actually the beans are cooked tender, then fried only once, being mashed in the process; served with practically everything in Mexico

guacamole avocado purée with onions, peppers, often fresh coriander (**cilantro**), and possibly chopped tomatoes; usually bland, it is sometimes made with hot **chiles**, so taste cautiously

migas bread bits fried in olive oil and flavored with garlic; a distinctively Spanish crouton

pan dulce literally sweet bread, this term covers a huge variety of pastries and sweet breads made in bakeries that seem to be on every corner; don't miss these delicious sweets, but buy only what you will eat in one day since they lose their bloom if kept longer

torta Mexico City only: a carved out bolillo filled with meat, avocado, tomato, etc.; a great takeout

Postres (Desserts)

Spanish desserts are relatively simple and not difficult to understand. Fruits are popular, sometimes in cream (**con crema**) or with whipped cream (**nata**, thicker than the American version). One can order a variety of pastries (**pastales** or, in Spain, **tortas**) or ice cream (**helado**).

arroz con leche rice pudding

chongos a kind of cross between custard and cheese made by letting gently heated milk separate into curds and whey, these are served with a sweet syrup; don't miss them

natillas universally available soft custard served cold

flan sometimes called **crème caramel**, this custard baked with caramel syrup on the bottom is probably the best known distinctly Spanish dessert; usually on every menu

Bebidas (Beverages)

atole a hot drink made with **masa harina**, rather like a thin cornmeal mush sweetened and flavored in various ways; not everybody's cup, but interesting to try — perhaps the chocolate version, called **champurrado**

café coffee; be careful how you order:

café americano American-style coffee

café con crema American-style coffee with cream (in small or very rural places, the cream may be evaporated milk, so be advised)

café con leche coffee with warm milk (**café au lait**)

café de olla coffee made in a clay pot served black flavored with stick cinnamon and sweetened with raw brown sugar

café solo espresso-style black coffee

chocolate spelled the same way but pronounced choco-LAHT-tay, this popular beverage in Mexico comes in many styles among which are mexicana (made with water) and francesca (made with milk and, possibly, an egg)

cerveza beer; light is **clara**, dark is **negra**; dark Mexican beer is labeled **oscura** and the very dark, once-a-year treat around Christmas is **nochebuena**

coñac brandy (no particular brand)

jerez sherry, our corruption of the name of the city that gave rise to the wine, Jerez, Spain, pronounced (both city and drink) *hereth*

jugo de naranja orange juice

Kalaúa the coffee-flavored, chocolatey liqueur of Mexico

refresco any soft drink, usually ordered by brand

tequila Mexican liquor distilled from the agave plant; other forms of agave products, including **mescal** and **pulque**; ask local advice

vino wine; red (**tinto**), rose (**rosado**), or white (**blanco**); local table wine is **vino corriente, vino de mesa,** or **vino del país**

English—Español

A

a, an [ə, ən] *art* un, -a.

aback [ə'bak] *adv* **be taken aback** quedar desconcertado.

abandon [ə'bandən] *v* abandonar. *n* abandono *m*.

abashed [ə'baʃt] *adj* avergonzado, confundido.

abate [ə'beit] *v* disminuir. **abatement** *n* disminución *f*.

abattoir ['abətwar] *n* matadero *m*.

abbey ['abi] *n* abadía *f*. **abbess** *n* abadesa *f*. **abbot** *n* abad *m*.

abbreviate [ə'briːvieit] *v* abreviar. **abbreviation** *n* abreviación *f*.

abdicate ['abdikeit] *v* abdicar. **abdication** *n* abdicación *f*.

abdomen ['abdəmən] *n* abdomen *m*. **abdominal** *adj* abdominal.

abduct [əb'dʌkt] *v* raptar. **abduction** *n* rapto *m*.

aberration [abə'reiʃən] *n* extravío *m*, engaño *m*. **aberrant** *adj* extraviado.

abet [ə'bet] *v* instigar, inducir.

abeyance [ə'beiəns] *n* **in abeyance** en suspenso.

abhor [ab'hor] *v* aborrecer, odiar. **abhorrence** *n* aborrecimiento *m*, odio *m*. **abhorrent** *adj* aborrecible.

***abide** [ə'baid] *v* residir, habitar; (*tolerate*) aguantar, sufrir. **abide by** atenerse a, cumplir con.

ability [ə'biləti] *n* habilidad *f*, capacidad *f*. **to the best of one's ability** lo mejor que pueda.

abject [,abdʒekt] *adj* abyecto.

ablaze [ə'bleiz] *adj* en llamas.

able ['eibl] *adj* capaz; (*talented*) hábil.

able-bodied *adj* entero. **able-bodied seaman** marinero de primera *m*. **be able** poder. **ably** *adv* hábilmente.

abnormal [ab'norml] *adj* anormal. **abnormality** *n* anormalidad *f*.

aboard [ə'bord] *adv*, *prep* a bordo (de). **all aboard!** ¡viajeros a bordo! **go aboard** embarcarse.

abode [ə'boud] *n* domicilio *m*.

abolish [ə'boliʃ] *v* abolir. **abolition** *n* abolición *f*.

abominable [ə'bominəbl] *adj* abominable. **abominate** *v* abominar (de). **abomination** *n* abominación *f*.

Aborigine [abə'ridʒini] *n* aborigen *m*.

abortion [ə'borʃən] *n* aborto *m*. **abort** *v* abortar.

abound [ə'baund] *v* abundar.

about [ə'baut] *adv* (*approximately*) casi, alrededor de, más o menos. **all about** por todas partes. *prep* (*place*) alrededor de; (*near*) cerca de; (*concerning*) de, acerca de.

above [ə'bʌv] *adv* encima, arriba. *prep* (*place*) encima de, sobre; (*number*) más de; (*rank*) superior a. **above-mentioned** *adj* susodicho, citado.

abrasion [ə'breiʒən] *n* raspadura *f*. **abrasive** *adj* raspante.

abreast [ə'brest] *adv* de frente. **keep abreast of** or **with** ir al paso de.

abridge [ə'bridʒ] *v* abreviar, resumir. **abridgement** *n* abreviación *f*, resumen *m*.

abroad [ə'brород] *adv* en el extranjero.

abrupt [ə'brʌpt] *adj* abrupto, brusco.

abscess ['abses] *n* absceso *m*.

abscond [əb'skond] *v* fugarse.

absent ['absənt] *adj* ausente. **absent-minded** *adj* distraído. **absent oneself** ausentarse. **absence** *n* ausencia *f*. **absentee** *n* ausente *m*, *f*. **absenteeism** *n* absentismo *m*.

absolute ['absəlutt] *adj* absoluto. **absolutely** *adv* absolutamente; *(interj)* categóricamente. **absolutism** *n* absolutismo *m*.

absolve [əb'zolv] *v* absolver. **absolution** *n* absolución *f*.

absorb [əb'zorb] *v* absorber. **be absorbed in** enfrascarse en. **absorbent** *adj* absorbente. **absorbing** *adj (coll)* sumamente interesante.

abstain [əb'stein] *v* abstenerse (de). **abstention** *n* abstención *f*. **abstinence** *n* abstinencia *f*.

abstemious [əb'stiːmiəs] *adj* abstemio.

abstract ['abstrakt; *v* ab'strakt] *adj* abstracto. *n* resumen *m*. *v* extractar. **abstractedly** *adv* distraídamente. **abstraction** *n* abstracción *f*.

absurd [əb'sɜːd] *adj* absurdo. **absurdity** *n* absurdidad *f*.

abundance [ə'bʌndəns] *n* abundancia *f*. **abundant** *adj* abundante.

abuse [ə'bjuːz; *n* ə'bjuːs] *v* abusar (de). *n* abuso *m*; injuria *f*. **abusive** *adj* abusivo; injurioso.

abyss [ə'bis] *n* abismo *m*. **abysmal** *adj* abismal; profundo.

academy [ə'kadəmi] *n* academia *f*. **academic** *adj* académico.

accede [ak'siːd] *v* acceder.

accelerate [ək'seləreit] *v* acelerar. **acceleration** *n* aceleración *f*. **accelerator** *n* acelerador *m*.

accent ['aksənt] *n* acento *m*. *v* acentuar.

accept [ək'sept] *v* aceptar. **acceptable** *adj* aceptable. **acceptance** *n* aceptación *f*.

access ['akses] *n* acceso *m*. **accessible** *adj* asequible.

accessory [ək'sesəri] *nm, adj* accesorio. *n (law)* cómplice *m, f*. **accessories** *pl n (mot, etc.)* complementos *m pl*.

accident ['aksidənt] *n* accidente *m*. **by accident** sin querer, por casualidad. **accidental** *adj* accidental.

acclaim [ə'kleim] *v* aclamar, aplaudir. *n also* **acclamation** aclamación *f*, aplauso *m*.

acclimatize [ə'klaimətaiz] *v* aclimatar.

accolade [ə'kəleid] *n* acolada *f*.

accommodate [ə'kɒmədeit] *v* acomodar; *(lodge)* alojar, hospedar; adaptar; *(provide)* proveer. **accommodating** *adj* complaciente. **accommodation** *n* alojamiento *m*.

accompany [ə'kʌmpəni] *v* acompañar. **accompaniment** *n* acompañamiento *m*. **accompanist** *n* acompañante, -a *m, f*.

accomplice [ə'kʌmplis] *n* cómplice *m, f*.

accomplish [ə'kʌmpliʃ] *v* cumplir. **accomplished** *adj (talented)* talentoso. **accomplishment** *n* efectuación *f*; talentos *m pl*.

accord [ə'kɔːd] *v* conceder; concordar. *n* acuerdo *m*. **of one's own accord** espontáneamente. **in accordance with** conforme a. **accordingly** *adv* en consecuencia. **according to** según.

accordion [ə'kɔːdiən] *n* acordeón *m*.

accost [ə'kost] *v* abordar.

account [ə'kaunt] *n (bank, etc.)* cuenta *f*; *(narrative)* relato *m*; *(status)* importancia *f*. **on account of** a causa de. **on no account** de ninguna manera. **take into account** tener en cuenta. **account for** dar una explicación de. **accountant** *n* contador *m*; *(chartered)* contador colegiado.

accrue [ə'kruː] *v* crecer.

accumulate [ə'kjuːmjuleit] *v* acumular. **accumulation** *n* acumulación *f*.

accurate ['akjurət] *adj* exacto. **accuracy** *n* precisión *f*.

accuse [ə'kjuːz] *v* acusar. **accusation** *n* acusación *f*. **the accused** acusado, -a *m, f*.

accustom [ə'kʌstəm] *v* acostumbrar.

ace [eis] *n* as *m*. **within an ace of** de dos dedos de.

ache [eik] *n* dolor *m*. *v* doler.

achieve [ə'tʃiːv] *v* ejecutar. **achievement** *n* ejecución *f*; *(feat)* hazaña *f*.

acid ['asid] *nm, adj* ácido. **acidity** *n* acidez *f*.

acknowledge [ək'nolidʒ] *v* reconocer, aceptar. **acknowledge receipt of** acusar recibo de. **acknowledgement** *n* reconocimiento *m*; acuse de recibo *m*.

acne ['akni] *n* acné *m*.

acorn ['eikɔːn] *n* bellota *f*.

acoustic [ə'kuːstik] *adj* acústico. **acoustics** *pl n* acústica *f sing*.

acquaint [ə'kweint] *v* informar, avisar. **acquaintance** *n (knowledge)* conocimiento *m*; *(person)* conocido, -a *m, f*. **be acquainted with** conocer(a).

acquiesce [akwi'es] *v* consentir, conformarse. **acquiescence** *n* conformidad *f*. **acquiescent** *adj* sumiso.

acquire [ə'kwaiə] *v* adquirir. **acquisition** *n* adquisición *f*. **acquisitive** *adj* adquisitivo; *(derog)* ahorrativo.

acquit [ə'kwit] v absolver. **acquit oneself** portarse. **acquittal** (*law*) absolución f.

acrid ['akrid] adj acre.

acrimony ['akrimənı] n acrimonia f. **acrimonious** adj áspero.

acrobat ['akrəbat] n acróbata m, f. **acrobatic** adj acrobático. **acrobatics** pl n acrobacia f sing.

across [ə'kros] adv a través, al través. prep a través de, al través de, de través de; al otro lado de, del otro lado de.

acrylic [ə'krilik] adj acrílico.

act [akt] v (*theatre*) representar; (*function*) funcionar, marchar; (*behave*) comportarse; (*take action*) obrar, tomar medidas; (*affect*) afectar. n acto m, acción f; obra f; (*law*) decreto; (*theatre*) acto m. **actor** n actor m. **actress** n actriz f.

action ['akʃən] n acción f, hecho m; (*mil*) acción f, batalla f; (*mech*) mecanismo m. **bring an action against** entablar demanda contra. **put out of action** inutilizar.

active ['aktiv] adj activo. **activate** v activar. **activist** n activista m, f. **activity** n actividad f; movimiento m.

actual ['aktʃuəl] adj verdadero, efectivo. **actually** adv en realidad.

actuate ['aktjueit] v mover; accionar.

acupuncture ['akjupʌŋktʃə] n acupuntura f.

acute [ə'kjut] adj agudo.

adamant ['adəmənt] adj firme, seguro.

Adam's apple [adəm'zapl] n nuez de la garganta f.

adapt [ə'dapt] v adaptar, ajustar; (*play, book*) refundir; (*music*) arreglar. **adaptable** adj adaptable. **adaptation** n adaptación f; refundición f; arreglo m. **adapter** n (*theatre*) refundidor m; (*elec*) enchufe de reducción m.

add [ad] v añadir; (*increase*) aumentar. **add up** sumar. **add up to** subir a. **addition** n el añadir m; (*math*) suma f, adición f. **additional** adj adicional.

addendum [ə'dendəm] n invar adenda f.

adder ['adə] n víbora f.

addict [adikt] n partidario, -a m, f; (*drugs*) toxicómano, -a m, f. **addiction** n adicción f; propensión f. **be addicted to** ser adicto a.

additive ['aditiv] n aditivo m.

address [ə'dres] v (*letter*) dirigir; (*meeting,*

etc.) pronunciar un discurso ante. **address oneself to** dirigirse. n (*postal*) dirección f; (*speech*) discurso m; (*envelope*) sobrescrito m. **addressee** n destinatario, -a m, f.

adenoids ['adənoidz] pl n amígdalas vegetaciones f pl.

adept [ə'dept] nm, adj experto.

adequate ['adikwət] adj adecuado, suficiente.

adhere [əd'hiə] v pegarse; (*to a policy*) adherirse a. **adherence** n adhesión f. **adhesive** adj adhesivo. **adhesive tape** esparadrapo m.

adherent [əd'hiərənt] n partidario, -a m, f.

adjacent [ə'dʒeisənt] adj próximo, contiguo.

adjective ['adʒiktiv] n adjetivo m.

adjoin [ə'dʒoin] v lindar (con). **adjoining** adj contiguo.

adjourn [ə'dʒəin] v aplazar; (*session*) levantar la sesión. **adjournment** n aplazamiento m; (*of a session*) suspensión f.

adjudicate [ə'dʒuidikeit] v adjudicar; (*law*) juzgar. **adjudication** n adjudicación f; (*law*) fallo m. **adjudicator** n árbitro m.

adjust [ə'dʒʌst] v arreglar; (*tech*) ajustar. **adjustment** n arreglo m; ajuste m.

ad-lib ['ad'lib] adv a voluntad, a discreción. v improvisar.

administer [əd'ministə] v administrar; (*law*) aplicar; (*med*) suministrar. **administration** n administración f; (*ministry*) gobierno m. **administrative** adj administrativo. **administrator** n administrador m.

admiral ['admərəl] n almirante m.

admire [əd'maiə] v admirar. **admirable** adj admirable. **admiration** n admiración f.

admit [əd'mit] v dar entrada a; (*concede*) conceder; (*acknowledge*) reconocer. **admission** n entrada f; (*acknowledgement*) confesión f.

adolescence [adə'lesns] n adolescencia f. **adolescent** n(m+f), adj adolescente.

adopt [ə'dopt] v adoptar; (*report*) aprobar. **adopted** adj (*child*) adoptivo. **adoption** n adopción f.

adore [ə'dot] v adorar. **adoration** n adoración f.

adorn [ə'doin] v adornar, embellecer. **adornment** n adorno m.

adrenaline [ə'drenəlin] n adrenalina f.

4

adrift [ə'drift] *adv* a la deriva.
adroit [ə'droit] *adj* diestro, hábil.
adulation [adju'leiʃən] *n* adulación *f*.
adult ['ʌdʌlt] *n, adj* adulto, -a.
adulterate [ə'dʌltəreit] *v* adulterar.
adultery [ə'dʌltəri] *n* adulterio *m*. **adulter-**
er *n* adúltero, -a *m, f*.
advance [əd'vɑːns] *v* adelantar; avanzar. *n*
progreso *m*, avance *m*, adelanto *m*;
(*cash*) anticipo *m*.
advantage [əd'vɑːntidʒ] *n* ventaja *f*. **take
advantage of** aprovecharse de. **advantageous** *adj* ventajoso.
advent ['ædvənt] *n* advenimiento *m*.
Advent *n* Adviento *m*.
adventure [əd'ventʃə] *n* aventura *f*;
(*comm*) especulación *f*. **adventurer** *n*
aventurero *m*. **adventurous** *adj* aventurero.
adverb ['ædvəːb] *n* adverbio *m*.
adversary ['ædvəsəri] *n* adversario, -a *m,
f*.
adverse ['ædvəːs] *adj* adverso. **adversity** *n*
adversidad *f*.
advertise ['ædvətaiz] *v* anunciar; publicar.
advertisement *n* anuncio *m*. **advertising** *n*
publicidad *f*.
advise [əd'vaiz] *v* aconsejar; avisar. **advisable** *adj* conveniente. **advisedly** *adv* con
intención. **adviser** *n* consejero *m*. **advice**
n consejo *m*.
advocate ['ædvəkeit] *v* recomendar.
aerial ['eəriəl] *adj* aéreo. *n* antena *f*.
aerodynamics [eərədai'namiks] *n* aerodinámica *f sing*.
aeronautics [eərə'nɔtiks] *n* aeronáutica *f
sing*.
aeroplane ['eərəplein] *n* avión *m*.
aerosol ['eərəsɔl] *n* aerosol *m*.
aesthetic [iːs'θetik] *adj* estético. **aesthetics**
n estética *f sing*.
affair [ə'feə] *n* asunto *m*; episodio *m*;
(*love*) aventura amorosa *f*. **affairs** (*business*) negocios *m pl*.
affect[1] [ə'fekt] *v* (*influence*) influir en;
(*move*) conmover.
affect[2] [ə'fekt] *v* (*pretend*) afectar.
affection [ə'fekʃən] *n* cariño *m*.
affiliate [ə'filieit] *v* afiliarse (a). **affiliation**
n afiliación *f*.
affinity [ə'finəti] *n* afinidad *f*.
affirm [ə'fəːm] *v* afirmar. **affirmation** *n*
afirmación *f*. **affirmative** *adj* afirmativo.
affix [ə'fiks] *v* fijar; añadir; pegar; poner.

afflict [ə'flikt] *v* afligir, aquejar. **affliction** *n*
aflicción *f*, dolor *m*.
affluent ['æfluənt] *adj* afluente, opulento.
affluence *n* afluencia *f*, opulencia *f*.
afford [ə'fɔːd] *v* tener medios; (*produce*)
dar; ofrecer.
affront [ə'frʌnt] *v* afrentar. *n* afrenta *f*,
ofensa *f*.
afloat [ə'flout] *adv* a flote.
afoot [ə'fut] *adv* a pie; (*fig*) en proyecto.
aforesaid [ə'fɔːsed] *adj* susodicho, men-
cionado.
afraid [ə'freid] *adj* temeroso, espantado.
be afraid tener miedo (*a or* de).
afresh [ə'freʃ] *adv* de nuevo.
Africa ['æfrikə] *n* África *f*. **African** *n, adj*
africano, -a.
aft [ɑːft] *adv* a popa.
after ['ɑːftə] *prep* (*time*) después de;
(*place*) detrás de; tras. *adv* (*time*)
después; (*place*) detrás. *conj* después (de)
que. **after all** con todo. **afterwards** *adv*
después. **after-effect** *n* consecuencia *f*.
aftershave *n* loción de afeitar *f*.
afternoon [ɑːftə'nuːn] *n* tarde *f*. **good
afternoon!** ¡buenas tardes!
again [ə'gen] *adv* de nuevo, otra vez;
además. **again and again** aún una y otra
vez. **now and again** de vez en cuando.
against [ə'genst] *prep* contra; (*touching*)
tocante.
age [eidʒ] *n* edad *f*; (*era*) época *f*. **of age**
mayor de edad. **under age** menor de
edad. *v* envejecer. **aged** *adj* de la edad
de; (*old*) viejo.
agency ['eidʒənsi] *n* agencia *f*; mediación
f.
agenda [ə'dʒendə] *n* agenda *f*.
agent ['eidʒənt] *n* agente *m, f*; (*comm*)
representante *m, f*.
aggravate ['ægrəveit] *v* agravar; (*coll*)
exasperar. **aggravation** *n* agravamiento
m; (*coll*) irritación *f*.
aggregate ['ægrigət] *m, adj* agregado. *v*
agregar, juntar.
aggression [ə'greʃən] *n* agresión *f*. **aggressive** *adj* agresivo. **aggressiveness** *n*
belicosidad *f*. **aggressor** *n* agresor, -a *m, f*.
aghast [ə'gɑːst] *adj* horrorizado.
agile ['ædʒail] *adj* ágil, ligero. **agility** *n*
agilidad *f*.
agitate ['ædʒiteit] *v* agitar, excitar. **agitate
for** luchar por. **agitation** *n* agitación *f*;
perturbación *f*.

agnostic [ag'nostik] *n, adj* agnóstico, -a. **agnosticism** *n* agnosticismo *m*.

ago [ə'gou] *adv* hace, ha. **long ago** hace mucho tiempo. **a short time ago** hace poco.

agog [ə'gog] *adj* ansioso.

agony ['agəni] *n* agonía *f*, angustia *f*. **agonize** *v* atormentar.

agree [ə'gri:] *v* estar de acuerdo, convenir (en); *(consent)* consentir (en); *(gram)* concordar; *(correspond)* estar conforme (con). **agreeable** *adj* agradable. **agreement** *n (pact)* pacto *m*; *(comm)* contrato *m*.

agriculture ['agrikʌltʃə] *n* agricultura *f*. **agricultural** *adj* agrícola.

aground [ə'graund] *adv* encallado. **run aground** encallar, varar.

ahead [ə'hed] *adv* delante, al frente. **be ahead** estar adelante. **go ahead!** ¡adelante!

aid [eid] *v* ayudar, socorrer. *n* ayuda *f*. **in aid of** en beneficio de. **first aid** primera cura. **go to the aid of** acudir en defensa de.

aim [eim] *v (weapon)* apuntar (a); *(remark)* dirigir (a). *n (weapon)* puntería *f*; *(fig)* propósito *m*, meta *f*, blanco *m*. **aimless** *adj* sin objeto. **aimlessly** *adv* a la ventura.

air [eə] *n* aire *m*; *(music)* aire *m*, tonada *f*; *(aspect)* aspecto *m*. *v* airear, ventilar. **airbed** ['eəbed] *n* colchón de viento *m*.

airborne ['eəbɔ:n] *adj* en el aire.

aircraft ['eəkra:ft] *n* avión *m*. **aircraft-carrier** *n* portaaviones *m invar*.

airfield ['eəfi:ld] *n* campo de aviación *m*.

air force *n* fuerza or flota aérea *f*.

air-hostess *n* azafata *f*.

air lift *n* puente aéreo *m*.

airline ['eəlain] *n* línea aérea *f*.

airmail ['eəmeil] *n* correo aéreo *m*.

airport ['eəpɔ:t] *n* aeropuerto *m*.

air-raid *n* bombardeo aéreo *m*.

airtight ['eətait] *adj* hermético, herméticamente cerrado.

airy ['eəri] *adj* aéreo; *(flippant)* frívolo.

aisle [ail] *n* nave lateral *f*.

ajar [ə'dʒa:] *adv* entreabierto, entornado.

alabaster ['aləba:stə] *n* alabastro *m*. *adj* alabastrino.

alarm [ə'la:m] *n* alarma *f*. *v* alarmar. **alarm clock** *n* despertador *m*.

alas [ə'las] *interj* ¡ay!

Albania [al'beinjə] *n* Albania *f*. **Albanian** *n, adj* albanés, -esa.

albatross ['albətrɔs] *n* albatros *m*.

albino [al'bi:nou] *n, adj* albino, -a.

album ['albəm] *n* álbum *m*.

alchemy ['alkəmi] *n* alquimia *f*. **alchemist** *n* alquimista *m*.

alcohol ['alkəhɔl] *n* alcohol *m*. **alcoholic** *n, adj* alcohólico, -a. **alcoholism** *n* alcoholismo *m*.

alcove ['alkouv] *n* nicho *m*, hueco *m*.

alderman ['ɔ:ldəmən] *n* teniente de alcalde *m*, concejal *m*.

ale [eil] *n* cerveza *f*.

alert [ə'lə:t] *adj* alerto, vivo, despierto. *v* poner sobre aviso, alertar.

algebra ['aldʒibrə] *n* álgebra *f*.

Algeria [al'dʒiəriə] *n* Argelia *f*. **Algerian** *n, adj* argelino, -a.

alias ['eiliəs] *nm, adv* alias.

alibi ['alibai] *n* coartada *f*.

alien ['eiljən] *n, adj* extranjero, -a. **alienate** *v* enajenar, alejar. **alienation** *n* alienación *f*.

alight[1] [ə'lait] *v* desmontar, bajar, apearse.

alight[2] [ə'lait] *adj* encendido, iluminado, en llamas.

align [ə'lain] *v* alinear. **alignment** *n* alineación *f*.

alike [ə'laik] *adj* igual, parecido, semejante. *adv* igualmente, del mismo modo.

alimentary canal [ali'mentəri] *n* tubo digestivo *m*.

alimony ['aliməni] *n* alimentos *m pl*.

alive [ə'laiv] *adj* vivo, activo. **alive to** sensible de. **alive with** rebosante de.

alkali ['alkəlai] *n* álcali *m*.

all [ɔ:l] *adj* todo. *pron* todo el mundo, todo, totalidad *f*. *adv* todo, enteramente. **all but** casi. **all right** está bien. **all the more** cuanto más. **all the same** sin embargo.

allay [ə'lei] *v* aliviar, calmar.

allege [ə'ledʒ] *v* alegar, afirmar.

allegiance [ə'li:dʒəns] *n* fidelidad *f*, lealtad *f*.

allegory ['aligəri] *n* alegoría *f*.

allergy ['alədʒi] *n* alergia *f*. **allergic** *adj* alérgico.

alleviate [ə'li:vieit] *v* aliviar. **alleviation** *n* alivio *m*.

alley ['ali] *n* callejuela *f*, paseo *m*. **blind alley** callejón sin salida *m*.

alliance [ə'laiəns] *n* alianza *f*.

allied ['alaid] *adj* aliado.

alligator ['æligeitə] *n* caimán *m*.

alliteration [əlitə'reiʃən] *n* aliteración *f*.

allocate ['æləkeit] *v* asignar, distribuir.

allocation *n* asignación *f*, repartimiento *m*.

allot [ə'lot] *v* asignar. **allotment** *n* ración *f*.

allow [ə'lau] *v* permitir, admitir. **allow for** tener en cuenta. **allowable** *adj* permisible, legítimo. **allowance** *n* ración *f*; pensión *f*. **monthly allowance** mesada *f*.

alloy ['aloi; *v* ə'loi] *n* aleación *f*; (*fig*) mezcla *f*. *v* alear, ligar.

allude [ə'luːd] *v* aludir. **allusion** *n* alusión *f*. **allusive** *adj* alusivo.

allure [ə'ljuə] *v* seducir, fascinar. **allurement** *n* incentivo *m*, anzuelo *m*. **alluring** *adj* halagüeño, tentador.

ally ['alai; *v* ə'lai] *n* aliado, -a *m*, *f*, asociado, -a *m*, *f*. *v* unir.

almanac ['oːlmənæk] *n* almanaque *m*.

almighty [oːl'maiti] *adj* omnipotente, todopoderoso.

almond ['aːmənd] *n* (*nut*) almendra *f*; (*tree*) almendro *m*.

almost ['oːlmoust] *adv* casi.

alms [aːmz] *n* limosna *f*. **almsgiving** *n* caridad *f*. **almshouse** *n* hospicio *m*.

aloft [ə'loft] *adv* en alto, arriba.

alone [ə'loun] *adj* solo, único. *adv* solamente, a solas. **leave alone** dejar en paz.

along [ə'loŋ] *prep* a lo largo de. **along with** en compañía de, junto con. **come along!** ¡ven! **alongside** *adv* al lado; (*naut*) al costado de.

aloof [ə'luːf] *adv* a distancia. *adj* altanero, reservado. **keep aloof** mantenerse alejado. **aloofness** *n* alejamiento *m*.

aloud [ə'laud] *adv* en voz alta, recio, alto.

alphabet ['alfəbit] *n* alfabeto *m*.

Alps [alps] *n* Alpes *m pl*.

already [oːl'redi] *adv* ya.

also ['oːlsou] *adv* también, además.

altar ['oːltə] *n* altar *m*. **high altar** altar mayor. **altar boy** monaguillo *m*. **altarpiece** retablo *m*.

alter ['oːltə] *v* cambiar, modificar, corregir, transformar; (*clothes*) arreglar. **alteration** *n* cambio *m*, modificación *f*; (*building*) reforma *f*.

alternate [oːl'təːnət; *v* 'oːltəneit] *adj* alterno. *v* alternar. **alternating current** corriente alterna.

alternative [oːl'təːnətiv] *n* alternativa *f*.

adj alternativo. **have no alternative but ...** no poder menos de ....

although [oːl'ðou] *conj* aunque.

altitude ['æltitjuːd] *n* altura *f*, altitud *f*.

altogether [oːltə'geðə] *adv* en total, en conjunto, del todo.

altruistic [altru'istik] *adj* altruista. **altruism** *n* altruismo *m*. **altruist** *n* altruista *m*, *f*.

aluminium [alju'miniəm] *n* aluminio *m*.

always ['oːlweiz] *adv* siempre.

am [am] *V* be.

amalgamate [ə'malgəmeit] *v* amalgamar, combinar, unir; combinarse, unirse. **amalgamation** *n* amalgamación *f*; mezcla *f*.

amass [ə'mas] *v* acumular, amontonar.

amateur ['amətə] *n*, *adj* aficionado, -a. **amateurish** *adj* de aficionado, superficial.

amaze [ə'meiz] *v* asombrar, sorprender, confundir. **amazement** *n* asombro *m*. **amazing** *adj* asombroso.

ambassador [am'basədə] *n* embajador *m*.

amber ['ambə] *n* ámbar *m*. *adj* ambarino.

ambidextrous [ambi'dekstrəs] *adj* ambidextro.

ambiguous [am'bigjuəs] *adj* ambiguo. **ambiguity** *n* ambigüedad *f*.

ambition [am'biʃən] *n* ambición *f*. **ambitious** *adj* ambicioso.

ambivalent [am'bivələnt] *adj* ambivalente.

amble ['ambl] *v* andar, andar lentamente. *n* paso de andadura *m*.

ambulance ['ambjuləns] *n* ambulancia *f*.

ambush ['ambuʃ] *n* emboscada *f*, asechanza *f*. *v* emboscar, asechar.

ameliorate [ə'miːliəreit] *v* mejorar. **amelioration** *n* mejora *f*.

amenable [ə'miːnəbl] *adj* tratable, dócil, sujeto.

amend [ə'mend] *v* enmendar, modificar, rectificar. **amendment** *n* enmienda *f*. **make amends** dar satisfacción, indemnizar.

amenity [ə'miːnəti] *n* amenidad *f*, comodidad *f*.

America [ə'merikə] *n* América *f*. **American** *n*, *adj* americano, -a *m*, *f*.

amethyst ['aməθist] *n* amatista *f*.

amiable ['eimiəbl] *adj* amistoso, afable.

amicable ['amikəbl] *adj* amigable.

amid [ə'mid] *prep* entre, rodeado por, en medio de.

amiss [ə'mis] *adv* mal, de más, impropiamente. **take amiss** llevar a mal.

ammonia [ə'mouniə] n amoníaco m.

ammunition [amju'niʃən] n municiones f pl.

amnesia [am'niziə] n amnesia f.

amnesty ['amnəsti] n amnistía f.

amoeba [ə'miːbə] n ameba f.

among [ə'mʌn] prep entre, en medio de.

amoral [ei'morəl] adj amoral.

amorous ['amərəs] adj amoroso.

amorphous [ə'mɔːfəs] adj amorfo.

amount [ə'maunt] n cantidad f, importe m, suma f. v llegar a, subir a, valer. **gross amount** importe bruto m. **net amount** importe neto m. **it amounts to this** se reduce a esto.

ampere ['ampeə] n amperio m.

amphetamine [am'fetəmin] n anfetamina f.

amphibian [am'fibiən] nm, adj anfibio.

amphitheatre ['amfiθiətə] n anfiteatro m.

ample ['ampl] adj amplio, abundante; (enough) bastante, suficiente.

amplify ['amplifai] v ampliar, amplificar, aumentar. **amplifier** n amplificador m.

amputate ['ampjuteit] v amputar. **amputation** n amputación f.

amuse [ə'mjuːz] v divertir, distraer, entretener. **amuse oneself** divertirse. **amusement** n diversión f, entretenimiento m, recreo m; (hobby) pasatiempo m. **amusement park** parque de atracciones m. **amusing** adj divertido, gracioso.

anachronism [ə'nakrənizəm] n anacronismo m. **anachronistic** adj anacrónico.

anaemia [ə'niːmiə] n anemia f. **anaemic** adj anémico.

anaesthetic [anəs'θetik] nm, adj anestésico.

anagram ['anəgram] n anagrama m.

analogy [ə'nalədʒi] n analogía f. **analogous** adj análogo.

analysis [ən'aləsis] n, pl -ses análisis m. **analyst** n analista m, f. **analytic(al)** adj analítico.

anarchy ['anəki] n anarquía f. **anarchic** adj anárquico. **anarchist** n anarquista m, f.

anathema [ə'naθəmə] n anatema m, f.

anatomy [ə'natəmi] n anatomía f. **anatomical** adj anatómico.

ancestor ['ansestə] n antepasado m. **ancestral** adj ancestral, hereditario. **ancestry** n linaje m.

anchor ['aŋkə] n ancla f; (fig) áncora f. v anclar, fijar, fondear.

anchovy ['antʃəvi] n anchoa f.

ancient ['einʃənt] adj anciano, antiguo. **ancients** pl n los antiguos m pl. **from ancient times** de antiguo.

ancillary [an'siləri] adj auxiliar.

and [and] conj y, e.

anecdote ['anikdout] n anécdota f.

anemone [ə'nemani] n anémona f.

anew [ə'njuː] adv de nuevo, otra vez.

angel ['eindʒəl] n ángel m. **angelic** adj angélico.

anger ['aŋgə] n cólera f, ira f, enojo m. v enojar, enfadar, encolerizar. **angry** adj enojado, enfadado.

angina [an'dʒainə] n angina f. **angina pectoris** angina de pecho.

angle ['aŋgl] n ángulo m, rincón m; (viewpoint) punto de vista m.

angling ['aŋglin] n pesca con caña f. **angler** n pescador, -a m, f.

anguish ['aŋgwiʃ] n angustia f, agonía f, dolor m.

animal ['animəl] n animal m, bestia f. adj animal. **animal kingdom** reino animal m. **animal spirits** brío m, energía f, exuberancia vital f.

animate ['animeit; adj 'animət] v animar, alentar, vivificar. adj f viviente, animado. **animated** adj animado, vivo. **animated cartoon** dibujo animado.

animosity [ani'mosəti] n animosidad f, hostilidad f.

aniseed ['anisiːd] n grano de anís m.

ankle ['aŋkl] n tobillo m.

annals ['anlz] pl n anales m pl.

annex ['aneks; v ə'neks] n anexo m. v anexar, anexionar; unir, juntar. **annexation** n anexión f.

annihilate [ə'naiəleit] v aniquilar. **annihilation** n aniquilación f.

anniversary [ani'vɔːsəri] n aniversario m.

annotate ['anəteit] v anotar, acotar, glosar. **annotation** n anotación f, nota f.

announce [ə'nauns] v anunciar, publicar, proclamar. **announcement** n anuncio m, aviso m, publicación f; (of engagement) participación f. **announcer** n annunciador, -a m, f; (radio) locutor, -a m, f.

annoy [ə'noi] v molestar, irritar, fastidiar. **annoyance** n molestia f, disgusto m. **annoyed** adj enojado. **annoying** adj fastidioso, enojoso, molesto.

annual 8

annual ['anjuəl] *adj* anual. *n* (*book*) anuario *m*; (*plant*) planta anual *f*.

annul [ə'nʌl] *v* anular; (*law*) abrogar. **annulment** *n* anulación *f*.

Annunciation [ə,nʌnsi'eiʃən] *n* (*rel*) Anunciación *f*.

anode ['anoud] *n* ánodo *m*.

anomaly [ə'noməli] *n* anomalía *f*. **anomalous** *adj* anómalo.

anonymous [ə'noniməs] *adj* anónimo.

anorak ['anorak] *n* anorak *m*.

another [ə'nʌðə] *adj* otro. *pron* otro, -a *m, f*. **one after another** uno después de otro.

answer ['aːnsə] *n* contestación *f*, respuesta *f*; (*solution*) solución *f*; (*math*) resultado *m*. *v* contestar, responder; (*a bell*) acudir; (*door*) abrir. **answer back** replicar. **answer by return** contestar a vuelta de correo. **answerable** *adj* responsable.

ant [ant] *n* hormiga *f*.

antagonize [an'tagənaiz] *v* antagonizar, contender. **antagonism** *n* antagonismo *m*, oposición *f*. **antagonist** *n* antagonista *m, f*. **antagonistic** *adj* antagónico.

antecedent [anti'siːdənt] *nm, adj* antecedente.

antelope ['antəloup] *n* antílope *m*.

antenatal [anti'neitl] *adj* antenatal.

antenna [an'tenə] *n* antena *f*.

anthem ['anθəm] *n* motete *m*. **national anthem** himno nacional *m*.

anthology [an'θolədʒi] *n* antología *f*.

anthropology [anθrə'polədʒi] *n* antropología *f*.

anti-aircraft [anti'eəkraift] *adj* anti-aéreo.

antibiotic [antibai'otik] *nm, adj* antibiótico.

antibody ['anti,bodi] *n* anticuerpo *m*.

anticipate [an'tisipeit] *v* prever, esperar; anticiparse a. **anticipation** *n* anticipación *f*, esperanza *f*, adelantamiento *m*. **in anticipation of** en espera de.

anticlimax [anti'klaimaks] *n* anticlímax *m*.

anticlockwise [anti'klokwaiz] *adj* en dirección contraria a las agujas del reloj.

antics ['antiks] *pl n* cabriola *f sing*, travesura *f sing*, payasadas *f pl*.

anticyclone [anti'saikloun] *n* anticiclón *m*.

antidote ['antidout] *n* antídoto *m*, contraveneno *m*.

antifreeze ['antifriːz] *n* anticongelante *m*.

antipathy [an'tipəθi] *n* antipatía *f*, aversión *f*.

antique [an'tiːk] *n* antigualla *f*, antigüedad *f*. *adj* antiguo. **antique dealer** anticuario *m*. **antique shop** tienda de antigüedades. **antiquity** *n* antigüedad *f*.

anti-Semitic [antisə'mitik] *adj* antisemítico. **anti-Semitism** *n* antisemitismo *m*.

antiseptic [anti'septik] *nm, adj* antiséptico.

antisocial [anti'souʃəl] *adj* antisocial.

anti-tank [anti'taŋk] *adj* antitanque.

antithesis [an'tiθəsis] *n, pl* **-ses** antítesis *f*.

antler ['antlə] *n* asta *f*, cuerno *m*.

antonym ['antənim] *n* antónimo *m*.

anus ['einəs] *n* ano *m*. **anal** *adj* anal.

anvil ['anvil] *n* yunque *m*.

anxious ['aŋkʃəs] *adj* ansioso, preocupado, inquieto. **anxiety** *n* inquietud *f*, ansiedad *f*, intranquilidad *f*.

any ['eni] *adv* cualquier; (*some*) algún, ningún; (*every*) todo. *pron* alguno, -a *m, f*; cualquiera *m, f*; ninguno, -a *m, f*. *adv* algo. **anybody** *or* **anyone** *pron* cualquiera, alguien, nadie. **anyhow** *adv* de cualquier modo. **anything** *n* algo *m*; (*negative*) nada *f*. **anywhere** *adv* dondequiera.

apart [ə'paːt] *adv* aparte.

apartment [ə'paːtmənt] *n* apartamento *m*, cuarto *m*, habitación *f*; (*flat*) piso *m*.

apathy ['apəθi] *n* apatía *f*, indiferencia *f*. **apathetic** *adj* apático.

ape [eip] *n* simio *m*, mono, -a *m, f*. *v* imitar.

aperitive [ə'peritiv] *nm, adj* aperitivo.

aperture ['apətjuə] *n* abertura *f*, orificio *m*, agujero *m*.

apex ['eipeks] *n* ápice *m*.

aphrodisiac [afrə'diziak] *n* afrodisíaco *m*.

apiece [ə'piːs] *adv* por persona, por cabeza, cada uno.

apology [ə'polədʒi] *n* disculpa *f*, apología *f*, excusa *f*. **apologize** *v* disculparse, pedir perdón; (*regret*) sentir.

apoplexy ['apəpleksi] *n* apoplejía *f*. **apoplectic** *adj* apoplético.

apostle [ə'posl] *n* apóstol *m*.

apostrophe [ə'postrəfi] *n* (*punctuation*) apóstrofo *m*; (*speech*) apóstrofe *m, f*.

appal [ə'poːl] *v* espantar, aterrar. **appalling** *adj* espantoso, horrible.

apparatus [apə'reitəs] *n* aparato *m*, máquina *f*.

apparent [ə'parənt] *adj* aparente; notable, obvio, evidente, claro. **apparently** *adv* al parecer.

apparition [apə'riʃən] *n* aparición *f*, fantasma *m*.

appeal [ə'piːl] *v* (*law*) apelar; (*attract*) atraer. *n* (*law*) apelación *f*; atractivo *m*. **appeal against** suplicar de.

appear [ə'piə] *v* aparecer; (*seem*) parecer; (*in court*) comparecer. **appearance** *n* aparición *f*; (*aspect*) apariencia *f*, aspecto *m*; (*arrival*) llegada *f*.

appease [ə'piːz] *v* aplacar, apaciguar. **appeasement** *n* aplacamiento *m*, apaciguamiento *m*.

appendix [ə'pendiks] *n* apéndice *m*. **appendicitis** *n* apendicitis *f*.

appetite ['apitait] *n* apetito *m*. **have an appetite** tener ganas. **appetizing** *adj* apetitoso.

applaud [ə'plɔːd] *v* aplaudir. **applause** *n* aplauso *m*.

apple ['apl] *n* (*fruit*) manzana *f*; (*tree*) manzano *m*. **apple sauce** compota de manzanas *f*.

apply [ə'plai] *v* dirigirse a, recurrir; aplicar; (*use*) emplear; (*for a job*) proponerse a. **apply oneself to** dedicarse a. **appliance** *n* aparato *m*. **applicable** *adj* aplicable. **applicant** *n* aspirante *m, f*. **application** *f* aplicación *f*.

appoint [ə'point] *v* nombrar, designar. **be appointed to** colocarse a. **be appointed as** ser nombrado *m*. **appointment** *n* puesto *m*, empleo *m*; (*assignation*) cita *f*. **make an appointment with** citar.

apportion [ə'pɔːʃən] *v* distribuir, repartir.

appraisal [ə'preizl] *n* valoración *f*, estimación *f*. **appraise** *v* valorizar, tasar.

appreciate [ə'priːʃieit] *v* apreciar, darse cuenta de; (*affection*) encarecer; (*in value*) tener en alza. **appreciation** *n* apreciación *f*, aprecio *m*; (*understanding*) percepción *f*; (*of shares, etc.*) aumento de valor *m*.

apprehend [apri'hend] *v* (*arrest*) prender, capturar; (*understand*) aprehender, percibir; (*fear*) temer. **apprehension** *n* (*arrest*) aprehensión *f*; (*understanding*) comprensión *f*; (*fear*) aprensión *f*. **apprehensive** *adj* aprensivo.

apprentice [ə'prentis] *n* aprendiz *m*. **apprenticeship** *n* aprendizaje *m*.

approach [ə'proutʃ] *v* acercarse a, aproximar; (*speak to*) hablar con. *n* acercamiento *m*, aproximación *f*; (*arrival*) llegada *f*; (*entrance*) entrada *f*.

appropriate [ə'prouprieit] *adj* ə'proupriət] *v* tomar posesión de, apropiar; (*assign*) asignar, destinar. *adj* propio, pertinente, correspondiente, conveniente *f*. **appropriateness** *n* conveniencia *f*.

approve [ə'pruːv] *v* aprobar. **approval** *n* aprobación *f*. **on approval** a prueba. **approved** *adj* bien visto.

approximate [ə'prɔksimeit; *adj* ə'prɔksimət] *v* aproximar, aproximarse. *adj* aproximado. **approximately** *adv* poco más o menos.

apricot ['eiprikɔt] *n* (*fruit*) albaricoque *m*; (*tree*) albaricoquero *m*.

April ['eiprəl] *n* abril *m*.

apron ['eiprən] *n* delantal *m*; (*stage*) proscenio *m*.

apt [apt] *adj* apto; propenso; (*suitable*) apropiado.

aptitude ['aptitjuid] *n* aptitud *f*.

aqualung ['akwəlʌŋ] *n* aparato de aire comprimido *m*.

aquarium [ə'kweəriəm] *n* acuario *m*.

Aquarius [ə'kweəriəs] *n* Acuario *m*.

aquatic [ə'kwatik] *adj* acuático.

aqueduct ['akwidʌkt] *n* acueducto *m*.

Arab [ɑrab] *m*(*m+f*), *adj* árabe. **Arabia** *n* Arabia *f*. **Arabic** *adj* arábigo.

arable ['arəbl] *adj* arable.

arbitrary ['ɑːbitrəri] *adj* arbitrario.

arbitrate ['ɑːbitreit] *v* arbitrar. **arbitration** *n* arbitraje *m*. **arbiter** or **arbitrator** *n* árbitro *m*.

arc [ɑːk] *n* arco *m*. **arc lamp** lámpara de arco *f*.

arcade [ɑː'keid] *n* arcada *f*, galería *f*.

arch¹ [ɑːtʃ] *n* arco *m*. *v* arquear.

arch² [ɑːtʃ] *adj* (*chief*) principal; archi-.

archaeology [ɑːki'olədʒi] *n* arqueología *f*. **archaeologist** *n* arqueólogo *m*.

archaic [ɑː'keiik] *adj* arcaico, arcaizante.

archbishop [ɑːtʃ'biʃəp] *n* arzobispo *m*.

archduke [ɑːtʃ'djuːk] *n* archiduque *m*.

archery ['ɑːtʃəri] *n* tiro con arco *m*. **archer** *n* arquero, -a *m, f*.

archetype ['ɑːkitaip] *n* arquetipo *m*.

archipelago [ɑːki'peləgou] *n* archipiélago *m*.

architect ['ɑːkitekt] *n* arquitecto *m*. **architecture** *n* arquitectura *f*.

archives ['ɑːkaivz] *n pl* archivo *m sing*.

arctic ['ɑːktik] *adj* ártico. **the Arctic** el Ártico.

ardent ['ɑːdənt] *adj* ardiente, apasionado.

ardour ['aɪdə] n ardor m.

arduous ['aɪdjuəs] adj arduo.

are [aɪ] V be.

area ['eəriə] n área f. superficie f: extensión f.

arena [ə'riːnə] n arena f. liza f.

Argentina [aɪdʒən'tiːnə] n Argentina f. **Argentinian** n, adj argentino, -a.

argue ['aɪgjuː] v debatir, disputar, discutir. **argue against** oponer. **arguable** adj discutible. **argument** n argumento m. **argumentative** adj contencioso.

arid ['arid] adj árido, seco.

Aries ['eəriz] n (astrol) Aries m.

°arise [ə'raɪz] v elevarse, subir; (revolt) sublevarse; (from bed) levantarse.

aristocracy [ari'stokrəsi] n aristocracia f. **aristocrat** n aristócrata m, f. **aristocratic** adj aristocrático.

arithmetic [ə'riθmətik] n aritmética f.

ark [aɪk] n arca f. **Noah's Ark** arca de Noé f.

arm¹ [aɪm] n (limb) brazo m. **armchair** n sillón m. **arm in arm** de bracete, de bracero. **armpit** n sobaco m. **within arm's reach** al alcance del brazo.

arm² [aɪm] n arma f. v armar. **to arms!** ¡a las armas! **take up arms** alzarse en armas. **under arms** sobre las armas.

armistice ['aɪmistis] n armisticio m.

armour ['aɪmə] n armadura f. arnés m; (ships, vehicles) blindaje m. v blindar, acorazar. **armour-plate** n coraza f. **armoury** n armería f.

army ['aɪmi] n ejército m.

aroma [ə'roumə] n aroma m. fragancia f. **aromatic** adj aromático.

around [ə'raund] prep alrededor de, cerca de; a la vuelta de. adv alrededor, en torno, por todas partes.

arouse [ə'rauz] v despertar, excitar.

arrange [ə'reindʒ] v arreglar, disponer; organizar; (music) adaptar; concertarse. **arrangement** n arreglo m; (agreement) acuerdo m; (music) adaptación f. **arrangements** pl n preparativos m pl.

array [ə'rei] v ataviar, poner en orden de batalla. n (dress) atavío m; (troops) formación f.

arrears [ə'riəz] pl n atrasos m pl. **in arrears** atrasado en pagos.

arrest [ə'rest] v arrestar, detener. n (stop) parada f; (detention) detención f. **under arrest** bajo arresto.

arrive [ə'raiv] v llegar. **arrival** n llegada f. venida f. **on arrival** al llegar.

arrogant ['arəgənt] adj arrogante, altanero. **arrogance** n arrogancia f.

arrow ['arou] n flecha f. saeta f.

arse [aɪs] n (vulgar) culo m, ojete m.

arsenal ['aɪsənl] n arsenal m.

arsenic ['aɪsnik] n arsénico m.

arson ['aɪsn] n incendiarismo m, incendio premeditado m.

art [aɪt] n arte m; (cunning) artificio m. **art gallery** museo de pinturas m. **artful** adj artero, mañoso.

artery ['aɪtəri] n arteria f.

arthritis [aɪ'θraitis] n artritis f.

artichoke ['aɪtiʃouk] n alcachofa f.

article ['aɪtikl] n artículo m; (object) objeto m.

articulate [aɪ'tikjuleit; adj aɪ'tikjulət] v articular. adj claro, distinto.

artifice ['aɪtifis] n artificio m.

artificial [aɪti'fiʃəl] adj artificial, falso. **artificiality** n lo artificial. **artificial respiration** respiración artificial f.

artillery [aɪ'tiləri] n artillería f.

artisan [aɪti'zan] n artesano, -a m, f.

artist ['aɪtist] n artista m, f. **artistic** adj artístico.

as [az] adv tan. prep, conj como, ya que, según, a medida que; (when) cuando; (since) puesto que; (because) porque; (although) aunque. **as a rule** por regla general. **as far as** en cuanto a. **as from** desde. **as good as** tan bueno como. **as if** como si. **as it were** en cierto modo. **as soon as** en cuanto. **as soon as possible** cuanto antes. **as usual** como de costumbre. **as well** también. **as well as** además de.

asbestos [az'bestos] n asbesto m.

ascend [ə'send] v subir. **ascendancy** n. **be in the ascendant** ir en aumento. **ascension** n subida f. **ascent** n subida f; (slope) cuesta f.

ascetic [ə'setik] adj ascético. n asceta m, f.

ash¹ [aʃ] n (cinder) ceniza f, cenizas f pl. **ashtray** n cenicero m.

ash² [aʃ] n (tree) fresno m.

ashamed [ə'ʃeimd] adj avergonzado.

ashore [ə'ʃoɪ] adv a tierra. **go ashore** desembarcar.

Ash Wednesday n miércoles de ceniza m.

Asia ['eiʃə] n Asia f. **Asian** n, adj asiático, -a.

aside [ə'said] adv aparte, a un lado. n (theatre) aparte m.

ask [aɪsk] v preguntar, pedir, invitar. **ask for trouble** buscárscla. **for the asking** sin más que pedirlo.

askew [ə'skjuː] adj oblicuamente, a un lado.

asleep [ə'sliːp] adj, adv dormido. **fall asleep** dormirse.

asparagus [ə'spærəgəs] n espárrago m.

aspect ['aspekt] n aspecto m, vista f.

asphalt ['asfalt] n asfalto m.

asphyxiate [əs'fiksieit] v asfixiar.

aspire [ə'spaiə] v aspirar. **aspiration** n aspiración f.

aspirin ['aspərin] n aspirina f.

ass [as] n asno m. **asinine** adj asnal.

assail [ə'seil] v atacar. **assailant** n asaltador, -a m, f.

assassinate [ə'sasineit] v asesinar. **assassin** n asesino m, f. **assassination** n asesinato m.

assault [ə'soːlt] n asalto m. v asaltar.

assemble [ə'sembl] v (people) convocar; (things) juntar; (machines) armar. **assemblage** n reunión f, ensamblaje m. **assembly** n asamblea f. **assembly line** línea de montaje f.

assent [ə'sent] v asentir. n asentimiento m.

assert [ə'səːt] v afirmar, declarar. **assertion** n afirmación f, aserción f.

assess [ə'ses] v evaluar, asesorar. **assessment** n valoración f.

asset ['aset] n ventaja f. **assets** pl n activo m sing, haber m sing, bienes m pl.

assiduous [ə'sidjuəs] adj asiduo, aplicado.

assign [ə'sain] v asignar, señalar; (law) consignar; (goods) traspasar. **assignment** n asignación f.

assimilate [ə'simileit] v asimilar, incorporarse. **assimilation** n asimilación f.

assist [ə'sist] v asistir, ayudar. **assistance** n ayuda f. **assistant** n ayudante m, colaborador m.

associate [ə'sousiət] v [ə'sousieit] n socio, -a m, f. compañero, -a m, f. cómplice m, f. v asociar, juntar. **associate with** ir con con. **association** n asociación f, sociedad f.

assorted [ə'soːtid] adj surtido, mezclado. **assortment** n clasificación f, mezcla f.

assume [ə'sjuːm] v asumir, tomar; (suppose) suponer. **assumed** adj fingido.

assuming that dado que. **assumption** n asunción f.

assure [ə'ʃuə] v asegurar, garantizar. **assurance** n seguridad f, certeza f; (comm) seguro m. **assuredly** adv seguramente.

asterisk ['astərisk] n asterisco m.

asthma ['asmə] n asma f.

astonish [ə'stoniʃ] v asombrar. **astonishment** n asombro m.

astound [ə'staund] v aturdir. **be astounded** quedarse muerto.

astray [ə'strei] adv desviado. **go astray** perderse.

astride [ə'straid] adv a horcajadas. prep a horcajadas sobre.

astringent [ə'strindʒənt] adj astringente.

astrology [ə'strolədʒi] n astrología f. **astrologer** n astrólogo, -a m, f.

astronaut ['astrənoːt] n astronauta m, f.

astronomy [ə'stronəmi] n astronomía f. **astronomer** n astrónomo m. **astronomical** adj astronómico.

astute [ə'stjuːt] adj astuto, agudo. **astuteness** n astucia f, sagacidad f.

asunder [ə'sʌndə] adv separadamente, en dos.

asylum [ə'sailəm] n (refuge) asilo m; (for the insane) manicomio m.

at [at] prep a, en.

ate [et] V eat.

atheism ['eiθiizəm] n ateísmo m. **atheist** n ateo, -a m, f.

Athens ['aθinz] n Atenas f. **Athenian** n(m+f), adj ateniense.

athlete ['aθliːt] n atleta m, f. **athletic** adj atlético. **athletics** n atletismo m.

Atlantic [ət'lantik] n Atlántico m. adj atlántico.

atlas ['atləs] n atlas m.

atmosphere ['atməsfiə] n atmósfera f, aire m; (feeling) ambiente m. **atmospheric** adj atmosférico. **atmospherics** pl n perturbaciones atmosféricas f pl.

atom ['atəm] n átomo m. **atomic** adj atómico.

atone [ə'toun] v expiar. **atonement** n expiación f.

atrocious [ə'trouʃəs] adj atroz. **atrocity** n atrocidad f.

attach [ə'tatʃ] v atar, adherir, pegar. **attach oneself to** asociarse con. **attachment** n unión f; (hook) enganche m; (friendship) amistad f.

attaché [əˈtaʃei] n agregado m. **attaché case** maletín m.

attack [əˈtak] v atacar. n ataque m; (mil) ofensiva f. **attacker** n atacador, -a m, f.

attain [əˈtein] v lograr, alcanzar. **attainable** adj asequible, realizable. **attainment** n logro m. **attainments** pl n prendas f pl.

attempt [əˈtempt] n tentativa f. v procurar, tratar de.

attend [əˈtend] v atender, servir; concurrir; (the sick) asistir; (listen) escuchar. **attendance** n servicio m, asistencia f; (audience) auditorio m. **attendant** n criado, -a m, f, servidor, -a m, f.

attention [əˈtenʃən] n atención f. **call attention to** destacar, hacer presente. **pay attention** prestar atención. **attentive** adj atento, cortés. **attentiveness** n cuidado m.

attic [ˈatik] n desván m, sotabanco m.

attire [əˈtaiə] n atavío m, ropaje m, traje m, adorno m. v ataviar, vestir.

attitude [ˈatitjud] n actitud f, postura f, ademán m.

attorney [əˈtəːni] n (agent) apoderado, -a m, f; (solicitor) abogado, -a m, f. **power of attorney** poderes m pl.

attract [əˈtrakt] v atraer, llamar. **attraction** n atracción f, imán m. **attractive** adj atractivo, atrayente.

attribute [ˈatribjut; v əˈtribjut] n atributo m. v atribuir. **attributable** adj atribuible. **attribution** n atributo m.

attrition [əˈtriʃən] n atrición f.

atypical [eiˈtipikl] adj atípico.

aubergine [ˈoubəʒiːn] n berenjena f.

auburn [ˈɔːbən] adj castaño rojizo.

auction [ˈɔːkʃən] n remate m, almoneda f, subasta f. v rematar, subastar. **auctioneer** n subastador m.

audacious [ɔːˈdeiʃəs] adj audaz, arrojado. **audacity** n audacia f, arrojo m, atrevimiento m.

audible [ˈɔːdəbl] adj audible. **audibility** n audibilidad f.

audience [ˈɔːdjəns] n audiencia f; oyentes m pl.

audiovisual [ɔːdiouˈviʒuəl] adj audiovisual.

audit [ˈɔːdit] v intervenir. n intervención f, ajuste (de cuentas) m. **auditor** n inteventor m, contador m.

audition [ɔːˈdiʃən] n audición f. v dar audición.

auditorium [ɔːdiˈtɔːriəm] n auditorio m, sala de espectáculos f.

augment [ɔːgˈment] v aumentar, engrosar; acrecentarse.

august [ɔːˈgast] adj augusto.

August [ˈɔːgəst] n agosto m.

aunt [aːnt] n tía f. **great-aunt** n tía abuela f.

aura [ˈɔːrə] n aura f; exhalación f.

auspicious [ɔːˈspiʃəs] adj propicio.

austere [ɔːˈstiə] adj austero, severo. **austerity** n austeridad f, severidad f.

Australia [ɔːˈstreiljə] n Australia f. **Australian** n, adj australiano, -a.

Austria [ˈɔːstriə] n Austria f. **Austrian** n, adj austríaco, -a.

authentic [ɔːˈθentik] adj auténtico.

author [ˈɔːθə] n autor, -a m, f.

authority [ɔːˈθɔrəti] n autoridad f. **on good authority** de buena fuente. **authoritarian** adj autoritario.

authorize [ˈɔːθəraiz] v autorizar. **authorization** n autorización f.

autobiography [ɔːtoubaiˈɔgrəfi] n autobiografía f. **autobiographical** adj autobiográfico.

autocratic [ɔːtouˈkratik] adj autocrático. **autocrat** n autócrata m, f.

autograph [ˈɔːtəgraːf] n autógrafo m. v firmar, dedicar.

automatic [ɔːtəˈmatik] adj automático. **automation** n automatización f.

automobile [ˈɔːtəməbiːl] n automóvil m.

autonomous [ɔːˈtɔnəməs] adj autónomo.

autopsy [ˈɔːtɔpsi] n autopsia f.

autumn [ˈɔːtəm] n otoño m. **autumnal** adj otoñal.

auxiliary [ɔːgˈziljəri] adj auxiliar. n auxiliador m.

avail [əˈveil] v servir, valer, importar; aprovechar. **avail oneself of** aprovecharse de. **to no avail** en balde.

available [əˈveiləbl] adj útil, disponible. **availability** n utilidad f, disponibilidad f.

avalanche [ˈavəlɑːnʃ] n avalancha f, alud m.

avarice [ˈavəris] n avaricia f, codicia f. **avaricious** adj avariento.

avenge [əˈvendʒ] v vengar, vindicar. **avenge oneself** vengarse de. **avenger** n vengador, -a m, f.

avenue [ˈavinjuː] n avenida f.

average [ˈavəridʒ] n promedio m, término medio m. adj de promedio, corriente. v hallar el término medio. **on average** por regla general.

aversion [ə'vɜːʃən] *n* aversión *f.* **averse** *adj* opuesto. **be averse to** ser enemigo de.

avert [ə'vɜːt] *v* apartar; (*avoid*) evitar.

aviary ['eivɪəri] *n* averia *f.*

aviation [eivi'eiʃən] *n* aviación *f.* **aviator** *n* aviador, -a *m. f.*

avid ['avid] *adj* ávido, codicioso, voraz. **avidity** *n* avidez *f.* codicia *f.*

avocado [avə'kɑːdou] *n* aguacate *m.*

avoid [ə'void] *v* evitar, eludir, evadir. **avoidance** *n* evitación *f.*

await [ə'weit] *v* esperar, aguardar.

*awake [ə'weik] *v* despertar; despertarse. *adj* despierto, atento (a). **awakening** *n* despertamiento *m.*

award [ə'wɔːd] *n* fallo *m,* premio *m,* recompensa *f. v* otorgar, conceder, conferir.

aware [ə'weə] *adj* enterado, vigilante, consciente. **become aware of** darse cuenta de. **make aware of** hacer saber. **awareness** *n* conocimiento *m.*

away [ə'wei] *adv* a lo lejos, ausente, fuera, en otro lugar.

awe [ɔː] *n* temor *m,* pasmo *m;* reverencia *f. v* intimidar, atemorizar. **awesome** *adj* pavoroso, imponente.

awful ['ɔːful] *adj* tremendo, atroz, terrible, espantoso. **how awful!** ¡qué barbaridad! **awfully** *adv* (*coll*) muy.

awkward ['ɔːkwəd] *adj* difícil; (*clumsy*) desmañado; (*ungraceful*) sin gracia.

awl [ɔːl] *n* punzón *m,* lezna *f.*

awning ['ɔːniŋ] *n* toldo *m.*

axe [aks] *n* hacha *f.*

axiom ['aksiəm] *n* axioma *m.*

axis ['aksis] *n* eje *m.*

axle ['aksl] *n* eje *m,* peón *m,* árbol *m.*

B

babble ['babl] *v* balbucear; garlar. *n* murmullo *m,* cháchara *f.*

baboon [bə'buːn] *n* babuino *m.*

baby ['beibi] *n* bebé *m,* criatura *f,* nene *m;* (*animals*) crío *m.* **babyhood** *n* niñez *f.* **babyish** *adj* infantil.

bachelor ['batʃələ] *n* soltero *m;* (*of Arts or Science*) licenciado *m,* bachiller *m.*

back [bak] *n* (*anat*) espalda *f;* dorso *m;* (*sport*) defensa *f. adj* trasero, posterior, de atrás; (*of pay, etc.*) atrasado. *adv* atrás; detrás; otra vez, de nuevo. *v* retroceder; (*support*) apoyar; (*bet on*) apostar a. **back down** abandonar. **back out** echarse atrás; (*retract*) desdecirse.

backache ['bakeik] *n* dolor de espaldas *m.*

backbone ['bakboun] *n* espinazo *m.*

backdate [,bak'deit] *v* poner fecha atrasada.

backfire [,bak'faiə] *n* petardeo *m. v* petardear.

backgammon ['bakgamən] *n* chaquete *m.*

backhand ['bakhand] *n* (*sport*) revés *m.* **back-handed** *adj* de revés; (*fig*) ambiguo.

backing ['bakiŋ] *n* forro *m;* (*support*) apoyo *m;* (*lining*) refuerzo *m;* (*betting*) el apostar (a) *m.*

backlash ['baklaʃ] *n* reacción *f.*

backlog ['baklog] *n* atrasos *m pl.*

backside ['baksaid] *n* trasero *m,* parte trasera *f.*

backward ['bakwəd] *adj* atrasado, vuelto hacia atrás. **backwardness** *n* atraso *m,* torpeza *f.* **backward and forward** de acá para allá.

backwards ['bakwədz] *adv* hacia atrás, al revés.

backwater ['bakwɔtə] *n* (*pool*) remanso *m.*

bacon ['beikən] *n* tocino *m.*

bacteria [bak'tiəriə] *n pl* bacteria *f pl.*

bad [bad] *adj* malo; (*ill*) enfermo; (*rotten*) podrido; (*debt*) incobrable; (*dangerous*) peligroso; (*coin*) falso; (*pain*) fuerte; (*unlucky*) desgraciado. **bad-tempered** *adj* de mal genio. **from bad to worse** de mal en peor. **badly** *adv* mal; (*seriously*) gravemente.

badge [badʒ] *n* insignia *f.* marca *f.* divisa *f.*

badger ['badʒə] *n* tejón *m. v* molestar.

badminton ['badmintən] *n* volante *m,* badminton *m.*

baffle ['bafl] *v* frustrar, desconcertar, confundir. **baffling** *adj* desconcertante, difícil; (*person*) enigmático.

bag [bag] *n* bolsa *f,* saco *m,* valija *f.* (*sewing*) costurera *f;* (*suitcase*) maleta *f. v* ensacar; (*coll, esp. game*) matar, tomar. **pack one's bags** liar el petate. **baggage** *m* equipaje *m.*

baggy ['bagi] *adj* holgado.

bagpipes ['bagpaips] *n pl* gaita *f.*

bail¹ [beil] *n* (*law*) fianza *f,* caución *f. v* poner bajo fianza.

bail² *or* **bale** [beil] *v* **bail out** (*flooded boat*) achicar, baldear; (*from aircraft*) lanzarse en paracaídas.

bailiff ['beilif] *n* (*law*) alguacil *m;* (*of estate*) capataz *m.*

bait [beit] *n* (*fishing*) cebo *m,* anzuelo *m;* (*lure*) añagaza *f. v* cebar, azuzar; (*annoy*) molestar.

bake [beik] *v* cocer al horno. **baker's dozen** la docena del fraile *f.* **baker** *m* panadero *m.* **bakery** *n* panadería *f.* **baking powder** levadura en polvo *f.*

balance ['balans] *n* equilibrio *m;* (*scales*) balanza *f;* (*comm*) balance *m. v* equilibrar; (*comm*) saldar.

balcony ['balkəni] *n* balcón *m,* galería *f;* (*theatre*) anfiteatro *m.*

bald [bo:ld] *adj* calvo, pelado; (*tyre*) desgastado. **baldness** *n* calvicie *f.*

bale¹ [beil] *n* fardo *m,* bala *f. v* embalar.

bale² *V* **bail²**.

ball¹ [bo:l] *n* pelota *f,* globo *m,* bola *f;* (*shot*) bala *f;* (*of wool*) ovillo *m;* (*of the foot*) planta del pie *f.* **ball-and-socket joint** articulación esférica *f.* **ball bearings** cojinete de bolas *m sing.* **ball-point pen** bolígrafo *m.*

ball² [bo:l] *n* (*dance*) baile *m.* **fancy-dress ball** baile de disfraces. **ballroom** *n* salón de baile *m.*

ballad ['baləd] *n* balada *f,* romance *m,* trova *f;* (*music*) canción *f.*

ballast ['baləst] *n* lastre. *v* lastrar.

ballet [balei] *n* ballet *m,* danza *f.* **ballet dancer** bailarín, bailarina *m, f.*

ballistic [bə'listik] *adj* balístico. **ballistic missile** proyectil balístico *m.*

balloon [bə'lu:n] *n* globo *m.* **balloonist** *n* aeronauta *m, f.*

ballot ['balət] *n* votación *f,* sufragio *m. v* votar, balotar. **ballot-box** *n* urna electoral *f.*

bamboo [bam'bu:] *n* bambú *m.*

ban [ban] *n* prohibición *f,* interdicción *f. v* prohibir, proscribir.

banal [bə'na:l] *adj* trivial, trillado.

banana [bə'na:nə] *n* (*fruit and tree*) plátano *m;* (*S. Am.*) (*fruit*) banana, (*tree*) banano *m.*

band¹ [band] *n* (*troop*) grupo *m,* banda *f;* (*music*) orquesta *f,* banda *f. v* congregar, unir, asociar.

band² [band] *n* (*strip*) lista *f,* tira *f,* banda *f.*

bandage ['bandidʒ] *n* venda *f. v* vendar.

bandit ['bandit] *n* bandido *m.*

bandy ['bandi] *adj also* **bandy-legged** estevado. *v* trocar.

bang [baŋ] *n* golpazo *m,* detonación *f,* golpe *m. v* golpear, estallar.

bangle [baŋl] *n* ajorca *f,* pulsera *f,* brazalete *m.*

banish ['baniʃ] *v* desterrar, despedir, exilar, deportar. **banishment** *n* destierro *m.*

banister ['banistə] *n* baranda *f,* pasamano *m.*

banjo ['bandʒou] *n* banjo *m.*

bank¹ [baŋk] *n* (*of river, etc.*) ribera *f,* orilla *f,* margen *m.*

bank² [baŋk] *n* banco *m.* **bank account** cuenta bancaria *f.* **bank holiday** día festivo *m. v* depositar en el banco. **banker** *n* banquero *m.*

bankrupt ['baŋkrʌpt] *n* quebrado, -a *m, f. adj* insolvente, quebrado. **go bankrupt** hacer bancarrota, declararse en quiebra. **bankruptcy** *n* bancarrota *f,* quiebra *f.*

banner ['banə] *n* bandera *f,* estandarte *m.*

banns [banz] *n pl* amonestaciones *f pl.* **publish the banns** decir las amonestaciones.

banquet ['baŋkwit] *m* banquete *m. v* banquetear.

bantam ['bantəm] *n* gallina enana *f.* **bantamweight** *n* peso gallo *m.*

banter ['bantə] *n* burla *f,* chanza *f. v* burlarse, tomar el pelo a.

baptize [bap'taiz] *v* bautizar. **baptism** *n* bautismo *m.* **baptist** *n* bautista *m.* **baptistry** *n* baptisterio *m,* bautisterio *m.*

bar [ba:] *n* barra *f;* (*soap, chocolate, etc.*) pastilla *f;* (*music*) barra *f,* compás *m;* (*barrier*) barrera *f;* (*refreshments*) bar *m;* (*law*) foro *m,* curia *f;* (*bank*) atrancar, obstruir, impedir. **barman** *n* mozo de bar *m.* **barmaid** *n* camarera *f.*

barb [ba:b] *n* púa *f;* (*fish-hook*) lengüeta *f.* **barbarian** [ba:'beəriən] *n, adj* bárbaro, -a *m, f.* **barbaric** *adj* bárbárico. **barbarity** *n* barbaridad *f.*

barbecue ['ba:bikju:] *n* barbacoa *f.*

barber ['ba:bə] *n* barbero *m,* peluquero *m.* **barber's shop** barbería *f,* peluquería *f.*

barbiturate [ba:'bitjurət] *n* barbitúrico *m.*

bare [beə] *adj* desnudo, descubierto. *v* desnudar, descubrir. **barefaced** *adj*

descarado. **barefoot** *adj* descalzo. **bare-
headed** *adj* sin sombrero. **barely** *adv*
apenas.

bargain ['baɪgin] *n* (*cheap*) ganga *f*;
(*agreement*) pacto *m*, ajuste *m*, convenio
m. *v* negociar, regatear. **bargain sale**
saldo *m*. **into the bargain** por más señas.

barge [baɪdʒ] *n* barca *f*, bote *m*, barcaza
f. **barge in** irrumpir. **barge into** entremeterse.

baritone ['baritoun] *n* barítono *m*.

bark¹ [baɪk] *n* (*dog*) ladrido *m*. *v* ladrar.

bark² [baɪk] *n* (*tree*) corteza *f*.

barley ['baɪli] *n* cebada *f*. **barley water** *n*
hordiate *m*.

barn [baɪn] *n* granero *m*, pajar *m*.

barometer [bə'rɒmitə] *n* barómetro *m*.

baron ['barən] *n* barón *m*. **baroness** *n*
baronesa *f*. **baronet** *n* baronet *m*.

baroque [bə'rɒk] *adj* barroco.

barracks ['barəks] *pl n* cuartel *m*, barraca
f.

barrage ['baraɪʒ] *n* presa *f*; (*mil*)
bombardeo *m*, cortina de fuego *f*.

barrel ['barəl] *n* (*cask*) barril *m*; (*gun*,
etc.) cañón *m*. **barrel organ** organillo *m*.

barren ['barən] *adj* (*land*) yermo, árido;
estéril. **barrenness** *n* aridez *f*; esterilidad
f.

barricade [bari'keid] *n* barrera *f*, barricada *f*, empalizada *f*. *v* barrear, obstruir.

barrier ['bariə] *n* barrera *f*; impedimento
m; valla *f*.

barrister ['baristə] *n* abogado, -a *m*, *f*.

barrow ['barou] *n* carretilla *f*.

barter ['baɪtə] *v* cambiar, trocar. *n*
trueque *m*, cambio *m*, tráfico *m*.

base¹ [beis] *n* base *f*, fundamento *m*, pie
m. *v* fundar, apoyarse, basar. **baseless**
adj sin base.

base² [beis] *adj* bajo, vil, impuro. **base-
ness** *n* bajeza *f*, vileza *f*.

baseball ['beisbɔɪl] *n* béisbol *m*.

basement ['beismənt] *n* sótano *m*.

bash [baʃ] *n* golpe *m*. *v* golpear.

bashful ['baʃful] *adj* vergonzoso, tímido,
encogido. **bashfulness** *n* vergüenza *f*,
encogimiento *m*.

basic ['beisik] *adj* fundamental; (*chem*)
básico.

basil ['bazl] *n* albahaca *f*.

basilica [bə'zilikə] *n* basílica *f*.

basin ['beisin] *n* bacía *f*, jofaina *f*; (*wash-
basin*) palangana *f*; (*dock*) dársena *f*;
(*river*) cuenca *f*.

basis ['beisis] *n* base *f*, fundamento *m*.

bask [bask] *v* calentarse.

basket ['baskit] *n* cesta *f*, canasta *f*. **basketball** *n* baloncesto *m*.

Basque [bask] *n*, *adj* vasco, -a *m*, *f*; (*language*) vascuence *m*.

bas-relief ['basri,liɪf] *n* bajorrelieve *m*.

bass¹ [beis] *n* (*voice*) bajo *m*. **bass clef** *n*
clave de fa *f*.

bass² [bas] *n* (*freshwater*) róbalo *m*; (*sea*)
lobina *f*.

bassoon [bə'suɪn] *n* bajón *m*.

bastard ['baɪstəd] *n* bastardo, -a *m*, *f*.

baste [beist] *v* (*cookery*) enlardar, pringar; (*sewing*) bastear, hilvanar.

bastion ['bastjən] *n* bastión *m*, baluarte
m.

bat¹ [bat] *n* maza *f*, palo *m*; (*cricket*)
paleta *f*; (*table tennis*) pala *f*. *v* golpear
con le paleta.

bat² [bat] *n* (*zool*) murciélago *m*.

batch [batʃ] *n* grupo *m*; (*loaves*) hornada
f.

bath [baɪθ] *n* baño *m*. *v* bañar, lavar,
tomar un baño. **bath-chair** *n* cochecillo
de inválido *m*. **bathrobe** *n* albornoz *m*.
bathroom *n* cuarto de baño *m*. **bathtowel**
n toalla de baño *f*. **swimming baths** *n pl*
piscina *f* *sing*.

bathe [beið] *v* bañar, bañarse. **bathing cap**
gorra de baño *f*. **bathing costume** traje de
baño *m*. **bathing pool** piscina *f*. **bathing
trunks** pantalones de baño *m pl*.

baton ['batn] *n* (*mil*) bastón de mando *m*;
(*police*) porra *f*; (*music*) batuta *f*.

battalion [bə'taljən] *n* batallón *m*.

batter¹ ['batə] *v* apalear, golpear, derribar.

batter² ['batə] *n* (*cookery*) batido *m*, pasta
f.

battery ['batəri] *n* (*elec*) pila *f*, batería *f*;
(*mil*) batería; (*law*) agresión *f*. **storage
battery** acumulador *m*. **battery cell** pila
de batería eléctrica *f*.

battle ['batl] *n* batalla *f*, combate *m*. *v*
batallar, luchar. **battlefield** *n* campo de
batalla *m*. **battlement** *n* almenaje *m*. **bat-
tleship** *n* buque de guerra *m*.

bawdy ['bɔɪdi] *adj* obsceno, escabroso.

bawl [bɔɪl] *v* vocear.

bay¹ [bei] *n* (*geog*) bahía *f*.

bay² [bei] *v* (*cry*) aullar. **at bay** acor-
ralado.

bay³ [bei] *n* (*tree*) laurel *m*.

bayonet ['beiənit] *n* bayoneta *f*. *v* dar un bayonetazo.

bay window *n* mirador *m*.

bazaar [bə'zɑː] *n* bazar *m*.

*****be** [biː] *v* ser, existir; estar; (*place*) encontrarse, quedar.

beach [biːtʃ] *n* playa *f*; costa *f*. *v* varar, encallar en la costa.

beacon ['biːkən] *n* fanal *m*, faro *m*; (*naut*) boya *f*.

bead [biːd] *n* cuenta *f*, perla *f*, gota *f*. **beads** *n pl* rosario *m sing*.

beagle ['biːgl] *n* sabueso *m*.

beak [biːk] *n* pico *m*; punta *f*. **beaked** *adj* picudo.

beaker ['biːkə] *n* vaso *m*, copa *f*.

beam [biːm] *n* (*light*) rayo *m*, destello *m*; (*arch*) madero *m*; (*width of a ship*) manga *f*; (*smile*) sonrisa brillante *f*. *v* irradiar; (*smile*) sonreír radiantemente.

bean [biːn] *n* (*broad*) haba *f*; (*black*) fréjol *m*; (*kidney*) habichuela *f*, alubia *f*, judía *f*.

*****bear¹** [beə] *v* soportar, aguantar, sufrir; (*carry*) llevar; (*have*) tener, (*fruit*) dar; (*give birth to*) parir; (*a strain*) resistir. **bear in mind** tener presente. **bearing** *n* porte *m*, aspecto *m*; relación *f*.

bear² [beə] *n* oso *m*.

beard [biəd] *n* barba *f*. *v* enfrentarse con, mesar la barba a. **bearded** *adj* barbudo. **beardless** *adj* imberbe.

bearings ['beəriŋz] *n pl* situación *f sing*, relación *f sing*, camino *m sing*. **lose one's bearings** desorientarse, desatinar. **take one's bearings** orientarse.

beast [biːst] *n* bestia *f*; res *f*; (*wild*) fiera *f*. **beastly** *adj* bestial; desagradable.

*****beat** [biːt] *v* batir; (*games*) derrotar, vencer; (*with weapon*) golpear; (*carpet*) sacudir. **beat down** atropellar. *n* (*med*) latido *m*, pulsación *f*; golpe *m*; (*music*) compás *m*.

beauty ['bjuːti] *n* hermosura *f*, belleza *f*; (*coll*) lo mejor. **beauty spot** lunar *m*. **beautiful** *adj* bello, hermoso; guapo. **beautify** *v* embellecer.

beaver ['biːvə] *n* castor *m*.

because [bi'kɔz] *conj* porque. **because of** a causa de.

beckon ['bekən] *v* llamar con señas, atraer, invitar.

*****become** [bi'kʌm] *v* convenir; llegar a ser, ponerse; hacerse. **becoming** *adj* que sienta bien, propio, decoroso. **becomingly** *adv* con gracia.

bed [bed] *n* cama *f*, lecho *m*; (*coal, etc.*) yacimiento *m*; (*flowers*) macizo *m*. **bedding** *n* ropa de cama *f*. **bedroom** *n* dormitorio *m*. **bedsitter** *n* salón con cama *m*. **bedspread** *n* colcha *f*.

bedbug ['bedbʌg] *n* chinche *f*.

bedraggled [bi'dragld] *adj* mojado y sucio, enlodado.

bee [biː] *n* abeja *f*. **bee line** línea recta *f*. **beehive** *n* colmena *f*. **bumble-bee** *n* abejorro *m*.

beech [biːtʃ] *n* (*tree*) haya *f*; (*nut*) hayuco *m*.

beef [biːf] *n* carne de vaca *f*. **roast beef** rosbif *m*.

been [biːn] *V* be.

beer [biə] *n* cerveza *f*.

beetle ['biːtl] *n* (*zool*) escarabajo *m*; (*tech*) pisón *m*. **death-watch beetle** carcoma *f*. **beetle-browed** *adj* cejijunto.

beetroot ['biːtruːt] *n* remolacha *f*.

before [bi'fɔː] *adv* delante; al frente; (*time*) antes; (*already*) ya. *prep* delante de; frente de; (*time*) ante; (*rather than*) antes de. *conj* antes (que). **beforehand** *adv* de antemano.

befriend [bi'frend] *v* favorecer, amistar, proteger, ayudar.

beg [beg] *v* pedir, suplicar; mendigar. **I beg your pardon?** ¿cómo dice? **I beg your pardon!** ¡Vd dispense! **beg the question** dejar a un lado. **beggar** *n* mendigo *m*.

*****begin** [bi'gin] *v* comenzar, empezar, iniciar. **to begin with** en primer lugar. **beginner** *n* principiante, -a *m, f*. **beginning** *n* principio *m*.

begrudge [bi'grʌdʒ] *v* envidiar; conceder de mala gana.

beguile [bi'gail] *v* engañar; (*charm*) encantar.

behalf [bi'hɑːf] *n* provecho *m*. **on behalf of** en nombre de, a favor de.

behave [bi'heiv] *v* comportarse, manejarse, portarse; funcionar, obrar. **behaviour** *n* comportamiento *m*, conducta *f*; funcionamiento *m*.

behead [bi'hed] *v* decapitar.

behind [bi'haind] *adv* atrás, detrás, hacia atrás; (*time*) después; (*late*) con retraso. *prep* detrás de, por detrás de. *n* (*coll*) trasero *m*. **fall behind** retrasarse. **behind the times** pasado de moda.

*behold [bi'hould] v mirar, contemplar. interj ¡aquí está!, ¡he aquí!

beige [beiʒ] adj beige.

being ['biiŋ] n ser m, existencia f, estado m. human being ser humano m. well-being n bienestar m.

belated [bi'leitid] adj tardío.

belch [beltʃ] n eructo m. v eructar, arrojar.

belfry ['belfri] n campanario m.

Belgium ['beldʒəm] m Bélgica f. Belgian n(m+f). adj belga.

believe [bi'liːv] v creer, pensar; opinar. believer n creyente m, f, fiel m. belief n, pl -s creencia f; opinión f.

bell [bel] n campana f, campanilla f; (electric) timbre m; (hand) esquila f.

belligerent [bi'lidʒərənt] n, adj beligerante, -a m, f.

bellow ['belou] v bramar, rugir. n bramido m.

bellows ['belouz] n pl fuelle m sing.

belly ['beli] n barriga f, panza f, vientre m. bellyful n hartón m.

belong [bi'loŋ] v pertenecer, tocar a. belong to ser de. belongings n pl bienes m pl.

beloved [bi'lʌvid] n amado, -a m, f, querido, -a m, f. favorito, -a m, f.

below [bi'lou] adv abajo, debajo. prep (por) debajo de.

belt [belt] n cinturón m, cinto m, faja f; (tech) correa f; (geog) zona f. v ceñir, rodear, fajar.

bench [bentʃ] n banco m, banca f, escaño m, (law) tribunal m.

*bend [bend] v torcer, doblar; inclinar, encorvar. n recodo m, curva f.

beneath [bi'niːθ] adv abajo, debajo. (prep) bajo, debajo de. beneath regard indigno de consideración.

benefactor ['benəfæktə] n bienhechor m, patrono m.

benefit ['benəfit] n beneficio m, provecho m. v beneficiar. beneficial adj ventajoso. beneficiary n beneficiario m.

benevolent [bi'nevələnt] adj benévolo; caritativo. benevolence n benevolencia f, caridad f.

benign [bi'nain] adj benigno.

bent [bent] adj torcido, encorvado; (on a course of action) resuelto (a); (fam) invertido. n talento m, inclinación f.

bequeath [bi'kwiːð] v legar; transmitir. bequest n legado m.

bereaved [bi'riːvd] adj afligido. bereave v quitar; afligir. bereavement n pérdida f, aflicción f.

beret ['berei] n boina f.

berry ['beri] n baya f, grano m.

berserk [bə'sɑːk] adj demente.

berth [bəːθ] n camarote m; (dock) fondeadero m. v fondear. give a wide berth to apartarse de.

beside [bi'said] prep junto a, cerca de. beside oneself fuera de sí. beside the point no venir al caso. besides adv (as well) también; (moreover) además.

besiege [bi'siːdʒ] v asediar, sitiar.

bespoke [bi'spouk] adj hecho a medida. bespeak v reservar.

best [best] adj, adv mejor. at best a lo mejor. do one's best hacer todo lo posible. make the best of sacar el mayor provecho de. best man padrino de boda m. best-seller n éxito de librería m.

bestow [bi'stou] v conferir, otorgar.

*bet [bet] v apostar; jugar. n apuesta f, postura f. better, bettor n apostador, -a m, f. betting shop establecimiento de apuesta m.

betray [bi'trei] v traicionar; engañar; revelar. betrayal n traición f.

better ['betə] adj, adv mejor. get better mejorarse. better half (coll) media naranja f. better off mejor situado. so much the better tanto mejor. v mejorarse.

between [bi'twiːn] prep entre. adv entre los dos. far between a grandes intervalos. between ourselves entre nosotros.

beverage ['bevəridʒ] n bebida f, brebaje m.

*beware [bi'weə] v tener cuidado de. interj ¡atención!

bewilder [bi'wildə] v desconcertar, aturrullar, aturdir. bewilderment n aturdimiento m, anonadamiento m.

beyond [bi'jond] adv más allá, más lejos. prep superior a, fuera de. beyond doubt fuera de duda. beyond measure sobremanera. beyond question indiscutible.

bias ['baiəs] n sesgo m, través m; propensión f, prejuicio m. v influir, predisponer. biased adj predispuesto. cut on the bias contar al sesgo.

bib [bib] n babero m, pechera f.

Bible ['baibl] n Biblia f. **biblical** adj bíblico.

bibliography [bibli'ɔgrəfi] n bibliografía f. **bibliographer** n bibliógrafo m. **bibliographical** adj bibliográfico.

biceps ['baiseps] n bíceps m.

bicker ['bikə] v disputar, reñir, altercar. **bickering** n altercado m.

bicycle ['baisikl] n bicicleta f.

*****bid** [bid] v ofrecer, pujar; (command) mandar; rogar. n oferta f; (attempt) tentativa f. **make a bid for** procurar. **no bid** (cards) paso. **bidder** n postor m.

bidet ['biːdei] n bidé m.

biennial [bai'eniəl] adj bienal, bianual.

bifocals [bai'foukəlz] pl n lentes bifocales m pl.

big [big] adj grande; grueso; abultado; importante.

bigamy ['bigəmi] n bigamia f. **bigamist** n bígamo, -a m, f. **bigamous** adj bígamo.

bigot ['bigət] n beatón, -ona m, f. fanático, -a m, f. **bigoted** adj fanático, intolerante. **bigotry** n fanatismo m, intolerancia f.

bikini [bi'kiːni] n bikini m.

bilingual [bai'lingwəl] adj bilingüe.

bilious ['biljəs] adj bilioso. **bile** n bilis f.

bill¹ [bil] n (comm) cuenta f, factura f; (poster) cartel m; (pol) proyecto de ley m; anuncio m. **billboard** n cartelera f. **bill of lading** conocimiento de embarque m. **bill of sale** escritura de venta f. v enviar una cuenta; anunciar. **bill and coo** arrullar; (coll) besuquearse.

bill² [bil] n (beak) pico m.

billiards ['biljədz] n billar m.

billion ['biljən] n (10¹²) billón m; (10⁹) mil millones m pl.

bin [bin] n arcón m, hucha f; papelera f; (wine) estante m.

binary ['bainəri] adj binario.

*****bind** [baind] v atar; ligar, unir; (bandage) vendar; (sheaves) agavillar, (books) encuadernar; (captive) aprisionar; (sewing) ribetear; (oblige) comprometer. **binding** n (books) encuadernación f; atadura f. adj válido; obligatorio.

binge [bindʒ] n (coll) parranda f. **go on the binge** ir de parranda.

binoculars [bi'nɔkjuləz] pl n binóculos m pl, prismáticos m pl, gemelos m pl.

biography [bai'ɔgrəfi] n biografía f. **biographer** n biógrafo, -a m, f. **biographical** adj biográfico.

biology [bai'ɔlədʒi] n biología f. **biological** adj biológico. **biologist** n biólogo m.

birch [bəːtʃ] n abedul m. v varear.

bird [bəːd] n pájaro m, ave f; (slang) chica f. **bird's eye view** vista de pájaro f. **birdcage** n jaula f. **birdseed** n alpiste m.

birth [bəːθ] n nacimiento m, parto m; linaje m; comienzo m. **give birth to** dar a luz; parir. **birth certificate** partida de nacimiento f. **birth control** anticoncepcionismo m. **birthday** n cumpleaños m. **birthplace** n lugar de nacimiento m. **birthrate** n natalidad f. **birthright** n herencia f.

biscuit ['biskit] n bizcocho m, galleta f.

bishop ['biʃəp] n obispo m; (chess) alfil m.

bison ['baisən] n bisonte m.

bit¹ [bit] n (drill) barrena f, taladro m; (horse) bocado m. **take the bit between one's teeth** desbocarse.

bit² [bit] n pedazo m, poco m, trocito m; (time) ratito m; (jot) jota f. **bit by bit** poco a poco. **not a bit** nada de eso.

bitch [bitʃ] n (dog) perra f; (slang) zorra f.

*****bite** [bait] v morder; (insect, etc.) picar. n mordedura f; picadura f. **biting** adj (remark, etc.) mordaz.

bitter ['bitə] adj amargo, áspero. **to the bitter end** hasta la muerte. **bitterness** n amargura f.

bizarre [bi'zaː] adj extravagante, grotesco.

black [blak] n, adj negro, -a m, f. **blacken** v ennegrecer; (character) denigrar.

blackberry ['blakbəri] n (bush) zarza f; (fruit) zarzamora f.

blackbird ['blakbəːd] n mirlo m.

blackboard ['blakbɔːd] n pizarra f.

blackcurrant [,blak'kʌrənt] n grosella negra f.

black eye n ojo a la funerala m.

blackhead ['blakhed] n espinilla f.

blackleg ['blakleg] n esquirol m.

blackmail ['blakmeil] n chantaje m. v hacer chantaje. **blackmailer** n chantajista m, f.

black market n mercado negro m.

blackout ['blakaut] n apagón m, apagamiento m; (fainting) desmayo m.

black pudding n morcilla f.

blacksmith ['blaksmiθ] n herrero m.

bladder ['bladə] n vejiga f.

blade [bleid] n (grass) brizna f; (razor) hoja f; (propeller) paleta f; (oar) pala f.

blow

blame [bleim] *n* culpa *f*. *v* culpar. **blameless** *adj* inculpable. **blameworthy** *adj* culpable.

bland [bland] *adj* afable; dulce.

blank [blaŋk] *adj* en blanco; (*empty*) vacío; confuso. *n* blanco *m*, hueco *m*; vacío *m*. **blank cartridge** cartucho para salvas *m*. **blank verse** verso libre *m*, verso suelto *m*.

blanket ['blaŋkit] *n* manta *f*, frazada *f*; (*of dust*) capa *f*. *v* cubrir con manta. *adj* comprensivo.

blare [bleə] *v* vociferar, rugir. *n* trompetazo *m*, fragor *m*; estrépito *m*.

blaspheme [blas'fi:m] *v* blasfemia. **blasphemer** *n* blasfemador, -a *m, f*. **blasphemous** *adj* blasfemo. **blasphemy** *n* blasfemia *f*.

blast [blast] *n* explosión *f*; (*trumpet*) trompetazo *m*; (*wind*) ráfaga *f*. *v* (*rocks*) barrenar; (*wither*) marchitar; (*curse*) maldecir. **full blast** en plena marcha. **blast furnace** alto horno *m*.

blatant ['bleitant] *adj* discarado, vocinglero, llamativo.

blaze [bleiz] *n* incendio *m*, llamarada *f*, conflagración *f*. *v* llamear, flamear; arder. **blaze a trail** abrir un camino. **blaze of colour** masa de color *f*. **blazer** *n* chaqueta deportiva *f*.

bleach [bli:tʃ] *v* blanquear, descolorar. *n* lejía *f*.

bleak [bli:k] *adj* desabrido, desierto, crudo; (*prospect*) sombrío.

bleat [bli:t] *v* balar. *n* balido *m*.

*****bleed** [bli:d] *v* sangrar. **bleed to death** morir desangrado. **bleeding** *n* hemorragia *f*.

blemish ['blemiʃ] *n* mácula *f*, defecto *m*, mancha *f*. *v* empañar, manchar.

blend [blend] *v* mezclar, combinar, fundir; (*colour*) matizar. *n* mezcla *f*, combinación *f*.

bless [bles] *v* bendecir; consagrar; favorecer. **blessedness** *n* felicidad *f*. **blessing** *n* bendición *f*; merced *f*; favor *m*.

blew [blu:] *V* blow².

blight [blait] *n* (*plants*) tizne *m*; (*fig*) influencia maligna *f*. *v* atizonar; (*fig*) malograr.

blind [blaind] *adj* ciego. *n* pretexto *m*; (*window*) persiana *f*. *v* cegar. **blindness** *n* ceguera *f*. **turn a blind eye** hacer la vista gorda.

blindfold ['blaindfould] *n* venda *f*. *v* vendar los ojos de.

blink [bliŋk] *v* parpadear, pestañear, guiñar. *n* parpadeo *m*, guiño *m*; (*of light*) destello *m*. **blinkers** *pl n* anteojeras *f pl*.

bliss [blis] *n* bienaventuranza *f*, felicidad *f*. **blissful** *adj* bienaventurado, feliz.

blister ['blistə] *n* vesícula *f*, ampolla *f*. *v* ampollar.

blizzard ['blizəd] *n* ventisca *f*.

bloated ['bloutid] *adj* abotagado.

blob [blob] *n* gota *f*, goterón *m*; borrón *m*.

bloc [blok] *n* (*pol*) bloque *m*.

block [blok] *n* bloque *m*; (*butcher's*) tajo *m*; (*houses*) manzana *f*; (*obstruction*) atasco *m*. *v* bloquear, obstruir, cerrar el paso. **block and tackle** polea con aparejo *f*.

blockade [blo'keid] *n* bloqueo *m*. *v* bloquear.

bloke [blouk] *n* (*coll*) tío *m*, fulano *m*.

blond [blond] *adj* rubio. **blonde** *n* rubia *f*.

blood [blʌd] *n* sangre *f*; (*lineage*) parentesco *m*. **bloodless** *adj* exangüe. **blood donor** donante de sangre *m, f*. **blood group** grupo sanguíneo *m*. **blood poisoning** envenenamiento de la sangre *m*. **blood pressure** *n* presión arterial *f*. **bloodshed** *n* matanza *f*. **bloodshot** *adj* inyectado de sangre. **bloodstream** *n* corriente sanguínea *f*. **bloodthirsty** *adj* sanguinario. **bloody** *adj* sangriento; (*slang*) maldito.

bloom [blum] *n* flor *f*; florecimiento *m*; (*prime*) lozanía *f*. *v* florecer. **in bloom** en flor. **blooming** *adj* floreciente.

blossom ['blosəm] *n* flor *f*. *v* florecer.

blot [blot] *n* borrón *m*; mancha *f*. *v* manchar, tachar; (*dry*) secar. **blot out** borrar. **blotter** *n* libro borrador *m*. **blotting paper** papel secante *m*.

blotch [blotʃ] *n* mancha *f*; (*med*) erupción *f*. *v* manchar, ennegrecer.

blouse [blauz] *n* blusa *f*.

blow¹ [blou] *n* (*hit*) golpe *m*, bofetada *f*; (*shock*) choque *m*; (*misfortune*) revés *m*. **come to blows** venir a las manos.

*****blow²** [blou] *n* soplido *m*. *v* soplar, hacer viento; (*pant*) jadear; (*fuse*) fundirse; (*music*) tocar. **blow away** disipar. **blow one's nose** sonarse las narices. **blow out** (*a light*) apagar soplando. **blow up** (*explode*) volar; (*inflate*) inflar.

blubber ['blʌbə] n grasa de ballena f. v gimotear.

blue [bluː] adj azul; (mournful) deprimido; (obscene) verde. **bluebell** n campanilla f. **bluebottle** n moscón m. **blueprint** n fotocopia f, plan m.

bluff [blʌf] v fanfarronear. n fanfarronada f; (cliff) morro m, tisco m, peñasco m. adj campechano, brusco.

blunder ['blʌndə] n desatino m, yerro m. v desatinar; tropezar (con); (coll) meter la pata. **blunderer** n desatinado m.

blunt [blʌnt] adj desafilado, embotado; (abrupt) franco, descortés; (plain) claro. v despuntar, desafilar, embotar; (pain) mitigar. **bluntness** n embotamiento m.

blur [bləː] v empañar; emborronar. n borrón m. **blurred** adj borroso.

blush [blʌʃ] v ruborizarse, enrojecerse. n rubor m, sonrojo m; (of shame) bochorno m.

boar [boː] n jabalí m.

board [boːd] n tabla f; (chess, draughts) tablero m; (for notices) tablón m; (table) mesa f; (food) comida f; (committee) junta f, tribunal m; (naut) bordo m. v (carpentry) enmaderar, entablar; (embark) embarcarse en.

boast [boust] n jactancia f, alarde m, baladronada f. v jactarse, presumir. **boastful** adj jactancioso.

boat [bout] n bote m, lancha f, barca f; buque m, barco m. v navegar, ir en bote. **boatman** n barquero m. **boatswain** n contramaestre m. **lifeboat** n lancha de socorro f.

boater ['boutə] n (hat) canotié m, canotier m.

bob [bob] v bambolear, menear. n balanceo m; borla f.

bobbin ['bobin] n (sewing-machine, loom) bobina f.

bobsleigh ['bobslei] n trineo doble m. v ir en trineo.

bodice ['bodis] n corpiño m.

body ['bodi] n cuerpo m, masa f, entidad f; (corpse) cadáver m; (mot) carrocería f. **bodyguard** n guardia de corps f.

bog [bog] n pantano m.

bogus ['bougəs] adj espurio, fingido, falso.

bohemian [bə'hiːmiən] adj bohemio.

boil¹ [boil] v hervir. n hervor m. **boil over** irse. **boiler** n caldera f. **boiling point** punto de ebullición m.

boil² [boil] n divieso m, grano m, furúnculo m.

boisterous ['boistərəs] adj borrascoso, bullicioso. **boisterousness** n bullicio m.

bold [bould] adj osado, arrojado, atrevido; resuelto; (showy) llamativo. **bold-faced** adj descarado. **bold-faced type** letra negra f. **boldness** n temeridad f, intrepidez f.

Bolivia [bə'liviə] n Bolivia f. **Bolivian** adj, n boliviano, -a m, f.

bolster ['boulstə] n travesaño m; almohada f. v estribar, levantar, apoyar.

bolt [boult] n (door) cerraja f, cerrojo m; (for nut) perno m; rayo m. v (run) huir; (secure) empernar; (food) zampar. **bolt upright** enhiesto. **thunderbolt** n rayo m.

bomb [bom] n bomba f. v bombardear.

bombard [bəm'baːd] v bombardear. **bombardment** n bombardeo m.

bonafide [bounə'faidi] adj fidedigno.

bond [bond] n lazo m, unión f, vínculo m; (comm) obligación f; (security) fianza f; (customs) depósito m. v unir, ligar; dar fianza. **bonds** n pl cadenas f pl. **bondage** n esclavitud f.

bone [boun] n hueso m; (fish) espina f. v desosar. **bony** adj huesudo. **all skin and bones** estar en los huesos. **pick a bone with** arreglar las cuentas con.

bonfire ['bonfaiə] n hoguera f.

bonnet ['bonit] n capota f, gorra f; (mot) capó m.

bonus ['bounəs] n extra m, prima f.

booby trap ['buːbi ,træp] n trampa f; (mil) mina f.

book [buk] n libro m; tomo m. v (a seat) tomar; (reserve) reservar; (engage) contratar. **bookcase** ['bukkeis] n librería f. **book-ends** ['bukendz] n pl sujetalibros m pl. **booking** ['bukiŋ] n taquilla f. **book-keeper** ['buk,kiːpə] n tenedor de libros m. **booklet** ['buklit] n folleto m. **bookmark** ['bukmaːk] n marcador m. **bookseller** ['bukselə] n librero m. **bookshop** ['bukʃop] n librería f.

boom [buːm] n (noise) ruido m; (econ) auge repentino m. v (comm) prosperar, estar en bonanza; sonar, bramar.

boost [buːst] v (advertise) dar bombo (a); (coll) empujar. n (coll) empujón m.

boot [buːt] *n* (*shoe*) bota *f*; (*mot*) maleta *f*. **get the boot** ser despedido.

booth [buːð] *n* cabina *f*, quiosco *m*.

booze [buːz] *n* (*coll*) bebida alcohólica *f*. *v* (*coll*) emborracharse, coger una turca.

border ['bɔːdə] *n* confín *m*; frontera *f*; margen *m*; (*sewing*) ribete *m*; (*garden*) arriate *m*. *v* lindar con. **borderline** *n* límite *m*.

bore¹ [bɔː] *v* (*hole, etc.*) perforar, horadar, taladrar. *n* taladro *m*, barreno *m*; (*gun*) calibre *m*.

bore² [bɔː] *v* aburrir, fastidiar. *n* aburrimiento *m*; (*person*) pelmazo *m*. **boredom** *n* tedio *m*, hastío *m*. **boring** *adj* aburrido, tedioso.

bore³ [bɔː] *V* **bear¹**.

born [bɔːn] *adj* nacido, nato. **be born** nacer.

borne [bɔːn] *V* **bear¹**.

borough ['bʌrə] *n* municipio *m*.

borrow ['borou] *v* tomar prestado, pedir prestado. **borrower** *n* prestatario *m*.

bosom ['buzəm] *n* seno *m*; pecho *m*.

boss [bos] *n* amo *m*, jefe *m*, patrón *m*; (*political*) cacique *m*. *v* dominar, dirigir.

botany ['botəni] *n* botánica *f*. **botanical** *adj* botánico. **botanist** *n* botánico, -a *m, f*.

both [bouθ] *adj*, *pron* ambos, los dos.

bother ['boðə] *v* molestar; (*worry*) preocuparse. *n* molestia *f*; preocupación *f*.

bottle ['botl] *n* botella *f*, frasco *m*; (*water*) cantimplora *f*; (*wine*) porrón *m*. *v* embotellar.

bottom ['botəm] *n* fondo *m*; casco *m*; (*anat*) trasero *m*, (*vulgar*) culo *m*; (*river*) lecho *m*; (*page*) pie *m*; (*chair*) asiento *m*. *adj* más bajo. **bottomless** *adj* sin fondo.

boudoir ['buːdwaː] *n* tocador *m*, gabinete *m*.

bough [bau] *n* rama *f*.

bought [bɔːt] *V* **buy**.

boulder ['bouldə] *n* peñasco *m*, pedrusco *m*.

bounce [bauns] *v* rebotar, botar, saltar; (*cheque*) ser rechazado. *n* rebote *m*, respingo *m*.

bound¹ [baund] *v* (*leap*) saltar, brincar. *n* salto *m*, brinco *m*.

bound² [baund] *n* límite *m*. **within bounds** dentro del límite.

bound³ [baund] *V* **bind**.

bound⁴ [baund] *adj* **bound for** destinado a, con rumbo a.

boundary ['baundəri] *n* lindero *m*, término *m*.

bouquet [buːkei] *n* ramo *m*, ramillete *m*; perfume *m*; (*wine*) nariz *f*.

bourgeois ['buəʒwɑ] *adj* burgués.

bout [baut] *n* turno *m*; (*illness*) ataque *m*.

bow¹ [bau] *v* (*bend*) inclinarse, saludar; (*submit*) someterse (a). *n* inclinación *f*; reverencia *f*.

bow² [bou] *n* (*music, weapon*) arco *m*; (*ribbon*) lazo *m*. **bow-legged** *adj* patiestevado. **bow window** ventana arqueada *f*.

bow³ [bau] *n* (*naut*) proa *f*.

bowels ['bauəlz] *n pl* intestinos *m pl*, entrañas *f pl*.

bowl¹ [boul] *n* receptáculo *m*; (*soup*) escudilla *f*; (*washing*) jofaina *f*.

bowl² [boul] *v* tirar; (*cricket*) sacar. **bowl over** (*fig*) desconcertar. **bowls** *pl n* juego de bolos *m sing*.

bowler hat *n* hongo *m*.

box¹ [boks] *n* caja *f*, cajón *m*; (*luggage*) baúl *m*; (*theatre*) palco *m*; (*sentry*) garita *f*, casilla *f*. *v* encajonar. **box office** taquilla *f*. **post-office box** apartado de correos *m*.

box² [boks] *v* (*sport*) boxear. **boxer** *n* boxeador *m*, pugilista *m*. **boxing** *n* boxeo *m*, pugilato *m*.

Boxing Day *n* Día de San Esteban *m*.

boy [boi] *n* muchacho *m*, niño *m*, chico *m*. **boyfriend** *n* novio *m*. **boy scout** muchacho explorador *m*. **boyhood** niñez *f*.

boycott ['boikot] *n* boicot *m*. *v* boicotear.

bra [braː] *n* (*coll*) sostén *m*.

brace [breis] *n* refuerzo *m*; (*tech*) abrazadera *f*; (*pair*) par *m*. *v* reforzar; refrescar. **braces** *n pl* tirantes *m pl*. **bracing** *adj* tónico.

bracelet ['breislit] *n* pulsera *f*; brazalete *m*.

bracken ['brakən] *n* helecho *m*.

bracket ['brakit] *n* soporte *m*; (*writing*) paréntesis *m*, corchete *m*.

brag [brag] *v* jactarse. *n* jactancia *f*.

Braille [breil] *n* Braille *m*, alfabeto para los ciegos *m*.

brain [brein] *n* cerebro *m*, sesos *m pl*. *v* romper la crisma. **brains** *n pl* talento *m sing*. **brainwash** *v* lavar el cerebro. **brainwave** *n* idea luminosa *f*. **brainy** *adj* sesudo. **rack one's brains** devanarse los sesos.

braise [breiz] v estofar.

brake [breik] n freno m. v frenar.

bramble ['bræmbl] n zarza f. maleza f. **bramble patch** breña f. matorral m.

bran [bræn] n salvado m.

branch [braintʃ] n rama f; (of learning) ramo m; (river) tributario m; (road, rail) ramal m; (company) dependencia f. v echar ramas, dividirse.

brand [brænd] n (manufacture) marca f; (animals) hierro m; (fire) tizón m; (stigma) estigma m. v marcar; tildar. **brand-new** adj enteramente nuevo.

brandish ['brændiʃ] v blandir.

brandy ['brændi] n coñac m.

brass [brais] n latón m; (music) cobre m, metal m; (coll) pasta f. **brassy** adj de latón; (coll) presuntuoso.

brassière ['bræsiə] V **bra**.

brave [breiv] adj valiente, intrépido. v desafiar. **bravery** n valentía f.

brawl [broil] n alboroto m, riña f. v alborotar.

brawn [broin] n carnosidad f, músculo m; (food) carne de cerdo adobada f. **brawny** adj musculoso.

brazen ['breizn] adj (metal) de latón; (fig) desahogado.

Brazil [brə'zil] n (el) Brasil m. **Brazilian** n, adj brasileño, -a m, f. **Brazil nut** nuez del Brasil f.

breach [briitʃ] n brecha f. v abrir brecha; romper. **breach of promise** infracción f. **breach of the peace** alteración de orden público f.

bread [bred] n pan m. **breadcrumb** n migaja f. **breadcrumbs** n pl pan rallado m sing. **slice of bread** rebanada f.

breadth [bredθ] n anchura f.

*break [breik] v romper; quebrar; quebrantar; (burst) reventar; (violate) infringir. **break away** desprenderse. **break down** (mech) averiarse; (cry) deshacerse en lágrimas. **break in** forzar la entrada. **break out** estallar. **break up** desmenuzar. n ruptura f, rotura f; (opening) abertura f; (interruption) interrupción f. **breakdown** n colapso m. **breakthrough** n avance m.

breakfast ['brekfəst] n desayuno m. v desayunar.

breast [brest] n pecho m; (female) mama f, teta f. **breastbone** n esternón m. **breast pocket** bolsillo de pecho m. **breaststroke** n brazada de pecho f.

breath [breθ] n respiración f, aliento m; (breeze) soplo m. **breathless** adj sin aliento. **under one's breath** en voz baja.

breathalyser ['breθəlaizə] n alcohómetro m.

breathe [briiδ] v respirar, exhalar, inspirar. **breathing** n respiración f.

*breed [briid] v criar, engendrar. n raza f, casta f. **breeding** n cría f, reproducción f; (upbringing) crianza f, educación f.

breeze [briiz] n brisa f. **breezy** adj fresco; (of manner) animado.

brew [bru] v (infuse) infusionar; (beer) fabricar. n poción f. **brewery** n fábrica de cerveza f.

bribe [braib] n soborno m. v sobornar. **bribery** n soborno m.

brick [brik] n ladrillo m. v enladrillar. **bricklayer** n albañil m. **brickyard** n ladrillar m.

bride [braid] n novia f, desposada f. **bridal** adj nupcial. **bridegroom** m novio m, desposado m. **bridesmaid** n dama de honor f, madrina de boda f.

bridge¹ [bridʒ] n puente m. **drawbridge** n puente levadizo m. **suspension bridge** puente colgante m. v pontear.

bridge² [bridʒ] n (cards) bridge m.

bridle ['braidl] n brida f, freno m. v enfrenar; picarse.

brief [briif] adj breve. n resumen m; (law) escrito m, relacion f. v (law) instruir. **briefcase** n cartera f. **briefly** adv brevemente.

brigade [bri'geid] n brigada f.

bright [brait] adj brillante; (intelligent) inteligente. **brighten** v hacer brillar; (make happy) alegrar; (polish) pulir; (weather) aclarar. **brightness** n brillantez f; (intelligence) talento m.

brilliant ['briljənt] adj brillante. **brilliance** n brillo m, fulgor m.

brim [brim] n (of a container) borde m; (hat) ala f.

brine [brain] n salmuera f.

*bring [brin] v traer, llevar, conducir. **bring about** causar, ocasionar. **bring down** rebajar. **bring in** introducir. **bring off** lograr, conseguir. **bring out** sacar; publicar. **bring together** reunir. **bring to light** descubrir. **bring up** criar, educar.

brink [brink] n borde m. **on the brink of a** dos dedos de.

brisk [brisk] *adj* animado, vivo.

bristle ['brisl] *n* cerda *f*. *v* erizarse. **bristly** *adj* erizado.

Britain ['britn] *n* Gran Bretaña *f*. **British** *adj* británico. **Briton** *n* británo, -a *m*, *f*. británico, -a *m*, *f*.

brittle ['britl] *adj* quebradizo.

broad [brood] *adj* ancho; (*fig*) lato, amplio; (*accent*) fuerte. **broad-minded** *adj* tolerante. **broaden** *v* ensanchar. **broadly** *adv* en general. **broadness** *n* anchura *f*.

broadcast ['broodkaist] *n* emisión *f*, radiodifusión *f*; *v* emitir, radiar. **broadcasting station** *n* emisora *f*.

broccoli ['brokəli] *n* bróculi *m*, brécol *f*.

brochure ['brouʃuə] *n* folleto *m*.

broke [brouk] *V* **break**. *adj* (*coll*) pelado, sin blanca.

broken ['broukn] *V* **break**.

broker ['broukə] *n* corredor de bolsa *m*.

bronchitis [broŋ'kaitis] *m* bronquitis *f*.

bronze [bronz] *n* bronce *m*.

brooch [broutʃ] *n* broche *m*.

brood [brood] *n* (*chickens*) pollada *f*; (*birds*) nidada *f*; (*other animals*) cría *f*. *v* empollar. **brood over** ruminar.

brook [bruk] *n* arroyo *m*.

broom [bruum] *n* escoba *f*; (*bot*) retama *f*.

broth [broθ] *n* caldo *m*.

brothel ['broθl] *n* burdel *m*, lupanar *m*.

brother ['brʌðə] *n* hermano *m*. **brother-in-law** *n* cuñado *m*. **brotherhood** *n* fraternidad *f*. **brotherly** *adv* fraternal.

brow [brau] *n* frente *f*; (*hill*) cumbre *f*. **browbeat** *v* intimidar verbalmente.

brown [braun] *adj* castaño, moreno. *v* (*cookery*) dorar; (*tan*) tostar. **brown paper** papel de estraza *m*. **brownish** *adj* pardusco.

browse [brauz] *v* pacer.

bruise [bruuz] *n* contusión *f*, magulladura *f*. *v* magullar.

brunette [bru'net] *n* morena *f*.

brush [brʌʃ] *n* cepillo *m*; (*broom*) escoba *f*; (*for painting*) pincel *m*; (*undergrowth*) matorral *m*. *v* cepillar; (*sweep*) barrer; (*touch*) rozar. **brush aside** echar a un lado. **brush off** sacudir(se).

brusque [brusk] *adj* brusco, rudo.

Brussels ['brʌsəlz] *n* Bruselas. **Brussels sprouts** coles de Bruselas *f pl*.

brute [bruut] *n* bruto *m*, bestia *m*, *f*. **brutal** *adj* brutal, bestial. **brutality** *n* brutalidad *f*.

bubble ['bʌbl] *n* burbuja *f*; borbollón *m*. *v* burbujear, borbollar.

buck [bʌk] *n* gamo *m*. *v* encorvarse. **buck up** animarse.

bucket ['bʌkit] *n* cubo *m*, balde *m*.

buckle ['bʌkl] *n* hebilla *f*. *v* enhebillar; doblarse.

buck-tooth *n* diente saliente *m*.

bud [bʌd] *n* brote *m*. *v* brotar, germinar.

budge [bʌdʒ] *v* mover, moverse, menearse.

budgerigar ['bʌdʒərigaː] *n* periquito *m*.

budget ['bʌdʒit] *n* presupuesto *m*. *v* presupuestar.

buffalo ['bʌfəlou] *n* búfalo *m*.

buffer ['bʌfə] *n* parachoque *m*.

buffet[1] ['bʌfit] *n* (*blow*) bofetón *m*, bofetada *f*. *v* abofetear, golpear.

buffet[2] ['bufei] *n* fonda *f*, bar *m*.

bug [bʌg] *n* chinche *m*. *v* (*coll*) ocultar un micrófono en.

bugger ['bʌgə] *n* sodomita *m*. *v* cometer sodomía. *interj* ¡joder! **bugger off!** ¡vete a la mierda! **buggery** *n* sodomía *f*.

bugle ['bjuːgl] *n* corneta *f*. **bugler** *n* trompetero *m*.

*****build** [bild] *v* construir; edificar; fundar. **building** *n* edificio *m*. **building site** *n* solar *m*. **built-up area** *n* zona urbana *f*.

bulb [bʌlb] *n* (*elec*) bombilla *f*; (*bot*) bulbo *m*.

Bulgaria [bʌl'geəriə] *n* Bulgaria *f*. **Bulgarian** *n*, *adj* búlgaro, -a *m*, *f*.

bulge [bʌldʒ] *n* hinchazón *f*, bulto *m*. *v* hincharse. **bulging** *adj* hinchado (de).

bulk [bʌlk] *n* bulto *m*; masa *f*; (*larger part*) grueso *m*. **in bulk** (*comm*) en bruto. **bulky** *adj* voluminoso.

bull [bul] *n* toro *m*. **bullfight** *n* corrida de toros *f*. **bullfighter** *n* torero *m*. **bull in a china shop** un caballo loco en una cacharrería *m*. **bullring** *n* plaza de toros *f*. **bull's-eye** *n* centro del blanco *m*.

bulldozer ['buldouzə] *n* bulldozer *m*, excavadora *f*.

bullet ['bulit] *n* bala *f*. **bullet-proof** *adj* a prueba de balas.

bulletin ['bulətin] *n* boletín *m*.

bullion ['buliən] *n* (*gold*) oro en barras *m*; (*silver*) plata en barras *f*.

bully ['buli] *n* valentón *m*, rufián *m*. *v* intimidar.

bum [bʌm] *n* (*coll*) posaderas *f pl*. *v* holgazanear.

bump [bʌmp] n (swelling) hinchazón f; (blow) golpe m. v chocar, golpear.

bumper [bʌmpə] n (mot) parachoques m invar. adj abundante.

bun [bʌn] n buñuelo m; (hair) moño m.

bunch [bʌntʃ] n (flowers) ramo m; (fruit) racimo m; (coll: gang) pandilla f. v agruparse.

bundle [bʌndl] n fardo m, bulto m. v enfardar, liar.

bungalow [bʌŋgəlou] n chalet m, casa de un solo piso f.

bungle [bʌŋgl] v estropear, chapucear. n chapucería f. **bungler** n chapucero, -a m, f. **bungling** adj chapucero.

bunion [bʌnjən] n juanete m.

bunk [bʌŋk] n litera f; (coll: nonsense) palabrería f. **do a bunk** pirarse.

bunker [bʌŋkə] n (refuge) refugio m; (coal) carbonera f; (golf) bunker m, hoya de arena f.

buoy [boi] n boya f. **buoyancy** n fluctuación f. **buoyant** adj boyante.

burden [bəːdn] n carga f. v cargar.

bureau [bjuərou] n (desk) escritorio m; (office) oficina f; departamento m.

bureaucracy [bju'rokrəsi] n burocracia f. **bureaucrat** n burócrata m, f. **bureaucratic** adj burocrático.

burglar [bəːglə] n ladrón m. **burglar alarm** alarma contra ladrones f. **burglary** n robo m. **burgle** v robar.

*burn [bəːn] v quemar, incendiar. n quemadura f. **burner** n quemador m. **burning** adj ardiente.

burrow [bʌrou] n madriguera f. v amadrigar, minar.

*burst [bəːst] n estallido m, explosión f. v reventar, estallar. **burst into tears** romper a llorar. **burst open** forzar.

bury [beri] v enterrar, sepultar. **burial** n entierro m.

bus [bʌs] n autobús m, ómnibus m. **double-decker bus** ómnibus de dos pisos m. **bus station** término m. **bus-stop** n parada de autobús or ómnibus m.

bush [buʃ] n arbusto m; (undergrowth) maleza f. **bushy** adj denso, espeso, matoso.

business [biznis] n negocio m, comercio m; ocupación f. **business hours** horas de trabajo f pl. **businesslike** adj práctico,

sistemático. **businessman** n hombre de negocios m. **mean business** estar resuelto. **mind one's own business** no meterse donde no le llaman.

bust[1] [bʌst] n (anat) pecho m; (art) busto m.

bust[2] [bʌst] adj (fam) quebrado, reventado. **go bust** quebrar.

bustle [bʌsl] n animación f. v menearse, dar prisa (a).

busy [bizi] adj ocupado; activo, diligente. **busybody** n entrometido m.

but [bʌt] conj pero, sino. prep excepto. adv solamente. **but for** a no ser por. **nothing but** nada más que.

butane [bjuːtein] n butano m.

butcher [butʃə] n carnicero m. **butcher's shop** carnicería f. v matar, destrozar.

butler [bʌtlə] n mayordomo m.

butt[1] [bʌt] n (gun) culata f; (cigarette, etc.) colilla f.

butt[2] [bʌt] n (of jokes, etc.) objeto m.

butt[3] [bʌt] v topar, acornear. **butt in** entrometerse.

butter [bʌtə] n mantequilla f; v untar con mantequilla.

buttercup [bʌtəkʌp] n ranúnculo m.

butterfly [bʌtəflai] n mariposa f.

butterscotch [bʌtəskotʃ] n dulce de azúcar y mantequilla m.

buttocks [bʌtəks] n pl nalgas f pl.

button [bʌtn] n botón m. v abotonear. **buttonhole** n ojal m. v (coll) importunar.

buttress [bʌtris] n estribo m, contrafuerte m; (fig) apoyo m. v estribar.

*buy [bai] v comprar. n compra f. **buy up** acaparar. **buyer** n comprador, -a m, f.

buzz [bʌz] v zumbar. n zumbido m. **buzzer** n zumbador m; (bell) timbre m.

by [bai] prep por, de, a; (near) cerca de. adv al lado, cerca; aparte. **by all means** naturalmente. **by and large** en general. **by the way** de paso.

bye-law [bailɔː] n reglamento m.

by-election [baii,lekʃən] n elección parcial f.

bypass [bai,pais] n desviación f. v desviar.

by-product [baiprodəkt] n subproducto m.

bystander [bai,standə] n espectador, -a m, f.

C

cab [kab] *n* taxi *m*; (*lorry*) cabina *f*.

cabaret ['kabərei] *n* cabaret *m*; (*show*) attracciones *f pl*.

cabbage ['kabidʒ] *n* col *f*, repollo *m*.

cabin ['kabin] *n* cabaña *f*; (*naut*) camarote *m*; (*aircraft, etc.*) cabina *f*. **cabin cruiser** *n* motonave *f*.

cabinet ['kabinit] *n* (*cupboard*) armario *m*; (*display*) vitrina *f*; (*pol*) gabinete *m*, consejo de ministros *m*. **medicine cabinet** botiquín *m*. **cabinet-maker** *n* ebanista *m*.

cable ['keibl] *n* (*rope, wire*) cable *m*; (*message*) cablegrama *m*. **cable address** dirección telegráfica *f*. **cable car** funicular *m*. *v* cablegrafiar.

cackle ['kakl] *v* carcarear. *n* carcareo *m*.

cactus ['kaktəs] *n pl* -**i** *or* -**uses** cacto *m*.

caddie ['kadi] *n* caddy *m*; (*trolley*) carrito *m*.

cadence ['keidəns] *n* cadencia *f*.

cadet [kə'det] *n* cadete *m*.

café ['kafei] *n* café *m*, restaurante *m*.

cafeteria [kafə'tiəriə] *n* cafetería *f*, restaurante de autoservicio *m*.

caffeine ['kafiin] *n* cafeína *f*.

cage [keidʒ] *n* jaula *f*. *v* enjaular.

cake [keik] *n* pastel *m*; (*soap*) pastilla *f*. **Christmas cake** tarta de Navidad *f*. **a piece of cake** (*coll*) ser pan comido. **sell like hot cakes** (*coll*) venderse como rosquillas. **take the cake** (*coll*) llevarse la palma. *v* endurecerse.

calamine ['kaləmain] *n* calamina *f*.

calamity [kə'laməti] *n* calamidad *f*.

calcium ['kalsiəm] *n* calcio *m*.

calculate ['kalkjuleit] *v* calcular; (*guess, suppose*) confiar en. **calculated** *adj* intencional, deliberado. **calculating** *adj* calculador. **calculation** *n* cálculo *m*. **calculator** *n* calculador *m*.

calendar ['kaləndə] *n* calendario *m*. **calendar month** mes civil *m*.

calf¹ [kaf] *n* (*zool*) becerro *m*, ternero *m*.

calf² [kaf] *n* (*anat*) pantorrilla *f*.

calibre ['kalibə] *n* (*measurement*) calibre *m*; (*talent*) capacidad *f*, talento *m*.

call [koːl] *n* llamada *f*; llamamiento *m*; (*cry*) grito *m*; (*visit*) visita *f*. **on call** de guardia. **trunk call** conferencia *f*. *v* llamar. **call for** pedir. **call off** cancelar. **call on** visitar. **call up** evocar; convocar.

callous ['kaləs] *adj* insensible, duro.

calm [kaːm] *adj* calmoso, sosegado, tranquilo. *n* calma *f*, tranquilidad *f*. *v* calmar, sosegar.

calorie ['kaləri] *n* caloría *f*.

came [keim] *V* **come**.

camel ['kaməl] *n* camello *m*.

camera ['kamərə] *n* máquina fotográfica *f*. **in camera** a puerta cerrada. **cameraman** *n* cameraman *m*.

camouflage ['kaməflaːʒ] *n* camuflaje *m*. *v* camuflar.

camp¹ [kamp] *n* (*site*) campamento *m*. **camp-bed** *n* cama plegable *f*. **holiday camp** campamento de vacaciones *m*. *v* acampar.

camp² [kamp] *adj* (*coll*) afeminado; afectado; homosexual.

campaign [kam'pein] *n* campaña *f*. **advertising campaign** campaña publicitaria *f*. **election campaign** campaña electoral *f*. *v* hacer (una) campaña.

campus ['kampəs] *n* recinto universitario *m*, campus *m*, ciudad universitaria *f*.

*can¹ [kan] *v* (*be able*) poder; (*know how to*) saber.

can² [kan] *n* (*container*) lata *f*. **can-opener** *n* abrelatas *m invar*. *v* enlatar, conservar en lata. **canned** *adj* enlatado.

Canada ['kanədə] *n* Canadá *m*. **Canadian** *n*(*m+f*), *adj* canadiense.

canal [kə'nal] *n* canal *m*.

canary [kə'neəri] *n* canario *m*.

Canary Islands *n pl* (islas) Canarias *f pl*.

cancel ['kansəl] *v* (*contract, decree, etc.*) cancelar; (*cheque, order, invitation*) anular; (*delete*) tachar; (*maths*) eliminar. **cancel out** anularse. **cancellation** *n* cancelación *f*; anulación *f*.

cancer ['kansə] *n* cáncer *m*. **cancerous** *adj* canceroso.

Cancer ['kansə] *n* Cáncer *m*.

candid ['kandid] *adj* franco, sincero.

candidate ['kandidət] *n* candidato *m*. **candidacy** *n* candidatura *f*.

candle ['kandl] *n* vela *f*; (*in a church*) cirio *m*. **burn the candle at both ends** hacer de la noche día. **candlestick** *n* candelero *m*.

candour ['kandə] *n* franqueza *f*, sinceridad *f*.

candy ['kandi] *n* caramelo *m*. *v* escarchar, cristalizar.

cane [kein] *n* caña *f*; (*walking stick*) bastón *m*; (*school*) palmeta *f*, vara *f*. **sugar cane** caña de azúcar *f*. **cane furniture** muebles de mimbre *m pl*. *v* castigar con la palmeta *o* vara.

canine ['keinain] *adj* canino. **canine tooth** diente canino *m*.

cannabis ['kænəbis] *n* marijuana *f*.

cannibal ['kænibəl] *n*(*m*+*f*). *adj* caníbal. **cannibalism** *n* canibalismo *m*.

cannon ['kænən] *n* cañón *m*. **cannonball** *n* bala de cañón *f*.

canoe [kə'nuː] *n* canoa *f*. *v* ir en canoa.

canon ['kænən] *n* canónigo *m*. **canonical** *adj* canónico. **canonize** *v* canonizar. **canonization** *n* canonización *f*.

canopy ['kænəpi] *n* (*awning*) toldo *m*; (*over a bed*) dosel *m*, baldaquín *m*.

canteen [kæn'tiːn] *n* (*restaurant*) cantina *f*; (*flask*) cantimplora *f*; (*cutlery*) juego de cubiertos *m*.

canter ['kæntə] *n* medio galope *m*. *v* ir a medio galope.

canton ['kæntən] *n* cantón *m*.

canvas ['kænvəs] *n* (*fabric*) lona *f*; (*art*) lienzo.

canvass ['kænvəs] *v* solicitar votos de; (*comm*) buscar clientes; (*public opinion*) sondear.

canyon ['kænjən] *n* cañón *m*.

cap [kæp] *n* gorra *f*; (*military or bathing*) gorro *m*; (*cover*) tapa *f*; (*bottle*) chapa *f*; (*pen*) capuchón *m*. *v* (*fig: crown*) coronar; (*do better than*) superar.

capable ['keipəbl] *adj* capaz, hábil. **capability** *n* capacidad *f*, habilidad *f*.

capacity [kə'pæsəti] *n* capacidad *f*; (*mot*) cilindrada *f*.

cape¹ [keip] *n* (*cloak*) capa *f*; (*cycling*) impermeable de hule *m*.

cape² [keip] *n* (*geog*) cabo *m*.

caper ['keipə] *n* (*jump*) cabriola *f*; (*prank*) travesura *f*; (*cookery*) alcaparra *f*.

capillary [kə'piləri] *n* capilar *m*.

capital ['kæpitl] *adj* capital. **capital punishment** pena capital *f*. *n* (*letter*) mayúscula *f*; (*city*) capital *f*; (*money*) fondo de operaciones *m*. **capitalism** *n* capitalismo *m*. **capitalist** *n* capitalista *m*, *f*. **capitalistic** *adj* capitalista. **capitalize** *v* capitalizar. **capitalization** *n* capitalización *f*.

capitulate [kə'pitjuleit] *v* capitular. **capitulation** *n* capitulación *f*.

capricious [kə'priʃəs] *adj* caprichoso. **caprice**, **capriciousness** *n* capricho *m*.

Capricorn ['kæprikɔːn] *n* Capricornio *m*.

capsicum ['kæpsikəm] *n* pimiento *m*, chile *m*.

capsize [kæp'saiz] *v* volcar, zozobrar.

capsule ['kæpsjuːl] *n* cápsula *f*.

captain ['kæptin] *n* capitán *m*. *v* capitanear. **captaincy** *n* capitanía *f*.

caption ['kæpʃən] *n* encabezamiento *m*, pie *m*. *v* poner pie a.

captive ['kæptiv] *n*, *adj* cautivo, -a. **captivate** *v* cautivar. **captivity** *n* cautividad *f*.

capture ['kæptʃə] *v* capturar; (*place*) tomar; (*market*) acaparar; (*fig*) atraer. *n* captura *f*, apresamiento *m*; (*place*) toma *f*.

car [kaː] *n* coche *m*, automóvil *m*; (*rail*) vagón *m*; (*cable*) cabina *f*. **car park** aparcamiento *m*. **car wash** lavado de coches *m*. **dining car** coche comedor *m*. **racing car** coche de carreras *m*. **sleeping car** coche cama *m*.

caramel ['kærəmel] *n* caramelo *m*, azúcar quemado *m*.

carat ['kærət] *n* quilate *m*.

caravan ['kærəvæn] *n* (*mot*) remolque *m*; (*travellers*) caravana *f*; (*gipsy*) carromato *m*.

caraway ['kærəwei] *n* (*seed*) carvi *m*; (*plant*) alcaravea *f*.

carbohydrate [kaːbə'haidreit] *n* carbohidrato *m*.

carbon ['kaːbən] *n* (*chem*) carbono *m*; carbón *m*. **carbon dioxide** bióxido de carbono *m*. **carbon paper** papel carbón *m*.

carbuncle ['kaːbʌŋkl] *n* (*med*) carbunco *m*, carbunclo *m*.

carburettor ['kaːbjuretə] *n* carburador *m*.

carcass ['kaːkəs] *n* (*animal*) res muerta *f*.

card [kaːd] *n* tarjeta *f*; (*visiting*) tarjeta de visita *f*; (*postcard*) tarjeta postal *f*; (*playing card*) carta *f*, naipe *m*; (*membership*) carnet *m*; (*thin cardboard*) cartulina *f*; (*coll*) gracioso, -a *m*, *f*. **cardboard** *n* cartón *m*. **card index** fichero *m*.

cardiac ['kaːdiak] *adj* cardiaco.

cardigan ['kaːdigən] *n* rebeca *f*.

cardinal ['kaːdənl] *n* (*church, bird*) cardenal *m*. *adj* cardinal, esencial. **cardinal number** número cardinal *m*.

care [keə] *n* cuidado *m*, atención *f*; (*worry*) inquietud *f*; (*responsibility*) cargo *m*. **medical care** asistencia médica *f*. **care of** para entregar a. **handle with care** frágil. **take care!** ¡ojo! *v* importar, preocuparse por. **take care of** guardar, tener cuidado de. **careful** adj cuidadoso. **carefulness** n cuidado m, esmero m. **careless** adj descuidado, desatento.

career [kə'riə] n carrera f, curso m. v correr a toda velocidad.

caress [kə'res] n caricia f. v acariciar.

cargo ['kaɪgou] n carga f, cargamento m.

caricature ['karikətjuə] n caricatura f. v caricaturizar.

carnage ['kaɪnidʒ] n carnicería f.

carnal ['kaɪnl] adj carnal. **carnality** n carnalidad f.

carnation [kaɪ'neiʃən] n clavel m.

carnival ['kaɪnivəl] n carnaval m.

carnivorous [kaɪ'nivərəs] adj carnívoro. **carnivore** n carnívoro -a m, f.

carol ['karəl] n villancico m.

carpenter ['kaɪpəntə] n carpintero m. **carpentry** n carpintería f.

carpet ['kaɪpit] n alfombra f; (fitted) moqueta f. **carpet-sweeper** n escoba mecánica f. v alfombrar.

carriage ['karidʒ] n carruaje m, carro m; vagón m; (posture) manera de andar f; (comm) porte m. **carriageway** n calzada f. **dual carriageway** carretera de doble calzada f.

carrier ['kariə] n portador m; (comm) empresa de transportes f; (med) portador, -a m, f.

carrot ['karət] n zanahoria f.

carry ['kari] v llevar; (bring) traer; (a load) transportar; (by pipes) conducir; (sustain) sostener. **carry forward** (comm) pasar. **carry out** realizar. **carrycot** n cuna portátil f.

cart [kaɪt] n carro m; (handcart) carro de mano m; (trolley) carrito m. v carretear. **cart horse** caballo de tiro m.

cartilage ['kaɪtilidʒ] n cartílago m.

cartography [kaɪ'tografi] n cartografía f.

carton ['kaɪtən] n cartón m, caja de cartón f.

cartoon [kaɪ'tuɪn] n caricatura f, chiote m; (art) cartón m; (film) dibujos animados m pl. **cartoonist** n caricaturista m, f, humorista m.

cartridge ['kaɪtridʒ] n cartucho m; (blank) cartucho sin bala m.

carve [kaɪv] v (meat) trinchar; (cut) cortar; (sculpture) tallar. **carve up** (divide) dividir; (stab) acuchillar. **carving knife** cuchillo de trinchar m.

cascade [kas'keid] n cascada f, salto de agua m. v caer en cascada.

case¹ [keis] n caso m; (affair) asunto m. **in any case** en todo caso. **in case** en caso. **in no case** de ningún modo. **in the case of** en cuanto a. **it's not a case of . . .** no se trata de . . . . **just in case** por si acaso. **state the case** exponer los hechos.

case² [keis] n (box) caja f; (rigid) estuche m; (soft) funda. **suitcase** n maleta f. v encajonar, embalar.

cash [kaʃ] n dinero al contante m, (comm) pago al contado m. **cash account** cuenta de caja f. **cash book** libro de caja m. **cash discount** descuento por pago al contado m. **cash on delivery** envío contra reembolso m. **cash register** caja registradora f. **petty cash** dinero para gastos menores m.

cashier¹ [kaˈʃiə] n (bank) cajero, -a m, f.

cashier² [kaˈʃiə] v (mil) dar de baja.

cashmere [kaʃ'miə] n cachemira f.

casing ['keisiŋ] n cubierta f; (wrapping) envoltura f; (cylinder) camisa f.

casino [kə'siɪnou] n casino m.

cask [kaɪsk] n barril m.

casket ['kaɪskit] n joyero m, cofre m.

casserole ['kasəroul] n (dish) cacerola f; (food) cazuela f.

cassette [kə'set] n (tape) cassette m; (phot) cartucho m.

cassock ['kasək] n sotana f.

***cast** [kaɪst] n (acting) reparto m; (throw) lanzamiento m; (appearance) aspecto m; (tech) molde m; (squint) estrabismo m; (plaster) escayola f. v echar, arrojar; (tech) moldear, fundir. **castaway** n náufrago m. **cast aside** desechar. **cast down** bajar. **cast iron** hierro colado m. **cast off** abandonar; (naut) desamarrar.

castanets [kastə'nets] pl n castañuelas f pl.

caste [kaɪst] n casta f.

castle ['kaɪsl] n castillo m.

castor ['kaɪstə] n (wheel) ruedecilla f.

castor oil n aceite de ricino m.

castrate [kə'streit] v castrar. **castration** n castración f.

casual ['kaʒuəl] adj casual, informal; (carefree) despreocupado. **casual clothes** ropa de sport f sing. **casually** adv de paso.

casualty ['kaʒuəlti] n accidente m; víctima f; (mil) baja f.

cat [kat] n gato, -a m. f. **let the cat out of the bag** descubrir el pastel.

catalogue ['katəlog] n catálogo m. v catalogar.

catalyst ['katəlist] n catalizador m.

catapult ['katəpʌlt] n catapulta f. honda f. v catapultar.

cataract ['katərakt] n catarata f.

catarrh [kə'tɑ:] n catarro m.

catastrophe [kə'tastrəfi] n catástrofe f. **catastrophic** adj catastrófico.

****catch** [katʃ] v (seize) agarrar, coger; (capture) prender, atrapar; (disease) contraer; (hook) enganchar. **catch on** (coll) comprender. **catch out** sorprender. **catch up** alcanzar. n (act of catching) cogida f; (prey) presa f; (bolt) pestillo m; (buckle) hebijón m; (drawback) trampa f; (trick) truco m. **safety catch** fiador m. **catching** adj contagioso. **catchy** adj pegadizo.

category ['katəgəri] n categoría f. **categorical** adj categórico, rotundo. **categorize** v clasificar.

cater ['keitə] v proveer de comida. **cater for** atender a. **caterer** n proveedor, -a m. f. **catering** n abastecimiento m.

caterpillar ['katəpilə] n oruga f.

cathedral [kə'θi:drəl] n catedral f.

cathode ['kaθoud] n cátodo m. **cathode-ray tube** tubo de rayos catódicos m.

catholic ['kaθəlik] n, adj católico, -a. adj universal; ortodoxo. **catholicism** n catolicismo m. **catholicity** n catolicidad f.

catkin ['katkin] n candelilla f.

cattle [katl] n ganado m.

catty ['kati] adj malicioso.

caught [kɔ:t] V catch.

cauliflower ['koliflauə] n coliflor m.

cause [kɔ:z] n causa f, motivo m. v causar, provocar. **in the cause of** por.

causeway ['kɔ:zwei] n terraplén m.

caustic ['kɔ:stik] adj cáustico, mordaz.

caution ['kɔ:ʃən] n cautela f, cuidado m; (warning) advertencia f. v (reprimand) amonestar; (warn) advertir. **cautionary** adj amonestador. **cautious** adj cauteloso, precavido.

cavalry ['kavəlri] n caballería f.

cave [keiv] n cueva f, caverna f. **cave in** derrumbarse. **cavernous** adj cavernoso.

caviar ['kaviɑ:] n caviar m.

cavity ['kavəti] n cavidad f; (dental) cavies f invar.

cayenne [kei'en] n pimentón m.

cease [si:s] v cesar. **cease-fire** n alto el fuego. **ceaseless** adj incesante.

cedar ['si:də] n cedro m.

cedilla [si'dilə] n cedilla f.

ceiling ['si:liŋ] n techo m; (aero) altura f; (fig) tope m, límite m. **hit the ceiling** subirse por las paredes.

celebrate ['seləbreit] v celebrar, festejar. **celebrated** adj célebre. **celebration** n celebración f. **celebrant** n celebrante m.

celery ['seləri] n apio m.

celestial [sə'lestiəl] adj celestial; (astron) celeste.

celibate ['selibət] n(m+f), adj célibe. **celibacy** n celibato m.

cell [sel] n celda f; (biol) célula f; (elec) pila f.

cellar ['selə] n sótano m; (wine) bodega f.

cello ['tʃelou] n violoncelo m. **cellist** n violoncelista m, f.

cellular ['seljulə] adj celular.

cement [sə'ment] n cemento. v (tech) cementar; (fig) cimentar.

cemetery ['semətri] n cementerio m.

cenotaph ['senətɑ:f] n cenotafio m.

censor ['sensə] n censor m. v censurar; (delete) tachar. **censorious** adj censorador. **censorship** n censura f.

censure ['senʃə] n censura f. v censurar. **censurable** adv censurable.

census ['sensəs] n censo m. **take a census of** empadronar.

cent [sent] n centavo m.

centenary [sen'ti:nəri] nm, adj centenario. **centenarian** n, adj centenario, -a. **centennial** adj centenario.

centigrade ['sentigreid] adj centígrado.

centimetre ['sentimi:tə] n centímetro m.

centipede ['sentipi:d] n ciempiés m invar.

centre ['sentə] n centro m. **community centre** centro social m. v centrar. **central** adj central, céntrico. **central heating** calefacción central f. **centralize** v centralizar. **centralization** n centralización f.

centrifugal [sen'trifjugəl] adj centrífugo.

century ['sentʃuri] n siglo m.

ceramic [sə'ramik] adj cerámico. **ceramics** n cerámica f sing.

cereal ['siəriəl] nm, adj cereal.

ceremony ['serəməni] n ceremonia f. **stand on ceremony** andarse con ceremonias. **ceremonial** nm, adj ceremonial. **ceremonious** adj ceremonioso.

certain ['sə:tn] adj cierto, seguro. **make certain** asegurarse. **certainly** adv desde luego, naturalmente. **certainly not de** ninguna manera. **certainly** n certeza f. certidumbre f; seguridad f.

certificate [sə'tifikət] n certificado m; (academic) título m, diploma f. **birth certificate** partida de nascimiento f. **death certificate** partida de defunción f. **marriage certificate** partida de matrimonio f. **certify** v certificar; garantizar.

cesspool ['sespul] n pozo negro m.

chafe [tʃeif] v (rub) rozar; (irritate) irritar; (for warmth) frotar; (fig) enfadar. n rozadura f; irritación f.

chaffinch ['tʃafintʃ] n pinzón m.

chain [tʃein] n cadena f. **chain store** sucursal m. v encadenar.

chair [tʃeə] n silla f. (university) cátedra f; (meeting) presidencia f. **folding chair** silla plegable f. **take the chair** tomar la presidencia. **chairman** n presidente m. v presidir.

chalet ['ʃalei] n chalet m.

chalk [tʃɔːk] n (geol) creta f; (for writing) tiza f. **not by a long chalk** ni mucho menos. v marcar con tiza. **chalk up** apuntarse. **chalky** adj cretáceo, yesoso.

challenge ['tʃalindʒ] n reto m, desafío m; (sentry) alto m; (incentive) estímulo m; (law) recusación f. v desafiar, retar. **challenger** n desafiador m, retador m.

chamber ['tʃeimbə] n (room, legislative body) cámara f; (tech) recámara f. **chambermaid** n doncella f, camarera f. **chamber music** música de cámara f. **chamber pot** orinal m.

chameleon [kəmilliən] n camaleón m.

chamois ['ʃamwai] n gamuza f.

champagne [ʃam'pein] n champaña f.

champion ['tʃampiən] n, adj campeón, -ona. v defender, hacerse el campeón de. **championship** n campeonato m.

chance [tʃains] n casualidad f, suerte f, azar m; oportunidad f, ocasión f; posibilidad f; riesgo m. adj casual, fortuito. v arriesgar; probar; (happen) acaecer. **chance upon** tropezar con.

chancellor ['tʃainsələ] n canciller m. **chancellery** n cancillería f.

chandelier [ʃandə'liə] n araña f.

change [tʃeindʒ] n cambio m; (money) suelto m; (clothes) muda f. **for a change** para variar. v cambiar; mudar. **changeable** adj (character, weather) variable; (inconsistent) cambiadizo; (able to be

changed) cambiable. **changing room** vestuario m.

channel ['tʃanl] n canal m; (of a river) cauce m; (fig) vía f; (groove) ranura f. **English Channel** Canal de la Mancha m.

chant [tʃaint] n canción f, canto m. v cantar; entonar.

chaos ['keios] n caos m. **chaotic** adj caótico.

chap¹ [tʃap] v (skin) agrietar. n grieta f.

chap² [tʃap] n (coll) tipo m, sujeto m.

chapel ['tʃapəl] n capilla f.

chaperon ['ʃapəroun] n carabina f. v acompañar.

chaplain ['tʃaplin] n capellán m.

chapter ['tʃaptə] n capítulo m; (rel) cabildo m. **quote chapter and verse** citar literalmente.

char¹ [tʃaɪ] v (burn) carbonizar.

char² [tʃaɪ] n (charwoman) asistenta f.

character ['karəktə] n carácter m; (person) personaje m; (role) papel m; (coll) tipo m. **character reference** informe m. **characterize** v caracterizar. **characterization** n caracterización f.

characteristic [karəktə'ristik] adj característico. n característica f.

charcoal ['tʃaɪkoul] n carbón de leña m.

charge [tʃaɪdʒ] n (responsibility) cargo m; (task) tarea f; (battery, explosive, attack) carga f. **charge account** cuenta a cargo f. **in charge of** encargado de. **take charge of** hacerse cargo de. v (accuse) acusar; (bill) cobrar; (mil) atacar.

chariot ['tʃariət] n carro m.

charity ['tʃarəti] n caridad f; (alms) limosna f; (society) sociedad benéfica f. **charitable** adj caritativo.

charm [tʃaɪm] n encanto m; (spell) hechizo m. v encantar; hechizar. **charming** adj encantador, simpático.

chart [tʃaɪt] n (naut) carta marina f; (map) mapa m; (table) tabla f; (graph) gráfico m. v tabular; trazar.

charter ['tʃaɪtə] n (law) carta; (comm) flete m, fletamento m, fletamiento m; (transport) alquiler m. v fletar; alquilar; (grant a charter) conceder carta a. **charter flight** vuelo charter' m. **charter member** socio fundador m.

chase [tʃeis] v perseguir; (hunt) cazar. **chase after** ir detrás de. **chase away/off** ahuyentar. n persecución f; caza f.

chasm ['kazəm] n sima f, abismo m.

chassis ['ʃasi] n (mech) chasis m.

chaste [tʃeist] adj casto; (style) sobrio. **chastity** n castidad f.

chastise [tʃas'taiz] v castigar.

chat [tʃat] n charla f. v charlar. **chatty** adj charlador.

chatter ['tʃatə] v chacharear, parlotear; (teeth) castañetear. n cháchara f. parloteo m; castañeteo m. **chatterbox** n charlatán, -ana m, f.

chauffeur ['ʃoufə] n chófer m, conductor, -a m, f.

chauvinism ['ʃouvinizəm] n chauvinismo m. **chauvinist** n(m+f). adj chauvinista.

cheap [tʃiːp] adj barato. **dirt cheap** baratísimo adj, adv. **cheapen** v abaratar.

cheat [tʃiːt] v (swindle) timar, estafar; (deceive) engañar; (at games) hacer trampas; (in exams) copiar. n timador, -a m, f. estafador. -a m, f; tramposo, -a m, f; (trick) trampa f.

check [tʃek] v parar, detener; (restrain) reprimir, refrenar; (inspect) inspeccionar; (facts) comprobar; (mark) poner contraseña a; (chess) dar jaque a. **check in** registrarse. **check on** averiguar. **check with** cotejar con. n parada f, detención f; (restraint) restricción f; (control) inspección f; (pattern) cuadro m; (chess) jaque m. **checkmate** v dar el mate; n jaque mate m. **checkpoint** n control m. **check-up** n (med) reconocimiento general m.

cheek [tʃiːk] n carrillo m, mejilla f; (coll) caradura f. **turn the other cheek** poner la otra mejilla. **cheekbone** n pómulo m. **cheeky** adj descarado.

cheer [tʃiə] v (shout) vitorear, aclamar; (gladden) alegrar. **cheer on** animar. **cheer up** alentar. n (shout) viva m; (comfort) consuelo m; (joy) ánimo m. **cheers!** interj ¡a su salud! **cheerful** adj alegre, animado. **cheerfulness** n alegría f. **cheerio!** interj ¡hasta luego! **cheerless** adj triste.

cheese [tʃiːz] n queso m. **cheesecake** n pastel de queso m. **cheesecloth** n estopilla f.

cheetah ['tʃiːtə] n leopardo cazador m.

chef [ʃef] n jefe de cocina m.

chemistry ['kemistri] n química f. **chemical** adj químico. **chemist** n químico m; farmacéutico m. **chemist's shop** farmacia f.

cheque [tʃek] n cheque m. **chequebook** n talonario de cheques m. **cheque card**

tarjeta de crédito f. **traveler's check** cheque de viaje m.

cherish ['tʃeriʃ] v (love) querer; (nourish) abrigar; (take care of) cuidar.

cherry ['tʃeri] n (fruit) cereza f; (tree) cerezo m.

chess [tʃes] n ajedrez m. **chessboard** n tablero de ajedrez m. **chessman** n pieza de ajedrez f.

chest [tʃest] n (anat) pecho m; (box) caja f. **chest of drawers** n cómoda f. **chesty** adj (cough) delicado de los broncios.

chestnut ['tʃesnʌt] n (fruit) castaña f; (tree) castaño m. adj (hair) castaño.

chew [tʃuː] v masticar. **chewing gum** chicle m. **chew the cud** rumiar. **chew up** estropear.

chick pea ['tʃik,piː] n garbanzo m.

chicken ['tʃikin] n pollo m. **chickenpox** n varicela f. **chicken out** (slang) ser una gallina.

chicory ['tʃikəri] n (coffee) achicoria f; (salad) escarola f.

chief [tʃiːf] n pl -s jefe m, f. adj principal. **chiefly** adv principalmente; sobre todo.

chilblain ['tʃilblein] n sabañón m.

child [tʃaild] n pl -ren niño, -a m, f. **childbirth** n parto m. **childhood** n niñez f. **childish** adj infantil, pueril. **childless** adj sin hijos.

Chile ['tʃili] n Chile m. **Chilean** n, adj chileno, -a.

chill [tʃil] n frío m; (med) tiritona f; (shiver) escalofrío m; (fig) frialdad f. v enfriar. **chilled to the bone** enfriado hasta los huesos. **chilly** adj fresco.

chilli ['tʃili] n chile m.

chime [tʃaim] v sonar, repicar. **chime in** intervenir. n carillón m.

chimney ['tʃimni] n chimenea f. **chimney pot** cañón de chimenea m. **chimney sweep** deshollinador m.

chimpanzee [tʃimpən'ziː] n chimpancé m.

chin [tʃin] n barbilla f, mentón m.

china ['tʃainə] n porcelana f.

China ['tʃainə] n China f. **Chinese** n, adj chino, -a. **the Chinese** los chinos.

chink¹ [tʃiŋk] n (fissure) raja f, grieta m.

chink² [tʃiŋk] n (sound) sonido metálico m. v hacer tintinear.

chip [tʃip] n (fragment) pedacito m; (in cup, etc.) desportilladura f; (gambling) ficha f. **chipboard** n madera aglomerada f. **chips** pl n (cookery) patata frita f. v astillar. **chip in** (*interrupt*) interrumpir; (*contribute money*) poner.

chiropodist [ki'rɔpədist] *n* pedicuro, -a *m, f.* **chiropody** *n* quiropodia *f.*

chirp [tʃɜːp] *v* (*birds*) gorjear; (*crickets*) chirriar. *n* gorjeo *m*; chirrido *m*. **chirpy** *adj* animado.

chisel ['tʃizl] *n* cincel *m. v* cincelar.

chivalry ['ʃivəlri] *n* caballerosidad *f.* **chivalrous** *adj* caballeroso.

chive [tʃaiv] *n* cebolleta *f.*

chlorine ['klɔːriːn] *n* cloro *m. v* tratar con cloro. **chlorinate** *v* tratar con cloro.

chloroform ['klɔrəfɔːm] *n* cloroformo *m. v* cloroformizar.

chlorophyll ['klɔrəfil] *n* clorofila *f.*

chocolate ['tʃɔkələt] *n* chocolate *m.* **drinking chocolate** chocolate a la taza *m.*

choice [tʃois] *n* elección *f*, selección *f*; preferencia *f. adj* (*best*) flor y nata.

choir ['kwaiə] *n* coro *m*, coral *f.* **choirboy** *n* niño de coro *m.* **choirmaster** *n* director de coro *m.*

choke [tʃouk] *v* (*strangle*) estrangular; (*block*) obstruir. *n* (*mot*) estrangulador *m.*

cholera ['kɔlərə] *n* cólera *m.*

**choose [tʃuːz] v escoger, elegir.

chop[1] [tʃop] *n* (*meat*) chuleta *f*; (*blow*) golpe *m. v* (*cut*) cortar; (*mince*) picar; (*lop*) tronchar. **chop down** talar. **chopper** *n* hacha *f*; (*slang*) helicóptero *m.*

chop[2] [tʃop] *v* **chop and change** cambiar de opinión. **choppy** *adj* (*sea*) picado.

chops [tʃops] *pl n* (*jaws*) morros *m pl.* **lick one's chops** relamerse.

chopstick ['tʃopstik] *n* palillo *m.*

chord [kɔːd] *n* (*music*) acorde *m*; (*anat*) cuerda *f.*

chore [tʃɔː] *n* (*unpleasant*) tarea penosa *f.* **chores** *pl n* (*household*) faenas de la casa *f pl.*

choreography [kɔri'ɔgrɔfi] *n* coreografía *f.* **choreographer** *n* coreógrafo *m.*

chorus ['kɔːrəs] *n* (*refrain*) estribillo *m*; (*singers*) coro *m.* **chorus girl** corista *f.* **choral** *adj* coral. **choral society** orfeón *m.*

chose [tʃouz] *V* **choose.**

christen ['krisn] *v* bautizar; (*nickname*) llamar. **christening** *n* bautismo *m.*

Christian ['kristʃən] *n, adj* cristiano, -a *m, f.* **Christian name** nombre de pila *m.* **Christianity** *n* cristianismo *m.*

Christmas ['krisməs] *n* Navidad *f.* **Christmas Day** día de Navidad *m.* **Christmas Eve** Nochebuena *f.*

chromatic [krə'matik] *adj* cromático.

chrome [kroum] *n* cromo *m.*

chromium ['kroumiəm] *n* cromo *m.* **chromium-plated** *adj* cromado.

chronic ['kronik] *adj* crónico; (*coll: dreadful*) terrible.

chronicle ['kronikl] *n* crónica *f.*

chronological [kronə'lodʒikəl] *adj* cronológico.

chrysalis ['krisəlis] *n* crisálida *f.*

chrysanthemum [kri'sanθəməm] *n* crisantemo *m.*

chubby ['tʃʌbi] *adj* gordinflón.

chuck [tʃʌk] *v* (*coll: throw*) tirar; (*give up*) abandonar.

chuckle ['tʃʌkl] *v* reir entre de dientes. *n* risa *f.*

chunk [tʃʌŋk] *n* pedazo *m*; (*large amount*) cantidad grande *f.*

church [tʃɜːtʃ] *n* iglesia *f.* **church service** oficio religioso *m.* **churchyard** *n* cementerio *m.*

churn [tʃɜːn] *n* mantequera *f. v* batir. **churn out** producir en profusión.

chute [ʃuːt] *n* tolva *f.*

cider ['saidə] *n* sidra *f.*

cigar [si'gaː] *n* cigarro puro *m.*

cigarette [sigə'ret] *n* cigarillo *m.* **cigarette case** pitillera *f.* **cigarette holder** boquilla *f.* **cigarette lighter** encendedor *m*, mechero *m.* **cigarette paper** papel de fumar *m.*

cinder ['sində] *n* carbonilla *f*, ceniza *f.*

cinema ['sinəmə] *n* cine *m.* **cinematography** *n* cinematografía *f.*

cinnamon ['sinəmən] *n* canela *f.*

circle ['sɜːkl] *n* círculo *m*; (*theatre*) piso principal *m.* **go round in circles** dar vueltas. *v* rodear; (*surround*) circundar. **circular** *adj, n* circular *f.*

circuit ['sɜːkit] *n* (*route*) circuito *m*; (*perimeter*) perímetro *m*; (*law*) distrito *m*; (*cinemas, theatres*) cadena *f.* **short circuit** cortocircuito *m.* **circuitous** *adj* indirecto.

circulate ['sɜːkjuleit] *v* circular. **circulation** *n* circulación *f.*

circumcise ['sɜːkəmsaiz] *v* circuncidar. **circumcision** *n* circuncisión *f.*

circumference [sə'kʌmfərəns] *n* circunferencia *f.*

circumflex ['sɜːkəmfleks] *n* circunflejo *m.*

circumscribe ['sɜːkəmskraib] *v* circunscribir. **circumscription** *n* circunscripción *f*.

circumstance ['sɜːkəmstəns] *n* circunstancia *f*. **extenuating circumstances** circunstancias atenuantes *f pl.* **under no circumstances** de ninguna manera. **under the circumstances** en estas circunstancias. **circumstantial** *adj* (*incidental*) circunstancial; (*detailed*) circunstanciado. **circumstantial evidence** testimonio indirecto *m*.

circus ['sɜːkəs] *n* circo *m*.

cistern ['sistən] *n* cisterna *f*, aljibe *m*.

cite [sait] *v* citar. **citation** *n* citación *f*; (*mil*) mención *f*.

citizen ['sitizn] *n* ciudadano, -a *m, f*. **citizenship** *n* ciudadanía *f*.

citrus ['sitrəs] *n* cidro *m*. **citrus fruit** *n* agrios *m pl*. **citric acid** ácido cítrico *m*.

city ['siti] *n* ciudad *f*.

civic ['sivik] *adj* cívico.

civil ['sivl] *adj* civil; (*polite*) cortés. **civil engineering** ingeniería civil *f*. **civil rights** derechos civiles *m pl*. **civil servant** funcionario, -a *m, f*. **civil service** administración pública *f*. **civil war** guerra civil *f*.

civilian [sə'viljən] *adj* civil, de paisano. *n* paisano, -a *m, f*.

civilization [,sivilai'zeiʃən] *n* civilización *f*. **civilize** *v* civilizar.

clad [klad] *adj* vestido (de).

claim [kleim] *v* (*damages*) exigir; (*a right*) reclamar; (*assert*) declarar; (*need*) requerir. *n* (*right*) derecho *m*; (*demand*) demanda *f*, reclamación *f*; (*statement*) declaración *f*; (*land*) propiedad *f*. **claimant** (*law*) *n* demandante *m, f*; (*pretender*) pretendiente *m, f*.

clairvoyant [kleə'voiənt] *n(m+f)*, *adj* clarividente. **clairvoyance** *n* clarividencia *f*.

clam [klam] *n* almeja *f*.

clamber ['klambə] *v* trepar.

clammy ['klami] *adj* pegajoso.

clamour ['klamə] *n* clamor *m*. *v* clamar, vociferar.

clamp [klamp] *n* abrazadera *f*. *v* sujetar con abrazadera. **clamp down on** suprimir.

clan [klan] *n* clan *m*. **clannish** *adj* exclusivista.

clandestine [klan'destin] *adj* clandestino.

clang [klaŋ] *v* sonar estrepitosamente. *n* sonido metálico *m*.

clap [klap] *v* aplaudir, dar palmadas. *n* (*with hands*) palmada *f*; (*noise*) ruido seco *m*. **clap of thunder** trueno *m*.

claret ['klarət] *n* clarete *m*.

clarify ['klarəfai] *v* aclarar; (*liquid*) clarificar. **clarification** *n* aclaración *f*; clarificación *f*.

clarinet [klarə'net] *n* clarinete *m*.

clarity ['klarəti] *n* claridad *f*.

clash [klaʃ] *v* (*collide*) chocar; (*cymbals*) golpear; (*interests*) estar en desacuerdo; (*dates*) coincidir; (*colours*) matarse. *n* ruido metálico *m*; (*encounter*) choque *m*; (*interests*) conflicto *m*; coincidencia *f*; disparidad *f*.

clasp [klɑːsp] *v* (*grasp*) agarrar; (*fasten*) abrochar. *n* (*hands*) apretón *m*; (*fastening*) cierre *m*; (*belt*) broche *m*.

class [klɑːs] *n* clase *f*.

classic ['klasik] *adj* clásico. **classical** *adj* clásico. **classics** *n pl* clásicas *f pl*.

classify ['klasifai] *v* clasificar. **classification** *n* clasificación *f*. **classified advertisement** anuncio por palabras *m*.

clatter ['klatə] *n* estruendo *m*; (*hooves*) chacoloteo *m*. *v* sonar con estrépito; chacolotear.

clause [klɔːz] *n* (*law*) cláusula *f*; (*gramm*) oración *f*.

claustrophobia [klɔːstrə'fəubiə] *n* claustrofobia *f*.

claw [klɔː] *n* (*talon*) garra *f*; (*cat*) uña *f*; (*crab*) pinza *f*; (*tech*) garfio *m*. *v* agarrar; arañar; (*tear*) desgarrar.

clay [klei] *n* arcilla *f*, barro *m*.

clean [kliːn] *adj* limpio; (*irreproachable*) sin tacha. *v* limpiar. **clean out** (*empty*) vaciar. **clean up** (*tidy*) ordenar; (*win*) ganarse. **clean-cut** *adj* bien hecho, perfilado. **cleaner** (*person*) *n* asistenta *f*. **cleanliness** *n* limpieza *f*. **clean-shaven** *adj* bien afeitado.

cleanse [klenz] *v* limpiar, purificar.

clear [kliə] *adj* claro, transparente; (*conscience*) tranquilo; evidente; (*free*) libre; (*unobstructed*) despejado; (*profit*) neto. *adv* claramente. *v* aclarar; despejar; (*law*) absolver, despejar; *n* margen *m*; despeje *m*; acreditación *f*. **clearance** *n* espacio *m*, altura libre *f*. **clearance sale** liquidación *f*.

clef [klef] *n* clave *f*.

clench [klentʃ] *v* apretar, sujetar.

clergy ['klɜːdʒi] *n* clero *m*. **clergyman** *n* clérigo *m*.

clerical ['klerikəl] *adj* (*clerk*) de oficina; (*rel*) clerical. **clerical error** error de copia *m*.

clerk [klɑːk] *n* oficinista *m, f*; (*law*) escribano *m*.

clever ['klevə] *adj* listo; inteligente; (*skilful*) hábil; (*cunning*) astuto. **cleverness** *n* habilidad *f*; ingenio *m*.

cliché ['kliːʃei] *n* cliché *m*, clisé *m*.

click [klik] *n* chasquido *m*; taconeo *m*. *v* chascar, chasquear; taconear.

client ['klaiənt] *n* cliente *m, f*.

cliff [klif] *n* (*coast*) acantilado *m*; (*crag*) risco *m*.

climate ['klaimət] *n* clima *m*; (*atmosphere*) ambiente *m*. **climatic** *adj* climático.

climax ['klaimaks] *n* punto culminante *m*; clímax *m*. *v* llevar al punto culminante.

climb [klaim] *v* subir, escalar; (*plant*) trepar. *n* subida *f*, escalada *f*. **climber** *n* escalador, -a *m, f*; (*mountaineer*) alpinista *m, f*; (*plant*) planta trepadora *f*.

*cling [kliŋ] *v* agarrarse; (*stick to*) adherirse a, pegarse a. **clinging** *adj* ceñido; pegajoso.

clinic ['klinik] *n* dispensario *m*; clínica *f*. **clinical** *adj* clínico.

clip¹ [klip] *v* (*trim*) recortar; (*animals*) esquilar; (*ticket*) picar; (*coll*: *cuff*) abofetear. *n* (*film*) fragmento; (*cuff*) bofetada *f*.

clip² [klip] *v* (*fasten*) sujetar. *n* grapa *f*; sujetapapeles *m invar*; (*hair*) horquilla *f*; (*pen, pencil*) prendedor *m*.

cloak [klouk] *n* capa *f*; (*fig*) manto *m*; (*mil*) capote *f*. **cloak-and-dagger** *adj* de capa y espada. **cloakroom** *n* guardarropa *m*; (*toilet*) servicios *m pl*. *v* encubrir, cubrir, encapotar.

clock [klok] *n* reloj *m*. **against the clock** contra reloj. **alarm clock** despertador *m*. **around the clock** durante 24 horas. **clockwise** *adj* en el sentido de las agujas del reloj. **clockwork** *n* aparato de relojería *m*. *v* registrar.

clog [klog] *n* zueco *m*. *v* atascar, obstruir.

cloister ['kloistə] *n* claustro *m*. *v* enclaustrar.

close [klouz; *adj, adv* klous] *v* cerrar; (*block*) tapar; (*end*) acabar; (*account*) saldar; (*distance*) acortar. **close in** acercarse. *n* conclusión *f*; final *m*. *adj* cercano; íntimo; (*air*) cargado; (*game*) reñido. *adv* cerca. **close-up** *n* primer plano *m*.

closet ['klozit] *n* (*WC*) retrete *m*, water *m*; armario *m*.

clot [klot] *n* (*blood*) coágulo *m*; (*liquid*) grumo *m*. *v* coagular, cuajar.

cloth [kloθ] *n* (*rag*) trapo *m*; (*fabric*) paño *m*; (*tablecloth*) mantel *m*.

clothe [klouð] *v* vestir; (*cover*) cubrir.

clothes [klouðz] *pl n also clothing* ropa *f sing*; vestidos *m pl*. **clothes basket** cesta de la ropa sucia *f*. **clothes brush** cepillo de la ropa *m*. **clothes line** tendedero *f*. **clothes peg** pinza *f*.

cloud [klaud] *n* nube *f*; (*gas*) capa *f*. *v* nublar; (*darken*) ensombrecer, oscurecer. **cloudburst** *n* chaparrón *m*. **cloudiness** *n* nubosidad *f*. **cloudless** *adj* despejado. **cloudy** *adj* nuboso; nublado.

clove¹ [klouv] *n* (*spice*) clavo *m*.

clove² [klouv] *n* (*of garlic, etc.*) diente *m*.

clover ['klouvə] *n* trébol *m*.

clown [klaun] *n* payaso *m*. *v* hacer el payaso.

club [klʌb] *n* (*association*) club *m*; (*stick*) porra *f*, garrote *m*; (*golf*) palo *m*. *v* (*beat*) aporrear. **clubfoot** *n* pie zopo *m*.

clue [kluː] *n* (*police lead*) pista *f*; (*piece of evidence*) indicio *m*.

clump [klʌmp] *n* (*trees*) grupo *m*; (*flowers*) matar *f*; (*earth*) terrón *m*; (*noise*) pisada fuerte *f*. *v* agrupar; andar con pisadas fuertes.

clumsy ['klʌmzi] *adj* (*awkward*) torpe; (*unskilful*) desmañado; (*tactless*) sin tacto. **clumsiness** *n* torpeza *f*; desmaña *f*.

cluster ['klʌstə] *n* grupo *m*; (*fruits*) racimo *m*. *v* agruparse, arracimarse.

clutch [klʌtʃ] *v* agarrar, apretar. *n* (*grip*) agarrón *m*; (*mot*) embrague *m*. **engage the clutch** embragar.

clutter ['klʌtə] *n* desorden *m*, confusión *f*. *v* desordenar, atentar.

coach [koutʃ] *n* (*carriage*) coche *m*; (*ceremonial carriage*) carroza *f*; (*mot*) autocar *m*; (*tutor*) profesor particular *m*; (*trainer*) entrenador *m*. *v* dar clases particulares; entrenar.

coagulate [kou'agjuleit] *v* coagular. **coagulation** *n* coagulación *f*.

coal [koul] *n* carbón *m*, hulla *f*. **coal cellar** carbonera *f*. **coalman** *n* carbonero *m*. **coalmine** *n* mina de carbón *f*. **coalminer** *n* minero de carbón *m*. **coal scuttle** cubo para el carbón *m*.

coalesce [kouə'les] v (unite) unirse; (merge) fusionarse.

coalition [kouə'lifən] n coalición f.

coarse [kɔɪs] adj (gross) grosero; (ill-made) basto. **coarse-grained** adj de grano grueso. **coarseness** n grosería f; basteza f.

coast [koust] n costa f. **the coast is clear** no hay moros en la costa. v (freewheel) deslizarse cuesta abajo. **coastguard** n guardacostas m invar. **coastline** n litoral m.

coat [kout] n chaqueta f; (overcoat) abrigo m; (animal) pelo m. **coat-hanger** percha f. **coat of arms** escudo de armas m. **coat of paint** mano de pintura f. v cubrir; dar una mano de pintura; (cookery) rebozar. **coating** n capa f; mano f; rebozo m.

coax [kouks] v engatusar.

cobbler ['koblə] n zapatero m.

cobra ['koubrə] n cobra f.

cobweb ['kobweb] n telaraña f.

cocaine [kə'kein] n cocaína f.

cock¹ [kok] n (male fowl) gallo m; (male bird) macho m; (impol: penis) polla f. **cocky** adj engreído.

cock² [kok] v (gun) amartillar; (ears) aguzar el oído.

cockle ['kokl] n berberecho m.

cockpit ['kokpit] n (aero) cabina del piloto f; (cockfighting) reñidero m.

cockroach ['kokroutʃ] n cucaracha f.

cocktail ['kokteil] n cóctel m. **cocktail shaker** coctelera f.

cocoa ['koukou] n cacao m.

coconut ['koukənʌt] n coco m. **coconut palm** cocotero m.

cocoon [kə'kuɪn] n capullo m.

cod [kod] n bacalao m.

code [koud] n código m; (signals) cifra f, clave f; (area code) prefijo m. **highway code** código de la circulación m. **Morse code** alfabeto Morse m. v cifrar.

codeine ['koudiɪn] n codeína f.

coeducation [kouedju'keifən] n coeducación f.

coerce [kou'əɪs] v forzar, obligar.

coexist [kouig'zist] v coexistir. **coexistence** n coexistencia f.

coffee ['kofi] n café m. **black/white coffee** café solo/con leche m. **coffee bean** grano de café m. **coffee pot** cafetera f. **coffee table** mesita de café f.

coffin ['kofin] n ataúd m.

cog [kog] n diente m; (wheel) rueda dentada f.

cognac ['konjak] n coñac m.

cohabit [kou'habit] v cohabitar, vivir juntos. **cohabitation** n cohabitación f.

cohere [kə'hiə] v adherirse, pegarse. **coherence** n coherencia f. **coherent** adj coherente.

coil [koil] n (rope) rollo m; (smoke) espiral m; (elec) carrete m. **coil spring** muelle en espiral m. v enrollar, arrollar.

coin [koin] n moneda f. **toss a coin** echar a cara o cruz. v acuñar; inventar. **coinage** n moneda f.

coincide [kouin'said] v coincidir. **coincidence** n coincidencia f. **coincidental** adj coincidente.

colander ['koləndə] n escurridor m.

cold [kould] adj frío. **be cold** (person) tener frío; (weather) hacer frío. **cold front** frente frío m. **cold storage** conservación f. **cold war** guerra fría f. **catch a cold** resfriarse. **cold-blooded** adj (biol) de sangre fría; (fig) insensible.

colic ['kolik] n cólico m.

collaborate [kə'labəreit] v colaborar. **collaboration** n colaboración f. **collaborator** n (colleague) colaborador, -a m, f; (pol) colaboracionista m, f.

collapse [kə'laps] v derrumbar; (med) sufrir un colapso. n derrumbamiento m; colapso; (failure) fracaso m. **collapsible** adj plegable.

collar ['kolə] n cuello m; (dog, etc.) collar m. **collarbone** n clavícula f. v (seize) agarrar por el cuello; (put a collar on) acollarar.

collate [ko'leit] v cotejar. **collation** n (food) colación f; (texts) cotejo m.

colleague ['koliig] n colega m, f.

collect [kə'lekt] v (bring together) juntar, reunir; (hobby) coleccionar; (funds) allegar; (taxes) recaudar; (bills) cobrar; (gather) recoger. **collected works** obras completas f pl. **collection** (hobby) colección f; (charity) colecta f; (people) grupo m; (things) reunión f; (rent, bills) cobro m; (taxes) recaudación f; (postal) recogida f. **collective** adj colectivo. **collector** n (tax) recaudador, -a m, f; (bills, rent) cobrador m; (hobbies) coleccionista m, f.

college ['kolidʒ] n colegio m. **collegiate** adj colegiado.

collide [kə'laid] v chocar. **collision** n choque m.

colloquial [kə'loukwiəl] adj familiar, popular. **colloquialism** n expresión familiar f.

Colombia [kə'lombiə] n Colombia f. **Colombian** n, adj colombiano, -a.

colon ['koulɒn] n dos puntos m pl; (anat) colon m.

colonel ['kɜːnl] n coronel m.

colony ['kɒləni] n colonia f. **colonial** adj colonial. **colonialist** m(m+f), adj colonialista. **colonist** n colono m. **colonization** n colonización f. **colonize** v colonizar.

colossal [kə'lɒsəl] adj colosal.

colour ['kʌlə] n color m. **colour bar** barrera racial f. **colour-blind** adj daltoniano. **colourful** adj animado. **fast colour** color sólido m. **in colour** en colores. v colorear; (dye) teñir.

colt [koult] n potro m.

column ['kɒləm] n columna f. **columnist** n columnista m, f.

coma ['koumə] n coma m.

comb [koum] n peine m; (honey) panal m. v peinar.

combat ['kɒmbat] n combate m. v combatir, luchar contra. **combatant** n(m+f), adj combatiente.

combine [kəm'bain; n 'kɒmbain] v combinar, reunir. n (comm) cártel m. **combination** n combinación f, asociación f.

combustion [kəm'bʌstʃən] n combustión f. **combustible** adj combustible.

*****come** [kʌm] v venir, llegar; proceder; salir. **come about** ocurrir. **come across** dar con. **come along!** ¡vamos! **come back** volver. **comeback** n restablecimiento m. **come off** desprender; (succeed) tener éxito. **come out** salir. **come to** (from faint) volver en sí; (total) ascender a.

comedy ['kɒmədi] n comedia f. **comedian** n cómico m.

comet ['kɒmit] n cometa m.

comfort ['kʌmfət] n (relief) alivio m; (consolation) consuelo m; (well-being) bienestar m; (convenience) comodidad f. v aliviar; consolar; animar. **comfortable** adj cómodo; agradable. **comfortably** adv cómodamente; confortablemente.

comic ['kɒmik] adj cómico, divertido. n (magazine) tebeo m. **comical** adj cómico.

comma ['kɒmə] n coma f. **inverted commas** comillas f pl.

command [kə'maind] n (order) orden f; (authority) mando m; (mastery) dominio m. v mandar, ordenar; dominar. **commandant** n comandante m. **commander** n comandante m; (leader) jefe m. **commander-in-chief** n comandante-en-jefe m. **commandment** n mandamiento m.

commandeer [kɒmən'diə] v expropiar.

commando [kə'maindou] n comando m.

commemorate [kə'meməreit] v conmemorar. **commemoration** n conmemoración f. **commemorative** adj conmemorativo.

commence [kə'mens] v empezar, comenzar. **commencement** n comienzo m.

commend [kə'mend] v (recommend) recomendar; (entrust) encomendar; (praise) alabar. **commendable** adj recomendable. **commendation** n alabanza f, elogio m, encomio m.

comment ['kɒment] n observación f; (explanation) comentario m. **no comment** sin comentarios. v comentar, hacer observaciones. **commentary** n comentario m, observación f. **running commentary** reportaje en directo m.

commerce ['kɒmɜːs] n comercio m. **commercial** adj comercial. **commercial traveller** agente comercial m. **commercialism** n mercantilismo m. **commercialize** v comercializar.

commiserate [kə'mizəreit] v compadecerse. **commiseration** n conmiseración f.

commission [kə'miʃən] n (profit) comisión f; (to a post, etc.) nombramiento m; (assignment) cometido m; (charge) encargo; (crime) ejecución f; (mil) grado de oficial m. v comisionar; encargar; (mil) nombrar. **commissionaire** n portero m. **commissioner** n comisionado m. **High Commissioner** alto comisario m.

commit [kə'mit] v (crime) cometer; (entrust) confiar; (imprison) encarcelar. **commit oneself** comprometerse. **commitment** n (assignment) cometido m; (pledge) compromiso m.

committee [kə'miti] n comité m, comisión f.

commodity [kə'mɒdəti] n mercancía f, producto m, artículo m.

common ['kɒmən] adj común; público; ordinario; frecuente. **commoner** n plebeyo, -a m, f. **Common Market** Mercado Común m. **commonness** n frecuencia f; vulgaridad f. **commonplace**

adj común, trivial. **commonsense** *adj* lógico. **commonwealth** *n* república *f*.

commotion [kə'mouʃən] *n* disturbio *m*; tumulto *m*.

commune[1] [kə'mjuɪn] *v* (*communicate*) comunicarse; (*meditate*) meditar. **communion** *n* comunión *f*.

commune[2] ['komjuɪn] *n* comuna *f*. **communal** *adj* comunal.

communicate [kə'mjuɪnikeit] *v* comunicar. **communication** *n* comunicación *f*. **communicative** *adj* comunicativo.

communism ['komjunizəm] *n* comunismo *m*. **communist** *n*(*m*+*f*), *adj* comunista.

community [kə'mjuɪnəti] *n* comunidad *f*. **community centre** centro social *m*.

commute [kə'mjuɪt] *v* (*travel*) viajar; (*law*) conmutar. **commuter** *n*, *adj* viajero, -a.

compact[1] [kəm'pakt] *adj* compacto; recogido; conciso; denso. *v* condensar; comprimir.

compact[2] ['kompakt] *n* pacto *m*; (*powder*) polvera *f*.

companion [kəm'panjən] *n* compañero, -a *m*, *f*; (*professional*) acompañante *m*, *f*. **companionship** *n* compañerismo *m*.

company ['kʌmpəni] *n* (*comm*) compañía *f*, empresa *f*; (*companionship*) compañerismo *m*, sociedad *f*.

compare [kəm'peə] *v* comparar. **comparable** *adj* comparable. **comparative** *adj* relativo; (*gram*) comparativo. **comparison** *n* comparación *f*.

compartment [kəm'paɪtmənt] *n* compartimiento *m*, departamento *m*.

compass ['kʌmpəs] *n* (*naut*) brújula *f*; (*extent*) extensión *f*. **compasses** *n pl* (*maths*) compás *m*.

compassion [kəm'paʃən] *n* compasión *f*. **compassionate** *adj* compasivo.

compatible [kəm'patəbl] *adj* compatible. **compatibility** *n* compatibilidad *f*.

compel [kəm'pel] *v* compeler, obligar. **compelling** *adj* convincente.

compensate ['kompənseit] *v* (*make up for*) compensar; (*repay*) indemnizar. **compensation** *n* compensación *f*; indemnización *f*; (*reward*) recompensa *f*.

compete [kəm'piɪt] *v* competir. **competition** *n* competición *f*; (*contest*) concurso *m*; (*comm*) competencia *f*. **competitive** *adj* competitivo; (*spirit*) de competencia. **competitor** *n* competidor, -a *m*, *f*. (*contestant*) concursante *m*, *f*.

competent ['kompətənt] *adj* competente; (*suitable*) adecuado. **competence** *n* competencia *f*, aptitud *f*.

compile [kəm'pail] *v* compilar. **compilation** *n* compilación *f*. **compiler** *n* compilador, -a *m*, *f*.

complacent [kəm'pleisnt] *adj* complaciente. **complacence**, **complacency** *n* satisfacción de sí mismo *f*.

complain [kəm'plein] *v* quejarse. **complaint** *n* queja *f*; (*med*) enfermedad *f*; (*law*) demanda *f*.

complement ['kompləmənt] *n* complemento *m*. *v* complementar. **complementary** *adj* complementario.

complete [kəm'pliɪt] *adj* completo; (*finished*) acabado, concluido, terminado; (*entire*) entero. *v* completar; terminar; (*fill in*) llenar. **completion** *n* cumplimiento *m*; terminación *f*.

complex ['kompleks] *adj* complejo, complicado. *n* complejo *m*. **complexity** *n* complejidad *f*.

complexion [kəm'plekʃən] *n* tez *f*, cutis *m*; aspecto *m*.

complicate ['komplikeit] *v* complicar. **complicated** *adj* complicado. **complication** *n* complicación *f*.

complicity [kəm'plisəti] *n* complicidad *f*.

compliment ['kompləmənt] *n* cumplido *m*. **compliments** *n pl* saludos *m pl*. **complimentary** *adj* elogioso; (*gratis*) de favor.

comply [kəm'plai] *v* conformarse; (*obey*) obedecer.

component [kəm'pounənt] *nm*, *adj* componente.

compose [kəm'pouz] *v* componer; calmar. **composed** *adj* sereno. **be composed of** constar de. **composer** *n* compositor, -a *m*, *f*. **composite** *adj* compuesto. **composition** *n* composición *f*.

compost ['kompost] *n* abono *m*.

composure [kəm'pouʒə] *n* calma *f*, serenidad *f*.

compound[1] [kəm'paund; *n*, *adj* 'kompaund] *v* componer; mezclar. *nm*, *adj* compuesto. **compound fracture** fractura complicada *f*.

compound[2] ['kompaund] *n* (*enclosure*) recinto cercado *m*.

comprehend [kompri'hend] *v* comprender. **comprehensible** *adj* comprensible. **comprehension** *n* comprensión *f*.

comprehensive *adj* extenso, amplio. **comprehensive insurance** seguro a todo riesgo *m*. **comprehensive school** colegio integrado *m*.

compress ['kompres; *v* kəm'pres] *n* (*med*) compresa *f*. *v* comprimir; (*condense*) condensar. **compression** *n* compresión *f*.

comprise [kəm'praiz] *v* comprender.

compromise ['komprəmaiz] *n* compromiso *m*, arreglo *m*. *v* (*agree*) llegar a un arreglo; (*yield*) transigir; (*endanger*) comprometer. **compromising** *adj* comprometedor.

compulsion [kəm'pʌlʃən] *n* obligación *f*; (*coercion*) coacción *f*; (*impulse*) impulso *m*. **compulsive** *adj* compulsivo. **compulsory** *adj*

computer [kəm'pjuttə] *n* computador *m*, computadora *f*, ordenador *m*. **compute** *v* computar, calcular. **computerize** *v* tratar.

comrade ['komrid] *n* camarada *m, f* compañero, -a *m, f*. **comradeship** *n* camaradería *f*.

concave [kon'keiv] *adj* cóncavo. **concavity** *n* concavidad *f*.

conceal [kən'siil] *v* ocultar. **concealed** *adj* oculto. **concealment** *n* encubrimiento *m*.

concede [kən'siid] *v* conceder; (*admit*) reconocer. **concede victory** darse por vencido.

conceit [kən'siit] *n* presunción *f*, vanidad *f*. **conceited** *adj* engreído, vanidoso.

conceive [kən'siiv] *v* concebir. **conceive of** imaginarse. **conceivable** *adj* concebible.

concentrate ['konsəntreit] *v* concentrar. *n* concentrado. **concentration** *n* concentración *f*. **concentration camp** campo de concentración *m*.

concentric [kən'sentrik] *adj* concéntrico.

concept ['konsept] *n* concepto *m*. **conception** *n* concepción *f*; idea *f*.

concern [kən'səin] *n* asunto *m*; (*interest*) interés *m*; (*business*) empresa *f* (*worry*) preocupación *f*. *v* (*have as a subject*) tratar de; (*affect*) afectar; (*be related to*) referirse a. **concerned** *adj* preocupado. **concerning** *prep* con respecto a.

concert ['konsət; *v* kən'sətt] *n* concierto *m*. *v* concertar.

concertina [konsə'tiinə] *n* concertina *f*.

concerto [kən'tʃəttou] *n* concierto *m*.

concession [kən'seʃən] *n* concesión *f*.

conciliate [kən'silieit] *v* conciliar. **conciliation** *n* conciliación *f*. **conciliator** *n* conciliador, -a *m, f*. **conciliatory** *adj* conciliatorio.

concise [kən'sais] *adj* conciso.

conclude [kən'kluid] *v* acabar, terminar; (*treaty*) concertar; (*deduce*) concluir. **conclusion** *n* conclusión *f*. **conclusive** *adj* conclusivo; concluyente.

concoct [kən'kokt] *v* (*mix*) confeccionar; (*plot*) urdir; inventar. **concoction** *n* (*mixture*) mezcla *f*; (*lies*) fabricación *f*.

concrete ['konkriit] *n* hormigón *m*. **concrete mixer** hormigonera *f*. **reinforced concrete** hormigón armado *m*. *adj* concreto; (*tech*) de hormigón.

concussion [kən'kʌʃən] *n* conmoción cerebral *f*. **concuss** *v* conmocionar.

condemn [kən'dem] *v* condenar; (*building*) declarar en ruina. **condemnation** *n* condenación *f*. **condemnatory** *adj* condenatorio. **condemned** *adj* condenado.

condense [kən'dens] *v* (*cut*) abreviar, resumir; (*physics*) condensar. **condensation** *n* condensación *f*; (*vapour*) vaho *m*; (*abbreviation*) resumen *m*. **condenser** *n* condensador *m*.

condescend [kondi'send] *v* condescender, dignarse. **condescending** *adj* condescendiente, superior. **condescension** *n* condescendencia *f*.

condition [kən'diʃən] *n* condición *f*, estado *m*. *v* condicionar, determinar. **conditional** *adj* condicional. **conditionally** *adv* con reservas. **conditioning** *n* condicionamiento *m*.

condolence [kən'douləns] *n* condolencia *f*, pésame *m*. **condole** *v* condolerse, dar el pésame.

condom ['kondom] *n* condón *m*.

condone [kən'doun] *v* condonar, perdonar.

conducive [kən'djuusiv] *adj* conducivo; (*helpful*) propicio.

conduct ['kondʌkt; *v* kən'dʌkt] *n* conducta *f*, comportamiento *m*. *v* (*lead*) conducir; (*music, business*) dirigir; (*behave*) comportarse. **conductance** *n* conductancia *f*. **conduction** *n* conducción *f*. **conductivity** *n* conductividad *f*.

conductor [kən'dʌktə] *n* (*music*) director, -a *m, f*; (*guide*) guía *m*; (*bus*) cobrador *m*; (*physics*) conductor *m*. **lightning conductor** pararrayos *m sing*.

cone [koun] *n* cono *m*; (*bot*) piña *f*; (*ice*

cream) cucurucho de helado *m.* **cone-shaped** *adj* cónico.

confectioner [kən'fekʃənə] *n* confitero, -a *m, f.* **confection** *n* dulce *m.* **confectionery** *n (sweets)* dulces *m pl; (shop)* confitería *f; (cake shop)* repostería *f.*

confederate [kən'fedərət] *nm, adj* confederado. *v* confederar. **confederation** *n* confederación *f.*

confer [kən'fəː] *v* consultar, conferir; *(hold a conference)* conferenciar. **conference** *n* consulta *f; (meeting)* conferencia *f; (talks)* entrevista *f.*

confess [kən'fes] *v* confesar. **confession** *n* confesión *f.* **confessional** *n (rel)* confesionario *m.* **confessor** *n* confesor *m; (priest)* director espiritual *m.*

confetti [kən'feti] *n* confeti *m.*

confide [kən'faid] *v* confiar. **confidence** *n (trust)* confianza *f; (secret)* confidencia *f; (self-reliance)* seguridad en sí mismo *f.* **confidence trick** estafa *f.* **confident** *adj* lleno de confianza. **confidential** *adj* confidencial. **confidentially** *adv* en confianza.

confine [kən'fain] *n* confín *m;* límite *m.* *v* confinar; limitar; *(med)* estar de parto. **confined** *adj* reducido. **confinement** *n* encierro *m; (med)* parto *m.*

confirm [kən'fəːm] *v* confirmar; *(treaty)* ratificar. **confirmation** *n* confirmación *f;* ratificación *f.* **confirmed** *adj* confirmado; *(inveterate)* empedernido.

confiscate ['konfiskeit] *v* confiscar. **confiscation** *n* confiscación *f.*

conflict ['konflikt; *v* kən'flikt] *n* conflicto *m.* *v* luchar; *(clash)* chocar. **conflicting** *adj* contrapuesto.

conform [kən'fɔːm] *v* conformarse. **conformist** *n(m+f), adj* conformista. **conformity** *n* conformidad *f.*

confound [kən'faund] *v* confundir; *(foil)* frustrar; *(disconcert)* desconcertar.

confront [kən'frʌnt] *v* hacer frente a; *(present with)* presentarse; *(bring face to face)* enfrentar, confrontar. **confrontation** *n* confrontación *f.*

confuse [kən'fjuːz] *v* confundir; desconcertar; complicar. **confused** *adj* confuso; perplejo. **confusing** *adj* confuso; desconcertante. **confusion** *n* confusión *f.* desorden *m.*

congeal [kən'dʒiːl] *v* congelar; coagular.

congenial [kən'dʒiːniəl] *adj (pleasant)* agradable; *(suitable)* conveniente; *(similar)* compatible.

congenital [kən'dʒenitl] *adj* congénito.

congested [kən'dʒestid] *adj* congestionado; *(crowded)* superpoblado. **congestion** *n* congestión *f;* superpoblación *f.*

conglomeration [kənglɔmə'reiʃən] *n* conglomeración *f.* **conglomerate** *v* conglomerar.

congratulate [kən'gratjuleit] *v* felicitar, dar la enhorabuena. **congratulations** *pl n* felicitaciones *f pl; interj* ¡felicidades!

congregate ['kongrigeit] *v* congregarse. **congregation** *n* congregación *f,* asamblea *f; (rel)* feligreses *m pl.*

congress ['kongres] *n* congreso *m.*

conical ['konikəl] *adj* cónico.

conifer ['konifə] *n* conífera *f.* **coniferous** *adj* conífero.

conjecture [kən'dʒektʃə] *n* conjetura *f.* *v* conjeturar. **conjectural** *adj* conjetural.

conjugal ['kondʒugəl] *adj* conyugal.

conjugate ['kondʒugeit] *v* conjugar. **conjugation** *n* conjugación *f.*

conjunction [kən'dʒʌŋkʃən] *n (gramm)* conjunción *f.* **conjunctive** *adj* conjuntivo.

conjunctivitis [kəndʒʌŋkti'vaitis] *n* conjuntivitis *f.*

conjure ['kandʒə; *(appeal to)* kən'dʒuə] *v (magic)* hacer juegos de manos; *(appeal to)* conjurar. **conjurer** *n* ilusionista *m,* prestidigitador *m.* **conjuring trick** juego de manos *m.*

connect [kə'nekt] *v (join)* unir, juntar; *(relate)* relacionar; *(elec)* conectar. **connected** *adj (joined)* conectado, unido; *(related)* emparentado; *(associated)* relacionado; coherente. **connection** *n* relación *f; (transport)* empalme *m; (elec)* conexión *f; (joint)* unión *f; (relative)* pariente *m.* **in connection with** con respecto a.

connoisseur [konə'səː] *n* experto, -a *m, f.* conocedor, -a *m, f.*

connotation [konə'teiʃən] *n* connotación *f.*

conquer ['koŋkə] *v* vencer, triunfar. **conquering** *adj* victorioso. **conqueror** *n* conquistador *m,* vencedor, -a *m, f.* **conquest** *n* conquista *f.*

conscience ['konʃəns] *n* conciencia *f.*

conscientious [konʃi'enʃəs] *adj* concienzudo. **conscientious objector** objetor de conciencia *m.* **conscientiousness** *n* escrupulosidad *f.*

conscious ['kɔnʃəs] *adj* (*aware*) consciente; (*deliberate*) intencional. **be conscious** tener conocimiento. **be conscious** of tener conciencia de. **become conscious** volver en si. **become conscious of** darse cuenta de. **consciousness** *n* conocimiento *m*.

conscript ['kɔnskript] *n* recluta *m*.

consecrate ['kɔnsikreit] *v* consagrar. **consecration** *n* consagración *f*.

consecutive [kən'sekjutiv] *adj* consecutivo.

consensus [kən'sensəs] *n* consenso *m*.

consent [kən'sent] *n* consentimiento *m*. **by common consent** de acuerdo mutuo. *v* consentir (en).

consequence ['kɔnsikwəns] *n* consecuencia *f*, resultado *m*. **consequent** *adj* consiguiente. **consequently** *adv* consecuentemente, por lo tanto.

conserve [kən'sɔːv] *v* conservar. *n* conserva *f*. **conservation** *n* conservación *f*. **conservative** *adj* conservador, moderado. **conservatory** *n* (*plants*) invernadero *m*; (*music*) conservatorio *m*.

consider [kən'sidə] *v* considerar; (*think*) pensar (en); (*study*) examinar; (*realize*) darse cuenta de; (*take into account*) tener en cuenta. **considerable** *adj* considerable. **considerably** *adv* considerablemente. **consideration** *n* consideración *f*; (*payment*) retribución *f*. **considerate** *adj* considerado.

consign [kən'sain] *v* consignar; (*send*) enviar; (*entrust*) confiar. **consignee** *n* consignatario *m*. **consignment** *n* consignación *f*; envío *m*.

consist [kən'sist] *v* consistir; (*made up of*) constar, componerse. **consistency** *n* (*density*) consistencia *f*; (*agreement*) conformidad *f*. **consistent** *adj* de acuerdo, firme. **consistently** *adv* constantemente; consecuentemente.

console¹ ['kɔnsoul] *n* (*table, organ*) consola *f*; (*support*) ménsula *f*; mesa de control *f*; pupitre *m*.

console² [kən'soul] *v* consolar. **consolation** *n* consuelo *m*. **consolation prize** premio de consolación *m*.

consolidate [kən'sɔlideit] *v* consolidar. **consolidation** *n* consolidación *f*.

consommé [kən'somei] *n* consomé *m*, caldo *m*.

consonant ['kɔnsənənt] *n* consonante *f*. *adj* conforme.

consortium [kən'sɔːtiəm] *n* consorcio *m*.

conspicuous [kən'spikjuəs] *adj* visible; (*remarkable*) notable; (*attracting attention*) llamativo.

conspire [kən'spaiə] *v* conspirar. **conspiracy** *n* conspiración *f*. **conspirator** *n* conspirador, -a *m*, *f*.

constable ['kɔnstəbl] *n* policía *m*, guardia *m*. **constabulary** *n* policía *f*.

constant ['kɔnstənt] *adj* (*continuous*) constante; (*faithful*) fiel, leal. **constancy** *n* constancia *f*; fidelidad *f*, lealdad *f*.

constellation [kɔnstə'leiʃən] *n* constelación *f*.

constipation [kɔnsti'peiʃən] *n* estreñimiento *m*. **constipated** *adj* estreñido.

constitute ['kɔnstitjuːt] *v* constituir. **constituency** *n* distrito electoral *m*. **constituent** *n* (*component*) componente *m*; (*pol*) votante *m*. *adj* (*component*) constitutivo, constituyente; electoral. **constitution** *n* constitución *f*. **constitutional** *adj* constitucional. *n* (*coll*) paseo *m*.

constraint [kən'streint] *n* (*restriction*) encierro *m*; (*compulsion*) coacción *f*; (*inhibition*) turbación *f*. **constrain** *v* encerrar; (*compel*) constreñir; (*inhibit*) incomodar.

constrict [kən'strikt] *v* (*narrow*) estrechar; (*compress*) oprimir. **constricted** *adj* estrecho. **constriction** *n* constricción *f*.

construct [kən'strʌkt] *v* construir. **construction** *n* construcción *f*; (*structure*) estructura *f*; (*meaning*) interpretación *f*. **constructive** *adj* constructivo. **constructor** *n* constructor *m*.

consul ['kɔnsəl] *n* cónsul *m*. **consular** *adj* consular. **consulate** *n* consulado *m*.

consult [kən'sʌlt] *v* consultar. **consultant** *n* (*adviser*) asesor *m*; (*med*) especialista *m*; (*tech*) consejero técnico *m*. **consultation** *n* consulta *f*. **consulting room** consultorio *m*.

consume [kən'sjuːm] *v* consumir; (*time*) tomar; (*food*) comerse; (*drink*) beberse. **consumer** *n* consumidor, -a *m*, *f*. **consumer goods** bienes de consumo *m pl*. **consumption** *n* consumo *m*; (*med: tuberculosis*) tisis *f*. **consumptive** *n*, *adj* (*med*) tísico, -a.

contact ['kɔntækt] *n* contacto *m*. **contact lens** lente de contacto *f*. *v* ponerse en contacto con.

contagious [kən'teidʒəs] *adj* contagioso. **contagion** *n* contagio *m*.

contain [kən'tein] *v* contener. **container** *n* (*package*) envase *m*; (*receptacle*) recipiente *m*. (*transport*) contenedor *m*. **containment** *n* contención *f*.

contaminate [kən'tæməneit] *v* contaminar. **contamination** *n* contaminación *f*.

contemplate ['kontəmpleit] *v* contemplar; (*expect*) contar con; (*consider*) considerar. **contemplation** *n* contemplación *f*, meditación *f*; consideración *f*. **contemplative** *adj* contemplativo.

contemporary [kən'tempərəri] *nm*, *adj* contemporáneo.

contempt [kən'tempt] *n* desprecio *m*, desdén *m*. **contempt of court** desacato a los tribunales *m*. **hold in contempt** despreciar. **contemptible** *adj* despreciable, desdeñable. **contemptuous** *adj* despreciativo, desdeñoso.

contend [kən'tend] *v* (*struggle*) contender; (*compete*) competir; (*dispute*) disputir; (*affirm*) afirmar. **contender** *n* competidor, -a *m, f.* **contention** *n* contienda *f*; (*argument*) discusión *f*; (*opinion*) opinión *f*. **contentious** *adj* (*person*) pendenciero; (*issue*) discutible. **contentiousness** *n* carácter pendenciero *m*.

content[1] ['kontent] *n* contenido *m*.

content[2] [kən'tent] *adj* also **contented** contento, satisfecho. **be contented with** contentarse con. **contentment** *n* contento *m*.

contest [kən'test; *n* 'kontest] *v* (*dispute*) disputar; (*question*) impugnar. *n* (*struggle*) contienda *f*; (*competition*) competición *f*; (*controversy*) controversia *f*. **contestant** *n* contrincante *m*; (*election*) candidato, -a *m, f.*

context ['kontekst] *n* contexto *m*.

continent ['kontinənt] *n* continente *m*. **the Continent** el continente europeo *m*. **continental** *adj* continental.

contingency [kən'tindʒənsi] *n* (*possibility*) contingencia *f*, eventualidad *f*; (*event*) acontecimiento fortuito *m*. **contingent** *adj* (*accidental*) fortuito; (*probable*) contingente; (*incidental*) derivado; (*dependent*) subordinado; (*dependent on chance*) aleatorio.

continue [kən'tinju] *v* continuar, seguir; (*extend*) prolongar. **continual** *adj* continuo. **continually** *adv* constantemente.

continuation *n* continuación *f*. **continuity** *n* continuidad *f*; (*cinema, radio*) guión *m*. **continuous** *adj* continuo.

contort [kən'tort] *v* retorcer, torcer. **contortion** *n* contorsión *f*; deformación *f*. **contortionist** *n* contorsionista *m, f.*

contour ['kontuə] *n* (*map*) curva de nivel *f*; (*outline*) contorno *m*.

contraband ['kontrəbænd] *n* contrabando *m. adj* de contrabando.

contraception [kontrə'sepʃən] *n* contracepción *f*. **contraceptive** *nm, adj* contraceptivo. **contraceptive pill** píldora contraceptiva *f*.

contract ['kontrakt; *v* kən'trakt] *n* contrato *m. v* (*shrink*) contraer; (*make a contract*) contratar; (*ailment*) coger. **contraction** *n* contracción *f*. **contractor** *n* contratista *m*. **contractual** *adj* contractual.

contradict [kontrə'dikt] *v* contradecir. **contradiction** *n* contradicción *f*. **contradictory** *adj* contradictorio.

contralto [kən'traltou] *n* contralto *m, f.*

contraption [kən'trapʃən] *n* (*coll*) chisme *m*.

contrary ['kontrəri] *adj* contrario. **on the contrary** al contrario.

contrast [kən'traist; *n* 'kontraist] *v* contrastar. *n* contraste *m*. **in contrast** por contraste. **in contrast to** a diferencia de. **contrasting** *adj* contrastante.

contravene [kontrə'vim] *v* contravenir. **contravention** *n* contravención *f*.

contribute [kən'tribjut] *v* contribuir (con); (*write*) escribir; (*give information*) aportar. **contribution** *n* contribución *f*; artículo *m*; aportación *f*; (*to conversation*) intervención *f*. **contributive** *adj* contributivo. **contributor** *n* contribuyente *m, f*; (*writer*) colaborador, -a *m, f*. **contributory** *adj* contribuyente.

contrive [kən'traiv] *v* idear, inventar; (*manage*) conseguir. **contrived** *adj* artificial. **contrivable** *adj* realizable; imaginable. **contrivance** *n* aparato *m*; invención *f*; (*resourcefulness*) ingenio *m*.

control [kən'troul] *n* control *m*; autoridad *f*; dominación *f*; (*standard of comparison*) testigo *m*. **remote control** mando a distancia *m*. **controls** *pl n* mandos *m pl. v* controlar; tener autoridad sobre; (*direct*) dirigir; (*regulate*) regular; (*vehicle*)

41

manejar. **controller** n director m. **air traffic controller** controlador del tráfico aéreo m. **controlling** adj predominante; (decisive) determinante.

controversy [kən'trɔvəsi] n controversia f. **controversial** adj discutible.

convalesce [kɔnvə'les] v convalecer. **convalescence** n convalecencia f.

convector [kən'vektə] n estufa de convección f. **convection** n convección f.

convenience [kən'viːnjəns] n conveniencia f; (comfort) comodidad f; (advantage) ventaja f; (useful object) dispositivo útil m. **at your convenience** cuando le sea posible. **public convenience** servicios m pl. **convenient** adj (handy) cómodo; (suitable) conveniente; (place) bien situado; (time) oportuno.

convent ['kɔnvənt] n convento m.

convention [kən'venʃən] n (usage) convención f; (assembly) asamblea f; (international agreement) convenio m. **conventions** n pl conveniencias f pl. **conventional** (not original) convencional; (traditional) clásico.

converge [kən'vəːdʒ] v convergir. **converger. convergence** n convergencia f. **converging** adj convergente.

converse[1] [kən'vəːs] v conversar, hablar. **conversant** adj versado, familiarizado. **conversation** n conversación f.

converse[2] ['kɔnvəːs] n lo opuesto m. adj opuesto, contrario.

convert [kən'vəːt; v kən'vəːt] n converso, -a m. f. v convertir. **conversion** n conversión f; transformación f.

convertible [kən'vəːtəbl] adj convertible; transformable. n (mot) descapotable m.

convex ['kɔnveks] adj convexo.

convey [kən'vei] v (carry) llevar, transportar; (suggest) sugerir, dar a entender; (transmit) transmitir; (meaning) expresar. **conveyance** n transporte m; transmisión f; (deed) escritura de traspaso f. **conveyancer** n notario que hace escritura de traspaso m. **conveyancing** n redacción de una escritura de traspaso f.

convict ['kɔnvikt; v kən'vikt] n presidiario, -a m. f. v (prove guilty) condenar; (betray) traicionar.

conviction [kən'vikʃən] n condena f; (belief) convicción f.

convince [kən'vins] v convencer. **convincing** adj convincente.

convivial [kən'viviəl] adj alegre, sociable, festivo.

convoy ['kɔnvɔi] n convoy m. v convoyar.

convulsion [kən'vʌlʃən] n (med) convulsión f; (laughter) carcajadas f pl. **convulse** v convulsionar.

cook [kuk] v cocinar; (coll: the books) falsificar. n cocinero, -a m. f. **cooker** n cocina f; olla f. **pressure cooker** olla de presión f. **cookery** n arte de cocina m; cocción f; cocina f. **cookery book** libro de cocina m. **do the cooking** guisar.

cool [kuːl] adj fresco; (calm) tranquilo; (unenthusiastic) frío. v enfriar; calmar. **cooler** n enfriador m. **cooling** adj refrescante. **cooling system** n sistema de refrigeración m. **coolish** adj fresquito. **coolly** adv fríamente; tranquilamente. **coolness** n frescor m; frialdad f; serenidad f; sangre fría f.

coop [kuːp] n (poultry) gallinero m. **coop up** encerrar.

cooperate [kou'ɔpəreit] v cooperar. **cooperation** n cooperación f. **cooperative** adj cooperativo.

coordinate [kou'ɔːdineit] n coordenada f. adj igual. v coordinar. **coordination** n coordinación f.

cope[1] [koup] v arreglárselas; dar abasto; poder con.

cope[2] [koup] n (rel) capa pluvial f.

Copenhagen [koupən'heigən] n Copenhague.

copious ['koupiəs] adj copioso, abundante.

copper[1] ['kɔpə] n (metal) cobre m. adj de cobre; (colour) cobrizo. **copper plate** plancha de cobre f.

copper[2] ['kɔpə] n also **cop** (slang) poli m.

copulate ['kɔpjuleit] v copular. **copulation** n cópula f.

copy ['kɔpi] n copia f; (book) ejemplar m; (pattern) modelo m; (reportage) asunto m. **carbon copy** papel carbón m. **fair copy** copia en limpio f. **rough copy** borrador m. v copiar; imitar. **copyright** n propiedad literaria.

coral ['kɔrəl] n coral m. adj coralino.

cord [kɔːd] n (string, rope) cuerda f; (insulated wire) cordón m. **spinal cord** médula espinal f. **umbilical cord** cordón umbilical m. **vocal cords** cuerdas vocales f pl.

cordial ['kɔːdiəl] adj, nm cordial. **cordiality** n cordialidad f.

cordon ['kɔɪdn] *n* cordón *m*. **cordon off** acordonar.

corduroy ['kɔɪdərɔɪ] *n* pana *f*.

core [kɔɪ] *n* (*fruit*) corazón *m*; (*geol*) núcleo; (*fig*) centro *m*. esencia *f*. *v* quitar el corazón de.

cork [kɔɪk] *n* (*bot*) corcho *m*; (*stopper*) tapón *m*. **cork tree** alcornoque *m*. **cork-tipped** *adj* con boquilla de corcho. *v* taponar. **uncork** *v* (*bottle*) descorchar. **corked** *adj* (*bottle*) taponado; (*wine*) que sabe a corcho. **corkscrew** *n* sacacorchos *m invar*.

corn[1] [kɔɪn] *n* (*wheat*) trigo *m*; (*maize*) maíz *m*; (*cereals*) granos cereales *m pl*. **corn on the cob** maíz in la mazorca *m*.

corn[2] [kɔɪn] *n* (*med*) callo *m*.

corner ['kɔɪnə] *n* (*inside angle*) rincón *m*; (*outside angle*) esquina *f*; (*of an object*) pico *m*. **cut corners** tomar atajos. *v* poner en un aprieto; (*accost*) abordar; (*mot*) tomar una curva; (*comm*) monopolizar.

cornet ['kɔɪnit] *n* corneta *f*; (*ice cream*) cucurucho *m*.

coronary ['kɔɪənəri] *adj* coronario. **coronary thrombosis** trombosis coronaria *f*.

coronation [kɔɪə'neiʃən] *n* coronación *f*.

corporal[1] ['kɔɪpərəl] *adj* corporal. **corporal punishment** castigo corporal *m*.

corporal[2] ['kɔɪpərəl] *n* (*mil*) cabo *m*.

corporation [kɔɪpə'reiʃən] *n* corporación *f*; sociedad anónima *f*. **municipal corporation** ayuntamiento *m*. **corporate** *adj* colectivo, corporativo.

corps [kɔɪ] *n* cuerpo *m*. **corps de ballet** cuerpo de ballet. **diplomatic corps** cuerpo diplomático.

corpse [kɔɪps] *n* cadáver *m*.

correct [kə'rekt] *adj* (*accurate*) exacto; (*behaviour*) correcto; (*right*) justo. *v* corregir. **correction** *n* corrección *f*. **corrective** *adj* correctivo. **correctness** *n* corrección *f*; exactitud *f*; (*judgment*) rectitud *f*.

correlate ['kɔɪəleit] *v* correlacionar. **correlation** *n* correlación *f*.

correspond [kɔɪə'spɔnd] *v* corresponder; (*write*) escribirse. **correspondence** *n* correspondencia *f*. **correspondent** *n* corresponsal *m*. *adj* (*newspaper*) corresponsal *m*. **correspond-ing** *adj* correspondiente *m, f*; (*newspaper*) corresponsal *m, f*.

corridor ['kɔɪidɔɪ] *n* pasillo *m*, corredor *m*.

corroborate [kə'rɔbəreit] *v* corroborar. **corroboration** *n* corroboración *f*.

corrode [kə'roud] *v* corroer. **corrosion** *n* corrosión *f*. **corrosive** *adj* corrosivo.

corrugated ['kɔrəgeitid] *adj* ondulado.

corrupt [kə'rʌpt] *adj* corrupto; corrompido; (*rotten*) estragado; (*perverted*) pervertido; (*bribable*) venal. *v* corromper; (*bribe*) sobornar. **corruptible** *adj* corruptible. **corruption** *n* corrupción *f*.

corset ['kɔɪsət] *n* faja *f*.

Corsica ['kɔɪsikə] *n* Córcega *f*. **Corsican** *n, adj* corso, -a *m, f*.

cosmetic [kɔz'metik] *nm, adj* cosmético.

cosmic ['kɔzmik] *adj* cósmico.

cosmopolitan [kɔzmə'pɔlitən] *n(m+f)*. *adj* cosmopolita.

*****cost** [kɔst] *n* costo *m*, coste *m*; (*price*) precio *m*; (*expenses*) gastos *m pl*. costes *pl* *n* (*law*) costas *f pl*. **at all costs** cueste lo que cueste. **cost of living** coste de vida *m*. **to one's cost** a expensas de uno. *v* costar; valer. **costly** *adj* caro.

Costa Rica [kɔstə'rikə] *n* Costa Rica. **Costa Rican** *n(m+f)*. *adj* costarriqueñse; *n, adj* costarriqueño, -a *m, f*.

costume ['kɔstjuɪm] *n* traje *m*. **bathing costume** traje de baño. **costume jewellery** bisutería *f*.

cosy ['kɔuzi] *adj* confortable; (*place*) acogedor.

cot [kɔt] *n* cuna *f*.

cottage ['kɔtidʒ] *n* casa de campo *f*; chalet *m*. **cottage cheese** requesón *m*.

cotton ['kɔtn] *n* algodón *m*. *adj* de algodón. **cotton-wool** *n* algodón hidrófilo *m*.

couch [kautʃ] *n* sofá *m*; (*bed*) lecho *m*. *v* (*express*) expresar.

cough [kɔf] *n* tos *f*. *v* toser. **cough up** (*coll*) cascar.

could [kud] *V* **can**[1].

council ['kaunsəl] *n* consejo *m*; (*assembly*) ayuntamiento *m*. **council house** vivienda protegida *f*. **town council** concejo municipal *m*. **councillor** *n* concejal *m*.

counsel ['kaunsəl] *n* consejo *m*; (*lawyer*) abogado *m*; (*legal adviser*) asesor jurídico *m*. *v* aconsejar; pedir consejo.

count[1] [kaunt] *v* contar, calcular; (*consider*) considerar. **count against** ir en contra de. **count for** valer por. **countable** *adj* contable. **countdown** *n* cuenta atrás *f*. **countless** *adj* incontable. *n* cuenta *f*, cálculo *m*; (*sum*) total *m*; (*votes*) escrutinio *m*.

count² [kaunt] n (noble) conde m. **countess** n condesa f.

countenance ['kauntinəns] n semblante m, cara f. v (approve) aprobar; (support) apoyar.

counter¹ ['kauntə] n (disc) ficha f; (table top) mostrador m, contador m. **Geiger counter** contador Geiger m. **under the counter** bajo mano.

counter² ['kauntə] adj (opposed) contrario, opuesto. v contraatacar; oponerse. **go counter to** ir en contra de.

counterattack ['kauntərə,tak] n contraataque m. v contraatacar.

counterfeit ['kauntəfit] adj falso, falsificado. v falsificar. n falsificación f.

counterfoil ['kauntə,foil] n talón m.

counterpart ['kauntə,part] n contraparte f.

country ['kʌntri] n (state) país m; (out of town) campo. **country estate** finca f. **country house** casa de campo f. **countryman** n campesino m; compatriota m. **countryside** n campo m; (landscape) paisaje m.

county ['kaunti] n condado m. **county council** diputación provincial f.

coup [ku] n golpe m. **coup d'état** golpe de estado m.

couple ['kʌpl] n par m; (married, engaged, etc.) pareja f. v emparejar; (associate) asociar; (vehicles) enganchar; (elec) conectar; (copulate) copular.

coupon ['kupon] n cupón m; (pools) boleto m.

courage ['kʌridʒ] n valor m, valentía f. **pluck up courage** armarse de valor. **take courage** cobrar ánimo. **courageous** adj valiente.

courgette [kuə'ʒet] n calabacín m.

courier ['kuriə] n guía m, f; agente de turismo m, f; mensajero, -a m, f.

course [kos] n (direction) dirección f, rumbo m; (progress) curso m; (way, means) camino m; (action, conduct) línea f; (meal) plato m; (track) pista f; (golf) campo m. **in due course** a su debido tiempo. **main course** plato fuerte m. **of course** claro, por supuesto. **set course for** hacer rumbo a. v (hunt) cazar; (run: liquid) correr.

court [kot] n (royalty) corte f; (alley) callejón sin salida m; (law) audiencia f, tribunal m; (sport) cancha f. **court order** orden judicial f. **go to court** acudir a los tribunales. **courtyard** n patio m. v (woo)

cortejar, hacer la corte a; buscar; pedir, solicitar. **courtier** n cortesano m. **courtly** adj cortés. **court-martial** n consejo de guerra m. **courtship** n noviazgo m.

courteous ['kɜtiəs] adj cortés. **courtesy** n cortesía f.

cousin ['kʌzn] n primo, -a m, f. **first cousin** primo, -a carnal m, f.

cove [kouv] n cala f; (slang) tío m.

cover ['kʌvə] n cubierta f; (lid) tapa f; (bed) colcha f; (table) tapete m; (refuge) refugio m; (parcel) envoltura f; (envelope) sobre m; (pretence) excusa f; (protection) amparo m. **cover charge** precio del cubierto m. **take cover** ponerse a cubierto. v cubrir, tapar. **coverage** n alcance m.

cow [kau] n vaca f; (female animal) hembra f. v intimidar. **cowboy** n vaquero m, (Amer) gaucho m. **cowshed** n establo m. **cowslip** n prímula f.

coward ['kauəd] n cobarde m, f. **cowardice** n cobardía f. **cowardly** adj cobarde.

cower ['kauə] v encogerse; agacharse.

coy [koi] adj (shy) tímido; (demure) remilgado.

crab [krab] n cangrejo m. **crab apple** manzana silvestre f. **crabbed** adj (bad-tempered) malhumorado; (writing) indescifrable.

crack [krak] n (noise) restallido m, chasquido m; (opening) abertura f; (split) raja f; (in walls, etc.) hendidura f; (slit) rendija f; (blow) golpe m; (coll: joke) chiste m. **crack of dawn** al amanecer. **have a crack** at intentar. v restallar, chasquear; golpear; (break) romper; (a nut) cascar; hender; rajar; (burst) reventar; (give in) ceder; (break down) hundirse; (coll: joke) bromear; (coll: safe) forzar. **get cracking** darse prisa. **crackpot** n, adj (coll) chiflado. -a m, f.

cracker ['krakə] n (Christmas) sorpresa f; (firework) buscapiés m invar; (biscuit) galleta f.

crackle ['krakl] n crepitación f, crujido m. v crepitar, crujir. **crackling** n (cookery) chicharrón m.

cradle ['kreidl] n cuna f; soporte m. v acunar; (in one's arms) mecer; soportar.

craft [kraft] n (trade) trabajo manual m; (skill) arte m; (guild) gremio m; (cunning) astucia f, maña f; (ship) embarcación f; (aircraft) avión m. **craftily** adv astutamente. **craftsman** n artesano m.

craftsmanship n artesanía f. **crafty** adj astuto, socarrón.

cram [kram] v (fill up) aborratar; (force in) meter a la fuerza; (for exam) empollar.

cramp [kramp] n (med) calambre m. v dar calambre a. **cramped** adj (crowded) apiñado; (writing) apretado.

cranberry ['kranbəri] n arándano m.

crane [krein] n (hoist) grúa f; (bird) grulla f. v (neck) estirar.

crank [kraŋk] n (tech) manivela f; (fool) chiflado, -a m. f. v arrancar con la manivela. **crankcase** n cárter m. **crankiness** n irritabilidad f; excentricidad f; chifladura f. **crankshaft** n cigueñal m.

crap [krap] n (slang: nonsense) disparate; (impol) mierda f. v (impol) cagar.

crash [kraʃ] n accidente m. choque m; (noise) estrépito m; (aircraft) caída f; (business) quiebra f. **crash course** curso intensivo m. **crash helmet** casco protector m. v chocar; caer; quebrar; (make a loud noise) retumbar. **crash-land** hacer un aterrizaje de emergencia.

crate [kreit] n cajón de embalaje m. v embalar.

crater ['kreitə] n cráter m.

crave [kreiv] v (desire) ansiar; (beg) suplicar; (attention) reclamar. **craving** n ansia f.

crawl [krɔːl] v arrastrarse, andar a gatas; (move slowly) andar lentamente. n arrastramiento m; marcha lenta f.

crayfish ['kreifiʃ] n ástaco m. cangrejo de río m.

crayon ['kreiən] n lápiz de tiza m. v dibujar al pastel.

craze [kreiz] n (wild enthusiasm) locura f; (fad) manía f; (fashion) moda f. v enloquecer. **craziness** n locura f. **crazy** adj loco.

creak [kriːk] n crujido m. v crujir. **creaky** adj que cruje.

cream [kriːm] n nata f, crema f. **whipped cream** nata batida. adj color crema. v (beat) batir; (skim) desnatar. **cream cheese** queso de nata m.

crease [kriːs] n (fold) pliegue m; (wrinkle) arruga f; (trousers) raya f. **crease-resistant** adj inarrugable. v plegar; arrugar; hacer la raya de.

create [kriˈeit] v crear. **creation** n creación f. **creator** n creador, -a m. f.

credentials [kriˈdenʃəlz] pl n credenciales f pl.

credible ['kredəbl] adj creíble. **credibility** n credibilidad f.

credit ['kredit] n crédito m; (comm) haber m; (prestige) honor m. **credits** pl n (film) ficha técnica f sing. **credit balance** saldo acreedor m. **credit card** tarjeta de crédito f. **credit rating** solvabilidad f. **on credit** a plazos. **we do not give credit** no se fía.

credit² ['kredit] v (believe) creer; (fig) atribuir; (an account) abonar en cuenta. **creditable** adj (believable) digno de crédito; (praiseworthy) encomiable; (well spoken of) de buena reputación. **creditably** adv honrosamente. **creditor** n acreedor, -a m. f.

credulous ['kredjuləs] adj crédulo.

creed [kriːd] n credo m.

***creep** [kriːp] v deslizarse, arrastrarse; (flesh) ponerse a uno la carne de gallina. n (coll) pelotillero, -a m. f. **creepy** adj horripilante.

cremate [kriˈmeit] v incinerar. **cremation** n incineración f. **crematorium** n horno crematorio m.

crescent ['kresnt] n medialuna f, luna creciente f. adj creciente.

cress [kres] n berro m.

crest [krest] n (on animal's head, wave) cresta f; (hill) cima f, cumbre f; (heraldry) timbre m. **crested** adj crestado. **crestfallen** adj alicaído.

crevice ['krevis] n grieta f; hendedura f.

crew [kruː] n (body of workers) equipo m; (ship, aircraft) tripulación f; (mob) banda f. **ground crew** personal de tierra m.

crib [krib] n (rack) pesebre m; (small cot) cuna f; (coll: exam) chuleta f. v plagiar.

cricket¹ ['krikit] n (insect) grillo m.

cricket² ['krikit] n (sport) criquet m.

crime [kraim] n crimen m; criminalidad f. **criminal** nm. adj criminal.

crimson ['krimzn] nm. adj carmesí.

cringe [krindʒ] v agacharse, encogerse. **cringing** adj servil.

crinkle ['kriŋkl] n arruga f. v arrugarse.

cripple ['kripl] n. adj tullido, -a m. f. v (person) tullir; (object) estropear; (fig) paralizar.

crisis ['kraisis] n pl -ses crisis f invar.

crisp [krisp] adj fresco; (bread) curruscante; (style) crespo; (snow) crujiente; (talk) animado. v encrespar, rizar. **potato**

crisp patata frita a la inglesa f. **crispness** n encrespado m.

criterion [krai'tiəriən] n pl -a criterio m.

criticize ['kriti,saiz] v criticar. **critic** (fault-finder) criticón, -ona m. f; (reviewer) crítico m. **critical** adj crítico. **criticism** n crítica f.

crochet ['krouʃei] n croché m, ganchillo m. v hacer a ganchillo.

crockery ['krokəri] n loza f, vajilla f.

crocodile ['krokə,dail] n cocodrilo m.

crocus ['kroukəs] n azafrán m.

crook [kruk] n (shepherd's) cayado m; (bishop's) báculo m; (coll) ladrón m, timador m.

crooked ['krukid] adj (bent) curvado; (twisted) torcido; (path) sinuoso; (nose) ganchudo; (coll) poco limpio. **crookedness** n sinuosidad f; (coll) falta de honradez f.

crop [krop] n (harvest) cosecha f; (cultivated produce) cultiva f; (whip) fusta f; (bird) buche m; (haircut) corte de pelo m. **crop rotation** rotación de cultivos f. v (graze) pacer; (ears) desorejar; (tail) cortar la cola de; (hair) cortar muy corto. **come a cropper** darse un batacazo.

croquet ['kroukei] n croquet m.

cross [kros] n cruz f; (breeding) cruce f. **make the sign of the cross** santiguarse. adj cruzado; (angry) enfadado. v (move) atravesar; (limbs) cruzar; (oppose) contrariar; (mark) marcar con una cruz. **cross out** tachar. **cross one's mind** ocurrírsele a.

cross-country adj a campo traviesa.

cross-current n contracorriente f.

cross-examination n repregunta f.

cross-eyed adj bizco.

crossfire ['kros,faiə] n fuego cruzado m.

crossing ['krosin] n (intersection) cruce f; (voyage) travesía f; (pedestrian) paso de peatones m.

cross-purposes pl n fines opuestos m pl.

cross-reference n remisión f.

crossroads ['kros,roudz] pl n cruce f sing; (fig) encrucijada f sing.

cross section n sección transversal f.

crossword ['kros,wəid] n crucigrama m.

crotchet ['krotʃit] n (music) negra f. **crotchety** adj de mal genio.

crouch [krautʃ] v agacharse, encogerse.

crow¹ [krou] n (bird) cuervo m. **as the crow flies** en línea recta. **crowbar** n palanca f.

crow² [krou] v cantar; cacarear. n cacareo m.

crowd [kraud] n muchedumbre f, multitud f. v amontonar; congregarse. **crowded** adj lleno.

crown [kraun] n corona f; (hat) copa f; (hill) cumbre f; (head) coronilla f. **crown jewels** joyas reales f pl. **crown prince** príncipe heredero m. v coronar. **to crown it all** para rematarlo todo. **crowning** adj supremo.

crucial ['kruʃəl] adj crucial, decisivo.

crucify ['krusi,fai] v crucificar. **crucifix** n crucifijo m. **crucifixion** n crucifixión f.

crude [kruːd] adj (raw) crudo; (steel) bruto; (oil) sin refinar; (vulgar) basto; (ill-made) tosco. **crudeness, crudity** n crudeza f; tosquedad f.

cruel ['kruəl] adj cruel. **cruelty** n crueldad f.

cruise [kruːz] n crucero m. v hacer un crucero; (patrol) patrullar; (at cruising speed) ir a una velocidad de crucero. **cruiser** n (naut) crucero m.

crumb [krʌm] n migaja f, miga f.

crumble ['krʌmbl] v desmenuzar; desmigar. **crumbly** adj desmenuzable.

crumple ['krʌmpl] v arrugar, ajar. **crumple up** desplomarse.

crunch [krʌntʃ] n crujido m; (coll) punto decisivo m. v crujir; mascar. **crunchy** adj crujiente.

crusade [kruː'seid] n cruzada f; (fig) campaña f. v hacer una cruzada. **crusader** n cruzado m.

crush [krʌʃ] n aplastamiento m; (crowd) aglomeración f; (squeeze) apretón m. **have a crush on** (coll) estar loco perdido por. v aplastar; apretar; (pulverize) machacar; (overwhelm) abrumar. **crushing** adj aplastante.

crust [krʌst] n (of a loaf) corteza f. **upper crust** la flor y nata f. **crusty** adj de corteza dura; (coll) brusco.

crutch [krʌtʃ] n (support) muleta f; (fig) apoyo m.

crux [krʌks] n quid m.

cry [krai] n grito m. v (call) gritar; (weep) llorar. **cry out** clamar.

crypt [kript] n cripta f. **cryptic** adj secreto; enigmático.

crystal ['kristl] n cristal m. adj de cristal. **crystal clear** cristalino. **crystallize** v cristalizar.

cub [kʌb] n (bear, lion, tiger, wolf) cachorro m. (other animals) cría f. **cub scout** niño explorador m.

Cuba [ˈkjuːbə] n Cuba f. **Cuban** n, adj cubano, -a.

cube [kjuːb] n (math) cubo m; (sugar, etc.) terrón m. v (math) cubicar. **cube root** raíz cúbica f. **cubic** adj cúbico.

cubicle [ˈkjuːbikl] n cubículo m; (for sleeping) cubilla f; (for changing) caseta f.

cuckoo [ˈkukuː] n cuco m, cuclillo m.

cucumber [ˈkjuːkʌmbə] n pepino m.

cuddle [ˈkʌdl] n abrazo m. v abrazar. **cuddly** adj mimoso.

cue¹ [kjuː] n (theatre) señal f; entrada f. v indicar.

cue² [kjuː] n (billiards) taco m.

cuff¹ [kʌf] n (shirt) puño m. **cufflinks** pl n gemelos m pl. **off the cuff** de improviso.

cuff² [kʌf] n (hit) bofetada f. v abofetear.

culinary [ˈkʌlinəri] adj culinario.

culminate [ˈkʌlmineit] v culminar. **culmination** n culminación f.

culprit [ˈkʌlprit] n culpado, -a m, f; culpable m, f.

cult [kʌlt] n culto m.

cultivate [ˈkʌltiveit] v cultivar. **cultivated** adj (land) cultivado; (person) culto. **cultivation** n cultivo m.

culture [ˈkʌltʃə] n cultura f; cultivo m. **cultured** adj culto.

cumbersome [ˈkʌmbəsəm] adj molesto; (annoying) incómodo.

cunning [ˈkʌniŋ] adj (sly) taimado; (clever) astuto; (skilful) mañoso. n astucia f; maña f.

cup [kʌp] n taza f; (prize) copa f.

cupboard [ˈkʌbəd] n armario m.

curate [ˈkjuərət] n cura m.

curator [kjuəˈreitə] n conservador, -a m, f.

curb [kəːb] v contener, refrenar. n (obstacle) estorbo m; (fig) freno m.

curdle [ˈkəːdl] v cuajar, cuajarse. **curd** cuajada f.

cure [kjuə] n (course of treatment; smoking food) cura f; (remedy) remedio m; (of leather) curtido m; (salting) salazón m. v curar; remediar; salar; curtir. **cure-all** n curalotodo m.

curfew [ˈkəːfjuː] n toque de queda m.

curious [ˈkjuəriəs] adj curioso. **curiosity** n curiosidad f.

curl [kəːl] n (hair) bucle m; (smoke) voluta f; (twist) torcedura f; serpenteo m.

v (hair) rizar. **curl oneself up** hacerse un ovillo. **curler** n rulo m. **curly** adj rizado; sinuoso; en espiral.

currant [ˈkʌrənt] n (dried grape) pasa f; (berry) grosella f; (bush) grosellero m.

currency [ˈkʌrənsi] n moneda f; (general use) uso corriente m.

current [ˈkʌrənt] n corriente f; curso m. **alternating/direct current** corriente alterna/continua f. adj (general) corriente, prevalente; (now) actual; (accepted) admitido. **current account** cuenta corriente f. **current affairs** actualidades f pl. **current rate of exchange** cambio del día m. **current year** año en curso. **currently** adv corrientemente; actualmente.

curry [ˈkʌri] n cari m, curry m. v preparar con cari. **curry powder** especias en polvo f pl.

curse [kəːs] n maldición f. v maldecir; (swear) decir palabrotas; (blaspheme) blasfemar.

curt [kəːt] adj brusco. **curtness** n brusquedad f.

curtail [kəːˈteil] v (cut short) abreviar; (expenses) reducir. **curtailment** n abreviación f; reducción f.

curtain [ˈkəːtn] n cortina f; (theatre) telón m. **curtain call** llamada a escena f. **draw the curtain** correr la cortina. v poner cortinas en; encubrir.

curtsy [ˈkəːtsi] n reverencia f. v hacer una reverencia.

curve [kəːv] n curva f; vuelta f. v doblar; encorvar. **curvature** n curvatura f; (earth) esfericidad f; (spine) encorvamiento m. **curved** adj curvo; doblado.

cushion [ˈkuʃən] n cojín m, almohadón m. v amortiguar, acolchar.

custard [ˈkʌstəd] n natillas f pl.

custody [ˈkʌstədi] n custodia f, guardia f; prisión f. **in custody** bajo custodia. **take into custody** detener. **custodian** n custodio m; guardián, -ana m, f.

custom [ˈkʌstəm] n (habit) costumbre f; (customers) clientela f sing. **customs** n derechos de aduana m pl. **customary** adj de costumbre. **custom-built** adj hecho de encargo. **customer** n cliente m, f.

*cut [kʌt] n corte m; (wound) herida f; (notch) muesca f; (reduction) reducción f; (med) incisión f. **short cut** atajo m. **cut-and-dried** adj previsto. **cut and thrust** la lucha f. v cortar; reducir; (reap) segar; (shorten) acortar. **cut short** cortar en

seco. *adj* cortado; reducido. **cut-price** *adj* a precio reducido.

cute [kjuːt] *adj* (*attractive*) mono, lindo; (*clever*) astuto. **cuteness** *n* monería *f*; astucia *f*.

cuticle ['kjuːtikl] *n* cutícula *f*.

cutlery ['kʌtləri] *n* cubiertos *m pl*.

cutlet ['kʌtlit] *n* chuleta *f*.

cycle ['saikl] *n* ciclo *m*; bicicleta *f*. *v* pasar por un ciclo; ir en bicicleta. **cyclical** *adj* cíclico. **cycling** *n* ciclismo *m*. **cyclist** *n* ciclista *m*, *f*.

cyclone ['saikloun] *n* ciclón *m*.

cylinder ['silində] *n* cilindro *m*. **cylinder block** bloque de cilindros *m*. **cylindrical** *adj* cilíndrico.

cymbal ['simbəl] *n* címbalo *m*, platillo *m*.

cynic ['sinik] *n*, *adj* cínico, -a *m*, *f*. **cynical** *adj* cínico. **cynicism** *n* cinicismo *m*.

cypress ['saiprəs] *n* ciprés *m*.

Cyprus ['saiprəs] *n* Chipre. **Cypriot** *n*(*m*+*f*). *adj* chipriota.

cyst [sist] *n* quiste *m*. **cystitis** *n* cistitis *f*.

Czechoslovakia [,tʃekəslə'vakiə] *n* Checoslovaquia *f*. **Czechoslovakian, Czechoslovak, Czech** *n*, *adj* checoslovaco, -a.

D

dab [dab] *n* (*light blow*) golpe ligero *m*; (*touch*) toque *m*; (*bit*) pizca *f*. *v* golpear ligeramente; dar unos toques de. *adj* **be a dab hand at** ser un hacha en.

dabble ['dabl] *v* (*splash*) salpicar; (*wet*) mojar. **dabble in** (*water*) chapotear; (*participation*) meterse en.

dad [dad] *n* (*coll*) papá *m*.

daffodil ['dafədil] *n* narciso *m*.

daft [daːft] *adj* (*coll*) tonto.

dagger ['dagə] *n* daga *f*; puñal *m*.

daily ['deili] *adj* diario, cotidiano. *adv* diariamente, cada día. *n* (*coll: newspaper*) diario *m*.

dainty ['deinti] *adj* (*taste*) delicado, fino; (*fussy*) difícil. **daintiness** *n* delicadeza *f*; elegancia *f*.

dairy ['deəri] *n* lechería *f*. **dairy cattle** vacas lecheras *f pl*. **dairy farm** granja de vacas *f*. **dairy products** productos lácteos *m pl*.

daisy ['deizi] *n* margarita *f*.

dam [dam] *n* (*barrier*) dique *m*; (*reservoir*) embalse *m*; (*zool*) madre *f*. *v* construir un dique; embalsar.

damage ['damidʒ] *n* daño *m*; (*fig*) perjuicio *m*. **damages** *pl n* (*law*) daños y perjuicios *m pl*. *v* dañar; perjudicar; (*spoil*) estropear.

damn [dam] *v* (*condemn*) condenar; (*curse*) maldecir. **damn!** (*interj*) ¡mechacis! **damnable** *adj* condenable, detestable. **damnation** *n* condenación *f*; (*interj*) ¡maldición! **damned** *adj* condenado; (*coll*) maldito; tremendo. *adv* sumamente.

damp [damp] *adj* húmedo. *n* humedad *f*. **damp course** aislante hidráfugo *m*. *v* (*also* **dampen**) humedecer; (*extinguish*) apagar, sofocar; (*discourage*) desanimar; (*sound*) amortiguar. **damper** *n* humedecedor *m*; (*chimney*) regulador *m*. **put a damper on** caer como un jarro de agua fría en.

damson ['damzən] *n* (*fruit*) ciruela damascena *f*; (*tree*) ciruelo damasceno *m*.

dance [daːns] *n* baile *m*; (*ritual*) danza *f*. **dance band** orquesta de baile *f*. **dance floor** pista de baile *f*. **dance hall** sala de baile *f*. *v* bailar. **dancer** *n* bailarín, -ina *m*, *f*.

dandelion ['dandi,laiən] *n* diente de león *m*.

dandruff ['dandrəf] *n* caspa *f*.

Dane [dein] *n* danés, -esa *m*, *f*. **Danish** *nm*, *adj* danés. **Great Dane** perro danés *m*.

danger ['deindʒə] *n* peligro *m*. **danger zone** área de peligro. **dangerous** *adj* peligroso.

dangle ['dangl] *v* (*hang*) colgar, dejar colgado; (*swing*) balancear en el aire.

dare [deə] *v* (*challenge*) desafiar; (*have the impudence to*) atreverse a. **I dare say** quizás. *n* desafío *m*, reto *m*. **daredevil** *n* temerario, -a *m*, *f*. **daring** *adj* atrevido; osado. *n* osadía *f*.

dark [daːk] *adj* oscuro; (*hair, complexion*) moreno; (*sombre*) triste; (*menacing*) amenazador; (*mysterious*) misterioso. **Dark Ages** edad de las tinieblas *f*. **dark room** cámara oscura *f*. **grow dark** anochecer. *n* oscuridad *f*. **after dark** después del anochecer. **be in the dark** estar a oscuras. **darken** *v* oscurecer; entristecer. **darkness** *n* oscuridad *f*.

darling ['dɑːlɪŋ] *n, adj* querido, -a *m, f.*
darn [dɑːn] *v* zurcir. *n* zurcido *m.* **darning needle** aguja de zurcir *f.*
dart [dɑːt] *n* (*missile*) dardo *m*; (*movement*) movimiento rápido *m. v* lanzar. **dartboard** *n* blanco *m.* **darts** *pl n* (*sport*) dardos *m pl.*
dash [daʃ] *n* (*rush*) carrera *f*; (*printing*) guión *m*; (*cookery*) poco *m*, gotas *f pl*; (*verve*) brío *m. v* (*rush*) precipitarse, ir de prisa; (*hopes*) defraudar. **dash off** (*letter, etc.*) escribir deprisa. **dashboard** *n* salpicadero *m.* **dashing** *adj* gallardo.
data ['deɪtə] *pl n* datos *m pl.* **data processing** proceso de datos *m.*
date¹ [deɪt] *n* (*calendar*) fecha *f*; época *f.* **be up to date** estar al día. **out of date** anticuado. **to date** hasta la fecha. **date line** meridiano de cambio de fecha *m. v* fechar.
date² [deɪt] *n* (*fruit*) dátil *m.* **date palm** palmera datilera *f.*
dative ['deɪtɪv] *nm, adj* dativo.
daughter ['dɔːtə] *n* hija *f.* **daughter-in-law** *n* nuera *f*, hija política *f.*
daunt [dɔːnt] *v* (*dishearten*) desanimar; (*intimidate*) intimidar. **dauntless** *adj* intrépido.
dawdle ['dɔːdl] *v* (*loiter*) holgazanear; (*waste time*) malgastar; (*walk slowly*) andar despacio.
dawn [dɔːn] *n* alba *m*, amanecer *m*; (*fig*) alborear *m.* **from dawn to dusk** de sol a sol. *v* alborear, amanecer.
day [deɪ] *n* día *m*; (*of work*) jornada *f.* **all day** todo el día. **every day** todos los días. **the day after tomorrow** pasado mañana. **the day before yesterday** anteayer. **from day to day** de día en día. **daybreak** *n* amanecer *m.* **daydream** *n* ensueño *m; v* soñar despierto. **daylight** *n* luz del día *f.* **in broad daylight** en pleno día. **good day!** ¡buenos días!
daze [deɪz] *n* aturdimiento *m. v* aturdir. **be in a daze** estar aturdido.
dazzle ['dazl] *n* brillo *m. v* deslumbrar. **dazzling** *adj* deslumbrante, deslumbrador.
dead [ded] *adj* muerto; (*absolute*) absoluto; (*insensible*) insensible; (*battery*) descargado; (*extinguished*) apagado. **deadline** *n* fecha *f.* **deadly** *adj* mortal; (*unerring*) absoluto; (*habit*) pernicioso.
deaden ['dedn] *v* (*sound, etc.*) amortiguar;

(*pain*) calmar; (*feeling*) embotar. **deadening** *adj* (*tech*) aislante.
deaf [def] *adj* sordo. **turn a deaf ear** hacerse el sordo. **deaf-and-dumb** *adj* sordomudo. **deafen** *v* ensordecer. **deafening** *adj* ensordecedor. **deafness** *n* sordera *f.*
deal [diːl] *v* repartir, distribuir. **deal in** comerciar en. *n* transacción *f*, negocio *m*; (*treatment*) trato *m*; (*agreement*) convenio *m*; (*amount*) cantidad *f*; (*cards*) reparto *m*; (*wood*) abeto *m.* **it's a deal!** ¡trato hecho! **your deal** te toca. **dealer** *m* comerciante *m, f*; (*cards*) mano *f.* **dealing** *n* trato *m*; (*behaviour*) conducta *f.* **dealings** *pl n* relaciones *f pl.*
dean [diːn] *n* (*rel*) deán *m*; (*academic*) decano *m.*
dear [dɪə] *adj* querido; (*costly*) caro, costoso. **dear me!** ¡Dios mío! **dear sir** estimado señor. **dearly** *adv* (*affectionately*) cariñosamente; (*costly*) caro.
death [deθ] *n* muerte *f*; (*formal*) fallecimiento *m.* **death certificate** certificado de defunción *m.* **death duty** derechos de sucesión *m pl.* **deathless** *adj* inmortal. **deathly** *adj* (*appearance*) cadavérico; (*silence*) sepulcral. **death penalty** pena de muerte *f.* **death rate** mortalidad *f.*
debase [dɪ'beɪs] *v* degradar; (*coins*) alterar. **debasement** *n* degradación *f*; alteración *f.*
debate [dɪ'beɪt] *n* debate *m*, discusión *f*; controversia *f. v* discutir; controvertir; considerar. **debatable** *adj* discutible. **debating society** asociación que organiza debates *f.*
debit ['debɪt] *n* (*entry of account*) débito *m*; (*left-hand side of account*) debe *m. v* cargar en cuenta.
debris ['deɪbriː] *n* escombros *m pl.*
debt [det] *n* deuda *f.* **run into debt** contraer deudas. **debtor** *n* deudor, -a *m, f.*
decade ['dekeɪd] *n* decenio *m.*
decadent ['dekədənt] *n(m+f), adj* decadente. **decadence** decadencia *f.*
decant [dɪ'kant] *v* decantar. **decanter** *n* garrafa *f*, jarra *f.*
decapitate [dɪ'kapɪteɪt] *v* decapitar. **decapitation** *n* decapitación *f.*
decay [dɪ'keɪ] *n* decomposición *f*; (*teeth*) caries *f invar*; decadencia *f*; (*physics*) desintegración progresiva *f. v* descomponerse; cariarse; decaer.

decease [di'siis] n fallecimiento m. v fallecer. **deceased** n, adj difunto, -a.

deceit [di'siit] n (cheating) engaño m; fraude m; decepción; (lying) mentira f. **deceitful** adj engañoso; fraudulento; mentiroso. **deceitfulness** n lo engañoso m; falsedad f.

deceive [di'siiv] v engañar; defraudar. **deceiver** n embustero, -a m, f.

December [di'sembə] n diciembre m.

decent ['diisənt] adj decente; (satisfactory) razonable; (coll) bueno, simpático. **decency** n decencia f, decoro m.

deceptive [di'septiv] adj engañoso. **deceptiveness** n apariencia engañosa f.

decibel ['desi,bel] n decibel m, decibelio m.

decide [di'said] v decidir; (line of action) determinar; (conflict) resolver; (choose) optar por. **decided** adj decidido; determinado; resuelto; (difference) marcado.

deciduous [di'sidjuas] adj de hoja caduca.

decimal ['desiməl] nf, adj decimal. **decimal point** coma de decimales f.

decipher [di'saifə] v descifrar.

decision [di'siʒən] n decisión f. **decisive** adj decisivo; concluyente; (manner) decidido; (tone) tajante. **decisively** adv con decisión.

deck [dek] n (ship) cubierta f; (bus) piso m. **deck chair** tumbona f.

declare [di'kleə] v declarar; proclamar. **declaration** n declaración f; proclamación f. **declaratory** adj declaratorio.

decline [di'klain] n (decrease) disminución f; (life) ocaso m; (decay) decaimiento; (number) baja f. v (to act) negarse (a); (an offer) rehusar; (gramm) declinar; bajar; (med) debilitarse. **declining** adj declinante.

decompose [,diikəm'pouz] v (break up) descomponer; (rot) pudrir. **decomposition** n descomposición f; putrefacción f.

decorate ['dekə,reit] v decorar, adornar; (medal) condecorar; (paint) pintar. **decoration** n (medal) condecoración f; (ornament) adorno m; (décor) decoración f. **decorative** adj decorativo. **decorator** n decorador, -a m, f.

decoy ['diikoi] n señuelo m.

decrease [di'kriis] v disminuir, reducir. n disminución f; reducción f. **decreasing** adj decreciente.

decree [di'krii] n decreto m. v decretar; pronunciar.

decrepit [di'krepit] adj decrépito.

dedicate ['dedi,keit] v (book, life, etc.) dedicar; (church) consagrar. **dedication** n (devotion) dedicación f; (inscription) dedicatoria f. **dedicatory** adj dedicatorio.

deduce [di'djuus] v deducir.

deduct [di'dʌkt] v descontar. **deductible** adj deducible. **deduction** n (discount) deducción f, rebaja f, descuento m; (conclusion) conclusión f, deducción f.

deed [diid] n acto m, acción f; (something done) hecho m; (feat) hazaña f; (law) escritura f.

deep [diip] adj profundo, hondo. **a hole a metre deep** un pozo de un metro de hondo. **deep in debt** cargado de deudas. **go off the deep end** perder los estribos. n (sea) piélago m. **deepfreeze** n congelador m.

deer [diə] n ciervo m.

deface [di'feis] v desfigurar; multilar. **defacement** n desfiguración f; mutilación f.

default [di'foilt] n (debt) falta de pago; (absence) falta f; (law) contumacia f, rebeldía f. **judgment by default** sentencia en rebeldía f. **win by default** ganar por incomparecencia del adversario. v dejar de pagar; condenar en rebeldía; (a contest) perder por incomparecencia.

defeat [di'fiit] n derrota f. v derrotar, vencer. **defeatism** n derrotismo m. **defeatist** n(m+f), adj derrotista.

defect ['diifekt; v di'fekt] n defecto m. v desertar. **defection** n deserción f. **defective** adj defectuoso; incompleto; (gramm) defectivo. **defectiveness** n imperfección f.

defend [di'fend] v defender. **defence** n defensa f. **self-defence** n autodefensa f. **defenceless** adj indefenso. **defendant** n (civil) demandado, -a m, f; (criminal) acusado, -a m, f. **defender** n defensor, -a m, f. **defensible** adj defensible; justificable. **defensive** adj defensivo. **on the defensive** a la defensiva.

defer [di'fəi] v (postpone) diferir; (submit) someter; (delay) tardar. **deference** n deferencia f. **in deference to** por respeto a. **deferential** adj deferente, respetuoso. **deferment** n aplazamiento m; (mil) prórroga f. **deferrable** adj diferible. **deferred** adj diferido; aplazado.

defiant [di'faiənt] *adj* provocativo; (*challenging*) desafiante. **defiance** *n* desafío *m*. **in defiance of** con desprecio de.

deficient [di'fiʃənt] *adj* deficiente; (*med*) atrasado.

deficit ['defisit] *n* déficit. *adj* deficitario.

define [di'fain] *v* definir; caracterizar; formular; determinar. **definition** *n* definición *f*; (*phot*) claridad *f*.

definite ['definit] *adj* definido; determinado; claro; definitivo; seguro. **definitely** *adv* claramente; categóricamente; (*without doubt*) seguramente.

deflate [di'fleit] *v* desinflar; (*comm*) provocar la deflación de; (*hopes*) reducir. **deflation** *n* desinflado *m*; (*comm*) deflación *f*.

deform [di'foːm] *v* deformar, desfigurar. **deformation** *n* deformación *f*.

defraud [di'frɔːd] *v* defraudar, estafar.

defrost [di'frɔst] *v* deshelar.

deft [deft] *adj* hábil, diestro. **deftness** *n* habilidad *f*, destreza *f*.

defunct [di'fʌŋkt] *adj* difunto.

defy [di'fai] *v* (*challenge*) desafiar, retar; (*resist*) resistir a.

degenerate [di'dʒenə,reit; *n*, *adj* di'dʒenərit] *v* degenerar. *n*, *adj* degenerado, -a. **degeneration** *n* degeneración *f*. **degenerative** *adj* degenerativo.

degrade [di'greid] *v* (*humiliate, reduce in rank*) degradar; (*quality*) rebajar; (*morals*) envilecer. **degradation** *n* degradación *f*. **degrading** *adj* degradante.

degree [di'griː] *n* (*stop*) grado *m*; categoria *f*; (*university*) título *m*. **bachelor's degree** licenciatura *f*. **by degrees** poco a poco. **doctor's degree** doctorado *m*. **to some degree** hasta cierto punto.

dehydrate [diː'haidreit] *v* deshidratar. **dehydration** *n* deshidratación *f*.

de-icer [diː'aisə] *n* descongelador *m*.

deity ['diːəti] *n* deidad *f*.

dejected [di'dʒektid] *adj* descorazonado, desanimado. **dejection** *n* desaliento *m*, abatimiento *m*.

delay [di'lei] *n* dilación *f*, retraso *m*; (*wait*) demora *f*. *v* retrasar; (*postpone*) aplazar. **delaying** *adj* dilatorio.

delegate ['deləgit; *v* 'deləgeit] *n* delegado, -a *m*, *f*. *v* delegar. **delegation** *n* delegación *f*.

delete [di'liːt] *v* tachar, borrar. **deletion** *n* supresión *f*.

deliberate [di'libərət; *v* di'libəreit] *adj*

(*intentional*) deliberado; (*unhurried*) lento; (*premeditated*) premeditado; (*cautious*) prudente. *v* deliberar; (*ponder*) reflexionar. **deliberately** *adv* (*on purpose*) a propósito; prudentemente; lentamente. **deliberation** *n* deliberación *f*; lentitud *f*; reflexión *f*.

delicate ['delikət] *adj* delicado; (*food*) exquisito; refinado; escrupuloso; (*touch*) ligero; (*health*) frágile. **delicacy** *n* delicadeza *f*, fragilidad *f*.

delicious [di'liʃəs] *adj* delicioso.

delight [di'lait] *n* deleite *m*; encanto *m*. *v* deleitar; encantar. **delightful** *adj* delicioso; encantador.

delinquency [di'liŋkwənsi] *n* delincuencia *f*. **delinquent** *n*(*m*+*f*), *adj* delincuente.

delirious [di'liriəs] *adj* delirante. **be delirious** delirar. **delirium** *n* delirio *m*.

deliver [di'livə] *v* (*hand over*) entregar; (*goods, post*) repartir; (*message*) dar; (*opinion*) expresar; (*speech*) pronunciar; (*baby*) asistir para dar a luz; (*free*) liberar. **deliverance** *n* liberación *f*. **delivery** *n* entrega *f*; reparto *m*; pronunciación *f*; lanzamiento *m*; (*med*) parto *m*; manera de expresarse *f*. **delivery service** servicio a domicilio *m*. **delivery van** furgoneta de reparto *f*. **take delivery of** recibir.

delta ['deltə] *n* delta *m*.

delude [di'luːd] *v* engañar. **delusion** *n* engaño, *m*, error *m*, ilusión *f*.

deluge ['deljuːdʒ] *n* diluvio *m*. *v* inundar; (*fig*) abrumar.

delve [delv] *v* cavar. **delve into** ahondar.

demand [di'maːnd] *n* (*comm*) demanda *f*; (*request*) petición *f*; (*for payment*) reclamación *f*. *v* (*require*) requerir; (*ask urgently*) exigir; reclamar. **demanding** *adj* (*tiring*) agotador; (*absorbing*) absorbente; (*person*) exigente.

demented [di'mentid] *adj* demente, loco. **dementia** *n* demencia *f*.

democracy [di'mokrəsi] *n* democracia *f*. **democrat** *n* demócrata *m*, *f*. **democratic** *adj* democrático.

demolish [di'moliʃ] *v* (*building*) demoler, derribar; (*fig*) destruir. **demolition** *n* demolición *f*, derribo *m*; destrucción *f*.

demon ['diːmən] *n* demonio *m*, diablo *m*.

demonstrate ['demən,streit] *v* demostrar, probar; (*show how something operates*) mostrar; (*pol*) hacer la manifestación. **demonstration** *n* demostración *f*, prueba *f*; manifestación *f*. **demonstrative** *adj* demostrativo. **demonstrator** n ayudante m, f; (protester) manifestante m, f.

demoralize [di'morə,laiz] v desmoralizar. **demoralization** n desmoralización f. **demoralizing** adj desmoralizador, desmoralizante.

demure [di'mjuə] adj recatado.

den [den] n (of animals, etc.) guardia f; (study) estudio m.

denial [di'naiəl] n (refusal) negativa f; (disavowal) negación f; (rejection) rechazamiento m. **self-denial** abnegación f.

denim ['denim] n mahón m.

Denmark ['denmɑːk] n Dinamarca f.

denomination [di,nɔmi'neiʃən] n (measure) denominación f; (rel) secta f, confesión f; (coins) valor m; (type) clase f, tipo m. **denominational** adj sectario. **denominator** n (math) denominador m.

denote [di'nout] v denotar.

denounce [di'nauns] v denunciar.

dense [dens] adj (thick) denso; (coll: person) torpe. **densely** adv densamente. **density** n densidad f; torpeza f.

dent [dent] n abolladura f. v abollar.

dental ['dentl] adj dental.

dentist ['dentist] n dentista m, f. **dentistry** n odontología f.

denture ['dentʃə] n dentadura f, postiza f.

denude [di'njuːd] v desnudar.

denunciation [din∧nsi'eiʃən] n denuncia f; (condemnation) condena f; (criticism) censura f.

deny [di'nai] v (refuse, dispute) negar; (request) denegar; (give the lie to) desmentir; (repudiate) repudiar.

deodorant [diː'oudərənt] n desodorante m.

depart [di'pɑːt] v (go away) marcharse; (set off) salir; (deviate) apartarse. **departed** adj pasado; (dead) difunto. **departure** n marcha f; salida f; desviación f.

department [di'pɑːtmənt] n (in a shop) departamento m; (in a business) servicio m; (college, university) sección f; (ministry) negociado m; (branch) ramo m; (fig: sphere) esfera f. **department store** gran almacén m. **departmental** adj departamental.

depend [di'pend] v depender. **dependence** n dependencia f. **dependent** adj dependiente; subordinado.

depict [di'pikt] v (art) pintar; (fig)

describir. **depiction** n pintura f; descripción f.

deplete [di'pliːt] v vaciar, agotar. **depletion** n agotamiento m.

deplore [di'plɔː] v deplorar, lamentar. **deplorable** adj deplorable, lamentable.

deport [di'pɔːt] v expulsar. **deport oneself** comportarse. **deportation** n expulsión f. **deportment** n porte m; conducta f.

depose [di'pouz] v deponer.

deposit [di'pozit] n (bank) depósito m; (substance) sedimento m, poso m; (pledge) señal f; (on accommodation) entrada f. v depositar; (money in account) ingresar; dar de señal. **deposit account** cuenta de depósitos a plazo f.

depot [di'pou] n (store) almacén m; (bus) cochera f; (mil) depósito m.

deprave [di'preiv] v depravar. **depravity** n depravación f.

depreciate [di'priːʃi,eit] v (belittle, money) despreciar; (goods) abaratar; (price) bajar. **depreciation** n depreciación f; abaratamiento m; (fig) desprecio m.

depress [di'pres] v (dishearten) deprimir; (weaken) debilitar; (lessen) disminuir; (lower) bajar; (push down) presionar; (pedal) pisar. **depressed** adj deprimido; (indigent) necesitado; (comm) de depresión. **depressing** adj deprimente. **depression** n (dejection) abatimiento m; (geog, med, comm) depresión f.

deprive [di'praiv] v privar, desposeer. **deprivation** n privación f; (loss) pérdida f.

depth [depθ] n profundidad f; (colour) intensidad f; (sound) gravedad f. **out of one's depth** perder pie; (fig) no entender nada.

deputy ['depjuti] n delegado m; (substitute) suplente m; (politician) diputado m. **deputation** n delegación f. **deputize** v diputar; delegar; sustituir.

derail [di'reil] v hacer descarrilar. **derailment** n descarrilamiento m.

derelict ['derilikt] adj abandonado. n (neut) derrelicto m; (person) deshecho m. **dereliction** n abandono m; (negligence) negligencia f.

deride [di'raid] v ridicular. **derision** n mofas f pl. **derisive** or **derisory** adj (mocking) mofador; (petty) irrisorio.

derive [di'raiv] v derivar; (profit) sacar. **derivation** n derivación f. **derivative** nm, adj derivado.

derogatory [di'rogǝtǝri] *adj* despectivo, rebajante.

descend [di'send] *v* descender, bajar. **descendant** *n (m+f)*, *adj* descendiente. **descent** *n* descenso *m*, bajada *f*; *(slope)* declive *m*; *(lineage)* descendencia *f*.

describe [di'skraib] *v* describir; *(draw)* trazar. **describe oneself as** presentarse como. **description** *n* descripción *f*; *(sort)* clase *f*. **descriptive** *adj* descriptivo.

desert[1] ['dezǝt] *n (land)* desierto *m*.

desert[2] [di'zǝːt] *v* abandonar; *(mil)* desertar de. **deserter** *n* desertor *m*. **desertion** *n (mil)* deserción *f*; abandono *m*.

deserts [di'zǝːts] *pl n* get one's deserts llevarse su merecido.

deserve [di'zǝːv] *v* merecer; ser digno de. **deserving** *adj* digno; *(deed)* meritorio.

design [di'zain] *n (intention)* propósito *m*; *(plan)* proyecto *m*; *(drawing)* dibujo *m*; *(style)* estilo *m*. **have designs on** haber puesto sus miras en. *v (prepare plans for)* diseñar; dibujar; proyectar; inventar; *(create)* crear; imaginar. **designer** *n* diseñador, -a *m, f*. *(draughtsman)* delineante *m*. **dress designer** modista *m*. **designing** *adj* intrigante.

designate ['dezigneit] *v (name for a duty)* designar; *(name)* denominar; *(appoint)* nombrar; *(point out)* señalar. *adj* designado; nombrado. **designation** *n* designación *f*; denominación *f*; nombramiento *m*.

desire [di'zaiǝ] *n* deseo *m*; *(request)* petición *f*. *v* desear; pedir; *(want)* querer. **desirable** *adj* deseable; atractivo. **desirability** *n* lo atractivo; conveniencia *f*. **desirous** *adj* deseoso.

desk [desk] *n (office)* escritorio *m*; *(school)* pupitre *m*.

desolate ['desǝlǝt] *adj (waste)* desolado; solitario; desierto; disconsolado. *v (lay waste)* asolar; abandonar; desconsolar. **desolating** *adj* desolador. **desolation** *n* desolación *f*; soledad *f*.

despair [di'speǝ] *n* desesperación *f*, desesperanza *f*. *v* desesperar.

desperate ['despǝrǝt] *adj* desesperado; *(resistance)* enérgico; *(urgent)* apremiante. **desperation** *n* desesperación *f*.

despise [di'spaiz] *v* despreciar. **despicable** *adj* despreciable. **despicableness** *n* bajeza *f*.

despite [di'spait] *prep* a pesar de.

despondent [di'spondǝnt] *adj* desanimado, desalentado. **despondency** *n* desánimo *m*, desaliento *m*.

despot ['despot] *n* déspota *m*. **despotic** *adj* despótico. **despotism** *n* despotismo *m*.

dessert [di'zǝːt] *n* postre *m*. **dessertspoon** *n* cuchara de postre *f*.

destine ['destin] *v* destinar. **destination** *n* destinación *f*. **destiny** *n* destino *m*.

destitute ['destitjuːt] *adj* indigente, menesteroso. **be destitute** estar en la miseria. **destitution** *n* indigencia *f*, miseria *f*.

destroy [di'stroi] *v* destruir, destrozar. **destroyer** *n (naut)* destructor *m*. **destruction** *n* destrucción *f*; ruina *f*. **destructive** *adj* destructivo.

detach [di'tatʃ] *v* despegar; separar. **detachable** *adj* separable; *(collar)* postizo. **detached** *adj* independiente; *(untroubled)* indiferente. **detachment** *n* separación *f*; indiferencia *f*; *(mil)* destacamento *m*.

detail ['diːteil] *n* detalle *m*. *v* detallar; *(itemize)* enumerar; *(mil)* destacar.

detain [di'tein] *v* retener; *(law)* detener. **detention** *n* detención *f*; arresto *m*.

detect [di'tekt] *v (discover)* descubrir; *(perceive)* percibir; *(note)* advertir; *(tech)* detectar. **detection** *n* descubrimiento *m*; detección *f*. **detective** *n* detective *m*. **detective story** novela policíaca *f*. **detector** *n* detector *m*. **lie detector** detector de mentiras *m*.

deter [di'tǝː] *v* desuadir. **deterrent** *adj* disuasivo. *n* fuerza de disuasión *f*.

detergent [di'tǝːdʒǝnt] *nm*, *adj* detergente.

deteriorate [di'tiǝriǝreit] *v (wear out)* deteriorar; *(become worse)* empeorar; *(in value)* depreciar. **deterioration** *n* deterioro *m*; empeoramiento *m*; *(decline)* decadencia *f*.

determine [di'tǝːmin] *v (fix)* determinar; *(cause)* provocar; *(limits)* definir; *(decide)* decidir; resolver. **determination** *n* determinación *f*; resolución *f*; decisión *f*. **determined** *adj* resuelto; decidido; determinado.

detest [di'test] *v* destestar, odiar. **detestable** *adj* detestable, odioso. **detestation** *n* odio *m*.

detonate ['detǝneit] *v* detonar. **detonating** *adj* detonante. **detonation** *n* detonación *f*.

detour ['diːtuǝ] *n* desvío *m*, desviación *f*; vuelta *f*. **make a detour** dar un rodeo.

detract [di'trakt] v (*take away*) quitar, reducir; (*denigrate*) denigrar. **detraction** n denigración f.

detriment ['detrimənt] n detrimento m, perjuicio m. **detrimental** adj perjudicial.

devalue [di:'valju:] v devaluar, desvalorizar. **devaluation** n devaluación f.

devastate ['devə,steit] v devastar. **devastating** adj devastador. **devastation** n devastación f.

develop [di'veləp] v (*expand*) desarrollar; (*business*) explotar; (*land*) urbanizar; (*resources*) aprovechar; (*promote*) fomentar; (*taste*) adquirir; (*ailment*) contraer; (*tendency*) manifestar; (*talent*) mostrar; (*phot*) revelar. **developer** n (*phot*) revelador m. **development** n desarrollo m; evolución f; progreso m.

deviate ['di:vi,eit] v desviarse. **deviation** n desviación f; (*from truth*) alejamiento m; (*sexual*) inversión f. **deviationism** n desviacionismo m. **deviationist** n desviacionista m, f.

device [di'vais] n (*tech*) mecanismo; ingenio; (*scheme*) ardid m; estratagema f.

devil ['devl] n diablo. **devilish** adj diabólico. **devil's advocate** abogado del diablo m.

devise [di'vaiz] v inventar; (*plan*) concebir; (*plot*) tramar.

devoid [di'void] adj desprovisto.

devolution [,di:və'lu:ʃən] n (*powers*) delegación f. **devolve** v delegar; transmitir.

devote [di'vout] v dedicar. **devoted** adj dedicado; (*loyal*) leal; (*devout*) devoto. **devotion** n dedicación f; lealtad f; devoción f. **devotional** adj piadoso.

devour [di'vauə] v devorar. **devouring** adj devorador.

devout [di'vaut] adj devoto; sincero. **devoutness** n devoción f.

dew [dju:] n rocío m.

dexterous ['dekstrəs] adj diestro, hábil. **dexterity** n destreza f, habilidad f.

diabetes [,diəˈbi:ti:z] n diabetes f. **diabetic** n, adj diabético, -a.

diagnose [,diəgˈnouz] v diagnosticar. **diagnosis** n diagnóstico m.

diagonal [daiˈagənəl] nf, adj diagonal. **diagonally** adv diagonalmente.

diagram ['daiə,gram] n (*math*) figura; (*chart*) gráfico m; (*sketch*) esquema; (*explanatory*) diagrama m. **diagrammatic** adj esquemático.

dial ['daiəl] n (*clock*) esfera f; (*selector*) botón m; (*telephone*) disco m. v marcar. **dialling tone** señal para marcar f.

dialect ['diaəlekt] n dialecto m.

dialogue ['daiəlog] n diálogo m.

diameter [daiˈamitə] n diámetro m. **diametrically** adv diametralmente.

diamond ['daiəmənd] n diamante m. **diamond-shaped** adj romboidal.

diaper ['daiəpə] n (*US*) pañal m.

diaphragm ['daiə,fram] n diafragma m.

diarrhoea [,daiəˈriə] n diarrea f.

diary ['daiəri] n diario m; (*for appointments*) agenda f.

dice [dais] n pl dados m pl. ∴ jugar a los dados. **dice with death** jugar con la muerte.

dictate [dikˈteit] v dictar; (*order*) mandar; (*impose*) imponer. n mandato m. **dictation** n dictado m. **dictator** n dictador m. **dictatorial** adj dictatorial. **dictatorship** n dictadura f.

dictionary ['dikʃənəri] n diccionario m.

did [did] V **do**.

die [dai] v morrir, fallecer. **die away** (*sound*) desvanecer. **die down** (*fire*) apagarse; (*wind*) amainar; (*conversation*) decaer. **die out** desaparecer.

diesel ['di:zəl] nm, adj diesel. **diesel engine** motor diesel m. **diesel oil** gasoil m.

diet ['daiət] n dieta f, régimen m. v poner a dieta or régimen. **dietary** adj dietético. **dietetics** n dietética f. **dietician** n dietético m.

differ ['difə] v ser diferente, ser distinto. **difference** n diferencia f; (*disagreement*) desacuerdo m. **different** adj diferente, distinto. **differential** nf, adj diferencial. **differentiate** v diferenciar, distinguir.

difficult ['difikəlt] adj difícil. **difficulty** n dificultad f.

*dig [dig] v cavar; excavar; (*coal, etc.*) extraer. **dig in** enterrar. **dig into** clavar. **dig up** desenterrar. n (*in the ribs*) golpe m; excavación arqueológica f; (*fig*) pinchazo m.

digest [daiˈdʒest] n resumen m. v digerir; (*summarize*) resumir; (*fig*) asimilar. **digestible** adj digerible. **digestion** n digestión f. **digestive** adj digestivo. **digestive system** aparato digestivo m.

digit ['didʒit] n (*finger, toe*) dedo m; (*math*) dígito m. **digital** adj digital.

dignified 54

dignified ['digni faid] *adj* digno; solemne. **dignify** *v* dignificar.

dignity ['digniti] *n* dignidad *f*. **dignitary** *n* dignatorio *m*.

digress [dai'gres] *v* desviarse, apartarse. **digression** *n* digresión *f*.

digs [digz] *n pl* (*coll*) pensión *f sing.*

dilapidated [di'lapi deitid] *adj* (*building*) ruinoso; (*clothes*) muy estropeado. **dilapidate** *v* deteriorar; estropear. **dilapidation** *n* estado ruinoso *m*.

dilate [dai'leit] *v* dilatar.

dilemma [di'lema] *n* dilema *m*.

diligent ['dilidʒent] *adj* diligente. **diligence** *n* diligencia *f*.

dilute [dai'luːt] *v* diluir, aguar; (*fig*) atenuar. *adj* diluido; atenuado. **dilution** *n* dilución *f*.

dim [dim] *adj* oscuro; (*memory*) lejano; (*sound*) sordo; (*sight*) turbio; (*light*) débil; (*vague*) borroso; (*colour*) apagado; (*slang*) tonto. **take a dim view of** ver con malos ojos. *v* (*light*) bajar; (*sight*) nublar. **dimly** *adv* vagamente; poco iluminado.

dimension [di'menʃən] *n* dimensión *f*.

diminish [di'miniʃ] *v* disminuir.

diminutive [di'minjutiv] *adj* diminuto. *nm*. *adj* (*gramm*) diminutivo.

dimple [dimpl] *n* hoyuelo *m*. *v* formar hoyuelos en.

din [din] *n* estrépito *m*, alboroto *m*.

dine [dain] *v* cenar. **dining car** coche restaurante *m*. **diningroom** *n* comedor *m*.

dinghy ['diŋgi] *n* bote *m*.

dingy ['dindʒi] *adj* sucio, sórdido.

dinner ['dinə] *n* (*evening*) cena *f*; (*midday*) comida *f*. **dinner jacket** esmoquin *m*. **dinner party** cena *f*. **dinner table** mesa de comedor *f*.

dinosaur ['dainəsoɪ] *n* dinosaurio *m*.

diocese ['daiəsis] *n* diócesis *f*. **diocesan** *n*, *adj* diocesano, -a.

dip [dip] *v* (*wet*) mojar; (*immerse*) sumergir; (*someone*) zambullir; (*scoop*) sacar; (*put a hand in*) meter; (*flag*) inclinar; (*headlights*) poner luz de cruce; (*road*) bajar; *n* baño *m*; (*slope*) declive *f*.

diphthong ['difθɒŋ] *n* diptongo *m*.

diploma [di'plouma] *n* diploma *m*.

diplomacy [di'plouməsi] *n* diplomacia *f*. **diplomat** *n* diplomático *m*. **diplomatic** *adj* diplomático. **diplomatic corps** cuerpo diplomático *m*. **diplomatic immunity** inmunidad diplomática *f*.

dipstick ['dipstik] *n* varilla graduada *f*.

dire [daiə] *adj* extremo; terrible.

direct [di'rekt] *adj* (*straight*) directo; (*blunt*) tajante; (*frank*) franco. **direct current** corriente continua *f*. *v* dirigir; (*order*) mandar; (*show the way*) indicar; (*gaze, attention*) señalar. **direction** *n* dirección *f*. **directions** *n pl* instrucciones *f pl*. **directive** *n* instrucción *f*. **directly** *adv* directamente; (*at once*) en seguida. **directness** *n* franqueza *f*. **director** *m* director *m*. **board of directors** consejo de administración *n*. **managing director** director gerente *m*.

dirt [dəɪt] *n* suciedad *f*; (*filth*) mugre *f*; (*rubbish*) basura *f*. **dirt-cheap** *adj* baratísimo. **dirty** *adj* sucio; (*obscene: person*) verde; (*language*) grosero. **dirty trick** mala pasada *f*.

disability [disə'biləti] *n* incapacidad *f*. **disable** *v* incapacitar; (*cripple*) lisiar. **disabled** *adj* inválido. **disablement** *n* incapacidad *f*.

disadvantage [disəd'vɑːntidʒ] *n* desventaja *f*. **be at a disadvantage** estar en situación desventajosa.

disagree [disə'griː] *v* discrepar; no estar de acuerdo. **disagreeable** *adj* desagradable. **disagreement** *n* desacuerdo *m*.

disappear [disə'piə] *v* desaparecer. **disappearance** *n* desaparición *f*.

disappoint [disə'point] *v* decepcionar; defraudar. **disappointing** *adj* decepcionante. **disappointment** *n* decepción *f*; disgusto *m*.

disapprove [disə'pruːv] *v* desaprobar; estar en contra. **disapproval** *n* desaprobación *f*. **disapproving** *adj* desaprobador. **disapprovingly** *adv* con desaprobación.

disarm [dis'ɑːm] *v* desarmar. **disarmament** *n* desarme *m*.

disaster [di'zɑːstə] *n* desastre *m*. **disastrous** *adj* desastroso.

disband [dis'band] *v* disolver; (*mil*) licenciar.

disc *or US* **disk** [disk] *n* disco *m*. **disc jockey** presentador de discos *m*.

discard [dis'kɑːd; 'diskɑːd] *v* (*cast away*) desechar; (*cards*) descartar; (*fig*) renunciar. *n* descarte *m*.

discern [di'səːn] *v* discernir. **discernible** *adj* perceptible. **discerning** *adj* perspicaz.

discharge [dis'tʃɑːdʒ] *v* descargar; (*debt*) saldar; (*gun*) disparar; (*sack*) despedir;

(law) absolver; *(duty)* desempeñar; *(prisoner)* liberar; *(patient)* dar de alta; *(bankrupt)* rehabilitar. *n* descarga *f*; *(debt)* descargo; *(gas)* escape *m*; liberación *f*; rehabilitación *f*; absolución *f*; desempeño *m*; alta *f*; disparo *m*.

disciple [di'saipl] *n* discipulo, -a *m, f*.

discipline ['disiplin] *n* disciplina *f*. *v* castigar. **disciplinarian** *n* disciplinario, -a *m, f*. **disciplinary** *adj* disciplinario.

disclaim [dis'kleim] *v* rechazar; *(law)* renunciar. **disclaimer** *n* *(denial)* denegación *f*; *(law)* renuncia *f*.

disclose [dis'klouz] *v* revelar. **disclosure** *n* revelación *f*; descubrimiento *m*.

discolour [dis'kʌlə] *v* descolorar; *(stain)* manchar. **discolouration** *n* descoloración *f*.

discomfort [dis'kʌmfət] *n* molestia *f*; incomodidad *f*; malestar. *v* molestar.

disconcert [diskən'səːt] *v* desconcertar, perturbar. **disconcerting** *adj* desconcertante.

disconnect [diskə'nekt] *v* *(elec)* desconectar; *(separate)* separar. **disconnection** *n* desconexión *f*; separación *f*.

disconsolate [dis'konsəlat] *adj* desconsolado. **disconsolateness** *n* desconsuelo *m*.

discontinue [diskən'tinjuː] *v* discontinuar, interrumpir; suspender. **discontinuance** *or* **discontinuation** *n* cesación *f*; suspensión *f*. **discontinuity** *n* discontinuidad *f*; interrupción *f*. **discontinuous** *adj* discontinuo.

discord ['diskoid] *n* discordia *f*; *(music)* disonancia *f*. **discordant** *adj* discordante; *(music)* discorde.

discotheque ['diskətek] *n* discoteca *f*.

discount ['diskaunt] *n* descuento *m*; *(reduction)* rebaja *f*. *v* descontar, rabajar; *(disregard)* no hacer caso de.

discourage [dis'kʌridʒ] *v* desanimar. **discourage from** recomendar que no. **discouragement** *n* desánimo *m*. **discouraging** *adj* desalentador.

discover [dis'kʌvə] *v* descubrir; *(realize)* darse cuenta de. **discoverer** *n* descubridor, -a *m, f*. **discovery** *n* descubrimiento *m*.

discredit [dis'kredit] *v* desacreditar; *(disbelieve)* dudar de; *(dishonour)* deshonrar. *n* descrédito *m*; duda *f*. **discreditable** *adj* indigno; vergonzoso.

discreet [dis'kriːt] *adj* discreto; prudente.

discretion *n* discreción; circunspección *f*. **at your discretion** a su gusto. **discretionary** *adj* discrecional.

discrepancy [di'skrepənsi] *n* discrepancia *f*; diferencia *f*. **discrepant** *adj* discrepante; diferente.

discrete [di'skriːt] *adj* discreto.

discriminate [di'skrimi,neit] *v* distinguir. **discriminate against** discriminar contra. **discriminating** *adj* *(law)* discriminatorio; *(taste)* muy bueno. **discrimination** *n* discriminación *f*; discernimiento *m*; buen gusto *m*. **discriminatory** *adj* discriminatorio.

discus ['diskəs] *n* disco *m*.

discuss [di'skʌs] *v* discutir; hablar de. **discussion** *n* discusión *f*.

disease [di'ziːz] *n* enfermedad *f*. **diseased** *adj* enfermo.

disembark [disim'baːk] *v* desembarcar. **disembarkation** *n* *(people)* desembarco *m*; *(cargo)* desembarque *m*.

disengage [disin'geidʒ] *v* *(detach)* soltar; *(unhook)* desenganchar; *(free)* liberar; *(mil)* retirar; *(gears)* desengranar; *(clutch)* desembragar. **disengagement** *n* liberación *f*; retirada *f*; desembrague *m*.

disfigure [dis'figə] *v* desfigurar; *(spoil)* afear. **disfigurement** *n* desfiguración *f*; afeamiento *m*.

disgrace [dis'greis] *n* *(disfavour)* desgracia *f*; *(cause of shame)* vergüenza *f*; deshonra *f*; ignominia *f*. *v* deshonrar. **disgraceful** *adj* deshonroso; vergonzoso.

disgruntled [dis'grʌntld] *adj* malhumorado.

disguise [dis'gaiz] *v* disfrazar. *n* disfraz *m*.

disgust [dis'gʌst] *n* repugnancia *f*. *v* repugnar.

dish [diʃ] *n* plato *m*; *(serving vessel)* fuente *f*. *v* servir. **dish out** dar. **dishwasher** *n* lavaplatos *m*.

dishearten [dis'haːtn] *v* descorazonar, desanimar. **disheartening** *adj* descorazonador.

dishevelled [di'ʃevəld] *adj* despeinado; desarreglado.

dishonest [dis'onist] *adj* fraudulento.

dishonour [dis'onə] *n* deshonra *f*. deshonor *m*. *v* deshonrar.

disillusion [disi'luːʒən] *v* desilusionar. *n* desilusión *f*.

disinfect [disin'fekt] *v* desinfectar. **disinfectant** *nm, adj* desinfectante.

disinherit [disin'herit] v desheredar. **disinheritance** n desheredamiento m.

disintegrate [dis'intigreit] v desintegrar. **disintegration** n desintegración f.

disinterested [dis'intristid] adj desinteresado; imparcial. **disinterest** n desinterés m.

disjointed [dis'dʒointid] adj desarticulado; (incoherent) inconexo.

disk V **disc**.

dislike [dis'laik] v aborrecer, tener aversión a. n aversión f. antipatía f.

dislocate ['disləkeit] v (joint) dislocar; (plans) desarreglar. **dislocation** n dislocación f; desarreglo m.

dislodge [dis'lodʒ] v desalojar. **dislodgement** n desalojamiento f.

disloyal [dis'loiəl] adj desleal. **disloyalty** n deslealtad f.

dismal [dizməl] adj triste; (face) sombrío; (voice) lúgubre.

dismantle [dis'mantl] v desmantelar; desmontar.

dismay [dis'mei] n consternación f; (fright) espanto m. v consternar; espantar; (discourage) desalentar.

dismiss [dis'mis] v despedir; (discharge) licenciar; (assembly) disolver; (mil) romper filas; (idea) descartar. **dismissal** n (employee) despido m; abandono m.

dismount [dis'maunt] v desmontar.

disobey [disə'bei] v desobedecer. **disobedience** n desobediencia f. **disobedient** adj desobediente.

disorder [dis'oɪdə] n desorden m; (riot) disturbio m; (illness) trastorno m. v desordenar. **disorderliness** n desorden m. **disorderly** adj (person) desordenado; (place) desarreglado; (meeting) alborotado.

disorganize [dis'oɪɡənaiz] v desorganizar. **disorganization** n desorganización f.

disown [dis'oun] v repudiar; (deny) negar; no reconocer.

disparage [di'sparidʒ] v desacreditar; (belittle) menospreciar; (denigrate) denigrar. **disparagement** n descrédito m; menosprecio m; denigración f. adj despectivo; menospreciativo; denigrante. **disparagingly** adv con desprecio.

disparity [dis'pariti] n disparidad f. **disparate** adj dispar.

dispassionate [dis'paʃənit] adj desapasionado; imparcial.

dispatch [dis'patʃ] n (message) despacho

m, expedición f; (messenger, parcels) envío m; (promptness) diligencia f. v despachar; enviar; matar.

dispel [di'spel] v disipar.

dispense [di'spens] v (drugs) preparar; (justice) administrar; (distribute) distribuir; (laws) aplicar. **dispense with** prescindir de. **dispensable** adj prescindible. **dispensary** n dispensario m; farmacia f. **dispensation** n distribución f; administración f; (exemption) dispensa f.

disperse [di'spəɪs] v dispersar. **dispersal** n dispersión f.

displace [dis'pleis] v desplazar; (oust) quitar el puesto; (remove from office) destituir. **displacement** n desplazamiento m; destitución f; reemplazo m.

display [dis'plei] v exhibir; demostrar. n exhibición f; demostración f; despliegue m; (emotion) alarde m; (show) exposición f; (parade) desfile m; (tech) representación visual f.

displease [dis'pliz] v desagradar, disgustar. **displeasing** adj desagradable. **displeasure** n desagrado m, disgusto m.

dispose [di'spouz] v (arrange) disponer; determinar; inclinar; mover. **dispose of** tirar; (transfer) traspasar; (argument) echar por tierra; (kill) liquidar; (sell) vender; (consume) consumir. **disposable** adj disponible; (to be thrown away) para tirar. **disposal** n (arrangement) disposición f; eliminación f; resolución f; traspaso m; venta f. **disposition** n disposición f; traspaso m; predisposición f.

disprove [dis'pruv] v refutar.

dispute [di'spjuɪt] n disputa f; discusión f; controversia f; (law) litigio m. v disputar; discutir; (question) poner en duda. **disputation** n discusión f; controversia f.

disqualify [dis'kwolifai] v (render unfit) incapacitar; (competitor) descalificar. **disqualification** n incapacidad f; descalificación f.

disregard [disrə'ɡaɪd] v (neglect) descuidar; desatender. n descuido m; indiferencia f.

disreputable [dis'repjutəbl] adj (shabby) lamentable; (not respectable) de mala fama. **disrepute** n descrédito m.

disrespect [disrə'spekt] n falta de respeto f. **disrespectful** adj irrespetuoso.

disrupt [dis'rapt] v (upset) trastornar; (interrupt) interrumpir; (break up) romper; desorganizar. **disruption** n trastorno *m*; ruptura *f*; interrupción *f*; desorganización *f*. **disruptive** *adj* perjudicial.

dissatisfy [di'sætisfai] *v* no satisfacer. **dissatisfaction** *n* descontento *m*.

dissect [di'sekt] *v* disecar. **dissection** *n* disección *f*.

dissent [di'sent] *n* disensión *f*; (*disagreement*) disentimiento *m*. *v* (*disagree*) disentir. **dissension** *n* disensión *f*.

dissident ['disidənt] *n*(*m+f*). *adj* disidente. **dissidence** *n* disidencia *f*.

dissimilar [di'similə] *adj* desigual; distinto. **dissimilarity** *n* desigualdad *f*.

dissociate [di'souʃieit] *v* disociar. **dissociation** *n* disociación *f*.

dissolute ['disəluːt] *adj* disoluto. **dissolution** *n* (*society, marriage, melting*) disolución *f*.

dissolve [di'zolv] *v* disolver; (*disintegrate*) descomponer; disipar; (*law; contract*) rescindir.

dissuade [di'sweid] *v* disuadir. **dissuasion** *n* disuasión *f*. **dissuasive** *adj* disuasivo.

distance ['distəns] *n* distancia *f*. *v* distanciar. **distant** *adj* distante, lejano.

distaste [dis'teist] *n* disgusto *m*, aversión *f*. **distasteful** *adj* desagradable.

distemper [dis'tempə] *n* (*dogs*) moquillo *m*; (*paint*) temple *m*.

distend [di'stend] *v* distender. **distension** *n* distensión *f*.

distil [di'stil] *v* destilar. **distillation** *n* destilación *f*. **distillery** *n* destilería *f*.

distinct [di'stiŋkt] *adj* (*clear*) claro; (*different*) distinto; (*definite*) bien determinado. **distinction** *n* distinción *f*. **distinctive** *adj* distintivo. **distinctness** *n* claridad *f*; diferencia *f*.

distinguish [di'stiŋgwiʃ] *v* distinguir. **distinguishable** *adj* distinguible. **distinguished** *adj* (*elegant*) distinguido; (*eminent*) eminente.

distort [di'stoːt] *v* torcer; (*fig*) desvirtuar. **distortion** *n* torcimiento *m*; desvirtuación *f*.

distract [di'strækt] *v* (*divert attention*) distraer; (*confuse*) aturdir; (*madden*) enloquecer. **distraction** *n* distracción *f*; aturdimiento *m*; locura *f*.

distraught [di'stroːt] *adj* distraído; enloquecido.

distress [di'stres] *n* aflicción *f*; (*poverty*) miseria *f*; (*danger*) peligro *m*. *v* afligir; angustiar. **distressed** *adj* afligido; en la miseria; en peligro. **distressing** *adj* angustioso.

distribute [di'stribjut] *v* distribuir, repartir. **distribution** *n* distribución *f*; reparto *m*. **distributor** *n* distribuidor, -a *m, f*; (*mot*) distribuidor *m*.

district ['distrikt] *n* (*pol*) distrito *m*; (*town*) barrio *m*; (*region*) región *f*. **district manager** representante regional *m*.

distrust [dis'trʌst] *n* desconfianza *f*. *v* desconfiar. **distrustful** *adj* desconfiado.

disturb [di'stəːb] *v* molestar; perturbar; agitar; preocupar. **disturbance** *n* molestia *f*; perturbación *f*; agitación *f*; preocupación *f*; (*row*) alboroto *m*; (*public disorder*) disturbio *m*. **disturbing** *adv* molesto; perturbador; preocupante.

disuse [dis'juːs] *n* desuso *m*; abandono *m*.

ditch [ditʃ] *n* (*trench*) zanja *f*; (*roadside*) cuneta *f*; (*irrigation*) acequia *f*; (*drainage*) canal *m*. *v* (*coll: get rid of*) tirar; (*coll: abandon*) abandonar.

ditto ['ditou] *n* ídem *m*.

divan [di'van] *n* diván *m*.

dive [daiv] *n* zambullida *f*. *v* zambullirse; saltar; bajar en picado; sumergirse. **diver** *n* buzo *m*; saltador, -a *m, f*.

diverge [dai'vəːdʒ] *v* divergir; desviar. **divergence** *n* divergencia *f*. **divergent** *adj* divergente.

diverse [dai'vəːs] *adj* diverso; distinto; diferente; variado. **diversity** *n* diversidad *f*.

divert [dai'vəːt] *v* (*reroute*) desviar; (*distract*) distraer; (*amuse*) divertir. **diversion** *n* desviación *f*; diversión *f*.

divide [di'vaid] *v* dividir. **division** *n* división *f*; separación *f*; distribución *f*; sección *f*; (*fig: opinions*) discrepancia *f*; (*fig: discord*) desunión *f*.

dividend ['dividend] *n* dividendo *m*.

divine [di'vain] *adj* divino. *v* adivinar. **divinity** *n* divinidad *f*; teología *f*.

divorce [di'voːs] *n* divorcio *m*. **sue for a divorce** pedir el divorcio. *v* divorciar; divorciarse de. **divorcee** *n* divorciado, -a *m, f*.

divulge [dai'vʌldʒ] *v* divulgar.

dizzy ['dizi] *adj* mareado; (*height, speed*) vertiginoso. **dizziness** *n* mareo *m*, vértigo *m*.

•do [duː] *v* (*act*) hacer; (*deal with*) ocuparse de; (*fulfil*) cumplir con; (*serve*) venir bien; (*feel*) estar, sentirse; (*be suitable*) valer; (*work*) trabajar; **do away with**

suprimir. **do for** llevar la casa a; **do up** (buttons, belt, etc.) abrocharse; (laces) atarse; (renovate) renovar. **do well** ir bien, salir bien; recuperarse. **do without** prescindir de. **doesn't do** to no conviene. **how do you do?** (after being introduced) encantado; (how are you?) ¿cómo está usted? **make do with** arreglárselas con. **please do** por supuesto, por favor.

docile ['dousail] adj dócil. **docility** n docilidad f.

dock¹ [dok] n (wharf) dársena f; v (ship) atracar al muelle; (arrive) llegar.

dock² [dok] n (law) banquillo de los acusados m.

dock³ [dok] v (cut, shorten) cortar; reducir; (coll: deduct) descontar; (coll: fine) multar.

doctor ['doktə] n médico, -a m, f; (university title) doctor, -a m, f. v atender; adulterar; falsificar. **doctorate** n doctorado m.

doctrine ['doktrin] n doctrina f. **doctrinaire** doctrinario. **doctrinal** adj doctrinal.

document ['dokjumənt] n documento m. v documentar. **documentary** nm, adj documental.

dodge [dodʒ] v esquivarse; eludir; (hide) echarse; (avoid) evitar. n (manoeuvre) regate m; (trick) truco m. **dodgy** (coll) adj astuto; (unreliable) incierto.

dog [dog] n perro m. **beware of the dog** cuidado con el perro. **v** seguir; perseguir. **dog biscuit** n galleta de perro f.

dog days n pl canícula f sing.

dog-eared adj sobado.

dogged ['dogid] adj tenaz. **doggedness** n tenacidad f.

doggerel ['dogərəl] n aleluyas f pl.

dogma ['dogmə] n dogma m. **dogmatic** adj dogmático.

do-it-yourself [ˌdu:itjɔ'self] adj hágalo usted mismo.

dole [doul] n (alms) limosna f; (unemployment pay) subsidio de paro m. **be on the dole** estar parado. **dole out** repartir.

doleful ['doulful] adj triste. **dolefulness** n tristeza f.

doll [dol] n muñeca f.

dollar ['dolə] n dólar m.

dolphin ['dolfin] n delfín m.

domain [də'mein] n dominio m; (fig) campo m.

dome [doum] n (arch) cúpula f, domo m.

domestic [də'mestik] adj doméstico; (home-loving) hogareño; (market) nacional. **domestic animal** animal doméstico m. **domestic help** doméstico, -a m, f. **domesticate** domesticar. **domestication** n domesticación f. **domesticity** n domesticidad f.

dominate ['domineit] v dominar. **dominant** adj dominante. **domineering** adj dominante.

dominion [də'minjən] n dominio m.

domino ['dominou] n dominó m. **play dominoes** jugar al dominó.

don [don] v ponerse. n catedrático m.

donate [də'neit] v donar. **donation** n donativo m.

done [dʌn] V **do**.

donkey ['doŋki] n burro m.

donor ['dounə] n donante m, f.

doom [du:m] n perdición f. v condenar. **doomsday** n día del juicio final m.

door [dɔ:] n puerta f. **next door** en la casa de al lado.

doorbell ['dɔ:bel] n timbre m.

door-keeper n portero m; conserje m.

door-handle n mano de la puerta f.

doorknob ['dɔ:nob] n tirador de puerta m.

door-knocker n llamador m.

doormat ['dɔ:mat] n felpudo m.

doorstep ['dɔ:step] n peldaño m; (threshold) umbral m.

doorway ['dɔ:wei] n portal m.

dope [doup] n (coll: drug) droga f; (coll: varnish) barniz m; (coll: information) informes m pl. v drogar.

dormant ['dɔ:mənt] adj letárgico; inactivo; latente.

dormitory ['dɔ:mitəri] n dormitorio m.

dormouse ['dɔ:maus] n lirón m.

dose [dous] n dosis f invar. v dar la dosis. **dosage** n dosis f invar.

dot [dot] n punto m. **on the dot** puntualmente. v poner el punto a; (scatter) salpicar.

dote [dout] v chochear. **dote on** estar chocho por. **dotage** n chochez f. **doting** adj chocho.

double ['dʌbl] nm, adj, adv doble. v doblar.

double bass n contrabajo m.

double bed n cama de matrimonio f.

double-breasted [ˌdʌbl'brestid] adj cruzado.

double-cross [,dʌbl'kros] n traición f. v traicionar.

double-edged [,dʌbl'edʒd] adj de dos filos.

double-entendre [dublã'tãdr] n expresión con doble sentido f.

double entry n (comm) partida doble f.

doubt [daut] n duda f. **no doubt** sin duda. v dudar. **doubtful** adj dudozo; sospechoso. **doubtless** adv indudablemente.

dough [dou] n masa f. **doughnut** n buñuelo m.

dove [dʌv] n paloma f.

dowdy ['daudi] adj desaliñado. **dowdiness** n desaliño m.

down¹ [daun] adv hacia abajo. prep abajo. adj descendente, bajo. **down payment** al contado. v derribar; tirar al suelo; (food) tragar; (drink) vaciar de un trago.

down² [daun] n plumón m; (fine hair) vello m; (upland) loma f.

downcast ['daun,kɑist] adj (sad) abatido; (in a downward direction) bajo.

downfall ['daun,foil] n ruina f; perdición f; caída f; (rain) chaparrón m.

downhearted [,daun'hɑitid] adj descorazonado.

downhill [,daun'hil] adj en pendiente. adv cuesta abajo.

downpour ['daun,poi] n aguacero m, chaparrón m.

downright ['daun,rait] adj categórico; sincero; evidente; verdadero. adv categóricamente; verdaderamente; completamente.

downstairs [,daun,steəz; adv ,daun'steəz] adj de abajo. adv abajo.

downstream [,daun'striim] adj, adv río abajo.

downtrodden ['daun,trodn] adj (fig) oprimido.

downward ['daunwəd] adj descendente. adv hacia abajo.

downwards ['daunwədz] adv hacia abajo.

dowry ['dauəri] n dote f.

doze [douz] v dormitar. n cabezada f.

dozen ['dʌzn] n docena f. **baker's dozen** docena del fraile f.

drab [drab] adj pardo; monótono.

draft [drɑift] n (version) redacción f; (drawing) esbozo m; (plan) bosquejo m; (payment) libramiento m; (bill) letra de cambio f; (naut) calado m; (conscription) quinta f. v hacer un proyecto; (draw up) redactar; esbozar; (conscript) reclutar.

drag [drag] v arrastrar; (river, etc.) dragar. **drag down** hundir. n (tow) arrastre m; (that which hinders) estorbo m; (device for dragging rivers, etc.) rastra f; (theatre) disfraz de mujer m; (aero) resistencia aerodinámica; (tech: brake) galga f. **what a drag!** ¡qué lata!

dragon ['dragən] n dragón m. **dragonfly** n libélula f.

drain [drein] n desaguadero m; (sewer inlet) sumidero m; (strength) pérdida f. v desaguar; (drink empty) vaciar; (marshes) desecar; (strength) agotar. **drainage** n desagüe m; desecación f. **drawing board** escurridero m. **drainpipe** n tubo de desagüe m.

drama ['drɑimə] n drama m. **dramatic** adj dramático. **dramatics** n pl teatro m. **dramatist** n dramaturgo, -a m, f. **dramatize** v adaptar al teatro.

drape [dreip] v cubrir con ropa, adornar con colgaduras. n colgadura f. **draper** n pañero, -a m, f. **drapery** n telas f pl.

drastic ['drastik] adj drástico.

draught [drɑift] n (air) corriente de aire f; (plan) bosquejo m; (drink) trago m. adj (animals) de tiro. **draughtboard** n tablero de damas m. **draughtsman** n delineante m. **draughtsmanship** n dibujo lineal m.

*draw [droi] n (sport) empate m; (lots) sorteo m; (lottery) lotería f. v (pull) tirar de; (extract) extraer; (attract) atraer; (art) dibujar; (a line) trazar; (nail, water, confession, profits, etc.) sacar; (comparisons) hacer; (breath) tomar; (earn) cobrar; (cheque) librar; (prize) ganar; sortear; (close curtains) descorrer; (blinds) bajar; (cards) robar. **draw attention** llamar la atención. **draw up** (document) redactar a.

drawback ['drotbak] n (disadvantage) desventaja f; (shortcoming) inconveniente m.

drawer ['droiə] n (container) cajón m; (art) dibujante m, f.

drawing ['droiŋ] n (art) dibujo m; (extraction) extracción f. **drawing board** tablero de dibujo m. **drawing pin** chincheta f. **drawing room** salón m.

drawl [droil] n voz lenta f. v arrastrar las palabras.

drawn [droin] adj (weary) cansado. **drawn to** atraído por.

dread 60

dread [dred] n miedo; terror. v temer.
dreadful adj terrible; espantoso.
*dream [drim] v soñar; imaginarse. n
sueño m. bad dream pesadilla f. daydream n ensueño m. dream up inventar.
dreary ['driəri] adj triste; monótono;
(boring) aburrido. dreariness n tristeza f;
monotonía f.
dredge [dredʒ] v dragar. n draga f.
dregs [dregz] n pl heces f pl.
drench [drentʃ] v empapar, mojar.
drenched to the skin estar mojada hasta
los huesos.
dress [dres] n (frock) vestido m; (clothing)
ropa; (evening dress: men) traje de etiqueta m, (women) traje de noche m;
(wedding) traje de novia m. v vestir. dress
up poner de tiros largos. dress up as dis-
frazarse de.
dress circle n piso principal m.
dress coat n frac m.
dress designer n modelista m, f.
dresser ['dresə] n aparador m.
dressing ['dresiŋ] n (act) vestir m;
(clothes) ropa f; (med) vendaje m;
(cookery) aliño m; (agriculture) abono m.
dressing gown bata f.
dressmaker ['dresmeikə] n modista m, f.
dressmaking n costura f.
dress rehearsal n ensayo general m.
dress shirt n camisa de frac f.
dressy ['dresi] adj elegante.
dribble ['dribl] n goteo m. v gotear.
drier ['draiə] n secador m; (for clothes)
secadora f.
drift [drift] n arrastramiento m; (snow)
ventisquero m; (sand) montón m; (naut,
aero) deriva f. v ser arrastrado;
amontonarse; derivar; (fig) vivir sin
rumbo. drift along vagar. drifter n
(vagrant) vagabundo m; (boat) trainera f.
drill [dril] n (tech) taladro m; (dental)
fresa f; (mil) instrucción f. v (mil)
ejercitar; (bore) taladrar, perforar. drill-
ing n instrucción f; perforación f.
*drink [driŋk] v beber; tomar; (toast)
brindar por. drink down beber de um
trago. drink in beberse. drink up bebér-
selo todo. n bebida f; (alcoholic) copa;
(water, milk) vaso m; algo de beber. soft
drink bebida no alcohólica f. have a
drink tomar algo.
drinkable ['driŋkəbl] adj potable.
drinker ['driŋkə] n bebedor, -a m, f.

drinking ['driŋkiŋ] n beber m; bebida f.
drinking fountain fuente de agua potable
f. drinking water agua potable f.
drip [drip] n goteo m; (drop) gota f. v
gotear. drip-dry adj de lava y pon.
*drive [draiv] v (push onwards) empujar;
(control a vehicle) conducir; (carry in a
vehicle) llevar; (some distance) recorrer;
(force someone out) echar; (compel) obligar. drive at (physically) dirigirse hacia;
(fig) insinuar. drive away irse; alejar.
drive by passar (por). drive in entrar;
clavar. drive into chocar contra. drive on
seguir su camino. drive up llegar. n paseo
m; excursión f; (journey) viaje m; (fig)
vigor m; (mil) ofensiva f; (tennis, golf)
drive m; (mot) tracción f; transmisión f;
propulsión f; (instinct) instinto m. driver
n conductor, -a m, f; chófer m; (taxi)
taxista m, f; (train) maquinista m. drive-
way n camino de entrada m.
drivel ['drivl] n tonterías f pl. v decir
tonterías.
driving ['draiviŋ] n conducción f. driving
licence carnet de conducir m. driving
school autoescuela f. driving test examen
para sacar el carnet de conducir m.
drizzle ['drizl] n llovizna f. v lloviznar.
drone [droun] n (noise) zumbido m;
(voices) murmullo m; (bee) zángano m;
(aero) teledirigido m. v zumbar;
murmurar.
droop [drup] n (shoulders) encorvamiento
m; (head) inclinación f. v estar
encorvado; inclinarse; (flowers)
marchitarse; (eyelids) caerse; (fig)
desanimarse; debilitarse.
drop [drop] n gota f. (sweet) pastilla f;
(bit) pizca f; (fall) caída f; (in value) disminución f; (in prices) baja f; (in temperature) descenso m. v (release) soltar; (let
fall) dejar caer; (tears) derramar; (a
friend) dejar; (prices, eyes, voice) bajar;
(give up a habit) dejar de; (leave behind)
despegarse de. drop behind quedarse
atrás. drop dead caerse muerto. drop in
on pasar por casa de. drop off dormirse.
dropout ['dropaut] n abandono m;
marginado, -a m, f.
dropsy ['dropsi] n hidropesía f.
drought [draut] n sequía f.
drown [draun] v ahogar.
drowsy ['drauzi] adj soñoliento. be drowsy tener sueño. drowse v dormitar.

drudge [drʌdʒ] n esclavo m. v currelar.
drudgery n trabajo penoso m.

drug [drʌg] n droga f; medicamento m. v drogar. **drug addict** drogadicto, -a m, f. **drug addiction** toxicomanía f.

drum [drʌm] n (music) tambor m; (container) bidón m; (ear) tímpano m. v tocar el tambor; (fingers) tamborilear. **drummer** n tambor m; batería f. **drumstick** n palillo de tambor m.

drunk [drʌŋk] adj borracho; (fig) ebrio. **get drunk** emborracharse. **drunkard** n borracho, -a m, f. **drunkenness** n embriaguez f.

dry [drai] adj seco; (measure) para áridos; (boring) aburrido; (thirsty) sediento; (wit) agudo; (subject) árido. v secar. **dry-clean** v limpiar en seco. **dry cleaner** tintorero, -a m, f.

dual ['djuəl] adj doble. **dual carriageway** pista doble f. **dual-purpose** adj de dos usos.

dubbed ['dʌbd] adj (named) apodado; (knighted) armado; (film) doblado. v apodar; armar; doblar.

dubious ['djuːbiəs] adj dudoso; ambiguo; indeciso; discutible; sospechoso.

duchess ['dʌtʃis] n duquesa f.

duck[1] [dʌk] n (bird) pata f; (drake) pato m; (dodging) esquiva f; (in water) zambullida f.

duck[2] [dʌk] v (crouch) agachar; zambullir.

duckling ['dʌkliŋ] n patito m.

duct [dʌkt] n (anat) canal m; (gas) conducto m; (elec) tubo m.

dud [dʌd] n (coll) desastre m; (mil) projectil fallido m. adj falso; inútil; defectuoso; (cheque) sin fondos.

due [djuː] adj (care, time) debido; (payable) pagadero. **due date** vencimiento m. **be due to** deberse a. n merecido m. adv derecho hacia. **dues** pl n derechos m pl. **duly** adv debidamente; a su debido tiempo.

duel ['djuəl] n duelo m. v batirse en duelo. **duellist** n duelista m.

duet [dju'et] n dúo m.

duke [djuːk] n duque m.

dull [dʌl] adj monótono; (obtuse) torpe; (slow) tardo; (tedious) pesado; (colour) apagado; (surface) mate; (weather) gris; (sullen) sombrío; (blunt) embotado. v (emotions) enfriarse; (pain) aliviar; (sound) apagar. **dullness** n monotonía f;

torpeza f; pesadez f. **dully** adv torpemente; lentamente.

dumb [dʌm] adj mudo; (coll) estúpido. **dumbbell** n pesa f. **dumbfound** v dejar sin habla. **dumbfounded** adj confuso, atónito. **dumbwaiter** n carrito m.

dummy ['dʌmi] n (teat) chupete m; (tailor's) maniquí m; (puppet) muñeco m; (cards) muerto m; (coll) lobo, -a m, f. adj ficticio, falso. v (sport) fintar.

dump [dʌmp] n (rubbish dump) depósito de basura m; (heap) montón m; (scrapheap) vertedero m; (coll: wretched place) tugurio m. v (throw away) tirar; (get rid of) deshacerse de; (unload) descargar. **dumping** n descarga f. **dumpy** adj regordete.

dumpling ['dʌmpliŋ] n masa hervida f.

dunce [dʌns] n tonto m, burro m.

dune [djuːn] n duna f.

dung [dʌŋ] n excrementos m pl; (manure) estiércol m.

dungarees [ˌdʌŋgə'riːz] pl n mono m sing.

dungeon ['dʌndʒən] n calabozo m, mazmorra f.

duplicate ['djuːplikət; v 'djuːplikeit] n copia f, doble m, duplicado m. adj duplicado. v duplicar; multicopiar. **duplicating machine** multicopista f. **duplication** n duplicación f; copia f.

durable ['djuərəbl] adj duradero. **durability** n durabilidad f.

duration [dju'reiʃən] n duración f.

during ['djuriŋ] prep durante.

dusk [dʌsk] n crepúsculo m. **dusky** adj oscuro; (complexion) moreno.

dust [dʌst] n polvo m. v (clean) limpiar el polvo; (powder) espolvorear. **dustbin** n cajón de basura m. **duster** (cloth) trapo m; (feather) plumero m. **dustman** n basurero m. **dustpan** n recogedor m. **dusty** adj polvoriento; cubierto de polvo.

duty ['djuːti] n deber m, obligación f; (tax) impuesto m. (at customs) derechos de aduana m pl. **off duty** estar libre. **on duty** de servicio. **dutiful** adj obediente; deferente. **duty-free** adj libre de derechos de aduana.

duvet ['duːvei] n colcha de plumón f.

dwarf [dwɔːf] n, adj enano, -a. v achicar. *

dwell [dwel] v vivir. **dwell on** (emphasize) insistir en; (a subject) extenderse en. **dwelling** n vivienda f.

dwindle ['dwindl] v disminuir, menguar.

dye [dai] n (*colouring substance*) tinte m; (*colour*) fast dye color sólido m. v teñir.

dyke [daik] n (*ditch*) zanja f; (*bank*) dique m.

dynamic [dai'namik] adj dinámico.

dynamite ['dainəmait] n dinamita f. v dinamitar.

dynamo ['dainəmou] n dínamo f.

dynasty ['dinəsti] n dinastía f. **dynastic** adj dinástico.

dysentery ['disəntri] n disentería f.

dyslexia [dis'leksiə] n dislexia f.

dyspepsia [dis'pepsiə] n dispepsia f. **dyspeptic** adj dispéptico.

E

each [iitʃ] adj cada. pron cada uno, cada una. **each other** el uno al otro.

eager ['iːgə] adj ávido; ansioso; impaciente. **eagerness** n ansia f; impaciencia f.

eagle ['iːgl] n águila f. **eagle-eyed** adj tener ojos de lince.

ear[1] [iə] n oreja f. (*fig*) oído m. **earache** n dolor de oído m. **eardrum** n tímpano m. **earmark** v reservar; destinar. **earring** n pendiente m; **earshot** n alcance del oído m.

ear[2] [iə] n (*grain*) espiga f.

earl [əːl] n conde m.

early ['əːli] adv temprano; pronto; al principio. adj temprano; próximo; pronto.

earn [əːn] v ganar; merecer. **earnings** pl n (*income*) ingresos m pl; (*salary*) sueldo m sing.

earnest ['əːnist] adj sincero; aplicado; serio. **in earnest** en serio.

earth [əːθ] n tierra f. **earthenware** n alfarería f.

earwig ['iəwig] n tijereta f.

ease [iːz] n facilidad f; naturalidad f; (*comfort*) comodidad f; (*from pain*) alivio m. v facilitar; aliviar; tranquilizar; (*tension*) relajar.

easel ['iːzl] n caballete m.

east [iist] n este m. adj also **easterly**, **eastern** oriental; del este; adv al este, hacia el este. **eastward** adj, adv hacia el este.

Easter ['iistə] n Pascua de Resurrección f. **Easter egg** huevo de Pascua m.

easy ['iːzi] adj fácil. **easy chair** sillón m. **easy-going** adj acomodadizo; indolente. **take it easy!** ¡tómatelo con calma! **easiness** n facilidad f.

*****eat** [iit] v comer. **eat up** comerse. **eatable** adj also **edible** comestible.

eavesdrop ['iːvzdrop] v fisgonear. **eavesdropper** n fisgón, -ona f.

ebb [eb] n reflujo m, menguante m. v menguar; decaer. **ebb tide** marea menguante f.

ebony ['ebəni] n ébano m.

eccentric [ik'sentrik] n, adj excéntrico, -a. **eccentricity** n excentricidad f.

ecclesiastical [iklizii'astikl] adj also **ecclesiastic** eclesiástico.

echo ['ekou] n eco m; resonancia f; repetición f. v resonar; repetir; imitar.

eclair [ei'kleə] n relámpago m.

eclipse [i'klips] n eclipse m. v eclipsar.

ecology [i'kolədʒi] n ecología f. **ecological** adj ecológico. **ecologist** n ecólogo m.

economy [i'konəmi] n economía f. **economic** adj also **economical** económico. **economics** n economía f. **economist** n economista m, f. **economize** v economizar.

ecstasy ['ekstəsi] n éxtasis m. **ecstatic** adj extático. **go into ecstasies over** extasiarse ante.

Ecuador ['ekwədoi] n Ecuador m. **Ecuadorean, Ecuadorean,** or **Ecuadorian** n, adj ecuatoriano, -a.

eczema ['eksimə] n eczema m.

edge [edʒ] n borde m; (*blade*) filo m, corte m. **have the edge on** llevar ventaja a. **be on edge** tener los nervios de punta. v bordear; mover poco a poco. **edging** n (*sewing*) orla f; (*path*) borde m. **edgy** adj nervioso.

edible ['edəbl] adj comestible.

Edinburgh ['edinbərə] n Edimburgo m.

edit ['edit] v (*text*) redactar; (*film*) montar; (*direct a paper, magazine*) dirigir. **editor** n radactor m; director m. **editorial** n editorial m; artículo de fondo m. **editorial staff** redacción f.

edition [i'diʃən] n edición f; tirada f.

educate ['edjuˌkeit] v educar. **educated** adj culto. **education** n educación f; (*teaching*) enseñanza f; (*specific*) instrucción f. **educational** adj educativo; (*teaching*) docente.

eel [iːl] *n* anguila *f*.

eerie ['iəri] *adj* misterioso; espantoso.

effect [i'fekt] *n* efecto *m*; resultado *m*; impresión *f*; (*meaning*) significado *m*. **side effect** efecto secundario. **take effect** (*drugs, etc.*) surtir efecto; (*law, etc.*) tener efecto. *v* efectuar. **effective** *adj* (*efficient*) eficaz; (*real*) efectivo; (*in force*) vigente. **effectiveness** *n* eficacia *f*; efecto *m*; vigencia *f*.

effeminate [i'feminət] *adj* afeminado.

effervescent [,efə'vesənt] *adj* efervescente. **effervesce** *v* estar en efervescencia.

efficient [i'fiʃənt] *adj* eficaz, eficiente. **efficiency** *n* eficacia *f*, eficiencia *f*.

effigy ['efidʒi] *n* efigie *f*.

effort ['efət] *n* esfuerzo *m*. **effortless** *adj* sin esfuerzo.

egg [eg] *n* huevo *m*. **bad egg** huevo podrido. **boiled egg** huevo pasado por agua. **hard-boiled egg** huevo duro. **new-laid egg** huevo fresco. **poached egg** huevo escalfado. **scrambled eggs** huevos revueltos *m pl*. **eggcup** *n* huevera *f*. **egg-shaped** *adj* oviforme. **eggshell** *n* cascarón de huevo *m*. **egg on** incitar.

egotism ['egətizm] *n* egotismo *m*. **egotist** *n* (*self-important person*) ègotista *m, f*; (*selfish person*) egoísta *m, f*.

Egypt ['iːdʒipt] *n* Egipto *m*. **Egyptian** *n, adj* egipcio, -a.

eiderdown ['aidədaun] *n* edredón *m*.

eight [eit] *nm, adj* ocho. **eighth** *n, adj* octavo, -a.

eighteen [ei'tiːn] *nm, adj* dieciocho. **eighteenth** *n, adj* decimoctavo, -a.

eighty ['eiti] *nm, adj* ochenta. **eightieth** *n, adj* octogésimo, -a.

either ['aiðə] *adj* cada, ambos. *pron* uno u otro; cualquiera de los dos. *adv* tampoco. *conj* o. **either ... or ... o ... o ...**

ejaculate [i'dʒakjuleit] *v* exclamar; (*med*) eyacular. **ejaculation** *n* exclamación *f*; eyaculación *f*.

eject [i'dʒekt] *v* expulsar; echar; (*tenant*) desahuciar. **ejection** *n* expulsión *f*; desahucio *m*. **ejector seat** asiento eyectable *m*.

eke [iːk] *v* **eke out** (*add to*) complementar; (*make last*) escatimar.

elaborate [i'labərət; *v* i'labəreit] *adj* complicado; detallado. *v* elaborar. **elaborate on** ampliar. **elaborately** *adv* cuidadosamente; complicadamente; detalladamente. **elaboration** *n* elaboración *f*; explicación *f*; complicación *f*.

elapse [i'laps] *v* transcurrir.

elastic [i'lastik] *adj* elástico. **elastic band** goma elástica *f*. **elasticity** *n* elasticidad *f*.

elated [i'leitid] *adj* jubiloso; exaltado. **elation** *n* júbilo *m*; exaltación *f*.

elbow ['elbou] *n* codo *m*. **elbow grease** fuerza de puños *f*. **elbow room** espacio suficiente *m*.

elder¹ ['eldə] *nm, adj* mayor. **elderly** *adj* mayor de edad. **eldest** *adj* mayor.

elder² ['eldə] *n* (*bot*) saúco *m*. **elderberry** *n* baya del saúco.

elect [i'lekt] *v* elegir. *adj* elegido. **election** *n* elección *f*. **electoral** *adj* electoral. **electorate** *n* electorado *m*.

electric [ə'lektrik] *adj also* **electrical** eléctrico. **electric blanket** manta eléctrica *f*. **electric fire** estufa eléctrica *f*. **electric shock** electrochoque *m*. **electrician** *n* electricista *m, f*. **electricity** *n* electricidad *f*. **electrify** *v* (*rail, industry*) electrificar; (*produce electricity*) electrizar; (*fig*) entusiasmar.

electrocute [i'lektrəkjut] *v* electrocutar. **electrocution** *n* electrocución *f*.

electrode [i'lektroud] *n* electrodo *m*.

electronic [elək'tronik] *adj* electrónico. **electronics** *n* electrónica *f*.

elegant ['eligənt] *adj* elegante; bello. **elegance** *n* elegancia *f*.

elegy ['elidʒi] *n* elegía *f*.

element ['eləmənt] *n* elemento *m*; factor *m*. **elementary** *adj* elemental; fundamental.

elephant ['elifənt] *n* elefante *m*.

elevate ['eliveit] *v* elevar; (*voice, eyes*) levantar; (*honour*) enaltecer. **elevation** *n* elevación *f*; (*hill*) altura *f*; (*thought*) nobleza *f*.

elevator ['eliveitor] *n* ascensor *m*.

eleven [i'levn] *nm, adj* once. **eleventh** *n, adj* undécimo, -a *m, f*; *adj* onceavo.

elf [elf] *n* duende *m*.

eligible ['elidʒəbl] *adj* elegible; atractivo.

eliminate [i'limineit] *v* eliminar. **elimination** *n* eliminación *f*.

elite [ei'liːt] *n* élite *f*.

ellipse [i'lips] *n* elipse *f*. **elliptical** *adj* elíptico.

elm [elm] *n* olmo *m*.

elocution [elə'kjuʃən] n elocución f; declamación f.

elope [i'loup] v fugarse. **elopement** n fuga f.

eloquent ['eləkwənt] adj elocuente. **eloquence** n elocuencia f.

else [els] adv más, de otra manera. **or else** si no. **elsewhere** adv otro sitio.

elude [i'lud] v eludir, escapar; (a blow) evitar. **elusive** adj escurridizo.

emaciated [i'meisieitid] adj demacrado. **emaciation** n demacración f.

emanate ['eməneit] v emanar. **emanation** n emanación f.

emancipate [i'mansipeit] v emancipar. **emancipation** n emancipación f.

embalm [im'baːm] v embalsamar.

embankment [im'baŋkmənt] n (road, rail) terraplén m; (river) dique m.

embargo [im'baːgou] n prohibición f.

embark [im'baːk] v embarcar. **embark on** emprender. **embarkation** n (people) embarco m; (cargo) embarque m.

embarrass [im'barəs] v desconcertar; molestar. **embarrassment** n desconcierto m; molestia f. **financial embarrassment** apuros de dinero m pl.

embassy ['embasi] n embajada f.

embellish [im'beliʃ] v embellecer; adornar. **embellishment** n embellecimiento m; adorno m.

ember ['embə] n ascua f.

embezzle [im'bezl] v malversar. **embezzlement** n malversación f. **embezzler** n malversador, -a m, f.

embitter [im'bitə] v (person) amargar. **embittered** adj amargado; rencoroso.

emblem ['embləm] n emblema m. **emblematic** adj emblemático.

embody [im'bodi] v personificar; materializar; incluir. **embodiment** n personificación f; incorporación f.

emboss [im'bos] v grabar en relieve; (paper) gofrar; (leather, silver) repujar. **embossed** adj (letterhead) gofrado.

embrace [im'breis] v abrazar; (encompass) abarcar; (opportunity) aprovecharse de. n abrazo m.

embroider [im'broidə] v bordar; (fig) adornar. **embroidery** n bordado m; adorno m.

embryo ['embriou] n embrión m. **in embryo** en embrión. **embryonic** adj embrionario.

emerald ['emərəld] n esmeralda f.

emerge [i'məːdʒ] v salir; sacarse. **emergence** n salida f.

emergency [i'məːdʒənsi] n emergencia f; (med) urgencia f. **emergency exit** salida de emergencia f. **emergency landing** aterrizaje forzoso m. **in case of emergency** en caso de emergencia.

emigrate ['emigreit] v emigrar. **emigrant** (m+f), adj emigrante. **emigration** n emigración f.

eminent ['eminənt] adj eminente. **eminence** n eminencia f.

emit [i'mit] v (light, sound) emitir; (cry) dar; (heat) desprender; (smoke) echar; (smell) despedir. **emission** n emisión f.

emotion [i'mouʃən] n emoción f. **emotional** adj (concerning the emotions) emocional; (occasion, person) emotivo. **emotionally** adv con emoción.

empathy ['empəθi] n empatía f.

emperor ['empərə] n emperador m. **empress** n emperatriz f.

emphasis ['emfəsis] n, pl -ses (fig) énfasis m; importancia f; (stress) acento m. **emphasize** v subrayar; (stress) acentuar. **emphatic** adj enfático; enérgico; categórico.

empire ['empaiə] n imperio m.

empirical [im'pirikəl] adj empírico. **empiricism** n empirismo m.

employ [im'ploi] v emplear. n also **employment** empleo m. **employee** n empleado, -a m, f. **employer** n empresario, -a m, f; empleador, -a m, f. **employment agency** agencia de colocaciones f.

empower [im'pauə] v autorizar, habilitar.

empty ['empti] adj vacío; vacante; desocupado; desierto. **empty-handed** adj con las manos vacías. **empty-headed** adj casquivano. v vaciar; (river) desaguar. **emptiness** n vacío m; vacuidad f.

emu ['iːmjuː] n emú m.

emulate ['emjuleit] v emular. **emulation** n emulación f.

emulsion [i'mʌlʃən] n emulsión f. **emulsify** v emulsionar.

enable [i'neibl] v permitir; capacitar.

enact [i'nakt] v (represent) representar; (a law) promulgar; (decree) decretar; (do) hacer. **enactment** n promulgación f; decreto m.

enamel [i'naməl] n esmalte m. v esmaltar.

enamour [i'namə] v enamorar. **be enamoured of** estar enamorado de.

encase [in'keis] v (enclose) encerrar; (box) encajonar.

enchant [in'tʃɑːnt] v encantar. **enchanter** n (magician) hechicero m; encanto m. **enchanting** adj encantador. **enchantment** n (charm) encanto m; (magic) hechizo m. **enchantress** n hechicera f; encanto m.

encircle [in'səːkl] v cercar, rodear.

enclose [in'klouz] v (shut in) encerrar; (surround) rodear; (in a letter) adjuntar. **enclosed** adj adjunto. **enclosure** n encierro m; carta adjunta f.

encore [ɔŋkɔː] interj ¡bis! ¡otra vez! n repetición f. v pedir la repetición; repetir.

encounter [in'kauntə] v encontrarse con; enfrentarse a. n encuentro m.

encourage [in'kʌridʒ] v animar, alentar; estimular; incitar. **encouragement** n ánimo m, aliento m; estimulación f; incitación f. **encouraging** adj alentador; prometedor.

encroach [in'kroutʃ] v invadir; usurpar. **encroachment** n invasión f; usurpación f.

encumber [in'kʌmbə] v (humper) estorbar; (load) cargar; (block) obstruir. **encumbrance** n estorbo m; obstáculo m.

encyclopaedia [insaiklə'piːdiə] n enciclopedia f.

end [end] n (tip) punta f; (tail end) cabo m; (finish) fin m, final m. **end product** (comm) producto final m; (result) resultado m. **make ends meet** pasar con lo que se tiene. v acabar, terminar. **ending** n fin m, final m. **endless** adj interminable.

endanger [in'deindʒə] v arriesgar, poner en peligro.

endeavour [in'devə] n esfuerzo m, empeño m. v esforzarse, procurar.

endemic [en'demik] adj endémico.

endive ['endiv] n escarola f, endibia f.

endorse [in'dɔːs] v (cheque, etc.) endosar; (approve) aprobar. **endorsement** n endoso m; aprobación f; (mot) nota de inhabilitación f.

endow [in'dau] v dotar; (prize, etc.) fundar. **endowment** n dotación f; fundación f.

endure [in'djuə] v (support) aguantar; (last) durar. **endurable** adj soportable. **endurance** n aguante m; resistencia f. **enduring** adj resistente; duradero.

enemy ['enəmi] n enemigo, -a m, f.

energy ['enədʒi] n energía f. **energetic** adj enérgico.

enfold [in'fould] v envolver; abrazar.

enforce [in'fɔːs] v (discipline) imponer; (law) hacer cumplir.

engage [in'geidʒ] v (employ) ajustar; (pledge) comprometer; (attention) llamar; (keep busy) ocupar; (clutch) embragar. **engaged** adj prometido; ocupado. **get engaged** comprometerse. **engagement** n compromiso m; (appointment) cita f; (encounter) encuentro m. **engagement ring** sortija de pedida f.

engine ['endʒin] n motor m; máquina f. **engine driver** maquinista m. **engine room** sala de máquinas f.

engineer [endʒi'niə] n ingeniero m; (workman) mecánico m. **engineering** n ingeniería f.

England ['inglənd] n Inglaterra f. **English** nm, adj inglés. **the English** los ingleses. **English Channel** n Canal de la Mancha m.

engrave [in'greiv] v grabar. **engraver** n grabador, -a m, f. **engraving** n grabado m.

engross [in'grous] v absorber. **engrossing** adj absorbente.

engulf [in'gʌlf] v tragarse; (sink) hundir.

enhance [in'hɑːns] v (prices, etc.) aumentar; (beauty) realzar. **enhancement** n aumento m; realce m.

enigma [i'nigmə] n enigma m. **enigmatic** adj enigmático.

enjoy [in'dʒɔi] v (like) gustar; (delight in, have the use of) gozar de, disfrutar de; (party) divertirse en. **enjoyable** adj agradable; divertido. **enjoyment** n placer m; diversión f.

enlarge [in'lɑːdʒ] v ampliar, agrandar; (expand) extender. **enlargement** n aumento m; extensión f; (phot) ampliación f. **enlarger** n (phot) ampliadora f.

enlighten [in'laitn] v iluminar; (inform) informar; aclarar. **enlightenment** n aclaración f.

enlist [in'list] v alistar; alistarse; (obtain support) conseguir. **enlistment** n alistamiento m.

enmity ['enməti] n enemistad f.

enormous [i'nɔːməs] adj enorme. **enormity** n enormidad f. **enormously** adv enormemente.

enough [i'nʌf] *adj. adv* bastante. *n* lo bastante. **enough is enough** basta y sobra. **curiously enough** por extraño que parezca. **sure enough** más que seguro. **that's enough** con eso basta.

enquire [in'kwaiə] *V* inquire.

enrage [in'reidʒ] *v* enfurecer.

enrich [in'ritʃ] *v* enriquecer; (*soil*) fertilizar. **enrichment** *n* enriquecimiento *m*; fertilización *f*.

enrol [in'roul] *v* inscribir; registrar; matricular; (*mil*) alistar. **enrolment** *n* inscripción *f*; registro *m*; matriculación *f*; alistamiento *m*.

ensign [ensain] *n* (*flag*) enseña *f*; (*badge*) insignia *f*; (*naut*) bandera de popa *f*.

enslave [in'sleiv] *v* esclavizar. **enslavement** *n* esclavitud *f*.

ensue [in'sju:] *v* seguir; resultar. **ensuing** *adj* siguiente; resultante.

ensure [in'ʃuə] *v* asegurar.

entail [in'teil] *v* (*involve*) suponer; (*follow as a result of*) acarrear; (*law*) vincular. **entailment** *n* vinculación *f*.

entangle [in'taŋgl] *v* enredar; complicar. **entanglement** *n* enredo *m*; (*fig*) lío *m*.

enter ['entə] *v* entrar en; penetrar; meterse en; registrar; matricular; presentar. **enter for** tomar parte en. **enter into** empezar; establecer; comprender.

enterprise ['entə,praiz] *n* empresa *f*; iniciativa *f*. **enterprising** *adj* emprendedor.

entertain [,entə'tein] *v* (*host*) recibir; (*amuse*) divertir; (*ideas*) abrigar. **entertainer** *n* artista *m*, *f*. **entertaining** *adj* divertido, entretenido. **entertainment** *n* entretenimiento *m*.

enthral [in'θrɔːl] *v* encantar. **enthralling** *adj* cautivador.

enthusiasm [in'θuːzi,azəm] *n* entusiasmo *m*. **enthusiast** *n* entusiasta *m*, *f*. **enthusiastic** *adj* (*person*) entusiasta; (*praise, etc.*) entusiástico.

entice [in'tais] *v* tentar, seducir. **enticing** *adj* tentador; atractivo. **enticement** *n* atracción *f*; seducción *f*.

entire [in'taiə] *adj* entero, completo. **entirety** *n* totalidad *f*.

entitle [in'taitl] *v* (*authorize*) dar derecho a; (*written work*) titular. **be entitled** tener derecho.

entity ['entəti] *n* entidad *f*, ente *m*.

entrails ['entreilz] *pl n* entrañas *f pl*.

entrance[1] ['entrəns] *n* entrada *f*; ingreso *m*. **entrance examination** examen de ingreso *m*. **entrance hall** vestíbulo *m*. **tradesmen's entrance** entrada de servicio *f*.

entrance[2] [in'trains] *v* arrebatar. **entrancing** *adj* encantador.

entrant ['entrant] *n* participante *m*, *f*.

entreat [in'triːt] *v* suplicar, implorar. **entreaty** *n* súplica *f*, imploración *f*.

entrée ['ontrei] *n* entrada *f*.

entrench [in'trentʃ] *v* atrincherar. **entrenchment** *n* atrincheramiento *m*; (*encroachment*) invasión *f*.

entrepreneur [,ontrəprə'nəɪ] *n* empresario *m*; intermediario *m*.

entrust [in'trʌst] *v* (*commit*) confiar; (*someone*) encargar.

entry ['entri] *n* (*entrance*) entrada *f*; (*into profession*) ingreso *m*; (*in a book*) anotación *f*; (*book-keeping*) asiento *m*. **no entry** dirección prohibida *f*.

entwine [in'twain] *v* entrelazar.

enunciate [i'nʌnsi,eit] *v* enunciar. **enunciation** *n* enunciación *f*.

envelop [in'veləp] *v* envolver. **enveloping** *adj* envolvente.

envelope ['envə,loup] *n* sobre *m*.

environment [in'vaiərənmənt] *n* ambiente *m*. **environmental** *adj* ambiental.

envisage [in'vizidʒ] *v* (*imagine*) imaginarse; (*foresee*) prever.

envoy ['envoi] *n* enviado *m*.

envy ['envi] *n* envidia *f*. *v* envidiar. **enviable** *adj* envidiable. **envious** *adj* envidioso. **enviously** *adv* con envidia.

enzyme ['enzaim] *n* enzima *f*.

epaulet ['epəlet] *n* charretera *f*.

ephemeral [i'femərəl] *adj* efímero.

epic ['epik] *n* poema épica *f*. *adj* épico.

epidemic [epi'demik] *n* epidemia. *adj* epidémico.

epilepsy ['epilepsi] *n* epilepsia *f*. **epileptic** *n*, *adj* epiléptico, -a. **epileptic fit** ataque epiléptico *m*.

Epiphany [i'pifəni] *n* Epifanía *f*.

episcopal [i'piskəpəl] *adj* episcopal.

episode ['episoud] *n* episodio *m*. **episodic** *adj* episódico.

epitaph ['epi,taɪf] *n* epitafio *m*.

epitome [i'pitəmi] *n* epítome *m*; (*fig*) personificación *f*. **epitomize** *v* compendiar; ser la personificación de.

epoch ['iːpok] *n* época *f*.

equable ['ekwəbl] *adj* uniforme; *(calm)* tranquilo.

equal ['iːkwəl] *n (m+f)*. *adj* igual. *v* igualar. **equality** *n* igualdad *f*. **equalize** *v* igualar; *(draw)* empatar.

equanimity [ekwə'nimiti] *n* ecuanimidad *f*.

equate [i'kweit] *v* igualar; comparar; poner en ecuación. **equation** *n* ecuación *f*.

equator [i'kweitə] *n* ecuador *m*. **equatorial** *adj* ecuatorial.

equestrian [i'kwestriən] *adj* ecuestre. *n* caballista *m*.

equilateral [ˌiːkwi'latərəl] *n* figura equilátera *f*. *adj* equilátero.

equilibrium [ˌiːkwi'libriəm] *n* equilibrio *m*.

equinox ['ekwinoks] *n* equinoccio *m*. **equinoctial** *adj* equinoccial.

equip [i'kwip] *v* equipar. **equipment** *n* equipo *m*; *(tools)* herramientas *f pl*.

equity ['ekwəti] *n* equidad *f*, justicia *f*.

equivalent [i'kwivələnt] *nm*, *adj* equivalente.

era ['iərə] *n* era *f*.

eradicate [i'radiˌkeit] *v* erradicar. **eradication** *n* erradicación *f*.

erase [i'reiz] *v* borrar. **eraser** *n* goma de borrar. **erasure** *n* borradura *f*.

erect [i'rekt] *adj* erguido. *v* erigir; *(assemble)* montar. **erection** *n* erección *f*; *(building)* construcción *f*; montaje *m*.

ermine ['əːmin] *n* armiño *m*.

erode [i'roud] *v* corroer; *(wear away)* erosionar. **erosion** *n* corrosión *f*; erosión *f*. **erosive** *adj* erosivo.

erotic [i'rotik] *adj* erótico. **eroticism** *n* erotismo *m*.

err [əː] *v* errar, desviarse; *(sin)* pecar. **erring** *adj* extraviado; pecaminoso.

errand ['erənd] *n* recado *m*. **run an errand** hacer un recado. **errand boy** recadero *m*.

erratic [i'ratik] *adj* desigual; errático.

error ['erə] *n (mistake)* error *m*; *(wrongdoing)* extravío *m*.

erudite ['erudait] *adj* erudito. **erudition** *n* erudición *f*.

erupt [i'rʌpt] *v* estar en erupción, salir con fuerza. **eruption** *n* erupción *f*. **eruptive** *adj* eruptivo.

escalate ['eskəˌleit] *v* intensificar, agravar. **escalation** *n* intensificación *f*. **escalator** *n* escalera mecánica *f*.

escalope ['eskəlop] *n* escalope *m*.

escape [is'keip] *n (flight)* fuga *f*; *(liquid)* salida *f*; *(gas)* escape *m*; *(responsibilities, etc.)* evasión *f*. **escape hatch** escotilla de salvamento *f*. **fire escape** escalera de incendios *f*. *v* escapar de; evadir; eludir. **escape notice** pasar inadvertido. **escapism** *n* evasión *f*.

escort ['eskoːt; *v* is'koːt] *n* acompañante *m*; *(mil)* escolta *f*. *v* acompañar; *(mil)* escoltar.

esoteric [esə'terik] *adj* esotérico.

especial [i'speʃəl] *adj* especial, particular; excepcional. **especially** *adv* especialmente, sobre todo.

espionage ['espiəˌnaːʒ] *n* espionaje *m*.

esplanade [ˌesplə'neid] *n* explanada *f*, bulevar *m*, paseo *m*.

essay ['esei] *n* ensayo *m*; composición *f*; *(attempt)* intento *m*. *v* probar; intentar. **essayist** *n* ensayista *m*, *f*.

essence ['esns] *n* esencia *f*. **essential** *adj* esencial, imprescindible; fundamental. *n* lo esencial. **essentials** *pl n* elementos esenciales *m pl*.

establish [i'stabliʃ] *v* establecer. **establishment** *n* establecimiento *m*. **The Establishment** clase dirigente *f*.

estate [i'steit] *n (property)* propiedad *f*; *(land)* finca *f*, *(S. Am.)* hacienda *f*, estancia *f*; *(inheritance)* herencia *f*; *(fortune)* fortuna *f*; *(social class)* estado *m*; *(of the deceased)* testamentaría *f*. **estate agency** agencia inmobiliaria *f*. **estate agent** agente inmobiliario *m*. **estate car** furgoneta *f*.

esteem [i'stiːm] *v* estimar, apreciar. *n* estima *f*, aprecio *m*.

estimate ['estimət; *v* 'estiˌmeit] *n (valuation)* estimación *f*; *(statement of cost)* presupuesto *m*. *v* estimar; hacer un presupuesto de. **estimation** *n* juicio *m*; *(esteem)* aprecio *m*.

estuary ['estjuəri] *n* estuario *m*.

eternal [i'təːnl] *adj* eterno. **eternity** *n* eternidad *f*.

ether ['iːθə] *n* éter *m*. **ethereal** *adj* etéreo.

ethical ['eθikl] *adj* ético. **ethics** *pl n* ética *f sing*.

ethnic ['eθnik] *adj* étnico.

etiquette ['etiˌket] *n* etiqueta *f*.

etymology [ˌeti'molədʒi] *n* etimología *f*. **etymologist** *n* etimólogo, -a *m*, *f*.

Eucharist ['juːkərist] *n* Eucaristía *f*.

eunuch ['juːnək] *n* eunuco *m*.

euphemism ['juːfəˌmizəm] *n* eufemismo *m*. **euphemistic** *adj* eufemístico.

euphoria [juˈfɔːriə] *n* euforia *f*. **euphoric** *adj* eufórico.

Europe ['juərəp] *n* Europa *f*. **European** *n*, *adj* europeo, -a. **European Economic Community (EEC)** *n* Comunidad Económica Europea (CEE) *f*.

euthanasia [juːθəˈneiziə] *n* eutanasia *f*.

evacuate [iˈvækjuˌeit] *v* evacuar. **evacuation** *n* evacuación *f*. **evacuee** *n* evacuado, -a *m*, *f*.

evade [iˈveid] *v* evadir, eludir. **evasion** *n* evasión *f*. **evasive** evasivo.

evaluate [iˈvæljuˌeit] *v* evaluar. **evaluation** *n* evaluación *f*.

evangelical [ˌiːvanˈdʒelikəl] *adj* evangélico. **evangelist** *n* evangelizador, -a *m*, *f*.

evaporate [iˈvæpəˌreit] *v* evaporar; deshidratar. **evaporated milk** leche evaporada *f*. **evaporation** *n* evaporación *f*; deshidratación *f*.

eve [iːv] *n* víspera *f*. **Christmas Eve** Nochebuena *f*. **New Year's Eve** Noche Vieja *f*. **on the eve of** en vísperas de.

even ['iːvən] *adj* (*surface*) uniforme; (*smooth*) suave; (*calm*) ecuánime; (*fair*) justo; (*same level*) a nivel; (*equal*) igual; (*number*) par. **break even** quedar igual. **get even** desquitarse. *adv* siquiera; incluso. **even if** incluso si. **even so** aun así. **even though** aunque. **even-tempered** *adj* sereno. *v* nivelar; igualar. **evenly** *adv* uniformemente; imparcialmente.

evening ['iːvniŋ] *n* tarde *f*; anochecer *m*. **evening class** clase nocturna *f*. **evening dress** (*man*) traje de etiqueta *m*; (*woman*) traje de noche *m*. **good evening!** (*early*) ¡buenas tardes! (*late*) ¡buenas noches!

event [iˈvent] *n* (*occurrence*) acontecimiento *m*; (*case*) caso *m*; (*outcome*) consecuencia *f*; (*in a programme*) número *m*; (*sport*) prueba *f*. **in the event of** en caso de. **eventful** *adj* agitado; memorable. **eventual** *adj* final; consiguiente. **eventuality** *n* eventualidad *f*. **eventually** *adv* finalmente; con el tiempo.

ever ['evə] *adv* (*always*) siempre; nunca, jamás. **we hardly ever go out** casi nunca salimos. **not ever** nunca jamás. **ever after** desde (que).

evergreen ['evəgriːn] *adj* de hoja perenne.

everlasting [ˌevəˈlaːstiŋ] *adj* eterno; perpetuo.

every ['evri] *adj* (*all*) todo; (*each*) cada. **everybody** *also* **everyone** *pron* todo el mundo. **everyday** *adj* diario. **every other day** cada dos días. **everything** *pron* todo. **everywhere** *adv* por *also* en todas partes.

evict [iˈvikt] *v* desahuciar. **eviction** *n* desahucio *m*.

evidence ['evidəns] *n* evidencia *f*; (*sign*) indicio *m*; (*law: proof*) prueba *f*; (*law: testimony*) testimonio *m*. *v* evidenciar. **give evidence** declarar como testigo. **evident** *adj* evidente, patente.

evil ['iːvl] *adj* malo; perverso; maligno. *n* mal *m*; desgracia *f*. **evildoer** *n* malhechor, -a *m*, *f*. **evil-minded** *adj* malpensado.

evoke [iˈvouk] *v* evocar. **evocation** *n* evocación *f*. **evocative** *adj* evocador.

evolve [iˈvolv] *v* evolucinar; (*develop*) desarrollarse. **evolution** *n* evolución *f*; desarrollo *m*. **evolutionary** *adj* evolutivo.

ewe [juː] *n* oveja *f*.

exacerbate [igˈzasəˌbeit] *v* exacerbar. **exacerbation** *n* exacerbación *f*.

exact [igˈzakt] *adj* exacto. *v* exigir. **exacting** *adj* (*person*) exigente; (*condition*) severo; (*work*) duro. **exactly** *adv* exactamente; precisamente.

exaggerate [igˈzadʒəˌreit] *v* exagerar; acentuar. **exaggerated** *adj* exagerado. **exaggeration** *n* exageración *f*.

exalt [igˈzolt] *v* exaltar, elevar; (*praise*) glorificar. **exaltation** *n* exaltación *f*; (*ecstasy*) arrobamiento. **exalted** *adj* exaltado, eminente.

examine [igˈzamin] *v* examinar; (*search*) reconocer; (*by touch*) palpar; (*law*) interrogar. **examination** *n* examen *m*; (*law*) interrogatorio *m*. **sit an exam** examinarse. **written exam** prueba escrita *f*. **examiner** *n* examinador, -a *m*, *f*; inspector, -a *m*, *f*.

example [igˈzampl] *n* ejemplo *m*. **follow someone's example** tomar ejemplo de uno. **for example** por ejemplo. **set an example** dar ejemplo.

exasperate [igˈzaspəˌreit] *v* exasperar. **exasperation** *n* exasperación *f*.

excavate ['ekskəˌveit] *v* excavar. **excavation** *n* excavación *f*. **excavator** (*person*) excavador *m*; (*tech*) excavadora *f*.

exceed [ikˈsiːd] *v* exceder. **exceedingly** *adv* sumamente.

excel [ik'sel] *v* superar, sobresalir. **excellence** *n* excelencia *f*. **His Excellency** su Excelencia *m*. **excellent** *adj* excelente.

except [ik'sept] *prep* excepto, salvo, con excepción de. **except for** excepto. *v* excluir, exceptuar. **exception** *n* exclusión *f*; excepción *f*. **take exception to** ofenderse por. **exceptional** *adj* excepcional.

excerpt ['eksɔɪpt] *n* extracto *m*. *v* extractar.

excess [ik'ses] *n* exceso *m*. *adj* excedente. **excess fare** suplemento *m*. **excess luggage** exceso de equipaje *also* peso *m*. **excessive** *adj* excesivo. **excessively** *adv* excesivamente.

exchange [iks'tʃeindʒ] *v* (*change*) cambiar; (*interchange*) intercambiar; (*courtesies*) hacerse; (*prisoners*) canjear; (*blows*) darse. *n* cambio *m*; intercambio *m*. **exchange control** control de divisas. **exchange rate** tipo de cambio *m*. **Stock Exchange** bolsa de valores *f*. **telephone exchange** central telefónica *f*.

exchequer [iks'tʃekə] *n* (*finances*) hacienda *f*; tesoro público *m*. **Chancellor of the Exchequer** Ministro de Hacienda *m*.

excise ['eksaiz] *n* impuestos sobre el consumo *m pl*.

excite [ik'sait] *v* (*stimulate*) excitar; emocionar; entusiasmar; (*irritate*) poner nervioso; (*urge*) incitar; (*imagination*) despertar; (*admiration, etc.*) provocar. **get excited** emocionarse; entusiasmarse. **excitement** *n* excitación *f*; emoción *f*; entusiasmo *m*; agitación *f*. **exciting** *adj* excitante; emocionante; apasionante.

exclaim [ik'skleim] *v* exclamar. **exclamation** *n* exclamación *f*. **exclamation mark** punto de admiración *m*.

exclude [ik'sklu:d] *v* excluir. **exclusion** *n* exclusión *f*. **exclusive** *adj* (*policy*) exclusivista; (*sole*) exclusivo; (*select*) selecto.

excommunicate [ekskə'mju:nikeit] *v* excomulgar. **excommunication** *n* excomunión *f*.

excrete [ik'skri:t] *v* excretar. **excrement** *n* excremento *m*. **excretion** *n* excreción *f*.

excruciating [ik'skru:ʃieitiŋ] *adj* (*noise*) intolerable; (*pain*) atroz.

excursion [ik'skɔːʃən] *n* excursión *f*.

excuse [ik'skju:z] *n* excusa *f*, disculpa *f*. *v* excusar, disculpar, perdonar; (*duty*) dispensar de. **excuse me!** ¡perdón! ¡discúlpeme! **excusable** *adj* excusable, disculpable, perdonable.

execute ['eksi,kju:t] *v* (*order, will, criminal*) ejecutar; (*carry out*) llevar a cabo. **execution** *n* ejecución *f*; (*of order*) cumplimiento *m*. **executioner** *n* verdugo *m*.

executive [ig'zekjutiv] *adj* (*power*) ejecutivo; (*function*) dirigente; (*ability*) de ejecución. *n* (*government branch*) poder ejecutivo *m*; (*person*) ejecutivo *m*.

exemplify [ig'zempli,fai] *v* ilustrar con ejemplos. **exemplification** *n* ejemplificación *f*.

exempt [ig'zempt] *adj* exento. *v* exentar, dispensar. **exemption** *n* exención *f*.

exercise ['eksə,saiz] *n* ejercicio *m*; gimnasia *f*. **exercise book** *n* cuaderno *m*. **take exercise** hacer ejercicio. *v* (*rights, etc.*) ejercer; (*physically*) ejercitarse; (*patience*) usar de.

exert [ig'zɔ:t] *v* ejercer. **exert oneself** esforzarse. **exertion** *n* esfuerzo *m*; (*of strength*) empleo *m*.

exhale [eks'heil] *v* exhalar; (*breathe out*) espirar. **exhalation** *n* exhalación *f*; espiración *f*.

exhaust [ig'zɔ:st] *v* agotar. *n* (*system*) escape *m*. **exhaust pipe** tubo de escape *m*. **exhausting** *adj* agotador. **exhaustion** *n* agotamiento *m*. **exhaustive** *adj* exhaustivo. **exhaustively** *adv* exhaustivamente.

exhibit [ig'zibit] *v* (*display*) mostrar; (*paintings, etc.*) exponer; (*documents*) presentar. *n* objeto expuesto *m*. **exhibition** *n* exposición *f*. **make an exhibition of oneself** ponerse en ridículo. **exhibitor** *n* expositor *m*.

exhilarate [ig'zilə,reit] *v* alegrar, animar. **exhilarating** *adj* estimulante. **exhilaration** *n* alegría *f*, regocijo *m*.

exile ['eksail] *n* exilio *m*, destierro *m*; (*person*) exiliado, -a *m, f*; desterrado, -a *m, f*. **go into exile** exiliarse, exilarse. *v* exiliar, exilar, desterrar.

exist [ig'zist] *v* existir; (*live*) vivir. **existence** *n* existencia *f*. **existent** *also* **existing** *adj* existente; (*present*) actual. **existentialism** *n* existencialismo *m*. **existentialist** *n* (*m+f*), *adj* existencialista.

exit ['egzit] *n* salida *f*; (*theatre*) mutis *m*. *v* (*theatre*) hacer mutio.

exonerate [ig'zonə,reit] *v* (*from blame*)

disculpar; (from obligation) dispensar de. **exoneration** n disculpa f; dispensa f.

exorbitant [ig'zɔːbitant] adj exorbitante.

exorcize ['eksɔːsaiz] v exorcizar. **exorcism** n exorcismo m. **exorcist** n exorcista m, f.

exotic [ig'zɔtik] adj exótico. **exoticism** n exotismo m.

expand [ik'spænd] v (cause to increase) desarrollar; (make larger) dilatar; (add to) ampliar. **expansion** n expansión f; desarollo m; dilatación f; ampliación f. **expansive** adj (person) expansivo; (wide) extenso. **expansiveness** n expansibilidad f.

expanse [ik'spæns] n extensión f; (wings) envergadura f.

expatriate [eks'peitriət; v eks'peitrieit] n, adj expatriado, -a. v desterrar. **expatriation** n expatriación f.

expect [ik'spekt] v (anticipate, hope for, require) esperar; (suppose) suponer. **expectant** adj expectante. **expectant mother** futura madre f. **expectation** n expectación f; (hope) esperanza f; (anticipation) previsión f.

expedient [ik'spiːdiənt] adj expeditivo, oportuno. n expediente. **expedience** also **expediency** n conveniencia f.

expedition [ˌekspiˈdiʃən] n expedición f.

expel [ik'spel] v expulsar.

expenditure [ik'spenditʃə] n gasto m. **expend** v gastar; (effort) dedicar. **expendable** adj (objects) gastable; (people) prescindible.

expense [ik'spens] n gasto m. **at the expense of** a costa de. **expense account** cuenta de gastos de representación f. **expensive** adj caro, costoso.

experience [ik'spiəriəns] n experiencia f. v experimentar; (difficulty) tener. **experienced** adj experimentado; experto.

experiment [ik'sperimənt] n experimento m. v hacer experimentos, experimentar. **experimental** adj experimental.

expert ['ekspəːt] n, adj experto, -a. **expertise** [ˌekspəˈtiːz] n pericia f.

expire [ik'spaiə] v (finish, die) expirar; (become void) caducar; (expel air) espirar. **expiration** also **expiry** n expiración f; (comm) vencimiento m.

explain [ik'splein] v explicar. **explanation** n explicación f. **explanatory** adj explicativo.

expletive [ek'spliːtiv] n (gramm) expletiva f; (oath) taco m.

explicit [ik'splisit] adj explícito.

explode [ik'spləud] v estallar, hacer explotar; (myth) refutar; (rumour) desmentir. **explosion** n explosión f. **explosive** nm, adj explosivo.

exploit[1] ['eksplɔit] n hazaña f.

exploit[2] [ik'splɔit] v explotar. **exploitation** n explotación f.

explore [ik'splɔː] v explorar. **exploration** n exploración f. **exploratory** adj exploratorio. **explorer** n explorador, -a m, f.

exponent [ik'spəunənt] n exponente m, f.

export ['ekspɔːt; v ik'spɔːt] n exportación f. v exportar. **exporter** n exportador, -a m, f.

expose [ik'spəuz] v (leave uncovered) exponer; (reveal) revelar; (plot, etc.) descubrir; (phot) exponer. **exposure** n exposición f; revelación f; descubrimiento m; (denunciation) denuncia f; (phot) fotografía f. **exposure meter** exposímetro m. **indecent exposure** exhibicionismo m.

expound [ik'spaund] v exponer; comentar.

express [ik'spres] v expresar; (press) exprimir. n (train) rápido m; (mail) correo urgente m. adj, adv expreso; rápido. **expression** n expresión f. **expressive** adj expresivo; (mot) expressway autopista f.

expulsion [ik'spʌlʃən] n expulsión f.

exquisite ['ekswizit] adj exquisito; intenso.

extend [ik'stend] v extender, aumentar; (widen) ampliar; (lengthen) prolongar; (stretch) estirar; (invitation) enviar; (aid) ofrecer; (hand) tender; (time-limit) prorragar. **extension** n extensión f; prolongación f; aumento m; prórroga f. **telephone extension** extensión f. **extensive** adj extenso.

extent [ik'stent] n (length) extensión f; (degree) punto m; (scope) alcance m.

exterior [ik'stiəriə] nm, adj exterior.

exterminate [ik'stɔːmi,neit] v exterminar. **extermination** n exterminio m.

external [ik'stɔːnl] adj externo. **for external use only** sólo para uso externo.

extinct [ik'stiŋkt] adj extinto; (fire, volcano) extinguido. **extinction** n extinción f.

extinguish [ik'stiŋgwiʃ] v extinguir; apagar; (hope) destruir. **extinguisher** n (fire) extintor.

fade

extort [ik'stɔtt] v arrancar, sacar por fuerza. **extortion** n extorsión f. **extortionate** adj exorbitante.

extra ['ekstrə] adj extra; de más; adicional; extraordinario; no incluido. n (extra charge) recargo m; (actor) extra m, f. adv extraordinariamente.

extract [ik'strakt; n 'ekstrakt] v extraer; (obtain, parts of books, etc.) sacar. n extracto m. **extraction** n extracción f; (descent) origen m.

extradite ['ekstrə,dait] v conceder la extradición de; obtener la extradición de. **extradition** n extradición f.

extramural [,ekstrə'mjuərəl] adj para estudiantes libres.

extraordinary [ik'strɔːdənəri] adj extraordinario; raro.

extravagant [ik'stravəgənt] adj (lavish) pródigo; (wasteful) despilfarrador; (taste) dispendioso; (language, ideas) extravagante. **extravagance** n prodigalidad f; despilfarro m; extravagancia f.

extreme [ik'striːm] nm, adj extremo. **go to extremes** llegar a extremos. **extremist** n (m+f), adj extremista. **extremity** n (end) extremidad f; (necessity) apuro m.

extrovert ['ekstrəvɜːt] n, adj extrovertido, -a.

exuberant [ig'zjuːbərənt] adj exuberante; enfórico. **exuberance** n exuberancia f; enforia f.

exude [ig'zjuːd] v exudar.

exult [ig'zʌlt] v exultar. **exult over** triunfar sobre. **exultant** adj exultante. **exultation** n exultación f.

eye [ai] n ojo m. **an eye for an eye** ojo por ojo. **private eye** detective m. **make eyes at** echar miradas a. **see eye to eye with** ver con los mismos ojos que. **turn a blind eye** cerrar los ojos. **up to one's eyes in work** estar hasta aquí en trabajo. **with an eye to** con miras a. **with the naked eye** a simple vista. v mirar.

eyeball ['aibɔːl] n globo del ojo m.

eyebrow ['aibrau] n ceja f.

eye-catching ['aikatʃiŋ] adj llamativo.

eyelash ['ailaʃ] n pestaña f.

eyelid ['ailid] n párpado m.

eye shadow n sombreador de ojos m.

eyesight ['aisait] n vista f.

eyesore ['aisɔː] n algo que ofende la vista.

eyewitness ['ai,witnis] n testigo ocular m.

F

fable ['feibl] n fábula f.

fabric ['fabrik] n (cloth) tejido m; estructura f, construcción f. **fabricate** v (invent) fingir. **fabrication** n fabricación f; invención f.

fabulous ['fabjuləs] adj fabuloso; (coll) macanudo.

façade [fə'saːd] n fachada f.

face [feis] n cara f, rostro m; (side) lado m; (aspect) aspecto m; (grimace) mueca f; (surface) superficie f; (clock) esfera f. **face down** boca abajo. **face up** boca arriba. **face to face** cara a cara. **on the face of it** a primera vista. **fly in the face of** burlarse de. **in the face of** frente a. **keep a straight face** mantenerse impávido. **lose face** quedar mal. **pull faces** hacer muecas. **save face** salvar las apariencias. v mirar hacia, dar a; estar en frente de; enfrentarse con; presentarse ante; (consequences) arrostrar; (stand) aguantar; (resurface) revestir.

face cloth n paño m.

facelift ['feislift] n (coll) lavado m.

face pack n mascarilla de belleza f.

face powder n polvos para la cara m pl.

facet ['fasit] n faceta f.

facetious [fə'siːʃəs] adj chistoso; gracioso.

face value n (bill) valor nominal m; (stamps) valor facial. **take something at face value** creer algo a pie juntillas.

facing ['feisiŋ] n (sewing) guarnición f; (building) revestimiento m. adj de enfrente.

facsimile [fak'simili] nm, adj facsímil.

fact [fakt] n hecho m; realidad f. **as a matter of fact** en realidad. **in fact** en verdad. **factual** adj objetivo.

faction ['fakʃən] n facción f. **factious** adj faccioso.

factor ['faktə] n factor m, elemento m; (comm) agente m.

factory ['faktəri] n fábrica f.

faculty ['fakəlti] n (university) facultad f; (gift) facilidad f.

fad [fad] n manía f; novedad f. **faddish** adj maniático.

fade [feid] v (colour) descolorarse; (light) apagarse; (sound) desvanecerse; (interest) decaer. **faded** adj descolorido; marchito.

fag [fag] *n* (*coll*: *cigarette*) pitillo *m*. **fag end** sobras *f pl*; (*cigarette*) colilla *f*. **fagged out** rendido.

fail [feil] *v* fallar; (*not succeed*) fracasar, no lograr; (*hopes*) frustrarse; (*run out*) acabarse; (*weaken*) decaer; (*exams*) ser suspendido; (*neglect*) dejar (de). **without fail** sin falta. **failing** *n* defecto *m*. **failure** *n* fracaso *m*; fallo *m*; suspenso *m*; (*break-down*) avería *f*.

faint [feint] *adj* (*near collapse*) mareado; (*weak*) débil; (*colour*) pálido; (*timid*) timorato; (*slight*) ligero; vago; indistinto. *v* desmayarse. *n* desmayo *m*.

fair¹ [feə] *adj* bello; hermoso; (*skin*) blanco; (*hair*) rubio; (*just*) justo; (*reputation, weather*) bueno; (*prospects*) favorable; (*play*) razonable; (*price*) razonable; (*comment*) acertado; (*average*) mediano. **by fair means or foul** por las buenas o por las malas. **fairly** *adv* con justicia; (*reasonably*) bastante. **fairness** *n* belleza *f*; justicia *f*.

fair² [feə] *n* (*amusements*) verbena *f*; (*market*) feria *f*. **fun fair** parque de atracciones *m*. **fairground** *n* real *m*.

fairy ['feəri] *n* hada *f*. *adj* de hada. **fairy lights** bombillas de colores *f pl*.

faith [feiθ] *n* confianza *f*. **have faith in** fiarse de. **religious faith** fe religiosa *f*. **faithful** *adj* fiel; exacto. **faithfulness** *n* fidelidad *f*; exactitud *f*. **faithless** *adj* desleal; infiel.

fake [feik] *n* falsificación *f*; impostor *m*. *adj* falso; falsificado; (*feigned*) fingido. *v* falsificar; fingir.

falcon ['foːlkən] *n* halcón *m*.

*fall [foːl] *v* caer; (*prices, temperature, water*) bajar; (*wind*) amainar; (*decay*) decaer; (*task, duty, privilege*) tocar; (*accent*) recaer. **fall apart** caerse a pedazos. **fall back on** echar mano a. **fall behind** retrasarse. **fall in love** enamorarse. **fall out** (*quarrel*) reñir. **fall through** venirse abajo. *n* (*body, earth, leaves*) caída *f*; (*prices*) baja *f*; (*slope*) declive *m*; (*US*: *season*) otoño *m*.

fallacy ['faləsi] *n* falacia *f*; (*deception*) engaño *m*. **fallacious** *adj* erróneo.

fallible ['faləbl] *adj* falible. **fallibility** *n* falibilidad *f*.

fallow ['falou] *adj* (*land*) en barbecho; inculto.

false [foːls] *adj* falso; erróneo. **false alarm** falsa alarma *f*. **false pretences** estafa *f*.

false teeth dientes postizos *m pl*. **falsehood** *n* falsedad *f*; mentira *f*. **falseness** *n* falsedad *f*; inexactitud *f*; perfidia *f*. **falsify** *v* falsificar; desvirtuar. **falsification** *n* falsificación *f*.

falsetto [foːl'setou] *n* falsete *m*. *adj* de falsete.

falter ['foːltə] *v* (*action*) vacilar; (*voice*) titubear. **faltering** *adj* vacilante; titubeante. **falteringly** *adv* con paso vacilante; con voz titubeante.

fame [feim] *n* fama *f*.

familiar [fə'miljə] *adj* familiar, conocido. **be familiar with** estar familiarizado con. **familiarity** *n* familiaridad *f*. **familiarize** *v* familiarizar.

family ['faməli] *n* familia *f*. **family allowance** subsidio familiar *m*. **family doctor** médico de cabecera *m*. **family planning** planificación familiar *f*. **family tree** árbol genealógico *m*.

famine ['famin] *n* (*general scarcity*) escasez *f*; (*food*) hambre *f*.

famished ['famiʃt] *adj* famélico. **be famished** estar muerto de hambre.

famous ['feiməs] *adj* famoso, célebre.

fan¹ [fan] *n* (*hand*) abanico *m*; (*tech*) ventilador *m*. **fan belt** correa del ventilador *f*. *v* abanicar; agitar.

fan² [fan] *n* aficionado, -a *m*, *f*; admirador, -a *m*, *f*. **fan club** club de admiradores *m*. **fan mail** correspondencia de los admiradores *f*.

fanatic [fə'natik] *n*, *adj* fanático, -a. **fanaticism** *n* fanatismo *m*.

fancy ['fansi] *adj* de adorno; de fantasía. *n* fantasía *f*; (*whim*) capricho *m*; (*desire*) afición *f*; (*delusion*) ilusión *f*; (*taste*) gusto *m*. *v* imaginarse; suponer; gustar; (*suspect*) parecerle(a); (*desire*) apetecer. **fancy oneself** ser un creído. **fancy that!** ¡imagínate! **fancy dress** disfraz *m*. **fancied** *adj* favorito; imaginario. **fanciful** *adj* imaginario; caprichoso.

fanfare ['fanfeə] *n* fanfarria *f*.

fang [fan] *n* colmillo *m*; (*snake*) diente *m*.

fantastic [fan'tastik] *adj* fantástico.

fantasy ['fantəsi] *n* fantasía *f*; capricho *m*.

far [faː] *adv* lejos; (*much*) mucho; muy. *adj* lejano; distante. **as far as** hasta; por lo que. **far and wide** por todas partes. **far away** lejos. **far-away** *adj* remoto. **Far East** Extremo Oriente *m*. **far-fetched** *adj* inverosímil. **far-reaching** *adj* de mucho alcance. **so far so good** hasta ahora todo va bien.

farce [fɑːs] n farsa f. **farcical** adj ridículo, absurdo.

fare [feə] n precio del billete m, tarifa f; (boat) pasaje m; (passenger) pasajero, -a; (in a taxi) cliente m, f; (in a bus) viajero, -a m, f; (food) comida f. v (get on) irle bien (a uno).

farewell ['feə'wel] (interj) ¡adiós! **say farewell** decir adiós, despedirse de. adj de despedida.

farm [fɑːm] n also **farmhouse** granja f, finca f; (S. Am.) estancia f, hacienda f. **farmhand** n peón m. **farmland** n tierras de labrantío f pl. **farmyard** n corral m. v cultivar. **farm out** mandar hacer fuera. **farmer** n agricultor m; granjero m. **farming** n labranza f; agricultura f.

fart [fɑːt] (impol) n pedo m. v peerse.

farther ['fɑːðə] adv (space) más lejos; (time) más adelante. adj (space, time) más lejano.

farthest ['fɑːðist] adv más lejos. adj (most distant) más lejano; (longest) más largo.

fascinate ['fasi,neit] v fascinar. **fascinating** adj fascinador. **fascination** n fascinación f.

fascism ['faʃizəm] n fascismo m. **fascist** n(m+f). adj fascista.

fashion ['faʃən] n manera f, modo m; moda f. **after a fashion** en cierto modo. **fashion show** desfile de modas m. **in fashion** de moda. **out of fashion** pasado de moda. v hacer; formar; (mould) moldear.

fast[1] [fɑːst] adj rápido, veloz; (colour) sólido; (clock, etc.) adelantado; (secure) seguro; firme. **fast asleep** profundamente dormido. **make fast** sujetar, atar. **pull a fast one** jugar una mala jugada. **stuck fast** (in mud) completamente atascado.

fast[2] [fɑːst] n ayuno m. v ayunar.

fasten ['fɑːsn] v (fix) fijar; (attach) sujetar; (dress) abrochar; (close) cerrar. **fastener** or **fastening** n corchete m; fijación f.

fastidious [fa'stidiəs] adj quisquilloso; (demanding) exigente. **fastidiousness** n melindre m.

fat [fat] n grasa f; (on meat) gordo m. adj grueso; gordo. **fatten** v (person) engordar; (animal) cebar. **fattening** adj que engorda.

fatal ['feitl] adj fatal, mortal. **fatality** n fatalidad f.

fate [feit] n destino m; suerte f. **fated** adj

predestinado; condenado. **fateful** adj profético; fatal.

father ['fɑːðə] n padre m. **Father Christmas** Papa Noel m. **father-in-law** n suegro m. **fatherland** n patria f. **fatherless** adj huérfano de padre m. **fatherly** adj paternal.

fathom ['faðəm] n braza f. v (water depth) sondar, sondear; (unravel) desentrañar. **fathomless** adj insondable.

fatigue [fə'tiːg] n fatiga f. v fatigar.

fatuous ['fatjuəs] adj fatuo; necio. **fatuity** or **fatuousness** n fatuidad f; necedad f.

fault [fɔːlt] n culpa f; defecto m; error m; falta f; (geol) falla f. **be at fault** tener la culpa. **faultless** n imperfección f. **faultless** adj perfecto. **faulty** adj malo; erróneo; defectuoso.

fauna ['fɔːnə] n fauna f.

favour ['feivə] n favor m; favoritismo m; (gift) obsequio m; (comm) carta f. atenta f. **be in favour of** estar a favor de. v favorecer. **favourable** adj favorable. **favourite** n, adj favorito, -a.

fawn [fɔːn] n cervato m. adj color de gamuza m. **fawn on** or **upon** adular.

fear [fiə] n miedo m; temor m. v temer; tener miedo de or a. **fearful** adj (frightening) espantoso; (frightened) temeroso. **fearless** adj intrépido, audaz.

feasible ['fiːzəbl] adj factible. **feasibility** n viabilidad f.

feast [fiːst] n fiesta f; banquete m. **feast day** día festivo m.

feat [fiːt] n hazaña f.

feather ['feðə] n pluma f. **feather bed** colchón de plumas m.

feature ['fiːtʃə] n característica f; (shape) figura f; (face) rasgo m; (written article) artículo principal m. **feature film** película principal f. v presentar; representar; (emphasize) destacar.

February ['februəri] n febrero m.

fed [fed] V **feed**.

federal ['fedərəl] adj federal.

federate ['fedə,reit] v federar. **federation** n federación f.

fee [fiː] n (professional) honorarios m pl; (club) cuota f. **entrance fee** entrada f.

feeble ['fiːbl] adj débil; (unconvincing) de poco peso. **feebleness** n debilidad f.

*feed [fiːd] v alimentar; dar de comer; (eat) comer. **be fed up with** (coll) estar harto de. **feed on** alimentarse con. n (for babies) comida f; (fodder) foraje m;

(tech) alimentación *f.* **feedback** *n* reaprovechamiento *m*; *(tech)* realimentación *f.*

*feel [fiːl] *v* tocar; mirar; sentir; *(realize)* darse cuenta de; *(caress)* sobar; *(think)* pensar. *n* tacto *m*; sensación *f*; atmósfera *f*; sentido *m.* **feeler** *n* antena *f*; tentáculo *m.* **feeling** *n* sentimiento *m*; sentido *m*; sensación *f*; opinión *f*; impresión *f.*

feet [fiːt] *V* **foot.**

feign [fein] *v* fingir; inventar.

feline ['fiːlain] *nm, adj* felino.

fell¹ [fel] *V* **fall.**

fell² [fel] *v* derribar; *(trees)* talar.

fellow ['felou] *n* hombre *m*; compañero; *(coll)* tipo *m*; *(of a society)* miembro *m.* **fellowship** *n* comunidad *f*; asociación *f.*

felony ['feləni] *n* delito grave *m.* **felon** *n* criminal *m.*

felt¹ [felt] *V* **feel.**

felt² [felt] *n* fieltro *m.* **felt-tip pen** rotulador *m.*

female ['fiːmeil] *adj* hembra; femenino. *n* *(animal)* hembra *f*; *(person)* mujer *f.*

feminine ['feminin] *nm, adj* femenino. **femininity** *n* feminidad *f.* **feminism** *n* feminismo *m.* **feminist** *n(m+f), adj* feminista.

fence [fens] *n* cerca *f*, valla *f. v* cercar, vallar; *(sport)* practicar la esgrima. **fencing** *n* *(sport)* esgrima *f.*

fend [fend] *v* **fend for oneself** arreglárselas. **fend off** desviar.

fender ['fendə] *n* guardafuegos *m invar*; *(US: car)* guardabarros *m invar.*

fennel ['fenl] *n* hinojo *m.*

ferment [fə'ment; *n* 'fɑːment] *v* fermentar. *n* fermento *m*; agitación *f.* **fermentation** *n* fermentación *f.*

fern [fəːn] *n* helecho *m.*

ferocious [fə'rouʃəs] *adj* feroz. **ferocity** *n* ferocidad *f.*

ferret ['ferit] *n* hurón *m.* **ferret out** conseguir, descubrir.

ferry ['feri] *n* transbordador *m. v* transportar.

fertile ['fəːtail] *adj* fértil; *(person)* fecundo. **fertility** *n* fertilidad *f*; fecundidad *f.* **fertilization** *n* fertilización *f*; fecundación *f.* **fertilize** *v* abonar; fecundar. **fertilizer** *n* abono *m.*

fervent ['fəːvənt] *adj* ferviente. **fervour** *n* fervor *m.*

fester ['festə] *v* supurar; *(fig)* enconarse.

festival ['festəvəl] *n* fiesta *f.*

festoon [fə'stuːn] *v* festonear. *n* guirnalda *f.*

fetch [fetʃ] *v* *(bring)* traer; *(procure)* buscar; *(reach)* alcanzar. **fetching** *adj* atractivo.

fête [feit] *n* fiesta *f. v* festejar.

fetid ['fiːtid] *adj* fétido.

fetish ['fetiʃ] *n* fetiche *m.*

fetter ['fetə] *v* encadenar. **fetters** *pl n* grilletes *m pl*; *(fig)* trabas *f pl.*

feud [fjuːd] *n* enemistad hereditaria *f. v* pelear, reñir.

feudal ['fjuːdl] *adj* feudal. **feudalism** *n* feudalismo *m.*

few [fjuː] *adj* poco. *n* pocos, -as *pl.* **a few** algunos, unos, unos pocos. **quite a few** bastante. **fewer** *adj* menos. **the fewer the better** cuantos menos mejor. **fewest** *adj* menos.

fiancé [fi'onsei] *n* novio *m.* **fiancée** *n* novia *f.*

fiasco [fi'askou] *n* fiasco *m.*

fib [fib] *n* mentirijilla *f. v* decir una mentirijilla.

fibre ['faibə] *n* fibra *f.* **fibreglass** *n* fibra de vidrio *f.*

fickle ['fikl] *adj* inconstante, veleidoso.

fiction ['fikʃən] *n* *(stories)* novela *f*; *(invention)* ficción *f.* **fictional** *or* **fictitious** *adj* novelesco; ficticio.

fiddle ['fidl] *n* violín *m*; *(coll: trick)* trampa *f. v* tocar el violín; *(coll: cheat)* camelar; *(coll: falsify)* amañar. **fiddle with** juguetear con. **fiddling** *adj* trivial; fútil.

fidelity [fi'deləti] *n* fidelidad *f.*

fidget ['fidʒit] *v* agitar nerviosamente. **fidgety** *adj* nervioso, agitado.

field [fiːld] *n* campo *m*; *(fig)* esfera *f.* **field glasses** gemelos *m pl.* **field marshal** mariscal de campo *m.* **fieldwork** *n* trabajo en el terreno *m.*

fiend [fiːnd] *n* demonio *m*, diablo *m*; *(coll)* fanático, -a *m, f.* **fiendish** *adj* diabólico.

fierce [fiəs] *adj* feroz, fiero; *(person)* violento; *(heat)* intenso; *(battle)* encarnizado. **fierceness** *or* **ferocity** *n* ferocidad *f*; violencia *f*; furia *f*; intensidad *f.*

fiery ['faiəri] *adj* *(burning)* ardiente; *(flaming)* llameante; *(passionate)* apasionado; *(temper)* fogoso.

fifteen [fifˈtiːn] *nm, adj* quince. **fifteenth** *n, adj* decimoquinto, -a.

fifth [fifθ] *n, adj* quinto, -a.

fifty [ˈfifti] *nm, adj* cincuenta. **go fifty-fifty** ir a medias. **fiftieth** *n, adj* quincuagésimo, -a. **fiftyish** *adj* cincuentón.

fig [fig] *n (fruit)* higo *m*; *(tree)* higuera *f*.

*fight [fait] *v* luchar contra, combatir. *n* lucha *f*, pelea *f*.

figment [ˈfigmənt] *n* invención *f*.

figure [ˈfigə] *n (number)* número *m*, cifra *f*; *(price)* precio *m*; *(statue, design, personage)* figura *f*; *(human)* línea *f*. **figurehead** *n* mascarón de proa *m*; *(fig)* testaferro *m*. **figure skating** patinaje artístico *m*. *v (math)* poner en cifras; *(calculate)* calcular. **figure out** comprender; resolver.

filament [ˈfiləmənt] *n* filamento *m*.

file¹ [fail] *n (folder)* carpeta *f*; *(card index)* fichero *m*; *(document holder)* archivador *m*; *(dossier)* expediente *m*. *v* archivar; *(a claim)* presentar. **file in/out** entrar/salir en fila. **file past** desfilar ante. **in single file** en fila de a uno. **filing** *n* clasificación *f*. **filing cabinet** archivo *m*. **filing clerk** archivero, -a *m, f*, archivista *m, f*.

file² [fail] *n (tool)* lima *f*. *v* limar. **filings** *pl n* limaduras *f pl*.

filial [ˈfiliəl] *adj* filial.

fill [fil] *v* llenar; *(space, time)* ocupar; *(vacancy)* cubrir; *(tooth)* empastar; *(hole)* tapar; *(cookery)* rellenar; *(requirements)* satisfacer. **fill in** *(form)* rellenar. **fill up** llenar. **filling** *n* relleno *m*; empaste *m*. **filling station** estación de servicio *f*.

fillet [ˈfilit] *n* filete *m*. *v* cortar en filetes.

film [film] *n (phot, cinema)* película *f*; *(layer)* capa *f*; *(eye)* nube *f*; *(mist, etc.)* velo *m*. **roll of film** rollo de película *m*. **filmgoer** *n* aficionado al cine *m*. **film star** astro de cine *m*, estrella de cine *f*.

filter [ˈfiltə] *n* filtro *m*. *v* filtrar. **filtering** *n* filtración *f*. **filter-tipped** *adj* con filtro, emboquillado.

filth [filθ] *n* inmundicia *f*, suciedad *f*; *(fig)* obscenidades *f pl*. **filthy** *adj* asqueroso, inmundo; obsceno.

fin [fin] *n* aleta *f*.

final [ˈfainl] *adj (last)* último; decisivo; definitivo. *n* final *f*. **finalist** *n* finalista *m, f*. **finalize** *v* finalizar. **finally** *adv* finalmente.

finance [faiˈnans] *n* finanzas *f pl*. *v*

finanzar. **financial** *adj* financiero. **financial year** año económico *m*. **financier** *n* financiero *m*.

finch [fintʃ] *n* pinzón *m*.

*find [faind] *v* encontrar, hallar. **find out** averiguar; descubrir. *n* hallazgo *m*. **findings** *pl n* hallazgos *m pl*; resultados *m pl*.

fine¹ [fain] *adj* excelente; elegante; *(pleasant)* agradable; bueno; fino; delicado. **that's fine!** ¡muy bien! *adv* en trozos pequeños; fino; muy bien. **fine arts** bellas artes *f pl*. **finely** *adv (small)* finamente; *(well)* primorosamente. **finery** *n* galas *f pl*.

fine² [fain] *n* multa *f*. *v* multar.

finesse [fiˈnes] *n* fineza *f*, delicadeza *f*; tácto *m*; *(bridge)* impás *m*.

finger [ˈfingə] *n* dedo *m*. **little finger** meñique *m*. *v* tocar. **fingernail** *n* uña *f*. **fingerprint** *n* huella dactilar *f*. **fingertip** *n* punta del dedo *f*. **have at one's fingertips** saberse al dedillo.

finish [ˈfiniʃ] *v* terminar, acabar; *(sport)* llegar. **finish off** rematar. *n* fin *m*, conclusión *f*; *(surface)* acabado *m*; *(sport)* llegada. **finishing line** meta *f*. **finishing touch** última mano *f*.

finite [ˈfainait] *adj* finito.

Finland [ˈfinlənd] *n* Finlandia *f*. **Finn** *n* finlandés, -esa *m, f*. **Finnish** *nm, adj* finlandés.

fir [fəː] *n* abeto *m*. **fir cone** piña *f*.

fire [ˈfaiə] *n* fuego *m*; *(uncontrolled)* incendio *m*; *(electric or gas)* estufa *f*. **be on fire** estar ardiendo. **catch fire** encenderse. **set on fire, set fire to** pegar fuego, incendiar. *v (with enthusiasm, etc.)* infundir (a); *(gun)* disparar; *(salute)* tirar; *(missile)* lanzar; *(sack)* echar. **fire on** hacer fuego sobre.

fire alarm *n* alarma de incendios *f*.

firearm [ˈfaiəˌaːm] *n* arma de fuego *f*.

fire brigade *n* cuerpo de bomberos *m*.

fire door *n* puerta incombustible *f*.

fire drill *n* ejercicios para casos de incendio *m pl*.

fire engine *n* bomba de incendios *f*.

fire-escape *n* escalera de incendios *f*.

fire-extinguisher *n* extintor *m*.

firefly [ˈfaiəflai] *n* luciérnaga *f*.

fire-guard *n* guardafuego *m*.

firelight [ˈfaiəˌlait] *n* lumbre *m*.

fireman [ˈfaiəmən] *n* bombero *m*.

fireplace ['faiə‚pleis] n chimenea f.

fireproof ['faiə‚pruːf] adj ininflamable, incombustible.

fireside ['faiə‚said] n hogar m.

fire station n parque de bomberos m.

firewood ['faiə‚wud] n leña f.

firework ['faiə‚wəːk] n fuego de artificio m.

firing squad n pelotón de ejecución m.

firm¹ [fəːm] adj firme, sólido; estable. **firmness** n firmeza f.

firm² [fəːm] n empresa f, firma f.

first¹ [fəːst] adj primero; básico; elemental. **first aid** primeros auxilios m pl. **first-class** adj de primera clase. **first cousin** primo hermano m. **first edition** edición príncipe m. **first floor** primer piso m. **first name** nombre de pila m. **first-rate** adj de primera calidad. **in the first place** en primer lugar.

first² [fəːst] adv antes, primero. **first and foremost** antes que nada. **first and last** en todos los aspectos. **travel first** viajar en primera. **you go first** usted primero.

first³ [fəːst] n primero, -a m, f; sobresaliente m. **at first** al principio. **be the first to** ser el primero en. **get a first** sacar sobresaliente.

fiscal ['fiskəl] adj fiscal.

fish [fiʃ] n (food) pescado m; (in water) pez m. **fish and chips** pescado frito con patatas fritas. v pescar. **fishy** adj (coll) sospechoso.

fishbone ['fiʃ‚boun] n espina f.

fish-bowl n pecera f.

fisherman ['fiʃəmən] n pescador m.

fish fingers n filete de pescado empanado m.

fish hook n anzuelo m.

fishing ['fiʃiŋ] n pesca f. **fishing line** sedal m. **fishing net** red de pesca f. **fishing rod** caña de pescar f. **fishing tackle** aparejo de pescar m. **go fishing** ir de pesca.

fish market n mercado de pescado.

fishmonger ['fiʃ‚mʌŋgə] n pescadero m. **fishmonger's** n pescadería f.

fission ['fiʃən] n fisión f, escisión f.

fissure ['fiʃə] n grieta f.

fist [fist] n puño m. **fistful** n puñado m.

fit¹ [fit] adj conveniente; apto; adecuado; (qualified) capacitado; (competent) capaz; (worthy) digno; (healthy) sano. **not fit to eat** no se puede comer. **see fit** juzgar conveniente. v (try on) probar; (qualify) capacitar; (tally with) cuadrar

con; adaptar; preparar; unir; (supply with) equipar con; (clothes) sentar bien a; (tailor) entallar. **fitness** n conveniencia f; salud f; aptitud f. **fitter** n (tailor) probador, -a m, f; (tech) ajustador m. **fitting** adj oportuno; digno; apropiado; propio. **fitting room** cuarto de pruebas m. **fittings** pl n muebles m pl; accesorios m pl.

fit² [fit] n (med) ataque m.

five [faiv] nm, adj cinco.

fix [fiks] v fijar; sujetar; (decide) establecer; (date) señalar; (hopes) poner; (coll: put right) arreglar. n aprieto m; (coll) una dosis de froga f. **fixation** n obsesión f. **fixed** adj fijo; (coll: rigged) amañado. **fixture** n instalación f; (sport) partido m; (coll) permanencia f.

fizz [fiz] n burbujeo m; (coll) gaseosa f. v burbujear.

flabbergasted ['flæbə‚gɑːstid] adj pasmado.

flabby ['flæbi] adj fláccido; (spineless) blandengue. **flabbiness** n flaccidez f; blandura f.

flag¹ [flæg] n bandera f; (stone) baldosa f. **flag down** detener haciendo señales. **flagpole** n asta de bandera f. **flagship** n buque insignia m.

flag² [flæg] v (weaken) flaquear; (interest) decaer. **flagging** adj flojo; desmadejado.

flagon ['flægən] n (jug) jarra f; (bottle) botella (de dos litros) f.

flagrant ['fleigrənt] adj flagrante; escandaloso.

flair [fleə] n don m; instinto m; talento m.

flake [fleik] n (snow) copo m; (soap) escama f; (paint) desconchón m. v caer en copos; desconchar. **flaky** adj escamoso. **flaky pastry** hojaldre m.

flamboyant [flæm‚bɔiənt] adj llamativo. **flamboyance** n extravagancia f.

flame [fleim] n llama f. **burst into flames** incendiarse. v llamear. **flammable** adj inflamable.

flamingo [flə‚miŋgou] n flamenco m.

flan [flæn] n flan m.

flank [flæŋk] n (animal) ijada f; (person) costado m; (mil) flanco m. v bordear.

flannel ['flænl] n (fabric) franela f; (face cloth) paño para lavarse la cara m. **flannels** pl n pantalones de franela m pl.

flap [flæp] v (shake) sacudir; (arms) agitar; (wings) batir. n (pocket) carterita f; (envelope, etc.) solapa f; (table) ala abatible f; (coat) faldón m; (aero) alerón m; (coll) crisis f.

flare [fleə] n (blaze) llamarada f; (signal) cohete de señales m; (widening) ensanchamiento m. v llamear; ensanchar; (clothes) acampanar. **flare up** (anger) ponerse furioso.

flash [flaʃ] n destello m, (sparkle) centelleo m; (phot) flash m; (moment) instante m; (inspiration) ráfaga f; (genius) rasgo m; (hope) resquicio m. **flashback** n escena retrospectiva f. **flash bulb** bombilla de magnesio f. **flashlight** n linterna f. v despedir; lanzar; encender; destellar; centellear. **flashing** adj intermitente.

flask [flɑːsk] n frasco m. (vacuum) termo m.

flat¹ [flat] adj plano, llano, chato; horizontal; (fig) categórico; monótono; (boring) pesado; (rate) fijo; (below pitch) desafinado; (tyre) desinflado; (battery) descargado; (horse racing) sin obstáculos. **flat beer** cerveza muerta f. **flat-footed** adj de pies planos. **be flat broke** estar sin blanca. **go flat out** ir a todo gas. **flatly** adv categóricamente; completamente. n (music) bemol m; (land) llano m; (tyre) pinchazo m. **flatten** v (make flat) aplanar; (crush) aplastar; (smooth) alisar.

flat² [flat] n apartamento m. **flatlet** n piso pequeño m.

flatter [flatə] v adular, halagar; favorecer. **flatterer** n adulador, -a m, f. **flattering** adj (words) halagüeño; (person) halagador; (clothes) favorecedor. **flattery** n halago m, adulación f.

flatulence [flatjuləns] n flatulencia f.

flaunt [flɔːnt] v ostentar. **flaunt oneself** pavonearse.

flautist [flɔːtist] n flautista m, f.

flavour [fleivə] n sabor m, gusto m; (cookery) sazón m, sainete m. v saborear; condimentar. **flavouring** n condimento m, sainete m.

flaw [flɔː] n defecto m; (error) fallo m. v (crack) agrietar; (spoil) estropear. **flawed** adj falto; imperfecto. **flawless** adj sin tacha; perfecto.

flax [flaks] n lino m. **flaxen** adj de lino; (hair) rubio.

flea [fliː] n pulga f. **fleabite** n picadura de pulga f.

fleck [flek] n (speck) mota f; (colour)

mancha f; (dust) partícula f. v motear; (paint) salpicar.

fled [fled] V **flee**.

***flee** [fliː] v evitar; escapar de.

fleece [fliːs] n (wool) lana f; (sheared wool) velón m. v (coll) pelar. **fleecy** adj (woolly) lanoso.

fleet [fliːt] n flota f; (navy) armada f. adj veloz. **fleeting** adj fugaz, breve.

Flemish [flemiʃ] nm, adj flamenco. **Fleming** n flamenco, -a m, f.

flesh [fleʃ] n carne f. **flesh-coloured** adj de color carne. **flesh-eating** adj carnívoro. **flesh wound** herida superficial f. **in the flesh** en carne y hueso. **fleshy** adj gordo.

flew [fluː] V **fly**.

flex [fleks] n flexible m. v doblar. **flexibility** n flexibilidad f. **flexible** adj (pliable) flexible; (fig) elástico.

flick [flik] v dar un golpecito a. **flick through** (book) hojear. n (whip) latigazo suave m; (light stroke) golpecito m; (duster) pasada f; (wrist) movimiento rápido m. **the flicks** (coll) el cine m.

flicker [flikə] v (light) parpadear; (flames) vacilar. n parpadeo m; (flame) llama vacilante f; (hope, etc.) requicio m.

flight¹ [flait] n (birds) bandada f; (aircraft) escuadrilla f; (act of flying) vuelo m; (distance flown) recorrido m. **flight crew** tripulación f. **flight deck** cubierta de aterrizaje f. **flight of stairs** tramo de escalera m. **flight path** trayectoria de vuelo f. **in flight** en vuelo. **flightiness** n ligereza f. **flightless** adj incapacitado para volar. **flighty** adj volátil; caprichoso.

flight² [flait] n (escape) huida f, fuga f.

flimsy [flimzi] adj (lacking substance) poco sólido; (fragile) frágil; (weak) débil; (paper) fino; (cloth) ligero; (excuse) flojo. **flimsiness** n fragilidad f; debilidad f; finura f; ligereza f.

flinch [flintʃ] v (draw back) retroceder; (hesitate) vacilar; (muscular movement) encogerse.

***fling** [fliŋ] v arrojar, tirar; (dash) precipitarse. **fling aside** dejar de lado. n (throw) lanzamiento m; (wild tune) juerga f.

flint [flint] n pedernal m; (of lighter) piedra de mechero f.

flip [flip] v (flick) dar un capirotazo. (coin) echar a cara o cruz. n capirotazo m. **flipper** n aleta f.

flippant [flipənt] adj frívolo. **flippancy** n ligereza f.

flirt [flɜːt] n (female) coqueta f; (male) mariposón m. v flirtear, coquetear. **flirtation** n coqueteo m.

flit [flit] v revolotear.

float [fləut] v flotar; (support) hacer flotar. n flotador m; (angling) corcho m; (carnival) carroza f.

flock[1] [flɒk] n (sheep, goats) rebaño m; (birds) bandada f; (people) muchedumbre f. v congregarse.

flock[2] [flɒk] n (filling) borra f.

flog [flɒg] v (beat) azotar; (coll: sell) vender. **flogging** n paliza f; flagelación f.

flood [flʌd] v inundar; irrigar; (overflow) desbordar. n inundación f; flujo m; diluvio m. in flood crecido.

*****floodlight** [ˈflʌdlait] n foco m. v iluminar con focos. **floodlighting** n iluminación con focos f.

floor [flɔː] n suelo m, piso m; (ocean) fondo m; (dance) pista f. first floor primer piso m. ground floor planta baja f. take the floor (speak) tomar la palabra. v (knock down) echar al suelo. **floorboard** n tabla del suelo f. **floorcloth** n trapo m. **flooring** n solado m. floor polish cera para el suelo f. floor show espectáculo de cabaret m. **floorwalker** n supervisor de división m.

flop [flɒp] v desplomarse; (fail) fracasar. n (coll) fracaso m. **floppy** adj flojo; colgante.

flora [ˈflɔːrə] n flora f.

florist [ˈflɒrist] n florista m, f. **florist's shop** florería f.

flounce[1] [flauns] v flounce in/out entrar/salir enfadado. n movimiento brusco m.

flounce[2] [flauns] n (of dress) volante m.

flounder [ˈflaundə] v forcejar; confundirse.

flour [flauə] n harina f. v enharinar. flour mill molino harinero m. floury adj (covered with flour) enharinado; (like flour) harinoso.

flourish [ˈflʌriʃ] v (prosper) florecer; (wave) agitar; (brandish) esgrimir. n ostentación f; (gesture) ademán m; (writing) rasgo m. **flourishing** adj floreciente.

flout [flaut] v burlarse de.

flow [fləu] v (liquid) fluir; (tears) correr; (blood in the body) circular; (blood from the body) derramarse; (tide) subir. flow away irse. flow from salir de. flow in/out entrar/salir a raudales. flow into

desembocar. n circulación f; movimiento m. flow chart organigrama m. **flowing** adj (river) fluente; (style) fluido; (hair) suelto; (beard) largo.

flower [flauə] n flor f. flower arrangement ramillete m. flower bed arriate m. **flowerpot** n maceta f. flower shop florería f. flower show exposición de flores f. v florecer. **flowering** adj floreciente; n florecimiento m. **flowery** adj florido.

flown [fləun] V fly.

flu [fluː] n gripe f.

fluctuate [ˈflʌktjueit] v fluctuar; vacilar. **fluctuation** n fluctuación f.

flue [fluː] n chimenea f; conducto de humo m.

fluent [ˈfluːənt] adj (language) bueno; (writing) fluido. **fluency** n facilidad f; dominio m. **fluently** adv (speech) con soltura; (writing) con fluidez.

fluff [flʌf] n pelusa f; mota f; masa esponjosa f. fluffy adj (pillow, cushion) mullido; (downy) velloso; (cloth) que tiene pelusa.

fluid [ˈfluːid] nm, adj fluido.

fluke [fluːk] n chiripa f. **fluky** adj de suerte.

flung [flʌŋ] V fling.

fluorescent [fluəˈresnt] adj fluorescente. **fluorescence** n fluorescencia f.

fluoride [ˈfluəraid] n fluoruro m. **fluoridation** n fluoración f.

flurry [ˈflʌri] n (excitement) agitación f; (snow) borrasca f; (rain) chaparrón m; (wind) ráfaga f.

flush[1] [flʌʃ] n (blush) rubor m; (fever) sofoco m; (lavatory) cisterna f. v ruborizarse; tener sofocos; (light) resplandecer. flush the toilet tirar de la cadena. flushed adj rebosante.

flush[2] [flʌʃ] adj (abundant) copioso; (lavish) liberal; (coll: well off) adinerado. flush with (level) a nivel con.

fluster [ˈflʌstə] v poner nervioso. n agitación f.

flute [fluːt] n flauta f.

flutter [ˈflʌtə] v (leaves, etc.) revolotear; (wings) batir; (curtains, flags) ondular; (heart) palpitar; (flap) agitar. n ondulación f; (wings) aleteo m; agitación f; (eyelids) parpadeo m; palpitación f.

flux [flʌks] n (flow) flujo m; (changes) cambios frecuentes m pl. be in a state of flux estar siempre cambiando.

*fly¹ [flai] v volar; (*escape*) huir; (*time*) pasar volando; (*kite*) echar a volar; (*aircraft*) pilotar; (*flag*) izar, enarbolar; (*go across*) atravesar; (*mileage*) recorrer. **fly away** emprender el vuelo. **fly over** sobrevolar. **fly past** desfilar. **flies** pl n (*trousers*) bragueta f.

fly² [flai] n mosca f.

fly-blown adj cochambroso.

fly-fishing n pesca con moscas f.

flying ['flaiiŋ] adj volador; volante. n aviación f.

flying colours pl n éxito rotundo m.

flying field n campo de aviación m.

flying fish n pez volador m.

flying saucer n platillo volante m.

flying squirrel n ardilla volante f.

flying start n salida lanzada f; (*fig*) principio feliz m.

flyleaf ['flailif] n guarda f.

flyover ['flai,ouvə] n paso elevado m.

fly-paper n papel matamoscas m.

fly swatter n matamoscas m invar.

flyweight ['flaiweit] n peso mosca m.

flywheel ['flaiwiil] n volante m.

foal [foul] n potro. v a m, f. v parir.

foam [foum] n espuma f. v espumar; (*animal*) espumajear. **foam rubber** gomespuma f. **foaming** adj espumoso.

focal ['foukəl] adj focal. **focal point** punto focal.

focus ['foukəs] n foco m. **in focus** enfocado. **out of focus** fuera de foco. v enfocar; concentrar.

fodder ['fodə] n forraje m.

foe [fou] n enemigo, -a m, f.

foetus ['fiitəs] n feto m. **foetal** adj fetal.

fog [fog] n niebla f, bruma f. **fogbound** adj (*foggy*) cubierto de niebla; (*immobilized*) detenido por la niebla. **foghorn** n sirena de niebla f. **foglamp** or **foglight** (*mot*) faro antiniebla m. **fogginess** n nebulosidad f. **foggy** adj nebuloso, brumoso.

foible ['foibl] n extravagancia f; (*fad*) manía f.

foil¹ [foil] v frustrar.

foil² [foil] n hoja fina de metal f; (*fig*) contraste m.

foil³ [foil] n (*fencing*) florete m.

foist [foist] v colar; meter.

fold¹ [fould] n (*crease*) pliegue m; (*wrinkle*) arruga f. v doblar, plegar; (*surround*) envolver; (*coll: close down*) liquidarse. **fold one's arms** cruzar los brazos. **folder**

n carpeta f. **folding** adj plegable. **folding door** puerta de fuelle f.

fold² [fould] n (*sheep*) redil m; (*religion*) grey f.

foliage ['fouliidʒ] n follaje m.

folk [fouk] pl n gente f sing; pueblo m. **folks** pl n (*coll*) familia f sing. **folk art** arte popular. **folk dance** baile folklórico m. **folklore** n folklore m. **folk music** música popular f. **folk singer** cantante de canciones populares. **folk song** canción popular f.

follicle ['folikl] n folículo m.

follow ['folou] v seguir; (*pursue*) perseguir; (*practise*) ejercer; (*ensue*) resultar. **follow up** investigar sobre; reforzar. **follower** n seguidor, -a m, f; discípulo m; aficionado, -a m, f. **following** adj siguiente. n partidarios m pl.

folly ['foli] n locura f.

fond [fond] adj cariñoso; indulgente. **be fond of** tenerle cariño a. **fondly** adj cariñosamente. **fondness** n cariño m.

fondle ['fondl] v acariciar; mimar.

font [font] n (*baptismal*) pila f; (*printing*) fundición f.

food [fuɪd] n comida f, alimento m; comestibles m pl. **food and drink** comida y bebida f. **food poisoning** intoxicación alimenticia f. **food shop** tienda de comestibles f. **foodstuff** n producto alimenticio m.

fool [fuɪl] n tonto, -a m, f; bobo, -a m, f; idiota m, f; (*jester*) bufón m. **foolproof** adj infalible. v (*deceive*) engañar; (*joke*) bromear. **fool about** or **around** juguetear. **foolhardy** adj temerario. **foolhardiness** n temeridad f. **foolish** adj insensato; tonto. **foolishly** adv neciamente. **foolishness** n insensatez f; tontería f.

foolscap ['fuɪlskap] n papel de barba m.

foot [fut] n, pl **feet** pie m; (*animal*) pata f. **from head to foot** de pies a cabeza. **on foot** a pie. **get cold feet** tener miedo. **football** ['fut,boɪl] n fútbol m; (*ball*) pelota f. **football pools** pl n quinielas f pl. **foot brake** n freno de pedal m.

footbridge ['fut,bridʒ] n pasarela f.

foothills ['futhilz] pl n estribaciones f pl.

foothold ['fut,hould] n punto de apoyo para el pie m; (*fig*) posición f.

footing ['futiŋ] n pie m, equilibrio m; condición f; posición f. **on an equal footing** en un pie de igual.

footlights ['fut,laits] *pl n* candilejas *f pl.*

footloose ['futlu:s] *adj* libre.

footnote ['fut,nout] *n* nota *f.*

footpath ['fut,pa:θ] *n* senda *f;* (*pavement*) acera *f.*

footprint ['fut,print] *n* pisada *f.*

footstep ['fut,step] *n* paso *m.*

for [fo:] *prep* para; por; de; (*time*) desde; durante; (*in favour of*) en favor de; (*in honour of*) en honor de; (*in place of*) en lugar de; (*as regards*) en cuanto a; (*against*) contra; (*in order that*) para que. *conj* pues, puesto que, ya que.

forage ['forid3] *v* forrajear; (*fig: seek*) buscar. *n* forraje *m.*

****forbear** [fo:'beə] *v* contenerse; abstenerse. **forbearance** *n* abstención *f;* indulgencia *f;* paciencia *f.*

****forbid** [fə'bid] *v* prohibir; (*prevent*) impedir. **forbidding** *adj* impresionante; inhóspito; severo; (*threatening*) amenazador.

force [fo:s] *n* fuerza *f;* (*mil*) cuerpo *m.* **in force** en vigor. **sales force** vendedores *m pl.* **join forces** unirse. *v* forzar; obligar; (*tech*) inyectar. **be forced to** verse obligado a. **forceful** *adj* fuerte; contundente.

forceps ['fo:seps] *pl n* fórceps *m sing.*

ford [fo:d] *n* vado *m. v* vadear.

fore [fo:] *adj* delantero; anterior. *adv* delante. *n* (*naut*) proa *f.* **come to the fore** empezar a destacar. *interj* (*golf*) ¡cuidado!

forearm ['fo:ra:m] *n* antebrazo *m. v* prevenir.

forebears ['fo:beəz] *pl n* antepasados *m pl.*

foreboding [fo:'boudiŋ] *n* presentimiento *m.*

****forecast** ['fo:ka:st] *n* previsión *f;* pronóstico *m;* plan *m. v* pronosticar. **weather forecast** pronóstico meteorológico *m.*

forecourt ['fo:ko:t] *n* antepatio *m.*

forefather ['fo:fa:ðə] *n* antepasado *m.*

forefinger ['fo:fiŋgə] *n* dedo índice *m.*

forefront ['fo:frʌnt] *n* delantera *f;* sitio de mayor importancia *m.*

foregone ['fo:gon] *adj* conocido de antemano. **foregone conclusion** conclusión inevitable *f.*

foreground ['fo:graund] *n* primer plano *m;* primer término *m.*

forehand ['fo:hænd] *n* (*tennis*) golpe derecho *m.*

forehead ['forid] *n* frente *f.*

foreign ['forən] *adj* extranjero; ajeno. **foreign affairs** asuntos extranjeros *m pl.* **foreign trade** comercio exterior *m.* **foreign exchange** cambio exterior *m.* **foreign legion** legión extranjera *f.* **foreigner** *n* extranjero, -a *m, f.*

foreleg ['fo:leg] *n* pata delantera *f.*

foreman ['fo:mən] *n* capataz *m.*

foremost ['fo:moust] *adj* delantero; principal. **first and foremost** ante todo.

forename ['fo:neim] *n* nombre de pila *m.*

forensic [fə'rensik] *adj* forense. **forensic medicine** medicina legal *f.*

forerunner ['fo:rʌnə] *n* precursor, -a *m, f;* (*herald*) anunciador, -a *m, f.*

****foresee** [fo:'si:] *v* prever. **foreseeable** *adj* previsible.

foreshadow [fo:'ʃadou] *v* presagiar; prefigurar.

foresight ['fo:sait] *n* previsión *f.*

foreskin ['fo:skin] *n* prepucio *m.*

forest ['forist] *n* selva *f;* bosque *m.* **forester** *n* guardabosque *m.* **forestry** *n* silvicultura *f.* **Forestry Commission** administración de montes *f.*

****forestall** [fo:'sto:l] *v* prevenir; impedir; anticiparse a.

foretaste ['fo:teist] *n* anticipación *f.*

****foretell** [fo:'tel] *v* predecir; presagiar.

forethought ['fo:θo:t] *n* premeditación *f.*

forever [fo:'evə] *adv* siempre, para siempre. **forever more** por siempre jamás.

forewarn [fo:'wo:n] *v* avisar, advertir. **forewarning** *n* aviso *m,* advertencia *f.*

foreword ['fo:wə:d] *n* prefacio *m;* prólogo *m.*

forfeit ['fo:fit] *v* (*right*) perder; (*property*) comisar.

forge[1] [fo:d3] *v* (*counterfeit*) falsificar; (*metal*) fraguar. *n* fragua *f.* **forger** *n* falsificador *m;* (*metal*) herrero *m.* **forgery** *n* falsificación *f;* (*things forged*) documento falsificado *m;* moneda falsificada *f.*

forge[2] [fo:d3] *v* **forge ahead** hacer grandes progresos.

****forget** [fə'get] *v* olvidar, olvidarse de. **forget-me-not** *n* nomeolvides *f.* **forgetful** *adj* olvidadizo; descuidado. **forgetfulness** *n* olvido *m;* descuido *m.*

****forgive** [fə'giv] *v* perdonar; dispensar. **forgiveness** *n* perdón *m;* remisión *f.* **forgiving** *adj* indulgente, clemente.

****forgo** [fo:'gou] *v* abstenerse; renunciar.

fork [foık] *n* (*cutlery*) tenedor *m*; (*gardening*) horca *f*; (*tree*) horcadura *f*; (*road*) bifurcación *f*; (*river*) horcajo *m*. **tuning fork** diapasón *m*. *v* bifurcarse. **forked** *adj* bifurcado.

forlorn [fə'loın] *adj* desamparado; triste.

form [foım] *n* (*shape*) forma *f*; (*figure*) figura *f*; (*type*) tipo *m*; (*document*) formulario *m*; (*school year*) curso *m*. *v* (*make*) hacer; (*model*) modelar; (*habit*) crear; (*constitute*) constituir; (*put together*) formar. **form a queue** ponerse en cola. **formation** *n* formación *f*. **formative** *adj* de formación, formativo.

formal ['foımal] *adj* formal; solemne; (*person*) formalista; ceremonioso; de cortesía; en debida forma. **formality** *n* (*requirement*) formalidad *f*; ceremonia *f*; rigidez *f*.

format ['foımat] *n* formato *m*.

former ['foımə] *adj* (*previous*) anterior; (*ex-*) antiguo, pasado. *pron* ése, ésa, aquél, equélla, el primero, la primera. **formerly** *adv* anteriormente; antiguamente.

formidable ['foımidəbl] *adj* formidable.

formula ['foımjulə] *n, pl* **-ae** fórmula *f*.

formulate ['foımjuleit] *v* formular. **formulation** *n* formulación *f*.

***forsake** [fə'seik] *v* abandonar.

fort [foıt] *n* fuerte *m*, fortaleza *f*.

forte ['foıtei] *n* fuerte *m*.

forth [foıθ] *adv* en adelante. **and so forth** y así sucesivamente. **forthcoming** *adj* próximo; (*approaching*) venidero; (*person*) abierto. **forthright** *adj* franco. **forthwith** *adv* en seguida; en el acto.

fortify ['foıtifai] *v* (*health, moral strength*) fortalecer; (*town*) fortificar; (*wine*) encabezar; (*argument*) reforzar. **fortification** *n* fortalecimiento *m*; fortificación *f*; reforzamiento *m*.

fortitude ['foıtitjuıd] *n* fortaleza *f*; firmeza *f*.

fortnight ['foıtnait] *n* quincena *f*. **fortnightly** *adj* quincenal. *adv* quincenalmente.

fortress ['foıtris] *n* fortaleza *f*.

fortuitous [fə'tjuıitəs] *adj, adv* casual.

fortunate ['foıtʃənət] *adj* afortunado; oportuno. **fortunately** *adv* afortunadamente.

fortune ['foıtʃən] *n* (*fate*) fortuna *f*; (*luck*) suerte *f*. **cost a fortune** costar un dineral. **stroke of fortune** golpe de suerte *m*. **fortune-teller** *n* adivino, -a *m, f*.

forty ['foıti] *nm, adj* cuarenta. **fortieth** *nm, adj* cuarentavo.

forum ['foırəm] *n* foro *m*; (*meeting*) tribuna *f*.

forward ['foıwəd] *adj* (*front*) delantero; (*movement*) hacia adelante; (*progressive*) avanzado; (*impertinent*) impertinente. *v* (*send*) expedir; (*promote*) promover. **please forward** remítase al destinario. *n* (*football*) delantero *m*. **forwards** *adv* adelante.

fossil ['fosl] *nm, adj* fósil. **fossilized** *adj* fosilizado.

foster ['fostə] *v* (*child*) criar; (*idea*) abrigar; (*project*) patrocinar; (*favour*) favorecer. *adj* adoptivo.

fought [foıt] *V* **fight**.

foul [faul] *adj* asqueroso; (*dirty*) sucio; (*air*) viciado; (*language*) grosero; (*smell*) fétido. **foul play** jugada sucia *f*. *n* falta *f*. *v* ensuciar; (*reputation*) manchar; (*sport*) cometer una falta.

found¹ [faund] *V* **find**.

found² [faund] *v* fundar; construir; (*opinion*) fundamentar. **foundation** *n* (*establishment*) fundación *f*; (*building*) cimientos *m pl*; (*fig*) fundamento *m*. **founder** *n* fundador, -a *m, f*.

founder ['faundə] *v* (*ship*) hundirse; (*fall*) derrumbarse.

foundry ['faundri] *n* fundición *f*.

fountain ['fauntin] *n* fuente *f*. **fountainhead** *n* manantial *m*. **fountain pen** pluma estilográfica *f*.

four [foı] *nm, adj* cuatro. **fourth** *m, adj* cuarto, -a *m, f*.

fourteen [foı'tiın] *nm, adj* catorce. **fourteenth** *n, adj* decimocuarto, -a *m, f*.

fowl [faul] *n* aves de corral *f pl*; (*cock*) gallo *m*; (*hen*) gallina *f*; (*chicken*) pollo *m*.

fox [foks] *n* zorro, -a *m, f*. *v* (*baffle*) desconcertar; (*trick*) engañar. **foxglove** *n* digital *f*. **foxhound** *n* perro raposero *m*. **foxhunting** *n* caza de zorros *f*.

foyer ['foiei] *n* foyer *m*.

fraction ['frakʃən] *n* fracción *f*; pequeña parte *f*. **fractional** *adj* fraccionario.

fracture ['fraktʃə] *n* fractura *f*. *v* fracturarse.

fragile ['fradʒail] *adj* frágil. **fragility** *n* fragilidad *f*.

fragment ['fragmənt] n fragmento m. v fragmentar.

fragrant ['freigrənt] adj fragante. **fragrance** n fragancia f.

frail [freil] adj frágil; débil; delicado. **frailty** n fragilidad f; debilidad f; delicadez f.

frame [freim] n (building) armazón f; (picture) marco m; (bicycle) cuadro m; (spectacles) montura f; (film) imagen f. **frame of mind** estado de ánimo m. v (enclose) enmarcar; (devise) elaborar; (shape) formar; hacer la armazón de.

France [frains] n Francia f.

franchise ['frantʃaiz] n derecho de voto m.

frank [frank] adj franco; abierto. **frankness** n franqueza f.

frankfurter ['frankfɔːtə] n salchicha alemana f.

frantic ['frantik] adj frenético; loco.

fraternal [frə'təːnl] adj fraternal. **fraternity** n (brotherhood) fraternidad f; (association) asociación f; (religious) hermandad f. **fraternize** v fraternizar.

fraud [frɔːd] n (law) fraude m; (deception) engaño m; (person) impostor m. **fraudulent** adj fraudulento.

fraught [frɔːt] adj **fraught with** cargado de.

fray[1] [frei] v raer, desgastar.

fray[2] [frei] n (brawl) riña f; (fight) combate m.

freak [friːk] n capricho m; fantasís f; monstruosidad f. adj imprevisto; extraño.

freckle ['frekl] n peca f. **freckled** adj pecoso.

free [friː] adj libre; gratis; (loose) suelto; generoso; sincero; (manner) desenvuelto. **free and easy** poco ceremonioso.

freedom ['friːdəm] n libertad f; soltura f.

free-for-all n refriega f.

freehand ['friːhand] adj a pulso.

freehold ['friːhould] n propiedad absoluta f.

freelance ['friːlaɪns] n persona que trabaja independientemente f.

freely ['friːli] adj libremente; voluntariamente; gratuitamente.

freemason ['friːmeisn] n francmasón. **freemasonry** n francmasonería f.

freesia ['friːziə] n fresia f.

freestyle ['friːstail] n estilo libre m.

free trade n librecambio m.

free will n libre albedrío m.

*__**freeze** [friːz] v (preserve) congelar; (chill) refrigerar; (from cold) helarse; (prices, etc.) bloquear; (turn to ice) helar; (stand still) quedarse inmóvil. n helada f; (blo-queo m. **freezer** n congelador m. **freezing** adj glacial. **freezing point** punto de congelación.

freight [freit] n (load) carga f; (transportation) transporte m; (by ship, plane) flete m; (other) mercancías f pl. **freight train** tren de mercancías m. **freighter** n (ship) buque de carga m; (aircraft) avión de carga m.

French [frentʃ] nm, adj francés. **the French** los franceses. **French bean** judía verde f. **French horn** trompa de llaves f. **French polish** barniz de muebles m. **french fries** patata frita f. v

frenzy ['frenzi] n frenesí m, delirio m. **frenzied** adj frenético.

frequent ['friːkwənt; v fri'kwent] adj frecuente; (usual) común. v frecuentar. **frequency** n frecuencia f. **frequently** adv frecuentemente.

fresco ['freskou] n fresco m.

fresh [freʃ] adj fresco; (bread) tierno; (water) dulce; (air) puro; (complexion) de buen color; (new) nuevo. adv recientemente. **freshwater** adj (fish) de agua dulce. **freshen up** refrescarse. **freshness** n frescura f; novedad f.

fret[1] [fret] v irritar; (complain) quejarse. **fretful** adj mal humorado; (upset) apenado.

fret[2] [fret] n (music) traste m. v adornar con calados. **fretsaw** n sierra de calar f. **fretwork** n calado m.

friar ['fraiə] n fraile m, monje m. **friary** n monasterio m.

friction ['frikʃən] n fricción f.

Friday ['fraidei] n viernes m. **Good Friday** Viernes Santo m.

fridge [fridʒ] n (coll) nevera f.

fried [fraid] adj frito.

friend [frend] n amigo, -a m, f. **make friends with** hacerse amigo de. **the best of friends** muy amigos. **friendliness** n simpatía f. **friendly** adj simpático; amistoso. **friendship** n amistad f.

frieze [friːz] n friso m.

frigate ['frigit] n fragata f.

fright [frait] n susto m; miedo m; terror m. **frighten** v asustar. **be frightened** tener miedo. **frightening** adj espantoso. **frightful** adj horrible; (fig) tremendo.

frigid ['fridʒid] adj glacial; (manner) frío; (med) frígido. **frigidity** n frialdad f; (med) frigidez f.

frill [fril] n (shirt) pechera f; (fluting) encañonado m; (flared edge) volante m; (ruff) gorguera f. **frilly** adj con volantes.

fringe [frindʒ] n franja f; (edge) borde m. **fringe benefits** beneficios complementarios m pl. v franjar.

frisk [frisk] v brincar; (coll: search) cachear. **friskiness** n viveza f. **frisky** adj juguetón.

fritter¹ ['fritə] v fritter away malgastar.

fritter² ['fritə] n (cookery) buñuelo m.

frivolity [fri'voliti] n frivolidad f. **frivolous** adj frívolo; trivial.

frizz [friz] v (hair) rizar. **frizzy** adj crespo.

fro [frou] adv to and fro de un lado a otro. **go to and fro** ir y venir.

frock [frok] n vestido m.

frog [frog] n rana f. **frogman** n hombre rana m. **frogs' legs** ancas de rana f pl. **have a frog in one's throat** tener carraspera.

frolic ['frolik] n juego m; diversión f. v juguetear; divertirse. **frolicsome** adj juguetón.

from [from] prep de; desde; (made from) con; (steal, buy, take, etc.) a; (drink, learn) en; (speak, act) por; (according to) según.

front [frʌnt] n (building) fachada f; (shop) escaparate m; parte delantera f; principio m; (face) cara f; (weather) frente m. **in front of** delante de. adj delantero; principal; primero.

frontier ['frʌntiə] n frontera f. adj fronterizo.

frost [frost] n escarcha f; helada f. **frostbite** n congelación f. **frostbitten** adj congelado. v cubrir de escarcha. **frosted glass** vidrio deslustrado m. **frosty** adj escarchado; helado.

froth [froθ] n espuma f; (fig) frivolidad f. v espumar. **frothy** adj espumoso; frívolo.

frown [fraun] n ceño m. v fruncir el entrecejo. **frown on** or **upon** desaprobar. **frowning** adj severo; amenazador.

froze [frouz] V freeze.

frozen ['frouzn] adj congelado, helado. **frozen food** comestibles congelados m pl.

frugal ['frugəl] adj frugal; sobrio. **frugality** n frugalidad f; sobriedad f.

fruit [frut] n (on tree) fruto m, (as food) fruta f. **fruit cake** pastel de fruta m. **fruit machine** máquina tragaperras f. **fruit salad** ensalada de frutas f. v dar fruto. **fruitful** adj fructífero; (fig) fructuoso. **fruition** n fruición f; realización f; (bot) fructificación f.

frustrate [frʌ'streit] v (plans, etc.) frustrar; impedir.

***fry** [frai] v freír. **frying pan** sartén f.

fuchsia ['fjuʃə] n fucsia f.

fuck [fʌk] v (impol) joder.

fudge [fʌdʒ] v fallar; inventar.

fuel ['fjuəl] n combustible m; gasolina f; (mot) carburante f. **fuel gauge** indicador del nivel de gasolina m. **fuel pump** gasolinera f. v (mot) echar gasolina a; (furnace) alimentar; (ship) abastecer de combustible.

fugitive ['fjudʒitiv] n, adj fugitivo, -a.

fulcrum ['fulkrəm] n fulcro m.

fulfil [ful'fil] v (promise, obligation) cumplir; (ambition) realizar; (purpose) servir; (wishes) satisfacer; (function) desempeñar; (plan) llevar a cabo. **fulfilment** n cumplimiento m; realización f; satisfacción f; (instructions) ejecución f.

full [ful] adj lleno; completo; (text) íntegro; (whole) entero; (price) sin descuento; (extensive) extenso; (daylight, development) pleno; (speed) todo; (capacity) máximo; (measure, weight) exacto; (flavour) mucho. **full employment** pleno empleo m. **full up** completamente lleno. **I'm full** no puedo más. **in full colour** a todo color.

full-blooded adj (thoroughbred) de pura sangre; (robust) vigoroso; (true blue) verdadero.

full-bodied adj (wine) de mucho cuerpo.

full-dress adj de etiqueta; de gala.

full-grown adj crecido; adulto.

full-hearted adj completo.

full house n (theatre or cinema notice) no hay localidades.

full-length adj de cuerpo entero.

full-scale adj de tamaño natural.

full stop n punto m.

full-time adj de jornada completa.

fumble ['fʌmbl] v tojetear; (drop) dejar caer; (feel) hurgar; (search) buscar.

fume [fjum] v (fig) bufar de cólera. **fumes** pl n numo m.

fun [fʌn] n alegría f; gracia f; diversión f. **for fun** en broma. **funfair** n parque de atracciones m. **have fun** divertirse. **make fun of** reírse de. **what fun!** ¡qué divertido!

function ['fʌŋkʃən] n función f; acto m; recepción f. v funcionar. **functional** adj funcional.

fund [fʌnd] n fondo m; (source) fuente f.

fundamental [fʌndə'mentl] adj fundamental.

funeral ['fjumərəl] n funeral m; (state) exequias nacionales f pl. **funeral parlour** funeraria f. **funeral procession** cortejo fúnebre m. **funeral service** misa de cuerpo presente f.

fungus ['fʌŋgəs] n, pl -i (bot) hongo m; (med) fungo m.

funnel ['fʌnl] n (pourer) embudo; (smokestack) chimenea f. v verter por un embudo; (direct) encauzar.

funny ['fʌni] adj divertido; gracioso; (curious) extraño. **taste funny** tener un sabor extraño. **funny business** cosas varas f pl. **funny-bone** hueso de la alegría m. **funnily** adv graciosamente.

fur [fəɪ] n pelo m; (pelt) piel f; (kettle) sarro m; (tongue) saburra f. **fur coat** abrigo de pieles m. v forrar con pieles; incrustar; cubrir de sarro. **furrier** n peletero m; (shop) peletería f. **furry** adj peludo; sarroso.

furious ['fjuəriəs] adj furioso; violento.

furnace ['fəɪnis] n horno m; (domestic) estufa f; (boiler) hogar m.

furnish ['fəɪniʃ] v (house) amueblar; (supply) suministrar; (give) facilitar; (opportunity) dar; (proof) aducir. **furnishings** pl n muebles m pl; mobiliario f.

furniture ['fəɪnitʃə] n muebles m pl. **furniture van** camión de mudanzas m.

furrow ['fʌrou] n (ploughing) surco m; (forehead) arruga f; (groove) ranura f. v surcar; arrugar.

further ['fəɪðə] adj (distant, additional) otro; (another) nuevo; (later) posterior; (education) superior. adv más; más lejos, más allá; (moreover) además. v favorecer. **furtherance** n adelantamiento m; fomento m. **furthermore** adv además. **furthermost** adj más lejano. **furthest** adj más lejano; extremo.

furtive ['fəɪtiv] adj furtivo.

fury ['fjuəri] n furia f; furor m.

fuse¹ [fjuɪz] n (elec) fusible m. **fuse box**

caja de fusibles f. v (join) fusionar; (melt) fundir.

fuse² [fjuɪz] n (explosives) mecha f; (detonator) espoleta f.

fuselage ['fjuɪzə,lɑɪʒ] n fuselaje m.

fusion ['fjuɪʒən] n fusión f.

fuss [fʌs] n (trouble) lío m; (commotion) alboroto m; (complaints) quejas f pl. **a lot of fuss about nothing** mucho ruido y pocas nueces. v agitarse; quejarse; preocuparse; molestar. **fussiness** n agitación f. **fussy** adj escrupuloso; exigente; melindroso.

futile ['fjuitail] adj vano; frívolo.

future ['fjuitʃə] n futuro m; porvenir m. adj futuro; venidero.

fuzz [fʌz] n (on face) vello m; (fluff) pelusa f. **fuzzy** adj velloso; (blurred) borroso.

G

gabble ['gabl] v chacharear. n cháchara f. **gabbler** n chacharero, -a m, f.

gable ['geibl] n gablete m.

gadget ['gadʒit] n aparato m; accesorio m.

gag¹ [gag] v amordazar. n mordaza f.

gag² [gag] n (joke) broma f; chiste m.

gaiety ['geiəti] n alegría f; jovialidad f.

gain [gein] n ganancia f; provecho m; aumento m. v ganar; avanzar.

gait [geit] n modo de andar m.

gala ['gɑɪlə] n fiesta f, gala f.

galaxy ['galəksi] n galaxia f.

gale [geil] n vendaval m.

gallant ['galənt] adj (to women) galante; (brave) valiente; (stately) elegante. **gallantry** n galantería f; valor m; (courtesy) cortesía f.

gall-bladder ['gɔil,bladə] n vesícula biliar f.

galleon ['galiən] n galeón m.

gallery ['galəri] n galería f; (spectators) tribuna f; (theatre) gallinero m.

galley ['gali] n (ship) galera f; (kitchen) cocina f.

gallon ['galən] n galón m.

gallop ['galəp] n galope m. v galopar.

gallows ['galouz] pl n cadalso m sing.

gallstone ['gɔːlstoun] n cálculo biliar m.

galore [gə'lɔː] adj, adv en cantidad.

galvanize ['gælvənaiz] v galvanizar.

gamble ['gæmbl] v (bet) apostar; (risk) arriesgar. **gamble on** contar con. n (risky enterprise) empresa arriesgada f; (game) jugada f. **gambler** n jugador, -a m, f. **gambling** n juego m. **gambling den** garito m.

game [geim] n juego m; (sport) deporte m; (of football, tennis, etc.) partido m; (cards, chess, etc.) partida f; (hunting) caza f. **game bird** ave de caza f. **gamekeeper** n guardabosque m. **play the game** jugar limpio. adj (coll) valiente.

gammon ['gæmən] n jamón ahumado m.

gang [gæŋ] n (band) cuadrilla f; (of gangsters) banda f. v **gang up on** conspirar contra. **gangster** n gángster m.

gangrene ['gæŋgriːn] n gangrena f. **gangrenous** adj gangrenoso.

gangway ['gæŋwei] n (passage) pasillo m; (naut) pasarela f.

gaol V jail.

gap [gæp] n (empty space) vacío m; (breach) brecha f; (cavity) hueco m; (in a wall) portillo m; (between hills) quebrada f; (in education) laguna f; (crack) resquicio m; (in a wood) claro m.

gape [geip] v (stare) quedarse boquiabierto; (open wide) abrirse mucho.

garage ['gæraːdʒ] n garaje m.

garbage ['gɑːbidʒ] n basura f. **garbage can** cubo de la basura m. **garbage disposal** vertedero de basuras m. **garbage man** basurero m.

garble ['gɑːbl] v amañar; mutilar. **garbled** adj amañado; mutilado.

garden ['gɑːdn] n jardín m; huerto m. v cultivar un huerto. **garden city** ciudad jardín f. **garden party** recepción al aire libre f. **garden produce** hortalizas f pl. **gardener** n jardinero, -a m, f. **gardening** n jardinería f.

gargle ['gɑːgl] v hacer gárgaras. n gárgaras f pl.

garland ['gɑːlənd] n guirnalda f. v enguirnaldar.

garlic ['gɑːlik] n ajo m.

garment ['gɑːmənt] n prenda f, traje m, vestido m.

garnish ['gɑːniʃ] v adornar, embellecer; (cookery) aderezar. n adorno m; aderezo m.

garrison ['gærisn] n guarnición f. v guarnecer.

garter ['gɑːtə] n liga f. **Order of the Garter** orden de la jarretera f.

gas [gæs] n gas m; (petrol) gasolina f. **bencina** f. **step on the gas** (coll) acelerar. v asfixiar con gas. **gaseous** adj gaseoso. **gas burner** n mechero de gas m. **gas fire** n estufa de gas f. **gas main** n cañería maestra de gas f. **gasmask** n máscara para gases f. **gas meter** n contador de gas m. **gaspipe** n cañería de gas f. **gas-ring** n fogón de gas m. **gas stove** n cocina de gas f. **gasworks** n fábrica de gas f.

gash [gæʃ] n herida f; cuchillada f. v acuchillar.

gasket ['gæskit] n junta de culata f.

gasoline ['gæsəliːn] n gasolina f.

gasp [gɑːsp] n (breathing difficulty) jadeo m; (surprise) boqueada f. v jadear; boquear.

gastric ['gæstrik] adj gástrico. **gastric fever** fiebre gástrica f. **gastric juice** jugo gástrico. **gastric ulcer** úlcera gástrica f. **gastritis** n gastritis f. **gastroenteritis** n gastroenteritis f.

gastronomic [gæstrə'nomik] adj gastronómico. **gastronomy** n gastronomía f.

gate [geit] n puerta f, entrada f; (metal) verja f; (level-crossing) barrera f. **gatecrash** v asistir sin invitación. **gatekeeper** n portero, -a m, f. **gatepost** n soporte de la puerta m. **gateway** n entrada f, paso m.

gateau ['gætou] n tarta f.

gather ['gæðə] v coger, amontonar; (strength) cobrar; (harvest) cosechar; (understand) colegir; (money) recaudar; (sewing) fruncir. **gather together** reunirse, congregarse. **gathering** n reunión f, afluencia f.

gaudy ['gɔːdi] adj chillón, cursi.

gauge [geidʒ] n (rail) entrevía f; (gun) calibre m; (measure) indicador m; (fig) medida f. v medir, juzgar; calibrar. **broad/narrow gauge railway** ferrocarril de vía ancha/estrecha m. **pressure gauge** manómetro m.

gaunt [gɔːnt] adj demacrado; (grim) feroz; (fig) lúgubre.

gauze [gɔːz] n gasa f.

gave [geiv] V give.

gay [gei] adj alegre; gozoso; (dress) guapo; (event) festivo; (coll) homosexual. n (coll: homosexual) maricón m.

gaze 86

gaze [geiz] v mirar fijamente. n mirada fija f.
gazelle [gə'zel] n gacela f.
gazetteer [gazə'tiə] n gacetero m.
gear [giə] n (mech) engranaje m, juego m, marcha f; (dress) traje m; (tackle) aparejo m. **gearbox** caja de velocidades f. **gear lever** palanca de cambio de velocidad. **in gear** engranado. v aparejar; engranar; adaptar.
geese [gits] V goose.
gelatine ['dʒelə,tiːn] n gelatina f.
gelignite ['dʒelignait] n gelignita f.
gem [dʒem] n joya f, gema f; (delight) preciosidad f.
Gemini ['dʒemini] pl n Géminis m.
gender ['dʒendə] n género m; sexo m.
gene [dʒiːn] n gene m.
genealogy [dʒiːni,alədʒi] n genealogía f. **genealogical** adj genealógico.
general ['dʒenərəl] nm, adj general. **general election** elección general f. **general opinion** voz común f. **general practitioner** médico, -a general m, f. **in general** generalmente. **generalization** n generalización f. **generalize** v generalizar.
generate ['dʒenəreit] v producir; (elec) generar. **generation** n generación f. **generator** n generador m; dínamo m.
generic [dʒi'nerik] adj genérico.
generous ['dʒenərəs] adj generoso; magnánimo. **generosity** n generosidad f; liberalidad f.
genetic [dʒi'netik] adj genético. **genetics** n genética f.
Geneva [dʒi'niːvə] n Ginebra f. **Lake Geneva** Lago de Ginebra.
genial ['dʒiːniəl] adj genial, cordial.
genital ['dʒenitl] adj genital. **genitals** pl n genitales m pl.
genitive ['dʒenitiv] nm, adj genitivo.
genius ['dʒiːmjəs] n genio m.
genteel [dʒen'tiːl] adj fino; melindroso.
gentle ['dʒentl] adj (light) ligero; (mild) suave; (slow) lento; (tame) manso; (moderate) moderado; (friendly) amable; (kind) bondadoso. **gentleman** n caballero m, señor m. **gentlemen** pl n (in correspondence) muy señores míos, muy señores nuestros m pl. **gentleness** n amabilidad f; bondad f; suavidad f.
gentry ['dʒentri] n pequeña nobleza f.
gents [dʒents] n (sign) caballeros m pl.

genuine ['dʒenjuin] adj puro; genuino; verdadero; auténtico.
genus ['dʒiːnəs] n género m.
geography [dʒi'ogrəfi] n geografía f. **geographer** n geógrafo m. **geographic** adj also **geographical** geográfico.
geology [dʒi'olədʒi] n geología f. **geological** adj geológico. **geologist** n geólogo m.
geometry [dʒi'omətri] n geometría f. **geometrical** adj geométrico.
geranium [dʒə'reiniəm] n geranio m.
geriatric [dʒeri'atrik] adj geriátrico. **geriatrics** n geriatría f.
germ [dʒəːm] n (med) bacilo m; microbio m; (fig) germen m.
Germany ['dʒəːməni] n Alemania f. **German** n, adj alemán, -ana m, f. **German measles** rubéola f. **Germanic** adj germánico.
germinate ['dʒəːmineit] v germinar, brotar. **germination** n germinación f.
gerund ['dʒerənd] n gerundio m.
gesticulate [dʒe'stikju,leit] v gesticular. **gesticulation** n gesticulación f.
gesture ['dʒestʃə] v gesticular. n gesto m.
*get [get] v obtener; tener; recibir; (fetch) buscar; (buy) comprar; (call) llamar; (find) encontrar; (catch, reproduce) coger; (bring) llevar; (extract) sacar; (succeed) conseguir; (coll: understand) llegar a comprender; (coll: kill) matar. **get about** desplazarse. **get across** (cross) atravesar; hacer comprender. **getaway** n huida f. **get at** (reach) alcanzar; (tease) meterse con. **get back** (return) volver; (recover) récobrar. **get by** (manage) arreglárselas. **get down** (descend) bajar; (write) poner por escrito. **get down to** ponerse a. **get off** bajarse de; escapar. **get on** (mount) subir a; (progress) progresar; (agree) llevarse bien; (grow old) envejecer. **get out** (fig) sacar. **get up** (arise) levantarse; (climb) subirse.
geyser ['giːzə] n (hot spring) géiser m; (water-heater) calentador de agua m.
ghastly ['gaːstli] adj horroroso; (pale) de una palidez mortal.
gherkin ['gəːkin] n cohombrillo m.
ghetto ['getou] n judería f.
ghost [goust] n fantasma m; espectro; (spirit) alma f. **ghost writer** escritor fantasma m. **Holy Ghost** Espíritu Santo m. **give up the ghost** entregar el alma. **ghostly** adj espectral. **ghostliness** n espiritualidad f.

giant ['dʒaɪənt] nm, adj gigante.

gibberish ['dʒɪbərɪʃ] n galimatías m invar.

gibe [dʒaɪb] n mofa f. v jibe at mofarse de.

giblets ['dʒɪblɪts] pl n menudillos m pl.

giddy ['gɪdɪ] adj (dizzy) mareado; (height) vertiginoso; (scatter-brained) frívolo. giddiness n mareo m, vértigo m.

gift [gɪft] n regalo m; (talent) don m; (offering) ofrenda f. gift-token vale para comprar un regalo m. gifted adj dotado; talentoso.

gigantic [dʒaɪ'gantɪk] adj gigantesco.

giggle ['gɪgl] v reirse tontamente. n risita f. the giggles la risa tonta f sing.

gill [gɪl] n (fish) branquia f; (plant) laminilla f; (measure) medida de líquidos f.

gilt [gɪlt] nm, adj dorado. gilt-edged (book) con cantos dorados. gilt-edged securities valores de máxima garantía m pl.

gimmick ['gɪmɪk] n (coll: gadget) artefact m; (coll: trick) truco m.

gin [dʒɪn] n ginebra f.

ginger ['dʒɪndʒə] n jengibre m. ginger beer gaseosa f. gingerbread n pan de jengibre m. adj (hair) rojizo. v (coll) animar.

gingerly ['dʒɪndʒəlɪ] adv delicadamente.

gipsy ['dʒɪpsɪ] n gitano, -a m, f.

giraffe [dʒɪ'raɪf] n jirafa f.

girder ['gəːdə] n viga f.

girdle ['gəːdl] n (belt) cinturón m; (corset) faja f. v ceñir; (fig) rodear.

girl [gəːl] n niña f, chica f; muchacha f; señorita f. girlfriend n amiguita f, novia f. girlhood n niñez f; juventud f. girlish adj de niña f; (of boys) afeminado.

girth [gəːθ] n circunferencia f; (waist, etc.) gordura f; (saddle) cincha f.

gist [dʒɪst] n esencia f, importe m.

*give [gɪv] v dar; (offer as a present) regalar; (deliver) entregar; (hand over) pasar; (provide with) proveer de; (grant) conceder; (infect) contagiar; (communicate) comunicar; (a speech) pronunciar; (med: administer) poner; (telephone: connect with) poner con. give-and-take n toma y daca m. give away distribuir; regalar; revelar. giveaway n revelación f. give back devolver. give in darse por vencido; ceder; (hand in) entregar. give off despedir. give out distribuir; emitir; anunciar; divulgar; (run out) agotarse.

give up abandonar; renunciar a; rendirse; entregar; ceder. give way to retirarse ante; abandonarse a.

glacier ['glasɪə] n glaciar m. glaciation o glaciación f.

glad [glad] adj feliz, alegre. be glad alegrarse. gladden v regocijar. gladly adv alegremente.

glamour [glamə] n encanto m. glamorous adj encantador.

glance [glans] n (look) vistazo m, ojeada f; (light) vislumbre f; (projectile) desviación f. v echar un vistazo, ojear; relumbrar; desviarse.

gland [gland] n glándula f. glandular adj glandular. glandular fever fiebre glandular f.

glare [gleə] n (look) mirada feroz f; (dazzle) deslumbramiento m. v mirar con ferocidad; deslumbrar. glaring adj feroz; deslumbrante; (conspicuous) manifiesto.

glass [glas] n vidrio m; cristal m; (for drinking) vaso m; (mirror) espejo m; (lens) lente f. glasses pl n gafas f pl. glassware n cristalería f. glassworks n fábrica de cristal y vidrio f. glassy adj vítreo; (eyes) vidrioso; (smooth) liso.

glaze [gleɪz] v (pottery) vidriar; (window) poner cristales a; (cookery) glasear. n vidriado m; brillo m. glazier n vidriero m.

gleam [gliːm] n rayo m. v relucir. gleaming reluciente.

glean [gliːn] v espigar.

glee [gliː] n alegría f. gleeful adj alegre.

glib [glɪb] adj locuaz; fácil. glibly adv con labia.

glide [glaɪd] v (aero) planear; (slide) resbalar. glide away escurrirse. n planeo m; (slide) deslizamiento m. glider n planeador m.

glimmer ['glɪmə] n luz trémula f; (fig) vislumbre m. v brillar con luz trémula.

glimpse [glɪmps] v entrever. n vistazo m. catch a glimpse of vislumbrar.

glint [glɪnt] n destello m. v destellar.

glisten ['glɪsn] v relucir. glistening adj reluciente.

glitter ['glɪtə] v brillar. n brillo m. glittering adj brillante.

gloat [glout] v recrearse con.

globe [gloub] n globo m. globe artichoke alcachofa f. globe-trotter n trotamundos m invar. global adj global; mundial.

gloom [gluːm] n obscuridad f; (fig) melancolía f. **gloomy** adj obscuro; melancólico.

glory ['glɔːri] n gloria f; esplendor. **glorify** v glorificar. **glorious** adj glorioso; espléndido.

gloss [glɔs] n brillo m; lustre m; (fig) apariencia f. v **gloss over** disculpar.

glossary ['glɔsəri] n glosario m.

glove [glʌv] n guante m. **boxing gloves** pl n guantes de boxeo m pl. **glovecompartment** guantera f. **fit like a glove** sentar como anillo al dedo. **hand in glove with** juntar diestra con diestra. v enguantar.

glow [glou] v (shine) brillar.

glucose ['gluːkous] n glucosa f.

glue [gluː] n cola f. v pegar.

glum [glʌm] adj deprimido, sombrío.

glut [glʌt] n exceso m. v hartar.

glutton ['glʌtən] n glotón, -ona m, f. **gluttonous** adj glotón. **gluttony** n glotonería f.

gnarled [naːld] adj nudoso; (persons) curtido.

gnash [naʃ] v **gnash one's teeth** crujir los dientes.

gnat [nat] n mosquito m.

gnaw [nɔː] v roer. **gnawing** adj roedor.

gnome [noum] n gnomo m.

go [gou] v ir; (depart) irse; (lead to) conducir a; (go towards) dirigirse a; (leave) dejar; (vanish) desaparecer; (be removed) quitarse; (turn, become) ponerse; (function) funcionar. **go off** (leave) marcharse; (rot) estropearse; (gun) dispararse. **go out** salir; (lights, fire, etc.) apagarse. **go round** dar la vuelta. **go with** acompañar; (harmonize) hacer juego con. **go without** (manage) arreglárselas. n (coll) energía f. **it's your go** te toca a ti. **on the go** ocupado. **go-between** n intermediario, -a m, f.

goad [goud] v aguijar; (fig) incitar; n garrocha f; (fig) estímulo m.

goal [goul] n (structure) meta f; (score) gol m; (destination) destinación f; (purpose) objeto m. **goalkeeper** n portero m. **goalpost** n poste m.

goat [gout] n (nanny) cabra f; (billy) cabrón m.

gobble [gobl] v engullir.

goblin ['goblin] n trasgo m, duende m.

god [god] n dios m. **by God!** ¡vive Dios! **for God's sake** por el amor de dios. **goddaughter** n ahijada f. **godfather** padrino

m. **godmother** n madrina f. **godsend** n don del cielo m. **godson** n ahijado m. **goddess** n diosa f.

goggles ['goglz] pl n anteojos m pl.

goings-on [,gouiŋz'on] pl n (coll) tejemanejes m pl.

gold [gould] n oro m. **golden** adj dorado; de oro.

goldfinch ['gouldfintʃ] n jilguero m.

goldfish ['gouldfiʃ] n pez de colores m. **goldfish bowl** pecera f.

goldsmith ['gouldsmiθ] n orfebre m.

golf [golf] n golf m. **golf course** campo de golf m. **golfer** n golfista m, f.

gondola ['gondələ] n góndola f. **gondolier** n gondolero m.

gone [gon] V **go**.

gong [goŋ] n gong m.

gonorrhoea [gonə'riə] n gonorrea f.

good [gud] adj bueno; (before m sing nouns) buen; (wholesome) sano; (pleasant) amable; (genuine) legítimo; (virtuous) virtuoso. n bien m. **no good** inútil. **for good** para siempre. **goodness** n bondad f. **good-looking** adj guapo.

good afternoon interj buenas tardes f pl.

goodbye [gud'bai] interj ¡adiós!

good evening interj buenas tardes f pl.

good-for-nothing n(m+f). adj inútil.

Good Friday n Viernes Santo.

good morning interj buenos días m pl.

good night interj buenas noches f pl.

goods [gudz] pl n (comm) artículos m pl; (possessions) bienes m pl. **goods and chattels** muebles y enseres m pl. **goods train** tren de mercancías m.

goose [guːs], n. pl **geese** ganso m, oca f.

gooseberry ['guzbəri] n (fruit) grosella espinosa f; (bush) grosellero espinoso m.

gore[1] [gɔː] v cornear.

gore[2] [gɔː] n sangre f.

gorge [gɔːdʒ] n cañón m. v hartarse.

gorgeous ['gɔːdʒəs] adj magnífico.

gorilla [gə'rilə] n gorila m.

gorse [gɔːs] n tojo m.

gory [gɔːri] adj ensangrentado.

gospel ['gospəl] n evangelio m.

gossip ['gosip] n (chat) charla f; (unkind) chisme; (person) murmurador, -a m, f; chismoso, -a m, f. **gossip column** ecos de sociedad m pl. v (talk scandal) cotillear; (chatter) charlar.

got [gɒt] V **get**.
Gothic ['gɒθik] adj gótico.
goulash ['guːlaʃ] n estofado húngaro m.
gourd [guəd] n calabaza f.
gourmet ['guəmei] n gastrónomo m.
gout [gaut] n gota f.
govern ['gʌvən] v (rule) gobernar; (administer) dirigir; (determine) guiar; (restrain) dominar; (prevail) prevalecer. **governess** n aya f. **government** n gobierno m. **governor** n gobernador m; administrador m; (coll: boss) jefe m.
gown [gaun] n traje largo m; (law, university) toga f. **dressing gown** bata f.
grab [grab] v agarrar, arrebatar. n asimiento m, presa f; (mech) gancho m.
grace [greis] n gracia f, elegancia; (courtesy) cortesía f; (kindness) bondad f; (forgiveness) perdón m; (before meals) bendición mesa f; (favour) favor; (delay) plazo m. **graceful** adj elegante; gracioso; cortés. **gracious** adj gracioso; grato.
grade [greid] n grado m; (persons, things) clase f; (mark) nota f; (gradient) pendiente f. v graduar; (goods) clasificar.
gradient ['greidiənt] n (declivity) decline m; (slope) cuesta f.
gradual ['gradjuəl] adj gradual.
graduate ['gradjuət; v 'gradjueit] n, adj graduado, -a. v graduarse; diplomarse.
graft [graːft] n injerto m. v injertarse.
grain [grein] n grano m; (wood) fibra f.
gram [gram] n gramo m.
grammar ['gramə] n gramática f. **grammar school** instituto de segunda enseñanza m. **grammatical** adj gramático.
gramophone ['graməfoun] n gramófono m; tocadiscos m invar.
granary ['granəri] n granero m.
grand [grand] adj magnífico; grande; importante; esplendido. **grandiose** adj grandioso.
grand-dad n also **grandpa** (coll) abuelito m.
grandchild ['grantʃaild] n nieto, -a m, f.
grandfather ['gran‚faːðə] n abuelo m.
grandma ['granmaː] n also **granny** (coll) abuelita f.
grandmother ['gran‚mʌðə] n abuela f.
grandparent ['gran‚peərənt] n abuelo, -a m, f.
grand piano n piano de cola m.
grandstand ['granstand] n tribuna f.
granite ['granit] n granito m. adj granítico.

grant [graːnt] v conceder; (agree to) acceder; (bestow) otorgar; (assume) suponer. n concesión f; otorgamiento m; (student) beca f.
granule ['granjuːl] n gránulo m. **granulated sugar** azúcar en polvo m.
grape [greip] n uva f. **grapevine** n vid f; (coll) rumores m pl.
grapefruit ['greipfruːt] n pomelo m.
graph [graf] n gráfica f. **graph paper** papel cuadriculado m. **graphic** adj gráfico.
grapple ['grapl] v **grapple with** (fight) luchar cuerpo a cuerpo; (fig) intentar a resolver.
grasp [graːsp] v agarrar; (fig) comprender. n agarro m; (reach) alcance m. **grasping** adj avaro.
grass [graːs] n hierba f; (pasture) pasto m; (lawn) césped m. **grasshopper** n saltamontes m. **grass snake** culebra f. **grassy** adj cubierto de hierba; (like grass) herbáceo.
grate¹ [greit] n parrilla f. **grating** n rejilla f.
grate² [greit] v rallar; (teeth) hacer rechinar. **grater** n rallador m.
grateful ['greitful] adj agradecido.
gratify ['gratifai] v satisfacer; (please) agradar. **gratifying** adj satisfactorio; agradable.
gratitude ['gratitjuːd] n agradecimiento m.
gratuity [grə'tjuːti] n propina f.
grave¹ [greiv] n sepultura f; (monument) tumba f. **gravedigger** n sepulturero m. **gravestone** n lápida sepulcral. **graveyard** n cementerio m.
grave² [greiv] adj grave, serio.
gravel ['gravəl] n grava f.
gravity ['graviti] n (force) gravedad f; (seriousness) solemnidad f.
gravy ['greivi] n salsa f.
graze¹ [greiz] v (scrape) raspar; (rub) rozar. n rozadura f.
graze² [greiz] v pastar.
grease [griːs] n grasa f. **greasepaint** n maquillaje m. **greaseproof paper** papel vegetal m. v engrasar. **greasy** adj grasiento; (slippery) resbaladizo.
great [greit] adj gran, grande; famoso; poderoso; magnífico. **greatly** adv grandemente, enormemente. **greatness** n grandeza f.
great-aunt n tía abuela f.

Great Britain n Gran Bretaña f.

Great Dane n perro danés m.

great-grandchild n biznieto, -a m, f.

great-grandfather n bisabuelo m.

great-grandmother n bisabuela f.

great-uncle n tío abuelo m.

Greece [griis] n Grecia f. **Greek** n, adj griego, -a m, f.

greed [griid] n avaricia f; (for food) glotonería f. adj avaro; glotón.

green [griin] adj verde; (inexperienced) novato; (fresh) fresco; (recent) nuevo. n (colour) verde m; (meadow) prado m; (lawn) césped m. **greens** pl n verduras f pl. **greenery** n verdor m.

greenfly ['griinflai] n pulgón m.

greengage ['griingeidʒ] n ciruela claudia f.

greengrocer ['griingrousə] n verdulero m. **greengrocery** n verdulería f.

greenhouse ['griinhaus] n invernadero m.

Greenland ['griinlənd] n Groenlandia f. **Greenlander** n groenlandés, -esa m, f.

greet [griit] v saludar. **greeting** n salutación f. **greetings** pl n recuerdos m pl.

gregarious [gri'geəriəs] adj gregario.

grew [gru] V **grow**.

grey [grei] nm, adj gris; (hair) cano. **grey-haired** adj canoso. **greyhound** n galgo m. **go grey** (hair) encanecer.

grid [grid] n rejilla f; (elec) red f.

grief [griif] n pena f, dolor m. **grief-stricken** adj desconsolado.

grieve [griiv] v afligir; lamentar. **grieve for** echar de menos. **grievous** adj doloroso; grave; apenado; lamentable. **grievous bodily harm** daños corporales m pl.

grill [gril] v (cook) asar a la parrilla. (interrogate) interrogar. n arilla f; (meal) asado a la parrilla m. **grillroom** n parrilla f.

grille [gril] n reja f; rejilla f.

grim [grim] adj feroz; severo; horrible; (coll) desagradable. **grimly** adv severamente; horriblemente.

grimace [gri'meis] n mueca f. v hacer muecas.

grime [graim] n mugre f. **grimy** adj mugriento.

*****grind** [graind] v (coffee, etc.) moler; (sharpen) afilar; (teeth) crujir. n (coll) trabajo pesado m. **grinder** n afilador m. **grindstone** n muela f. **keep one's nose to the grindstone** batir al yunque.

grip [grip] n (of hand) mano f; (hold) agarro m; (bag) maleta f; (understanding) comprensión f. v **asir**; (wheels) agarrarse; (press) apretar; (the attention) atraer. **gripping** adj impresionante.

gripe [graip] v retortijón m. v (coll) quejarse.

grisly ['grizli] adj espantoso; horroroso; repugnante.

gristle ['grisl] n cartílago m.

grit [grit] n cascajo m; polvo m; (coll: courage) valor m. v (teeth) rechinar.

groan [groun] n gemido m; (dismay) gruñido m. v gemir; gruñir.

grocer ['grousə] n tendero, -a m, f. **groceries** pl n comestibles m pl. **grocery** n tienda de comestibles f.

groin [groin] n ingle f.

groom [grum] n (horse) mozo de caballos m; (of bride) novio m. v (horse) almohazar; (smarten) arreglar.

groove [gruv] n ranura f, muesca f; (record) surco m; (fig) rutina f. v hacer ranuras en; estriar. **grooved** adj acanalado; estriado. **groovy** adj (coll) fenómeno.

grope [group] v andar a tientas. **grope for** buscar a tientas. **gropingly** adv a tientas.

gross [grous] adj (not net) bruto; (coarse) grosero; grueso, denso. n gruesa f.

grotesque [grə'tesk] nm, adj grotesco.

grotto ['grotou] n gruta f.

ground¹ [graund] V **grind**.

ground² [graund] n suelo m; (earth) tierra f; (sport) campo m; (basis) base f; (background) fondo m; (fig) terreno m. v poner en tierra; (teach) enseñar los rudimentos de. **grounds** pl n jardines m pl; (sediment) sedimento m sing; (reason) causa f sing.

ground control n control desde tierra m.

ground floor n planta baja f.

grounding ['graundiŋ] n **have a good grounding in** tener una buena base en.

groundless ['graundlis] adj sin fundamento.

ground level n nivel del suelo m.

ground rent n alquiler del terreno m.

groundsheet ['graundʃiit] n tela impermeable f.

groundwork ['graundwək] n base f.

group [grup] n grupo m. v agrupar.

grouse¹ [graus] n ortega f.

grouse² [graus] v (coll) quejarse.

grove [grouv] n boscaje m.

grovel ['grovl] v arrastrarse; (fig) humillarse.

*grow [grou] v crecer; (increase) aumentar; (become) hacerse; (turn) ponerse; (develop) desarrollarse; (cultivate) cultivar. **grown-up** n adulto, -a m, f. **growth** n crecimiento m; aumento m; desarrollo m; (med) bulto m; vegetación f.

growl [graul] v gruñir. n gruñido m.

grub [grʌb] n larva f; (coll: food) comida f. v cavar. **grubby** adj sucio.

grudge [grʌdʒ] v envidiar. n rencor m. **bear a grudge** tener ojeriza. **grudging** adj mezquino. **grudgingly** adv de mala gana.

gruelling ['grualiŋ] adj penoso; agotador.

gruesome ['grusəm] adj pavoroso, macabro.

gruff [grʌf] adj (manner) brusco; (voice) bronco. **gruffness** n brusquedad f; bronquedad f.

grumble ['grʌmbl] v quejarse. n queja f.

grumpy ['grʌmpi] adj malhumorado. **grumpiness** n malhumor f.

grunt [grʌnt] v gruñir. n gruñido m.

guarantee [garən'tiː] n garantía f. v garantizar. **guarantor** n garante m, f.

guard [gaid] n (soldier) guardia m; (sentry) centinela m; (escort) escolta f; (keeper) guardián m; (train) jefe de tren m; (protection) defensa f; (watchfulness) vigilancia f. **be on guard** estar de guardia. **guard dog** perro de guardia m. **guard's van** furgón de equipajes m. v guardar; proteger. **guard against** protegerse contra. **guarded** adj (cautious) cauteloso.

guardian n (custodian) guardián; (of an orphan) tutor, -a m, f. **guardian angel** ángel de la Guardia m.

guerrilla [gə'rilə] n guerrillero m. **guerrilla warfare** guerrilla f.

guess [ges] n cálculo m; conjetura f; suposición f. **at a guess** a primera vista. **guesswork** n conjetura f. v adivinar; suponer; acertar.

guest [gest] n invitado, -a m, f; (hotel) huésped. -a m, f. **be my guest** yo invito. **guest of honour** invitado de honor m. **guest-house** n casa de huéspedes f. **guest-room** cuarto de huéspedes m.

guide [gaid] n guía m, f; (counsellor) consejero, -a m, f. **girl guide** exploradora f. v guiar; conducir; dirigir. **guidance** n consejo m.

guided missile projectil teledirigido m. **guided tour** visita acompañada f.

guild [gild] v (association) gremio m; (craftsmen, etc.) guilda f.

guillotine ['gilətiːn] n guillotina f. v guillotinar.

guilt [gilt] n culpabilidad f. **guilty** adj culpable. **plead guilty** confesarse culpable.

guinea pig ['ginipig] n conejillo de Indias m.

guitar [gi'taː] n guitarra f. **guitarist** n guitarrista m, f.

gulf [gʌlf] n golfo m; (abyss) abismo m.

gull [gʌl] n gaviota f.

gullet [gʌlit] n esófago m; (throat) garganta f.

gullible [gʌlibl] adj crédulo. **gullibility** n credulidad f.

gully ['gʌli] n hondonada f.

gulp [gʌlp] v tragar. n (drink) trago m; (food) bocado m.

gum¹ [gʌm] n goma f. v engomar.

gum² [gʌm] n (mouth) encía f.

gun [gʌn] n (weapon) arma f; revólver m; pistola f; (hunting) escopeta f; rifle m; cañón m. **gunfire** n cañonazos m pl. **gunman** n pistolero m. **gunpowder** pólvora f. **gun-running** n contrabanda de armas f. **gunshot** n disparo m.

gurgle ['gəigl] n (water) borboteo m; (child) gorjeo m. v borbotear; gorjear.

gush [gʌʃ] v derramar. n chorro m; (fig) efusión f. **gushing** adj (person) efusivo.

gust [gʌst] n (wind) ráfaga f; (smoke) bocanada f; (rain) aguacero m; (laughter, anger) accesión f. **gusty** adj borrascoso.

gusto ['gʌstou] n placer m; brío m; entusiasmo m.

gut [gʌt] n (anat) intestino m, tripa f. **guts** pl n (coll) agallas f pl. v destripar; vaciar.

gutter ['gʌtə] n (roof) canal m; (street) arroyo m.

guy¹ [gai] n (coll) tipo m.

guy² [gai] n (rope) tirante m.

gymnasium [dʒim'neiziəm] n gimnasio m. **gymnast** n gimnasta m, f. **gymnastic** adj gimnástico. **gymnastics** n gimnasia f.

gynaecology [gainə'kɔlədʒi] n ginecología f. **gynaecological** adj ginecológico. **gynaecologist** n ginecólogo, -a m, f.

gypsum ['dʒipsəm] n yeso m.

gyrate [dʒai'reit] v girar. **gyration** n giro m.

gyroscope ['dʒairəˌskoup] giroscopio *m.*

H

haberdasher ['habədaʃə] *n* mercero, -a *m, f.* **haberdashery** *n* mercería *f.*
habit ['habit] *n* costumbre *f;* (*clothes*) traje *m.* **habitual** *adj* acostumbrado.
habitable ['habitəbl] *adj* habitable.
habitat ['habitat] *n* medio *m,* habitación *f.*
hack¹ [hak] *v* acuchillar, cortar; (*kick*) dar un puntapié. *n* corte *m;* puntapié *m.* **hacking** *adj* (*cough*) seco.
hack² [hak] *n* (*horse*) rocín *m;* (*writer*) escritorzuelo *m.*
hackneyed ['haknid] *adj* usado, trillado.
had [had] *V* have.
haddock ['hadək] *n* eglefino *m.*
haemorrhage ['heməridʒ] *n* hemorragia *f.*
haemorrhoids ['hemərɔidz] *pl n* hemorroides *f pl.*
hag [hag] *n* (*coll*) bruja *f.*
haggard ['hagəd] *adj* ojeroso; extraviado.
haggle ['hagl] *v* regatear. **haggle** *n* regateo *m.*
Hague, The [heig] *n* La Haya.
hail¹ [heil] *n* granizo *m.* **hailstone** *n* granizo *m,* piedra *f.* **hailstorm** *n* granizada *f.*
hail² [heil] *v* (*salute*) saludar; (*coll*) llamar. **hail from** proceder de.
hair [heə] *n* pelo *m;* (*human head*) cabello *m.* **comb one's hair** peinarse. **have one's hair done** ir a la peluquería. **let one's hair down** (*coll*) soltarse el pelo. **split hairs** hilar muy fino. **tear one's hair out** tirarse de los pelos. **hairy** *adj* peludo.
hairbrush ['heəbrʌʃ] *n* cepillo (para el pelo) *m.*
haircut ['heəkʌt] *n* corte de pelo *m.* **have a haircut** cortarse el pelo.
hairdresser ['heəˌdresə] *n* peluquero, -a *m, f.* **hairdresser's** *n* peluquería *f.* **hairdressing** *n* peluquería *f.*
hair dryer *n* secador (para el pelo) *m.*
hairnet ['heənet] *n* redecilla *f.*
hairpiece ['heəpiːs] *n* postizo *m.*
hairpin ['heəpin] *n* horquilla *f.*
hair-remover *n* depilatorio *m.*
hairspray ['heəsprei] *n* fijador (para el pelo) *m.*
hairstyle ['heəstail] *n* peinado *m.*

Haiti ['heiti] *n* Haiti *m.* **Haitian** *n, adj* haitiano, -a.
half [haːf] *n* mitad *f;* medio *m;* (*division of a match*) tiempo *m.* **by half** con mucho. **half-and-half** mitad y mitad. **in half** por la mitad. **go halves with** ir a medias con. *adj* medio. **half an hour** media hora. **half a dozen** media docena. *adv* a medias; media. **half as many** or **much** la mitad. **half as much again** la mitad más. **not half!** (*coll*) ¡no poco!
half-baked [ˌhaːfˈbeikt] *adj* (*coll: idea*) mal concebido; (*coll: person*) disparatado.
half-breed ['haːfbriːd] *n* mestizo, -a *m, f.*
half-brother ['haːfˌbrʌðə] *n* hermanastro *m.*
half-hearted [ˌhaːfˈhaːtid] *adj* poco entusiasta.
half-mast [ˌhaːfˈmaːst] *n* **at half-mast** a media asta.
half-price [ˌhaːfˈprais] *adj, adv* a mitad de precio.
half-sister ['haːfˌsistə] *n* hermanastra *f.*
half-time [ˌhaːfˈtaim] *n* (*sport*) descanso *m. adj* (*work*) de media jornada.
halfway ['haːfwei] *adv* a medio camino. **meet halfway** (*compromise*) partir la diferencia (con). *adj* medio.
half-wit ['haːfwit] *n* tonto, -a *m, f.*
halibut ['halibət] *n* halibut *m.*
hall [hɔːl] *n* (*entrance*) vestíbulo *m;* (*room*) sala *f.* **hall porter** conserje *m.* **hall-stand** *n* perchero *m.*
hallmark ['hɔːlmaːk] *n* contraste *m;* (*fig*) sello *m. v* contrastar.
hallowed ['haloud] *adj* santo. **hallow** santificar.
Hallowe'en [halouˈiːn] *n* víspera del Día de todos los Santos *f.*
hallucination [həˌluːsiˈneiʃən] *n* alucinación *f.*
halo ['heilou] *n* halo *m;* (*rel*) aureola *f.*
halt [hɔːlt] *n* alto *m,* parada *f. v* parar; interrumpir.
halter ['hɔːltə] *n* cabestro *m.*
halve [haːv] *v* compartir; partir en dos; reducir a la mitad.
ham [ham] *n* jamón *m.*
hamburger ['hambəːgə] *n* hamburguesa *f.*
hammer ['hamə] *n* martillo *m;* (*firearm*) percursor *m.* **come under the hammer** salir a subasta. *v* martillar, martillear; (*nail*) clavar; (*iron*) batir. **hammer out** (*disputes, etc.*) elaborar.

hammock ['hamək] *n* hamaca *f*.

hamper¹ ['hampə] *v* impedir; embarazar.

hamper² ['hampə] *n* canasta *f*.

hamster ['hamstə] *n* hámster *m*.

hamstring ['hamstriŋ] *v* (*coll*) paralizar.

hand [hand] *n* mano *f*; (*watch, etc.*) aguja *f*; (*worker*) trabajador *m*; (*writing*) escritura *f*; (*applause*) ovación *f*; (*measure*) palmo *m*; (*naut*) marinero *m*. **at first hand** de primera mano. **at hand** a mano. **by hand** en mano. **hand and foot** de pies y manos. **hand in hand** de la mano. **hands up!** ¡arriba las manos! **hand to hand** cuerpo a cuerpo. **keep one's hand in** no perder la práctica. **on the other hand** por otra parte. *v* dar. **hand down** transmitir. **hand in** entregar. **hand over** ceder. **handful** *n* puñado *m*.

handbag ['handbag] *n* bolso *m*.

handbook ['handbuk] *n* manual *m*; guía *f*.

handbrake ['handbreik] *n* freno de mano *m*.

handcuff ['handkʌf] *v* poner las esposas a. **handcuffs** *pl n* esposas *f pl*.

handicap ['handikap] *n* desventaja *f*; (*sport*) handicap *m*. *v* perjudicar.

handicraft ['handikraːft] *n* mano de obra *f*.

handiwork ['handiwəːk] *n* obra *f*.

handkerchief ['haŋkətʃif] *n* pañuelo *m*.

handle ['handl] *n* (*cup, bag, etc.*) asa *f*; (*grip of a tool*) mango *m*; (*stick, door knob*) pomo *m*; (*door lever*) tirador *m*; (*lever*) brazo *m*. *v* tocar; (*naut*) dirigir; (*mot*) conducir; (*tool*) manejar; (*lift, shift*) manipular; (*cope*) poder con; (*deal with*) ocuparse de. **handle with care** frágil. **handlebars** *pl n* manillar *m sing*.

handmade [,hand'meid] *adj* hecho a mano.

hand-out ['handaut] *n* (*leaflet*) prospecto *m*; (*charity*) limosna *f*. **hand out** dar; distribuir.

hand-pick [hand'pik] *v* (*people*) escoger a dedo; (*objects*) escoger con sumo cuidado.

handrail ['handreil] *n* pasamano *m*.

handshake ['handʃeik] *n* apretón de manos *m*.

handsome ['hansəm] *adj* hermoso, bello; guapo.

handstand ['hand,stand] *n* pino *m*.

handwriting ['hand,raitiŋ] *n* escritura *f*. **handwritten** *adj* escrito a mano.

handy ['handi] *adj* (*near*) a mano; (*skilful*) mañoso; diestro; (*convenient*) cómodo; (*manageable*) manejable; (*useful*) útil. **come in handy** venir bien.

*****hang** [han] *v* colgar, suspender; (*execute*) ahorcar; (*head*) bajar; (*wallpaper*) empapelar; (*of clothes*) caer. **hang about** *or* **around** vagar. **hang fire** estar en suspenso. **hang-gliding** *n* vuelo libre *m*. **hangman** *n* verdugo *m*. **hang on** mantenerse firme; (*remain*) quedarse; (*hold on*) agarrarse; (*depend upon*) depender de. **hangover** *n* (*slang*) resaca *f*. **hang-up** *n* (*coll*) complejo *m*.

hangar ['haŋə] *n* hangar *m*.

hanker ['haŋkə] *v* **hanker for** *or* **after** anhelar. **hankering** *n* anhelo *m*.

haphazard [,hap'hazəd] *adj* fortuito.

happen ['hapən] *v* acontecer, suceder; (*take place*) tener lugar; (*arise*) sobrevenir. **happening** *n* suceso *m*, ocurrencia *f*.

happy ['hapi] *adj* feliz, alegre. **happy birthday!** ¡feliz cumpleaños! **happy Christmas!** ¡felices Pascuas! **happy-go-lucky** *adj* descuidado. **happiness** *n* alegría *f*. **happily** *adv* felizmente.

harass ['harəs] *v* hostigar. **harassment** *n* hostigamiento *m*.

harbour ['haːbə] *n* puerto *m*; (*haven*) asilo *m*. *v* dar refugio a; (*cherish*) abrigar.

hard [haːd] *adj* duro; firme; violento; inflexible; cruel; (*unjust*) opresivo; (*weather*) severo; (*stiff*) tieso. *adv* duro; de firme; vigorosamente; (*raining*) a cántaros; (*closely*) de cerca; (*badly*) mal; (*heavily*) pesadamente. **hard-and-fast** *adj* (*rule*) inalterable. **hard-bitten** *adj* also **hard-boiled** (*fig*) duro, tenaz. **hard-hearted** *adj* insensible. **hard labour** trabajos forzados *m pl*. **hard up** (*coll*) apurado. **hardware** *n* ferretería *n*. **harden** *v* endurecer; (*make callous*) hacer insensible. **hardness** *n* dureza *f*; inhumanidad *f*; tiesura *f*; dificultad *f*. **hardship** *n* penas *f pl*; sufrimiento *m*; privación *f*.

hardy ['haːdi] *adj* audaz; fuerte; (*bot*) resistente.

hare [heə] *n* liebre *f*. **hare-brained** *adj* casquivano. **hare-lip** *n* labio leporino *m*.

haricot ['harikou] *n* judía *f*.

harm [haːm] *n* mal *m*; daño *m*. **harmful** *adj* malo; dañino. **harmless** *adj* inofensivo; inocuo.

harmonic [haɪ'mɒnik] *nm. adj* armónico.
harmonica [haɪ'mɒnikə] *n* armónica *f.*
harmonize ['haɪmənaiz] *v* armonizar.
harmony ['haɪmənɪ] *n* armonia *f.* **harmonious** *adj* armonioso.
harness ['haɪnis] *n* guarniciones *f pl.* *v* enjaezar; (*power, etc.*) represar.
harp [haɪp] *n* arpa *f.* *v* **harp on** volver a repetir. **harpist** *n* arpista *m. f.*
harpoon [haɪ'puɪn] *n* arpón *m. v* arponear.
harpsichord ['haɪpsɪ,kɔɪd] *n* arpicordio *m.* clavicémbalo *m.*
harrowing ['harouɪŋ] *adj* atormentador, patibulario.
harsh [haɪʃ] *adj* (*features*) duro; (*voice*) ronco; (*sound*) discordante; (*texture*) áspero.
harvest ['haɪvist] *n* cosecha *f.* *v* cosechar.
has [haz] *V* have.
hash [haʃ] *n* (*food*) picadillo *m*; (*coll*) lio *m.* **make a hash of** estropear por completo. *v* (*food*) picar.
hashish ['haʃiɪʃ] *n* hachis *m* invar.
haste [heist] *n* prisa *f.* **hasten** *v* dar prisa a; apresurar. **hastily** *adv* de prisa; (*rashly*) a la ligera. **hasty** *adj* precipitado; (*rash*) apresurado.
hat [hat] *n* sombrero *m.* **bowler hat** sombrero hongo *m.* **Panama hat** jipijapa *m.* **top hat** sombrero de copa *m.* **take one's hat off** to descubrirse ante.
hatch[1] [hatʃ] *v* hacer salir del cascarón; (*coll: plot*) maquinar.
hatch[2] [hatʃ] *n* (*serving*) ventanilla *f*; (*naut*) escotilla *f*; (*trapdoor*) trampa *f.*
hatchet ['hatʃit] *n* hacha *f.*
hate [heit] *v* odiar, aborrecer. *n also* **hatred** odio *m.* **pet hate** pesadilla *f.* **hateful** *adj* odioso.
haughty ['hɔɪtɪ] *adj* altanero. **haughtiness** *n* altaneria *f.*
haul [hɔɪl] *v* (*drag*) arrastrar; (*transport*) acarrear. *n* (*pull*) tirón *m*; (*journey*) recorrido *m*; (*fish*) redada *f*; (*loot*) botín *m.* **haulage** *n* acarreo *m*, transporte *m.*
haunt [hɔɪnt] *v* (*ghost*) aparecer en; (*follow*) perseguir; (*frequent*) frecuentar; (*memories*) obsesionar. *n* lugar predilecto *m.* **haunting** *adj* obsesionante.
°have [hav] *v* tener; (*receive*) recibir; (*drink, food*) tomar; (*get*) conseguir; (*coll: deceive*) engañar. **have on** (*wear*) llevar; (*coll: tease*) tomar el pelo a. **have to** tener que.

haven ['heivn] *n* abrigo *m*; (*fig*) refugio *m.*
haversack ['havsak] *n* mochila *f.*
havoc ['havək] *n* estragos *m pl.* **play havoc with** hacer estragos en.
hawk [hɔɪk] *n* halcón *m.*
hawthorn ['hɔːθɔɪn] *n* espino *m.*
hay [hei] *n* heno *m.* **make hay while the sun shines** hacer su agosto. **hay fever** fiebre del heno *f.* **haystack** *n* almiar *m.* **go haywire** (*machine*) estropearse; (*plans*) desorganizarse.
hazard ['hazəd] *n* peligro *m*; (*chance*) azar *m. v* arriesgar; (*guess*) aventurar. **hazardous** *adj* arriesgado, peligroso.
haze [heiz] *n* neblina *f*; (*fig*) confusión *f.* **hazy** *adj* nebuloso; (*fig*) confuso.
hazel ['heizl] *n* avellano *m.* **hazel-nut** *n* avellana *f.* *adj* de avellano.
he [hiɪ] *pron* él.
head [hed] *n* cabeza *f*; (*chief*) jefe *m*; (*school*) director, -a *m. f*; (*bed, table, river*) cabecera *f*; (*coin*) cara *f*; (*spear, arrows*) punta *f*; (*steam*) presión *f*; (*hammer*) cotillo *m. v* (*demonstration, list, etc.*) encabezar; (*lead*) estar a la cabeza de; dirigir; conducir; (*goal*) meter de cabeza. **head off** cortar el paso a. **head for** dirigirse hacia. **headed** *adj* (*notepaper*) con membrete. **heading** *n* título *m.* **heady** *adj* embriagador.
headache ['hedeik] *n* dolor de cabeza *m.*
headfirst [,hed'fɜɪst] *adv* de cabeza.
headlamp ['hedlamp] *or* **headlight** *n* (*mot*) faro *m.*
headland ['hedlənd] *n* punta *f*, promontorio *m.*
headline ['hedlain] *n* (*book*) título *m*; (*newspaper*) titular *m.* **make the headlines** estar en primera plana.
headlong ['hedlɒŋ] *adv* (*headfirst*) de cabeza; (*rush*) precipitado.
headmaster [,hed'maɪstə] *n* director *m.* **headmistress** *n* directora *f.*
head-on [,hed'ɒn] *adj, adv* de frente.
headphones ['hedfounz] *pl n* auriculares *m pl.*
headquarters [,hed'kwɔɪtəz] *n* (*mil*) cuartel general *m*; (*firm*) domicilio social *m*; (*organization*) sede *f.*
headrest ['hedrest] *n* cabecero *m*, cabezal *m.*
headscarf ['hedskaɪf] *n* pañuelo *m.*
headstrong ['hedstrɒŋ] *adj* testarudo.

headway ['hedwei] *n* progreso *m*.

heal [hiːl] *v* (*disease*) curar, sanar; (*wound*) cicatrizar.

health [helθ] *n* salud *f*. **health certificate** certificado médico *m*. **health food** alimentos naturales *m pl*. **health officer** inspector de sanidad *m*. **health resort** balneario *m*. **Ministry of Health** Dirección General de Sanidad *f*. **public health** sanidad pública *f*. **your health!** ¡a su salud! **healthy** *adj* sano, saludable, salubre. **healthy appetite** buen apetito *m*.

heap [hiːp] *n* montón *m*, pila *f*; (*people*) muchedumbre *f*. *v* amontonar, apilar.

*****hear** [hiə] *v* oír; (*listen*) escuchar; (*attend*) asistir a; (*give audience*) dar audiencia; (*news*) enterarse de. **hear from** enterarse de. **hear hear!** ¡¡ muy bien! **hear about** *or* **of** oír hablar de. **hearing** (*sense*) oído *m*; (*act of hearing*) audición *f*. **hearing aid** aparato para sordos *m*. **hearsay** *n* rumor *m*.

hearse [hɜːs] *n* coche fúnebre *m*.

heart [hɑːt] *n* (*anat*) corazón *m*; (*feelings*) entrañas *f pl*; (*courage*) ánimo *m*; (*soul*) alma *f*; (*cards*) copas *f pl*; (*lettuce*) repollo *m*. **by heart** de memoria. **to one's heart's content** hasta quedarse satisfecho. **a man after my own heart** un hombre de los que me gustan. **hearten** *v* animar. **heartless** *adj* cruel. **hearty** *adj* (*welcome*) cordial; (*meal*) abundante.

heart attack *n* ataque cardíaco *m*.

heartbeat ['hɑːtbiːt] *n* latido del corazón *m*.

heart-breaking ['hɑːtbreikiŋ] *adj* desgarrador. **heart-broken** *adj* acongojado.

heartburn ['hɑːtbɜːn] *n* acedía *f*.

heart failure *n* colapso cardíaco *m*.

heartfelt ['hɑːtfelt] *adj* de todo corazón.

hearth [hɑːθ] *n* hogar *m*. **hearthrug** *n* alfombra *f*.

heart-throb ['hɑːtθrob] *n* ídolo *m*.

heart-to-heart *adj* franco, sincero. **have a heart-to-heart talk** tener una conversación íntima.

heartwarming ['hɑːtwɔːmiŋ] *adj* caluroso.

heat [hiːt] *n* calor *m*; (*animals*) celo *m*; (*fig*) vehemencia *f*; (*passion*) ardor *m*; (*of a race*) carrera eliminatoria *f*. *v* calentar; excitar; (*annoy*) irritar. **heatstroke** *n* insolación *f*. **heatwave** *n* onda de calor *f*. **in the heat of the moment** en el calor del momento. **heated** *adj* calentado; (*argument*) apasionado. **heater** *n* calentador *m*. **heating** *n* calefacción *f*. **central heating** calefacción central *f*.

heath [hiːθ] *n* (*plant*) brezo *m*; (*land*) brezal *m*.

heathen ['hiːðən] *n, adj* pagano, -a.

heather ['heðə] *n* brezo *m*.

heave [hiːv] *n* (*lift*) gran esfuerzo *m*; (*pull*) tirón *m*; (*sea*) movimiento *m*; (*breast*) palpitación *f*; (*retching*) náusea *f*. *v* (*pull*) tirar de; (*lift*) levantar; (*sigh*) exhalar; (*waves*) subir y bajar; (*retch*) tener náusea; (*breast*) palpitar. **heave to** ponerse al pairo.

heaven ['hevn] *n* cielo *m*, paraíso *m*. **heavenly** *adj* celeste; (*fig*) delicioso.

heavy ['hevi] *adj* pesado, torpe; (*slow*) lento; (*thick*) grueso; (*hard*) duro; (*strong*) fuerte; (*oppressive*) opresivo; (*cold*) malo; (*sky*) anublado; (*meal*) abundante; (*food*) indigesto; (*soil*) recio. **heavyweight** *nm, adj* peso pesado. **heaviness** *n* peso *m*; torpor *m*; tristeza *f*; ponderosidad *f*.

Hebrew ['hiːbruː] *n* (*people*) hebreo, -a *m, f*; (*language*) hebreo *m*. *adj* hebreo.

heckle ['hekl] *v* interrumpir. **heckler** *n* perturbador, -a *m, f*. **heckling** *n* interrupción *f*.

hectare ['hektɑː] *n* hectárea *f*.

hectic ['hektik] *adj* agitado.

hedge [hedʒ] *n* seto *m*. *v* cercar con un seto; (*fig*) vacilar; (*a bet*) compensar.

hedgehog ['hedʒhog] *n* erizo *m*.

heed [hiːd] *v* atender. *n* atención *f*, cuidado *m*. **heedless** *adj* desatento; negligente.

heel [hiːl] *n* (*anat*) talón *m*; (*shoe*) tacón *m*. *v* poner tacón a.

hefty ['hefti] *adj* (*heavy*) pesado; (*robust*) robusto.

heifer ['hefə] *n* novilla *f*.

height [hait] *n* altura *f*; (*people*) estatura *f*; (*hill*) colina *f*; (*fig*) colmo *m*; cumbre *f*. **heighten** *v* elevar; (*fig*) aumentar.

heir [eə] *n* heredero *m*. **heiress** *n* heredera *f*. **heirloom** *n* reliquia de familia *f*.

held [held] *V* **hold**.

helicopter ['helikoptə] *n* helicóptero *m*.

hell [hel] *n* infierno *m*. **go to hell!** (*impol*) ¡vete al infierno! **go hell for leather** ir como si se llevara el diablo. **to hell with it!** ¡qué diablos! **hellish** *adj* infernal; (*fig*) horrible.

hello [hə'ləu] *interj* (*greeting*) ¡hola!; (*attract attention*) ¡oye!; (*phone*) ¡oiga!; (*answering the phone*) ¡diga!

helm [helm] *n* caña del timón *f*. **be at the helm** empuñar el timón.

helmet ['helmit] *n* casco *m*; (*of motorcyclist, labourer, etc.*) careta *f*.

help [help] *n* ayuda *f*; socorro *m*; auxilio *m*; remedio *m*; (*employee*) empleado *m*; (*servant*) criado, -a *m, f. interj* ¡socorro! *v* ayudar; auxiliar; socorrer; (*relieve*) aliviar; (*serve*) servir; (*avoid*) evitar; (*facilitate*) facilitar; (*prevent oneself from*) no poder menos que. **help yourself!** ¡sírvese! **it can't be helped!** ¡no hay más remedio! **helper** *n* ayudante *m*. **helpful** *adj* útil; provechoso; amable. **helping** *n* porción *f*. **helpless** *adj* desamparado.

hem [hem] *n* dobladillo *m*. *v* hacer un dobladillo en. **hem in** (*fig*) rodear. **hemline** *n* bajo *m*.

hemisphere ['hemisfiə] *n* hemisferio *m*.

hemp [hemp] *n* cáñamo *m*.

hen [hen] *n* (*chicken*) gallina *f*; (*female of other birds*) hembra *f*. **henhouse** *n* gallinero *m*. **hen party** (*coll*) reunión de mujeres *f*. **henpecked** *adj* dominado por su mujer.

hence [hens] *adv* por eso, por lo consiguiente; (*time*) de ahora; (*place*) de aquí. **henceforth** *adv* desde aquí en adelante.

henna ['henə] *n* alheña *f*.

her [hə] *pron* ella; (*direct object*) la; (*indirect object*) le, a ella. *adj su (pl* sus).

herald ['herəld] *n* heraldo *m*. *v* proclamar. **heraldic** *adj* heráldico. **heraldry** *n* heráldica *f*.

herb [həb] *n* hierba *f*. **herbal** *adj* herbario.

herd [həd] *n* rebaño *m*, manada *f*. *v* (*round up*) reunir en manada; (*drive*) conducir; (*fig*) agrupar.

here [hiə] *adv* aquí. **hereafter** *adv* en lo futuro; en adelante. **here and now** ahora mismo. **here and there** aquí y allá. **here goes!** ¡vamos a ver! **here is/are** aquí está/están.

hereditary [hi'reditəri] *adj* hereditario. **heredity** [hi'rediti] *n* herencia *f*.

heresy ['herəsi] *n* herejía *f*. **heretic** *n* hereje *m, f*. **heretical** *adj* herético.

heritage ['heritidʒ] *n* herencia *f*.

hermit ['həmit] *n* ermitaño *m*.

hernia ['hɜniə] *n* hernia *f*.

hero ['hiərəu] *n* héroe *m*. **heroine** *n* heroína *f*. **hero-worship** *n* culto a los héroes *m*. **heroic** *adj* heroico. **heroism** *n* heroísmo *m*.

heroin ['herəuin] *n* heroína *f*.

heron ['herən] *n* garza *f*.

herring ['heriŋ] *n* arenque *m*. **red herring** (*coll*) pista falsa *f*.

hers [həz] *pron* suyo, suya.

herself [hə'self] *pron* (*reflexive*) se; (*emphatic*) ella misma. **by herself** a solas.

hesitate ['heziteit] *v* vacilar. **hesitant** *adj* vacilante. **hesitation** *n* vacilación *f*.

heterosexual [hetərə'sekʃuəl] *n(m+f), adj* heterosexual.

hexagon ['heksəgən] *n* hexágono *m*. **hexagonal** *adj* hexagonal.

heyday ['heidei] *n* auge *m*, apogeo *m*.

hiatus [hai'eitəs] *n* laguna *f*.

hibernate ['haibəneit] *v* hibernar. **hibernation** *n* hibernación *f*.

hiccup ['hikʌp] *n* hipo *m*. **have the hiccups** tener hipo. *v* hipar.

*hide¹ [haid] *v* esconder. **hide something from someone** ocultar algo a alguien. **hide-and-seek** *n* escondite *m*. **hide-out** *n* escondrijo *m*.

hide² [haid] *n* piel *f*; (*leather*) cuero *m*.

hideous ['hidiəs] *adj* horroroso.

hiding¹ ['haidiŋ] *n* **be in hiding** estar escondido. **go into hiding** esconderse. **hiding place** escondite *m*.

hiding² ['haidiŋ] *n* (*beating*) paliza *f*.

hierarchy ['haiərɑki] *n* jerarquía *f*. **hierarchical** *adj* jerárquico.

hi-fi ['hai,fai] *n* alta fidelidad *f*.

high [hai] *adj* alto; de alto; (*speed, hopes, number*) grande; (*post*) importante; (*wind*) fuerte; (*altar, Mass*) mayor; (*voice*) agudo; (*quality*) superior; (*river*) crecido; (*noon*) pleno; (*game*) manido; (*shine, polish*) brillante; (*colour*) subido. **highbrow** ['haibrau] *n(m+f), adj* intelectual.

high chair *n* silla alta para niño *f*.

high frequency *adj* de alta frecuencia.

high-heeled *adj* de tacón alto.

high jump *n* salto de altura *m*.

highland ['hailənd] *n* tierras altas *f pl. adj* montañoso.

highlight ['hailait] *v* destacar. *n* (*art*) toque de luz *m*; (*fig*) atracción principal *f*.

Highness ['hainis] n Alteza f.

high-pitched adj de tono alto.

high-rise block n torre f.

high-speed adj de gran velocidad.

high-spirited adj brioso.

high street n calle principal f.

highway ['haiwei] n camino real m, carretera f. **highway code** código de la circulación m. **highwayman** n salteador de caminos m.

hijack ['haidʒak] v (aircraft) secuestrar; (people) asaltar; (goods) robar. n secuestro m; asalto m.

hike [haik] n excursión a pie f. v ir de excursión. **hiker** n excursionista m, f. **hiking** n excursionismo m.

hilarious [hi'leəriəs] adj (funny) hilarante; (merry) alegre. **hilarity** n hilaridad f.

hill [hil] n colina f. cerro m; (slope) cuesta f. **hillside** n ladera f. **hilly** adj montañoso.

him [him] pron él; (direct object) le, lo.

himself [him'self] pron (reflexive) se; sí, sí mismo; (emphatic) él mismo. **by himself** a solas.

hind [haind] adj trasero, posterior. **hindquarters** pl n cuarto trasero m sing. **hindsight** n percepción retrospectiva f.

hinder ['hində] v impedir; interrumpir. **hindrance** n impedimento m; obstáculo m.

Hindu [hin'du:] n(m+f), adj hindú. **Hinduism** n hinduismo m.

hinge [hindʒ] n bisagra f; (stamps) fijasellos m invar. v **hinge on** depender de.

hint [hint] n indirecta f; (tip) consejo m; (clue) pista f; indicación f; (trace) pizca f. **broad hint** una insinuación muy clara. **take the hint** (pejorative) darse por aludido; (follow advice) aprovechar el consejo. v insinuar; soltar indirectas.

hip [hip] n cadera f.

hippopotamus [hipə'potəməs] n hipopótamo m.

hire [haiə] v alquilar; (person) contratar. **hire out** alquilar. n (house, etc.) alquiler m; (engagement) contratación f; (wages) sueldo m. **for hire** de alquiler; (taxi) libre. **hire purchase** compra a plazos f.

his [hiz] adj su (pl sus); de él. pron suyo, suya.

hiss [his] n silbido m. v silbar.

history ['histəri] n historia f. **historian** n historiador, -a m, f. **historic** adj histórico.

*****hit** [hit] v golpear, pegar a; (target) dar

en; (wound) herir; (collide) chocar con. **hit home** dar en el blanco. **hit it off with** hacer buenas migas con. n golpe m; (mil) impacto m; (success) exito m. **hit-or-miss** adv a la buena de Dios.

hitch [hitʃ] n obstáculo m; problema m; (knot) vuelta de cabo m. v (travel) hacerse llevar en coche; (tie) atar; (link) enganchar. **hitch-hike** v hacer autostop. **hitch-hiker** n autostopista m, f. **hitch-hiking** n autostop m.

hitherto [hiðə'tu:] adv hasta ahora.

hive [haiv] n colmena f.

hoard [hoːd] n acumulación f; tesoro m. v acumular, amasar.

hoarding ['hoːdiŋ] n (fence) valla f; (advertising) cartelera f.

hoarse [hoːs] adj ronco. **hoarsely** adv roncamente. **hoarseness** n ronquera f.

hoax [houks] n estafa f; engaño m; burla f. v estafar; engañar; burlar.

hobble ['hobl] v cojear. n (gait) cojera f.

hobby ['hobi] n pasatiempo m.

hock¹ [hok] n (pork, etc.) pernil m.

hock² [hok] n vino del Rín m.

hockey ['hoki] n hockey m. **hockey stick** bastón de hockey m.

hoe [hou] n azadón m. v azadonar.

hog [hog] n cerdo m, puerco m. v (coll) acaparar.

hoist [hoist] v (heavy objects) levantar; (sails, flag) izar. n (lifting) levantamiento m; (crane) grúa f; (lift) montacargas m invar; (lifting mechanism) cabria f.

*****hold** [hould] v tener; mantener; agarrar; (believe) creer; (keep) guardar; (sustain) sostener; (opinion) defender. **hold back** reprimir. **hold forth** perorar. **hold on** sujetar; (wait) aguantar; (grip) agarrarse. **hold out** (hand) tender, ofrecer; (last) durar; (resist) resistir. **hold up** (raise) levantar; (support) sostener; (delay) retrasar. n (grip) asimiento m, agarro m; (handhold) asidero m; (control) autoridad f. dominio m. **get hold of** coger, agarrar. **hold-up** n interrupción f; (robbery) atraco a mano armada m; (traffic jam) embotellamiento m. **holder** n (person) poseedor, -a m, f; (object) receptáculo m.

hold² [hould] n (naut) bodega f.

hole [houl] n agujero m; (from digging) hoyo m; (in garments) boquete m; (mouse) ratonera f; (rabbit) madriguera f.

holiday ['hɔlədi] n (day) fiesta f; (several days) vacaciones f pl. **holiday resort** centro de turismo m.

Holland ['hɔlənd] n Holanda f.

hollow ['hɔlou] n hueco m; (in ground) hondonada f. adj, adv hueco. v ahuecar.

holly ['hɔli] n acebo m.

hollyhock ['hɔlihɔk] n malva loca f.

holster ['houlstə] n pistolera f.

holy ['houli] adj santo; sacro; sagrado; (bread, water) bendito. **holiness** n santidad f.

homage ['hɔmidʒ] n homenaje m. **pay homage** rendir homenaje.

home [houm] n casa f; hogar m; domicilio m; (fig) morada f. **at home** en casa. **make yourself at home** está usted en su casa. adv a casa. **go home** volver a casa. **homeless** adj sin casa ni hogar. **home address** dirección privada f. **homesick** adj nostálgico.

homicide ['hɔmisaid] n (act) homicidio m; (person) homicida m, f. **homicidal** adj homicida.

homogeneous [hɔmə'dʒiiniəs] adj homogéneo.

homosexual [hɔmə'seksuəl] n(m+f). adj homosexual. **homosexuality** n homosexualidad f.

honest ['ɔnist] adj honrado; sincero; franco. **honesty** n honradez f; sinceridad f; rectitud f.

honey ['hʌni] n miel f. **honeycomb** n panal m. **honeymoon** n luna de miel f. **honeysuckle** n madreselva f.

honour ['ɔnə] n honor m; rectitud f. v honrar. **honorary** adj honorario. **honourable** adj honorable.

hood [hud] n capucha f; (car, pram) capota f.

hoof [huf] n casco m; (cloven) pezuña f.

hook [huk] n gancho m; (fish) anzuelo m; (dress) corchete m; (hanger) colgadero m. v enganchar; (fish) pescar; (dress) abrochar; colgar. **hooked** adj (shaped) ganchudo. **get hooked on** (coll) enviciarse en.

hooligan ['huːligən] n rufián m. **hooliganism** n rufianería f.

hoop [huːp] n (toy) aro m; (barrel) fleje m.

hoot [huːt] n (owl) ululato m; (person) silbato m; (shout) grito m; (boat, factory) toque de sirena m. v ulular; silbar; dar

un bocinazo; gritar; dar un toque de sirena; (boo) abuchear.

hop¹ [hɔp] v saltar; brincar; saltar con un pie. n salto m; brinco m; (coll: dance) baile m; (coll: stage in a journey) etapa f.

hop² [hɔp] n (bot) lúpulo m.

hope [houp] n esperanza f. v esperar. **hopeful** adj lleno de esperanzas; confiado. **hopeless** adj desesperado; (coll) inútil.

horde [hɔid] n horda f.

horizon [hə'raizn] n horizonte m.

horizontal [hɔri'zɔntl] adj horizontal.

hormone ['hɔimoun] n hormona f.

horn [hɔin] n cuerno m; (mot) bocina f.

hornet ['hɔinit] n avispón m.

horoscope ['hɔrəskoup] n horóscopo m.

horrible ['hɔribl] adj horrible, espantoso.

horrid ['hɔrid] adj horroroso, odioso.

horrify ['hɔrifai] v horrorizar. **horrific** adj horrífico, horrendo.

horror ['hɔrə] n horror m. adj (film, story, etc.) de miedo.

hors d'œuvres [ɔi'dəivr] pl n entremeses m pl.

horse [hɔis] n caballo m. **on horseback** a caballo. **horsepower** n caballo de vapor m. **horseradish** n rábano picante m. **horse show** concurso hípico m.

horticulture ['hɔitikʌltʃə] n horticultura f. **horticultural** adj horticultural.

hose [houz] n manga f; manguera f; (stockings) medias f pl. v regar con una manga.

hosiery ['houziəri] n medias f pl; (business) calcetería f.

hospitable [hɔ'spitəbl] adj hospitalario.

hospital ['hɔspitl] n hospital m. **hospitalize** v hospitalizar.

hospitality [hɔspi'taliti] n hospitalidad f.

host¹ [houst] n huésped m. **hostess** n huéspeda f.

host² [houst] n (crowd) muchedumbre f.

hostage ['hɔstidʒ] n rehén m.

hostel ['hɔstal] n hostería f; residencia f. **youth hostel** albergue juvenil m.

hostile ['hɔstail] adj hostil; enemigo. **hostility** n hostilidad f; enemistad f.

hot [hɔt] adj caliente; (climate) cálido; (sun) abrasador; (day) caluroso; (spicy) picante; (temper) vivo; (issue) controvertido; (pursuit) porfiado. **be hot** (person) tener calor; (weather) hacer calor. **hot dog** perro caliente m. **hot-house** invernadero m. **hotplate** n calientaplato

m invar. **hot-tempered** *adj* enfadadizo.
hot-water bottle bolsa de agua caliente *f*.
hotel [hou'tel] *n* hotel *m*.
hound [haund] *n* perro de caza *m*. *v* (*fig*) perseguir.
hour ['auə] *n* hora *f*. **after hours** fuera de horas. **by the hour** por horas. **hour by hour** de hora en hora. **peak hours** horas de mayor consumo. **rush hour** hora punta. **small hours** altas horas. **zero hour** hora H. **hourly** *adv* de cada hora.
house [haus; *v* hauz] *n* casa *f*; (*theatre*) sala *f*; (*audience*) público *m*. *v* (*hold*) alojar; (*put up*) albergar.
houseboat ['hausbout] *n* casa flotante *f*.
housecoat ['hauskout] *n* bata *f*.
household ['haushould] *n* casa *f*, familia *f*. *adj* casero.
housekeeper ['haus,kipə] *n* (*paid*) ama de llaves *f*; (*housewife*) ama de casa *f*. **housekeeping** *n* (*work*) quehaceres domésticos *m pl*; (*money*) dinero para gastos domésticos *m*.
housemaid ['hausmeid] *n* criada *f*.
house-to-house *adj, adv* de casa en casa.
house-trained ['haustreind] *adj* enseñado.
house-warming ['haus,wɔːmiŋ] *n* **have a house-warming party** inaugurar la casa.
housewife ['hauswaif] *n* ama de casa *f*.
housing ['hauziŋ] *n* alojamiento *m*. **housing estate** urbanización *f*.
hovel ['hɔvəl] *n* casucha *f*.
hover ['hɔvə] *v* cernerse; (*fig*) rondar. **hovercraft** *n* aerodeslizador *m*.
how [hau] *adv* (*as*) como; (*in what way*) cómo; (*in exclamation before adv or adj*) qué. **how are you?** *or* **how do you do?** ¿cómo está usted? **how much?** ¿cuánto?
however [hau'evə] *conj* sin embargo. *adv* de cualquier manera que.
howl [haul] *v* (*dog, wolf*) aullar; (*wind*) bramar; (*pain*) dar alaridos; (*child*) berrear. *n* aullido *m*; bramido *m*; alarido *m*; grito *m*; berrido *m*.
hub [hʌb] *n* (*wheel*) cubo *m*; (*fig*) centro *m*. **hubcap** *n* (*mot*) tapacubos *m invar*.
huddle ['hʌdl] *v* amontonar. *n* grupo *m*.
hue [hjuː] *n* color *m*.
huff [hʌf] *n* **in a huff** enojado.
hug [hʌg] *v* abrazar. *n* abrazo *m*.
huge [hjuːdʒ] *adj* enorme.
hulk [hʌlk] *n* (*ship*) carraca *f*; (*derog: person*) armatoste *m*. **hulking** *adj* voluminoso.
hull [hʌl] *n* (*naut*) casco *m*.

hum [hʌm] *n* (*bees, engines*) zumbido *m*; (*a tune*) canturreo *m*. *v* zumbar; canturrear; (*fig: with activity*) hervir. **humming-bird** *n* colibrí *m*.
human ['hjuːmən] *nm, adj* humano. **human being** ser humano *m*. **human nature** naturaleza humana *f*.
humane [hjuˈmein] *adj* humano.
humanity [hjuˈmanəti] *n* humanidad *f*. **humanitarian** *adj* humanitario.
humble ['hʌmbl] *adj* humilde. *v* humillar.
humdrum ['hʌmdrʌm] *adj* monótono.
humid ['hjuːmid] *adj* húmedo. **humidity** *n* humedad *f*.
humiliate [hjuˈmilieit] *v* humillar. **humiliation** *n* humillación *f*.
humility [hjuˈmiləti] *n* humildad *f*.
humour ['hjuːmə] *n* humor *m*; (*temperament*) disposición *f*. *v* complacer. **humorist** *n* humorista *m, f*. **humorous** *adj* humorístico.
hump [hʌmp] *n* horoba *f*. *v* (*coll: carry*) cargar con.
hunch [hʌntʃ] *v* encorvarse. *n* (*coll*) presentimiento *m*. **hunchback** *n* jorobado, -a *m, f*.
hundred ['hʌndrəd] *n* ciento *m*; centenar *m*; centena *f*. *adj* cien, ciento. **hundredth** *nm, adj* centésimo.
hung [hʌŋ] *V* hang.
Hungary ['hʌŋgəri] *n* Hungría *f*. **Hungarian** *n, adj* húngaro, -a.
hunger ['hʌŋgə] *n* hambre *f*. *v also* **be hungry** tener hambre, estar hambriento. **hunger for** desear. **hungrily** *adv* hambrientamente.
hunt [hʌnt] *n* caza *f*; (*search*) busca *f*. *v* cazar; buscar. **hunting** *n* caza *f*. **huntsman** *n* cazador *m*.
hurdle ['həːdl] *n* (*sport*) valla *f*; (*fig*) obstáculo *m*. *v* vallar.
hurl [həːl] *v* lanzar, arrojar; (*abuse*) soltar.
hurricane ['hʌrikən] *n* huracán *m*.
hurry ['hʌri] *n* prisa *f*. **be in a hurry** llevar prisa. *v* dar prisa (a), apresurar. **hurried** *adj* apresurado. **hurriedly** *adv* apresuradamente.
*hurt [həːt] *v* (*cause pain*) doler; (*wound*) herir; (*damage*) hacer daño (a); ofender; (*feelings*) mortificar. *n* herida *f*; daño *m*; mal *m*. *adj* lastimado; herido. **hurtful** *adj* dañoso; perjudicial; (*words*) hiriente.
husband ['hʌzbənd] *n* marido *m*, esposo *m*.

hush [hʌʃ] *n* silencio *m*. *interj* ¡calla! *v* silenciar. **hush up** echar tierra a. **hushed** *adj* callado.

husk [hʌsk] *n* (*cereals*) cáscara *f*; (*peas and beans*) vaina *f*; (*chestnut*) erizo *m*. *v* descascarar; desvainar; pelar.

husky ['hʌski] *n* (*dog*) perro esquimal *m*. *adj* (*hoarse*) ronco; (*strong*) fuerte. **huskily** *adv* con voz ronca. **huskiness** *n* ronquera *f*.

hussar [hə'zaɪ] *n* húsar *m*.

hustle ['hʌsl] *v* empujar; (*fig*) precipitar. *n* (*energy*) empuje *m*; (*hurry*) prisa *f*; (*push*) empujón *m*. **hustle and bustle** trajín y vaivén *m*.

hut [hʌt] *n* choza *f*, cabaña *f*.

hutch [hʌtʃ] *n* (*rabbit*) conejera *f*.

hyacinth ['haiəsinθ] *n* jacinto *m*.

hybrid ['haibrid] *nm, adj* híbrido. **hybridization** *n* hibridación *f*.

hydraulic [hai'drɔːlik] *adj* hidráulico.

hydrocarbon [,haidrə'kaɪbən] *n* hidrocarburo *m*.

hydro-electric *adj* hidroeléctrico.

hydrofoil ['haidrəfoil] *n* aerodeslizador *m*.

hydrogen ['haidrədʒən] *n* hidrógeno *m*.

hyena [hai'iːnə] *n* hiena *f*.

hygiene ['haidʒiːn] *n* higiene *f*. **hygienic** *adj* higiénico.

hymn [him] *n* himno *m*. **hymn-book** or **hymnal** *n* himnario *m*.

hyphen ['haifən] *n* guión *m*.

hypnosis [hip'nousis] *n* hipnosis *f*. **hypnotic** *adj* hipnótico. **hypnotism** *n* hipnotismo *m*. **hypnotist** *n* hipnotizador, -a *m, f*. **hypnotize** *v* hipnotizar.

hypochondria [haipə'kɔndriə] *n* hipocondría *f*. **hypochondriac** *n, adj* hipocondríaco, -a *m, f*.

hypocrisy [hi'pɔkrəsi] *n* hipocresía *f*. **hypocrite** *n* hipócrita *m, f*. **hypocritical** *adj* hipócrita.

hypodermic [haipə'dəɪmik] *adj* hipodérmico. *n* jeringa hipodérmica *f*.

hypothesis [hai'pɔθəsis] *n, pl* -ses hipótesis *f*. **hypothetical** *adj* hipotético.

hysterectomy [,histə'rektəmi] *n* histerectomía *f*.

hysteria [hi'stiəriə] *n* histeria *f*. **hysterical** *adj* histérico. **hysterics** *n* histerismo *m*; ataque histérico *m*.

I

I [ai] *pron* yo.

Iberian [ai'biəriən] *adj* ibérico. *n* ibero, -a *m, f*.

ice [ais] *n* hielo *m*. **iceberg** *n* iceberg *m*. **icebreaker** *n* rompehielos *m invar*. **ice-cold** *adj* helado. **ice cream** helado *m*. **ice-skate** *n* patín de cuchilla *m*. *v* (*turn into ice*) helar; (*chill*) enfriar. **icing** *n* escarchado *m*. **icing sugar** azúcar en polvo *m, f*. **icy** *adj* (*wind, place*) glacial; (*hand, foot*) helado.

Iceland ['aisland] *n* Islandia *f*. **Icelander** *n* islandés, -esa *m, f*. **Icelandic** *adj* islandés.

icicle ['aisikl] *n* carámbano *m*.

icon ['aikon] *n* icono *m*.

idea [ai'diə] *n* idea *f*.

ideal [ai'diəl] *nm, adj* ideal. **idealist** *n* idealista *m, f*. **idealistic** *adj* idealista.

identical [ai'dentikəl] *adj* idéntico. **identical twins** gemelos homólogos *m pl*.

identify [ai'dentifai] *v* identificar. **identify with** identificarse con. **identification** *n* identificación *f*; (*papers*) documentos de identidad *m pl*.

identity [ai'dentiti] *n* identidad *f*. **identity card** carnet de identidad *m*.

ideology [aidi'olədʒi] *n* ideología *f*.

idiom ['idiəm] *n* (*expression*) idiotismo *m*; (*language*) idioma *m*. **idiomatic** *adj* idiomático.

idiosyncrasy [,idiə'siŋkrəsi] *n* idiosincrasia *f*.

idiot ['idiət] *n* imbécil *m, f*, idiota *m, f*. **idiotic** *adj* idiota.

idle ['aidl] *adj* (*lazy*) perezoso; (*at leisure*) ocioso; (*unemployed*) desocupado; (*machine*) parado; (*talk*) frívolo; (*fears*) infundado. *v* (*waste time*) perder el tiempo; (*be lazy*) holgazanear; (*mechanism*) girar loco. **idleness** *n* (*laziness*) holgazanería *f*; (*leisure*) ociosidad *f*; (*unemployment*) paro *m*.

idol ['aidl] *n* ídolo *m*. **idolatry** *n* idolatría *f*. **idolize** *v* idolatrar.

idyllic [i'dilik] *adj* idílico.

if [if] *conj* si. **as if** como si. **if not** si no. **if only** ¡ojalá que! **if so** si es así.

ignite [ig'nait] *v* encender, prender fuego a.

ignition [ig'niʃən] *n* ignición *f*; (*mot*)

encendido m. **ignition key** llave de contacto f. **ignition switch** interruptor del encendido m.

ignorant ['ignərənt] adj ignorante. **ignorance** n ignorancia f.

ignore [ig'nɔː] v (warning) no hacer caso de; (person) no hacer caso a; (leave out) pasar por alto.

ill [il] adj (sick) enfermo; (bad) malo. nm, adv mal. **ill-advised** adj malaconsejado. **ill-at-ease** adj molesto. **ill-mannered** adj mal educado. **ill health** mala salud f. **ill-treat** v maltratar. **ill will** mala voluntad f. **illness** n enfermedad f.

illegal [i'liːgəl] adj ilegal.

illegible [i'ledʒəbl] adj ilegible.

illegitimate [,ili'dʒitimit] adj ilegítimo. **illegitimacy** n ilegitimidad f.

illicit [i'lisit] adj ilícito.

illiterate [i'litərit] n, adj analfabeto, -a. **illiteracy** n analfabetismo m.

illogical [i'lɒdʒikəl] adj ilógico.

illuminate [i'luːmiːneit] v (light up) iluminar; (clear) aclarar. **illumination** n iluminación f; aclaración f.

illusion [i'luːʒən] n ilusión f.

illustrate ['iləstreit] v ilustrar; (demonstrate) demostrar. **illustration** n ilustración f; ejemplo m. **illustrator** n ilustrador, -a m, f.

illustrious [i'lʌstriəs] adj ilustre.

image ['imidʒ] n imagen f; (fig) reputación f. **be the image of** ser el retrato de. **imagery** n imágenes f pl.

imagine [i'mædʒin] v imaginar. **imaginary** adj imaginario. **imagination** n imaginación f. **imaginative** adj imaginativo.

imbalance [im'baləns] n desequilibrio m.

imbecile ['imbəsiːl] n imbécil m, f.

imitate ['imiteit] v imitar. **imitation** n imitación f.

immaculate [i'makjulit] adj inmaculado.

immaterial [,imə'tiəriəl] adj indiferente; no importa.

immature [,imə'tjuə] adj inmaduro. **immaturity** n inmadurez f.

immediate [i'miːdiət] adj inmediato; (near) cercano. **immediately** adv inmediatamente; directamente.

immense [i'mens] adj inmenso, enorme.

immerse [i'məːs] v sumergir. **immersion** n sumersión f. **immersion heater** calentador de inmersión m.

immigrate ['imigreit] v inmigrar. **immigrant** n(m+f), adj inmigrante. **immigration** n inmigración f.

imminent ['iminənt] adj inminente.

immobile [i'moubail] adj inmóvil. **immobilize** v inmovilizar.

immoral [i'mɔrəl] adj inmoral. **immorality** n inmoralidad f.

immortal [i'mɔːtl] adj inmortal. **immortality** n inmortalidad f. **immortalize** v inmortalizar.

immovable [i'muːvəbl] adj inmóvil; (steadfast) inflexible.

immune [i'mjuːn] adj inmune. **immunity** n inmunidad f. **immunization** n inmunización f. **immunize** v inmunizar.

imp [imp] n diablillo m.

impact ['impakt] n impacto m.

impair [im'peə] v dañar. **impairment** n daño m.

impale [im'peil] v atravesar.

impart [im'paːt] v (give) impartir; (grant) conceder; (make known) comunicar.

impartial [im'paːʃəl] adj imparcial. **impartiality** n imparcialidad f.

impasse [am'paːs] n callejón m.

impassive [im'pasiv] adj impasible.

impatient [im'peiʃənt] adj impaciente. **become impatient** perder la paciencia. **impatience** n impaciencia f.

impeach [im'piːtʃ] v acusar; (prosecute) encausar; (a witness) recusar. **impeachment** n acusación f; (prosecution) enjuiciamiento m; recusación f.

impeccable [im'pekəbl] adj impecable.

impede [im'piːd] v estorbar; impedir.

impediment [im'pedimənt] n estorbo m; obstáculo m; defecto m.

impel [im'pel] v impeler; mover; (push) empujar; obligar.

impending [im'pendiŋ] adj inminente; próximo.

imperative [im'perətiv] adj (peremptory) perentorio; (urgent) imperioso; (necessary) indispensable.

imperfect [im'pəːfikt] adj imperfecto; incompleto. n (gramm) imperfecto m.

imperial [im'piəriəl] adj imperial; (fig) señorial. **imperialism** n imperialismo m.

impersonal [im'pəːsənl] adj impersonal.

impersonate [im'pəːsəneit] v hacerse pasar por; (theatre) imitar. **impersonation** n imitación f.

impertinent [im'pəːtinənt] adj impertinente. **impertinence** n impertinencia f.

impervious [im'pɔːviəs] *adj* impenetrable; (*to criticism, pain, etc.*) insensible.

impetuous [im'petjuəs] *adj* impetuoso.

impetus ['impətəs] *n* (*force*) ímpetu *m*; (*fig*) impulso *m*; estímulo *m*.

impinge [im'pindʒ] *v* **impinge on** tropezar con; usurpar.

implement ['implimənt]; *v* ['impliment] *n* (*tool*) herramienta *f*; (*utensil*) utensilio; **implements** *pl n* (*writing*) artículos *m pl*; (*agr*) aperos *m pl*. *v* llevar a cabo; (*law*) aplicar.

implication [impli'keiʃən] *n* implicación *f*; complicidad *f*; consecuencia *f*. **implicate** *v* implicar; comprometer.

implicit [im'plisit] *adj* implícito; absoluto.

implore [im'ploɪ] *v* suplicar. **imploring** *adj* suplicante.

imply [im'plai] *v* implicar; presuponer; significar; dar a entender. **implied** *adj* implícito.

impolite [impə'lait] *adj* descortés.

import [im'poɪt] *n* (*comm*) artículo importado *m*; (*meaning*) sentido *m*; importancia *f*. *v* (*comm*) importar; significar.

importance [im'poɪtəns] *n* importancia *f*. **important** *adj* importante.

impose [im'pouz] *v* imponer; (*tax*) gravar con. **impose on** abusar de. **imposing** *adj* imponente. **imposition** *n* imposición *f*; abuso *m*; (*tax*) impuesto *m*.

impossible [im'posəbl] *adj* imposible.

impostor [im'postə] *n* impostor, -a *m*, *f*.

impotent ['impətənt] *adj* impotente. **impotence** *n* impotencia *f*.

impound [im'paund] *v* confiscar.

impoverish [im'povəriʃ] *v* (*people*) empobrecer; (*land*) agotar.

impregnate [im'pregneit] *v* fecundar; (*saturate*) empapar. **impregnable** *adj* inexpugnable. **impregnation** *n* fecundación *f*; impregnación *f*.

impress [im'pres] *v* impresionar; (*print*) imprimir. **impression** *n* impresión *f*. **impressive** *adj* impresionante.

imprint ['imprint; *v* im'print] *n* impresión *f*. *v* imprimir.

imprison [im'prizn] *v* encarcelar. **imprisonment** *n* encarcelamiento *m*.

improbable [im'probəbl] *adj* improbable; (*story, etc.*) inverosímil.

impromptu [im'promptjuɪ] *adv* improvisadamente. *adj* improvisado.

improper [im'propə] *adj* indecente; indecoroso; incorrecto.

improve [im'pruːv] *v* mejorar; favorecer; perfeccionar. **improvement** *n* mejora *f*; progreso *m*; reforma *f*.

improvise ['imprəvaiz] *v* improvisar. **improvisation** *n* improvisación *f*.

impudent ['impjudənt] *adj* impudente. **impudence** *n* impudencia *f*.

impulse ['impʌls] *n* impulso *m*. **impulsive** *adj* impulsivo.

impure [im'pjuə] *adj* impuro. **impurity** *n* impureza *f*.

in [in] *prep* en; de; durante; a. *adv* dentro. **be in** (*at home*) estar en casa. **be in on** estar enterado de.

inability [inə'biləti] *n* incapacidad *f*.

inaccessible [inak'sesəbl] *adj* inaccesible. **inaccessibility** *n* inaccesibilidad *f*.

inaccurate [in'akjurit] *adj* inexacto. **inaccuracy** *n* inexactitud *f*.

inactive [in'aktiv] *adj* inactivo. **inaction** *n* inacción *f*. **inactivity** *n* inactividad *f*.

inadequate [in'adikwit] *adj* insuficiente. **inadequacy** *n* insuficiencia *f*.

inadvertent [inəd'vəːtənt] *adj* inadvertido; descuidado. **inadvertently** *adv* por inadvertencia.

inane [in'ein] *adj* (*futile*) inane; (*silly*) necio. **inanity** *n* inanidad *f*; necedad *f*.

inanimate [in'animit] *adj* inanimado.

inarticulate [inaɪ'tikjulit] *adj* (*sound*) inarticulado; (*person*) incapaz de expresarse.

inasmuch [inəz'mʌtʃ] *adv* **inasmuch as** puesto que, visto que.

inaudible [in'ɔidəbl] *adj* inaudible.

inaugurate [i'nɔɪgjuˌreit] *v* inaugurar. **inaugural** *adj* inaugural. **inauguration** *n* inauguración *f*.

inborn [inˈbɔɪn] *adj* innato; (*med*) congénito.

incapable [in'keipəbl] *adj* incapaz.

incendiary [in'sendiəri] *adj* incendiario. **incendiary bomb** bomba incendiaria *f*.

incense[1] ['insens] *n* incienso *m*.

incense[2] [in'sens] *v* encolerizar.

incentive [in'sentiv] *n* incentivo *m*, estímulo *m*.

incessant [in'sesənt] *adj* incesante, continuo.

incest ['insest] *n* incesto *m*. **incestuous** *adj* incestuoso.

inch [intʃ] *n* pulgada *f*. **inch by inch** poco a poco. **within an inch of** a dos pasos de. *v* **inch forward** avanzar poco a poco.

incident ['insidənt] *n* incidente *m*; *(in a story)* episodio *m*. **incidental** *adj* incidente; incidental; imprevisto; *(expense)* accesorio *m*; *(music)* de fondo; *(secondary)* secundario; *(casual)* fortuito. **incidentally** *adv (by the way)* a propósito.

incinerator [in'sinə,reitə] *n* quemador de basuras *m*. **incinerate** *v* quemar. **incineration** *n* incineración *f*.

incite [in'sait] *v* incitar; provocar. **incitement** *n* incitamiento *m*; estímulo *m*.

incline [in'klain] *v* inclinar. **be inclined to** inclinarse a. *n* pendiente *f*. **inclination** *n* *(tilt)* inclinación *f*; *(slope)* pendiente *f*; *(leaning)* tendencia *f*.

include [in'kluːd] *v* incluir; *(enclose in a letter)* adjuntar. **including** *adj* incluso. **inclusion** *n* inclusión *f*. **inclusive** *adj* inclusivo.

incognito [,inkog'niːtou] *adv* de incógnito.

incoherent [,inkə'hiərənt] *adj* incoherente. **incoherence** *n* incoherencia *f*. **incoherently** *adv* de modo incoherente.

income ['inkʌm] *n* ingresos *m pl*. **income tax** impuesto de utilidades *m*.

incomparable [in'kompərəbl] *adj* incomparable. **incomparably** *adv* incomparablemente.

incompatible [inkəm'patəbl] *adj* incompatible. **incompatibility** *n* incompatibilidad *f*.

incompetent [in'kompitənt] *adj* incompetente. **incompetence** *n* incompetencia *f*.

incomplete [,inkəm'pliːt] *adj* incompleto; sin terminar.

incomprehensible [in,kompri'hensəbl] *adj* incomprensible.

inconceivable [inkən'siːvəbl] *adj* inconcebible.

incongruous [in'kongruəs] *adj* incongruo; incompatible. **incongruity** *n* incongruidad *f*.

inconsiderate [,inkən'sidərit] *adj (thoughtless)* inconsiderado; *(lacking consideration for others)* desconsiderado.

inconsistent [,inkən'sistənt] *adj (substance)* inconsistente; *(actions, thoughts)* inconsecuente. **inconsistency** *n* inconsistencia *f*; inconsecuencia *f*.

incontinence [in'kontinəns] *n* incontinencia *f*. **incontinent** *adj* incontinente.

inconvenient [inkən'viːnjənt] *adj (place)* incómodo; *(time)* inoportuno. **inconvenience** *n* inconvenientes *m pl*, molestia *f*. *v* incomodar, molestar.

incorporate [in'kotpə,reit] *v* incorporar, incluir; *(contain)* contener; *(comm)* constituir en sociedad.

incorrect [inkə'rekt] *adj* incorrecto; erróneo.

increase [in'kriːs] *v* aumentar. *n* aumento *m*. **increasing** *adj* creciente. **increasingly** *adv* cada vez más.

incredible [in'kredəbl] *adj* increíble.

incredulous [in'kredjuləs] *adj* incrédulo. **incredulity** *n* incredulidad *f*.

increment ['inkrəmənt] *n* aumento *m*.

incriminate [in'krimineit] *v* incriminar. **incriminating** *adj* acriminador.

incubate ['inkju,beit] *v* incubar. **incubation** *n* incubación *f*. **incubator** *n* incubadora *f*.

incur [in'kəː] *v* incurrir; *(debt)* contraer; *(loss)* sufrir.

incurable [in'kjuərəbl] *adj* incurable.

indebted [in'detid] *adj (owing money)* endeudado (con); *(fig)* agradecido. **indebtedness** *n* deuda *f*; agradecimiento *m*.

indecent [in'diːsnt] *adj* indecente. **indecency** *n* indecencia *f*.

indeed [in'diːd] *adv* en efecto; realmente. **yes indeed!** ¡ya lo creo!

indefinite [in'definit] *adj* indefinido; impreciso.

indelible [in'deləbl] *adj* indeleble.

indemnity [in'demnəti] *n (security)* indemnidad *f*; reparación *f*.

indent [in'dent] *v (dent)* abollar; *(notch)* dentar; *(comm)* pedir; *(print)* sangrar. **indentation** *n (notch)* muesca *f*; *(print)* sangría *f*.

independent [,indi'pendənt] *adj* independiente. **independence** *n* independencia *f*.

index ['indeks] *n* índice *m*; *(math)* exponente *m*. **index finger** dedo índice *m*. **cost-of-living index** el índice del coste de la vida. *v (file)* clasificar; *(a book)* poner un índice a.

India ['indjə] *n* India *f*. **Indian** *n* indio, -a *m, f*; *(language)* indio *m*. *adj* indio. **Indian ink** tinta china *f*. **Indian summer** veranillo de San Martín *m*. **India paper** papel de China *m*. **India rubber** goma de borrar *f*.

indicate ['indikeit] *v* indicar, señalar. **indication** *n* indicación *f*, señal *f*. **indicative** *nm, adj* indicativo. **indicator** *n* indicador *m*.

indict [in'dait] v acusar. **indictment** n acusación f.

indifferent [in'difrənt] adj indiferente; insignificante; (mediocre) regular. **indifference** n indiferencia f.

indigenous [in'didʒinəs] adj indígena.

indigestion [,indi'dʒestʃən] n indigestión f. **indigestible** adj indigesto.

indignant [in'dignənt] adj indignado. **get indignant** indignarse. **indignantly** adv con indignación. **indignation** n indignación f.

indignity [in'dignəti] n (lack of dignity) indignidad f; (outrage) afrenta f.

indirect [,indi'rekt] adj indirecto.

indiscreet [,indi'skriːt] adj indiscreto. **indiscretion** n indiscreción f.

indiscriminate [,indi'skriminit] adj indistinto; universal; (person) sin criterio.

indispensable [,indi'spensəbl] adj indispensable.

indisposed [,indi'spouzd] adj (ill) indispuesto, enfermo; (reluctant) maldispuesto. **indisposition** n indisposición f; aversión f.

individual [,indi'vidjuəl] adj individual; personal. n individuo m. **individuality** n individualidad f.

indoctrinate [in'doktrineit] v adoctrinar. **indoctrination** n adoctrinamiento m.

indolent ['indələnt] adj indolente. **indolence** n indolencia f.

indoor ['indoː] adj interior. **indoor pool** piscina cubierta f. **indoors** adv dentro; en casa.

induce [in'djuːs] v (convince) inducir, persuadir; (cause) causar, provocar. **inducement** n incentivo m; (motive) móvil m.

indulge [in'dʌldʒ] v (pamper) mimar; (give way to) ceder a. **indulge in** entregarse a. **indulgence** n indulgencia f; satisfacción f; tolerancia f; (self-indulgence) desenfreno m. **indulgent** adj indulgente.

industry ['indəstri] n industria f; diligencia f. **industrial** adj industrial. **industrial relations** relaciones profesionales f pl. **industrialist** n industrial m. **industrialize** v industrializar. **industrious** adj trabajador.

inebriated [in'niːbrieitid] adj ebrio.

inedible [in'edibl] adj incomible.

inefficient [,ini'fiʃnt] adj ineficaz; incompetente. **inefficiency** n ineficacia f; incompetencia f.

inept [i'nept] adj inepto.

inequality [,ini'kwoləti] n desigualdad f; injusticia f.

inert [i'nəːt] adj inerte. **inertia** n inercia f.

inevitable [in'evitəbl] adj inevitable. **inevitability** n inevitabilidad f.

inexpensive [,inik'spensiv] adj poco costoso, barato.

inexperienced [,inik'spiəriənst] adj inexperto.

infallible [in'faləbl] adj infalible.

infamous ['infəməs] adj de mala fama; odioso. **infamy** n infamia f.

infancy ['infənsi] n infancia f, niñez f.

infant ['infənt] n niño, -a m, f. adj naciente. **infantile** adj infantil.

infantry ['infəntri] n infantería f.

infatuate [in'fatjueit] v be infatuated with (person) estar chiflado por; (idea) estar encaprichado por. **infatuation** n enamoramiento m.

infect [in'fekt] v infectar; contaminar. **infection** n infección f; contaminación f. **infectious** adj infeccioso; contagioso.

infer [in'fəː] v deducir. **inference** n deducción f.

inferior [in'fiəriə] nm, adj inferior. **inferiority** n inferioridad f. **inferiority complex** complejo de inferioridad m.

infernal [in'fəːnl] adj infernal; (coll) maldito.

infest [in'fest] v infestar. **infestation** n infestación f.

infidelity [,infi'deliti] n infidelidad f.

infiltrate [in'filtreit] v infiltrarse. **infiltration** n infiltración f.

infinite ['infinit] nm, adj infinito. **infinity** n infinidad f; (math) infinito m.

infinitive [in'finitiv] nm, adj infinitivo.

infirm [in'fəːm] adj débil. **infirmity** n debilidad f; (illness) enfermedad f. **infirmary** [in'fəːməri] n enfermería f; hospital m.

inflame [in'fleim] v (set on fire) inflamar; (passion) avivar; (anger) encender. **inflammable** adj inflamable. **inflammation** n inflamación f. **inflammatory** adj incendiario.

inflate [in'fleit] v hinchar; (prices) provocar la inflación de. **inflation** n (air) inflado m; (comm) inflación f. **inflationary** adj inflacionista.

inflection [in'flekʃən] n inflexión f.

inflict [in'flikt] v infligir, imponer. **infliction** n (punishment) castigo m.

influence ['influəns] *n* influencia *f.* **under the influence of** bajo los efectos de. *v* (*person*) influenciar; (*decision*) influir en. **influential** *adj* influyente.

influenza [‚influ'enzə] *n* gripe *f.*

influx ['inflʌks] *n* (*gas, etc.*) entrada *f;* (*people*) afluencia *f.*

inform [in'fɔːm] *v* informar. **informative** *adj* informativo. **informer** *n* denunciante *m, f.*

informal [in'fɔːml] *adj* sin ceremonia; (*person*) sencillo; (*tone*) familiar; (*unofficial*) no oficial. **informality** *n* ausencia de ceremonia *f;* sencillez *f.*

information [‚infə'meiʃən] *n* información *f.* **information bureau** centro de informaciones *m.* **information desk** informaciones *f pl.*

infra-red [‚infrə'red] *adj* infrarrojo.

infringe [in'frindʒ] *v* infringir, violar. **infringe on** usurpar. **infringement** *n* infracción *f;* usurpación *f.*

infuriate [in'fjuəri‚eit] *v* enfurecer; exasperar. **infuriating** *adj* exasperante.

ingenious [in'dʒiːnjəs] *adj* ingenioso. **ingenuity** *n* ingeniosidad *f.*

ingot ['ingət] *n* lingote *m.*

ingredient [in'griːdjənt] *n* ingrediente *m.*

inhabit [in'habit] *v* (*occupy*) habitar; (*live in*) vivir en. **inhabitant** *n* habitante *m.*

inhale [in'heil] *v* inhalar; (*smoke*) tragar.

inherent [in'hiərənt] *adj* inherente.

inherit [in'herit] *v* heredar. **inheritance** *n* herencia *f;* sucesión *f.*

inhibit [in'hibit] *v* (*restrain*) inhibir; (*prevent*) impedir. **inhibition** *n* inhibición *f.*

inhuman [in'hjuːmən] *adj* inhumano; insensible. **inhumanity** *n* inhumanidad *f.*

iniquity [i'nikwəti] *n* iniquidad *f.* **iniquitous** *adj* inicuo.

initial [i'niʃl] *adj* inicial, primero. *n* inicial *f;* (*used as abbreviation*) siglas *f pl.* *v* poner iniciales a. **initially** *adv* al principio.

initiate [i'niʃi‚eit] *v* iniciar; (*proceedings*) entablar; (*membership*) admitir. **initiation** *n* iniciación *f.*

initiative [i'niʃiətiv] *n* iniciativa *f.*

inject [in'dʒekt] *v* inyectar. **injection** *n* inyección *f.*

injure ['indʒə] *v* herir; lastimar; ofender. **injury** *n* herida *f;* daño *m;* ofensa *f.* **injurious** *adj* injurioso; ofensivo.

injustice [in'dʒʌstis] *n* injusticia *f.*

ink [ink] *n* tinta *f.* **ink-well** *n* tintero *m.* *v* entintar.

inkling ['inkliŋ] *n* idea *f;* algo *m;* sospecha *f;* indicio *m.*

inland ['inlənd; *adv* in'land] *adj* interior. **Inland Revenue** fisco *m.* *adv* hacia el interior.

in-laws ['in‚lɔːz] *pl n* (*coll*) familia política *f sing.*

*inlay [in'lei; *n* 'inlei] *v* incrustar; adornar con marquetería. *n* incrustación *f;* (*with coloured woods*) taracea *f.*

inlet ['inlet] *n* cala *f;* brazo de mar *m;* (*tech*) entrada *f.*

inmate ['inmeit] *n* (*prison*) preso *m;* (*asylum*) internado, -a *m, f;* (*hospital*) enfermo, -a *m, f.*

inn [in] *n* posada *f;* taberna *f.* **innkeeper** *n* posadero, -a *m, f;* tabernero, -a *m, f.*

innate [i'neit] *adj* innato.

inner ['inə] *adj* interior; íntimo. **inner tube** cámara de neumático *f.*

innocent ['inəsnt] *adj* inocente. **innocence** *n* inocencia *f.*

innocuous [i'nokjuəs] *adj* inocuo; inofensivo.

innovation [inə'veiʃən] *n* innovación *f.*

innuendo [‚inju'endou] *n* insinuación *f.*

innumerable [i'njuːmərəbl] *adj* innumerable.

inoculate [i'nokju‚leit] *v* inocular. **inoculation** *n* inoculación *f.*

inorganic [‚inɔː'ganik] *adj* inorgánico.

input ['input] *n* entrada *f;* (*computer*) input *m.*

inquest ['inkwest] *n* encuesta *f.*

inquire [in'kwaiə] *v* informarse de; preguntar. **inquire into** investigar. **inquiring** *adj* (*mind*) curioso; (*look*) inquisidor. **inquiry** *n* pregunta *f;* (*official*) investigación *f;* (*request for information*) petición de información *f.* **inquiry office** oficina de informaciones *f.* **inquiries** *pl n* (*sign*) información *f sing.*

inquisition [‚inkwi'ziʃən] *n* investigación *f.* **the Inquisition** la Inquisición *f.*

inquisitive [in'kwizətiv] *adj* preguntón; curioso. **inquisitiveness** *n* curiosidad *f.*

insane [in'sein] *adj* loco. **insane asylum** manicomio *m.* **insanity** *n* locura *f.*

insatiable [in'seiʃəbl] *adj* insaciable.

inscribe [in'skraib] *v* inscribir; (*engrave*) grabar. **inscription** *n* inscripción *f.*

insect ['insekt] *n* insecto *m;* (*coll*) bicho *m.* **insecticide** *n* insecticida *f.*

insecure [ˌinsiˈkjuə] *adj* inseguro; (*unstable*) inestable. **insecurity** *n* inseguridad *f.*

inseminate [inˈsemineit] *v* inseminar. **insemination** *n* inseminación *f.*

insensitive [inˈsensətiv] *adj* insensible. **insensitivity** *n* insensibilidad *f.*

inseparable [inˈsepərəbl] *adj* inseparable.

insert [inˈsəːt; *n* ˈinsəːt] *v* introducir; (*advert*) insertar; (*between pages*) intercalar. *n* (*in a book*) encarte *m.* **insertion** *n* inserción *f*; encarte *m*; (*advert*) anuncio *m.*

inshore [ˌinˈʃɔː] *adj* cercano a la orilla.

inside [ˌinˈsaid] *adv* dentro,· adentro. *prep* dentro de. *adj* interior; confidencial. *n* interior *m*; parte de adentro *f.* **inside out** al revés.

insidious [inˈsidiəs] *adj* insidioso. **insidiousness** *n* insidia *f.*

insight [ˈinsait] *n* perspicacia *f.*

insignificant [ˌinsigˈnifikənt] *adj* insignificante. **insignificance** *n* insignificancia *f.*

insincere [ˌinsinˈsiə] *adj* insincero; hipócrita. **insincerity** *n* insinceridad *f*; hipocresía *f.*

insinuate [inˈsinjueit] *v* insinuar. **insinuation** *n* insinuación *f.*

insipid [inˈsipid] *adj* insípido, soso.

insist [inˈsist] *v* insistir, empeñarse. **insistence** *n* insistencia *f*, empeño *m.* **insistent** *adj* insistente. **insistently** *adv* insistentemente.

insolent [ˈinsələnt] *adj* insolente. **insolence** *n* insolencia *f.*

insoluble [inˈsoljubl] *adj* insoluble.

insomnia [inˈsomniə] *n* insomnio *m.* **insomniac** *m(m+f)*, *adj* insomne.

inspect [inˈspekt] *v* inspeccionar, examinar. **inspection** *n* inspección *f*, examen *m.* **inspector** *n* inspector *m*, *f.*

inspire [inˈspaiə] *v* inspirar. **inspiration** *n* inspiración *f.* **inspirational** *adj* inspirador.

instability [ˌinstəˈbiləti] *n* inestabilidad *f*, instabilidad *f.*

install [inˈstɔːl] *v* instalar. **installation** *n* instalación *f.*

instalment [inˈstɔːlmənt] *n* (*payment*) plazo *m*; (*serial*) fascículo *m.* **monthly instalment** mensualidad *f.*

instance [ˈinstəns] *n* ejemplo *m.* **for instance** por ejemplo.

instant [ˈinstənt] *n* instante *m*, momento *m.* *adj* (*coffee, soup, etc.*) instantáneo; urgente; inmediato; inminente; (*this*

month) corriente. **instantaneous** *adj* instantáneo. **instantly** *adv* al instante.

instead [inˈsted] *adv* en su lugar. **instead of** en vez de.

instep [ˈinstep] *n* empeine *m.*

instigate [ˈinstigeit] *v* instigar, incitar; fomentar. **instigation** *n* instigación *f.* **instigator** *n* instigador, -a *m, f.*

instil [inˈstil] *v* instilar; inculcar.

instinct [ˈinstiŋkt] *n* instinto *m.* **instinctive** *adj* instintivo.

institute [ˈinstitjuːt] *n* instituto *m.* *v* instituir, establecer; (*start*) empezar. **institution** *n* institución *f*; establecimiento *m.*

instruct [inˈstrʌkt] *v* (*teach*) instruir; (*order*) mandar. **instruction** *n* instrucción *f.* **instructive** *adj* instructivo. **instructor** *n* instructor *m*; profesor *m*; maestro *m.*

instrument [ˈinstrəmənt] *n* instrumento *m.* **instrumental** *adj* instrumental. **be instrumental in** contribuir a.

insubordinate [ˌinsəˈbɔːdənət] *adj* insubordinado. **insubordination** *n* insubordinación *f.*

insufficient [ˌinsəˈfiʃənt] *adj* insuficiente. **insufficiency** *n* insuficiencia *f.*

insular [ˈinsjulə] *adj* insular; (*outlook*) estrecho de miras.

insulate [ˈinsjuleit] *v* aislar. **insulation** *n* aislamiento *m*; (*material*) aislador *m.*

insulin [ˈinsjulin] *n* insulina *f.*

insult [inˈsʌlt; *n* ˈinsʌlt] *v* insultar. *n* insulto *m.*

insure [inˈʃuə] *v* asegurar. **insurance** *n* seguro *m.* **insurance broker** corredor de seguros *m.* **insurance policy** póliza de seguro *f.* **fully comprehensive insurance** seguro a todo riesgo *m.* **third party insurance** seguro contra terceros *m.* **national insurance** seguros sociales *m pl.* **take out insurance** hacerse un seguro.

intact [inˈtakt] *adj* intacto.

intake [ˈinteik] *n* (*air, water*) toma *f*; (*mot*) entrada *f*; (*fuel, steam*) válvula de admisión *f*; (*food*) ración *f*; (*school*) número de personas admitidas *m*; (*thing taken in*) consumo *m.*

intangible [inˈtandʒəbl] *adj* intangible. **intangibility** *n* intangibilidad *f.*

integral [ˈintigrəl] *adj* (*part*) integrante; (*complete*) integral. *n* integral *f.*

integrate [ˈintigreit] *v* integrar. **integration** *n* integración *f.*

integrity [in'tegrəti] *n* integridad *f.*

intellect ['intilekt] *n* intelecto *m*, inteligencia *f.* **intellectual** *n*(*m*+*f*), *adj* intelectual.

intelligent [in'telidʒənt] *adj* inteligente. **intelligence** *n* inteligencia *f*; (*information*) noticia *f*; (*secret information*) información *f.*

intelligible [in'telidʒəbl] *adj* inteligible.

intend [in'tend] *v* proponerse.

intense [in'tens] *adj* intenso; fuerte; profundo; ardiente; enorme. **intensify** *v* intensificar; aumentar. **intensity** *n* intensidad *f.* **intensive** *adj* intensivo. **intensive care** asistencia intensiva *f.*

intent[1] [in'tent] *n* intención *f.* propósito *m.*

intent[2] [in'tent] *adj* atento; profundo; constante.

intention [in'tenʃən] *n* intención *f.* **intentional** *adj* intencional.

inter [in'tɔː] *v* enterrar. **interment** *n* entierro *m.*

interact [,intər'akt] *v* actuar recíprocamente. **interaction** *n* interacción *f.*

intercede [,intə'siːd] *v* interceder. **intercession** *n* intercesión *f.*

intercept [,intə'sept] *v* (*message*) interceptar; (*stop someone*) parar. **interception** *n* intercepción *f*, interceptación *f.*

interchange [,intə'tʃeindʒ] *n* intercambio *m*; cambio *m.* **interchangeable** *adj* intercambiable.

intercom ['intəkom] *n* interfono *m.*

intercourse ['intəkɔːs] *n* (*social*) trato *m*; (*pol, comm*) relaciones *f pl*; (*sexual*) contacto sexual *m.*

interest ['intrist] *n* interés *m*; (*advantage*) beneficio *m.* **business interests** negocios *m pl.* *v* interesar. **be interested** interesarse en.

interfere [,intə'fiə] *v* entrometerse. **interfere with** (*hinder*) estorbar; (*touch*) tocar; (*interests*) oponerse a. **interference** *n* intromisión *f*; obstrucción *f*; (*radio*) parásitos *m pl.* **interfering** *adj* (*person*) entrometido; interferente.

interim ['intərim] *n* interín *m.* *adj* provisional.

interior [in'tiəriə] *nm*, *adj* interior.

interjection [,intə'dʒekʃən] *n* interjección *f.*

interlude ['intəluːd] *n* intervalo *m*; (*theatre*) entremés *m*; (*music*) interludio *m.*

intermediate [,intə'miːdiət] *adj* intermedio. **intermediary** *n* intermediario, -a *m, f.*

interminable [in'təːminəbl] *adj* interminable.

intermission [,intə'miʃən] *n* (*interruption*) intermisión *f*; (*theatre*) entreacto *m*; (*cinema*) descanso *m.*

intermittent [,intə'mitənt] *adj* intermitente. **intermittently** *adv* a intervalos.

intern [in'tɔːn] *n* interno *m.* *v* internar. **internment** *n* internamiento *m.*

internal [in'tɔːnl] *adj* interno. **internal combustion engine** motor de combustión interna *m.*

international [,intə'naʃənl] *adj* internacional. **international date line** línea de cambio de fecha *f.*

interpose [,intə'pouz] *v* interponer; intervenir. **interposition** *n* interposición *f.*

interpret [in'təːprit] *v* interpretar. **interpretation** *n* interpretación *f.* **interpreter** *n* intérprete *m, f.*

interrogate [in'terəgeit] *v* interrogar. **interrogation** *n* interrogatorio *m.* **interrogator** *n* interrogador, -a *m, f.*

interrogative [,intə'rogətiv] *adj* (*sentence*) interrogativo; (*look*) interrogador. *n* palabra interrogativa *f.*

interrupt [,intə'rapt] *v* interrumpir. **interruption** *n* interrupción *f.*

intersect [,intə'sekt] *v* cruzar; (*math*) cortar. **intersection** *n* (*mot*) cruce *m*; (*math*) intersección *f.*

intersperse [,intə'spəːs] *v* esparcir.

interval ['intəvəl] *n* (*time, space, music*) intervalo *m*; (*theatre*) entreacto *m*; (*cinema*) descanso *m.*

intervene [,intə'viːn] *v* intervenir; (*happen*) ocurrir; (*time*) transcurrir; (*distance*) mediar. **intervention** *n* intervención *f.*

interview ['intəvjuː] *n* entrevista *f*, interviú *f.* *v* entrevistar. **interviewer** *n* entrevistador, -a *m, f.*

intestine [in'testin] *n* intestino *m.* **intestinal** *adj* intestinal.

intimate[1] ['intimət] *adj* íntimo; (*individual*) personal; (*loving*) amoroso; (*detailed*) profundo. **intimacy** *n* relaciones íntimas *f pl.*

intimate[2] ['intimeit] *v* insinuar; anunciar. **intimation** *n* insinuación *f*; indicación *f*; indicio *m.*

intimidate [in'timideit] v intimidar. **intimidation** n intimidación f.

into ['intu] prep en; a; hacia; contra; dentro.

intolerable [in'tolərəbl] adj intolerable.

intolerant [in'tolərənt] adj intolerante. **intolerance** n intolerancia f.

intonation [,intə'neiʃən] n entonación f. **intone** v entonar.

intoxicate [in'toksikeit] v embriagar, emborrachar. **intoxicated** adj borracho, ebrio. **intoxication** n embriaguez f, borrachera f.

intransitive [in'transitiv] nm, adj intransitivo.

intravenous [,intrə'vinəs] adj intravenoso.

intrepid [in'trepid] adj intrépido.

intricate [in'trikət] adj intrincado; complejo. **intricacy** n intrincamiento m; complejidad f.

intrigue ['intrig; v in'trig] n intriga f. v intrigar.

intrinsic [in'trinsik] adj intrínseco.

introduce [,intrə'djuːs] v presentar; introducir; (acquaint) iniciar. **introduction** n presentación f; introducción f. **introductory** adj introductorio.

introspective [,intrə'spektiv] adj introspectivo. **introspection** n introspección f.

introvert ['intrə,vɜːt] n introvertido, -a m, f. **introverted** adj introvertido.

intrude [in'truːd] v imponer; meter por fuerza. **intruder** n intruso, -a m, f. **intrusion** n entremetimiento m.

intuition [,intju'iʃən] n intuición f. **intuitive** adj intuitivo.

inundate ['inʌndeit] v inundar. **inundation** n inundación f.

invade [in'veid] v invadir. **invader** n invasor, -a m, f. **invasion** n invasión f.

invalid¹ [in'vælid] nm, adj (disabled) inválido; (sick) enfermo.

invalid² [in'vælid] adj (not valid) nulo.

invaluable [in'væljuəbl] adj inestimable.

invariable [in'veəriəbl] adj invariable. **invariably** adv invariablemente; constantemente.

invective [in'vektiv] n invectiva f.

invent [in'vent] v inventar. **invention** n invención f. **inventive** adj inventivo. **inventor** n inventor, -a m, f.

inventory ['inventri] n inventario m.

invert [in'vɜːt] v invertir. **inverted commas** comillas f pl. **inversion** n inversión f.

invertebrate [in'vɜːtibrət] nm, adj invertebrado.

invest [in'vest] v invertir; (install) investir. **invest in** (fig) comprarse. **invest with** (fig) envolver en. **investment** n inversión f. **investor** n inversionista m, f.

investigate [in'vestigeit] v investigar, examinar; estudiar. **investigation** n investigación f; estudio m.

invigorating [in'vigəreitiŋ] adj tónico, estimulante. **invigorate** v vigorizar, estimular.

invincible [in'vinsəbl] adj invencible.

invisible [in'vizəbl] adj invisible. **invisibility** n invisibilidad f.

invite [in'vait] v invitar, convidar; (questions) solicitar; (ask for) pedir; (cause) provocar. **invitation** n invitación f. **inviting** adj atractivo; seductor; tentador; apetitoso.

invoice ['invois] n factura f. v facturar.

invoke [in'vouk] v invocar; (ask for) pedir; (fall back on) recurrir. **invocation** n invocación f.

involuntary [in'voləntəri] adj involuntario. **involuntarily** adv sin querer.

involve [in'volv] v (concern) concernir; (imply) suponer; (affect) afectar; (entail) ocasionar; (draw somebody in) comprometer; mezclar; (require) exigir; (complicate) complicar. **involved** adj complicado. **involvement** n envolvimiento m; participación f; compromiso m.

inward ['inwəd] adj interior, interno; (thoughts) íntimo. **inwardly** adv interiormente. **inwards** adv hacia dentro.

iodine ['aiədiːn] n yodo m.

ion ['aiən] n ion m.

irate [ai'reit] adj furioso.

Ireland ['aiələnd] n Irlanda f. **Irish** nm, adj irlandés. **the Irish** los irlandeses m pl.

iris ['aiəris] n lirio m.

irk [ɜːk] v molestar. **irksome** adj molesto.

iron ['aiən] n (metal) hierro m; (for pressing) plancha f. (golf) palo de golf m. **cast iron** hierro colado m. **Iron Curtain** telón de acero m. **wrought iron** hierro forjado m. **ironmonger's** n quincallería f. v planchar. **iron out** (fig) allanar. **ironing** n planchado m. **ironing board** tabla de planchar.

irony ['aiərəni] n ironía f. **ironic** adj irónico.

irrational [i'raʃənl] adj irracional. n (math) número irracional m.

irregular [i'regjulə] *adj* irregular. **irregularity** *n* irregularidad *f*.

irrelevant [i'reləvənt] *adj* (*remark*) fuera de propósito; (*beside the point*) no pertinente.

irreparable [i'repərəbl] *adj* irreparable.

irresistible [,iri'zistəbl] *adj* irresistible.

irrespective [,iri'spektiv] *adj* **irrespective of** sin tener en cuenta.

irresponsible [,iri'sponsəbl] *adj* irresponsable; irreflexivo.

irrevocable [i'revəkəbl] *adj* irrevocable.

irrigate ['irigeit] *v* irrigar. **irrigation** *n* irrigación *f*.

irritate ['iriteit] *v* irritar. **irritable** *adj* irritable. **irritation** *n* irritación *f*.

is [iz] *V* be.

island ['ailənd] *n* isla; (*traffic*) refugio *m*.

isolate ['aisəleit] *v* aislar. **isolation** *n* aislamiento *m*.

issue ['iʃu] *n* (*stamps, shares, etc.*) emisión *f*; (*publication*) publicación *f*; (*edition*) tirada *f*; (*copy*) número *m*; (*passport*) expedición *f*; (*distribution*) reparto *m*; (*outcome*) resultado *m*; (*question*) cuestión *f*; (*affair*) asunto *m*; (*offspring*) progenie *f*. **take issue with** estar en desacuerdo con. *v* salir; resultar; publicar; distribuir; (*give*) dar; emitir; (*decree*) promulgar; (*warrant, cheque*) extender; (*tickets*) expender; (*licence*) facilitar.

isthmus ['isməs] *n* istmo *m*.

it [it] *pron* él, ella ello; (*direct object*) lo, la; (*indirect object*) le.

italic [i'talik] *adj* itálico. **italics** *pl n* bastardilla *f sing*.

Italy ['itəli] *n* Italia *f*. **Italian** *n, adj* italiano, -a.

itch [itʃ] *n* picazón *f*; (*desire*) ganas *f pl. v* picar.

item ['aitəm] *n* artículo *m*; noticia *f*; detalle *m*; punto *m*. **itemize** *v* detallar.

itinerary [ai'tinərəri] *n* itinerario *m*.

its [its] *adj* su (*pl* sus).

itself [it'self] *pron* se; él/ello mismo, ella misma; (*after prep*) sí mismo, -a. **by itself** aislado; (*alone*) solo.

ivory ['aivəri] *n* marfil *m*.

ivy ['aivi] *n* hiedra *f*, yedra *f*.

J

jab [dʒab] *v* (*stab*) pinchar; (*elbow*) dar un codazo a. *n* pinchazo *m*; codazo *m*; (*blow*) golpe seco *m*; (*coll: injection*) inyección *f*.

jack [dʒak] *n* (*mot*) gato *m*; (*cards*) valet *m*, jota *f*; (*Spanish cards*) sota *f*. *v* **jack up** levantar con el gato.

jackal ['dʒakotl] *n* chacal *m*.

jackdaw ['dʒakdɔt] *n* grajilla *f*.

jacket ['dʒakit] *n* chaqueta *f*; (*book*) sobrecubierta *f*; (*tech: cylinder, pipe, etc.*) camisa *f*.

jackpot ['dʒakpot] *n* premio gordo *m*.

jade [dʒeid] *nm, adj* jade *m*.

jaded ['dʒeidid] *adj* cansado.

jagged ['dʒagid] *adj* dentado.

jaguar ['dʒagjuə] *n* jaguar *m*.

jail [dʒeil] *n* cárcel *f*. *v* encarcelar. **jailer** *n* carcelero *m*.

jam[1] [dʒam] *v* (*force in*) meter a la fuerza; (*squash*) apretar; (*catch*) pillar; (*pack*) atestar; (*clog*) atorar; (*block*) bloquear; (*moving part*) atascar; (*radio*) interferir; (*become wedged*) atrancarse. *n* atasco *m*; (*people*) aglomeración *f*; (*traffic*) embotellamiento *m*. **be in a jam** (*coll*) estar en un apuro.

jam[2] [dʒam] *n* mermelada *f*.

janitor ['dʒanitə] *n* portero *m*.

January ['dʒanjuəri] *n* enero *m*.

Japan [dʒə'pan] *n* Japón *m*. **Japanese** *nm, adj* japonés.

jar[1] [dʒɑt] *n* (*vessel*) vasija *f*; (*jam pot*) tarro *m*; (*large pot*) tinaja *f*.

jar[2] [dʒɑt] *v* (*sound*) chirriar; (*shake*) sacudir; (*colours*) chocar; (*music*) sonar mal; (*nerves*) irritar.

jargon ['dʒɑɪgən] *n* jerga *f*.

jasmine ['dʒazmin] *n* jazmín *m*.

jaundice ['dʒɔɪndis] *n* icterícia *f*; (*fig*) celos *m pl*.

jaunt [dʒɔɪnt] *n* paseo *m*.

jaunty ['dʒɔɪnti] *adj* vivaz; desenvuelto.

javelin ['dʒavəlin] *n* jabalina *f*.

jaw [dʒɔɪ] *n* (*person*) mandíbula *f*; (*animal*) quijada *f*. **jawbone** *n* mandíbula *f*; quijada *f*.

jazz [dʒaz] *n* jazz *m*. **jazz band** orquesta de jazz *f*.

jealous ['dʒeləs] *adj* celoso; envidioso. **jealousy** *n* celos *m pl*; envidia *f*.

jeans [dʒiːns] *pl n* pantalones vaqueros *m pl.*

jeep [dʒiːp] *n* jeep *m.*

jeer [dʒiə] *v* (*boo*) abuchear; (*mock*) mofarse de. *n* abucheo *m;* mofa *f.*

jelly [dʒeli] *n* jalea *f.* **jellyfish** *n* medusa *f.*

jeopardize [dʒepədaiz] *v* arriesgar. **jeopardy** *n* riesgo *m,* peligro *m.*

jerk [dʒəːk] *n* sacudida *f;* (*shove*) empujón *m;* (*pull*) tirón. *v* sacudir; mover a tirones. **jerkily** *adv* con sacudidas. **jerky** *adj* espasmódico.

jersey [dʒəːzi] *n* jersey *m.*

jest [dʒest] *v* bromear. *n* broma *f.* **jester** *n* bromista *m, f.*

jet [dʒet] *n* (*liquid*) chorro *m;* (*flame*) llama *f;* (*plane*) avión de reactor *m.* **jet-propelled** *adj* de reacción.

jetty [dʒeti] *n* muelle *m.*

Jew [dʒuː] *n* judío, -a *m, f.* **Jewish** *adj* judío.

jewel [dʒuːəl] *n* joya *f;* piedra preciosa *f;* (*in a watch*) rubí *m.* **jeweller** *n* joyero *m.* **jeweller's** *n* joyería *f.* **jewellery** *n* joyería *f.*

jig [dʒig] *n* giga *f. v* bailar la giga; dar saltitos.

jigsaw [dʒigsɔː] *n* (*puzzle*) rompecabezas *m invar;* (*saw*) sierra de vaivén *f.*

jilt [dʒilt] *v* dejar plantado a.

jingle [dʒiŋgl] *n* tintineo *m;* (*verse*) copla *f. v* tintinear.

jinx [dʒiŋks] *n* (*coll*) maleficio *m.* **put a jinx on** echar mal de ojo a.

job [dʒɔb] *n* trabajo *m,* empleo *m.* **job lot** colección miscelánea *f.* **make a good job of** (*something*) hacer (algo) bien. **odd-job man** factótum *m.*

jockey [dʒɔki] *n* jinete *m;* jockey *m.*

jocular [dʒɔkjulə] *adj* jocoso; bromista.

jodhpurs [dʒɔdpəz] *pl n* pantalones de montar *m pl.*

jog [dʒɔg] *n* sacudida *f;* (*with elbow*) codazo *m.* **jogtrot** *n* trote corto *m. v* sacudir; (*memory*) refrescar. **jog someone's elbow** darle en el codo a uno. **jogging** *n* jogging *m.*

join [dʒɔin] *v* juntar, unir; (*roads*) ir a dar a; (*friends*) reunirse con; (*a company*) ingresar en; (*a club*) hacerse socio de; (*a political party*) afiliarse a; (*hands*) darse la mano; (*two pieces*) ensamblar; (*rivers*) confluir. **join in** participar en. **join up** (*mil*) alistarse. **joiner** carpintero *m.*

joint [dʒɔint] *n* juntura *f,* unión *f;* (*anat*) articulación *f;* (*meat*) corte para asar; (*slang: place*) antro *m. adj* unido; colectivo; conjunto; mutuo. **jointly** *adv* en común.

joist [dʒɔist] *n* vigueta *f.*

joke [dʒouk] *n* chiste *m;* (*prank*) broma *f. v* contar chistes; bromear. **joker** *n* chistoso, -a *m, f;* bromista *m, f;* (*fool*) payaso, -a *m, f;* (*cards*) comodín *m.*

jolly [dʒɔli] *adj* alegre, jovial; divertido. *adv* (*coll: emphatic*) muy. **jollity** *n* alegría *f,* jovialidad *f.*

jolt [dʒoult] *v* sacudir; (*vehicle*) traquetear. *n* sacudida *f;* choque *m;* (*fig: shock*) susto *m.*

jostle [dʒɔsl] *v* (*push*) empujar; (*elbow*) codear. *n* empujones *m pl.*

jot [dʒɔt] *n* jota *f. v* **jot down** apuntar.

journal [dʒəːnl] *n* (*newspaper*) periódico *m;* (*magazine*) revista *f;* (*diary*) diario *m;* (*of a learned society*) boletín *m.* **journalism** *n* periodismo *m.* **journalist** *n* periodista *m, f.*

journey [dʒəːni] *n* viaje *m. v* viajar.

jovial [dʒouviəl] *adj* jovial. **joviality** *n* jovialidad *f.*

joy [dʒɔi] *n* alegría *f;* placer *m.* **joyful** *or* **joyous** *adj* alegre, gozoso.

jubilant [dʒuːbilənt] *adj* jubiloso. **jubilation** *n* júbilo *m.*

jubilee [dʒuːbiliː] *n* jubileo *m.*

Judaism [dʒuːdeiizəm] *n* judaísmo *m.*

judge [dʒʌdʒ] *n* juez *m;* árbitro *m. v* juzgar; arbitrar. **judging by** a juzgar por. **judgement** *n* (*trial*) juicio; (*legal sentence*) sentencia *f;* apreciación *f.*

judicial [dʒuːdiʃəl] *adj* judicial.

judicious [dʒuːdiʃəs] *adj* juicioso.

judo [dʒuːdou] *n* judo *m.*

jug [dʒʌg] *n* jarra *f;* (*slang: prison*) chirona *f.*

juggernaut [dʒʌgənɔːt] *n* camión grande *m.*

juggle [dʒʌgl] *v* hacer juegos malabares. **juggler** *n* malabarista *m, f.* **juggling** *n* juegos malabares *m pl.*

jugular [dʒʌgjulə] *adj* yugular.

juice [dʒuːs] *n* jugo *m.* **juicy** *adj* jugoso.

jukebox [dʒuːkbɔks] *n* máquina de discos *f.*

July [dʒuˈlai] *n* julio *m.*

jumble [dʒʌmbl] *v* embrollar; mezclar. *n* embrollo *m;* mezcolanza *f.* **jumble sale** venta de caridad *f.*

jump [dʒʌmp] n salto m. v saltar. **jump at** (offer, etc.) aprovechar. **make someone jump** sobresaltar a uno. **jumpy** adj (coll) nervioso.

jumper ['dʒʌmpə] n (garment) jersey m.

junction ['dʒʌŋkʃən] n (join) unión f; (rail) empalme m; (road) cruce f.

juncture ['dʒʌŋkʃə] n coyuntura f. **at this juncture** en esta coyuntura.

June [dʒuːn] n junio m.

jungle ['dʒʌŋgl] n selva f.

junior ['dʒuːnjə] adj (younger) hijo; (lower rank) subalterno. n menor m, f; subalterno, -a m, f; (in school) pequeño, -a m, f.

juniper ['dʒuːnipə] n enebro m. **juniper berry** enebrina f.

junk[1] [dʒʌŋk] n trastos viejos m pl; (coll: rubbish) porquería f. **junk-shop** n baratillo m.

junk[2] [dʒʌŋk] n (naut) junco m.

jurisdiction [dʒuəris'dikʃən] n jurisdicción f.

jury ['dʒuəri] n jurado m. **juror** n jurado, -a m, f.

just [dʒʌst] adv justo; justamente; precisamente. **have just** acabar de. adj justo; exacto.

justice ['dʒʌstis] n justicia f. **Justice of the Peace** juez de paz m.

justify ['dʒʌstifai] v justificar. **justifiable** adj justificable. **justification** n justificación f.

jut [dʒʌt] v **jut out** sobresalir.

jute [dʒuːt] n yute m.

juvenile ['dʒuːvənail] n joven m, f. adolescente m, f; menor m, f. adj juvenil; infantil. **juvenile delinquent** delincuente juvenil m, f.

juxtapose [dʒʌkstə'pouz] v yuxtaponer. **juxtaposition** n yuxtaposición f.

K

kaftan ['kaftan] n caftán m.

kaleidoscope [kə'laidəskoup] n calidoscopio m.

kangaroo [kaŋgə'ruː] n canguro m.

karate [kə'rɑːti] n karate m.

kebab [ki'bab] n pincho m.

keel [kiːl] n quilla f. **keel over** (naut) zozobrar; (coll: faint) desplomarse.

keen [kiːn] adj entusiasta; fuerte; vivo; penetrante; (prices) competitivo; (mind) agudo; (sharp) afilado. **keenly** adv con entusiasmo; profundamente. **keenness** n entusiasmo m; deseo m; profundidad f; agudeza f; finura f.

*keep [kiːp] v guardar; tener. (promise) cumplir; (appointment) acudir a; (hang on to) quedarse; (support) mantener; (hold) reservar; (detain) detener; (look after) cuidar; (continue) seguir. **keep at** seguir con. **keep away** mantener a distancia. **keep down** contener. **keep fit** mantenerse en forma. **keep out!** ¡prohibida la entrada! **keep up with** seguir. **keeper** n guarda m.

keg [keg] n barril m.

kennel ['kenl] n perrera f.

kerb [kəːb] n bordillo m.

kernel ['kəːnl] n (nut) pepita f; (seed) grano.

kerosene ['kerəsiːn] n queroseno m.

ketchup ['ketʃəp] n salsa de tomate f.

kettle ['ketl] n hervidor m. **kettledrum** n timbal m.

key [kiː] n llave f; (for a code) clave f; (music) tono m; (piano, typewriter) tecla f. **keyboard** n teclado m. **keyhole** n ojo de la cerradura m. **key-ring** n llavero m. adj clave.

khaki ['kɑːki] nm, adj caqui.

kick [kik] n patada f, puntapié m; (animal) coz f; (recoil) culatazo m; (fig: energy) fuerza f. v dar una patada a; dar una coza. **kick off** (football) hacer el saque del centro; (fig) comenzar. **kick-off** n saque del centro m; (coll) comienzo m. **kick out** (coll) poner de patitas en la calle.

kid[1] [kid] n (goat) cabrito m; (leather) cabritilla f; (coll: child) niño, -a m, f.

kid[2] [kid] v (coll) tomar el pelo.

kidnap ['kidnap] v secuestrar, raptar. **kidnapper** n secuestrador, -a m, f. raptor, -ora m, f. **kidnapping** n secuestro m, rapto m.

kidney ['kidni] n riñón m.

kill [kil] v matar; (fig: hopes) arruinar. n muerte f; caza f. **killjoy** n aguafiestas m, f invar. **killer** n asesino, -a m, f. **killing** n (murder) asesinato m; (slaughter) matanza f.

kiln [kiln] n horno m.

kilo ['kiːləu] n kilo m.

kilogram ['kiləgræm] n kilogramo m.

kilometre ['kiləmiːtə] n kilómetro m.

kin [kin] n parientes m pl. **kinship** n parentesco m.

kind[1] [kaind] adj amable; bueno. **kind-hearted** adj bondadoso. **kindness** n amabilidad f; bondad f.

kind[2] [kaind] n clase f, tipo m; género m; especie f. **in kind** en especie.

kindergarten ['kindəgɑːtn] n jardín de la infancia m.

kindle ['kindl] v encender; despertar.

kindred ['kindrid] n parientes m pl. adj (related) emparentado; (similar) semejante. **kindred spirits** almas gemelas f pl.

kinetic [kin'etik] adj cinético.

king [kiŋ] n rey m; (draughts) dama f. **kingfisher** n martín pescador m. **kingdom** n reino m. **king-size** adj enorme, gigante.

kink [kiŋk] n (rope) retorcimiento m; (hair) rizo m. v retorcer. **kinky** adj retorcido; (coll) extraño.

kiosk ['kiɒsk] n quiosko m, kiosko m.

kipper ['kipə] n arenque ahumado m.

kiss [kis] v besar. n beso m. **kiss of life** respiración boca a boca f.

kit [kit] n (tools) herramientas f pl; (sport) equipo m; (first aid) botiquín m; (model for assembling) maqueta f. **kit out** equipar.

kitchen ['kitʃin] n cocina f. **kitchen sink** fregadero m.

kite [kait] n cometa f; (bird) milano m.

kitten ['kitn] n gatito m.

kitty ['kiti] n plato m, platillo m.

kleptomania [kleptə'meiniə] n cleptomanía f. **kleptomaniac** n(m+f), adj cleptómano.

knack [nak] n facilidad f; tino m; habilidad f. **get the knack of** coger el tino de.

knapsack ['napsak] n mochila f.

knead [niːd] v amasar.

knee [niː] n rodilla f. **kneecap** n rótula f. ***kneel** [niːl] v arrodillarse.

knew [njuː] V know.

knickers ['nikəz] pl n bragas f pl.

knife [naif] n cuchillo m. v (stab) apuñalar.

knight [nait] n caballero m. v armar caballero. **knighthood** n título de caballero m.

knit [nit] v tejer. **knit together** juntar;

(bones) soldarse. **knitting** n tejido de punto m. **knitting machine** máquina de hacer punto f. **knitting needle** aguja de hacer punto f.

knob [nob] n bulto m; (door) pomo m; (radio, etc.) botón m; (drawer) tirador m; (butter) pedazo m.

knobbly ['nobli] adj nudoso.

knock [nok] n golpe m, toque m. v golpear, pegar; (fig: criticize) meterse con. **knock down** (price) rebajar; (person) atropellar; (object) derribar. **knock-kneed** adj patizambo. **knock out** (stun) dejar K.O.; (from contest) eliminar. **knockout** n (boxing) knock out m, K.O. m. **knock over** tirar. **knocker** n aldaba f, aldabón m.

knot [not] n nudo m. v anudar. **knotty** (problem) espinoso.

***know** [nou] v (facts) saber; (people, places) conocer; (recognize) reconocer; (distinguish) distinguir. **know-all** n (coll) sabelotodo m, f. **know-how** n (coll) habilidad f; conocimientos m pl. **knowing** adj astuto; (look) de entendimiento.

knowledge ['nolidʒ] n conocimiento m. **knowledgeable** adj entendido; erudito.

knuckle ['nʌkl] n nudillo m. **knuckle down to** ponerse seriamente a. **knuckle under** someterse.

L

label ['leibl] n etiqueta f. v poner etiqueta a.

laboratory [lə'borətəri] n laboratorio m.

labour ['leibə] n (work) trabajo m; (task) tarea f; (effort) esfuerzo m; (childbirth) parto m; (manpower) trabajadores m pl. **labour-saving** adj que ahorra trabajo. v trabajar; esforzarse. **laborious** adj laborioso. **labourer** n obrero m; peón m.

labyrinth ['labərinθ] n laberinto m.

lace [leis] n (fabric) encaje m. (shoe) cordón m. v atar; (drink) rociar.

lacerate ['lasəreit] v lacerar. **laceration** n laceración f.

lack [lak] n falta f, carencia f. **for lack of** por falta de. v carecer de, faltar a; necesitar.

lackadaisical [ˌlakəˈdeizikəl] *adj* apático; descuidado; tardo.

lacquer [ˈlakə] *n* (*hair*) laca *f*; (*paint*) pintura al duco *f*. *v* echar laca a; pintar al duco.

lad [lad] *n* (*coll*) chico *m*, muchacho *m*.

ladder [ˈladə] *n* escalera de mano *f*; (*stocking*) carrera *f*. **ladderproof** *adj* indesmallable.

laden [leidn] *adj* cargado.

ladle [ˈleidl] *n* cucharón *m*.

lady [ˈleidi] *n* señora *f*. **ladies** (*sign*) servicios de señoras *m pl*. **ladies and gentlemen!** ¡señoras y señores! **ladybird** *n* mariquita *f*. **lady-in-waiting** *n* dama de honor *f*. **ladylike** *adj* distinguida.

lag¹ [lag] *v* (*be behind time*) retrasarse; (*trail*) quedarse atrás. *n* intervalo *m*; (*delay*) retraso *m*.

lag² [lag] *v* poner un revestimiento calorífugo a. **lagging** *n* revestimiento calorífugo *m*.

lager [ˈlaigə] *n* cerveza dorada *f*.

lagoon [ləˈguːn] *n* laguna *f*.

laid [leid] *V* **lay¹**.

lain [lein] *V* **lie¹**.

lair [leə] *n* guarida *f*.

laity [ˈleiəti] *n* laicado *m*.

lake [leik] *n* lago *m*.

lamb [lam] *n* cordero *m*. **lamb chop** chuleta de cordero *f*.

lame [leim] *adj* cojo; (*excuse, etc.*) malo. **lame duck** incapaz *m, f*. *v* dejar cojo. **lamely** *adv* cojeando. **lameness** *n* cojera *f*; debilidad *f*.

lament [ləˈment] *n* lamento *m*. *v* lamentar, llorar. **lamentable** *adj* lamentable. **lamentation** *n* lamentación *f*.

laminate [ˈlamineit] *v* laminar. **laminated** *adj* laminado.

lamp [lamp] *n* lámpara *f*; (*street*) farol *m*; (*mot*) faro *m*. **lamppost** *n* poste de alumbrado *m*. **lampshade** *n* pantalla *f*.

lance [laɪns] *n* lanza *f*. *v* (*med*) abrir.

land [land] *n* tierra *f*; (*country*) país *m*. **landlady** *n* patrona *f*, dueña *f*. **landlord** *n* patrón *m*, dueño *m*. **landmark** *n* señal *f*. **landscape** *n* paisaje *m*. *v* desembarcar; (*aircraft*) aterrizar; (*fall*) caer; (*arrive*) llegar. **landing** *n* (*passengers*) desembarco *m*; (*cargo*) desembarque *m*; aterrizaje *m*. (*staircase*) rellano *m*. **landing stage** desembarcadero *m*.

lane [lein] *n* camino *m*; (*motorway*) banda *f*; (*running, swimming*) calle *f*.

language [ˈlaŋgwidʒ] *n* (*means of expression*) lenguaje *m*; (*of a nation*) lengua *f*. **bad** *or* **foul language** palabrotas *f pl*.

languish [ˈlaŋgwiʃ] *v* languidecer.

lanky [ˈlaŋki] *adj* larguirucho.

lantern [ˈlantən] *n* farol *m*, linterna *f*.

lap¹ [lap] *n* (*sport*) vuelta *f*. *v* dar una vuelta; (*fold*) doblar; (*wrap*) envolver.

lap² [lap] *v* (*drink*) chapotear; beber a lengüetadas.

lap³ [lap] *n* rodillas *f pl*.

lapel [ləˈpel] *n* solapa *f*.

lapse [laps] *n* (*time*) lapso *m*; (*failure*) fallo *m*; (*moral error*) desliz *m*; (*fall*) caída *f*. *v* (*time*) transcurrir; cometer un desliz; caer.

larceny [ˈlaɪsəni] *n* ratería *f*.

larch [laɪtʃ] *n* alerce *m*.

lard [laɪd] *n* manteca de cerdo *f*.

larder [ˈlaɪdə] *n* despensa *f*.

large [laɪdʒ] *adj* grande, amplio. **at large** libre. **large-scale** *adj* en gran escala. **largely** *adv* en gran parte.

lark¹ [laɪk] *n* (*zool*) alondra *f*.

lark² [laɪk] (*coll*) *n* juerga *f*; (*joke*) broma *f*. **lark about** hacer el tonto.

larva [ˈlaɪvə] *n, pl* **larvae** larva *f*.

larynx [ˈlaɪriŋks] *n* laringe *f*. **laryngitis** *n* laringitis *f*.

laser [ˈleizə] *n* láser *m*.

lash [laʃ] *n* (*whip*) azote *m*; (*tail*) coletazo *m*; (*waves*) embate *m*; (*eyelash*) pestaña *f*. *v* azotar; (*wind*) sacudir; (*bind*) atar. **lash out** repartir golpes a diestro y siniestro; (*coll: money*) gastar. **lashing** *n* flagelación *f*; **lashings** *pl n* (*coll*) montones *m pl*.

lass [las] *n* chica *f*, muchacha *f*.

lassitude [ˈlasitjuːd] *n* lasitud *f*.

lasso [laˈsuː] *n* lazo *m*. *v* coger con el lazo.

last [laɪst] *adj* último. **last-minute** *adj* de última hora. **last night** anoche. *adv* el último, la última, lo último; por última vez; finalmente. *n* último. -a *m, f*; final *m*. **at least** por fin. **lastly** *adv* por último. *v* durar; permanecer; aguantar. **last out** resistir. **lasting** *adj* duradero.

latch [latʃ] *n* picaporte *m*. *v* cerrar.

late [leit] *adj* tardío; (*recent*) reciente; (*last*) último; (*delayed*) retrasado; (*former*) antiguo; (*dead*) fallecid. *adv* (*not on time*) tarde; (*after the appointed time*) con retraso; recientemente; anteriormente. **lately** *adv* hace poco. **lateness** *n* retraso *m*. **later** *adj* más tarde. **see you**

later! ¡hasta luego! latest adj (most recent) último. at the latest a más tardar.
latent ['leitənt] adj latente.
lateral ['latərəl] adj lateral.
lathe [leið] n torno m.
lather ['laiðə] n (soap) espuma f; (horse) sudor m. v enjabonar.
Latin ['latin] n, adj latino. -a. n (language) latín m.
Latin America n América Latina f. Latin American n, adj latinoamericano. -a m, f.
latitude ['latitjuid] n latitud f.
latrine [lə'triin] n letrina f, retrete m.
latter ['latə] adj último. the latter éste, ésta.
lattice ['latis] n celosía f; enrejado m.
laugh [laif] v reír, reírse. laugh at reírse de. n risa f. laughable adj ridículo. it's no laughing matter no es cosa de risa. laughing-stock n hazmerreír m invar. laughter n risa f, risas f pl.
launch¹ [lointʃ] v (ship) botar; (lifeboat) echar al mar; (missile) lanzar; (issue) emitir; (an attack) emprender; (a company) fundar; (film, play) estrenar. launching n botadura f; lanzamiento m; fundación f; iniciación f.
launch² [lointʃ] n lancha f. motor launch lancha motora f.
launder ['loində] v lavar. launderette n lavandería automática f. laundry n (place) lavandería f.
laurel ['lorəl] n laurel m.
lava ['laivə] n lava f.
lavatory ['lavətəri] n retrete m; servicios m pl.
lavender ['lavində] n espliego m.
lavish ['laviʃ] adj pródigo; generoso; abundante; lujoso. v prodigar.
law [loi] n ley f. (profession) derecho m, leyes f pl. law-abiding adj respetuoso de las leyes. lawsuit n proceso m. lawful adj legal; lícito. lawyer n jurista m, f; abogado m.
lawn [loin] n césped m. lawn-mower n cortacéspedes m invar.
lax [laks] adj flojo; elástico; negligente. laxity n laxitud f; elasticidad f; negligencia f; flojedad f.
laxative ['laksətiv] nm, adj laxante.
*lay¹ [lei] v (place) poner; (table) cubrir. layabout n holgazán, -ana m. lay-by n área de aparcamiento f. lay off (workers)

despedir. lay on (provide) proveer de. lay-out n (arrangement) disposición f; (printing) composición f; (money) gasto m.
lay² [lei] adj laico. layman n seglar m.
lay³ [lei] V lie.
layer [leiə] n capa f.
lazy ['leizi] adj perezoso. laze around holgazanear. laziness n pereza f.
*lead¹ [liid] v llevar, conducir; remitir; (orchestra) dirigir; ir a la cabeza. lead on (encourage) animar; (seduce) seducir a. lead up to conducir a; preparar el terreno para. n (role) primer papel m; supremacía f; (clue) pista f; ejemplo; primer lugar; (advantage) ventaja f; (elec) cable m; (newspaper) noticia más importante f. leader n guía m, f; jefe m, f; caudillo m; editorial m. leadership n dirección f; mando m; jefatura f. leading adj primero principal; que encabeza.
lead² [led] n plomo m; (pencil) mina f.
leaf [liif] n hoja f; página f; (table) hoja abatible f. v leaf through hojear. leaflet n (pamphlet) folleto m.
league [liig] n liga f. in league with asociado con.
leak [liik] n gotera f; (hole) agujero m; (gas, liquid) fuga f, salida f; (information) filtración f. v gotear; (boat) hacer agua; salirse; perder; filtrarse.
*lean¹ [liin] v inclinarse. lean back reclinarse. lean on apoyarse. lean over backwards to (coll) no escatimar esfuerzos para. leaning (liking) predilección f; (tendency) tendencia f.
lean² [liin] adj magro, sin grasa; (person) flaco. n carne magra f. leanness n magrez f; flaqueza f.
*leap [liip] v saltar; lanzarse. n salto m, brinco m. by leaps and bounds a pasos agigantados. leapfrog n pídola f. leap year año bisiesto m.
*learn [ləin] v aprender. learn of enterarse de. learned (adj) instruido; erudito. learner n principiante m, f; (driver) aprendiz, -a m, f. learning n erudición f, saber m.
lease [liis] n arrendamiento m. v arrendar. leasehold adj arrendado m.
leash [liiʃ] n correa f.
least [liist] adj menor. pron lo menos. adv menos. at least por lo menos.
leather ['leðə] n cuero m, piel f. patent leather charol m. leathery adj (meat) correoso; (skin) curtido.

*leave¹ [liiv] v irse, marcharse; (abandon) dejar; (go out of) salir de. be left quedar. leave off dejar de. leave out omitir. left-luggage office consigna f. left-overs pl n sobras f pl.

leave² [liiv] n permiso m. be on leave estar de permiso. take leave of despedirse de.

lecherous ['letʃərəs] adj lascivo. lecher n lascivo, -a m, f. lechery n lascivia f.

lectern ['lektən] n atril m.

lecture ['lektʃə] n conferencia f. lecture hall sala de conferencias f. v dar una conferencia; dar clase. lecturer n conferenciante m, f; (university) profesor, -a m, f.

led [led] V lead¹.

ledge [ledʒ] n saliente m; (window) antepecho m; (shelf) repisa f.

ledger ['ledʒə] n libro mayor f.

lee [lii] n (shelter) abrigo m; (naut) sotavento m. leeward adj, adv a sotavento.

leech [liitʃ] n sanguijuela f; (person) lapa f.

leek [liik] n puerro m.

leer [liə] v mirar de soslayo. n mirada de soslayo f. leering adj de soslayo.

leeway ['liiwei] n (naut) deriva f; (fig) campo m.

left¹ [left] V leave¹.

left² [left] adj izquierdo. n izquierda f. adv a or hacia la izquierda. left-handed adj zurdo. left-wing adj izquierdista.

leg [leg] n (person) pierna f; (animal) pata f; (furniture) pie m; (trousers) pernera f; (cookery: lamb) pierna f; (chicken) muslo m; (pork, venison) pernil m; (sport, journey) etapa f.

legacy ['legəsi] n legado m, herencia f.

legal ['liigəl] adj jurídico; legal; legítimo; lícito. legality n legalidad f. legalize v legalizar.

legend ['ledʒənd] n leyenda f. legendary adj legendario.

legible ['ledʒəbl] adj legible. legibility n legibilidad f.

legion ['liidʒən] n legión f.

legislate ['ledʒisleit] v legislar; establecer por ley. legislation n legislación f. legislature n legislatura f.

legitimate [lə'dʒitimət] adj legítimo; válido; auténtico. legitimacy n legitimidad f.

leisure ['leʒə] n ocio m; tiempo libre m.

lemon ['lemən] n (fruit) limón m; (tree) limonero m; (colour) amarillo limón m. lemonade n limonada f. lemon squeezer exprimelimones m invar.

*lend [lend] v prestar. lending library biblioteca de préstamo f.

length [lenθ] n longitud f, largo m; (distance) distancia f; (space) espacio m; (piece) pedazo m; lengthen v alargar; prolongar. lengthy adj largo; prolongado.

lenient ['liiniənt] adj indulgente, clemente. leniency n indulgencia f, clemencia f.

lens [lenz] n lente f; (magnifying glass) lupa f; (photo) objetivo m; (eye) cristalino m. contact-lens lente de contacto f.

lent [lent] V lend.

Lent [lent] n Cuaresma f.

lentil ['lentil] n lenteja f.

Leo ['liiou] n (astrol) León m.

leopard ['lepəd] n leopardo m.

leotard ['liiətaid] n leotardo m.

leper ['lepə] n leproso, -a m, f. leprosy n lepra f. leprous adj leproso.

lesbian ['lezbiən] nf, adj lesbiana. lesbianism n lesbianismo m.

less [les] adj menos; menor; inferior. adv, prep menos. n menor m, f. less and less cada vez menos. lessen v disminuir, reducir. lesser adj menor.

lesson ['lesn] n lección f; clase f.

lest [lest] conj de miedo que; para no.

*let [let] v permitir, dejar; (rent) alquilar. let down (lower) bajar, descender; (disappoint) fallar. let-down n decepción f. let in dejar entrar; hacer entrar. let out dejar salir; (clothes) ensanchar.

lethal ['liiθəl] adj mortífero.

lethargy ['leθədʒi] n letargo m. lethargic adj letárgico.

letter ['letə] n (character) letra f; (message) carta f. letter-box n buzón m.

lettuce ['letis] n lechuga f.

leukaemia [lu'kiimiə] n leucemia f.

level ['levl] adj horizontal; (flat) llano; (even) a nivel; (equal) igual; (spoonful) raso; uniforme. be level with al nivel de. level crossing paso a nivel m. level-headed adj juicioso. n nivel m. on the level (coll) honrado. v nivelar, allanar.

lever ['liivə] n palanca f. leverage n apalancamiento m.

levy ['levi] n exacción f; impuesto m. v exigir; imponer.

lewd [luːd] adj lascivo.

liable ['laiəbl] adj sujeto; (law) responsable. liable to capaz de. liability n responsabilidad f; inconveniente m; (nuisance) estorbo m.

liaison [liːˈeizon] n enlace m.

liar ['laiə] n mentiroso, -a m, f.

libel ['laibəl] n (act) difamación f; (writing) escrito difamatorio m. v difamar. libellous adj difamatorio.

liberal ['libərəl] adj liberal; libre; generoso.

liberate ['libəreit] v liberar. liberation n liberación f.

liberty ['libəti] n libertad f. at liberty libre.

Libra ['liːbrə] n Libra f.

library ['laibrəri] n biblioteca f. librarian n bibliotecario, -a m, f.

libretto [li'bretou] n libreto m.

lice [lais] V louse.

licence ['laisəns] n licencia f, permiso m, autorización f; (driving) carnet de conducir m. licence number matrícula f. v conceder una licencia; autorizar. licensed adj autorizado. licensee n concesionario m.

lichen ['laikən] n liquen m.

lick [lik] v lamer. n lamedura f, lamido m.

lid [lid] n tapa f, tapadera f.

*lie¹ [lai] v acostarse; echarse. lie around estar tirado. lie down acostarse. lie in quedarse en la cama.

lie² [lai] n mentira f. v mentir.

lieutenant [lefˈtenənt] n (mil) teniente m; (deputy) lugarteniente m.

life [laif] n vida f. lifeless adj sin vida, muerto.

lifebelt ['laifbelt] n cinturón salvavidas m.

lifeboat ['laifbout] n bote salvavidas m.

lifebuoy ['laifboi] n boya salvavidas f.

lifeguard ['laifgaid] n vigilante m.

life insurance n seguro de vida m.

life-jacket n chaleco salvavidas m.

lifelike ['laiflaik] adj natural; parecido.

lifeline ['laiflain] n (diver's) cordel de señales m; (fig) cordón umbilical m.

lifelong ['laifloŋ] adj de toda la vida.

life-size adj de tamaño natural.

lifetime ['laiftaim] n vida f.

lift [lift] n ascensor m; (act of lifting) levantamiento m; (upward support) empuje m. give someone a lift llevar en coche. v levantar; alzar; coger; elevar.

ligament ['ligəmənt] n ligamento m.

*light¹ [lait] v (set fire to) encender; (room, etc.) iluminar. n luz f; lámpara f; (mot) faro m. adj claro; luminoso. light bulb bombilla f. lighthouse n faro m. light meter fotómetro m. light-year n año luz m. lighten v aclarar. lighter (cigarette) n mechero m. lighting n alumbrado m; iluminación f.

light² [lait] adj liviano; ligero. light-headed adj mareado; delirante. light-hearted adj alegre. lightweight adj ligero, de poco peso. lighten v alijerar; aliviar. lightness n ligereza f.

*light³ [lait] v light upon posarse.

lightning ['laitniŋ] n relámpago m. lightning conductor pararrayos m invar.

like¹ [laik] adj parecido; semejante; igual; mismo. prep como, igual que. be or look like parecerse a. liken v comparar. likeness n semejanza f; forma f; retrato m. likewise adv del mismo modo.

like² [laik] v gustarle (a uno); querer a; (want) querer. likeable adj amable, simpático. liking n cariño m; simpatía f; gusto m.

likely ['laikli] adj probable; posible; plausible. be likely to ser probable que. adv probablemente. likelihood n probabilidad f.

lilac ['lailək] n lila f; (colour) lila m. adj de color lila.

lily ['lili] n azucena f. lily-of-the-valley n lirio de los valles m.

limb [lim] n miembro m.

limbo ['limbou] n (rel) limbo m; (fig) olvido m.

lime¹ [laim] n cal f. limestone n piedra caliza f.

lime² [laim] n (fruit) lima f; (tree) limero m. lime juice jugo de lima m.

limelight ['laimlait] n in the limelight en el candelero.

limerick ['limərik] n quintilla humorística f.

limit ['limit] n límite m. v limitar. limitation n limitación f. limitless adj ilimitado.

limousine ['liməziːn] n limusina f.

limp¹ [limp] v cojear.

limp² [limp] adj flácido. limpness n flojedad f.

limpet ['limpit] n lapa f.

line [lain] n línea f, rayo m, trazo m; (wrinkle) arruga f; (row) fila f; (wire) cable m; (people) cola f; (of poem) verso *m; (rope)* cuerda *f; (flex)* cordón *m; (of communication)* vía *f; (shipping)* compañía *f. v* rayar; arrugar; alinearse por; bordear; *(provide an inner layer)* forrar; *(brakes)* guarnecer. **line up** poner en fila. **linear** *adj* lineal.

linen ['linin] *n* hilo *m*, lino *m; (sheets, etc.)* ropa blanca *f.* **linen basket** canasta de la ropa *f.*

liner ['lainə] *n* transatlántico *m.*

linger ['liŋgə] *v (person)* quedarse; *(memory, etc.)* persistir; *(dawdle)* rezagarse; *(loiter)* callejear.

lingerie ['lãʒərii] *n* ropa interior *f.*

linguist ['liŋgwist] *n* lingüista *m, f.* **linguistic** *adj* lingüístico. **linguistics** *n* lingüística *f.*

lining ['lainiŋ] *n (clothes)* forro *m; (brakes)* guarnición *f.*

link [liŋk] *n (chain)* eslabón *m; (cuff)* gemelos *m pl; (fig)* vínculo *m. v* unir; acoplar; conectar.

linoleum [li'nouliəm] *n also* lino linóleo *m.*

linseed ['lin,siid] *n* linaza *f.* **linseed oil** aceite de lino *m.*

lint [lint] *n* hilas *f pl.*

lion ['laiən] *n* león *m.* **lioness** *n* leona *f.*

lip [lip] *n* labio *m; (jug)* pico *m; (cup)* borde *m.* **lip-read** *v* leer en los labios. **lipstick** *n* barra de labios *f.*

liqueur [li'kjuə] *n* licor *m.*

liquid ['likwid] *nm, adj* líquido. **liquidate** *v* liquidar. **liquidation** *n* liquidación *f.*

liquor ['likə] *n* bebida alcohólica *f.*

liquorice ['likəris] *n* regaliz *m.*

Lisbon ['lizbən] *n* Lisboa.

lisp [lisp] *n* ceceo *m. v* decir ceceando.

list[1] [list] *v* hacer una lista de; enumerar. *n* lista *f;* catálogo *m.*

list[2] [list] *v (naut)* escorar. *n* escora *f.*

listen ['lisn] *v* escuchar, oír. **listener** *n* oyente *m, f.*

listless ['listlis] *adj* decaído, apático.

lit [lit] *V* **light**.

litany ['litəni] *n* letanía *f.*

literacy ['litərəsi] *n* capacidad de leer y escribir *f.* **be literate** saber leer y escribir.

literal ['litərəl] *adj* literal.

literary ['litərəri] *adj* literario.

literature ['litrətʃə] *n* literatura *f; (advertising matter)* folletos publicitarios *m pl.*

litigation [liti'geiʃən] *n* litigio *m.*

litre ['liitə] *n* litro *m.*

litter ['litə] *n* basura *f;* desorden *m; (zool)*

camada *f; (bedding for animals)* pajaza *f; (stretcher)* camilla *f.* **litter-bin** *n* papelera *f. v* ensuciar; cubrir; desordenar.

little ['litl] *adj (small)* pequeño; *(quantity)* poco. *nm, adv* poco. **little by little** poco a poco.

liturgy ['litədʒi] *n* liturgia *f.* **liturgical** *adj* litúrgico.

live[1] [liv] *v* vivir. **live down** conseguir que se olvide. **live up to** cumplir con.

live[2] [laiv] *adj* vivo; *(broadcast)* en directo; *(coal)* en ascuas; *(elec)* cargado. *adv* en directo.

livelihood ['laivlihud] *n* sustento *m.*

lively ['laivli] *adj* vivo; enérgico; activo. **liveliness** *n* viveza *f;* animación *f.*

liven ['laivn] *v* **liven up** animar.

liver ['livə] *n* hígado *m.*

livestock ['laivstok] *n* ganado *m.*

livid ['livid] *adj* lívido; *(coll)* furioso.

living ['liviŋ] *adj* vivo, viviente. *n* vida *f;* vivos *m pl.* **living room** sala de estar *f.*

lizard ['lizəd] *n* lagarto *m.*

load [loud] *n (burden)* carga *f; (animals, vehicles)* cargamento *m; (fig)* peso *m. v* cargar. **loaded** *adj* cargado; *(coll: rich)* podrido de dinero.

loaf[1] [louf] *n* pan *m.*

loaf[2] [louf] *v* **loaf around** callejear. **loafer** *n (coll)* holgazán, -ana *m, f.*

loan [loun] *n* préstamo *m. v* prestar.

loathe [louð] *v* aborrecer. **loathing** *n* aborrecimiento *m.* **loathsome** *adj* asqueroso.

lob [lob] *n* volear. *n* volea alta *f,* lob *m.*

lobby ['lobi] *n* pasillo *m;* vestíbulo *m;* grupo de presión *m. v* ejercer presiones sobre.

lobe [loub] *n* lóbulo *m.*

lobster ['lobstə] *n* langosta *f.*

local ['loukəl] *adj* local; vecinal. *n (coll: pub)* bar del barrio *m.* **the locals** *(coll: people)* la gente del lugar *f,* localidad *n (neighbourhood)* localidad *f; (place)* lugar *m.* **localize** *v* localizar. **locally** *adv* localmente; en el sitio.

locate [lə'keit] *v (find)* encontrar; *(look for and discover)* localizar; situar. **location** *n* localización *f;* colocación *f;* situación *f; (cinema)* exteriores *m pl.* **film on location** *v* rodar.

lock[1] [lok] *n (on door, box, etc.)* cerradura *f; (canal)* esclusa *f. v* cerrarse con llave; *(mech)* bloquearse. **lock away** guardar bajo llave. **lock in** encerrar. **lock out** cerrar la puerta a. **lock up** *(house)* cerrar;

lock 118

(money) dejar bajo llave; (imprison) encarcelar.

lock² [lɒk] n (of hair) mecha f, mechón m.

locker ['lɒkə] n (shelf) casillero m, (cupboard) armario m.

locket ['lɒkit] n relicario m.

locomotive [ˌlɒukə'mɒutiv] n locomotiva f. adj locomotor. **locomotion** n locomoción f.

locust ['lɒukəst] n langosta f.

lodge [lɒdʒ] n (porter's) portería f; (caretaker's) casa del guarda f; (hunting) pabellón m. v alojar; (place) colocar; presentar; (appeal) interponer. **lodger** n huésped, -a m, f. **lodgings** pl n habitación f. **board and lodging** pensión completa f.

loft [lɒft] n (for hay) pajar m; (attic) desván m. **lofty** adj (high) alto; (principles) elevado; (haughty) arrogante.

log [lɒg] n tronco m. **logbook** n (naut) cuaderno de bitácora m; (aero) diario de vuelo m. v anotar, apuntar.

logarithm ['lɒgəriθəm] n logaritmo m.

loggerheads ['lɒgəhedz] pl n **be at loggerheads** estar a mal.

logic ['lɒdʒik] n lógica f. **logical** adj lógico.

loins [lɒinz] pl n lomos m pl.

loiter ['lɒitə] v callejear.

lollipop ['lɒlipɒp] n chupón m.

London ['lʌndən] n Londres.

lonely ['lɒunli] adj solo; aislado; solitario. **loneliness** n soledad f.

long¹ [lɒŋ] adj (length) largo; (memory) bueno; (time) mucho; (long-lasting) viejo. **as long as** mientras. **long-range** adj de larga distancia. **long-sighted** adj hipermétrope; (having foresight) previsor. **long-sleeved** adj de mangas largas. **longstanding** adj de muchos años. **long-term** adj a largo plazo. **long-winded** adj (person) prolijo; (speech) interminable.

long² [lɒŋ] v **long for** desear con ansia. **long to** tener muchas ganas de. **longing** n anhelo m.

longevity [lɒn'dʒevəti] n longevidad f.

longitude ['lɒndʒitjuːd] n longitud f. **longitudinal** adj longitudinal.

loo [luː] n (coll) retrete m.

look [luk] n (glance) mirada f; (inspection) ojeada f; aspecto m. v mirar; parecer; representar. **look after** cuidar a, cuidar de; (watch over) vigilar. **look at** mirar. **look down on** mirar despectivamente.

look for buscar. **look forward to** esperar. **look out** tener cuidado. **look up** levantar los ojos; (improve) ponerse mejor; (research) consultar, buscar. **look up to** apreciar.

loom¹ [luːm] v perfilarse; surgir.

loom² [luːm] n telar m.

loop [luːp] n lazo m; (belt) presilla f. v hacer un lazo en.

loophole ['luːphɒul] v (fig) escapatoria f.

loose [luːs] adj suelto; (fitting) holgado; (knot) flojo; (translation) libre; (tooth) que se mueve; get **loose** escaparse. **let loose** soltar. **loose change** dinero suelto m. **loose-leaf** adj de hojas sueltas. v (free) soltar; (untie) desatar. **loosely** adv sin apretar; aproximadamente; vagamente. **loosen** v aflojar, soltar.

loot [luːt] n botín m. **looter** n saqueador, -a m, f. **looting** saqueo m.

lop [lɒp] v cortar.

lopsided ['lɒp'saidid] adj ladeado; desequilibrado.

lord [lɔːd] n señor m.

lorry ['lɒri] n camión m. **lorry-driver** n camionero m.

*lose [luːz] v perder; (watch, clock) atrasar. **loser** n perdedor, -a m, f. **lost property** objetos perdidos m pl.

loss [lɒs] n pérdida f; (damage) daño m. (defeat) derrota f. **be at a loss** estar perdido. **sell at a loss** vender con pérdida.

lost [lɒst] V **lose**.

lot [lɒt] n destino m; porción f; (auction) lote m; (ground) parcela f. **a lot** mucho. **lots of** cantidades de. **quite a lot of** bastante.

lotion ['lɒuʃən] n loción f.

lottery ['lɒtəri] n lotería f.

lotus ['lɒutəs] n loto m.

loud [laud] adj fuerte; alto; ruidoso; sonoro; (colours) chillón; vulgar. adv (laugh) estrepitosamente. **loud-hailer** n megáfono m. **loud-mouthed** adj fanfarrón, -ona m, f. **loudspeaker** n altavoz m. **loudly** adv en voz alta. **loudness** n fuerza f.

lounge [laundʒ] n salón m. **lounge suit** traje de calle m. v (lazy posture) repantigarse; (idle) gandulear. **lounger** n tumbona f.

louse [laus] n, pl **lice** piojo m. **lousy** adj piojoso; (slang) malísimo.

lout [laut] *n* bruto *m*. **loutish** *adj* bruto.

love [lʌv] *n* amor *m*; cariño *m*; pasión *f*; (*tennis*) cero *m*. **fall in love with** enamorarse de. **love affair** amorío *m*. **make love** hacer el amor con. **with love from** (*in letter*) abrazos *m pl*. v amar, querer. **lovable** *adj* adorable. **lover** *n* amante *m, f*; (*enthusiast*) aficionado, -a *m, f*. **loving** *adj* cariñoso; amoroso.

lovely ['lʌvli] *adj* encantador; delicioso; precioso.

low [lou] *adj* bajo; pequeño; (*scarce*) escaso; (*weak*) débil; (*downhearted*) desanimado. **lowland** *n* tierra baja *f*. **low-lying** *adj* bajo. **low-paid** *adj* mal pagado. **low-priced** *adj* barato. **lowly** *adj* humilde.

lower ['louə] *adj* inferior; más bajo. v bajar. **lower oneself** rebajarse.

loyal ['lɔiəl] *adj* leal; fiel. **loyalty** *n* lealtad *f*; fidelidad *f*.

lozenge ['lɔzindʒ] *n* pastilla *f*.

lubricate ['luːbrikeit] *v* lubrificar, lubricar. **lubricant** *n* lubrificante *m*, lubricante *m*. **lubrication** *n* lubrificación *f*, lubricación *f*, engrase *m*.

lucid ['luːsid] *adj* lúcido; claro. **lucidity** *n* lucidez *f*; claridad *f*.

luck [lʌk] *n* suerte *f*; destino *m*. **bad luck** mala suerte *f*. **good luck** buena suerte *f*. **lucky** *adj* afortunado; oportuno. **be lucky** tener mucha suerte.

lucrative ['luːkrətiv] *adj* lucrativo.

ludicrous ['luːdikrəs] *adj* ridículo, absurdo.

lug [lʌg] *v* arrastrar.

luggage ['lʌgidʒ] *n* equipaje *m*; maletas *f pl*. **luggage label** etiqueta *f*. **luggage rack** portaequipajes *m invar*. **luggage van** furgón de equipajes *m*.

lukewarm ['luːkwɔːm] *adj* tibio.

lull [lʌl] *n* (*in storm*) calma *f*; (*fig*) tregua *f*. *v* sosegar.

lullaby ['lʌləbai] *n* canción de cuna *f*.

lumbago [lʌm'beigou] *n* lumbago *m*.

lumber¹ ['lʌmbə] *n* (*wood*) maderos *m pl*; (*junk*) trastos viejos *m pl*. **lumberjack** *n* leñador *m*. **lumber yard** depósito de madera *m*. v. **lumber with** (*coll*) hacer que cargue con.

lumber² ['lʌmbə] *v* moverse pesadamente.

luminous ['luːminəs] *adj* luminoso.

lump [lʌmp] *n* pedazo *m*, trozo *m*; (*mass*) masa *f*; (*clay*) pella *f*; (*stone*) bloque *m*; (*earth, sugar*) terrón *m*; (*med*) chichón.

lump sum cantidad total *f*. **lumpy** *adj* lleno de bultos.

lunar ['luːnə] *adj* lunar.

lunatic ['luːnətik] *n, adj* loco, -a *m, f*. **lunacy** *n* locura *f*.

lunch [lʌntʃ] *n* almuerzo *m*. v almorzar. **lunchtime** *n* hora de comer *f*.

lung [lʌŋ] *n* pulmón *m*.

lunge [lʌndʒ] *v* embestir, lanzarse. *n* embestida *f*.

lurch¹ [ləːtʃ] *v* dar bandazos. **lurch along** ir dando bandazos. *n* bandazo *m*.

lurch² [ləːtʃ] *n* **leave in the lurch** dejar en la estacada.

lure [luə] *v* atraer. *n* aliciente *m*; encanto *m*; (*decoy*) cebo *m*.

lurid ['luərid] *adj* espeluznante; sensacional.

lurk [ləːk] *v* (*lie in wait*) estar al acecho; (*be hidden*) esconderse; (*fig: be always around*) rondar. **lurking** *adj* vago; oculto.

luscious ['lʌʃəs] *adj* exquisito; apetitoso; voluptuoso.

lush [lʌʃ] *adj* lozano, exuberante.

lust [lʌst] *n* (*sexual*) lascivia *f*; (*for power, etc.*) anhelo *m*. *v* **lust after** (*object*) codiciar; (*person*) desear. **lusty** *adj* robusto, fuerte.

lustre ['lʌstə] *n* lustre *m*.

lute [luːt] *n* laúd *m*.

Luxembourg ['lʌksəmˌbəːg] *n* Luxemburgo *m*.

luxury ['lʌkʃəri] *n* lujo *m*. **luxuriant** *adj* exuberante. **luxurious** *adj* lujoso.

lynch [lintʃ] *v* linchar.

lynx [links] *n* lince *m*.

lyre [laiə] *n* lira *f*.

lyrical ['lirikəl] *adj* lírico.

lyrics ['liriks] *pl n* letra *f sing*. **lyricist** *n* autor de la letra de una canción *m*.

M

mac [mak] *n* (*coll*) impermeable *m*.

macabre [mə'kaːbr] *adj* macabro.

macaroni [makə'rouni] *n* macarrones *m pl*.

mace¹ [meis] *n* (*staff*) maza *f*.

mace² [meis] *n* (*spice*) macis *f*.

machine [mə'ʃiːn] *n* máquina *f*. **machine-**

gun *n* ametralladora *f*. **machinery** *n* maquinaria *f*; mecanismo *m*.

mackerel ['makrəl] *n* caballa *f*.

mackintosh ['makin.tɒʃ] *n* impermeable *m*.

mad [mad] *adj* loco, demente; rabioso; *(angry)* furioso. **madden** *v* enloquecer; enfurecer. **maddening** *adj* desesperante. **madly** *adv* locamente; furiosamente. **madness** *n* locura *f*; rabia *f*; furia *f*. **madam** ['madəm] *n* señora *f*.

made [meid] *V* **make**.

Madeira [mə'diərə] *n (island)* Madera *f*; *(wine)* madera *m*.

magazine [.magə'zim] *n (publication)* revista *f*; *(warehouse)* almacén *m*; *(explosives store)* polvorín *m*; *(rifle)* recámara *f*.

maggot ['magət] *n* gusano *m*, cresa *f*. **maggoty** *adj* gusanoso.

magic ['madʒik] *n* magia *f*. *adj also* **magical** mágico. **magician** *n* ilusionista *m, f*.

magistrate ['madʒistreit] *n* magistrado *m*; juez municipal *m*.

magnanimous [mag'naniməs] *adj* magnánimo. **magnanimity** *n* magnanimidad *f*.

magnate ['magneit] *n* magnate *m*.

magnet ['magnət] *n* imán *m*. **magnetic** magnético; atractivo. **magnetism** *n* magnetismo *m*. **magnetize** *v* magnetizar; atraer.

magnificent [mag'nifisnt] *adj* magnífico. **magnificence** *n* magnificencia *f*.

magnify ['magnifai] *v* magnificar; aumentar; exagerar. **magnifying glass** lupa *f*. **magnification** *n* aumento *m*; exageración *f*.

magnitude ['magnitjud] *n* magnitud *f*.

magnolia [mag'nouliə] *n* magnolia *f*.

magpie ['magpai] *n* urraca *f*.

mahogany [mə'hogəni] *n* caoba *f*.

maid [meid] *n (servant)* criada *f*; muchacha *f*. **old maid** solterona *f*.

maiden ['meidən] *n* doncella *f*. *adj* virgen; soltera; inaugural. **maiden name** apellido de soltera *m*.

mail [meil] *n (letters)* correspondencia *f*; *(service)* correo *m*. **mailbag** *n* saca de correspondencia *f*. **mail order** pedido hecho por correo *m*.

maim [meil] *v* mutilar.

main [mein] *adj* principal. **main course** plato principal *m*. **mainland** *n* continente *m*. **main line** línea principal *f*. **main road** carretera general *f*. **mainstay** *n* estay

mayor *m*. *n (gas, water)* cañería principal *f*. **in the main** por lo general. **mains** *n (elec)* la red eléctrica *f*.

maintain [mein'tein] *v* mantener; conservar. **maintenance** *n* mantenimiento *m*; conservación *f*. **maintenance allowance** pensión alimenticia *f*.

maisonette [meizə'net] *n* casita *f*.

maize [meiz] *n* maíz *m*.

majesty ['madʒəsti] *n* majestad *f*. **majestic** *adj* majestuoso.

major ['meidʒə] *adj* mayor; principal. *n (mil)* comandante *m*.

majority [mə'dʒoriti] *n* mayoría *f*. **overwhelming majority** mayoría abrumadora *f*.

★**make** [meik] *v* hacer, efectuar; ser; llegar a. *n* marca *f*; hechura *f*. **make-believe** *n* simulación *f*. **make out** *(draw up)* hacer; *(cheque)* extender. **make do with** arreglárselas con. **makeshift** *n* improvisado. **make up** inventar; completar; recuperar; *(face)* maquillarse. **make-up** *n* maquillaje *m*; carácter *m*. **make up for** compensar. **maker** *n* fabricante *m*. **making** *n* fabricación *f*.

maladjusted [malə'dʒʌstid] *adj* inadaptado. **maladjustment** *n* inadaptación *f*.

malaria [mə'leəriə] *n* malaria *f*, paludismo *m*.

male [meil] *nm, adj* macho.

malevolent [mə'levələnt] *adj* malévolo. **malevolence** *n* malevolencia *f*.

malfunction [mal'fʌŋkʃən] *n* funcionamiento defectuoso *m*. *v* funcionar defectuosamente.

malice ['malis] *n* malicia *f*. **malicious** *adj* malicioso.

malignant [mə'lignənt] *adj* malvado; malo; *(med)* maligno. **malignancy** *n* maldad *f*; malignidad *f*.

malinger [mə'liŋgə] *v* fingirse enfermo.

mallet ['malit] *n* mazo *m*.

malnutrition [malnju'triʃən] *n* desnutrición *f*.

malt [mɔilt] *n* malta *f*.

Malta ['mɔiltə] *n* Malta. **Maltese** *n, adj* maltés, -esa.

maltreat [mal'trit] *v* maltratar. **maltreatment** *n* maltrato *m*.

mammal ['maməl] *n* mamífero *m*.

mammoth ['maməθ] *n* mamut *m*. *adj* gigantesco.

man [man] *n, pl* **men** hombre *m. v* armar; ocupar. **manhood** *n* virilidad *f.* **manly** *adj* masculino.

manage ['manidʒ] *v* (*business, affairs, etc.*) dirigir; (*instrument*) manejar; (*property*) administrar. **manage to** conseguir, arreglárselas. **manageable** *adj* manejable; (*undertaking*) factible; (*animal, person*) dócil. **management** *n* gestión *f.*, administración *f.*, dirección *f.*; (*board of directors*) junta directiva. **manager** *n* gerente *m.*, director *m.* **managerial** *adj* directorial. **managing director** director gerente *m.*

mandarin ['mandərin] *n* mandarín *m. adj* mandarino. **mandarin orange** mandarina *f.*; (*tree*) mandarino *m.*

mandate ['mandeit] *n* mandato *m.* **mandatory** *adj* obligatorio.

mandolin ['mandəlin] *n* mandolina *f.*

mane [mein] *n* crin *f.*, crines *f pl.*

mange [meindʒ] *n* sarna *f.* **mangy** *adj* sarnoso; (*coll*) asqueroso.

manger ['meindʒə] *n* pesebre *m.*

mangle¹ ['maŋgl] *n* (*wringer*) escurridor *m. v* pasar por el escurridor.

mangle² ['maŋgl] *v* despedazar; (*fig*) deformar.

mango ['maŋgou] *n* mango *m.*

manhandle [man'handl] *v* (*person*) maltratar; (*goods*) manipular.

manhole ['manhoul] *n* registro *m.*

mania ['meiniə] *n* manía *f.* **maniac** *n* maníaco, -a *m, f*; (*fig*) fanático, -a *m, f.*

manicure ['manikjuə] *n* manicura *f. v* hacer la manicura a. **manicurist** *n* manicuro, -a *m, f.*

manifest ['manifest] *adj* manifiesto, evidente. *v* mostrar, manifestarse. **manifestation** *n* manifestación *f.*

manifesto [mani'festou] *n* manifiesto *m.*

manifold ['manifould] *adj* múltiple; diverso. *n* **exhaust manifold** (*mot*) colector de escape *m.*

manipulate [mə'nipjuleit] *v* manipular. **manipulation** *n* manipulación *f.*

mankind [man'kaind] *n* raza humana *f.*, humanidad *f.*

man-made [man'meid] *adj* sintético, artificial.

manner ['manə] *n* manera *f.*, modo *m.*; clase *f.*; aire *m.* **manners** *pl n* modales *m pl.*

mannerism ['manərizəm] *n* amaneramiento *m.*

manoeuvre [mə'nuːvə] *n* maniobra *f. v* maniobrar.

manor ['manə] *n* señorío *m.* **manor house** casa solariega *f.*

manpower ['man,pauə] *n* mano de obra *f.*

mansion ['manʃən] *n* (*country*) gran casa de campo *f.*; (*town*) palacete *m.*

manslaughter ['man,slɔːtə] *n* homicidio sin premeditación *m.*

mantelpiece ['mantlpiːs] *n* repisa de chimenea *f.*

mantle ['mantl] *n* (*cloak*) capa *f.*; (*gaslamp*) manguito *m.*

manual ['manjuəl] *nm, adj* manual. **manually** *adv* a mano.

manufacture [manju'faktʃə] *n* (*product*) producto manufacturado; (*act*) fabricación *f. v* manufacturar, fabricar. **manufacturer** *n* fabricante *m.*

manure [mə'njuə] *n* estiércol *m.*, abono. *v* estercolar, abonar.

manuscript ['manjuskript] *nm* manuscrito.

many ['meni] *adj* muchos, mucho, un gran número de. *pron* muchos. **as many as** hasta. **how many?** ¿cuántos? ¿cuántas? **so many** tantos, tantas. **too many** demasiado.

map [map] *n* mapa *m*; (*town*) plano *m. v* levantar un mapa de. **map out** proyectar.

maple ['meipl] *n* arce *m.*

mar [maː] *v* estropear; frustrar.

marathon ['marəθən] *nm, adj* maratón.

marble ['maːbl] *n* mármol *m*; (*toy*) bola *f. v* jaspear.

march [maːtʃ] *v* marchar. *n* marcha *f.*

March [maːtʃ] *n* marzo *m.*

marchioness [maːʃə'nes] *n* marquesa *f.*

mare [meə] *n* yegua *f.*

margarine [maːdʒə'riːn] *n* margarina *f.*

margin ['maːdʒin] *n* borde *m.*, lado *m.*; orilla *f.*; margen *m.* **marginal** *adj* marginal. **marginally** *adv* por muy poco.

marguerite [maːgə'riːt] *n* margarita *f.*

marigold ['marigould] *n* caléndula *f.*

marijuana [mari'waːnə] *n* marijuana *f.*, marihuana *f.*

marina [mə'riːnə] *n* puerto deportivo *m.*

marinade [mari'neid] *n* adobo *m. v* adobar.

marine [mə'riːn] *adj* marino. *n* (*mil*) soldado de infantería de marina. **merchant marine** marina mercante *f.*

marital ['maritl] *adj* marital, matrimonial.

maritime ['maritaim] *adj* marítimo.

marjoram ['maɪdʒərəm] *n* mejorana *f*.

mark[1] [maɪk] *n* marca *f*; señal *f*; mancha *f*; (*school*) nota *f*; calificación *f*; (*trace*) huella *f*. **marksman** *n* tirador *m*. *v* marcar; señalar; calificar. **marked** *adj* marcado; pronunciado; sensible.

mark[2] [maɪk] *n* (*currency*) marco *m*.

market ['maɪkit] *n* mercado *m*; (*demand*) salida *f*. **market day** día de mercado *m*. **market place** plaza de mercado *f*. **market research** estudio de mercados *m*. **market value** valor corriente *m*. *v* poner en venta, vender. **marketing** *n* comercialización.

marmalade ['maɪmǝleid] *n* mermelada *f* de naranja *f*.

maroon[1] [mǝ'ruɪn] *adj* castaño.

maroon[2] [mǝ'ruɪn] *v* abandonar.

marquee [maɪkiɪ] *n* gran tienda de campaña *f*.

marquess ['maɪkwis] *n* marqués *m*.

marquetry ['maɪkǝtri] *n* marquetería *f*.

marriage ['maridʒ] *n* matrimonio *m*; (*wedding*) boda *f*. **marriage certificate** partida de casamiento *f*.

marrow ['marou] *n* (*bone*) médula *f*. **vegetable marrow** calabacín *m*.

marry ['mari] *v* casar; (*get married*) casarse. **married** *adj* casado. **married couple** matrimonio *m*. **married name** apellido de casada *m*.

Mars [maɪz] *n* Marte *m*. **Martian** *n, adj* marciano, -a.

marsh [maʃ] *n* pantano *m*. **marshmallow** *n* (*bot*) malvavisco *m*; (*cookery*) melcocha *f*. **marshy** *adj* pantanoso.

marshal ['maɪʃǝl] *n* (*mil*) mariscal *m*; (*organizer*) maestro de ceremonias *m*. *v* poner en orden; (*mil*) formar.

martial ['maɪʃǝl] *adj* marcial.

martin ['maɪtin] *n* avión *m*.

martyr ['maɪtǝ] *n* mártir *m*, *f*. *v* martinizar. **martyrdom** *n* martirio *m*.

marvel ['maɪvǝl] *n* maravilla *f*. *v* maravillarse. **marvellous** *adj* maravilloso.

marzipan ['maɪzi'pan] *n* mazapán *m*.

mascara [ma'skaɪrǝ] *n* rímel *m*.

mascot ['maskǝt] *n* mascota *f*.

masculine ['maskjulin] *adj* masculino. **masculinity** *n* masculinidad *f*.

mash [maʃ] *v* machacar. *n* (*animal feed*) afrecho remojado *m*.

mask [maɪsk] *n* máscara *f*, careta *f*. *v* enmascarar.

masochist ['masǝkist] *n* masoquista *m*, *f*. **masochism** *n* masoquismo *m*. **masochistic** *adj* masoquista.

mason ['meisn] *n* albañil *m*. **masonry** *n* albañilería.

masquerade [maskǝ'reid] *n* (*pretence*) mascarada *f*. *v* **masquerade as** hacerse pasar por.

mass[1] [mas] *n* masa *f*. **mass media** medios informativos *m pl*. **mass meeting** mitin popular *m*. **mass-produce** *v* fabricar en serie. **mass production** fabricación en serie *f*. *v* agrupar.

mass[2] [mas] *n* (*rel*) misa *f*.

massacre ['masǝkǝ] *n* matanza *f*. *v* matar en masa.

massage ['masaɪʒ] *n* masaje *m*. *v* dar un masaje. **masseur, masseuse** *n* masajista *m*, *f*.

massive ['masiv] *adj* sólido; masivo.

mast [maɪst] *n* (*naut*) palo *m*, mástil *m*; (*radio, etc.*) poste *m*.

master ['maɪstǝ] *n* (*owner*) dueño *m*; (*college*) director *m*; (*secondary school*) profesor *m*; (*primary school*) maestro; (*graduate*) licenciado, -a *m*, *f*; (*household*) señor *m*; (*work force*) patrón *m*; (*ship*) capitán *m*. **master copy** original *m*. **master key** llave maestra *f*. **master of ceremonies** maestro de ceremonias *m*. **masterpiece** *n* obra maestra *f*. *v* (*passions, language*) dominar; (*an animal*) domar; (*difficulties*) vencer. **mastery** *n* dominio *m*; maestría *f*.

masturbate ['mastǝbeit] *v* masturbarse. **masturbation** *n* masturbación *f*.

mat [mat] *n* (*floor*) estera *f*; (*door*) esterilla *f*; (*table*) salvamanteles *m invar*; (*doily*) tapete *m*. **matted** *adj* (*hair*) enmarañado.

match[1] [matʃ] *n* fósforo *m*, cerilla *f*. **matchbox** *n* caja de fósforos *or* cerillas *f*.

match[2] [matʃ] *n* (*sport*) partido *m*; (*equal*) igual *m*; (*pair*) pareja *f*. *v* igualar; (*colours*) casar; (*gloves, etc.*) parear; (*clothes, furnishings*) hacer juego con; (*fit*) encajar; corresponder. **matchless** *adj* sin igual.

mate [meit] *n* (*animals*) macho, hembra *m*, *f*; amigo, -a *m*, *f*; camarada *m*, *f*; (*spouse*) compañero, -a *m*, *f*. *v* acoplar; casar; (*chess*) dar jaque mate a.

material [mǝ'tiǝriǝl] *n* material *m*; (*cloth*) tela *f*. **materials** *pl n* (*building*) materiales *m pl*; (*teaching*) material *m*; artículos *m* *pl. adj* material; esencial. **materialist** *n(m+f)*. *adj* materialista. **materialize** *v* materializar; realizar.

maternal [mə'tɜɪnl] *adj* maternal; *(relation)* materno.

maternity [mə'tɜɪnəti] *n* maternidad *f*. **maternity hospital** casa de maternidad *f*.

mathematics [mæθə'mætiks] *n* matemáticas *f pl*. **mathematical** *adj* matemático. **mathematician** *n* matemático, -a *m, f*.

matinée ['mætinei] *n (cinema)* primera sesión *f*; *(theatre)* función de la tarde *f*. **matinée idol** ídolo del público *m*.

matins ['mætinz] *n* maitines *m pl*.

matriarch ['meitriɑːk] *n* mujer que manda *f*. **matriarchal** *adj* matriarcal.

matrimony ['mætriməni] *n* matrimonio *m*. **matrimonial** *adj* matrimonial.

matrix ['meitriks] *n* matriz *f*.

matron ['meitrən] *n* matrona *f*; *(hospital)* enfermera jefe *f*; *(school)* ama de llaves *f*.

matt [mæt] *adj* mate.

matter ['mætə] *n* materia *f*; material *m*; asunto *m*; cuestión *f*; tema *m*. **as a matter of fact** en realidad. **matter-of-fact** *adj* prosaico. **what's the matter?** ¿qué pasa? *v* importar. **it doesn't matter** no importa.

mattress ['mætris] *n* colchón *m*. **spring-mattress** *n* colchón de muelles *m*.

mature [mə'tjuə] *adj* maduro. *v* madurar. **maturity** *n* madurez *f*.

maudlin ['mɔːdlin] *adj* sensiblero.

maul [mɔːl] *v* maltratar; herir gravemente.

mausoleum [mɔːsə'liəm] *n* mausoleo *m*.

mauve [mouv] *nm, adj* malva.

maxim ['mæksim] *n* máxima *f*.

maximum ['mæksiməm] *nm, adj* máximo.

*may [mei] *v* poder.

May [mei] *n* mayo *m*. **May Day** primero de mayo *m*.

maybe ['meibi] *adv* quizás, quizá.

mayday ['meidei] *n* señal de socorro *f*.

mayonnaise [meiə'neiz] *n* mayonesa *f*.

mayor [meə] *n* alcalde *m*. **mayoress** *n* alcaldesa *f*.

maze [meiz] *n* laberinto *m*.

me [miː] *pron* me; *(after prep)* mí.

mead [miːd] *n (drink)* aguamiel *f*.

meadow ['medou] *n* prado *m*.

meagre ['miːgə] *adj* escaso, pobre.

meal¹ [miːl] *n (food)* comida *f*.

meal² [miːl] *n (flour)* harina *f*.

*mean¹ [miːn] *v (signify)* tener la intención de, querer decir.

mean² [miːn] *adj (humble)* humilde; *(petty)* mezquino; *(stingy)* agarrado; *(character)* vil; *(unkind)* malo. **meanness** *n* humildad *f*; mezquindad *f*; *(stinginess)* tacañería *f*; vileza *f*; maldad *f*.

mean³ [miːn] *n (average)* promedio; *(math)* media *f*. *adj* medio; mediano.

meander [mi'ændə] *v (river)* serpentear; *(person)* vagar. *n* meandro *m*.

meaning ['miːnin] *n* significación *f*; sentido *m*; pensamiento *m*. **meaningful** *adj* significativo. **meaningless** *adj* sin sentido; insignificante.

means [miːnz] *n (way)* medio *m*, manera *f*; *(wealth)* fondos *m pl*. **by all means!** ¡por supuesto! **by means of** por medio de. **by no means** de ningún modo.

meanwhile ['miːnwail] *adv* mientras tanto.

measles ['miːzlz] *n* sarampión *m*.

measure ['meʒə] *v* medir. *n* medida *f*. **made to measure** hecho a la medida. **measurement** *n* medida *f*.

meat [miːt] *v* carne *f*. **cold meat** fiambre *m*. **meatball** *n* albóndiga *f*. **meat pie** empanada *f*.

mechanic [mi'kænik] *n* mecánico *m*. **mechanical** *adj* mecánico. **mechanics** *n* mecánica *f sing*. **mechanism** *n* mecanismo *m*. **mechanize** *v* mecanizar.

medal ['medl] *n* medalla *f*. **medallion** *n* medallón *m*. **medallist** *n* condecorado con una medalla.

meddle ['medl] *v* **meddle in** meterse en; **meddle with** toquetear. **meddlesome** *adj* entremetido.

media ['miːdiə] *pl n* medios *m pl*.

mediate ['miːdieit] *v* ser mediador en; mediar. **mediation** *n* mediación *f*. **mediator** *n* mediador, -a *m, f*.

medical ['medikl] *adj* médico; de medicina. **medical consultant** médico consultor *m*. **medical school** facultad de medicina *f*. **medicate** *v* medicinar. **medicated** *adj* medicinal.

medicine ['medsən] *n (art and drug)* medicina *f*; *(coll)* purga *f*. **medicine cabinet** botiquín *m*. **medicinal** *adj* medicinal.

medieval [medi'iːvl] *adj* medieval.

mediocre [miːdi'oukə] *adj* mediocre. **mediocrity** *n* mediocridad *f*.

meditate ['mediteit] *v* meditar. **meditation** *n* meditación *f*. **meditative** *adj* meditativo.

Mediterranean [,meditə'reiniən] *adj* mediterráneo. *n* Mediterráneo *m*.

medium ['miːdiəm] *n* (*environment*) medio ambiente *m*; (*means*) medio *m*; (*spiritualism*) médium *m*, *f*. **happy medium** justo medio *m*. *adj* mediano. **medium wave** (*radio*) onda media *f*.

medley ['medli] *n* mezcla *f*; (*music*) popurrí *m*.

meek [miːk] *adj* dócil, manso; humilde. **meekness** *n* docilidad *f*, mansedumbre *f*.

*meet [miːt] *v* (*encounter*) encontrar, encontrarse a; (*come together*) entrevistarse con; (*come across*) cruzarse con; (*roads*) desembocar en; (*correspond to*) empalmar con; satisfacer; (*requirement, engagement*) cumplir con; (*expenses*) costear; (*claims*) acceder a. **meet someone half-way** llegar a un arreglo con alguien. **pleased to meet you!** ¡mucho gusto! **meeting** *n* encuentro *m*; reunión *f*; sesión *f*; (*interview*) cita *f*; (*official*) entrevista *f*.

megaphone ['megəfoun] *n* megáfono *m*.

melancholy ['melənkəli] *n* melancolía *f*. *adj also* **melancholic** melancólico.

mellow ['melou] *adj* (*ripe*) maduro; (*wine*) añejo; (*voice*) suave. *v* madurar; suavizar.

melodrama ['melədraːmə] *n* melodrama *m*. **melodramatic** *adj* melodramático.

melody ['melədi] *n* melodía *f*. **melodious** *adj* melodioso.

melon ['melən] *n* melón *m*.

melt [melt] *v* fundir; derretir; (*fig*) ablandar. **melting** *n* fusión *f*, fundición *f*.

member ['membə] *n* miembro *m*. **membership** *n* calidad de miembro *f*. **membership fee** cuota de socio *f*.

membrane ['membrein] *n* membrana *f*. **membranous** *adj* membranoso.

memento [mə'mentou] *n* recuerdo *m*.

memo ['memou] *n* (*coll*) memorándum *m*.

memoirs ['memwaːz] *pl n* memorias *f pl*.

memorable ['memərəbl] *adj* memorable.

memorandum [memə'randəm] *n* memorándum *m*.

memory ['meməri] *n* memoria *f*; (*thing remembered*) recuerdo *m*. **memorize** *v* memorizar, aprender de memoria.

men [men] *V* **man**.

menace ['menis] *n* amenaza *f*. *v* amenazar.

menagerie [mi'nadʒəri] *n* casa de fieras *f*.

mend [mend] *v* remendar; reparar; (*improve*) mejorar. **be on the mend** (*coll*) estar mejorando.

menial ['miːniəl] *adj* (*of a servant*) doméstico; (*mean*) bajo. *n* (*servant*) criado, -a *m*, *f*.

meningitis [menin'dʒaitis] *n* meningitis *f*.

menopause ['menəpoːz] *n* menopausia *f*.

menstrual ['menstruəl] *adj* menstrual. **menstruate** *v* menstruar. **menstruation** *n* menstruación *f*.

mental ['mentl] *adj* mental; (*coll: mad*) chiflado. **mental arithmetic** cálculo mental *m*. **mental deficiency** deficiencia mental *f*. **mental home** *or* **hospital** manicomio *m*. **mentality** *n* mentalidad *f*. **mentally** *adj* mentalmente. **mentally handicapped** anormal.

menthol ['menθəl] *n* mentol *m*.

mention ['menʃən] *v* mencionar, hablar de. **don't mention it!** ¡de nada! ¡no hay de qué! **not to mention** por no decir nada de. *n* mención *f*.

menu ['menjuː] *n* carta *f*, lista de platos *f*.

mercantile ['məːkəntail] *adj* mercantil; mercante.

mercenary ['məːsinəri] *nm*, *adj* mercenario.

merchandise ['məːtʃəndaiz] *n* mercancías *f pl*. **merchandizing** *n* comercio mercantil *f*.

merchant ['məːtʃənt] *n* comerciante *m*, *f*, negociante *m*, *f*; (*shopkeeper*) tendero, -a *m*, *f*. **merchant navy** marina mercante *f*.

mercury ['məːkjuri] *n* mercurio *m*.

mercy ['məːsi] *n* misericordia *f*, merced *f*. **at the mercy of** a merced de. **merciful** *adj* clemente; misericordioso. **merciless** *adj* despiadado.

mere [miə] *adj* mero.

merge [məːdʒ] *v* (*parties, companies*) fusionar; (*join*) unir; (*colours*) fundir. **merger** *n* fusión *f*; unión *f*.

meridian [mə'ridiən] *nm*, *adj* meridiano.

meringue [mə'raŋ] *n* merengue *m*.

merit ['merit] *n* mérito *m*. *v* merecer.

mermaid ['məːmeid] *n* sirena *f*.

merry ['meri] *adj* alegre; divertido; (*coll: slightly drunk*) achispado. **merry-go-round** *n* tiovivo *m*. **merriment** *n* alegría *f*; diversión *f*.

mesh [meʃ] *n* mella *f*; (*gears*) engranaje *m*. *v* engranar (con).

mesmerize ['mezməraiz] *v* hipnotizar.

mess [mes] *n* confusión *f*, desorden *m*; (*dirt*) porquería *f*, suciedad *f*; (*awkward situation*) lío *m*; (*mil*) comedor de la tropa *m*. **make a mess of** desordenar;

ensuciar. **what a mess!** ¡qué asco! ¡qué porquería! ¡qué lío! **mess up** desordenar; ensuciar. **messy** *adj* confuso; desordenado; sucio.

message ['mesɪdʒ] *n* recado *m*; (*official communication*) mensaje *m*; (*errand*) encargo *m*. **messenger** *n* mensajero, -a *m, f*.

met [met] *V* meet.

metal ['metl] *n* metal *m. adj* de metal. **metallic** *adj* metálico. **metallurgist** *n* metalúrgico *m*. **metallurgy** *n* metalurgia *f*.

metamorphosis [metə'mɔːfəsis] *n* metamorfosis *f*.

metaphor ['metəfə] *n* metáfora *f*. **metaphorical** *adj* metafórico.

metaphysics [metə'fiziks] *n* metafísica *f*. **metaphysical** *adj* metafísico. **metaphysician** *n* metafísico *m*.

meteor ['miːtiə] *n* meteoro. **meteoric** *adj* meteórico. **meteorite** *n* meteorito *m*.

meteorology [miːtiə'rolədʒi] *n* meteorología *f*. **meteorological** *adj* meteorológico. **meteorologist** *n* meteorologista *m, f*.

meter ['miːtə] *n* contador *m*.

methane ['miːθein] *n* metano *m*.

method ['meθəd] *n* método *m*; técnica *f*. **methodical** *adj* metódico.

Methodist ['meθədist] *n* metodista *m, f*. **Methodism** *n* metodismo *m*.

methylated spirits ['meθileitid] *pl n* alcohol desnaturalizado *m*.

meticulous [mi'tikjuləs] *adj* meticuloso.

metre ['miːtə] *n* metro *m*. **metric** *adj* métrico.

metronome ['metrənoum] *n* metrónomo *m*.

metropolis [mə'tropəlis] *n* metrópoli *f*. **metropolitan** *adj* metropolitano.

Mexico ['meksikou] *n* Méjico, México. **Mexican** *n, adj* mejicano, -a, mexicano, -a.

mice [mais] *V* **mouse**.

microbe ['maikroub] *n* microbio *m*.

microfilm ['maikrəfilm] *n* microfilm *m*.

microphone ['maikrəfoun] *n* micrófono *m*.

microscope ['maikrəskoup] *n* microscopio *m*. **microscopic** *adj* microscópico.

microwave ['maikrəweiv] *n* microonda *f*.

mid [mid] *adj* medio; mediados.

mid-air [mid'eə] *n* **in mid-air** entre cielo y tierra.

midday [mid'dei] *n* mediodía *m*.

middle ['midl] *n* medio *m*, centro *m*; mitad *f*. **in the middle** en el centro. *adj* central; mediano; de en medio; medio; intermedio. **middle-aged** *adj* de mediano edad. **the Middle Ages** Edad Media *f sing*. **middle-class** *adj* de la clase media; burgués. **Middle East** Oriente Medio *m*. **middleman** *n* intermediario *m*. **middle-of-the-road** *adj* centrista, moderado. **middleweight** *n* peso medio *m*. **middling** *adj* regular, mediano.

midge [midʒ] *n* mosca enana *f*.

midget ['midʒit] *n* enano, -a *m, f*.

midnight ['midnait] *n* medianoche *f*.

midriff ['midrif] *n* diafragma *m*.

midst [midst] *n* **in our midst** entre nosotros. **in the midst of** en medio de.

midstream [mid'striːm] *n* **in midstream** en medio del río.

midsummer ['mid,sʌmə] *n* pleno verano *m*. **Midsummer Day** el día de San Juan *m*.

midway [mid'wei] *adv, adj* a medio camino.

midweek [mid'wiːk] *n* medio de la semana *m*.

midwife ['midwaif] *n* comadrona *f*, partera *f*. **midwifery** *n* obstetricia *f*.

midwinter [mid'wintə] *n* pleno invierno *m*.

might[1] [mait] *V* **may**.

might[2] [mait] *n* poder *m*; fuerza *f*. **mighty** ['maiti] *adj* poderoso; fuerte; enorme. *adv* (*coll*) muy.

migraine ['miːgrein] *n* migraña *f*.

migrate [mai'greit] *v* emigrar. **migration** *n* migración. *adj* migratoria.

mike [maik] *n* (*coll: microphone*) micro *m*.

mild [maild] *adj* (*person*) dulce, apacible; (*weather*) templado; (*wind*) suave; (*disease*) benigno. **mildness** *n* dulzura *f*; suavidad *f*; benignidad *f*.

mildew ['mildjuː] *n* moho *m*; (*vine*) mildeu *m*; (*plants*) tizón *m*.

mile [mail] *n* milla *f*. **mileage** recorrido en millas *m*. **milestone** *n* mojón *m*; (*fig*) jalón *m*.

militant ['militənt] *adj* belicoso; (*pol*) militante. *n* militante *m, f*.

military ['militəri] *adj* militar.

milk [milk] *n* leche *f*. **milk chocolate** *n* chocolate con leche *m*. **milkman** *n* lechero *m*. **milk of magnesia** *n* leche de magnesia *f*. *v* ordeñar; (*fig*) exprimir.

milkiness *n* aspecto lechoso *m.* **milking** *n* ordeño *m.* **milky** *adj* lechoso.
Milky Way *n* Vía Láctea *f.*
mill [mil] *n* molino *m.;* (*grinder*) molinillo *m.;* (*factory*) fábrica *f.* **millstone** *n* muela *f.;* (*burden*) cruz *f.* *v* moler. **miller** *n* molinero, -a *m. f.*
millennium [mi'leniəm] *n* milenario *m.*
millet ['milit] *n* mijo *m.*
milligram ['miligram] *n* miligramo *m.*
millimetre ['mili,miitə] *n* milímetro *m.*
milliner ['milinə] *n* sombrerero, -a *m. f.* **milliner's** *n* sombrerería *f.* **millinery** *n* sombreros de señora *m pl.*
million ['miljən] *n* millón *m.* **millionaire** *n* millonario, -a *m. f.* **millionth** *n, adj* millonésimo, -a *m. f.*
mime [maim] *n* mimo *m,* pantomima *f.* *v* actuar de mimo.
mimic ['mimik] *adj* mímico; imitativo. *n* mimo *m;* imitador, -a *m. f.* *v* imitar, remedar. **mimicry** *n* mímica *f;* (*zool*) mimetismo *m.*
minaret [minə'ret] *n* minarete *m.*
mince [mins] *n* (*meat*) carne picada *f.* **mincemeat** *n* conserva de fruta picada y especias *f.* **mince pie** pastel con frutas picadas *m.* *v* picar; (*walk*) andar con pasos menuditos. **mince words** tener pelos en la lengua. **mincer** *n* máquina de picar carne *f.* **mincing** *adj* afectado.
mind [maind] *n* mente *f.* **bear in mind** tener en cuenta. **go out of one's mind** perder el juicio. **have a good mind to** tener ganas de. **keep in mind** acordarse de. **make up one's mind** decidirse. **read someone's mind** adivinar el pensamiento de alguien. **to my mind** a mi parecer. *v* (*look out*) tener cuidado; (*guard*) cuidar; (*rules*) cumplir; (*pay attention*) prestar atención. **do you mind?** ¿le importa? **I don't mind** a mí no me importa. **never mind** no se preocupe.
mine¹ [main] *pron* (el) mío, (la) mía, (lo) mío.
mine² [main] *n* mina *f.* **minefield** *n* campo de minas *m.* **mineshaft** *n* pozo de extracción. *m.* **minesweeper** *n* dragaminas *m invar.* *v* minar; (*mil*) sembrar minas en. **miner** *n* minero *m.* **mining** *n* minería *f.* **mining engineer** ingeniero de minas *m.*
mineral ['minərəl] *nm, adj* mineral. **minerals** (*coll: drinks*) *pl n* gaseosas *f pl.*
mingle ['mingl] *v* mezclar.
miniature ['minitfə] *nf, adj* miniatura.

minim ['minim] *n* mínima *f,* blanca *f.*
minimum ['miniməm] *nm, adj* mínimo. **minimal** *adj* mínimo. **minimize** *v* minimizar.
minister ['ministə] *n* ministro *m.* *v* **minister to** atender a. **ministerial** *adj* ministerial. **ministry** *n* ministerio *m.*
mink [mink] *n* visón *m.*
minor ['mainə] *adj* menor, más pequeño; secundario; de poca importancia. *n* menor de edad *m, f.*
minority [mai'noriti] *n* minoría *f.* **in the minority** en la minoría. *adj* minoritario.
minstrel ['minstrəl] *n* trovador.
mint¹ [mint] *n* (*bot*) menta *f.*
mint² [mint] *n* casa de la moneda *f. adj* nuevo. *v* acuñar.
minuet [minju'et] *n* minué *m.*
minus ['mainəs] *prep* menos. *adj* negativo. **minus sign** signo menos *m.*
minute¹ ['minit] *n* minuto *m.* **minutes** *pl n* actas *f pl.*
minute² [mai'njurt] *adj* (*tiny*) diminuto; (*detailed*) minucioso.
miracle ['mirəkl] *n* milagro *m.* **miraculous** *adj* milagroso.
mirage ['mirair3] *n* espejismo *m.*
mirror ['mirə] *n* espejo *m;* (*mot*) retrovisor *m.* *v* reflejar.
mirth [mə:θ] *n* alegría *f;* hilaridad *f.*
misadventure [misəd'ventfə] *n* desgracia *f.*
misanthropist [miz'anθrəpist] *n* misántropo *m.* **misanthropic** *adj* misantrópico. **misanthropy** *n* misantropía *f.*
misapprehension [misapri'henfən] *n* malentendido *m.*
misbehave [misbi'heiv] *v* portarse mal. **misbehaviour** *n* mala conducta *f.*
miscalculate [mis'kalkjuleit] *v* calcular mal. **miscalculation** *n* cálculo erróneo *m.*
miscarriage [mis'karid3] *n* (*med*) aborto *m;* (*plans, etc.*) fracaso *m.* **miscarriage of justice** error judicial *m.*
miscellaneous [misə'leiniəs] *adj* diverso.
mischief ['mistfif] *n* (*evil*) maldad *f;* (*of child*) travesura *f;* (*damage*) daño *m.* **get into mischief** hacer tonterías. **make mischief** sembrar la discordia. **mischievous** *adj* malo; travieso; dañino.
misconception [miskən'sepfən] *n* concepto falso *m.*
misconduct [mis'kondəkt] *n* (*mis-behaviour*) mala conducta *f;* (*mismanagement*) mala administración *f.*

misconstrue [miskən'stru:] v interpretar mal.

misdeed [mis'di:d] n delito m.

misdemeanour [misdi'mi:nə] n (law) infracción f; (misbehaviour) mala conducta f.

miser ['maizə] n avaro, -a m, f. **miserly** adj mezquino.

miserable ['mizərəbl] adj (sad) triste; (sick) mal; (unfortunate) desgraciado; (wretched) miserable; (distressing) de pena.

misery ['mizəri] n tristeza f; (pain) dolor m; desgracia f; miseria f; (coll: person) aguafiestas m, f.

misfire [mis'faiə] v fallar; (mot) tener fallos. n fallo m.

misfit ['misfit] n inadaptado, -a m, f.

misfortune [mis'fɔ:tʃən] n desgracia f.

misgiving [mis'givɪŋ] n recelo m; inquietud f.

misguided [mis'gaidid] adj descaminado; poco afortunado.

mishap ['mishap] n contratiempo m.

misinterpret [misin'tə:prit] v interpretar mal. **misinterpretation** n interpretación errónea f.

misjudge [mis'dʒʌdʒ] v juzgar mal. **misjudgment** n estimación errónea f.

*__mislay__ [mis'lei] v extraviar.

*__mislead__ [mis'li:d] v engañar; equivocar. **misleading** adj engañoso.

misnomer [mis'noumə] n nombre inapropiado m.

misogynist [mi'sodʒənist] n misógino m.

misplace [mis'pleis] v colocar mal; (lose) extraviar.

misprint ['misprint] n errata f.

miss[1] [mis] v fallar; no dar en; (train, bus, etc.) perder; (a meeting) no asistir a; (long for) echar de menos. **miss out** omitir. n tiro errado m; (failure) fracaso m. **missing** adj (lacking) que falta; perdido; ausente; desaparecido.

miss[2] [mis] n señorita.

misshapen [mis'ʃeipən] adj (object) deformado; (person) deforme.

missile ['misail] n proyectil m. **guided missile** proyectil teledirigido m.

mission ['miʃən] n misión f. **missionary** n, adj misionero, -a.

mist [mist] n (haze) calina f; (fog) neblina f; (at sea) bruma f; (on glasses) vaho m. **mist over** or **up** empañar. **misty** adj de niebla; brumoso; vago; empañado.

*__mistake__ [mi'steik] v (be wrong) equivocarse en; (the way) equivocarse de; (misunderstand) entender mal. n error m; equivocación f; falta f. **by mistake** sin querer. **make a mistake** equivocarse. **mistaken** adj equivocado; erróneo; mal comprendido. **be mistaken** estar equivocado.

mistletoe ['misltou] n muérdago m.

mistress ['mistris] n (of the house) señora f; (owner) dueña f; (lover) amante f; (teacher) profesora f.

mistrust [mis'trʌst] n desconfianza f; (suspicion) recelo m. v desconfiar de; recelar de. **mistrustful** adj desconfiado; receloso.

*__misunderstand__ [misʌndə'stand] v entender mal. **misunderstanding** n malentendido m.

misuse [mis'ju:s; v mis'ju:z] n mal uso m; abuso m; maltrato m; mal empleo m. v abusar de; maltratar; emplear mal.

mitigate ['mitigeit] v mitigar; aliviar; atemar. **mitigation** n mitigación f; alivio m; atenuación f.

mitre ['maitə] n (rel) mitra f; (carpentry) inglete m. v unir con ingletes.

mitten ['mitn] n mitón m.

mix [miks] v mezclar; (drinks) preparar; (salad) aliñar; (flour, cement, etc.) amasar. **mix up** mezclar; confundir. **mix-up** n lío m; confusión f. **mixed feelings** sentimientos contradictorios m pl. **mixed grill** plato combinado m. **mixer** n (elec) mezclador m; (cement) mezcladora f. **mixture** n mezcla f; (med) mixtura f.

moan [moun] v gemir; (coll: complain) quejarse. n gemido m; queja f.

moat [mout] n foso m.

mob [mob] n multitud f; (rabble) chusma f. v acosar.

mobile ['moubail] nm, adj móvil. **mobility** n movilidad f. **mobilize** v movilizar.

moccasin ['mokəsin] n mocasín m.

mock [mok] v burlarse de; ridiculizar. adj simulado; falso; imitado. **mockery** n burla f; simulacro m; imitación f. **mocking** adj burlón.

mode [moud] n modo m, manera f; (fashion) moda f.

model ['modl] n modelo m; (of a statue) maqueta f; (fashion) maniquí m; (dressmaking pattern) patrón m. v modelar; (dress) presentar.

moderate ['modərət; v 'modəreit] n, adj moderado, -a. v moderar; aplacar. **moderately** adv moderadamente; (fairly) mediocremente. **in moderation** con moderación.

modern ['modən] adj moderno. **modern languages** lenguas vivas f pl. **modernization** n modernización f. **modernize** v modernizar.

modest ['modist] adj modesto; discreto. **modesty** n modestia f.

modify ['modifai] v modificar. **modification** n modificación f.

modulate ['modjuleit] v modular. **modulation** n modulación f.

module ['modjul] n módulo m.

mohair ['mouheə] n moer m.

moist [moist] adj húmedo. **moisten** v numedecer, mojar. **moisture** n humedad f. **moisturize** v humedecer. **moisturizing cream** crema hidratante f.

molasses [mə'lasiz] n melaza f.

mole[1] [moul] n (on skin) lunar m.

mole[2] [moul] n (zool) topo m. **molehill** n topera f.

molecule ['molikjul] n molécula f. **molecular** adj molecular.

molest [mə'lest] v molestar, importunar.

mollusc [mɔ'ləsk] n molusco m.

molten ['moultən] adj fundido.

moment ['moumənt] n momento m. **at the moment** de momento. **momentary** adj momentáneo. **momentarily** adv momentáneamente. **momentous** adj de gran importancia.

momentum [mə'mentəm] n momento m; ímpetu m; impulso m.

monarch ['monək] n monarca m. **monarchist** n, adj monárquico, -a. **monarchy** n monarquía f.

monastery ['monəstəri] n monasterio m. **monastic** adj monacal.

Monday ['mʌndi] n lunes m.

money ['mʌni] n dinero m. **get one's money's worth** sacar jugo a su dinero. **moneylender** n prestamista m, f.

mongol ['mongəl] n, adj (med) mongol, -a. **mongolism** n mongolismo m.

mongrel ['mʌngrəl] n (dog) perro mestizo m.

monitor ['monitə] n monitor m; instructor m; (tech) radioescucha m. v controlar.

monk [mʌnk] n monje m.

monkey ['mʌnki] n mono m. **monkey around** entretenerse, perder el tiempo.

monogamy [mə'nogəmi] n monogamia f. **monogamous** adj monógamo.

monogram ['monəgram] n monograma m.

monologue ['monəlog] n monólogo m.

monopolize [mə'nopəlaiz] v monopolizar. **monopoly** n monopolio m.

monosyllable ['monəsiləbl] n monosílabo m. **monosyllabic** adj (word) monosílabo; (statement) monosilábico.

monotone ['monətoun] n monotonía f. **monotonous** adj monótono. **monotony** n monotonía f.

monsoon [mon'sum] n monzón m.

monster ['monstə] n monstruo m. **monstrosity** n monstruosidad f. **monstrous** adj monstruoso.

month [mʌnθ] n mes m. **calendar month** mes civil m. **monthly** n, adj mensual. adv mensualmente.

monument ['monjumənt] n monumento m. **monumental** adj monumental; enorme.

mood[1] [mud] n humor m. **moody** adj malhumorado; caprichoso.

mood[2] [mud] n (gramm) modo m.

moon [mum] n luna f. **crescent moon** media luna f. **full moon** luna llena f. **new moon** luna nueva f. **moonbeam** n rayo de luna m. **moonlight** n claro de luna m. **moonlighting** n (coll) pluriempleo m.

moor[1] [muə] n páramo m.

moor[2] [muə] v marrrar.

mop [mop] n (floor) fregona f; (hair) pelambrera f. v fregar. **mop up** limpiar.

mope [moup] v tener ideas negras.

moped ['mouped] n ciclomotor m.

moral ['morəl] adj moral; virtuoso. **moral support** apoyo moral m. n (fable) moraleja f. **morals** pl n moralidad f sing. **moralist** n moralista m, f. **moralize** v moralizar.

morale [mə'ral] n moral f.

morbid ['morbid] adj mórbido.

more [mor] adj más; superior; mayor. pron. adv más. **all the more** aún más. **and what's more** y lo que es más. **even more** más aún. **more and more** cada vez más. **more than ever** más que nunca. **once more** una vez más.

moreover [mor'rouvə] adv además, también; por otra parte.

morgue [morg] n depósito de cadáveres m.

morning ['mɔːnɪŋ] n mañana f. adj de la mañana. **morning coat** chaqué m. **morning sickness** náuseas f pl.

moron ['mɔːrɒn] n retrasado mental m; (coll) imbécil m. f. **moronic** adj retrasado mental; (coll) idiota.

morose [mə'rous] adj malhumorado.

morphine ['mɔːfiːn] n morfina f.

Morse code [mɔːs] n morse m.

morsel ['mɔːsəl] n bocado m.

mortal ['mɔːtl] nm, adj mortal. **mortality** n mortalidad f.

mortar ['mɔːtə] n mortero m.

mortgage ['mɔːgɪdʒ] n hipoteca f.

mortify ['mɔːtifai] v mortificar. **mortification** n mortificación f.

mortuary ['mɔːtjuəri] n depósito de cadáveres m.

mosaic [mə'zeiik] n mosaico m. adj de mosaico.

Moscow ['mɒskou] n Moscú.

mosque [mɒsk] n mezquita f.

mosquito [mə'skiːtou] n mosquito m. **mosquito bite** picadura de mosquito f. **mosquito net** mosquitero m.

moss [mɒs] n musgo m. **mossy** adj musgoso.

most [moust] adj más; la mayoría de. pron la mayoría; la mayor parte; lo máximo. adv más; (very) de lo más. **at most** a lo sumo. **make the most of** sacar el mayor provecho de. **mostly** adv principalmente, sobre todo; en general.

motel [mou'tel] n motel m.

moth [mɒθ] n mariposa nocturna f; clothes moth polilla f. **mothball** bola de naftalina f. **moth-eaten** adj apolillado; (fig) anticuado.

mother ['mʌðə] n madre f. **mother-in-law** n suegra f. **mother-of-pearl** n madreperla f. **Mothers' Day** día de la Madre m. **mother-to-be** futura madre f. **motherly** adj maternal.

motion ['mouʃən] n movimiento m; (signal) señas f pl; (indication) ademán m; (of a machine) mecanismo m; (med) deposición f; (at a meeting) moción f. set in motion poner en marcha. v indicar con la mano; hacer señas. **motionless** adj inmóvil.

motivate ['moutiveit] v motivar. **motivation** n motivo m.

motive ['moutiv] n (reason) motivo m; (law) móvil m. adj motor, motriz.

motor ['moutə] n motor m. **motorbike** n (coll) moto f. **motorboat** n lancha motora f. **motorcar** n automóvil m, coche m. **motorcyclist** n motociclista m. f. **motoring** n automovilismo m. **motorist** n automovilista m. f. **motorway** n autopista f.

mottled ['mɒtld] adj abigarrado.

motto ['mɒtou] n lema m.

mould¹ [mould] n (container) molde m; (shape) forma f; (pattern) modelo m. v moldear; formar.

mould² [mould] n (fungus) moho m. **mouldy** adj mohoso. **go mouldy** enmohecerse.

moult [moult] v mudar. n muda f.

mound [maund] n (natural) montículo m; (artificial) terraplén m; (heap) montón m; (burial) túmulo m.

mount¹ [maunt] v subir; montar a caballo. **mount up** aumentar. n (horse) montura f; (base) soporte m; (phot) borde m; (drawing) fondo m.

mount² [maunt] n monte m.

mountain ['mauntən] n montaña f. **mountaineer** n montañero, -a m, f. **mountaineering** n montañismo m. **mountainous** adj montañoso.

mourn [mɔːn] v lamentar. **mournful** adj triste; afligido. **mourning** n luto m, duelo m.

mouse [maus] n, pl **mice** ratón m. **mousetrap** n ratonera f. **mousy** adj (coll: hair) pardusco; (coll: shy) tímido.

mousse [muːs] n crema batida f.

moustache [mə'staːʃ] n bigote m.

mouth [mauθ] n boca f; (opening) abertura f; (entrance) entrada f; (bottle) gollete m; (river) desembocadura f. **mouthpiece** n (music) boquita f; (phone) micrófono m; (spokesman) portavoz m. **mouthwash** n enjuague m. **mouth-watering** adj muy apetitoso. v articular.

move [muːv] v cambiar de; mudarse de; mover; transportar; (from one place to another) trasladar; poner en marcha; (emotionally) emocionar; (in debate) proponer. n (fig) paso m; marcha f; medida f; (house) mudanza f; (turn) turno m; (chess, etc.) jugada f. **movable** adj movible, móvil. **movement** n movimiento m; (gesture) ademán m; acto m; tendencia f; transporte m; traslado m; (vehicles) tráfico m; (tech) mecanismo m; (mil) maniobra f. **moving** adj móvil; en movimiento; (emotional) conmovedor.

movie ['muːvi] n (US) película f. **go to the movies** ir al cine.

****mow** [mou] v (lawn) cortar, segar. **mow down** barrer.

Mr ['mistə] n señor m; Sr.

Mrs ['misiz] n señora f; Sra.

much [mʌtʃ] adj, adv, pron mucho. **as much** tanto (como). **how much?** ¿cuánto? **much as** por mucho que. **so much** tanto. **too much** demasiado.

muck [mʌk] n (manure) estiércol m; (dirt) suciedad f. v **muck about** (coll) perder el tiempo. **mucky** adj asqueroso.

mucus ['mjuːkəs] n mucosidad f. **mucous** adj mucoso.

mud [mʌd] n barro m; (thick mud) fango m. **mudguard** n guardabarros m invar. **muddy** adj fangoso.

muddle ['mʌdl] n desorden m; confusión f. v confundir, embrollar. **muddle through** salir del paso. **muddleheaded** adj atontado.

muff [mʌf] n manguito m.

muffle ['mʌfl] v amortiguar. **muffle up** embozar. **muffler** n bufanda f.

mug [mʌg] n tazón m; (slang: face) jeta f; (slang: fool) primo, -a m, f. v asaltar. **mugging** n asalto m.

muggy ['mʌgi] adj bochornoso.

mulberry ['mʌlbəri] n (fruit) mora f; (tree) morera f, moral m.

mule[1] [mjuːl] n (animal) mulo, -a m, f. **mulish** adj testarudo.

mule[2] [mjuːl] n (slipper) babucha f.

multicoloured [ˌmʌlti'kʌləd] adj multicolor.

multilingual [ˌmʌlti'liŋgwəl] adj políglota.

multiple ['mʌltipl] adj múltiple. n múltiplo m. **multiple sclerosis** esclerosis en placas f.

multiply ['mʌltiplai] v multiplicar. **multiplication** n multiplicación f. **multiplication table** tabla de multiplicar f.

multiracial [ˌmʌlti'reiʃəl] adj multiracial.

multitude ['mʌltitjuːd] n multitud f, muchedumbre f.

mumble ['mʌmbl] v mascullar. n refunfuño m.

mummy[1] ['mʌmi] n momia f. **mummification** n momificación f. **mummify** v momificar.

mummy[2] ['mʌmi] n (coll: mother) mamá f.

mumps [mʌmps] n paperas f pl.

munch [mʌntʃ] v mascar.

mundane [mʌn'dein] adj mundano.

municipal [mjuː'nisipəl] adj municipal. **municipality** n municipio m.

mural ['mjuərəl] nm, adj mural.

murder ['məːdə] n homicidio m, asesinato m. **murderer** n asesino m. **murderess** n asesina f. **murderous** adj homicida, asesino.

murky ['məːki] adj oscuro; lóbrego.

murmur ['məːmə] v murmurar. n murmullo m.

muscle ['mʌsl] n músculo m. v **muscle in** (coll) meterse por fuerza en. **muscular** adj muscular; (person) musculoso.

muse [mjuːz] n musa f. v meditar, contemplar.

museum [mjuː'ziəm] n museo m.

mushroom ['mʌʃrum] n hongo m, seta f; (food) champiñón m. v crecer como hongos.

music ['mjuːzik] n música f. **music hall** music-hall m. **music stand** atril m. **musical** adj de música; (ear) musical; (person) aficionado a la música. **musical (comedy)** n comedia musical f. **musical instrument** instrumento de música m. **musician** n músico, -a m, f.

musk [mʌsk] n almizcle m.

musket ['mʌskit] n mosquete m. **musketeer** n mosquetero m.

Muslim ['mʌzlim] n, adj musulmán, -ana.

muslin ['mʌzlin] n muselina f.

mussel ['mʌsl] n mejillón m.

****must** [mʌst] v deber; tener que.

mustard ['mʌstəd] n mostaza f. **mustard pot** mostacera f.

muster ['mʌstə] v reunir; (mil) formar. n reunión f; asamblea f; (mil) revista f. **pass muster** ser aceptable.

musty ['mʌsti] adj mohoso. **smell musty** oler a cerrado.

mute [mjuːt] n, adj mudo, -a; (music) sordina f. v apagar; poner sordina a. **muted** adj sordo.

mutilate ['mjuːtileit] v mutilar. **mutilation** n mutilación f.

mutiny ['mjuːtini] n motín m, rebelión f. v amotinarse, rebelarse. **mutinous** adj amotinado; (fig) rebelde.

mutter ['mʌtə] v murmurar. n murmullo m. **muttering** n refunfuño m.

mutton ['mʌtn] n cordero m.

mutual ['mjuː'tʃuəl] adj mutuo; común.

muzzle ['mʌzl] n (nose) hocico m; (device) bozal m; (gun) boca f. v abozalar.

my [mai] *adj* mi (*pl* mis), mío, mía (*pl* míos, mías).

myself [mai'self] *pron* (*reflexive*) me; (*emphatic*) yo mismo, -a; (*after prep*) mí. **by myself** (completamente) solo, -a.

mystery ['mistəri] *n* misterio *m*. **mysterious** *adj* misterioso.

mystic [mistik] *n* iniciado, -a *m, f*; místico, -a *m, f*. *adj also* **mystical** místico; esotérico; oculto; sobrenatural. **mystify** ['mistifai] *v* oscurecer; desconcertar; desorientar; (*deceive*) engañar. **mystification** *n* mistificación *f*; complejidad *f*; confusión *f*.

mystique [mi'stiik] *n* mística *f*.

myth [miθ] *n* mito *m*. **mythical** *adj* mítico. **mythological** *adj* mitológico. **mythology** *n* mitología *f*.

N

nag [nag] *v* regañar. *n* (*horse*) rocín *m*.

nail [neil] *n* (*metal*) clavo *m*; (*anat*) uña *f*; (*claw*) garra *f*. **nailbrush** *n* cepillo de uñas *m*. **nail-file** *n* lima de uñas *f*. **nail polish** esmalte de uñas *m*. **nail-scissors** *n* tijeras para las uñas *f pl*. *v* clavar.

naive [nai'iiv] *adj* ingenuo. **naivety** *n* ingenuidad *f*.

naked ['neikid] *adj* desnudo. **nakedness** *n* desnudez *f*.

name [neim] *n* nombre *m*; (*surname*) apellido *m*; *fama f*; título *m*. **my name is ... me llamo .... namesake** *n* tocayo, -a *m, f*. **what's your name?** ¿cómo se llama? *v* llamar; nombrar. **nameless** *adj* sin nombre; anónimo. **namely** *adv* a saber.

nanny ['nani] *n* niñera *f*.

nap¹ [nap] *n* sueño ligero *m*. *v* dormitar. **be caught napping** estar desprevenido.

nap² [nap] *n* (*of cloth*) lanilla *f*.

nape [neip] *n* nuca *f*.

napkin ['napkin] *n* servilleta *f*.

nappy [napi] *n* pañal *m*.

narcotic [nar'kotik] *nm, adj* narcótico.

narrate [nə'reit] *v* contar. **narration** *n* narración *f*. **narrator** *n* narrador, -a *m, f*.

narrative ['narətiv] *n* narrativa *f*. *adj* narrativo.

narrow ['narou] *adj* estrecho. **narrow-gauge** *adj* de vía estrecha. **narrow-minded** *adj* de miras estrechas. *v* estrechar. **narrow down** reducir. **narrowly** *adv* (*only just*) por muy poco; estrechamente. **narrowness** *n* estrechez *f*.

nasal ['neizəl] *adj* nasal. **nasalize** *v* nasalizar.

nasturtium [nə'stəːʃəm] *n* capuchina *f*.

nasty ['naisti] *adj* sucio; repugnante; (*unfriendly*) antipático; grosero; desagradable.

nation ['neiʃən] *n* nación *f*. **national** *nm, adj* nacional. **national anthem** himno nacional *m*. **nationalism** *n* nacionalismo *m*. **nationalist** *n(m+f)*. *adj* nacionalista. **nationality** *n* nacionalidad *f*. **nationalization** *n* nacionalización *f*. **nationalize** *v* nacionalizar.

native ['neitiv] *adj* (*country, town*) natal; (*inhabitant*) nativo; (*language*) materno; (*product*) del país. *n* natural *m, f*; nativo, -a *m, f*.

nativity [nə'tivəti] *n* nacimiento *m*.

natural ['natʃərəl] *adj* natural. **naturalism** *n* naturalismo *m*. **naturalist** *n* naturalista *m, f*. **naturally** *adv* naturalmente; por naturaleza.

nature ['neitʃə] *n* naturaleza *f*; (*character*) natural *m*; esencia *f*.

naughty ['notti] *adj* travieso; malvado. **naughtiness** *n* travesura *f*.

nausea ['noːziə] *n* náusea *f*. **nauseate** *v* dar asco.

nautical ['nottikəl] *adj* marítimo, náutico.

naval ['neivəl] *adj* naval; de marina. **naval officer** oficial de marina *m*.

navel ['neivəl] *n* ombligo *m*. **navel orange** naranja navel *f*.

navigate ['navigeit] *v* navegar; (*steer*) gobernar. **navigable** *adj* navegable. **navigation** *n* navegación *f*. **navigator** *n* navegante *m*.

navy ['neivi] *n* marina *f*. **navy blue** azul marino *m*.

near [niə] *adv* cerca. *prep* cerca de. *adj* cercano. *v* acercarse a; aproximarse a. **the near future** el futuro próximo. **nearby** *adv* cerca. **nearly** *adv* casi. **not nearly** ni con mucho. **very nearly** casi casi.

neat [niit] *adj* limpio; bien cuidado; ordenado; (*drink*) solo. **neaten** *v* limpiar; ordenar. **neatly** *adv* con cuidado; (*dress*) con gusto; (*skilfully*) hábilmente. **neatness** *n* limpieza *f*; orden *m*; gusto *m*.

necessary ['nesisəri] *adj* necesario. **if necessary** si es preciso. **it is necessary es** preciso. **necessitate** *v* necesitar. **necessity** *n* necesidad *f*.

neck [nek] *n* (*human, garment*) cuello *m*; (*animal*) pescuezo *m*; (*bottle*) gollete *m*. **neck and neck** parejas. **necklace** *n* collar *m*.

nectar ['nektə] *n* néctar *m*.

need [niːd] *n* necesidad *f*; (*lack*) carencia *f*. *v* necesitar; hacer falta a uno. **needless** *adj* innecesario; inútil. **needy** *adj* necesitado. *n* **the needy** los necesitados *m pl*.

needle ['niːdl] *n* aguja *f*. **darning needle** aguja de zurcir. **knitting needle** aguja de hacer punto. **needlework** *n* costura *f*. *v* (*coll*) pinchar.

negative ['negətiv] *adj* negativo. *n* (*gramm*) negación *f*; (*phot*) negativo *m*; (*reply*) contestación negativa *f*.

neglect [ni'glekt] *v* no cumplir con; dejar de; no observar; descuidar; abandonar. *n* negligencia *f*; abandono *m*; inobservancia *f*; dejadez *f*. **neglected** *adj* descuidado; abandonado.

negligée ['negliʒei] *n* negligé *m*.

negligence ['neglidʒəns] *n* negligencia *f*; descuido *m*. **negligent** *adj* negligente; descuidado.

negotiate [ni'gouʃieit] *v* negociar; (*obstacle*) franquear; (*hill*) subir; (*bend*) tomar. **negotiable** *adj* negociable; franqueable. **negotiation** *n* negociación *f*.

Negro ['niːgrou] *nm, adj* negro.

neigh [nei] *v* relinchar. *n* relincho *m*.

neighbour ['neibə] *n* vecino, -a *m, f*. **neighbourhood** *n* vecindad *f*; (*district*) barrio *m*. **neighbouring** *adj* vecino; (*near*) cercano. **neighbourly** *adj* de buena vecindad.

neither ['naiðə] *adv* tampoco. **neither ... nor ...** ni ... ni ... *conj* ni, tampoco. *pron* ninguno, -a *m, f*. *adj* ninguno de los dos.

neon ['niːon] *n* neón *m*.

nephew ['nefjuː] *n* sobrino *m*.

nepotism ['nepətizəm] *n* nepotismo *m*.

nerve [nəːv] *n* nervio *m*; valor *m*; (*coll: cheek*) cara *f*. **get on someone's nerves** crisparle los nervios a uno. **lose one's nerve** (*coll*) rajarse. **nerve-wracking** *adj* crispante; horribilante. **nerves** *pl* (*coll*) nerviosismo *m*. **nervous** *adj* nervioso;

(*apprehensive*) miedoso. **nervous breakdown** depresión nerviosa *f*.

nest [nest] *n* nido *m*. *v* anidar.

nestle ['nesl] *v* arrellanarse; acurrucarse.

net[1] [net] *n* red *f*. **net curtains** visillo *m sing*. **network** *n* red *f*. *v* coger.

net[2] [net] *adj* neto. **net weight** peso neto *m*.

Netherlands ['neðələndz] *pl n* Países Bajos *m pl*.

nettle ['netl] *n* ortiga *f*. **nettle rash** urticaria *f*. *v* irritar.

neuralgia [njuˈraldʒə] *n* neuralgia *f*. **neuralgic** *adj* neurálgico.

neurosis [njuˈrousis] *n* neurosis *f*. **neurotic** *n, adj* neurótico, -a.

neuter ['njuːtə] *nm, adj* neutro.

neutral ['njuːtrəl] *adj* neutro. *n* (*mot*) punto muerto *m*. **neutrality** *n* neutralidad *f*. **neutralize** *v* neutralizar.

never ['nevə] *adv* nunca, jamás. **never-ending** *adj* sin fin. **nevermore** *adv* nunca más.

nevertheless [nevəðəˈles] *adv* sin embargo, no obstante.

new [njuː] *adj* nuevo; fresco.

newcomer ['njuːkʌmə] *n* recién llegado, -a *m, f*.

new-born ['njuːbɔːn] *adj* recién nacido, -a *m, f*.

new-fangled ['njuːˌfaŋgəld] *adj* recién inventado.

new-laid ['njuːˈleid] *adj* (*egg*) recién puesto.

newly-wed ['njuːliˌwed] *adj* recién casado, -a *m, f*.

news [njuːz] *n* noticias *f pl*; actualidad *f*; (*radio*) diario hablado *m*; (*TV*) telediario *m*; (*film*) noticiario *m*. **news agency** agencia de información *f*. **newsagent** *n* vendedor de periódicos *m*. **news flash** noticia de última hora *f*. **news item** noticia *f*. **newsletter** *n* boletín *m*. **newspaper** *n* periódico *m*, diario *m*. **newsstand** *n* quiosco de periódicos *m*.

newt [njuːt] *n* tritón *m*.

New Testament *n* Nuevo Testamento *m*.

New Year *n* Año Nuevo *m*. **Happy New Year!** ¡feliz Año Nuevo! **New Year's Eve** nochevieja *f*.

New Zealand [njuːˈziːlənd] *n* Nueva Zelanda *f*, Nueva Zelandia *f*. **New Zealander** neocelandés, -esa *m, f*, neozelandés, -esa *m, f*.

next [nekst] *adj* próximo; siguiente; que viene; (*adjoining*) vecino. *adv* luego, después; la proxima vez; ahora. *prep* junto a, cerca de. **the next day el día siguiente** *m*. **next-door** *adj* de al lado. **next to al lado de. next-of-kin** *n* pariente más cercano *m*. **who's next?** ¿a quién le toca?

nib [nib] *n* plumilla *f*.

nibble ['nibl] *v* mordiscar, mordisquear. *n* mordisqueo *m*.

nice [nais] *adj* (*kind*) amable; (*agreeable*) agradable; (*likeable*) simpático; (*pretty*) bonito; (*pleasant*) ameno; precioso; escrupuloso; (*weather*) bueno; (*point*) delicado. **nicely** *adv* amablemente; agradablemente; bien. **nicety** *n* precisión *f*; delicadeza *f*.

niche [nit∫] *n* nicho *m*, hornacina *f*.

nick [nik] *n* (*notch*) muesca *f*; (*cut*) rasguño *m*. **in the nick of time** justo a tiempo. *v* hacer muescas; cortar; (*slang: steal*) birlar; (*slang: arrest*) pescar.

nickel ['nikl] *n* níquel *m*.

nickname ['nikneim] *n* apodo *m*. *v* apodar.

nicotine ['nikətin] *n* nicotina *f*.

niece [nis] *n* sobrina *f*.

niggle ['nigl] *v* ocuparse de menudencias. **niggling** *adj* de poca monta; molesto.

night [nait] *n* noche *f*. **good night!** ¡buenas noches! **last night** anoche *f*. **tomorrow night** mañana por la noche *f*. **night cap** *n* (*garment*) gorro de dormir; (*coll: drink*) bebida tomada antes de acostarse *f*.

nightclub ['naitklʌb] *n* night club *m*.

nightdress ['naitdres] *n* camisón *m*, camisa de dormir *f*.

nightfall ['naitfɔl] *n* anochecer *m*.

nightingale ['naitiŋgeil] *n* ruiseñor *m*.

night-life ['naitlaif] *n* vida nocturna *f*.

night-light ['naitlait] *n* lamparilla *f*.

nightly ['naitli] *adj* nocturno. *adv* por las noches; todas las noches.

nightmare ['naitmeə] *n* pesadilla *f*.

night-school ['nait,skul] *n* escuela nocturna *f*.

nightshade ['naitʃeid] *n* **deadly nightshade** belladona *f*.

night shift *n* turno de noche *m*.

night-watchman [,nait'wɔtʃmən] *n* guarda nocturno *m*; sereno *m*.

nil [nil] *n* nada *f*; ninguno, -a *m, f*; (*sport*) cero *m*.

nimble ['nimbl] *adj* ágil; (*mind*) vivo. **nimbleness** *n* agilidad *f*; vivacidad *f*.

nine [nain] *nm, adj* nueve. **dressed up to the nines de punta en blanco. ninth** *n, adj* noveno, -a.

nineteen [nain'tin] *nm, adj* diecinueve. **nineteenth** *n, adj* decimonoveno, -a.

ninety ['nainti] *nm, adj* noventa. **ninetieth** *n, adj* nonagésimo, -a.

nip¹ [nip] *v* (*pinch*) pellizcar; (*bite*) morder; (*coll: go quickly*) pegar un salto. **nip in the bud** cortar de raíz. *n* pellizco *m*; mordisco *m*. **nippy** *adj* rápido; (*chilly*) fresquito.

nip² [nip] *n* (*drop*) gota *f*; (*drink*) trago *m*.

nipple ['nipl] *n* (*female*) pezón *m*; (*male*) tetilla *f*; (*bottle*) tetina *f*.

nit [nit] *n* liendre *f*; (*coll*) papanatas *m* invar.

nitrogen ['naitrədʒən] *n* nitrógeno *m*.

no [nou] *adv* no. *adj* ninguno. **no longer or more** ya no. **no parking** prohibido aparcar. **no smoking** prohibido fumar. **no thoroughfare** calle sin salida.

noble ['noubl] *n(m+f)*, *adj* noble. **nobility** *n* nobleza *f*.

nobody ['noubodi] *pron* nadie.

nocturnal [nok'tɔːnəl] *adj* nocturno.

nod [nod] *v* inclinar; asentir con la cabeza; saludar con la cabeza; (*sleepily*) dar cabezadas. *n* inclinación de cabeza *f*; saludo con. la cabeza *m*; cabezada *f*.

noise [noiz] *n* ruido *m*. **noiseless** *adj* silencioso. **noisy** *adj* ruidoso.

nomad ['noumad] *n* nómada *m, f*. **nomadic** *adj* nómada.

nominal ['nominl] *adj* nominal.

nominate ['nomineit] *v* (*appoint*) nombrar; (*propose*) designar. **nomination** *n* nombramiento *m*, designación *f*.

nonchalant ['nonʃələnt] *adj* imperturbable; indiferente. **nonchalance** *n* imperturbabilidad *f*; indiferencia *f*.

nonconformist [nonkən'fɔːmist] *n(m+f)*, *adj* disidente.

nondescript ['nondiskript] *adj* indescriptible.

none [nʌn] *pron* nadie; ninguno, -a. *adv* de ningún modo, de ninguna manera.

nonentity [non'entəti] *n* nulidad *f*.

nonetheless [,nʌnðə'les] *adv* sin embargo, no obstante.

non-existent [nonig'zistənt] *adj* inexistente.

non-fiction [non'fikʃən] n literatura no novelesca f.

non-resident [non'rezidənt] n(m+f), adj no residente.

nonsense ['nonsəns] n tonterías f pl. **nonsensical** adj disparatado.

non-stop [non'stop] adj directo; continuo; sin escalas. adv sin parar; directamente.

noodles ['nuːdlz] pl n fideos m pl.

noon [nuːn] n mediodía m.

no-one ['nouwʌn] pron nadie.

noose [nuːs] n nudo corredizo m; lazo m; (hangman's) soga f.

nor [noː] conj ni; tampoco.

norm [noːm] n norma f.

normal ['noːməl] adj normal. n lo normal m.

north [noːθ] n norte m. adj also **northerly**, **northern** del norte, norteño; (facing north) que da al norte. adv hacia el norte. **northbound** adj de dirección norte. **north-east** nm, adj nordeste. **north-west** nm, adj noroeste.

Norway ['noːwei] n Noruega f. **Norwegian** n, adj noruego, -a.

nose [nouz] n nariz f; (sense of smell) olfato m; (aircraft, car) morro m. **blow one's nose** sonarse. **have a nosebleed** sangrar por la nariz. **nosey** adj (coll) entremetido.

nostalgia [no'staldʒə] n nostalgia f. **nostalgic** adj nostálgico.

nostril ['nostrəl] n ventanilla de la nariz f; (horse) ollar m. **nostrils** pl n narices f pl.

not [not] adv no; ni; como no; sin. **certainly not!** ¡de ninguna manera! **not at all** (acknowledging thanks) no hay de qué.

notable ['noutəbl] adj notable. **notably** adv notablemente, señaladamente.

notary ['noutəri] n notario m.

notch [notʃ] n (cut) muesca f; (degree) grado m. v hacer una muesca en.

note [nout] n nota f; (key of piano, organ) tecla f; (sound) sonido m; (money) billete m; (music) tono m; (renown) renombre m; marca. **notebook** n cuaderno m. **notepaper** papel de escribir m. **noteworthy** adj notable. v tomar nota de; darse cuenta de; anotar, apuntar. **noted** adj notable; célebre.

nothing ['nʌθiŋ] pron nada; no ... nada. n cero m. **nothing but** sólo.

notice ['noutis] n (advert) anuncio m; (poster) cartel m; (sign) letrero m; atención f; (warning) aviso m; (dismissal) despido m; (resignation) dimisión f. **notice to quit** desahucio m. v darse cuenta de; fijarse en; observar; ver; prestar atención. **noticeable** adj notable; evidente. **notice-board** n tablón de anuncios m. **at short notice** a corto plazo.

notify ['noutifai] v avisar, notificar.

notion ['nouʃən] n idea f, concepto m.

notorious [nou'toːriəs] adj notorio. **notoriety** n notoriedad f.

notwithstanding [notwiθ'standiŋ] prep a pesar de. adv sin embargo. conj por más que.

nougat ['nuːgaː] n turrón de almendras m.

nought [noːt] n cero m.

noun [naun] n nombre m, sustantivo m.

nourish ['nʌriʃ] v alimentar. **nourishing** adj alimenticio. **nourishment** n alimento m.

novel[1] ['novəl] n novela f. **novelist** n novelista m, f.

novel[2] ['novəl] adj nuevo; original. **novelty** n novedad f.

November [nə'vembə] n noviembre m.

novice ['novis] n novicio, -a m, f.

now [nau] adv ahora; ya; ya ahora; actualmente; inmediatamente. **from now on** de ahora en adelante. **nowadays** adv hoy día. **now and again** de vez en cuando. **up to now** hasta ahora.

nowhere ['nouweə] adv por ninguna parte; en ninguna parte; a ninguna parte.

noxious ['nokʃəs] adj nocivo.

nozzle ['nozl] n boca f, boquilla f.

nuance ['njuːãs] n matiz m.

nuclear ['njuːkliə] adj nuclear.

nucleus ['njuːkliəs] n núcleo m.

nude [njuːd] nm, adj desnudo. **nudism** n nudismo m. **nudist** n(m+f), adj nudista. **nudity** n desnudez f.

nudge [nʌdʒ] v dar un codazo a. n codazo m.

nugget ['nʌgit] n pepita f.

nuisance ['njuːsns] n (thing) molestia f; (person) molesta f. **be a nuisance** ponerse pesado. **what a nuisance!** (coll) ¡qué pesadez!

null [nʌl] adj nulo. **null and void** nulo y sin valor.

numb [nʌm] adj entumecido; (with fear) petrificado. v entumecer; dejar helado.

numbness n entumecimiento m; parálisis f.

number ['nʌmbə] n número m. **number plate** (mot) matrícula f. v numerar; contar.

numeral ['njuːmərəl] n número m, cifra f.

numeration [ˌnjuːməˈreɪʃn] n numeración f. **numerator** n numerador m.

numerical [njuːˈmerɪkl] adj numérico.

numerous ['njuːmərəs] adj numeroso.

nun [nʌn] n monja f.

nurse [nəːs] n enfermera f; (nanny) niñera f. v (the sick) cuidar; (suckle) criar; (cradle) mecer; (hopes) abrigar; (plans) acariciar. **nursing home** clínica f.

nursery ['nəːsəri] n (room) habitación de los niños f; (day nursery) guardería infantil f; (plants) vivero m. **nursery rhyme** poesía infantil f. **nursery school** escuela de párvulos f.

nurture ['nəːtʃə] v nutrir, alimentar; (rear) criar.

nut [nʌt] n (bot) nuez f; (tech) tuerca f; (person) loco, -a m, f. **in a nutshell** en pocas palabras. **nutcracker** n.cascanueces m invar. **nutmeg** n nuez moscada f.

nutrient ['njuːtriənt] n alimento nutritivo m.

nutrition [njuːˈtrɪʃən] n nutrición f. **nutritious** adj nutritivo.

nuzzle ['nʌzl] v hocicar.

nylon ['naɪlon] n nilón m.

nymph [nimf] n ninfa f.

O

oak [ouk] n roble m.

oar [ɔː] n remo m. **oarsman** n remero m.

oasis [ouˈeisis] n oasis m invar.

oath [ouθ] n (law) juramento m; (expletive) blasfemia f. **take the oath** prestar juramento.

oats [outs] pl n avena f sing. **oatmeal** n harina de avena f.

obedient [əˈbiːdiənt] adj obediente. **obedience** n obediencia f.

obese [əˈbiːs] adj obeso. **obesity** n obesidad f.

obey [əˈbei] v obedecer.

obituary [əˈbitjuəri] n necrología f.

object ['obʒikt; v əˈbʒekt] n objeto m;

(gramm) complemento m; (aim) meta f. v oponerse; objetar; protestar. **objection** n objeción m; reparo m. **objectionable** adj censurable; desagradable. **objective** nm, adj objetivo.

oblige [əˈblaidʒ] v (compel) obligar; (please) complacer; (assist) hacer un favor. **be obliged to** (have to) verse obligado a; (be grateful) estar agradecido a. **obligation** n obligación f; (comm) compromiso m. **obligatory** adj obligatorio.

oblique [əˈbliːk] adj sesgado; indirecto.

obliterate [əˈblitəreit] v borrar; cancelar. **obliteration** n borrado m; cancelación f.

oblivion [əˈblivian] n olvido m. **oblivious** adj olvidadizo; ignorante.

oblong ['oblon] adj oblongo. n cuadrilongo m.

obnoxious [əbˈnokʃəs] adj ofensivo; execrable.

oboe ['oubou] n oboe m. **oboist** n oboe m, oboísta m, f.

obscene [əbˈsiːn] adj obsceno. **obscenity** n obscenidad f.

obscure [əbˈskjuə] adj oscuro; confuso. v oscurecer; (hide) esconder. **obscurity** n oscuridad f.

observe [əbˈzəːv] v observar; ver; decir. **observant** adj observador; atento. **observation** n (remark) observación f; (of rules) observancia f. **observatory** n observatorio m.

obsess [əbˈses] v obsesionar. **obsession** n obsesión f.

obsolescent [obsəˈlesnt] adj que cae en desuso. **obsolescence** n caída en desuso f.

obsolete ['obsəliːt] adj anticuado.

obstacle ['obstəkl] n obstáculo m.

obstetrics [obˈstetriks] n obstetricia f. **obstetrician** n tocólogo m.

obstinate ['obstinit] adj obstinado; terco; rebelde. **obstinacy** n obstinación f; terquedad f.

obstruct [əbˈstrʌkt] v obstruir; (hinder) estorbar. **obstruction** n obstrucción f; estorbo m.

obtain [əbˈtein] v obtener, lograr; (acquire) adquirir; (extract) sacar.

obtrusive [əbˈtruːsiv] adj importuno, molesto; (meddlesome) entrometido. **obtrusion** n intrusión f.

obtuse [əbˈtjuːs] adj obtuso.

obverse ['obvəːs] n anverso m. adj del anverso.

obvious ['ɒbviəs] adj obvio.
occasion [ə'keiʒən] n ocasión f, oportunidad f; (cause) motivo m; circunstancia f. v ocasionar; incitar. **occasional** adj ocasional. **occasionally** adv de vez en cuando.
occult ['ɒkʌlt] adj oculto. n **the occult** ciencias ocultas f pl.
occupy ['ɒkjupai] v ocupar; emplear. **occupant** n (place) ocupante m, f; (position) posesor, -a m, f. **occupation** n ocupación f; profesión f; trabajo m. **occupational** adj profesional. **occupational hazard** gajes del oficio m pl.
occur [ə'kəː] v (happen) ocurrir, acontecer; producirse; (opportunity) presentarse; (take place) tener lugar. **occurrence** n acontecimiento m; caso m.
ocean ['ouʃən] n océano m. **oceanic** adj oceánico.
ochre ['oukə] n ocre m.
o'clock [ə'klɒk] adv **one o'clock** la una. **two/three/etc. o'clock** las dos/tres/etc.
octagon ['ɒktəgən] n octágono m. **octagonal** adj octagonal.
octane ['ɒktein] n octano m.
octave ['ɒktiv] n octava f.
October [ɒk'toubə] n octubre m.
octopus ['ɒktəpəs] n pulpo m.
oculist ['ɒkjulist] n oculista m, f.
odd [ɒd] adj (number) extraño, raro; impar; (left over) sobrante; (occasional) alguno. **odd jobs** pequeños arreglos m pl. **oddity** n (thing) curiosidad f; (quality) singularidad f. **oddment** n saldo m. **odds** pl n (betting) apuesta f sing; (chances) posibilidades f pl. **be at odds with** estar peleado con uno. **it makes no odds** no importa. **odds and ends** pedazos m pl.
ode [oud] n oda f.
odious ['oudiəs] adj odioso.
odour ['oudə] n olor m; perfume m. **odourless** adj inodoro.
oesophagus [iː'sɒfəgəs] n esófago m.
of [ɒv] prep de.
off [ɒf] adj (substandard) malo; (fruit, vegetables, meat, fish) pasado; (wine) agriado; (cancelled) suspendido; (elec) apagado; (water) cortado; (brake) suelto. prep de; fuera de; a ... de; desde; en.
offal ['ɒfəl] n asadura f.
off-chance [ˌɒf'tʃɑins] n **on the off-chance** (coll) por si acaso.
off-colour [ɒf'kʌlə] adj **be off-colour** (coll) encontrarse indispuesto.

offend [ə'fend] v ofender; escandalizar; (eyes, ears) herir. **offence** n ofensa f; escándalo m; (law) delito m. **take offence** ofenderse por. **offender** n ofensor, -a m, f; delincuente m, f. **offensive** adj ofensivo; chocante; insultante.
offer ['ɒfə] v ofrecer; (proposal) proponer; presentarse. n oferta f; propuesta f. **offering** n (action) oferta f; (gift) regalo m.
offhand [ɒf'hand] adj improvisado; brusco. adv sin pensarlo; bruscamente.
office ['ɒfis] n (place) oficina f; (service) oficio m; (public office) cargo m; (function) funciones f pl. **take office** entrar en funciones. **officer** n (mil) oficial m; (public appointee) funcionario, -a m, f; (police) policía f.
official [ə'fiʃəl] adj oficial. n funcionario, -a m, f.
officious [ə'fiʃəs] adj oficioso.
offing ['ɒfin] n **in the offing** en perspectiva.
off-licence ['ɒflaisns] n bodega f.
off-peak [ɒf'piːk] adj, adv de menos tráfico; (elec) de menor consumo.
off-season [ɒf'siːzn] n estación muerta f. adv, adj fuera de temporada.
offset [ɒf'set; n 'ɒfset] v compensar; desviar. n (printing) offset m.
offshore [ɒf'ʃoi] adj de la costa.
offside [ɒf'said] n (mot: right) lado derecho m; (mot: left) lado izquierdo m; (sport) fuera de juego m.
offspring ['ɒfsprin] n progenitura f; (fig) fruto m.
offstage ['ɒfsteidʒ] adv, adj entre bastidores.
off-the-cuff [ɒfðə'kʌf] adj espontáneo. adv de proviso.
off-white [ɒf'wait] adj blancuzco.
often ['ɒfn] adv a menudo. **as often as not** la mitad de las veces. **every so often** alguna que otra vez.
ogre ['ougə] n ogro m.
oil [oil] n aceite m; petróleo m; (painting) óleo m; fuel m. **oily** adj (tech) grasiento; (food) aceitoso; (skin) graso; (fig: manner) zalamero.
oilcan ['oilkan] n aceitera f; (for storage) bidón de aceite m.
oilcloth ['oilklɒθ] n hule m.
oil colour n óleo m.

oilfield ['ɔilfiːld] n yacimiento pertrolífero m.

oil-fired [ɔil'faiəd] adj alimentado con mazut.

oilskin ['ɔilˌskin] n impermeable de hule m.

oil stove n estufa de mazut f.

oil tanker n petrolero m.

oil well n pozo de petróleo m.

ointment ['ɔintmənt] n ungüento m.

O.K. [ou'kei] interj ¡de acuerdo!

old [ould] adj viejo; antiguo; (adult) mayor; (clothes) usado; (wine) añejo; (other food) pasado; (familiar) conocido. **I am six years old** tengo seis años. **how old is he?** ¿cuántos años tiene? **old age** vejez f. **old-age pensioner** pensionista m, f. **old-fashioned** adj chapado a la antigua; pasado de moda. **old maid** solterona f.

olive ['ɔliv] n (fruit) aceituna f, oliva f; (tree) olivo m. **olive green** nm, adj verde oliva m. **olive oil** aceite de oliva m.

Olympic [ə'limpik] adj olímpico. **Olympic Games** juegos olímpicos m pl.

omelette ['ɔmlit] n tortilla f.

omen ['oumən] n presagio m, augurio m.

ominous ['ɔminəs] adj amenazador.

omit [ou'mit] v omitir; suprimir. **omission** n omisión f; olvido m.

omnipotent [ɔm'nipətənt] adj omnipotente. **omnipotence** n omnipotencia f.

on [ɔn] pron en, sobre; a. **oncoming** adj venidero. **onlooker** n espectador, -a m, f. **onset** n principio m; ataque m. **onshore** adj hacia la tierra. **onslaught** n ataque violento m. **onward(s)** adj, adv hacia adelante. **from now onwards** de ahora en adelante.

once [wʌns] adv una vez; (formerly) antes, hace tiempo. conj una vez que. **at once** en seguida. **once again** una vez más. **once and for all** de una vez para siempre.

one [wʌn] n, pron, adj uno, -a m, f. **be one up** on marcar un tanto a costa de. **one by one** uno por uno. **one-sided** adj parcial; desigual. **one-way** adj de dirección única. **that one** ése or aquél, ésa or aquélla. **this one** éste, ésta. **which one?** ¿cuál?

oneself [wʌn'self] pron se; sí; sí mismo, -a; (emphatic) uno mismo, una misma. **by oneself** solo, -a.

onion ['ʌnjən] n cebolla f.

only ['ounli] adj solo; único. adv sólo, solamente. conj pero, sólo que.

onus ['ounəs] n responsabilidad f.

onyx ['ɔniks] n ónice m, f.

ooze [uːz] v rezumar; exudar.

opal ['oupəl] n ópalo m.

opaque [ə'peik] adj opaco; oscuro. **opacity** n opacidad f; oscuridad f.

open ['oupən] v abrir; (exhibition) inaugurar; iniciar. adj abierto; (unfolded) desplegado; (frank) franco; (meeting) público; (unsolved) pendiente; (post) vacante; (free) libre; (sea) alta. **open-air** adj al aire libre. **open-handed** adj generoso. **open-minded** adj imparcial. **open-mouthed** adj, adv boquiabierto.

opening ['oupəniŋ] n abertura f; inauguración f; oportunidad f; vacante f; principio m; (act of opening) apertura f; (breach) brecha f. adj inaugural. **opening night** noche de estreno f.

opera ['ɔpərə] n ópera f. **opera glasses** prismáticos m pl. **opera house** ópera f. **opera singer** cantante de ópera m, f. **operatic** adj operístico. **operetta** n opereta f, zarzuela f.

operate ['ɔpəreit] v (machine) manjar; (hacer) funcionar; (direct) dirigir; (med) operar. **operable** adj operable. **operating table** quirófano m. **operation** n funcionamiento m; manejo m; maniobra f; aplicación f; actividad f. **in operation** en vigor; en funcionamiento. **operational** adj operacional. **operative** adj en vigor; operativo; eficaz. **operator** n operario, -a m, f; maquinista m, f; telefonista m, f; (tour) agente de viajes; (wireless) radiotelegrafista m.

ophthalmic [ɔf'θalmik] adj oftálmico.

opinion [ə'pinjən] n opinión f. **in my opinion** a mi parecer. **public opinion poll** sondeo de la opinión pública m.

opium ['oupiəm] n opio m.

opponent [ə'pounənt] n adversario, -a m, f; contrario, m.

opportune [ɔpə'tjuːn] adj oportuno. **opportunism** n oportunismo m. **opportunist** (m+f), adj oportunista.

opportunity [ɔpə'tjuːnəti] n oportunidad f.

oppose [ə'pouz] v oponerse a. **opposed** adj opuesto. **be opposed to** oponerse a. **opposition** n oposición f; resistencia f.

opposite ['ɔpəzit] adj opuesto; contrario. **the opposite sex** el otro sexo. prep enfrente de, frente a. *n* lo opuesto, lo contrario.

oppress [ə'pres] *v* oprimir. **oppression** *n* opresión *f*. **oppressive** *adj* opresor, opresivo; (*heat*) sofocante; (*mentally*) agobiante. **oppressor** *n* opresor, -a *m, f*.

opt [opt] *v* **opt out** *of* no meterse. **opt to** optar por.

optical ['optikl] *adj* óptico. **optical illusion** ilusión óptica *f*. **optician** *n* óptico *m*.

optimism ['optimizəm] *n* optimismo *m*. **optimist** *n* optimista *m, f*. **optimistic** *adj* optimista.

optimum ['optiməm] *adj* óptimo. *n* lo óptimo.

option ['opʃən] *n* opción *f*; posibilidad *f*; elección *f*. **optional** *adj* facultativo.

opulent ['opjulənt] *adj* opulento; abundante. **opulence** *n* opulencia *f*.

or [oɪ] *conj* o; (*negative*) ni. **or else** si no. **or not** o no.

oracle ['orəkl] *n* oráculo *m*.

oral ['oɪrəl] *nm, adj* oral.

orange ['orɪndʒ] *n* (*fruit*) naranja *f*; (*tree*) naranjo *m*; (*colour*) naranja *m*. *adj* naranja. **orangeade** *n* naranjada *f*.

orator ['orətə] *n* orador, -a *m, f*. **orate** *v* perorar. **oration** *n* oración *f*. **oratory** *n* oratoria *f*.

orbit ['oɪbit] *n* órbita *f*. *v* estar en órbita; dar vueltas.

orchard ['oɪtʃəd] *n* huerto *m*; (*apple*) manzanal *m*; (*pear*) peral *m*.

orchestra ['oɪkəstrə] *n* orquesta *f*. **orchestral** *adj* orquestal. **orchestrate** *v* orquestar. **orchestration** *n* orquestación *f*.

orchid ['oɪkid] *n* orquídea *f*.

ordain [oɪ'dein] *v* (*rel*) ordenar; (*fate*) destinar. **ordination** *n* ordenación *f*.

ordeal [oɪ'diɪl] *n* sufrimiento *m*.

order ['oɪdə] *n* orden *m*; (*rel*) orden *f*; (*comm*) pedido *m*; (*medal*) condecoración *f*. **in order** (*correct*) en regla. **in order to** para. **out of order** no funcionar. *v* ordenar; organizar; clasificar; pedir; mandar.

orderly ['oɪdəli] *adj* ordenado; metódico; disciplinado. *n* (*mil*) ordenanza *m*.

ordinal ['oɪdinl] *adj* ordinal.

ordinary ['oɪdənəri] *adj* corriente, usual; (*mediocre*) ordinario; simple; (*average*) medio. *n* lo corriente, lo ordinario. **out of the ordinary** extraordinario, excepcional.

ore [oɪ] *n* mineral *m*.

oregano [ori'gaɪnou] *n* orégano *m*.

organ ['oɪgən] *n* órgano *m*. **organist** *n* organista *m, f*.

organic [oɪ'ganik] *adj* orgánico.

organism ['oɪgənizəm] *n* organismo *m*.

organize ['oɪgənaiz] *v* organizar. **organization** *n* organización *f*. **organizer** *n* organizador, -a *m, f*.

orgasm ['oɪgazəm] *n* orgasmo *m*.

orgy ['oɪdʒi] *n* orgía *f*.

oriental [oɪri'entl] *n*(*m*+*f*), *adj* oriental.

orientate ['oɪriənteit] *v* orientar. **orientation** *n* orientación *f*.

orifice ['orifis] *n* orificio *m*.

origin ['oridʒin] *n* origen *m*. **originate** *v* originar, provocar; comenzar. **originate from** ser descendiente de. **originator** *n* autor, -a *m, f*; creador, -a *m, f*.

original [ə'ridʒinl] *adj* original; (*first*) primero. *n* original *m*. **originally** *adv* al principio; con originalidad.

ornament ['oɪnəmənt] *n* ornamento *m*, adorno *m*. *v* ornamentar, adornar. **ornamental** *adj* ornamental, de adorno.

ornate [oɪ'neit] *adj* recargado.

ornithology [oɪni'θolədʒi] *n* ornitología *f*. **ornithological** *adj* ornitológico. **ornithologist** *n* ornitólogo *m*.

orphan ['oɪfən] *n, adj* huérfano, -a. *v* dejar huérfano. **orphanage** *n* orfanato *m*.

orthodox ['oɪθədoks] *adj* ortodoxo. **orthodoxy** *n* ortodoxia *f*.

orthopaedic [oɪθə'piɪdik] *adj* ortopédico.

oscillate ['osileit] *v* oscilar; fluctuar. **oscillation** *n* oscilación *f*; fluctuación *f*.

ostensible [o'stensəbl] *adj* aparente. **ostensibly** *adv* aparentemente.

ostentatious [osten'teiʃəs] *adj* ostentoso. **ostentation** *n* ostentación *f*.

osteopath ['ostiəpaθ] *n* osteópata *m, f*.

ostracize ['ostrəsaiz] *v* condenar al ostracismo. **ostracism** *n* ostracismo *m*.

ostrich ['ostritʃ] *n* avestruz *m*.

other ['ʌðə] *pron, adj* otro, -a. **other than** de otra manera que.

otherwise ['ʌðəwaiz] *adj* distinto. *adv* de otra manera; a parte de eso.

otter ['otə] *n* nutria *f*.

***ought** [oɪt] *v* deber; tener que.

our [auə] *pron* nuestro, -a; el nuestro, la nuestra. *adj* nuestro.

ours [auəz] *pron* nuestro, -a; el nuestro, la nuestra.

ourselves [auə'selvz] *pron* nos; nosotros, nosotras; (*emphatic*) nosotros mismos, nosotras mismas. **by ourselves** solos, solas.

oust [aust] *v* expulsar, echar.

out [aut] *adj* fuera; (*light, fire, etc.*) apagado; (*games*) eliminado. **out loud** en voz alta. **out of** fuera de; (*through*) por; (*from*) de; (*without*) no tener, sin.

outboard ['autboid] *adj* fuera borda, fuera bordo.

outbreak ['autbreik] *n* (*start*) comienzo *m*; (*disease*) epidemia *f*; (*spots*) erupción *f*; (*violence, crime*) ola *f*; (*revolution*) motín *m*; (*temper*) arrebato *m*.

outbuilding ['autbildiŋ] *n* dependencia *f*.

outburst ['autbəist] *n* explosión *f*; (*applause*) salvo *m*; (*temper*) arrebato *m*.

outcast ['autkaist] *n* proscrito, -a *m, f*; paria *m, f*.

outcome ['autkʌm] *n* resultado *m*; consecuencias *f pl*.

outcry ['autkrai] *n* (*noise*) alboroto *m*; protesta *f*.

*****outdo** [aut'duɪ] *v* superar.

outdoor ['autdoɪ] *adj* al aire libre; (*clothes*) de calle. **outdoors** *adv* fuera; al aire libre.

outer ['autə] *adj* externo, exterior. **outer space** espacio exterior *m*.

outfit ['autfit] *n* (*gear*) equipo *m*; (*clothes*) ropa *f*; (*lady's costume*) conjunto *m*.

outgoing ['autgouiŋ] *adj* saliente; (*manner*) sociable. **outgoings** *pl n* gastos *m pl*.

*****outgrow** [aut'grou] *v* crecer más que; (*lose*) perder con la edad. **outgrowth** *n* excrecencia *f*.

outing ['autiŋ] *n* excursión *f*; paseo *m*.

outlandish [aut'landiʃ] *adj* extraño; apartado.

outlaw ['autloɪ] *n* proscrito, -a *m, f*. *v* proscribir; declarar ilegal.

outlay ['autlei] *n* gastos *m pl*.

outlet ['autlit] *n* salida *f*; (*drain*) desaguadero *m*; (*elec*) toma *f*; (*comm*) mercado *m*.

outline ['autlain] *n* contorno *m*; perfil *m*; silueta *f*; (*draft*) bosquejo *m*; (*summary*) resumen *m*; (*map*) trazado *m*. *v* (*sketch*) esbozo *m*. *v* perfilar; bosquejar; resumir; trazar.

outlive [aut'liv] *v* sobrevivir.

outlook ['autluk] *n* vista *f*; punto de vista *m*.

outlying ['autlaiiŋ] *adj* exterior; remoto.

outnumber [aut'nʌmbə] *v* exceder en número.

out-of-date [autəv'deit] *adj* anticuado; pasado de moda.

outpatient ['autpeiʃənt] *n* paciente no internado *m*.

outpost ['autpoust] *n* puesto avanzado *m*.

output ['autput] *n* producción *f*; (*tech*) rendimiento *m*; (*power*) potencia *f*.

outrage ['autreidʒ] *n* ultraje *m*; desafuero *m*. *v* ultrajar.

outrageous [aut'reidʒəs] *adj* ultrajante; escandaloso.

outright [aut'rait; *adj* 'autrait] *adv* francamente; (*entirely*) en su totalidad; (*at once*) en el acto. *adj* completo; absoluto; categórico; franco.

outset ['autset] *n* principio *m*. **at the outset** al principio.

outside [aut'said; *adj* 'autsaid] *adv* fuera, afuera. *prep* fuera de; más allá de. *n* exterior *m*. *adj* exterior, externo; al aire libre; remoto; independiente. **outsider** *n* (*to a group*) intruso, -a *m, f*; (*to a place*) forastero, -a *m, f*; (*horse racing*) caballo no favorito *m*.

outsize ['autsaiz] *adj* de talla muy grande.

outskirts ['autskəitz] *pl n* afueras *f pl*; cercanías *f pl*.

outspoken [aut'spoukən] *adj* franco. **outspokenness** *n* franqueza *f*.

outstanding [aut'standiŋ] *adj* destacado, notable; (*features*) sobresaliente; (*success*) excepcional; (*debt*) pendiente; (*still to be done*) por hacer.

outstrip [aut'strip] *v* dejar atrás.

outward ['autwəd] *adj* exterior; (*journey*) de ida. **outward bound** que sale. **outwardly** *adv* exteriormente; aparentemente. **outwards** *adv* hacia fuera.

outweigh [aut'wei] *v* pesar más que; (*value*) valer más que.

outwit [aut'wit] *v* burlar.

oval [ouvəl] *adj* oval, ovalado. *n* óvalo *m*.

ovary ['ouvəri] *n* ovario *m*.

ovation [ou'veiʃən] *n* ovación *f*.

oven ['ʌvn] *n* horno *m*. **ovenproof** *adj* de horno.

over ['ouvə] *adv* encima, por encima; (*too much*) demasiado; al otro lado. *adj* (*finished*) terminado. *prep* sobre, encima de; al otro lado; superior a; durante.

overall ['ouvərɔil] *adj* de conjunto; total. *adv* en conjunto; por todas partes. **overalls** *pl n* guardapolvo *m sing*.

overbalance [ouvə'baləns] v (hacer) perder el equilibrio.

overbearing [ouvə'beəriŋ] adj dominante, autoritario.

overboard ['ouvəbɔid] adv (fall) por la borda. **go overboard** (coll) pasarse de la raya. **man overboard!** ¡hombre al agua!

overcast [ouvə'kaist] adj nublado.

overcharge [ouvə'tʃaidʒ] v cobrar un precio excesivo; (overload) sobrecargar.

overcoat ['ouvəkout] n abrigo m, sobretodo m.

*****overcome** [ouvə'kʌm] v vencer; triunfar. **be overcome by** estar muerto de.

overcrowded [ouvə'kraudid] adj atestado; superpoblado. **overcrowding** n atestamiento m; superpoblación f.

*****overdo** [ouvə'dui] v exagerar; (exhaust) fatigarse demasiado.

overdose ['ouvədous] n dosis excesiva f.

overdraft ['ouvədraift] n giro en descubierto m.

*****overdraw** [ouvə'drɔi] v girar en descubierto. **be overdrawn** adj tener un descubierto en su cuenta.

overdue [ouvə'djui] adj (train, etc.) atrasado; (comm) vencido y sin pagar.

overestimate [ouvə'estimeit] v sobreestimar.

overexpose [ouvəik'spouz] v (phot) sobreexponer.

overflow [ouvə'flou; n 'ouvəflou] v (flow over) derramarse; (flood) inundar. n desbordamiento m; derrame m; inundación f; (pipe) cañería de desagüe f.

overgrown [ouvə'groun] adj cubierto de hierba; (too big) demasiado crecido para su edad.

*****overhang** [ouvə'djui; n 'ouvəhaŋ] v sobresalir. n saliente m. **overhanging** adj saliente. sobresaliente.

overhaul [ouvə'hɔil] v investigar; revisar. n examen m, revisión f; arreglo m.

overhead [ouvə'hed] adv arriba. adj de arriba. **overheads** pl n gastos generales m pl.

*****overhear** [ouvə'hiə] v oír (por casualidad); sorprender.

overheat [ouvə'hiit] v recalorar; (fig) acalorar.

overjoyed [ouvə'dʒɔid] adj contentísimo.

overland [ouvə'land] adv por vía terrestre. adj terrestre.

overlap [ouvə'lap; n 'ouvəlap] v traslapar. n traslapo m.

*****overlay** [ouvə'lei; n 'ouvəlei] v revestir. n revestimiento m; cubierta f.

overleaf [ouvə'liif] adv a la vuelta.

overload [ouvə'loud; n 'ouvəloud] v sobrecargar. n sobrecarga f.

overlook [ouvə'luk] v (miss) no notar; (ignore) no darse cuenta de; (excuse) perdonar; (command a view) dar a; dominar.

overnight [ouvə'nait] adv (during the night) por la noche; (suddenly) de la noche a la mañana. **stay overnight** pasar la noche. adj (journey) de noche; (stay) por una noche.

overpower [ouvə'pauə] v subyugar; (smell, etc.) trastornar; dominar. **overpowering** adj (desire) irresistible; abrumador.

overrated [ouvə'reitid] adj sobreestimado.

*****override** [ouvə'raid] v (ride over) pasar por encima de; dominar; (fig) anular, rechazar. **overriding** adj principal.

overrule [ouvə'ruil] v denegar, no admitir.

*****overrun** [ouvə'rʌn] v (exceed) rebasar; (overflow) derramarse; (invade) invadir; (flood) inundar; (infest) plagar.

overseas [ouvə'siiz] adv en ultramar. adj de ultramar; (foreign) extranjero; (comm) exterior.

overseer [ouvə'siə] n capataz m; inspector, -a m, f.

overshadow [ouvə'ʃadou] v sombrear; (fig) eclipsar.

*****overshoot** [ouvə'ʃuut] v ir más allá de.

oversight ['ouvəsait] n descuido m; omisión f. **through an oversight** por descuido.

*****oversleep** [ouvə'sliip] v dormir demasiado.

overspill ['ouvəspil] n exceso m.

overt [ou'vəit] adj abierto; manifiesto. **overtly** adv evidentemente.

*****overtake** [ouvə'teik] v (pass) adelantar; (catch up) alcanzar.

*****overthrow** [ouvə'θrou; n 'ouvəθrou] v (overturn) volcar; (plans) desbaratar; (government) derrocar; (empire) derrumbar. n desbaratamiento m; derrocamiento m; derrumbamiento m.

overtime ['ouvətaim] n horas extraordinarias f pl.

overtone ['ouvətoun] n (music) armónico m; (fig) alusión f.

overture ['ouvətjuə] n (music) obertura f; (proposal) propuesta f.

overturn [ouvə'tə:n] v (car) volcar; (government. etc.) derrocar.

overweight [ouvə'weit] adj be overweight pesar demasiado.

overwhelm [ouvə'welm] v (conquer) vencer; (with grief) postrar; (work) inundar; (in argument) confundir; (joy) rebosar. **overwhelming** adj (desire) irresistible; (defeat) aplastante; (work) abrumador.

overwork [ouvə'wə:k] v usar demasiado; hacer trabajar demasiado. n exceso de trabajo m.

overwrought [ouvə'rɔ:t] adj sobreexcitado, nerviosísimo.

ovulation [ɔvju'leiʃn] n ovulación f.

owe [ou] v deber; tener deudas. **owing** adj que se debe. **owing to** debido a.

owl [aul] n lechuza f.

own [oun] v tener, poseer; (acknowledge) reconocer. **own up** confesar. adj propio. **get one's own back** desquitarse. **on one's own** solo, sola. **owner** n dueño, -a m, f; poseedor, -a m, f. **ownership** n propiedad f; posesión f.

ox [ɔks] n, pl **oxen** buey m. **oxtail** n rabo de buey m.

oxygen [ˈɔksidʒən] n oxígeno m. **oxygen tent** cámara de oxígeno f.

oyster [ˈɔistə] n ostra f.

P

pace [peis] n paso m; (gait) andar m; (horse) andadura f; (speed) velocidad f. **keep pace with** ajustarse al paso de; (events) mantenerse al corriente de. v andar; recorrer. **pace up and down** dar vueltas.

pacific [pə'sifik] adj pacífico.

Pacific Ocean n Océano Pacífico m.

pacifism [ˈpasifizəm] n pacifismo m. **pacifist** n(m+f). adj pacifista.

pacify [ˈpasifai] v pacificar; calmar.

pack [pak] n (gang) partida f; (hounds) jauría f; (cards) baraja f; (bundle) bulto m; (med) paño m, compresa f. **packhorse** n caballo de carga m. v embalar; envasar; (suitcase) hacer; (cram) apretar. **pack it in** (coll) dejarlo. **packing** n embalaje m; envase m.

package [ˈpakidʒ] n paquete m; (bundle) fardo m. adj (deal) acuerdo global m; (holiday, tour) viaje todo comprendido m. v embalar; envasar.

packet [ˈpakit] n paquete m; (tea, etc.) sobre m; (cigarettes) cajetilla f.

pact [pakt] n pacto m.

pad¹ [pad] n (paper) bloc m; (blotting) carpeta f; (ink) tampón m; (cushion) almohadilla f; (launching) plataforma de lanzamiento f. v acolchar; rellenar. **pad out** (coll) meter paja en. **padding** n acolchado m; relleno m; (fig) paja f.

pad² [pad] v andar a pasos quedos.

paddle¹ [ˈpadl] n (oar) canalete m; (waterwheel) álabe m. **paddle boat** or **steamer** vapor de ruedas m. v remar con canalete.

paddle² [ˈpadl] v (wade) chapotear.

paddock [ˈpadək] n paddock m.

padlock [ˈpadlɔk] n candado m. v cerrar con candado.

paediatric [piːdi'atrik] adj pediátrico. **paediatrician** n pediatra m, pediatra m. **paediatrics** n pediatría f.

pagan [ˈpeigən] n, adj pagano, -a.

page¹ [peidʒ] n (book) página f.

page² [peidʒ] n also **page-boy** (hotel) botones m invar; (court, wedding) paje m. v (person) hacer llamar por un paje.

pageant [ˈpadʒənt] n desfile histórico m. **pageantry** n aparato m, pompa f.

paid [peid] V pay.

pail [peil] n cubo m.

pain [pein] n dolor m. **painkiller** n calmante m. **pains** pl n (effort) esfuerzo m. **painstaking** adj concienzudo; cuidadoso. v doler; afligir. **painful** adj doloroso; (embarrassing) difícil. **painless** adj sin dolor; (easy) fácil.

paint [peint] n pintura f. **paintbox** n caja de pinturas f. **paintbrush** (artist) pincel m; (house painter) brocha f. **paint roller** rodillo m. v pintar; (fig) describir. **painter** n pintor, -a m, f. **painting** n pintura f; (picture) cuadro m.

pair [peə] n (objects) par m; (people, animals) pareja f; (oxen) yunta f; (horses) tronco m. v (socks, etc.) emparejar; (mate) aparearse. **pair off** (people) formar pareja.

pal [pal] n (coll) amigote m; camarada m, f.

palace [ˈpaləs] n palacio m. **palatial** adj magnífico; suntuoso.

palate ['palit] n paladar m. **palatable** adj sabroso; (fig) agradable.

pale [peil] adj pálido. v palidecer. **paleness** n palidez f.

palette ['palit] n paleta f.

pall[1] [pɔːl] v perder el sabor; aburrirse (de).

pall[2] [pɔːl] n (of coffin) paño mortuorio m; (smoke) cortina f; (snow) capa f.

pallid ['palid] adj pálido.

palm[1] [pɑːm] n (hand) palma f. **palm off** (coll) colar. **palmist** n quiromántico. -a m, f. **palmistry** n quiromancia f.

palm[2] [pɑːm] n (tree) palma f. palmera f.

palpitate ['palpiteit] v palpitar. **palpitation** n palpitación f.

paltry ['pɔːltri] adj miserable.

pamper ['pampə] v mimar.

pamphlet ['pamflit] n folleto m.

pan [pan] n cacerola f.

Panama [panə'mɑː] n Panamá m. **Panama City** n Panamá.

pancake ['pankeik] n pancake m. **Pancake Tuesday** n martes de carnaval.

pancreas ['paŋkriəs] n páncreas m. **pancreatic** adj pancreático.

panda ['pandə] n panda m.

pandemonium [pandi'mouniəm] n pandemonio m.

pander ['pandə] v **pander to** complacer.

pane [pein] n vidrio m, cristal m.

panel ['panl] n (door) panel m; (wall) lienzo m; (dress) paño m; (control) tablero m; (experts) grupo m; (judges) jurado m. v revestir con paneles; artesonar. **panelist** n miembro del jurado m. **panelling** n revestimiento de madera m; artesonado m.

pang [paŋ] n (pain, hunger) punzada f; (jealousy) angustia f; (love) herida f; (conscience) remordimiento m.

panic ['panik] n pánico m. **panic-stricken** adj preso de pánico. v asustarse.

panorama [panə'rɑːmə] n panorama m. **panoramic** adj panorámico.

pansy ['panzi] n pensamiento m.

pant [pant] v jadear, n jadeo m.

panther ['panθə] n pantera f.

pantomime ['pantəmaim] n (mime) pantomima f.

pantry ['pantri] n despensa f.

pants [pants] pl n (underpants) calzoncillos m pl; (coll: trousers) pantalones m pl.

papal ['peipl] adj papal.

paper ['peipə] n papel m; (news) periódico m, diario m; (blotting) papel secante m; (brown) papel de estraza m; (carbon) papel carbón m; (drawing) papel de dibujo m; (greaseproof) papel vegetal m; (tissue) papel de seda m; (toilet) papel higiénico m; (writing) papel de escribir m; (identity) documentación f. v (walls) empapelar.

paperback ['peipəbak] n libro en rústica m.

paper bag n saco de papel m.

paper-boy n repartidor de periódicos m.

paper-clip n sujetapapeles m invar.

paper-knife n cortapapeles m invar.

paper-mill n fábrica de papel f.

paper shop n (coll) vendedor de periódicos m.

paperweight ['peipəweit] n pisapapeles m invar.

paperwork ['peipəwərk] n papeleo m.

paprika ['paprikə] n paprika f.

par [pɑː] n igualdad f; (comm) par f; (golf) recorrido normal m. **be on a par with** correr parejas con. **feel below par** (coll) no sentirse bien.

parable ['parəbl] n parábola f.

parachute ['parəʃuːt] n paracaídas m invar. v saltar con paracaídas. **parachutist** n paracaidista m, f.

parade [pə'reid] n alarde m; (mil) desfile m; (promenade) paseo público m. v (display) hacer alarde de; hacer desfilar; (placard) pasear.

paradise ['parədais] n paraíso m.

paradox ['parədoks] n paradoja f. **paradoxical** adj paradójico.

paraffin ['parəfin] n (solid) parafina f; (fuel) petróleo m.

paragraph ['parəgrɑːf] m párrafo m. **new paragraph** punto y aparte.

parallel ['parəlel] adj paralelo. n paralela f. **parallelogram** n paralelogramo m.

paralyse ['parəlaiz] v paralizar. **paralysis** n parálisis f. **paralytic** n, adj paralítico. -a. adj (coll: drunk) como una cuba.

paramilitary [parə'militəri] adj paramilitar.

paramount ['parəmaunt] adj supremo.

paranoia [parə'noiə] n paranoia f. **paranoid** n, adj paranoico, -a.

parapet ['parəpit] n parapeto m.

paraphernalia [parəfə'neiliə] n avíos m pl.

paraphrase ['pærəfreiz] n paráfrasis f. v parafrasear.

paraplegic [,pærə'pli:dʒik] n, adj parapléjico, -a.

parasite ['pærəsait] n parásito m. **parasitic** adj parásito.

parasol ['pærəsol] n parasol m.

paratrooper ['pærə,tru:pə] n soldado paracaidista m.

parcel ['pɑːsəl] n paquete m; (portion) parcela f. **parcel office** despacho de paquetes m. **parcel post** servicio de paquetes m. v also **parcel up** empaquetar.

parch [pɑːtʃ] v (land) resecar; (person) abrasar; **be parched with thirst** abrasarse de sed.

parchment ['pɑːtʃmənt] n pergamino m.

pardon ['pɑːdn] n perdón m; (law) indulto m; (rel) indulgencia f. v perdonar; disculpar; indultar. **pardon?** ¿cómo? **I beg your pardon** dispénseme.

pare [peə] v reducir; (vegetables) pelar; (fruit) mondar.

parent ['peərənt] n padre, madre m, f. **parents** pl n padres m pl. **parental** adj de los padres. **parenthood** n paternidad f, maternidad f.

parenthesis [pə'renθəsis] n paréntesis m invar. **in parentheses** entre paréntesis.

Paris ['pæris] n París.

parish ['pæriʃ] n parroquia f; (civil) municipio m. **parish church** iglesia parroquial f. **parishioner** n parroquiano, -a m, f.

parity ['pæriti] n paridad f.

park [pɑːk] n parque (público) m. **car park** aparcamiento de coches m. v aparcar. **parking** n estacionamiento m. **parking meter** parcómetro m. **parking ticket** multa por aparcamiento indebido f.

parliament ['pɑːləmənt] n parlamento m. **parliamentary** adj parlamentario.

parlour ['pɑːlə] n salón m; sala de recibir f.

parochial [pə'roukiəl] adj parroquial; (derog) pueblerino.

parody ['pærədi] n parodia f. v parodiar.

parole [pə'roul] n libertad bajo palabra f.

paroxysm ['pærəksizəm] n paroxismo m; (joy, anger, etc.) ataque m.

parrot ['pærət] n loro m. **parrot fashion** como un loro.

parsley ['pɑːsli] n perejil m.

parsnip ['pɑːsnip] n pastinaca f.

parson ['pɑːsn] n (priest) cura m; (Protestant) pastor m. **parsonage** n casa del cura f.

part [pɑːt] n parte f; (role) papel m; (tech) pieza f. **on my part** di mi parte. **part exchange** cambio de un objeto por otro pagando la diferencia. **part-time** adv a media jornada; adj de media jornada. v dividir; separar; (leave) despedirse. **part one's hair** hacerse la raya. **part with** tener que separarse de. **parting** n separación f; despedida f; (hair) raya f. **partly** adv en parte.

*partake [pɑːteik] v **partake of** compartir.

partial ['pɑːʃəl] adj parcial. **be partial to** ser aficionado a. **partiality** n parcialidad f; inclinación f.

participate [pɑː'tisipeit] v participar. **participant** n participe m, f. **participation** n participación f.

participle ['pɑːtisipl] n participio m.

particle ['pɑːtikl] n partícula f; (dust, etc.) grano m; (fig) pizca f.

particular [pə'tikjulə] adj particular; detallado; exigente. n detalle m. **in particular** particularmente. **I'm not particular** me da igual. **full particulars** información completa f.

partisan [pɑːti'zan] n partidario, -a m, f; (mil) guerrillero m. **partisanship** n partidismo m.

partition [pɑː'tiʃən] n división f; (section) parte f. v dividir; repartir.

partner ['pɑːtnə] n (comm) asociado, -a m, f, socio, -a m, f; (dancing) pareja f; (cards, etc.) compañero, -a m, f; (marriage) cónyuge m, f. v asociarse con; ser pareja de. **partnership** n asociación f; (firm) sociedad f. **go into partnership with** asociarse con.

partridge ['pɑːtridʒ] n perdiz f.

party ['pɑːti] n (pol) partido m; (law) parte f; (reception) fiesta f; (gathering) reunión f. **party line** (phone) línea telefónica compartida entre abonados f; (pol) línea política del partido f.

pass [pɑːs] v pasar; (exam) aprobar; (be acceptable) aceptarse; **pass away** or **on** (die) pasar a mejor vida. **pass out** (faint) desmayarse. **pass round** (detour) dar la vuelta a; (distribute) pasar de mano en mano. **pass up** (decline) rechazar. n (permit) pase m; (exam) aprobado m; (mountain) desfiladero m; (sport) pase m.

passage ['pæsidʒ] n (way) pasaje m; (alley) callejón m; (house) corredor m; (time) paso m; (literature) trozo m; (bill) aprobación f; (sea voyage) travesía f.

passenger ['pæsindʒə] n pasajero, -a m, f.

passer-by [,pɑsə'baɪ] n transeúnte m, f.

passion ['pæʃən] n pasión f; (anger) cólera f. **passionate** adj apasionado; colérico.

passive ['pæsɪv] adj pasivo. n (gramm) voz pasiva f. **passiveness** also **passivity** n pasividad f.

Passover ['pɑːsəʊvə] n pascua (de los Judíos) f.

passport ['pɑːspɔːt] n pasaporte m.

password ['pɑːswəd] n contraseña f.

past [pɑːst] nm, adj pasado. prep por delante de; (beyond) más allá de; (time) más de. **twenty past nine** las nueve y veinte. **go past** pasar.

pasta ['pæstə] n pastas f pl.

paste [peɪst] n (meat) pasta f; (glue) engrudo m; (jewellery) estrás m. v pegar.

pastel ['pæstəl] n pastel m.

pasteurize ['pæstʃəraɪz] v pasteurizar. **pasteurization** n pasteurización f.

pastime ['pɑːstaɪm] n pasatiempo m.

pastoral ['pɑːstərəl] adj pastoril; (rel) pastoral.

pastry ['peɪstri] n (dough) pasta f; (cakes) pasteles m pl. **puff pastry** hojaldre m. **pastry-cook** n pastelero m.

pasture ['pɑːstʃə] n (grass) pasto m; (field) prado m. v apacentar.

pasty¹ ['peɪsti] adj pastoso; (face) pálido.

pasty² ['pæsti] n empanada f.

pat [pæt] v dar palmaditas; (a pet) acariciar. n palmadita f; caricia f; (of butter) porción f. adj adecuado. adv oportunamente.

patch [pætʃ] n (clothes) pieza f, remiendo m; (for puncture, wound, etc.) parche m; (land) parcela f. **patchwork** n labor de retazos m. v remendar; poner un parche. **patchy** adj desigual.

patent ['peɪtənt] adj patente, evidente; patentado. **patent leather** charol m. v patentar. n patente f. **patently** adv evidentemente.

paternal [pə'tɜːnl] adj paterno, paternal. **paternity** n paternidad f.

path [pɑːθ] n (way) camino m, sendero m; (star, sun) curso m.

pathetic [pə'θetɪk] adj patético.

pathology [pə'θɒlədʒi] n patología f. **pathological** adj patológico. **pathologist** n patólogo m.

patient ['peɪʃənt] adj paciente. n enfermo, -a m, f. **patience** n paciencia f; (game) solitario m.

patio ['pætɪəʊ] n patio m.

patriarchal ['peɪtrɪɑːkl] adj patriarcal.

patriot ['pætrɪət] n patriota m, f. **patriotic** adj patriótico. **patriotism** n patriotismo m.

patrol [pə'trəʊl] n patrulla f. **patrol car** coche patrulla m. v patrullar.

patron ['peɪtrən] n patrocinador, -a m, f; (saint) patrón, -ona m, f, patrono m; (arts) mecenas m; (customer) cliente m, f. **patronage** n (sponsorship) patrocinio m; (royal) patronato m. **patronize** v (comm) patrocinar; (arts) fomentar; (artist) proteger; (be condescending) tratar con condescencia. **patronizing** adj de superioridad.

patter¹ ['pætə] v (rain) repiquetear; (footsteps) corretear. n golpecitos m pl; repiqueteo m.

patter² ['pætə] n (salesman) charlatanería f. v chapurrear.

pattern ['pætən] n (design) dibujo m; (needlework) patrón m; (sample) muestra f; (example) ejemplo m. v diseñar; (cloth) estampar. **patterned** adj adornado con dibujos.

paunch [pɔːntʃ] n panza f, barriga f.

pauper ['pɔːpə] n pobre m, f.

pause [pɔːz] n pausa f; silencio m. v hacer una pausa; descansar; vacilar; pararse.

pave [peɪv] v empedrar, enlosar. **pave the way for** facilitar el paso de. **pavement** n acera f. **paving** n pavimento m. **paving stone** adoquín m.

pavilion [pə'vɪljən] n pabellón m.

paw [pɔː] n pata f; (cat) garra f. v tocar con la pata; (coll) manosear.

pawn¹ [pɔːn] v empeñar. n prenda f. **pawnbroker** n prestamista m, f. **pawnshop** n casa de empeños f.

pawn² [pɔːn] n peón m.

*****pay** [peɪ] v pagar; dar; (compliment, visit) hacer; (attention) prestar. **pay back** (money) reembolsar; (avenge) devolver. **pay in** ingresar. **pay off** (debt) saldar; (creditor) reembolsar; (mortgage) redimir; (be worthwhile) merecer la pena; (be fruitful) dar resultado. n paga f;

salario *m.* **pay-as-you-earn** *n* deducción del sueldo para los impuestos *f.* **payday** *n* día de paga *m.* **pay rise** aumento de sueldo *m.* **pay-roll** *n* nómina *f.* **pay-slip** *n* hoja de paga *f.* **payable** *adj* pagadero. **payee** *n* beneficiario, -a *m. f.* **payment** *n* pago *m.*; recompensa *f.*

pea [piː] *n* guisante *m.*

peace [piːs] *n* paz *f.* **peacemaker** *n* pacificador, -a *m. f.* **peace offering** sacrificio propiciatorio *m.* **peaceful** *adj* pacífico.

peach [piːtʃ] *n* (*fruit*) melocotón *m.*; (*tree*) melocotonero *m.*

peacock ['piːkɒk] *n* pavo real *m.*

peak [piːk] *n* punta *f.*; peñasco *m.*; (*cap*) visera *f.* **peak hours** horas punta *f pl.*

peal [piːl] *n* (*bells*) ripiqueteo *m.*; (*laughter*) carcajada *f.*; (*thunder*) trueno *m.* v repiquetear; (*thunder*) retumbar; (*laugh*) resonar.

peanut ['piːnʌt] *n* cacahuete *m.*

pear [peə] *n* (*fruit*) pera *f.*; (*tree*) peral *m.*

pearl [pɜːl] *n* perla *f.* **pearly** *adj* nacarado.

peasant ['peznt] *n, adj* campesino, -a.

peat [piːt] *n* turba *f.*

pebble ['pebl] *n* guijarro *m.* **pebbly** *adj* guijarroso.

peck [pek] *v* picotear; picar. *n* picotazo *m.*; (*coll: kiss*) besito *m.*

peckish ['pekiʃ] *adj* **feel peckish** (*coll*) tener gazuza.

peculiar [pi'kjuːljə] *adj* raro; extraño; característico; propio; especial. **peculiarity** *n* particularidad *f.*; rareza *f.*; característica *f.*

pedal ['pedl] *n* pedal *m.* v pedalear.

pedantic [pi'dantik] *adj* pedante.

peddle ['pedl] *v* vender de puerta en puerta.

pedestal ['pedistl] *n* pedestal *m.*

pedestrian [pi'destriən] *n* peatón *m.* **pedestrian crossing** paso de peatones *m.* **pedestrian precinct** zona reservada para peatones *f. adj* (*style*) prosaico.

pedigree ['pedigriː] *n* (*ancestry*) linaje *m.*; (*animals*) pedigrí *m.* **pedigree animal** animal de raza *m.*

pedlar ['pedlə] *n* vendedor ambulante *m.*

peel [piːl] *v* pelar. **peel off** quitar, despegar. *n* (*potatoes, oranges*) monda *f.*, cáscara *f.*; (*candied*) piel confitada *f.* **potato-peeler** *n* pelapatatas *m invar.* **peelings** *pl n* peladuras *f pl.*

peep [piːp] *n* ojeada *f.* v echar una ojeada (a). **peeping Tom** mirón *m.* **peep out** asomar.

peer¹ [piə] *v* entornar los ojos. **peer into** mirar dentro de.

peer² [piə] *n* (*nobility*) par *m.*; (*equal*) igual *m.* **peerage** *n* pares *m pl.* **peerless** *adj* sin par.

peevish ['piːviʃ] *adj* displicente; enojadizo.

peg [peg] *n* (*hats, coats*) percha *f.*; (*clothes*) pinza *f.*; (*tent*) estaca *f.* **off the peg** *adj* de confección. v enclavijar; (*prices*) estabilizar.

pejorative [pə'dʒɒrətiv] *adj* pejorativo.

Peking [.piː'kiŋ] *n* Pekín, Pequín.

pelican ['pelikən] *n* pelícano *m.*

pellet ['pelit] *n* bolita *f.*; (*gun*) perdigón *m.*; (*med*) píldora *f.*

pelmet ['pelmit] *n* galería *f.*

pelt¹ [pelt] *v* tirar, arrojar; (*with questions*) acribillar; (*rain*) llover a cántaros; (*coll: run*) ir a todo correr. **at full pelt** a toda mecha.

pelt² [pelt] *n* pellejo *m.*, piel *f.*

pelvis ['pelvis] *n* pelvis *f.* **pelvic** *adj* pélvico.

pen¹ [pen] *n* pluma *f.* **penknife** *n* cortaplumas *m invar.* **pen-name** *n* seudónimo *m.*

pen² [pen] *n* (*farm animals*) corral *m.*; (*sheep*) redil *m.*; (*pigs*) pocilga *f.* v scorralar.

penal ['piːnl] *adj* penal. **penal colony** penal *m.* **penalize** *v* penar, castigar. **penalty** *n* pena *f.*; (*football*) penalty *m.*; (*fig*) castigo *m.*

penance ['penəns] *n* penitencia *f.*

pencil ['pensl] *n* lápiz *m.* **pencil-sharpener** *n* sacapuntas *m invar.* v escribir con lápiz.

pendant ['pendənt] *n* colgante *m.*

pending ['pendiŋ] *adj* pendiente. *prep* hasta; durante.

pendulum ['pendjuləm] *n* péndulo *m.*

penetrate ['penitreit] *v* penetrar. **penetrable** *adj* penetrable. **penetration** *n* penetración *f.*

penguin ['peŋgwin] *n* pingüino *m.*

penicillin [peni'silin] *n* penicilina *f.*

peninsula [pə'ninsjulə] *n* península *f.* **peninsular** *adj* peninsular.

penis ['piːnis] *n* pene *m.*

penitent ['penitənt] *n(m+f)*, *adj* penitente. **penitence** *n* penitencia *f.*

pennant ['penənt] n (*small flag*) banderín m; (*naut*) gallardete m.

penniless ['penilis] adj sin dinero.

pension ['penʃən] n (*old age, retirement*) jubilación f; (*allowance*) pensión f. **pension fund** caja de jubilaciones f. v pensionar. **pension off** jubilar. **pensioner** n pensionista m, f.

pensive ['pensiv] adj pensativo.

pentagon ['pentəgən] n pentágono m. **pentagonal** adj pentagonal.

penthouse ['penthaus] n ático m.

pent-up ['pent'ʌp] adj reprimido.

penultimate [pi'nʌltimət] adj penúltimo.

people ['piːpl] n personas f pl; gente f sing; (*nation*) nación f sing; pueblo m sing; habitantes m pl; (*coll*) familia f sing. v poblar.

pepper ['pepə] n (*spice*) pimienta f; (*vegetable*) pimiento m. **peppercorn** n grano de pimiento m. **peppermint** n (*plant*) hierbabuena f; (*flavour*) menta f; (*sweet*) pastilla de menta f. **pepper-pot** n pimentero m. v sazonar con pimienta. **peppery** adj picante.

per [pəː] prep por. **per cent** por ciento. **percentage** n porcentaje m.

perceive [pə'siːv] v percibir; (*notice*) notar.

perceptible [pə'septibl] adj perceptible; sensible. **perceptibly** adv sensiblemente. **perception** [pə'sepʃən] n percepción f; sensibilidad f. **perceptive** adj perceptivo; perspicaz.

perch [pəːtʃ] n percha f. v (*bird*) posarse; encaramar.

percolate ['pəːkəleit] v filtrar. **percolator** n cafetera de filtro f.

percussion [pə'kʌʃən] n percusión f.

perennial [pə'reniəl] adj perenne. n planta perenne.

perfect ['pəːfikt; v pə'fekt] adj perfecto; absoluto. n (*gramm*) pretérito perfecto m. v perfeccionar. **perfection** n perfección f; (*perfecting*) perfeccionamiento m. **perfectionist** n(m+f). adj perfeccionista.

perforate ['pəːfəreit] v perforar. **perforation** n perforación f.

perform [pə'fɔːm] v llevar a cabo, ejecutar; (*duty*) cumplir; (*functions*) desempeñar; (*act*) representar. **performance** n ejecución f; cumplimiento m; desempeño m; representación f; (*machine*) funcionamiento m; m; celebración f; (*sport*) actuación f.

perfume ['pəːfjuːm] n perfume m. v perfumar.

perhaps [pə'haps] adv quizá, quizás, tal vez.

peril ['peril] n peligro m. **perilous** adj peligroso.

perimeter [pə'rimitə] n perímetro m.

period ['piəriəd] n período m; época f; edad f; tiempo m; (*school*) clase f; (*menstrual*) regla f. **periodic** adj periódico. **periodical** nm, adj periódico.

peripheral [pə'rifərəl] adj periférico. **periphery** n periferia f.

periscope ['periskoup] n periscopio m.

perish ['periʃ] v perecer. **perishable** adj perecedero.

perjure ['pəːdʒə] v perjure oneself perjurarse. **perjurer** n perjuro, -a m, f. **perjury** n perjurio m. **commit perjury** jurar en falso.

perk [pəːk] v **perk up** animarse. **perky** adj descarado; fresco.

perm [pəːm] n (*coll*) permanente f. **have a perm** hacerse la permanente.

permanent ['pəːmənənt] adj permanente. **permanence** n permanencia f. **permanently** adv permanentemente, para siempre.

permeate ['pəːmieit] v penetrar; (*soak*) impregnar. **permeable** adj permeable.

permit [pə'mit; n 'pəːmit] v permitir; dar permiso; tolerar. n permiso m; licencia f; pase m. **permissible** adj permisible. **permission** n permiso m; licencia f. **permissive** adj permisivo; tolerante.

permutation [pəːmju'teiʃən] n permutación f.

pernicious [pə'niʃəs] adj (*med*) pernicioso; (*evil*) funesto.

perpendicular [,pəːpen'dikjulə] nf, adj perpendicular.

perpetrate ['pəːpitreit] v perpetrar; cometer. **perpetration** n perpetración f; comisión f. **perpetrator** n (*law*) perpetrador, -a m, f; (*author*) autor, -a m, f.

perpetual [pə'petjuəl] adj perpetuo. **perpetuate** [pə'petjueit] v perpetuar. **perpetuation** n perpetuación f.

perplex [pə'pleks] v dejar perplejo, confundir. **perplexed** adj perplejo; confuso. **perplexing** adj confuso; complicado; difícil. **perplexity** n perplejidad f; confusión f.

persecute ['pəːsikjuːt] v perseguir; molestar. **persecution** n persecución f.

147

persevere [,pɜːsiˈviə] v perseverar. **perseverance** n perseverancia f. **persevering** adj perseverante.

persist [pəˈsist] v persistir. **persistence** n persistencia f. **persistent** adj persistente; continuo.

person [ˈpɜːsn] n persona f. **personal** adj personal; en persona. **personality** n personalidad f. **personally** adv personalmente.

personify [pəˈsonifai] v personificar. **personification** n personificación f.

personnel [,pɜːsəˈnel] n personal m.

perspective [pəˈspektiv] n perspectiva f.

perspire [pəˈspaiə] v transpirar, sudar. **perspiration** n transpiración f, sudor m.

persuade [pəˈsweid] v persuadir. **persuasion** n persuasión f. **persuasive** adj persuasivo; convincente.

pert [pɜːt] adj impertinente; alegre; animado.

pertain [pəˈtein] v pertenecer; ser propio de. **pertinent** adj pertinente. **pertinent to** relacionado con.

perturb [pəˈtɜːb] v perturbar. **perturbation** n perturbación f.

Peru [pəˈruː] n Perú m.

peruse [pəˈruːz] v leer atentamente; examinar. **perusal** n lectura atenta f; examen m.

pervade [pəˈveid] v penetrar; saturar.

perverse [pəˈvɜːs] adj obstinado; contrario; (wicked) perverso. **perversity** n obstinación f; perversidad f.

pervert [pəˈvɜːt; n ˈpɜːvɜːt] v (person) pervertir; (facts) desnaturalizar. n pervertido (-a) sexual m, f. **perversion** n perversión f; desnaturalización f.

pessimism [ˈpesimizəm] n pesimismo m. **pessimist** n pesimista m, f. **pessimistic** adj pesimista.

pest [pest] n animal or insecto nocivo m; (coll: person) lata f. **pesticide** n pesticida m.

pester [ˈpestə] v importunar, molestar.

pet [pet] n animal doméstico m; (person) preferido, -a m, f; my pet! ¡mi cielo! adj mimado. **pet hate** pesadilla f. **pet name** nombre cariñoso m. **pet subject** tema preferido m. v minar; (caress) acariciar.

petal [ˈpetl] n pétalo m.

petition [pəˈtiʃən] n petición f. v suplicar; pedir.

petrify [ˈpetrifai] v petrificarse; quedarse seco.

petrol [ˈpetrəl] n gasolina f; (S.Am.) nafta f. **petrol pump** surtidor de gasolina m. **petrol station** gasolinera f. **petrol tank** depósito de gasolina m.

petroleum [pəˈtrouliəm] n petróleo m.

petticoat [ˈpetikout] n enaguas f pl, enagua f.

petty [ˈpeti] adj pequeño; insignificante. **petty cash** dinero suelto m. **petty-minded** mezquino. **petty officer** contramaestre m. **pettiness** n pequeñez f; insignificancia f.

petulant [ˈpetjulənt] adj malhumorado, irritable. **petulance** n mal humor m, irritabilidad f.

pew [pjuː] n banco de iglesia m.

pewter [ˈpjuːtə] n estaño m, peltre m.

phantom [ˈfantəm] n fantasma m.

pharmacy [ˈfɑːməsi] n farmacia f. **pharmaceutical** adj farmacéutico. **pharmacist** n farmacéutico, -a m, f.

pharynx [ˈfariŋks] n faringe f. **pharyngitis** n faringitis f.

phase [feiz] n fase f. **phase in** introducir progresivamente. **phase out** reducir progresivamente.

pheasant [ˈfeznt] n faisán m.

phenomenon [fəˈnomənən] n, pl **-ena** fenómeno m. **phenomenal** adj fenomenal.

phial [ˈfaiəl] n frasco m.

philanthropy [fiˈlanθrəpi] n filantropía f. **philanthropic** adj filantrópico. **philanthropist** n filántropo, -a m, f.

philately [fiˈlatəli] n filatelia f. **philatelic** adj filatélico. **philatelist** n filatelista m, f.

philosophy [fiˈlosəfi] n filosofía f. **philosopher** n filósofo, -a m, f. **philosophical** adj filosófico. **philosophize** v filosofar.

phlegm [flem] n flema f. **phlegmatic** adj flemático.

phobia [ˈfoubiə] n fobia f.

phone [foun] n (coll) teléfono m. v telefonear.

phonetic [fəˈnetik] adj fonético. **phonetics** n fonética f.

phoney [ˈfouni] adj (coll) falso, espurio.

phosphate [ˈfosfeit] n fosfato m.

phosphorescence [fosfəˈresəns] n fosforescencia f. **phosphorescent** adj fosforescente.

phosphorus [ˈfosfərəs] n fósforo m. **phosphorous** adj fosforoso.

photo [ˈfoutou] n (coll) foto f.

photocopy [ˈfoutouˌkopi] n fotocopia f. v fotocopiar. **photocopier** n fotocopiadora f. **photocopying** n fotocopiaje m.

photogenic [,foutou'dʒenik] adj fotogénico.

photograph ['foutəgra:f] n fotografía f. **photograph album** álbum de fotografías m. v fotografiar. **photographer** n fotógrafo, -a m,f. **photographic** adj fotográfico. **photography** n fotografía f.

phrase [freiz] n frase f, expresión f; (gramm) locución f. **phrase-book** n repertorio de expresiones m. v expresar.

physical ['fizikəl] adj físico; n (coll) reconocimiento médico m.

physician [fi'ziʃən] n médico m.

physics ['fiziks] n física f. **physicist** n físico m.

physiology [,fizi'olədʒi] n fisiología f. **physiological** adj fisiológico. **physiologist** n fisiólogo, -a m, f.

physiotherapy [,fiziou'θerəpi] n fisioterapia f. **physiotherapist** n fisioterapeuta m, f.

physique [fi'zi:k] n constitución f; (appearance) físico m.

piano [pi'anou] n piano m. **pianist** n pianista m, f.

pick¹ [pik] n elección f, selección f. **take one's pick** elegir a su gusto. v escoger; seleccionar; (fruit) recoger; (flowers) coger; (lock) abrir con ganzúa. **pick at** (food) picar (la comida). **pick-me-up** n (coll) tónico. m. **pick out** escoger; distinguir; (highlight) hacer resaltar. **pick-pocket** n ratero, -a m, f. **pick up** levantar; recoger; (improve) mejorarse; (learn) aprender; (arrest) detener.

pick² [pik] n (tool) piqueta f; (music) plectro m.

picket ['pikit] n piquete m; (person) huelguista m, f. v estar de guardia.

pickle ['pikl] v conservar en vinagre. n encurtido m.

picnic ['piknik] n merienda campestre f. v merendar en el campo.

pictorial [pik'tɔ:riəl] adj pictórico, ilustrado.

picture ['piktʃə] n ilustración f; (portrait) retrato m; (painting) cuadro m; (film) película f. **picture frame** marco m. **picture gallery** museo de pintura m. **pictures** n (coll) cine m. v describir; imaginarse.

picturesque [piktʃə'resk] adj pintoresco.

pidgin ['pidʒən] n lengua macarrónica f.

pie [pai] n (fruit) pastel m; (meat) pastel de carne m.

piece [pi:s] n pedazo m, trozo m; parte f; (material) pieza f. **piecemeal** adv hecho por partes. **piecework** n trabajo a destajo m. v **piece together** juntar.

pier [piə] n malecón m; (landing-stage) muelle m.

pierce [piəs] v penetrar; perforar; (go through) traspasar. **piercing** adj penetrante; (wind) cortante.

piety ['paiəti] n piedad f.

pig [pig] n puerco m, cerdo m. **pigskin** n piel de cerdo f. **pigsty** n pocilga f. **pigtail** n coleta f.

pigeon ['pidʒən] n paloma f. **pigeonhole** n casilla f.

pigment ['pigmənt] n pigmento m.

pike [paik] n (fish) lucio m.

pilchard ['piltʃəd] n sardina arenque f.

pile¹ [pail] n (heap) pila f, montón m. v amontonar. **pile up** acumular. **pile-up** n accidente múltiple m.

pile² [pail] n (post) poste m.

pile³ [pail] n (of carpet, etc.) pelo m.

piles [pailz] pl n (med) hemorroides f pl.

pilfer ['pilfə] v (coll) sisar. **pilferage** n sisa f.

pilgrim ['pilgrim] n peregrino, -a m, f. **pilgrimage** n peregrinación f.

pill [pil] n píldora f.

pillage ['pilidʒ] n saqueo m. v saquear.

pillar ['pilə] n pilar m, columna f. **pillar-box** n buzón m.

pillion ['piljən] n grupa f. **ride pillion** ir a la grupa.

pillow ['pilou] n almohada f. **pillowcase** n funda de almohada f.

pilot ['pailət] n piloto m. **pilot-light** n piloto m. v guiar; conducir.

pimento [pi'mentou] n pimienta de Jamaica f.

pimp [pimp] n chulo m.

pimple ['pimpl] n espinilla f. **pimply** adj espinilloso.

pin [pin] n alfiler m; (hairpin) horquilla f; (safety pin) imperdible m; (tech) pezonera f; (bolt) perno m. **pincushion** n almohadilla f. **pin-money** n alfileres m pl. **pinpoint** v localizar con toda precisión. **pins and needles** hormigueo m. **pinstripe** n raya muy fina f. v prender con alfileres. **pin down** (fix) sujetar; (find) encontrar; (enemy) inmovilizar. **pin up** (notice) fijar.

pinafore ['pinəfɔ:] n (apron) delantal m. **pinafore dress** falda con peto f.

149   plan

pincers ['pinsəz] *pl* *n* (*tool*) tenazas *f pl*; (*zool*) pinzas *f pl*.

pinch [pintʃ] *n* pellizco *m*; (*salt. etc.*) pizca *f*. **at a pinch** en caso de necesidad. **feel the pinch** empezar a pasar apuros. *v* pellizcar; (*shoes, etc.*) apretar; (*coll: steal*) mangar.

pine¹ [pain] *n* pino *m*. **pine-cone** *n* piña *f*.

pine² [pain] *v* languidecer. **pine for** anhelar.

pineapple ['painapl] *n* ananás *m*, piña *f*.

ping-pong ['piŋpoŋ] *n* ping-pong *m*, tenis de mesa *m*.

pinion ['pinjən] *n* ala *f*. *v* maniatar.

pink [piŋk] *n* (*colour*) rosa *m*; (*flower*) clavel *m*. *adj* rosa.

pinnacle ['pinəkl] *n* pináculo *m*.

pioneer [,paiə'niə] *n* pionero *m*, iniciador *m*.

pious ['paiəs] *adj* pío, devoto.

pip¹ [pip] *n* (*seed*) pepita *f*.

pip² [pip] *n* (*phone. etc.*) señal *f*.

pipe [paip] *n* (*gas, water, etc.*) tubo *m*, tubería *f*, cañería *f*; (*tobacco*) pipa *f*; (*music*) caramillo *m*. **pipe-cleaner** limpiapipas *m invar*. **pipeline** *n* (*oil*) oleoducto *m*; (*gas*) gasoducto *m*; (*water*) tubería *f*. *v* conducir por tubería; transportar por oleoducto. **pipe down** (*coll*) callarse. **pipe** *n* (*music*) sonido de la gaite *m*; (*sewing*) ribete; tubería *f*.

piquant ['piːkənt] *adj* picante. **piquancy** *n* picante *m*.

pique [piːk] *n* pique *m*. *v* picar; herir.

pirate ['paiərət] *n* pirata *m*. *v* piratear. **piracy** *n* piratería *f*.

pirouette [,piru'et] *n* pirueta *f*. *v* hacer piruetas.

Pisces ['paisiz] *n* Piscis *m*.

piss [pis] *n* (*impol*) meada *f*. *v* mear. **piss off!** ¡vete al cuerno! **pissed** *adj* (*drunk*) trompa. **be pissed off** estar furioso (con).

pistachio [pi'staʃiou] *n* pistacho *m*.

pistol ['pistl] *n* pistola *f*.

piston ['pistən] *n* émbolo *m*, pistón *m*.

pit [pit] *n* (*hole*) pozo *m*, hoyo; mina; (*orchestra*) foso de la orquesta *m*; (*of the stomach*) boca *f*; *v* llenar de hojitos; (*oppose*) oponer. **pit oneself against** medirse con.

pitch¹ [pitʃ] *n* (*throw*) lanzamiento *m*; (*sport*) campo *m*; (*music*) tono *m*; (*gradient*) grado de inclinación *m*; (*of a ship*) cabezada *f*. *v* lanzar, echar; entonar; (*of a ship*) cabecear; (*tent*) armar; (*fall*)

caerse. **pitchfork** *n* horca *f*. *v* (*fig*) catapultar.

pitch² [pitʃ] *n* pez *f*, brea *f*. **pitch-black** *adj* negro como el carbón.

pitfall ['pitfoːl] *n* escollo *m*; trampa *f*.

pith [piθ] *n* médula *f*; (*fig*) meollo *m*. **pithy** *adj* conciso, expresivo.

pittance ['pitəns] *n* miseria *f*.

pituitary [pi'tjuitəri] *n* glándula pituitaria *f*.

pity ['piti] *n* compasión *f*; lástima *f*. **take pity on** tener lástima de. **what a pity!** ¡qué lástima! *v* compadecerse de. **pitiful** *adj* lastimoso; (*bad*) lamentable. **pitiless** *adj* despiadado.

pivot ['pivət] *n* pivote *m*; eje *m*. *v* girar sobre su eje.

placard ['plakaːd] *n* cartel *m*. *v* fijar carteles.

placate [plə'keit] *v* aplacar. **placatory** *adj* placativo.

place [pleis] *n* sitio *m*, lugar *m*; (*post*) puesto *m*; local *m*; posición *f*. **all over the place** por todas partes. **in place** en su sitio. **in place of** en lugar de. **out of place** fuera de lugar. **take place** suceder, ocurrir. **take the place of** sustituir a. *v* colocar; poner; situar; (*an order*) hacer. **be well placed** estar en buena posición.

placenta [plə'sentə] *n* placenta *f*.

placid ['plasid] *adj* plácido. **placidity** *n* placidez *f*.

plagiarize ['pleidʒəraiz] *v* plagiar. **plagiarism** *n* plagio *m*. **plagiarist** *n* plagiario, -a *m, f*.

plague [pleig] *n* (*disease*) peste *f*; (*social scourge*) plaga *f*; (*nuisance*) molestia *f*. *v* importunar.

plaice [pleis] *n* platija *f*.

plaid [plad] *n* tartán *m*. *adj* escocés.

plain [plein] *adj* (*clear*) claro; simple; puro; completo; (*frank*) franco; natural; (*unattractive*) sin atractivo. **plain-clothes** *adj* en traje de calle. **make plain** poner de manifiesto. *n* llanura *f*.

plaintiff ['pleintif] *n* demandante *m, f*.

plaintive ['pleintiv] *adj* quejumbroso.

plait [plat] *n* (*fold*) pliegue *m*; (*hair*) trenza *f*. *v* plisar; trenzar.

plan [plan] *n* (*map*) plano *m*; (*scheme*) plan *m*, proyecto *m*. *v* (*for the future*) hacer planes para; (*holidays*) hacer el plan de; (*design*) hacer el plano de; (*action*) planear; (*production*) planificar. **planning** *n* planificación *f*.

plane[1] [plein] n plano m; (coll: aeroplane) avión m. adj plano.

plane[2] [plein] n (tool) cepillo m. v cepillar.

plank [plaŋk] n tabla n.

plankton ['plaŋktən] n plancton m.

plant [plaint] n (bot) planta f; (tech) maquinaria f; (factory) fábrica f; (installation) instalación f. v plantar. **plantation** n plantación f; hacienda f.

plaque [plaik] n placa f.

plasma ['plazmə] n plasma m.

plaster ['plaistə] n (walls) yeso m; (for wounds) emplasto m. **plaster of Paris** yeso blanco m. v enyesar; cubrir. **plasterer** yesero m.

plastic ['plastik] nm, adj plástico. **plastic surgery** cirugía plástica f.

plate [pleit] n (dish) plato m; (of metal) chapa f; (tableware) vajilla f; (in book) lámina f. v chapar; (silver) platear; (gold) dorar. **plateful** n plato m.

plateau ['platou] n meseta f.

platform ['platfoim] n plataforma f; (rail) andén m; (stage) estrado m; (builders) andamio m; (pol) programa m. **platform ticket** billete de andén m.

platinum ['platinəm] n platino m.

platonic [pləˈtonik] adj platónico.

platoon [pləˈtuin] n (mil) pelotón m.

plausible ['plɔizəbl] adj plausible; (person) convincente. **plausibility** n plausibilidad f.

play [plei] n juego m, diversión f. (theatre) obra de teatro f; (manoeuvre) jugada f. v jugar. **player** n jugador, -a m, f; (music) intérprete m, f; (theatre) actor, actriz m, f. **playful** adj juguetón. **playfulness** n carácter juguetón m.

playback ['pleibak] n reproducción f. **play back** v volver a poner.

playground ['pleigraund] n campo de juegos m.

playhouse ['pleihaus] n teatro m.

playing card n carta f, naipe m.

playing field n campo de deportes m.

plaything ['pleiθiŋ] n juguete m.

playwright ['pleirait] n autor de teatro m.

plea [plii] n súplica f; petición f; (law) alegato m.

plead [pliid] v suplicar; implorar; intervenir; hacer un alegato.

pleasant ['pleznt] adj agradable.

please [pliiz] v gustar, agradar. **if you please** por favor. **pleased** adj contento. **pleasing** adj agradable.

pleasure ['pleʒə] n placer m, gusto m. **pleasurable** adj grato.

pleat [pliit] n pliegue m. v plisar.

plectrum ['plektrəm] n plectro m.

pledge [pledʒ] n prenda f; promesa f. v dar en prenda; prometer.

plenty ['plenti] n abundancia f; cantidad f. **plenty of** bastante. **plentiful** adj abundante, copioso.

pleurisy ['pluərisi] n pleuresía f.

pliable ['plaiəbl] adj flexible; (person) dócil. **pliability** n flexibilidad f; docilidad f.

pliers ['plaiəz] pl n alicates m pl.

plight [plait] n aprieto m; crisis f.

plimsolls ['plimsəlz] pl n zapatos de tenis m pl.

plod [plod] v andar con paso pesado; (coll: work) trabajar con ahínco. **plodder** n empollón, -ona m, f.

plonk [plonk] n (coll) pirriaque m.

plop [plop] n plaf m. v hacer plaf.

plot[1] [plot] n (story, etc.) argumento m; (conspiracy) conspiración f; v tramar, maquinar; (route) trazar.

plot[2] [plot] n (land) terreno m; (garden) cuadro m.

plough [plau] n arado m. v arar. **plough one's way through** abrirse paso. **ploughman** n arador.

pluck [plʌk] n valor m; (music) plectro m; (pull) tirón m. v (pull) arrancar; (music) puntear; (fruit) coger; (fowl) desplumar; (eyebrows) depilarse. **pluck out** arrancar. **pluck up courage** armarse de valor. **plucky** adj valiente.

plug [plʌg] n (stopper) taco m; (sink, bath) tapón m; (elec) enchufe m; (mot) bujía f. v taponar; tapar; enchufar; (block up) atascar; (coll: advertise) dar publicidad a. **plug away at** perseverar en. **plug in** enchufar.

plum [plʌm] n (fruit) ciruela f; (tree) ciruelo m.

plumage ['pluimidʒ] n plumaje m.

plumb [plʌm] n plomada f, plomo m. **plumbline** n cuerda de plomada f; (in water) sonda f. adj vertical. adv a plomo. v aplomar; sondar. **plumber** n fontanero m. **plumbing** n fontanería f; instalación de cañerías f.

plume [pluim] n (feather) pluma f; (smoke) penacho m. v emplumar.

plummet ['plʌmit] n plomo m. v (bird, aircraft) caer en picado; (person, thing) caer a plomo; (prices) caer verticalmente.

plump[1] [plʌmp] adj (person) rellenito; (animal) gordo. **plumpness** n gordura f.

plump[2] [plʌmp] v caer de golpe. **plump for** decidirse por.

plunder ['plʌndə] v saquear; robar. n saqueo m; (loot) botín m. **plunderer** n saqueador m. **plundering** n saqueo m.

plunge [plʌndʒ] n (fall) caída f; (short dive) zambullida f; (high dive) salto m. **take the plunge** aventurarse. v (knife, etc.) meter; sumergir; (into despair) hundirse; (launch oneself) lanzarse; (fall) caer.

pluperfect [pluːˈpəfikt] n pluscuamperfecto m.

plural ['pluərəl] nm, adj plural.

plus [plʌs] prep más. n cantidad positiva f; (sign) signo más m. adj positivo.

plush [plʌʃ] adj afelpado; (fig) lujoso. n felpa f.

ply[1] [plai] v (tool) manejar; (trade) ejercer; (questions) acosar; (ship, etc.) hacer el trayecto de. **ply between** hacer el servicio entre.

ply[2] [plai] n (wood) chapa f; (wool) cabo m; (fabric) capa f. **plywood** n contrapachado m.

pneumatic [njuːˈmatik] adj neumático. **pneumatic drill** barreno neumático m.

pneumonia [njuːˈmouniə] n pulmonía f.

poach[1] [poutʃ] v cazar or pescar en vedado. **poacher** n cazador or pescador furtivo m. **poaching** n caza or pesca furtiva f.

poach[2] [poutʃ] v (egg) escalfar.

pocket ['pokit] n bolsillo m. **pocket-money** n dinero de bolsillo m. v embolsarse.

pod [pod] n vaina f.

podgy ['podʒi] adj (coll) gordo.

poem ['pouim] n poema m.

poet ['pouit] n poeta m. **poetess** n poetisa f. **poetic** adj poético. **poetry** n poesía f.

poignant ['poinjənt] adj conmovedor.

point [point] n punto m.; (sharp end) punta f; (decimal) coma f; (elec) contacto m; (meaning) sentido m; motivo; (headland) cabo m. **points** pl n (railway) agujas f pl. **beside the point** que no viene al caso. **come** or **get to the point** ir al grano. **make a point of** insistir en. **point-blank** adv (shoot) a quema ropa;

(demand) sin rodeos; (refuse) categóricamente. **what's the point?** ¿para qué sirve? v señalar; (a weapon) apuntar. **point out** señalar; advertir. **pointed** adj (sharpened) afilado; (shape) puntiagudo. (remark) directo. **pointless** adj inútil.

poise [poiz] n equilibrio m; (bearing) porte m; elegancia f; serenidad f. v poner en equilibrio; preparar. **be poised** estar en equilibrio; estar preparado.

poison ['poizən] n veneno m. v envenenar. **poisoning** n envenenamiento m. **poisonous** adj venenoso; tóxico.

poke [pouk] n empujón con el dedo; (with elbow) codazo m; (fig) hurgonada f. v dar con la punta del dedo; dar un codazo; hurgar. **poker** n hurgón m.

poker ['poukə] n (cards) póker m. **poker-faced** adj de cara inmutable.

Poland ['poulənd] n Polonia f. **Pole** n polaco, -a m, f. **Polish** nm, adj polaco.

polar ['poulə] adj polar. **polar bear** oso blanco. **polarize** v polarizar.

pole[1] [poul] n (wood) palo m; (metal) barra f; (telegraphs) poste m; (flag) asta f. **pole-vault** n salto de pértiga m.

pole[2] [poul] n (geog, elec) polo m. **pole star** estrella polar f.

police [pəˈliːs] n policía f. **the police force** el cuerpo de policía. **policeman** n policía m, guardia m. **police station** comisaría de policía f. **policewoman** n mujer policía f.

policy[1] ['poləsi] n (government) política f; principio m; táctica f.

policy[2] ['poləsi] n (insurance) póliza f.

polio ['pouliou] n polio f.

polish ['poliʃ] n (shine) brillo m; (act) pulimento m; (furniture) cera f; (shoes) betún m; (nails) esmalte m; (fig) elegancia f. v (shoes) limpiar; (metal) pulir; (floors) encerar. **polish off** zampar. **polish up** dar brillo a; (improve) perfeccionar.

polite [pəˈlait] adj cortés. **politeness** n cortesía f.

politics ['politiks] n polítca f. **political** adj político. **politician** n político.

polka ['polkə] n polca f.

poll [poul] n votación f; elecciones f pl; (survey) sondeo m. v obtener; sondear. **polling booth** cabina electoral f; **polling day** día de elecciones m. **polling station** central electoral m.

pollen ['polən] n polen m. **pollen count**

índice de polen *m*. **pollinate** *v* polinizar. **pollination** *n* polinización *f*.

pollute [pə'luːt] *v* contaminar. **pollution** *n* contaminación *f*.

polo ['pəuləu] *n* polo *m*. **water polo** polo acuático *m*. **polo-neck** *n* cuello vuelto *m*.

polyester [ˌpɒli'estə] *n* poliéster *m*.

polygamy [pə'ligəmi] *n* poligamia *f*.

polygon ['pɒligən] *n* polígono *m*.

polystyrene [ˌpɒli'staiəriːn] *n* poliestireno *m*.

polytechnic [ˌpɒli'teknik] *n* escuela politécnica *f*.

polythene ['pɒliθiːn] *n* polietileno *m*.

pomegranate ['pɒmigrænit] *n* (*fruit*) granada *f*; (*tree*) granado *m*.

pomp [pɒmp] *n* pompa *f*. **pompous** *adj* pomposo.

pond [pɒnd] *n* charca *f*; (*artificial*) estanque *m*.

ponder ['pɒndə] *v* considerar; meditar.

pony ['pəuni] *n* poney *m*. **pony-tail** *n* cola de caballo *f*.

poodle ['puːdl] *n* perro de lanas *m*.

poof [puf] *n* (*derog*) marica *m*.

pool[1] [puːl] *n* (*liquid*) charco *m*; (*swimming*) piscina *f*.

pool[2] [puːl] *n* (*money*) banca *f*; (*things*) recursos comunes *m pl*; (*reserve*) reserva *f*; (*comm*) fondos comunes *m pl*; (*typing*) servicio de mecanografía *m*. **pools** *pl n* (*football*) quinielas *f pl*. *v* aunar; reunir; poner en un fondo común.

poor [puə] *adj* pobre; mediocre.

poorly ['puəli] *adj* pobremente; mal. **be poorly** estar malo.

pop[1] [pɒp] *n* taponazo *m*; (*drink*) gaseosa *f*. **popcorn** *n* rosetas de maíz *f pl*. *v* pinchar; (*cork*) hacer saltar; (*put*) meter. **pop in** entrar un momento.

pop[2] [pɒp] *adj* popular. **pop music** música pop *f*.

pope [pəup] *n* papa *m*.

poplar ['pɒplə] *n* álamo *m*.

poplin ['pɒplin] *n* popelina *f*.

poppy ['pɒpi] *n* amapola *f*.

popular ['pɒpjulə] *adj* popular. **popularity** *n* popularidad *f*. **popularize** *v* popularizar.

population [ˌpɒpju'leiʃən] *n* población *f*. **populate** *v* poblar.

porcelain ['pɔːslin] *n* porcelana *f*.

porch [pɔːtʃ] *n* pórtico *m*.

porcupine ['pɔːkjupain] *n* puerco espú *m*.

pore[1] [pɔː] *n* (*anat*) poro *m*.

pore[2] [pɔː] *v* **pore over** estar absorto en.

pork [pɔːk] *n* cerdo *m*.

pornography [pɔː'nɒgrəfi] *n* pornografía *f*. **pornographic** *adj* pornográfico.

porous ['pɔːrəs] *adj* poroso.

porpoise ['pɔːpəs] *n* marsopa *f*.

porridge ['pɒridʒ] *n* gachas de avena *f pl*.

port[1] [pɔːt] *n* (*harbour*) puerto *m*.

port[2] [pɔːt] *n* (*naut*: *left*) babor *m*.

port[3] [pɔːt] *n* (*wine*) oporto *m*.

portable ['pɔːtəbl] *adj* portátil.

portent ['pɔːtent] *n* presagio *m*.

porter ['pɔːtə] *n* (*attendant*) mozo *m*; (*doorman*) portero; (*in government buildings*) conserje *m*.

portfolio [pɔːt'fəuliəu] *n* (*folder*) carpeta *f*; (*pol*) cartera *f*.

porthole ['pɔːthəul] *n* portilla *f*.

portion ['pɔːʃən] *n* porción *f*; parte *f*.

portrait ['pɔːtrət] *n* retrato *m*.

portray [pɔː'trei] *v* retratar; representar. **portrayal** *n* retrato *m*; representación *f*.

Portugal ['pɔːtjugl] *n* Portugal *m*. **Portuguese** *nm, adj* portugués. **the Portuguese** los portugueses.

pose [pəuz] *n* postura *f*; afectación *f*. *v* colocar; (*question*) formular; (*problem*) plantear. **pose as** dárselas de.

posh [pɒʃ] *adj* elegante, de lujo; afectado.

position [pə'ziʃən] *n* posición *f*; sitio *m*; situación *f*; opinión *f*; (*job*) empleo *m*. *v* situar, disponer.

positive ['pɒzətiv] *adj* seguro; categórico; verdadero; afirmativo; positivo.

possess [pə'zes] *v* poseer. **possession** *n* posesión *f*. **possessive** *nm, adj* posesivo.

possible ['pɒsəbl] *adj* posible. **possibility** *n* posibilidad *f*. **possibly** *adv* (*perhaps*) tal vez.

post[1] [pəust] *n* (*pole*) poste *m*. *v* pegar.

post[2] [pəust] *n* (*sentry*, *job*) puesto *m*. *v* (*a sentry*) apostar; (*mil*: *send*) destinar.

post[3] [pəust] *n* (*mail*) correo *m*; (*letters*) cartas *f pl*. *v* mandar, enviar; echar. **postage** *n* franqueo *m*. **postage stamp** sello *m*. **postal** *adj* postal. **postal order** giro postal *m*.

postbox ['pəustbɒks] *n* buzón *m*.

postcard ['pəustkaːd] *n* tarjeta postal *f*.

post-code *n* código postal *m*.

poster ['pəustə] *n* cartel *m*.

poste restante [pəust'restãt] *n* lista de correos *f*.

posterior [po'stiəriə] *adj* posterior. *n* (*coll*) trasero *m*.

posterity [po'sterəti] *n* posteridad *f*.

postgraduate [poust'grædjuit] *n*, *adj* postgraduado, -a.

post-haste *adv* a toda prisa.

posthumous ['postjuməs] *adj* póstumo.

postman ['pousmən] *n* cartero *m*.

postmark ['pousmɑːk] *n* matasellos *m invar*. *v* matasellar.

postmaster ['pousmɑːstə] *n* administrador de correos *m*. **postmistress** *n* administradora de correos *f*.

post-mortem *n* autopsia *f*.

post office *n* correos *m* pl.

postpone [pous'poun] *v* aplazar. **post-ponement** *n* aplazamiento *m*.

postscript ['pousskript] *n* posdata *f*.

postulate ['postjuleit; *n* 'postjulət] *v* postular. *n* postulado *m*.

posture ['postʃə] *n* postura *f*, actitud *f*.

pot [pot] *n* (*cooking*) olla *f*; (*flowers*) tiesto *m*; (*preserves*) tarro *m*. **pot roast** carne asada *f*. **pots and pans** batería de cocina *f*. *v* (*plant*) poner en tiesto.

potassium [pə'tasjəm] *n* potasio *m*.

potato [pə'teitou] *n* patata *f*.

potent ['poutənt] *adj* poderoso; (*drink*) fuerte.

potential [pə'tenʃəl] *adj* posible; (*phys*) potencial. *n* posibilidad *f*; (*phys*) potencial *m*; (*elec*) voltaje *m*.

pot-hole ['pothoul] *n* (*in road*) bache *m*; (*underground*) cueva *f*. **pot-holer** *n* espeleólogo *m*. **pot-holing** *n* espeleología *f*.

potion ['pouʃən] *n* dosis *f*, poción *f*.

potter¹ ['potə] *v* (*coll*) **potter about** *or around* no hacer nada de particular.

potter² ['potə] *n* alfarero *m*. **potter's wheel** torno de alfarero *m*.

pottery ['potəri] *n* (*shop, craft*) alfarería *f*; (*pots*) cacharros de barro *m* pl.

potty ['poti] *n* (*coll*: *baby's*) orinal *m*. *adj* (*coll*: *crazy*) chiflado.

pouch [pautʃ] *n* bolsa *f*; (*tobacco*) petaca *f*.

poultice ['poultis] *n* cataplasma *f*.

poultry ['poultri] *n* aves de corral *f* pl.

pounce [pauns] *v* saltar. *n* salto *m*, ataque *m*.

pound¹ [paund] *v* aporrear; martillear; azotar.

pound² [paund] *n* libra *f*.

pour [poː] *v* verter; echar; servir; (*rain*) diluviar; (*flow*) fluir; (*people*) salir en tropel.

pout [paut] *n* mala cara *f*. *v* poner mala cara.

poverty ['povəti] *n* pobreza *f*.

powder ['paudə] *n* polvo *m*; (*cosmetic*) polvos *m* pl; (*gun*) pólvora *f*. **powder puff** borla *f*. **powder room** cuarto tocador *m*. *v* pulverizar. **powdery** *adj* en polvo; pulverizado.

power ['pauə] *n* poder *m*; (*elec*) potencia *f*; (*tech*) fuerza *f*; (*energy*) energía *f*. **power station** central eléctrica *f*. *v* accionar, impulsar. **powerful** *adj* poderoso; potente. **powerless** *adj* impotente; sin autoridad.

practicable ['praktikəbl] *adj* practicable; utilizable; realizable. **practicability** *n* practicabilidad *f*.

practical ['praktikəl] *adj* práctico. **practical joke** broma pesada *f*.

practice ['praktis] *n* práctica *f*; (*music*) ejercicios *m* pl; (*training*) entrenamiento *m*; (*profession*) ejercicio *m*.

practise ['praktis] *v* practicar; (*professionally*) ejercer; (*exercise*) ejercitarse; (*patience, etc.*) tener; (*music*) hacer ejercicios en.

practitioner [prak'tiʃənə] *n* (*med*) médico *m*. **general practitioner** internista *m*.

pragmatic [prag'matik] *adj* pragmático; dogmático.

Prague [prɑːg] *n* Praga.

prairie ['preəri] *n* llanura *f*, pradera *f*.

praise [preiz] *n* alabanza *f*, elogio *m*. *v* alabar, elogiar. **praiseworthy** *adj* laudable.

pram [pram] *n* cochecito de niño *m*.

prance [prɑːns] *v* caracolear, encabritarse.

prank [praŋk] *n* (*joke*) broma *f*; (*mischief*) travesura *f*.

prattle ['pratl] *v* (*chatter*) charlar; (*of a child*) balbucear. *n* chácara *f*; balbuceo *m*.

prawn [proːn] *n* gamba *f*.

pray [prei] *v* orar, rezar. **prayer** *n* oración *f*, rezo *m*. **prayer book** devocionario *m*.

preach [priːtʃ] *v* predicar. **preacher** *n* predicador, -a *m, f*. **preaching** *n* predicación *f*.

precarious [pri'keəriəs] *adj* precario.

precaution [pri'koːʃən] *n* precaución *f*. **take precautions** tomar precauciones.

precede [pri'siːd] *v* preceder, anteceder.

precedence *n* precedencia *f*; prioridad *f*.
precedent *n* precedente *m*.
precinct ['priisiŋkt] *n* recinto *m*; frontera *f*; zona *f*. **shopping precinct** zona comercial *f*.
precious ['preʃəs] *adj* precioso.
precipice ['presipis] *n* precipicio *m*.
precipitate [pri'sipiteit; *adj* pri'sipitət] *v* (*throw*) precipitar, arrojar; (*hasten*) acelerar; (*cause*) causar. *adj* precipitado.
precipitation *n* precipitación *f*.
précis ['preisi] *n* resumen *m*.
precise [pri'sais] *adj* preciso; exacto. **precision** *n* precisión *f*; exactitud *f*.
preclude [pri'kluːd] *v* excluir; evitar; impedir.
precocious [pri'kouʃəs] *adj* precoz. precociousness *or* precocity *n* precocidad *f*.
preconceive [ˌpriːkən'siːv] *v* preconcebir. preconception *n* preconcepción *f*.
precursor [ˌpri'kəːsə] *n* precursor, -a *m, f*.
predator ['predətə] *n* animal de rapiña *m*; (*person*) depredador, -a *m, f*.
predecessor ['priːdisesə] *n* predecesor, -a *m, f*.
predestine [pri'destin] *v* predestinar. **predestination** *n* predestinación *f*.
predicament [pri'dikəmənt] *n* situación difícil *f*.
predicate ['predikət] *n* predicado *m*. *v* afirmar; implicar.
predict [pri'dikt] *v* predecir. **predictable** *adj* previsible. **prediction** *n* predicción *f*.
predominate [pri'domineit] *v* predominar. **predominance** *n* predominio *m*. **predominant** *adj* predominante.
pre-eminent [pri'eminənt] *adj* preeminente. **pre-eminence** *n* preeminencia *f*.
preen [prin] *v* limpiar. **preen oneself** pavonearse.
prefabricate [priː'fabrikeit] *v* prefabricar. **prefabrication** *n* prefabricación *f*. **prefab** *n* (*coll*) casa prefabricada *f*.
preface ['prefis] *n* prólogo *m*. *v* (*introduce*) introducir.
prefect ['priːfekt] *n* (*school*) alumno/alumna responsable de disciplina *m, f*.
prefer [pri'fəː] *v* preferir. **preferable** *adj* preferible. **preference** *n* preferencia *f*. **preferential** *adj* preferente.
prefix ['priːfiks] *n* prefijo *m*. *v* poner un prefijo; anteponer.
pregnant ['pregnənt] *adj* (*woman*)

embarazada, encinta; (*animal*) preñada.
pregnancy *n* embarazo *m*.
prehistoric [ˌpriːhi'storik] *adj* prehistórico.
prejudice ['predʒədis] *n* prejuicio *m*; parcialidad *f*. *v* predisponer; (*damage*) perjudicar. **prejudiced** *adj* predispuesto; parcial. **prejudicial** *adj* perjudicial.
preliminary [pri'liminəri] *adj* preliminar. **preliminaries** *pl n* preliminares *m pl*.
prelude ['preljuːd] *n* preludio *m*.
premarital [priː'maritl] *adj* premarital.
premature [premə'tʃuə] *adj* prematuro.
premeditate [priː'mediteit] *v* premeditar. **premeditation** *n* premeditación *f*.
premier ['premiə] *adj* primero. *n* primer ministro *m*.
première ['premieə] *n* estreno *m*.
premise ['premis] *n* premisa *f*. **premises** *pl n* local *m sing*; edificio *m sing*.
premium ['priːmiəm] *n* (*comm*) prima *f*; (*award*) premio *m*. **at a premium** a premio.
premonition [ˌpremə'niʃən] *n* premonición *f*.
preoccupied [priː'okjupaid] *adj* preocupado. **preoccupation** *n* preocupación *f*.
prepare [pri'peə] *v* preparar, disponer. **preparation** *n* preparación *f*. **preparations** *pl n* preparativos *m pl*. **preparatory** *adj* preparatorio; preliminar. **preparatory school** escuela preparatoria *f*.
preposition [ˌprepə'ziʃən] *n* preposición *f*.
preposterous [pri'postərəs] *adj* ridículo, absurdo.
prerogative [pri'rogativ] *n* prerrogativa *f*.
prescribe [pri'skraib] *v* prescribir; (*med*) recetar. **prescription** *n* (*med*) receta *f*, prescripción *f*.
presence ['prezns] *n* presencia *f*.
present* ['preznt] *adj* presente. *n* presente *m*, actualidad *f*. **at present** ahora, en la actualidad. **those present** los presentes. **presently** *adv* luego.
present* [pri'zent; *n* 'preznt] *v* presentar; regalar; (*a problem*) plantear; (*an argument*) exponer. *n* regalo *m*. **presentable** *adj* presentable. **presentation** *n* presentación *f*; (*gift*) regalo *m*; (*ceremony*) entrega *f*.
preserve [pri'zəːv] *v* (*food*) conservar; (*protect*) preservar. **preserved** *adj* en conserva. **preserves** *pl n* conservas *f pl*; (*jam*) confitura *f*. **preservation** *n* conservación

f; (*protection*) preservación *f*. **preservative** *n* producto de conservación *m*.

preside [pri'zaid] *v* presidir.

president ['prezidənt] *n* presidente, -a *m*, *f*. **presidency** *n* presidencia *f*. **presidential** *adj* presidencial.

press [pres] *n* (*newspapers*) prensa *f*; (*printing*) imprenta *f*. **press conference** rueda de prensa *f*. **press cutting** recorte de periódico *m*. *v* (*mechanical*) prensar; (*push*) apretar; (*iron*) planchar; (*button*) dar a; (*squeeze*) estrujar; (*urge*) urgir. **press for** pedir con insistencia. **pressing** *adj* urgente.

pressure ['preʃə] *n* presión *f*; (*weight*) peso *m*; (*strength*) fuerza *f*; (*elec, med*) tensión *f*. **pressure cooker** olla de presión *f*. **pressure gauge** manómetro *m*. **pressurize** *v* (*cabin, etc.*) presurizar; (*coll: force*) acozar.

prestige [pre'stiːʒ] *n* prestigio *m*.

presume [pri'zjuːm] *v* suponer; permitirse. **presumption** *n* presunción *f*; (*daring*) atrevimiento *m*. **presumptuous** *adj* presuntuoso; atrevido.

pretend [pri'tend] *v* fingir; (*claim*) pretender; (*imagine*) suponer. **pretence** *n* fingimiento *m*; pretexto *m*; pretexto *m*; apariencia *f*. **pretension** *n* pretensión *f*. **pretentious** *adj* pretencioso; (*showy*) presumido.

pretext ['priːtekst] *n* pretexto *m*.

pretty ['priti] *adj* bonito, lindo. *adv* bastante.

prevail [pri'veil] *v* prevalecer, triunfar; predominar. **prevail upon** convencer. **prevailing** *adj* (*wind*) predominante, reinante; (*present*) actual. **prevalent** *adj* predominante; (*present-day*) actual; (*common*) común; extendido.

prevent [pri'vent] *v* impedir; (*avoid*) evitar. **prevention** *n* prevención *f*; impedimento *m*. **preventive** *adj* preventivo.

preview ['priːvjuː] *n* preestreno *m*. *v* ver antes que los demás.

previous ['priːviəs] *adj* anterior. **previously** *adv* antes.

prey [prei] *n* presa *f*; víctima *f*. **be a prey to** ser víctima de. *v* **prey on** (*animals*) alimentarse de. **prey on one's mind** preocupar mucho.

price [prais] *n* precio *m*. **fixed price** precio fijo *m*. **full price** precio fuerte *m*. **price list** tarifa *f*. **sale price** precio de venta *m*.

v poner precio a; valorar. **priceless** *adj* inestimable.

prick [prik] *n* pinchazo *m*. *v* pinchar. **prick up one's ears** aguzar el oído.

prickle ['prikl] *n* espina. *v* picar. **prickly** *adj* espinoso.

pride [praid] *n* orgullo *m*; dignidad *f*. **pride oneself on** enorgullecerse de.

priest [priːst] *n* sacerdote *m*. **priesthood** *n* (*office*) sacerdocio *m*; (*clergy*) clero *m*.

prim [prim] *adj* (*fussy*) remilgado; (*demure*) recatado.

primary ['praiməri] *adj* primario; básico; primero.

primate ['praimət] *n* (*zool*) primate *m*; (*rel*) primado *m*.

prime [praim] *adj* primero; principal; original; selecto; (*math*) primo. **prime minister** primer ministro *m*. *v* preparar; (*person*) informar. **primer** *n* (*book*) cartilla *f*. **primer coat** primera mano *f*.

primitive ['primitiv] *adj* primitivo.

primrose ['primrouz] *n* primavera *f*.

prince [prins] *n* príncipe *m*. **princely** *adj* principesco. **princess** *n* princesa *f*.

principal ['prinsəpəl] *adj* principal. *n* (*school*) director, -a *m*, *f*.

principle ['prinsəpl] *n* principio *m*. **on principle** por principio.

print [print] *n* (*finger*) huella *f*; (*impression*) marca *f*; (*phot*) prueba *f*; (*edition*) tirada *f*; (*type*) tipo *m*; (*picture*) grabado *m*. **out of print** agotado. *v* imprimir; (*phot*) sacar. **printed matter** impresos *m pl*. **printer** *n* impresor *m*. **printing** *n* impresión *f*; (*phot*) tiraje *m*. **printing press** prensa *f*.

prior ['praiə] *adj* anterior; preferente. **prior to** antes de. **priority** *n* prioridad *f*.

prise [praiz] *v* **prise off/open** abrir; levantar por fuerza.

prism ['prizm] *n* prisma *m*.

prison ['prizn] *n* cárcel *f*. **prisoner** *n* preso, -a *m*, *f*.

private ['praivət] *adj* privado; personal; reservado; (*house, car, lessons, etc.*) particular; confidencial. *n* soldado raso *m*. **privacy** *n* intimidad *f*; aislamiento *m*. **privately** *adv* en privado; personalmente.

privet ['privət] *n* alheña *f*.

privilege ['privilidʒ] *n* privilegio *m*. **privileged** *adj* privilegiado.

privy ['privi] *n* letrina *f*.

prize [praiz] *n* premio *m*. **prizewinner** *n*

premiado, -a *m, f. adj* premiado. *v* estimar.
probable ['probəbl] *adj* probable; (*credible*) verosímil. **probability** *n* probabilidad *f.* **probably** *adv* probablemente.
probation [prə'beiʃən] *n* (*law*) libertad vigilada *f*; (*trial period*) período de prueba m. **on probation** a prueba. **probationary** *adj* de prueba.
probe [proub] *n* (*act*) sondeo *m*; (*med*) sonda *f*. *v* sondear; explorar.
problem ['probləm] *n* problema m. **problematic** *adj* problemático.
proceed [prə'sid] *v* seguir; proceder; avanzar. **proceed to** ponerse a. **procedure** *n* procedimiento m. **proceedings** *pl n* debates m *pl*; (*law*) proceso m *sing.*
process ['prouses] *n* proceso m; procedimiento m; método m. **in the process** of en curso de. *v* tratar; (*phot*) revelar.
procession [prə'seʃən] *n* procesión *f*, desfile m.
proclaim [prə'kleim] *v* proclamar; declarar. **proclamation** *n* proclamación *f*; declaración *f.*
procreate ['proukrieit] *v* procrear. **procreation** *n* procreación *f.*
procure [prə'kjuə] *v* conseguir.
prod [prod] *n* golpecito m. *v* punzar; (*urge*) estimular.
prodigal ['prodigəl] *adj* pródigo.
prodigy ['prodidʒi] *n* prodigio m. **prodigious** *adj* prodigioso.
produce [prə'djus; *n* 'prodjus] *v* producir; (*manufacture*) fabricar; causar. *n* productos m *pl*. **producer** *n* productor, -a *m, f*; (*theatre*) escenógrafo m. **product** *m* producto m. **production** *n* producción *f*; fabricación *f*; presentación *f*; (*theatre*) dirección *f*. **productive** *adj* productivo; fecundo. **productivity** *n* productividad *f.*
profane [prə'fein] *adj* profano. *v* profanar. **profanity** *n* lo profano; impiedad *f.*
profess [prə'fes] *v* (*state*) declarar; (*claim*) pretender; (*affirm*) afirmar.
profession [prə'feʃən] *n* profesión *f*. **professional** *n*(*m+f*), *adj* profesional.
professor [prə'fesə] *n* catedrático, -a *m, f.* **professorship** *n* cátedra *f.*
proficient [prə'fiʃənt] *adj* competente; experto. **proficiency** *n* competencia *f*; pericia *f.*
profile ['proufail] *n* perfil m; (*biography*) reseña *f.*

profit ['profit] *n* (*financial*) ganancia *f*; (*fig*) provecho m. **profit-making** *adj* productivo. *v* **profit by** or **from** beneficiarse de. **profitable** *adj* provechoso.
profound [prə'faund] *adj* profundo. **profoundly** *adv* profundamente.
profuse [prə'fjus] *adj* profuso; abundante. **profusely** *adv* profusamente. **profusion** *n* profusión *f*; abundancia *f.*
programme ['prougram] *n* programa m. *v* programar. **programmer** *n* programador, -a *m, f.* **programming** *n* programación *f.*
progress ['prougres] *n* progreso m. **in progress** en curso. **make progress** hacer progresos. *v* progresar, avanzar, hacer progresos. **progression** *n* progresión *f.* **progressive** *adj* progresivo; (*political, social*) progresista.
prohibit [prə'hibit] *v* prohibir; impedir. **prohibition** *n* prohibición *f.*
project ['prodʒekt; *v* prə'dʒekt] *n* proyecto m. *v* proyectar; (*protrude*) hacer resaltar. **projectile** *n* proyectil m. **projecting** *adj* saliente. **projection** *n* proyección *f*; saliente m. **projector** *n* proyector m; (*planner*) proyectista m, *f.*
proletarian [proulə'teəriən] *n*, *adj* proletario, -a. **proletariat** *n* proletariado m.
proliferate [prə'lifəreit] *v* proliferar. **proliferation** *n* proliferación *f.*
prolific [prə'lifik] *adj* prolífico.
prologue ['proulog] *n* prólogo m.
prolong [prə'loŋ] *v* prolongar. **prolongation** *n* prolongación *f.*
promenade [promə'naid] *n* paseo m. *v* pasear, pasearse.
prominent ['prominənt] *adj* prominente; saliente; preeminente. **prominence** *n* prominencia *f*; importancia *f.*
promiscuous [prə'miskjuəs] *adj* promiscuo; (*person*) libertino. **promiscuity** *n* promiscuidad *f.*
promise ['promis] *n* promesa *f*. *v* prometer. **promising** *adj* que promete.
promontory ['proməntəri] *n* promontorio m.
promote [prə'mout] *v* promover, ascender; (*comm*) promocionar; (*encourage, stir up*) fomentar; financiar. **promotion** *n* ascenso m; promoción *f*; fomento m.
prompt [prompt] *adj* pronto; rápido; inmediato; puntual. *v* incitar; inspirar;

157

sugerir; (*theatre*) apuntar. **prompter** *n* apuntador, -a *m, f*.

prone [proun] *adj* propenso; (*lying*) boca abajo.

prong [proŋ] *n* diente *m*, púa *f*.

pronoun ['prounaun] *n* pronombre *m*.

pronounce [prə'nauns] *v* pronunciar; declarar. **pronouncement** *n* declaración *f*. **pronunciation** *n* pronunciación *f*.

proof [pruːf] *n* prueba *f*; (*alcohol*) graduación normal *f*. *adj* resistente (a); al abrigo de. **proof-read** *v* corregir pruebas. **proof-reading** *n* corrección de pruebas *f*.

prop[1] [prop] *n* puntal *m*; (*fig*) sostén *m*, apoyo *m*. *v* (*lean*) apoyar; (*support*) mantener.

prop[2] [prop] *n* (*coll: theatre*) accesorio *m*.

propaganda [propə'gandə] *n* propaganda *f*.

propagate ['propəgeit] *v* propagar. **propagation** *n* propagación *f*.

propel [prə'pel] *v* propulsar, impulsar. **propeller** *n* propulsor *m*; (*aircraft, ship*) hélice *f*. **propelling pencil** portaminas *m* invar.

proper ['propə] *adj* propio; correcto; decente; formal; justo; (*suitable*) apto; (*true*) verdadero; (*characteristic*) peculiar. **proper noun** nombre propio *m*. **properly** *adv* propiamente; bien; decentemente; correctamente.

property ['propəti] *n* (*estate*) hacienda *f*; (*possessions*) bienes *m pl*, propiedad *f*; (*quality*) cualidad *f*.

prophecy ['profəsi] *n* profecía *f*. **prophesy** *v* profetizar. **prophet** *n* profeta *m*. **prophetic** *adj* profético.

proportion [prə'poːʃən] *n* proporción *f*; parte *f*. **out of proportion** desproporcionado. *v* proporcionar; distribuir. **proportional** *adj* proporcional, en proporción.

propose [prə'pouz] *v* proponer; (*marriage*) declararse; (*toast*) brindar; (*intend*) intentar. **proposal** *n* proposición *f*; (*marriage*) oferta de matrimonio *f*; (*plan*) proyecto *m*. **proposition** *n* proposición *f*; proyecto *m*.

proprietor [prə'praiətə] *n* propietario, -a *m, f*; dueño *m, f*.

propriety [prə'praiəti] *n* decoro *m*; conveniencia *f*; oportunidad *f*; corrección *f*.

propulsion [prə'pʌlʃən] *n* propulsión *f*.

prose [prouz] *n* prosa *f*.

prosecute ['prosikjuːt] *v* proseguir; (*law*)

procesar. **prosecution** *n* (*of duty*) cumplimiento *m*; (*continuation*) continuación *f*; (*action of prosecuting*) procesamiento *m*; (*trial*) proceso *m*; (*party*) parte acusadora *f*.

prospect [prospekt; *v* prə'spekt] *n* perspectiva *f*; vista *f*. **prospects** *pl n* (*of a job, etc.*) perspectivas *f pl*. *v* prospectar. **prospective** *adj* eventual; futuro.

prospectus [prə'spektəs] *n* prospecto *m*.

prosper [prə'spə] *v* prosperar. **prosperity** *n* prosperidad *f*. **prosperous** *adj* próspero.

prostitute ['prostitjuːt] *n* prostituta *f*. *v* prostituir. **prostitution** *n* prostitución *f*.

prostrate ['prostreit; *v* pro'streit] *adj* (*lying down*) boca abajo; (*exhausted*) postrado. *v* postrar. **prostrate oneself** postrarse. **prostration** *n* prostración *f*; prosternación *f*.

protagonist [prou'tagənist] *n* protagonista *m, f*.

protect [prə'tekt] *v* proteger. **protection** *n* protección *f*. **protective** *adj* protector.

protégé ['protəʒei] *n* protegido *m*. **protégée** *n* protegida *f*.

protein ['proutiːn] *n* proteína *f*.

protest ['proutest; *v* prə'test] *n* protesta *f*. *v* protestar. **protester** *n* (*on march*) manifestador, -a *m, f*.

Protestant ['protistənt] *n(m+f), adj* protestante.

protocol ['proutəkol] *n* protocolo *m*.

prototype ['proutətaip] *n* prototipo *m*.

protractor [prə'traktə] *n* transportador *m*.

protrude [prə'truːd] *v* sacar; sobresalir. **protruding** *adj* saliente, sobresaliente.

proud [praud] *adj* orgulloso; soberbio.

prove [pruːv] *v* probar; demostrar; (*show*) mostrar.

proverb ['provəːb] *n* proverbio *m*. **proverbial** *adj* proverbial.

provide [prə'vaid] *v* proveer; dar; preparar (por); proporcionar medios de vida (a). **provided that** si siempre que.

provident ['providənt] *adj* próvido. **providence** *n* providencia *f*. **providential** *adj* providencial.

province ['provins] *n* provincia *f*; esfera *f*. **the provinces** la provincia *f*. **provincial** *adj* provincial.

provision [prə'viʒən] *n* (*supply*) suministro *m*; (*providing*) provisión *f*; (*of treaty, law, etc.*) disposición *f*. **make provision for** prever. **provisions** *pl n* provisiones *f pl*. **provisional** *adj* provisional.

proviso [prə'vaizou] n condición f; estipulación f.

provoke [prə'vouk] v provocar. **provocation** n provocación f. **provocative** adj provocador.

prow [prau] n proa f.

prowess ['prauis] n valor m; proeza f.

prowl [praul] v rondar. **prowler** n rondador, -a m, f.

proximity [prok'siməti] n proximidad f.

proxy ['proksi] n poder m, procuración f. **by proxy** por poderes.

prude [pruːd] n mojigato, -a m, f. **prudish** adj mojigato.

prudent ['pruːdənt] adj prudente. **prudence** n prudencia f.

prune¹ [pruːn] n (fruit) ciruela pasa f.

prune² [pruːn] v podar; cortar; reducir.

pry [prai] v fisgar, fisgonear. **pry into** entrometerse en. **prying** adj fisgón.

psalm [saːm] n salmo m.

pseudonym ['sjuːdənim] n pseudónimo m.

psychedelic [,saikə'delik] adj psiquedélico.

psychiatry [sai'kaiətri] n psiquiatría f.

psychic ['saikik] adj psíquico. n medium m.

psychoanalysis [,saikouə'naləsis] n psicoanálisis m. **psychoanalyse** v psicoanalizar. **psychoanalyst** n psicoanalista m, f.

psychology [sai'kolədʒi] n psicología f. **psychological** adj psicológico. **psychologist** n psicólogo, -a m, f.

psychopath ['saikəpaθ] n psicópata m, f. **psychopathic** adj psicopático.

psychosis [sai'kousis] n psicosis f. **psychotic** adj psicopático. n psicópata m, f.

psychosomatic [,saikəsə'matik] adj psicosomático.

psychotherapy [,saikə'θerəpi] n psicoterapia f.

pub [pʌb] n taberna f. **pub crawl** chateo m.

puberty ['pjuːbəti] n pubertad f.

pubic ['pjuːbik] adj púbico.

public ['pʌblik] nm, adj público.

publication [,pʌbli'keiʃən] n publicación f.

publicity [pʌb'lisəti] n publicidad f.

publicize ['pʌblisaiz] v publicar.

public library n biblioteca de préstamo f.

public relations n colegio privado de enseñanza media m.

public-spirited adj de espíritu cívico.

public transport n servicio de transportes m.

publish ['pʌbliʃ] v publicar. **publisher** n editor, -a m, f. **publishing** n publicación f. **publishing house** casa editora f.

pucker ['pʌkə] v (wrinkle) arrugar; (pleat) fruncir. n (pleat) frunce m.

pudding ['pudiŋ] n pudín m, budín m.

puddle ['pʌdl] n charco m.

puerile ['pjuərail] adj pueril.

Puerto Rico [,pwəːtou'riːkou] n Puerto Rico.

puff [pʌf] n (breath) resoplido m; (air) soplo m; (wind) ráfaga f; (smoke) bocanada f; v (blow) soplar; (pant) jadear; (smoke) echar bocanadas. **puff out** or **up** hinchar. **puffy** adj hinchado.

pull [pul] n tracción f; (pull) arrastre m; esfuerzo m; (influence) enchufe m; atracción f. v (open) tirar de; (drag) arrastrar; (uproot) arrancar; (tooth) sacar; (trigger) apretar; (attract) atraer. **pull ahead** destacarse. **pull away** separar, apartar. **pull down** bajar; echar abajo. **pull in** entrar; llegar. **pull oneself together** serenarse. **pull out** (mot) salirse; sacar; arrancar; (mil) retirarse. **pull through** sacar de un apuro. **pull together** aunar sus esfuerzos. **pull up** (mot) parar; (socks) subirse; (a chair) acercar.

pulley ['puli] n polea f.

pullover ['pul,ouvə] n jersey m.

pulp [pʌlp] n pulpa f. v reducir a pulpa.

pulpit ['pulpit] n púlpito m.

pulsate [pʌl'seit] v palpitar; vibrar; brillar. **pulsation** n pulsación f; vibración f.

pulse [pʌls] n (med) pulso m; (phys) pulsación f. v latir; vibrar.

pulverize ['pʌlvəraiz] v pulverizar. **pulverization** n pulverización f.

pump [pʌmp] n bomba f; (petrol) surtidor m; (plimsoll) zapato de lona m. v bombear; sacar. **pump up** inflar.

pumpkin ['pʌmpkin] n calabaza f.

pun [pʌn] n retruécano m.

punch¹ [pʌntʃ] n puñetazo m; golpe m. v dar um puñetazo.

punch² [pʌntʃ] n (drink) ponche m.

punch³ [pʌntʃ] n (tool) sacabocados m invar; perforadora f. v taladrar; perforar; picar.

punctual ['pʌŋktʃuəl] adj puntual. **punctuality** n puntualidad f.

punctuate ['pʌŋktʃueit] v puntuar. **punctuation** n puntuación f.

puncture ['pʌŋktʃə] n (tyre) pinchazo m; (leather, skin) perforación f. **have a puncture** tener un pinchazo. v pinchar; perforar.

pungent ['pʌndʒənt] adj (smell) acre; (taste) picante. **pungency** n acritud f; lo picante; mordazidad f.

punish ['pʌniʃ] v castigar. **punishment** n castigo m.

punt¹ [pʌnt] n (boat) batea f.

punt² [pʌnt] v (bet) apostar. **punter** n jugador m.

puny ['pjuːni] adj escuchimizado.

pupil¹ ['pjuːpil] n alumno, -a m, f.

pupil² ['pjuːpil] n (eye) pupila f.

puppet ['pʌpit] n títere m; marioneta f.

puppy ['pʌpi] m cachorro m.

purchase ['pəːtʃəs] n compra f. **purchase tax** impuesto sobre la venta m. v comprar.

pure ['pjuə] adj puro. **purify** v purificar. **purist** n purista m, f. **purity** n pureza f.

purée ['pjuərei] n puré m.

purgatory ['pəːgətəri] n purgatorio m.

purge [pəːdʒ] v purgar; purificar. n purga f. **purgative** nm, adj purgante.

puritan ['pjuəritən] n, adj puritano, -a. **puritanical** adj puritano.

purl [pəːl] v ribetear; hacer al revés. n (on lace) puntilla f; (thread) hilo de oro o de plata f.

purple ['pəːpl] nm, adj morado.

purpose ['pəːpəs] n propósito m, objetivo m; destino m; determinación f; uso m; utilidad f. **on purpose** a propósito. **purposeful** adj decidido; (person) resuelto; útil.

purr [pəː] v ronronear. n ronroneo m.

purse [pəːs] n monedero m, portamonedas m invar; (prize) premio m. v **purse one's lips** apretar los labios.

purser ['pəːsə] n contador m.

pursue [pə'sjuː] v perseguir. **pursuer** n perseguidor, -a m, f. **pursuit** n persecución f; profesión f; ocupación f; pasatiempo m.

pus [pʌs] n pus m.

push [puʃ] n empujón m; (force) empuje m. v empujar; presionar; (notice on doors) empujen. **be pushed for time** tener prisa. **pushing** adj ambicioso.

*****put** [put] v poner; meter; echar; (question) hacer; (state) decir. **put away**

guardar; (money) ahorrar. **put back** volver a poner; (clock) atrasar. **put down** bajar; (in writing) apuntar; (repress) reprimir; (kill) sacrificar. **put off** (postpone) aplazar; (disgust) censar; (revolt) asquear; disuadir. **put on** (clothes) ponerse; (a show) representar; (pretend) fingir. **put up** levantar; (hang) colgar; (resistance) oponer; (build) construir. **put up with** aguantar; conformarse con. **put upon** engañar.

putrid ['pjuːtrid] adj pútrido; podrido.

putt [pʌt] n put m. v tirar al hoyo. **putter** n putter m.

putty ['pʌti] n masilla f.

puzzle ['pʌzl] n enigma f; (game) rompecabezas m invar. v dejar perplejo. **puzzle out** resolver; descifrar. **puzzling** adj enigmático; misterioso.

pyjamas [pə'dʒɑːməz] pl n pijama m sing.

pylon ['pailən] n poste m.

pyramid ['pirəmid] n pirámide f.

python ['paiθən] n pitón m.

Q

quack¹ [kwak] n (duck) graznido m. v graznar.

quack² [kwak] n charlatán m.

quadrangle ['kwodraŋgl] n (courtyard) patio m; (math) cuadrángulo m.

quadrant ['kwodrənt] n cuadrante m.

quadrilateral [kwodrə'latərəl] nm, adj cuadrilátero.

quadruped ['kwodruped] nm, adj cuadrúpedo.

quadruple [kwod'ruːpl] adj cuádruple.

quadruplets [kwo'druːplits] pl n cuatrillizos, -as m, f pl.

quagmire ['kwagmaiə] n pantano m.

quail¹ [kweil] n (zool) codorniz f.

quail² [kweil] v acobardarse.

quaint [kweint] adj pintoresco; excéntrico.

quake [kweik] v estremecerse. n estremecimiento m. **quake with fear** temblar de miedo.

qualify ['kwolifai] v (entitle) capacitar; calificar; modificar; limitar. **qualification** n reserva f; aptitud f; requisito m. **qualifications** pl n títulos m pl. **qualified** adj competente; capacitado; titulado; con reservas.

quality ['kwolǝti] n (*attribute*) cualidad f; calidad f.

qualm [kwɑːm] n escrúpulo m.

quandary ['kwondǝri] n incertidumbre f; dilema m.

quantify ['kwontifai] v determinar la cantidad de.

quantity ['kwontǝti] n cantidad f.

quarantine ['kworǝntiːn] n cuarentena f. v someter a cuarentena.

quarrel ['kworǝl] n disputa f; pelea f. v disputar, pelear. **quarrelsome** adj peleador.

quarry[1] ['kwori] n (*stone, etc.*) cantera f. v explotar una cantera.

quarry[2] ['kwori] n presa f.

quarter ['kwoːtǝ] n cuarto m; cuarta parte f; (*of year*) trimestre m; (*district*) barrio m. **quarter-final** n cuarto de final m. **quartermaster** n (*naut*) cabo de la marina m. **quarter past four** las cuatro y quince. **quarters** pl n (*mil*) cuartel m sing. **at close quarters** de cerca. **quarter to four** las cuatro menos cuarto. v dividir en cuatros; (*mil*) acuartelar. **quarterly** adj trimestral.

quartet [kwoːˈtet] n cuarteto m.

quartz [kwoːts] n cuarzo m.

quash [kwoʃ] v amular; ahogar; (*rebellion*) reprimir.

quaver ['kweivǝ] n (*music*) corchea f; temblor m. v temblar.

quay [kiː] n muelle m.

queasy ['kwiːzi] adj (*sick*) mareado; (*upset*) delicado. **queasiness** n náuseas f pl.

queen [kwiːn] n reina f; (*cards*) dama f. **Queen Mother** reina madre f.

queer [kwiǝ] adj raro; curioso; (*unwell*) indispuesto; (*slang: homosexual*) maricón. n (*slang*) maricón m, marica f.

quell [kwel] v reprimir.

quench [kwentʃ] v (*flames*) apagar; (*thirst*) aplacar; (*desire*) sofocar.

query ['kwiǝri] n pregunta f; duda f. v preguntar; dudar (de).

quest [kwest] n búsqueda f.

question ['kwestʃǝn] n pregunta f; cuestión f; problema m. **begging the question** petición de principio f. **beside the question** que no viene al caso. **out of the question** imposible. **question mark** signo de interrogación m. **without question** sin

duda. v preguntar; interrogar; poner en duda. **questionable** adj dudoso; discutible. **questioning** n interrogatorio m. **questionnaire** n cuestionario m.

queue [kjuː] n cola f. v hacer cola.

quibble ['kwibl] n pega f; subterfugio m. v sutilizar; (*find fault*) ser quisquilloso.

quick [kwik] adj rápido; (*reply*) pronto; (*lively*) vivo; (*clever*) agudo; (*on feet*) ligero. **quicksand** n avena movediza f. **quick-tempered** adj irascible. **quick-witted** adj agudo. **quicken** v acelerar; estimular. **quickly** adv rápidamente.

quid [kwid] n (*coll*) libra f.

quiet ['kwaiǝt] adj silencioso; callado; (*step*) ligero; tranquilo; (*dress*) sobrio. n also **quietness** tranquilidad f; silencio m; reposo m. **quieten** v callar; calmar. **quietly** adv silenciosamente; tranquilamente.

quill [kwil] n (*feather*) pluma f; (*pen*) cálamo m; (*porcupine*) púa f.

quilt [kwilt] n colcha f; (*eiderdown*) edredón m. v acolchar.

quince [kwins] n membrillo m.

quinine [kwiˈniːn] n quinina f.

quinsy ['kwinzi] n angina f.

quintet [kwinˈtet] n quinteto m.

quirk [kwǝːk] n peculiaridad f.

quit [kwit] v (*job*) abandonar; (*place*) dejar; (*leave*) irse de.

quite [kwait] adv completamente, enteramente; exactamente; verdaderamente; (*fairly*) bastante.

quiver[1] ['kwivǝ] v temblar; estremecerse. n temblor m; estremecimiento m.

quiver[2] ['kwivǝ] n (*for arrows*) aljaba f.

quiz [kwiz] n (*inquiry*) encuesta f; (*questioning*) interrogatorio m; examen m. v interrogar.

quizzical ['kwizikl] adj curioso; (*bantering*) burlón.

quota ['kwoutǝ] n cupo m; (*share*) cuota f.

quote [kwout] v citar; dar; (*comm*) cotizar. **quotation** n cita f; (*comm*) cotización f. **quotation marks** comillas f pl.

R

161

rancour

rabbi ['rabai] n rabino m.

rabbit ['rabit] n conejo m.

rabble ['rabl] n gentío m; (derog) populacho m.

rabies ['reibiz] n rabia f. **rabid** adj rabioso.

race[1] [reis] n carrera f; (yacht) regata f. **racehorse** n caballo de carreras m. v (person) competir con; (horse) hacer correr; (pulse) latir a ritmo acelerado.

race[2] [reis] n raza f; familia f. **racial** adj racial. **racialism** n also **racism** racismo m. **racialist** n(m+f), adj also **racista**.

rack [rak] n (shelf) estante m; (coats, etc.) percha f; (plates) escurreplatos m invar; (car roof) baca f; (torture) potre m. v atormentar. **rack one's brains** devanarse los sesos.

racket[1] ['rakit] n (sport) raqueta f.

racket[2] ['rakit] n (noise) alboroto m, barullo m; (coll: crime) tráfico m; timo m.

radar ['reidɑː] n radar m.

radial ['reidiəl] adj radial. **radial tyre** neumático radial m.

radiant ['reidiənt] adj resplandeciente. **radiance** n resplandor m.

radiate ['reidieit] v (heat) irradiar; (rays) emitir; (spread) difundir. **radiation** n radiación f. **radiator** n radiador m.

radical ['radikəl] nm, adj radical.

radio ['reidiou] n radio f. **radio beacon** radiofaro m. **radio contact** radiocomunicación f. **radio control** teledirección f. **radio station** emisora f. **radio wave** onda f. v transmitir por radio.

radioactive [reidiou'aktiv] adj radioactivo. **radioactivity** n radioactividad f.

radiography [reidi'ɔɡrəfi] n radiografía f. **radiographer** n radiógrafo m.

radiology [reidi'ɔlədʒi] n radiología f. **radiologist** n radiólogo m.

radiotherapy [reidiou'θerəpi] n radioterapia f.

radish ['radiʃ] n rábano m.

radium ['reidiəm] n radio m.

radius ['reidiəs] n radio m.

raffia ['rafiə] n rafia f.

raffle ['rafl] n rifa f. v rifar.

raft [rɑːft] n balsa f.

rafter ['rɑːftə] n viga f.

rag[1] [rag] n (waste piece) harapo m; (cleaning) trapo m; (derog: newspaper) periodicucho m. **ragamuffin** n golfo m.

ragged adj (clothes) hecho jirones; (edge) mellado.

rag[2] [rag] v (coll) tomar el pelo a. n payasadas f pl. **ragtime** n música sincopada f.

rage [reidʒ] n (anger) cólera f, rabia f; (of elements) furia f; (fashion) moda f. **be all the rage** hacer furor. v (be angry) estar furioso; (wind, fire, beasts) bramar; (sea) alborotarse. **raging** adj (person) furioso; (pain) muy fuerte; (storm) encrespado.

raid [reid] n (mil) correría f; (aerial) ataque m; (police) redada f; (robbery) asalto m. v hacer una redada; asaltar. **raider** n invasor m; (thief) ladrón m.

rail [reil] n (stairs) barandilla f; (bridge) antepecho m; (balcony) baranda f; (bar) barra f; (fence) cerco m; (train, tram) vía férrea f. **by rail** por ferrocarril. **railway** or US **railroad** n ferrocarril m.

railings ['reilinz] pl n barandilla f sing.

rain [rein] n lluvia f. **rainbow** n arco iris m. **raincoat** n impermeable m. **raindrop** n gota de lluvia f. **rainfall** n precipitación f. **rainwater** n agua de lluvia f. v llover. **rainy** adj lluvioso.

raise [reiz] v alzar, levantar; (increase) aumentar; provocar; (problem) plantar; (animals) criar.

raisin ['reizən] n pasa f.

rake [reik] n rastro m. v rastrillar. **rake together** reunir a duras penas.

rally ['rali] n reunión f; (pol) mitin político m; (mot) rallye m; (tennis) peloteo m. v reunir; (recover) recuperarse. **rally round** tomar el partido de.

ram [ram] n carnero m; (battering ram) ariete m. v (earth, etc.) apisonar; (fist, head) dar con; (pack) meter a la fuerza.

ramble ['rambl] n excursión f. v pasear; (fig) divagar.

ramp [ramp] n rampa f.

rampage ['rampeidʒ] n **be on the rampage** alborotar.

rampant ['rampənt] adj (plant) exuberante; (heraldry) rampante; (aggressive) violento. **be rampant** estar difundido.

rampart ['rampɑːt] n terraplén m, muralla f.

ramshackle ['ramʃakl] adj desvenajado.

ran [ran] V **run**.

ranch [rɑːntʃ] n rancho m; hacienda f.

rancid ['ransid] adj rancio.

rancour ['raŋkə] n rencor m.

random ['rændəm] n **at random** al azar. *adj* hecho al azar. **random sample** muestra cogida al azar f.

rang [ræŋ] V **ring**.

range [reindʒ] n (*row*) fila f; (*mountains*) sierra f; (*area*) extensión f; (*distance*) alcance m; (*of an aircraft*) autonomía f; (*mil: firing*) campo de tiro m; (*voice*) registro m; (*colours, prices*) gama f; (*subjects*) variedad f; (*grazing land*) dehesa f; (*cooking stove*) cocina económica f. v (*place*) colocar; (*put in a row*) alinear; clasificar; (*wander*) recorrer.

rank[1] [ræŋk] n fila f; grado m; categoría f. **the rank and file** la tropa f; (*ordinary people*) gente del montón f. v (*estimate*) situar, poner; figurar; (*mil*) alinear.

rank[2] [ræŋk] *adj* lozano; rancio.

rankle ['ræŋkl] v escocer.

ransack ['rænsæk] v saquear; (*search*) registrar.

ransom ['rænsəm] n rescate m. **hold to ransom** exigir rescate. v rescatar.

rap [ræp] v golpear. n golpecito m.

rape [reip] n violación f. v violar. **rapist** n violador m.

rapid ['ræpid] *adj* rápido. **rapids** pl n rápidos m pl. **rapidity** n rapidez f.

rapier ['reipiə] n estoque m.

rapport [ræ'pɔt] n relación f; armonía f.

rapture ['ræptʃə] n éxtasis m invar. **go into raptures over** extasiarse por.

rare[1] [reə] *adj* raro. **rarity** n rareza f.

rare[2] [reə] *adj* (*cookery*) poco hecho.

rascal ['raːskəl] n bribón m, pícaro m.

rash[1] [ræʃ] *adj* temerario. **rashness** n temeridad f.

rash[2] [ræʃ] n (*med*) erupción f.

rasher ['ræʃə] n loncha f.

raspberry ['raːzbəri] n (*fruit*) frambuesa f; (*bush*) frambueso m.

rat [ræt] n rata f. **rat poison** matarratas m invar. **rat race** competencia f.

rate [reit] n proporción f; índice m; velocidad f; ritmo m; precio; (*discount, interest*) tipo m; (*pulse*) frecuencia f. **at any rate** de todos modos. **ratepayer** n contribuyente m, f. **rates** pl n contribución municipal f sing. v valorar; considerar; clasificar; estimar. **rateable** *adj* valorable.

rather ['raːðə] *adv* más bien; bastante; (*fairly*) algo. **I would rather ...** prefiero ....

ratify ['rætifai] v ratificar. **ratification** n ratificación f.

ratio ['reiʃou] n razón f, relación f.

ration ['ræʃən] n ración f. v racionar. **rationing** n racionamiento m.

rational ['ræʃənl] *adj* racional; razonable; lógico. **rationale** n razón fundamental f. **rationalize** v racionalizar.

rattle ['rætl] n (*toy*) sonajero m; (*football fan's*) carraca f; ruido de sonajero; (*train noise*) traqueteo m; (*chains*) ruido metálico m; (*door, window*) golpe m; (*teeth*) castañeteo m; (*machine gun*) tableteo m; v hacer sonar; traquetear; hacer un ruido metálico; golpetear; castañetear; tabletear; (*put off*) desconcertar.

raucous ['rɔːkəs] *adj* ronco.

ravage ['rævidʒ] n estrago m. v asolar.

rave [reiv] v delirar, desvariar. **rave over** entusiasmarse por. **raving** *adj* delirante.

raven ['reivən] n cuervo m.

ravenous ['rævənəs] *adj* hambriento. **be ravenous** tener un hambre canina.

ravine [rə'viːn] n desfiladero m.

ravish ['ræviʃ] v violar; raptar. **ravishing** *adj* encantador.

raw [rɔː] *adj* (*uncooked*) crudo; (*unrefined*) bruto; (*inexperienced*) novato; (*nerves*) a flor de piel; (*flesh*) vivo; (*weather*) frío y húmedo. **raw deal** (*coll*) injusticia f. **raw materials** materias primas f pl. **rawness** n crudeza f.

ray [rei] n rayo m; (*line, fish*) raya f.

rayon ['reion] n rayón m.

razor ['reizə] n navaja f; (*safety*) maquinilla de afeitar f; (*elec*) máquina de afeitar eléctrica f. **razor blade** hoja de afeitar f.

reach [riːtʃ] v (*arrive at*) llegar a; (*achieve*) lograr; (*stretch out*) extender; alcanzar. n alcance m; poder m; capacidad f. **out of reach** fuera del alcance. **within reach** al alcance.

react [ri'ækt] v reaccionar. **reaction** n reacción f. **reactionary** n, *adj* reaccionario, -a. **reactor** n reactor m.

*****read** [riːd] v leer; estudiar; (*public address*) decir; (*riddle*) interpretar; (*meter, etc.*) marcar. **reader** n lector, -a m, f; (*university*) profesor, -a m, f; (*book*) libro de lectura m. **reading** n lectura f; estudio m; interpretación f. **reading-glass** n lente para leer m. **reading-lamp** lámpara de sobremesa f.

readjust [riːəˈdʒʌst] v reajustar. **readjustment** n reajuste m.

ready [ˈredi] adj listo; pronto; a mano. **get ready** prepararse. **ready cash** dinero contante m. **ready-made** adj hecho. **readily** adv fácilmente; en seguida. **readiness** n prontitud f; facilidad f.

real [riəl] adj real, verdadero. **realism** n realismo m. **realist** n realista m, f. **reality** n realidad f, verdad f. **really** adv realmente, en verdad. **really?** ¿de veras?

realize [ˈriəlaiz] v (understand) darse cuenta de; (achieve) llevar a cabo; (make real) realizar. **realization** n comprensión f; realización f.

realm [relm] n reino m; (fig) esfera f.

reap [riːp] v segar; (fig) cosechar. **reaping** n siega f; cosecha f. **reaping machine** segadora mecánica f.

reappear [riːəˈpiə] v reaparecer. **reappearance** n reaparición f.

rear[1] [riə] adj posterior, de atrás. **rear-admiral** n contraalmirante m. **rearguard** n retaguardia f. **rear-view mirror** retrovisor m. n parte posterior f, parte de atrás f; (of a column) cola f. **bring up the rear** cerrar la marcha.

rear[2] [riə] v (family) criar; (lift up) alzar, levantar; (horse, etc.) empinarse.

rearrange [riːəˈreindʒ] v arreglar de otra manera; volver a arreglar. **rearrangement** n nuevo arreglo m.

reason [ˈriːzn] n razón f. v razonar. **reasonable** adj razonable. **reasoning** n razonamiento m.

reassure [riːəˈʃuə] v asegurar de nuevo; confortar. **reassurance** n confianza restablecida f. **reassuring** adj tranquilizador.

rebate [ˈriːbeit] n rebaja f, descuento m.

rebel [ˈrebl] n(m+f), adj rebelde. v rebelarse. **rebellion** n rebelión f. **rebellious** adj rebelde.

rebound [riˈbaund; n ˈriːbaund] v rebotar. n rebote m.

rebuff [riˈbʌf] v rechazar. n desaire m.

*****rebuild** [riˈbild] v reedificar.

rebuke [riˈbjuːk] v censura f, reproche m. v censurar, reprochar.

recall [riˈkɔːl] v llamar; recordar. n llamada f; (dismissal) destitución f.

recant [riˈkant] v retractar.

recap [ˈriːkap] v (coll) recapitular. n recapitulación f.

recapture [riˈkaptʃə] v reconquistar; (recreate) hacer revivir. n reconquista f.

recede [riˈsiːd] v retroceder; (tide) descender.

receipt [rəˈsiːt] n (act of receiving) recepción f; (slip of paper) recibo m.

receive [rəˈsiːv] v recibir; aceptar. **receiver** n (of loot) recibidor, -a m, f; (law) síndico m; (phone) auricular m.

recent [ˈriːsnt] adj reciente. **recently** adv recientemente.

receptacle [rəˈseptəkl] n receptáculo m.

reception [rəˈsepʃən] n recepción f; acogida f. **receptionist** n recepcionista m, f. **receptive** adj receptivo.

recess [riˈses] n (hollow) hueco m; (niche) nicho m; (parliament) período de clausura m; (rest) descanso m.

recession [rəˈseʃən] n (comm) recesión f; (retreat) retroceso m.

recharge [riˈtʃaːdʒ] v recargar.

recipe [ˈresəpi] n receta f.

recipient [rəˈsipiənt] n (receiver) receptor, -a m, f; (cheque, letter, etc.) destinatario, -a m, f.

reciprocate [rəˈsiprəkeit] v corresponder; intercambiar. **reciprocating engine** motor alternativo m. **reciprocal** adj recíproco.

recite [rəˈsait] v recitar. **recital** n (a relating) relato m; (music) recital m. **recitation** n relato m; recitación f.

reckless [ˈrekləs] adj temerario; audaz. **recklessness** n temeridad f; audacia f.

reckon [ˈrekən] v calcular; contar; considerar; (coll) creer. **reckoning** n cálculo m; cuenta f; (fig) retribución f.

reclaim [riˈkleim] v (land) ganar; (reform) reformar; (by-product) regenerar. **reclamation** n (claiming back) reclamación f; (moral) enmienda f; (land) aprovechamiento m; regeneración f.

recline [rəˈklain] v apoyar; recostar.

recluse [rəˈkluːs] n recluso, -a m, f.

recognize [ˈrekəgnaiz] v reconocer; confesar. **recognition** n reconocimiento m. **recognizable** adj identificable.

recoil [rəˈkɔil; n ˈriːkɔil] v echarse atrás; (gun) dar culatazo; (spring) aflojarse. n culatazo m; aflojamiento m; (repugnance) asco m.

recollect [rekəˈlekt] v acordarse de. **recollection** n recuerdo m.

recommence [riːkəˈmens] v empezar de nuevo.

recommend [rekəˈmend] v recomendar; aconsejar. **recommendation** n recomendación f.

recompense ['rekəmpens] *n* recompensa *f*; (*law*) compensación *f*. *v* recompensar; compensar.

reconcile [rekənsail] *v* (*dispute*) arreglar; (*individuals*) reconciliar; (*ideas*) conciliar. **reconcile oneself to** resignarse a. **reconciliation** *n* arreglo *m*; reconciliación *f*; conciliación *f*.

reconstruct [riːkən'strʌkt] *v* (*building*) reconstruir; (*crime*) reconstituir. **reconstruction** *n* reconstrucción *f*; reconstitución *f*.

record [rə'koːd; *n* 'rekoːd] *v* registrar; tomar nota de; (*sound*) grabar. *n* registro *m*; anotación *f*; grabación *f*; disco *m*; (*account*) relación *f*; (*minutes*) actas *f pl*; (*personal history*) historial *m*; (*sport*) récord *m*. **long-playing record** disco de larga duración *m*. **record-player** *n* tocadiscos *m invar*. **recorded** *adj* grabado; registrado. **recorded delivery** entrega registrada *f*. **recorder** *n* archivista *m, f*; (*music*) flauta *f*. **recording** *n* (*music*) grabación *f*.

recount [ri'kaunt; *n* 'riːkaunt] *v* contar. *n* recuento *m*.

recoup [ri'kuːp] *v* (*recover*) recuperar; (*compensate*) indemnizar.

recover [rə'kʌvə] *v* (*get back*) recuperar; (*get well*) recobrar; ganar; obtener. **recovery** *n* recuperación *f*; (*med*) restablecimiento *m*.

recreation [rekri'eiʃən] *n* recreación *f*; (*school break*) recreo *m*.

recrimination [rəkrimi'neiʃən] *n* recriminación *f*. **recriminate** *v* recriminar.

recruit [rə'kruːt] *n* recluta *m*. *v* reclutar. **recruitment** *n* reclutamiento *m*.

rectangle ['rektæŋgl] *n* rectángulo *m*. **rectangular** *adj* rectangular.

rectify ['rektifai] *v* rectificar.

rectum ['rektəm] *n* recto *m*.

recuperate [rə'kjuːpəreit] *v* recuperar; (*health*) recobrar. **recuperation** *n* recuperación *f*; (*health*) restablecimiento *m*.

recur [ri'kəː] *v* volver; repetirse. **recurrence** *n* vuelta *f*; repetición *f*; reaparición *f*. **recurrent** *adj also* **recurring** periódico; que vuelve; (*med*) recurrente.

red [red] *n* rojo *m*, colorado *m*. **in the red** deber dinero. *adj* rojo, colorado. **go red** ruborizarse. **Red Cross** Cruz Roja *f*. **redcurrant** grosella *f*. **red-handed** *adv* con las manos en la masa. **redhead** *n* pelirrojo, -a *m, f*. **red-hot** *adj* al rojo; ardiente. **red-letter day** día memorable

m. red-light district barrio de mala fama *m*. **red tape** (*coll*) papeleo *m*. **redness** *n* color rojo *m*.

redeem [rə'diːm] *v* (*promise*) cumplir; (*mortgage*) amortizar; (*pawn*) desempeñar; (*fault*) expiar; (*rescue*) rescatar. **redemption** *n* cumplimiento *m*; amortización *f*; desempeño *m*; expiación *f*; rescate *m*; (*rel*) redención *f*. **beyond redemption** sin redención, irremediable.

redirect [riːdai'rekt] *v* (*letter, etc.*) remitir al destinatario.

redress [rə'dres] *v* rectificar. *n* reparación *f*.

reduce [rə'djuːs] *v* reducir; rebajar; (*slim*) adelgazar. **reduction** *n* reducción *f*; (*length*) acortamiento *m*; (*width*) estrechamiento; (*weight*) adelgazamiento *m*; (*rank*) degradación *f*; (*prices*) disminución *f*; (*discount*) rebaja *f*; (*temperature*) baja *f*.

redundant [rə'dʌndənt] *adj* excesivo, superfluo. **be made redundant** perder su empleo. **redundancy** *n* desempleo *m*.

reed [riːd] *n* caña *f*; (*of wind instrument*) lengüeta *f*.

reef [riːf] *n* arrecife *m*.

reek [riːk] *v* apestar. *n* tufo *m*.

reel[1] [riːl] *n* (*cotton*) carrete *m*, bobina *f*; (*film*) cinta *f*; (*fishing*) carretel *m*. **reel off** (*recite*) recitar de un tirón.

reel[2] [riːl] *v* (*sway*) hacer eses, dar vueltas.

refectory [rə'fektəri] *n* refectorio *m*.

refer [rə'fəː] *v* remitir; enviar; (*date, event*) situar; atribuir. **reference** *n* referencia *f*; alusión *f*; relación *f*; (*source of information*) fuente *f*; (*person*) fiador *m*. **reference book** libro de consulta *m*. **reference library** biblioteca de consulta *f*. **reference number** número de referencia *m*. **terms of reference** mandato *m*. **make reference to** referirse a. **without reference to** sin consultar. **with reference to** en cuanto a.

referee [refə'riː] *n* árbitro *m*; (*guarantor of character*) garante *m*. *v* arbitrar.

referendum [refə'rendəm] *n* referéndum *m*.

refill [riː'fil; *n* 'riːfil] *v* rellenar. *n* recambio *m*; carga *f*.

refine [rə'fain] *v* refinar; purificar; (*technique*) perfeccionar; (*style*) pulir. **refinement** *n* (*person*) refinamiento *m*; (*manners*) finura *f*; (*sugar, oil*) refinado *m*;

(*metal*) purificación *f*; (*technique*) perfeccionamiento *m*; (*style*) elegancia *f*. **refinery** *n* refinería *f*.

reflect [rə'flekt] *v* reflejar; (*think*) reflexionar. **reflection** *n* (*image*) reflejo *m*; (*act*) reflexión; meditación *f*; crítica *f*.

reflex ['ri:fleks] *nm*, *adj* reflejo. **reflexive** *adj* reflexivo.

reform [rə'fɔ:m] *v* reformar; formar de nuevo. *n* reforma *f*. **reformation** *n* reformación *f*. **reformed** *adj* reformado.

refract [rə'frakt] *v* refractar. **refraction** *n* refracción *f*.

refrain¹ [rə'frein] *v* abstenerse.

refrain² [rə'frein] *n* estribillo *m*.

refresh [rə'freʃ] *v* refrescar. **refresher course** cursillo de repaso *m*. **refreshing** *adj* refrescante. **refreshments** *pl n* refrescos *m pl*.

refrigerator [rə'fridʒəreitə] *n* refrigerador *m*, nevera *f*. **refrigerate** *v* refrigerar. **refrigeration** *n* refrigeración *f*.

refuel [ri:'fjuəl] *v* repostar(se).

refuge ['refju:dʒ] *n* refugio *m*; asilo *m*. **take refuge** refugiarse en. **refugee** *n* refugiado, -a *m, f*.

refund [ri'fʌnd] *v* reembolsar. *n* 'ri:fʌnd] reembolso *m*.

refuse¹ [rə'fju:z] *v* negar. **refusal** *n* negativa *f*; (*rejection*) rechazo *m*.

refuse² ['refju:s] *n* basura *f*, desecho *m*, desperdicios *m pl*.

refute [ri'fju:t] *v* refutar.

regain [ri'gein] *v* recobrar; (*return to*) volver a.

regal ['ri:gəl] *adj* real, regio.

regard [rə'ga:d] *v* mirar; observar; considerar. **as regards** con respecto a. *n* mirada *f*; atención *f*; respeto *m*; aprecio *m*. **regards** *pl n* (*in a letter*) saludos *m pl*. **regarding** *prep* con respecto a. **regardless** *adv* a pesar de todo. **regardless of** sin tener en cuenta.

regatta [rə'gatə] *n* regata *f*.

regent ['ri:dʒənt] *n* regente *m, f*. **regency** *n* regencia *f*.

regime [rei'ʒi:m] *n* régimen *m*.

regiment ['redʒimənt] *n* regimiento *m*. **regimental** *adj* del regimiento.

region ['ri:dʒən] *n* región *f*. **regional** *adj* regional.

register ['redʒistə] *n* registro *m*; lista *f*. *v* registrar; (*a complaint*) presentar; (*luggage*) facturar; (*letter*) certificar; (*birth*,

death) declarar. **registrar** *n* registrador *m*; (*med*) doctor. -a *m, f*. **registration** *n* (*trademark*) registro *m*; inscripción *f*; declaración *f*; certificación *f*; facturación *f*; matrícula *f*. **registration number** número de matrícula *m*. **registration plate** placa de matrícula *f*. **registry office** registro civil *m*.

regress [ri'gres] *v* retroceder. **regression** *n* regresión *f*.

regret [rə'gret] *v* sentir, lamentar. *n* sentimiento *m*; pesar *m*; arrepentimiento *m*; excusas *f pl*. **regrettable** *adj* lamentable; doloroso.

regular ['regjulə] *adj* regular; normal; habituado. *n* (*mil*) regular; (*bar*) asiduo, -a *m, f*. **regularity** *n* regularidad *f*.

regulate ['regjuleit] *v* regular; ajustar.

regulation [regju'leiʃən] *n* regulación *f*; regla *f*. *adj* reglamentario.

rehabilitate [ri:hə'biliteit] *v* (*reputation*) rehabilitar; (*for work*) restaurar. **rehabilitation** *n* reconstrucción *f*; (*med*) reeducación *f*.

rehearse [rə'hə:s] *v* ensayar. **rehearsal** *n* ensayo *m*.

reign [rein] *n* reinado *m*; dominio *m*. *v* reinar.

reimburse [ri:im'bə:s] *v* reembolsar. **reimbursement** *n* reembolso *m*.

rein [rein] *n* rienda *f*; (*fig*) riendas *f pl*.

reincarnation [ri:inkə'neiʃən] *n* reencarnación *f*.

reindeer ['reindiə] *n* reno *m*.

reinforce [ri:in'fɔ:s] *v* reforzar. **reinforcement** *n* refuerzo *m*. **reinforced concrete** hormigón armado *m*.

reinstate [ri:in'steit] *v* reinstalar; restablecer. **reinstatement** *n* reintegración *f*, restablecimiento *m*.

reinvest [ri:in'vest] *v* reinvertir. **reinvestment** *n* reinversión *f*.

reissue [ri:'iʃu:] *v* (*book*) reeditar; (*shares*, *stamps*) volver a emitir.

reject [rə'dʒekt; *n* 'ri:dʒekt] *v* rechazar. *n* cosa defectuosa *f*. **rejection** *n* rechazamiento *m*; (*a reject*) cosa rechazada *f*.

rejoice [rə'dʒois] *v* alegrar, regocijar. **rejoicing** *n* alegría *f*, regocijo *m*.

rejoin [rə'dʒoin] *v* (*reply*) replicar; (*club*, *society*, *etc*.) reincorporarse a; (*friends*) reunirse con; (*two objects*) volver a unirse a.

rejuvenate [rə'dʒurvəneit] v rejuvenecer. **rejuvenation** n rejuvenecimiento m.

relapse [rə'laps] n recaída f; (med) recidiva f. v recaer; reincidir.

relate [rə'leit] v (tell) contar; (be connected) relacionar. **related** adj (subjects) relacionado; (by birth or marriage) emparentado. **relating to** lo que tiene que ver con.

relation [rə'leiʃn] n (account) narración f; (relative) pariente, -a m, f; (connection) relación f. **relationship** n relación f; (kinship) parentesco m.

relative ['relativ] adj relativo. n pariente, -a m, f. **relatively** adv relativamente. **relativity** n relatividad f.

relax [rə'laks] v relajar; (loosen) aflojar. **relaxation** n relajación f; descanso m; distracción f. **relaxing** adj relajante.

relay [ri'lei; n 'rilei] v transmitir. n relevo m. **relay race** carrera de relevos f.

release [rə'liis] n liberación f; (exemption) exención f; (film, record) salida f; (information) anuncio m; (gas, steam) escape m. v liberar; (film, record) estrenar; anunciar; (let go) soltar; (mechanism) disparar.

relegate ['religeit] v relegar. **relegation** n relegación f.

relent [rə'lent] v ceder; enternecerse. **relentless** adj inexorable.

relevant ['reləvənt] adj pertinente; relativo; aplicable. **relevance** n pertinencia f; aplicabilidad f.

reliable [ri'laiəbl] adj de confianza; seguro. **reliability** n seguridad f; formalidad f.

reliance [rə'laiəns] n dependencia f; (trust) confianza f.

relic ['relik] n reliquia f; vestigio m.

relief [rə'liif] n alivio m; (aid) socorro m; (for the poor) auxilio m; (substitute worker) relevo m; (geog, art) relieve m. adj suplementario.

relieve [rə'liiv] v aliviar; liberar; (replace) relevar; (help) socorrer.

religion [rə'lidʒən] n religión f. **religious** adj religioso.

relinquish [rə'liŋkwiʃ] v renunciar.

relish ['reliʃ] v (food) saborear; (enjoy) disfrutar. n gusto m; atracción f; entusiasmo m; (food) condimento m.

relive [ri'liv] v volver a vivir, revivir.

reluctant [rə'lʌktənt] adj maldispuesto.

reluctance n resistencia f. **reluctantly** adv de mala gana.

rely [rə'lai] v **rely on** contar con, confiar en.

remain [rə'mein] v quedarse. **remainder** n residuo m; resto m. **remains** pl n restos m pl; ruinas f pl.

remand [rə'maind] v reencarcelar. n reencarcelamiento m. **on remand** estar detenido.

remark [rə'maik] n observación f; comentario m. v observar, notar; hacer una observación. **remarkable** adj notable.

remarry [ri'mari] v volver a casarse. **remarriage** n segundas nupcias f pl.

remedy ['remədi] n remedio m. v remediar. **remedial** adj remediador; reparador.

remember [ri'membə] v recordar, acordarse de. **remembrance** n recuerdo m.

remind [rə'maind] v recordar. **reminder** n advertencia f; (comm) notificación f.

reminiscence [remə'nisəns] n reminiscencia f. **reminisce** v recordar el pasado. **reminiscent** adj evocador. **be reminiscent of** recordar.

remiss [rə'mis] adj descuidado.

remission [rə'miʃn] n remisión f, perdón m; exoneración f.

remit [rə'mit] v (send) remitir; (forgive) perdonar; (return to a lower court) devolver a un tribunal inferior. **remittance** n remesa f.

remnant ['remnənt] n resto m; (fabric) retal m.

remorse [rə'mois] n remordimiento m. **remorseful** adj arrepentido. **remorseless** adj sin remordimientos.

remote [rə'mout] adj (distant) lejano; (in time or space) remoto; (slight) ligero; (out-of-the-way) retirado; (stand-offish) distante. **remote control** mando a distancia m.

remove [rə'muiv] v quitar; sacar; separar; (move house) mudar. **removal** n mudanza f; (transfer) traslado m; (from office) despido m.

remunerate [rə'mjuunəreit] v remunerar. **remuneration** n remuneración f. **remunerative** adj remunerador.

renaissance [rə'neisəns] n renacimiento m.

rename [ri'neim] v poner un nuevo nombre a.

render ['rendə] v (comm) rendir; dar; (a service) hacer; (assistance) prestar; interpretar; (fat) derretir. **rendering** n also **rendition** interpretación f.

rendezvous ['rondivu:] n cita f. v reunir.

renegade ['renigeid] n, adj renegado, -a.

renew [rə'nju:] v renovar; (extend) prorogar; (efforts) reanudar. **renewal** n renovación f; prórroga f; (continuation after interruption) reanudación f.

renounce [ri'nauns] v renunciar. **renunciation** n renunciación f.

renovate ['renəveit] v renovar; reformar. **renovation** n renovación f; reforma f.

renown [rə'naun] n renombre m, fama f. **renowned** adj renombrado, afamado.

rent [rent] n alquiler m. **rent-free** sin pagar alquiler. v alquilar. **rental** n alquiler m.

reopen [ri:'oupən] v volver a abrir. **reopening** n reapertura f.

reorganize [ri:'ɔ:gənaiz] v reorganizar. **reorganization** n reorganización f.

rep [rep] n (coll) viajante m.

repair [ri'peə] v reparar; componer. n reparación f; compostura f; arreglo m. **beyond repair** no tener arreglo. **closed for repairs** cerrado por reformas.

repartee [repɑː'tiː] n respuesta aguda f; (coll) dimes y diretes m pl.

repatriate [ri:'pætrieit] v repatriar. **repatriation** n repatriación f.

***repay** [ri'pei] v (money) devolver; (debt) liquidar; (a person) compensar; (return) corresponder a. **repayment** n devolución f, pago m; (reward) recompensa f.

repeal [rə'pi:l] v revocar, abrogar. n revocación f, abrogación f.

repeat [rə'pi:t] v repitir; recitar. n repetición f.

repel [rə'pel] v repeler; rechazar. **repellent** adj repelente.

repent [rə'pent] v arrepentirse de. **repentance** n arrepentimiento m. **repentant** adj arrepentido.

repercussion [ri:pə'kʌʃən] n repercusión f.

repertoire ['repətwɑː] n also **repertory** repertorio m.

repetition [repə'tiʃn] n repetición f. **repetitive** adj reiterativo.

replace [rə'pleis] v (substitute) sustituir; (put back) reponer. **replacement** n repuesto m; (person) sustituto, -a m, f.

replay [ri:'plei; n 'ri:plei] v (sport) volver a

jugar; (music) volver a tocar. n (sport) repetición de un partido f; (television) repetición f.

replenish [rə'pleniʃ] v rellenar. **replenishment** n relleno m.

replica ['replikə] n réplica f, copia f.

reply [rə'plai] v responder, contestar. n respuesta f, contestación f.

report [rə'pɔ:t] n (spoken account) relato m; (piece of news) noticia f; (official) informe m; (newspaper or broadcast story) reportaje m; (reputation) fama f; (school) boletín m; (explosion) estampido m. v relatar; (for a newspaper) hacer la crónica de; (message) repetir; (denounce) denunciar; presentar un informe. **reporter** n reportero m, periodista m, f.

repose [rə'pouz] n reposo m, descanso m. v reposar, descansar.

represent [reprə'zent] v representar. **representation** n representación f.

representative [reprə'zentətiv] adj representativo. n representante m, f.

repress [rə'pres] v reprimir. **repression** n represión f. **repressive** adj represivo.

reprieve [rə'priːv] n (law) indulto m; (fig: relief) alivio m. v indultar; aliviar.

reprimand ['reprimɑːnd] n reprimenda f. v reprender.

reprint ['ri:print; v ri:'print] n reimpresión f. v reimprimir.

reprisal [rə'praizəl] n represalia f.

reproach [rə'proutʃ] v reprochar. n reproche m. **reproachful** adj reprensor, acusador.

reproduce [ri:prə'dju:s] v reproducir. **reproduction** n reproducción f. **reproductive** adj reproductor.

reprove [rə'pru:v] v reprobar, censurar. **reproof** n reprobación f, censura f.

reptile ['reptail] n reptil m.

republic [rə'pʌblik] n república f. **republican** n, adj republicano, -a.

repudiate [rə'pju:dieit] v (person) repudiar; (reject) rechazar; (contract) negarse a cumplir. **repudiation** n repudiación f; rechazo m; desconocimiento m.

repugnant [rə'pʌgnənt] adj repugnante. **repugnance** n repugnancia f.

repulsion [rə'pʌlʃn] n repulsión f. **repulsive** adj repulsivo. **repulsiveness** n carácter repulsivo m.

repute [rə'pju:t] n reputación f. **reputable** adj acreditado. **reputation** n reputación f. **reputed** adj supuesto.

request [ri'kwest] *n* ruego *m*; demanda *f*. **at the request of** a petición de. *v* rogar, pedir. **request stop** parada discrecional *f*.

requiem ['rekwiəm] *n* requiem *m*.

require [rə'kwaiə] *v* (*need*) requerir; (*demand*) exigir; (*desire*) desear. **requirement** *n* requisito *m*; necesidad *f*.

requisite ['rekwizit] *adj* necesario, indispensable.

requisition [,rekwi'ziʃən] *n* demanda *f*; pedido *m*. *v* requisar.

*reread [ri:'ri:d] *v* releer.

re-route [ri:'ru:t] *v* cambiar el itinerario de.

*rerun [ri:'rʌn; *n* 'ri:rʌn] *v* (*film*) restrenar; (*race*) correr de nuevo. *n* reestreno *m*.

resale [ri:'seil] *n* reventa *f*.

rescue ['reskju:] *n* rescate *m*. **rescue operations** operaciones de salvamento *f pl*. **go to the rescue of** ir en auxilio de. *v* rescatar, salvar. **rescuer** *n* rescatador, -a *m, f*; salvador, -a *m, f*.

research [ri'sə:tʃ] *n* investigación *f*. *v* investigar. **researcher** *n* investigador, -a *m, f*.

*resell [ri:'sel] *v* revender.

resemble [rə'zembl] *v* parecerse a. **resemblance** *n* parecido *m*.

resent [ri'zent] *v* tomar a mal; ofenderse por. **resentful** *adj* resentido; ofendido. **resentment** *n* resentimiento *m*.

reserve [rə'zə:v] *n* reservar. *n* reserva *f*; (*mil*) reservista *m*. **reservation** *n* reserva *f*. **reserved** *adj* reservado.

reservoir ['rezəvwa:] *n* represa *f*, embalse *m*.

reside [rə'zaid] *v* residir. **residence** *n* (*building*) residencia *f*; (*stay*) permanencia *f*. **resident** *n(m+f)*, *adj* residente. **residential** *adj* residencial.

residue ['rezidju:] *n* residuo *m*. **residual** *adj* residual.

resign [rə'zain] *v* renunciar; (*hand over*) ceder. **resign oneself** to resignarse a. **resignation** *n* renuncia *f*; (*from a post*) dimisión *f*; resignación *f*. **resigned** *adj* resignado.

resilient [rə'ziliənt] *adj* elástico; (*human body*) resistente; (*person*) de carácter fuerte. **resilience** *n* elasticidad *f*; resistencia *f*; fuerza moral *f*.

resin ['rezin] *n* resina *f*.

resist [rə'zist] *v* resistir; (*bear*) aguantar;

(*impede*) impedir. **resistance** *n* resistencia *f*; aguante *f*. **resistant** *adj* resistente.

*rest [ri'sit] *v* (*exam*) representarse.

resolute ['rezəlu:t] *adj* resuelto.

resolve [rə'zolv] *v* resolverse. **resolution** *n* resolución *f*.

resonant ['rezənənt] *adj* resonante. **resonance** *n* resonancia *f*. **resonate** *v* resonar.

resort [rə'zo:t] *n* estación *f*; centro *m*; recurso *m*. **as a last resort** como último recurso. *v* **resort to** recurrir a.

resound [rə'zaund] *v* resonar; (*fig*) tener resonancias. **resounding** *adj* resonante; sonoro; (*fig*) tremendo.

resource [rə'zo:s] *n* recurso *m*; expediente *m*. **resourceful** *adj* ingenioso, inventivo. **resourcefulness** *n* ingenio *m*, inventiva *f*.

respect [rə'spekt] *n* respeto *m*; consideración *f*; (*aspect*) aspecto *m*. **pay one's respects to** presentar sus respetos a. **with respect to** con respecto a. *v* respetar. **respectable** *adj* respetable; decente. **respectful** *adj* respetuoso. **respective** *adj* respectivo.

respiration [respə'reiʃn] *n* respiración *f*.

respite ['respait] *n* respiro *m*.

respond [rə'spond] *v* contestar; responder; reaccionar. **response** *n* respuesta *f*. **responsive** *adj* sensible.

responsible [rə'sponsəbl] *adj* responsable. **responsibility** *n* responsabilidad *f*.

rest[1] [rest] *n* descanso *m*; reposo *m*; (*music*) pausa *f*; tranquilidad *f*; (*support*) apoyo *m*. *v* descansar; (*stop*) pararse; (*stay*) quedar; (*decision*) depender de; (*lean*) apoyar. **restful** *adj* descansado; tranquilo. **restive** *adj* inquieto. **restless** *adj* desasosegado.

rest[2] [rest] *n* (*remainder*) resto *m*. **the rest** lo demás.

restaurant ['restront] *n* restaurant(e) *m*, restorán *m*. **restaurant car** coche restaurante *m*.

restore [rə'sto:] *v* restaurar; restablecer; (*return*) restituir; (*repair*) reformar; (*to former rank*) rehabilitar. **restoration** *n* restauración *f*; restablecimiento *m*; (*returning*) restituición *f*.

restrain [rə'strein] *v* impedir; limitar; (*repress*) contener. **restraint** *n* restricción *f*; limitación *f*; (*feelings*) represión *f*; moderación *f*.

restrict [rə'strikt] *v* restringir. **restricted** *adj* restringido; (*outlook*) estrecho.

restriction *n* restricción *f*. **restrictive** *adj* restrictivo.

result [rə'zʌlt] *n* resultado *m*. *v* resultar. **result from** derivarse de. **result in** tener por resultado. **resultant** *adj* resultante.

resume [rə'zjuːm] *v* reanudar. **resumption** *n* reanudación *f*.

résumé ['rezumei] *n* resumen *m*.

resurgence [ri'sɜːdʒəns] *n* resurgimiento *m*.

resurrect [rezə'rekt] *v* resucitar. **resurrection** *n* resurrección *f*.

resuscitate [rə'sʌsəteit] *v* resucitar. **resuscitation** *n* resucitación *f*.

retail ['riːteil] *n* venta al por menor. *adj*, *adv* al por menor. *v* vender al por menor; (*relate*) contar. **retailer** *n* vendedor al por menor.

retain [rə'tein] *v* (*keep*) quedarse con; conservar; retener.

retaliate [rə'talieit] *v* vengarse. **retaliation** *n* venganza *f*. **in retaliation** para vengarse.

retard [rə'taid] *v* retardar, retrasar. **retarded** *adj* atrasado.

reticent ['retisənt] *adj* reservado. **reticence** *n* reserva *f*.

retina ['retinə] *n* retina *f*.

retinue ['retinjuː] *n* comitiva *f*.

retire [rə'taiə] *v* (*from work*) jubilarse; (*draw back*) retirarse; (*go to bed*) cogerse. **retired** *adj* (*trader, soldier*) retirado; (*civilian*) jubilado. **retirement** *n* retiro *m*; jubilación *f*.

retort[1] [rə'tɔːt] *v* replicar. *n* réplica *f*.

retort[2] [rə'tɔːt] *n* (*chem*) retorta *f*.

retrace [ri'treis] *v* volver a trazar; repasar. **retrace one's steps** desandar lo andado.

retract [rə'trakt] *v* retractar. **retraction** *n* retractación *f*, retracción *f*.

retreat [rə'triːt] *v* retirarse; retroceder. *n* retirada *f*; (*place*) retiro *m*.

retrial [ri'traiəl] *n* nuevo juicio *m*.

retrieve [rə'triːv] *v* recuperar; (*from ruin*) salvar; (*hunting*) cobrar. **retrieval** *n* recuperación *f*. **retriever** *n* (*dog*) perro cobrador *m*.

retrograde ['retrəgreid] *adj* a retrógrado.

retrospect ['retrəspekt] *n* **in retrospect** retrospectivamente. **retrospective** *adj* retrospectivo.

return [rə'tɜːn] *v* devolver; (*refund*) reembolsar; (*lost or stolen property*) restituir; (*investment*) dar; (*elect*) elegir; (*come*

back) volver. **return a call** devolver una visita. *n* vuelta *f*. retorno *m*; (*reward*) recompensa *f*; restitución *f*; (*profit*) ganancias *f pl*; (*interest*) interés *m*; (*tax*) declaración *f*; (*ballot*) resultados *m pl*. **many happy returns!** ¡feliz cumpleaños! **return ticket** billete de ida y vuelta *m*. **in return** en recompensa. **on sale or return** en depósito.

reunite [riːju'nait] *v* reunir. **reunion** *n* reunión *f*.

rev [rev] (*mot*) *n* revolución *f*. **rev counter** cuentarrevoluciones *m invar*. **rev up** acelerar.

reveal [rə'viːl] *v* revelar, descubrir. **revealing** *adj* revelador. **revelation** *n* revelación *f*.

revel ['revl] *v* jaranear, ir de juerga. *n* jarana *f*, juerga *f*. **revelry** *n* jolgorio *m*.

revenge [rə'vendʒ] *n* venganza *f*. *v* vengar. **take revenge for** vengarse de.

revenue ['revinjuː] *n* (*from taxes*) rentas públicas *f pl*; (*income*) entrada *f*.

reverberate [rə'vɜːbəreit] *v* reverberar, reflejar. **reverberation** *n* reverberación *f*.

reverence ['revərəns] *n* reverencia *f*, veneración *f*. **revere** *v* reverenciar, venerar. **reverent** *adj* reverente, respetuoso.

reverse [rə'vɜːs] *n* lo contrario; (*cloth*) revés *m*; (*coin*) cruz *f*; (*printed form*) dorso *m*; (*mot: gear*) marcha atrás *f*. *adj* opuesto; contrario; inverso. *v* invertir; (*turn the other way round*) volver al revés; (*decision*) revocar; (*car*) dar marcha atrás. **reverse the charges** (*phone*) poner una conferencia a cobro revertido. **reversal** *n* inversión *f*. **reversible** *adj* reversible.

revert [rə'vɜːt] *v* volver; revertir.

review [rə'vjuː] *n* examen *m*; crítica *f*; (*mil, theatre*) revista *f*. *v* examinar; volver a examinar; hacer una crítica de. **reviewer** *n* crítico, -a *m*, *f*.

revise [rə'vaiz] *v* revisar; corregir. **revision** *n* repaso *m*; corrección *f*.

revive [rə'vaiv] *v* (*med*) reanimar, resucitar; (*trade*) reactivar; (*play*) reponer; (*custom*) restablecer; (*interest*) renovar; (*hopes*) despertar. **revival** *n* reanimación *f*; resucitación *f*; reactivación *f*; restablecimiento *f*; (*interest*) renacimiento *m*.

revoke [rə'vouk] *v* revocar; (*withdraw*) suspender.

revolt

170

revolt [rə'vəult] n rebelión f. v (offend) dar asco a; rebelarse. revolting adj asqueroso.

revolution [revə'luːʃən] n revolución f. revolutionary n, adj revolucionario, -a. revolutionize v revolucionar.

revolve [rə'vɒlv] v girar. revolver n revólver m. revolving door puerta giratoria f.

revue [rə'vjuː] n revista f.

revulsion [rə'vʌlʃən] n repulsión f.

reward [rə'wɔːd] n premio m, recompensa f. v premiar, recompensar.

*rewind [riː'waind] v (film, tape) rebobinar. rewinding n rebobinado m.

*rewrite [riː'rait] v volver a escribir; volver a redactar.

rhesus ['riːsəs] n macaco de la India m. rhesus factor factor Rhesus m.

rhetoric ['retərik] n retórica f. rhetorical adj retórico.

rheumatism ['ruːmətizəm] n reumatismo m, reúma m. rheumatic adj reumático.

rhinoceros [rai'nɒsərəs] n rinoceronte m.

rhododendron [roudə'dendrən] n rododendro m.

rhubarb ['ruːbaːb] n ruibarbo m.

rhyme [raim] n rima f. v rimar.

rhythm ['riðəm] n ritmo m. rhythmic adj rítmico.

rib [rib] n costilla f; (umbrella) varilla f. (knitting) cordoncillo m.

ribbon ['ribən] n cinta f. in ribbons hecho jirones.

rice [rais] n arroz m.

rich [ritʃ] adj rico. riches pl n riqueza f sing. richness n abundancia f; fertilidad f.

rickety ['rikəti] adj tambaleante.

*rid [rid] v librar, desembarazar. get rid of deshacerse de. riddance n libramiento m. good riddance! ¡menudo alivio!

riddle¹ ['ridl] n enigma m; acertijo m.

riddle² ['ridl] v cribar.

*ride [raid] v montar; (horse) montar a caballo. ride a bicycle/motorbike montar en bicicleta/motocicleta. n vuelta f, paseo m; (journey) viaje m. rider n (horse) jinete m; (addition) cláusula adicional f. riding n equitación f.

ridge [ridʒ] n (hills) cadena f; (crest) cumbre f; (surface) ondulación f; (roof) caballete m.

ridicule ['ridikjuːl] n ridículo m. v ridiculizar. ridiculous adj ridículo.

rife [raif] adj abundante.

rifle¹ ['raifl] n fusil m. rifle range campo de tiro m.

rifle² ['raifl] v saquear.

rift [rift] n (fissure) grieta f; (in clouds) claro m; (fig) ruptura f.

rig [rig] n (naut) aparejo m. v (mast) enjarciar; preparar; arreglar; equipar; (election) amañar. rig out ataviar. rig up improvisar. rigging n aparejo m; montaje m; equipo m.

right [rait] adj (not left) derecho; bueno; bien; justo; correcto; exacto. be right tener razón. adv a la derecha; (straight) derecho; bien; correctamente; exactamente; inmediatamente. n bien m; justicia f; (divine, to the throne, etc.) derecho m; (right hand) derecha f. civil rights pl n derechos civiles m pl. right angle ángulo recto m. right-handed adj que usa la mano derecha. right-of-way n (public) servidumbre de paso m; (roads) prioridad f. right-wing adj (pol) derechista.

righteous ['raitʃəs] adj justo, honrado.

rightful ['raitfəl] adj legítimo.

rigid ['ridʒid] adj rígido; severo. rigidity n rigidez f; severidad f.

rigmarole ['rigmərəul] n (coll) galimatías m invar.

rigour ['rigə] n rigor m; severidad f. rigorous adj riguroso; severo.

rim [rim] n (cup) borde m; (wheel) llanta f.

rind [raind] n (fruit) cáscara f; (cheese, bacon) corteza f.

ring¹ [rin] n (finger) anillo m, sortija f; círculo m; (napkin) aro m; (keys) llavero m. v formar círculo. ringleader n cabecilla m. ring road carretera de circunvalación f.

*ring² [rin] v (bell) sonar; llamar (por teléfono); (ears) zumbar. ring off (phone) colgar. ring up (phone) llamar (por teléfono); (curtain) subir. n (phone) llamada f; (sound) sonido m; (large bell) campaneo m; (electric bell) toque m; (alarm clock) timbre m; (laughter) cascabeleo m.

rink [rink] n (ice-skating) pista de hielo f; (roller-skating) pista de patinaje f.

rinse [rins] n v aclarar. n aclarado m.

riot ['raiət] n revuelta f. run riot desmandarse. v alborotar. rioter n alborotador, -a m, f. riotous adj alborotado.

rip [rip] v rasgar. **rip off** or **out** arrancar. n rasgón m, rasgadura f.

ripe [raip] adj maduro. **ripen** v madurar. **ripeness** n madurez f.

ripple ['ripl] n rizo m; (sound of water) chapoteo m; (conversation) murmullo m. v rizar.

*rise [raiz] v (get up) levantarse; (in the air) elevarse; (temperature, slope) subir; (in rank) ascender; salir; crecer; desarrollarse; (revolt) sublevarse. **rising** adj naciente; ascendente; creciente. n (sun, moon) salida f; (tide) flujo m; (water level) crecida f; (slope, temperature, curtain) subida f; (hill) elevación f; (development) desarrollo m; (prices, rate, pressure) aumento m. **give rise to** provocar.

risk [risk] n riesgo m, peligro m. **at risk** a riesgo. v arriesgar. **risky** adj arriesgado.

rissole ['risoul] n croqueta f.

rite [rait] n rito m.

ritual ['ritʃuəl] nm, adj ritual.

rival ['raivəl] n(m+f), adj rival. v competir con. **rivalry** n rivalidad f, competencia f.

river ['rivə] n río m. **riverside** n ribera f.

River Plate n Río de la Plata m.

rivet ['rivit] n remache m, roblón m. v (tech) remachar; (fig) fijar; (fig) cautivar. **rivetting** adj cautivador.

road [roud] n camino m; carretera f; (in town) calle f. **road-block** n barricada f. **road-side** n borde de la carretera m. **road sign** señal de tráfico f. **roadway** n calzada f. **roadworks** pl n obras f pl.

roam [roum] v rondar, vagar por.

roar [ro] v (lion) rugir; (bull, sea, wind) bramar; (engine) zumbar; (shout) vociferar. **roar with anger** rugir de cólera. **roar with laughter** reírse a carcajadas. n rugido m; bramido m; zumbido m; (crowd) clamor m; vociferaciones f pl.

roast [roust] v (meat) asar; (coffee) tostar. nm, adj asado.

rob [rob] v robar, hurtar. **robber** n ladrón, -ona m, f. **robbery** n robo m, hurto m.

robe [roub] n (judge's) toga f; (dressing gown) bata f; (costume) traje m; (monk's) hábito m. v vestir.

robin ['robin] n petirrojo m.

robot ['roubot] n robot m.

robust [rə'bʌst] adj robusto, vigoroso.

rock[1] [rok] n roca f; (in the sea) peña f; (stone) piedra f; (sweet) pirulí m.

rock[2] [rok] v (cradle) mecer; (move) balancear; (shake) sacudir. n (music) rock m. **rocking chair** mecedora f. **rocking-horse** n caballito de balancín m.

rocket ['rokit] n cohete m. v (prices) subir vertiginosamente.

rod [rod] n (pole) barra f; (fishing) caña f; (curtain) varilla f.

rode [roud] V **ride**.

rodent ['roudənt] n roedor m.

roe [rou] n (fish eggs) hueva f. **soft roe** lechas f pl.

rogue [roug] n granuja m, pícaro m. **roguish** adj pícaro, picaresco. **roguishness** n picardía f.

role [roul] n papel m.

roll [roul] n (paper, film, butter, tobacco) rollo m; (bread) panecillo m; (cloth) pieza f; (register) registro m; (list of names) nómina f; (thunder) fragor m; (drum) redoble m. **roll-call** n lista f. **roll of honour** lista de honor f. v hacer rodar; (cigarettes) liar; (waves) arrastrar. **roll along** rodar por. **roll over** dar una vuelta. **roller** n (lawn) rodillo m. **roller-coaster** n montaña rusa f. **roller-skate** n patín de ruedas m. **rolling-pin** n rodillo m.

romance [rou'mans] n (love) amores m pl; aventura amorosa f; (story) novela romántica f. adj (language) romance. v fantasear. **romantic**, **-a** adj romántico.

Rome [roum] n Roma. **Roman** n, adj romano, -a. **Roman Catholic** n, adj católico romano, católica romana. **Roman numeral** número romano m.

romp [romp] n retozo m. v retozar.

roof [ruf] n, pl **roofs** (building) tejado m; (cave, car, etc.) techo m. **roof of the mouth** cielo de la boca m. **roof rack** baca f.

rook [ruk] n (bird) grajo m; (chess) torre f.

room [rum] n cuarto m; (public) sala f; (hotel) habitación de hotel f; (space) sitio m; (accommodation) alojamiento m. **double room** habitación de matrimonio f. **make room for** dejar sitio. **room and board** cama y comida f, pensión completa f. **room-mate** n compañero/compañera de habitación m, f. **room service** servicio de habitaciones m. **single room** habitación individual f. **roomy** adj espacioso.

roost [rust] n percha f; gallinero m. v posarse. **rooster** n gallo m.

root[1] [ruːt] n raíz f; origen m. v echar raíces; (*become fixed*) arraigar.

root[2] [ruːt] v (*pigs*) hozar.

rope [roup] n cuerda f; (*pearls*) sarta f. **know the ropes** estar al tanto. **learn the ropes** ponerse al tanto. v (*tie*) amarrar; (*lasso*) coger con lazo. **rope off** acordonar. **ropy** *adj* (*coll*) malo.

rosary ['rouzəri] n rosario m.

rose[1] [rouz] n rosa f. **rose-bush** n rosal m. **rose garden** rosaleda f. **rosewood** n palisandro m. **rosy** *adj* rosado.

rose[2] [rouz] V **rise**.

rosemary ['rouzməri] n romero m.

rosette [rou'zet] n escarapela f.

*****rot** [rot] v pudrirse. n putrefacción f; (*substance*) podredumbre f; (*coll: rubbish*) bobadas f pl. **rotten** *adj* podrido; (*coll: bad*) pésimo; (*coll: ill*) fatal.

rota ['routə] n lista f.

rotate [rou'teit] v (*hacer*) girar, (*hacer*) dar vueltas; (*crops*) alternar. **rotary** *adj* rotatorio, rotativo. **rotation** n giro m; revolución f.

rouge [ruːʒ] n colorete m.

rough [rʌf] *adj* (*surface*) áspero; (*coarse*) tosco; duro; brutal; (*draft*) aproximado. **rough-and-ready** *adj* improvisado. **rough copy or draft** borrador m. v **rough it** (*coll*) vivir sin comodidades. **roughly** *adv* más o menos. **roughness** n aspereza f; tosquedad f; brutalidad f; dureza f.

roulette [ruːlet] n ruleta f.

round [raund] *adj* redondo. *prep* alrededor de. n círculo m; esfera f; (*slice*) rodaja f; (*patrol, drinks*) ronda f; (*ammunition*) andanada f; (*applause*) salva f. v redondear; dar la vuelta; doblar. **round off** acabar. **round up** acorralar; reunir; (*figure*) redondear.

roundabout ['raundəbaut] n (*mot*) plaza circular f; (*fair*) tiovivo m. *adj* indirecto.

rouse [rauz] v despertar; animar.

route [ruːt] n ruta f, itinerario m.

routine [ruːˈtiːn] *adj* rutinario. n rutina f.

rove [rouv] v vagar, errar.

row[1] [rou] n (*file*) fila f; (*knitting*) vuelta f.

row[2] [rou] v (*boat*) remar; (*a person*) llevar a remo. **rowing** n remo m. **rowing boat** n bote de remos m.

row[3] [rau] n (*quarrel*) bronca f; (*fuss*) jaleo m; (*noise*) alboroto m. v reñir.

rowdy ['raudi] *adj* camorrista. **rowdiness** n alboroto m; ruido m.

royal ['roiəl] *adj* real, regio. **royalist** n

monárquico, -a m, f. **royalties** pl n derechos de autor m pl. **royalty** n realeza f.

rub [rʌb] n frotamiento m. v frotar. **rubbing** n (*brass, etc.*) frotamiento m.

rubber ['rʌbə] n caucho m, goma f; (*eraser*) goma de borrar f. **rubber band** goma f. **rubber stamp** sello de goma m. **rubber tree** gomero m. **rubbery** *adj* parecido a la goma.

rubbish ['rʌbiʃ] n (*refuse*) basura f; (*waste*) desperdicios m pl; (*derog*) porquería f; (*nonsense*) tonterías f pl.

rubble ['rʌbl] n escombros m.

ruby ['ruːbi] n rubí m.

rucksack ['rʌksak] n mochila f.

rudder ['rʌdə] n timón m.

rude [ruːd] *adj* (*coarse*) grosero; (*impolite*) descortés; (*rough*) tosco; (*hard*) duro; (*painful*) penoso; (*health*) robusto. **rudeness** n grosería f; descortesía f; indecencia f.

rudiment ['ruːdimənt] n rudimento m. **rudimentary** *adj* rudimentario.

rueful ['ruːfəl] *adj* contrito; vergonzoso; triste. **ruefully** *adv* tristemente. **ruefulness** n tristeza f, aflicción f.

ruff [rʌf] n (*dress*) gorguera f; (*on animals*) collarín m.

ruffian ['rʌfiən] n rufián m.

ruffle ['rʌfl] v (*disturb*) agitar; (*hair*) desgreñar; (*feathers*) erizar; (*cloth*) fruncir; (*wrinkle*) arrugar; (*worry*) perturbar.

rug [rʌg] n (*carpet*) alfombra f; (*small carpet*) tapete m; (*blanket*) manta de viaje f.

rugged ['rʌgid] *adj* (*rock*) escarpado; (*ground*) accidentado; (*character*) desabrido; (*face*) duro; (*climate*) riguroso. **ruggedness** n lo escarpado; lo accidentado; desabrimiento m; dureza f.

ruin ['ruːin] n ruina f. v arruinar. **ruinous** *adj* ruinoso.

rule [ruːl] n regla f; mando m, gobierno m. **as a rule** por regla general. **rule of the road** reglamento del tráfico m. **rules and regulations** reglamento m *sing*. v mandar, gobernar; (*lines*) tirar (una línea). **rule out** excluir. **ruler** n gobernante m, f; soberano, -a m, f; (*measuring*) regla f. **ruling** n (*law*) decisión f.

rum [rʌm] n ron m.

rumble ['rʌmbl] n nido sordo m; (*stomach*) borborigmo m. v retumbar; (*stomach*) sonar.

rummage ['rʌmidʒ] v revolver. **rummage sale** venta de prendas usadas f.

rumour ['ruːmə] n rumor m. **it is rumoured (that)** se rumorea (que).

rump [rʌmp] n (quadruped) ancas f pl; (person) trasero m; (cookery) cuarto trasero m.

*run [rʌn] v correr; circular; (theatre) estar en cartel; (leak) salirse; (car) marchar; (machine) funcionar; (melt) derretirse; (colours) desteñirse; (road) pasar; (stockings) hacerse una carrerilla. n (race) carrera f; (short trip) paseo m; (of a train, etc.) trayecto m; (series) serie f; (ski) pista f; (print) tirada f. **in the long run** a la larga.

run away v escaparse. **runaway** nm, adj fugitivo.

run down v (knock over) atropellar; (criticize) poner por los suelos. **run-down** adj (exhausted) agotado. **rundown** n informe detallado m.

rung[1] [rʌn] V **ring**.

rung[2] [rʌn] n peldaño m.

run in v (mot) rodar; (arrest) detener.

runner ['rʌnə] n (athlete) corredor, -a m, f; (sledge) patín m. **runner bean** judía escarlata f. **runner-up** n subcampeón, -ona m, f.

run out v acabarse.

run over v (hit) pillar; (rehearse) volver a ensayar; (text) echar un vistazo a; (overflow) rebosar.

run up v (make quickly) hacer rápidamente; (flag) izar. **run up against** tropezar con.

runway ['rʌnwei] n pista f.

rupture ['rʌptʃə] n ruptura f; (med) hernia f. v romper.

rural ['ruərəl] adj rural, campestre.

ruse [ruːz] n ardid m.

rush[1] [rʌʃ] n ímpetu m; prisa f; carrera precipitada f. v hacer precipitadamente; meter prisa. **rush hour** hora punta f.

rush[2] [rʌʃ] n (bot) junco m.

rusk [rʌsk] n galleta dura f.

Russia ['rʌʃə] n Rusia f. **Russian** n, adj ruso, -a.

rust [rʌst] n orín m. herrumbre f. v oxidar. **rusty** adj oxidado.

rustic ['rʌstik] adj rústico.

rustle ['rʌsl] v (leaves) susurrar; (paper) crujir. n susurro m; crujido m.

rut [rʌt] n rodera f.

ruthless ['ruːθlis] adj despiadado, implacable.

rye [rai] n centeno m.

S

sabbatical [sə'batikəl] adj sabático. **sabbatical year** año de permiso m.

sable ['seibl] n cebellina f.

sabotage ['sabətɑːʒ] n sabotaje m. v sabotear. **saboteur** n saboteador, -a m, f.

sabre ['seibə] n sable m.

saccharin ['sakərin] n sacarina f. adj sacarino.

sachet ['saʃei] n saquito m.

sack [sak] n saco m. **get the sack** (coll) recibir el pasaporte. v (coll) despedir.

sacrament ['sakrəmənt] n sacramento m.

sacred ['seikrid] adj sagrado.

sacrifice ['sakrifais] n sacrificio m. v sacrificar.

sacrilege ['sakrəlidʒ] n sacrilegio m. **sacrilegious** adj sacrílego.

sad [sad] adj triste. **sadden** v entristecer. **sadly** adv tristemente; (unfortunately) desgraciadamente. **sadness** n tristeza f.

saddle ['sadl] n (horse) silla f; (bicycle) sillín m. **saddle-bag** n (horse) alforja f; (bicycle) cartera f. **saddle with** cargar con. **saddler** n guarnicionero m. **saddlery** n guarniciones f pl.

sadism ['seidizəm] n sadismo m. **sadist** n sádico, -a m, f. **sadistic** adj sádico.

safari [sə'fɑːri] n safari m. **safari park** reserva f.

safe [seif] adj (unhurt) sano y salvo; (undamaged) intacto; (secure) seguro; (harmless) inofensivo; (trustworthy) de fiar. n caja de caudales f. **safekeeping** n custodia f. **be on the safe side** para mayor seguridad. **safely** adv a buen puerto; sin peligro. **safety** n seguridad f; salvamento m. **safety belt** cinturón de seguridad m. **safety pin** imperdible m.

safeguard ['seifgɑːd] n salvaguardia f. v salvaguardar.

saffron ['safrən] n azafrán m. adj azafranado.

sag [sag] v doblegarse; flaquear. n hundimiento m; flexión f.

saga ['sɑːgə] n saga f.

sage[1] [seidʒ] nm, adj sabio.

sage[2] [seidʒ] n (bot) salvia f.

Sagittarius [sadʒi'teəriəs] n Sagitario m.

said [sed] V say.

sail [seil] n vela f; (trip) paseo m; (windmill) brazo m. **sailcloth** n lona f. **set sail** hacerse a la mar. v (leave) salir; (cross) atravesar; (boat) navegar. **sail through** (coll) hacer muy fácilmente. **sailing** n (navigation) navegación f; (departure) salida f. **sailing boat** barco de vela m. **sailor** n marinero m.

saint [seint] n santo, -a m, f.

sake [seik] n **for the sake of** por; para; por amor de.

salad ['saləd] n ensalada f. **salad cream** mayonesa f. **salad dressing** vinagreta f.

salami [sə'lɑːmi] n salchichón m.

salary ['saləri] n sueldo m.

sale [seil] n venta f; (reductions) liquidación f. **for** or **on sale** en venta. **sale-room** n sala de subasta f. **salesman** n (shop) dependiente m; (rep) representante m. **salesmanship** n arte de vender m.

saline ['seilain] adj salino. **salinity** n salinidad f.

saliva [sə'laivə] n saliva f. **salivary** adj salival. **salivate** v salivar.

sallow ['salou] adj cetrino.

salmon ['samən] n salmón m.

salon [seint] n salón m.

saloon [sə'luːn] n salón m; sala f. **saloon bar** salón interior m. **saloon car** coche salón m.

salt [soɪlt] n sal f. **salt-cellar** n salero m. v salar. **salty** adj salado.

salute [sə'luːt] n saludo m; (gun) salva f. v saludar.

salvage ['salvidʒ] n salvamento m; objetos salvados m pl. v salvar.

salvation [sal'veiʃən] n salvación f.

same [seim] adj mismo; igual. pron el mismo, la misma. adv de la misma forma. **all the same** sin embargo. **at the same time** al mismo tiempo.

sample ['sɑːmpl] n muestra f; prueba f; ejemplo m. v probar; (drinks) catar.

sanatorium [sanə'toːriəm] n sanatorio m.

sanctify ['saŋktifai] v santificar. **sanctification** n santificación f.

sanctimonious [saŋkti'mouniəs] adj santurrón.

sanction ['saŋkʃən] n sanción f. v sancionar; autorizar.

sanctity ['saŋktəti] n santidad f; inviolabilidad f.

sanctuary ['saŋktʃuəri] n santuario m; (refuge) refugio m; (animal) reserva f.

sand [sand] n arena f. **sandbag** n saco terrero m. **sand dune** duna f. **sandpaper** n papel de lija m. v (with sandpaper) lijar. **sandy** adj (beach) arenoso; (hair) rubio rojizo.

sandal ['sandl] n sandalia f.

sandwich ['sanwidʒ] n bocadillo m. v intercalar.

sane [sein] adj sano; razonable. **sanity** n juicio m; (sensibleness) sensatez f.

sang [saŋ] V sing.

sanitary ['sanitəri] adj sanitario; higiénico. **sanitary towel** paño higiénico m.

sank [saŋk] V sink.

sap [sap] n savia f.

sapphire ['safaiə] n zafiro m.

sarcasm ['saːkazəm] n sarcasmo m.

sardine [saː'diːn] n sardina f.

Sardinia [saː'dinjə] n Cerdeña f. **Sardinian** n, adj sardo, -a m, f.

sardonic [saː'donik] adj sardónico.

sash[1] [saʃ] n faja f; (chest ribbon) banda f; (waist) fajín m.

sash[2] [saʃ] n (frame) marco m. **sash window** ventana de guillotina f.

sat [sat] V sit.

Satan [seitən] n Satán m, Satanás m. **satanic** adj satánico.

satchel ['satʃəl] n cartera f.

satellite ['satəlait] n satélite m.

satin ['satin] n raso m.

satire ['sataiə] n sátira f. **satirical** adj satírico. **satirize** v satirizar.

satisfy ['satisfai] v satisfacer; convencer. **satisfaction** n satisfacción f. **satisfactory** adj satisfactorio.

saturate ['satʃəreit] v saturar; (soak) empapar. **saturation** n saturación f. **reach saturation point** llegar al punto de saturación.

Saturday ['satədi] n sábado m.

sauce [soɪs] n salsa f; (slang) insolencia f. **saucy** adj descarado; coquetón.

saucepan ['soɪspən] n cacerola f.

saucer ['soɪsə] n platillo m. **flying saucer** platillo volante m.

sauerkraut ['sauəkraut] n sauerkraut m.

sauna ['soɪnə] n sauna f.

saunter ['soɪntə] v pasearse. n paso lento m; paseo m.

sausage ['sosidʒ] n salchicha f. **sausage-meat** n carne de salchicha f. **sausage roll** empanadilla de salchicha f.

savage ['savidʒ] adj (fierce) feroz; (primitive) salvaje; cruel; violento. n salvaje m, f. v embestir. **savagery** n salvajada f; ferocidad f.

save[1] [seiv] v salvar; (put aside) ahorrar; (keep till later) guardar; (protect) proteger; (goal) parar. **savings** pl n ahorros m pl. **savings bank** caja de ahorros f.

save[2] [seiv] prep salvo, excepto. conj a no ser que.

saviour ['seivjə] n salvador, -a m, f.

savoir-faire [ˌsavwaːˈfeə] n desparpajo m; sentido común m.

savour ['seivə] v saborear; tener sabor de. n sabor m, gusto m. **savoury** adj sabroso; salado. n entremés salado m.

saw[1] [soː] V see.

*** saw**[2] [soː] n (tool) sierra f; (proverb) refrán m. **sawdust** n aserrín m. **sawmill** n aserradero m. v aserrar.

saxophone ['saksəfoun] n saxofón m.

*** say** [sei] v decir; recitar. **I have no say** no tener ni voz ni voto. **saying** n (act) decir m; (maxim) refrán m.

scab [skab] n costra f, postilla f; (derog: blackleg) esquirol m.

scaffold ['skafəld] n (platform) tarina f; (gallows) cadalso m. **scaffolding** n andamio m.

scald [skoːld] v escaldar; (instruments) esterilizar. n escaldadura f. **scalding** adj hirviendo, hirviente.

scale[1] [skeil] n (fish, etc.) escama f; (tartar) sarro m. **scaly** adj escamoso; sarroso.

scale[2] [skeil] n (music, measurement) escala f; (damage, etc.) amplitud f. **scale drawing** dibujo hecho a escala m. v (climb) escalar. **scale down** reducir a escala.

scales [skeilz] pl n balanza f sing.

scallop ['skaləp] n (zool) venera f; (cookery) escalope m; (sewing) festón m. **scallop shell** concha f. v festonear.

scalp [skalp] n cuero cebelludo m. v escalpar.

scalpel ['skalpəl] n escalpelo m.

scamper ['skampə] v corretear.

scampi ['skampi] n gamba grande f.

scan [skan] v recorrer con la mirada; escrutar; (tech) explorar; (poetry) escandir.

scandal ['skandl] n escándalo m; (gossip) chismorreo m; (law) difamación f. **scandalize** v escandalizar. **scandalous** adj escandaloso.

Scandinavia [ˌskandiˈneivjə] n Escandinavia f. **Scandinavian** n, adj escandinavo, -a.

scant [skant] adj also **scanty** insuficiente. **scantily** adv muy ligeramente.

scapegoat ['skeipgout] n cabeza de turco f.

scar [skaː] n cicatriz f. v cicatrizar; (fig) marcar.

scarce [skeəs] adj escaso; insuficiente; raro. **scarcely** adv apenas; casi. **scarcity** n escasez f.

scare [skeə] n susto m; alarma f. v asustar, espantar. **be scared** tener miedo. **scarecrow** n espantapájaros m invar.

scarf [skaːf] m (woollen) bufanda f; (light) pañuelo m.

scarlet ['skaːlit] adj escarlato. **scarlet fever** escarlatina f.

scathing ['skeiðiŋ] adj cáustico, mordaz.

scatter ['skatə] v esparcir; (sprinkle) salpicar; (put to flight) derrotar; dispersar; (squander) desparramar. **scatter-brained** adj atolondrado.

scavenge ['skavindʒ] v recoger; buscar entre. **scavenger** n barrendero m; animal que se alimenta de carroña m.

scene [siːn] n escena f; (place) lugar m; espectáculo m; vista f. **scenic** adj escénico; pintoresco.

scenery ['siːnəri] n (landscape) paisaje m; (theatre) decorado m.

scent [sent] n perfume m; (smell) olor m; (track) rastro m. v perfumar; (smell) oler.

sceptic ['skeptik] n escéptico, -a m, f. **sceptical** adj escéptico. **scepticism** n escepticismo m.

sceptre ['septə] n cetro m.

schedule ['ʃedjuːl] n programa m; (timetable) horario m. v programar; fijar.

scheme [skiːm] n plan m; proyecto m, esquema m; (plot) intriga f. v proyectar; intrigar, conspirar.

schizophrenia [ˌskitsəˈfriːniə] n esquizofrenia f. **schizophrenic** n, adj esquizofrénico, -a.

scholar ['skolə] n (learned person) erudito, -a m, f; (schoolchild) colegial, -a m, f, alumno, -a m, f; (student) estudiante m, f. **scholarly** adj erudito. **scholarship** n (award) beca f; erudición f.

scholastic [skə'lastik] *adj* escolar, escolástico.

school¹ [skuːl] *n* escuela *f*; (*private or secondary*) colegio *m*. **schoolboy** *n* alumno *m*, colegial *m*. **schoolgirl** *n* alumna *f*, colegiala *f*. **schooling** *n* educación *f*, enseñanza *f*. **schoolmaster** *n* (*primary*) maestro *m*; (*secondary*) profesor *m*. **schoolmistress** *n* maestra *f*; profesora *f*. **school-room** *n* clase *f*; sala de clase *f*.

school² [skuːl] *n* (*of fish*) banco *m*.

schooner ['skuːnə] *n* goleta *f*.

sciatica [sai'atikə] *n* ciática *f*. **sciatic** *adj* ciático.

science ['saiəns] *n* ciencia *f*. **science fiction** ciencia ficción *f*. **scientific** *adj* científico. **scientist** *n* científico, -a *m*, *f*.

scintillating ['sintileitiŋ] *adj* relumbrante; (*fig*) brillante.

scissors ['sizəz] *pl n* tijeras *f pl*.

scoff¹ [skof] *v* burlarse.

scoff² [skof] *v* (*coll: eat*) zamparse.

scold [skould] *v* reñir, reprender. *n* virago *f*. **scolding** *n* reprensión *f*.

scone [skon] *n* bollo *m*.

scoop [skuːp] *n* pala de mano *f*; (*press*) éxito periodístico *m*. *v* sacar con pala; (*dig*) excavar.

scooter ['skuːtə] *n* (*motor*) scooter *m*; (*child's*) patinete *m*.

scope [skoup] *n* (*range*) alcance *m*; (*opportunity*) libertad *f*; (*field of action*) esfera *f*.

scorch [skoːtʃ] *n* quemadura *f*. *v* quemar; (*singe*) chamuscar.

score [skoː] *n* (*number of points*) tanteo *m*; (*result*) resultado *m*; (*test marks*) calificación *f*; (*twenty*) veintena *f*; (*music*) partitura *f*; (*notch*) muesca *f*. **scoreboard** *n* marcador *m*. *v* (*point, goal*) marcar; orquestar; hacer una muesca en. **scorer** *n* (*scorekeeper*) tanteador *m*; (*football*) goleador *m*.

scorn [skoːn] *n* desdén *m*, desprecio *m*. *v* desdeñar, despreciar. **scornful** *adj* desdeñoso, despreciativo.

Scorpio ['skoːpiou] *n* Escorpión *m*.

scorpion ['skoːpiən] *n* escorpión *m*.

Scotland ['skotlənd] *n* Escocia *f*. **Scot** *n* escocés, -esa *m*, *f*. **Scotch** *n* whisky escocés *m*. **Scots** *nm*, *adj* escocés. **Scottish** *adj* escocés.

scoundrel ['skaundrəl] *n* sinvergüenza *m*.

scour¹ [skauə] *v* (*clean*) fregar. **scourer** *n* (*pad*) estropajo *m*.

scour² [skauə] *v* (*search*) recorrer, batir.

scout [skaut] *n* explorador *m*. **scoutmaster** *n* jefe de exploradores *m*.

scowl [skaul] *v* fruncir el entrecejo. *n* ceño *m*.

scramble ['skrambl] *v* (*climb*) trepar; (*struggle*) pelearse; (*mix*) mezclar; (*eggs*) revolver. *n* lucha *f*, pelea *f*.

scrap [skrap] *n* (*piece*) trozo *m*; (*metal*) chatarra *f*; (*coll: fight*) pelea *f*. **scrapbook** *n* álbum de recortes *m*. papel para apuntes *m*. **scraps** *pl n* restos *m pl*, sobras *f pl*. *v* desechar; (*coll*) pelear.

scrape [skreip] *n* (*noise*) chirrido *m*; (*act*) raspado *m*; (*mark*) arañazo *m*; (*graze*) rasguño *m*; (*coll: trouble*) apuro *m*. *v* raspar; (*graze*) arañar; (*drag*) arrastrar.

scratch [skratʃ] *n* arañazo *m*; raya *f*; rasguño *m*; cero *m*.

scrawl [skroːl] *v* garabatear. *n* garabato *m*.

scream [skriːm] *n* grito *m*, chillido *m*. *v* gritar, chillar.

screech [skriːtʃ] *v* chillar, gritar; (*brakes*) chirriar. *n* chillido *m*, grito *m*; chirrido *m*.

screen [skriːn] *n* (*TV, film*) pantalla *f*; (*folding*) biombo *m*; (*fig*) cortina *f*. **screen-play** *n* guión *m*. **screen test** prueba cinematográfica *f*. *v* (*film*) proyectar; (*shelter*) proteger; (*sift*) tamizar.

screw [skruː] *n* tornillo *m*; (*propeller*) hélice *f*. **screwdriver** *n* destornillador *m*. *v* atornillar. **screw up** (*paper*) arrugar.

scribble ['skribl] *v* garabatear. *n* garabato *m*.

script [skript] *n* (*film*) guión *m*; (*theatre*) argumento *m*; (*writing*) escritura *f*.

scripture ['skriptʃə] *n* (*school*) religión *f*; (*holy*) Sagrada Escritura *f*.

scroll [skroul] *n* rollo *m*; (*arch*) voluta *f*.

scrounge [skraundʒ] (*coll*) *v* sablear; gorronear. **scrounger** *n* sablista *m*, *f*; gorrón, -ona *m*, *f*.

scrub¹ [skrʌb] *n* fregado *m*; fricción *f*. *v* fregar; restregar; (*coll: cancel*) cancelar. **scrubbing brush** cepillo de fregar *m*.

scrub² [skrʌb] *n* matorral *m*; maleza *f*.

scruff [skrʌf] *n* **by the scruff of the neck** por el cogote.

scruffy ['skrʌfi] *adj* desaliñado. **scruffiness** *n* desaliño *m*.

scrum [skrʌm] *n* melée *f*.

scruple ['skruːpl] *n* escrúpulo *m*. **scrupulous** *adj* escrupuloso.

scrutiny ['skruːtənɪ] *n* escrutinio *m*. **scrutinize** *v* escudriñar.

scuffle ['skʌfl] *n* pelea *f*, refriega *f*. *v* pelear, reñir.

scull [skʌl] *n* remo *m*.

scullery ['skʌlərɪ] *n* trascocina *f*.

sculpt [skʌlpt] *v* esculpir. **sculptor** *n* escultor, -a *m, f*. **sculpture** *n* escultura *f*.

scum [skʌm] *n* espuma *f*; (*derog*) escoria *f*.

scurf [skəːf] *n* caspa *f*.

scurvy ['skəːvɪ] *n* escorbuto *m*.

scuttle¹ ['skʌtl] *n* (*coal*) cubo del carbón *m*.

scuttle² ['skʌtl] *v* (*naut*) barrenar.

scuttle³ ['skʌtl] *v* escabullirse.

scythe [saɪð] *n* guadaña *f*. *v* guadañar.

sea [siː] *n* mar *m, f*.

sea-bed *n* fondo del mar *m*.

seaborne ['siːbɔːn] *adj* transportado por mar.

seafood ['siːfuːd] *n* mariscos *m pl*.

seafront ['siːfrʌnt] *n* paseo marítimo *m*.

seagoing ['siːɡouɪŋ] *adj* (*ship*) de alta mar; (*person*) marinero.

seagull ['siːɡʌl] *n* gaviota *f*.

seahorse ['siːhɔːs] *n* caballo de mar *m*.

seal¹ [siːl] *n* sello *m*. *v* sellar; (*close*) cerrar; (*fate*) decidir. **sealing wax** lacre *m*.

seal² [siːl] *n* (*zool*) foca *f*. **sealskin** *n* piel de foca *f*.

sea-level *n* nivel del mar *m*.

sea-lion *n* león marino *m*.

seam [siːm] *n* (*sewing*) costura *f*; (*coal*) vena *f*; (*geol*) capa *f*. **seamy** *adj* (*fig*) sórdido.

seaman ['siːmən] *n pl* **seamen** marinero *m*.

séance ['seɪɑ̃s] *n* sesión de espiritismo *f*.

sear [sɪə] *v* (*scorch*) abrasar; (*wither*) marchitar. **searing** *adj* (*pain*) punzante.

search [səːtʃ] *n* investigación *f*; (*to find something*) búsqueda *f*; (*house, car*) registro *m*. **searchlight** *n* reflector *m*. **search-party** *n* equipo de salvamento *m*. **search warrant** *n* mandamiento de registro *m*. *v* buscar; registrar; investigar. **searching** *adj* (*look*) penetrante; (*examination*) minucioso.

sea shell *n* concha marina *f*.

seashore ['siːʃɔː] *n* playa *f*; costa *f*.

seasick ['siːsɪk] *adj* **be seasick** marearse. **sea sickness** mareo *m*.

seaside ['siːsaɪd] *n* playa *f*; costa *f*. **seaside resort** estación balnearia *f*.

season ['siːzn] *n* estación *f*; temporada *f*; época *f*. **season ticket** abono *m*. *v* (*food*) sazonar; (*wood*) secar. **seasonal** *adj* estacional; (*work*) temporal. **seasoning** *n* condimento *m*.

seat [siːt] *n* asiento *m*; silla *f*; localidad *f*; centro *m*. **seat-belt** *n* cinturón de seguridad *m*. *v* sentar; colocar; tener cabida para.

seawater ['siːwɔːtə] *n* agua de mar *f*.

seaweed ['siːwiːd] *n* alga *f*.

seaworthy ['siːwəːðɪ] *adj* marinero. **seaworthiness** *n* navegabilidad *f*.

second¹ ['sekənd] *n* (*time*) segundo *m*. **second hand** segundero *m*.

second² ['sekənd] *n* segundo, -a *m, f*. (*gear*) segunda *f*. **seconds** *pl n* artículos de segunda clase *m pl. adj* segundo. **on second thoughts** pensándolo bien. **second-class** *adj* de segunda clase. **travel second-class** viajar en segunda. **second-hand** *adj* de segunda mano, usado. **second-rate** *adj* de segunda categoría. *v* (*in debate*) apoyar. **secondly** *adv* en segundo lugar.

secondary ['sekəndərɪ] *adj* secundario. **secondary school** instituto de enseñanza media *m*.

secret ['siːkrɪt] *nm, adj* secreto. **secrecy** *n* secreto *m*. **secretive** *adj* reservado; callado. **secretly** *adv* en secreto.

secretary ['sekrətərɪ] *n* secretario, -a *m, f*. **secretarial** *adj* de secretario.

secrete [sɪ'kriːt] *v* (*hide*) esconder; (*med*) secretar. **secretion** *n* secreción *f*.

sect [sekt] *n* secta *f*. **sectarian** *adj* sectario.

section ['sekʃən] *n* sección *f*; parte *f*.

sector ['sektə] *n* sector *m*.

secular ['sekjulə] *adj* profano; secular; laico.

secure [sɪ'kjuə] *adj* seguro. *v* asegurar; cerrar firmemente; garantizar; conseguir; reservar; consolidar. **security** *n* seguridad *f*; (*for loan*) garantía *f*.

sedate [sɪ'deɪt] *adj* sosegado; tranquilo. **sedation** *n* sedación *f*. **sedative** *nm, adj* sedante.

sediment ['sedimənt] *n* (*geol*) sedimento *m*; (*liquid*) poso *m*.

seduce [si'djuːs] *v* seducir. **seduction** *f*. seducción *f*. **seductive** *adj* seductor.

*see[1] [siː] *v* ver; comprender; mirar; visitar; recibir. **see off** ir a despedir. **see through** (*not be deceived*) calar. **see to** ocuparse de. **see you later!** ¡hasta luego!

see[2] [siː] *n* (*rel*) obispado *m*.

seed [siːd] *n* semilla *f*; (*fruit*) pepita *f*; (*sperm*) semen *m*. **seedless** *adj* sin semillas; sin pepitas. **seedling** *n* plantón *m*. **seedy** *adj* granado; (*coll*: *ill*) pachucho.

*seek [siːk] *v* buscar; tratar; solicitar.

seem [siːm] *v* parecer. **seeming** *adj* aparente. **seemingly** *adv* al parecer, por lo visto.

seep [siːp] *v* rezumarse. **seepage** *n* filtración *f*.

seesaw ['siːsɔː] *n* columpio *m*, subibaja *m*. *v* columpiarse.

seethe [siːð] *v* borbotar. **seething** *adj* (*coll*) bufando de cólera.

segment ['segmənt] *n* segmento *m*; (*orange, etc.*) gajo *m*.

segregate ['segrigeit] *v* segregar. **segregation** *n* segregación *f*.

seize [siːz] *v* tomar; (*grab firmly*) agarrar; (*a person*) detener. **seize up** (*tech*) agarrotarse. **seizure** *n* asimiento *m*; detención *f*; (*property*) embargo *m*; (*in war*) toma *f*; (*med*) ataque *m*.

seldom ['seldəm] *adv* raramente.

select [sə'lekt] *v* escoger, elegir. *adj* escogido; (*exclusive*) selecto. **selection** *n* selección *f*. **selective** *adj* selectivo.

self [self] *n* sí mismo *m*, sí misma *f*; personalidad *f*.

self-addressed *adj* con su propia dirección.

self-adhesive *adj* autoadhesivo.

self-assured *adj* seguro de sí mismo. **self-assurance** *n* confianza en sí mismo *f*.

self-centred *adj* egocéntrico.

self-confident *adj* seguro de sí mismo. **self-confidence** *n* seguridad en sí mismo *f*.

self-conscious *adj* cohibido. **self-consciousness** *n* turbación *f*.

self-contained *adj* independiente.

self-control *n* dominio de sí mismo *m*. **self-controlled** *adj* sereno.

self-defence *n* (*technique*) autodefensa *f*; (*law*) legítima defensa *f*.

self-determination *n* autodeterminación *f*.

self-discipline *n* autodisciplina *f*.

self-educated *adj* autodidacto.

self-employed *adj* que trabaja por cuenta propia.

self-esteem *n* amor propio *m*.

self-evidence *adj* patente, manifiesto.

self-explanatory *adj* que se explica por sí mismo.

self-expression *n* expresión de la propia personalidad *f*.

self-interest *n* interés propio *m*.

selfish ['selfiʃ] *adj* egoísta. **selfishness** *n* egoísmo *m*.

selfless ['selflis] *adj* desinteresado.

self-made *adj* and **self-made man** hijo de sus propias obras *m*.

self-opinionated *adj* obstinado.

self-pity *n* lástima de sí mismo *f*.

self-portrait *n* autorretrato *m*.

self-possessed *adj* seguro de sí mismo.

self-respect *n* dignidad *f*.

self-righteous *adj* farisaico. **self-righteousness** *n* fariseísmo *m*.

self-rule *n* autonomía *f*.

self-sacrifice *n* sacrificio de sí mismo *m*.

selfsame ['selfseim] *adj* mismísimo *m*.

self-satisfied *adj* satisfecho de sí mismo.

self-service *n* autoservicio *m*.

self-sufficient *adj* independiente. **self-sufficiency** *n* independencia *f*.

self-willed *adj* obstinado.

self-winding *adj* de cuerda automática.

*sell [sel] *v* vender(se); hacer vender. **sell off** liquidar. **seller** *n* vendedor, -a *m*, *f*; (*dealer*) comerciante *m*.

semantic [sə'mantik] *adj* semántico. **semantics** *n* semántica *f*.

semaphore ['seməfɔː] *n* semáforo *m*.

semblance ['sembləns] *n* apariencia *f*.

semen ['siːmən] *n* semen *m*.

semibreve ['semibriːv] *n* semibreve *f*.

semicircle ['semisəːkl] *n* semicírculo *m*. **semicircular** *adj* semicircular.

semicolon [,semi'koulən] *n* punto y coma *m*.

semiconscious [semi'kɔnʃəs] *adj* semiconsciente.

semi-detached house *n* casa doble *f*.

semifinal [semi'fainl] *n* semifinal *f*.

seminar ['seminɑː] *n* seminario *m*.

semi-precious *adj* fino; semiprecioso.

semiquaver ['semikweivə] *n* semicorchea *f*.

semitone ['semitoun] *n* semitono *m*.

semolina [semə'liinə] *n* sémola *f*.

senate ['senit] *n* senado *m*. **senator** *n* senador *m*.

*send [send] *v* enviar, mandar; remitir; echar; transmitir. **send back** devolver. **send for** llamar a; (*mail-order*) escribir pidiendo.

senile ['siinail] *adj* senil. **senility** *n* senilidad *f*.

senior ['sinjə] *adj* (*age*) mayor; (*rank*) superior. *n* (*school*) mayor *m, f*. **seniority** *n* antigüedad *f*.

sensation [sen'seifən] *n* sensación *f*. **sensational** *adj* sensacional.

sense [sens] *n* sentido *m*; significado *m*; sensación *f*; sentimiento *m*; (*consensus*) sentir *m*. **senses** *pl n* (*reason*) juicio *m sing*; (*consciousness*) sentido *m*. *v* sentir. **senseless** *adj* (*unconscious*) sin sentido; (*silly*) insensato.

sensible ['sensəbl] *adj* sensato; razonable; (*clothes*) práctico.

sensitive ['sensitiv] *adj* sensible; (*easily hurt*) susceptible. **sensitivity** *n* sensibilidad *f*; susceptibilidad *f*.

sensual ['sensjuəl] *adj* sensual. **sensuality** *n* sensualidad *f*.

sensuous ['sensjuəs] *adj* sensual.

sent [sent] *V* send.

sentence ['sentəns] *n* (*gramm*) frase *f*; (*law*) sentencia *f*. *v* sentenciar, condenar.

sentiment ['sentimənt] *n* sentimiento *m*; (*sentimentality*) sentimentalismo *m*; opinión *f*. **sentimental** *adj* sentimental.

sentry ['sentri] *n* centinela *m*.

separate ['seprət]; *v* 'sepəreit] *adj* separado; distinto; independiente; (*room*) particular. *v* separar; dividir; distinguir entre. **separation** *n* separación *f*.

September [sep'tembə] *n* septiembre *m*, setiembre *m*.

septic ['septik] *adj* séptico.

sequel ['siikwəl] *n* consecuencia *f*; secuela *f*.

sequence ['siikwəns] *n* sucesión *f*; serie *f*; orden *m*.

sequin ['siikwin] *n* lentejuela *f*.

serenade [serə'neid] *n* serenata *f*. *v* dar una serenata a.

serene [sə'riin] *adj* sereno. **serenity** *n* serenidad *f*.

serf [səif] *n* siervo, -a *m, f*.

sergeant ['saidʒənt] *n* (*mil*) sargento *m*; (*police*) cabo *m*. **sergeant-major** *n* sargento mayor *m*.

serial ['siəriəl] *n* serial *m*. *adj* de serie; seriado. **serialize** *v* publicar por entregas.

series ['siəriz] *n* serie *f*.

serious ['siəriəs] *adj* serio; grave. **seriousness** *n* seriedad *f*; gravedad *f*.

sermon ['səimən] *n* sermón *m*.

serpent ['səipənt] *n* serpiente *f*.

serrated [sə'reitid] *adj* serrado; dentado.

servant ['səivənt] *n* criado, -a *m, f*; sirviente, -a *m, f*; empleado, -a *m, f*; funcionario, -a *m, f*.

serve [səiv] *v* servir; atender. **it serves you right** te está bien empleado. *n* (*tennis*) saque *m*.

service ['səivis] *n* servicio *m*; favor *m*; (*mot*) revisión *f*; (*tea*) juego *m*; (*tennis*) saque *m*. **service charge** servicio *m*. **serviceman** *n* militar *m*. **service station** (*mot*) estación de servicio *f*. *v* (*check*) revisar; (*maintain*) mantener. **serviceable** *adj* utilizable; práctico.

serviette [səivi'et] *n* servilleta *f*.

servile ['səivail] *adj* servil. **servility** *n* servilismo *m*.

session ['sefən] *n* sesión *f*; junta *f*.

*set [set] *v* poner; colocar; fijar; (*clock*) regular; (*bones*) reducir; (*type*) componer; (*to music*) poner en música; (*sun*) ponerse. **set about** ponerse (a). **setback** *n* revés *m*; contratiempo *m*. **set off** (*leave*) partir; (*explode*) hacer estallar; (*cause*) hacer. **set out** partir; disponer. **set up** erigir; montar; establecer. *n* grupo *m*; (*tools, china, etc.*) juego *m*; (*kitchen implements*) batería *f*; (*books*) colección *f*; (*people*) clase *f*; (*clothes*) caída *f*; (*sun, etc.*) puesta *f*; (*radio, etc.*) aparato *m*; (*tennis*) set *m*; (*theatre*) decorado *m*. *adj* fijo; inmóvil; asignado; establecido. **setting** *n* (*adjustment*) ajuste *m*; (*theatre*) decorado *m*.

settee [se'tii] *n* canapé *m*.

settle ['setl] *v* (*solve*) resolver; calmar; (*country*) colonizar. **settle down** instalarse; calmarse. **settle up** (*bill*) pagar. **settlement** *n* colonización *f*; arreglo *m*; liquidación *f*; satisfacción *f*.

seven ['sevn] *nm, adj* siete. **seventh** *n, adj* séptimo, -a..

seventeen [sevn'tiin] *nm, adj* diecisiete. **seventeenth** *n, adj* decimoséptimo, -a.

seventy ['sevntɪ] *nm, adj* setenta. **seventieth** *n, adj* septuagésimo, -a.

sever ['sevə] *v* cortar.

several ['sevrəl] *adj, pron* varios.

severe [sə'vɪə] *adj* severo; duro; (*pain*) agudo; (*illness*) grave. **severity** *n* severidad *f*; gravedad *f*; (*weather*) inclemencia *f*.

*sew [səu] *v* coser. **sewing** *n* costura *f*. **sewing machine** máquina de coser *f*.

sewage ['sjuːɪdʒ] *n* aguas residuales *f pl*.

sewer ['sjuə] *n* alcantarilla *f*, albañal *m*.

sex [seks] *n* sexo *m*. **sexual** *adj* sexual. **sexual intercourse** relaciones sexuales *f pl*. **sexuality** *n* sexualidad *f*. **sexy** *adj* provocativo.

sextet [seks'tet] *n* sexteto *m*.

shabby ['ʃabɪ] *adj* andrajoso; (*behaviour*) mezquino.

shack [ʃak] *n* choza *f*.

shade [ʃeɪd] *n* sombra *f*; (*lamp*) pantalla *f*; (*colour*) tono *m*; (*meaning*) matiz *m*. *v* dar sombra; (*art*) sombrear. **shady** *adj* sombreado; (*person*) dudoso.

shadow ['ʃadəu] *n* sombra *f*. **shadow cabinet** gabinete fantasma *m*. *v* (*follow*) seguir. **shadowy** *adj* indistinto; misterioso.

shaft [ʃaːft] *n* (*handle*) mango *m*; (*lift*) hueco *m*; (*light*) rayo *m*; (*ventilation*) pozo de ventilación *m*; (*mine*) pozo *m*; (*spear*) asta *f*.

shaggy ['ʃagɪ] *adj* peludo.

*shake [ʃeɪk] *v* sacudir; (*bottle*) agitar; (*head*) menear; (*brandish*) esgrimir. **shake hands** darse la mano. **shake off** librarse de. *n* sacudida *f*; meneo *m*; movimiento *m*; temblor *m*. **shaky** *adj* tembloroso; (*weak*) poco sólido.

shall [ʃal] *aux* translated by future tense.

shallot [ʃə'lot] *n* chalote *m*.

shallow ['ʃaləu] *adj* poco profundo; superficial.

sham [ʃam] *adj* fingido, simulado; falso. *n* (*person*) impostor, -a *m, f*; (*object*) impostura *f*. *v* fingir, simular.

shame [ʃeɪm] *n* vergüenza *f*; deshonra *f*; pena *f*. *v* avergonzar; deshonrar. **shamefaced** *adj* avergonzado; tímido. **shameful** *adj* vergonzoso. **shameless** *adj* desvergonzado; sinvergüenza.

shampoo [ʃam'puː] *n* champú *m*. *v* dar un champú a.

shamrock ['ʃamrok] *n* trébol *m*.

shandy ['ʃandɪ] *n* cerveza con gaseosa *f*.

shanty[1] ['ʃantɪ] *n* (*hut*) chabola *f*. **shanty town** barrio de las latas *m*.

shanty[2] ['ʃantɪ] *n* (*music*) saloma *f*.

shape [ʃeɪp] *n* forma *f*; figura *f*; aspecto *m*. *v* dar forma a; labrar; cortar; (*idea*) formular. **shapeless** *adj* informe. **shapely** *adj* bien proporcionado.

share [ʃeə] *n* parte *f*; (*comm*) acción *f*. **shareholder** *n* accionista *m, f*. *v* compartir.

shark [ʃaːk] *n* tiburón *m*.

sharp [ʃaːp] *adj* (*edge*) afilado; (*point*) punzante; (*bend*) brusco; (*phot*) nítido; (*outline*) definido; (*pain*) agudo; (*taste*) picante; (*clever*) vivo. *n* (*music*) sostenido *m*. **sharpen** *v* (*knife*) afilar; (*pencil*) sacar punta a. **sharpness** *n* lo afilado; agudeza *f*; (*clarity*) nitidez *f*.

shatter ['ʃatə] *v* destrozar; (*health*) quebrantar; (*fig*) echar por tierra. **shattered** *adj* destrozado; roto; quebrantado. **shattering** *adj* demoledor; fulgurante.

shave [ʃeɪv] *v* afeitarse. **shaving** *n* (*of wood, metal*) viruta *f*. **shaving brush** brocha de afeitar *f*. **shaving cream** crema de afeitar *f*.

shawl [ʃoːl] *n* chal *m*.

she [ʃiː] *pron* ella. **she who** la que, aquella que, quien.

sheaf [ʃiːf] *n* (*corn*) gavilla *f*; (*arrows*) haz *m*; (*papers*) fajo *m*.

*shear [ʃɪə] *v* esquilar. **shears** *pl n* tijeras *f pl*.

sheath [ʃiːθ] *n* (*umbrella, knife, etc.*) funda *f*; (*sword*) vaina *f*. **sheathe** *v* envainar; cubrir.

*shed[1] [ʃed] *v* (*drop*) deshacerse de.

shed[2] [ʃed] *n* cobertizo *m*; barraca *f*.

sheen [ʃiːn] *n* brillo *m*; (*silk*) viso *m*.

sheep [ʃiːp] *n* oveja *f*. **sheepdog** *n* perro pastor *m*. **sheepskin** *n* piel de carnero *f*. **sheepish** *adj* vergonzoso.

sheer[1] [ʃɪə] *adj* completo; total; puro; (*cliff*) cortado a pico; (*stockings*) diáfano.

sheer[2] [ʃɪə] *v* (*naut*) guiñar.

sheet [ʃiːt] *n* (*bed*) sábana *f*; (*paper, glass*) hoja *f*; (*ice*) capa *f*; (*metal*) chapa; (*water*) extensión *f*. **sheet lightning** fucilazo *m*. **sheet music** música en hojas sueltas *f*.

sheikh [ʃeɪk] *n* jeque *m*.

shelf [ʃelf] *n* estante *m*.

shell [ʃel] *n* concha *f*; (*crustacean*) caparazón *m*; (*egg, nut*) cáscara *f*; (*pea*) vaina *f*; (*cannon*) proyectil *m*. **shellfish** *pl*

n mariscos *m pl.* *v* (*mil*) bombardear; (*peas, shrimps*) pelar; (*nuts*) descascarar.
shelter ['ʃeltə] *n* abrigo *m*; asilo *m*. *v* abrigar; proteger; dar asilo.
shelve [ʃelv] *v* (*project*) dar carpetazo a. **shelving** *n* estantería *f*.
shepherd ['ʃepəd] *n* pastor *m*.
sheriff ['ʃerif] *n* sheriff *m*.
sherry ['ʃeri] *n* jerez *m*.
shield [ʃiːld] *n* escudo *m*; (*fig*) defensa *f*. *v* escudar; proteger.
shift [ʃift] *n* cambio *m*; movimiento *m*; (*work*) turno *m*. **shift key** tecla de mayúsculas *f*. **shift work** trabajo por turnos *m*. *v* cambiar; mover. **shifty** *adj* furtivo.
shimmer ['ʃimə] *v* relucir. *n* luz trémula *f*.
shin [ʃin] *n* espinilla *f*.
*****shine** [ʃain] *v* brillar. *n* brillo *m*, lustre *m*. **shiny** *adj* lustroso, brillante.
shingle ['ʃiŋgl] *n* (*pebbles*) guijarros *m pl.* **shingles** *n* (*med*) herpes *m, f pl.*
ship [ʃip] *n* barco *m*, navío *m*, buque *m*. **shipshape** *adj* en buen orden. **shipwreck** *n* naufragio *m*. *v* embarcar; transportar; (*send*) enviar. **shipment** *n* cargamento *m*. **shipping** *n* barcos *m pl.* buques *m pl.*
shirk [ʃəːk] *v* esquivar. **shirker** *n* gandul, -a *m, f.*
shirt [ʃəːt] *n* camisa *f*. **in one's shirt sleeves** en mangas de camisa. **shirt-tail** *n* faldón *m*.
shit [ʃit] *nf*, *interj* (*vulgar*) mierda. *v* cagar.
shiver ['ʃivə] *v* temblar; estremecerse. *n* temblor *m*; estremecimiento *m*.
shoal [ʃoul] *n* (*fish*) banco *m*.
shock [ʃɔk] *n* choque *m*; (*elec*) descarga *f*. **shock absorber** amortiguador *m*. **shock-proof** *adj* a prueba de choques. *v* conmocionar; escandalizar. **shocking** *adj* escandaloso; espantoso; (*news*) aterrador.
shoddy ['ʃɔdi] *adj* inferior. **shoddiness** *n* fabricación inferior *f*.
*****shoe** [ʃuː] *v* (*horse*) herrar. *n* zapato *m*. **shoelace** *n* cordón *m*. **shoemaker** *n* zapatero *m*. **shoe repairer's** zapatería de viejo *f*. **shoe shop** zapatería *f*.
shone [ʃɔn] *V* **shine**.
shook [ʃuk] *V* **shake**.
*****shoot** [ʃuːt] *v* (*fire*) lanzar, tirar; (*kill*) matar; (*wound*) herir; (*film*) filmar; (*hunt*) cazar. *n* (*bot*) brote *m*. **shooting** *n* tiro *m pl*; (*hunting*) caza *f*.
shop [ʃɔp] *n* tienda *f*; (*larger*) almacén *m*.

shop assistant *n* dependiente, -a *m, f.*
shopkeeper ['ʃɔpkiːpə] *n* comerciante *m, f.*
shoplifter ['ʃɔpliftə] *n* ratero, -a *m, f.* **shoplifting** *n* ratería *f.*
shopper ['ʃɔpə] *n* comprador, -a *m, f.*
shopping ['ʃɔpiŋ] *n* compras *f pl.* **go shopping** ir de compras. **shopping bag** bolsa de la compra *f.* **shopping centre** centro comercial *m.* **shopping trolley** carrito *m.*
shop steward *n* enlace sindical *m.*
shore [ʃɔː] *n* (*beach*) playa *f*; (*edge of sea*) orilla *f*; (*coast*) costa *f.*
short [ʃɔːt] *adj* corto; pequeño; (*not tall*) bajo; (*brusque*) seco; (*temper*) vivo. **in short** en resumen. **shortage** *n* falta *f*, escasez *f.* **shorten** *v* acortar; disminuir; abreviar. **shortly** *adv* dentro de poco.
shortbread ['ʃɔːtbred] *n* mantecada *f.*
short-circuit *n* cortocircuito. *v* ponerse en cortocircuito.
shortcoming ['ʃɔːtkʌmiŋ] *n* defecto *m.*
short cut *n* atajo *m.*
shorthand ['ʃɔːthand] *n* taquigrafía *f.* **shorthand typist** taquimecanógrafo, -a *m, f.*
short list *n* lista de los posibles *f.*
short-lived *adj* efímero.
shorts [ʃɔːts] *pl n* pantalones cortos *m pl.*
short-sighted *adj* miope.
short story *n* novela corta *f.*
short-tempered *adj* de mal genio.
short-term *adj* de corto plazo.
short wave *n* onda corta *f. adj* de onda corta.
shot[1] [ʃɔt] *V* **shoot**.
shot[2] [ʃɔt] *n* bala *f*; tiro *m*; tirador, -a *m, f*; (*sport*) peso *m*; (*med*) inyección *f*. **shotgun** *n* escopeta *f.*
should[1] [ʃud] *v* deber, tener que.
should[2] [ʃud] *aux translated by conditional tense.*
shoulder ['ʃouldə] *n* hombro *m.* **shoulder-blade** *n* omóplato *m*; (*animal*) paletilla *f.* *v* llevar al hombro.
shout [ʃaut] *n* grito *m*. *v* gritar.
shove [ʃʌv] *n* empujón *m*. *v* empujar.
shovel ['ʃʌvl] *n* pala *f*. *v* traspalar.
*****show** [ʃou] *v* mostrar; descubrir; revelar; exhibir; indicar; demostrar; probar. *n* exposición *f*; espectáculo *m*; (*appearance*) apariencia *f*; (*ostentation*) pompa *f.*
show business *n* mundo del espectáculo *m.*

shower ['ʃauə] *n* (*rain*) chubasco *m*; (*bath*) ducha *f*. *v* llover; ducharse; (*pour*) derramar.

show in *v* hacer pasar.

show jumping *n* concurso hípico *m*.

show off *v* (*coll*) darse pisto.

showpiece ['ʃoupiːs] *n* modelo *m*; obra maestra *f*.

showroom ['ʃourum] *n* sala de muestras *f*.

show up *v* (*coll: arrive*) aparecer; (*embarrass*) poner en evidencia.

showy ['ʃoui] *adj* ostentoso.

shrimp [ʃrimp] *n* camarón *m*.

shrine [ʃrain] *n* capilla *f*; santuario *m*; altar *m*.

*****shrink** [ʃriŋk] *v* (*clothes*) encoger. **shrink from** repugnarse de. **shrinkage** *n* encogimiento *m*.

shrivel ['ʃrivl] *v* secar, marchitar. **shrivel up** apergaminarse.

shroud [ʃraud] *n* sudario *m*, mortaja *f*; (*fig*) velo *m*. *v* amortajar; (*fig*) envolver.

Shrove Tuesday [ʃrouv] *n* martes de carnaval *m*.

shrub [ʃrʌb] *n* arbusto *m*. **shrubbery** *n* arbustos *m pl*, matorrales *m pl*.

shrug [ʃrʌg] *v* encogimiento de hombros *m*. *v* encogerse de hombros.

shudder ['ʃʌdə] *n* repeluzno *m*; (*engine*) vibración *f*. *v* estremecerse.

shuffle ['ʃʌfl] *n* arrastramiento de los pies *m*; (*cards*) barajada *f*. *v* arrastrar; barajar.

shun [ʃʌn] *v* evitar, rehuir.

shunt [ʃʌnt] *v* (*trains*) desviar.

*****shut** [ʃʌt] *v* cerrar. **shut in** encerrar. **shut out** no admitir. **shut up** (*coll*) callarse; hacer callar.

shutter ['ʃʌtə] *n* (*window*) postigo *m*; (*phot*) obturador *m*.

shuttle ['ʃʌtl] *n* lanzadera *f*. **shuttlecock** *n* volante *m*. **shuttle service** servicio regular de ida y vuelta *m*.

shy [ʃai] *adj* tímido. *v* (*horse*) espantarse. **shyness** *n* timidez *f*.

Siamese [ˌsaiə'miːz] *adj* (*cat, twin*) siamés.

sick [sik] *adj* enfermo. **be sick** vomitar. **be sick of** (*coll*) estar harto de. **feel sick** tener náuseas. **sickbed** *n* lecho de enfermo *m*. **sick benefit** subsidio de enfermedad *m*. **sicken** *v* poner enfermo. **sickening** *adj* nauseabundo; (*distressing*) deprimente. **sickly** *adj* (*person*) enfermizo; (*taste*) empalagoso. **sickness** *n* enfermedad *f*; (*sea, air*) mareo *m*.

sickle ['sikl] *n* hoz *f*.

side [said] *n* lado *m*; (*edge*) borde; (*team*) equipo *m*. **side with** ponerse de parte de. *adj* lateral; secundario; indirecto.

sideboard ['saidbord] *n* aparador *m*.

sideburns ['saidbəːnz] *pl n* patillas *f pl*.

sidecar ['saidkaː] *n* sidecar *m*.

side effects *pl n* efectos secundarios *m pl*.

sidelight ['saidlait] *n* (*mot*) luz de posición *f*.

sideline ['saidlain] *n* negocio accesorio *m*; (*sport*) banquillo *m*.

sidelong ['saidloŋ] *adj, adv* de reojo.

side-splitting *adj* divertidísimo.

side-step *v* evitar.

side street *n* calle lateral *f*.

side-track *v* despistar.

sideways ['saidweiz] *adv* oblicuamente. *adj* de lado.

siding ['saidiŋ] *n* (*rail*) vía muerta *f*.

sidle ['saidl] *v* avanzar furtivamente. **sidle up** to acercarse furtivamente.

siege [siːdʒ] *n* sitio *m*, asedio *m*.

sieve [siv] *n* tamiz *m*, scolador *m*. *v* tamizar.

sift [sift] *v* tamizar; (*sprinkle*) espolvorear; (*evidence*) examinar cuidadosamente. **sift out** encontrar; seleccionar. **sifter** cedazo *m*.

sigh [sai] *n* suspiro *m*. *v* suspirar.

sight [sait] *n* vista *f*; espectáculo *m*. **sightseeing** *n* turismo *m*. *v* avistar; (*aim*) apuntar.

sign [sain] *n* señal *f*; indicio *m*; (*notice*) anuncio *m*; muestra *f*. **signpost** *n* letrero *m*. *v* firmar.

signal ['signəl] *n* señal *f*. *v* hacer señales; indicar.

signature ['signətʃə] *n* firma *f*.

signify ['signifai] *v* significar. **significance** *n* significado *m*. **significant** *adj* significativo.

silence ['sailəns] *n* silencio *m*. *v* callar; hacer callar. **silencer** (*mot, gun*) *n* silenciador *m*. **silent** *adj* silencioso; callado.

silhouette [silu'et] *n* silueta *f*. **be silhouetted against** destacarse contra.

silk [silk] *n* seda *f*. **silkworm** *n* gusano de seda *m*. **silky** *adj* (*fabric*) sedoso; (*voice, manner*) suave.

sill [sil] *n* antepecho *m*, alféizar *m*.

silly ['sili] *adj* tonto, bobo. **silliness** *n* tontería *f*, bobería *f*.

skim

silt [silt] n cieno m, limo m. **silt up**
encenagar.

silver ['silvə] n plata f; (coll: change)
suelto m. adj de plata; (like silver)
plateado. **silver plate** baño de plata m.
silversmith n platero m. v platear. **silvery**
adj plateado; (voice) argentino.

similar ['similə] adj semejante, parecido.
similarity n semejanza f.

simile ['simɪli] n símil m.

simmer ['simə] v hervir a fuego lento;
(fig) germentar. **simmer down** calmarse.

simple ['simpl] adj sencillo; natural; fácil;
simple; puro; inocente; (simple-minded)
necio. **simpleton** n simplón, -ona m, f.
simplicity n sencillez f; simpleza f. **simplify** v simplificar. **simply** adv sencilla-
mente; meramente.

simulate ['simjuleit] v similar. **simulation**
n simulación f.

simultaneous [,siml'teinjəs] adj
simultáneo.

sin [sin] n pecado m. v pecar. **sinful** adj
(person) pecador; pecaminoso. **sinner** n
pecador, -a m, f.

since [sins] adv desde entonces. prep
desde. conj desde que; (because) ya que.

sincere [sin'siə] adj sincero. **sincerity** n
sinceridad f.

sinew ['sinjuɪ] n tendón m.

sing [siŋ] v cantar. **singer** n cantor, -a m,
f, cantante m, f. **singing** n canto m.

singe [sindʒ] v chamuscar. n chamus-
quina f.

single ['siŋgl] adj solo; único; (copy)
suelto; (not double) individual; (unmarried) soltero. **single bed** cama individual
f. **single file** fila de a uno f. **single-handed**
adv sin ayuda. **single-minded** adj
resuelto. **single room** habitación individual f. **single (ticket)** billete de ida m. **sin-
gles** n (sport) individual m. **single out**
separar, distinguir.

singular ['siŋgjulə] nm, adj singular.

sinister ['sinistə] adj siniestro.

sink [siŋk] v hundir, sumergir; (mine)
cavar; (voice) bajar; (collapse) dejarse
caer; (go down) descender. **sink in** (idea,
etc.) darse cuenta de. n (kitchen) fregadero; (bathroom, bedroom) lavabo m.

sinuous ['sinjuəs] adj sinuoso.

sinus ['sainəs] n seno m. **sinusitis** n sinusitis f.

sip [sip] n sorbo m. v sorber, beber a
sorbos.

siphon ['saifən] n sifón m. v trasegar con
sifón. **siphon off** sacar con un sifón.

sir [səi] n señor m, caballero m.

siren ['saiərən] n sirena f.

sirloin ['səɪlɔin] n solomillo m.

sister ['sistə] n hermana f; (hospital)
enfermera f; (nun) monja f; (religious
title) sor f. **sister-in-law** n cuñada f.

sit [sit] v sentar; (exam) presentarse a;
(committee) ser miembro. **baby-sit** v
cuidar niños. **sit down** sentarse. **sit up**
incorporarse; (stay up) no acostarse. **sitting** n sentada f; sesión f; (meal) servicio
m. **sittingroom** n sala de estar f.

site [sait] n lugar m, sitio m; (building)
solar m; camping m.

situation [sitju'eifən] n situación f; (job)
empleo m. **situate** v situar.

six [siks], nm, adj seis. **sixth** n, adj sexto,
-a; (date) seis m.

sixteen [siks'tiin] nm, adj dieciséis. **sixteenth** n, adj decimosexto, -a.

sixty ['siksti] nm, adj sesenta. **sixtieth** n,
adj sexagésimo, -a.

size [saiz] n tamaño m; (person, clothes)
talla f; (gloves, shoes) número m. **size up**
evaluar, juzgar. **sizeable** adj grande; considerable.

sizzle ['sizl] v chisporrotear. n chisporroteo m.

skate[1] [skeit] n patín m. v patinar.
skateboard n skateboard m. **skater** n
patinador, -a m, f. **skating** n patinaje m.
skating-rink n pista de patinaje f.

skate[2] [skeit] n (fish) raya f.

skeleton ['skelitn] n esqueleto m. adj
(staff, etc.) muy reducido. **skeleton key**
llave maestra f.

sketch [sketf] n dibujo m; (rough) croquis
m; (theatre) sketch m. v dibujar; hacer
un croquis de. **sketch-book** n bloc de
dibujo m. **sketchy** adj incompleto;
impreciso.

skewer ['skjuə] n brocheta f. v espetar.

ski [skiː] n esquí m. **ski-lift** telesquí m. v
esquiar. **skier** n esquiador, -a m, f. **skiing**
n esquí m.

skid [skid] n patinazo m. v patinar.

skill [skil] n habilidad f; destreza f. **skilful**
adj hábil; diestro. **skilled** diestro;
experto; (worker) cualificado.

skim [skim] v (milk) desnatar; (surface)
rozar. **skim through** hojear.

skimp [skimp] v escatimar; chapucear. **skimpy** adj escaso; pequeño; corto.

skin [skin] n piel f.; (face) cutis m; (milk) nata f. **skin-diving** n natación submarina f. **skin-tight** adj muy ajustado. v (an animal) despellejar. **skinny** adj flaco, descarnado.

skip [skip] n pequeño salto m, brinco m. v saltar, brincar; saltar a la comba; (miss) saltarse.

skipper ['skipə] n capitán m.

skirmish ['skə:miʃ] n escaramuza f. v escaramuzar.

skirt [skə:t] n falda f. v dar la vuelta a. **skirting board** zócalo m.

skittle ['skitl] n bolo m. **skittles** n juego de bolos m.

skull [skʌl] n cráneo m. **skull and cross-bones** calavera f.

skunk [skʌŋk] n mofeta f.

sky [skai] n cielo m. **sky-blue** nm, adj azul celeste. **skylark** n alondra f. **skylight** n claraboya f. **skyline** n horizonte m. **sky-scraper** n rascacielos m invar.

slab [slab] n (lump) trozo m; (cake) porción f.; (block) bloque m; (stone) losa f.; (metal) plancha f.; (chocolate) tableta f.

slack [slak] adj (loose) flojo; (lazy) perezoso; (trade) encalmado. **slacken** v aflojar; disminuir.

slacks [slaks] pl n pantalones m pl.

slag [slag] n escoria f. **slag heap** escorial m.

slam [slam] n golpe m; (door) portazo m; (bridge) slam m. v hacer golpear; cerrar de un golpe. **slam on the brakes** dar un frenazo.

slander ['slɑːndə] n calumnia f.; (law) difamación f. v calumniar; difamar. **slanderous** adj calumnioso; difamatorio.

slang [slaŋ] n germanía f., argot m; jerga f.

slant [slɑːnt] n inclinación f., sesgo m. v inclinar. **slanting** adj inclinado, al sesgo.

slap [slap] n palmada f.; (on face) bofetada f. v pegar con la mano; (put) poner violentamente. **slapdash** adj (person) descuidado; (work) chapucero. **slapstick** n payasada f.

slash [slaʃ] n (knife) cuchillada f.; (whip) latigazo m. v acuchillar; dar latigazos a; (coll: prices) sacrificar.

slat [slat] n tablilla f.

slate [sleit] n pizarra f. v empizarrar.

slaughter ['slɔːtə] n matanza f. **slaughter-house** n matadero m. v matar; exterminar.

slave [sleiv] n esclavo, -a m, f. v trabajar como un negro. **slavery** n esclavitud f.

sledge [sledʒ] n trineo m.

sledgehammer ['sledʒhamə] n almádena f.

sleek [sliːk] adj liso; pulcro.

*****sleep** [sliːp] v dormir; (spend the night) pasar la noche. n sueño m. **go to sleep** dormirse. **sleeper** (rail) traviesa f. **sleeping-bag** n saco de dormir m. **sleeping-pill** n somnífero m. **sleepless night** noche en blanco f. **sleepy** adj soñoliento.

sleet [sliːt] n aguanieve f. v caer aguanieve.

sleeve [sliːv] n manga f.; (record) funda f. **sleeveless** adj sin manga.

sleigh [slei] n trineo m.

slender ['slendə] adj (thin) delgado, fino; (light and graceful) esbelto; (resources) escaso; (excuse) pobre; (hopes) ligero.

slice [slais] n tajada f.; (bread) rebanada f.; (fruit) raja f.; (implement) pala f. v cortar; partir en tajadas/rebanadas/rajas.

slick [slik] adj (derog) astuto; resbaladizo. n (oil) capa de aceite f.

*****slide** [slaid] v deslizar; hacer resbalar. n (children's) tobogán m; (act of sliding) deslizamiento m; (microscope) portaobjeto m; (phot) diapositiva f. **slide-rule** n regla de cálculo f. **sliding** adj (door) corredera; (roof) corredizo; (scale) móvil.

slight [slait] adj pequeño; insignificante; (person) débil; frágil. v despreciar. n desprecio m. **slightest** adj lo más mínimo. **slightly** adv ligeramente.

slim [slim] adj delgado; esbelto. v adelgazar. **slimming** adj (diet, etc.) que no engorda, para adelgazar.

slime [slaim] n limo m; (fig) cieno m. **slimy** adj limoso; (person) rastrero.

*****sling** [sliŋ] v lanzar; suspender. n (med) cabestrillo m; (weapon) honda f.

*****slink** [sliŋk] v **slink away** escurrirse.

slip [slip] n (error) falta f; (oversight) inadvertencia f.; (skid) patinazo m; (stumble) traspiés m; (moral lapse) desliz m; (petticoat) combinación f.; (pillow) funda f; (paper) trozo. **slip of the tongue** or **pen** lapsus m. v resbalar; pasar; poner; descorrer; escurrirse.

slipper ['slɪpə] n zapatilla f.

slippery ['slɪpəri] adj resbaladizo; (person) escurridizo.

*slit [slɪt] v cortar; rasgar. n cortadura f; resquicio m.

slither ['slɪðə] v resbalar; deslizarse.

slobber ['slɒbə] v babosear. n baba f.

sloe [slou] n endrina f.

slog [slɒg] n (coll) pesadez f. v (coll) sudar tinta.

slogan ['slougən] n slogan m.

slop [slɒp] v (splash) salpicar; (pour) derramar.

slope [sloup] n inclinación f; (hill) falda f. v inclinarse. **sloping** adj inclinado; (shoulders) caídos.

sloppy ['slɒpi] adj (food) aguoso; (garment) muy ancho; (careless) capucero; (sentimental) sensiblero. **sloppiness** n (sentiment) sensiblería f.

slot [slɒt] n ranura f, muesca f. v encajar; hacer una ranura.

slouch [slautʃ] v andar cabizbajo.

slovenly ['slʌvnli] adj desaliñado.

slow [slou] adj despacio; lento; (clock) atrasado; (stupid) tardo; (boring) aburrido. in slow motion a cámara lenta. slow down ir más despacio.

slug [slʌg] n (zool) babosa f; (bullet) posta f.

sluggish ['slʌgiʃ] adj perezoso; lento.

sluice [sluːs] n esclusa f. v regar; lavar.

slum [slʌm] n barrio bajo m. the slums tugurios m pl.

slumber ['slʌmbə] n sueño tranquilo m. v dormir tranquilo.

slump [slʌmp] n (fig) baja f; (comm) baja repentina f; depresión económica f. v desplomarse.

slung [slʌŋ] V sling.

slunk [slʌŋk] V slink.

slur [sləː] n baldón m; borrón m; (music) ligado m. v articular mal.

slush [slʌʃ] n nieve sucia y deshecha f.

slut [slʌt] n marrana f.

sly [slai] adj astuto; disimulado.

smack¹ [smak] n golpe m; bofetada f; (sound) chasquido m. v dar una bofetada; dar una palmada; pegar con la mano.

smack² [smak] v smack of saber a; (fig) oler a.

small [smɔːl] adj pequeño; poco; chico; escaso. small change dinero suelto m.

smallpox n viruela f. **small talk** charla f. **n the small of the back** región lumbar f.

smart [smaːt] adj vivo; rápido; (clever) listo; de moda; majo. v picar. smarten up ponerse elegante. **smartness** n viveza f; elegancia f.

smash [smaʃ] n (sound) estrépito m; accidente m; (blow) puñetazo m; ruina f. v quebrar, romper; destruir; aplastar; chocar con. **smashing** adj (slang) estupendo.

smear [smiə] n mancha f; (med) frotis m; (fig) calumnia f. v manchar; (bread) untar; calumniar.

*smell [smel] v oler; tener olor. n olor m; (sense) olfato m. **smelly** adj maloliente.

smile [smail] n sonrisa f. v sonreír.

smirk [sməːk] n sonrisa afectada f. v sonreír afectadamente.

smock [smɒk] n blusa f.

smog [smɒg] n niebla espesa con humo f.

smoke [smouk] n humo m. **smoke-screen** n cortina de humo f. v humear; (tobacco) fumar. **smoker** n fumador, -a m, f. **no smoking** se prohíbe fumar. **smoky** adj que huele a humo.

smooth [smuːð] adj liso; suave; llano; uniforme; (person) suavón. v alisar; suavizar. **smooth over** exculpar. **smoothly** adv lisamente; con suavidad.

smother ['smʌðə] v sofocar; apagar.

smoulder ['smouldə] v arder sin llama.

smudge [smʌdʒ] n mancha f; tiznón m. v manchar; tiznar.

smug [smʌg] adj pagado de sí mismo.

smuggle ['smʌgl] v pasar de contrabando; matutear. **smuggler** n contrabandista m, f. **smuggling** n contrabando m.

snack [snak] n bocado m, tentempié m. **snack bar** cafetería f.

snag [snag] n pega f, obstáculo m. v enganchar; estorbar.

snail [sneil] n caracol m.

snap [snap] n (fingers) castañeteo m; (bones, teeth, mouth) crujido m; (breaking wood) chasquido m; (bite) mordisco m; (phot) instantánea f. adj instantáneo; rápido. **snapdragon** n dragón m. **snapshot** n instantánea f. v (bones) romper; (branch) partir; (joints) hacer crujir; (dog) intentar morder; (person) regañar.

snare [sneə] n trampa f, lazo m. v atrapar.

snarl [snaːl] n gruñido m. v gruñir.

snatch [snatʃ] n fragmento m; (thefi) robo m. v agarrar; tomar.

sneak [sniːk] v hacer furtivamente. **sneak in/out** entrar/salir furtivamente. n (slang) chivato, -a m, f.

sneer [snɪə] v decir con desprecio. n desprecio m. **sneering** adj burlón.

sneeze [sniːz] n estornudo m. v estornudar.

sniff [snif] n aspiración f; inhalación f. v (smell) oler; aspirar.

snigger [ˈsnigə] n risa disimulada f. reírse por lo bajo.

snip [snip] v cortar de un tijeretazo. n (coll: bargain) ganga f.

snipe [snaip] n agachadiza f. v **snipe at** (mil) tirotear. **sniper** n paco m.

snivel [ˈsnivl] v lloriquear. **snivelling** adj llorón; mocoso.

snob [snob] n snob m, esnob m. **snobbish** adj snob, esnob.

snooker [ˈsnuːkə] n snooker m.

snoop [snuːp] v fisgonear; entrometerse.

snooty [ˈsnuːti] adj (coll) presumido.

snooze [snuːz] n siesta f; sueñecito m. v dormitar.

snore [snoː] n ronquido m. v roncar. **snoring** n ronquido m.

snorkel [ˈsnoːkəl] n (swimmer's) tubo de respiración m; (submarine's) esnórquel m.

snort [snoːt] n resoplido m. v resoplar.

snout [snaut] n hocico m.

snow [snou] n nieve f. v nevar. **be snowed under with** estar abrumado de. **snowy** adj nevoso.

snowball [ˈsnoubɔːl] n bola de nieve f. v tirar bolas de nieve; acumularse.

snowbound [ˈsnoubaund] adj bloqueado por la nieve.

snowdrift [ˈsnoudrift] n ventisquero m.

snowdrop [ˈsnoudrop] n campanilla blanca f.

snowfall [ˈsnoufɔːl] n nevada f.

snowflake [ˈsnoufleik] n copo de nieve m.

snowstorm [ˈsnoustɔːm] n tormenta de nieve f.

snub [snʌb] n repulsa f. v repulsar.

snuff [snʌf] n rapé m. **snuff-box** n tabaquera f. v (extinguish) despabilar.

snug [snʌg] adj cómodo; abrigadito.

snuggle [ˈsnʌgl] v arrimarse; apretarse.

so [sou] adv así; tan; también; tanto; por lo tanto. conj así que, de modo que, de

manera que. **and so on** y así sucesivamente. **if so** de ser así. **is that so?** ¿de veras? ... **or so** a poco más o menos ... . **so as to** de manera que. **so-called** adj llamado. **so much** or **many** tanto, tantos. **so-so** adj (coll) así así. **so that** para que. **so what?** ¿y qué?

soak [souk] v empapar. **soak in** penetrar en. **soak up** absorber. **soaking** n remojo m. **soaking wet** calado hasta los huesos.

soap [soup] n jabón m. **soap dish** jabonera f. **soap powder** jabón en polvo m. **soapsuds** pl n jabonaduras f pl. v jabonar. **soapy** adj jabonoso.

soar [soː] v remontarse; (fig) elevarse.

sob [sob] n sollozo m. v sollozar.

sober [ˈsoubə] adj moderado; serio; (not drunk) sobrio. v **sober up** serenarse.

soccer [ˈsokə] n fútbol m.

sociable [ˈsouʃəbl] adj sociable.

social [ˈsouʃəl] adj social; (friendly) amistoso. **social science** sociología f. **social security** seguridad social f. **socialism** n socialismo m. **socialist** n(m+f), adj socialista. **socialize** v socializar.

society [səˈsaiəti] n sociedad f.

sociology [sousiˈolədʒi] n sociología f. **sociological** adj sociológico. **sociologist** n sociólogo, -a m, f.

sock [sok] n calcetín m.

socket [ˈsokit] n hueco m; (elec) enchufe m.

soda [ˈsoudə] n (chem) sosa f; (water) agua de seltz f.

sodden [ˈsodn] adj empapado, saturado.

sofa [ˈsoufə] n sofá m.

soft [soft] adj blando; suave; (low) bajo. **soft-boiled** adj (egg) pasado por agua. **soften** v ablandar; suavizar; bajar; **softness** n blandura f; suavidad f; dulzura f; debilidad f; estupidez f.

soggy [ˈsogi] adj empapado; (bread) pastoso.

soil[1] [soil] n tierra f.

soil[2] [soil] v ensuciar.

solar [ˈsoulə] adj solar.

sold [sould] V **sell**.

solder [ˈsoldə] n soldadura f. v soldar. **soldering-iron** n soldador m.

soldier [ˈsouldʒə] n soldado m.

sole[1] [soul] n adj solo, único.

sole[2] [soul] n (of shoe) suela f; (of foot) planta f. v solar.

sole[3] [soul] n (fish) lenguado m.

solemn ['sɒləm] adj solemne. **solemnity** n solemnidad f.

solicitor [sə'lisitə] n abogado, -a m, f.

solicitude [sə'lisitjuːd] n solicitud f.

solid ['sɒlid] adj sólido; firme; continuo. n sólido m. **solids** pl n alimentos sólidos m pl. **solidarity** n solidaridad f. **solidify** v solidificarse; congelarse.

solitary ['sɒlitəri] adj solitario; solo, único.

solitude ['sɒlitjuːd] n soledad f.

solo ['souləu] nm, adv solo. **soloist** n solista m.

solstice ['sɒlstis] n solsticio m.

soluble ['sɒljubl] adj soluble.

solution [sə'luːʃən] n solución f.

solve [sɒlv] v resolver; acertar.

solvent ['sɒlvənt] adj (finance) solvente. n (chem) disolvente m. **solvency** n solvencia f.

sombre ['sɒmbə] adj sombrío.

some [sʌm] adj algún, alguno, algunos; unos, varios. pron algunos; unos; un poco; parte. adv bastante; unos. **somebody** or **someone** pron alguien. **somehow** adv de algún modo; por alguna razón. **something** pron algo. **sometime** adv alguna vez, algún día. **sometimes** adv a veces, de vez en cuando. **somewhat** adv algo, algún tanto. **somewhere** adv en alguna parte. **somewhere else** en alguna otra parte.

somersault ['sʌməsɔːlt] n salto mortal m. v dar un salto mortal.

son [sʌn] n hijo m. **son-in-law** n yerno m.

sonata [sə'nɑːtə] n sonata f.

song [sɒn] n (art) canto m; (composition) canción f.

sonic ['sɒnik] adj sónico.

sonnet ['sɒnit] n soneta m.

soon [suːn] adv pronto, dentro de poco; (early) temprano. **as soon as** tan pronto como. **sooner or later** tarde o temprano.

soot [sut] n hollín m.

soothe [suːð] v tranquilizar, calmar. **soothing** adj tranquilizador, calmante.

sophisticated [sə'fistikeitid] adj sofisticado; mundano; (machinery) complejo.

sopping ['sɒpin] adj empapadísimo.

soprano [sə'prɑːnou] n soprano m, f.

sordid ['sɔːdid] adj sórdido.

sore [sɔː] adj malo; dolorido; (fig) doloroso. **sore point** tema delicado m. **sorely** adv (bitterly) profundamente; (very) muy. **soreness** n dolor m.

sorrow ['sɒrou] n pesar m; tristeza f. v afligirse. **sorrowful** adj afligido; triste.

sorry ['sɒri] adj afligido; triste; apenado; lastimoso. **feel sorry for** compadecer. interj ¡perdóneme! ¡disculpe!

sort [sɔːt] n clase f; especie f; tipo m; modo m; persona f. v separar de; clasificar. **sort out** apartar; (problems) arreglar. **sorting office** sala de batalla f.

soufflé ['suːflei] n soufflé m.

sought [sɔːt] V seek.

soul [soul] n alma f. **soulful** adj expresivo; conmovedor.

sound¹ [saund] n (noise) sonido m, ruido m. **sound barrier** barrera del sonido f. **sound effects** efectos sonoros m pl. **soundproof** adj insonoro. **sound-track** n pista sonora f. v sonar, resonar; (seem) parecer.

sound² [saund] adj sano; (reasonable) lógico; (argument) válido; (policy) prudente; (investment) seguro; (comm) solvente. **be sound asleep** estar profundamente dormido.

sound³ [saund] v (depth) sondar; (opinion) sondear.

soup [suːp] n sopa f. **clear soup** consomé m. **thick soup** puré m. **soup plate** plato sopero m. **soup spoon** cuchara sopera f.

sour [sauə] adj ácido, agrio. v agriar. **sourness** n acidez f, agrura f.

source [sɔːs] n fuente f; origen m.

south [sauθ] n sur m. adj also **southerly**, **southern** del sur. adv hacia el sur. **southbound** adj con rumbo al sur. **south-east** nm, adj sudeste. **south-west** nm, adj sudoeste.

South America n Sudamérica f, América del Sur f. **South American** sudamericano, -a m, f.

souvenir [suːvə'niə] n recuerdo m.

sovereign ['sɒvrin] n, adj soberano, -a.

***sow¹** [sou] v sembrar; esparcir.

sow² [sau] n cerda f, puerca f.

soya ['sɔiə] n soja f. **soya bean** soja f. **soy sauce** salsa picante de soja f.

spa [spɑː] n balneario m; manantial mineral m.

space [speis] n espacio m; (place) sitio m; (time) temporada f. **spaceman** n astronauta m, cosmonauta m. **spaceship** n nave espacial f. v espaciar. **spacious** adj espacioso; amplio.

spade [speid] n pala f.
spades [speidz] pl n (cards) picos m pl; (Spanish cards) espadas f pl.
spaghetti [spə'geti] n espaguetis m pl.
Spain [spein] n España f. **Spaniard** n español, -a m, f. **Spanish** nm, adj español.
span [span] n (time) espacio m, duración f; (wings) envergadura f; (space) distancia f; (bridge) tramo m. v atravesar; medir.
spaniel ['spanjəl] n perro de aguas m; (cocker) sabueso m.
spank [spaŋk] v dar una azotaina. **spanking** n azotaina f.
spanner ['spanə] n llave f.
spare [speə] adj de reserva; de sobra; disponible. **spare part** (mot) recambio m. **spare-ribs** pl n (cookery) costillas de cerdo f pl. **spare room** cuarto de los invitados m. **spare time** ratos libres m pl. **spare tyre** neumático de repuesto m. v (do without) pasarse sin; (avoid) evitar; (expense) escatimar. **sparing** adj (words) parco; limitado; escaso; frugal.
spark [spaɪk] n chispa f. v chispear. **spark off** provocar. **sparking-plug** n bujía f.
sparkle ['spaɪkl] n centelleo m; (fig) brillo m. v centellear; (fig) brillar. **sparkling** adj (drink) espumoso.
sparrow ['spærou] n gorrión m.
sparse [spaɪs] adj escaso, poco denso. **sparsely** adv escasamente.
spasm ['spazəm] n espasmo m; (fit) ataque m. **spasmodic** adj espasmódico.
spastic ['spastik] n, adj espástico, -a.
spat [spat] V spit.
spatial ['speiʃl] adj espacial.
spatula ['spatjulə] n espátula f.
spawn [spoɪn] n (fish) freza f, hueva f; (frog) huevos m pl. v frezar; depositar.
*****speak** [spiɪk] v decir; hablar. **speak up** hablar más fuerte. **speak up for** hablar en favor de. **speaker** n orador, -a m, f; (loudspeaker) altavoz m.
spear [spiə] n lanza f. v traspasar. **spearhead** n vanguardia f.
special ['speʃəl] adj especial; particular; extraordinario. **specialist** n especialista m, f. **speciality** n especialidad f. **specialize** v especializar.
species ['spiɪʃiɪz] n especie f.
specify ['spesifai] v especificar. **specific** adj específico. **specification** n especificación f; estipulación f; requisito m.

specimen ['spesimin] n (biol) espécimen m; modelo m; (sample) muestra f; (example) ejemplar m.
speck [spek] n manchita f; pizca f. **speckle** v motear.
spectacle ['spektəkl] n espectáculo m. **spectacles** pl n gafas f pl. **spectacular** adj espectacular.
spectator [spek'teitə] n espectador, -a m, f.
spectrum ['spektrəm] n espectro m.
speculate ['spekjuleit] v especular; conjeturar. **speculation** n especulación f; conjetura f. **speculative** adj especulativo; conjetural.
speech [spiɪtʃ] n (address) discurso m; (faculty) habla f; (lecture) conferencia f; conversación f; pronunciación f. **speechless** adj mudo.
*****speed** [spiɪd] v (mot) ir a toda velocidad. **speed along** apresurarse. **speed up** acelerar. **speeding** n exces de velocidad m. **speedy** adj veloz. n prisa f; velocidad f; rapidez f. **speedboat** n lancha motora f. **speed limit** velocidad máxima f. **speedometer** n velocímetro m.
*****spell**[1] [spel] v escribir; deletrear; significar. **spelling** n ortografía f.
spell[2] [spel] n (magic) hechizo m, encanto m. **spellbound** adj encantado.
spell[3] [spel] n período m; turno m.
*****spend** [spend] v (money) gastar; (time) pasar. **spending** n gasto m. **spending money** dinero para gastos menudos m.
sperm [spəɪm] n esperma f.
spew [spjuɪ] v vomitar.
sphere [sfiə] n esfera f; (province) competencia f. **spherical** adj esférico.
spice [spais] n especia f. v especiar. **spicy** adj especiado, picante; (fig) sabroso.
spider ['spaidə] n araña f. **spider's web** telaraña f.
spike [spaik] n escarpia f.
*****spill** [spil] v derramar. n (coll: fall) caída f.
*****spin** [spin] v girar, dar vueltas; dar efecto a; (cotton, silk, etc.) hilar; (web) tejer; (fig: a yarn) contar. **spin-dryer** n secador centrífugo m. **spin out** prolongar. **spinning** n hilado m. **spinning wheel** rueca f. n giro m.
spinach ['spinidʒ] n espinaca f.
spindle ['spindl] n (axle, shaft) eje m; (of a lathe) mandril m; (of a spinning wheel) huso m. **spindly** adj larguirucho.

spine [spain] *n* (*anat*) espina dorsal *f*; (*zool*) púa *f*; (*book*) lomo *m*. **spinal** *adj* espinal. **spiny** *adj* espinoso.

spinster ['spinstə] *n* soltera *f*.

spiral ['spaiərəl] *adj* espiral. *n* espiral *f*. *v* dar vueltas en espiral.

spire ['spaiə] *n* aguja *f*.

spirit ['spirit] *n* espíritu *m*, alma *f*; (*ghost*) fantasma *m*; (*courage*) valor *m*; (*liveliness*) ánimo; (*mood*) humor *m*; alcohol *m*. **spirited** *adj* animado, vigoroso. **spirited** *adj* espiritual. **spiritualism** *n* espiritualismo *m*. **spiritualist** *n*(*m*+*f*), *adj* espiritualista.

*spit¹ [spit] *v* escupir. *n* saliva *f*, escupitajo *m*.

spit² [spit] *n* (*cookery*) espetón *m*, asador *m*; (*geog*) lengua de tierra *f*.

spite [spait] *n* rencor *m*, malevolencia *f*. **in spite of** a pesar de. *v* mortificar. **spiteful** *adj* rencoroso.

splash [splaʃ] *n* salpicadura *f*; (*sound*) chapoteo; (*mark*) mancha *f*. *v* salpicar.

spleen [spliːn] *n* (*anat*) bazo *m*; (*fig*) mal humor *m*.

splendid ['splendid] *adj* espléndido; excelente. **splendour** *n* resplandor *m*.

splice [splais] *v* empalmar; (*coll*: *marry*) unir, casar.

splint [splint] *n* férula *f*.

splinter ['splintə] *n* (*wood*) astilla *f*; (*bomb*) casco *m*; (*bone*) esquirla *f*; (*piece*) fragmento *m*. *v* astillar.

*split [split] *v* hender, partir; rajar; dividir; separar; (*atom*) desintegrar. *n* partido *m*, hendido *m*; división *f*; (*in cloth*) rasgón *m*; (*quarrel*) ruptura *f*. **split second** fracción de segundo *f*.

splutter ['splʌtə] *v* (*person*) farfullar; (*flame*) chisporrotear. *n* farfulla *f*; chisporroteo *m*.

*spoil [spoil] *v* estropear, echar a perder; (*child*) mimar; (*damage*) dañar. **spoilsport** *n* aguafiestas *m*, *f invar*. **spoils** *pl n* botín *m sing*.

spoke¹ [spouk] *V* **speak**.

spoke² [spouk] *n* reyo *m*.

spokesman ['spouksmən] *n* portavoz *m*.

sponge [spʌndʒ] *n* esponja *f*; (*cake*) bizcocho esponjoso *m*. **sponge bag** esponjera *f*. *v* limpiar con esponja; (*coll*: *cadge*) sacar de gorra. **spongy** *adj* esponjoso.

sponsor ['sponsə] *n* (*for financial support*) patrocinador, -a *m*, *f*; (*warrantor*) fiador,

-a *m*, *f*; (*for club membership*) padrino, -a *m*, *f*; *v* patrocinar; fiar; apadrinar. **sponsorship** *n* patrocinio *m*.

spontaneous [spon'teinjəs] *adj* espontáneo. **spontaneity** *n* espontaneidad *f*.

spool [spuːl] *n* bobina *f*.

spoon [spuːn] *n* cuchara *f*. **spoonful** *n* cucharada *f*.

sporadic [spə'radik] *adj* esporádico.

sport [spoːt] *n* deporte *m*; (*plaything*) juguete *m*; (*amusement*) bula *f*. **sports car** coche deportivo *m*. **sports jacket** chaqueta de sport *f*. **sportsman/woman** *n* deportista *m*, *f*. *v* llevar; ostentar. **sporting** *adj* deportivo; caballeroso. **sportive** *adj* juguetón; bromista.

spot [spot] *n* (*med*) grano *m*; espinilla *f*; (*mark*) mancha *f*; (*pattern*) lunar *m*; (*place*) sitio *m*; (*liquid*) gota *f*; parte *f*; punto *m*; (*coll*) poco *m*. **on the spot** en el momento; en el acto. **spot check** inspección repentina *f*. **spotlight** *n* foco *m*. *v* manchar; reconocer; notar. **spotless** *adj* inmaculado. **spotted** *adj* (*speckled*) moteado; con manchas; de lunares. **spotty** *adj* espinilloso.

spouse [spaus] *n* esposo, -a *m*, *f*.

spout [spaut] *n* (*teapot*) pitorro *m*; (*jug*) pico *m*; (*rainwater pipe*) caño *m*; (*jet*) chorro *m*; (*waterspout*) tromba *f*. *v* echar; (*coll*) soltar.

sprain [sprein] *n* torcedura *f*. *v* torcer.

sprawl [sproːl] *n* postura desgarbada *f*. *v* extender.

spray¹ [sprei] *n* (*water*) rociada *f*; (*sea*) espuma *f*; (*sprayer*) pulverizador *m*. *v* (*sprinkle*) rociar; pulverizar; (*crops*) fumigar; vaporizarse.

spray² [sprei] *n* (*flowers*) ramo *m*, ramillete *m*.

*spread [spred] *v* extender; (*on the ground*) exponer; (*marmalade, butter, etc*.) untar; propagar; difundir; (*wings*) desplegar. **spread out** esparcir. *n* propagación *f*, difusión *f*; (*town*) extensión *f*; (*span*) enyergadura *f*; (*range*) gama *f*.

spree [spriː] *n* juerga *f*.

sprig [sprig] *n* ramito *m*.

sprightly ['spraitli] *adj* despierto, vivo.

*spring [spriŋ] *v* saltar. **spring up** brotar; surgir. *n* (*season*) primavera *f*; (*leap*) salto *m*, brinco *m*; (*water*) fuente *f*; (*coil*) muelle *m*. **springboard** *n* trampolín *m*. **spring-cleaning** *n* limpieza general *f*.

spring onion cebolleta f. **springy** adj elástico.

sprinkle ['sprɪŋkl] v (water) rociar; (sugar, salt, etc.) salpicar. **sprinkler** n regadera f; (fire) extintor m.

sprint [sprɪnt] n sprint m, esprint m. v sprintar, esprintar.

sprout [spraut] n brote m, retoño m. **Brussels sprouts** coles de Bruselas f pl.

spruce [spruːs] n (bot) pícea f. adj elegante. **spruce up** acicalar.

spun [spʌn] V **spin**.

spur [spəː] n espuela f; (fig) estímulo m. **on the spur of the moment** sin pensarlo. v espolear. **spur on** estimular.

spurious ['spjuəriəs] adj espurio, falso.

spurn [spəːn] v desdeñar, rechazar.

spurt [spəːt] n (water) chorro m; (energy) gran esfuerzo m. v chorrear; hacer un gran esfuerzo; acelerar.

spy [spaɪ] n espía m, f. v espiar; observar. **spying** n espionaje m.

squabble ['skwɔbl] n riña f. v disputar.

squad [skwɔd] n escuadra f; (mil) pelotón m.

squadron ['skwɔdrən] n (mil) escuadrón m; (naut) escuadra f; (aero) escuadrilla f.

squalid ['skwɔlid] adj mugriento; escuálido; miserable. **squalor** n mugre f; miseria f.

squall [skwɔːl] n ráfaga f.

squander ['skwɔndə] v malgastar.

square [skweə] n (shape) cuadrado m; (pattern) cuadro m; (chessboard) casilla f; (in a town) plaza f. adj cuadrado; rectangular; (coll: old-fashioned) anticuado. v cuadrar; (settle) arreglar.

squash [skwɔʃ] n (sport) juego de pelota m; (drink) limonada f, naranjada f; (crushing) aplastamiento m. v (crush) aplastar; (squeeze) apretar.

squat [skwɔt] n posición en cuchillas f. adj rechoncho. v agacharse. **squatter** n persona que ocupe ilegalmente un sitio f.

squawk [skwɔːk] n graznido m. v graznar.

squeak [skwiːk] n (mice, etc.) chillido m; (hinge) chirrido m. v chillar; chirriar.

squeal [skwiːl] n chillido m. v chillar.

squeamish ['skwiːmɪʃ] adj remilgado; delicado.

squeeze [skwiːz] n presión f; (hug) abrazo m; (hand) apretón m; (crowd) gentío m. v abrazar; apretar; (extract) exprimir.

squid [skwɪd] n calamar m.

squint [skwɪnt] n (med) estrabismo m;

(coll: glance) ojeada f. v entrecerrar los ojos.

squirm [skwəːm] v retorcerse.

squirrel ['skwirəl] n ardilla f.

squirt [skwəːt] n chorro m. v lanzar; chorrear.

stab [stab] n puñalada. v apuñalar.

stabilize ['steɪbilaɪz] v estabilizar. **stabilizer** n estabilizador m.

stable[1] ['steɪbl] n cuadra f.

stable[2] ['steɪbl] adj estable; fijo. **stability** n estabilidad f; firmeza f.

staccato [stə'kɑːtou] adv staccato. adj (voice, style, etc.) entrecortado.

stack [stak] n (hay, etc.) almiar m; (pile) montón m; (chimney) cañón m. **stacks of** (coll) un montón de m sing. v hacinar; amontonar.

stadium ['steɪdiəm] n estadio m.

staff [stɑːf] n vara f; palo m; (flag) asta f; personal m. **staff-room** n (school) sala de profesores f. v proveer de personal.

stag [stag] n venado m, ciervo m. **stag party** reunión de hombres f.

stage [steɪdʒ] n (theatre) escenario m; (platform) estrado m; (point) etapa f; (phase) fase f. **stage manager** regidor de escena m. v representar; efectuar; organizar.

stagger ['stagə] n tambaleo m. v tambalearse; (amaze) asombrar; (payments, etc.) escalonar. **staggering** adj asombroso.

stagnant ['stagnənt] adj estancado. **stagnate** v estancarse. **stagnation** n estancamiento m.

staid [steɪd] adj serio; formal.

stain [steɪn] n mancha f; tinte m. **stain remover** quitamanchas m invar. v manchar; (wood) teñir. **stained-glass window** vidriera f.

stair [steə] n escalón m. **staircase** n also **stairs** pl n escalera f sing.

stake[1] [steɪk] n (post) poste m; estaca f; (for plants) rodrigón m; (for execution) hoguera f. v estacar.

stake[2] [steɪk] n (bet) apuesta f; (investment) intereses m pl. **at stake** en juego. v apostar.

stale [steɪl] adj (bread) duro; (egg) poco fresco; (food) rancio; (air) viciado. **staleness** n ranciedad f.

stalemate ['steɪlmeɪt] n (chess) ahogado m; (fig) punto muerto m.

stalk¹ [stoːk] *n* (*stem*) tallo *m*.

stalk² [stoːk] *v* acechar. **stalk in/out** entrar/salir con paso airado.

stall¹ [stoːl] *n* (*market*) puesto *m*; (*theatre*) butaca *f*; (*exhibition*) caseta *f*. *v* (*engine*) parar.

stall² [stoːl] *v* (*delay*) andar con rodeos. **stall off** dar largas a.

stallion [staljən] *n* semental *m*.

stamina [ˈstaminə] *n* vigor *m*; aguante *m*.

stammer [ˈstamə] *n* tartamudez *f*. *v* tartamudear.

stamp [stamp] *n* sello *m*, timbre *m*; marca *f*; impresión *f*; (*with foot*) zapatazo *m*. **stamp-collecting** *n* filatelia *f*. *v* estampar; sellar; imprimir; (*one's foot*) patear.

stampede [stamˈpiːd] *n* desbocamiento *m*; desbandada *f*. *v* provocar la desbandada de.

*stand [stand] *v* (*on feet*) estar de pie; (*place*) poner; resistir; soportar; (*trial*) someterse a; (*remain*) permanecer; (*pay for*) sufragar. *n* posición *f*; plataforma *f*; (*coats, hats*) percha *f*; (*fig*) postura *f*. **stand for** significar; representar. **stand out** sobresalir. **standstill** *n* parada *f*. **come to a standstill** pararse. **stand up for** defender.

standard [ˈstandəd] *n* (*weight, length, money*) patrón *m*; (*of living*) nivel *m*; modelo *m*; criterio *m*. *adj* normal; oficial; legal; (*comm*) standard. **standard lamp** lámpara de pie *f*. **standardize** *v* estandardizar; normalizar.

standing [ˈstandiŋ] *adj* de pie; vertical; clásico; fijo. **standing order** (*bank*) pedido regular *m*. *n* posición *f*; situación *f*; reputación *f*; duración *f*.

stank [staŋk] *V* **stink**.

stanza [ˈstanzə] *n* estancia *f*, estrofa *f*.

staple¹ [ˈsteipl] *n* (*papers*) grapa *f*; (*of wool, cotton*) fibra *f*. *v* sujetar con una grapa.

staple² [ˈsteipl] *adj* básico; principal.

star [staː] *n* (*astron, cinema*) estrella *f*; asterisco *m*. **stars** *pl n* (*astrol*) astros *m pl*. **starfish** *n* estrella de mar *f*. *v* estrellar; ser protagonista. **stardom** *n* estrellato *m*. **starry** *adj* estrellado.

starboard [ˈstaːbəd] *n* estribor *m*.

starch [staːtʃ] *n* almidón *m*. *v* almidonar. **starchy** *adj* almidonado.

stare [steə] *n* mirada fija *f*. *v* mirar fijamente.

stark [staːk] *adj* (*bleak*) desolado; (*stiff*)

rígido; completo; puro; absoluto. **stark naked** completamente desnudo.

starling [ˈstaːliŋ] *n* estornino *m*.

start [staːt] *n* comienzo *m*; (*of a race*) salida *f*; (*jump*) sobresalto *m*; (*fright*) susto *m*. *v* comenzar, empezar; (*clock*) poner en marcha; (*car*) arrancar; (*establish*) fundar; (*rumour*) lanzar; provocar; sobresaltar. **starter** *n* (*mot*) arranque *m*; (*meal*) entremés *m*.

startle [ˈstaːtl] *v* asustar. **startling** *adj* sorprendente; alarmante.

state [steit] *n* estado *m*; condición *f*; (*luxury*) lujo *m*; gran pompa *f*. **statesman** *n* estadista *m*. *v* afirmar, declarar; dar; decir; consignar; exponer. **stately** *adj* majestuoso. **statement** *n* declaración *f*; informe *m*; comunicado *m*; (*bank*) balance mensual *m*.

static [ˈstatik] *adj* estático. *n* (*radio*) parásitos *m pl*.

station [ˈsteiʃən] *n* (*rail, radio*) estación *f*; (*position*) puesto *m*; (*place*) lugar *m*; (*social*) posición *f*. *v* apostar; estacionar.

stationary [ˈsteiʃənəri] *adj* estacionario; inmóvil.

stationer [ˈsteiʃənə] *n* papelero *m*. **stationer's** *n* papelería *f*. **stationery** *n* objetos de escritorio *m pl*; papel de escribir y sobres *m*.

statistics [stəˈtistiks] *n* (*science*) estadística *f*. *pl n* (*data*) estadísticas *f pl*. **statistical** *adj* estadístico.

statue [ˈstatjuː] *n* estatua *f*.

stature [ˈstatʃə] *n* estatura *f*; (*fig*) talla *f*.

status [ˈsteitəs] *n* (*standing*) categoría *f*; (*state*) estado *m*; (*social standing*) posición *f*.

statute [ˈstatjuːt] *n* estatuo *m*. **statutory** *adj* establecido por la ley.

staunch¹ [stoːntʃ] *adj* fiel; inquebrantable.

staunch² [stoːntʃ] *v* restañar.

stay [stei] *n* estancia *f*; (*support*) apoyo *m*. *v* (*remain*) quedarse; (*postpone*) aplazar; (*endure*) resistir; (*support*) apoyar.

steadfast [ˈstedfaːst] *adj* constante; fijo.

steady [ˈstedi] *adj* constante, firme; regular; continuo. *v* estabilizar; calmar; sostener. **steadily** *adv* firmemente; regularmente; sin parar. **steadiness** *n* firmeza *f*; estabilidad *f*; uniformidad *f*; regularidad *f*.

steak [steik] *n* (*beefsteak*) bistec *m*; (*of other meat or fish*) filete *m*.

*steal [stiil] v robar. stealing n robo m.

stealthy ['stelθi] adj furtivo.

steam [stiim] n vapor m. let off steam (coll) desahogarse. v echar vapor; (cookery) cocinar al vapor.

steel [stiil] n acero m. steel wool estropajo m. steelworks pl n acería f sing. steely adj acerado; inflexible.

steep¹ [stiip] adj escarpado.

steep² [stiip] v empapar.

steeple ['stiipl] n aguja f. steeplechase n carrera de obstáculos f. steeplejack n reparador de chimeneas m.

steer [stiə] v (ship) gobernar; (vehicle) dirigir; (bicycle) llevar; (course) seguir; (car) manejar. steering n (naut) gobierno m; (mot) conducción f. steering-wheel n volante m.

stem¹ [stem] n tallo m; (glass) pie m. stem from derivarse de.

stem² [stem] v (stop) detener, contener.

stench [stent∫] n tufo m.

stencil ['stensl] n estarcido m. v (typing) cliché de multicopista m.

step [step] n paso m; (stairs, ladder) peldaño m; (doorway) umbral m; (degree) escalón m; (measure) medida f. stepladder n escalera de tijera f. v dar un paso; ir. step up subir; aumentar.

stepbrother ['stepbrʌðə] n hermanastro m.

stepdaughter ['stepdɔːtə] n hijastra f.

stepfather ['stepfɑːðə] n padrastro m.

stepmother ['stepmʌðə] n madrastra f.

stepsister ['stepsistə] n hermanastra f.

stepson ['stepsʌn] n hijastro m.

stereo ['steriou] nf, adj estéreo. stereophonic adj estereofónico.

stereotype ['steriətaip] n estereotipo m. v estereotipar.

sterile ['sterail] adj estéril. sterility n esterilidad f. sterilization esterilización f. sterilize v esterilizar.

sterling ['stəːliŋ] n libra esterlina f. adj (silver) plata de ley f; (character) excelente.

stern¹ [stəːn] adj severo.

stern² [stəːn] n (naut) popa f.

stethoscope ['steθəskoup] n estetoscopio m.

stew [stjuː] n estofado m. v (meat) estofar; (fruit) cocer.

steward ['stjuəd] n camarero m; despensero m. shop steward enlace sindical m.

stewardess n (ship) camarera f; (air) azafata f.

stick¹ [stik] n madero m; estaca f; palo m; (club) garrote m; (walking) bastón m.

*stick² [stik] v fijar; (thrust) clavar; (penetrate) pinchar; (glue) pegar; (stay) quedarse. stick out sacar; sobresalir. stick up for (coll) defender. sticky adj pegajoso; (coll) difícil.

stickler ['stiklə] n be a stickler for dar mucha importancia a.

stiff [stif] adj rígido; (manner) distante; (person) severo. stiffen v atiesarse; endurecerse. stiffness n rigidez f; frialdad f; obstinación f.

stifle ['staifl] v ahogar, sofocar; (smile, etc.) suprimir. stifling adj sofocante.

stigma ['stigmə] n estigma m.

stile [stail] n portilla con escalones f.

still¹ [stil] adv todavía, aún; (always) siempre; (nevertheless) sin embargo; (sit, stand) quieto. adj tranquilo; inmóvil; silencioso. stillborn adj nacido muerto. still life bodegón m. n calma f; (phot) vista fija f.

still² [stil] n alambique m; destilería f.

stilt [stilt] n zanco m. stilted adj campanudo.

stimulus ['stimjuləs] n, pl -li estímulo m; incentivo m. stimulant nm, adj estimulante. stimulate v estimular. stimulation n estímulo m.

*sting [stiŋ] v picar; herir; (coll: overcharge) clavar. n (insect) aguijón m; (wound) picadura f; (pain) escozor m.

*stink [stiŋk] v heder, oler mal. n hedor m.

stint [stint] n sesión de trabajo f. v escatimar; limitar.

stipulate ['stipjuleit] v estipular. stipulation n estipulación f.

stir [stəː] n agitación f; sensación f; conmoción f. v (tea, etc.) revolver; mezclar; (move) mover; excitar. stir up provocar; fomentar.

stirrup ['stirəp] n estribo m.

stitch [stit∫] n (sewing) puntada f; (knitting) punto m; (med) punto de sutura m; (pain) dolor de costado m. v coser; (med) suturar.

stoat [stout] n armiño m.

stock [stok] n (supply) reserva f; (farm) ganado m; (cookery) caldo m; (lineage) linaje m; (race) raza f; (tree) tronco m. stockbroker n corredor de Bolsa m. stock

exchange Bolsa f. **stockpile** n reservas f pl. **stocktaking** n inventario m. v surtir, abastecer.

Stockholm ['stokhoum] n Estocolmo.

stocking ['stokiŋ] n media f.

stocky ['stoki] adj rechoncho.

stodge [stodʒ] n (coll) comida indigesta f. **stodgy** adj indigesto.

stoical ['stouikl] adj estoico.

stoke [stouk] v alimentar.

stole[1] [stoul] V steal.

stole[2] [stoul] n estola f.

stomach ['stʌmək] n estómago m. **stomach-ache** n dolor de estómago m. v soportar.

stone [stoun] n piedra f; (fruit) hueso m; (med) cálculo m. **stone-cold** adj helado. v (throw) apedrear. **stony** adj pedregoso.

stood [stud] V stand.

stool [stuːl] n taburete m.

stoop [stuːp] n espaldas encorvadas f pl. v encorvarse; agacharse. **stoop** to rebajarse a.

stop [stop] n parada f; cesación f; suspensión f; (stay) estancia f; (gramm) punto m. v parar; impedir; interrumpir; evitar; dejar de; (a hole) tapar; (a gap) rellenar; cesar. **stop-watch** n cronómetro m. **stoppage** n (blockage) obstrucción f; (strike) huelga f. **stopper** n tapón m.

store [stoː] n (supply) provisión f; (warehouse) depósito m; (large shop) almacén m; (smaller shop) tienda f. v (keep) guardar; almacenar; (supply) suministrar. **storage** n almacenaje m.

storey ['stoːri] n piso m.

stork [stoːk] n cigüeña f.

storm [stoːm] n tempestad f; (thunderstorm) tormenta f. v (mil) asaltar; (wind) ser tempestuoso; (fig) fabiar. **stormy** adj tempestuoso; violento.

story ['stoːri] n historia f; cuento m.

stout [staut] adj fuerte; intrépido; gordo; grueso. n cerveza negra f.

stove [stouv] n (cooker) cocina f; (heater) estufa f.

stow [stou] v colocar, meter. **stow away** guardar; esconder. **stowaway** n polizón m.

straddle ['stradl] v estar a caballo sobre; montar a horcajadas.

straggle ['stragl] v (leg) rezagarse; (spread) desparramarse. **straggler** n rezagado, -a m, f.

straight [streit] adj derecho; recto; en orden; (hair) lacio. adv derecho; directamente. **straight ahead** todo recto. **straight away** en seguida. **straightforward** adj sincero; (simple) sencillo. **straighten** v enderezar; arreglar.

strain[1] [strein] n tensión f; esfuerzo m; (med) torcedura f. v (stretch) estirar; forzar; (sprain) torcer; (filter) filtrar; (cookery) colar. **strainer** n colador m.

strain[2] [strein] n raza f; tendencia f.

strait [streit] n estrecho m.

strand[1] [strand] n (hair) trenza f; (rope) cabo m; (thread) hebra f.

strand[2] [strand] n (shore) playa f; (river) ribera f. v (ship) encallar. **be stranded** hallarse abandonado.

strange [streindʒ] adj extraño; raro; inesperado; (unknown) desconocido. **stranger** n desconocido, -a m, f.

strangle ['straŋgl] v estrangular. **stranglehold** n collar de fuerza m. **strangler** n estrangulador, -a m, f.

strap [strap] n correa f; (on garment) tirante m. v atar con correa; (med) vendar. **strapping** adj robusto.

strategy ['stratədʒi] n estrategia f. **strategic** adj estratégico.

stratum ['straːtəm] n, pl -ta estrato m, capa f.

straw [stroː] n paja f. **it's the last straw!** ¡es el colmo!

strawberry ['stroːbəri] n (plant and fruit) fresa f.

stray [strei] n animal extraviado m. adj perdido; extraviado; aislado. v errar; desviarse; perderse.

streak [striːk] n raya f; vena f; (light) rayo m. v rayar; ir como un rayo. **streaky** adj rayado.

stream [striːm] n río m; arroyo m; corriente f. **streamlined** adj aerodinámico; (mot) carenado; (efficient) eficaz. v correr, fluir. **streamer** n serpentina f.

street [striːt] n calle f.

strength [streŋθ] n fuerza f. **strengthen** v fortalecer; reforzar; confirmar.

strenuous ['strenjuəs] adj arduo; enérgico.

stress [stres] n tensión f; presión f; (gramm) acento tónico m. v (emphasize) subrayar; insistir en; acentuar.

stretch [stretʃ] n (scope) alcance m; (of arms, distance) extensión f; (time) período m; (of road) trecho m. **home**

stretch última etapa *f. v* estirar; tender; extender. **stretcher** *n* camilla *f.*

stricken ['strikən] *adj* afligido.

strict [strikt] *adj* severo; exacto. **strictly** *adv* severamente; exactamente. **strictly speaking** en realidad. **strictness** *n* severidad *f;* exactitud *f.*

*°***stride** [straid] *v* dar zancadas; andar a pasos largos. *n* zancada *f;* tranco *m.*

strident ['straidənt] *adj* estridente; llamativo.

strife [straif] *n* disputa *f,* lucha *f.*

*°***strike** [straik] *n* (*industry*) huelga *f;* (*hit*) golpe *m;* (*oil. etc.*) descubrimiento *m. v* (*hit*) golpear; pegar; declararse en huelga; (*clock*) sonar; (*a bargain*) cerrar; descubrir; (*a match*) encender. **striker** *n* huelguista *m, f.* **striking** *adj* impresionante; en huelga.

*°***string** [striŋ] *v* (*beads*) ensartar; (*hang*) enristrar. *n* cuerda *f;* (*of cars*) fila *f.* **string bean** judía verde *f.* **string quartet** cuarteto de cuerdas *m.* **stringy** *adj* fibroso.

stringent ['strindʒənt] *adj* estricto, riguroso.

strip[1] [strip] *v* quitar; (*undress*) desnudar; (*bed*) deshacer.

strip[2] [strip] *n* (*of land*) zona *f;* (*of wood*) listón *m;* (*tatter, scrap*) tira *f.*

stripe [straip] *n* raya *f;* azote *m.* **striped** *adj* con rayas.

*°***strive** [straiv] *v* esforzarse (a).

strode [stroud] *V* **stride.**

stroke[1] [strouk] *n* golpe *m,* choque *m;* (*swimming*) braza *f;* (*clock*) campanada *f;* (*mark*) trazo *m;* (*med*) ataque *m;* (*lightning*) rayo *m.*

stroke[2] [strouk] *v* acariciar. *n* caricia *f.*

stroll [stroul] *n* vuelta *f,* paseo *m. v* dar un paseo, pasearse.

strong [stroŋ] *adj* fuerte; robusto. **strong muy bien. stronghold** *n* fortaleza *f;* (*fig*) baluarte *m.* **strong-minded** *adj* resuelto. **strong-room** *n* cámara acorazada *f.*

struck [strʌk] *V* **strike.**

structure ['strʌktʃə] *n* estructura *f;* construcción *f.* **structural** *adj* estructural; de construcción.

struggle ['strʌgl] *n* lucha *f. v* luchar; (*to escape*) forcejear. **struggle in/out** entrar/salir penosamente.

strum [strʌm] *v* (*guitar*) rasguear; (*other instruments*) rascar. *n* (*guitar*) rasgueo *m.*

strung [strʌŋ] *V* **string.**

strut[1] [strʌt] *v* pavonearse.

strut[2] [strʌt] *n* (*arch*) puntal *m;* (*aero*) montante *m.*

stub [stʌb] *n* (*tree*) tocón *m;* (*cigarette*) colilla *f;* (*cheque*) talón *m;* (*ticket*) resguardo *m;* (*pencil, candle*) cabo *m. v* (*toe*) tropezar con. **stub out** apagar.

stubble ['stʌbl] *n* rastrojo *m;* (*chin*) barba *f.*

stubborn ['stʌbən] *adj* terco; inflexible. **stubbornness** *n* terquedad *f;* tenacidad *f.*

stuck [stʌk] *V* **stick.**

stud[1] [stʌd] *n* (*collar*) botón de camisa *m;* (*boot*) taco *m;* (*nail, rivet*) tachón *m. v* tachonar. **studded with** sembrado de, lleno de.

stud[2] [stʌd] *n* (*place*) cuadra *f;* (*animal*) semental *m.* **stud horse** caballo padre *m.*

student ['stjudənt] *n* estudiante *m, f;* (*pupil*) alumno, -a *m, f.*

studio ['stjudiou] *n* estudio *m.*

study ['stʌdi] *n* estudio *m;* (*room*) gabinete *m. v* estudiar; examinar. **studious** *adj* estudioso; solícito.

stuff [stʌf] *n* material *m,* materia *f;* cosas *f pl;* (*cloth*) tejido *m. v* llenar; (*cram*) atestar; (*cookery*) rellenar. **stuffing** *n* (*furniture*) rehenchimiento *m;* (*cookery*) relleno *m;* (*padding*) paja *f.* **stuffy** *adj* mal ventilado; (*person*) pomposo.

stumble [stʌmbl] *v* tropezar.

stump [stʌmp] *n* (*tree*) tocón *m;* (*limb*) muñón *m;* (*pencil, etc.*) cabo *m;* (*cricket*) poste *m. v* (*fig*) dejar perplejo.

stun [stʌn] *v* aturdir; (*amaze*) pasmar. **stunning** *adj* aturdidor; (*coll*) fenomenal.

stung [stʌŋ] *V* **sting.**

stunk [stʌŋk] *V* **stink.**

stunt[1] [stʌnt] *v* impedir el crecimiento de. **stunted** *adj* atrofiado.

stunt[2] [stʌnt] *n* hazaña *f;* truco publicitario *m.* **stunt man** doble especial *m.*

stupid ['stjupid] *adj* estúpido. **stupidity** *n* estupidez *f.*

stupor ['stjupə] *n* estupor *m.*

sturdy ['stədi] *adj* robusto, vigoroso. **sturdiness** *n* robustez *f;* vigor *m.*

sturgeon ['stədʒən] *n* esturión *m.*

stutter ['stʌtə] *n* tartamudeo *m. v* tartamudear.

sty [stai] *n* (*pig*) pocilga *f;* (*med*) orzuelo *m.*

style [stail] *n* estilo *m;* (*kind*) tipo *m;* manera *f;* (*fashion*) moda *f;* (*clothes*) hechura f; (hair) peinado m. v (design) diseñar. **stylish** adj elegante.

stylus ['stailəs] n (tool) estilete m; (record player) aguja f.

suave [swɑːv] adj afable, urbano.

subconscious [sʌb'kɔnʃəs] nm, adj subconsciente.

subcontract [sʌbkən'trækt] v subcontratar. **subcontractor** n subcontratista m.

subdivide [sʌbdɪ'vaɪd] v subdividir(se). **subdivision** n subdivisión f.

subdue [səb'djuː] v (riot, etc.) sojuzgar; (sound, light) atenuar; (voice) bajar; (pain) aliviar; (feelings) contener. **subdued** adj sojuzgado; atenuado; bajo; aliviado; contenido.

subject ['sʌbdʒɪkt, v səb'dʒɛkt] n sujeto m; (school) asignatura f; (theme) tema m; motivo m; (people) súbdito, -a m, f. **subject to** sujeto a; propenso a. v sojuzgar; (to an examination) someter. **subjection** n sujeción f. **subjective** adj subjetivo.

subjunctive [səb'dʒʌŋktɪv] nm, adj subjuntivo.

sublet [sʌb'lɛt] v subarrendar.

sublime [sə'blaɪm] adj sublime. n lo sublime.

submarine ['sʌbmərɪn] n submarino m.

submerge [səb'mɜːdʒ] v sumergir. n sumersión f.

submit [səb'mɪt] v someter. **submission** n sumisión f. **submissive** adj sumiso.

subnormal [sʌb'nɔːml] adj subnormal.

subordinate [sə'bɔːdɪnət] adj (gramm) subordinado; subalterno. n subordinado, -a m, f; subalterno, -a m, f. v subordinar. **subordination** n subordinación f.

subscribe [səb'skraɪb] v **subscribe to** aprobar; (newspaper) subscribirse a. **subscriber** n suscriptor, -a m, f; abonado, -a m, f. **subscription** n suscripción f; abono m; (membership fee) cuota f.

subsequent ['sʌbsɪkwənt] adj subsiguiente; posterior.

subservient [səb'sɜːvɪənt] adj subordinado; servil.

subside [səb'saɪd] v (land) hundirse; (flood) bajar; (excitement) calmarse; (wind) amainar. **subsidence** n hundimiento m.

subsidiary [səb'sɪdɪərɪ] adj subsidiario; secundario; (comm) afiliado. n (comm) filial f.

subsidize ['sʌbsɪdaɪz] v subvencionar. **subsidy** n subvención f.

subsist [səb'sɪst] v subsistir. **subsistence** n subsistencia f.

substance ['sʌbstəns] n sustancia f. **substantial** adj sustancial; sustancioso; importante.

substandard [sʌb'stændəd] adj inferior.

substitute ['sʌbstɪtjuːt] n (person) sustituto, -a m, f; substituto, -a m, f; (thing) sucedáneo m. v sustituir, reemplazar. **substitution** n sustitución f.

subtitle ['sʌbtaɪtl] n subtítulo m. v subtitular.

subtle ['sʌtl] adj sutil; delicado. **subtlety** n sutileza f; delicadeza f.

subtract [səb'trækt] v restar, sustraer. **subtraction** n resta f, sustracción f.

suburb ['sʌbɜːb] n suburbio m. **the suburbs** las afueras f pl. **suburban** adj suburbano.

subvert [səb'vɜːt] v derribar; corromper. **subversion** n subversión f. **subversive** adj subversivo.

subway ['sʌbweɪ] n pasaje subterráneo m; (US) metro m.

succeed [sək'siːd] v triunfar; (follow) suceder; (inherit) heredar. **succeeding** adj sucesivo; venidero. **success** n éxito m; triunfo m. **successful** adj que tiene éxito; próspero. **successfully** adv con éxito. **succession** n sucesión f; herencia f. **successive** adj sucesivo. **successor** n sucesor, -a m, f.

succinct [sək'sɪŋkt] adj sucinto.

succulent ['sʌkjulənt] adj suculento; (plant) carnoso. n planta carnosa f.

succumb [sə'kʌm] v sucumbir.

such [sʌtʃ] adj tal; semejante, parecido; tan, tanto. **such as** como. adv tan, tanto. pron los que, las que; lo que; todo lo que; esto, éste, ésta. **as such** en sí.

suck [sʌk] v chupar; (baby) mamar. **suck up to** (slang) dar coba a.

sucker ['sʌkə] n (bot) chupón m; (device) émbolo m; (slang: simpleton) primo m.

suction ['sʌkʃən] n succión f.

sudden ['sʌdən] adj súbito; inesperado; repentino. **all of a sudden** de repente.

suds [sʌdz] pl n jabonaduras f pl.

sue [suː] v proceder contra.

suede [sweɪd] n ante m.

suet ['suːɪt] n sebo m.

suffer ['sʌfə] v sufrir, padecer; tolerar; dejar; (undergo) aguantar. **suffering** n sufrimiento m, padecimiento m; dolor m.

sufficient [sə'fiʃənt] *adj* suficiente; bastante. **suffice** *v* ser suficiente, bastar. **sufficiently** *adv* suficientemente, bastante.

suffix ['sʌfiks] *n* sufijo *m*.

suffocate ['sʌfəkeit] *v* ahogar, sofocar. **suffocation** *n* ahogo *m*; asfixia *f*.

sugar ['ʃugə] *n* azúcar *m*. **sugar bowl** azucarero *m*. **sugar cane** caña de azúcar *f*. **sugar lump** terrón de azúcar *m*.

suggest [sə'dʒest] *v* sugerir; indicar. **suggestion** *n* sugerencia *f*; indicación *f*. **suggestive** *adj* sugestivo; evocador.

suicide ['suisaid] *n* (*act*) suicidio *m*; (*person*) suicida *m*, *f*. **commit suicide** suicidarse. **suicidal** *adj* suicida.

suit [suit] *n* traje *m*; (*woman's*) conjunto *m*; (*law*) pleito *m*; (*cards*) palo *m*. **suitcase** *n* maleta *f*. *v* convenir; venir bien a. **suitable** *adj* conveniente; apropiado.

suite [swit] *n* (*in hotel*) suite *f*; (*furniture*) juego *m*.

sulk [sʌlk] *v* enfurruñarse. *n* enfurruñamiento *m*. **sulky** *adj* enfurruñado.

sullen ['sʌlən] *adj* taciturno; malhumorado. **sullenness** *n* taciturnidad *f*; mal humor *m*.

sulphur ['sʌlfə] *n* azufre *m*. **sulphuric** *adj* sulfúrico.

sultan ['sʌltən] *n* sultán *m*.

sultana [sʌl'tɑnə] *n* pasa de Esmirna *f*.

sultry ['sʌltri] *adj* (*weather*) sofocante; (*person*) sensual.

sum [sʌm] *n* suma *f*; cantidad *f*; cálculo *m*. *v* **sum up** recapitular; resumir; (*person*) evaluar.

summarize ['sʌməraiz] *v* resumir, recapitular. **summary** *n* resumen *m*; *adj* sumario.

summer ['sʌmə] *n* verano *m*. **summer holidays** vacaciones de verano *f pl*. **summerhouse** *n* cenador *m*.

summit ['sʌmit] *n* cumbre *f*, cima *f*; (*fig*) apogeo *m*.

summon ['sʌmən] *v* llamar, convocar; mandar; hacer venir. **summon up** evocar. **summons** ['sʌmənz] *pl n* llamamiento *m*; (*law*) citación *f*. *v* citar.

sumptuous ['sʌmptʃuəs] *adj* suntuoso.

sun [sʌn] *n* sol *m*. **sunny** *adj* bañado de sol.

sunbathe ['sʌnbeið] *v* tomar el sol. **sunbathing** *n* baños de sol *m pl*.

sunbeam ['sʌnbiːm] *n* rayo de sol *m*.

sunburn ['sʌnbəːn] *n* (*tan*) bronceado *m*; (*pain*) quemadura del sol *f*. **sunburnt** *adj* bronceado; quemado por el sol.

Sunday ['sʌndi] *n* domingo *m*.

sundial ['sʌndaiəl] *n* reloj de sol *m*.

sundry ['sʌndri] *adj* varios. **all and sundry** todo el mundo. **sundries** *pl n* artículos diversos *m pl*.

sunflower ['sʌnˌflauə] *n* girasol *m*.

sun-glasses ['sʌnˌɡlɑːsiz] *pl n* gafas de sol *f pl*.

sunk [sʌŋk] *V* **sink**.

sunlight ['sʌnlait] *n* luz del sol *f*.

sunrise ['sʌnraiz] *n* salida del sol *f*.

sunset ['sʌnset] *n* puesta del sol *f*.

sunshine ['sʌnʃain] *n* sol *m*.

sunstroke ['sʌnstrouk] *n* insolación *f*.

sun-tan ['sʌntan] *n* bronceado *m*. **sun-tan lotion** loción bronceadora *f*.

super ['suːpə] *adj* (*coll*) estupendo; formidable.

superannuation [ˌsuːpərænju'eiʃən] *n* jubilación *f*.

superb [su'pəːb] *adj* soberbio; magnífico.

supercilious [ˌsuːpə'siliəs] *adj* altanero; desdeñoso.

superficial [ˌsuːpə'fiʃəl] *adj* superficial.

superfluous [su'pəːfluəs] *adj* superfluo.

superhuman [suːpə'hjuːmən] *adj* sobrehumano.

superimpose [ˌsuːpərim'pouz] *v* sobreponer. **superimposed** *adj* (*photo, etc.*) superpuesto.

superintendent [ˌsuːpərin'tendənt] *n* superintendente *m*, *f*; director, -a *m*, *f*; (*police*) subjefe de la policía *m*.

superior [su'piəriə] *n*, *adj* superior, -a. **superiority** *n* superioridad *f*.

superlative [su'pəːlətiv] *adj* superlativo; supremo. (*gramm*) *nm*, *adj* superlativo.

supermarket ['suːpəˌmɑːkit] *n* supermercado *m*.

supernatural [ˌsuːpə'natʃərəl] *adj* sobrenatural. *n* lo sobrenatural.

supersede [ˌsuːpə'siːd] *v* sustituir, reemplazar.

supersonic [ˌsuːpə'sonik] *adj* supersónico.

superstition [ˌsuːpə'stiʃən] *n* superstición *f*. **superstitious** *adj* supersticioso.

supervise ['suːpəvaiz] *v* supervisar; vigilar. **supervision** *n* superintendencia *f*. **supervisor** *n* supervisor, -a *m*, *f*; director, -a *m*, *f*.

supper ['sʌpə] *n* cena *f*.

supple ['sʌpl] *adj* flexible, elástico. **suppleness** *n* flexibilidad *f*.

supplement ['sʌpləmənt] *n* suplemento *m*. *v* suplir, complementar. **supplementary** *adj* suplementario.

supply [sə'plai] *n* (*stock*) surtido *m*; provisión *f*; (*act of supplying*) suministro *m*. **supplies** *pl n* material *m sing*; provisiones *f pl*; (*stores*) víveres *m pl*. *v* alimentar; proveer; abastecer; presentar.

support [sə'poːt] *n* apoyo *m*; sostén *m*; soporte *m*. *v* apoyar; sostener; defender; (*financially*) mantener. **supporter** *n* partidario, -a *m*, *f*; (*sport*) aficionado, -a.

suppose [sə'pouz] *v* suponer. **supposed** *adj* supuesto. **be supposed to** deber. **supposedly** *adv* según se supone. **supposing** *conj* si, suponiendo (que). **supposition** *n* suposición *f*.

suppress [sə'pres] *v* suprimir; (*yawn, laugh, etc.*) contener; (*passion*) dominar; (*fact*) disimular; (*revolt*) sofocar; (*publication*) prohibir; (*news*) ocultar. **suppression** *n* supresión *f*; dominio *m*; represión *f*; prohibición *f*; ocultación *f*.

supreme [su'priːm] *adj* supremo. **supremacy** *n* supremacía *f*.

surcharge ['səːtʃaːdʒ] *n* sobrecarga *f*.

sure [ʃuə] *adj* seguro, cierto. **sure enough** efectivamente. **sure-footed** *adj* de pie firme. **surely** *adv* seguramente; sin duda.

surety ['ʃuərəti] *n* garantía *f*, fianza *f*.

surf [səːf] *n* resaca *f*; (*foam*) espuma *f*. **surf-board** *n* tabla hawaiana *f*. **surfing** *n* surf *m*.

surface ['səːfis] *n* superficie *f*. **on the surface** en apariencia. *v* (*road*) revestir; (*swimmer*) salir a la superficie; (*submarine*) sacar a la superficie.

surfeit ['səːfit] *n* exceso *m*.

surge [səːdʒ] *n* oleada *f*; (*anger*) ola *f*. *v* (*sea*) levantarse; (*crowd*) bullir.

surgeon ['səːdʒən] *n* cirujano *m*. **surgery** *n* (*skill*) cirugía *f*; (*place*) consultorio *m*. **surgical** *adj* quirúrgico.

surly ['səːli] *adj* malhumorado.

surmount [sə'maunt] *v* vencer, superar.

surname ['səːneim] *n* apellido *m*.

surpass [sə'paːs] *v* superar, sobrepasar.

surplus ['səːpləs] *n* excedente *m*. *adj* sobrante.

surprise [sə'praiz] *n* sorpresa *f*. *adj* de sorpresa. *v* sorprender.

surrealism [sə'riəlizəm] *n* surrealismo *m*. **surrealist** *n*(*m*+*f*). *adj* surrealista. **surrealistic** *adj* surrealista.

surrender [sə'rendə] *v* rendir; (*give up*) ceder; entregar. *n* rendición *f*; capitulación *f*.

surreptitious [,sʌrəp'tiʃəs] *adj* subrepticio.

surround [sə'raund] *v* cercar, rodear. *n* borde *m*. **surrounding** *adj* circundante. **surroundings** *pl n* (*environment*) medio ambiente *m*; (*environs*) alrededores *m pl*.

survey ['səːvei; *v* sə'vei] *n* inspección *f*; (*report*) informe *m*; (*of a question*) examen *m*; panorama *m*; (*land*) medición *f*. *v* inspeccionar; estudiar; examinar; contemplar; medir. **surveying** *n* inspección *f*; agrimensura *f*. **surveyor** *n* (*land*) agrimensor *m*; (*house*) inspector *m*.

survive [sə'vaiv] *v* sobrevivir a. **survival** *n* supervivencia *f*. **survivor** *n* sobreviviente *m*, *f*.

susceptible [sə'septəbl] *adj* susceptible; sensible.

suspect ['sʌspekt; *v* sə'spekt] *n*, *adj* sospechoso, -a. *v* sospechar.

suspend [sə'spend] *v* suspender. **suspender** *n* liga *f*. **suspense** *n* incertidumbre *f*; (*book, film*) suspense *m*. **in suspense** pendiente. **suspension** *n* suspensión *f*. **suspension bridge** puente colgante *m*.

suspicion [sə'spiʃən] *n* sospecha *f*. **suspicious** *adj* (*suspecting*) suspicaz; (*suspected*) sospechoso.

sustain [sə'stein] *v* sostener; mantener; apoyar; (*suffer*) recibir.

swab [swob] *n* (*mop*) estropajo *m*; (*med: pad*) tapón *m*. *v* fregar con estropajo; limpiar con tapón.

swagger ['swagə] *n* pavoneo *m*. *v* pavonearse; darse importancia.

swallow[1] ['swolou] *v* tragar. **swallow up** tragarse. *n* trago *m*; (*amount*) bocado *m*.

swallow[2] ['swolou] *n* (*bird*) golondrina *f*.

swam [swam] *V* swim.

swamp [swomp] *n* pantano *m*; marisma *f*. *v* sumergir; inundar. **swampy** *adj* pantanoso.

swan [swon] *n* cisne *m*.

swank [swaŋk] *n* (*coll*) fanfarronada *f*; (*person*) fanfarrón, -ona *m*, *f*. *v* fanfarronear. **swanky** *adj* fanfarrón.

swap *or* **swop** [swop] *n* cambio *m*, treque *m*. *v* cambiar, trocar.

swarm [swoːm] *n* (*bees*) enjambre *m*; (*fig*) multitud *f*. *v* enjambrar; (*fig*) pulular.

swarthy ['swoːði] *adj* moreno.

swat [swot] *v* aplastar.

sway [swei] n balanceo m; oscilación f; dominio m. v balancearse; oscilar; (influence) influir.

*****swear** [sweə] v jurar. **swear in** tomar juramento a. **swear-word** n palabrota f.

sweat [swet] n sudor m. v sudar.

sweater n suéter m.

swede [swiid] n naba f.

Sweden [swiidn] n Suecia f. **Swede** n sueco, -a m, f. **Swedish** nm, adj sueco.

*****sweep** [swiip] v deshollinar; barrer; explorar. **sweep in/out** entrar/salir rápidamente. **sweep through** difundirse. n (chimney) deshollinador m; (a cleaning) barrido m; (curve) curva f. **make a clean sweep** llevárselo todo. **sweeping** adj aplastante; demasiado general. **sweeping statement** declaración demasiado general f.

sweet [swiit] adj (taste) dulce; (air, breath, etc.) fresco; (smell) bueno; (friendly) encantador; (kind) bondadoso. n (toffee) caramelo m; (dessert) postre m. **sweetbread** n mollejas f pl. **sweet corn** maíz tierno m. **sweetheart** n novio, -a m, f. **sweet potato** patata boniato f. **sweetshop** n confitería f. **sweeten** v azucarar, endulzar. **sweetly** adv dulcemente; (sound) melodiosamente. **sweetness** n dulzor m; (character) dulzura f.

*****swell** [swel] v hinchar; inflarse. n inflado m; hinchazón m; curvatura f. **swelling** n inflamiento m.

swelter ['sweltə] v sofocarse de calor. **sweltering** adj sofocante.

swerve [swəːv] v desviar; (vehicle) dar un viraje. n viraje m.

swift [swift] adj rápido; pronto. n (bird) vencejo m. **swiftness** rapidez f; prontitud f.

swill [swil] v lavar con much agua; (drink) beber a tragos. n (for pigs) bazofia f.

*****swim** [swim] v nadar. n baño m. **swimmer** n nadador, -a m, f. **swimming** n natación f. **swimming baths** or **pool** piscina f. **swimming costume** traje de baño m.

swindle ['swindl] n estafa f. v estafar. **swindler** n estafador, -a m, f.

swine [swain] n cerdo m, puerco m; (impol) canalla m, f.

*****swing** [swin] v hacer girar; balancear; oscilar; virar. n (amusement) columpio m; oscilación f; impulso m; (pol) viraje m. **in full swing** a toda velocidad.

swipe [swaip] (coll) n golpetazo m. v golpear con fuerza; (steal) afanar.

swirl [swəːl] n remolino m. v arremolinarse.

swish [swiʃ] n silbo m; (of water) susurro m; (of garment) crujido m. v (cane) blandir; (tail) menear.

Swiss [swis] n, adj suizo, -a. **Swiss roll** brazo de gitano m.

switch [switʃ] n (elec) interruptor m, conmutador m; (change) paso m; (stick) varilla f. **switchboard** n centralita de teléfonos f. v (opinion, policy) cambiar de; (places) cambiar; (a train) desviar. **switch off** desconectar. **switch on** encender.

Switzerland ['switsələnd] n Suiza f.

swivel ['swivl] n pivote m. v girar sobre un eje; dar una vuelta.

swollen ['swoulən] V **swell**.

swoop [swuip] n calada f; redada f. **at one fell swoop** de un solo golpe. v calarse, abatirse.

swop V **swap**.

sword [soid] n espada f. **swordfish** n pez espada m.

sworn [swoin] V **swear**.

swot [swot] (coll) n empollón, -ona m, f. v empollar **swotting** n estudio m.

swum [swʌm] V **swim**.

swung [swʌn] V **swing**.

sycamore ['sikəmoi] n sicomoro m.

syllable ['siləbl] n sílaba f. **syllabic** adj silábico.

syllabus ['siləbəs] n programa m.

symbol [simbl] n símbolo m, emblema m. **symbolic** adj simbólico. **symbolism** n simbolismo m. **symbolize** v simbolizar.

symmetry ['simitri] n simetría f. **symmetrical** adj simétrico.

sympathy ['simpəθi] n pésame m; compasión f. **sympathetic** adj compasivo; comprensivo; favorable. **sympathize with** compadecerse de.

symphony ['simfəni] n sinfonía f. **symphonic** adj sinfónico.

symposium [sim'pouziəm] n simposio m.

symptom ['simptəm] n síntoma m. **symptomatic** adj sintomático.

synagogue ['sinəgog] n sinagoga f.

synchromesh ['sinkroumeʃ] n sincronizador.

synchronize ['sinkrənaiz] v sincronizar. **synchronization** n sincronización f.

syncopate ['siŋkəpeit] n sincopar. **syncopation** n síncopa f.

syndicate ['sindikit] n sindicato m.

syndrome ['sindroum] n síndrome m.

synonym ['sinənim] n sinónimo m. **synonymous** adj sinónimo.

synopsis [si'nopsis] n, pl **-ses** sinopsis f invar.

syntax ['sintaks] n sintaxis f.

synthesis ['sinθisis] n, pl **-ses** síntesis f invar. **synthesize** v sintetizar.

syphilis ['sifilis] n sífilis f.

syringe [si'rindʒ] n jeringa f. v jeringar.

syrup ['sirəp] n (med) jarabe m; (fruit) almíbar m. **syrupy** adj almibarado.

system ['sistəm] n sistema m; método m. **systematic** adj sistemático.

T

tab [tab] n etiqueta f. **keep tabs on** (coll) tener controlado.

tabby ['tabi] n gato atigrador m.

table ['teibl] n mesa f. **table-cloth** n mantel m. **table-mat** n salvamanteleo m invar. **table-napkin** n servilleta f. **tablespoon** n cucharón m. **tablespoonful** cucharada f. **table tennis** tenis de mesa m. **clear the table** levantar la mesa. **set the table** poner la mesa.

table d'hôte [taiblə'dout] n menú m.

tablet ['tablit] n (med, soap) pastilla f; (stone, chocolate) tableta f; (writing-paper) bloc m.

taboo [tə'buː] nm, adj tabú.

tabulate ['tabjuleit] v tabular.

tacit ['tasit] adj tácito.

taciturn ['tasitəm] adj taciturno.

tack [tak] n (nail) tachuela f; (sewing) hilván m; (naut: change of direction) virada f; (distance sailed) bordada f. v clavar con tachuelas; hilvanar; virar de bordo.

tackle ['takl] n (ropes) jarcias f pl; (rigging) aparejo m; (equipment) trastos m pl; (sport) placaje m. v placar; (seize) agarrar; (fig) abordar, emprender.

tact [takt] n tacto m. **tactful** adj con tacto, discreto. **tactless** adj falto de tacto, indiscreto.

tactics ['taktiks] pl n táctica f sing. **tactical** adj táctico.

tadpole ['tadpoul] n renacuajo m.

taffeta ['tafitə] n tafetán m.

tag [tag] n etiqueta f; (shoelace) herrete m; (game) pillapilla m. **tag along** (coll) seguir.

tail [teil] n cola f; rabo m; (coat, shirt) faldón m. **tail-end** n zaga f, rabera f. **tails** pl n (coin) cruz f sing. v (coll) seguir.

tailor ['teilə] n sastre m. v entallar; (fig) adaptar.

taint [teint] v (stain) manchar; (food) corromper; (air) viciar; (fig) mancillar. n mancha f; corrupción f; contaminación f.

*****take** [teik] v tomar; llevarse; (carry) cargarse; (phot) sacar; (shoe size) calzar; (occupy) ocupar; (responsibility) asumir; (bear) aguantar; (suppose) suponer. **take after** parecerse a. **take along** llevarse. **take away** quitar; (subtract) restar. **take back** (return) devolver; (retract) retirar. **take down** (pictures, curtains) descolgar; (from a shelf) bajar; (write) apuntar. **take someone down a peg** (coll) bajarle los humos a alguien. **take in** acoger; (situation) entender; (clothes) achicar; (coll: deceive) engañar. **take off** (clothes) quitarse; (aero) despegar. **take-off** n despegue m; (coll) imitamonos m invar. **take on** (employ) contratar; (challenge) competir con. **take-over** (comm) adquisición f.

talcum powder ['talkəm] n talco m.

tale [teil] n cuento m. **fairy tales** cuentos de hadas m pl. **tell tales** (coll) contar chismes.

talent ['talənt] n talento m. **talented** adj talentoso, talentudo.

talk [toːk] n conversación f; charla f; (lecture) conferencia f; (speech) discurso m. v decir; hablar. **talk back** replicar. **talk down to** ponerse al alcance de. **talk into** convencer para que. **talk over** discutir. **talkative** adj hablador. **talking** n conversación f. **talking point** tema de conversación m.

tall [toːl] adj alto; grande. **tallboy** n cómoda alta f. **tallness** n altura f; lo alto.

tally ['tali] n tarja f; cuenta f. v tarjar; cuadrar.

talon ['talən] n garra f.

tambourine [tambə'riːn] n pandereta f, pandero m.

tame [teim] *adj* manso; domesticado; (*not exciting*) aburrido. *v* domesticar; amansar.

tamper ['tampə] *v* **tamper with** (*text*) amañar; (*spoil*) estropear.

tampon ['tampɒn] *n* tapón *m*.

tan [tan] *n* bronceado *m*, color tostado *m*. *adj* bronceado, tostado. (*hide*) curtir; (*sun*) broncear. tostar.

tandem ['tandəm] *n* tándem *m*.

tangent ['tandʒənt] *nf*, *adj* tangente. **go off at a tangent** salirse por la tangente.

tangerine [tandʒə'riːn] *n* (*fruit*) mandarina *f*.

tangible ['tandʒəbl] *adj* tangible.

tangle ['tangl] *v* enmarañar; enredar. *n* maraña *f*; enredo *m*.

tank [taŋk] *n* tanque *m*, cisterna *f*. depósito *m*; (*mil*) tanque *m*. **tanker** *n* (*lorry*) camión cisterna *m*; (*ship*) petrolero *m*.

tankard ['taŋkəd] *n* jarro *m*.

tantalize ['tantəlaiz] *v* atormentar. **tantalizing** *adj* que atormenta.

tantamount ['tantəmaunt] *adj* **be tantamount to** ser equivalente a.

tantrum ['tantrəm] *n* berrinche *m*, rabieta *f*. **fly into a tantrum** coger una rabieta.

tap[1] [tap] *n* golpecito *m*. **tap-dance** *n* zapateado *m*. *v* golpear ligeramente.

tap[2] [tap] *n* (*water*) grifo *m*; (*barrel*) espita *f*. *v* poner una espita a; (*phone*) interceptar; (*fig*: *draw on*) utilizar.

tape [teip] *n* cinta *f*; (*recording*) cinta magnetofónica *f*. **tape-measure** *n* cinta métrica *f*. **tape-recorder** *n* magnetófono *m*. **tapeworm** *n* tenia *f*. *v* (*record*) grabar; (*fasten*) atar con cinta.

taper ['teipə] *n* (*candle*) vela *f*; (*narrowing*) estrachamiento *m*. *v* estrechar. **tapering** *adj* cónico.

tapestry ['tapəstri] *n* tapiz *m*.

tapioca [tapi'oukə] *n* tapioca *f*.

tar [taɪ] *n* alquitrán *m*. *v* alquitranar.

tarantula [tə'rantjulə] *n* tarántula *f*.

target ['taɪgit] *n* blanco *m*; (*fig*) objeto *m*.

tariff ['tarif] *n* tarifa *f*.

tarmac ['taɪmak] *n* superficie alquitranada *f*.

tarnish ['taɪniʃ] *v* deslustrar. *n* deslustre *f*.

tarpaulin [taɪ'pɔːlin] *n* lona alquitranada *f*.

tarragon ['tarəgən] *n* estragón *m*.

tart[1] [taɪt] *adj* agrio; ácido.

tart[2] [taɪt] *n* tarta *f*; (*slang*) fulana *f*.

tartar ['taɪtə] *n* (*chem*) tártaro *m*; (*on teeth*) sarro *m*.

task [taɪsk] *n* tarea *f*. **taskmaster** *n* capataz *m*.

tassel ['tasəl] *n* borla *f*.

taste [teist] *n* (*sense*) gusto *m*; sabor *m*. *v* probar; saber. **taste of** saber a. **tasteful** *adj* de buen gusto. **tasteless** *adj* insípido; (*in bad taste*) de mal gusto. **tasty** *adj* sabroso.

tattered ['tatəd] *adj* andrajoso.

tattoo[1] [tə'tuː] *n* (*on skin*) tatuaje *m*. *v* tatuar.

tattoo[2] [tə'tuː] *n* (*mil*) desfile militar *m*; (*drumming*) repiqueteo *m*.

tatty ['tati] *adj* (*coll*) en mal estado.

taunt [tɔːnt] *v* mofarse de. *n* mofa *f*. **taunting** *adj* burlón; provocante.

Taurus ['tɔːrəs] *n* Tauro *m*.

taut [tɔːt] *adj* tenso, tirante. **tautness** *n* tensión *f*, tirantez *f*.

tavern ['tavən] *n* (*bar*) taberna *f*; (*inn*) venta *f*.

tawny ['tɔːni] *adj* leonado.

tax [taks] *n* impuesto *m*, contribución *f*. **tax-free** *adj* exento de impuestos. **tax evasion** evasión fiscal *f*. **tax haven** refugio fiscal *m*. **taxpayer** *n* contribuyente *m*, *f*. **tax return** declaración de renta *f*. *v* gravar con un impuesto; imponer contribuciones; (*try*) poner a prueba. **taxable** *adj* imponible. **taxation** *n* impuestos *m pl*; (*system*) sistema tributario *m*.

taxi ['taksi] *n* taxi *m*. **taxi-driver** *n* taxista *m*, *f*. **taximeter** *n* taxímetro *m*. **taxi rank** parada de taxis *f*. *v* (*aero*) rodar por la pista.

tea [tiː] *n* té *m*; (*snack*) merienda *f*. **teacup** *n* tasa de té *f*. **teapot** *n* tetera *f*. **teaspoon** *n* cucharilla *f*. **teaspoonful** *n* cucharadita *f*. **tea towel** trapo de cocina *m*.

***teach** [tiːtʃ] *v* enseñar. **teacher** *n* (*primary*) maestro, -a *m*, *f*; (*secondary*) profesor, -a *m*, *f*. **teaching** *n* enseñanza *f*.

teak [tiːk] *n* teca *f*.

team [tiːm] *n* (*yoked animals*) yunta *f*; (*horses*) tronco *m*; (*people*) equipo *m*. **team-mate** *n* compañero de equipo *m*. **team spirit** espíritu de equipo *m*. **teamwork** *n* trabajo de equipo *m*. *v* **team up** agruparse.

201

tense

tear¹ [teə] v desgarrar; (*snatch*) arrancar. **tear along/out** ir a toda velocidad. **tear down** demoler. **tear off** (*coupon*) cortar. n rasgón m.

tear² [tiə] n lágrima f. **tear gas** gas lacrimógeno m. **tear-jerker** (*coll*) n obra sentimental f. **tearful** adj lloroso.

tease [tiiz] v provocar. n broma f; (*person*) bromista m, f. **teasing** n bromas f pl.

teat [tiit] n pezón m; (*animals*) teta f.

technique [tek'niik] n técnica f. **technical** adj técnico. **technicality** n detalle técnico m. **technician** n técnico, -a m, f. **technological** adj tecnológico. **technology** n tecnología f.

teddy bear ['tedi,beə] n osito de felpa m.

tedious ['tiidiəs] adj latoso. **tediousness** n also **tedium** pesadez f, tedio m.

tee [tii] n tee m. v **tee off** dar el primer golpe.

teem [tiim] v pulular, hormiguear.

teenage ['tiineidʒ] adj adolescente. **teenager** n adolescente m, f. **teens** pl n adolescencia f sing.

teeth [tiiθ] V tooth.

teethe [tiið] v echar los dientes. **teething** n dentición f.

teetotaller [tii'toutələ] n abstemio, -a m, f.

telecommunications [,telikəmjuː ni'keiʃənz] pl n telecomunicaciones f pl.

telegram ['teligram] n telegrama m.

telegraph ['teligraːf] n telégrafo m. **telegraph pole** poste telegráfico m. v telegrafiar. **telegraphic** adj telegráfico.

telepathy [tə'lepəθi] n telepatía f. **telepathic** adj telepático.

telephone ['telifoun] n teléfono m. **telephone box** or **kiosk** cabina telefónica f. **telephone call** llamada telefónica f. **telephone directory** guía de teléfonos f. **telephone exchange** central telefónica f. **telephone number** número de teléfono m. **telephone operator** or **telephonist** telefonista m, f. v telefonear.

telescope ['teliskoup] n telescopio m. **telescopic** adj telescópico.

television ['teliviʒən] n televisión f. **television set** televisor m. **televise** v televisar.

telex ['teleks] n télex m.

tell [tel] v decir; (*story*) contar; comunicar; mandar; (*identify*) reconocer; (*distinguish*) distinguir; (*deduce*) deducir;

(*observe*) notar. **tell against** perjudicar. **tell of** hablar de. **tell off** (*coll*) regañar. **tell on** afectar a. **telltale** adj revelador.

temper ['tempə] n (*anger*) cólera f; temperamento m; humor m. **lose one's temper** enfadarse. v templar.

temperament ['tempərəmənt] n temperamento m. **temperamental** adj caprichoso.

temperate ['tempərət] adj templado.

temperature ['temprətʃə] n temperatura f; (*med*) fiebre f.

tempestuous [tem'pestjuəs] adj tempestuoso.

temple¹ ['templ] n (*rel*) templo m.

temple² ['templ] n (*anat*) sien f.

tempo ['tempou] n (*music*) tiempo m; (*fig*) ritmo m.

temporary ['tempərəri] adj temporal, provisional. **temporary worker** temporario, -a m, f.

tempt [tempt] v tentar; seducir. **temptation** n tentación f.

ten [ten] nm, adj diez m. **tenth** n, adj décimo, -a.

tenacious [tə'neiʃəs] adj tenaz. **tenaciousness** also **tenacity** n tenacidad f.

tenant ['tenənt] n habitante m, f, ocupante m, f. **tenancy** n alquiler m, arrendamiento m.

tend¹ [tend] v tender, tener tendencia a. **tendency** n tendencia f.

tend² [tend] v (*look after*) cuidar; manejar.

tender¹ ['tendə] adj tierno; delicado; (*kind*) cariñoso; compasivo; (*sensitive*) sensible; (*painful*) dolorido. **tenderize** v ablandar. **tenderness** n (*affection*) ternura f; (*meat*) lo tierno.

tender² ['tendə] v ofertar, hacer una oferta. n oferta f. **legal tender** moneda corriente f.

tendon ['tendən] n tendón m.

tendril ['tendril] n zarcillo m.

tenement ['tenəmənt] n casa de vecindad f.

tennis ['tenis] n tenis m. **tennis ball** pelota de tenis f. **tennis court** campo de tenis m. **tennis player** tenista m, f. **tennis shoes** zapatos de tenis m pl.

tenor ['tenə] n (*music*) tenor m; (*sense*) significado m; (*course*) curso m.

tense¹ [tens] adj tenso; estirado. v tensar. **tension** n tensión f.

tense² [tens] n tiempo m.

tent [tent] n tienda de campaña f. **pitch a tent** armar una tienda de campaña.
tentacle ['tentəkl] n tentáculo m.
tentative ['tentətiv] adj provisional; de tanteo; indeciso.
tenterhooks ['tentəhuks] pl n **be on tenterhooks** estar sobre ascuas.
tenuous ['tenjuəs] adj tenue; delgado.
tepid ['tepid] adj templaducho; (fig) tibio. **tepidness** n also **tepidity** tibieza f.
term [təːm] n periodo m; (comm) plazo m; (school) trimestre m; curso m; (end) término m. **terms** pl n condiciones f pl; (terminology) términos m pl; (comm) tarifa f sing; (relationship) relaciones f pl. **come to terms with** llegar a un acuerdo con. **on good/bad terms with** en buenas/malas relaciones con. **terms of reference** mandato m sing. v llamar, calificar.
terminal ['təːminəl] adj terminal, final. n final de línea m; (extremity) extremidad f; (elec) borne m.
terminate ['təːmineit] v terminar, concluir. **termination** n terminación f.
terminology [təːmi'nolədʒi] n terminología f.
terminus ['təːminəs] n término m.
terrace ['terəs] n terraza f; (houses) hilera de casas f.
terrain [tə'rein] n terreno m.
terrestrial [tə'restriəl] adj terrestre.
terrible ['terəbl] adj terrible; atroz; horrible. **terribly** adv terriblemente. **terribly bad** malísimo. **terribly good** buenísimo.
terrier ['teriə] n terrier m.
terrify ['terifai] v aterrorizar. **terrific** adj (coll: excellent) estupendo; (coll: extreme) terrible; enorme.
territory ['teritəri] n territorio m. **territorial** adj territorial.
terror ['terə] n terror m. **terrorism** n terrorismo m. **terrorist** n(m+f), adj terrorista. **terrorize** v aterrorizar, aterrar.
terse [təːs] adj conciso.
terylene ® ['terəliːn] n terylene ® m.
test [test] n prueba f; examen m; (med) análisis m. **test case** (law) juicio que hace jurisprudencia m. **test match** partido internacional m. **test paper** examen m. **test pilot** piloto de pruebas m. **test tube** tubo de ensayo m. v probar; poner un examen a; analizar; (sight) graduar; (weight) comprobar.
testament ['testəmənt] n testamento m.

the New Testament el Nuevo Testamento m. **the Old Testament** el Antiguo Testamento m.
testicle ['testikl] n testículo m.
testify ['testifai] v testificar; dar testimonio.
testimony ['testiməni] n testimonio m. **testimonial** n testimonio m; recomendación f.
tetanus ['tetənəs] n tétanos m.
tether ['teðə] n traba f, atadura f. **at the end of one's tether** hartísimo. v trabar, atar.
text [tekst] n texto m. **textbook** n libro de texto m. **textual** adj textual.
textile ['tekstail] nm, adj textil.
texture ['tekstjuə] n textura f.
than [ðən] conj que; de; cuando; del que.
thank [θaŋk] v agradecer. **thank you** gracias. **thanksgiving** n acción de gracias f. **thanks to** gracias a. **thankful** adj agradecido. **thankless** adj desagradecido; ingrato.
that [ðat] adj ese, esa; aquel, aquella; el, la. pron ése, ésa; aquél, aquélla; (neuter) eso; (neuter: farther away) aquello; (before relative pron or of) el, la, lo; (who, which) que; el que, la que; quien; el cual, la cual; (neuter) lo que. adv así de; tan; tanto. conj que; de que; para que; porque.
thatch [θatʃ] n (straw) paja f; (roof) techo de paja m. v cubrir con un tejado de paja.
thaw [θɔː] n (ice) deshielo m; (snow) derretimiento m. v deshelar; derretir.
the [ðə] art el, la (pl los, las); (neuter) lo.
theatre ['θiətə] n teatro m. **theatrical** adj teatral, de teatro.
theft [θeft] n hurto, robo.
their [ðeə] adj su, sus; suyo, suya.
theirs [ðeəz] pron el suyo, la suya.
them [ðem] pron ellos, ellas; (direct object) los, las; (indirect object) les.
theme [θiːm] n tema m. **thematic** adj temático.
themselves [ðəm'selvz] pl pron se; ellos mismos, ellas mismas; sí mismos, sí mismas. **by themselves** solos.
then [ðen] adv (that time) entonces; (afterwards) después, luego; (furthermore) además; (despite that) a pesar de eso; (consequently) por lo tanto. n entonces; ese momento. conj en ese caso; entonces.

theology [θi'olədʒi] n teología f. **theologian** n teólogo, -a m, f. **theological** adj teológico.

theorem ['θiərəm] n teorema m.

theory ['θiəri] n teoría f. **theoretical** adj teórico.

therapy ['θerəpi] n terapia f. **therapeutic** adj terapéutico. **therapist** n terapeuta m, f.

there [ðeə] adv ahí; allí; allá. **thereabouts** adv (place) por ahí, por allí; (degree) más o menos. **thereafter** adv después, más tarde. **thereby** adv por eso, por ello. **therefore** adv por lo tanto. **therein** adv allí dentro; en eso. **there is** or **are** hay. **thereof** adv de eso; su. **thereto** adv a eso, a ello. **thereupon** adv immediatamente después; sobre eso. **therewith** adv con eso. **there you are** eso es.

thermal ['θəːməl] adj termal; (tech) térmico. n corriente de aire caliente que sube.

thermodynamics [θəːmoudai'namiks] n termodinámica f.

thermometer [θə'momitə] n termómetro m.

thermonuclear [θəːmou'njukliə] adj termonuclear.

Thermos ® ['θəːmɒs] n termo ® m, termos ® m.

thermostat ['θəːməstat] n termostato m. **thermostatic** adj termostático.

these [ðiːz] pl adj estos, estas. pl pron éstos, éstas.

thesis ['θiːsis] n, pl -ses tesis f invar.

they [ðei] pl pron ellos, ellas.

thick [θik] adj grueso; espeso; denso; (coll) torpe. **thick-skinned** adj (fig) insensible. **thicken** v espesar(se). **thickness** n espesor m.

thief [θiːf] n ladrón, -ona m, f.

thigh [θai] n muslo m.

thimble ['θimbl] n dedal m.

thin [θin] adj (person) flaco; delgado; fino; (hair) ralo; (audience) escaso; (air) enrarecido; (beer) aguado; (voice) débil; (liquid) claro; (excuse) flojo. v adelgazar; (dilute) diluir. **thinness** n delgadez f, flaqueza f.

thing [θiŋ] n cosa f; objeto m; artículo m; (coll) chisme m. **things** pl n (affairs, belongings) cosas f pl.

think [θiŋk] v pensar; meditar; imaginar. **I think so** creo que sí. **think about** pensar en. **think over** pensar bien.

third [θəːd] adj tercero. n tercero, -a m, f; (fraction) tercio m; (music) tercera f. **third-party insurance** seguro contra tercera persona m. **third-rate** adj de poca calidad.

thirst [θəːst] n sed f. v tener sed. **be thirsty** tener sed.

thirteen [θəː'tiːn] nm, adj trece. **thirteenth** n, adj decimotercero, -a m, f.

thirty ['θəːti] nm, adj treinta. **thirtieth** n, adj trigésimo, -a m, f.

this [ðis] adj este, esta. pron éste, ésta. adv tan; así de.

thistle ['θisl] n cardo m.

thong [θɒŋ] n correa f.

thorn [θɔːn] n espina f. **thorny** adj espinoso.

thorough ['θʌrə] adj (search, etc.) minucioso; (person) concienzudo; a fondo; completo. **thoroughbred** n pura sangre m, f. **thoroughfare** n vía pública f. **thoroughly** adv a fondo; completamente. **thoroughness** n minuciosidad f.

those [ðouz] adj esos, esas; aquellos, aquellas. pron ésos, ésas; aquéllos, aquéllas.

though [ðou] conj aunque. adv sin embargo. **as though** como si.

thought [θɔːt] n pensamiento m; idea f; consideración f; intención f; opinión f. **thoughtful** adj pensativo; serio; (mindful) cuidadoso; (considerate) solícito. **thoughtless** adj irreflexivo; descuidado; desconsiderado.

thousand ['θauzənd] nm, adj mil. **thousandth** adj milésimo. n (fraction) milésima parte f; (position) número mil m.

thrash [θraʃ] v dar una paliza a. **thrash about** revolcarse. **thrash out** discutir a fondo. **thrashing** n paliza f.

thread [θred] n hilo m; (screw) rosca f, filete m. v ensartar, enhebrar. **threadbare** adj raído, gastado.

threat [θret] n amenaza f. **threaten** v amenazar.

three [θriː] nm, adj tres. **three-cornered** adj triangular. **three-dimensional** adj tridimensional. **threefold** adj triple. **three-legged** adj de tres patas. **three-piece** tresillo m. **three-ply** adj contrar. **three-quarter** adj tres cuartos.

thresh [θreʃ] v trillar. **threshing** trilladora f.

threshold ['θreʃould] n umbral m.

threw [θruː] V throw.

thrift [θrɪft] n economía f. **thrifty** adj económico.

thrill [θrɪl] n emoción f; (quiver) estremecimiento m. v estremecer. **thriller** n novela or película escalofriante f. **thrilling** adj emocionante; escalofriante.

thrive [θraɪv] v crecer; desarrollarse; tener buena salud; prosperar. **thriving** adj lozano; próspero.

throat [θrout] n garganta f. **clear one's throat** aclararse la voz. **throaty** adj gutural.

throb [θrob] n (heart) latido m, palpitación f; (engine) zumbido m; (pulse) pulsación f; (pain) punzada f. v latir; pulsar; zumbar; dar punzadas.

thrombosis [θrom'bousis] n trombosis f invar.

throne [θroun] n trono m.

throng [θroŋ] n multitud f, muchedumbre f. v atestar; afluir.

throttle ['θrotl] v estrangular. n (tech) regulador m; (mot) acelerador m.

through [θruː] adj directo; continuo. adv de parte a parte; completamente. prep (via) por; (time) durante; (place) a través de. **no through road** calle sin salida f. **through traffic** tránsito m. **throughout** prep (place) por todo, en todo; (time) durante todo. adv hasta el final.

*****throw** [θrou] n tiro m, lanzamiento m; (wrestling) tumbado m. v lanzar, tirar, arrojar; (a blow) dar; (light) proyectar. **throw away** tirar; (get rid of) desechar; (money) despilfarrar. **throw off** (a habit) renunciar a; (the scent) despistar. **throw out** expulsar, echar; rechazar. **throw up** (job) dejar; (vomit) devolver.

thrush [θrʌʃ] n tordo m.

*****thrust** [θrʌst] v empujar, clavar; meter; poner. n empujón m; (stab) estocada f.

thud [θʌd] n ruido sordo m. v caer con un ruido sordo.

thumb [θʌm] n pulgar m. v also **thumb through** hojear. **thumb a lift** (coll) hacer autostop. **thumb index** uñeros m pl.

thump [θʌmp] n (blow) porrazo m; (noise) ruido sordo m. v (strike) golpear; (heart) latir con fuerza.

thunder ['θʌndə] n trueno m; (fig) estruendo m. **thunderstorm** n tormenta f. **thunderstruck** adj atónito. v tronar.

Thursday ['θəːzdi] n jueves m.

thus [ðʌs] adv así; de este modo.

thwart [θwɔːt] v frustrar, impedir.

thyme [taim] n tomillo m.

thyroid ['θairoid] adj tiroides f invar. adj tiroideo.

tiara [ti'ɑːrə] n tiara f.

tick¹ [tik] n (mark) marca f; (sound) tictac m. **tick off** (coll) reprender.

tick² [tik] n (zool) garrapata f.

ticket ['tikit] n (price) etiqueta f; (entrance) entrada f; (transport) billete m; (permit) pase m. **cloakroom ticket** número del guardarropa m. **complimentary ticket** entrada de favor f. **parking ticket** multa por aparcamiento indebido f. **return ticket** billete de ida y vuelta m. **single ticket** billete de ida m. **ticket agency** agencia de venta de billetes f. **ticket office** taquilla f.

tickle ['tikl] v hacer cosquillas a. n cosquilleo m. **ticklish** adj cosquilloso.

tide [taid] n marea f. **tide-mark** n línea de la marea alta f; (coll) lengua del agua f. v **tide over** sacar de apuro.

tidy ['taidi] adj ordenado; (appearance) arreglado; (clean) limpio. v ordenar; limpiar. **tidily** adv bien; aseadamente. **tidiness** n orden m; aseo m.

tie [tai] v atar; (lace) lacear; (knot) hacer; (unite) unir; (link) ligar; (sport) empatar. n (neck) corbata f; (knot) nudo m; (bond) lazo m; (sport) empate m; (fig) atadura f.

tier [tiə] n grada f; (row) fila f; (cake) piso m.

tiger ['taigə] n tigre m.

tight [tait] adj (bolt, knot, etc.) apretado; (clothes) ajustado; (taut) tirante; (control) estricto; (seal) hermético; (bend) cerrado; (coll: drunk) borracho; (coll: mean) agarrado. **tight-fisted** adj tacaño. **tight-lipped** adj callado. **tightrope** n cuerda de volatinero f. adv also **tightly** bien; herméticamente. **hold tight!** ¡agárrense bien! **tighten** (screw, etc.) apretar; (rope, etc.) tensar; (control) estrechar. **tighten one's belt** (coll) apretarse el cinturón. **tights** pl n mallas f pl.

tile [tail] n (roof) teja f; (floor) baldosa f. v tejar; embaldosar.

till¹ [til] V until.

till² [til] n caja f.

till³ [til] v labrar, cultivar.

tiller ['tilə] *n* (*naut*) caña del timón *f*.

tilt [tilt] *n* inclinación *f*. **at full tilt** en toda mecha. *v* inclinar. **tilt at** arremeter contra.

timber ['timbə] *n* madera de construcción *f*. **timbered** (*house*) enmaderado.

time [taim] *n* tiempo *m*, momento *m*; época *f*; período *m*; (*season*) estación *f*; (*clock*) hora *f*; (*occasion*) vez *f*; (*fixed time period*) plazo *m*; (*music*) duración *f*; (*music: tempo*) compás *m*; (*sport*) final *m*. **a long time** mucho tiempo. **a short time** poco tiempo. **at the same time** al mismo tiempo. **from time to time** de vez en cuando. **in time** a tiempo. **on time** a la hora. **timeless** *adj* eternal. **timely** *adj* oportuno.

time exposure *n* exposición *f*.

time limit *n* límite de tiempo *m*.

timepiece ['taimpiːs] *n* reloj *m*.

timesaving ['taimˌseiviŋ] *adj* que ahorra tiempo.

time signal *n* señal horaria *f*.

timetable ['taimteibl] *n* horario *m*; (*transport*) guía *f*.

time zone *n* huso horario *m*.

timid ['timid] *adj* tímido. **timidity** *n* timidez *f*.

tin [tin] *n* estaño *m*; (*tinplate*) hojalata *f*; (*can*) lata *f*; (*baking*) molde *m*. **tinfoil** *n* papel de estaño *m*, abrelatas *m invar*. **tinny** *adj* (*sound, taste*) metálico.

tinge [tindʒ] *n* tinte *m*. *v* teñir.

tingle ['tiŋgl] *v* sentir hormigueo. *n* hormigueo *m*.

tinker ['tiŋkə] *n* calderero *m* *v* componer, arreglar. **tinker with** jugar con.

tinkle ['tiŋkl] *n* tintineo *m*. *v* hacer tintinear.

tinsel ['tinsəl] *n* oropel *m*.

tint [tint] *n* (*hair*) tinte *m*; tono *m*; matiz *m*. *v* teñir; matizar.

tiny ['taini] *adj* diminuto.

tip[1] [tip] *n* punta *f*; (*cigarette*) filtro *m*. **on tiptoe** de puntillas.

tip[2] [tip] *v* (*tilt*) inclinar; (*pour*) verter; (*upset*) volcar.

tip[3] [tip] *n* (*hint*) consejo *m*, información *f*; (*money*) propina *f*. *v* dar una propina a. **tip-off** *n* (*coll*) información *f*.

tipsy ['tipsi] *adj* (*coll*) achispado.

tire[1] [taiə] *v* cansar(se). **tire out** agotar. **tired** *adj* cansado. **be tired of** estar harto de. **tiredness** *n* cansancio *m*. **tiresome** *adj* pesado.

tire[2] *V* tyre.

tissue ['tiʃuː] *n* (*anat*) tejido *m*; (*cloth*) tisú *m*; (*handkerchief*) pañuelo de papel *m*. **tissue paper** papel de seda *m*.

title ['taitl] *n* título *m*; derecho *m*. **title deed** título de propiedad *m*. **title page** portada *f*. *v* titular. **titled** *adj* con título de nobleza.

titter ['titə] *n* risita *f*. *v* reírse nerviosamente.

to [tu] *prep* a; (*direction*) hacia; (*as far as*) hasta; (*time*) menos; (*destination, purpose*) para; (*according to*) según; (*in juxtaposition*) contra; (*compared with*) en comparación con; (*in*) por; (*in memory of*) en honor a. **to-do** *n* (*coll*) follón *m*.

toad [toud] *n* sapo *m*. **toadstool** *n* hongo venenoso *m*.

toast [toust] *n* pan tostado *m*; (*speech*) brindis *m invar*. **toast-rack** *n* portatostadas *m invar*. *v* tostar. **toaster** *n* tostador *m*.

tobacco [tə'bakou] *n* tabaco *m*. **tobacconist's** *n* estanco *m*.

toboggan [tə'bogən] *n* tobogán *m*. *v* deslizarse en tobogán.

today [tə'dei] *nm*, *adj* hoy.

toddler ['todlə] *n* niño pequeño *m*; niña pequeña *f*.

toe [tou] *n* dedo del pie. **big toe** dedo gordo *m*. **toenail** *n* uña (del dedo del pie) *f*. **toe the line** (*coll*) conformarse.

toffee ['tofi] *n* caramelo *m*. **toffee-apple** *n* manzana garrapiñada *f*.

together [tə'geðə] *adv* juntos; (*at the same time*) a la vez; (*agreed*) de acuerdo. **togetherness** *n* solidaridad *f*.

toil [toil] *n* trabajo agotador *m*. *v* trabajar duro.

toilet ['toilit] *n* (*lavatory*) retrete *m*; (*washing, etc.*) arreglo *m*. **toilet paper** papel higiénico *m*. **toilet soap** jabón de tocador *m*. **toilet water** agua de Colonia *f*.

token ['toukən] *n* (*sign*) muestra *f*, prueba *f*; (*symbol*) símbolo *m*; (*keepsake*) recuerdo *m*; (*disc*) ficha *f*; (*book, record*) vale *m*. **as a token of** como prueba de. *adj* simbólico.

told [tould] *V* tell.

tolerate ['toləreit] *v* tolerar, soportar; admitir; respetar. **tolerable** *adj* tolerable; (*fair*) mediano. **tolerance** *n* *also* **toleration** tolerancia *f*. **tolerant** *adj* tolerante.

toll¹ [toul] *n* (*road*) peaje *m*; (*bridge*) pontaje *m*; (*victims*) bajas *f pl*. **toll-gate** *n* barrera de peaje *f*.

toll² [toul] *v* tocar, tañar.

tomato [tə'maɪtou] *n* tomate *m*.

tomb [tuːm] *n* tumba *f*. **tombstone** *n* piedra sepulcral *f*.

tomorrow [tə'morou] *nm, adv* mañana. **the day after tomorrow** pasado mañana *m*.

ton [tʌn] *n* tonelada *f*.

tone [toun] *n* tono *m*; estilo *m*. *v* (*colour*) matizar. **tone down** atenuarse.

tongs [toŋz] *pl n* (*coal*) tenazas *f pl*; (*sugar*) tenacillas *f pl*.

tongue [tʌŋ] *n* lengua *f*. **tongue-tied** *adj* mudo.

tonic ['tonik] *adj* tónico. *n* (*med*) tónico *m*; (*music*) tónica *f*.

tonight [tə'nait] *n, adv* esta noche.

tonsil ['tonsil] *n* amígdala *f*. **tonsillitis** *n* amigdalitis *f*.

too [tuː] *adv* demasiado; (*also*) también; (*moreover*) además.

took [tuk] *V* **take**.

tool [tuːl] *n* herramienta *f*; utensilio *m*. **toolshed** *n* cobertizo para herramientas *m*.

tooth [tuːθ] *n, pl* **teeth** diente *m*; (*back tooth*) muela *f*. **toothache** *n* dolor de muelas *m*. **tooth-brush** *n* cepillo de dientes *m*. **toothpaste** *n* pasta dentífrica *f*. **toothpick** *n* palillo de dientes *m*. **toothless** *adj* desdentado.

top¹ [top] *n* parte de arriba *f*, lo alto *m*; (*of mountain*) cima *f*; (*of tin, pan, bottle, etc.*) tapa *f*; (*of page*) cabeza *f*; (*of the head*) coronilla *f*; (*surface*) superficie *f*. *adj* de arriba; (*best*) mejor; (*first*) primero. *v* (*cover*) cubrir; (*exceed*) superar. **top up** llenar completamente.

top² [top] *n* (*toy*) peón *m*, trompo *m*.

topaz ['toupaz] *n* topacio *m*.

topcoat ['topkout] *n* abrigo *m*.

topdressing ['top.dresiŋ] *n* abono *m*.

top hat *n* chistera *f*.

top-heavy *adj* inestable.

topic ['topik] *n* tema *m*, asunto *m*. **topical** *adj* de actualidad.

topography [tə'pografi] *n* topografía *f*. **topographical** *adj* topográfico.

topple ['topl] *v* derribar, volcar, hacer caer.

top-secret *adj* confidencial.

topsoil ['topsoil] *n* tierra vegetal *f*.

topsy-turvy [topsi'tərvi] *adj* revuelto.

torch [toːtʃ] *n* (*electric*) linterna *f*; (*burning*) antorcha *f*.

tore [toː] *V* **tear**.

torment [toːment; *v* toːˈment] *n* tormento *m*, suplicio *m*. *v* atormentar.

tornado [toːˈneidou] *n* tornado *m*.

torpedo [toːˈpiːdou] *n* torpedo *m*. *v* torpedear.

torrent ['torənt] *n* torrente *m*. **torrential** *adj* torrencial.

torso ['toːsou] *n* torso *m*.

tortoise ['toːtəs] *n* tortuga *f*. **tortoise-shell** *n* carey *m*.

tortuous ['toːtʃuəs] *adj* tortuoso.

torture ['toːtʃə] *n* tortura *f*. *v* torturar. **torturer** *n* torcionario *m*.

toss [tos] *v* (*throw*) lanzamiento *m*; (*fall*) caída *f*; (*head*) sacudida *f*; (*coin*) sorteo a cara o cruz *m*; (*bull*) cogida *f*. *v* lanzar; sacudir; (*coin*) echar a cara o cruz; (*salad*) dar vueltas *f*.

tot¹ [tot] *n* (*child*) nene *m*; (*drink*) trago *m*.

tot² [tot] *v* **tot up** sumar.

total ['toutl] *nm, adj* total. *v* (*add up*) sumar; (*add up to*) totalizar. **totalitarian** *n, adj* totalitario, -a.

totter ['totə] *v* bambolearse.

touch [tʌtʃ] *n* (*sense*) tacto *m*; (*contact*) contacto *m*; (*light stroke*) toque *m*; (*tap*) golpe ligero *m*; (*brush*) roce *m*. *v* tocar; rozar; (*reach*) alcanzar; (*affect*) afectar; (*move*) enternecer; (*food*) tomar. **touchy** *adj* susceptible.

tough [tʌf] *adj* (*hard*) duro; resistente; (*character*) tenaz; (*job*) difícil. **toughen** *v* endurecer. **toughness** *n* dureza *f*; resistencia *f*; dificultad *f*.

toupee ['tuːpei] *n* tupé *m*.

tour [tuə] *n* excursión *f*; visita *f*; viaje *m*; (*theatre*) gira *f*. **package tour** viaje todo comprendido *m*. **tour of duty** turno de servicio *m*. *v* recorrer. **touring** *n also* **tourism** turismo *m*. **tourist** *n* turista *m, f*. **tourist agency** agencia de viajes *f*.

tournament ['tuənəmənt] *n* torneo *m*.

tousled ['tauzld] *adj* (*hair*) despeinado.

tow [tou] *n* remolque *m*. *v* remolcar; (*from towpath*) sirgar. **towpath** *n* camino de sirga *m*. **tow-rope** *n* remolque *m*.

towards [tə'woːdz] *prep* hacia; (*for*) para; (*with*) con; (*with regard to*) con respecto a.

towel ['tauəl] *n* toalla *f*; (*bath*) toalla de baño *f*; (*sanitary*) paño higiénico *m*. **towel-rail** *n* toallero *m*. **towelling** *n* felpa *f*.

tower ['tauə] *n* torre *f*. **control tower** torre de control *f*. **tower over** dominar. **towering** *adj* sobresaliente.

town [taun] *n* (*large*) ciudad *f*; (*small*) pueblo *m*. **new town** pueblo nuevo *m*. **town hall** ayuntamiento *m*. **town planning** urbanismo *m*.

toxic ['toksik] *adj* tóxico.

toy [toi] *n* juguete *m*. *adj* de juguete. **v toy with** toquetear; (*idea*) acariciar.

trace [treis] *n* (*trail*) rastro *m*; (*indication*) indicio *m*; (*a little*) pizca *f*. **v** (*plan*) trazar; (*through paper*) calcar; (*trail*) rastrear; (*find*) encontrar. **tracing** *n* calco *m*. **tracing paper** papel de calcar *m*.

track [trak] *n* (*of animals, people*) huella *f*; (*of things*) rastro *m*; (*path*) sendero *m*; (*rail*) vía *f*; (*course*) curso *m*; (*racing*) pista *f*; (*tank, tractor*) oruga *f*. **track suit** *n* mono de entrenamiento *m*. **v** (*hunt*) rastrear; (*pursue*) seguir la pista de. **track down** acorralar. **tracker** *n* perseguidor *m*.

tract¹ [trakt] *n* (*region*) trecho *m*; (*anat*) aparato *m*.

tract² [trakt] *n* (*pamphlet*) folleto *m*.

tractor ['traktə] *n* tractor *m*.

trade [treid] *n* comercio *m*; (*job*) ramo *m*. **trademark** *n* marca de fábrica *f*. **tradesman** *n* comerciante *m*. **trade union** sindicato *m*. **trade unionist** sindicalista *m*, *f*. **v** comerciar; negociar; cambiar. **trade in** tomar como entrada. **trader** *n* comerciante *m*, *f*; negociante *m*, *f*.

tradition [trə'diʃən] *n* tradición *f*. **traditional** *adj* tradicional.

traffic ['trafik] *n* (*mot*) circulación *f*, tráfico *m*; (*tourist*) tránsito *m*; (*trade*) comercio *m*. **traffic jam** embotellamiento *m*. **traffic-light** *n* semáforo *m*. **traffic warden** guardián del tráfico *m*.

tragedy ['tradʒədi] *n* tragedia *f*. **tragic** *adj* trágico.

trail [treil] *n* (*path*) camino *m*, sendero *m*; (*person or animal*) huellas *f* pl; (*smoke*) estela *f*; (*blood*) reguero *m*. **v** (*drag*) arrastrar; (*chase*) perseguir; (*an animal*) rastrear; (*lag*) ir detrás de; (*hang down*) colgar. **trailer** *n* (*mot*) remolque *m*; (*film*) trailer *m*.

train [trein] *n* (*railway*) tren *m*; (*procession*) desfile *m*; (*series*) serie *f*; (*dress*) cola *f*. **v** (*teach*) educar; (*someone for a job*) formar, capacitar; (*animal*) amaestrar; (*horse*) domar; (*sport*) entrenar. **trainee** *n* aprendiz, -a *m*, *f*. **trainer** *n* (*sport*) entrenador, -a *m*, *f*; (*boxing*) cuidador *m*; (*animals*) amaestrador, -a *m*, *f*; (*horses*) domador, -a *m*, *f*.

trait [treit] *n* rasgo *m*.

traitor ['treitə] *n* traidor, -a *m*, *f*.

tram [tram] *n* tranvía *m*.

tramp [tramp] *n* (*person*) vagabundo, -a *m*, *f*; (*hike*) caminata *f*; (*sound*) ruido de pasos *m*. **v** patear; vagabundear.

trample ['trampl] **v** pisotear, pisar.

trampoline ['trampəlin] *n* cama elástica *f*.

trance [trams] *n* trance *m*.

tranquil ['trankwil] *adj* tranquilo. **tranquility** *n* tranquilidad *f*. **tranquillize v** tranquilizar. **tranquillizer** *n* tranquilizante *m*.

transact [tran'zakt] **v** (*negotiate*) tratar; (*perform*) llevar a cabo. **transaction** *n* (*business*) negociación *f*; (*deal*) transacción *f*.

transcend [tran'send] **v** exceder, superar. **transcendental** *adj* trascendental.

transcribe [tran'skraib] **v** transcribir. **transcription** *n* transcripción *f*.

transept [tran'sept] *n* transepto *m*.

transfer [trans'fəː; *n* 'transfəː] **v** trasladar; transferir. **transfer** *n* traslado *m*; (*law*) cesión *f*; (*picture*) calcomanía *f*. **transferable** *adj* transferible. **not transferable** (*right*) inalienable; (*ticket*) intransferible.

transfix [trans'fiks] **v** traspasar.

transform [trans'fom] **v** transformar. **transformation** *n* transformación *f*. **transformer** *n* (*elec*) transformador *m*.

transfuse [trans'fjuz] **v** transfundir. **transfusion** *n* transfusión *f*.

transient ['tranziənt] *adj* transitorio.

transistor [tran'zistə] *n* transistor *m*. **transistorize v** transistorizar.

transit ['transit] *n* tránsito *m*. **in transit** de tránsito.

transition [tran'ziʃən] *n* transición *f*. **transitional** *adj* transitorio.

transitive ['transitiv] *adj* transitivo.

transitory ['transitəri] *adj* transitorio.

translate [trans'leit] **v** traducir. **translation** *n* traducción *f*. **translator** *n* traductor, -a *m*, *f*.

translucent [trans'lusnt] *adj* translúcido. **translucence** *n* translucidez *f*.

transmit [tranz'mit] v transmitir, trasmitir. **transmission** n transmisión f. trasmisión f. **transmitter** n (apparatus) transmisor m; (station) emisora f.

transparent [trans'peərənt] adj transparente. **transparency** n transparencia f; (phot) transparente m.

transplant [trans'plaint; n 'transplaint] v trasplantar. n trasplante m.

transport [transport; v trans'port] n transporte m. v transportar. **transportation** n transporte m; (convicts) deportación f.

transpose [trans'pouz] v transponer; (music) transportar. **transposition** n transposición f; transporte m.

transverse ['tranzvərs] adj transverso.

transvestite [tranz'vestait] n travestido m.

trap [trap] n trampa f; (mice, rats) ratonera f; (vehicle) cabriolé m; (tech) sifón de depósito m; (theatre) escotillón m. **trapdoor** n trampa f. v coger; coger en una trampa; rodear; pillar; bloquear.

trapeze [trə'piːz] n trapecio m. **trapeze artist** trapecista m, f.

trash [traʃ] n basura f; (coll) cachivaches m pl.

trauma ['trɔːmə] n trauma f. **traumatic** adj traumático.

travel ['travl] v recorrer; viajar por. **travels** pl n viajes m pl. **travel agency** agencia de viajes f. **travel-sickness** n mareo m. **traveller** n viajero, -a m, f; (comm) viajante de comercio m. **traveller's cheque** cheque de viaje m.

travesty ['travəsti] n parodia f.

trawler ['trɔːlə] n barco rastreador m. **trawling** n pesca a la rastrea f.

tray [trei] n bandeja f.

treachery ['tretʃəri] n traición f. **treacherous** adj (person) traidor; (action) traicionero.

treacle ['triːkl] n melaza f.

°tread [tred] v pisar; (walk) andar por. **tread on** (crush) pisotear. n paso m; (step of a staircase) huella f; (tyre) banda de rodadura f.

treason ['triːzn] n traición f.

treasure ['treʒə] n tesoro m. v valorar; guardar en la memoria. **treasurer** n tesorero, -a m, f. **treasury** n tesorería f.

treat [triːt] v tratar; tomar; (a patient) atender; (pay for) invitar, comprar. n invitación f; placer m. **treatment** n trato m; (med) tratamiento m.

treatise ['triːtiz] n tratado m.

treaty ['triːti] n tratado m; acuerdo m.

treble ['trebl] n (music) tiple m, soprano m. adj triple; (music) de tiple. v triplicar. adv tres veces.

tree [triː] n árbol m.

trek [trek] v caminar trabajosamente. n expedición f; caminata f.

trellis ['trelis] n enrejado m; espaldera f. v poner un enrejado.

tremble ['trembl] v temblar. n temblor m.

tremendous [trə'mendəs] adj tremendo, enorme; extraordinario; (coll: excellent) formidable.

tremor ['tremə] n temblor m.

trench [trentʃ] n zanja f; (mil) trinchera f.

trend [trend] n tendencia f; dirección f; orientación f. **trendy** adj (coll) modernísimo.

trespass ['trespəs] n entrada ilegal f. v violar; abusar; invadir. **trespasser** n intruso, -a m, f. **trespassers will be prosecuted** prohibido el paso.

trestle ['tresl] n caballete m. **trestle table** mesa de caballete f.

trial ['traiəl] n (law) juicio m; (experiment) prueba f, ensayo m; (annoyance) molestia f; (hardship) dificultad f. adj de prueba.

triangle ['traiangl] n triángulo m. **triangular** adj triangular.

tribe [traib] n tribu f. **tribal** adj tribal. **tribesman** n miembro de una tribu m.

tribunal [trai'bjuːnl] n tribunal m.

tributary ['tribjutəri] n afluente m. adj tributario.

tribute ['tribjuːt] n tributo m.

trick [trik] n (stratagem) truco m; (ruse) astucia f; (practical joke) broma f; (cards) baza f. **trick photography** trucaje m. **trick question** pega f. v engañar. **trickery** n engaño m; astucia f. **tricky** adj difícil; delicado.

trickle ['trikl] n hilo m, chorrito m. v verter poco a poco; gotear.

tricycle ['traisikl] n triciclo m.

trifle ['traifl] n nadería f. v **trifle with** jugar con. **trifling** adj insignificante.

trigger ['trigə] n gatillo m. v accionar. **trigger off** provocar.

trigonometry [trigə'nomətri] n trigonometría f.

trill [tril] n trino m. v trinar.

trim [trim] adj aseado; (neat) arreglado; elegante. v arreglar; (reduce) cercenar; (hair) entresacar; (nails) recortar; (hedge) podar; (*sails*) orientar. **trimmings** *pl n* recortes *m pl*; accesorios *m pl*.

trinket ['trɪŋkɪt] *n* dije *m*.

trio ['trɪːou] *n* trío *m*.

trip [trɪp] *n* (*voyage, effect of drugs*) viaje *m*; (*stumble*) tropezón *m*. *v* dar un traspié; tropezar; (*make someone fall*) echar la zancadilla.

tripe [traɪp] *n* callos *m pl*; (*coll*) bobadas *f pl*.

triple ['trɪpl] *nm, adj* triple. *v* triplicar. *adv* tres veces.

triplet ['trɪplɪt] *n* (*music*) tresillo *m*; (*poetry*) terceto *m*; (*person*) trillizo, -a *m, f*.

tripod ['traɪpɒd] *n* trípode *m*.

trite [traɪt] *adj* trillado, trivial. **triteness** *n* lo trillado; trivialidad *f*.

triumph ['traɪʌmf] *n* triunfo *m*. *v* triunfar. **triumphant** *adj* triunfante. **triumphantly** *adv* triunfantemente.

trivial ['trɪvɪəl] *adj* trivial. **trivia** *pl n* also **trivialities** trivialidades *f pl*.

trod [trɒd] *V* tread.

trolley ['trɒlɪ] *n* (*shopping*) carretilla *f*; (*tea*) carrito *m*; (*in mines*) vagoneta *f*.

trombone [trɒm'boun] *n* trombón *m*.

troop [truːp] *n* (*people*) banda *f*, grupo *m*; (*animals*) manada *f*. **troops** *pl n* (*mil*) tropas *f pl*. *v* **troop in/out** entrar/salir en tropel.

trophy ['troufɪ] *n* trofeo *m*.

tropic ['trɒpɪk] *n* trópico *m*. **Tropic of Cancer** Trópico de Cáncer. **Tropic of Capricorn** Trópico de Capricornio. **tropical** *adj* tropical.

trot [trɒt] *n* trote *m*. **on the trot** (*coll*) seguidos, seguidas. *v* trotar. **trotter** *n* mano *f*.

trouble ['trʌbl] *n* (*worry*) preocupación *f*; apuro *m*; pena *f*; (*misfortune*) desgracia *f*; problema *m*; disturbios *m pl*. **be in trouble** estar en un apuro. **look for trouble** buscar camorra. **what's the trouble?** ¿qué pasa? **troublemaker** *n* alborotador, -a *m, f*. **troublesome** *adj* molesto. *v* preocupar; perturbar; afectar; molestar.

trough [trɒf] *n* (*food*) pesebre *m*; (*drinking*) abrevadero *m*; (*depression*) depresión *f*.

trousers ['trauzəz] *pl n* pantalón *m sing*.

trout [traut] *n* trucha *f*.

trowel ['trauəl] *n* palustre *m*; (*gardening*) desplantador *m*.

truant ['truːənt] *n* **play truant** hacer novillos. **truancy** *n* rabona *f*.

truce [truːs] *n* tregua *f*. **call a truce** acordar una tregua.

truck [trʌk] *n* camión *m*; (*rail*) batea *f*. **truck driver** conductor de camión *m*.

trudge [trʌdʒ] *v* andar con dificultad.

true [truː] *adj* verdadero; (*faithful*) fiel; legítimo; (*real*) auténtico; (*accurate*) exacto. **true to life** conforme a la realidad. **truly** *adv* verdaderamente.

truffle ['trʌfl] *n* trufa *f*.

trump [trʌmp] *n* (*cards*) triunfo *m*. *v* fallar. **trump up** inventar.

trumpet ['trʌmpɪt] *n* trompeta *f*. *v* (*elephant*) barritar. **trumpeter** *n* trompetista *m, f*.

truncate [trʌŋ'keɪt] *v* truncar.

truncheon ['trʌntʃən] *n* matraca *f*; (*police*) porra *f*.

trunk [trʌŋk] *n* (*anat, bot*) tronco *m*; (*elephant*) trompa *f*; (*case*) baúl *m*. **trunk call** conferencia telefónica *f*. **trunk road** carretera principal *f*. **trunks** *pl n* calzoncillos cortos *m pl*; (*mot*) maleta

truss [trʌs] *n* (*hay*) haz *m*; (*fruit*) racimo *m*; (*med*) braguero *m*. *v* atar.

trust [trʌst] *n* confianza *f*; (*law*) fideicomiso *m*; (*comm*) trust *m*; (*expectation*) esperanza *f*. **trustworthy** *adj* digno de confianza; fidedigno. *v* tener confianza en; confiar; esperar; creer. **trustee** *n* guardián *m*; (*law*) fideicomisario, -a *m, f*. **trusting** *adj* confiado. **trusty** *adj* leal, seguro.

truth [truːθ] *n* verdad *f*. **truthful** *adj* veraz; verdadero. **truthfulness** *n* veracidad *f*.

try [traɪ] *n* tentativa *f*, prueba *f*; (*rugby*) ensayo *m*. *v* probar; intentar; ensayar; (*law*) ver; (*strain*) poner a prueba; (*annoy*) molestar; (*tire*) cansar; (*afflict*) hacer sufrir. **try on** (*garment*) probarse. **try it on** (*coll*) intentar dar el pego. **trying** *adj* molesto.

tsar [zaː] *n* zar *m*.

T-shirt ['tiːʃəːt] *n* camiseta *f*.

tub [tʌb] *n* tina *f*; (*bath*) bañera *f*.

tuba ['tjuːbə] *n* tuba *f*.

tube [tjuːb] *n* tubo *m*; (*coll*: *underground*) metro *m*. **tubeless** *adj* (*tyre*) sin cámara.

tuber ['tjuːbə] *n* tubérculo *m*.

tuberculosis [tjuːbəːkjuˈlousis] *n* tuberculosis *f*.

tuck [tʌk] *n* (*sewing*) alforza *f*; (*food*) comida *f*; (*sweets*) cucherías *f pl*. *v* meter; (*sheets*) remeter; (*fold*) alforzar. **tuck up** (*in bed*) arropar.

Tuesday ['tjuːzdi] n martes m.

tuft [tʌft] n (plants) mata f; (feathers) penacho m; (hair) mechón m.

tug [tʌg] n tirón m; (boat) remolcador m. **tug-of-war** n juego de la cuerda m. v (pull) tirar; (tow) remolcar; (drag) arrastrar.

tuition [tjuˈiʃən] n enseñanza f.

tulip ['tjuːlip] n tulipán m.

tumble ['tʌmbl] n caída f; (acrobatics) voltereta f. v caerse; dar volteretas; (knock over) derribar. **tumbledown** adj ruinoso. **tumble-dryer** n secadora al aire caliente f. **tumbler** n (glass) vaso m; (acrobat) voltalinero, -a f.

tummy ['tʌmi] n (coll) barriga f.

tumour ['tjuːmə] n tumor m.

tumult ['tjuːmʌlt] n tumulto m. **tumultuous** adj tumultuoso.

tuna ['tjuːnə] n atún m.

tune [tjuːn] n aire m. **in tune** afinado. **out of tune** desafinado. v (music) afinar; (mot) poner a punto. **tune in to** (radio) sintonizar con. **tuneful** adj melodioso. **tuneless** adj discordante. **tuner** n (person) afinador m; (radio) sintonizador m. **tuning** afinación f; sintonización f; puesta a punto f. **tuning fork** diapasón m.

tunic ['tjuːnik] n túnica f.

tunnel ['tʌnl] n túnel m. v hàcer un túnel en; (dig) cavar.

turban ['təːbən] n turbante m.

turbine ['təːbain] n turbina f.

turbot ['təːbət] n rodaballo m.

turbulent ['təːbjulənt] adj turbulento. **turbulence** n turbulencia f.

tureen [təˈriːn] n sopera f.

turf [təːf] n cesped m; (sport) turf m. v encespedar. **turf out** (coll) echar.

turkey ['təːki] n pavo m.

Turkish ['təːkiʃ] nm, adj turco. **Turkish bath** baño turco m.

turmeric ['təːmərik] n cúrcuma f.

turmoil ['təːmoil] n desorden m; agitación f; alboroto m.

turn [təːn] n vuelta f; (road) curva f; (body) movimiento m; (opportunity) turno m; (change) cambio m; (change in situation) viraje m; (fright) susto m. **take turns** at turnarse en. v dar vueltas; dar la vuelta a; (body) volver; (corner) doblar; (page) pasar; cambiar. **turn down** (lower) bajar; (reject) rechazar. **turn off** cerrar; (light) apagar; (engine) parar. **turn on**

(light, radio) encender; (current) conectar; (coll: excite) excitar. **turn out** (end up) resultar; (light) apagar. **turnover** n (comm) volumen de negocios m. **turnstile** n torniquete m. **turntable** n (record-player) plato giratorio m. **turn up** presentarse; (appear) aparecer. **turning** n vuelta f; curva f; (side road) bocacalle f. **turning point** momento crucial m.

turnip ['təːnip] n nabo m.

turpentine ['təːpəntain] n trementina f.

turquoise ['təːkwoiz] n (stone) turquesa f; (colour) azul turquesa m.

turret ['tʌrit] n torreón m; (mil) torreta f.

turtle ['təːtl] n tortuga de mar f. **turtle-neck** n (jumper collar) cuello que sube ligeramente m.

tusk [tʌsk] n defensa f.

tussle ['tʌsl] n pelea f; lucha f. v pelearse.

tutor ['tjuːtə] n (private) profesor particular m; (university) tutor m. v dar clases privadas.

tuxedo [tʌkˈsiːdou] n smoking m.

tweed [twiːd] n tweed m.

tweezers ['twiːzəz] pl n pinzas f pl.

twelve [twelv] nm, adj doce. **twelfth** n, adj duodécimo, -a.

twenty ['twenti] nm, adj veinte. **twentieth** n, adj vigésimo, -a.

twice [twais] adv dos veces.

twiddle ['twidl] v dar vueltas a. **twiddle one's thumbs** estar mano sobre mano.

twig [twig] n ramita f.

twilight ['twailait] n crepúsculo m.

twin [twin] n, adj gemelo, -a. **twin beds** camas gemelas f pl.

twine [twain] n bramante m. v (twist) retorcer; (interlace) trenzar; (embrace) rodear con.

twinge [twindʒ] n (pain) punzada f; (fig) arrebato m.

twinkle ['twiŋkl] n centelleo m; (brightness) brillo m. v centellear; (eyes) brillar.

twirl [twəːl] v dar vueltas a. n vuelta f.

twist [twist] v torcer; retorcer. n torcimiento m, torsión f; (tobacco) rollo m; vuelta f; deformación f; contorsión f; inclinación f; (warp) abarquillamiento m; (ankle) torcedura f; (swindle) trampa f.

twit [twit] n (slang) imbécil m, f.

twitch [twitʃ] n (pull) tirón m; (med) tic m. v tirar bruscamente de; (nervously) crispar.

twitter ['twɪtə] v gorjear. n gorjeo m.

two [tuː] nm, adj dos. **two-faced** adj falso. **two-legged** adj bípedo.

tycoon [taiˈkuːn] n magnate m.

type [taɪp] n (sort) tipo m, clase f; (print) carácter m, tipo m. **typesetting** n composición f. **typewriter** n máquina de escribir f. v escribir a máquina. **typical** adj típico. **typing** n mecanografía f. **typist** n mecanógrafo, -a m, f.

typhoid ['taifoid] n fiebre tifoidea f.

typhoon [taiˈfuːn] n tifón m.

tyrant ['taɪrənt] n tirano m. **tyrannical** adj tiránico. **tyranny** n tiranía f.

tyre or US **tire** ['taiə] n neumático m.

U

ubiquitous [juːˈbɪkwɪtəs] adj ubicuo.

udder ['ʌdə] n ubre f.

ugly ['ʌgli] adj feo; repugnante. **ugliness** n fealdad f.

ulcer ['ʌlsə] n úlcera f.

ulterior [ʌlˈtɪəriə] adj ulterior. **ulterior motive** segunda intención f.

ultimate ['ʌltimət] adj último; fundamental. **ultimately** adv por fin, al final; esencialmente. **ultimatum** n ultimátum m.

ultraviolet [ʌltrəˈvaiələt] adj ultravioleta.

umbilical [ʌmˈbilikəl] adj umbilical. **umbilical cord** cordón umbilical m.

umbrage ['ʌmbridʒ] n resentimiento m, enfado m. **take umbrage at** ofenderse por.

umbrella [ʌmˈbrelə] n paraguas m invar.

umpire ['ʌmpaiə] n árbitro m. v arbitrar.

umpteen [ʌmpˈtiːn] (coll) adj muchísimos. **umpteenth** adj enésimo.

unable [ʌnˈeibl] adj incapaz. **be unable to** (physical) ser incapaz de; (due to circumstances) no poder hacer.

unabridged [ʌnəˈbridʒd] adj íntegro.

unacceptable [ʌnəkˈseptəbl] adj inaceptable.

unaccompanied [ʌnəˈkʌmpənid] adj solo, sin compañía; (music) sin acompañamiento.

unaided [ʌnˈeidid] adj sin ayuda, solo.

unadulterated [ʌnəˈdʌltəreitid] adj no adulterado, sin mezcla.

unanimous [juːˈnaniməs] adj unánime. **unanimity** n unanimidad f.

unarmed [ʌnˈaːmd] adj (person) sin armas; desarmado.

unattached [ʌnəˈtatʃt] adj (loose) suelto; libre; independiente.

unattractive [ʌnəˈtraktiv] adj poco atrayente, desagradable.

unauthorized [ʌnˈɔːθəraizd] adj no autorizado.

unavoidable [ʌnəˈvoidəbl] adj inevitable.

unaware [ʌnəˈweə] adj inconsciente; ignorante. **be unaware of** ignorar. **unawares** adv sin querer; de improviso.

unbalanced [ʌnˈbalənst] adj desequilibrado; (mentally) trastornado.

unbearable [ʌnˈbeərəbl] adj insoportable, intolerable, insufrible.

unbelievable [ʌnbiˈliːvəbl] adj increíble.

***unbend** [ʌnˈbend] v (straighten) desencorvar; (fig) relajar. **unbending** adj inflexible.

unbiased [ʌnˈbaiəst] adj imparcial.

unbreakable [ʌnˈbreikəbl] adj irrompible.

unbridled [ʌnˈbraidld] adj (fig) desenfrenado.

unbutton [ʌnˈbʌtn] v desabrochar; (fig) desahogarse.

uncalled-for [ʌnˈkɔːldfɔː] adj innecesario; injustificado; gratuito.

uncanny [ʌnˈkani] adj extraño; misterioso.

uncertain [ʌnˈsəːtn] adj incierto. **uncertainty** n incertidumbre f.

uncle ['ʌŋkl] n tío m.

uncomfortable [ʌnˈkʌmfətəbl] adj incómodo; (anxious) inquieto; (awkward) difícil.

uncommon [ʌnˈkɔmən] adj poco común, raro.

uncompromising [ʌnˈkɔmprəmaiziŋ] adj inflexible; irreconciliable.

unconditional [ʌnkənˈdiʃənl] adj incondicional.

unconscious [ʌnˈkɔnʃəs] adj (med) inconsciente; (unaware) ignorante.

unconventional [ʌnkənˈvenʃənl] adj poco convencional.

uncooked [ʌnˈkukt] adj no cocido, crudo.

uncouth [ʌnˈkuːθ] adj grosero.

uncover [ʌnˈkʌvə] v descubrir; (reveal) revelar; (take the lid off) destapar.

uncut [ʌnˈkʌt] adj no cortado.

undecided [ʌndi'saidid] *adj* indeciso; irresoluto.

undeniable [ʌndi'naiəbl] *adj* incontestable.

under ['ʌndə] *adv* debajo; abajo; más abajo; (*insufficient*) insuficiente; (*for less*) para menos. *prep* debajo de; bajo; por debajo de; menos de; (*age*) menor de; (*lower in rank*) por debajo de; (*repair, construction, etc.*) en; (*according to*) según; conforme a.

underarm ['ʌndəraɪm] *adj*, *adv* por debajo del brazo; sobacal.

undercharge [ʌndə'tʃaɪdʒ] *v* cobrar menos de lo debido.

underclothes ['ʌndəklouðz] *pl n* ropa interior *f sing*.

undercoat ['ʌndəkout] *n* (*paint*) primera capa *f*.

undercover [ʌndə'kʌvə] *adj* secreto; clandestino.

undercut [ʌndə'kʌt] *v* vender más barato que.

underdeveloped [ʌndədi'veləpt] *adj* de desarrollo atrasado; (*phot*) no revelado lo suficiente.

underdog ['ʌndədog] *n* desvalido *m*.

underdone [ʌndə'dʌn] *adj* (*meat*) poco hecho.

underestimate [ʌndə'estimeit] *v* tasar en menos; menospreciar. *n also* **underestimation** infravaloración *f*; menosprecio *m*.

underfoot [ʌndə'fut] *adv* debajo de los pies.

undergo [ʌndə'gou] *v* sufrir, pasar por.

undergraduate [ʌndə'gradjuət] *n* estudiante no licenciado, -a *m, f*.

underground ['ʌndəgraund; *adv* ʌndə'graund] *adj* subterráneo; oculto, secreto. *adv* bajo tierra; clandestinamente.

undergrowth ['ʌndəgrouθ] *n* maleza *f*.

underhand [ʌndə'hand] *adj* bajo mano; secreto.

***underlie** [ʌndə'lai] *v* estar debajo de; servir de base a. **underlying** *adj* básico, fundamental.

underline [ʌndə'lain] *v* subrayar. **underlining** *n* subrayado *m*.

undermine [ʌndə'main] *v* socavar, minar.

underneath [ʌndə'niɪθ] *prep* bajo, debajo de. *adv* debajo, por debajo. *adj* inferior, de abajo.

underpaid [ʌndə'peid] *adj* mal pagado.

underpants ['ʌndəpants] *pl n* calzoncillos *m pl*.

underpass ['ʌndəpaɪs] *n* paso subterráneo *m*.

underprivileged [ʌndə'privilidʒd] *adj* menesteroso.

underrate [ʌndə'reit] *v* subestimar.

underskirt ['ʌndəskəɪt] *n* enaguas *f pl*.

understaffed [ʌndə'staɪft] *adj* falto de personal.

***understand** [ʌndə'stand] *v* entender, comprender; (*believe*) creer. **understandable** *adj* comprensible. **understanding** *n* entendimiento *m*; comprensión *f*; (*reason*) razón *f*; interpretación *f*; (*knowledge*) conocimientos *m pl*; (*agreement*) acuerdo *m*.

understate *v* quitar importancia a. **make an understatement** describir sin énfasis. **that's an understatement!** ¡y usted que lo diga!

understudy ['ʌndəstʌdi] *n* suplente *m, f*. *v* suplir, doblar.

***undertake** [ʌndə'teik] *v* emprender; prometer. **undertaker** *n* empresario de pompas funebres *m*. **undertaking** *n* empresa *f*; compromiso *m*.

undertone ['ʌndətoun] *n* **in an undertone** en voz baja.

underwater [ʌndə'wɔɪtə] *adj* submarino.

underwear ['ʌndəweə] *n* ropa interior *f*.

underweight [ʌndə'weit] *adj* de peso insuficiente.

underworld ['ʌndəwɔɪld] *n* (*criminal*) hampa *f*; (*hell*) infierno *m*.

***underwrite** [ʌndə'rait] *v* (*sign, bonds*) subscribir; (*guarantee*) garantizar; (*insure*) asegurar.

undesirable [ʌndi'zaiərəbl] *adj* no deseable; pernicioso. *n* indeseable *m, f*.

***undo** [ʌn'duɪ] *v* (*open*) abrir; (*knot*) desatar; (*a tie*) desanudar; (*button*) desabrochar; (*parcel*) deshacer; (*zip*) bajar; (*ruin*) arruinar. **undoing** *n* ruina *f*. **come undone** desatarse.

undoubted [ʌn'dautid] *adj* indudable.

undress [ʌn'dres] *v* desnudar(se).

undue [ʌn'djuɪ] *adj* excesivo; impropio. **unduly** *adv* excesivamente; impropiamente.

undulate ['ʌndjuleit] *v* ondular. **undulating** *adj* ondulante. **undulation** *n* ondulación *f*.

unearth [ʌn'ɔːθ] v desenterrar; descubrir.
unearthly adj sobrenatural; misterioso; espantoso. **unearthly hour** (coll) hora intempestiva f.

uneasy [ʌn'iːzi] adj inquieto; molesto; agitado; preocupado.

uneducated [ʌn'edjukeitid] adj ineducado.

unemployed [ʌnem'ploid] adj parado, desempleado. **the unemployed** los parados m pl. **unemployment** n paro m, desempleo m.

unenthusiastic [ʌnenθjuːzi'astik] adj sin entusiasmo.

unequal [ʌn'iːkwəl] adj desigual; (inadequate) inadecuado; (med) irregular.

uneven [ʌn'iːvn] adj accidentado; (unequal) desigual; (number) impar.

uneventful [ʌni'ventfəl] adj sin acontecimientos.

unexpected [ʌneks'pektid] adj inesperado.

unfailing [ʌn'feiliŋ] adj infalible; (inexhaustible) inagotable; (unceasing) constante.

unfair [ʌn'feə] adj injusto. **unfairness** n injusticia f.

unfaithful [ʌn'feiθfəl] adj infiel. **unfaithfulness** n infidelidad f.

unfamiliar [ʌnfə'miljə] adj desconocido; extraño.

unfasten [ʌn'faːsn] v (open) abrir; (dress, button) desabrochar; (knot) desatar; (set free) soltar; (loosen) aflojar.

unfavourable [ʌn'feivərəbl] adj desfavorable, adverso.

unfinished [ʌn'finiʃt] adj inacabado, no terminado.

unfit [ʌn'fit] adj incapaz; no apto; incompetente; impropio; (ill) enfermo, malo.

unfold [ʌn'fould] v desplegar; (plans) revelar; (thoughts) desarrollarse.

unforeseen [ʌnfor'siːn] adj imprevisto.

unforgivable [ʌnfə'givəbl] adj imperdonable.

unfortunate [ʌn'fortʃənət] adj desafortunado; desgraciado.

unfounded [ʌn'faundid] adj infundado, sin fundamento.

unfriendly [ʌn'frendli] adj hostil; desfavorable.

unfurnished [ʌn'fəːniʃd] adj desamueblado.

ungainly [ʌn'geinli] adj desgarbado.

ungrateful [ʌn'greitfəl] adj ingrato.

unhappy [ʌn'hapi] adj infeliz; triste. **unhappiness** n infelicidad f.

unhealthy [ʌn'helθi] adj (person) enfermo; (place) malsano.

unheard-of [ʌn'həːdov] adj inaudito; sin precedente.

unhoped-for [ʌn'houptfoː] adj inesperado.

unhurt [ʌn'həːt] adj indemne, ileso.

unhygienic [ʌnhai'dʒiːnik] adj antihigiénico.

unicorn [juːnikorn] n unicornio m.

unidentified flying object [ʌnai'dentifaid] n also UFO objeto volador no identificado m, OVNI m.

uniform ['juːniform] nm, adj uniforme. **uniformity** n uniformidad f.

unify ['juːnifai] v unificar. **unification** n unificación f.

unilateral [juːni'latərəl] adj unilateral.

unimaginative [ʌni'madʒinətiv] adj poco imaginativo.

unimportant [ʌnim'portnt] adj poco importante.

uninhabited [ʌnin'habitid] adj inhabitado.

uninhibited [ʌnin'hibitid] adj sin inhibición.

unintentional [ʌnin'tenʃənl] adj involuntario.

uninterested [ʌn'intristid] adj indiferente; desinteresado. **uninteresting** adj poco interesante.

union ['juːnjən] n unión f; (trade) sindicato m.

unique [juː'niːk] adj único.

unisex [juːni,seks] adj (coll) unisexo invar.

unison ['juːnisn] n unisonancia. **in unison** al unísono.

unite [juː'nait] v unir; reunir; juntarse. **united** adj unido. **United Kingdom** Reino Unido m. **United Nations** Naciones Unidas f pl. **United States of America** Estados Unidos de América m pl.

unity ['juːniti] m unidad f.

universe ['juːnivəːs] m universo m. **universal** adj universal.

university [juːni'vəːsəti] n universidad f. adj universitario.

unjust [ʌn'dʒʌst] adj injusto.

unkempt [ʌn'kempt] adj descuidado; (hair) despeinado.

unkind [ʌn'kaind] adj poco amable; severo; cruel. **unkindness** n falta de amabilidad f; severidad f; crueldad f.

unknown [ʌn'noun] *n*, *adj* desconocido, -a.

unlawful [ʌn'lɔtfəl] *adj* ilegal; ilegítimo.

unless [ʌn'les] *conj* a no ser que, a menos que.

unlike [ʌn'laik] *adj* diferente, distinto. *prep* a diferencia de.

unlikely [ʌn'laikli] *adj* improbable; (*unexpected*) inverosímil.

unlimited [ʌn'limitid] *adj* ilimitado.

unload [ʌn'loud] *v* descargar; (*get rid of*) deshacerse de.

unlock [ʌn'lɔk] *v* abrir.

unlucky [ʌn'lʌki] *adj* desgraciado; (*day, number, etc.*) funesto.

unmarried [ʌn'marid] *adj* soltero.

unnatural [ʌn'natʃərəl] *adj* antinatural; anormal; artificial.

unnecessary [ʌn'nesəsəri] *adj* innecesario, inútil.

unnerving [ʌn'nərviŋ] *adj* desconcertante.

unnoticed [ʌn'noutist] *adv* inadvertido; desapercibido. **go** *or* **pass unnoticed** pasar desapercibido.

unobtainable [ʌnəb'teinəbl] *adj* que no se puede conseguir.

unobtrusive [ʌnəb'trusiv] *adj* discreto, modesto.

unoccupied [ʌn'ɔkjupaid] *adj* (*at leisure*) desocupado; (*untenanted*) deshabitado; (*seat*) libre.

unofficial [ʌnə'fiʃəl] *adj* no oficial.

unorthodox [ʌn'ɔːθədɔks] *adj* poco ortodoxo.

unpack [ʌn'pak] *v* (*box*) desembalar; (*suitcase*) deshacer.

unpaid [ʌn'peid] *adj* impagado; (*bill*) por pagar; (*worker*) no retribuido.

unpleasant [ʌn'pleznt] *adj* (*weather*) desagradable; (*unfriendly*) antipático; (*annoying*) molesto.

unpopular [ʌn'pɔpjulə] *adj* impopular.

unprecedented [ʌn'presidentid] *adj* sin precedentes.

unpredictable [ʌnprə'diktəbl] *adj* que no se puede prever; (*capricious*) antojadizo.

unqualified [ʌn'kwɔlifaid] *adj* sin título; (*without reservation*) sin reserva.

unravel [ʌn'ravəl] *v* (*wool*) deshacer; (*untangle*) desenredar; (*mystery*) desembrollar.

unreal [ʌn'riəl] *adj* irreal.

unreasonable [ʌn'rizzənəbl] *adj* irrazonable; extravagante; excesivo.

unrelenting [ʌnri'lentiŋ] *adj* implacable.

unreliable [ʌnri'laiəbl] *adj* (*character*) inconstante; (*person*) poco seguro; (*machine*) poco fiable; (*service*) dudoso.

unrest [ʌn'rest] *n* desasosiego *m*, agitación *f*.

unruly [ʌn'ruːli] *adj* ingobernable; rebelde.

unsafe [ʌn'seif] *adj* inseguro; peligroso.

unsatisfactory [ʌnsatis'faktəri] *adj* poco satisfactorio.

unscrew [ʌn'skruː] *v* destornillar.

unscrupulous [ʌn'skruːpjuləs] *adj* poco escrupuloso.

unselfish [ʌn'selfiʃ] *adj* desinteresado; generoso.

unsettle [ʌn'setl] *v* perturbar; (*mentally*) desequilibrar. **unsettled** *adj* perturbado; agitado; desequilibrado; (*weather*) incierto.

unsightly [ʌn'saitli] *adj* feo, repugnante.

unskilled [ʌn'skild] *adj* no cualificado; no especializado. **unskilled worker** obrero no cualificado *m*.

unsound [ʌn'saund] *adj* (*unhealthy*) enfermizo; (*mentally*) demente; (*morally*) corrompido; (*goods*) imperfecto; (*foundations*) poco sólido; (*business*) poco seguro; (*argument*, *opinion*) falso.

unspeakable [ʌn'spiːkəbl] *adj* indecible.

unspecified [ʌn'spesifaid] *adj* no especificado.

unstable [ʌn'steibl] *adj* inestable.

unsteady [ʌn'stedi] *adj* inestable; inconstante.

unstuck [ʌn'stʌk] *adj* **come unstuck** despegarse; (*hopes*, *plans*) fracasar.

unsuccessful [ʌnsək'sesfəl] *adj* sin éxito; (*person*, *attempt*, *etc.*) fracasado; (*candidate*) suspendido. **be unsuccessful** fracasar. **unsuccessfully** *adv* sin éxito; infructuosamente.

unsuitable [ʌn'suːtəbl] *adj* inapropiado; inconveniente; inoportuno.

untangle [ʌn'taŋgl] *v* desenmarañar.

untidy [ʌn'taidi] *adj* desarreglado; (*person*) desordenado. **untidiness** *n* desorden *m*.

untie [ʌn'tai] *v* desatar.

until [ən'til] *prep* hasta. *conj* hasta que.

untoward [ʌntə'wɔːd] *adj* insumiso; adverso; desafortunado.

untrue [ʌn'truː] *adj* falso, mentiroso; imaginario; infiel.

unusual [ʌn'juːʒuəl] adj desacostumbrado; extraño; excepcional.

unwanted [ʌn'wontid] adj no deseado; superfluo.

unwell [ʌn'wel] adj indispuesto, enfermo.

*unwind [ʌn'waind] v desenrollar; (relax) descansar.

unwise [ʌn'waiz] adj imprudente; indiscreto.

unworthy [ʌn'wəːði] adj indigno.

unwrap [ʌn'ræp] v desenvolver; (parcel) deshacer.

up [ʌp] adv arriba; hacia arriba; al aire; en el aire; (louder) más fuerte; (out of bed) levantado; (standing) de pie, en pie. be up to ser capaz de. prep arriba; en; contra; en el fondo de. walk up and down pasearse a lo largo y a lo ancho. ups and downs los altibajos m pl. up-and-coming adj joven y prometedor.

upbringing ['ʌpbriŋiŋ] n educación f.

update [ʌp'deit] v (bring up to date) poner al día; (modernize) modernizar.

upheaval [ʌp'hiːvl] n (geol) levantamiento m; (fig) agitación f.

uphill [ʌp'hil] adj ascendente; (struggle) arduo.

*uphold [ʌp'hould] v sostener; defender; confirmar.

upholster [ʌp'houlstə] v entapizar. upholstery n (material) tapicería f; (filling) relleno m.

upkeep ['ʌpkiːp] n mantenimiento m.

uplift [ʌp'lift] n (geol) elevación f; (fig) inspiración f.

upon [ə'pon] prep sobre, encima de.

upper ['ʌpə] adj alto; superior. upper-class adj de la clase alta. upper hand dominio m. uppermost adj más alto; predominante.

upright ['ʌprait] adj vertical; derecho; (fig) recto. adv en posición vertical.

uprising ['ʌpraiziŋ] n sublevación f.

uproar ['ʌproː] n alboroto m, tumulto m. uproarious adj tumultuoso; ruidoso.

uproot [ʌp'ruːt] v desarraigar; (fig) arrancar.

*upset [ʌp'set; n 'ʌpset] v (knock over) volcar; (spill) derramar; (plans, etc.) trastornar; desconcertar; (displease) enfadar. adj (worried) preocupado; (ill) indispuesto; (nerves) desquiciado; enfadado; (stomach) trastornado. n vuelco m; trastorno m; (illness) malestar m; dificultad f; (trouble) molestia f.

upshot ['ʌpʃot] n resultado m.

upside down [ʌpsai'daun] adv, adj al revés.

upstairs [ʌp'steəz] adv arriba. go upstairs subir. adj de arriba.

upstream [ʌp'striːm] adv río arriba, aguas arriba; (swim) a contracorriente.

up-to-date adj moderno.

upward ['ʌpwəd] adj ascendente. upwards adv hacia arriba.

uranium [ju'reiniəm] n uranio m.

urban ['əːbən] adj urbano.

urchin ['əːtʃin] n pilluelo m.

urge [əːdʒ] v incitar; exhortar; requerir. n vivo deseo m; impulso m.

urgent ['əːdʒənt] adj urgente; insistente. urgency n urgencia f; insistencia f.

urine ['juərin] n orina f. urinate v orinar.

urn [əːn] n urna f.

Uruguay ['juərəgwai] n Uruguay m. Uruguayan n, adj uruguayo, -a.

us [ʌs] pron nos; nosotros.

usage ['juːzidʒ] n (custom) usanza f; (treatment) tratos m pl; (gramm) uso m.

use [juːs; v juːz] n uso m; empleo m; (tool) manejo m. it's no use es inútil. what's the use? ¿para qué? v usar, emplear; consumir; tomar; utilizar. use up agotar. used de segunda mano. be used for servir para. be used to estar acostumbrado a. get used to habituarse a. useful adj útil. useless adj inútil. user n usuario, -a m, f.

usher ['ʌʃə] n (law) ujier m; (theatre) acomodador m. v usher in anunciar; hacer pasar. usherette n acomodadora f.

usual ['juːʒuəl] adj normal; habitual; acostumbrado. as usual como siempre. usually adv normalmente.

usurp [ju'zəːp] v usurpar.

utensil [ju'tensl] n utensilio m.

uterus ['juːtərəs] n útero m.

utility [ju'tiləti] n utilidad f. adj utilitario.

utilize ['juːtilaiz] v utilizar.

utmost ['ʌtmoust] adj mayor; supremo; extremo; más lejano. n máximo m. do one's utmost hacer todo lo posible.

utter¹ ['ʌtə] v decir; (cries) lanzar; (sigh) dar; (sentiments) expresar.

utter² ['ʌtə] adj absoluto; completo.

U-turn ['juːtəːn] n media vuelta f.

V

vacant adj (empty) vacío; deshabitado; (free) libre; (absent-minded) distraído; vago; estúpido. **vacancy** (job) vacante f; (room) habitación libre f. **no vacancies** completo.

vacate v dejar vacío.

vacation n vacaciones f pl.

vaccine n vacuna f. **vaccinate** v vacunar. **vaccination** n vacunación f.

vacillate v vacilar; oscilar. **vacillation** n vacilación f.

vacuum n vacío m. **vacuum cleaner** aspiradora f. **vacuum flask** termo m. v pasar la aspiradora en.

vagina n vagina f.

vagrant n, adj vagabundo, -a. **vagrancy** n vagabundeo m.

vague adj vago, indistinto; incierto.

vain adj vano, inútil; (conceited) vanidoso. **in vain** en vano.

valiant adj valeroso.

valid adj válido. **validity** n validez f.

valley n valle m.

value n valor m; precio m; importancia f. v (appraise) valorar, tasar; estimar; apreciar. **valuable** adj valioso; precioso; costoso. **valuables** pl n objetos de valor m pl. **valuation** n valuación f; estimación f.

valve n válvula f.

vampire n vampiro m.

van n (road) camión m; (removal) carro de mudanzas m; (guard's) furgón de equipajes m; (leading section) vanguardia f.

vandal n vándalo, -a m, f. **vandalism** n vandalismo m. **vandalize** v destrozar.

vanilla n vainilla f.

vanish v desaparecer.

vanity n vanidad f. **vanity case** neceser m.

vapour n vapor m. **vapourize** v vaporizar.

varicose veins pl n varices f pl.

variety n variedad f; diversidad f. **variety show** función de variedades f.

various adj diverso; vario.

varnish n barniz m. v barnizar.

vary v variar; cambiar; modificar. **vary from** diferenciarse de. **variable** nf, adj variable. **variant** nf, adj variante. **variation** n variación f.

vase n vaso m; jarrón m.

vasectomy n vasectomía f.

vast adj vasto. **vastness** n inmensidad f.

vat n tinaja f.

Vatican n Vaticano m. **Vatican City** Ciudad del Vaticano f.

vault[1] n (cellar) sótano m; (arch) bóveda f; (tomb) panteón m; (bank) cámara acorzada f.

vault[2] v saltar. n salto m. **vaulting horse** potro m.

veal n ternera f.

veer v (wind) girar; (ship) virar; (fig) cambiar.

vegetable n (bot) vegetal m; (cookery) verdura f, legumbre f. adj vegetal. **vegetable garden** huerto m, huerta f. **vegetarian** n, adj vegetariano, -a. **vegetation** n vegetación f.

vehement adj vehemente; violento. **vehemence** n vehemencia f; violencia f. **vehemently** adv con vehemencia.

vehicle n vehículo m.

veil n velo m. v velar.

vein n vena f.

velocity n velocidad f.

velvet n terciopelo m. adj de terciopelo. **velvety** adj aterciopelado.

vending machine n distribuidor automático m.

veneer n chapa f; (fig: gloss) barniz m. v chapear.

venerate v venerar. **venerable** adj venerable. **veneration** n veneración f.

venereal disease n enfermedad venérea f.

Venetian blind n persiana veneciana f.

Venezuela [veni'zweilə] n Venezuela f. **Venezuelan** n, adj venezolano, -a.

vengeance n venganza f. **with a vengeance** (coll) de verdad.

venison n venado m.

venom n veneno m. **venomous** adj venenoso.

vent n (hole) agujero m, abertura f; (airhole) respiradero m; (tube) conducto de ventilación m. **give vent to** dar libre curso a. v desahogar.

ventilate v ventilar. **ventilation** n ventilación f.

ventriloquist n ventrílocuo, -a m, f. **ventriloquism** n ventriloquía f.

venture n aventura f, empresa arriesgada f. v aventurar; arriesgar.

venue n lugar de reunión m.

veranda n also **verandah** veranda f. galería f.

verb n verbo. **verbal** adj verbal.

verdict n veredicto m.

verge n margen m, borde m; (lake) orilla f. **on the verge of** (fig) a punto de, a dos dedos de. v **verge on** rayar en.

verify v verificar. **verification** n verificación f.

vermin n (rats, mice, etc.) bichos m pl; (fleas, people) sabandijas f pl. **verminous** adj (lousy) piojoso.

vermouth n vermut m.

vernacular adj vernáculo. n lenguaje vulgar m.

versatile adj de talentos variados; (mind) flexible. **versatility** n diversos talentos m pl; flexibilidad f.

verse n (poetry) poesía f; (stanza) estrofa f; (Bible) versículo m.

version n versión f.

versus prep contra.

vertebra n, pl -brae vértebra f. **vertebral** adj vertebral. **vertebrate** nm, adj vertebrado.

vertical nf, adj vertical.

vertigo n vértigo m.

very adv muy; mucho, mucha. **very much** mucho, muchísimo. adj mismo; propio; (real) verdadero; puro.

vessel n (container) vasija f; (ship) nave f.

vest n camiseta f.

vestibule n vestíbulo m.

vestige n vestigio m, rastro m.

vestry n vestuario m, sacristía f.

vet n (coll) veterinario m. v (coll) corregir, revisar.

veteran nm, adj veterano. **veteran troops** tropas aguerridas f pl.

veterinary surgeon n veterinario m.

veto n veto m. v vetar, poner el veto.

vex v molestar; enfadar. **vexation** n molestia f; disgusto m.

via prep por, por la vía de.

viable adj viable. **viability** n viabilidad f.

viaduct n viaducto m.

vibrate v vibrar. **vibration** n vibración f.

vicar n vicario m; (of a parish) cura m. **vicarage** n casa del cura f.

vicarious adj vicario.

vice[1] n (evil) vicio m; (defect) defecto m.

vice[2] n (tool) tornillo de banco m.

vice-chancellor n rector m.

vice-consul n vicecónsul m.

vice-president n vicepresidente m.

vice versa adv viceversa.

vicinity n vecindad f; (nearness) cercanía f.

vicious adj (of vice) vicioso; (bad) malo; (depraved) pervertido; (taste) corrompido; (life) disoluto; (crime) atroz. **vicious circle** círculo vicioso m. **viciousness** n lo vicioso; maldad f; perversidad f.

victim n víctima f. **victimize** v perseguir; tomar como víctima. **victimization** n persecución f.

victory n victoria f. **victorious** adj victorioso.

video-tape n cinta magnética video f. v grabar programas de televisión.

vie v competir, rivalizar.

Vienna n Viena f.

view n vista f; panorama m; inspección f; idea f. **viewfinder** n visor m. **viewpoint** punto de vista m. v mirar; visitar; considerar. **viewer** n (TV) telespectador, -a m, f; (onlooker) espectador, -a m, f; (for slides) visionadora f.

vigil n vela f, vigilia f. **vigilance** n vigilancia f. **vigilant** adj vigilante.

vigour n vigor m. **vigorous** adj vigoroso.

vile adj vil; horrible.

villa n chalet m; (country house) casa de campo f.

village n aldea f, pueblo m. **villager** n aldeano, -a m, f.

villain n canalla m. **villainy** n villanía f.

vindictive adj vengativo.

vine n vid f; parra f. **vineyard** n viña f.

vinegar n vinagre m.

vintage adj (season) vendimia f; (crop) cosecha f. **vintage wine** vino añejo m.

vinyl n vinilo m.

viola n (music) viola f.

violate v (ravish) violar; (desecrate) profanar; (infringe) contravenir. **violation** n violación f; profanación f; contravención f.

violence n violencia f. **violent** adj violente.

violet n (flower, colour) violeta. adj violado.

violin n violín m. **violinist** n violinista m, f.

viper n víbora f.

virgin nf, adj virgen. **virginity** n virginidad f.

Virgo

218

Virgo n Virgo m.
virile adj viril. **virility** n virilidad f.
virtually adv virtualmente; práctica-
mente.
virtue n virtud f; (advantage) ventaja f.
by virtue of debido a. **virtuous** adj virtuoso.
virus n virus m.
visa n visado m.
viscount n vizconde m. **viscountess** vizcondesa f.
visible adj visible. **visibility** n visibilidad f.
vision n (sight, apparition) visión f;
(capacity to see) vista f; (dream) sueño m.
visionary n, adj visionario, -a m, f.
visit n visita f. v (go to, call on) visitar;
(stay in) pasar una temporada en. **visitor**
n visitante m, f; visita f.
visor n visera f.
visual adj visual. **visualize** v imaginarse.
vital adj vital. **vitality** n vitalidad f. **vitally**
adv vitalmente.
vitamin n vitamina f.
vivacious adj vivo; vivaracho. **vivacious-
ness** n also **vivacity** viveza f, vivacidad f.
vivid adj vivo; (description) gráfico. **vivid-
ness** n (colour) viveza f, intensidad f;
(style) fuerza f.
vivisection n vivisección f.
vixen n zorra f, raposa f.
vocabulary n vocabulario m.
vocal adj vocal; (fig) ruidoso. **vocalist** n
cantante m, f.
vocation n vocación f. **vocational** adj
profesional.
vociferous adj ruidoso.
vodka n vodca m.
voice n voz f. v hablar; expresar.
void n vacío m. adj (empty) vacío; (job)
vacante; (law) nulo.
volatile adj (chem) volátil; (fig) voluble.
volcano n volcán m. **volcanic** adj volcánico.
volley n (bullets) andanada f; (arrows,
stones) lluvia f; (applause) salva f; (sport)
voleo m. v (missile) lanzar; (sport) volear.
volt n voltio m. **voltage** n voltaje m.
volume n (space, sound) volumen m;
(book) tomo m, volumen m. **voluminous**
adj voluminoso; abundante.
volunteer nm, adj voluntario. v ofrecer;
(remark) hacer; (information) dar.
voluptuous adj voluptuoso. **voluptuousness** n voluptuosidad f.
vomit n vómito m. v vomitar.

voodoo n vodú m.
voracious adj voraz. **voraciousness** n also
voracity voracidad f.
vote n voto m; (action) votación f. **vote of
confidence** voto de confianza f. **vote of
thanks** voto de gracias m. v votar; elegir;
proponer; declarar. **voter** n votante m, f;
elector, -a m, f.
vouch v **vouch for** (thing) responder de,
garantizar; (person) responder por.
voucher n (comm) bono m, vale m. **lunch-
eon voucher** vale de comida f.
vow n voto m; promesa solemne f. v
jurar; prometer.
vowel n vocal f.
voyage n viaje m. v viajar (por mar).
vulgar adj común; ordinario; grosero.
vulgarity n vulgaridad f; grosería f.
vulnerable adj vulnerable.
vulture n buitre m.

W

wad n (bung) tapón m; (notes) rollo m;
(cotton wool) bolita f. **wadding** n (cotton
wool) guata f; (filling) relleno m.
waddle v anadear. n anadeo m.
wade v vadear. **wade through** (book, etc.)
estudiar detenidamente.
wafer n (for ices) barquillo m. **wafer-thin**
adj finísimo.
waft v llevar por el aire; flotar. n ráfaga f.
wag v agitar; (tail) menear. n (tail)
coleada f; movimiento m; (joker)
bromista m, f.
wage n salario m, paga f. v **wage war**
hacer guerra.
wager n apuesta f. v apostar.
waggle v menear, agitar. n meneo m.
wagon n carro m; carreta f; (rail) vagón
m.
waif n niño abandonado m.
wail n lamento m, gemido. v lamentarse,
gemir.
waist n cintura f, talle m. **waistband** n
pretina f. **waistcoat** n chaleco m. **waist-
line** n cintura f.
wait n espera f. **lie in wait for** acechar. v
esperar; (at table) atender. **waiter** n mozo
m, camarero m. **waiting** n espera f;
servicio m. **waiting-list** n lista de espera f.

waiting-room n sala de espera f. **waitress** n camarera f.

waive v renunciar a; desitir de.

wake¹ n velatorio m.

*wake² v also wake up despertar(se).

Wales n el País de Gales.

walk n paseo m; camino m; (gait) andar m; (pace) paso m. v (go on foot) recorrer a pie; (distance) hacer a pie; (take out) pasear; (escort) acompañar. **walkout** n huelga f. **walkover** n victoria fácil f. **walker** n paseante m, f. **walking** n andar m. **walking-stick** n bastón m.

wall n pared f; muro m. v murar; amurallar.

wallet n cartera f.

wallflower n alhelí m. **be a wallflower** quedarse en el poyete.

wallop (coll) n golpazo m, trompazo m. v zurrar. **walloping** n paliza f.

wallow v revolcarse.

wallpaper n papel pintado m. v empapelar.

walnut n (nut) nuez f; (tree, wood) nogal m.

walrus n morsa f.

waltz n vals m. v valsar.

wan adj macilento.

wand n (magic) varita f; vara f.

wander v vagar por; (stroll) pasearse; (mentally) desvariar.

wane v (moon) menguar; (fig) decaer.

wangle v conseguir con trampas. (coll) n trampa f.

want n (lack) falta f; (need) necesidad f; (poverty) miseria f; (wish) deseo m; (gap) vacío m. **for want of** por falta de. v querer; desear; necesitar; (ask) pedir; (look for) buscar. **wanted** adj buscado (por la policía). **wanting** adj (absent) ausente; (lacking) deficiente.

wanton adj lascivo; (promiscuous) libertino; (senseless) sin sentido. **wantonness** n libertinaje f; crueldad f; exuberancia f; (lack of moderation) desenfreno m.

war n guerra f. **be on the warpath** (coll) estar buscando guerra. **warfare** n guerra f. **warhead** n cabeza de guerra f. **war memorial** monumento a los Caídos m. **War Office** Ministerio de la Guerra m. **warship** n buque de guerra m. **wartime** n tiempo de guerra m.

warble v gorjear, trinar. n gorjeo m, trino m.

ward n (hospital) sala f; (pol) distrito electoral m; (law: guardianship) custodia f; (minor) pupilo m. v **ward off** evitar.

warden n guarda m; vigilante m; director m.

warder n carcelero m; guardián m.

wardrobe n guardarropa m; (theatre) vestuario m.

warehouse n almacén m. v almacenar.

warm adj tibio; caliente; (climate) cálido; (fire) acogedor; (welcome) caluroso; (kind) cariñoso. v calentar; acalorar. **warm up** calentar; (reheat) recalentar. **warming-pan** n calentador de cama m. **warmth** n calor m; cordialidad f.

warn v advertir; aconsejar; (rebuke) amonestar. **warning** n advertencia f, aviso m; alarma f; ejemplo m; amonestación f. **warning light** lámpara indicadora f.

warp v (wood) alabear; (yarn) urdir; (fig) deformar. n alabeo m; urdimbre f; deformación f.

warrant n (police) orden f; (law) autorización legal f; justificación f; garantía f. v autorizar; justificar; garantizar. **warranty** n garantía f.

warren n (rabbit) conejal m; (fig) colmena f.

warrior n guerrero m.

Warsaw [ˈwɔːsɔː] n Varsovia.

wart [wɔːt] n verruga f.

wary [ˈwɛəri] adj cauto, precavido.

was [wɔz] V be.

wash [wɔʃ] v lavar; (dishes) fregar. **wash away** quitar. **wash down** (swallow) tragar. **wash up** fregar. **washable** adj lavable. **wash-and-wear** adj de lava y pon. **washbasin** n lavabo m. **washboard** n tabla de lavar f. **washer** n arandela f. **washing** n lavado m; colada f; fregado m. **washing machine** lavadora f. **washing powder** jabón en polvo m. **washing-up bowl** barreño m. **washout** n (slang) desastre m.

wasp [wɔsp] n avispa f.

waste [weist] n pérdida f; (food) desperdicios m pl; (rubbish) basura f. **waste disposal unit** vertedero de basuras m. **waste land** yermo m; erial m. **waste paper** papel usado m. **waste-paper basket** papelera f. v malgastar, despilfarrar; perder; (use up) consumir; (by disuse) desperdiciar. **waste away** consumirse. **wasteful** adj (person) despilfarrador, -a *m, f;* ruinoso. **waster** *n also* **wastrel** derrochador, -a *m, f.*

watch [wotʃ] *n* (*wrist*) reloj de la pulsera *m;* (*pocket*) reloj de bolsillo *m;* (*naut*) guardia *f;* vigilancia *f.* **keep watch** estar de guardia. **watch chain** cadena de reloj *f.* **watchdog** *n* perro guardián *m.* **watchmaker** *n* relojero *m.* **watchman** *n* vigilante *m.* **watch spring** muelle *m.* **watch strap** correa de reloj *f.* **watchword** *n* consigna *f. v* mirar, ver, observar; (*pay attention to*) fijarse en; (*keep an eye on*) vigilar. **watchful** *adj* atento; vigilante.

water ['wɔːtə] *n* agua *f. v* (*wet*) humedecer; (*soak*) mojar; (*plants*) regar; (*eyes*) llorar. **water down** moderar. **watery** *adj* acuoso; aguado, insípido.

water-biscuit *n* galleta de harina y agua *f.*

water-closet *n* retrete *m,* wáter *m.*

water-colour *n* acuarela *f.*

watercress ['wɔːtəkres] *n* berro *m.*

waterfall ['wɔːtəfɔːl] *n* cascada *f;* catarata *f.*

water-ice *n* sorbete *m.*

watering-can *n* regadera *f.*

water lily *n* nenúfar *m.*

waterline ['wɔːtəlain] *n* línea de flotación *f.*

waterlogged ['wɔːtəlogd] *adj* (*wood*) empapado; (*med*) inundado.

water main *n* cañería principal *f.*

watermark ['wɔːtəmaːk] *n* filigrana *f;* (*tide*) marca del nivel de agua *f.*

watermelon ['wɔːtəmelən] *n* sandía *f.*

waterproof ['wɔːtəpruːf] *nm, adj* impermeable. *v* impermeabilizar.

watershed ['wɔːtəʃed] *n* (*fig*) momento decisivo *m;* (*geog*) línea divisoria de las aguas *f.*

water-ski *v* hacer esquí acuático. **water-skiing** *n* esquí acuático *m.*

water softener *n* ablandador del agua *m.*

watertight ['wɔːtətait] *adj* estanco; hermético; (*fig*) perfecto.

waterway ['wɔːtəwei] *n* vía navegable *f.*

waterworks ['wɔːtəwəːks] *n* sistema de abastecimiento de agua *m.*

watt [wot] *n* vatio *m.*

wave [weiv] *n* (*sea*) ola *f;* (*hair*) ondulación *f;* (*physics, radio, etc.*) onda *f;* (*hand*) señal *f.* **permanent wave** permanente *f.* **waveband** *n* banda de ondas *f.* **wavelength** *n* longitud de onda *f. v* agitar; (*hair*) ondular. **wavy** *adj* ondulado.

waver ['weivə] *v* vacilar; (*falter*) flaquear; (*totter*) titubear. **wavering** *adj* vacilante; tembloroso.

wax[1] [waks] *n* cera *f.* **waxwork** *n* figura de cera *f.* **waxworks** *n* museo de figuras de cera. *m. v* encerar. **waxy** *adj* ceroso.

wax[2] [waks] *v* crecer.

way [wei] *n* camino *m;* paso *m;* ruta *f;* senda *f;* dirección *f;* rumbo *m;* distancia *f;* (*journey*) viaje *m;* progreso *m;* modo *m,* manera *f;* (*means*) medio *m.* **be in the way** estar de por medio. **by the way** a propósito. **give way** ceder. **on the way** en camino. **this way** por aquí. **under way** en marcha; en preparación. **way in** entrada *f.* **way out** salida *f.*

*****waylay** [wei'lei] *v* abordar.

wayside ['weisaid] *n* borde del camino *m. adj* al borde del camino.

wayward ['weiwəd] *adj* voluntarioso; díscolo.

we [wiː] *pron* nosotros, -as.

weak [wiːk] *adj* débil; flaco; flojo. **weaken** *v* debilitar. **weakling** *n* persona débil *f;* cobarde *m.* **weakness** *n* debilidad *f;* (*point*) punto flaco *m.*

wealth [welθ] *n* riqueza *f;* abundancia *f.* **wealthy** *adj* rico.

wean [wiːn] *v* (*baby*) destetar. **wean from** apartar de.

weapon ['wepən] *n* arma *f.*

*****wear** [weə] *n* llevar; poner; gastar. **wear off** pasar(se). **wear out** usarse, consumirse. *n* uso *m;* gasto *m;* deterioro *m.* **wear and tear** desgaste *m.*

weary ['wiəri] *adj* fatigado, cansado, aburrido. *v* fatigar, causar; aburrir. **wearily** *adv* cansadamente. **weariness** *n* fatiga *f.*

weasel ['wiːzl] *n* comadreja *f.*

weather ['weðə] *n* tiempo *m.* **weatherbeaten** *adj* curtido. **weather chart** mapa meteorológico *m.* **weathercock** *n* veleta *f.* **weather forecast** boletín meteorológico *m. v* (*survive*) superar.

*****weave** [wiːv] *v* tejer; entrelazar; (*through traffic, etc.*) zigzaguear.

web [web] *n* (*spider*) tela de araña *f;* (*fabric*) tejido *m;* (*on feet*) membrana *f;* (*network*) red *f;* (*fig*) sarta *f.* **web-footed** *adj* palmípedo.

wed [wed] *v* casarse con; casar. **wedding** *n* boda *f,* casamiento *m.* **wedding dress** traje de novia *m.* **wedding ring** alianza *f.*

wedge [wedʒ] *n* cuña *f*; calzo *m*. *v* encajar; (*jam*) apretar.

Wednesday ['wenzdi] *n* miércoles *m*.

weed [wiːd] *n* mala hierba *f*. **weed-killer** *n* herbicida *m*. *v* desherbar. **weeding** *n* escarda *f*.

week [wiːk] *n* semana *f*. **a week today/tomorrow** hoy/mañana en ocho. **weekday** *n* día de trabajo *m*. **weekend** *n* fin de semana *m*. **weekly** *adv* semanal. **weekly** *n* semanario *m*.

*****weep** [wiːp] *v* llorar, lamentar. **weeping willow** sauce llorón *m*.

weigh [wei] *v* pesar. **weigh down** doblar bajo un peso. **weigh** *n* peso *m*. **pull one's weight** poner de su parte. **weightlifting** *n* halterofilia *f*. **weightlessness** *n* ingravidez *f*.

weird [wiəd] *adj* extraño; misterioso; fantástico. **weirdness** *n* misterio *m*; lo sobrenatural.

welcome ['welkəm] *adj* bienvenido; grato. **be welcome** ser oportuno. **you're welcome!** ¡eres el bienvenido!; (*after thanks*) ¡no hay de qué! *n* bienvenida *f*. *v* dar la bienvenida a; recibir; alegrarse por.

weld [weld] *v* soldar. **welder** *n* soldador *m*. **welding** *n* soldadura *f*.

welfare ['welfeə] *n* bienestar *m*, bien *m*. **welfare state** estado benefactor *m*.

well¹ [wel] *n* pozo *m*. **well up** brotar.

well² [wel] *adj*, *adv* bien. **as well** también. **well-advised** *adj* juicioso.

well-behaved *adj* bien educado.

well-being *n* bienestar *m*.

well-born *adj* de buena familia.

well-bred *adj* (*person*) bien educado; (*animal*) de raza pura.

well-built *adj* bien hecho.

well-dressed *adj* bien vestido.

well-informed *adj* muy documentado.

wellington ['welintən] *n* bota de agua *f*.

well-kept *adj* (*secret*) bien guardado; (*garden*) bien cuidado.

well-known *adj* bien conocido.

well-made *adj* bien hecho.

well-off *adj* rico.

well-paid *adj* bien pagado.

well-read *adj* leído.

well-spent *adj* (*time*) bien empleado.

well-spoken *adj* bienhablado.

well-timed *adj* oportuno.

well-to-do *adj* rico.

well-trodden *adj* trillado.

well-worn *adj* gastado.

Welsh [welʃ] *adj* galés. *n* (*language*) galés *m*; (*person*) galés, -esa *m*, *f*.

went [went] *V* go.

wept [wept] *V* weep.

were [wəː] *V* be.

west [west] *n* oeste *m*. **the West** el Mundo Occidental *m*. *adj* also **westerly** del oeste, occidental. *adv* al oeste, hacia el oeste. **westbound** *adj* con rumbo al oeste. **western** *adj* occidental, del oeste. *n* (*film*) western *m*.

wet [wet] *adj* mojado; húmedo; (*weather*) lluvioso; (*paint*) fresco. **wet blanket** aguafiestas *m*, *f invar*. **wet suit** traje de buzo *m*. *n* lluvia *f*. *v* mojar; humedecer.

whack [wak] *n* golpe *m*. *v* golpear, pegar.

whale [weil] *n* ballena *f*.

wharf [woːf] *n* muelle *m*.

what [wot] *pron* lo que; (*interrog*, *interj*) qué, cuál, cómo, cuánto. *adj* el que, la que, lo que; qué.

whatever [wot'evə] *pron* todo lo que; lo que; cualquier cosa que. *adj* cualquiera. **nothing/whatever** nada en absoluto.

wheat [wiːt] *n* trigo *m*.

wheel [wiːl] *n* rueda *f*; (*steering*) volante *m*. **wheelbarrow** *n* carretilla *f*. **wheelchair** *n* sillón de ruedas *m*. *v* hacer rodar; empujar; dar una vuelta.

wheeze [wiːz] *n* respiración dificultosa *f*. *v* respirar con dificultad. **wheezy** *adj* asmático.

whelk [welk] *n* buccino *m*.

when [wen] *adv* cuándo, a qué hora. *conj* cuando; en que; (*as soon as*) en cuanto. **whenever** *conj* cuando; cada vez que.

where [weə] *interrog adv* dónde; adónde; de dónde; por dónde; (*in what respect*) en qué. *relative adv* donde; en donde, en que, en el cual, la cual; adonde, a donde, al que, al cual, a la cual. *conj* donde. **whereabouts** *adv* dónde, por dónde; *n* paradero *m*. **whereas** *conj* mientras, en tanto que. **whereupon** *adv* después de lo cual. **wherever** *conj* dondequiera que; a dondequiera que.

whether ['weðə] *conj* si.

which [witʃ] *interrog pron* cuál; qué. **relative pron** que; el cual, la cual, el que, la que; lo cual, lo que. *adj* qué; cuál; cuyo; cómo. **of which** del que, de la que; del cual; de la cual. **whichever** *pron* el que, la que; cualquiera que; *adj* cualquier.

whiff [wif] *n* soplo *m*; olorcillo *m*.

while [wail] *conj* mientras; *(although)* aunque. *n* rato *m*, tiempo *m*. **while away** pasar.

whim [wim] *n* capricho *m*.

whimper ['wimpə] *n* quejido *m*, gemido *m*. *v* quejarse, gemir.

whimsical ['wimzikl] *adj* caprichoso; fantástico.

whine [wain] *n (animal)* gañido *m*; *(complaint)* queja *f*; *(pain)* quejido *m*; *(engine)* zumbido *m*. *v* gañir; quejarse; zumbar.

whip [wip] *n* azote *m*; *(riding)* látigo *m*. **whiplash** *n* latigazo *m*. **whip-round** *n (coll)* colecta *f*. *v* azotar; *(cookery)* batir. **whip up** avivar. **whipping** *n* azotamiento *m*.

whippet ['wipit] *n* lebrel *m*.

whirl [wəːl] *n* vuelta *f*, giro *m*; *(fig)* torbellino *m*. *v* dar vueltas, girar. **whirlpool** *n* remolino *m*.

whirr [wəː] *n (wings)* batir *m*; *(engine)* zumbido *m*. *v* girar; zumbar.

whisk [wisk] *n (cookery)* batidor. *v* batir.

whisker ['wiskə] *n* pelo del bigote *m*. **whiskers** *pl n* bigotes *m pl*.

whisky ['wiski] *n* whisky *m*.

whisper ['wispə] *n* cuchicheo *m*. *v* cuchichear.

whistle [wisl] *n* pito *m*; *(sound)* silbido *m*; pitido *m*. *v* silbar.

white [wait] *adj* blanco. **white elephant** *(fig)* objeto costoso e inútil *m*. *n* blanco *m*; *(person)* blanco, -a *m*, *f*. **whiten** *v* blanquear. **whiteness** *n* blancura *f*.

whitewash ['waitwoʃ] *n* cal *f*. *v* encalar; *(fig: cover up)* encubrir.

whiting ['waitiŋ] *n* pescadilla *f*.

whittle ['witl] *v* tallar. **whittle down** reducir poco a poco.

whizz [wiz] *n* zumbido *m*. **whizz-kid** *n (coll)* promesa *f*. **whizz past** pasar como un rayo.

who [huː] *relative pron* quien, el quel la que; que, el cual, la cual; que, a quien. *interrog pron* quién. **whoever** *pron* quienquiera que, cualquiera que, el que, la que, quien.

whole [houl] *adj* todo, completo, entero, total; íntegro, intacto. *n* todo *m*, total *m*, totalidad *f*. **on the whole** en general. **wholehearted** *adj* sin reservas. **wholeheartedly** *adv* incondicionalmente. **wholemeal** *adj* integral. **wholesome** *adj* saludable.

wholesale ['houlseil] *n* venta al por mayor *f*. *adj*, *adv* al por mayor; en masa.

whom [huːm] *relative pron* que, quien, a quien. *interrog pron* quién, a quién. **of whom** del cual, de la cual, de quien.

whooping cough ['huːpiŋ] *n* tos ferina *f*.

whore [hoː] *n (derog)* puta *f*.

whose [huːz] *relative pron* cuyo, cuya. *interrog pron* de quién.

why [wai] *adv (interrog)* por qué; *(on account of which)* por el cual, por la cual, por lo cual. *interj* ¡vaya! ¡toma! ¡pues bien!

wick [wik] *n* mecha *f*.

wicked ['wikid] *adj* malo, perverso, malicioso. **wickedness** *n* maldad *f*, perversidad *f*.

wicker ['wikə] *n* mimbre *m*. **wickerwork** *n* cestería *f*.

wicket ['wikit] *n (cricket)* palos *m pl*.

wide [waid] *adj* ancho; vasto; grande. *adv* lejos; mucho. **wide awake** completamente despierto. **widespread** *adj* general. **widely** *adv* muy; mucho; generalmente.

widow ['widou] *n* viuda *f*. **be widowed** quedar viuda. **widower** *n* viudo *m*.

width [widθ] *n* anchura *f*.

wield [wiːld] *v (tool)* manejar; *(weapon)* blandir; *(power)* ejercer.

wife [waif] *n* mujer *f*, esposa *f*.

wig [wig] *n* peluca *f*.

wiggle ['wigl] *v* menear. *n* meneo *m*. **wiggly** *adj (line)* ondulante.

wild [waild] *adj (animal, person)* salvaje; *(plant)* silvestre; *(bull)* bravo; *(character)* violento. **like wildfire** como un reguero de pólvora. **wildlife** *n* fauna *f*. **wildly** *adv* violentamente; locamente; frenéticamente; disolutamente.

wilderness ['wildənəs] *n* desierto *m*; soledad *f*.

wilful ['wilfəl] *adj (stubborn)* obstinado; *(headstrong)* voluntarioso; deliberado.

will¹ [wil] *aux translated by future tense.*

will² [wil] *n* voluntad *f*; testamento *m*. *v* disponer; desear; *(bequeath)* legar. **against one's will** de mal grado. **willpower** *n* fuerza de voluntad *f*. **willing** *adj* de buena voluntad; *(obliging)* complaciente. **be willing to** estar dispuesto a. **willingly** *adv* de buena gana. **willingness** *n* buena voluntad *f*.

willow ['wilou] *n* sauce *m*. **willowy** *adj* esbelto.

wilt [wilt] v marchitar(se); (*person*) languidecer.

wily ['waili] adj astuto, chuzón.

*win [win] n victoria f; (*amount won*) ganancia f. v ganar; conquistar; triunfar. **winner** n ganador, -a m, f; vencedor, -a m, f. **winning** adj ganador; (*smile, etc.*) encantador. **winnings** pl n ganancias f pl.

wince [wins] v hacer muecas. n mueca de dolar f.

winch [wintʃ] n torno m. v guindar.

wind¹ [wind] n viento m; (*breath*) aliento m; respiración f; (*med*) gases m pl. v dejar sin aliento. **windy** adj (*place*) expuesto al viento; (*day, night*) ventoso.

*wind² [waind] v devanar; envolver; enrollar; (*bend*) torcer; (*road*) serpentear; (*watch*) dar cuerda a. **wind up** terminar; (*comm*) liquidar. **winding** adj sinuoso; tortuoso.

wind-break n protección contra el viento f.

windfall ['windfoil] n fruta caída f; (*fig*) ganancia inesperada f.

wind instrument n instrumento de viento m.

windlass ['windləs] n torno m.

windmill ['wind,mil] n molino de viento m.

window ['windou] n ventana f; (*car*) ventanilla f; (*cashier's*) taquilla f; (*shop*) escaparate m. **window blind** persiana f. **window-box** n jardinera f. **window cleaner** n limpiacristales m invar. **window-sill** n antepecho m. **window-shopping** n contemplación de escaparates f.

windpipe ['windpaip] n tráquea f.

windproof ['windpruif] adj a prueba de viento.

windshield ['windʃiild] n parabrisas m invar. **windshield wiper** limpiaparabrisas m invar.

wind-sock n manga de aire f.

windswept ['windswept] adj (*hair*) despeinado.

wind tunnel n túnel aerodinámico m.

wine [wain] n vino m. **wineglass** n copa f. **wine list** lista de vinos f. **wine-taster** n catavinos m invar. **wine waiter** bodeguero m.

wing [wiŋ] n ala f. **wing chair** sillón de orejas m. **wing commander** teniente coronel m. **wing-mirror** n retrovisor m. **wing nut** palometa f. **wings** pl n (*theatre*) bastidores m pl. **wingspan** n envergadura f.

wink [wiŋk] n guiño m; (*light*) parpadeo m. v guiñar; (*light*) parpadear.

winkle ['wiŋkl] n bígaro m. **winkle out** sacar con dificultad.

winter ['wintə] n invierno m. v invernar. **wintry** adj de invierno; (*fig*) frío.

wipe [waip] v limpiar; (*mop*) enjugar; (*dry*) secar. **wipe out** destruir. n limpieza f.

wire [waiə] n alambre m; (*elec*) cordón m, cable m; hilo m; (*piano*) cuerda f; telegrama m. **barbed wire** alambrada f. **wire-brush** n cepillo metálico m. **wire-cutters** pl n cortalambres m invar. **wireless** n radio f. v telegrafiar; (*a house*) poner la instalación eléctrica de. **wiry** adj (*hair*) tieso; (*person*) enjuto y fuerte.

wise [waiz] adj sabio; juicioso; (*informed*) enterado. **wisdom** n sabiduría f; juicio m. **wisdom tooth** muela del juicio f.

wish [wiʃ] v querer; desear; gustar. n deseo m. **wishbone** n espoleta f. **wishful** adj deseroso. **wishful thinking** ilusiones f pl.

wisp [wisp] n (*straw*) manojo m; (*hair*) mechón m; (*smoke*) voluta f; (*trace*) vestigio m. **wispy** adj fino.

wistful ['wistfəl] adj triste; ansioso; pensativo. **wistfully** adv tristemente; con ansia.

wit [wit] n inteligencia f; agudeza f; (*humour*) gracia f; (*person*) persona aguda f. **be at one's wits' end** no saber qué hacer.

witch [witʃ] n bruja f. **witchcraft** n brujería f. **witch-doctor** n hechicero m. **witch-hunt** n persecución f.

with [wið] prep con; junto con; en manos de; más; en compañía de; (*because of*) de.

*withdraw [wiðdroi] v quitar; apartar; retirar; sacar. **withdrawal** n retirada f; (*bank*) salida f; renuncia f; retractación f; abandono m. **withdrawn** adj ensimismado.

wither ['wiðə] v (*plant*) marchitar(se); (*weaken*) debilitar. **withered** adj marchito; seco. **withering** adj (*look*) fulminante; (*remark*) mordaz.

*withhold [wiðhould] v (*refuse*) negar; (*hold back*) retener; (*hide*) ocultar.

within [wiðin] adv dentro; (*at home*) en casa. prep dentro de; en; al alcance de; (*less than*) a menos de.

without [wi'ðaut] *prep* sin; (*outside*) fuera de. *adv* fuera.

*****withstand** [wið'stand] *v* resistir, aguantar; oponerse a.

witness ['witnis] *n* (*person*) testigo *m*; (*evidence*) prueba *f*; (*testimony*) testimonio *m*. *v* (*be present at*) asistir a; (*document*) firmar como testigo. **witness to** atestiguar.

witty ['witi] *adj* salado, gracioso. **witticism** *n* rasgo de ingenio m, agudeza *f*.

wizard ['wizəd] *n* mago *m*.

wobble ['wobl] *v* tambalearse. *n* tambaleo *m*. **wobbly** *adj* tambaleante.

woke [wouk] *V* **wake.**

wolf [wulf] *n* lobo *m*. **wolfhound** *n* perro lobo *m*. **wolf-whistle** *n* silbido de admiración *m*. *v* **wolf down** (*coll*) zamparse.

woman ['wumən] *n, pl* **women** mujer *f*. **Women's Lib** (*coll*) Movimiento de la Liberación de la Mujer *m*. **womanhood** *n* mujeres *f pl*; femeneidad *f*. **womanly** *adj* femenino.

womb [wuum] *n* matriz *f*, útero *m*.

won [wʌn] *V* **win.**

wonder ['wʌndə] *n* maravilla *f*, milagro *m*; admiración *f*. **no wonder** no es de extrañar. *v* preguntarse; pensar; asombrarse. **wonderful** *adj* maravilloso; (*astonishing*) asombroso.

woo [wuu] *v* cortejar; (*fig*) solicitar. **wooing** *nm, adj* galanteo.

wood [wud] *n* (*forest*) bosque *m*; (*material*) madera *f*; (*stick*) palo *m*; (*firewood*) leña *f*. **wooden** *adj* de madera; (*stiff*) estirado. **woody** *adj* arbolado; (*stem*) leñoso.

woodcock ['wudkok] *n* chocha *f*, becada *f*.

woodcut ['wudkʌt] *n* grabado en madera *m*. **woodcutter** *n* (*forester*) leñador *m*.

woodland ['wudlənd] *n* bosque *m*.

woodpecker ['wudpekə] *n* pájaro carpintero *m*.

wood-pigeon *n* paloma torcaz *f*.

woodshed ['wudʃed] *n* leñera *f*.

woodwind ['wudwind] *n* (*music*) instrumentos de viento de madera *m pl*.

woodwork ['wudwəːk] *n* carpintería *f*.

woodworm ['wudwəːm] *n* carcoma *f*.

wool [wul] *n* lana *f*. **woollen** *adj* de lana. **woolly** *adj* lanoso; de lana; (*ideas*) borroso.

word [wəːd] *n* palabra *f*; (*gramm*) vocablo *m*. **in other words** en otras palabras; es

decir. *v* expresar; redactar. **wording** *n* redacción *f*; términos *m pl*. **wordy** *adj* verboso.

wore [woː] *V* **wear.**

work [wəːk] *n* trabajo *m*, obra *f*. **men at work** obras *f pl*. **out of work** parado. *a. v* trabajar. **work out** resolver. **workable** *adj* (*plan*) realizable.

worker ['wəːkə] *n* trabajador, -a *m, f*; obrero, -a *m, f*.

work-force *n* mano de obra *f*.

working ['wəːkiŋ] *n* trabajo *m*; funcionamiento *m*; manejo *m*; cultivo *m*. **working-class** *adj* de la clase obrera. **workings** *pl n* excavaciones *f pl*.

workman ['wəːkmən] *n* trabajador *m*; obrero *m*. **workmanship** *n* (*skill*) artesanía *f*; ejecución *f*.

work permit *n* permiso de trabajo *m*.

workshop ['wəːkʃop] *n* taller *m*.

work-to-rule *n* trabajo a ritmo lento *m*.

world [wəːld] *n* mundo *m*. **world-wide** *adj* mundial. **worldly** *adj* mundano; material.

worm [wəːm] *n* guzano *m*; (*earthworm*) lombriz *f*.

worn [woːn] *V* **wear.**

worry ['wʌri] *n* preocupación *f*. *v* preocupar(se); molestar. **don't worry!** ¡no te ocupes! **worried** *adj* preocupado.

worse [wəːs] *adj, adv* peor. **get worse** *or* **worsen** empeorar. **to make matters worse** para empeorar las cosas. *n* lo peor.

worship ['wəːʃip] *n* culto *m*; (*fig*) adoración *f*. *v* venerar; (*fig*) adorar.

worst [wəːst] *adj, adv* peor. el peor *m*, la peor *f*, lo peor. **at worst** en el peor de los casos.

worsted ['wustid] *n* estambre *m*.

worth [wəːθ] *n* valor *m*; mérito *m*; valía *f*; fortuna *f*. **be worth** valer. **be worth it** merecer la pena. **worthless** *adj* sin valor; inútil. **worthwhile** *adj* que vale la pena; útil.

would [wud] *aux translated by conditional or imperfect tense.*

wound[1] [waund] *V* **wind**[2].

wound[2] [wuːnd] *n* herida *f*. *v* herir.

wove [wouv] *V* **weave.**

wrangle ['raŋgl] *n* disputa *f*. *v* discutir.

wrap [rap] *v* envolver; cubrir. **wrap up** abrigarse. *n* (*shawl*) chal *m*. **wrapper** *n* envoltura *f*; (*book*) sobrecubierta *f*. **wrapping** *n* envoltura *f*. **wrapping-paper** *n* papel de envolver *m*.

wreath [riːθ] n guirnalda f; (funeral) corona f. **wreathe** v enguirnaldar; (wind) enroscar.

wreck [rek] n (ship) naufragio m; (train, car, plane) restos m pl; (accident) accidente m; (person) ruina f. v (ship) hundir; (building) destruir; destrozar; (hopes) estropear. **wreckage** n restos m pl; (building) escombros m pl.

wren [ren] n reyezuelo m.

wrench [rentʃ] n (tool) llave inglesa f; (pull) tirón m; (emotional) dolor m. v arrancar; (med) torcer.

wrestle ['resl] v luchar con or contra. **wrestler** n luchador, -a m, f. **wrestling** n lucha f.

wretch [retʃ] n desgraciado, -a m, f; miserable m, f. **wretched** adj desgraciado; (weather) miserable; horrible.

wriggle ['rigl] v menear; agitar; (fish) colear. n meneo m; serpenteo m.

***wring** [riŋ] v retorcer. **wringer** n escurridor m. **wringing wet** chorreando.

wrinkle ['riŋkl] n arruga f. v arrugar.

wrist [rist] n muñeca f.

writ [rit] n (law) orden f, mandato m. **issue a writ against someone** demandar a alguien en juicio.

***write** [rait] v escribir; redactar. **writer** n escritor, -a m, f; autor, -a m, f. **writing** n el escribir m; (handwriting) escritura f; (something written) escrito m. **in writing** por escrito. **writing-pad** n bloc de papel de escribir m. **writing-paper** n papel de escribir m.

writhe [raið] v retorcerse; angustiarse.

wrong [roŋ] adj malo; mal; (incorrect) equivocado; impropio; falso; erróneo. **be wrong** tener la culpa; (mistaken) estar equivocado. adv mal. n mal m; error m; daño m; injusticia f. **wrongful** adj injusto; ilegal.

wrote [rout] V **write**.

wrought iron [ˌrottˈaiən] n hierro forjado m.

wry [rai] adj torcido; doblado; (smile) forzado.

X

xenophobia n xenofobia f. **xenophobic** adj xenófobo.

Xerox ® n (machine) Xérox ® m, fotocopiadora f; (copy) xerografía f. v fotocopiar.

Xmas V **Christmas**.

X-ray n (photo) radiografía f. **X-rays** pl n rayos X m pl. v radiografiar.

xylophone n xilófono m.

Y

yacht n yate m. **yachting** n navegación a vela f.

yank n tirón m. v dar un tirón.

yap n ladrido m. v ladrar.

yard n patio m; (site) depósito m; (repair) taller m; (rail) estación f.

yarn n hilo m; (tale) cuento m.

yawn v bostezar; (hole) abrirse. n bostezo m.

year n año m. **yearbook** n anuario m. **yearly** adj anual.

yearn v anhelar, ansiar. **yearning** n anhelo m, ansia f.

yeast n levadura f; (fig) fermento m.

yell n grito m. v gritar.

yellow nm, adj amarillo. v volver amarillo.

yelp n gañido m. v gañir.

yes nm, adv sí.

yesterday nm, adv ayer. **the day before yesterday** anteayer.

yet adv todavía, aún; (already) ya. conj sin embargo, no obstante; (but) pero.

yew n tejo m.

yield v producir; entregar; dar; ceder; (interest) devengar. n producción f; (crop) cosecha f; (interest) rédito m.

yodel n canción tirolesa f. v cantar a la tirolesa.

yoga n yoga m.

yoghurt n yogur m.

yoke n (animals) yugo m; (oxen) yunta f; (dress) canesú m. v uncir. **yoke together** trabajar juntos.

yolk n yema f.

yonder adv allá, a lo lejos.

you pron (subject: fam) tú sing; (subject: fam) vosotros, vosotras pl; (after prep) ti; (direct and indirect object) te sing; (direct and indirect object) os pl; (subject and after prep: polite) usted, ustedes; (direct object) le, la; (indirect object) le; (indirect object with direct object pron) se sing, pl.

young adj joven. pl n (people) los jóvenes m pl; (of an animal) cría f sing. **youngster** n joven m, f.

your adj (fam) tu sing, vuestro pl; (polite) su, sus, de usted, de ustedes. **yours** pron (fam) el tuyo, la tuya, los tuyos, las tuyas, el vuestro, la vuestra, los vuestros, las vuestras; (polite) el suyo, la suya, el de usted, la de usted.

yourself pron (fam) tú mismo m, tú misma f; (after prep) ti m, f; (polite) usted mismo m, usted misma f. **by yourself** tú solo, usted solo. **yourselves** pl pron (fam) vosotros mismos m pl; vosotras mismas f pl; (polite) ustedes mismos m pl, ustedes mismas f pl.

youth n juventud f; (boy) joven m. **youth hostel** albergue de juventud m.

Yugoslavia [juːgə'slɑːviə] n Yugoslavia f.

Yugoslav n, adj yugoslavo, -a. **Yugoslavian** n, adj yugoslavo, -a.

Z

zany adj (coll) estrafalario.

zeal n celo m. **zealous** adj celoso.

zebra n cebra f. **zebra crossing** paso de peatones m.

zero n cero m. **zero hour** hora H f, momento decisivo m.

zest n ánimo m; brío m; sabor m. **zestful** adj animado; sabroso.

zigzag n zigzag m. v zigzaguear.

zinc n cinc m, zinc m.

zip n cremallera f. **zip code** (US) código postal m. v **zip up** subir la cremallera de.

zodiac n zodiaco m.

zone n zona f. v dividir en zonas.

zoo n zoo m, parque zoológico m.

zoology n zoología f. **zoological** adj zoológico. **zoologist** n zoólogo, -a m, f.

zoom n zumbido m. **zoom lens** zoom m. v zumbar. **zoom past** (coll) pasar zumbando.

Spanish—Inglés

A

a [a] *prep* to, at; on, in; by, by means of.
abacero [aβa'θero] *sm* grocer. **abacería** *sf* grocery.
abad [a'βað] *sm* abbot. **abadesa** *sf* abbess. **abadía** *sf* abbey.
abadejo [aβa'ðexo] *sm* codfish.
abajo [a'βaxo] *adv* underneath, below, down. ¡**abajo** ... ! *interj* down with ... ! **de abajo** *adj* lower.
abalanzar [aβalan'θar] *v* balance; hurl. **abalanzarse** a rush at.
abandonar [aβando'nar] *v* abandon; leave. **abandonarse** *v* give way; lose heart. **abandonado** *adj* abandoned; slovenly. **abandono** *sm* abandonment; neglect.
abanicar [aβani'kar] *v* fan. **abanico** *sm* fan.
abarcar [aβar'kar] *v* take in; comprise; undertake.
abarrotar [aβarro'tar] *v* stow; fill up; overload.
*abastecer [aβaste'θer] *v* supply, provide with. **abastecimiento** *sm* supply. **abasto** *sm* supply of provisions.
abatir [aβa'tir] *v* knock down; kill; humble. **abatido** *adj* dejected; depressed; dismayed. **abatimiento** *sm* depression; discouragement.
abdicar [aβði'kar] *v* abdicate. **abdicación** *sf* abdication.
abdomen [aβ'ðomen] *sm* abdomen.
abedul [aβe'ðul] *sm* birch-tree.
abeja [a'βexa] *sf* bee. **abeja machiega** honey bee.
aberración [aβerra'θjon] *sf* aberration.
abertura [aβer'tura] *sf* aperture, opening; gap.
abeto [a'βeto] *sm* fir.

abierto [a'βjerto] *adj* open; candid.
abigarrar [aβiɣar'rar] *v* variegate; fleck. **abigarrado** *adj* flecked; mottled; variegated.
abismo [a'βismo] *sm* abyss. **abismal** *adj* abysmal.
abjurar [aβxu'rar] *v* abjure, forswear. **abjuración** *sf* abjuration.
ablandar [aβlan'dar] *v* soften. **ablandarse** *v* mellow; relent.
*abnegarse [aβne'garse] *v* deny oneself; renounce.
abobado [aβo'βaðo] *adj* stupid, silly; stupefied.
abocarse [aβo'karse] *v* approach; meet by appointment.
abochornar [aβotʃor'nar] *v* overheat; *(fig)* shame. **abochornarse** *v* blush.
abofetear [aβofete'ar] *v* slap.
abogar [aβo'gar] *v* plead; advocate.
abolengo [aβo'lengo] *sm* ancestry; inheritance.
abolir [aβo'lir] *v* abolish.
abollar [aβo'ʎar] *v* dent. **abolladura** *sf* dent. **abollonar** *v* emboss.
abominar [aβomi'nar] *v* abominate. **abominable** *adj* abominable. **abominación** *sf* abomination.
abonar [aβo'nar] *v* guarantee; stand surety for; subscribe to; improve; *(agr)* manure. **abonado** *adj* safe; sure; trustworthy. *sm* subscriber; season-ticket holder. **abono** *sm* guarantee; subscription; fertilizer.
abordar [aβor'ðar] *v* approach; *(mar)* board ship; *(mar)* put into port.
aborigen [aβo'rixen] *s(m+f)*, *adj* aborigine, aboriginal.
*aborrecer [aβorre'θer] *v* hate. **aborrecimiento** *sm* hatred.
abortar [aβor'tar] *v* abort. **aborto** *sm* *(med)* abortion; *(fig)* failure.

abotonar [aβoto'nar] v button up.

abovedado [aβoβe'ðaðo] adj arched. **abovedar** v arch.

abrasar [aβra'sar] v burn; dry up. **abrasarse (de, en)** v (de, en amor) burn with. **abrasivo** adj abrasive.

abrazar [aβra'θar] v embrace, hug. **abrazo** sm embrace.

abrelatas [aβre'latas] sm invar tin-opener.

abreviar [aβre'βjar] v abbreviate; speed up. **abreviatura** sf abbreviation.

abrigar [aβri'gar] v shelter; wrap up. **abrigo** sm shelter; overcoat.

abril [a'βril] sm April.

abrir [a'βrir] v open; extend; unfold; reveal.

abrochar [aβro'tʃar] v fasten; button.

abrogar [aβro'gar] v repeal. **abrogación** sf repeal.

abrumar [aβru'mar] v oppress; weigh down; overwhelm; annoy. **abrumarse** v become foggy. **abrumador** adj overwhelming; annoying.

abrupto [a'βrupto] adj rugged; steep; abrupt.

absceso [aβs'θeso] sm abscess.

ábside ['aβsiðe] sm apse.

absolución [aβsolu'θjon] sf (rel) absolution; (jur) acquittal.

absoluto [aβso'luto] adj absolute; complete; (fig) overbearing. **en absoluto** absolutely.

*****absolver** [aβsol'βer] v absolve; acquit.

absorber [aβsor'βer] v absorb. **absorbente** adj absorbent. **absorción** sf absorption. **absorto** adj absorbed; amazed.

abstemio [aβs'temjo] adj abstemious.

*****abstenerse** [aβste'nerse] v abstain. **abstinencia** sf abstinence.

abstracto [aβs'trakto] adj abstract. **abstracción** sf abstraction. *****abstraer** v abstract; refrain from; become thoughtful. **abstraer de** exclude; do without. **abstraído** adj retired; preoccupied; absent-minded.

absurdo [aβ'surðo] adj absurd.

abuelo [a'βwelo] sm grandfather. **abuela** sf grandmother.

abultar [aβul'tar] v enlarge; increase; be bulky. **abultado** adj bulky; exaggerated. **abultamiento** sm bulkiness; exaggeration.

abundar [aβun'dar] v abound. **abundancia** sf abundance. **abundante** adj abundant.

aburrir [aβur'rir] v bore; (fam) spend time/money; grow bored; grow weary.

aburrido adj boring; weary. **aburrimiento** sm boredom; wearisomeness.

abusar [aβu'sar] v abuse; impose upon; go too far. **abuso** sm abuse; misuse.

abyecto [a'βjecto] adj abject. **abyección** sf degradation; misery.

acá [a'ka] adv here; now. **acá y allá** here and there.

acabar [aka'βar] v end; complete; kill; be destroyed. **acabar de** have just. **acabarse** v run out. **acabado** adj finished; perfect. sm finish.

academia [aka'ðemja] sf academy. **académico** adj academic.

*****acaecer** [akae'θer] v happen. **acaecimiento** sm happening.

acalorar [akalo'rar] v make warm; (fig) excite. **acalorarse** v become heated. **acalorado** adj hot.

acallar [aka'ʎar] v quieten; silence; (fig) ease.

acampar [akam'par] v camp.

acantilado [akanti'laðo] adj steep; rocky. sm cliff.

acaparar [akapa'rar] v monopolize; hoard. **acaparador** adj monopolistic; (fig) acquisitive.

acariciar [akari'θjar] v caress, fondle, stroke; (fig) cherish. **acariciador** adj caressing.

acarrear [akarre'ar] v transport; carry; (fig) cause; bring about.

acaso [a'kaso] sm chance. adv perhaps. **por si acaso** just in case.

acatar [aka'tar] v respect; heed; observe. **acatable** adj worthy of respect. **acatador** adj respectful. **acatamiento** sm respect.

acaudalar [akauða'lar] v accumulate, hoard. **acaudalado** adj wealthy.

acaudillar [akauði'ʎar] v lead, command. **acaudillamiento** sm leadership.

acceder [akθe'ðer] v accede, consent. **acceder a** agree to. **accesión** sf agreement.

acceso [ak'θeso] sm access; (med) fit.

accidente [akθi'ðente] sm accident. **accidental** adj accidental.

acción [ak'θjon] sf action. **acciones** s pl shares pl, stock sing. **accionar** v work, actuate. **accionista** s(m+f) shareholder.

acebo [a'θeβo] sm holly.

acechar [aθe'tʃar] v spy on; watch; ambush; stalk. **acecho** sm observation; lying in wait.

aceite [a'θeite] *sm* oil. **aceite de motor** engine oil. **aceitoso** *adj* oily. **aceituna** *sf* olive.

acelerar [aθele'rar] *v* accelerate; quicken. **acelerarse** *v* hurry. **acelerador** *sm* accelerator.

acendrar [aθen'drar] *v* (*metales*) refine; (*fig*) purify.

acentuar [aθen'twar] *v* accentuate; stress. **acento** *sm* accent; stress.

aceptar [aθep'tar] *v* accept. **aceptable** *adj* acceptable, passable. **aceptación** *sf* acceptance.

acequia [a'θekja] *sf* irrigation ditch; drain.

acera [a'θera] *sf* pavement.

acerbo [a'θerβo] *adj* harsh; sharp; sour; (*fig*) severe.

acerar [aθe'rar] *v* harden with steel; strengthen; (*fig*) fortify.

acerca de [a'θerka ðe] *adv* about.

acercar [aθer'kar] *v* approach; bring near. **acercarse** *v* approach, draw near. **acercamiento** *sm* approach; approximation; reconciliation.

acero [a'θero] *sm* steel.

acérrimo [a'θerrimo] *adj* very strong; extremely tenacious; stalwart.

*****acertar** [aθer'tar] *v* (*el blanco*) hit; guess; be right; find; succeed. **acertado** *adj* correct; apt.

acertijo [aθer'tixo] *sm* riddle.

aciago [a'θjago] *adj* unlucky; ill-fated.

acicalar [aθika'lar] *v* polish; bedeck; groom; (*fam*) spruce oneself up. **acicalado** *adj* spruce; dapper; polished. **acicaladura** *sf* also **acicalamiento** *smi* polishing; grooming; dressing up.

ácido [a'θiðo] *sm, adj* acid.

acierto [a'θjerto] *sm* success; good idea; skill.

aclamar [akla'mar] *v* acclaim; applaud. **aclamación** *sf* acclamation.

aclarar [akla'rar] *v* explain, clarify; (*color*) lighten; thin out; (*dudas*) remove; (*la ropa*) rinse. **aclaración** *sf* explanation. **aclarado** *sm* rinse.

aclimatizar [aklimati'θar] *v* acclimatize.

acné [ak'ne] *sm* acne.

acobardar [akoβar'ðar] *v* frighten; discourage.

acoger [ako'xer] *v* welcome; receive; shelter; accept. **acogerse** *v* take refuge. **acogedor** *adj* (*persona*) welcoming; (*ambiente*) friendly. **acogida** *sf* welcome.

acolchar [akol'tʃar] *v* pad; upholster; (*fig*) muffle. **acolchado** *adj* padded.

acólito [a'kolito] *sm* acolyte.

acometer [akome'ter] *v* attack; undertake; fill; occur to. **acometida** *sf* attack.

acomodar [akomo'ðar] *v* arrange; settle; accommodate; adjust; adapt; prepare; (*fig*) reconcile. **acomodación** *sf* arrangement; preparation. **acomodamente** *adv* conveniently; easily. **acomodadizo** *adj* accommodating; adaptable. **acomodado** *adj* convenient; prepared; well-to-do. **acomodador** *sm* usher. **acomodamiento** *sm* convenience; arrangement; preparation.

acompañar [akompa'nar] *v* accompany; escort. **acompañamiento** *sm* accompaniment; escort; (*cortejo*) funeral procession.

acondicionar [akondiθjo'nar] *v* set up; fix; prepare; improve. **acondicionarse** *v* condition oneself. **acondicionado** *adj* equipped. **aire acondicionado** air-conditioning.

acongojar [akongo'xar] *v* sadden; distress.

aconsejar [akonse'xar] *v* advise. **aconsejarse** *v* seek advice.

*****acontecer** [akonte'θer] *v* happen. **acontecimiento** *sm* event.

acopiar [ako'pjar] *v* store; collect. **acopiamiento** *sm* stock.

acoplar [ako'plar] *v* fit; connect; couple; (*animales*) mate. **acoplarse** *v* become friends again. **acoplado** *adj* well-matched. **acoplamiento** *sm* connection; coordination.

acorazar [akora'θar] *v* armour. **acorazado** *adj* armoured; (*fig*) hardened.

*****acordar** [akor'ðar] *v* agree; decide; remind. **acordarse** *v* remember; agree. **acordado** *adj* agreed to; wise.

acordeón [akorðe'on] *sm* accordion.

acordonar [akorðo'nar] *v* cordon off; (*los zapatos*) lace. **acordonado** *adj* cordoned off; ribbed.

acorralar [akorra'lar] *v* enclose; corner; round up.

acortar [akor'tar] *v* shorten; reduce. **acortarse** *v* become shorter; (*intimidarse*) be shy. **acortamiento** *sm* shortening; reduction.

acosar [ako'sar] *v* hound; pursue; harass; pester. **acoso** *sm* pursuit.

*acostar [akos'tar] v lay down; put to bed. acostarse v lie down; go to bed.

acostumbrar [akostum'brar] v accustom; be in the habit of. acostumbrarse a v become used to. acostumbrado adj usual.

acotar [ako'tar] v (terreno) demarcate; enclose; delimit; outline; accept. acotado adj enclosed. acotamiento sm demarcation; boundary mark; outline.

acre¹ ['akre] adj acrid; bitter.

acre² ['akre] sm acre.

*acrecentar [akreθen'tar] v increase. acrecentamiento sm increase; growth.

acreditar [akreδi'tar] v accredit; prove; vouch for; authorize; (com) credit. acreditado adj reputable.

acreedor [akree'δor] s(m+f) creditor. adj worthy.

acribillar [akriβi'ʎar] v riddle with holes.

acróbata [a'kroβata] s(m+f) acrobat.

acta ['akta] sf minutes of a meeting; official document.

actitud [akti'tuδ] sf posture, attitude.

activar [akti'βar] v speed up; stimulate; (quím) activate. actividad sf activity.

activo [ak'tiβo] adj active. sm (com) assets pl.

acto ['akto] n act, deed; ceremony; (teatro) act. salón de actos assembly hall. actor sm actor. actriz sf actress. actual adj present; topical; of this month. actualmente adv at present; nowadays.

actuar [ak'twar] v act; perform; behave. actuación sf action; performance; conduct. actuario sm (jur) clerk of the court.

acuarela [akwa'rela] sf watercolour.

acuario [a'kwario] sm aquarium.

acuático [a'kwatiko] adj aquatic.

acuciar [aku'θjar] v urge; pester; (anhelar) long for. acucioso adj urgent; diligent; desirous.

acuclillarse [akukli'ʎarse] v crouch, squat.

acuchillar [akutʃi'ʎar] v knife, stab, hack. acuchillado adj knifed; (fig) experienced.

acudir [aku'δir] v come; go; (a una cita) keep; answer; attend; help; (al médico) consult.

acueducto [akwe'δukto] sm aqueduct.

acuerdo [a'kwerδo] sm agreement. ¡de acuerdo! O.K.! ponerse de acuerdo come to an agreement.

acumular [akumu'lar] v accumulate; pile; store. acumulación sf accumulation.

acuñar [aku'ɲar] v (monedas) mint; (poner cuñas) wedge.

acuoso [aku'oso] adj watery. acuosidad sf wateriness.

acurrucarse [akurru'karse] v curl up.

acusar [aku'sar] v (jur) accuse; charge; blame; denounce; reveal; (com) acknowledge. acusación sf accusation. acusado sm (jur) defendant.

acústico [a'kustiko] adj acoustic. acústica sf acoustics.

achacar [atʃa'kar] v attribute.

achatar [atʃa'tar] v flatten.

achicar [atʃi'kar] v reduce; (mar) bale; (fig) humiliate. achicado adj childish.

achicoria [atʃi'korja] sf chicory.

achicharrar [atʃitʃar'rar] v burn; (molestar) annoy. achicharradero sm furnace.

achispado [atʃis'paδo] adj tipsy. achispar v make tipsy.

adalid [aδa'liδ] sm leader.

adaptar [aδap'tar] v adapt; adjust. adaptabilidad sf adaptability. adaptable adj adaptable. adaptación sf adaptation; (tecn) fitting.

adecuado [aδe'kwaδo] adj adequate; suitable.

adefesio [aδe'fesjo] (fam) sm nonsense; (traje) ridiculous garment; (persona) ridiculously dressed person.

adelantar [aδelan'tar] v advance; (reloj) put forward; speed up; gain; (auto) overtake. prohibido adelantar no overtaking. adelantarse v go forward. adelantado adj advanced. adelantamiento sm also adelanto advance. adelante adv ahead, forward. ¡adelante! come in! de hoy en adelante in future.

adelgazar [aδelga'θar] v make thin; slim. adelgazador adj slimming. adelgazamiento sm slimming. régimen de adelgazamiento diet.

ademán [aδe'man] sm expression; gesture. ademanes s pl manners.

además [aδe'mas] adv besides, furthermore. además de as well as.

adentro [a'δentro] adv within, inside. ¡adentro! come in! mar adentro out to sea. tierra adentro inland.

adepto [a'δepto] s(m+f) adept; supporter.

adestrar V adiestrar

aderezar [aδere'θar] v adorn; (culin) prepare; guide. aderezo sm adornment; cooking; seasoning; (de ensalada) dressing.

adeudar [aðeu'ðar] v owe; (com) charge; run into debt. **adeudado** adj owing; (persona) in debt. **adeudo** sm (deuda) debt; (com) charge.

*__adherir__ [aðe'rir] v adhere, stick. **adherirse** adhere to. **adherencia** sf (acción de pegar) adherence. **adhesión** sf (apoyo) support. **adhesivo** sm, adj adhesive.

adición [aðiˈθyon] sf addition. **adicional** adj additional. **adicionar** v add.

adicto [aˈðikto] adj devoted. s(m+f) supporter; addict.

adiestrar [aðjesˈtrar] v train, teach. **adiestrador**, -a sm, sf trainer. **adiestramiento** sm training.

adinerado [aðineˈraðo] adj wealthy. **adinerado**, -a sm, sf rich person. **adinerarse** v (fam) make one's fortune.

adiós [aˈðjos] interj, sm goodbye.

adivinar [aðiβiˈnar] v foretell; guess; (el pensamiento) read. **adivinable** adj foreseeable. **adivinación** sf also **adivinamiento** sm divination; guessing. **adivinador**, -a sm, sf fortune-teller.

adjetivo [aðxeˈtiβo] sm adjective.

adjudicar [aðxuðiˈkar] v award; adjudicate.

adjuntar [aðxunˈtar] v attach; enclose; give.

adjunto [aðˈxunto] adj attached; enclosed. sm assistant.

administrar [aðminisˈtrar] v administer, control; (fam) hand out. **administración** sf administration. **administrativo** adj administrative.

admirar [aðmiˈrar] v admire. **admirarse** v surprise, astonish. **admirable** adj admirable. **admiración** sf admiration.

admirador [aðmiraˈðor], -a sm, sf admirer. adj admiring.

admitir [aðmiˈtir] v admit; accept; allow; acknowledge. **admisible** adj admissible. acceptable. **admisión** sf admission; acceptance.

adobar [aðoˈβar] v pickle; season; cook.

*__adolecer__ [aðoleˈθer] v fall ill. **adolecer de** suffer from.

adolescencia [aðolesˈθenθja] sf adolescence. **adolescente** s(m+f), adj adolescent.

adonde ['aðonde] adv where. ¿**adónde**? where?

adoptar [aðopˈtar] v adopt; assume. **adopción** sf adoption. **adoptivo** adj adoptive.

adoquín [aðoˈkin] sm paving-stone; (fam) dunce. **adoquinar** v pave.

adorar [aðoˈrar] v adore; worship; pray. **adorable** adj adorable. **adoración** sf adoration; worship.

*__adormecer__ [aðormeˈθer] v make sleepy. **adormecerse** fall asleep. **adormecerse en** give oneself up to.

adormidera [aðormiˈðera] sf poppy.

adornar [aðorˈnar] v adorn, decorate; (trajes) trim; (coc) garnish; (fig) embellish. **adornarse** v dress up. **adorno** sm decoration; trimming; garnish.

*__adquirir__ [aðkiˈrir] v acquire, obtain. **adquisición** sf acquisition; (compra) purchase. **adquisitivo** adj acquisitive.

adrede [aˈðrede] adv on purpose.

adscribir [aðskriˈβir] v attribute, ascribe; assign. **adscripción** sf attribution; assignment. **adscripto** adj attributed; assigned.

aduana [aˈðwana] sf customs pl. derechos de aduana sm pl customs duty sing. **aduanero** sm customs officer.

*__aducir__ [aðuˈθir] v (razones) allege; (un texto) quote; (pruebas) offer as proof.

adueñarse [aðweˈɲarse] v appropriate.

adular [aðuˈlar] v flatter. **adulación** sf flattery.

adulterar [aðulteˈrar] v adulterate; commit adultery. **adulterio** sm adultery. **adúltero**, -a sm, sf adulterer, adulteress.

adulto [aˈðulto], -a s, adj adult.

adusto [aˈðusto] adj very hot; (fig) harsh.

advenedizo [aðβeneˈðiθo], -a s, adj upstart.

advenimiento [aðβeniˈmjento] sm advent; coming.

adverbio [aðˈβerβjo] sm adverb.

adversario [aðβerˈsarjo] sm adversary. **adversidad** sf adversity. **adverso** adj adverse; opposing.

*__advertir__ [aðβerˈtir] v warn; recommend; (señalar) point out; tell; (comprender) realize. **advertido** adj informed; experienced. **advertencia** sf also **advertimiento** sm warning.

adyacente [aðjaˈθente] adj adjacent.

aéreo [aˈereo] adj aerial.

aerodinámica [aeroðiˈnamika] sf aerodynamics. **aerodinámico** adj aerodynamic.

aeronáutica [aeroˈnautika] sf aeronautics. **aeronáutico** adj aeronautical.

aeroplano [aeroˈplano] sm aeroplane.

aeropuerto [aero'pwerto] *sm* airport.

aerosol [aero'sol] *sm* aerosol.

afable [a'faβle] *adj* pleasant; genial. **afabilidad** *sf* affability.

afamado [afa'maðo] *adj* famous.

afán [a'fan] *sm* (*trabajo penoso*) toil; (*deseo*) desire; (*entusiasmo*) zeal; (*preocupación*) anxiety. **afanador** *adj* enthusiastic. **afanar** *v* work hard; (*fig: robar*) steal. **afanarse** *v* exert oneself. **afanoso** *adj* laborious; hectic.

afección [afek'θjon] *sf* (*cariño*) affection; (*med*) complaint. **afeccionarse** *v* grow fond.

afectar [afek'tar] *v* affect; pretend; adopt; (*atañer*) concern; (*dañar*) damage. **afectado** *adj* spoiled; unnatural; upset. **afecto** [a'fekto] *adj* dear. **afecto a** fond of. *sm* affection.

afeitar [afei'tar] *v* shave. **afeitarse** *v* shave; make up one's face. **afeite** *sm* make-up, cosmetics *pl*.

afeminado [afemi'naðo] *adj* effeminate. *sm* effeminate person.

*****aferrar** [afer'rar] *v* seize; (*mar*) moor. **aferrarse** *v* cling.

afianzar [afjan'θar] *v* reinforce; establish; restore; guarantee; seize; support. **afianzarse** *v* steady oneself; become strong. **afianzamiento** *sm* surety; guarantee; establishment.

afición [afi'θjon] *sf* inclination; fondness; (*interés*) hobby. **la afición** *sf* the fans *pl*. **aficionado** [afiθjo'naðo], **-a** *sm, sf* fan; amateur; keen.

afilar [afi'lar] *v* sharpen; grind. **afilado** *adj* sharp. **afilador** *sm* (*persona*) knife-grinder; (*correa*) strop. **afilamiento** *sm* (*la nariz*) pointedness; (*los dedos*) slenderness.

afiliar [afi'ljar] *v* affiliate. **afiliación** *sf* affiliation.

afín [a'fin] *adj* adjacent; similar; related. **afinidad** *sf* similarity, affinity.

afinar [afi'nar] *v* polish; perfect; (*música*) tune. **afinarse** *v* become slimmer. **afinadura** *sf also* afinamiento *sm* tuning; (*fig*) refinement.

afirmar [afir'mar] *v* affirm; strengthen. **afirmarse** *v* steady oneself. **afirmación** *sf* statement; strengthening. **afirmativo** *adj* affirmative.

aflicción [aflik'θjon] *sf* affliction, grief. **afligido** *adj* distressed; (*por una muerte*) bereaved. **afligir** *v* grieve; distress; afflict.

aflojar [aflo'xar] *v* loosen, slacken; relax; (*fiebre*) abate; (*fam*) fork out, cough up. **aflojamiento** *sm* loosening, slackening; abatement; relaxation.

afluencia [aflu'enθja] *sf* crowd; (*tropel*) rush; influx; abundance.

*****afluir** [aflu'ir] *v* flow.

afónico [a'foniko] *adj* hoarse, voiceless. **afonía** *sf* loss of voice.

*****aforar** [afo'rar] *v* gauge, measure; appraise. **aforo** *sm* measurement; appraisal.

aforrar [afor'rar] *v* (*ropa, etc.*) line. **aforrarse** *v* wrap oneself up.

afortunado [afortu'naðo] *adj* fortunate; happy.

afrenta [a'frenta] *sf* insult; disgrace. **afrentar** *v* insult. **afrentarse** *v* be ashamed. **afrentador** *adj also* afrentoso insulting; offensive.

África ['afrika] *sf* Africa. **africano, -a** *s, adj* African.

afrontar [afron'tar] *v* confront; bring face to face. **afrontamiento** *sm* confrontation.

afuera [a'fwera] *adv* out, outside. **¡afuera!** get out! **afueras** *s pl* suburbs *pl*.

agachar [aga'tʃar] *v* lower, bend. **agacharse** *v* bend over; crouch; (*para evitar algo*) duck. **agachada** *sf* (*fam*) trick.

agalla [a'gaʎa] *sf* gill; (*fam*) pluck. **agallas** *s pl* tonsils *pl*.

agarrar [agar'rar] *v* seize, clutch; (*comprender*) grasp; get; take; win; (*fam*) stick. **agarro** *sm* hold, grasp. **agarradero** *sm* handle.

agarrotar [agarro'tar] *v* tighten; strangle. **agarrotarse** *v* (*motor*) seize up; (*músculo*) go numb. **agarrotado** *adj* bound; stiff; seized up.

agasajar [agasa'xar] *v* welcome warmly; entertain. **agasajo** *sm* gift; welcome. **agasajos** *sm pl* hospitality *sing*.

agazapar [agaθa'par] *v* (*fam*) nab, catch. **agazaparse** *v* crouch; duck.

agencia [a'xenθja] *sf* agency; office. **agencia de prensa** news agency. **agencia de turismo** *or* **viajes** travel agency. **agenciar** *v* get; (*fam*) wangle. **agente** *sm* agent; policeman. **agente de bolsa** stockbroker. **agente inmobiliario** estate agent.

agenda [a'xenda] *sf* diary.

ágil ['axil] *adj* agile. **agilidad** *sf* agility.

agitar [axi'tar] *v* wave; shake; upset; stir up. **agitarse** *v* sway; fidget. **agitación** *sf* waving; shaking; movement; excitement.

agitado adj agitated; rough. **agitador, -a** sm, sf agitator.

aglomerar [aglome'rar] v form a crowd; amass. **aglomeración** sf mass. **aglomeración de tráfico** traffic jam.

agobiar [ago'βjar] v weigh down; overwhelm; humiliate; depress. **agobiado** v bent down; overwhelmed; exhausted. **agobio** sm burden.

agolparse [agol'parse] v crowd together; amass. **agolpamiento** sm crowd; (cosas) pile.

agonía [ago'nia] sf (muerte) death; desire; agony. **agonizar** v be dying; suffer; annoy.

***agorar** [ago'rar] v predict. **agorero, -a** sm, sf fortune-teller.

agosto [a'gosto] sm August.

agotar [ago'tar] v drain; exhaust. **agotador** adj exhausting. **agotamiento** sm exhaustion.

agraciar [agra'θjar] v adorn; award; pardon. **agraciado** adj pretty; graceful.

agradar [agra'ðar] v please. **agradable** adj pleasant.

***agradecer** [agraðe'θer] v thank; be grateful for; be welcome. **agradecido** adj grateful. **¡muy agradecido!** much obliged! **agradecimiento** sm gratitude.

agrado [agra'ðo] sm pleasure; liking.

agrandar [agran'dar] v make larger; exaggerate. **agrandamiento** sm enlargement.

agravar [agra'βar] v aggravate; worsen. **agravación** sf also **agravamiento** sm aggravation. **agravante** adj aggravating.

agraviar [agra'βjar] v offend; insult; wrong; take offence. **agravio** sm insult; affront; wrong.

***agredir** [agre'ðir] v assault.

agregado [agre'gaðo] sm aggregate; assistant; attaché; addition. **agregar** join; incorporate. **agregarse** v be added; be incorporated.

agricultura [agrikul'tura] sf agriculture. **agrícola** adj agricultural.

agrietar [agrje'tar] v crack; chap.

agrio ['agrjo] adj sour; (carácter) bitter. sm (sabor) sourness.

agrupar [agru'par] v group; gather together. **agruparse** v come together.

agua [a'gwa] sf water. **agua abajo/arriba** down-/upstream. **agua dulce** fresh water. **entre dos aguas** sitting on the fence. **hacer agua** leak. **irse al agua** fall through.

aguacate [agwa'kate] sm avocado pear.

aguacero [agwa'θero] sm shower, downpour.

aguantar [agwan'tar] v tolerate, bear; (sostener) support; (esperar) wait, await; (durar) last. **aguante** sm patience; endurance.

aguar [a'gwar] v dilute; spoil. **aguarse** be ruined. **aguado** adj watered down.

aguardar [agwar'ðar] v wait for.

aguardiente [agwar'ðjente] sm liquor.

aguarrás [agwa'rras] sm turpentine.

aguazal [agwa'θal] sm mire.

agudeza [agu'deθa] sf (de los sentidos) sharpness; (del dolor) acuteness; (ingenio) wit. **agudizar** v sharpen; worsen. **agudo** adj sharp; acute; witty.

agüero [a'gwero] sm omen. **de buen agüero** lucky.

aguijar [agi'xar] v goad; hurry. **aguijón** sm (de un insecto) sting; stimulus. **aguijonada** sf sting; prick. **aguijonear** v goad; spur on.

águila ['agila] sf eagle. **águila ratonera** buzzard.

aguinaldo [agi'nalðo] sm Christmas present.

aguja [a'guxa] sf needle; (reloj) hand; (arq) spire. **agujas** s pl points pl.

agujero [agu'xero] sm hole; (alfiletero) pincushion.

agujetas [agu'xetas] sf pl stiffness sing. **lleno de agujetas** stiff all over.

aguzar [agu'θar] v sharpen; (estimular) encourage; (el apetito) whet. **aguzado** adj sharp; sharpened. **aguzado** adj sharpening.

ahí [a'i] adv there. **de ahí** thus, so. **por ahí** that way; thereabouts. **¡ahí es nada!** fancy that!

ahijada [ai'xaða] sf goddaughter; protégée. **ahijado** sm godson; protégé.

ahincar [ain'kar] v urge. **ahincarse** v hurry. **ahincadamente** adv tenaciously. **ahincado** adj insistent; eager. **ahínco** sm effort.

ahogar [ao'gar] v drown; flood; stifle; overwhelm. **ahogarse** v drown, be drowned. **ahogadero** sm Turkish bath. **ahogado** adj drowned; (por el gas) asphyxiated; strangled; (grito) muffled. **ahogador** adj suffocating. **ahogo** sm breathlessness; (angustia) distress.

ahora [a'ora] adv now. conj now, now then. **ahora bien** come now. **ahora mismo** right away.

ahorcar [aor'kar] v hang. **ahorcarse** v hang oneself. **ahorcadura** sf hanging.

ahorrar [aor'rar] v save; free; avoid. **ahorrador** adj thrifty. **ahorro** sm saving; thrift.

ahuecar [awe'kar] v hollow. **¡ahueca!** (fam) scram!

ahumar [au'mar] v (culin) smoke; (llenar de humo) fill with smoke. **ahumarse** v taste smoky; (fam: emborracharse) become tipsy. **ahumado** adj smoky; smoked; (fam) tipsy.

ahuyentar [aujen'tar] v frighten off; keep at bay; (fig) dismiss. **ahuyentarse** v flee.

airado [ai'raðo] adj vexed; immoral.

aire ['aire] sm air; (parecido) likeness; (aspecto) appearance; (porte) bearing; (música) time; (auto: estrangulador) choke. **hace aire** it's windy. **aire acondicionado** air conditioning. **aireación** sf ventilation. **airear** v ventilate. **airoso** adj ventilated; windy; (fig) graceful.

aislar [ai'slar] v isolate; (elec) insulate. **aislado** adj alone; remote; insulated. **aislador** adj insulating. **cinta aisladora** sf insulating tape. **aislamiento** sm isolation; insulation.

ajar [a'xar] v crumple; wrinkle; fade; (fig) age.

ajedrez [axe'ðreθ] sm chess.

ajeno [a'xeno] adj of other people; alien; free; detached; irrelevant.

ajetreo [axe'treo] sm rush; activity; bustle; exhaustion. **ajetreado** adj busy. **ajetrearse** v be busy; rush; exhaust oneself.

ajo ['axo] sm garlic. **ajo cebollino** chive. **ajo porro** leek. **diente de ajo** clove of garlic. **soltar ajos** swear.

ajuar [a'xwar] sm (de novia) trousseau; (de casa) furnishings pl.

ajustar [axus'tar] v adjust; arrange; tighten. **ajuste** sm adjustment; fitting.

ajusticiar [axusti'ðjar] v execute.

al [al] contraction of **a** el.

ala ['ala] sf wing; hat brim.

alabar [ala'βar] v praise. **alabarse** v (jactarse) boast. **alabanza** sf praise.

alabastro [ala'βastro] sm alabaster.

alacena [ala'ðena] sf larder; cupboard.

alacrán [ala'kran] sm scorpion.

alambicar [alambi'kar] v distil; complicate; (precio) minimize. **alambicado** adj elaborate; (estilo) subtle; affected; minimized. **alambique** sm still. **pasar algo por**

el **alambique** examine something very carefully.

alambre [a'lambre] sm wire. **alambrada** sf (de la guerra) barbed wire; (reja) wire netting.

alameda [ala'meða] sf (avenida) tree-lined walk; (de álamos) poplar grove.

álamo ['alamo] sm poplar. **álamo temblón** aspen.

alano [a'lano] sm mastiff.

alarde [a'larðe] sm parade; display. **alardear** v boast. **alardeo** sm boasting.

alargar [alar'gar] v lengthen, increase, enlarge; (posponer) defer; (dar) reach, hand; (la mano) stretch. **alargarse** v get longer. **alargado** adj elongated. **alargamiento** sm lengthening; extension.

alarido [ala'riðo] sm yell, shriek.

alarmar [alar'mar] v alarm; alert. **alarmarse** v be frightened. **alarma** sf alarm.

alba ['alβa] sf dawn.

albañil [alβa'ɲil] sm bricklayer.

albaricoque [alβari'koke] sm apricot.

albatros [alβa'tros] sm albatross.

albedrío [alβe'ðrio] sm will; (capricho) whim; custom. **libre albedrío** free will.

albergar [alβer'gar] v shelter; accommodate; (fig) cherish. **albergue** sm lodgings pl; (refugio) shelter; (posada) hostel.

albóndiga [al'βondiga] sf rissole.

albor [al'βor] sm dawn; (blancura) whiteness.

albornoz [alβor'noθ] sm bathrobe.

alborotar [alβoro'tar] v make a noise; disturb. **alborotarse** v (perturbarse) become upset; get excited; (una muchedumbre) riot. **alborotado** adj excited; (fig) eventful. **alborotador** adj noisy; rebellious. **alboroto** sm disturbance, uproar.

alborozar [alβoro'θar] v gladden; produce laughter. **alborozarse** v rejoice. **alborozado** adj overjoyed.

álbum ['alβum] sm album.

alcachofa [alka'tʃofa] sf artichoke.

alcahuete [alka'wete] sm pimp; (chismoso) gossip. **alcahueta** sf procuress; gossip.

alcalde [al'kalde] sm mayor. **alcaldesa** sf mayoress. **alcaldía** sf mayorship; (oficina) mayor's office.

alcance [al'kanθe] sm reach; (sonido, arma de fuego, etc.) range; scope; importance. **al alcance** within reach. **dar alcance a** catch up with. **alcanzar** v reach; catch up; understand; hit; affect; succeed; be enough; (durar) last.

alcantarilla [alkanta'riʎa] sf sewer; drain.

alcázar [al'kaθar] sm palace; fortress; (mar) quarterdeck.

alcoba [al'koβa] sf bedroom.

alcohol [alko'ol] sm alcohol. **alcohólico, -a** s, adj alcoholic.

alcornoque [alkor'noke] sm cork tree; (fig) nitwit.

aldaba [al'ðaβa] sf door knocker; (pestillo) latch, bolt. **tener buenas aldabas** (fam) have influential friends.

aldea [al'ðea] sf village.

aleación [alea'θjon] sf alloy.

alegar [ale'gar] v allege; state; emphasize; quote; (jur) plead, claim. **alegato** sm declaration; plea.

alegoría [alego'ria] sf allegory. **alegórico** adj allegorical.

alegrar [ale'grar] v gladden; make merry; be pleasing to; excite. **alegrarse** v be happy; (fam) become tipsy. **alegre** adj happy; bright; good; (fam) tipsy; (atrevido) daring. **alegría** sf joy; happiness. **¡qué alegría!** great!

alejar [ale'xar] v move away; keep away; avert. **alejarse** v go away. **alejado** adj far away; aloof. **alejamiento** sm removal; absence.

Alemania [ale'manja] sf Germany. **alemán, -ana** sm, sf German (person). **alemán** sm (idioma) German (language).

***alentar** [alen'tar] v breathe; (fig) glow; (animar) encourage. **alentado** adj encouraged; (orgulloso) proud; (valiente) brave. **alentador** adj encouraging.

alerce [a'lerθe] sm larch.

alergia [a'lerxja] sf allergy. **alérgico** adj allergic.

alero [a'lero] sm eaves pl. **estar en el alero** hang in the balance.

alerta [a'lerta] sm alert. adv on the alert. **¡alerta!** look out! **alertar** v alert, warn. **alerto** adj alert.

aleta [a'leta] sf (peces) fin; (foca) flipper.

aleve [a'leβe] adj also **alevoso** treacherous. **alevosía** sf treachery. **alevoso, -a** sm, sf traitor.

alfabeto [alfa'βeto] sm alphabet. **alfabético** adj alphabetical. **por orden alfabético** in alphabetical order. **alfabetizado** adj literate.

alfarero [alfa'rero] sm potter. **alfarería** sf pottery (art and workshop).

alférez [al'fereθ] sm (mil) second lieutenant.

alfil [al'fil] sm (ajedrez) bishop.

alfiler [alfi'ler] sm pin; brooch. **alfiler de la ropa** clothes-peg. **alfilerar** v pin. **alfilerazo** sm pinprick.

alfombra [al'fombra] sf carpet; rug. **alfombrar** v carpet.

alforja [al'forxa] sf rucksack.

alga ['alga] sf seaweed.

algarabía [algara'βia] sf Arabic; (fig) gibberish; (ruido) noise, row.

algazara [alga'θara] sf hubbub, uproar.

álgebra ['alxebra] sf algebra. **algebraico** adj also **algébrico** algebraic.

álgido ['alxiðo] adj icy cold; (fig) decisive.

algo ['algo] pron something; anything. adv rather, quite. **algo** sm something; (comida) snack.

algodón [algo'ðon] sm cotton. **algodón hidrófilo** cotton wool.

alguacil [algwa'θil] sm sheriff; city governor.

alguien ['algjen] pron someone, somebody; (interrog) anybody.

algún [al'gun] adj some, any. **algún tanto** a little.

alguno [al'guno] adj some, any. pron one, some; someone. **algunos** ms pl some, a few.

alhaja [al'axa] sf jewel; treasure.

alhelí [ale'li] sm, pl -líes wallflower.

alheña [a'leɲa] sf privet; blight, mildew. **alheñar** v (secarse) wither; become mildewed.

alhucema [alu'θema] sf lavender.

aliaga [ali'aga] sf gorse.

aliar [ali'ar] v ally. **aliado, -a** sm, sf ally. **alianza** sf alliance.

alicaído [alika'iðo] adj depressed; weak.

alicates [ali'kates] sm pl pliers, pincers pl.

aliciente [ali'θjente] sm lure; interest; encouragement.

alienar [alje'nar] v alienate. **alienación** sf alienation. **alienado** adj insane.

aliento [a'ljento] sm breath; (fig) courage. **cobrar aliento** catch one's breath.

aligerar [alixe'rar] v lighten; shorten; alleviate. **aligerarse** v get a move on.

alimentar [alimen'tar] v feed; supply; (promover) foster. **alimentación** sf food; feeding. **alimenticio** adj nourishing. **alimento** sm food.

alinear [aline'ar] v line up. **alinearse en** join. **alineación** sf also **alineamiento** sm alignment.

aliñar [ali'ɲar] v adorn; (culin) season; prepare. **aliño** sm adornment; seasoning; preparation.

alisar [ali'sar] v smooth; polish; level. **alisaduras** sf pl shavings pl.

alistar [alis'tar] v list; recruit; prepare. **alistado** adj enlisted. **alistamiento** sm enlistment.

aliviar [ali'βjar] v lighten; alleviate; help; console. **aliviarse** v feel better, recover. **alivio** sm lightening; relief. **... de alivio** (fam) a hell of a ....

alma ['alma] sf soul; spirit; person. **con el alma en la boca** at death's door.

almacén [alma'θen] sm warehouse; department store. **almacenaje** sm storage. **almacenero** sm storekeeper.

almanaque [alma'nake] sm almanac; diary.

almeja [al'mexa] sf clam.

almendra [al'mendra] sf almond. **almendro** sm almond tree.

almiar [al'mjar] sm haystack.

almíbar [al'miβar] sm syrup.

almidón [almi'ðon] sm starch.

almirante [almi'rante] sm admiral. **almirantazgo** sm admiralty.

almohada [almo'aða] sf pillow; cushion; (funda) pillowslip.

almoneda [almo'neða] sf auction; (a bajo precio) clearance sale.

almorranas [almor'ranas] sf pl haemorrhoids pl, piles pl.

***almorzar** [almor'θar] v lunch. **almuerzo** sm lunch.

alojar [alo'xar] v lodge, accommodate. **alojarse** v put up, stay. **alojamiento** sm accommodation, lodgings pl.

alondra [a'londra] sf lark.

alpargata [alpar'gata] sf rope-soled shoe. **alpargatería** sf shoe factory or shop.

Alpes ['alpes] sm pl Alps pl.

alpinismo [alpi'nismo] sm mountaineering. **alpinista** s(m+f) climber.

alpiste [al'piste] sm canary seed; (fam) drink; (fam) money.

alquería [alke'ria] sf farm; (aldea) village.

alquilar [alki'lar] v rent; hire; charter. **alquilarse** v be for hire; to be let. **se alquila** (casa) to rent; (coche) for hire. **alquiler** sm renting; letting; hiring.

alquileres sm pl rent sing. **exento de alquiler** rent-free.

alquimia [al'kimja] sf alchemy.

alquitrán [alki'tran] sm tar. **alquitranado** adj tarred.

alrededor [alreðe'ðor] adv round, around. **alrededor de** about, around. **alrededores** sm pl environs pl, outskirts pl.

alta ['alta] sf (del hospital) discharge; (ingreso) enrolment. **dar de alta** pass as fit. **darse de alta** enrol.

altanero [alta'nero] adj haughty, arrogant.

altar [al'tar] sm altar.

altavoz [alta'βoθ] sm loudspeaker.

alterar [alte'rar] v change, alter; disturb; (estropear) spoil. **alterarse** v go sour; change; be disturbed; get excited. **alteración** sf alteration; (altercado) quarrel.

altercar [alter'kar] v argue, quarrel. **altercación** sf argument, quarrel.

alternar [alter'nar] v alternate; be sociable. **alterno** adj alternating; alternate.

alternativa [alterna'tiβa] sf alternative choice; (trabajo) shift-work; (rotación de cosechas) rotation. **tomar la alternativa** qualify as a bullfighter.

alto¹ [alto] adj tall; high; upper; (fuerte) loud; advanced; noble. **lo alto** the top. adv high; high up; out loud. **en alto** (elevación) hill; (altura) height. **alteza** sf height; (título) highness; grandeur. **altitud** sf altitude; (geog) elevation.

alto² sm, interj halt. **hacer alto** stop.

alubia [a'luβja] sf French bean.

alucinación [aluθina'θjon] sf hallucination.

alud [a'luð] sm avalanche.

aludir [alu'ðir] v allude, mention. **aludido** adj in question. **no darse por aludido** turn a deaf ear.

alumbrar [alum'brar] v light; illuminate; give light; (descubrir) find; (parir) give birth; (brillar) shine. **alumbrarse** v (fam) become tipsy. **alumbramiento** sm lighting; illumination. **alumbrante** adj illuminating; (fig) enlightening.

aluminio [alu'minjo] sm aluminium.

alumno [a'lumno] sm pupil, student.

alzar [al'θar] v raise; lift. **alzarse** v rise; stand out. **alza** sf raise. **¡alza!** bravo! **alzamiento** sm increase; uprising.

allá [a'ʎa] adv there; long ago. **más allá** farther on. **vamos allá** let's go.

allanar [aʎa'nar] v level, flatten, smooth. **allanar el terreno** clear the way.

allegar [aʎe'gar] v collect, reap; add; unite. allegar fondos raise funds. allegarse v arrive; approach. allegarse a become attached to.

allegado [aʎe'gaðo], -a sm, sf relative; close friend. adj related, close. allegamiento sm collection; gathering; union; friendship; relationship.

allende [a'ʎende] adv beyond; besides. allende el mar overseas.

allí [a'ʎi] adv there; then. aquí y allí here and there. por allí over there.

ama ['ama] sf mistress of the house; (patrona) landlady.

amable [a'maβle] adj kind. amabilidad sf kindness.

amaestrar [amaes'trar] v train.

amagar [ama'gar] v threaten; show signs of. amagarse v (fam) hide.

amainar [amai'nar] v lessen; moderate. amainarse v yield.

amalgamar [amalga'mar] v amalgamate. amalgamación sf amalgamation.

amamantar [amaman'tar] v suckle, nurse. amamantador adj suckling. amamantamiento sm suckling.

*amanecer [amane'θer] v dawn; arrive at break of day. sm dawn, daybreak.

amansar [aman'sar] v break in; tame; (fig: dolor) ease.

amante [a'mante] sm, sf lover. adj fond.

amañado [ama'paðo] adj skilful; (falso) fake. amañar v fix; fake.

amapola [ama'pola] sf poppy.

amar [a'mar] v love.

amargar [amar'gar] v embitter; be or taste bitter. amargo adj bitter. amargor sm also amargura sf bitterness.

amarillo [ama'riʎo] adj yellow.

amarrar [amar'rar] v fasten; tie; moor. amarradero sm moorings pl. amarre sm fastening.

amartelar [amarte'lar] v (enamorar) make lovesick; (dar celos) make jealous. amartelarse de (fam) get a crush on.

amartillar [amarti'ʎar] v hammer.

amasar [ama'sar] v knead; mix; prepare; (med) massage; (fam) cook up; (fig) amass. amasijo sm (harina) dough; (fam) mixture, hotchpotch; plot.

amatista [ama'tista] sf amethyst.

ámbar ['ambar] sm amber.

ambición [ambi'θjon] sf ambition. ambicioso adj ambitious.

ambiente [am'bjente] sm atmosphere; environment. adj surrounding.

ambiguo [am'bigwo] adj ambiguous. ambigüedad sf ambiguity.

ámbito ['ambito] sm (recinto) enclosure; (alcance) scope; sphere; (extensión) expanse.

ambos ['ambos] adj, pron both.

ambulancia [ambu'lanθja] sf ambulance.

ambulante [ambu'lante] adj travelling; walking.

amedrentar [ameðren'tar] v frighten.

amenazar [amena'θar] v threaten. amenaza sf threat. amenazador adj threatening.

amenguar [amen'gwar] v lessen; (deshonrar) dishonour.

amenizar [ameni'θar] v make pleasant. amenidad sf pleasantness; amenity. ameno adj pleasant, delightful.

América [a'merika] sf America. América del Norte/Sur North/South America. América Latina Latin America. americano, -a s, adj American.

ametralladora [ametraʎa'ðora] sf machine gun.

amígdala [a'miɣðala] sf tonsil. amigdalitis sf tonsillitis.

amigo [a'migo] sm friend; boyfriend. amiga sf friend; girlfriend; mistress. amigo por correspondencia pen friend. amigo adj friendly.

amilanar [amila'nar] v frighten, terrify. amilanarse v become terrified.

aminorar [amino'rar] v lessen, reduce. aminoración sf lessening.

amistad [amis'taθ] sf friendship. amistades sf pl friends pl. hacer las amistades make up. amistar v reconcile. amistoso adj friendly.

amnesia [am'nesja] sf amnesia.

amnistía [amnis'tia] sf amnesty. amnistiar v grant an amnesty to.

amo ['amo] sm master; overseer; employer; proprietor; (fam) boss.

amodorrarse [amoðor'rarse] v become drowsy. amodorrado adj drowsy.

amohinar [amoi'nar] v irritate; fret. amohinarse v become irritated or peevish.

*amolar [amo'lar] v (cuchillo) grind, sharpen; (fam: fastidiar) annoy.

amoldar [amol'ðar] v mould; fit; shape. amoldarse v adapt oneself.

amonestar [amones'tar] v warn; advise; admonish; (*anuncio de bodas*) publish the banns of. **amonestación** sf warning, admonition. **correr las amonestaciones** publish the banns.

amontonar [amonto'nar] v pile up; accumulate. **amontonarse** v crowd together; heap up; (*fam*) become angry.

amor [a'mor] sm love; devotion. **amor interesado** love of money. **amor propio** self-esteem. **amoroso** adj affectionate.

amoratar [amora'tar] v (*frío*) make purple; (*golpes*) bruise. **amoratado** adj purple; black and blue.

amordazar [amorða'θar] v gag; (*un perro*) muzzle; (*fig*) gag, silence.

amorfo [a'morfo] adj amorphous.

amortiguar [amorti'gwar] v (*luz*) dim; (*ruido*) deaden; (*fuego*) damp; (*golpe*) cushion; (*fig*) mitigate. **amortiguación** sf also **amortiguamiento** sm dimming; deadening; mitigation.

amortiguador [amortigwa'ðor] sm (*auto*) shock absorber. adj dimming; deadening; mitigating.

amortizar [amorti'θar] v amortize; (*una máquina*) depreciate.

amotinar [amoti'nar] v incite to revolt; (*fig*) disturb. **amotinarse** v mutiny. **amotinado** adj also **amotinador** adj mutinous, rebellious. **amotinamiento** sm mutiny.

amparar [ampa'rar] v shelter; protect; (*ayudar*) help. **ampararse** v seek help or protection. **amparo** sm aid; protection; refuge.

ampliar [am'pljar] v enlarge; lengthen; expand; increase. **amplio** adj wide, full; spacious. **amplitud** sf width; fullness; spaciousness; extent.

amplificar [amplifi'kar] v amplify. **amplificación** sf amplification. **amplificador** sm amplifier; adj amplifying.

ampolla [am'poʎa] sf blister; (*redoma*) phial; (*frasco*) flask. **ampollar** v blister.

amputar [ampu'tar] v amputate. **amputación** sf amputation.

amueblar [amwe'βlar] v furnish.

amuleto [amu'leto] sm amulet.

anacronismo [anakro'nismo] sm anachronism.

anales [a'nales] sm pl annals pl. **analista** s(m+f) annalist.

analfabeto [anafa'βeto], -a s, adj illiterate.

análisis [a'nalisis] sm invar analysis. **analista** s(m+f) analyst. **analítico** adj analytical. **analizar** v analyse.

analogía [analo'xia] sf analogy. **análogo** adj analogous, similar.

ananás [ana'nas] sm pineapple.

anaquel [ana'kel] sm shelf. **anaquelería** sf shelving.

anarquía [anar'kia] sf anarchy. **anarquismo** sm anarchism. **anarquista** s(m+f), adj anarchist.

anatomía [anato'mia] sf anatomy. **anatómico** adj anatomical.

anca [anka] sf haunch; rump. **ancas** sf pl (*fam*) bottom sing.

anciano [an'θjano] adj old. sm old man. **ancianidad** sf old age.

ancla [ankla] sf anchor. **anclar** v also **echar anclas** anchor.

ancho [antʃo] adj wide, broad; thick; (*fig*) relieved. sm width. **a sus anchas** at ease. **anchura** sf width; fullness; (*media*) measurement; (*fig*: *frescura*) cheek.

anchoa [an'tʃoa] sf anchovy.

Andalucía [andalu'θia] sf Andalusia. **andaluz**, -a s, adj Andalusian.

andamio [an'damjo] sm scaffold; platform. **andamios** sm pl scaffolding sing.

***andar** [an'dar] v walk; go; come; (*máquina*) work; (*correr*) run. **¡anda!** go on! **andar en** be engaged in; rummage in. sm walk, gait.

andas [andas] sf pl (*para una imagen*) portable platform sing; (*féretro*) bier sing; (*para enfermo*) stretcher sing.

andén [an'den] sm station platform; (*de autopista*) hard shoulder.

Andorra [an'dorra] sf Andorra. **andorrano**, -a s, adj Andorran.

andrajo [an'draxo] sm rag. **estar hecho un andrajo** be in rags. **andrajoso** adj ragged, tattered.

anécdota [a'nekðota] sf anecdote. **anecdótico** adj anecdotal.

anegar [ane'gar] v flood; drown. **anegación** sf drowning; flooding.

anejo [a'nexo] adj joined, attached. sm annexe.

anemia [a'nemja] sf anaemia. **anémico** adj anaemic.

anestésico [anes'tesiko] sm, adj anaesthetic. **anestesista** s(m+f) anaesthetist.

anexar [anek'sar] v annex. **anexión** sf annexation.

anfibio [an'fiβjo] *sm* amphibian. *adj* amphibious.

anfiteatro [anfite'atro] *sm* amphitheatre; (*universidad*) lecture theatre; (*teatro*) gallery.

anfitrión [anfitri'on], **-ona** *sm, sf* host, hostess.

ángel ['anxel] *sm* angel. **tener ángel** be charming. **angelical** *adj* also **angélico** angelic. **angelito** *sm* cherub.

angina [an'xina] *sf* angina.

anglicano [angli'kano], **-a** *s, adj* Anglican.

angosto [an'gosto] *adj* narrow. **angostura** *sf* narrowness.

anguila [an'gila] *sf* eel.

ángulo ['angulo] *sm* angle; bend. **anguloso** *adj* angular.

angustiar [angus'tjar] *v* distress; worry. **angustia** *sf* anguish. **angustiado** *adj* distressed; miserable. **angustioso** *adj* distressing; anguished.

anhelar [ane'lar] *v* pant, gasp; (*desear*) yearn for, crave. **anhelo** *sm* panting; desire.

anidar [ani'ðar] *v* nest; (*fig*) shelter.

anillo [a'niʎo] *sm* ring. **anillo de boda** wedding ring. **anillo de compromiso** *or* **pedida** engagement ring. **anillar** *v* ring.

ánima ['anima] *sf* soul.

animal [ani'mal] *sm* animal, beast. *adj* animal. **animalada** *sf* stupid thing to do *or* say; (*grosería*) bad language.

animar [ani'mar] *v* animate; entertain; encourage; comfort. **animarse** *v* cheer up. **animación** *sf* animation. **animado** *adj* lively. **animador, -a** *sm, sf* entertainer; master of ceremonies; *adj* entertaining; encouraging.

ánimo ['animo] *sm* soul; spirit; mind; courage; intention. **¡ánimo!** come on! **animoso** *adj* spirited; courageous.

aniquilar [aniki'lar] *v* annihilate.

anís [a'nis] *sm* aniseed.

aniversario [aniβer'sarjo] *sm* anniversary.

ano ['ano] *sm* anus.

anoche [a'notʃe] *adv* last night.

*****anochecer** [anotʃe'θer] *v* grow dark. *sm* nightfall.

anomalía [anoma'lia] *sf* anomaly. **anómalo** *adj* anomalous.

anónimo [a'nonimo] *adj* anonymous. *sm* anonymous person.

anormal [anor'mal] *adj* abnormal. **anormalidad** *sf* abnormality.

anotar [ano'tar] *v* note, jot down. **anotación** *sf* note.

ansiar [an'sjar] *v* long for. **ansia** *sf* longing; (*pena*) anguish; (*fervor*) eagerness. **ansias** *sf pl* retching *sing*. **ansiedad** *sf* longing; anxiety; eagerness. **ansioso** *adj* anxious; eager; longing.

antagonismo [antago'nismo] *sm* antagonism. **antagonista** *adj* antagonistic. **antagonizar** *v* antagonize.

antaño [an'taɲo] *adv* last year; formerly.

antártico [an'tartico] *adj* antarctic. *sm* the Antarctic. **Antártica** *sf* Antarctica.

ante¹ ['ante] *prep* before; in the presence of; with regard to. **ante todo** to begin with.

ante² ['ante] *sm* suede.

anteanoche [antea'notʃe] *adv* the night before last.

anteayer [antea'jer] *adv* the day before yesterday.

antecedente [anteθe'ðente] *sm* antecedent. *adj* previous. **antecedencia** *sf* lineage. **anteceder** *v* precede.

antecesor [anteθe'sor], **-a** *sm, sf* predecessor; ancestor. *adj* antecedent.

antelación [antela'θjon] *sf* preference. **con antelación** in advance.

antemano [ante'mano] *adv* **de antemano** beforehand.

antena [an'tena] *sf* (*radio*) aerial; (*insecto*) antenna.

antenatal [antena'tal] *adj* antenatal.

anteojo [ante'oxo] *sm* small telescope. **anteojos** *sm pl* spectacles *pl*.

antepasado [antepa'saðo] *adj* previous. *sm* ancestor.

antepecho [ante'petʃo] *sm* (*de escalera*) handrail; (*de ventana*) window sill.

*****anteponer** [antepo'ner] *v* prefer. **anteponerse** *v* push forward.

anterior [ante'rjor] *adj* preceding, former; front.

antes ['antes] *adv* before, formerly; first; rather. **antes de** before. **antes que** rather than. **cuanto antes** as soon as possible.

antiaéreo [antja'ereo] *adj* anti-aircraft.

antibiótico [anti'bjotiko] *sm, adj* antibiotic.

anticiclón [antiθi'klon] *sm* anticyclone.

anticipar [antiθi'par] *v* anticipate; advance. **anticiparse a** (*con infinitivo*) to ... before. **anticipación** *sf* anticipation. **con anticipación** in advance. **anticipado**

adj early, premature. **anticipo** *sm* advance payment; foretaste.

anticoncepcional [antikonθepθjo'nal] *sm*, *adj* contraceptive. **anticonceptivo** *adj* contraceptive.

anticuado [anti'kwaðo] *adj* out of date; old-fashioned.

anticuario [anti'kwarjo], **-a** *sm*, *sf* antiquarian.

antídoto [an'tiðoto] *sm* antidote.

antieconómico [antieko'nomiko] *adj* uneconomic.

antiguo [an'tigwo] *adj* ancient, antique; senior; former. **de antiguo** of old. **antigualla** *sf* antique; (*persona*) old fogey; (*noticia*) stale news. **antiguamente** *adv* formerly. **antigüedad** *sf* antiquity; seniority.

antílope [an'tilope] *sm* antelope.

Antillas [an'tiʎas] *sf pl* West Indies.

antipatía [antipa'tia] *sf* antipathy; dislike; unfriendliness. **antipático** *adj* disagreeable; unfriendly; nasty.

antisemítico [antise'mitiko] *adj* anti-Semitic. **antisemitismo** *sm* anti-Semitism.

antiséptico [anti'septiko] *sm*, *adj* antiseptic.

antisocial [antiso'θjal] *adj* antisocial.

antítesis [an'titesis] *sf* antithesis.

antojarse [anto'xarse] *v* seem; imagine; fancy; take a fancy to. **antojársele a uno** take it into one's head to.

antojo [an'toxo] *sm* whim; (*lunar*) birthmark. **antojos** *sm pl* craving *sing*. **antojadizo** *adj* capricious.

antología [antolo'xia] *sf* anthology.

antorcha [an'tortʃa] *sf* torch.

antro ['antro] *sm* cave, den; (*fam: tasca*) low dive.

antropófago [antro'pofaɣo], **-a** *sm*, *sf* cannibal. *adj* cannibalistic. **antropofagia** *sf* cannibalism.

antropología [antropolo'xia] *sf* anthropology. **antropológico** *adj* anthropological. **antropólogo**, **-a** *sm*, *sf* anthropologist.

anual [a'nwal] *adj* annual. **anualidad** *sf* annuity. **anuario** *sm* yearbook.

anublar [anu'βlar] *v* cloud over, obscure. **anublarse** *v* become cloudy; fade away.

anudar [anu'ðar] *v* knot; join; tie; (*empezar*) begin. **anudarse** become knotted; (*plantas*) wither. **anudadura** *sf* also **anudamiento** *sm* knotting; withering.

anular [anu'lar] *v* (*cheque*) cancel; (*ley*)

repeal; (*fig: dominar*) overshadow. **anularse** *v* (*fig: renunciar*) give up everything. **anulación** *sf* cancellation; abrogation; repeal. **anulador** *adj* repealing.

anunciar [anun'θjar] *v* announce, proclaim; notify; (*hacer publicidad*) advertise; (*predecir*) foretell. **anunciador**, **-a** *sm*, *sf* announcer; advertiser; *adj* announcing; advertising. **anuncio** *sm* announcement; advertisement; omen; sign.

anzuelo [an'θwelo] *sm* fish-hook; (*fig: aliciente*) lure.

añadir [aɲa'ðir] *v* add; increase. **añadido** *sm* addition. **añadidura** *sf* addition; extra. **por añadidura** furthermore, besides.

añejo [a'ɲexo] *adj* mature; (*carne*) cured; very old.

añicos [a'ɲikos] *sm pl* pieces, bits. **hacerse añicos** wear oneself out.

añil [a'ɲil] *sm* indigo plant; indigo dye.

año ['aɲo] *sm* year. **al año** yearly. **tener ... años** be ... years old. **todos los años** every year.

añorar [aɲo'rar] *v* long for; be homesick. **añoranza** *sf* homesickness; nostalgia; yearning.

***apacentar** [apaθen'tar] *v* graze. **apacentadero** *sm* pasture. **apacentador**, **-a** *sm*, *sf* herdsman/woman.

apacible [apa'θiβle] *adj* mild; gentle; peaceful. **apacibilidad** *sf* mildness; peacefulness.

apaciguar [apaθi'gwar] *v* pacify; appease. **apaciguarse** *v* calm down. **apaciguador**, **-a** *sm*, *sf* peace-maker. **apaciguamiento** *sm* pacification; appeasement.

apagar [apa'gar] *v* (*fuego*) extinguish; switch off; muffle; (*sed*) quench; (*dolor*) soothe; (*disturbio*) calm down. **apagado** *adj* extinguished; dull; lifeless; muffled. **apagaincendios** *sm invar* fire-extinguisher.

apalear [apale'ar] *v* beat; (*grano*) thresh; (*maltratar*) thrash. **apaleo** *sm* beating; winnowing; thrashing.

apañar [apa'ɲar] *v* fix; arrange; repair; (*ataviar*) dress up; (*coger*) grab; (*fam: robar*) swipe; (*fam: preparar*) get ready. **apañado** *adj* handy; dressed up.

aparador [apara'ðor] *sm* sideboard; (*escaparate*) shop window.

aparato [apa'rato] *sm* apparatus; machine; ceremony.

*aparecer [apare'θer] v appear. **aparecido** sm ghost.

aparejar [apare'xar] v prepare; (caballos) harness, saddle; (cuadro) prime. **aparejador** sm quantity surveyor. **aparejo** sm preparation; equipment; harness.

aparentar [aparen'tar] v pretend; feign. **aparente** [apa'rente] adj apparent; evident; (adecuado) suitable.

aparición [apari'θjon] sf appearance; (visión) apparition; publication.

apariencia [apari'enθja] sf appearance; aspect; probability.

apartamento [aparta'mento] sm flat.

apartar [apar'tar] v separate; (quitar) remove; (clasificar) sort; (poner a un lado) put aside. **apartarse** v turn aside; (irse) leave. **apartado** adj separated; distant; sm paragraph; (habitación) spare room. **apartado de correos** post-office box. **apartamiento** sm separation; remoteness. **aparte** adv apart (from); aside.

apasionar [apasjo'nar] v rouse, stir. **apasionarse** v become excited. **apasionado** adj madly in love; passionate; (ardiente) fervent. **apasionamiento** sm passion.

apatía [apa'tia] sf apathy. **apático** adj apathetic.

apear [ape'ar] v get down; dismount. **apearse** v alight, get off.

apedrear [apeðre'ar] v stone. **apedrearse** v hail. **apedreo** sm stoning.

apelar [ape'lar] v appeal. **apelar a** appeal to. **apelar de** appeal against.

apellido [ape'λiðo] sm surname; (apodo) nickname. **apellido de soltera** maiden name.

apenar [ape'nar] v grieve.

apenas [a'penas] adv scarcely; no sooner than.

apéndice [a'penðiθe] sm appendix; supplement. **apendicitis** sf appendicitis.

apercibir [aperθi'βir] v prepare; (proveer) equip; (advertir) warn. **apercibirse de** equip oneself with. **apercibimiento** sm preparation; advice; (jur) summons.

aperitivo [aperi'tiβo] sm appetizer; apéritif. adj appetizing.

apero [a'pero] sm equipment; tools pl.

apertura [aper'tura] sf opening.

apesadumbrar [apesadum'brar] v grieve, afflict. **apesadumbrarse** v be upset.

apestar [apes'tar] v infect; (fig) vex; (fam)

stink. **apestado** adj (olor) foul; (que tiene peste) plague-ridden; infested.

*apetecer [apete'θer] v have a hankering for, fancy; (bienvenido) be welcome. **apetecible** adj desirable, tempting. **apetencia** sf desire; appetite.

apetito [ape'tito] sm appetite.

apiadarse [apja'ðarse] v have pity on.

ápice ['apiθe] sm apex; jot, iota.

apiñar [api'nar] v squeeze together. **apiñarse** v crowd, throng. **apiñadura** sf also **apiñamiento** sm congestion; throng.

apio ['apjo] sm celery.

apisonadora [apisona'ðora] sf steam roller. **apisonar** v flatten. **apisonamiento** sm flattening.

aplacar [apla'kar] v appease; calm. **aplacable** adj appeasable. **aplacamiento** sm appeasement. **aplacador** adj appeasing.

aplanar [apla'nar] v level, flatten; (fam) make dejected. **aplanador** adj levelling. **aplanadora** sf leveller. **aplanamiento** sm levelling, flattening; (fam) dejection.

aplastar [aplas'tar] v crush, flatten.

aplaudir [aplau'ðir] v applaud. **aplauso** sm applause.

aplazar [apla'θar] v postpone; (convocar) summon. **aplazamiento** sm postponement; summons.

aplicar [apli'kar] v apply; attach; (recursos, dinero) assign. **aplicarse** v apply oneself; be applicable. **aplicación** sf application. **aplicado** adj studious.

aplomo [a'plomo] sm aplomb, self-confidence. **aplomado** adj self-assured.

apocar [apo'kar] v lessen; belittle. **apocarse** v become cowed. **apocado** adj spineless, timid. **apocamiento** sm timidity.

apodar [apo'ðar] v nickname. **apodo** sm nickname.

apoderar [apoðe'rar] v authorize. **apoderarse de** take possession of. **apoderado** sm agent; sports manager.

apogeo [apo'xeo] sm climax; summit.

apolillarse [apoli'λarse] v become motheaten. **apolilladura** sf moth-hole.

apoplejía [aplople'xia] sf apoplexy. **apoplético, -a** s, adj apoplectic.

aportar [apor'tar] v bring, contribute; arrive. **aportación** sf contribution.

aposentar [aposen'tar] v lodge; give lodging to. **aposentarse** v take lodgings. **aposentamiento** sm lodging. **aposento** sm room; lodging.

apostar [apos'tar] v bet. **apostarse** v bet; take up one's post. **apostador, -a** sm, sf punter.

apóstol [a'postol] sm apostle. **apostólico** adj apostolic.

apóstrofo [a'postrofo] sm (gram) apostrophe.

apoyar [apo'jar] v support; back up; lean; rest. **apoyar en** lean against. **apoyarse en** lean on. **apoyo** sm support.

apreciar [apre'θjar] v appreciate; value. **apreciar en mucho** value highly. **apreciable** adj appreciable; estimable; (ruido) audible. **apreciación** sf appreciation; (valoración) appraisal. **apreciativo** adj appreciative. **aprecio** sm appraisal; esteem.

aprehender [apreen'der] v seize; understand. **aprehensible** adj understandable. **aprehensión** sf capture, arrest; understanding.

apremiar [apre'mjar] v press, urge; (obligar) force; (dar prisa) hurry. **apremiador** adj urgent. **apremio** sm urgency; compulsion.

aprender [apren'der] v learn. **aprendiz, -a** sm, sf apprentice. **aprendizaje** sm apprenticeship.

aprensión [apren'sjon] sf apprehension, fear. **aprensivo** adj apprehensive.

apresar [apre'sar] v seize, arrest. **apresamiento** sm seizure.

aprestar [apres'tar] v prepare; (telas) size. **aprestarse** v get ready. **apresto** sm preparation.

apresurar [apresu'rar] v hurry, quicken. **apresuradamente** adv hastily. **apresurado** adj hurried. **apresuramiento** sm haste.

*apretar [apre'tar] v squeeze; grip; tighten; (botón) press; (la mano) shake; (dolor) get worse; (comprimir) press down. **apretarse** v crowd together; huddle together. **apretado** adj tight; (colchón) hard; cramped; cluttered; difficult; (tacaño) miserly. **apretón** sm squeeze; (fam: aprieto) tight spot; (fam: accesidad natural) call of nature. **aprieto** sm awkward situation.

aprisa [a'prisa] adv quickly.

aprisionar [aprisjon'ar] v imprison.

*aprobar [apro'βar] v approve; approve of; (examen) pass. **aprobación** sf approval; pass. **aprobado** adj approved. sm pass.

apropiar [apro'pjar] v appropriate; adapt.

apropiarse de algo appropriate something. **apropiado** adj appropriate, suitable, able.

aprovechar [aproβe'tʃar] v profit by; be useful; make progress. **aprovecharse de** take advantage of. **aprovechado** adj thrifty; (apañado) resourceful; studious; (egoísta) selfish. **aprovechamiento** sm profit; exploitation; benefit.

aproximar [aproksi'mar] v bring nearer. **aproximarse** v approach. **aproximación** sf approximation; nearness. **aproximado** adj approximate.

aptitud [apti'tuð] sf aptitude; capacity. **apto** adj apt; suitable.

apuesta [a'pwesta] sf bet.

apuesto [a'pwesto] adj smart, spruce.

apuntar [apun'tar] v (señalar) point at; (arma) aim; (sugerir) point out; (anotar) make a note of; (demostrar) display; (sacar punta) sharpen; (jugar) bet; (teatro) prompt. **apuntarse** v put one's name down; (fam) enrol. **apuntado** adj pointed. **apunte** sm (nota) note; (puesta) stake; prompter; (teatro) cue; (dibujo) sketch.

apuñalar [apuɲa'lar] v stab.

apurar [apu'rar] v purify; (acabar) exhaust; (vaciar) drain; examine in detail; (dar prisa) rush, hurry. **apurarse** v (preocuparse) worry; hurry up. **apuradamente** adv with difficulty; (ser indigente) in want; (fam) exactly. **apurado** adj (pobre) hard up; (agotado) worn out; (avergonzado) embarrassed. **apuro** sm (dificultad) tight spot; embarrassment.

aquejar [ake'xar] v afflict. **aquejoso** adj afflicted.

aquel, aquella [a'kel, a'keʎa] adj that. **aquellos, aquellas** pl those. **aquél, aquélla** pron that; the one; the former.

aquí [a'ki] adv here. **de aquí en adelante** from now on. **heme aquí** here I am. **por aquí** this way.

aquietar [akje'tar] v quieten.

aquilatar [akila'tar] v test, examine closely.

Arabia [a'raβja] sf Arabia. **árabe** adj Arab, Arabian, Arabic; sm, sf Arab, Arabian; sm (lengua) Arabic. **arábico** adj also **arábigo** Arabic.

arancel [aran'θel] sm tariff, duty.

araña [a'raɲa] sf spider; (luz) chandelier.

arañar [ara'ɲar] v scratch. **arañada** sf scratch. **arañador** adj scratching, scraping. **arañazo** sm scratch.

arar [a'rar] v plough. **arado** sm plough.

arbitrar [arβi'trar] v arbitrate; referee. **arbitraje** sm arbitration. **arbitrario** adj arbitrary. **árbitro** sm referee, umpire.

arbitrio [ar'βitrjo] sm (voluntad) will; (recurso) means; (jur) judgment. **arbitrios** sm pl taxes pl.

árbol ['arβol] sm tree; (tecn) shaft; (palo) mast. **árbol de Navidad** Christmas tree. **arboleda** sf wood, spinney.

arbusto [ar'βusto] sm bush.

arca ['arka] sf box, chest. **arca de agua** reservoir.

arcada [ar'kaða] sf arcade. **arcadas** sf pl nausea sing.

arcaico [ar'kaiko] adj archaic. **arcaísmo** sm archaism.

arce ['arθe] sm maple.

arcilla [ar'θiʎa] sf clay.

arco ['arko] sm arc; arch; (arma, música) bow. **arco iris** rainbow.

archiduque [artʃi'ðuke] sm archduke. **archiduquesa** sf archduchess.

archipiélago [artʃi'pjelago] sm archipelago.

archivo [ar'tʃiβo] sm file; archives pl. **archivador** sm filing cabinet. **archivar** v file. **archivero, -a** sm, sf also **archivista** s(m+f) archivist.

arder [ar'ðer] v burn; (estiércol) rot; (fig) seethe. **arderse** v burn up. **ardiente** adj ardent, burning; feverish.

ardid [ar'ðið] sm trick, ruse.

ardilla [ar'ðiʎa] sf squirrel.

ardor [ar'ðor] sm ardour; (quemazón) burn; (fig) enthusiasm. **ardorosamente** adv ardently. **ardoroso** adj burning; feverish; fervent.

arduo ['arðuo] adj arduous, difficult.

área ['area] sf area.

arena [a'rena] sf sand; (en el circo) arena; (ruedo) bullring. **arena movediza** quicksand. **arenal** sm stretch of sand. **arenar** v sand.

arengar [aren'gar] v harangue. **arenga** sf harangue.

arenque [a'renke] sm herring.

argamasa [arga'masa] sf mortar. **argamasar** v mortar.

Argentina [arxen'tina] sf Argentina. **argentino** adj (de plata) silvery; Argentinian. **argentino, -a** sm, sf Argentine, Argentinian.

argolla [ar'goʎa] sf large metal ring, hoop.

argucia [ar'guθja] sf fallacy; subtlety.

****argüir** [ar'gwir] v (alegar) argue; indicate; demonstrate; (delatar) accuse; infer.

aria ['arja] sf aria.

argumento [argu'mento] sm argument; (cuento) plot. **argumentador** adj argumentative.

aridez [ari'ðeθ] sf dryness. **aridecer** v dry up. **aridecerse** v become dry. **árido** adj arid. **medida de áridos** sf dry measure.

arisco [a'risko] adj (tímido) shy; (huraño) unfriendly; (animales) wild.

aristocracia [aristo'kraθja] sf aristocracy. **aristócrata** s(m+f) aristocrat. **aristocrático** adj aristocratic.

aritmética [arit'metika] sf arithmetic. **aritmético** adj arithmetic, arithmetical.

armada [ar'maða] sf navy, fleet.

armar [ar'mar] v arm; prepare; reinforce; (proveer) provide; organize. **armarse** v arm oneself; prepare oneself; (estallar) break out. **arma** sf weapon. **armado** adj armed. **armadura** sf armour; framework. **armamento** sm armament.

armario [ar'marjo] sm cupboard; (para ropa) wardrobe.

armazón [arma'ðon] sm (anat) skeleton. sf (conjunto de piezas) framework.

armería [arme'ria] sf gunsmiths; (heráldica) heraldry.

armisticio [armis'tiθjo] sm armistice.

armonía [armo'nia] sf harmony. **armónico** adj also **armonioso** harmonious.

armónica [ar'monika] sf harmonica.

aro ['aro] sm (argolla) iron ring; (de tonel) hoop.

aroma [a'roma] sm aroma. **aromático** adj aromatic, fragrant. **aromatizante** adj flavouring. **aromatizar** v flavour.

arpa ['arpa] sf harp. **arpista** s(m+f) harpist.

arpón [ar'pon] sm harpoon.

arquear [arke'ar] v arch, curve. **arqueo** sm arching.

arqueología [arkeolo'xia] sf archaeology. **arqueológico** adj archaeological. **arqueólogo** sm archaeologist.

arquero [ar'kero] sm archer; (com) cashier.

arquitectura [arkitek'tura] sf architecture. **arquitecto** sm architect.

arrabal [arra'βal] sm suburb. **arrabales** sm pl outskirts pl.

arraigar [arrai'gar] v take root. **arraigarse** v settle down. **arraigado** adj deep-rooted. **arraigo** sm roots pl; influence.

arrancar [arran'kar] v root up, tear out, force out; (las flemas) expectorate; (suspiro) heave; (agarrar) snatch; (auto) start. **arrancarse** v begin. **arrancada** sf sudden start; jerk. **arrancado** adj uprooted; (fam) broke. **arrancadura** sf pulling; uprooting; (dientes) extraction. **arranque** sm (auto) starting; (carretera) beginning; (energía) burst; origin.

arrasar [arra'sar] v (llenar) fill to the brim; (edificio) demolish; (allanar) level. **arrasarse** v clear up. **arrasadura** sf levelling. **arrasamiento** sm levelling; demolition.

arrastrar [arras'trar] v pull, haul, drag; (viento) blow away; (provocar) give rise to; attract. **arrastrarse** v crawl, creep. **arrastre** sm dragging; haulage. **ser de mucho arrastre** to be highly influential.

arrebatar [arreβa'tar] v snatch; (viento) blow away; carry away; (arrancar) rip off; enrage; captivate. **arrebatarse** v get overcooked. **arrebatadamente** adv hurriedly. **arrebatadizo** adj short-tempered. **arrebatamiento** sm seizure; (éxtasis) rapture. **arrebato** sm (furor) rage; rapture.

arrebujarse [arreβu'xarse] v wrap oneself up.

arreciar [arre'θjar] v grow worse or stronger; increase in intensity.

arrecife [arre'θife] sm reef.

arreglar [arre'glar] v organize, regulate; (poner en orden) tidy; (disponer) arrange; (componer) mend; get ready; (rectificar) put right. **arreglarse** v be content; (vestirse) dress; (ponerse de acuerdo) agree; (ir tirando) get by. **arreglado** adj regulated; tidy; (bien vestido) smart; reasonable; (conducta) good. **arreglo** sm agreement; arrangement; repair.

arremeter [arreme'ter] v attack. **arremetida** sf assault.

*__arrendar__ [arren'dar] v let; (alquilar) rent. **arrendador** sm landlord; (que toma en alquiler) tenant. **arrendadores** sf landlady; tenant. **arrendamiento** sm letting; rent.

arreo [ar'reo] sm adornment. **arreos** sm pl harness sing.

*__arrepentirse__ [arrepen'tirse] v repent. **arrepentimiento** sm repentance.

arrestar [arres'tar] v arrest. **arrestarse** v rush boldly. **arrestado** adj imprisoned; (audaz) bold. **arresto** sm arrest; imprisonment. **arrestos** sm pl boldness sing.

arriar [ar'rjar] v (vela, bandera) strike, lower; (cable) slacken. **arriarse** v (inundarse) be flooded.

arriba [ar'riβa] adv up; upstairs; above. **de arriba abajo** from head to foot. **mano arriba!** hands up! **arriba** prep above.

arribar [arri'βar] v arrive. **arribar a** reach. **arribada** sf arrival.

arriendo [ar'rjendo] sm letting; renting; hiring.

arriesgar [arrjes'gar] v risk. **arriesgarse** v take a risk. **arriesgarse en** venture on. **arriesgado** adj dangerous.

arrimar [arri'mar] v (acercar) get near or close; put away. **arrimarse** v draw up; gather together; live together.

arrinconar [arrinko'nar] v corner; (desechar) discard; (fam: vivir solo) live in isolation. **arrinconado** adj (olvidado) forgotten; (abandonado) forsaken.

arroba [ar'roβa] sf weight of 11.5 kg.

arrobar [arro'βar] v entrance. **arrobado** adj in ecstasy. **arrobador** adj bewitching. **arrobamiento** sm also **arrobo** ecstasy, rapture.

arrodillarse [arroði'Aarse] v kneel. **arrodillamiento** sm kneeling.

arrogancia [arro'ganθja] sf arrogance. **arrogante** adj arrogant.

arrojar [arro'xar] v throw, hurl; emit. **arrojarse** v hurl oneself. **arrojado** adj bold. **arrojo** sm boldness, daring.

arrollar [arro'Aar] v (enrollar) roll up; (llevarse) sweep away; (atropellar) run over; (aniquilar) crush.

arropar [arro'par] v (abrigarse) wrap up; (en una cama) tuck up; cover.

arrostrar [arros'trar] v face up to, confront.

arroyo [ar'roAo] sm stream; (calle) gutter.

arroz [ar'roθ] sm rice.

arrugar [arru'gar] v wrinkle; (ropa) crease. **arruga** sf wrinkle; crease.

arruinar [arrui'nar] v ruin; destroy.

arrullar [arru'Aar] v lull to sleep; (paloma) coo. **arrullo** sm cooing.

arrumbar [arrum'bar] v discard; (fig) ignore.

arrurruz [arrur'ruθ] sm arrowroot.

arsenal [arse'nal] sm arsenal; (astillero) shipyard.

arsénico [ar'seniko] *sm* arsenic.

arte ['arte] *sm*, *sf* art; (*hechura*) workmanship; (*astucia*) cunning. **no tener arte ni parte en** have nothing to do with. **por buenas o malas artes** by fair means or foul.

artefacto [arte'fakto] *sm* device, appliance.

artejo [ar'texo] *sm* knuckle.

arteria [ar'terja] *sf* artery.

artesano [arte'sano] *sm* craftsman. **artesanía** *sf* craftsmanship.

ártico ['artiko] *adj* arctic. **Ártico** *sm* the Arctic. **Círculo Polar Ártico** *sm* Arctic Circle.

articular [artiku'lar] *v* articulate, join together. **articulación** *sf* articulation.

artículo [ar'tikulo] *sm* article; item; (*dictionary*) entry. **artículos** *sm pl* goods *pl*.

artificial [artifi'θjal] *adj* artificial.

artificio [arti'fiθjo] *sm* device; skill; (*truco*) trick.

artillería [artiʎe'ria] *sf* artillery. **artillero** *sm* gunner.

artimaña [arti'maɲa] *sf* (*trampa*) trap; (*astucia*) trick.

artista [ar'tista] *s(m+f)* artist; actor, actress. **artístico** *adj* artistic.

artritis [ar'tritis] *sf* arthritis.

arzobispo [arθo'βispo] *sm* archbishop.

as [as] *sm* ace.

asa ['asa] *sf* handle.

asado [a'saðo] *sm* (*culin*) roast (meat). *adj* roast, roasted. **asador** *sm* spit. **asar** *v* roast; (*fam*) pester.

asalariado [asala'rjaðo], -a *sm*, *sf* wage-earner. *adj* paid, wage-earning.

asaltar [asal'tar] *v* assault, attack; (*banco*) raid; (*fig*: *idea*) cross one's mind. **asalto** *sm* attack; (*boxeo*) round.

asamblea [asam'blea] *sf* assembly, meeting.

asbesto [as'βesto] *sm* asbestos.

ascendencia [asθen'ðenθja] *sf* ancestry; origin; (*predominio*) influence.

*ascender [asθen'der] *v* ascend; (*subir a*) add up; (*empleo*) be promoted; promote. **ascendiente** *sm* influence. **ascendientes** *sm pl* ancestors *pl*, ancestry *sing*. **ascensión** *sf* ascent; promotion. **ascensor** *sm* elevator.

asco ['asko] *sm* disgust, loathing. **dar asco** disgust. **hacer asco** turn one's nose up.

ascua ['askwa] *sf* ember. **estar sobre ascuas** be on tenterhooks.

asear [ase'ar] *v* clean; wash; decorate; (*arreglar*) tidy up. **asearse** *v* have a wash; spruce oneself up. **aseado** *adj* clean; tidy. **aseo** *sm* cleanliness; tidiness.

asechar [ase'tʃar] *v* ambush. **asecho** *sm* trap.

asediar [ase'ðjar] *v* besiege; (*fig*) bother. **asedio** *sm* siege.

asegurar [asegu'rar] *v* secure; safeguard; (*consolidar*) strengthen; (*confortar*) reassure; insure; assure. **asegurarse** *v* make sure. **asegurado** *adj* insured; assured. **asegurador** *sm* underwriter. **aseguramiento** *sm* securing; insurance; assurance.

asemejarse [aseme'xarse] *v* resemble, be alike.

*asentar [asen'tar] *v* place; seat; (*cimientos*) lay; (*polvo*) settle; (*campamento*) pitch; (*establecer*) found; (*afilar*) sharpen; (*convenir*) agree; (*acalmar*) calm down; (*ir bien*) be suitable. **asentarse** *v* sit down; settle down.

*asentir [asen'tir] *v* agree, assent. **asentimiento** *sm* assent.

asequible [ase'kiβle] *adj* reasonable; (*alcanzable*) obtainable; affable.

*aserrar [aser'rar] *v* saw. **aserradero** *sm* sawmill. **aserrado** *adj* serrated. **aserrín** *sm* sawdust.

aserto [a'serto] *sm* assertion.

asesinar [asesi'nar] *v* murder; assassinate. **asesinato** *sm* murder; assassination. **asesino** *adj* murderous.

asesorar [aseso'rar] *v* advise; take advice. **asesoramiento** *sm* advising; opinion.

asestar [ases'tar] *v* (*arma*) aim; (*golpe*) strike. **asestadura** *sf* aiming.

asfalto [as'falto] *sm* asphalt. **asfaltado** *adj* covered with asphalt. **asfaltar** *v* asphalt.

asfixiar [asfik'sjar] *v* suffocate. **asfixia** *sf* suffocation.

así [a'si] *adv* so, thus, in this way, in that way. **así así** so-so. **así como** just as; as well as. **así que** as soon as; therefore. **así sea** so be it.

Asia ['asja] *sf* Asia. **asiático**, -a *s*, *adj* Asiatic, Asian.

asidero [asi'ðero] *sm* handle; (*fig*) excuse.

asiduo [a'siðwo] *adj* assiduous, hardworking; frequent.

asiento [a'sjento] *sm* seat, chair; place; (*de botellas*, etc.) base, bottom; (*tratado*) treaty; note; stability; (*sentido común*) common sense. **asientos** *sm pl* seat *sing*, bottom *sing*. **asiento de estómago** attack of indigestion. **tomar asiento** sit down.

asignar [asig'nar] v assign; attribute; allocate. **asignación** sf (*atribución*) allocation; (*cita*) appointment; (*subsidio*) grant; (*sueldo*) wages.

asignatura [asigna'tura] sf (scholastic) subject.

asilo [a'silo] sm asylum; refuge; home; shelter.

asimilar [asimi'lar] v assimilate; compare. **asimilarse** v be assimilated; (*asemejarse*) resemble. **asimilación** sf assimilation; comparison.

asimismo [asi'mismo] adv in like manner, in the same way.

*asir [a'sir] v grasp; grip; (*plantas*) take root. **asirse de** hang on to.

asistir [asis'tir] v help; attend; be present; (*testigo*) witness. **asistencia** sf assistance; attendance; (*teatro, etc.*) audience; (*muchedumbre*) crowd; (*médica*) care; presence. **asistencias** sf pl maintenance *sing*. **asistenta** sf charlady; (*hotel*) chambermaid. **asistente** sm assistant; (*mil*) orderly; member of an audience.

asma ['asma] sf asthma.

asno ['asno] sm donkey; ass; (*fig*) idiot.

asociar [aso'θjar] v associate; (*com*) enter into partnership. **asociarse** v associate oneself; share. **asociación** sf association; (*com*) partnership. **asociado** sm member.

asolar [aso'lar] v destroy; (*arrasar*) flatten; (*color*) parch. **asolador** adj devastating. **asolamiento** sm devastation.

asolear [asole'ar] v put in the sun. **asolearse** v sunbathe.

asomar [aso'mar] v show, appear. **asomarse** v lean out; (*fam: archisparse*) become tipsy. **asomada** sf brief appearance. **asomo** sm appearance; (*sombra*) shadow; (*indicio*) hint.

asombrar [asom'brar] v astonish; (*dar sombra*) shade; (*color*) darken. **asombrador** adj astonishing. **asombramiento** sm also **asombro** sm astonishment; (*fam: aparecido*) ghost. **asombroso** adj astonishing; stupefying.

aspecto [as'pekto] sm aspect; appearance.

áspero ['aspero] adj (*tosco*) rough; (*agrio*) sour; (*persona*) gruff; (*voz*) harsh; (*clima*) hard; (*terreno*) rugged. **aspereza** sf roughness; sourness; harshness.

aspersión [asper'sjon] sf sprinkling; spraying. **asperjar** v sprinkle.

aspirar [aspi'rar] v inhale; (*fig*) aspire. **aspiración** sf inhalation; aspiration. **aspiradora** sf vacuum cleaner.

aspirina [aspi'rina] sf aspirin.

asqueroso [aske'roso] adj disgusting; vile; dirty; repulsive. **asquerosidad** sf filth; obscenity.

asta ['asta] sf (*arma*) spear; (*palo*) shaft; (*de la bandera*) staff; (*cuerno*) horn. **a media asta** at half mast.

asterisco [aste'risko] sm asterisk.

astil [as'til] sm handle; (*pluma*) quill.

astillar [asti'λar] v splinter; smash.

astillero [asti'λero] sm shipyard.

astringir [astrin'xir] v constrict; (*sujetar*) blind. **astringente** sm, adj astringent.

astro ['astro] sm star.

astrología [astrolo'xia] sf astrology. **astrólogo** sm astrologer.

astronauta [astro'nauta] s(m+f) astronaut. **astronáutica** sf astronautics.

astronomía [astrono'mia] sf astronomy. **astronómico** adj astronomical. **astrónomo** sm astronomer.

astucia [as'tuθja] sf (*habilidad*) cleverness; (*ingenio*) cunning. **astuto** adj clever; cunning.

asumir [asu'mir] v assume.

asunto [a'sunto] sm (*tema*) subject; (*cosa*) affair; (*negocio*) business; (*caso*) fact; (*cuestión*) matter. **asuntos a tratar** pl agenda *sing*. **asuntos exteriores** foreign affairs.

asustar [asus'tar] v frighten.

atacar [ata'kar] v attack; (*recalcar*) stuff; (*un botón*) fasten. **atacador, -a** sm, sf assailant. **ataque** sm attack; (*med*) fit. **ataque cardíaco** heart attack. **ataque fulminante** (*med*) stroke. ¶

atado [a'taðo] sm bundle. adj shy.

atajar [ata'xar] v intercept; (*detener*) check; (*impedir*) obstruct; (*tomar el camino más corto*) take a short cut. **atajador, -a** sm, sf interceptor. **atajo** sm short cut.

atar [a'tar] v tie; lace; bind. **loco de atar** raving mad. **atarse** v become confused. **atador** adj binding. **atadura** sf binding; (*cuerda*) rope; (*fig*: vínculo) bond.

*atardecer [atarðe'θer] v get late; grow dark. sm dusk.

atareado [atare'aðo] adj very busy. **atarear** v load with work.

atascar [atas'kar] v plug, stop (a leak); obstruct. **atascadero** sm mire; (fig) stumbling-block. **atasco** sm obstruction.

ataúd [ata'uð] sm coffin.

ataviar [ata'βjar] v dress up, adorn. **ataviarse** en or de dress oneself up in. **atavío** sm attire.

ateísmo [ate'ismo] sm atheism. **ateísta** s(m+f) atheist. **ateo, -a** sm, sf atheist.

atemorizar [atemori'θar] v frighten.

atención [aten'θjon] sf attention; courtesy; interest; (cariño) kindness. **prestar atención** pay attention. **atenciones** sf pl business affairs. **atento** adj attentive; kind; careful; special; (consciente) aware.

*__atender__ [aten'der] v attend to; (cuidar) look after; serve; (una máquina) service; (un aviso) listen to.

*__atenerse__ [ate'nerse] v abide, adhere; (a una persona) rely on.

atentar [aten'tar] v attempt; offend.

atenuar [ate'nwar] v attenuate; lessen; (la luz) dim. **atenuación** sf attenuation.

aterrar¹ [ate'rrar] v demolish.

aterrar² [ate'rrar] v frighten, terrify. **aterrador** adj terrifying.

aterrizar [aterri'θar] v (aviac) land. **aterrizaje** sm landing.

aterrorizar [aterrori'θar] v terrify; terrorize. **aterrorizador** adj terrifying.

atesorar [ateso'rar] v hoard; (fig) possess. **atesoramiento** sm hoarding.

*__atestar__ [ates'tar] v (llenar) stuff; (un tren) crowd, pack; (desordenar) clutter up. **atestado** adj full up; packed.

atestiguar [atesti'gwar] v testify.

ático ['atiko] sm attic.

atisbar [atis'βar] v (mirar) spy on; (vislumbrar) distinguish; (vigilar) watch for. **atisbo** sm spying; (fig) hint.

atizar [ati'θar] v (el fuego) poke, stir; (fig) stir up, incite. **atizador** sm poker.

Atlántico [at'lantiko] sm Atlantic. **atlántico** adj Atlantic.

atlas ['atlas] sm atlas.

atleta [at'leta] s(m+f) athlete. **atlético** adj athletic. **atletismo** sm athletics.

atmósfera [at'mosfera] sf atmosphere. **mala atmósfera** atmospherics pl. **atmosférico** adj atmospheric.

atolondrar [atolon'drar] v confuse; (aturdir) stun. **atolondrarse** v lose one's head. **atolondradamente** adv recklessly. **atolondramiento** sm recklessness; confusion.

atolladero [atoʎa'ðero] sm bog; (fig) impasse. **atollarse** v get bogged down.

átomo ['atomo] sm atom. **atómico** adj atomic.

atónito [a'tonito] adj astonished.

atontar [aton'tar] v (golpe) stun, daze; (dejar sin habla) dumbfound; (embrutecer) deaden; (drogas) make stupid. **atontado** adj stunned; bewildered; dumbfounded; stupid.

atormentar [atormen'tar] v torment; torture. **atormentador** sm tormentor; torturer.

atornillar [atorni'ʎar] v screw in/on/down.

atosigar [atosi'gar] v poison; (molestar) pester. **atosigarse** v toil. **atosigador** adj poisoning; pestering. **atosigamiento** sm poisoning; pestering.

atracar [atra'kar] v (robar) hold up; moor; (fam) gorge. **atracarse** v gorge oneself. **atracada** sf docking; (pelea) scuffle. **atracador** sm bandit.

atracción [atrak'θjon] sf attraction. **atracciones** sf pl entertainment sing. **atractivo** adj attractive.

*__atraer__ [atra'er] v attract. **atracción** sf attraction. **atracciones** sf pl entertainment sing.

atrancar [atran'kar] v (puerta) bar; block up. **atrancarse** v become blocked/stuck/jammed.

atrapar [atra'par] v catch, trap.

atrás [a'tras] adv behind; in the rear; back; backwards; backwards. **¡atrás!** get back! **atrasado** adj late; behind; in arrears; (reloj) slow; backward; in debt. **atrasar** v (diferir) postpone; put back; slow down; lose (time). **atrasarse** lag behind; be late; be slow. **atraso** sm delay; backwardness; slowness.

*__atravesar__ [atraβe'sar] v (poner) place or put across; (traspasar) pierce; penetrate; cross; (apostar) bet. **atravesarse** v stand or lie across; get stuck; interfere; quarrel. **atravesado** adj lying across; pierced; (fig) wicked.

atreverse [atre'βerse] v dare; venture; be insolent. **atrevido, -a** sm, sf daredevil; cheeky person. **atrevimiento** sm boldness; effrontery.

*__atribuir__ [atriβu'ir] v attribute. **atribución** sf attribution. **atributo** sm attribute.

atrocidad [atroθi'ðað] *sf* atrocity. **atroz** *adj* atrocious. **atrozmente** *adv* atrociously.

atrofia [a'trofja] *sf* atrophy. **atrofiar** *v* atrophy.

atropellar [atrope'ʎar] *v* knock down; (*pisotear*) trample on; (*ultrajar*) offend; (*agraviar*) bully; (*trabajo*) rush. **atropellar por ignore. atropellarse** *v* hurry. **atropelladamente** *adv* hurriedly. **atropellado** *adj* hasty. **atropellador** *adj* precipitate. **atropello** *sm* jostling, pushing; accident; outrage.

atún [a'tun] *sm* tunny, tuna.

aturdir [atur'ðir] *v* stun, daze; (*marear*) make dizzy; bewilder. **aturdido** *adj* dazed; (*imprudente*) thoughtless. **aturdidor** *adj* deafening. **aturdimiento** *sm* daze; giddiness; amazement.

aturrullar [aturru'ʎar] *v* confuse, bewilder. **aturrullarse** *v* become confused; panic.

atusar [atu'sar] *v* (*cortar*) trim; (*alisar*) smooth; (*acariciar*) stroke. **atusarse** *v* spruce oneself up.

audacia [au'ðaθja] *sf* audacity. **audaz** *adj* audacious.

audible [au'ðiβle] *adj* audible. **audibilidad** *sf* audibility.

audición [auði'ðjon] *sf* hearing; (*prueba*) audition.

audiencia [au'ðjenθja] *sf* audience; hearing; (*tribunal*) court.

audífono [au'ðifono] *sm* hearing aid.

audiovisual [auðjoβi'swal] *adj* audiovisual.

auge ['auxe] *sm* peak; progress.

augurar [augu'rar] *v* predict. **augurio** *sm* augury, omen.

aula ['aula] *sf* lecture hall; (*escuela*) classroom. **aula magna** assembly hall.

aullar [au'ʎar] *v* howl. **aullido** *sm* howl.

aumentar [aumen'tar] *v* increase; (*sueldo*) raise; magnify; (*mejorar*) get better; (*empeorar*) get worse. **aumento** *sm* increase; rise; magnification.

aun [a'un] *adv* even. **aun así** even so. **aun cuando** although. **aún** *adv* still, yet. **aún no** not yet.

aunque [a'unke] *conj* even though, although.

áureo ['aureo] *adj* gold(en).

aureola [aure'ola] *sf* halo.

auricular [auriku'lar] *adj* of the ear, aural.

sm (*dedo*) little finger; (*teléfono*) telephone receiver. **auriculares** *sm pl* headphones *pl*.

aurora [au'rora] *sf* dawn.

ausencia [au'senθja] *sf* absence. **ausente** *adj* absent; missing.

auspicio [aus'piθjo] *sm* auspice, omen; (*patrocinio*) patronage.

austero [aus'tero] *adj* austere. **austeridad** *sf* austerity.

austral [aus'tral] *adj* southern.

Australia [aus'tralja] *sf* Australia. **australiano, -a** *s, adj* Australian.

Austria ['austrja] *sf* Austria. **austríaco, -a** *s, adj* Austrian.

auténtico [au'tentiko] *adj* authentic. **autenticar** *v* authenticate. **autenticidad** *sf* authenticity.

autístico [au'tistiko] *adj* autistic.

auto¹ ['auto] *sm* (*fam*) car. **auto de choque** dodgem car.

auto² *sm* (*jur*) sentence; (*de un pleito*) judgment. **autos** *sm pl* proceedings *pl*.

autobiografía [autoβjoɣra'fia] *sf* autobiography. **autobiográfico** *adj* autobiographical.

autobús [auto'βus] *sm* bus.

autocar [auto'kar] *sm* motor coach.

autodominio [autoðo'minjo] *sm* self-control.

autoescuela [autoes'kwela] *sf* driving school.

autoexpresión [autoekspre'sjon] *sf* self-expression.

autógrafo [au'tografo] *sm, adj* autograph.

automata [au'tomata] *sm* robot.

automático [auto'matiko] *adj* automatic. **automización** *sf* automation.

automóvil [auto'moβil] *sm* motorcar. **automovilista** *s(m +f)* motorist.

autonomía [autono'mia] *sf* autonomy. **autónomo** *adj* autonomous.

autopista [auto'pista] *sf* expressway.

autopsia [au'topsja] *sf* autopsy, postmortem.

autor [au'tor], **-a** *sm, sf* author; creator.

autorizar [autori'θar] *v* authorize; approve. **autoridad** *sf* authority. **autoritario** *adj* authoritarian. **autorización** *sf* authorization. **autorizado** *adj* authorized, official; (*seguro*) reliable.

autorretrato [autorre'trato] *sm* self-portrait.

autoservicio [autoser'βiθjo] *sm* self-service restaurant; supermarket.

autostop [auto'stop] *sm* hitchhiking. **hacer el autostop** hitchhike. **autostopista** *s(m+f)* hitchhiker.

auxiliar [auksi'ljar] *v* help; attend. *sm, adj* assistant; auxiliary.

avalancha [aβa'lantʃa] *sf* avalanche.

avalorar [aβalo'rar] *v* (*realzar*) enhance; (*fig*) inspire.

avaluar [aβalu'ar] *v* value, appraise.

avanzar [aβan'θar] *v* advance, progress. **avance** *sm* advance; (*com*) balance. **avanzada** *sf* (*mil*) outpost.

avaricia [aβa'riθja] *sf* avarice. **avaricioso** *adj* greedy; miserly. **avaro** *adj* miserly, mean.

avasallar [aβasa'ʎar] *v* subjugate; dominate. **avasallarse** *v* submit.

ave [aβe] *sf* bird. **aves de corral** *pl* poultry *sing*.

avecinarse [aβeθi'narse] *v* approach.

avellana [aβe'ʎana] *sf* hazelnut.

avena [a'βena] *sf sing* oats *pl*.

avenencia [aβe'nenθja] *sf* agreement; (*arreglo*) compromise.

avenida [aβe'niða] *sf* avenue.

***avenir** [aβe'nir] *v* reconcile, bring together; (*suceder*) happen. **avenirse** *v* agree; adapt; correspond to. **avenimiento** *sm* agreement.

aventajar [aβenta'xar] *v* lead; come in front of; (*sobresalir*) surpass; prefer. **aventajado** *adj* outstanding; favourable.

aventura [aβen'tura] *sf* adventure; (*riesgo*) risk; (*amor*) affair. **aventurado** *adj* risky. **aventurar** *v* risk; venture. **aventurero, -a** *adj* adventurous.

***avergonzar** [aβerɣon'θar] *v* shame; (*poner en un apuro*) embarrass. **avergonzarse** *v* be ashamed. **avergonzado** *adj* ashamed; embarrassed.

avería [aβe'ria] *sf* aviary.

avería² [aβe'ria] *sf* (*coche*) breakdown; (*daño*) damage. **averiar** *v* damage; break down.

averiguar [aβeri'gwar] *v* investigate; (*examinar*) verify. **averiguación** *sf* investigation; verification. **averiguador** *adj* investigating; inquiring.

aversión [aβer'sjon] *sf* aversion.

avestruz [aβes'truθ] *sm* ostrich.

aviación [aβja'θjon] *sf* aviation; air force. **aviador, -a** *sm, sf* aviator.

ávido ['aβiðo] *adj* avid; (*con ganas*) eager. **avidez** *sf* avidity; eagerness.

avinagrar [aβina'grar] *v* sour, make bitter. **avinagrado** *adj* sour; (*fam*) peevish.

avión¹ [a'βjon] *sm* aircraft. **avión a reacción** jet plane. **por avión** by airmail.

avión² *sm* swift; martin.

avisar [aβi'sar] *v* inform; advise; admonish. **avisado** *adj* prudent. **mal avisado** rash. **avisador, -a** *sm, sf* adviser; informer; messenger. **aviso** *sm* notice; announcement; advice; (*advertencia*) warning; prudence.

avispa [a'βispa] *sf* wasp.

avivar [aβi'βar] *v* enliven; (*acelerar*) hasten; revive. **avivador** *adj* hastening; enlivening.

ay ['ai] *interj* alas!

aya ['aja] *sf* governess.

ayer [a'jer] *adv* yesterday; (*fig*) formerly, lately. *sm* the recent past. **de ayer acá** since yesterday.

ayo ['ajo] *sm* tutor.

ayudar [aju'ðar] *v* help. **ayudarse** *v* help each other; make use of. **ayuda** *sf* help. **ayudante, -a** *sm, sf* assistant.

ayunar [aju'nar] *v* fast. **ayuno** *sm* fast, fasting.

ayuntamiento [ajunta'mjento] *sm* union; joint; (*cópula*) copulation; (*institución*) town council; (*edificio*) town hall.

azada [a'θaða] *sf* hoe; spade.

azafata [aθa'fata] *sf* air hostess.

azafrán [aθa'fran] *sm* saffron.

azahar [aθa'ar] *sm* orange blossom; lemon blossom.

azar [a'θar] *sm* chance, accident; (*desgracia*) misfortune. **al azar** at random.

azogue [a'θoɣe] *sm* mercury.

azorar [aθo'rar] *v* upset, embarrass. **azorarse** *v* become flustered. **azoramiento** *sm* embarrassment; (*miedo*) fear.

azotar [aθo'tar] *v* beat; (*a un niño*) spank; (*látigo*) whip. **azote** *sm* whip; spanking; (*fig: verdugo*) scourge.

azotea [aθo'tea] *sf* flat roof.

azúcar [a'θukar] *sm or sf* sugar. **azúcar en terrón** lump sugar. **azúcar extra fina** castor sugar. **azúcar morena** brown sugar. **azucarado** *adj* sugary. **azucarero, -a** *sm, sf* sugar bowl.

azucena [aθu'θena] *sf* white lily.

azufre [a'θufre] *sm* sulphur.

azul [a'θul] *sm, adj* blue. **azul marino** navy blue. **azulado** *adj* blue, bluish.

azulejo [aθu'lexo] sm tile.

azuzar [aθu'θar] v (fig) incite; urge; cause trouble. azuzador, -a sm, sf trouble-maker.

B

baba ['baβa] sf saliva, spit. babero sm bib.

Babia ['baβja] sf estar en Babia have one's head in the clouds.

babor [ba'βor] sm (mar) port side.

babosa [ba'βosa] sf slug.

bacalao [baka'lao] sm cod.

bacía [ba'θia] sf (de barbero) shaving-bowl; (recipiente) metal basin.

bacteria [bak'terja] sf germ. bacterias sf pl bacteria pl.

bache ['batʃe] sm pothole.

bachiller [batʃi'ʎer] s(m+f) holder of a school-leaving certificate; (universidad) holder of a bachelor's degree. bachillerato sm school-leaving certificate; bachelor's degree.

bagaje [ba'gaxe] sm (mil) baggage; (animal) beast of burden.

bahía [ba'ia] sf bay.

bailar [bai'lar] v dance. bailarín, -ina sm, sf ballet dancer. baile sm dancing; dance; ball. baile de disfraces or trajes fancy-dress ball.

bajamar [baxa'mar] sf low tide.

bajar [ba'xar] v get down; lower; let down; take or bring down. baja sf fall, drop. bajada sf (caída) drop; (pendiente) slope; (descendimiento) descent.

bajo ['baxo] adj (estatura) short; low; lowered; (sonido) soft; (conducta) disgraceful. adv low; below; quietly, softly. prep under. bajeza sf base act; lowness.

bajón [ba'xon] sm (música) bassoon; (bajada) fall.

bala ['bala] sf (proyectil) bullet; (algodón) bale. balazo sm (tiro) shot; (herida) wound.

balada [ba'laða] sf ballad.

baladí [bala'ði] adj trivial, unimportant.

baladrón [bala'ðron], -ona sm, sf boaster, braggart. adj boastful.

balancear [balanθe'ar] v balance; (barco)

roll; (vacilar) hesitate. balancearse v roll; (en un columpio) swing. balance sm (com) balance sheet; (inventario) stocktaking. balanceo sm balancing; (oscilación) swaying. balanza sf scales pl.

balar [ba'lar] v bleat.

balaustrada [balaus'traða] sf balustrade.

balbucear [balβuθe'ar] v stammer, stutter. balbuceo sm stammer.

balcón [bal'kon] sm balcony.

baldar [bal'ðar] v cripple; (naipes) trump; (molestar) inconvenience. baldarse v wear oneself out. baldado, -a sm, sf cripple. baldadura sf infirmity.

balde¹ ['balðe] sm bucket.

balde² adv de balde free of charge. en balde in vain.

baldío [bal'ðio] sm wasteland. adj uncultivated; (fig) useless.

baldón [bal'ðon] sm (afrenta) affront; (deshonra) disgrace.

baldosa [bal'ðosa] sf paving tile.

balneario [balne'arjo] sm spa.

balón [ba'lon] sm ball, football; (com) bale. baloncesto sm basketball. balonvolea sm volleyball.

balsa¹ ['balsa] sf balsa.

balsa² sf raft.

balsa³ sf (agua) pond.

bálsamo ['balsamo] sm balsam; (fig) balm.

Báltico ['baltiko] sm Baltic Sea. báltico adj Baltic.

ballena [ba'ʎena] sf whale.

ballesta [ba'ʎesta] sf crossbow. ballestero sm archer.

ballet [ba'le] sm ballet.

bambolear [bambole'ar] v sway.

bambolla [bam'boʎa] sf show, ostentation. darse bambolla show off.

bambú [bam'bu] sm bamboo.

banana [ba'nana] sf banana. banano sm banana tree.

banasta [ba'nasta] sf large basket.

banca ['banka] sf (asiento) bench; (com) banking.

bancarrota [bankar'rota] sf bankruptcy. hacer bancarrota go bankrupt.

banco ['banko] sm bench; (iglesia) pew; (colegio) desk; (com) bank.

banda ['banda] sf group; (pandilla) gang; (faja) sash; (cinta) ribbon; (lado) side; (orilla) river bank. bandada sf flock.

bandeja [ban'dexa] sf tray.

bandera [ban'dera] *sf* flag, banner. **a banderas desplegadas** openly. **banderilla** *sf* bullfighter's dart. **banderillero** *sm* one who thrusts banderillas into the bull.

bandido [ban'diðo] *sm* bandit.

bando ['bando] *sm* proclamation; *(facción)* faction; party; *(pez)* shoal (of fish).

bandolero [bando'lero], **-a** *sm, sf* bandit.

banjo ['banxo] *sm* banjo.

banquete [ban'kete] *sm* banquet, feast.

bañar [ba'ɲar] *v* bathe. **bañarse** *v (en la bañera)* have a bath; *(en el mar)* bathe. **bañera** *sf* bathtub. **bañero** *sm* lifeguard. **bañista** *s(m+f)* bather. **baño** *sm* bath; *(en el agua)* dip, swim; *(cubierta)* coating. **cuarto de baño** bathroom.

baquetear [bakete'ar] *v (incomodar)* bother; *(maltratar)* treat harshly. **baquetazo** *sm* blow, knock. **baqueteo** *sm (traqueteo)* jolting; *(molestia)* bother.

bar [bar] *sm* bar.

baraja [ba'raxa] *sf* pack of cards. **barajar** *v* shuffle.

barandilla [baran'diʎa] *sf* rail, railing.

barato [ba'rato] *adj* cheap. **dar de barato** take for granted. **baratear** *v* undersell. **baratija** *sf* trinket. **baratijas** *sf pl* junk *sing*. **baratura** *sf* cheapness.

baraúnda [bara'unda] *sf (alboroto)* uproar; *(confusión)* chaos.

barba ['barβa] *sf* beard. **barba a barba** face to face. **barbado** *adj* bearded. **barbería** *sf* barber's shop. **barbero** *sm* barber. **barbudo** *adj* having a full beard.

bárbaro ['barβaro], **-a** *sm, sf* barbarian; *(fig)* lout. *adj* barbarous, barbaric; *(bruto)* rough; *(fam)* fantastic. **barbaridad** *sf* barbarity; *(ultraje)* outrage. **¡qué barbaridad!** fancy that! how terrible!

barbecho [bar'βetʃo] *sm* fallow land. **barbechar** *v* leave fallow.

barbilla [bar'βiʎa] *sf* chin.

barca ['barka] *sf* boat. **barca de pasaje** ferry boat.

barco ['barko] *sm* ship, boat. **ir en barco** go by boat.

barnizar [barni'θar] *v (madera)* varnish; *(cerámica)* glaze. **barniz** *sm* varnish; glaze.

barómetro [ba'rometro] *sm* barometer. **barométrico** *adj* barometric.

barón [ba'ron] *sm* baron. **baronesa** *sf* baroness. **baronet** *sm* baronet.

barquillo [bar'kiʎo] *sm* thin sweet wafer.

barra ['barra] *sf (metal, madera, chocolate, jabón, etc.)* bar; *(vara)* rod; *(joya)* pin; *(palanca)* lever; *(pan)* loaf; *(jur)* dock; *(mar)* tiller.

barraca [bar'raka] *sf* cabin, hut; *(feria)* stall.

barranco [bar'ranko] *sm* ravine, gully; *(fig)* obstacle.

barrenar [barre'nar] *v* drill, bore; *(leyes)* violate; *(una empresa)* foil. **barrena** *sf* drill.

barrer [bar'rer] *v* sweep.

barrera [bar'rera] *sf* barrier; obstacle; gate. **barrera de peaje** tollgate.

barricada [barri'kada] *sf* barricade.

barriga [bar'riga] *sf* belly.

barril [bar'ril] *sm* barrel.

barrio ['barrjo] *sm* district, quarter.

barro ['barro] *sm* mud. **barroso** *adj* muddy.

barroco [bar'roko] *sm* baroque period. *adj* baroque.

barruntar [barrun'tar] *v* have a feeling; *(suponer)* suppose. **barruntador** *adj* prophetic. **barrunte** *or* **barrunto** *sm* feeling; supposition; *(indicio)* sign.

bártulos ['bartulos] *sm pl* belongings, odds and ends. **liar los bártulos** pack one's bags.

barullo [ba'ruʎo] *sm* confusion; *(alboroto)* row. **a barullo** galore.

basar [ba'sar] *v* found; base. **basarse en** be based on. **base** *sf* base, basis. **a base de** by. **alimento base** staple food. **básico** *adj* basic, essential.

bastante [bas'tante] *adj* enough. *adv* enough, sufficiently; *(algo)* rather, fairly. **bastar** *v* suffice. **¡basta!** that's enough!

bastardo [bas'tardo], **-a** *s, adj* bastard. **bastardear** *v* degenerate. **bastardilla** *sf* italics *pl*. **bastardillo** *adj* italic.

bastidor [basti'ðor] *sm* frame; *(ventana)* sash. **entre bastidores** behind the scenes.

basto¹ ['basto] *adj* coarse, crude.

basto² *sm (arnés)* pack-saddle.

basto³ *sm (naipes)* ace of clubs. **bastos** *sm pl* clubs.

bastón [bas'ton] *sm* cane, stick.

basura [ba'sura] *sf* rubbish, litter. **basurero** *sm* dustman.

bata ['bata] *sm (de cama)* dressing gown; *(de médico, etc.)* overall.

batalla [ba'taʎa] *sf* battle. **campo de batalla** battlefield.

batata [ba'tata] *sf* sweet potato.
batea [ba'tea] *sf* (*barco*) punt; (*bandeja*) tray; (*vagón*) open wagon.
batería [bate'ria] *sf* battery; (*teatro*) footlights; (*música*) percussion. **batería de cocina** kitchen utensils *pl*.
batir [ba'tir] *v* (*huevos*) beat; (*las manos*) clap; (*vencer*) defeat; (*derribar*) knock down; (*culin*) whisk. **batirse** *v* fight. **batido** *sm* (*leche*) milk shake; (*culin*) batter. **batidor** *sm* whisk.
batuta [ba'tuta] *sf* (*música*) baton. **llevar la batuta** rule the roost.
baúl [ba'ul] *sm* trunk.
bautizar [bauti'θar] *v* baptize, christen; (*fam: vino, etc.*) water down. **bautismo** *sm* baptism, christening. **bautista** *sm* Baptist.
baya ['baja] *sf* berry.
bayeta [ba'jeta] *sf* baize; floorcloth; rag.
bayoneta [bajo'neta] *sf* bayonet.
baza ['baθa] *sf* (*naipes*) trick. **meter baza** intervene.
bazar [ba'θar] *sm* bazaar.
bazo ['baθo] *sm* spleen. *adj* brownish yellow.
beato [be'ato] *adj* pious; blessed; (*fam*) sanctimonious.
beber [be'βer] *v* drink. **beberse** *v* drink up. **bebida** *sf* drink.
beca ['beka] *sf* grant; scholarship.
becerro [be'θerro] *sm* yearling calf.
bedel [be'ðel] *sm* porter; beadle.
befar [be'far] *v* mock, taunt. **befa** *sf* jeer, taunt.
béisbol ['beisβol] *sm* baseball.
Belén [be'len] *s* Bethlehem. **belén** *sm* Nativity scene; (*fam*) bedlam.
Bélgica ['belxika] *sf* Belgium. **belga** *s*(*m+f*), *adj* Belgian.
bélico ['beliko] *adj* warlike. **belicosidad** *sf* bellicosity. **belicoso** *adj* bellicose.
beligerante [belixe'rante] *s*(*m+f*), *adj* belligerent. **beligerancia** *sf* belligerence.
bellaco [be'ʎako] *adj*, *-a sm*, *sf* rogue. *adj* cunning; wicked.
belleza [be'ʎeθa] *sf* beauty. **bellísimo** *adj* gorgeous. **bello** *adj* beautiful; noble.
bellota [be'ʎota] *sf* acorn.
bemol [be'mol] *sm*, *adj* (*música*) flat.
bencina [ben'θina] *sf* benzine.
*bendecir [benðe'θir] *v* bless; praise. **bendición** *sf* benediction; grace. **bendito** *adj* blessed; saintly; (*fam*) wretched.

beneficiar [benefi'θjar] *v* benefit; profit. **benefactor**, *-a sm*, *sf also* **bienhechor**, *-a* benefactor. **beneficencia** *sf* charity; welfare. **beneficiado**, *-a sm*, *sf also* **beneficiario**, *-a* beneficiary. **beneficio** *sm* benefit; gain. **beneficioso** *adj* beneficial.
benemérito [bene'merito] *adj* worthy, well-deserving.
beneplácito [bene'plaθito] *sm* consent, approval.
benevolencia [benevo'lenθja] *sf* benevolence. **benevolente** *or* **benévolo** *adj* benevolent.
benignidad [benigni'ðað] *sf* kindness; (*clima*) mildness. **benigno** *adj* kind; mild.
beodo [be'oðo], *-a sm*, *sf* drunkard. *adj* drunk.
berberecho [berβe'retʃo] *sm* cockle.
berenjena [beren'xena] *sf* eggplant.
bermejo [ber'mexo] *adj* vermilion; (*cabellos*) ginger.
bermellón [berme'ʎon] *sm* vermilion.
berrear [berre'ar] *v* bellow; yell. **berrearse** *v* (*fam*) spill the beans. **berrido** *sm* bellow; yell.
berrinche [ber'rintʃe] *sm* (*fam*) tantrum.
berro ['berro] *sm* watercress.
berza ['berθa] *sf* cabbage.
besar [be'sar] *v* kiss. **beso** *sm* kiss.
bestia ['bestja] *sf* beast, animal. *sm*, *sf* (*persona*) beast; idiot. **bestial** *adj* bestial; beastly; (*fam*) smashing; enormous. **bestialidad** *sf* bestiality; beastliness.
betún [be'tun] *sm* shoe polish; bitumen.
biblia ['biβlia] *sf* Bible. **bíblico** *adj* biblical.
bibliografía [biβliogra'fia] *sf* bibliography. **bibliográfico** *adj* bibliographic(al). **bibliógrafo**, *-a sm*, *sf* bibliographer.
biblioteca [biβlio'teka] *sf* library. **bibliotecario**, *-a sm*, *sf* librarian.
bíceps ['biθeps] *sm invar* biceps.
bicicleta [biθi'kleta] *sf* bicycle.
bicho ['bitʃo] *sm* small animal; insect; (*fam*) odd character; (*fam*) ugly person.
bieldo [bjel'ðo] *sm* pitchfork.
bien [bjen] *adv* well; right; properly; very; fully; easily; gladly. **ahora bien** nevertheless. **o bien** or else. **¿y bien?** so what? *sm* good; welfare; advantage; gain; darling. **bien que** *conj also* **si bien** although. **no bien** no sooner. **bienes** *sm pl* property *sing*, riches. **bienes inmuebles** real estate *sing*.

bienal [bje'nal] *sf, adj* biennial.

bienaventurado [bjenaβentu'raðo] *adj* happy; blessed; (*fig*) naïve.

bienestar [bjenes'tar] *sm* well-being; comfort.

bienhechor [bjene'tʃor], **-a** *sm, sf* benefactor.

bienio ['bjenjo] *sm* period of two years.

bienvenida [bjenβe'niða] *sf* welcome. **dar la bienvenida** a welcome.

bistec [bis'tek] *sm* steak.

bifurcarse [bifur'karse] *v* fork; branch off. **bifurcación** *sf* fork; junction.

bigamia [bi'gamja] *sf* bigamy. **bígamo, -a** *sm, sf* bigamist.

bigote [bi'gote] *sm* moustache.

bilingüe [bi'lingwe] *adj* bilingual.

bilis ['bilis] *sf* bile; (*fig*) bad temper.

billar [bi'ʎar] *sm* billiards. **billar ruso** snooker.

billete [bi'ʎete] *sm* ticket; (*dinero*) banknote; (*carta*) letter. **billete de abono** season ticket. **billete de ida** single ticket. **billete de ida y vuelta** return ticket. **sacar un billete** buy a ticket.

billón [bi'ʎon] *sm* billion.

binóculo [bi'nokulo] *sm* binoculars *pl*.

biografía [biogra'fia] *sf* biography. **biográfico** *adj* biographical. **biógrafo, -a** *sm, sf* biographer.

biología [biolo'xia] *sf* biology. **biológico** *adj* biological. **biólogo** *sm* biologist.

biombo ['bjombo] *sm* folding screen.

bióxido [bi'oksido] *sm* dioxide. **bióxido de carbono** carbon dioxide.

biplano [bi'plano] *sm* biplane.

birlar [bir'lar] *v* (*fam: robar*) pinch, swipe; (*fam: matar*) bump off.

bisabuela [bisa'βwela] *sf* great-grandmother. **bisabuelo** *sm* great-grandfather.

bisagra [bi'sagra] *sf* hinge.

bisiesto [bi'sjesto] *adj* **año bisiesto** leap year.

bisoño [bi'soɲo], **-a** *sm, sf* greenhorn, novice; (*mil*) rookie.

bizarría [biθar'ria] *sf* (*valor*) bravery; generosity.

bizcar [biθ'kar] *v* squint. **bizco** *adj* cross-eyed. **dejar bizco** (*fam*) dumbfound.

bizcocho [biθ'kotʃo] *sm* sponge cake. **bizcocho borracho** rum baba.

bizma ['biθma] *sf* poultice.

blanco ['blanko], **-a** *adj* white; blank; (*fam*) cowardly. *sm, sf* white man/woman; white colour; *sm* (*de tiro*)

target. **blanca** *sf* (*música*) minim. **no tener blanca** be completely broke. **blancura** *sf* whiteness. **dar en el blanco** be on target. **quedarse en blanco** be disappointed. **blanquear** *v* whiten; whitewash. **blanquecer** *v* whitewash; bleach.

blandir [blan'dir] *v* flourish, brandish.

blando ['blando] *adj* soft; mild; gentle. *adv* softly; gently. **blandura** *sf* softness; tenderness; (*carácter*) weakness.

blasfemar [blasfe'mar] *v* blaspheme; (*fig*) curse. **blasfemia** *sf* blasphemy; curse. **blasfemo, -a** *sm, sf* blasphemer.

blasón [bla'son] *sm* heraldry; (*escudo*) coat of arms. **hacer blasón de** boast about.

blindaje [blin'daxe] *sm* armour. **blindado** *adj* armoured; armour-plated.

bloquear [bloke'ar] *v* block; obstruct; (*mil*) blockade. **bloque** *sm* block; bloc. **bloqueo** *sm* blockade.

blusa ['blusa] *sf* blouse; (*guardapolvo*) overall.

boa ['boa] *sf* boa constrictor.

boato [bo'ato] *sm* pomp; show.

bobada [bo'baða] *sf* nonsense; foolish thing. **bobería** *sf* stupidity. **bobo, -a** *sm, sf* fool, idiot.

bobina [bo'bina] *sf* reel, spool.

boca ['boka] *sf* mouth; opening. **a boca de jarro** point-blank. **a boca de noche** at dusk. **boca abajo/arriba** face down/up. **¡punto en boca!** mum's the word!

bocacalle [boka'kaʎe] *sf* intersection.

bocadillo [boka'ðiʎo] *sm* sandwich; snack. **bocado** *sm* mouthful; bite.

boceto [bo'θeto] *sm* (*dibujo*) sketch; (*escrito*) draft.

bocina [bo'θina] *sf* trumpet; (*aut*) horn, hooter.

bochorno [bo'tʃorno] *sm* sultry weather; (*vergüenza*) embarrassment; (*mareo*) giddiness. **sufrir un bochorno** feel embarrassed. **bochornoso** *adj* sultry; thundery; embarrassing.

boda ['boða] *sf* wedding, marriage.

bodega [bo'ðega] *sf* wine cellar; wine shop; bar.

bofetada [bofe'taða] *sf* slap; blow.

boga ['boga] *sf* (*mar*) rowing; (*fig*) vogue. **estar en boga** be in fashion. **bogador, -a** *sm, sf* rower.

bohemio [bo'emjo], **-a** *s, adj* Bohemian; (*gitano*) gipsy.

boicotear [boikote'ar] v boycott. **boicot** or **boicoteo** sm boycott.

boina ['boina] sf beret.

bola ['bola] sf ball; (canica) marble; (betún) shoe polish; (del mundo) globe; (fig) fib. **bola de naftalina** mothball. **bolear** v fib; throw.

boleta [bo'leta] sf ticket; pass; (vale) voucher; (votación) ballot paper.

boleto [bo'leto] sm lottery ticket; betting slip; (fam) fib. **boletín** sm bulletin. **boletín de noticias** news bulletin. **boletín de precios** price list. **boletín meteorológico** weather forecast.

bolígrafo [bo'ligrafo] sm ballpoint pen.

Bolivia [bo'liβja] sf Bolivia. **boliviano, -a** s, adj Bolivian.

bolsa ['bolsa] sf bag; purse. **bolsillo** sm pocket.

bollo ['boʎo] sm roll, bun, small loaf.

bomba ['bomba] sf pump, bomb. **bomba de gasolina** petrol pump.

bombardear [bombarðe'ar] v bombard.

bombilla [bom'biʎa] sf (elec) light bulb; (tecn) small pump; glass tube.

bombo ['bombo] sm big drum; great praise. adj surprised.

bombón [bom'bon] sm sweet, chocolate.

bonachón [bona'tʃon] adj (fam) genial.

bondad [bon'dað] sf goodness; kindness. **tenga la bondad de ...** please ... . **bondadoso** adj warm-hearted; good.

bonete [bo'nete] sm academic cap. **gran bonete** important person.

bonito [bo'nito] adj pretty, nice, graceful.

bono ['bono] sm voucher; certificate; bond. **bono postal** money-order.

boquear [boke'ar] v gasp; utter; be dying. **boqueada** sf gasp.

boquerón [boke'ron] sm large opening; anchovy; whitebait. **boquete** sm small hole; gap.

boquiabierto [bokja'βjerto] adj open-mouthed; gaping.

boquilla [bo'kiʎa] sf mouthpiece; nozzle; pipe stem.

borboll(e)ar [borβo'ʎar] v bubble. **borbolleo** sm bubbling. **borbollón** sm bubble.

borbotar [borβo'tar] v bubble; boil; gush. **borbotón** sm bubbling; boiling.

bordar [bor'ðar] v embroider. **bordado** sm embroidery.

borde ['borðe] sm border, edge; rim. **bordear** v skirt, edge round.

bordillo [bor'ðiʎo] sm kerb.

bordo ['borðo] sm (mar) side of a ship; tack. **a bordo** on board. **de alto bordo** ocean-going.

boreal [bore'al] adj northern.

bornear [borne'ar] v bend, turn, twist; warp.

borra ['borra] sf coarse wool; nap; waste; (fam) idle chatter.

borracho [bor'ratʃo] adj drunk; (fam) crazy. **borrachera** or **borrachería** sf drunkenness; drunken spree.

borrador [borra'ðor] sm rough copy; blotter; scribbling pad.

borrar [bor'rar] v cross out; erase; blot. **goma de borrar** rubber. **borrable** adj erasable.

borrasca [bor'raska] sf storm; squall. **borrascoso** adj stormy; squally; (fig) boisterous.

borrico [bor'riko] sm ass. **puesto en el borrico** hellbent.

borrón [bor'ron] sm blot, smudge; blemish; stain. **borronear** v scribble (on). **borroso** adj blurred; smudged; stained; illegible.

bosque ['boske] sm forest, wood.

bosquejar [boske'xar] v make a rough sketch of. **bosquejo** sm outline; sketch.

bostezar [boste'θar] v yawn. **bostezo** sm yawn.

bota[1] ['bota] sf boot. **ponerse las botas a** do justice to (something).

bota[2] sf wineskin.

botánica [bo'tanika] sf botany. **botánico** adj botanical. **botanista** s(m+f) botanist.

botar [bo'tar] v throw, fling; launch.

bote[1] ['bote] sm thrust; blow; jump; bounce.

bote[2] sm jar; can.

bote[3] sm boat. **bote salvavidas** lifeboat.

botella [bo'teʎa] sf bottle.

botica [bo'tika] sf chemist's shop; medicine chest; medicines pl; shop, store. **hay de todo como en botica** there is everything under the sun. **boticario** sm chemist.

botija [bo'tixa] sf earthenware pot. **botijo** sm earthenware jug.

botín [bo'tin] sm booty, loot.

botón [bo'ton] sm button; (flor) bud; (puerta) knob. **botonar** v bud.

bóveda ['boβeða] sf vault. **bóveda de jardín** bower.

bucle

bovino [bo'βino] adj bovine.

boxear [bokse'ar] v box. **boxeador** sm boxer. **boxeo** sm boxing.

boya ['boja] sf buoy. **boyante** adj buoyant.

bozal [bo'θal] sm muzzle. s(m+f) (fam) greenhorn. adj (fam) stupid; foolish; untamed.

bracero [bra'θero], **-a** sm, sf hired hand; labourer.

braga ['braga] sf (cuerda) guy-rope; (de mujer) knickers pl; (de niño) nappy. **calzarse las bragas** wear the trousers.

bramar [bra'mar] v roar, bellow. **bramido** sm roar, bellow.

brasa ['brasa] sf live coal. **estar en brasas** be on edge. **brasero** sm brazier.

Brasil [bra'sil] sm Brazil. **brasileño, -a** s, adj Brazilian.

bravío [bra'βio] adj wild; fierce. sm fierceness.

bravo ['braβo] adj brave; fierce; (fam) rough; (fam) rude; (fam) luxurious. **mar bravo** rough sea. **¡bravo!** interj bravo! well done! **bravura** sf ferocity; courage; manliness.

brazada [bra'θaða] sf arm movement; stroke. **brazado** sm armful.

brazalete [braθa'lete] sm bracelet.

brazo ['braθo] sm arm; branch; (fig) strength, power. **brazo a brazo** hand to hand. **a brazo partido** with bare fists. **brazo derecho** right-hand man. **tener brazo** be tough.

brea ['brea] sf pitch, tar.

brebaje [bre'βaxe] sm concoction, potion.

brécol ['brekol] sm broccoli.

brecha ['bretʃa] sf breach, opening.

bregar¹ [bre'gar] v struggle; fight. **brega** sf struggle; quarrel. **andar a la brega** (fig) slog away.

bregar² v (amasar) knead.

Bretaña [bre'taɲa] sf Britain; Brittany. **Gran Bretaña** Great Britain. **bretón, -ona** s, adj Breton.

breve ['breβe] adj brief, short. **en breve** before long. sf (música) breve. **brevedad** sf brevity.

brezal [bre'θal] sm heath. **brezo** sm heather.

bribón [bri'βon], **-ona** sm, sf rascal; rogue; vagabond. adj rascally.

brida ['briða] sf bridle; rein; horsemanship. **a toda brida** hell for leather.

brigada [bri'gaða] sf brigade; gang; squad. sm sergeant-major.

brillar [bri'ʎar] v shine; sparkle; gleam. **brillante** adj brilliant; shining; glossy. **brillo** sm brilliance; brightness; glitter.

brincar [brin'kar] v bounce; jump; hop. **brinco** sm jump; hop; skip; bounce.

brindar [brin'ðar] v offer; drink someone's health. **brindis** sm invar toast.

brío ['brio] sm spirit; vigour; determination. **brioso** adj spirited; vigorous; determined; elegant.

brisa ['brisa] sf breeze.

británico [bri'taniko], **-a** sm, sf Briton. adj British. **los británicos** the British.

brocha ['brotʃa] sf paintbrush; (afeitar) shaving brush.

broche [brotʃe] sm brooch; clasp, clip. **broche de oro** finishing touch.

broma ['broma] sf joke; fun; trick. **broma pesada** practical joke. **en broma** as a joke. **sin broma** joking apart. **bromear** v joke. **bromista** s(m+f) practical joker; funny person.

bromuro [bro'muro] sm bromide.

bronca ['bronka] sf (fam) row; brawl; ticking off. **echar una bronca** tick off.

bronce ['bronθe] sm bronze. **bronceado** adj bronzed; sun-tanned.

bronco ['bronko] adj rough; brittle; (voz) harsh; (carácter) hard, rude.

bronquial [bronki'al] adj bronchial. **bronquitis** sf bronchitis.

brotar [bro'tar] v grow; bud; germinate; spring forth. **brote** sm bud; shoot; (agua) gushing; (fiebre) rise; (fig) outbreak.

bruja ['bruxa] sf witch. **brujo** sm sorcerer.

brújula ['bruxula] sf compass. **perder la brújula** lose one's grip.

bruma ['bruma] sf mist. **brumoso** adj misty.

bruno ['bruno] adj dark brown.

bruñir [bru'nir] v polish. **bruñido** sm shine, polish. **bruñidor** sm polisher.

brusco ['brusko] adj brusque; abrupt; rough.

Bruselas [bru'selas] sf Brussels.

bruto ['bruto] adj coarse; brutish; rough; gross. sm brute; beast. **en bruto** gross; rough; uncut. **brutal** adj brutal; savage. **brutalidad** sf brutality; brutishness.

bucear [buθe'ar] v dive; swim underwater. **buceo** sm dive; diving; skin diving.

bucle ['bukle] sm curl; ringlet.

buche [butʃe] *sm* craw; crop; stomach; *(fam)* belly; *(fam)* bosom, breast.

budismo [bu'ðismo] *sm* Buddhism. **budista** *s(m+f)*, *adj* Buddhist.

buenaventura [bwenaβen'tura] *sf* good luck, fortune.

bueno ['bweno] *adj also* **buen** good; right; sound; fine; *(fam)* funny; *(fam)* amazing. *interj, conj* well; all right. **a buenas** of one's own accord. **buena voluntad** goodwill. **de buena gana** willingly. **¡buenas!** hello! **buenas noches** good night. **buenas tardes** good afternoon; good evening. **buenos días** good morning. **de buenas a primeras** without warning; at first sight; straight away. **estar de buenas** be in a good mood.

buey [bwej] *sm* ox. **a paso de buey** at a snail's pace.

búfalo ['bufalo] *sm* buffalo.

bufanda [bu'fanda] *sf* scarf, muffler.

bufar [bu'far] *v* spit; snort; puff and blow.

bufete [bu'fete] *sm* *(mesa)* writing-desk; *(despacho)* solicitor's office; clientele.

buhardilla [bwar'ðiʎa] *sf* attic, garret; skylight.

búho ['buo] *sm* owl; *(fam)* recluse.

buhonero [bwo'nero] *sm* pedlar, hawker. **buhonería** *sf* hawking, peddling.

buitre ['bwitre] *sm* vulture.

bujía [bu'xia] *sf* candle; candlepower; *(aut)* sparking-plug.

bulbo [bulβo] *sm* *(bot)* bulb. **bulboso** *adj* bulbous.

Bulgaria [bul'garja] *sf* Bulgaria. **búlgaro, -a** *s, adj* Bulgarian.

bulto ['bulto] *sm* bulk, size; shape, form; bale, package; piece of luggage; *(med)* lump, swelling. **a bulto** approximately. **de bulto** obvious. **escoger a bulto** pick at random.

bulla ['buʎa] *sf* noise; bustle. **meter bulla** kick up a racket.

bullir [bu'ʎir] *v* boil; swarm; stir; bustle; abound; itch. **bullicio** *sm* bustle; uproar. **bullicioso** *adj* lively; noisy; bustling.

buñuelo [bu'ɲwelo] *sm* fritter; doughnut; *(fam)* mess.

buque [buke] *sm* ship, vessel. **buque de guerra** warship. **buque cargero** freighter.

burbujear [burβuxe'ar] *v* bubble. **burbuja** *sf* bubble.

burdel [bur'ðel] *sm* brothel.

burdo ['burðo] *adj* clumsy; coarse; crude.

burgués [bur'ges] *adj* bourgeois, middle-class. **burguesía** *sf* bourgeoisie, middle class.

burla ['burla] *sf* hoax; joke; trick; taunt. **burlar** *v* hoax; trick; mock. **burlarse de** make fun of. **burlería** *sf* fun; artifice; deceit; ridicule.

burocracia [buro'kraθja] *sf* bureaucracy. **burócrata** *s(m+f)* bureaucrat. **burocrático** *adj* bureaucratic.

burro ['burro] *sm* donkey; *(fam)* fool. **burro cargado de letras** pompous ass.

buscar [bus'kar] *v* search for, look for. **busca** *sf* search. **en busca de** in search of. **buscador, -a** *sm, sf* seeker. **búsqueda** *sf* search.

busto ['busto] *sm* bust.

butaca [bu'taka] *sf* theatre seat; armchair.

buzo [buθo] *sm* diver. **campana de buzo** diving-bell.

buzón [bu'θon] *sm* pillar box, letter box; plug, bung.

C

cabal [ka'βal] *adj* exact; complete; perfect. **a cabal** exactly; perfectly.

cábala ['kaβala] *sf* *(fig)* intrigue; divination.

cabalgar [kaβal'gar] *v* ride. **cabalgada** *sf* raid; cavalcade. **cabalgador** *sm* horseman.

caballa [ka'βaʎa] *sf* mackerel.

caballero [kaβa'ʎero] *sm* horseman; gentleman; knight. **caballeresco** *adj* chivalrous. **caballería** *sf* cavalry.

caballete [kaβa'ʎete] *sm* ridge; trestle; easel; bridge of the nose.

caballo [ka'βaʎo] *sm* horse; *(ajedrez)* knight; *(naipes)* queen. **a caballo** on horseback. **caballo de vapor** horsepower. **caballo entero** stallion. **caballito** *sm* pony.

cabaña [ka'βaɲa] *sf* cabin; herd, flock.

cabaret [kaβa're] *sm* cabaret; nightclub.

cabecear [kaβeθe'ar] *v* nod; shake one's head. **cabecera** *sf* *(de mesa, cama, etc.)* head; river's source.

cabello [ka'βeʎo] *sm* hair. **traído por los cabellos** far-fetched. **cabelludo** *adj* hairy; shaggy; downy.

*caber [ka'βer] v fit, find room; befall; be possible. **no cabe duda** there is no doubt.

cabestro [ka'βestro] sm halter; leading ox. **llevar del cabestro** lead by the nose. **cabestrillo** sm arm sling.

cabeza [ka'βeθa] sf head; chief; summit; capital. **cabeza de turco** scapegoat. **cabeza torcida** hypocrite. **cabezudo** adj big-headed.

cabida [ka'βiða] sf capacity, space. **dar cabida a** make room for. **tener cabida** be appropriate.

cabildo [ka'βilðo] sm town council; (rel) chapter.

cabina [ka'βina] sf cabin; telephone kiosk.

cabizbajo [kaβiθ'βaxo] adj downcast.

cable ['kaβle] sm cable, rope; cable(gram). **cablegrafiar** v cable. **cablegrama** sm cable(gram).

cabo [kaβo] sm cape, headland; end; stump; handle; rope; corporal; bit, piece. **al cabo de** at the end of. **llevar a cabo** carry out.

cabotaje [kaβo'taxe] sm coastal navigation.

cabra ['kaβra] sf goat.

cabria ['kaβrja] sf crane, hoist.

cabriola [ka'βrjola] sf gambol; hop; jump. **cabriolar** v jump; caper.

cacahuete [kaka'wete] sm peanut.

cacao [ka'kao] sm cocoa; cacao.

cacarear [kakare'ar] v crow, cackle; boast. **cacareo** sm crowing, cackling; boasting.

cacería [kaθe'ria] sf hunting; hunt.

cacerola [kaθe'rola] sf saucepan.

cacique [ka'θike] sm political boss; tyrant.

caco ['kako] sm pickpocket; thief; (fam) coward.

cacto ['kakto] sm cactus.

cacharrería [katʃarre'ria] sf crockery. **cacharro** sm earthenware vessel; thing; piece of junk. **lavar los cacharros** do the washing-up.

cachemir [katʃe'mir] sm cashmere.

cachete [ka'tʃete] sm blow, slap; cheek; swollen cheek. **cachetear** v slap.

cachivache [katʃi'βatʃe] sm pot; thing; utensil; bauble.

cacho ['katʃo] sm piece, chunk, slice.

cachorro [ka'tʃorro], **-a** sm, sf pup; cub; kitten.

cada ['kaða] adj invar each, every. **cada vez más** more and more.

cadáver [ka'ðaβer] sm corpse.

cadena [ka'ðena] sf chain. **cadena perpetua** life imprisonment. **estar en cadena** be in prison.

cadencia [ka'ðenθja] sf cadence, rhythm.

cadera [ka'ðera] sf hip.

cadete [ka'ðete] sm cadet.

caducar [kaðu'kar] v expire, lapse; become senile. **caduco** adj senile; in decline.

*caer [ka'er] v fall, drop, tumble; decline; fall due; fade; fit, suit; realize, understand; be located, lie. **caer en** or **sobre** fall upon. **caer en la cuenta** understand. **caer en saco roto** fall on deaf ears. **caída** sf fall; downfall; lapse.

café [ka'fe] sm coffee; café. **café con leche** white coffee. **café solo** black coffee. **cafeína** sf caffeine. **cafetera** sf coffee pot. **cafetería** sf coffee bar.

caimán [kai'man] sm alligator.

caja ['kaxa] sf box, case; safe; coffin; frame; hole, slot; cash box; cashier's office; cash; (música) drum; (auto) body. **caja de ahorros** savings bank. **cajero, -a** sm, sf cashier. **cajetilla** sf packet; small box. **cajón** sm large box; crate, chest; drawer; coffin.

cal [kal] sm lime.

calabaza [kala'βaθa] sf pumpkin; gourd; (fam) fool. **dar calabazas a** (examen) fail; jilt. **llevar calabazas** be jilted. **calabazada** sf (fam) blow on the head.

calabozo [kala'βoθo] sm prison cell; pruning knife.

calamar [kala'mar] sm squid.

calambre [ka'lambre] sm cramp.

calamidad [kalami'ðað] sf calamity.

calar [ka'lar] v soak; perforate; slice; size up; (fam) pick pockets. **calarse hasta los huesos** get soaked to the skin.

calavera [kala'βera] sf skull. **calaverada** sf wild escapade, tomfoolery. **calaverear** v act recklessly; live it up.

calcar [kal'kar] v trace; copy; trample upon. **calco** sm tracing; copy.

calce ['kalθe] sm (de rueda) rim; wedge.

calceta [kal'θeta] sf stocking; fetter. **hacer calceta** knit. **calcetero, -a** sm, sf hosier. **calcetín** sm sock.

calcinar [kalθi'nar] v burn, blacken.

calcio ['kalθjo] sm calcium.

calcular [kalku'lar] v calculate. **calcula-ción** sf calculation. **calculadora** sf calculating machine. **cálculo** sm calculation; estimate; (med) gallstone.

calda ['kalða] sf heating. **caldas** sf pl thermal springs pl.

caldera [kal'ðera] sf cauldron, boiling pan. **calderilla** sf small change.

caldo ['kalðo] sm broth; soup; salad dressing. **caldos** sm pl liquid foodstuffs pl; wines pl.

calefacción [kalefak'θjon] sf heating. **calefacción central** central heating.

calendario [kalen'darjo] sm calendar.

*calentar [kalen'tar] v heat, warm; (fam) thrash. **calentarse** v warm oneself; become excited. **calentador** sm heater. **calentura** sf fever. **caliente** adj hot, warm.

caletre [ka'letre] sm (fam) good sense, sound judgment.

calibrar [kali'βrar] v calibrate; gauge, measure. **calibre** sm calibre; gauge; (fig) importance.

calidad [kali'ðað] sf quality; (med) fever. **calidades** sf pl conditions pl; rules pl. **a calidad de que** on condition that. **en calidad de** in the capacity of.

cálido ['kaliðo] adj hot, warm.

calificar [kalifi'kar] v qualify; judge; distinguish; prove worthy. **calificarse** v give proof of nobility. **calificación** sf appreciation; distinction; judgment. **calificado** adj distinguished; suitable.

calina [ka'lina] sf mist, fog.

cáliz ['kaliθ] sm chalice, cup.

calmante [kal'mante] adj soothing. sm sedative.

calmar [kal'mar] v calm; be calm. **calmarse** v quieten down. **calma** sf calm, lull. **calmoso** adj calm.

calor [ka'lor] sm heat, warmth; fervour; fever. **hacer calor** (temperatura) be hot. **tener calor** (persona) be hot. **caluroso** adj hot, warm; (fig) ardent.

caloría [kalo'ria] sf calorie.

calvo ['kalβo] adj bald; bare; threadbare. **calvez** sf also **calvicie** baldness.

calzar [kal'θar] v put shoes on; wear (shoes, gloves, spurs); wedge. **calza** sf chock; (fam) stocking. **calzada** sf roadway.

calzón [kal'θon] sm trousers pl; safety belt. **calzones** sm pl trousers pl. **calzoncillos** sm pl underpants pl.

callar [ka'ʎar] v be silent; shut up. **callado** adj silent; reserved; secret. **de callado** quietly.

calle ['kaʎe] sf street, road. **dejar en la calle** leave penniless. **hacer calle** clear the way. **callejón** sm alley. **callejón sin salida** cul-de-sac. **callejuela** sf back street; (fig) loophole.

callo ['kaʎo] sm (med) corn, callus. **callos** sm pl tripe sing. **calloso** adj hard, callous.

cama ['kama] sf bed; litter; floor. **caer en cama** fall ill. **cama de campaña/matrimonio/soltero** camp/double/single bed.

camafeo [kama'feo] sm cameo.

camaleón [kamale'on] sm chameleon.

camandulero [kamandu'lero] adj (fam) sly; hypocritical.

cámara [ka'mara] sf room; loft; chamber; cine or TV camera; inner tube. **ayuda de cámara** sf valet. **música de cámara** sf chamber music.

camarada [kama'raða] sm comrade; colleague.

camarero [kama'rero] sm waiter; steward. **camarera** sf waitress; stewardess; chambermaid.

camarilla [kama'riʎa] sf clique; parliamentary lobby.

camarón [kama'ron] sm shrimp.

camarote [kama'rote] sm cabin.

cambiar [kam'bjar] v change; exchange. **cambiante** sm moneychanger. **cambio** sm change; alteration; small change. **a cambio de** in exchange for. **en cambio** on the other hand.

camelar [kame'lar] v (fam) flatter; woo. **cameleo** sm (fam) flattery.

camello [ka'meʎo] sm camel.

camilla [ka'miʎa] sf stretcher; litter; couch.

caminar [kami'nar] v walk; travel; move along. **caminante** s(m+f) traveller. **camino** sm path; road; route; way. **abrirse camino** make one's way. **camino adelante** straight on. **ponerse en camino** set out.

camión [ka'mjon] sm truck. **camión de bomberos** fire engine.

camisa [ka'misa] sf shirt; fruit skin; casing; lining; dust jacket; paper wrapper. **camisa de dormir** nightdress. **camisa de fuerza** straightjacket. **dejar sin camisa** ruin (someone). **camiseta** sf vest. **camisón** sm nightdress; nightshirt.

camorra [ka'morra] *sf* (*fam*) quarrel, fight. **buscar camorra** look for trouble.
campamento [kampa'mento] *sm* camp. **campar** *v* camp; excel.
campana [kam'pana] *sf* bell; mantelpiece; parish (church); curfew.
campante [kam'pante] *adj* proud; pleased; (*fam*) relaxed, cool.
campaña [kam'paɲa] *sf* plain; campaign.
campechano [kampe'tʃano] *adj* (*fam*) genial; frank. **campechanía** *sf* good nature; frankness.
campeón [kampe'on], **-ona** *sm, sf* champion. **campeón de venta** bestseller. **campeonato** *sm* championship. **de campeonato** (*fig, fam*) fantastic.
campo ['kampo] *sm* field; countryside; camp; pitch; background. **campo de aviación** airfield. **campo raso** open country. **campesino, -a** *s, adj* peasant, rustic.
can [kan] *sm* dog; trigger.
cana ['kana] *sf* white or grey hair. **peinar canas** be getting old.
Canadá [kana'ða] *sm* Canada. **canadiense** *s*(*m+f*), *adj* Canadian.
canal [ka'nal] *sm* canal; channel; ditch; tube. *sf* carcass. **canalón** *sm* drainpipe; gutter.
canalla [ka'naʎa] *sf* rabble, mob. *sm* swine, scoundrel.
canapé [kana'pe] *sm* couch, sofa; (*culin*) canapé.
Canarias [ka'narjas] *sf pl* Canary Islands *pl*. **canario, -a** *sm, sf* inhabitant of the Canary Islands.
canario [ka'narjo] *sm* canary.
canasta [ka'nasta] *sf* basket.
cancelar [kanθe'lar] *v* cancel, annul. **cancelación** *sf* cancellation.
cáncer ['kanθer] *sm* (*med*) cancer.
Cáncer *sm* (*astron*) Cancer.
canciller [kanθi'ʎer] *sm* chancellor.
canción [kan'θjon] *sf* song; tune; rhyme. **mudar de canción** change one's tune. **cancionero** *sm* song-book.
cancha ['kantʃa] *sf* football ground; tennis court; racecourse.
candado [kan'daðo] *sm* padlock.
candela [kan'dela] *sf* candle; candlestick; fire; blossom; (*fam*) light. **candela** *sm* candlestick; oil lamp. **poner en el candelero** make popular.
candente [kan'dente] *adj* red-hot, burning.

candidato [kandi'ðato] *sm* candidate. **candidatura** *sf* candidature.
cándido ['kandiðo] *adj* innocent, pure; gullible; candid. **candidez** *sf* candour; gullibility; stupid remark.
candil [kan'dil] *sm* oil lamp.
candor [kan'dor] *sm* innocence; candour; simplicity. **candoroso** *adj* ingenuous; innocent; frank.
canela [ka'nela] *sf* cinnamon.
canelón [kane'lon] *sm* gutter; spout; icicle.
cangrejo [kan'grexo] *sm* crab.
canguro [kan'guro] *sm* kangaroo.
caníbal [ka'niβal] *s*(*m+f*), *adj* cannibal. **canibalismo** *sm* cannibalism.
canilla [ka'niʎa] *sf* (*tecn*) bobbin, spool; (*med*) shinbone; tap, spout.
canino [ka'nino] *adj* canine. **hambre canina** ravenous hunger.
canjear [kanxe'ar] *v* exchange. **canje** *sf* exchange.
cano ['kano] *adj* white-haired, grey-haired; (*fig*) ancient.
canoa [ka'noa] *sf* canoe.
canon ['kanon] *sm* rule; levy; perfect example; (*rel, música*) canon.
canónigo [ka'nonigo] *sm* (*rel*) canon. **canónico** *adj* canonical. **canonización** *sf* canonization. **canonizar** *v* canonize.
cansar [kan'sar] *v* tire, fatigue. **cansado** *adj* tired, weary; tiresome. **vista cansada** weak eyesight. **cansancio** *sm* weariness, fatigue.
cantar [kan'tar] *v* sing; chant; praise; (*fam*) squeal, confess. *sm* song; tune; poem. **cantante** *s*(*m+f*) singer.
cántara ['kantara] *sf* pitcher; liquid measure.
cántaro ['kantaro] *sm* pitcher. **llover a cántaros** rain cats and dogs.
cantera [kan'tera] *sf* quarry; (*fig*) breeding ground, source. **cantería** *sf* masonry; building made of hewn stone. **cantero** *sm* stonemason; crust of bread; strip of land.
cantidad [kanti'ðað] *sf* quantity, amount.
cantimplora [kantim'plora] *sf* siphon; water bottle.
cantina [kan'tina] *sf* buffet; canteen; wine cellar; picnic basket.
canto[1] ['kanto] *sm* song; singing. **cantor, -a** *sf* singer.
canto[2] *sm* edge; border; crust; corner;

pebble. **al canto** (*fam*) in support. **de canto** edgeways.

caña ['kaɲa] *sf* cane; reed; walking stick; beer glass; shin bone. **caña de azúcar** sugar-cane. **caña de pescar** fishing-rod.

cañada [ka'ɲaða] *sf* glen, ravine.

cáñamo ['kaɲamo] *sm* hemp.

caño ['kaɲo] *sm* pipe; sewer. **cañería** *sf* drain; piping.

cañón [ka'ɲon] *sm* canyon; cannon, gun; gun barrel; pipe, tube.

caoba [ka'oβa] *sf* mahogany.

caos ['kaos] *sm* chaos. **caótico** *adj* chaotic.

capa ['kapa] *sf* cloak; cape; covering; lid.

capacidad [kapaθi'ðað] *sf* capacity; ability; opportunity.

capacha [ka'patʃa] *sf* also **capacho** *sm* shopping basket.

capar [ka'par] *v* castrate; (*fam*) reduce.

capataz [kapa'taθ] *sm* foreman; overseer.

capaz [ka'paθ] *adj* capable; able; spacious.

capellán [kape'ʎan] *sm* chaplain.

capilar [kapi'lar] *sm, adj* capillary.

capilla [ka'piʎa] *sf* chapel; choir; hood. **estar en capilla** (*fam*) be in suspense.

capital [kapi'tal] *sm* (*com*) capital. *sf* capital city. *adj* principal.

capitán [kapi'tan] *sm* captain, leader. **capitanear** *v* command; lead.

capitular [kapitu'lar] *v* capitulate; make an agreement. **capitulación** *sf* capitulation; agreement.

capítulo [ka'pitulo] *sm* (*libro*) chapter; town council meeting; (*rel*) chapter.

capón [ka'pon] *sm* capon; eunuch; gelding; bundle of sticks.

capote [ka'pote] *sm* cape; greatcoat. **capotear** *v* (*fig, fam*) shirk.

capricho [ka'pritʃo] *sm* caprice, whim. **caprichoso** *adj* capricious.

cápsula ['kapsula] *sf* capsule; cartridge case; metal cap.

captar [kap'tar] *v* win over; gain; grasp.

capturar [kaptu'rar] *v* capture; arrest. **captura** *sf* capture.

capucha [ka'putʃa] *sf* hood; circumflex accent.

capuchina [kapu'tʃina] *sf* nasturtium.

capullo [ka'puʎo] *sm* cocoon; bud. **en capullo** in embryo.

cara ['kara] *sf* face; appearance; surface. **cara adelante/atrás** forwards/backwards. **cara o cruz** heads or tails. **dar la cara**

face the music. **hacer cara** face up to. **tener cara de** look like.

carabina [kara'βina] *sf* carbine; rifle. **carabinero** *sm* rifleman.

caracol [kara'kol] *sm* snail; spiral.

carácter [ka'rakter] *sm* character; nature; condition; sign, mark. **característica** *sf* characteristic. **característico** *adj* characteristic. **caracterización** *sf* characterization; (*teatro*) make-up. **caracterizar** *v* characterize; confer an honour on; (*teatro*) make up.

¡caramba! [ka'ramba] *interj* damn it!

caramelo [kara'melo] *sm* sweet, toffee; caramel.

carapacho [kara'patʃo] *sm* shell, carapace.

carátula [ka'ratula] *sf* mask; (*fam*) theatre, stage.

caravana [kara'βana] *sf* caravan; group, crowd.

carbohidrato [karβoi'ðrato] *sm* carbohydrate.

carbón [kar'βon] *sm* coal; charcoal; carbon; carbon paper. **carbonera** *sf* coal cellar; coal scuttle; charcoal burner. **carbonería** *sf* coalyard. **carbono** *sm* carbon.

carbunclo [kar'βunklo] *sm* also **carbunco** (*med*) carbuncle.

carburador [karβura'ðor] *sm* carburettor.

carcajada [karka'xaða] *sf* burst of laughter.

cárcel ['karθel] *sf* prison. **carcelero, -a** *sm, sf* jailer, warder.

carcomer [karko'mer] *v* corrode, eat away; undermine.

cardar [kar'ðar] *v* (*tecn*) card, comb. **carda** *sf* (*tecn*) card, carding; (*fam*) reprimand.

cardenal [karðe'nal] *sm* cardinal; bruise.

cardíaco [kar'ðiako] *adj* cardiac.

cardinal [karði'nal] *adj* principal; cardinal.

cardo ['karðo] *sm* thistle.

carear [kare'ar] *v* confront; compare; come face to face. **carearse** *v* meet.

*****carecer** [kare'θer] *v* lack, need. **carencia** *sf* lack, shortage; deficiency.

carestía [kares'tia] *sf* shortage, scarcity; high price.

careta [ka'reta] *sf* mask. **careta antigás** gasmask.

carey [ka'rej] *sm* turtle; tortoiseshell.

cargar [kar'gar] *v* load; burden; charge; tax; blame; attack; (*fam*) vex; lean, incline. **cargarse de** become full; be overburdened; (fam) be fed up; (cielo) become dark. **carga** sf load, burden; charge; tax; pressure. **cargadero** sm loading bay. **cargador** sm freighter; loader; carrier. **cargamento** sm cargo, load.

cargo ['kargo] sm post; accusation; responsibility; (com) charge; freighter. **cuenta a cargo** sf charge account.

cariarse [ka'rjarse] v decay. **caries** sf invar caries.

caribe [ka'riβe] s(m+f), adj Caribbean. **Mar Caribe** sm Caribbean Sea.

caricatura [karika'tura] sf caricature.

caricia [ka'riθja] sf caress. **caricioso** adj caressing.

caridad [kari'ðað] sf charity. **caritativo** adj charitable.

cariño [ka'riŋo] sm love, affection. **cariñoso** adj affectionate, loving.

cariz [ka'riθ] sm appearance, aspect.

carmesí [karme'si] sm, adj crimson.

carmín [kar'min] sm, adj carmine.

carnada [kar'naða] sf bait.

carnaval [karna'βal] sm carnival.

carne ['karne] sf meat, flesh. **carne magra** lean meat. **carnal** adj carnal. **carnicería** sf butcher's shop. **carnicero** sm butcher.

carnero [kar'nero] sm sheep; ram; mutton; cemetery.

carpa ['karpa] sf carp.

caro ['karo] adj expensive; dear, beloved.

carpeta [kar'peta] sf folder, file; portfolio; briefcase; tablecloth. **dar carpetazo a** shelve.

carpintería [karpinte'ria] sf carpentry; carpenter's shop. **carpintero** sm carpenter, joiner.

carrera [ka'rrera] sf race; road; career; course; line; (media) ladder. **de carrera** swiftly. **hacer carrera** succeed.

carreta [ka'rreta] sf cart, wagon. **carretear** v cart, haul.

carrete [ka'rrete] sm reel, spool, bobbin.

carretera [karre'tera] sf road, highway. **carretera de circunvalación** by-pass.

carril [ka'rril] sm furrow, rut; narrow road; rail.

carro ['karro] sm cart; car; typewriter carriage. **carro blindado** armoured car. **carro de mudanzas** removal van.

carroña [ka'rroŋa] sf carrion.

carroza [ka'rroθa] sf carriage; state coach; float.

carta ['karta] sf letter; chart; map; playing card; charter, document. **carta certificada** registered letter. **carta de venta** bill of sale. **tomar cartas en** (fam) take part in.

cartel [kar'tel] sm placard, poster. **cartelera** sf hoarding.

cartera [kar'tera] sf wallet; purse; briefcase; notebook; portfolio; office of a cabinet minister.

cartero [kar'tero] sm postman.

cartílago [kar'tilago] sm cartilage.

cartón [kar'ton] sm cardboard; carton; cartoon.

cartucho [kar'tutʃo] sm cartridge; paper cone.

casa ['kasa] sf house, home; household; business; building; flat. **casa de empeños** pawnshop. **casa de huéspedes** boarding-house. **casa pública** brothel. **casa y comida** board and lodging. **en casa** at home. **un amigo de casa** a friend of the family.

casar [ka'sar] v give in marriage; join. **casarse con** marry, get married. **casamiento** sm marriage.

cascabel [kaska'βel] sm small bell. **serpiente de cascabel** sf rattlesnake. **cascabelada** sf (fam) foolish action.

cascada [kas'kaða] sf waterfall.

cascar [kas'kar] v crack; burst; split; break; (fam) beat up; (fam) cough up; (fam) chatter; (fam) kick the bucket.

cáscara [kas'kara] sf shell; peel; rind; husk; bark.

cascarón [kaska'ron] sm egg-shell.

casco ['kasko] sm skull; helmet; skin; segment; shrapnel. **cascotes** sm pl rubble sing.

caserío [kase'rio] sm group of houses; settlement; country house.

casero [ka'sero] adj home-made; familiar; informal; (fam) domestic. sm landlord; tenant; caretaker.

casi ['kasi] adv nearly, almost.

casilla [ka'siʎa] sf hut, cabin; lodge; pigeonhole; section.

caso ['kaso] sm case, matter; event; chance; occasion. **el caso es the** fact is. **en tal caso** in such a case. **en todo caso** in any case. **hacer caso a** pay attention to.

caspa ['kaspa] sf dandruff.

casta ['kasta] sf caste; breed; class.

castaño [kas'taŋo] sm chestnut-tree;

chestnut brown. *adj* chestnut. **castaña** *sf* chestnut; hair bun.

castañuela [kasta'ɲwela] *sf* castanet.

castellano [kaste'ʎano], **-a** *s, adj* Castilian. *sm* (*lengua*) Castilian.

castidad [kasti'ðað] *sf* chastity.

castigar [kasti'ɣar] *v* punish, chastise. **castigo** *sm* punishment.

Castilla [kas'tiʎa] *sf* Castile.

castillo [kas'tiʎo] *sm* castle.

castizo [kas'tiθo] *adj* pure; pure-blooded; traditional.

casto ['kasto] *adj* chaste, pure.

castor [kas'tor] *sm* beaver.

castrar [kas'trar] *v* castrate; (*agr*) prune. **castrado** *sm* eunuch.

castrense [kas'trense] *adj* military.

casual [ka'swal] *adj* chance, coincidental. **casualidad** *sf* chance; coincidence; accident. **por casualidad** by chance.

casucha [ka'sutʃa] *sf also* **casuca** hovel.

cataclismo [kata'klismo] *sm* cataclysm.

catacumbas [kata'kumbas] *sf pl* catacombs *pl*.

catadura[1] [kata'ðura] *sf* tasting. **catador** *sm* taster, sampler. **catar** *v* taste, sample.

catadura[2] *sf* (*fam*) expression, look.

catalejo [kata'lexo] *sm* telescope.

catálogo [ka'talogo] *sm* catalogue. **catalogar** *v* catalogue; classify.

Cataluña [kata'luɲa] *sf* Catalonia.

cataplasma [kata'plasma] *sf* poultice.

catarata [kata'rata] *sf* waterfall; (*med*) cataract.

catarro [ka'tarro] *sm* catarrh, common cold. **catarro pradial** hay fever. **coger un catarro** catch cold.

catástrofe [ka'tastrofe] *sf* catastrophe. **catastrófico** *adj* catastrophic.

catecismo [kate'θismo] *sm* catechism.

cátedra ['kateðra] *sf* lecture room; senior teaching post; (*puesto*) chair.

catedral [kate'ðral] *sf* cathedral.

categoría [katego'ria] *sf* category; class; rank. **categórico** *adj* categorical; strict.

caterva [ka'terβa] *sf* crowd; heap.

cátodo ['katoðo] *sm* cathode.

católico [ka'toliko], **-a** *s, adj* (Roman) Catholic. **catolicismo** *sm* (Roman) Catholicism.

catorce [ka'torθe] *sm, adj* fourteen. **catorceno** *adj* fourteenth.

catre ['katre] *sm* camp-bed; cot.

cauce ['kauθe] *sm* river bed; ditch.

caución [kau'θjon] *sf* caution; pledge; bail.

caucho ['kautʃo] *sm* rubber.

caudal [kau'ðal] *sm* wealth; abundance.

caudillo [kau'ðiʎo] *sm* leader, chief.

causar [kau'sar] *v* cause, create, occasion. **causa** *sf* cause, reason, motive; (*jur*) trial. **a causa de** owing to. **causa pública** public welfare.

cáustico ['kaustiko] *adj* caustic, burning; scathing.

cautela [kau'tela] *sf* care, caution; cunning. **cauteloso** *adj* cautious; cunning. **cauto** *adj* cautious, wary.

cautivar [kauti'βar] *v* capture; captivate; charm. **cautividad** *sf* captivity. **cautivo, -a** *sm, sf* captive.

cavar [ka'βar] *v* dig; excavate; (*agr*) dress; ponder. **cava** *sf* cultivation. **cavadura** *sf* digging; dressing.

caverna [ka'βerna] *sf* cavern, cave. **cavernoso** *adj* cavernous; (*fig*) deep.

cavidad [kaβi'ðað] *sf* cavity.

cavilar [kaβi'lar] *v* think deeply, meditate. **caviloso** *adj* pensive; worried.

cayado [ka'jaðo] *sm* shepherd's crook; walking-stick.

cazar [ka'θar] *v* hunt; chase; shoot; catch. **caza** *sf* hunt; chase; game. **cazador, -a** *sm, sf* hunter.

cazo ['kaθo] *sm* ladle; saucepan; gluepot. **cazo eléctrico** electric kettle.

cazoleta [kaθo'leta] *sf* small pan; pipe bowl.

cazuela [ka'θwela] *sf* casserole; (*teatro*) the gods.

cebada [θe'βaða] *sf* barley. **cebadar** *v* feed (animals).

cebar [θe'βar] *v* feed, fatten up; prime, charge; penetrate; long for. **cebarse en** vent one's rage on; gloat over.

cebolla [θe'βoʎa] *sf* onion; flower bulb. **cebolleta** *sf* chive. **cebolleta** *sf* leek.

cebra ['θeβra] *sf* zebra. **paso de cebra** *sm* zebra crossing.

cecear [θeθe'ar] *v* lisp. **ceceo** *sm* lisp. **ceceoso** *adj* lisping.

ceder [θe'ðer] *v* give up; yield; sag.

cedro ['θeðro] *sm* cedar.

cédula ['θeðula] *sf* charter; certificate; form; patent.

*****cegar** [θe'gar] *v* blind; go blind; block up; cover. **cegador** *adj* blinding. **cegarra** *adj* (*fam*) short-sighted. **cegarrita** *adj* (*fam*) peering. **ceguedad** *or* **ceguera** *sf* blindness.

ceja ['θexa] *sf* eyebrow; mountain top; rim; cloud-cap. **fruncir las cejas** knit one's brows. **quemarse las cejas** burn the midnight oil. **tener entre ceja y ceja** (*fam*) concentrate on.

celada [θe'laδa] *sf* helmet; trick; ambush.

celar [θe'lar] *v* check on; watch; conceal; protect. **celador** *sm* watchman.

celda ['θelδa] *sf* cell.

celebrar [θele'βrar] *v* celebrate; praise; acclaim; conduct; (*rel*) say mass. **celebrarse** *v* take place. **celebración** *sf* celebration; acclamation. **celebrante** *sm* celebrant priest. **célebre** *adj* famous. **celebridad** [θeleβri'δaδ] *sf* fame; celebration.

celeridad [θeleri'δaδ] *sf* speed.

celeste [θe'leste] *adj* heavenly.

celibato [θeli'βato] *sm* celibacy; (*fam*) bachelor. **célibe** *s(m+f)* single person; bachelor; spinster.

celo ['θelo] *sm* zeal; heat, rut. **celos** *sm pl* jealousy *sing*. **dar celos** a make jealous. **tener celos** be jealous. **celosía** *sf* window lattice; venetian blind; jealousy. **celoso** *adj* zealous; jealous.

celta ['θelta] *s(m+f)* Celt. *sm* (*lengua*) Celtic.

célula ['θelula] *sf* cell.

celuloide [θelu'loiδe] *sm* celluloid.

celulosa [θelu'losa] *sf* cellulose.

cementerio [θemen'terjo] *sm* cemetery.

cemento [θe'mento] *sm* cement. **cemento armado** reinforced concrete.

cenagal [θena'gal] *sm* marsh, swamp; (*fam*) tight spot, mess.

cenar [θe'nar] *v* dine on, have for supper/dinner. **cena** *sf* evening meal, supper, dinner.

cenefa [θe'nefa] *sf* border; edging; frieze.

ceniza [θe'niθa] *sf* ash, cinder. **convertir en cenizas** reduce to ashes. **cenicero** *sm* ashtray.

censo ['θenso] *sm* census; tax; annuity; pension; ground rent; (*fig*) burden. **censar** *v* take a census of. **censor** *sm* censor; auditor.

censurar [θensu'rar] *v* censor; censure; condemn. **censura** *sf* censoring; censorship. **censurable** *adj* blameworthy. **censurador** *sm* censor. **censurista** *s(m+f)* critic; fault-finder.

centellear [θenteʎe'ar] *v* *also* **centellar**

sparkle; flash; twinkle; flicker. **centella** *sf* flash; spark. **centelleo** *sm* gleam; glitter; sparkle.

centavo [θen'taβo] *sm* cent.

centena [θen'tena] *sf* hundred. **centenada** *sf* *also* **centenar** *sm* hundred. **a** *or* **por centenares** by the hundred. **centenario** *sm* centenary.

centeno[1] [θen'teno] *sm* rye.

centeno[2] *adj* hundred.

centésimo [θen'tesimo] *adj* hundredth. *sm* cent.

centígrado [θen'tigraδo] *adj* centigrade.

centímetro [θen'timetro] *sm* centimetre.

céntimo ['θentimo] *adj* hundredth. *sm* cent.

centinela [θenti'nela] *s(m+f)* guard, sentry.

centrar [θen'trar] *v* centre. **central** *adj* central. **central** *sf* head office; headquarters; power station; switchboard. **centro** *sm* centre, middle; aim, goal, objective.

centrífugo [θen'trifugo] *adj* centrifugal.

centroamérica [θentroa'merika] *sf* Central America. **centroamericano** *adj* Central American.

centuria [θen'turja] *sf* century.

*****ceñir** [θe'nir] *v* gird, surround, encircle; crown; frame; shorten, take in; be a tight fit for. **ceñirse** *v* limit; adapt oneself to; cling. **ceñido** *adj* tight-fitting. **ceñidor** *sm* belt.

ceño ['θeno] *sm* frown. **fruncir el ceño** frown. **ceñudo** *adj* frowning.

cepa ['θepa] *sf* tree stump; stock; root; origin.

cepillar [θepi'ʎar] *v* brush; plane. **cepillarse** *v* (*fam*) fail an exam; (*fam*) polish off. **cepillo** *sm* brush; plane.

cepo ['θepo] *sm* branch; stocks *pl*; collecting box; (*tecn*) clamp, socket.

cera ['θera] *sf* wax.

cerámico [θe'ramiko] *adj* ceramic. **cerámica** *sf* ceramics; pottery.

cerca ['θerka] *adv* near, close, nearby. **cerca de** close by; almost; about. **de cerca** closely. **cercanía** *sf* nearness. **cercanías** *sf pl* vicinity *sing*. neighbourhood *sing*. **cercano** *adj* near, close.

cercar [θer'kar] *v* enclose; fence; surround. **cerca** *sf* enclosure, wall, fence. **cercado** *sm* enclosure.

cerco ['θerko] *sm* ring; circle; enclosure; frame; siege.

cerda [ˈθerda] *sf* (*zool*) sow; bristle.
cerdear *v* (*animales*) be lame, limp. **cerdo** *sm* pig; pork. **cerdoso** *adj* bristly.

Cerdeña [θerˈðeɲa] *sf* Sardinia.

cereal [θereˈal] *sm, adj* cereal.

cerebro [θeˈreβro] *sm* brain. **cerebral** *adj* cerebral.

ceremonia [θereˈmonja] *sf* ceremony. **ceremonial** *adj* ceremonial. **ceremonioso** *adj* ceremonious.

cereza [θeˈreθa] *sf* cherry. **cerezo** *sm* cherry tree.

cerilla [θeˈriʎa] *sf* match.

*****cerner** [θerˈner] *v* sift; sieve; examine carefully; drizzle. **cernerse** *v* sway; waddle; hover; threaten.

cero [ˈθero] *sm* zero, nothing.

*****cerrar** [θerˈrar] *v* shut, close. **cerrarse** *v* close up; stand firm; heal; cloud over. **cerrar con llave** lock. **cerrar la boca** shut up. **cerrar la marcha** bring up the rear. **cerrado** *adj* closed; secretive; obtuse; overcast. **cerradura** *sf* lock; locking up. **cerraje** *sm* lock.

cerril [θerˈril] *adj* rough, rocky; wild; ill-bred.

cerro [ˈθerro] *sm* hill, ridge; animal's neck.

cerrojo [θerˈroxo] *sm* bolt.

certeza [θerˈteθa] *sf also* **certidumbre** certainty.

certificar [θertifiˈkar] *v* certify; register; guarantee. **certificado** *sm* certificate; registered letter.

cervato [θerˈβato] *sm* (*zool*) fawn.

cerveza [θerˈβeθa] *sf* beer.

cerviz [θerˈβiθ] *sf* nape of the neck, cervix. **bajar la cerviz** bow one's head.

cesar [θeˈsar] *v* cease, stop; leave one's job. **cesación** *sf* cessation, stoppage. **cesante** *adj* out of office, unemployed. **cesantía** *sf* suspension from office.

cesión [θeˈsjon] *sf* transfer; assignment; conveyance; resignation.

césped [ˈθespeð] *sm* turf, lawn. **césped inglés** lawn.

cesta [ˈθesta] *sf* basket, hamper. **cestería** *sf* basketwork, wickerwork. **cesto** *sm* basket.

cetro [ˈθetro] *sm* sceptre; (*fig*) power.

cheque [ˈtʃek] *s* check

cianuro [θjaˈnuro] *sm* cyanide.

ciática [θiˈatika] *sf* sciatica. **ciático** *adj* sciatic.

cicatería [θikateˈria] *sf* stinginess.

cicatriz [θikaˈtriθ] *sf* scar.

ciclismo [θiˈklismo] *sm* cycling. **ciclista** *s(m+f)* cyclist.

ciclo [ˈθiklo] *sm* cycle. **cíclico** *adj* cyclical.

ciclón [θiˈklon] *sm* cyclone.

cidra [ˈθiðra] *sf* citron. **cidro** *sm* citron tree.

ciego [ˈθjeɣo], **-a** *sm, sf* blind person. *adj* blind.

cielo [ˈθjelo] *sm* sky; heaven; ceiling; climate. **¡cielos!** good heavens!

ciempiés [θjemˈpjes] *sm invar* centipede.

ciénaga [ˈθjenaɣa] *sf* bog, marsh, swamp.

ciencia [ˈθjenθja] *sf* science; knowledge, learning. **ciencia ficción** science fiction.

científico [θjenˈtifiko], **-a** *sm, sf* scientist. *adj* scientific.

cieno [ˈθjeno] *sm* mud. **cienoso** *adj* muddy.

ciento [ˈθjento] *sm, adj also* **cien** hundred.

cierre [ˈθjerre] *sm* closing; fastening; lock.

cierto [ˈθjerto] *adj* certain. *adv* certainly. **de cierto** certainly. **por cierto** of course.

ciervo [ˈθjerβo] *sm* deer; stag. **cierva** *sf* hind.

cierzo [ˈθjerθo] *sm* north wind.

cifra [ˈθifra] *sf* number, figure; cipher; code; abbreviation. **en cifra** in short. **cifrar** *v* summarize; cipher; enclose. **cifrar las esperanzas en** set one's hopes on.

cigarro [θiˈɣarro] *sm* cigar. **cigarillo** *sm* cigarette.

cigüeña [θiˈɣwena] *sf* stork.

cilindro [θiˈlindro] *sm* cylinder. **cilíndrico** *adj* cylindrical.

cima [ˈθima] *sf* top; summit. **dar cima a** finish off. **por cima** at the top; superficially.

címbalo [ˈθimbalo] *sm* cymbal.

cimbrar [θimˈbrar] *v also* **cimbrear** vibrate; bend; sway.

*****cimentar** [θimenˈtar] *v* found; establish. **cimiento** *sm* foundation.

cinc [θink] *sm* zinc.

cincel [θinˈθel] *sm* chisel. **cincelador** *sm* engraver; stonecutter.

cinco [ˈθinko] *sm, adj* five.

cincuenta [θinˈkwenta] *sm, adj* fifty.

cinchar [θinˈtʃar] *v* girth; fasten with hoops. **cincha** *sf* girth, cinch. **cincho** *sm* belt; hoop.

cine [ˈθine] *sm* cinema.

cínico ['θiniko], **-a** *sm. sf* cynic. *adj* cynical; shameless. **cinismo** *sm* cynicism.

cinife [θinife] *sm* mosquito.

cinta ['θinta] *sf* ribbon; strip; tape; tape-measure. **cinteado** *adj* beribboned.

cintura [θin'tura] *sf* waist; belt. **meter a uno en cintura** make someone behave. **cinturón** *sm* belt; zone; circle. **cinturón de seguridad** safety belt.

ciprés [θi'pres] *sm* cypress.

circo ['θirko] *sm* circus.

circuito [θir'kwito] *sm* circuit.

circular [θirku'lar] *v* circulate; circularize; move. *adj* round, circular. **circulación** *sf* circulation; traffic.

circuncidar [θirkunθi'ðar] *v* circumcise. **circuncisión** *sf* circumcision. **circunciso** *adj* circumcised.

circundar [θirkun'dar] *v* surround, encircle.

circunferencia [θirkunfe'renθja] *sf* circumference.

circunflejo [θirkun'flexo] *sm* circumflex.

circunscribir [θirkunskri'βir] *v* circumscribe.

circunspecto [θirkun'spekto] *adj* circumspect. **circunspección** *sf* circumspection.

circunstancia [θirkun'stanθja] *sf* circumstance; condition; incident. **circunstancial** *adj* circumstantial. **circunstante** *adj* surrounding; present.

circunvecino [θirkunβe'θino] *adj* neighbouring.

ciruela [θi'rwela] *sf* plum. **ciruelo** *sm* plum-tree.

cirugía [θiru'xia] *sf* surgery. **cirujano** *sm* surgeon.

cisco ['θisko] *sm* coal dust; (*fam*) hubbub.

cisma ['θisma] *sm* schism; discord.

cisne ['θisne] *sm* swan.

cisterna [θis'terna] *sf* cistern, water tank.

cita ['θita] *sf* citation; appointment; quotation. **citar** *v* make an appointment; quote; (*jur*) summons.

ciudad [θju'ðað] *sf* city. **ciudadanía** *sf* citizenship. **ciudadano, -a** *sm, sf* citizen. **ciudadela** *sf* citadel.

cívico ['θiβiko] *adj* civic; patriotic.

civilizar [θiβili'θar] *v* civilize. **civil** *adj* civil. **civilización** *sf* civilization.

cizalla [θi'ðaʎa] *sf* shears *pl*; metal shavings *pl*.

clamar [kla'mar] *v* cry out; beseech. **clamor** [kla'mor] *sm* shout; cry. **clamorear** *v* cry out for; beseech. **clamoroso** *adj* noisy.

clandestino [klandes'tino] *adj* secret.

clara ['klara] *sf* white of egg; bald patch. **claraboya** [klara'βoja] *sf* skylight.

clarear [klare'ar] *v* clear; dawn; grow light; be transparent; (*fam*) reveal secrets.

clarete [kla'rete] *sm* claret.

clarificar [klarifi'kar] *v* clarify. **clarificación** *sf* clarification.

clarín [kla'rin] *sm* bugle.

clarinete [klari'nete] *sm* clarinet.

claro ['klaro] *adj* light; clear; distinct. *adv* clearly. *sm* opening; space; clearing. **claro que** of course. **claro que sí** certainly. **claridad** *sf* clarity; light; brightness.

clase ['klase] *sf* class, type; lesson; classroom. **clase media** middle class. **clase particular** private lesson.

clásico ['klasiko] *adj* classic(al). *sm* classic.

clasificar [klasifi'kar] *v* classify. **clasificación** *sf* classification.

claudicar [klauði'kar] *v* limp; (*fam*) yield; (*fig*) shirk; (*fig*) falter. **claudicación** *sf* limping; yielding; shirking.

claustro ['klaustro] *sm* cloister; teaching staff. **claustral** *adj* cloistered. **claustrofobia** [klaustro'foβja] *sf* claustrophobia.

cláusula ['klausula] *sf* clause.

clavar [kla'βar] *v* nail; fasten, fix; (*fam*) cheat. **clava** *sf* club, cudgel. **clavado en la cama** bed-ridden. **clavija** *sf* peg, pin. **clavo** *sm* nail; spike.

clave ['klaβe] *sf* key; clue; clef. *sm* harpsichord.

clavel [kla'βel] *sm* carnation.

clavícula [kla'βikula] *sf* collar bone.

clemencia [kle'menθja] *sf* mercy. **clemente** *adj* merciful.

clérigo ['klerigo] *sm* clergyman, priest. **clerical** *adj* clerical. **clericato** *sm* also **clero** clergy.

cliente ['kljente], **-a** *sm, sf* client, customer; patient. **clientela** *sf* clients *pl*, customers *pl*; practice.

clima ['klima] *sm* climate. **climático** *adj* climatic.

clínica ['klinika] *sf* clinic. **clínico** *adj* clinical.

clisé [kli'se] *sm* (*foto*) negative; (*fig*) cliché.

cloaca [klo'aka] *sf* sewer, drain.

cloro ['kloro] *sm* chlorine.

clorofila [kloro'fila] *sf* chlorophyll.

cloroformo [kloro'formo] *sm* chloroform. **cloroformar** *v* chloroform.

club [kluβ] *sm* club. **club de noche** nightclub.

coacción [koak'θjon] *sf* coercion. **coactivo** *adj* coercive.

coagular [koagu'lar] *v* coagulate; curdle; clot. **coagulación** *sf* coagulation; clotting.

coalición [koali'θjon] *sf* coalition.

coartada [koar'taða] *sf* alibi.

coartar [koar'tar] *v* hinder; prevent; limit; restrict.

cobarde [ko'βarðe] *s(m+f)* coward. *adj* cowardly. **cobardía** *sf* cowardice.

cobertizo [koβer'tiθo] *sm* garage; shed.

cobertura [koβer'tura] *sf* covering.

cobijar [koβi'xar] *v* cover, shelter. **cobijo** *sm* shelter.

cobrar [ko'βrar] *v* charge; earn; gain. **cobrarse** *v* (*med*) recover. **cobradero** *adj* recoverable. **cobrador, -a** *sm, sf* collector; conductor; receiver. **cobranza** *sf* collection; receipt.

cobre ['koβre] *sm* copper. **batirse el cobre** (*fam*) get on with it. **cobres** *sm pl* (*música*) brass.

*cocer [ko'θer] *v* cook. **cocido** *sm* stew.

cocinar [koθi'nar] *v* cook. **cocina** *sf* kitchen; cookery. **cocinero, -a** *sm, sf* cook.

coco ['koko] *sm* coconut; coconut palm; grub, larva; (*fam*) face; (*fam*) head. **hacer cocos** make faces.

cocodrilo [koko'ðrilo] *sm* crocodile.

cóctel [kok'tel] *sm* cocktail.

coche [kot'ʃe] *sm* car; coach; carriage. **coche cama** sleeper. **coche de alquiler** self-drive car. **coche fúnebre** hearse.

cochino [ko'tʃino] **-a** *sm, sf* pig, swine. *adj* (*fam*) rotten; filthy; disgusting. **cochinada** *sf* filth; filthy thing. **cochinera** *sf* pigsty.

codear [koðe'ar] *v* nudge, elbow. **codearse** *v* rub shoulders with. **codazo** *sm* nudge. **codo** *sm* elbow; bend.

codeína [koðe'ina] *sf* codeine.

codelincuente [koðelin'kwente] *s(m+f)* accomplice. **codelincuencia** *sf* complicity.

códice ['koðiθe] *sm* codex.

codiciar [koði'θjar] *v* covet. **codicia** *sf* greed. **codicioso** *adj* greedy.

codificar [koðifi'kar] *v* codify. **codificación** *sf* codification.

código ['koðigo] *sm* code. **código de carreteras** highway code.

codillo [ko'ðiʎo] *sm* forearm; (*culin*) shoulder.

codorniz [koðor'niθ] *sf* quail.

coercer [koer'θer] *v* coerce. **coerción** *sf* coercion.

coexistir [koeksis'tir] *v* coexist. **coexistencia** *sf* coexistence.

cofia ['kofja] *sf* coif; hair-net.

cofradía [kofra'ðia] *sf* fraternity; society.

cofre ['kofre] *sm* chest.

coger [ko'xer] *v* get; take; catch; seize; fit; collect. **cogida** *sf* gathering; (*tauromaquia*) goring. **cogido** *sm* fold, pleat.

cogote [ko'gote] *sm* nape of the neck. **ser tieso de cogote** be stiff-necked.

cohete [ko'ete] *sm* rocket.

cohibir [koi'βir] *v* inhibit; embarrass. **cohibidor** *adj* inhibiting. **cohibición** *sf* inhibition. **cohibido** *adj* restricted.

cohombrillo [koom'briʎo] *sm* gherkin. **cohombro** *sm* cucumber.

coincidencia [koinθi'ðenθja] *sf* coincidence. **coincidente** *adj* coincidental.

cojear [koxe'ar] *v* limp; hobble; (*fig*) waver; (*fig*) lapse. **cojera** *sf* lameness. **cojo** *adj* lame; lopsided.

cojín [ko'xin] *sm* cushion. **cojinete** *sm* small pillow; pad; (*tecn*) bearing. **cojinete de bolas** ball-bearing.

cok [kok] *sm* coke.

col [kol] *sf* cabbage. **coles de Bruselas** Brussels sprouts *pl*.

cola ['kola] *sf* tail; end; (*vestido*) train; queue; glue. **hacer cola** form a queue.

colaborar [kolaβo'rar] *v* collaborate. **colaboración** *sf* collaboration. **colaborador, -a** *sm, sf* collaborator.

colapso [ko'lapso] *sm* collapse, breakdown.

*colar [ko'lar] *v* strain; filter; wash; confer; (*fig, fam*) slip through. **colarse** *v* slip; gatecrash; jump the queue; err. **colada** *sf* washing. **coladero** *sm* colander, sieve.

colcha ['koltʃa] *sf* bedspread.

colchón [kol'tʃon] *sm* mattress.

colear [kole'ar] *v* wag the tail.

colección [kolek'θjon] *sf* collection. **colectivo** *adj* collective. **colectividad** *sf* collectivity; community.

colega [ko'lega] *sm* colleague.

colegio [ko'lexjo] *sm* college, school. **colegial** *sm* schoolboy.

colegir [kole'xir] *v* infer, conclude.

cólera ['kolera] *sf* anger. *sm* cholera. **colérico** *adj* angry.

coleta [ko'leta] *sf* pigtail; postscript.

*colgar [kol'gar] *v* hang, hang up, hang out. **colgadero** *sm* hook; peg; hanger. **puente colgante** *sm* suspension bridge.

coliflor [koli'flor] *sf* cauliflower.

colilla [ko'liʎa] *sf* cigarette stub.

colina [ko'lina] *sf* hill.

colindar [kolin'dar] *v* adjoin. **colindante** *adj* adjacent.

colisión [koli'sjon] *sf* collision.

colmar [kol'mar] *v* fill to overflowing. **colmado** *adj* plentiful.

colmena [kol'mena] *sf* beehive.

colmillo [kol'miʎo] *sm* tooth; fang; tusk. **enseñar los colmillos** (*fam*) threaten.

colmo ['kolmo] *sm* highest point; limit.

colocar [kolo'kar] *v* place; put in position; arrange; find employment for. **colocarse** *v* get a job. **colocación** *sf* employment; position; investment.

Colombia [ko'lombja] *sf* Colombia. **colombiano, -a** *s, adj* Colombian.

colonia [ko'lonja] *sf* colony. **colonial** *adj* colonial; imported. **colonialismo** *sm* colonialism. **colonización** *sf* colonization. **colonizar** *v* colonize. **colono** *sm* colonist, colonial.

coloquio [ko'lokjo] *sm* conversation.

color [ko'lor] *sm* colour; dye; paint; complexion. **colorado** *sm, adj* coloured; red. **ponerse colorado** blush. **colorar** *v* colour, dye. **colorear** *v* colour, dye; grow red; ripen. **colorete** *sm* rouge. **colorido** *sm* colour, colouring. **colorín** *sm* goldfinch; (*fam*) measles.

colosal [kolo'sal] *adj* colossal.

columbrar [kolum'brar] *v* glimpse; (*fig*) suspect.

columna [ko'lumna] *sf* column, pillar.

columpiar [kolum'pjar] *v* swing. **columpiarse** *v* sway; (*fam*) waddle; blunder. **columpio** *sm* swing.

collado [ko'ʎaðo] *sm* hill; fell.

collar [ko'ʎar] *sm* necklace; collar.

coma¹ ['koma] *sf* (*gram*) comma.

coma² *sm* (*med*) coma.

comadre [ko'maðre] *sf* midwife; godmother; (*fam*) neighbour, friend. **comadrear** *v* gossip. **comadreo** *sm* gossip.

comadreja [koma'ðrexa] *sf* weasel.

comadrona [koma'ðrona] *sf* midwife.

comandante [koman'dante] *sm* commander. **comandar** *v* command.

comandita [koman'dita] *sf* sleeping partnership. **socio comanditario** *sm* sleeping partner.

comarca [ko'marka] *sf* region, district.

comba ['komba] *sf* bend, curve; camber; sag. **combadura** *sf* curvature; camber.

combatir [komba'tir] *v* combat, fight. **combate** *sm* combat, battle, struggle. **combatiente** *sm* fighter; soldier.

combinar [kombi'nar] *v* combine; plan, arrange. **combinación** *sf* combination; project; permutation. **combinatorio** *adj* combining.

combustible [kombus'tiβle] *adj* combustible. *sm* fuel.

comedero [kome'ðero] *adj* edible. *sm* dining-room; feeding-trough.

comedia [ko'meðja] *sf* play; comedy; theatre. **comediante, -a** *sm, sf* actor/actress.

comediar [kome'ðjar] *v* divide into equal shares.

comedido [kome'ðiðo] *adj* polite, courteous; moderate. **comedir** *v* prepare. **comedirse** *v* restrain oneself.

comedor [kome'ðor] *sm* dining-room.

comensal [komen'sal] *sm* table companion.

comentar [komen'tar] *v* comment on; discuss. **comentario** *sm* commentary. **comentarista** *s*(*m*+*f*) commentator. **comento** *sm* comment.

*comenzar [komen'θar] *v* commence. **comienzo** *sm* beginning.

comer [ko'mer] *v* eat; corrode; erode. **no tener qué comer** have nothing to eat. **ser de buen comer** have a good appetite. **comerse** *v* swallow; eat up. **comestible** *adj* edible. **comestibles** *sm pl* food *sing*; groceries *pl*. **comida** *sf* food; meal; lunch.

comercio [ko'merθjo] *sm* commerce; trade; shop. **comercio al por mayor/menor** wholesale/retail trade. **comerciante** *sm* shopkeeper; merchant; tradesman. **comerciar** *v* trade.

cometa [ko'meta] *sf* kite. *sm* comet.

cometer [kome'ter] *v* commit. **cometido** *sm* task; assignment; mission.

comezón [kome'θon] *sf* itch; itching.

cómico ['komiko] *adj* comic(al). *sm* comedian.

comilón [komi'lon], **-ona** *sm, sf* glutton. *adj* gluttonous. *sf* feast.

comillas [ko'miʎas] *sf pl* inverted commas *pl.*

comisaría [komisa'ria] *sf* police station. **comisario** *sm* commissary; commissioner; police inspector.

comisión [komi'sjon] *sf* commission; mission; committee.

comiso [ko'miso] *sm* (*jur*) confiscation.

comité [komi'te] *sm* committee.

comitiva [komi'tiβa] *sf* retinue.

como ['komo] *adv* how; as; as if; why; when; so that; about, approximately. *conj* as, since, because; if. **así como** as soon as; in the same way that. **como quiera que sea** in one way or another. **tan pronto como** as soon as. ¿**cómo**? *adv* how? why? in what way? ¿**cómo**! *interj* what! why! eh! **el cómo y el porqué** the how and the why.

cómoda ['komoða] *sf* chest of drawers.

cómodo ['komoðo] *adj* convenient; comfortable. **comodidad** *sf* convenience, comfort. **a su comodidad** at your earliest convenience.

compacto [kom'pakto] *adj* compact, close.

*****compadecer** [kompaðe'θer] *v* pity. **compadecerse** *v* sympathize. **compadre** [kom'paðre] *sm* godfather; pal, crony.

compaginar [kompaxi'nar] *v* arrange; combine; join; match; agree.

compañero [kompa'ɲero], **-a** *sm, sf* companion, partner; one of a pair. **compañerismo** *sm* fellowship. **compañía** *sf* company, society.

comparar [kompa'rar] *v* compare. **comparación** *sf* comparison. **comparativo** *adj* comparative.

*****comparecer** [kompare'θer] *v* appear in court. **orden de comparecer** *sm* summons.

compartimiento [komparti'mjento] *sm* compartment; section; division. **compartir** *v* divide; share.

compás [kom'pas] *sm* (*mar*) compass; (*mat*) pair of compasses; rhythm; pattern, standard. **llevar el compás** beat time. **compasado** *adj* orderly, moderate. **compasar** *v* measure; regulate.

compasión [kompa'sjon] *sf* compassion. **compasivo** *adj* compassionate.

compatible [kompa'tiβle] *adj* compatible. **compatibilidad** *sf* compatibility.

compatriota [kompa'trjota] *s(m+f)* compatriot.

compeler [kompe'ler] *v* compel.

compendio [kom'pendjo] *sm* compendium; summary, précis. **en compendio** briefly. **compendir** *v* summarize.

compensar [kompen'sar] *v* compensate; offset; make amends. **compensación** *sf* compensation. **compensatorio** *adj* compensatory.

*****competir** [kompe'tir] *v* compete; contest. **competencia** *sf* competition; concern; competence. **competente** *adj* competent; able. **competición** *sf* competition. **competidor, -a** *sm, sf* competitor.

compilar [kompi'lar] *v* compile. **compilación** *sf* compilation.

compinche [kom'pintʃe] *s(m+f)* pal, chum; accomplice.

*****complacer** [kompla'θer] *v* please; oblige; humour. **complacerse** *v* be pleased, be glad (to). **complacencia** *sf* pleasure; indulgence. **complaciente** *adj* helpful; obliging.

complejo [kom'plexo] *adj, sm* complex. **complejidad** *sf* complexity.

complementario [komplemen'tarjo] *adj* complementary. **complemento** *sm* complement.

completar [komple'tar] *v* complete. **completo** *adj* complete.

complicar [kompli'kar] *v* complicate; be complicated *or* confused. **complicarse** *v* become confused *or* complicated. **complicación** *sf* complication. **complicado** *adj* complicated.

cómplice ['kompliθe] *s(m+f)* accomplice. **complicidad** *sf* complicity.

complot [kom'plot] *sm* plot; intrigue; (*fam*) understanding.

*****componer** [kompo'ner] *v* compose; form; repair; adjust; write. **componerse** *v* compose oneself; tidy oneself up; dress up; agree. **componerse de** consist of. **componedor, -a** *sm, sf* compositor; repairer; arbitrator. **componente** *sm* component; ingredient. **componible** *adj* adjustable.

comportar [kompor'tar] *v* tolerate; involve. **comportarse** *v* behave. **comportamiento** *sm* behaviour. **comporte** *sm* behaviour; bearing.

composición [komposi'θjon] *sf* composition; mixture; agreement; settlement. **compositor, -a** *sm, sf* composer.

compostura [kompos'tura] *sf* composition, structure; repair; neatness; adornment; agreement; composure; adjustment.

compota [kom'pota] *sf (culin)* compote.

comprar [kom'prar] *v* buy; bribe. **compra** *sf* purchase. **comprador, -a** *sm, sf* shopper.

comprender [kompren'der] *v* understand; include. **comprensibilidad** *sf* intelligibility. **comprensible** *adj* understandable. **comprensión** *sf* understanding; inclusion. **comprensivo** *adj* understanding; comprising.

comprimir [kompri'mir] *v* squeeze, compress. **comprimirse** *v* control oneself. **compresa** *sf* compress; sanitary towel. **compresión** *sf* compression.

*comprobar [kompro'βar] *v* verify, check. **comprobación** *sf* verification. **comprobante** *adj* verifying. *sm* voucher; receipt.

comprometer [komprome'ter] *v* risk; compromise; commit. **comprometido** *adj* embarrassing; committed; implicated. **compromiso** *sm* commitment; agreement; compromise.

compuesto [kom'pwesto] *sm* compound. *adj* compound; repaired; dressed-up.

compunción [kompun'θjon] *sf* compunction; contrition.

computar [kompu'tar] *v* compute, calculate. **computadora** *sf* computer.

comulgar [komul'gar] *v* give/take communion; *(fig)* share.

común [ko'mun] *adj* common; ordinary; vulgar. *sm* community, public toilet. **por lo común** generally. **comunal** *adj* communal.

comunicar [komuni'kar] *v* communicate; convey; transmit; *(dos cuartos)* connect. **comunicarse** *v* spread; keep in touch with; exchange. **comunicación** *sf* communication; message. **comunicativo** *adj* talkative; catching.

comunidad [komuni'ðað] *sf* community.

comunión [komu'njon] *sf* communion.

comunismo [komu'nismo] *sm* communism. **comunista** *sm (m+f)*, *adj* communist.

con [kon] *prep* with; by; in spite of; to, towards. **con que** *conj* whereupon; and so. **con tal que** provided that.

cóncavo ['konkaβo] *adj* concave. **concavidad** *sf* hollow, cavity.

*concebir [konθe'βir] *v* conceive; imagine; understand; take; *(med)* conceive.

concebible *adj* conceivable, imaginable. **concepción** *sf* conception, idea; *(med)* conception. **concepto** *sm* concept; idea; opinion; witticism.

conceder [konθe'ðer] *v* concede, grant; allow; spare; award. **concesión** *sf* concession; grant.

concejo [kon'θexo] *sm* council. **concejal** *sm* councillor. **concejil** *adj* municipal.

concentrar [konθen'trar] *v* concentrate. **concentración** *sf* concentration.

concernir [konθer'njente] *adj* concerning, regarding. **concernir** *v* concern.

*concertar [konθer'tar] *v* harmonize; agree; adjust; compare. **concertado** *adj* concerted.

conciencia [kon'θjenθja] *sf* conscience; consciousness; mind; conscientiousness. **concienzudo** *adj* conscientious.

concierto [kon'θjerto] *sm* concert; concerto; agreement; *(fig)* harmony. **de concierto** in agreement.

conciliar [konθi'ljar] *v* conciliate; reconcile; gain. *adj* of a council. *sm* councillor. **concilio** *sm* councillor; council.

conciso [kon'θiso] *adj* concise.

concitar [konθi'tar] *v* stir up.

*concluir [konklu'ir] *v* conclude; deduce; settle; convince. **conclusión** *sf* conclusion.

*concordar [konkor'ðar] *v* agree. **concordancia** *sf* agreement. **concorde** *adj* in agreement. **concordia** *sf* harmony.

concretar [konkre'tar] *v* bring together; limit; specify; state explicitly. **concretarse** *v* confine oneself; be definite; keep; take shape. **concreto** *adj* concrete, specific. **en concreto** in brief.

concubina [konku'βina] *sf* concubine.

concurrir [konkur'rir] *v* meet; attend; go; coincide; contribute; concur; compete. **concurrido** *adj* popular; crowded. **concurso** *sm* meeting; cooperation; help; competition.

concusión [konku'sjon] *sf* concussion.

concha ['kontʃa] *sf* shell.

condado [kon'daðo] *sm* earldom; county. **conde** *sm* earl. **condesa** *sf* countess.

condecorar [kondeko'rar] *v (persona)* decorate. **condecoración** *sf* medal, decoration.

condenar [konde'nar] *v* condemn; sentence; block up. **condena** *sf* sentence; conviction. **cumplir condena** serve a sentence. **condenación** *sf* condemnation;

damnation. **condenado, -a** *sm, sf* condemned person; wretch.

condensar [konden'sar] *v* condense. **condensación** *sf* condensation. **condensador** *sm* condenser.

***condescender** [kondesθen'der] *v* condescend; yield; comply. **condescendencia** *sf* condescension; compliance. **condescendiente** *adj* condescending; obliging.

condicionar [kondiθjo'nar] *v* condition; determine. **condición** *sf* condition; quality; temperament.

condimentar [kondimen'tar] *v* season. **condimento** *sm* seasoning, condiment.

condolerse [kondo'lerse] *v* condole, sympathize. **condolencia** *sf* condolence.

condonar [kondo'nar] *v* pardon, condone. *(deuda)* cancel. **condonación** *sf* pardon.

***conducir** [kondu'θir] *v* conduct; transport; guide; manage; *(auto)* drive; be suitable. **conducirse** *v* behave. **conducción** *sf* transport; guidance; direction, management. **conducción a izquierda** left-hand drive. **permiso de conducción** *sm* driving licence. **conducta** *sf* transport; conduct; direction; behaviour.

conducto [kon'dukto] *sm* conduit; pipe. **conductor** *sm* (*tecn*) conductor.

conectar [konek'tar] *v* connect; switch on. **conectador** *sm* connector. **conexión** *sf* connection.

conejo [ko'nexo] *sm* rabbit.

confabularse [konfaβu'larse] *v* plot. **confabulación** *sf* conspiracy.

confeccionar [konfekθjon'ar] *v* make, make up. **confección** *sf* making; tailoring; clothing. **confeccionado** *adj* ready-made, ready-to-wear.

confederar [konfeðe'rar] *v* confederate. **confederación** *sf* confederation, confederacy.

conferenciar [konferen'θjar] *v* talk, discuss. **conferencia** *sf* conference; lecture; telephone call. **conferencia a cobro revertido** reverse-charge call. **conferencia en la cumbre** summit conference. **conferencia interurbana** trunk call.

***conferir** [konfe'rir] *v* confer, consult; award, grant.

***confesar** [konfe'sar] *v* confess, admit. **confesar de plano** own up. **confesión** *sf* confession.

confeti [kon'feti] *sm pl* confetti *sing*.

confiar [kon'fjar] *v* entrust; trust; rely. **confiable** *adj* trustworthy. **confiado** *adj* confident; trusting. **confianza** *sf* confidence; reliability; informality.

confidencia [konfi'ðenθja] *sf* secret; confidence. **confidencial** *adj* confidential. **confidente** *adj* faithful.

confinar [konfi'nar] *v* confine; banish. **confinar con** border on. **confín** *sm* border, limit.

confirmar [konfir'mar] *v* confirm. **confirmarse** *v* be confirmed. **confirmación** *sf* confirmation.

confiscar [konfis'kar] *v* confiscate. **confiscación** *sf* confiscation.

confitar [konfi'tar] *v* coat with sugar; preserve in syrup. **confite** *sm* sweet. **confitería** *sf* sweet-shop. **confitura** *sf* candied fruit.

conflicto [kon'flikto] *sm* conflict.

***confluir** [konflu'ir] *v* converge, meet.

conformar [konfor'mar] *v* conform. **conformarse** *v* resign oneself. **conforme** *adj* in agreement; alike; according. **conforme a** in accordance with. **según y conforme** it all depends.

confortar [konfor'tar] *v* comfort; encourage. **confortable** *adj* comfortable. **conforte** *sm* solace, comfort.

confrontar [konfron'tar] *v* confront; compare. **confrontar con** border on; confront. **confrontación** *sf* confrontation.

confundir [konfun'dir] *v* confuse; mistake. **confusión** *sf* confusion. **confuso** *adj* confused; embarrassed.

congelar [konxe'lar] *v* freeze; congeal. **congelación** *sf* freezing. **congelación de salarios** wage freeze. **congelador** *sm* freezer.

congénito [kon'xenito] *adj* congenital.

congestionar [konxestjo'nar] *v* congest. **congestión** *sf* congestion.

conglomerarse [konglome'rarse] *v* conglomerate. **conglomeración** *sf* conglomeration.

congoja [kon'goxa] *sf* agony; distress.

congratular [kongratu'lar] *v* congratulate. **congratularse** *v* be delighted. **congratulación** *sf* congratulation; delight.

congregar [kongre'gar] *v* congregate. **congregación** *sf* congregation.

congreso [kon'greso] *sm* congress; assembly; conference.

congrio ['kongrjo] *sm* conger eel.

congruente [kongru'ente] *adj* congruent; suitable. **congruencia** *sf* congruence; suitability.

cónico ['koniko] *adj* conical.

conífero [ko'nifero] *adj* coniferous. **conífera** *sf* conifer.

conjeturar [konxetu'rar] *v* conjecture, guess. **conjetura** *sf* conjecture, guess.

conjugar [konxu'gar] *v* combine; (*gram*) conjugate. **conjugación** *sf* conjugation.

conjunto [kon'xunto] *sm* whole. *adj* joint. **en conjunto** as a whole. **conjunción** *sf* (*gram*) conjunction.

conjurar [konxu'rar] *v* bind by oath; implore; ward off; conspire; exorcise. **cónjura** *sf also* **conjuración** conspiracy. **conjurador** *sm* exorcist. **conjuro** *sm* exorcism; entreaty.

conmemorar [konmemo'rar] *v* commemorate. **conmemoración** *sf* commemoration. **conmemorativo** *adj* commemorative.

conmigo [kon'migo] *pron* with me, with myself.

conminar [konmi'nar] *v* threaten; warn. **conminativo** *adj* threatening; compulsory.

conmiseración [konmisera'θjon] *sf* commiseration.

conmoción [konmo'θjon] *sf* commotion; upheaval; shock. **conmoción cerebral** concussion.

conmover [konmo'βer] *v* disturb; touch. **conmoverse** *v* be moved. **conmovedor** *adj* moving, touching.

conmutar [konmu'tar] *v* exchange. **conmutador** *sm* switch.

connivencia [konni'βenθja] *sf* connivance.

connotar [konno'tar] *v* imply. **connotación** *sf* connotation.

cono ['kono] *sm* cone.

*****conocer** [kono'θer] *v* know; understand; recognize. **conocer de** know about. **conocer de** or **en** (*jur*) try (a case). **conocer de nombre** know by name. **conocerse** *v* meet; be acquainted with. **se conoce que** it is clear that. **conocedor, -a** *s, adj* expert. **conocido, -a** *sm, adj* acquaintance. **conocimiento** *sm* knowledge; good sense; consciousness; (*com*) bill of lading; proof of identity. **perder el conocimiento** lose consciousness.

conque ['konke] *conj* so. *sm* (*fam*) condition. **conqué** *sm* (*fam*) means.

conquistar [konkis'tar] *v* conquer; win;

win over. **conquista** *sf* conquest. **conquistador, -a** *sm, sf* conqueror.

consabido [konsa'βiðo] *adj* traditional; well known; aforementioned.

consagrar [konsa'grar] *v* consecrate; dedicate. **consagración** *sf* consecration; dedication.

consanguíneo [konsan'gineo] *adj* related by blood. **consanguinidad** *sf* blood relationship.

consciente [kons'θjente] *adj* conscious.

consecuencia [konse'kwenθja] *sf* consequence; outcome; consistency. **en** or **por consecuencia** consequently. **ser de consecuencia** be of importance. **traer como consecuencia** result in. **consecuente** *adj* consequent; consistent.

consecutivo [konseku'tiβo] *adj* consecutive.

*****conseguir** [konse'gir] *v* get; attain; procure; bring about; manage. **dar por conseguido** take for granted.

consejo [kon'sexo] *sm* advice, counsel; council. **consejo de guerra** court-martial. **entrar en consejo** begin consultation. **consejero** *sm* adviser; member of board of directors.

*****consentir** [konsen'tir] *v* allow; believe; tolerate; spoil; agree. **consentir en** consent to. **consentirse** *v* begin to crack; come loose. **consentido** *adj* pampered.

conserje [kon'serxe] *sm* porter, doorkeeper.

conservar [konser'βar] *v* conserve; preserve. **conservarse** *v* last, wear well. **conserva** *sf* preserved food; jam; pickles *pl*. **conservación** *sf* conservation; preserving. **conservador, -a** *sm, sf* (*pol*) Conservative; (*museo*) curator.

considerar [konsiðe'rar] *v* consider. **considerable** *adj* considerable; substantial. **consideración** *sf* consideration. **por consideración a** out of respect for. **ser de consideración** be important. **tener** or **guardar consideraciones** show consideration.

consignar [konsig'nar] *v* consign; assign; deposit; send. **consignación** *sf* consignment. **consigna** *sf* left-luggage office; password; slogan.

consigo [kon'sigo] *pron* with him/her/you/one.

consiguiente [konsi'gjente] *adj* consequent.

consistir [konsis'tir] v consist. **consistir en** consist of. **consistencia** sf consistency. **consistente** adj consistent.

*****consolar** [konso'lar] v console. **consolación** sf consolation.

consolidar [konsoli'ðar] v consolidate; strengthen. **consolidación** sf consolidation.

consonante [konso'nante] sm consonant. adj rhyming; harmonious. **consonancia** sf rhyme; harmony. **consonar** v rhyme; harmonize.

consorte [kon'sorte] s(m+f) consort; accomplice; companion. **consorcio** sm association; fellowship; consortium.

conspicuo [kons'pikwo] adj conspicuous.

conspirar [konspi'rar] v conspire, plot. **conspiración** sf conspiracy, plot.

constante [kons'tante] adj constant. **constancia** sf constancy.

constar [kons'tar] v be clear; be evident; be on record. **constar de** consist of. **constar en** appear; be recorded.

constelación [konstela'θjon] sf constellation; climate.

consternarse [konster'narse] v be dismayed. **consternación** sf consternation, dismay.

constiparse [konsti'parse] v catch a cold. **constipación** sf cold. **estar constipado** have a cold.

*****constituir** [konstitu'ir] v constitute; establish; compose. **constitución** sf constitution.

constreñir [konstre'ɲir] v constrain; force; constipate. **constreñimiento** sm constraint. **constricción** sf constriction.

*****construir** [konstru'ir] v construct. **construcción** sf construction. **constructor, -a** sm, sf builder, constructor.

consuelo [kon'swelo] sm consolation.

cónsul ['konsul] sm consul. **consulado** sm consulate.

consultar [konsul'tar] v consult. **consulta** sf consultation.

consumado [konsu'maðo] adj consummate; accomplished. **consumación** sf consummation; completion. **consumar** v accomplish; complete.

consumir [konsu'mir] v consume. **consumirse** v languish; be uneasy. **consumido** adj consumed; (fam) lean; (fam) timid. **consumo** sm consumption.

contabilidad [kontaβili'ðað] sf accounting; bookkeeping. **contable** sm bookkeeper; accountant.

contacto [kon'takto] sm contact.

contagiar [konta'xjar] v infect, contaminate; corrupt. **contagio** sm contagion. **contagioso** adj contagious.

contaminar [kontami'nar] v contaminate. **contaminación** sf contamination.

*****contar** [kon'tar] v count; relate. **contar con** count on; expect; possess. **contado** adj counted, limited. **al contado** cash down. **de contado** immediately. **por de contado** certainly. **contador** sm counter; cashier; (tecn) meter. **contador de aparcamiento** parking meter.

contemplar [kontem'plar] v contemplate. **contemplación** sf contemplation. **contemplativo** adj contemplative.

contemporáneo [kontempo'raneo], -a s, adj contemporary.

*****contender** [konten'der] v contend; struggle; argue. **contención** sf contention. **contencioso** adj contentious. **contendedor** sm contender, antagonist. **contendiente** s(m+f) litigant. **contienda** sf contest; dispute.

*****contener** [konte'ner] v contain; control; suppress; stop.

contenido [konte'niðo] adj reserved; moderate; contained. sm contents pl.

contentar [konten'tar] v satisfy, content. **contentarse** v be pleased. **contentamiento** sm contentment. **contento** adj content, satisfied.

contestar [kontes'tar] v answer; confirm; agree. **contestable** adj questionable. **contestación** sf reply; dispute.

contexto [kon'teksto] sm context.

contigo [kon'tigo] pron (fam) with you.

contiguo [kon'tigwo] adj contiguous; adjoining. **contigüidad** sf contiguity.

continente [konti'nente] sm continent; bearing; container. adj containing; continent. **continencia** sf continence. **continental** adj continental.

contingente [kontin'xente] adj contingent, accidental. sm contingent. **contingencia** sf contingency.

continuar [konti'nwar] v continue; remain; endure. **continuación** sf continuation. **a continuación de** following. **continuo** adj continuous.

contorno [kon'torno] sm contour, outline.

contornos *sm pl* environs *pl.* **en contorno** round about.

contra ['kontra] *prep* against; opposite; facing. **el pro y el contra** the pros and cons. **en contra de** in opposition to.

contrabajo [kontra'βaxo] *sm* double bass.

contrabando [kontra'βando] *sm* contraband; smuggling.

contracción [kontrak'θjon] *sf* contraction.

*****contradecir** [kontraðe'θir] *v* contradict. **contradicción** *sf* contradiction.

*****contraer** [kontra'er] *v* contract; enter into; be infected with. **contraer matrimonio con** marry.

contrafuerte [kontra'fwerte] *sm* buttress.

*****contrahacer** [kontraa'θer] *v* counterfeit; copy. **contrahacerse** *v* feign.

contrahecho [kontra'etʃo] *adj* deformed.

contramaestre [kontrama'estre] *sm* foreman; *(mar)* boatswain.

contramandar [kontraman'dar] *v* countermand.

contrapelo [kontra'pelo] *adv* **a contrapelo** against the grain.

contrapesar [kontrape'sar] *v* counterpoise, counterbalance; offset. **contrapeso** *sm* counterpoise.

contraponer [kontrapo'ner] *v* set against; oppose; contrast.

contrapunto [kontra'punto] *sm* counterpoint.

contrariar [kontra'rjar] *v* oppose. **contrariedad** *sf* opposition; setback; annoyance.

contrario [kon'trarjo], **-a** *sm, sf* opponent. **al contrario** on the contrary. **de lo contrario** otherwise. *adj* contrary, opposite.

contrarrestar [kontrares'tar] *v* counteract; oppose; resist; *(la pelota)* return.

contrarrevolución [kontrareβolu'θjon] *sf* counter-revolution. **contrarrevolucionario**, **-a** *s, adj* counter-revolutionary.

contrasentido [kontrasen'tiðo] *sm* contradiction; nonsense; mistranslation; misinterpretation.

contraseña [kontra'seɲa] *sf* countersign; password.

contrastar [kontras'tar] *v* contrast; resist; inspect. **contraste** *sm* contrast; opposition; hallmark; inspector. **en contraste con** in contrast to.

contrato [kon'trato] *sm* contract; covenant.

contraveneno [kontraβe'neno] *sm* antidote.

*****contravenir** [kontraβe'nir] *v* contravene. **contravención** *sf* contravention.

*****contribuir** [kontri'βwir] *v* contribute; pay tax. **contribución** *sf* contribution; tax. **contribuyente** *s(m + f)* tax-payer.

contrición [kontri'θjon] *sf* contrition.

contrincante [kontrin'kante] *sm* competitor; rival.

controversia [kontro'βersja] *sf* controversy. **controvertible** *adj* controversial. **controvertir** *v* dispute, argue.

contumacia [kontu'maθja] *sf* stubbornness, obstinacy; *(jur)* contempt of court. **contumaz** *adj* stubborn; perverse.

conturbar [kontur'βar] *v* perturb; disturb. **conturbación** *sf* perturbation.

contusión [kontu'sjon] *sf* contusion, bruise. **contusionar** *v* bruise.

*****convalecer** [konβale'θer] *v* convalesce. **convalecencia** *sf* convalescence.

convecino [konβe'θino] *adj* neighbouring.

convencer [konβen'θer] *v* convince. **convencido** *adj* convincing. **convencimiento** *sm* conviction.

*****convenir** [konβe'nir] *v* agree, be agreed; arrange; be convenient; be advisable. **me conviene** it suits me. **convención** *sf* convention; agreement; assembly. **convencional** *adj* conventional. **conveniente** *adj* docile. **conveniencia** *sf* convenience; conformity; usefulness; advantage. **conveniente** *adj* convenient; expedient; proper. **convenio** *sm* agreement; compact.

convento [kon'βento] *sm* convent.

converger [konβer'xer] *v also* **convergir** converge; *(fig)* agree. **convergencia** *sf* convergence. **convergente** *adj* convergent.

conversar [konβer'sar] *v* converse. **conversar con** talk to. **conversar sobre** talk about. **conversador** *adj* sociable. **conversación** *sf* conversation.

*****convertir** [konβer'tir] *v* convert. **convertirse** *v* become, turn into. **conversión** *sf* conversion. **convertible** *adj* convertible.

convexo [kon'βekso] *adj* convex. **convexidad** *sf* convexity.

convicción [konβik'θjon] *sf* conviction. **convicto** *adj* convicted.

convidar [konβi'ðar] *v* invite. **convidarse** *v* offer one's services. **convidada** *sf (fam)* invitation to a drink. **pagar la convidada** *(fam)* treat to a drink. **convidado**, **-a** *sm*, *sf* guest. **convidador, -a** *sm, sf* host/hostess.

convincente [konβin'θente] *adj* convincing.

convivir [konβi'βir] *v* coexist. **convivencia** *sf* coexistence.

convocar [konβo'kar] *v* convoke. **convocación** *sf* convocation. **convocador, -a** *sm, sf* convener. **convocatoria** *sf* summons.

convoy [kon'βoj] *sm* convoy. **convoyar** *v* convoy.

convulsión [konβul'sjon] *sf* convulsion. **convulsivo** *adj* convulsive.

conyugal [konju'gal] *adj* conjugal. **cónyuge** *s(m+f)* spouse.

coñac [ko'nak] *sm* cognac, brandy.

cooperar [koope'rar] *v* cooperate. **cooperación** *sf* cooperation. **cooperativa** *sf* cooperative.

coordinar [koorði'nar] *v* coordinate. **coordinación** *sf* coordination.

copa ['kopa] *sf* glass; cup; goblet. **sombrero de copa** top-hat. **tomar una copa** have a drink. **copas** *sf pl* (*naipes*) hearts. **copado** *adj* (*árbol*) bushy. **copera** *sf* cupboard; sideboard.

Copenhague [kope'nage] *sf* Copenhagen.

copete [ko'pete] *sm* tuft of hair; bun; (*pájaro*) crest; summit; (*fig*) haughtiness. **de alto copete** aristocratic.

copiar [ko'pjar] *v* copy; record. **copia** *sf* copy; duplicate; image; abundance. **copiador, -a** *sm, sf* copier. **copiante** *s(m+f)* copyist.

copla ['kopla] *sf* verse; song; ballad. **coplas de ciego** doggerel.

copo ['kopo] *sm* flake; ball of wool; clot; lump.

coque ['koke] *sm* coke.

coquetear [kokete'ar] *v* flirt. **coqueta** *sf* flirt. **coqueteo** *sm* flirtation. **coquetón** *sm* (*fam*) philanderer.

coraje [ko'raxe] *sm* courage; anger. **corajinoso** *adj* irate.

coral [ko'ral] *sm* coral. *adj* choral.

coraza [ko'raθa] *sf* armour.

corazón [kora'θon] *sm* heart. **de corazón** sincerely.

corbata [kor'βata] *sf* necktie.

corcovado [korko'βaðo], **-a** *sm, sf* hunchback. *adj* hunchbacked.

corchea [kor'tʃea] *sf* (*música*) quaver.

corchete [kor'tʃete] *sm* clasp.

corcho ['kortʃo] *sm* cork.

cordel [kor'ðel] *sm* thin rope, line. **a cordel** in a straight line.

cordero [kor'ðero] *sm* lamb.

cordial [kor'ðjal] *adj* invigorating, stimulating; cordial, friendly. **dedo cordial** *sm* middle finger. **cordialidad** *sf* cordiality.

cordillera [korði'ʎera] *sf* mountain range.

cordón [kor'ðon] *sm* string; cord; braid.

cordura [kor'ðura] *sf* prudence; discretion.

coreografía [koreogra'fia] *sf* choreography.

cornada [kor'nada] *sf* goring. **cornear** *v* gore.

corneja [kor'nexa] *sf* crow.

corneta [kor'neta] *sf* bugle; hunting horn. **corneta de llaves** cornet.

cornudo [kor'nuðo] *adj* horned; cuckolded. *sm* cuckold.

coro ['koro] *sm* chorus.

coronar [koro'nar] *v* crown. **corona** *sf* crown. **coronación** *sf* coronation.

coronel [koro'nel] *sm* colonel.

coronilla [koro'niʎa] *sf* crown of the head.

corporal [korpo'ral] *adj* corporal. **corporación** *sf* corporation. **corpóreo** *adj* corporeal. **corpulencia** *sf* corpulence. **corpulento** *adj* corpulent.

corpúsculo [kor'pusculo] *sm* corpuscle.

corral [kor'ral] *sm* yard; courtyard; corral; enclosure.

correa [kor'rea] *sf* leather strap; belt. **correa de ventilador** fan belt.

corredor [korre'ðor] *sm* corridor; runner; (*com*) broker.

***corregir** [korre'xir] *v* correct. **corregirse** *v* reform oneself. **corrección** *sf* correction; punishment. **correccional** *adj* reformatory. **correctivo** *sm, adj* corrective. **correcto** *adj* correct; well-bred.

correo [kor'reo] *sm* mail, post; post office; courier. **correo certificado** registered post. **a vuelta de correo** by return of post.

correr [kor'rer] *v* run; flow; pass; sail; cover; travel over. **correrse** *v* move; (*fam*) talk too much.

corresponder [korrespon'der] *v* correspond; concern; reply; repay; be grateful; belong to; match; suit; fit. **a quien corresponda** to whom it may concern. **corresponderse** *v* correspond; agree; like each other. **correspondencia** *sf* correspondence, letters *pl*; agreement; reciprocation. **corresponsal** *s(m+f)* newspaper correspondent.

corrida [kor'riða] *sf* sprint. **corrida de toros** bullfight.

corrido [kor'riðo] *adj* abashed; experienced; over the specified weight.

corriente [kor'rjente] *sf* current, flow. *adj* current; running; everyday; standard; fluent. **agua corriente** running water. **al corriente** informed, up-to-date. **corriente alterna/continua** alternating/direct current. **corriente de aire** draught.

corroborar [korroβo'rar] *v* corroborate; strengthen. **corroboración** *sf* corroboration.

*****corroer** [korro'er] *v* corrode. **corrosión** *sf* corrosion.

corromper [korrom'per] *v* corrupt; ruin; bribe. **corromperse** *v* putrefy; be corrupted. **corrupción** *sf* corruption; stink; bribery.

corsé [kor'se] *sm* corset.

cortabolsas [korta'bolsas] *sm invar (fam)* pickpocket.

cortaplumas [korta'plumas] *sm invar* penknife.

cortar [kor'tar] *v* cut; cut short; break in on; stop; switch off. **cortarse** *v* cut oneself; become embarrassed. **cortante** *adj* cutting; sharp. **corte** *sm* cut; cutting edge.

corte ['korte] *sf* (royal) court.

cortejar [korte'xar] *v* court; accompany. **cortejo** *sm* courtship; accompaniment; homage.

cortesía [korte'sia] *sf* courtesy. **cortés** *adj* courteous.

corteza [kor'teθa] *sf* bark; rind; crust.

cortijo [kor'tixo] *sm* farmhouse and farm.

cortina [kor'tina] *sf* curtain; screen; dregs *pl*. **cortina de hierro** iron curtain. **cortina de humo** smokescreen.

corto ['korto] *adj* short; defective; stupid; timid. **corto circuito** short circuit. **corto de vista** short-sighted.

corvo ['korβo] *adj* curved; bent; crooked.

cosa ['kosa] *sf* thing; something; affair. **cosa de oír/ver** something worth listening to/seeing. **no sea cosa que** lest.

cosecha [ko'setʃa] *sf* harvest. **cosechar** *v* reap, harvest.

coser [ko'ser] *v* sew; stitch; join. **coserse la boca** *(fam)* keep mum.

cosquillas [kos'kiʎas] *sf* tickling; ticklishness. **hacer cosquillas a** tickle. **cosquillear** *v* tickle. **cosquilloso** *adj* ticklish.

costa¹ ['kosta] *sf* coast. **costear** *v* sail along the coast. **costera** *sf* slope, hill. **costero** *adj* coastal.

costa² *sf* cost; expense. **a toda costa** at all costs. **costar** *v* cost; cause. **coste** *sm* cost, price.

costado [kos'taðo] *sm* side. **costados** *sm pl* lineage *sing*.

costilla [kos'tiʎa] *sf* rib; chop, cutlet. **costillas** *sf pl* shoulders *pl*.

costra ['kostra] *sf* scab; crust; *(fam)* filthiness.

costumbre [kos'tumbre] *sf* custom. **de costumbre** usual; usually.

costura [kos'tura] *sf* sewing; seam; dressmaking. **costurera** *sf* seamstress.

cotejar [kote'xar] *v* compare. **cotejo** *sm* comparison.

cotidiano [koti'ðjano] *adj* daily.

coto ['koto] *sm* enclosure; reserve; limit. **coto de caza** hunting reserve.

cotorra [ko'torra] *sf* parrot; magpie; *(fam)* chatterbox.

coyuntura [konjun'tura] *sf* joint; opportunity.

coz [koθ] *sf* recoil; kick.

cráneo ['kraneo] *sm* skull.

cráter ['krater] *sm* crater.

crear [kre'ar] *v* create; make; invent; found. **creación** *sf* creation. **creador, -a** *sm, sf* creator; inventor. **creativo** *adj also* **creador** creative.

*****crecer** [kre'θer] *v* grow. **crecerse** *v* become conceited; take courage. **creces** *sf pl* increase *sing*. **con creces** amply, with interest. **crecido** *adj* grown; high; large; in flood. **crecimiento** *sm* growth; increase; flooding.

credenciales [kreðen'θjales] *sf pl* credentials *pl*.

crédito ['kreðito] *sm* credit; credence; reputation. **carta de crédito** *sf* credit card.

credo ['kreðo] *sm* creed.

crédulo ['kreðulo] *adj* credulous.

*****creer** [kre'er] *v* believe; think. **¡créamelo!** believe me! **¡ya lo creo!** of course! **creíble** *adj* credible.

crema ['krema] *sf* cream; custard.

cremación [krema'θjon] *sf* cremation.

cremallera [krema'ʎera] *sf* zip-fastener.

crepúsculo [kre'puskulo] *sm* twilight.

crespo ['krespo] *adj* crispy; fuzzy; crinkled; (*fig*) obscure; (*fig*) angry.

cresta ['kresta] *sf* crest; comb; tuft.

creta ['kreta] *sf* chalk.

criar [kri'ar] *v* breed; create; beget. **criarse** *v* grow up; be raised or reared. **cría** *sf* act of breeding; litter; brood; young. **criada** *sf* maid. **criadero** *sm* (*plants*) nursery. **criado** *sm* manservant. **crianza** *sf* breeding; nursing. **buena/mala crianza** good/bad upbringing. **criatura** *sf* creature; infant.

cribar [kri'βar] *v* sieve; sift. **criba** *sf* sieve; screen.

crimen ['krimen] *sm* crime. **criminal** *sm, adj* criminal.

criollo [kri'oʎo], -a *s, adj* Creole.

cripta ['kripta] *sf* crypt.

crisálida [kri'saliða] *sf* chrysalis.

crisantemo [krisan'temo] *sm* chrysanthemum.

crisis ['krisis] *sf invar* crisis (*pl* -ses).

crisol [kri'sol] *sm* crucible.

crispar [kris'par] *v* cause to contract or twitch; contort; irritate. **crisparse** *v* twitch.

cristal [kris'tal] *sm* crystal; glass; window; mirror. **cristal de contacto** contact lens. **cristal tallado** cut glass. **cristal trasero** (*auto*) rear window. **cristalería** *sf* glassworks; glassware. **cristalero**, -a *sm, sf* glazier; glassblower. **cristalino** *adj* crystalline; (*fig*) limpid.

Cristo ['kristo] *sm* Christ. **cristiandad** *sf* Christianity. **cristianismo** *sm* Christianity. **cristiano**, -a *s, adj* Christian.

criterio [kri'terjo] *sm* criterion (*pl* -a); point of view; opinion.

criticar [kriti'kar] *v* criticize. **crítica** *sf* criticism; review.

crítico ['kritiko] *sm* critic. *adj* critical.

cromo ['kromo] *sm* chromium, chrome; picture card.

crónica ['kronika] *sf* chronicle; report. **cronista** *sm* chronicler; correspondent. **crónico** ['kroniko] *adj* chronic.

cronología [kronolo'xia] *sf* chronology. **cronológico** *adj* chronological.

cronómetro [kro'nometro] *sm* chronometer; stopwatch.

croqueta [kro'keta] *sf* croquette.

croquis ['krokis] *sm invar* sketch, rough draft.

crucero [kru'θero] *sm* cruiser; cruise; crossroads *pl*.

crucificar [kruθifi'kar] *v* crucify. **crucifijo** *sm* crucifix. **crucifixión** *sf* crucifixion.

crucigrama [kruθi'grama] *sm* crossword puzzle.

crudo ['kruðo] *adj* crude; raw; immature; (*fam*) boastful.

cruel [kru'el] *adj* cruel. **crueldad** *sf* cruelty.

cruento [kru'ento] *adj* bloody.

crujir [kru'xir] *v* creak; rustle; crackle. **crujido** *sm* creak; rustle; crackle.

crustáceo [krus'taθeo] *sm, adj* crustacean.

cruz [kruθ] *sf* cross. **en cruz** crosswise. **cruzada** *sf* crusade; crossroads *pl*. **cruzado** *sm* crusader; knight. **cruzar** *v* cross; cross oneself; pass or place across; dub. **cruzarse** *v* pass each other; exchange.

cuaderno [kwa'ðerno] *sm* notebook; exercise book; (*fam*) pack of cards.

cuadra ['kwaðra] *sf* stable; hut; large hall; hospital ward.

cuadragésimo [kwaðra'xesimo] *adj* fortieth.

cuadrante [kwa'ðrante] *adj* squaring. *sm* quadrant.

cuadrar [kwa'ðrar] *v* square. **cuadrado** *adj* square; stocky; perfect.

cuadrilla [kwa'ðriʎa] *sf* gang. **cuadrillero** *sm* foreman.

cuadro ['kwaðro] *sm* square; picture; sight, scene. **en cuadro** in a square.

cuadrúpedo [kwa'ðrupeðo] *sm, adj* quadruped.

cuajar [kwa'xar] *v* coagulate; congeal; clot; settle; fill with; (*fam*) catch on. **cuajado** *adj* curdled; congealed; (*fig*) dumbfounded. **cuajadura** *sf* curdling; congealing; coagulation.

cual [kwal] *pron* which; who. *adv* such as. **a cual más** equally. **¿cuál?** *pron interrog* which? what?

cualidad [kwali'ðað] *sf* quality.

cualquier [kwal'kjer] *adj* (*con sustantivo*) any. **cualquiera** *pron, pl* **cualesquiera** any; anyone; anybody.

cuan [kwan] *adv* how; as.

cuando ['kwando] *adv* when. **de vez en cuando** from time to time. **hasta cuando** until. **¿cuándo?** *adv interrog* when?

cuantía [kwan'tia] *sf* quantity.

cuanto ['kwanto] *adj* as much as; all; whatever. *adv* **en cuanto** as soon as. **en**

cuanto a as to. ¿cuánto? *pron interrog* how much? how long?

cuarenta [kwa'renta] *sm, adj* forty.

cuaresma [kwa'resma] *sf* Lent.

cuartear [kwarte'ar] *v* quarter; cut into joints. **cuartearse** *v* crack.

cuartel [kwar'tel] *sm* quarter; barracks.

cuarto ['kwarto] *adj* fourth. *sm* quarter; room. **cuarto de baño** bathroom. **cuarto de estar** livingroom.

cuarzo [kwar'θo] *sm* quartz.

cuatro ['kwatro] *sm, adj* four.

cuba ['kuba] *sf* barrel; tub; drunkard. **estar como una cuba** (*fam*) be drunk.

Cuba *sf* Cuba. **cubano, -a** *s, adj* Cuban.

cúbico ['kuβiko] *adj* cubic. **raíz cúbica** *sf* cube root.

cubículo [ku'βikulo] *sm* cubicle.

cubo ['kuβo] *sm* bucket.

cubrir [ku'βrir] *v* cover; drown; repay. **cubrirse** *v* cover oneself; put on one's hat; cloud over. **cubierta** *sf* cover; roof; tyre; bedspread; (*mar*) deck. **cubierto** *sm* cover; place-setting; menu. **bajo cubierto** under cover. **precio del cubierto** *sm* cover charge.

cucaracha [kuka'ratʃa] *sf* cockroach.

cuclillas [ku'kliʎas] *adv* en cuclillas squatting, on one's haunches.

cuclillo [ku'kliʎo] *sm* cuckoo; cuckold.

cuchara [ku'tʃara] *sf* spoon; ladle; trowel. **cucharada** *sf* spoonful. **cucharadita** *sf* teaspoonful. **cucharita** *sf* teaspoon; coffeespoon. **cucharón** *sm* ladle; scoop.

cuchichear [kutʃitʃe'ar] *v* whisper. **cuchicheo** *sm* whisper; whispering.

cuchilla [ku'tʃiʎa] *sf* kitchen knife; chopper; razor blade; range of mountains. **patines de cuchilla** *sm pl* ice skates *pl*. **cuchillada** *sf* slash; stab; knifing. **andar a cuchilladas** be at daggers drawn. **cuchillería** *sf* cutlery; cutlery shop. **cuchillo** *sm* knife.

cuello ['kweʎo] *sm* collar; neck; throat. **cuello de pico** V-neck. **cuello vuelto** polo neck.

cuenca ['kwenka] *sf* wooden bowl; eye socket; (*geog*) basin.

cuenta ['kwenta] *sf* account; bill; count; report. a cuenta on account. ¿a cuenta de qué? why? tener en cuenta bear in mind.

cuento ['kwento] *sm* tale; fib; fuss. **cuento chino** nonsense.

cuerda ['kwerða] *sf* cord; rope; string;

chain; (*anat*) chord. **cuerdas vocales** vocal chords *pl*.

cuerdo ['kwerðo], **-a** *sm, sf* sane person. *adj* sane.

cuerno ['kwerno] *sm* horn; antler; feeler.

cuero ['kwero] *sm* skin; hide; leather.

cuerpo ['kwerpo] *sm* body; piece, section; stage; corps. **cuerpo de casa** housework. **cuerpo entero** full-length. **cuerpo muerto** (*mar*) mooring buoy.

cuervo ['kwerβo] *sm* raven.

cuesta ['kwesta] *sf* slope; hill. a cuestas on one's back. **cuesta abajo/arriba** down/uphill.

cuestión [kwes'tjon] *sf* question; issue; dispute. **cuestionar** *v* question; argue.

cueva ['kweβa] *sf* cave; cellar; den.

cuidar [kwi'ðar] *v* take care of; pay attention to. **cuidar de que take care that. no cuidarse de** take no notice of. **cuidado** *sm* care; carefulness; affair; worry. ¡cuidado! beware! **cuidador** *adj* careful.

cuita ['kwita] *sf* worry; sorrow. **cuitado** *adj* worried; bashful.

culebra [ku'leβra] *sf* snake; (*fam*) practical joke. **culebrear** *v* wriggle; zigzag.

culinario [kuli'narjo] *adj* culinary.

culminar [kulmi'nar] *v* culminate. **culminación** *sf* culmination. **culminante** *adj* culminating.

culo ['kulo] *sm* (*fam*) bottom, arse. ir de culo go downhill.

culpar [kul'par] *v* blame. **culparse** *v* take the blame. **culpa** *sm* blame; fault; guilt. echar la culpa a lay the blame on. **culpabilidad** *sf* culpability. **culpable** *adj* guilty.

cultivar [kulti'βar] *v* cultivate; grow; develop. **cultivador, -a** *sm, sf* farmer; grower; *sf* (*máquina*) cultivator. **cultivación** *sf* cultivation; culture. **cultivo** *sm* cultivation; culture.

culto ['kulto] *adj* cultivated; cultured; civilized. *sm* worship; cult. **rendir culto a** worship. **cultura** *sf* culture, learning.

cumbre ['kumbre] *sf* peak, summit.

cumpleaños [kumple'aɲos] *sm invar* birthday. **feliz cumpleaños** happy birthday.

cumplir [kum'plir] *v* fulfil; reach; end; do one's duty. **cumplirse** *v* be realized. **cumplir años** have a birthday. por cumplir as a matter of form. **cumplido** *adj* plentiful;

faultless; polite. **cumplimentar** v compliment; fulfil. **cumplimentero** adj excessively formal. **cumplimiento** sm compliment; fulfilment; politeness.

cúmulo ['kumulo] sm heap; large amount; (nube) cumulus.

cuna ['kuna] sf cradle; (fig) origin; birthplace.

cundir [kun'dir] v spread; increase; grow.

cuneta [ku'neta] sf ditch; gutter; hard shoulder.

cuña ['kuɲa] sf wedge; chock. **tener cuña** (fam) have friends at court.

cuñado [ku'ɲaðo] sm brother-in-law

cuño ['kuɲo] sm die; die-stamp; (fig) impression.

cuota ['kwota] sf quota; contribution; dues pl.

cupón [ku'pon] sm coupon; ticket.

cúpula ['kupula] sf dome.

cura¹ ['kura] sm priest. **cura párroco** parish priest.

cura² sf cure; healing; remedy; treatment; dressing. **primera cura** first aid. **curación** sf cure. **curador, -a** sm, sf guardian; tutor; curator. **curativo** adj healing.

curioso [ku'rjoso] adj curious; neat; attentive. sm bystander. **curiosidad** sf curiosity.

cursar [kur'sar] v attend; study; frequent. **cursado** adj skilled. **cursante** s(m+f) student.

cursi ['kursi] adj pretentious; affected; vulgar. s(m+f) pretentious person; snob.

curso ['kurso] sm course; direction; school year. **curso acelerado** crash course.

curtir [kur'tir] v tan; harden. **curtirse** v become tanned; become hardened; accustom oneself. **curtidor** sm tanner. **curtiduría** sf tannery. **curtimiento** sm tanning.

curva [kur'βa] sf curve, bend. **curvar** v curve, bend. **curvatura** sf curvature. **curvo** adj curved, bent.

cúspide ['kuspiðe] sf peak, summit.

custodiar [kusto'ðjar] v take care of; guard; defend. **custodia** sf custody. **custodio** sm custodian.

cutis ['kutis] sm invar skin, complexion.

cuyo ['kujo] pron whose; of which; of whom.

CH

chabacano [tʃaβa'kano] adj vulgar, common. **chabacanería** sf vulgarity; vulgar remark.

chacal [tʃa'kal] sm jackal.

chafar [tʃa'far] v flatten; crush; crease; (en una discusión) stump.

chal [tʃal] sm shawl.

chalado [tʃa'laðo] adj (fam) crazy, dotty.

chalán [tʃa'lan] sm horse dealer; shady businessman.

chaleco [tʃa'leko] sm waistcoat.

chalupa [tʃa'lupa] sf canoe; launch.

chambelán [tʃambe'lan] sm chamberlain.

champaña [tʃam'paɲa] sm champagne.

champú [tʃam'pu] sm shampoo.

chamuscar [tʃamus'kar] v singe, scorch.

chancear [tʃanθe'ar] v joke. **chancearse** v make fun of. **chanza** sf joke.

chanchullo [tʃan'tʃuʎo] sm (fam) crooked deal.

chantaje [tʃan'taxe] sm blackmail. **chantajista** s(m+f) blackmailer.

chapa ['tʃapa] sf metal sheet; rouge; (fam) common sense.

chaparro [tʃa'parro] adj (fam) tubby.

chaparrón [tʃapar'ron] sm downpour, cloudburst.

chapón [tʃa'pon] sm ink blot.

chapotear [tʃapote'ar] v sponge; moisten; splash. **chapoteo** sm sponging; moistening; splashing.

chapucero [tʃapu'θero], **-a** sm, sf bungler; liar. adj crude, clumsy. **chapucear** v botch, bungle.

chapuzar [tʃapu'θar] v duck, plunge into water.

chaqueta [tʃa'keta] sf jacket.

charca ['tʃarka] sf pool.

charco ['tʃarko] sm puddle.

charlar [tʃar'lar] v (fam) chat, chatter; gossip. **charla** sf (fam) chatter, talk. **charlador, -a** sm, sf also **charlatán, -ana** sm, sf chatterbox. **charladuría** sf chatter; gossip.

charol [tʃa'rol] sm varnish; patent leather. **darse charol** boast. **charolar** v varnish.

charro ['tʃarro] adj (fam) churlish; ill-bred; tawdry. **charrada** sf boorishness.

chasquear [tʃaske'ar] v trick; disappoint. **chasco** sm trick; disappointment.

chato ['tʃato] adj flat-nosed; flat. sm small glass.

chaval [tʃa'βal] sm (fam) lad; kid. **chavala** sf (fam) lass; girl.

Checoslovaquia [tʃekoslo'βakja] sf Czechoslovakia. **checoslovaco, -a s, adj** Czechoslovak(ian).

cheque ['tʃeke] sm cheque. **cheque de viajero** traveller's cheque.

chicle ['tʃikle] sm chewing gum.

chico ['tʃiko] adj small. sm boy. **chica** sf girl.

chichón [tʃi'tʃon] sm lump, bump.

chiflar [tʃi'flar] v whistle; hiss; (fam) swig. **chiflarse por** be crazy about. **chifla** sf whistle; hissing. **chiflado, -a sm, sf** (fam) crackpot; (fam: aficionado) fan; adj (fam) crazy.

chile ['tʃile] sm chili, chilli.

Chile ['tʃile] sm Chile. **chileno, -a s, adj** Chilean.

chillar [tʃi'ʎar] v scream; howl; squeak; blare. **chillador** adj screaming; shrieking. **chillería** sf screaming; scolding. **chillido** sm scream; howl; squeak.

chimenea [tʃime'nea] sf chimney; fireplace.

chimpancé [tʃimpan'θe] sm chimpanzee.

china ['tʃina] sf porcelain; china.

China sf China. **chino, -a s, adj** Chinese.

chinche ['tʃintʃe] sf bedbug.

chingar [tʃin'gar] v (fam) drink; (fam) pester.

Chipre ['tʃipre] sm Cyprus. **chipriota** s(m+f), adj Cypriot.

chiripa [tʃi'ripa] sf fluke, lucky accident.

chirriar [tʃirri'ar] v creak; squeak; chatter. **chirrido** sm creaking; squeaking; chattering.

chisme ['tʃisme] sm gadget; contrivance; knick-knack. **chismes** sm pl gossip sing. **chismear** v gossip. **chismería** sf tittle-tattle. **chismoso** adj gossiping.

chispear [tʃispe'ar] v spark; sparkle; drizzle. **chispa** sf spark; little bit. **chispeante** adj sparkling.

chisporrotear [tʃisporrote'ar] v spark; sizzle. **chisporroteo** sm sparking; sizzling.

chistar [tʃis'tar] v speak; open one's lips. **no chistar** say not a word. **¡chite!** interj hush!

chiste ['tʃiste] sf joke. **tener chiste** be funny. **chistoso** adj funny; joking.

chivo ['tʃiβo], **-a sm, sf** (zool) kid.

chocar [tʃo'kar] v surprise; shock; collide. **choque** sm shock; jolt; crash; dispute.

chocolate [tʃoko'late] sm chocolate. **chocolatería** chocolate shop.

chochear [tʃotʃe'ar] v be in one's dotage. **chochera** sf dotage. **chocho** adj doddering.

chofer ['tʃofer] sm chauffeur.

chorizo [tʃo'riθo] sm spicy sausage.

chorrear [tʃorre'ar] v gush; spout; drip. **chorreo** sm gushing; spouting; dripping. **chorro** sm jet; gush; flow; stream.

choza ['tʃoθa] sf hut, hovel.

chubasco [tʃu'βasko] sm shower; squall; (fig) setback.

chuleta [tʃu'leta] sf chop, cutlet; (fam) slap.

chulo ['tʃulo] sm pimp; (fam) ruffian; (fam) spiv. adj cheeky; flashy; insolent. **chulada** sf cheek; vulgar thing; funny thing. **chulear** v get cheeky with.

chungar [tʃun'gar] v (fam) tease; tell jokes. **chunga** sf banter, fun.

chupar [tʃu'par] v suck; absorb. **chuparse** v become worn to a shadow. **chupada** sf suck, sucking. **chupadero** also **chupador** adj sucking; absorbent. **chupete** sm (para niños) dummy. **chupetear** v suck at.

churro [tʃurro] sm deep-fried batter; (fam) dead loss.

chusco ['tʃusko], **-a sm, sf** wag, wit. adj funny.

chusma ['tʃusma] sf rabble, riffraff.

chuzo ['tʃuβo] sm (arma) pike. **llover a chuzos** pour down.

D

dactilógrafo [dakti'lografo], **-a sm, sf** typist. **dactilografía** sf typing.

dádiva ['daðiβa] sf gift. **dadivoso** adj generous.

dado ['daðo] sm die (pl dice).

daga ['daga] sf dagger.

dama ['dama] sf lady; mistress; (ajedrez) queen; (juego de damas) king. **damas** sf pl draughts.

damasco [da'masko] sm damask.

damnificar [damnifi'kar] v injure, harm.

danés [da'nes], **-esa** sm, sf Dane. sm (lengua) Danish. adj Danish.

danzar [dan'θar] v dance. **danza** sf dance, dancing. **danzante**, **-a** sm, sf dancer.

dañar [da'ɲar] v harm; damage; spoil. **dañino** adj destructive. **daño** sm injury; damage; loss.

*dar [dar] v give; grant; yield; (reloj) strike; (naipes) deal. **dar a face; overlook. dar como** or **por** declare; consider. **dar con** meet. **lo mismo da** it makes no difference. **darse** v regard oneself; devote oneself; matter; occur. **darse cuenta** realize.

dardo ['darðo] sm dart.

dársena ['darsena] sm dock.

dátil ['datil] sm (fruto) date.

dato ['dato] sm fact; piece of information.

de [de] prep of; from.

debajo [de'βaxo] adv underneath. **debajo de** prep under, beneath, below.

debatir [deβa'tir] v debate, discuss. **debate** sm debate.

deber [de'βer] v owe; must; ought. sm duty; debt. **debidamente** adv fittingly. **debido** adj fitting; just. **debido a** due to. **débito** sm debt.

debilitar [deβili'tar] v weaken. **débil** adj weak. **debilidad** sf weakness.

*decaer [deka'er] v decline; decay. **decadencia** sf decadence; decline. **decadente** adj decadent.

decano [de'kano] sm dean.

decapitar [dekapi'tar] v decapitate. **decapitación** sf decapitation.

decena [de'θena] sf unit of ten.

decencia [de'θenθja] sf decency; modesty; cleanliness. **decente** adj decent; modest; clean.

decenio [de'θenjo] sm decade.

decepción [deθep'θjon] sf disappointment.

decidir [deθi'ðir] v decide. **decidirse** v make up one's mind. **decisión** sf decision. **decisivo** adj decisive.

décima ['deθima] sf tenth; tithe. **decimal** adj decimal. **décimo** adj tenth. **decimoctavo** adj eighteenth. **decimocuarto** adj fourteenth. **decimonono** or **decimonoveno** adj nineteenth. **decimoquinto** adj fifteenth. **decimoséptimo** adj seventeenth. **decimosexto** adj sixteenth. **decimotercio** adj thirteenth.

*decir [de'θir] v say; tell; speak; call. **¿diga?** (teléfono) hello!

declamar [dekla'mar] v declaim; speak out; recite. **declamación** sf declamation; oration. **declamador**, **-a** sm, sf orator.

declarar [dekla'rar] v declare; state; explain. **declararse** v declare oneself; (fuego, etc.) break out; (amor) propose. **declaración** sf declaration.

declinar [dekli'nar] v decay; fade; depart; (gram) decline. **declinación** sf decline; (gram) declension.

declive [de'kliβe] sm slope; (com) slump.

decorar [deko'rar] v decorate. **decoración** sf decoration. **decorador**, **-a** sm, sf decorator. **decorativo** adj decorative.

decoro [de'koro] sm decorum; dignity; respect.

*decrecer [dekre'θer] v decrease. **decremento** sm diminution.

decrépito [de'krepito] adj decrepit.

decretar [dekre'tar] v decree. **decreto** sm decree.

dedal [de'ðal] sm thimble.

dédalo ['deðalo] sm maze.

dedicar [deði'kar] v dedicate, devote. **dedicación** sf dedication. **dedicatoria** sf (libro) dedication.

dedillo [de'ðiʎo] sm **al dedillo** at one's fingertips.

dedo ['deðo] sm finger; toe. **dedo del corazón** middle finger. **dedo índice** forefinger. **dedo meñique** little finger. **dedo pulgar** thumb.

*deducir [deðu'θir] v deduce; allege; deduct. **deducción** sf deduction. **deductivo** adj deductive.

defectible [defek'tiβle] adj fallible; defective. **defecto** sm defect. **defectuoso** adj defective.

*defender [defen'der] v defend; prohibit; oppose. **defendible** adj defensible. **defendido**, **-a** sm, sf (jur) defendant. **defensa** sf defence; shelter. **defensa pasiva civil** defence. **defensivo** adj defensive. **defensor**, **-a** sm, sf protector; counsel.

deferencia [defe'renθja] sf deference. **deferente** adj deferential.

*deferir [defe'rir] v defer; delegate.

deficiencia [defi'θjenθja] sf deficiency. **deficiente** adj deficient.

definir [defi'nir] v define. **definición** sf definition. **definido** adj definite. **definitivo** adj definitive. **en definitiva** in short.

deformar [defor'mar] *v* deform; disfigure. **deformación** *sf* deformation; distortion. **deforme** *adj* deformed; abnormal. **deformidad** *sf* deformity; (*fig*) perversion.

defraudar [defrau'dar] *v* defraud; evade; disappoint; frustrate. **defraudar al fisco** evade taxes. **defraudación** *sf* fraud; deceit. **defraudador, -a** *sm, sf* tax evader; swindler.

defunción [defun'θjon] *sf* decease.

degenerar [dexene'rar] *v* degenerate. **degeneración** *sf* degeneration.

deglutir [deglu'tir] *v* swallow. **deglución** *sf* swallowing.

*degollar [dego'Aar] *v* cut the throat of; behead; (*fig*) ruin. **degollación** *sf* throat-cutting; decapitation. **degolladero** *sm* slaughter-house; scaffold. **degollador, -a** *sm, sf* executioner.

degradar [degra'ðar] *v* degrade. **degradación** *sf* degradation.

degustación [degusta'θion] *sf* tasting; sampling.

dehesa [de'esa] *sf* pasture.

deificar [deifi'kar] *v* deify. **deidad** *sf* deity. **deificación** *sf* deification.

dejar [de'xar] *v* leave; yield; drop; let; allow. **dejar de** leave off, stop; fail to. **dejarse** *v* neglect oneself. **dejarse vencer** give in to. **dejarse de** cease to.

del [del] *contraction of* **de el**.

delantal [delan'tal] *sm* apron.

delante [de'lante] *adv* before, in front, ahead. **delante de** before, in front of. **delantera** *sf* front; advantage; lead. **delantero** *adj* front; foremost.

delatar [dela'tar] *v* denounce; betray. **delator, -a** *sm, sf* informer.

delegar [dele'gar] *v* delegate. **delegación** *sf* delegation. **delegado** *adj* delegated.

deleitar [delei'tar] *v* delight; please. **deleitarse** *v* take delight. **deleite** *sm* delight; pleasure. **deleitoso** *adj* delightful.

deletrear [deletre'ar] *v* spell out; interpret. **deletreo** *sm* spelling out; decipherment.

deleznable [deleθ'naβle] *adj* brittle; fragile; frail.

delfín [del'fin] *sm* dolphin.

delgado [del'gaðo] *adj* thin; delicate; ingenious. **delgadez** *sf* thinness.

deliberar [deliβe'rar] *v* deliberate, consider. **deliberación** *sf* deliberation. **deliberado** *adj* deliberate.

delicado [deli'kaðo] *adj* delicate; tender; touchy. **delicadez** *sf* delicacy; tenderness; touchiness; frailty; squeamishness.

delicioso [deli'θjoso] *adj* delicious; delightful. **delicia** *sf* delight.

delimitar [delimi'tar] *v* delimit. **delimitación** *sf* delimitation.

delincuencia [delin'kwenθja] *sf* delinquency. **delincuente** *s(m+f)* delinquent; criminal.

delinear [deline'ar] *v* delineate; outline; sketch. **delineación** *sf* delineation. **delineante** *sm* draughtsman.

delirar [deli'rar] *v* be delirious; rave. **delirio** *sm* delirium.

delito [de'lito] *sm* crime.

delta [delta] *sm* delta.

demacrarse [dema'krarse] *v* waste away. **demacración** *sf* emaciation. **demacrado** *adj* emaciated.

demagogia [dema'goxja] *sf* demagogy. **demagogo** *sm* demagogue.

demandar [deman'dar] *v* request; desire; (*jur*) sue. **demanda** *sf* demand; appeal; petition; question. **demandando, -a** *sm, sf* (*jur*) defendant. **demandante** *s(m+f)* (*jur*) plaintiff.

demarcar [demar'kar] *v* demarcate. **demarcación** *sf* demarcation.

demás [de'mas] *adj* other; rest; remaining. **los demás, las demás** the others. **estar demás** be unwanted. **y demás etcetera**. **demasía** *sf* excess; outrage; insolence. **demasiado** *adj, adv* too much.

demencia [de'menθja] *sf* insanity. **demente** *adj* insane.

democracia [demo'kraθja] *sf* democracy. **demócrata** *adj* democratic. *s(m+f)* democrat. **democrático** *adj* democratic.

*demoler [demo'ler] *v* demolish. **demolición** *sf* demolition.

demonio [de'monjo] *sm* demon. **demoniaco** *adj* demoniac.

demorar [demo'rar] *v* delay; remain. **demora** *sf* delay.

*demostrar [demos'trar] *v* demonstrate; prove. **demostrable** *adj* demonstrable. **demostración** *sf* demonstration. **demostrativo** *adj* demonstrative.

*denegar [dene'gar] *v* deny, refuse. **denegación** *sf* denial, refusal.

denigrar [deni'grar] *v* denigrate; slander; insult. **denigración** *sf* denigration; disgrace.

denominar [denomi'nar] *v* name.
denominación *sf* denomination.

denotar [deno'tar] *v* denote; indicate.

denso ['denso] *adj* dense. **densidad** *sf* density.

dentado [den'taðo] *adj* toothed; jagged; (*tecn*) cogged. **dentadura** *sf* set of teeth. **dental** *adj* dental. **dentar** *v* furnish with teeth; cut one's teeth. **dentellar** *v* (*dientes*) chatter. **dentellear** *v* bite. **dentífrico** *sm* toothpaste. **dentista** *s(m+f)* dentist.

dentro ['dentro] *adv* inside, within. **dentro de poco** shortly.

denudar [denu'ðar] *v* denude.

denunciar [denun'θjar] *v* denounce; inform; accuse. **denuncia** *sf* denunciation; accusation.

departamento [departa'mento] *sm* department.

depender [depen'der] *v* depend. **dependencia** *sf* dependence; reliance. **dependiente, -a** *sm, sf* shop assistant. **dependiente** *de* dependent on.

deplorar [deplo'rar] *v* deplore; regret. **deplorable** *adj* deplorable.

*****deponer** [depo'ner] *v* lay down; lay aside; remove from office; depose; (*jur*) give evidence; defecate. **deponente** *s(m+f)* witness.

deportar [depor'tar] *v* deport. **deportación** *sf* deportation.

deporte [de'porte] *sm* sport. **deportismo** *sm* sport; enthusiasm for sport. **deportista** *s(m+f)* sportsman/woman. **coche deportivo** sports car.

depositar [deposi'tar] *v* deposit. **depósito** *sm* deposit; store; tank; tip.

depravar [depra'βar] *v* deprave; corrupt. **depravación** *sf* depravity. **depravado** *adj* depraved.

depreciar [depre'θjar] *v* depreciate, lessen in value. **depreciación** *sf* depreciation.

deprimir [depri'mir] *v* depress. **depresión** *sf* depression. **depresivo** *adj* depressing.

depurar [depu'rar] *v* purify. **depuración** *sf* purification.

derecha [de'retʃa] *sf* right; right hand. **a la derecha** on the right. **derecho** *sm* law; *adj* right; straight; upright.

derivar [deri'βar] *v* derive. **derivación** *sf* derivation.

derogar [dero'γar] *v* repeal; abolish; cancel. **derogación** *sf* repeal; abolition.

derramar [derra'mar] *v* spill; overflow; scatter; spread. **derramarse** *v* be scattered; overflow. **derrame** *sm* spilling; leakage; overflow; slope.

*****derretir** [derre'tir] *v* melt; dissipate. **derretirse** *v* be deeply in love; (*fam*) be impatient. **derretimiento** *sm* melting; (*fam*) consuming passion.

derribar [derri'βar] *v* tear down; knock down; throw down. **derribarse** *v* fall down. **derribo** *sm* demolition. **derribos** *sm pl* rubble *sing*.

derrocar [derro'kar] *v* hurl down; ruin.

derrochar [derro'tʃar] *v* squander. **derrochador, -a** *s, adj* prodigal; spendthrift.

derrotar [derro'tar] *v* defeat; ruin; put to flight. **derrota** *sf* defeat; failure. **derrotado** *adj* defeated; shabby.

derrumbar [derrum'bar] *v* knock down, hurl down, pull down. **derrumbarse** *v* collapse. **derrumbo** *sm* collapse; overthrow; demolition.

desabotonar [desaβoto'nar] *v* unbutton; blossom. **desabotonarse** *v* come undone.

desabrigar [desaβri'γar] *v* uncover; leave without shelter; take off clothing. **desabrigado** *adj* uncovered; unprotected; exposed. **desabrigo** *sm* uncovering; exposure.

desabrochar [desaβro'tʃar] *v* unfasten; undo. **desabrocharse** *v* come undone.

desacatar [desaka'tar] *v* be disrespectful; disobey. **desacato** *sm* disrespect; contempt.

*****desacertar** [desaθer'tar] *v* be wrong; act foolishly. **desacertado** *adj* mistaken; ill-advised; unsuccessful; unfortunate; clumsy. **desacierto** *sm* mistake, blunder.

desacomodar [desakomo'ðar] *v* inconvenience; dismiss. **desacomodarse** *v* lose one's job. **desacomodado** *adj* poor; inconvenient; unemployed. **desacomodamiento** *sm also* **desacomodo** *sm* discomfort; inconvenience.

desaconsejado [desakonse'xaðo] *adj* ill-advised. **desaconsejar** *v* advise against.

*****desacordar** [desakor'ðar] *v* put out of tune. **desacordarse** *v* get out of tune; be forgetful. **desacordado** *adj* discordant.

desacostumbrar [desakostum'brar] *v* break a habit. **desacostumbrado** *adj* unusual.

desacreditar [desakreði'tar] *v* discredit.

desacuerdo [desa'kwerðo] *sm* discord; disagreement; unconsciousness.

desafecto [desa'fekto] *adj* disaffected; indifferent; adverse.

desafinar [desafi'nar] *v* be out of tune; (*fig*) speak out of turn.

desafío [desa'fio] *sm* challenge.

desagradar [desagra'ðar] *v* displease; be unpleasant. **desagradable** *adj* unpleasant.

desagradecido [desagraðe'θiðo], **-a** *sm*, *sf* ingrate. *adj* ungrateful.

desagraviar [desagra'βjar] *v* make amends for. **desagravio** *sm* indemnity; compensation.

desaguar [desa'gwar] *v* drain. **desaguadero** *sm* drain; channel. **desagüe** *sm* drainage; outlet.

desahogar [desao'gar] *v* ease; console. **desahogarse** *v* recover; free oneself; speak one's mind; get out of debt. **desahogado** *adj* impudent; well-off; spacious; uncluttered. **desahogo** *sm* ease; comfort; relief.

desahuciar [desau'θjar] *v* evict; despair of. **desahucio** *sm* eviction.

desairar [desai'rar] *v* disregard; snub. **desairado** *adj* spurned; unattractive; awkward. **desaire** *sm* snub; rebuff; gracelessness.

desajustar [desaxus'tar] *v* disarrange. **desajustarse** *v* break down. **desajuste** *sm* breakdown.

desalado [desa'laðo] *adj* impatient; hasty; unsalted.

*****desalentar** [desalen'tar] *v* make breathless; discourage. **desalentarse** *v* lose heart.

desaliñar [desali'ɲar] *v* disturb; ruffle. **desaliñado** *adj* slovenly. **desaliño** *sm* slovenliness; uncleanness; negligence.

desalojar [desalo'xar] *v* remove; eject. **desalojarse** *v* move out. **desalojamiento** *sm* ejection.

desalquilado [desalki'laðo] *adj* vacant. **desalquilar** *v* vacate.

desamor [desa'mor] *sm* indifference; ingratitude.

desamparar [desampa'rar] *v* abandon. **desamparo** *sm* abandonment; helplessness.

desangrar [desaŋ'grar] *v* bleed; impoverish. **desangrarse** *v* lose much blood.

desanimar [desani'mar] *v* discourage. **desanimarse** *v* become discouraged. **desánimo** *sm* discouragement.

desanudar [desanu'ðar] *v* untie; disentangle.

desapacible [desapa'θiβle] *adj* disagreeable. **desapacibilidad** *sf* unpleasantness.

*****desaparecer** [desapare'θer] *v* disappear; hide; wear off. **desaparecido** *adj* missing. **desaparecimiento** *sm* disappearance.

desapegarse [desape'garse] *v* lose interest in. **desapego** *sm* lack of interest; coldness.

desapercibido [desaperθi'βiðo] *adj* unnoticed. **coger desapercibido** catch unawares.

desapoderar [desapoðe'rar] *v* dispossess; dismiss.

*****desapretar** [desapre'tar] *v* loosen.

*****desaprobar** [desapro'βar] *v* disapprove of. **desaprobación** *sf* disapproval.

desaprovechar [desaproβe'tʃar] *v* waste; lose ground. **desaprovechado** *adj* unprofitable; backward. **desaprovechamiento** *sm* waste; misuse.

desapuntar [desapun'tar] *v* unstitch.

desarmar [desar'mar] *v* disarm; disband; dismantle; calm. **desarme** *sm* disarmament.

desarraigar [desarrai'gar] *v* uproot. **desarraigado** *adj* uprooted; rootless.

desarreglar [desarre'glar] *v* upset; disarrange. **desarreglado** *adj* slovenly; faulty. **desarreglo** *sm* disorder; untidiness; trouble.

desarrollar [desarro'ʎar] *v* unfold; develop. **desarrollo** *sm* development.

desarrugar [desarru'gar] *v* smooth out.

desasear [desase'ar] *v* soil; disarrange. **desaseo** *sm* dirtiness; disorder.

*****desasir** [desa'sir] *v* loosen, undo. **desasirse de** get rid of.

*****desasosegar** [desasose'gar] *v* disturb. **desasosiego** *sm* disquiet; restlessness.

desastre [de'sastre] *sm* disaster. **desastrado** *adj* unlucky; dirty; disorderly. **desastroso** *adj* disastrous.

desatar [desa'tar] *v* undo; unravel. **desatarse** *v* break out; lose all reserve. **desatadura** *sf* untying.

*****desatender** [desaten'der] *v* ignore; slight. **desatención** *sf* inattention; discourtesy. **desatentado** *adj* absent-minded. **desatento** *adj* discourteous.

desatinar [desati'nar] *v* bewilder; rave; blunder. **desatinado** *adj* silly; rash. **desatino** *sm* absurdity; blunder; tactlessness.

*****desavenir** [desaβe'nir] *v* cause to quarrel. **desavenirse** *v* quarrel. **desavenido** *adj* incompatible.

desaventajado [desaβenta'xaθo] *adj* unfavourable; inferior.

desaviar [desa'βjar] *v* lead astray; deprive of necessities; inconvenience. **desavío** *sm* inconvenience; lack of means.

desayunar [desaju'nar] *v* breakfast. **desayuno** *sm* breakfast.

desazonar [desaθo'nar] *v* render tasteless; displease. **desazón** *sm* insipidity; displeasure. **desazonado** *adj* tasteless; displeased.

desbandarse [desβan'darse] *v* disband; disperse.

desbarajustar [desβaraxus'tar] *v* confuse. **desbarajuste** *sm* confusion.

desbaratar [desβara'tar] *v* ruin; spoil; waste; talk rubbish. **desbaratarse** *v* fall apart; get carried away. **desbaratado** *adj* wrecked; dissipated. **desbaratamiento** *sm* waste; disorder; wrecking.

desbordar [desβor'ðar] *v* flood; overflow; *(fig)* lose one's self-control. **desbordamiento** *sm* overflow.

descabezar [deskaβe'θar] *v* behead. **descabezarse** *v* rack one's brains. **descabezado** *adj* headless; rash.

descalabrar [deskala'βrar] *v* wound (in the head); maltreat; defeat. **descalabro** *sm* setback; defeat.

descalificar [deskalifi'kar] *v* disqualify. **descalificación** *sf* disqualification.

descalzar [deskal'θar] *v* take off one's shoes. **descalzo** *adj* barefoot.

descamisado [deskami'saðo] *adj* destitute. *sm* tramp.

descansar [deskan'sar] *v* rest; sleep; lean; depend. **descansado** *adj* rested. **descanso** *sm* rest; repose.

descarado [deska'raðo] *adj* brazen; cheeky; blatant.

descargar [deskar'gar] *v* unload; discharge; free; absolve. **descarga** *sf* discharge; unloading. **descargado** *adj* *(batería)* flat. **descargo** *sm* unloading; discharge of debt. **descargue** *sm* unloading of goods.

descartar [deskar'tar] *v* discard; leave out. **descartarse** *v* get out of. **descarte** *sm* discarding; rejection.

***descender** [desθen'der] *v* descend; flow; lower. **descendencia** *sf* lineage. **descendiente** *s(m + f)* descendant. **descenso** *sm* descent; fall; decline.

descentralizar [desθentrali'θar] *v* decentralize.

descifrar [desθi'frar] *v* decipher. **descifrable** *adj* decipherable.

***descolgar** [deskol'gar] *v* lower; *(teléfono)* pick up; take down. **descolgarse** *v* come down; slip; drop; surprise.

descolorar [deskolo'rar] *v* discolour. **descolorido** *adj* discoloured.

descomedido [deskome'ðiðo] *adj* immoderate; disproportionate; rude. **descomedirse** *v* go too far.

***descomponer** [deskompo'ner] *v* decompose; disturb. **descomponerse** *v* rot; become upset. **descomposición** *sf* decomposition. **descompuesto** *adj* broken; faulty; insolent.

***desconcertar** [deskonθer'tar] *v* disconcert; damage. **desconcierto** *sm* disorder; confusion.

desconectar [deskonek'tar] *v* disconnect.

desconfiar [deskon'fjar] *v* lack confidence. **desconfiar de** distrust. **desconfiado** *adj* distrustful. **desconfianza** *sf* mistrust, suspicion.

desconformar [deskonfor'mar] *v* disagree, dissent.

***desconocer** [deskono'θer] *v* fail to recognize; ignore; deny; disown. **desconocido** *adj* unknown; unrecognized; ungrateful. **desconocimiento** *sm* ignorance; ingratitude; repudiation.

desconsiderado [deskonside'raðo] *adj* inconsiderate.

***desconsolar** [deskonso'lar] *v* grieve, distress. **desconsolado** *adj* disconsolate. **desconsuelo** *sm* grief; affliction.

***descontar** [deskon'tar] *v* discount; deduct; take for granted.

descontento [deskon'tento] *adj* dissatisfied.

descontinuar [deskontinu'ar] *v* discontinue.

descorazonar [deskorazo'nar] *v* discourage.

descorchar [deskor'tʃar] *v* uncork. **descorchador** *sm* corkscrew.

descortés [deskor'tes] *adj* discourteous. **descortesía** *sf* discourtesy.

descreer [deskre'er] *v* disbelieve; discredit. **descrédito** *sm* discredit.

describir [deskri'βir] *v* describe. **descripción** *sf* description. **descriptivo** *adj* descriptive.

descuajar [deskwa'xar] *v* liquefy; uproot; dishearten.

285   desesperar

descubrir [desku'βrir] v discover; uncover; publish. **descubierto** adj exposed; manifest; hatless. **descubridor, -a** sm, sf discoverer. **descubrimiento** sm discovery.

descuento [des'kwento] sm discount.

descuidar [deskwi'ðar] v neglect; release; distract. **descuidar de** forget to. **¡descuida!** don't worry! **descuidarse** v be careless; neglect one's health. **descuidado** adj neglectful; careless; casual. **descuido** sm negligence; carelessness; thoughtlessness.

desde ['desðe] prep from; since; after. **desde luego** of course; immediately.

*****desdecir** [desðe'θir] v gainsay; be unworthy of. **desdecirse** v retract.

desdeñar [desðe'ɲar] v disdain; scorn. **desdén** sm disdain; scorn. **al desdén** nonchalantly. **desdeñoso** adj disdainful.

desdicha [des'ðitʃa] sf misfortune; misery. **desdichado** adj unfortunate; wretched.

desdoblar [desðo'βlar] v unfold; split.

desdorar [desðo'rar] v tarnish. **desdoro** sm stain; dishonour.

desear [dese'ar] v wish, desire. **deseable** adj desirable. **deseo** sm desire. **deseoso** adj desirous.

desecar [dese'kar] v dry up.

desechar [dese'tʃar] v refuse; reject. **desecho** sm residue; rubbish; contempt.

desembalar [desemba'lar] v unpack.

desembarazar [desembara'θar] v clear; extricate; vacate. **desembarazarse** v get rid of. **desembarazo** sm freedom; naturalness.

desembarcar [desembar'kar] v unload; disembark. **desembarcadero** sm landing-stage. **desembarco** sm disembarkation; landing.

desembocar [desembo'kar] v flow; empty. **desembocadura** sf mouth; outlet; opening.

desembolsar [desembol'sar] v pay out. **desembolso** sm payment. **desembolsos** sm pl expenses pl.

desembragar [desembra'gar] v disengage; release; (auto) declutch. **desembrague** sm disengaging; (auto) declutching; (auto) clutch pedal.

desembrollar [desembro'ʎar] v disentangle; sort out.

desempate [desem'pate] sm (fútbol) play-off.

desempeñar [desempe'ɲar] v (teatro) play

a role; release from debt. **desempeño** sm redemption of a pledge; freedom from an obligation.

desempleado [desemple'aðo] adj unemployed. **desempleo** sm unemployment.

desencantar [desenkan'tar] v disillusion. **desencanto** sm disillusionment.

desenfadar [desenfa'ðar] v appease. **desenfadarse** v calm down. **desenfadado** adj free, unencumbered. **desenfado** sm freedom; naturalness.

desenfrenar [desenfre'nar] v unbridle. **desenfrenarse** v give way to passion. **desenfrenado** adj unbridled. **desenfreno** sm licentiousness.

desenganchar [desengan'tʃar] v unfasten, unhook.

desengañar [desenga'ɲar] v disabuse, disillusion. **desengaño** sm disillusionment.

desenlace [desen'laθe] sm dénouement; outcome.

desenredar [desenre'ðar] v disentangle; straighten out. **desenredo** sm disentanglement.

desenrollar [desenro'ʎar] v unroll; unwind.

*****desentenderse** [desenten'derse] v pretend to be ignorant (of); take no part in.

*****desenterrar** [desenter'rar] v disinter; unearth; recall. **desenterramiento** sm disinterment; recollection.

desentonar [desento'nar] v be out of tune; humiliate; behave badly. **desentono** sm discord; bad behaviour.

desentrañar [desentra'ɲar] v disembowel; (fig) unravel.

desenvainar [desenβai'nar] v unsheath; (fig) bring into the open.

*****desenvolver** [desenβol'βer] v unwrap; unwind; develop; expand. **desenvolverse** v become unwrapped; fend for oneself; prosper. **desenvoltura** sf naturalness; cheerfulness; eloquence.

deseo [de'seo] V desear.

desequilibrar [desekili'βrar] v unbalance. **desequilibrado** adj off balance; mentally unbalanced. **desequilibrio** sm imbalance.

desertar [deser'tar] v desert. **desertor, -a** sm, sf deserter.

desesperar [desespe'rar] v (cause to) despair; exasperate. **desesperación** sf desperation; despair; anger. **desesperado** adj desperate; hopeless. **desesperanza** sf despair.

desestimar [desesti'mar] v undervalue; reject. **desestima** sf lack of esteem.

desfachatado [desfatʃa'taðo] adj brazen; shameless. **desfachatez** sf brazenness; impudence.

desfalcar [desfal'kar] v embezzle. **desfalco** sm embezzlement.

*desfallecer [desfaʎe'θer] v faint; weaken. **desfallecido** adj faint; weak. **desfallecimiento** sm weakness; faintness.

desfavorable [desfaβo'raβle] adj unfavourable.

desfigurar [desfigu'rar] v disfigure; disguise; distort. **desfiguramiento** sm disfigurement; distortion.

desfilar [desfi'lar] v parade. **desfiladero** sm gorge, defile. **desfile** sm parade. **desfile de modas** fashion show.

desgajar [desga'xar] v tear off; break off.

desganar [desga'nar] v spoil the appetite of. **desganarse** v lose one's appetite. **desgana** sf loss of appetite; reluctance. **desganado** adj lacking appetite; reluctant.

desgarbado [desgar'βaðo] adj gawky; ungainly.

desgarrar [desga'rrar] v rend; tear; (fig: corazón) break. **desgarrado** adj dissolute. **desgarro** sm tear; impudence.

desgastar [desgas'tar] v wear away; corrode; ruin. **desgaste** sm wear; corrosion; ruin.

desgraciar [desgra'θjar] v displease; prevent; spoil. **desgraciarse** v fail; lose favour. **desgracia** sf misfortune; accident; grief; disgrace; unfriendliness. **por desgracia** unfortunately. **desgraciado** adj unlucky; unhappy; in disgrace.

deshabitado [desaβi'taðo] adj uninhabited.

*deshacer [desa'θer] v undo; cancel; destroy; frustrate. **deshacerse** v get rid of; break; go to pieces. **deshacerse por** strive to.

*deshelar [dese'lar] v thaw; melt. **deshelamiento** sm de-icing. **deshielo** sm thawing; melting.

desheredar [desere'ðar] v disinherit. **desheredado** adj disinherited; underprivileged. **desheredamiento** sm disinheritance.

deshidratar [desiðra'tar] v dehydrate. **deshidratación** sf dehydration.

deshilar [desi'lar] v unravel. **deshilado** adj unravelled; frayed.

deshilvanado [desilβa'naðo] adj (fig: discurso) disjointed; disconnected.

deshinchar [desin'tʃar] v deflate; give vent to. **deshincharse** v go down; go flat; (fig) come off one's high horse. **deshinchado** adj flat; deflated. **deshinchadura** sf deflation.

deshojar [deso'xar] v defoliate.

deshollinar [desoʎi'nar] v sweep chimneys. **deshollinador** sm chimney-sweep.

deshonesto [deso'nesto] adj dishonest; indecent.

deshonrar [deson'rar] v dishonour. **deshonra** sf dishonour; affront. **deshonroso** adj shameful, disgraceful.

deshora [des'ora] adv a deshora at an inconvenient time.

deshuesar [deswe'sar] v (carne) bone; (fruta) stone.

desidia [de'siðja] sf carelessness; inertia. **desidioso** adj lazy.

desierto [de'sjerto] sm desert. adj deserted.

designar [desig'nar] v designate. **designación** sf designation. **designio** sm intention, idea.

desigual [desi'gwal] adj unequal; uneven; changeable; different. **desigualdad** sf inequality.

desilusionar [desilusjo'nar] v disillusion. **desilusión** sf disillusionment.

desinfectar [desinfek'tar] v disinfect. **desinfección** sf disinfection. **desinfectante** sm, adj disinfectant.

desinflar [desin'flar] v deflate.

desinterés [desinte'res] sm disinterest. **desinteresado** adj disinterested.

desistir [desis'tir] v desist.

desleal [desle'al] adj disloyal. **deslealtad** sf disloyalty.

deslenguado [deslen'gwado] adj foulmouthed; shameless. **deslenguarse** v (fam) use foul language.

desligar [desli'gar] v loosen; untie; (fig) absolve. **desligarse** v break away.

deslindar [deslin'dar] v define the limits of. **deslinde** sm delimitation.

deslizar [desli'θar] v slip; glide; slide. **desliz** sm skid; (fig) indiscretion. **deslizadero** sm slippery place.

*deslucir [deslu'θir] v tarnish.

deslumbrar [deslum'βrar] v dazzle; (fig) bewilder. **deslumbrador** adj dazzling. **deslumbramiento** sm dazzle; glare.

desmán [des'man] *sm* excess; misconduct; outrage.

desmandar [desman'dar] *v* countermand. **desmandarse** *v* stray; get out of hand.

desmantelar [desmante'lar] *v* dismantle.

desmayar [desma'jar] *v* falter; discourage. **desmayarse** *v* faint. **desmayado** *adj* faint, fainting. **desmayo** *sm* swoon.

*****desmedirse** [desme'ðirse] *v* forget oneself; lose self-control. **desmedido** *adj* excessive.

desmejorar [desmexo'rar] *v* weaken; impair. **desmejorarse** *v* deteriorate.

*****desmembrar** [desmem'brar] *v* dismember; divide. **desmembración** *sf* dismemberment.

*****desmentir** [desmen'tir] *v* contradict; deny; belie. **desmentirse** *v* go back on one's word.

desmenuzar [desmenu'θar] *v* crumble; sift.

desmerecer [desmere'θer] *v* be unworthy of; be inferior. **desmerecimiento** *sm* demerit.

desmesurado [desmesu'raðo] *adj* disproportionate; excessive. **desmesurarse** *v* go too far.

desmontar [desmon'tar] *v* clear; level; (*árbol*) fell; dismantle.

desmoralizar [desmorali'θar] *v* demoralize. **desmoralización** *sf* demoralization.

desmoronar [desmoro'nar] *v* cause to crumble away. **desmoronarse** *v* crumble.

desnatar [desna'tar] *v* (*leche*) skim; (*fig*) take the best of.

desnivel [desni'βel] *sm* unevenness; gradient; difference of level.

desnudar [desnu'ðar] *v* strip, denude. **desnudez** *sf* nakedness. **desnudo** *adj* naked.

*****desobedecer** [desoβeðe'θer] *v* disobey. **desobediencia** *sf* disobedience. **desobediente** *adj* disobedient.

desocupar [desoku'par] *v* vacate. **desocuparse** *v* leave work; retire. **desocupación** *sf* leisure; unemployment. **desocupado** *adj* idle; unemployed; free.

desolar [deso'lar] *v* lay waste; afflict. **desolarse** *v* grieve. **desolación** *sf* desolation. **desolado** *adj* desolate; disconsolate.

desodorante [desoðo'rante] *sm*, *adj* deodorant.

desorden [des'orðen] *sm* disorder. **desordenado** *adj* disordered.

desorganizar [desorgani'θar] *v* disorganize. **desorganización** *sf* disorganization.

desorientar [desorjen'tar] *v* mislead; (*fig*) confuse. **desorientarse** *v* lose one's bearings. **desorientación** *sf* disorientation; perplexity.

despabilado [despaβi'laðo] *adj* wide awake; alert. **despabilarse** *v* wake up.

despacio [des'paθjo] *adv* slowly; gradually.

despachar [despa'tʃar] *v* dispatch; attend to; dismiss. **despacharse** *v* get rid of; finish; hurry. **despacho** *sm* dispatch; customs clearance; study; office; warrant; telegram.

despachurrar [despatʃur'rar] *v* (*fam*) crush; squash; (*fig*) make a mess of.

desparpajo [despar'paxo] *sm* self-assurance; nonchalance. **desparpajado** *adj* self-assured. **desparpajar** *v* disarrange; (*fam*) prattle.

desparramar [desparra'mar] *v* scatter; squander.

despavorido [despaβori'ðo] *adj* terrified.

despectivo [despek'tiβo] *adj* contemptuous, scornful.

despechar [despe'tʃar] *v* drive to despair; slight; enrage; (*fam*) wean. **despecharse** *v* despair. **despecho** *sm* despair. **a despecho de** in spite of.

despedazar [despeða'θar] *v* tear to pieces; smash.

*****despedir** [despe'ðir] *v* dismiss; see off; give off; escort. **despedirse** *v* say goodbye. **despedida** *sf* dismissal; farewell.

despegar [despe'gar] *v* unstick. **despegarse** *v* become detached; become indifferent. **despegado** *adj* unstuck; (*fig*) cold.

despeinar [despei'nar] *v* disarrange the hair.

despejar [despe'xar] *v* free from obstructions. **despejarse** *v* be free and easy. **despejado** *adj* bright; clear. **despejo** *sm* brightness; self-confidence.

despellejar [despeʎe'xar] *v* skin, flay.

despensa [des'pensa] *sf* pantry; store of food.

despeñadero [despeɲa'ðero] *sm* precipice; (*fam*) risk. **despeñadizo** *adj* steep. **despeñar** *v* precipitate. **despeño** *sm* fall.

desperdiciar [desperði'θjar] *v* waste. **desperdiciador, -a** *sm*, *sf* squanderer.

desperezarse [despere'θarse] *v* stretch oneself; rouse oneself.

*despertar [desper'tar] v awaken. **despertarse** v wake up. **despertador** sm alarm clock; warning. **despertamiento** sm awakening. **despierto** adj awake; watchful.

despiadado [despja'ðaðo] adj cruel, pitiless.

despilfarrar [despilfar'rar] v squander. **despilfarrado** adj wasteful; shabby. **despilfarro** sm waste; slovenliness.

despintar [despin'tar] v take paint off; fade.

despistar [despis'tar] v throw off the scent. **despistarse** v get lost. **despiste** sm absent-mindedness.

*desplegar [desple'gar] v unfold; reveal; display. **desplegadura** sf unfolding.

desplomarse [desplo'marse] v tilt; collapse; drop. **desplomo** sm (pared, etc.) bulge.

despojar [despo'xar] v deprive; dispossess. **despojarse** v divest oneself. **despojo** sm plunder. **despojos** sm pl scraps pl, leavings pl.

desposado [despo'saðo] adj newly-wed. **desposanda** sf bride. **desposando** sm bridegroom. **desposar** v marry. **desposarse** v become engaged; get married.

desposeer [despose'er] v dispossess.

déspota ['despota] sm despot. **despótico** adj despotic. **despotismo** sm despotism.

despreciar [despre'θjar] v reject; ignore; despise. **despreciarse** de not deign to. **despreciable** adj despicable. **desprecio** sm scorn; contempt; snub.

desprender [despren'der] v separate, remove; give off. **desprenderse** v withdraw; renounce; be deduced. **desprendimiento** sm disinterestedness; generosity; separation. **desprendimiento de tierras** landslide.

desprevenido [despreβe'niðo] adj unprepared. **desprevención** sf lack of foresight.

desproporción [despropor'θjon] sf disproportion. **desproporcionado** adj disproportionate.

después [des'pwes] adv afterwards, after, next, later; since. **después de** after. **después que** after.

desquiciar [deski'θjar] v unhinge; disconnect. **desquiciarse** v lose control. **desquiciado** adj off balance; (fam) crazy.

desquitar [deski'tar] v compensate.

desquitarse v recoup; get one's revenge. **desquite** sm compensation; revenge.

destacar [desta'kar] v (mil) detach; stand out. **destacarse** v be conspicuous. **destacado** adj outstanding.

destajo [des'taxo] sm piecework. **destajar** v settle the terms for a job.

destapar [desta'par] v uncover. **destaparse** v reveal oneself.

destartalado [destarta'laðo] adj (casa) tumbledown; rambling.

destello [des'teλo] sm sparkling. **destellar** v sparkle.

destemplar [destem'plar] v disconcert. **destemplarse** v get out of tune; lose one's temper. **destemplado** adj out of tune; inharmonious.

*desteñir [deste'ɲir] v discolour; fade.

*desterrar [dester'rar] v banish; (fig) discard. **desterrarse** v go into exile. **destierro** sm exile.

destilar [desti'lar] v distil; filter; ooze. **destilación** sf distillation. **destilador** sm still.

destinar [desti'nar] v destine; assign. **destino** sm destiny; destination; job. **con destino a** bound for. **destinario** sm addressee.

*destituir [desti'twir] v dismiss; deprive of. **destitución** sf removal; dismissal.

destornillar [destorni'λar] v unscrew. **destornillarse** v (fam) go crazy. **destornillador** sm screwdriver.

destreza [des'treθa] sf skill, dexterity.

destronar [destro'nar] v dethrone; depose. **destronamiento** sm dethronement.

destrozar [destro'θar] v destroy; squander. **destrozo** sm destruction.

*destruir [destru'ir] v destroy. **destruirse** v (mat) cancel out. **destrucción** sf destruction. **destructivo** adj destructive. **destructor** adj destructive.

desunir [desu'nir] v separate; disunite. **desunión** sf separation.

desusar [desu'sar] v be unaccustomed to. **desusarse** v become obsolete. **desusado** adj obsolete. **desuso** sm disuse.

desvalido [desβali'ðo] adj helpless; destitute.

desvalijar [desβali'xar] v rifle; rob.

desván [des'βan] sm attic.

*desvanecer [desβane'θer] v make disappear; remove. **desvanecerse** v evaporate; disappear; faint. **desvanecido** adj smug;

vain; (med) faint. **desvanecimiento** sm disappearance; smugness; faint.

desvariar [desβa'rjar] v rave. **desvarío** sm delirium.

desvelar [desβe'lar] v stop from sleeping. **desvelarse** v stay awake; (fig) dedicate oneself. **desvelo** sm insomnia; effort; devotion. **gracias a mis desvelos** thanks to my efforts.

desventaja [desβen'taxa] sf disadvantage. **desventajoso** adj disadvantageous.

desventura [desβen'tura] sf misfortune. **desventurado** adj unfortunate; faint-hearted.

desvergonzado [desβergon'θaðo], -a sm, sf shameless person. adj shameless.

desviar [des'βjar] v deviate; turn aside. **desviarse** v branch off. **desvío** sm detour; deviation.

desvirtuar [desβir'twar] v impair; decrease in strength or merit.

desvivirse [desβi'βirse] v long for; go out of one's way to.

detallar [deta'ʎar] v (com) retail; tell in detail. **detalle** sm detail; nice gesture. **vender al detalle** sell retail. **detalladamente** adv in detail. **detallista** s(m+f) retailer.

detective [detek'tiβe] s(m+f) detective.

detener [dete'ner] v detain. **detenerse** v linger. **detención** sf arrest; delay; thoroughness. **detenido** adj under arrest; careful.

detergente [deter'xente] sm, adj detergent.

deteriorar [deterjo'rar] v deteriorate; damage. **deterioración** sf also **deterioro** sm deterioration.

determinar [determi'nar] v determine. **determinarse** v make up one's mind. **determinación** sf determination; decision. **determinado** adj determined; decided; definite.

detestar [detes'tar] v detest. **detestable** adj detestable. **detestación** sf detestation.

detonar [deto'nar] v detonate. **detonación** sf detonation.

detractar [detrak'tar] v defame. **detracción** sf defamation.

detraer [detra'er] v denigrate; withdraw.

detrás [de'tras] adv behind. **detrás de** prep behind. **por detrás de uno** behind someone's back.

detrimento [detri'mento] sm detriment;

damage. **en detrimento de** to the detriment of.

deuda ['deuða] sf debt; trespass. **deudor**, -a sm, sf debtor.

deudo ['deuðo], -a sm, sf relative. sm relationship.

devanar [deβa'nar] v wind, coil. **devanarse los sesos** (fam) rack one's brains.

devanear [deβane'ar] v rave. **devaneo** sm delirium; flirtation.

devastar [deβas'tar] v devastate. **devastación** sf devastation.

devengar [deβen'gar] v have due; (intereses) yield.

devoción [deβo'θjon] sf devotion. **devocionario** sm prayer book.

devolver [deβol'βer] v return. **devolución** sf return; refund.

devorar [deβo'rar] v devour.

devoto [de'βoto], -a sm, sf devotee. adj devout; devoted.

día ['dia] sm day. **¡buenos días!** good morning! **al día** fresh. **ocho días** a week. **todos los días** every day.

diablo ['djaβlo] sm devil. **diabólico** adj diabolical.

diafragma [dja'fragma] sm diaphragm.

diagnosticar [diagnosti'kar] v diagnose. **diagnosis** sf invar diagnosis. **diagnóstico** adj diagnostic.

diagonal [diago'nal] sf, adj diagonal.

diagrama [dia'grama] sm diagram.

dialecto [dia'lekto] sm dialect. **diálogo** [di'alogo] sm dialogue.

diamante [dia'mante] sm diamond. **diámetro** [di'ametro] sm diameter. **diametral** adj diametric.

diario [di'arjo] sm daily newspaper; diary. **diario hablado** news bulletin. adj daily. **de diario** for everyday use.

diarrea [dia'rrea] sf diarrhoea.

dibujar [diβu'xar] v draw. **dibujante** s(m+f) artist; designer; cartoonist; draughtsman. **dibujo** sm drawing; sketch; design.

dicción [dik'θjon] sf diction; word.

diccionario [dikθjo'narjo] sm dictionary.

diciembre [di'θjembre] sm December.

dictado [dik'taðo] sm dictation; title. **dictados** sm pl dictates pl. **dictador** sm dictator. **dictadura** sf dictatorship. **dictar** v dictate.

dictamen [dik'tamen] sm opinion; advice; report.

dicha ['ditʃa] *sf* happiness; good luck. **por dicha** luckily. **dichoso** *adj* happy; lucky; (*fam*) boring.

dicho ['ditʃo] *V* **decir**. *sm* saying; remark; proverb. **dicho y hecho** no sooner said than done.

diente ['djente] *sm* tooth.

diestra ['djestra] *sf* right hand. **diestro** *adj* right; skilful; sly.

dieta ['djeta] *sf* diet.

diez [djeθ] *sm, adj* ten. **diecinueve** *sm, adj* nineteen. **dieciocho** *sm, adj* eighteen. **dieciséis** *sm, adj* sixteen. **diecisiete** *sm, adj* seventeen. **diezmar** *v* decimate.

difamar [difa'mar] *v* defame, slander. **difamación** *sf* defamation. **difamatorio** *adj* defamatory.

diferencia [dife'renθja] *sf* difference. **a diferencia de** unlike. **diferenciar** *v* differentiate; differ. **diferenciarse** be different. **diferente** *adj* different.

***diferir** [dife'rir] *v* defer; differ.

difícil [di'fiθil] *adj* difficult. **dificultad** *sf* difficulty. **dificultar** *v* make difficult; hinder.

difidente [difi'ðente] *adj* mistrustful. **difidencia** *sf* mistrust.

difundir [difun'dir] *v* diffuse; broadcast; divulge; spread. **difusión** *sf* spread; broadcast; diffusion.

difunto [di'funto] *adj* dead. *sm* deceased person.

***digerir** [dixe'rir] *v* digest; (*fig*) endure. **digestible** *adj* digestible. **digestión** *sf* digestion.

dignarse [dig'narse] *v* deign, condescend. **dignidad** [digni'ðað] *sf* dignity; rank. **dignatario** *sm* dignitary. **digno** *adj* worthy.

digresión [digre'sjon] *sf* digression.

dilación [dila'θjon] *sf* delay.

dilatar [dila'tar] *v* dilate; expand; delay. **dilatarse** *v* speak at great length. **dilatación** *sf* extension; delay. **dilatado** *adj* numerous; long-winded. **dilatorio** *adj* dilatory.

dilema [di'lema] *sm* dilemma.

diligencia [dili'xenθja] *sf* diligence; (*fam*) job.

dilucidar [diluθi'ðar] *v* elucidate; solve.

diluir [dilu'ir] *v* dilute. **dilución** *sf* dilution.

diluvio [di'luβjo] *sm* deluge.

dimanar [dima'nar] *v* arise from; flow.

dimensión [dimen'sjon] *sf* dimension.

diminutivo [diminu'tiβo] *adj* diminutive. **diminuto** *adj* tiny.

dimitir [dimi'tir] *v* resign. **dimisión** *sf* resignation.

Dinamarca [dina'marka] *sf* Denmark. **dinamarqués, -esa** *sm, sf* Dane; *adj* Danish.

dinamita [dina'mita] *sf* dynamite.

dínamo ['dinamo] *sm* dynamo. **dinámico** *adj* dynamic.

dinastía [dinas'tia] *sf* dynasty.

dinero [di'nero] *sm* money. **de dinero** rich. **dinero suelto** loose change. **estar mal de dinero** be hard up.

dintel [din'tel] *sm* lintel.

dio [djo] *V* **dar**.

diócesi(s) [di'oθesi(s)] *sf invar* diocese.

dios [djos] *sm* god, idol. **diosa** *sf* goddess.

diploma [di'ploma] *sf* diploma.

diplomacia [diplo'maθja] *sf* diplomacy. **diplomático** *sm* diplomat; *adj* diplomatic.

diputado [dipu'taðo] *sm* deputy, delegate, representative.

dique ['dike] *sm* dike; dam; dry dock.

dirigir [diri'xir] *v* direct; govern; steer; regulate. **dirigirse** *v* go; speak; write. **dirección** *sf* direction; directorship; management; postal address. **directivo** *adj* directive; guiding. **directo** *adj* direct; straight. **director, -a** *sm, sf* director; editor. **directorio** *sm* directory.

***discernir** [disθer'nir] *v* discern. **discernimiento** *sm* discernment.

disciplina [disθi'plina] *sf* discipline; doctrine; obedience. **disciplinar** *v* discipline; train.

discípulo [dis'θipulo], **-a** *sm, sf* disciple; pupil.

disco ['disko] *sm* disc; record; discus.

disconforme [diskon'forme] *adj* in disagreement. **disconformidad** *sf* disagreement.

discontinuar [disconti'nwar] *v* discontin- ue. **discontinuación** *sf* discontinuation. **discontinuo** *adj* discontinuous.

discordia [dis'korðja] *sf* discord. **dis- cordante** *adj also* **discorde** discordant.

discoteca [disko'teka] *sf* disco; record library.

discreción [diskre'θjon] *sf* discretion. **a discreción** optional, at will.

discrepancia [diskre'panθja] *sf* discrepan- cy.

discreto [dis'kreto] *adj* discreet; moder- ate; sober; witty. -

disculpar [diskul'par] *v* excuse; forgive. *v* apologize. **disculpa** *sf* excuse; apology.

discurrir [disku'rrir] *v* ponder; speak; roam; invent.

discurso [dis'kurso] *sm* discourse; reason- ing; passage of time. **discursivo** *adj* dis- cursive.

discutir [disku'tir] *v* discuss; debate. **dis- cusión** *sf* discussion; argument. **discutido** *adj* controversial.

disecar [dise'kar] *v* dissect. **disección** *sf* dissection.

diseminar [disemi'nar] *v* scatter. **dis- eminarse** *v* spread. **diseminación** *sf* dis- semination.

disentería [disente'ria] *sf* dysentery.

*****disentir** [disen'tir] *v* dissent; differ. **dis- ensión** *sf* dissent; disagreement; quarrel.

diseñar [dise'nar] *v* sketch; design. **dis- eñador, -a** *sm, sf* designer. **diseño** *sm* sketch; design.

disfrazar [disfra'θar] *v* disguise. **disfraz** *sm* disguise; fancy dress.

disfrutar [disfru'tar] *v* possess; enjoy; receive. **disfrute** *sm* enjoyment.

disgregar [disgre'gar] *v* disintegrate; sepa- rate. **disgregación** *sf* disintegration; sepa- ration.

disgustar [disgus'tar] *v* upset; displease. **disgustarse** *v* become angry. **disgustado** *adj* annoyed; displeased; disappointed. **disgusto** *sm* annoyance; displeasure; repugnance; trouble.

disidente [disi'ðente] *s(m+f)*, *adj* dissi- dent. **disidir** *v* dissent.

disimular [disimu'lar] *v* pretend; dissem- ble; hide; tolerate. **disimulable** *adj* excus- able. **disimulo** *sm* concealment; indul- gence.

disipar [disi'par] *v* dissipate. **disiparse** *v* disperse; vanish; clear up. **disipación** *sf* dissipation. **disipado** *adj* dissipated.

dislocar [dislo'kar] *v* dislocate. **dislocación** *sf* dislocation.

*****disminuir** [disminu'ir] *v* diminish. **diminución** *sf* decrease; reduction.

disociar [diso'θjar] *v* dissociate. **disocia- ción** *sf* dissociation.

*****disolver** [disol'βer] *v* dissolve. **disoluble** *adj* dissoluble. **disolución** *sf* dissolution; *(fig)* dissoluteness. **disoluto** *adj* dissolute.

*****disonar** [diso'nar] *v* disagree; be inhar- monious. **disonancia** *sf* discord. **diso- nante** *adj* discordant.

disparar [dispa'rar] *v* fire; shoot; throw. **dispararse** *v* explode; fly off; race. **dis- paradamente** *adv* hurriedly; foolishly. **disparo** *sm* firing; shot; attack.

disparatado [dispara'taðo] *adj* absurd. **disparatar** *v* talk nonsense; act foolishly. **disparate** *sm* absurdity.

disparidad [dispari'ðað] *sf* disparity.

dispensar [dispen'sar] *v* dispense; pardon. **dispense usted** forgive me. **dispensa** *sf* dispensation; exemption. **dispensable** *adj* dispensable. **dispensario** *sm* dispensary.

dispersar [disper'sar] *v* disperse. **disper- sión** *sf* dispersal. **disperso** *adj* dispersed, scattered.

*****disponer** [dispo'ner] *v* dispose; arrange; decide; prepare. **disponer de** dispose of; have. **disponerse** *v* a get ready. **disponible** *adj* disposable; available. **disposición** *sf* disposition; instruction; inclination; determination. **tomar disposiciones** take steps. **ultima disposición** last will and tes- tament. **dispuesto** *adj* arranged; dis- posed; ready; willing.

disputar [dispu'tar] *v* dispute; debate. **dis- puta** *sf* dispute, argument.

distancia [dis'tanθja] *sf* distance. **distante** *adj* distant.

distinguir [distin'gir] *v* distinguish; esteem. **distinción** *sf* distinction; polite- ness. **distinguido** *adj* distinguished. **dis- tintivo** *adj* distinctive. **distinto** *adj* dis- tinct; different.

*****distraer** [distra'er] *v* distract; entertain. **distracción** *sf* distraction. **distraído** *adj* absent-minded; entertaining.

*****distribuir** [distriβu'ir] *v* distribute; deliv- er; allot. **distribución** *sf* distribution. **cuadro de distribución** *sm* switchboard. **distribuidor** *sm (auto)* distributor; agent. **distribuidor automático** slot machine.

distrito [dis'trito] *sm* district.
disturbar [distur'βar] *v* disturb. **disturbio** *sm* disturbance.
disuadir [diswa'ðir] *v* dissuade.
diurno [di'urno] *adj* daily.
divagar [diβa'gar] *v* digress; roam. **divagación** *sf* digression.
diván [di'βan] *sm* divan.
divergir [diβer'xir] *v* diverge; disagree. **divergencia** *sf* divergence. **divergente** *adj* divergent.
diverso [di'βerso] *adj* diverse. **diversos** *adj pl* various; many. **diversidad** *sf* diversity.
*divertir [diβer'tir] *v* entertain; divert. **divertido** *adj* amusing; entertaining.
dividir [diβi'ðir] *v* divide; split. **división** *sf* division; (*gram*) hyphen, dash. **divisor** *sm* divider. **divisorio** *adj* dividing.
divino [di'βino] *adj* divine. **divinidad** *sf* divinity.
divisa [di'βisa] *sf* emblem; (*com*) currency. **divisas** *sf pl* (*com*) foreign exchange *sing*. **control de divisas** (*com*) exchange control.
divisar [diβi'sar] *v* distinguish, discern.
divorciar [diβor'θjar] *v* divorce. **divorciarse** *v* get divorced. **divorciado, -a** *sm, sf* divorcee. **divorcio** *sm* divorce.
divulgar [diβul'gar] *v* divulge; circulate; spread. **divulgarse** *v* come out. **divulgación** *sf* disclosure.
doblar [do'βlar] *v* double; fold; bend; (*fig*) persuade; (*fig*) submit. **doblarse** *v* fold; buckle; stoop; yield. **dobladillo** *sm* hem; trouser turn-up. **dobladura** *sf* crease, fold. **doble** *adj also* **doblado** double; dual; stocky; deceitful. **el doble** twice as much.
doce ['doθe] *sm, adj* twelve. **docena** *sf* dozen.
docente [do'θente] *adj* educational. **personal docente** teaching staff.
dócil ['doθil] *adj* docile; obedient. **docilidad** *sf* docility.
doctor [dok'tor], **-a** *sm, sf* doctor. **docto** *adj* learned. **doctorado** *sm* doctorate.
doctrina [dok'trina] *sf* doctrine. **doctrinal** *adj* doctrinal.
documentar [dokumen'tar] *v* document. **documentación** *sf* documentation; identity papers *pl*.
dogal [do'gal] *sm* halter.
dogma ['dogma] *sm* dogma. **dogmático** *adj* dogmatic. **dogmatismo** *sm* dogmatism.

dogo ['dogo] *sm* bulldog.
*doler [do'ler] *v* hurt; ache; grieve. **dolerse de** feel the effects of; regret; pity. **dolor** *sm* grief; repentance. **dolorido** *adj* in pain; grief-stricken. **doloroso** *adj* painful; pitiful; sorrowful.
domar [do'mar] *v* tame; train. **doma** *sf* training.
doméstico [do'mestiko], **-a** *sm, sf* servant. *adj* domestic. **domesticar** *v* domesticate. **domesticidad** *sf* domesticity.
domiciliar [domiθi'ljar] *v* domicile. **domiciliarse** *v* take up residence. **domiciliado** *adj* resident. **domicilio** *sm* home.
dominar [domi'nar] *v* dominate; master. **dominación** *sf* domination; authority. **dominador** *adj* dominating, dominant. **dominante** *adj* dominating; dominant. **dominio** *sm* dominion; authority; supremacy.
domingo [do'mingo] *sm* Sunday. **hacer domingo** take a day off.
dominó [domi'no] *sm* (*juego*) dominoes *pl*.
don[1] [don] *sm* (*con nombre de pila*) Mr.
don[2] *sm* gift; talent. **donación** *sf* donation. **donador, -a** *sm, sf* donor. **donar** *v* give, bestow. **donativo** *sm* offering.
donaire [do'naire] *sm* charm, grace; wit. **donairoso** *adj* graceful; witty.
donde ['donðe] *adv* where. **dondequiera** *adv* wherever. **¿dónde?** where? **¿por dónde?** which way?
doña ['doɲa] *sf* (*con el nombre de pila de una señora o una viuda*) Mrs.
dorar [do'rar] *v* gild; (*culin*) brown. **dorado** *adj* gilt; golden.
*dormir [dor'mir] *v* sleep. **dormirse** *v* go to sleep. **dormilón, -ona** *sm, sf* sleepyhead. **dormitorio** *sm* dormitory.
dorso [dorso] *sm* back. **dorsal** *adj* dorsal.
dos [dos] *sm, adj* two. **dos veces** twice. **las dos** two o'clock. **los dos** both.
dosis ['dosis] *sf invar* dose. **dosificación** *sf* dosage. **dosificar** *v* dose.
dotar [do'tar] *v* endow; equip; staff. **dotación** *sf* endowment; foundation; personnel. **dotado** *adj* endowed; gifted. **dotador, -a** *sm, sf* donor. **dote** *sf* dowry. **dotes** *sf pl* endowments *pl*, talents *pl*.
draga ['draga] *sf* dredge. **dragado** *sm* dredging. **dragar** *v* dredge; (*minas*) sweep.

dragón [dra'gon] *sm* dragon.

drama ['drama] *sm* drama. **dramática** *sf* dramatic art. **dramático** *adj* dramatic. **dramatizar** *v* dramatize. **dramaturgo, -a** *sm, sf* playwright.

drenaje [dre'naxe] *sm* drainage. **drenar** *v* drain.

droga ['droga] *sf* drug. (*fam, fig*) trick, practical joke, fib. **drogadicto, -a** *s, adj* drug addict. **drogar** *v* drug, dope.

dual [dwal] *adj* dual. **dualidad** *sf* duality. **dualismo** *sm* dualism.

ducado [du'kaðo] *sm* duchy.

dúctil ['duktil] *adj* ductile; malleable.

ducha ['dutʃa] *sf* shower. **ducharse** *v* have or take a shower.

dudar [du'ðar] *v* doubt. **duda** *sf* doubt. **sin duda** doubtless. **dudoso** *adj* doubtful; dubious.

duelo[1] ['dwelo] *sm* sorrow; mourning.

duelo[2] *sm* duel.

duende ['dwende] *sm* imp; goblin; elf.

dueño ['dweɲo], **-a** *sm, sf* owner; master/mistress; landlord/landlady.

dulce ['dulθe] *sm* sweet. *adj* sweet; mild; gentle; soft; (*agua*) fresh. **dulcería** *sf* confectionery. **dulzura** *sf* sweetness; mildness.

dúo ['duo] *sm* duet.

duodécimo [duo'ðeθimo] *sm, adj* twelfth.

duplicar [dupli'kar] *v* duplicate. **duplicarse** *v* double. **duplicación** *sf* duplication; doubling. **duplicado, -a** *adj* duplicate. **duplicador** *sm* duplicator.

duplicidad [dupliθi'ðað] *sf* duplicity.

duque ['duke] *sm* duke. **duquesa** *sf* duchess.

durar [du'rar] *v* last, endure. **durable** *adj* durable. **duración** *sf* duration. **durante** *adv* during.

durazno [du'raθno] *sm* peach; peach tree.

durmiente [dur'mjente] *adj* sleeping.

duro ['duro] *adj* hard; firm. **dureza** *sf* hardness; severity.

E

e [e] *conj* and.

ébano ['eβano] *sm* ebony.

ebrio ['eβrjo] *adj* drunk.

eclesiástico [ekle'sjastiko] *adj, sm* ecclesiastic.

eclipse [e'klipse] *sm* eclipse. **eclipsar** *v* eclipse.

eco ['eko] *sm* echo.

economía [ekono'mia] *sf* economy. **económico** *adj* economical. **economista** *s(m+f)* economist. **economizar** *v* economize.

ecuador [ekwa'ðor] *sm* equator.

ecuestre [e'kwestre] *adj* equestrian.

echar [e'tʃar] *v* throw; emit; (*naipes*) deal/pour out; dismiss; begin; perform. **echar a** start to. **echar abajo** demolish. **echar a perder** spoil. **echar de ver** notice. **echarse** *v* lie down.

edad [e'ðað] *sf* age. **edad madura** middle age.

edicto [e'ðikto] *sm* edict.

edificar [eðifi'kar] *v* build; (*fig*) edify. **edificio** *sm* edifice.

editar [eði'tar] *v* publish. **edición** *sf* edition. **editor, -a** *sm, sf* publisher.

edredón [eðre'ðon] *sm* eiderdown.

educar [eðu'kar] *v* educate; bring up; train. **educación** *sf* education; upbringing. **educado** *adj* educated; well-mannered.

efectivo [efek'tiβo] *adj* effective; real. **dinero efectivo** *sm* cash. **efecto** *sm* effect; result; (*com*) document. **efectos** *sm pl* effects *pl*, assets *pl*. **efectos en cartera** holdings *pl*. **efectuar** *v* carry out.

efervescencia [eferβes'θenθja] *sf* effervescence. **efervescente** *adj* effervescent.

eficacia [efi'kaθja] *sf* efficacy; efficiency. **eficaz** *adj* efficacious; efficient. **eficiencia** *sf* efficiency. **eficiente** *adj* efficient.

efigie [e'fixje] *sf* effigy.

efímero [e'fimero] *adj* ephemeral.

efusión [efu'sjon] *sf* effusion.

Egipto [e'xipto] *sm* Egypt. **egipcio, -a** *s, adj* Egyptian.

egoísmo [ego'ismo] *sm* egoism. **egoísta** *s(m+f)* egoist. **egotismo** *sm* egotism. **egotista** *s(m+f)* egotist.

egregio [e'grexjo] *adj* eminent.

eje ['exe] *sm* axis; axle; (*fig*) core, hub. **eje del mundo** earth's axis.

ejecutar [exeku'tar] *v* execute; put to death; seize; perform. **ejecución** *sf* execution. **ejecutivo** *sm, adj* executive. **ejecutor, -a** *sm, sf* executor; executioner.

ejemplar [exem'plar] *sm* copy; model;

specimen; example. *adj* exemplary. **ejemplificar** *v* exemplify. **ejemplo** *sm* example. **dar ejemplo** set an example. **sin ejemplo** unprecedented.

ejercer [exer'θer] *v* practise; exercise. **ejercicio** *sm* exercise.

ejército [e'xerθito] *sm* army.

él [el] *art m* the.

él [el] *pron* he. it.

elaborar [elaβo'rar] *v* elaborate; make; manufacture. **elaboración** *sf* elaboration. **elaborado** *adj* elaborate.

elástico [e'lastiko] *sm, adj* elastic. **elasticidad** *sf* elasticity.

elección [elek'θjon] *sf* election; choice. selection. **elector, -a** *sm, sf* elector. **electorado** *sm* electorate. **electoral** *adj* electoral.

eléctrico [e'lektriko] *adj* electric(al). **electricidad** *sf* electricity. **electrizar** *v* electrify. **electrocutar** *v* electrocute. **electrodo** *sm* electrode. **electrónico** *adj* electronic.

elefante [ele'fante] *sm* elephant.

elegancia [ele'ganθja] *sf* elegance. **elegante** *adj* elegant.

***elegir** [ele'xir] *v* elect, choose. **elegible** *adj* eligible.

elemental [elemen'tal] *adj* elementary. **elemento** *sm* element. **elementos** *sm pl* elements; rudiments.

elevar [ele'βar] *v* elevate, lift, raise. **elevarse** *v* rise; soar; be elated. **elevación** *sf* elevation; rapture; pride. **elevado** *adj* lofty; sublime.

eliminar [elimi'nar] *v* eliminate. **eliminación** *sf* elimination.

elocución [eloku'θjon] *sf* elocution. **elocuencia** *sf* eloquence. **elocuente** *adj* eloquent.

elogiar [elo'xjar] *v* praise. **elogio** *sm* praise. **elogioso** *adj* laudatory.

elucidar [eluθi'ðar] *v* elucidate. **elucidación** *sf* elucidation.

eludir [elu'ðir] *v* elude.

ella ['eʎa] *pron* she, it.

ello ['eʎo] *pron* it.

emanar [ema'nar] *v* emanate. **emanación** *sf* emanation.

emancipar [emanθi'par] *v* emancipate. **emancipación** *sf* emancipation.

embajada [emba'xaða] *sf* embassy; (*fig*) errand. **embajador** *sm* ambassador.

embalar [emba'lar] *v* pack, bale. **embalaje** *sm* packing; bale.

embarazar [embara'θar] *v* embarrass; hinder; make pregnant. **embarazarse** *v* become pregnant. **embarazada** *adj* pregnant. **embarazo** *sm* embarrassment; obstacle; pregnancy. **embarazoso** *adj* embarrassing; awkward.

embarcar [embar'kar] *v* embark; ship; (*fam*) involve. **embarcarse** *v* go on board. **embarcación** *sf* boat; embarkation; voyage. **embarcadero** *sm* landing-stage. **embarco** *sm* embarkation.

embargar [embar'gar] *v* (*jur*) seize; (*fig*) overcome; blunt. **embargo** *sm* embargo. **sin embargo** nevertheless.

embarque [em'barke] *sm* shipment.

embarrar [embar'rar] *v* smear; cover with mud. **embarrarse** *v* get dirty.

embeber [embe'βer] *v* absorb, soak up; shrink. **embebecerse** *v* (*fig*) immerse oneself.

***embellecer** [embeʎe'θer] *v* embellish.

***embestir** [embes'tir] *v* attack; charge. **embestida** *sf* onslaught; charge.

emblema [em'blema] *sm* emblem. **emblemático** *adj* emblematic.

embobar [embo'βar] *v* stupefy; fascinate.

embocar [embo'kar] *v* put in the mouth; enter; (*fig*) swallow. **embocadura** *sf* mouth of a river; (*vino*) taste; (*caballo*) bit.

embolsar [embol'sar] *v* pocket.

emborrachar [emborra'tʃar] *v* intoxicate. **emborracharse** *v* get drunk.

emboscar [embos'kar] *v* ambush. **emboscarse** *v* lie in ambush. **emboscada** *sf* ambush.

embotar [embo'tar] *v* blunt, dull; pack in a jar. **embotarse** *v* become enervated. **embotadura** *sf also* **embotamiento** *sm* bluntness, dullness.

embotellar [embote'ʎar] *v* bottle. **embotellarse** *v* learn by heart. **embotellado** *adj* bottled; jammed. **embotellamiento** *sm* bottling; traffic jam.

embozar [embo'θar] *v* muffle; wrap up. **embozadamente** *adv* secretly. **embozo** *sm* fold; (*fig*) disguise. **quitarse el embozo** bare one's face.

embragar [embra'gar] *v* (*auto*) engage the clutch. **embrague** *sm* (*auto*) clutch.

embriagarse [embrja'garse] *v* get drunk. **embriagado** *adj* drunk.

embrión [em'brjon] *sm* embryo. **embriología** *sf* embryology.

embrollar [embro'ʎar] v muddle, confuse. **embrollarse** v get mixed up. **embrollo** sm confusion.

embrujar [embru'xar] v bewitch.

*embrutecer** [embrute'θer] v brutalize; stupefy.

embudo [em'buðo] sm funnel; crater; (fig) trick.

embuste [em'buste] sm lie; trick. **embustear** v lie; cheat. **embustería** sf deceit; imposture. **embustero, -a** sm, sf liar; cheat; adj lying; deceitful.

embutir [embu'tir] v stuff; cram; (tecn) inlay. **embutido** sm sausage.

emergencia [emer'xenθja] sf emergence; emergency. **emergente** adj emergent; resultant. **emerger** v emerge.

emigrar [emi'grar] v emigrate; migrate. **emigración** sf emigration; migration. **emigrado, -a** sm, sf emigrant. **emigrante** s(m+f), adj emigrant.

eminencia [emi'nenθja] sf eminence; height. **eminente** adj eminent.

emisario [emi'sarjo], -a sm, sf emissary.

emitir [emi'tir] v emit; broadcast; transmit. **emisión** sf emission; broadcast; programme. **emisor** sm transmitter. **emisora** sf radio station.

emoción [emo'θjon] sf emotion; thrill. **emocionante** adj moving; exciting.

empachar [empa'tʃar] v satiate; give indigestion; sicken; conceal; (fig) hinder. **empacharse** v have indigestion; become confused; get fed up. **empachado** adj clumsy; sick; fed up. **empacho** sm indigestion; (fig) embarrassment.

empadronar [empaðro'nar] v register. **empadronamiento** sm census.

empalagar [empala'gar] v cloy; vex. **empalagarse** v get fed up. **empalagoso** adj cloying.

empalar [empa'lar] v impale.

empalizada [empali'θaða] sf stockade. **empalizar** v fence.

empalmar [empal'mar] v splice; couple, join. **empalme** sm joint; junction.

empanada [empa'naða] sf meat pie.

empañar [empa'ɲar] v tarnish; swathe; obscure. **empañarse** v cloud over. **empañado** adj misty.

empapar [empa'par] v soak; drench. **empapamiento** sm soaking.

empapelar [empape'lar] v paper; wrap in paper.

empaquetar [empake'tar] v pack, package. **empaque** sm packing.

emparejar [empare'xar] v match; pair; draw level; catch up. **emparejadura** sf matching; levelling.

empastar [empas'tar] v paste; fill. **empastado** adj filled; (libro) clothbound.

empatar [empa'tar] v (juegos) tie, draw. **empate** sm tie, draw.

*empedernir** [empeðer'nir] v harden. **empedernido** adj hardened; inveterate.

*empedrar** [empe'ðrar] v pave. **empedrado** adj paved; cobbled.

empeine [em'peine] sm groin; instep; (med) impetigo.

empeñar [empe'ɲar] v pawn, pledge; commit; get involved. **empeñarse** v start; strive; get into debt. **empeñado** adj insistent. **empeño** sm pledge; contract; insistence; yearning. **casa de empeño** sf pawnshop. **en empeño** in pawn.

empeorar [empeo'rar] v make worse; worsen. **empeoramiento** sm deterioration.

*empequeñecer** [empekeɲe'θer] v dwarf; belittle.

emperador [empera'ðor] sm emperor. **emperatriz** sf empress.

*empezar** [empe'θar] v begin.

empinar [empi'nar] v straighten; exalt. **empinarse** v rear up; stand on tiptoe; tower. **empinado** adj erect; on tiptoe; haughty.

empírico [em'piriko] adj empirical. **empirismo** sm empiricism.

emplazar [empla'θar] v summon; locate. **emplazamiento** sm (jur) summons.

emplear [emple'ar] v employ; use; invest; spend. **empleado, -a** sm, sf employee. **empleador, -a** sm, sf employer. **empleo** sm employment; job; use.

*empobrecer** [empoβre'θer] v impoverish. **empobrecimiento** sm impoverishment.

empollar [empo'ʎar] v hatch; (fam) swot, mug up.

emponzoñar [empoɲθo'ɲar] v poison. **emponzoñamiento** sm poisoning.

empotrar [empo'trar] v embed. **empotramiento** sm embedding.

emprender [empren'der] v undertake; start; attack. **emprender con** accost. **emprendedor** adj enterprising.

empresa [em'presa] sf enterprise; (com) company; management. **empresario, -a** sm, sf impresario; contractor.

empréstito [em'prestito] *sm* loan.

empujar [empu'xar] *v* push; press; (*fig*) urge. **empuje** *sm* push; enterprise. a **empujes** by fits and starts.

empuñar [empu'ɲar] *v* seize; take up. **empuñadura** *sf* hilt.

emular [emu'lar] *v* emulate.

emulsión [emul'sjon] *sf* emulsion. **emulsionar** *v* emulsify.

en [en] *prep* on; in; into; onto. **en casa** at home. **en donde** where. **en tren** by train.

enaguas [e'nagwas] *sf pl* petticoat *sing*.

enajenar [enaxe'nar] *v* alienate; transfer; drive mad; enrapture. **enajenarse** *v* lose one's self-control. **enajenación** *sf also* **enajenamiento** *sm* alienation; absent-mindedness; rapture; panic.

enamorar [enamo'rar] *v* court; win the love of. **enamorarse** *v* fall in love. **enamorado, -a** *sm, sf* sweetheart.

enano [e'nano], **-a** *sm, sf* dwarf.

enarbolar [enarβo'lar] *v* hoist. **enarbolarse** *v* rear; lose one's temper.

***enardecer** [enarðe'θer] *v* inflame. **enardecerse** *v* become excited.

encabestrar [enkaβes'trar] *v* put a halter on.

encabezar [enkaβe'θar] *v* lead; head; take a census of; put a title to. **encabezamiento** *sm* headline; heading; census.

encadenar [enkaðe'nar] *v* chain, shackle. **encadenamiento** *sm* chaining; (*fig*) linking.

encajar [enka'xar] *v* fit; join; bear; pocket; drop; land. **encajarse** *v* get stuck; squeeze in. **encajadura** *sf* (*hueso*) setting. socket. **encaje** *sm* joint; setting; socket; lace.

encallar [enka'ʎar] *v* run aground. **encallarse** *v* harden. **encalladero** *sm* sandbank; reef.

encaminar [enkami'nar] *v* direct; guide. **encaminarse** *v* set out for.

encandilar [enkandi'lar] *v* dazzle; stimulate. **encandilarse** *v* (*ojos*) sparkle.

encantar [enkan'tar] *v* enchant; charm. **encantado** *adj* charmed; haunted. **¡encantado!** pleased to meet you! **encantador** *adj* charming. **encanto** *sm* charm; delight.

encapotar [enkapo'tar] *v* cover with a cloak. **encapotarse** *v* cloak oneself; look sullen; cloud over. **encapotado** *adj* overcast.

encapricharse [enkapri'tʃarse] *v* set one's mind on. **encapricharse por** or **con** become infatuated with.

encarar [enka'rar] *v* face up to; aim; confront. **encaramiento** *sm* encounter.

encarcelar [enkarθe'lar] *v* imprison. **encarcelamiento** *sm* imprisonment.

***encarecer** [enkare'θer] *v* raise the price of; praise; urge. **encarecidamente** *adv* earnestly. **encarecido** *adj* highly recommended. **encarecimiento** *sm* price increase; emphasis; recommendation.

encargar [enkar'gar] *v* (*com*) order; commission; entrust; charge; advise. **encargarse de** take charge of. **encargado** *sm* agent. **encargo** *sm* errand; job; order.

encarnar [enkar'nar] *v* personify; heal; pierce the flesh; bait. **encarnarse** *v* mix, join in. **encarnación** *sf* incarnation. **encarnado** *adj* incarnate; red; (*uña*) ingrowing.

encarnizar [enkarni'θar] *v* infuriate. **encarnizarse** *v* devour. **encarnizado** *adj* inflamed; bloody.

encasillar [enkasi'ʎar] *v* classify.

encauzar [enkau'θar] *v* channel; direct. **encauzamiento** *sm* channelling; (*fig*) guidance.

***encender** [enθen'der] *v* light; set on fire; turn on; arouse. **encendedor** *sm* lighter. **encendido** *adj* lit; burning; flushed. **encendimiento** *sm* burning; ardour.

***encerrar** [enθer'rar] *v* shut up; enclose; contain. **encerrarse** *v* live in seclusion. **encerramiento** *sm* enclosure; lock-up. **encierro** *sm* enclosure; prison.

encía [en'θia] *sf* (*anat*) gum.

enciclopedia [enθiklo'peðja] *sf* encyclopaedia. **enciclopédico** *adj* encyclopaedic.

encima [en'θima] *adv* above; overhead. **por encima** over; quickly; superficially. **encima de** on top of.

encina [en'θina] *sf* ilex, holm oak.

encinta [en'θinta] *adj* pregnant.

enclavar [enkla'βar] *v* locate; nail; pierce. **enclave** *sm* enclave; situation.

enclenque [en'klenke] *adj* sickly; feeble; skinny.

encoger [enko'xer] *v* shrink. **encogerse de hombros** shrug one's shoulders. **encogido** *adj* shrunk; (*fig*) timid. **encogimiento** *sm* shrinkage; shyness.

encolar [enko'lar] *v* glue. **encolamiento** *sm* gluing.

encomendar [enkomen'ðar] v entrust.
encomendarse v commend oneself.
encomienda sf assignment; tribute; land
concession.

encomiar [enko'mjar] v praise.
encomiador adj laudatory.

enconar [enko'nar] v inflame; infect.
enconarse v become inflamed; become
infected; get angry.

encontrar [enkon'trar] v find; meet.
encontrarse v find oneself; quarrel.
encontrado adj opposed.

encopetado [enkope'taðo] adj of noble
birth; aristocratic; presumptuous.

encorvar [enkor'βar] v curve. **encorvarse** v
become bent; (caballo) buck. **encorvado**
adj bent; stooped. **encorvamiento** sm
bend; stoop.

encrespar [enkres'par] v curl; make
rough; excite; irritate. **encresparse** v
curl; become rough; become entangled.

encrucijada [enkruθi'xaða] sf crossroads
pl.

encuadernar [enkwaðer'nar] v (libro)
bind. **encuadernación** sf bookbinding.

encuadrar [enkwa'ðrar] v frame; insert.
encuadre sm frame.

encubrir [enku'βrir] v conceal; (jur)
receive stolen goods. **encubierto** adj concealed. **encubrimiento** sm concealment.

encuentro [en'kwentro] sm encounter;
collision.

encumbrar [enkum'brar] v raise; ascend;
exalt. **encumbrado** adj high, lofty.
encumbramiento sm height; praise.

enchufar [entʃu'far] v plug in; connect.
enchufado, -a sm, sf (fam) wirepuller.
enchufe sm electric plug; joint; (fam)
cushy job. **enchufismo** sm (fam) wirepull-
ing.

endeble [en'deβle] adj frail. **endebles** sf
frailty.

endémico [en'demiko] adj endemic.

enderezar [endere'θar] v straighten;
guide; put right. **enderezarse** v stand up
straight. **enderezado** adj favourable.

endeudarse [endeu'ðarse] v get into debt.

endiablado [endja'βlaðo] adj devilish.
endiablar v bedevil.

endiosar [endjo'sar] v deify. **endiosarse** v
be conceited. **endiosado** adj deified; conceited.

endosar [endo'sar] v also **endorsar**
endorse. **endoso** sm also **endorso** sm
endorsement.

endulzar [endul'θar] v sweeten.
endulzadura sf sweetening.

endurecer [endure'θer] v harden.
endurecido adj hardened. **endurecimiento**
sm hardening.

enebro [e'neβro] sm juniper.

enemigo [ene'miɣo], -a sm, sf enemy. adj
hostile. **enemistar** v make an enemy of.

energía [ener'xia] sf energy. **enérgico** adj
energetic; vigorous; drastic.

enero [e'nero] sm January.

enfadar [enfa'ðar] v anger. **enfado** sm
anger; annoyance. **enfadoso** adj annoying.

énfasis [enfasis] s(m or f) emphasis.
enfático adj emphatic.

enfermar [enfer'mar] v make ill; fall ill.
enfermedad sf illness. **enfermedad profesional** occupational disease. **enfermería**
sf infirmary. **enfermera**, -o sf, sm nurse.
enfermo adj ill.

enfilar [enfi'lar] v line up.

enflaquecer [enflake'θer] v weaken;
make thin; grow thin. **enflaquecimiento**
sm weakening; emaciation.

enfocar [enfo'kar] v focus; approach,
tackle. **enfoque** sm focus; approach.

enfrascar [enfras'kar] v bottle. **enfrascarse**
v become involved; become engrossed.

enfrentar [enfren'tar] v confront; face;
resist. **enfrentarse** v face up to. **enfrente**
adv opposite. **enfrente de** prep opposite.

enfriar [enfri'ar] v cool. **enfriarse** v cool
down. **enfriadero** sm coldroom.
enfriamiento sm cooling.

enfurecer [enfure'θer] v infuriate.
enfurecerse v rage. **enfurecimiento** sm
fury.

enganchar [engan'tʃar] v hook; hitch;
hang up; harness. **enganche** sm hook;
coupling; harnessing; enlistment.

engañar [enga'nar] v deceive. **engaño** sm
deceit. **engañoso** adj deceitful.

engatusar [engatu'sar] v coax; flatter.
engatusamiento sm coaxing.

engendrar [enxen'drar] v engender;
breed. **engendrador** adj generating.
engendramiento sm generating. **engendro**
sm foetus; abortion; monster;
brainchild.

englobar [englo'βar] v include; embrace.

engordar [engor'ðar] v fatten; gain
weight. **engorde** sm (animales) fattening
up.

engorro [en'gorro] *sm* nuisance. **engorroso** *adj* troublesome.

engranar [engra'nar] *v* put in gear, mesh, interlock. **engranaje** *sm* gear; cogs; connection.

*****engrandecer** [engrande'θer] *v* enlarge; exaggerate; promote. **engrandecimiento** *sm* enlargement; increase; exaggeration.

engrasar [engra'sar] *v* grease. **engrase** *sm* greasing.

engreído [engre'iðo] *adj* conceited. **engreimiento** *sm* conceit. **engreír** *v* make conceited.

*****engrosar** [engro'sar] *v* fatten; thicken; increase. **engrosarse** *v* enlarge. **engrosamiento** *sm* fattening; thickening.

*****engullir** [engu'ʎir] *v* gobble; gulp down.

enhiesto [e'njesto] *adj* erect; upright. **enhestar** *v* erect. **enhestarse** *v* rise; straighten oneself up.

enhorabuena [enora'βwena] *sf* congratulations *pl.* **dar la enhorabuena** congratulate. **enhorabuena** *adv* inopportunely.

enigma [e'nigma] *sm* enigma. **enigmático** *adj* enigmatic.

enjabonar [enxaβo'nar] *v* soap. **enjabonadura** *sf* lathering.

enjambre [en'xambre] *sm* swarm. **enjambrar** *v* swarm.

enjaular [enxau'lar] *v* cage.

enjuagar [enxwa'gar] *v* rinse. **enjuague** *sm* rinse, rinsing; *(fig)* plot.

enjugar [enxu'gar] *v* dry; wipe; cancel. **enjugador** *sm* clothes-drier.

enjuiciar [enxwi'θjar] *v* (*jur*) sue; try; prosecute; judge. **enjuiciamiento** *sm* trial; lawsuit; judgment.

enlace [en'laθe] *sm* link; connection; liaison; marriage. **enlazar** *v* join; connect; relate. **enlazarse** *v* marry.

*****enloquecer** [enloke'θer] *v* madden. **enloquecido** *adj* mad. **enloquecimiento** *sm* madness.

enlosar [enlo'sar] *v* tile; pave. **enlosado** *sm* tiling; paving.

enlucir [enlu'θir] *v* plaster; polish. **enlucido** *sm* plaster. **enlucimiento** *sm* plastering; polishing.

enlutar [enlu'tar] *v* dress in mourning; *(fig)* sadden. **enlutado** *adj* in mourning.

enmarañar [enmara'ɲar] *v* entangle; muddle; confuse. **enmarañamiento** *sm* tangle; confusion.

enmascarar [enmaska'rar] *v* mask. **enmascararse** *v* go in disguise. **enmascaramiento** *sm* camouflage.

*****enmendar** [enmen'dar] *v* amend; correct; reform. **enmendadura** *sf* correction. **enmienda** *sf* rectification; repair; amendment.

*****enmohecer** [enmoe'θer] *v* rust; make mouldy. **enmohecerse** *v* get rusty; grow mouldy. **enmohecimiento** *sm* rusting; mouldering.

*****enmudecer** [enmuðe'θer] *v* silence. **enmudecerse** *v* fall silent; become dumb.

*****ennoblecer** [ennoβle'θer] *v* ennoble; do honour to. **ennoblecimiento** *sm* ennobling.

enojar [eno'xar] *v* annoy; offend. **enojarse** *v* get cross. **enojado** *adj* angry. **enojo** *sm* annoyance; anger.

*****enorgullecer** [enorguʎe'θer] *v* make proud. **enorgullecerse** *v* grow proud. **enorgullecerse de** pride oneself on. **enorgullecimiento** *sm* pride.

enorme [e'norme] *adj* enormous. **enormidad** *sf* hugeness; enormity.

*****enrarecer** [enrare'θer] *v* make rare; rarefy. **enrarecerse** *v* become scarce. **enrarecido** *adj* rarefied. **enrarecimiento** *sm* scarcity.

enredar [enre'ðar] *v* catch; entangle; compromise; involve. **enredarse** *v* become involved. **planta enredadera** *sf* climbing plant. **enredador** *adj* mischievous. **enredo** *sm* tangle; mess; love affair. **enredoso** *adj* complicated; mischievous. **enrevesado** [enreβe'saðo] *adj* complicated, involved.

*****enriquecer** [enrike'θer] *v* enrich.

*****enrojecer** [enroxe'θer] *v* redden; cause to blush. **enrojecerse** *v* blush. **enrojecimiento** *sm* glowing; blush.

enrollar [enro'ʎar] *v* coil up. **enrollamiento** *sm* rolling up; coiling.

*****enronquecer** [enronke'θer] *v* make hoarse. **enronquecimiento** *sm* hoarseness.

enroscar [enros'kar] *v* twist, curl. **enroscarse** *v* curl up. **enroscadura** *sf* twisting, curling.

ensalada [ensa'laða] *sf* salad.

ensalmar [ensal'mar] *v* (*huesos*) set; cure. **ensalmador, -a** *sm, sf* quack; bonesetter. **ensalmado** *sm* quack remedy.

ensalzar [ensal'θar] *v* praise. **ensalzarse** *v* boast. **ensalzamiento** *sm* praise.

ensamblar [ensam'blar] *v* assemble; join.

ensamblado *sm* joint. **ensamblador** *sm* joiner. **ensamblaje** *sm* joining; joint.

ensanchar [ensan'tʃar] *v* grow broader; enlarge; stretch. **ensancharse** *v* put on airs. **ensanche** *sm* enlargement; extension; new suburb.

ensañar [ensa'ɲar] *v* infuriate. **ensañarse** *v* be merciless.

ensayar [ensa'jar] *v* test; try; rehearse. **ensayarse** *v* practise; rehearse. **ensayo** *sm* test; trial; essay; rehearsal. **ensayo general** dress rehearsal.

ensenada [ense'naða] *sf* cove; inlet.

enseñar [ense'ɲar] *v* show; teach. **bien/mal enseñado** well/ill-bred. **enseñanza** *sf* teaching; education.

enseres [en'seres] *sm pl* goods and chattels; equipment *sing*.

ensillar [ensi'ʎar] *v* saddle.

ensimismarse [ensimis'marse] *v* become lost in thought. **ensimismado** *adj* lost in thought. **ensimismamiento** *sm* pensiveness.

***ensordecer** [ensorðe'θer] *v* deafen. **ensordecerse** *v* grow deaf. **ensordecedor** *adj* deafening. **ensordecimiento** *sm* deafness.

ensuciar [ensu'θjar] *v* dirty. **ensuciador** *adj* dirtying. **ensuciamiento** *sm* dirtiness, dirt.

ensueño [en'sweɲo] *sm* dream; fantasy. **¡ni por ensueño!** not likely!

entablar [enta'βlar] *v* begin; open; establish; board up; put in a splint; (*juegos*) set up. **entablado** *sm* planking; wooden floor.

entallar [enta'ʎar] *v* carve; notch; engrave; fit to the body. **entalladura** *sf* notch; mortise; carving.

ente ['ente] *sm* entity; (*fam*) fellow.

***entender** [enten'der] *v* understand; believe; mean. **entenderse** *v* make oneself understood. **entendedor, -a** *sm, sf* expert. **entendidamente** *adv* cleverly. **entendido** *adj* understood; well informed; clever. **¡entendido!** O.K.!

enterar [ente'rar] *v* inform; instruct. **enterarse** *v* become aware. **enterado** *adj* aware.

***enternecer** [enterne'θer] *v* soften. **enternecerse** *v* be moved; relent.

entero [en'tero] *adj* entire, whole; perfect; pure; strong. **por entero** completely. **enteramente** *adv* entirely.

***enterrar** [enter'rar] *v* bury. **enterrador**

sm gravedigger. **entierro** *sm* burial; funeral.

entidad [enti'ðað] *sf* society; company; significance; entity.

entonar [ento'nar] *v* tune; intone; sing in tune. **entonación** *sf* intonation. **entonado** *adj* in tune; haughty.

entonces [en'tonθes] *adv* then; in that case; and so.

entornar [entor'nar] *v* (*ojos, puerta*) half close; tilt.

***entorpecer** [entorpe'θer] *v* benumb; obstruct. **entorpecimiento** *sm* numbness; sluggishness; obstruction.

entrada [en'traða] *sf* entrance; doorway; admission; (*deporte*) gate; ticket; income; takings *pl*. **derechos de entrada** *sm pl* import duty *sing*. **de entrada** to begin with. **entrar** *v* enter; flow into; fit; join; introduce; invade. **el año que entra** the coming year.

entrambos [en'trambos] *pl adj* both.

entraña [en'traɲa] *sf* essence; core; disposition. **entrañas** *sf pl* entrails, bowels. **no tener entrañas** be heartless. **entrañable** *adj* dear, beloved. **entrañar** *v* bury deep; involve. **entrañarse** *v* penetrate to the core.

entre ['entre] *prep* between; among. **entre semana** on weekdays. **entretanto** *adv* meanwhile.

entreabierto [entrea'βjerto] *adj* half-open.

entrecejo [entre'θexo] *sm* frown.

entregar [entre'gar] *v* deliver; surrender. **entrega** *sf* delivery; (*fascículo*) instalment.

entrelazar [entrela'θar] *v* entwine.

entremés [entre'mes] *sm* (*culin*) hors d'oeuvre; (*teatro*) short farce.

entremeter [entreme'ter] *v* also **entrometer** mix; insert. **entremeterse** *also* **entrometerse** *v* interfere. **entremetido, -a** *sm, sf also* **entrometido, -a** busybody.

entrenar [entre'nar] *v* train; coach. **entrenador, -a** *sm, sf* trainer; coach. **entrenamiento** *sm* training; coaching.

entresacar [entresa'kar] *v* select; prune; thin out.

entresuelo [entre'swelo] *sm* mezzanine.

entretejer [entrete'xer] *v* interweave.

***entretener** [entrete'ner] *v* entertain; delay; maintain. **entretenerse** *v* pass the time. **entretenido** *adj* entertaining; busy. **entretenimiento** *sm* entertainment; pastime; delaying.

*entrever [entre'βer] v make out; foresee.

entrevista [entre'βista] sf interview. entrevistar v interview. entrevistarse v hold an interview.

*entristecer [entriste'θer] v sadden. entristecerse v grow sad. entristecimiento sm sadness.

*entumecer [entume'θer] v numb. entumecerse v go numb; (mar) surge. entumecido adj numb. entumecimiento sm numbness.

enturbiar [entur'βjar] v make cloudy; muddy. enturbiarse v be in disorder.

entusiasmar [entusjas'mar] v fill with enthusiasm. entusiasmarse v be very keen. entusiasmo sm enthusiasm. entusiasta s(m+f) enthusiast; adj enthusiastic. entusiástico adj enthusiastic.

enumerar [enume'rar] v enumerate. enumeración sf enumeration.

enunciar [enun'θjar] v enunciate. state. enunciación sf statement. enunciation.

envainar [enβai'nar] v sheathe.

*envanecer [enβane'θer] v make vain. envanecimiento sm vanity.

envasar [enβa'sar] v pack; wrap; bottle. envasador sm packer; large funnel. envase sm packing; bottling; container.

*envejecer [enβexe'θer] v age. envejecerse v grow old. envejecido adj aged. envejecimiento sm ageing.

envenenar [enβene'nar] v poison. envenenador adj poisonous. envenenamiento sm poisoning; pollution.

envergadura [enβerga'ðura] sf wingspan; (fig) scope.

enviar [en'βjar] v send. enviado, -a sm, sf messenger; representative; envoy.

envidiar [enβi'ðjar] v envy. envidia sf envy. envidioso adj envious.

*envilecer [enβile'θer] v debase. envilecimiento sm debasement; degradation.

envío [en'βio] sm dispatch; shipment; remittance.

*envolver [enβol'βer] v envelop; wrap up; involve; imply; (mil) encircle. envoltura sf wrapping; envelope.

enzarzar [enθar'θar] v cover with brambles; set at odds. enzarzarse v get caught up in brambles; (fig) squabble.

enzima [en'θima] sf enzyme.

épico ['epiko] adj epic.

epidemia [epi'ðemja] sf epidemic. epidémico adj epidemic.

epígrafe [e'pigrafe] sm epigraph.

epílogo [e'pilogo] sm epilogue.

episcopado [episko'paðo] sm bishopric; episcopate. episcopal adj episcopal.

episodio [epi'soðjo] sm episode.

epitafio [epi'tafjo] sm epitaph.

época ['epoka] sf epoch.

equidad [eki'ðað] sf equity; fairness.

equilibrar [ekili'βrar] v balance. equilibrio sm equilibrium; balance; poise. equilibrismo sm acrobatics. equilibrista s(m+f) acrobat.

equinoccio [eki'nokθjo] sm equinox. equinoccial adj equinoctial.

equipar [eki'par] v equip. equipaje sm luggage; equipment. equipo sm team; equipment; trousseau.

equitación [ekita'θjon] sf riding; horsemanship.

equitativo [ekita'tiβo] adj fair, equitable.

equivalencia [ekiβa'lenθja] sf equivalence. equivalente adj equivalent. equivaler v be equivalent.

equivocar [ekiβo'kar] v mistake. equivocarse v be mistaken. equivocación sf mistake. equivoco adj ambiguous.

era¹ ['era] sf era.

era² ['era] V ser.

eremita [ere'mita] sm also ermitaño sm hermit.

eres ['eres] V ser.

*erguir [er'gir] v raise, erect. erguirse v straighten up. erguimiento sm raising.

erigir [eri'xir] v erect; build; establish. erigirse v set oneself up. erección sf erection; establishment. erecto adj erect.

erizar [eri'θar] v bristle. erizarse v bristle; (pelo) stand on end. erizado adj bristly. erizo [e'riθo] sm hedgehog.

erradicar [erraði'kar] v eradicate; uproot. erradicación sf eradication.

*errar [er'rar] v miss; fail; wander. errarse v be mistaken. erradizo adj wandering. errado adj mistaken. errante adj wandering; nomadic. erróneo adj erroneous, mistaken. error sm error.

eructar [eruk'tar] v belch. eructo sm belch.

erudición [eruði'θjon] sf erudition. erudito, -a sm, sf scholar; adj erudite.

erupción [erup'θjon] sf eruption; (med) rash. eruptivo adj eruptive.

esbelto [es'βelto] adj slim. esbeltez sf slimness.

esbozar [esβo'θar] v sketch. **esbozo** sm sketch.

escabechar [eskaβe'tʃar] v (culin) pickle; (fam) fail an exam; (fam) bump off. **escabeche** sm pickle.

escabroso [eska'βroso] adj rough; crude; harsh; (fig) difficult. **escabro** sm (med) scab. **escabrosidad** sf roughness; crudity; harshness.

*escabullirse [eskaβu'ʎirse] v sneak away or out.

escala [es'kala] sf ladder; scale; port of call. **en gran escala** on a large scale. **escala franca** free port. **hacer escala en** put in at. **escalar** v climb; escalate. **escalamiento** sm escalation.

escaldar [eskal'ðar] v scald; make red hot. **escaldado** adj scalded; cautious.

escalera [eska'lera] sf stairs pl. **escalera móvie** escalator.

escalfar [eskal'far] v (culin) poach. **escalfado** adj poached. **escalfador** sm poacher.

escalofrío [eskalo'frio] sm shiver. **escalofriante** adj bloodcurdling.

escalón [eska'lon] sm rung; step. **escalonar** v space; stagger. **escalonado** adj spread out; staggered. **escalonamiento** sm spacing; staggering.

escalonia [eska'lonja] sf also **escaloña** shallot.

escalpelo [eskal'pelo] sm scalpel.

escama [es'kama] sf (jabón) flake; (animal) scale. **escamado** adj (fam) suspicious. **escamar** v scale; (fam) make suspicious. **escamarse** v (fam) become suspicious. **escamoso** adj scaly; (fam) suspicious.

escamot(e)ar [eskamo't(j)ar] v make disappear; shirk. **escamoteo** sm (fam) swindle. **escamoteador, -a** sm, sf conjurer; (fam) swindler.

escampar [eskam'par] v clear out; stop raining. **escampada** sf clear spell.

escándalo [es'kandalo] sm scandal; uproar; viciousness. **dar un escándalo** make a scene. **escandalizar** v scandalize. **escandalizarse** v be shocked. **escandaloso** adj scandalous; turbulent.

escaño [es'kaɲo] sm bench; seat in Parliament.

escapar [eska'par] v escape. **escaparse** v escape; leak. **escapada** sf escape; escapade. **escape** sm escape; leakage. a escape at full speed. **tubo de escape** exhaust pipe.

escaparate [eskapa'rate] sm shop window.

escarabajo [eskara'βaxo] sm beetle; (fam) dwarf.

escaramuza [eskara'muθa] sf skirmish. **escaramucear** v skirmish.

escarbar [eskar'βar] v scratch; scrape; pry into. **escarbo** sm scraping; scratching.

escarcha [es'kartʃa] sf frost.

escarlata [eskar'lata] sf, adj scarlet.

*escarmentar [eskarmen'tar] v punish; learn from experience; be warned. **escarmiento** sm punishment; warning.

*escarnecer [eskarne'θer] v mock. **escarnecimiento** sm scorn; derision.

escarola [eska'rola] sf endive.

escarpa [es'karpa] sf slope.

escasear [eskase'ar] v skimp; be scarce. **escasamente** adv scantily. **escasez** sf scarcity. **escaso** adj scarce; skimpy.

escena [es'θena] sf scene; stage. **poner en escena** stage. **escénico** adj scenic.

escéptico [es'θeptiko] s, adj sceptic(al). **escepticismo** sm scepticism.

*esclarecer [esklare'θer] v brighten; clear; dawn. **esclarecido** adj illustrious. **esclarecimiento** sm illumination; splendour; dawn.

esclavitud [esklaβi'tuð] sf slavery. **esclavizar** v enslave. **esclavo, -a** sm, sf slave.

esclusa [es'klusa] sf lock; floodgate. **esclusa de aire** airlock.

escoba [es'koβa] sf broom, brush. **escobar** v sweep, brush.

*escocer [esko'θer] v smart, sting. **escocerse** v chafe. **escocedor** adj painful. **escocedura** sf sting.

escoger [esko'xer] v choose. **escogido** adj chosen, choice. **escogimiento** sm choice, selection.

escolar [esko'lar] s(m+f) schoolboy/girl. adj scholastic. **escolástica** sf scholasticism. **escolástico** adj scholastic.

escolta [es'kolta] sf escort. **escoltar** v escort.

escollo [es'koʎo] sm reef; difficulty; danger.

escombro [es'kombro] sm mackerel; débris; rubbish.

esconder [eskon'der] v hide. **esconderse** v conceal oneself. **escondidamente** adv secretly. **escondite** sm hiding place; (juego) hide-and-seek.

escopeta [esko'peta] sf shotgun; rifle. **escopeta de aire comprimido** airgun.

escoplo [es'koplo] sm chisel. **escoplear** v chisel; gouge.

escoria [es'korja] sf slag; dross; (fig) scum. **escorial** sm slag heap.

escorpión [eskor'pjon] sm scorpion.

escotado [esko'taðo] adj (vestido) low-cut. **escotar** v lower the neckline; scoop out.

escotilla [esko'tiʎa] sf (mar) hatch.

escribano [eskri'βano] sm clerk; notary.

escribir [eskri'βir] v write. **escribir a máquina** type. **escribirse** v spell. **escribido** adj (fam) well read. **escribiente** s(m+f) clerk. **escrito a mano** handwritten. sm writing; document; letter. **escritor, -a** sm, sf writer. **escritorio** sm bureau; office. **escritura** sf writing; script; (jur) deed.

escrúpulo [es'krupulo] sm scruple; conscientiousness. **escrupuloso** adj scrupulous.

escrutinio [eskru'tinjo] sm scrutiny. **escrutar** v scrutinize.

escuadra [es'kwaðra] sf carpenter's square; (mil) squad; (mar) corporal; (mar) squadron; (fig) gang. **a escuadra** at right angles. **escuadrar** v square.

escuálido [es'kwaliðo] adj squalid; weak; skinny. **escualidez** sf squalor; weakness; emaciation.

escuchar [esku'tʃar] v listen to; hear. **escucharse** v pay too much attention to oneself. **escucha** sf listening; sentry; chaperone. **a la escucha** on the alert. **escuchador, -a** sm, sf listener.

escudero [esku'ðero] sm squire, page. **escudar** v shield. **escudo** sm shield.

escudriñar [eskuðri'nar] v scrutinize. **escudriñador** adj examining; curious. **escudriñamiento** sm investigation; search.

escuela [es'kwela] sf school.

esculpir [eskul'pir] v sculpture; engrave. **escultor, -a** sm, sf sculptor. **escultura** sf sculpture.

escupir [esku'pir] v spit. **escupidura** sf spittle.

escurrir [esku'rir] v drain; wring out; drip; slip; ooze. **escurrirse** v drain; sneak off. **escurridizo** adj slippery. **escurridor** sm plate rack; colander; draining board; wringer. **escurriduras** sf pl dregs pl. **escurrimiento** sm draining; dripping.

ese [ese] adj also **esa** that.

ése ['ese] pron also **ésa** that one; the former.

esencia [e'senθja] sf essence. **esencial** adj essential.

esfera [es'fera] sf sphere. **esférico** adj spherical.

esfinge [es'finxe] sf sphinx.

esforzar [esfor'θar] v invigorate; strengthen; encourage. **esforzarse** v make an effort. **esforzado** adj vigorous. **esfuerzo** sm effort.

esgrimir [esgri'mir] v brandish; fence. **esgrima** sf fencing. **esgrimidor, -a** sm, sf fencer.

eslabón [esla'βon] sm link. **eslabonamiento** sm linking. **eslabonar** v link.

esmaltar [esmal'tar] v enamel; (las uñas) varnish. **esmalte** sm varnish.

esmerado [esme'raðo] adj careful, painstaking. **esmerar** v polish; take great pains.

esmeralda [esme'ralða] sf emerald.

esnórquel [es'norkel] sm snorkel.

eso ['eso] pron that, that thing. **en eso** at that moment. **eso es** that's right. **eso mismo** just so. **por eso** because of that. **esos** adj pl also **esas** those. **ésos** pron pl also **ésas** those; the former.

espabilar [espaβi'lar] v (vela) snuff. **espabilarse** v (fam) look sharp.

espaciar [espa'θjar] v space out; spread. **espaciarse** v expatiate; enjoy oneself. **espacial** adj space. **nave espacial** spaceship. **espaciamiento** sm spacing. **espacio** sm space. **espacioso** adj spacious.

espada [es'paða] sf sword; swordsman. sm matador. **pez espada** swordfish.

espalda [es'palða] sf shoulder; back. **a espaldas** behind someone's back. **volver las espaldas** turn tail.

espantapájaros [espanta'paxaros] sm invar scarecrow.

espantar [espan'tar] v scare. **espantarse** v take fright. **espanto** sm fright; terror. **espantoso** adj frightful; amazing.

España [es'paɲa] sf Spain.

español [espa'ɲol], -a sm, sf Spaniard. (lengua) Spanish. adj Spanish.

esparcir [espar'θir] v scatter; spread. **esparcirse** v amuse oneself. **esparcidamente** adv separately. **esparcido** adj cheerful; amusing; scattered. **esparcimiento** sm scattering; pastime.

espárrago [es'parrago] *sm* asparagus.

espasmo [es'pasmo] *sm* spasm. espasmódico *adj* spasmodic.

especia [es'peθja] *sf* spice.

especial [espe'θjal] *adj* special; particular. en especial especially. especialidad *sf* speciality. especialista *s(m+f)*, *adj* specialist. especializarse *v* specialize.

especie [es'peθje] *sf* species; kind; affair; appearance.

específico [espe'θifiko] *adj* specific. *sm* (*med*) patent medicine. especificación *sf* specification. especificación normalizada standard specification. especificar *v* specify.

espectáculo [espek'takulo] *sm* spectacle; entertainment. espectacular *adj* spectacular. espectador, -a *sm*, *sf* spectator.

espectro [es'pektro] *sm* spectre.

espejo [es'pexo] *sm* mirror. espejo retrovisor (*auto*) rear-view mirror. espejismo *sm* mirage.

esperar [espe'rar] *v* hope; expect; await. esperar a que wait until. espera *sf* waiting; expectation; delay. sala de espera waiting room. esperanza *sf* hope. esperanzador *adj* encouraging.

esperpento [esper'pento] *sm* fright; grotesqueness; absurdity.

espesar [espe'sar] *v* thicken; tighten. espeso *adj* thick; greasy. espesamiento *sm* thickening.

espetar [espe'tar] *v* (*culin*) skewer; pierce. espetarse *v* be pompous.

espía [es'pia] *s(m+f)* spy. espiar *v* spy upon. espionaje *sm* espionage.

espiga [es'piga] *sf* (*bot*) ear. spike. espigado *adj* gone to seed. spike. espigar *v* glean.

espín [es'pin] *sm* porcupine.

espina [es'pina] *sf* thorn; spine; splinter; fishbone. espina dorsal backbone.

espinaca [espi'naka] *sf* spinach.

espiral [espi'ral] *sf*, *adj* spiral.

espíritu [es'piritu] *sm* spirit; soul; ghost; wit; breathing. espiritado *adj* possessed; (*fam*) skinny. espiritismo *sm* spiritualism. espiritista *s(m+f)* spiritualist. espirituoso *adj* spirited. espiritual *adj* spiritual. espiritualidad *sf* spirituality.

espléndido [es'plendiðo] *adj* splendid; magnificent. esplendor *sm* splendour.

espliego [es'pljego] *sm* lavender.

esplín [es'plin] *sm* spleen.

espolear [espole'ar] *v* spur. spur on. espoleo *sm* spurring.

esponja [es'ponxa] *sf* sponge. esponjar *v* make spongy; puff up. esponjarse *v* become spongy; (*fig*) become puffed up with pride; glow with health.

esponsales [espon'sales] *sm pl* betrothal *sing*.

espontáneo [espon'taneo] *adj* spontaneous. espontaneidad *sf* spontaneity.

esporádico [espo'raðiko] *adj* sporadic.

esposa [es'posa] *sf* wife. esposas *sf pl* handcuffs. esposado *adj* newly married; handcuffed.

espuela [es'pwela] *sf* spur. echar la espuela have one for the road.

espuma [es'puma] *sf* foam; froth; lather. espumadera *sf* strainer. espumajear *v* foam at the mouth. espumajoso *adj* foaming; frothy. espumar *v* skim; froth; lather; sparkle. espumoso *adj* frothy; sparkling.

esquela [es'kela] *sf* note; short letter; obituary.

esqueleto [eske'leto] *sm* skeleton.

esquema [es'kema] *sm* scheme. esquemático *adj* schematic.

esquí [es'ki] *sm*, *pl* esquíes *or* esquís ski. esquiador, -a *sm*, *sf* skier. esquiar *v* ski.

esquilar [eski'lar] *v* shear, clip. sin esquilar unshorn.

esquimal [eski'mal] *sm*, *adj* Eskimo.

esquina [es'kina] *sf* (*afuera*) corner. doblar la esquina turn the corner. esquinar *v* form a corner with.

esquirol [eski'rol] *sm* (*fam*) strike-breaker, blackleg.

esquivar [eski'βar] *v* avoid, shun; disappear. esquivarse *v* shy away. esquivo *adj* unsociable.

estabilidad [estaβili'ðað] *sf* stability. estabilizar *v* stabilize. estable *adj* stable.

*establecer [estaβle'θer] *v* establish. establecerse *v* settle down; set up. establecido *adj* established. establecimiento *sm* establishment.

establo [es'taβlo] *sm* cowshed.

estaca [es'taka] *sf* stake. post. estacada *sf* fence; stockade. estacar *v* fence; stake out.

estación [esta'θjon] *sf* station; season. estacionamiento *sm* parking. estacionar *v* park.

estadio [es'taðjo] *sm* stadium; (*med*) phase.

estado [es'taðo] *sm* state; status; order; estate; statement. **estado de ánimo** state of mind. **estar en estado** be pregnant. **hombre de estado** statesman.

Estados Unidos [es'taðos u'niðos] *sm pl* United States (of America). **estadounidense** *s(m + f)*, *adj* American.

estafa [es'tafa] *sf* swindle. **estafador**, **-a** *sm*, *sf* swindler. **estafar** *v* swindle.

estafeta [esta'feta] *sf* courier; sub-post office.

estallar [esta'ʎar] *v* explode; burst; erupt. **estallido** *sm* explosion; crash.

estampar [estam'par] *v* stamp; print; imprint. **estampa** *sf* print; engraving; impression; footprint.

estampida [estam'piða] *sf* stampede; explosion, bang. **estampido** *sm* explosion, bang.

estancar [estan'kar] *v* stem; block; delay; monopolize. **estancarse** *v* stagnate. **estancación** *sf* stagnation. **estancado** *adj* stagnant; blocked. **estanco** *sm* monopoly; state tobacco shop. **estanquero**, **-a** *sm*, *sf* tobacconist.

estandarte [estan'darte] *sm* banner.

estanque [es'tanke] *sm* reservoir; ornamental pond.

estante [es'tante] *sm* shelf. **estantería** *sf* shelving; bookcase.

estaño [es'taɲo] *sm* tin. **estañar** *v* solder.

***estar** [es'tar] *v* be. **está bien** (it's all right). **estar para** be about to. **no está he** *or* **she** is not at home. **ya que estamos** while we're at it.

estático [es'tatiko] *adj* static.

estatua [es'tatwa] *sf* statue.

estatura [esta'tura] *sf* stature, height.

estatuto [esta'tuto] *sm* statute. **estatuario** *adj* statutory.

este¹ ['este] *adj also* **esta** this; the latter. **este²** *sm*, *adj* east.

éste ['este] *pron also* **ésta** this.

estela [es'tela] *sf (mar)* wake; trail.

estelar [este'lar] *adj* stellar.

estepa [es'tepa] *sf* steppe.

estera [es'tera] *sf* matting.

estereofónico [estereo'foniko] *adj* stereophonic.

estereotipo [estereo'tipo] *sm* stereotype.

estéril [es'teril] *adj* sterile; pointless. **esterilizar** *v* sterilize.

esterlina [ester'lina] *adj* sterling. **libra esterlina** pound sterling.

estético [es'tetiko] *adj* aesthetic. **estética** *sf* aesthetics.

estetoscopio [esteto'skopjo] *sm* stethoscope.

estiércol [es'tjerkol] *sm* manure.

estigma [es'tigma] *sm* stigma. **estigmatizar** *v* stigmatize.

estilar [esti'lar] *v* be accustomed; *(documento)* draw up; be in use; be in fashion. **estilístico** *adj* stylistic. **estilizado** *adj* stylized. **estilo** *sm* style; type; fashion.

estimar [esti'mar] *v* esteem; estimate. **estima** *sf* esteem. **estimable** *adj* estimable. **estimación** *sf* estimate; estimation.

estimular [estimu'lar] *v* stimulate. **estimulante** *adj* stimulating; *sm (med)* stimulant. **estímulo** *sm* stimulus.

estipular [estipu'lar] *v* stipulate. **estipulación** *sf* stipulation.

estirar [esti'rar] *v* stretch; extend. **estirado** *adj* affected; miserly. **estirón** *sm* jerk.

estirpe [es'tirpe] *sf* lineage; stock.

esto ['esto] *pron* this. **en esto** whereupon.

estofa [es'tofa] *sf (fig)* quality; class; brocade. **estofado** *adj* quilted; *(culin)* stewed. **estofar** *v* quilt; stew.

estoico [es'toiko], **-a** *s*, *adj* stoic. **estoicismo** *sm* stoicism.

estómago [es'tomago] *sm* stomach. **estomagar** *v* give indigestion.

estorbar [estor'βar] *v* hinder; be in the way. **estorbo** *sm* hindrance; obstruction.

estornino [estor'nino] *sm* starling.

estornudar [estornu'ðar] *v* sneeze. **estornudo** *sm* sneeze.

estoy [es'toi] *V* **estar**.

estrafalario [estrafa'larjo] *adj* outlandish; extravagant; slovenly.

estrada [es'traða] *sf* road, highway.

estragar [estra'gar] *v* corrupt; destroy. **estrago** *sm* ruin, havoc. **hacer estragos** wreak havoc.

estrangular [estrangu'lar] *v* strangle. **estrangulación** *sf* strangulation. **estrangulador** *sm* strangler; *(auto)* choke.

estratagema [estrata'xema] *sf* stratagem. **estrategia** *sf* strategy. **estratégico** *adj* strategic.

estrechar [estre'tʃar] *v* make smaller; tighten; bring closer together. **estrecharse** *v* become narrower; squeeze together; shake hands; make economies. **estrechamente** *adv* narrowly. **estrechamiento** *sm* narrowing; taking-in;

tightening; handshake. **estrecho** adj narrow; cramped; tight; strict.

estrella [es'treʎa] sf star. **estrellado** adj starry.

estrellar [estre'ʎar] v smash (to pieces).

*estremecer [estreme'θer] v shake; startle. **estremecerse** v shudder; tremble. **estremecimiento** sm shake; shudder; tremble.

estrenar [estre'nar] v wear for the first time; (teatro) perform for the first time. **estreno** sm inauguration; first night; dress rehearsal.

estrenuo [es'trenwo] adj strong; courageous.

estreñido [estre'niðo] adj constipated. **estreñimiento** sm constipation.

estrépito [es'trepito] sm noise, din; fuss. **estrepitoso** adj noisy; resounding.

estribo [es'triβo] sm stirrup; step; running-board. **perder los estribos** lose one's head.

estribor [estri'βor] sm (mar) starboard.

estricto [es'trikto] adj strict.

estridente [estri'ðente] adj strident.

estropajo [estro'paxo] sm scourer; rubbish. **estropajoso** adj thick; stringy; slovenly.

estropear [estrope'ar] v spoil; break; maim; age.

estructura [estruk'tura] sf structure; framework. **estructural** adj structural. **estructurar** v organize; construct.

estruendo [es'trwendo] sm din; uproar; bustle; pomp. **estruendoso** adj noisy.

estrujar [estru'xar] v squeeze; crush. **estrujadura** sf pressure. **estrujón** sm squeeze.

estuario [es'twarjo] sm estuary.

estuche [es'tutʃe] sm box; case; casket; sheath.

estudiar [estu'ðjar] v study. **estudiante** s(m+f) student. **estudio** sm study; research; studio. **estudioso** adj studious.

estufa [es'tufa] sf stove; fire; hothouse.

estupefacto [estupe'fakto] adj stupefied; astonished. **estupefacción** sf stupefaction; astonishment.

estupefaciente [estupefa'θjente] adj stupefying; astonishing. sm (med) narcotic.

estupendo [estu'pendo] adj stupendous.

estúpido [es'tupiðo] adj stupid. **estupidez** sf stupidity. **estupor** sm stupor.

esturión [estu'rjon] sm sturgeon.

etapa [e'tapa] sf (de un viaje) stage; period.

éter ['eter] sm ether. **etereo** adj ethereal.

eternidad [eterni'ðað] sf eternity. **eterno** adj eternal. **eternizar** v perpetuate.

ética ['etika] sf ethics. **ético** adj ethical.

etimología [etimolo'xia] sf etymology. **etimológico** adj etymological.

etiqueta [eti'keta] sf etiquette; label; tag. **etiquetero** adj formal.

eucalipto [euka'lipto] sm eucalyptus.

eufemismo [eufe'mismo] sm euphemism. **eufemístico** adj euphemistic.

eunuco [eu'nuko] sm eunuch.

Europa [eu'ropa] sf Europe. **europeo, -a** s, adj European.

eutanasia [euta'nasja] sf euthanasia.

evacuar [eβa'kwar] v evacuate; fulfil. **evacuación** sf evacuation. **evacuado, -a** sm, sf evacuee.

evadir [eβa'ðir] v evade. **evadirse** v escape. **evadido, -a** sm, sf fugitive. **evasión** sf escape; flight. **evasivo** adj evasive.

evaluar [eβa'lwar] v evaluate; value. **evaluación** sf evaluation.

evangélico [eβan'xeliko] adj evangelical. **evangelio** sm gospel. **evangelista** sm evangelist.

evaporar [evapo'rar] v evaporate. **evaporación** sf evaporation.

evento [e'βento] sm (unforeseen) event. **eventual** [even'twal] adj temporary; possible; accidental. **eventualidad** sf contingency.

evidencia [evi'ðenθja] sf certainty; proof; evidence. **evidenciar** v make evident. **evidente** adj evident.

evitar [eβi'tar] v avoid. **evitable** adj avoidable.

evocar [evo'kar] v evoke. **evocación** sf evocation. **evocativo** adj evocative.

evolución [evolu'θjon] sf evolution. **evolucionar** v evolve. **evolutivo** adj evolutionary.

exacerbar [eksaðer'βar] v exacerbate, exasperate. **exacerbación** sf exacerbation.

exactitud [eksakti'tuð] sf exactitude; accuracy. **exacto** adj exact; correct.

exagerar [eksaxe'rar] v exaggerate. **exagerado** adj exaggerated. **exageración** sf exaggeration.

exaltar [eksal'tar] v exalt; raise; praise. **exaltarse** v get worked up; get heated. **exaltación** sf exaltation. **exaltado** adj hotheaded.

examinar [eksami'nar] *v* examine; inspect; test. **examinarse** *v* take an examination. **examen** *sm* examination; inquiry; investigation. **examen de conductor** driving test. **examinador, -a** *sm, sf* examiner.

exangüe [ek'sangwe] *adj* bloodless; weak.

exánime [ek'sanime] *adj* lifeless; unconscious; weak. **caer exánime** fall in a faint.

exasperar [eksaspe'rar] *v* exasperate; vex. **exasperarse** *v* become annoyed. **exasperación** *sf* exasperation. **exasperante** *adj* exasperating.

excavar [ekska'βar] *v* excavate; dig. **excavación** *sf* excavation.

exceder [eksθe'ðer] *v* exceed. **excederse** *v* forget oneself. **excedente** *adj* exceeding; excessive.

excelencia [eksθe'lenθja] *sf* excellence. **excelente** *adj* excellent; first-rate.

excéntrico [eks'θentriko] *adj, sm* eccentric. **excentricidad** *sf* eccentricity.

excepción [eksθep'θjon] *sf* exception. **a excepción de** with the exception of. **estado de excepción** state of emergency. **excepcional** *adj* exceptional. **excepto** *prep* excepting.

excerpta [ek'θerpta] *sf* excerpt.

excesivo [eksθe'siβo] *adj* excessive. **exceso** *sm* excess; surplus. **exceso de equipaje** excess luggage.

excitar [eksθi'tar] *v* excite; stir up. **excitabilidad** *sf* excitability. **excitable** *adj* excitable. **excitante** *adj* exciting.

exclamar [ekskla'mar] *v* exclaim. **exclamarse contra** protest against. **exclamación** *sf* exclamation. **exclamatorio** *adj* exclamatory.

*****excluir** [eksklu'ir] *v* exclude. **exclusivo** *adj* exclusive. **exclusión** *sf* exclusion.

excomulgar [ekskomul'gar] *v* excommunicate. **excomulgación** *sf* excommunication. **excomulgado** *adj* excommunicated; *(fam)* accused.

excreción [ekskre'θjon] *sf* excretion. **excremento** *sm* excrement. **excretar** *v* excrete.

excursión [ekskur'sjon] *sf* excursion. **excursión a pie** hike. **ir de excursión** go on an outing. **excursionista** *s(m+f)* tripper; hiker.

excusar [eksku'sar] *v* excuse; avoid; exempt. **excusarse** *v* apologize. **excusa** *sf* excuse; apology. **excusable** *adj* pardonable. **excusadamente** *adv* unnecessarily. **excusado** *adj* excused; unnecessary; exempt; concealed; private. **excusado es decir** needless to say. **excusado** *sm* toilet.

exentar [eksen'tar] *v* exempt. **exención** *sf* exemption. **exento** *adj* exempt.

exequias [ek'sekjas] *sf pl* funeral rites.

exhalar [eksa'lar] *v* exhale; emit; utter. **exhalación** *sf* exhalation; vapour; shooting star; lightning flash.

exhausto [ek'sausto] *adj* exhausted. **exhaustivo** *adj* exhaustive.

exhibir [eksi'βir] *v* exhibit. **exhibición** *sf* exhibition. **exhibicionismo** *sm* exhibitionism. **exhibicionista** *s(m+f)* exhibitionist.

exhortar [eksor'tar] *v* exhort. **exhortación** *sf* exhortation.

exigir [eksi'xir] *v* demand. **exigencia** *sf* demand; requirement. **exigente** *adj* exacting.

exiguo [ek'sigwo] *adj* scanty. **exigüidad** *sf* scantiness.

eximir [eksi'mir] *v* exempt; excuse. **eximente** *adj* exempting.

existir [eksis'tir] *v* exist. **existencia** *sf* existence. **en existencia** in stock. **existente** *adj* existent; extant; in stock.

éxito ['eksito] *sm* success; result. **tener éxito** be successful.

éxodo [eksoðo] *sm* exodus, emigration.

exonerar [eksone'rar] *v* exonerate; relieve; dismiss. **exoneración** *sf* exoneration; relief.

exorbitante [eksorβi'tante] *adj* exorbitant, excessive.

exorcizar [eksorθi'θar] *v* exorcize. **exorcismo** *sm* exorcism. **exorcista** *sm* exorcist.

exótico [ek'sotiko] *adj* exotic.

expansión [ekspan'sjon] *sf* expansion; recreation. **expansionarse** *v* give vent to one's feelings. **expansivo** *adj* expansive.

expatriar [ekspatri'ar] *v* exile. **expatriación** *sf* banishment.

expectación [ekspekta'θjon] *sf* expectation. **expectante** *adj* expectant.

expedición [ekspeði'θjon] *sf* expedition; party; shipment; dispatch; speed.

*****expedir** [ekspe'ðir] *v* send, dispatch; issue. **expediente** *sm (jur)* proceedings *pl*; dossier; inquiry; record. **expediente** *adj* expedient.

expendedor [ekspenðe'ðor], **-a** *sm, sf*

dealer; retailer; ticket agent. *adj* spending.

experiencia [ekspe'rjenθja] *sf* experience; experiment.

experimentar [eksperimen'tar] *v* experiment; test; feel. **experimentado** *adj* experienced. **experimental** *adj* experimental. **experimento** *sm* experiment.

experto [eks'perto] *sm, adj* expert.

expiar [eks'pjar] *v* atone for. **expiación** *sf* atonement.

expirar [ekspi'rar] *v* expire; die; die down. **expiración** *sf* expiration.

explanar [ekspla'nar] *v* level; (*fig*) explain. **explanación** *sf* levelling; (*fig*) explanation.

explicar [ekspli'kar] *v* explain; justify; lecture. **explicarse** *v* speak plainly; understand. **explicación** *sf* explanation. **explicativo** *adj* explanatory.

explícito [eks'pliθito] *adj* explicit.

explorar [eksplo'rar] *v* explore, investigate. **exploración** *sf* exploration. **explorador** *sm* explorer; (*mil*) scout; boy scout; *adj* exploratory.

explosión [eksplo'sjon] *sf* explosion. **explosivo** *sm, adj* explosive.

explotar [eksplo'tar] *v* exploit; develop; cultivate; explode. **explotación** *sf* exploitation; operation; development; cultivation.

*exponer [ekspo'ner] *v* expose; set out; explain. **exponerse** *v* lay oneself open. **exponente** *s(m+f)* exponent; example; proof.

exportar [ekspor'tar] *v* export. **exportación** *sf* export. **exportador, -a** *sm, sf* exporter.

exposición [eksposi'θjon] *sf* exhibition; display; statement; explanation; risk; (*foto*) exposure. **sala de exposición** showroom.

exprés [eks'pres] *sm* (*tren*) express; (*café*) espresso.

expresar [ekspre'sar] *v* express, convey. **expresarse** *v* express oneself; state. **expresamente** *adv* specifically; explicitly. **expresión** *sf* expression. **expresiones** *sf pl* greetings; regards. **expresivamente** *adv* expressively; affectionately. **expresivo** *adj* expressive; affectionate. **expreso** *adj* expressed; express.

exprimir [ekspri'mir] *v* squeeze; exploit. **exprimidor** *sm* squeezer.

expuesto [eks'pwesto] *adj* on display; exposed; explained.

expulsar [ekspul'sar] *v* expel, throw out.

exquisito [ekski'sito] *adj* exquisite; delightful; refined.

éxtasis ['ekstasis] *sm invar* ecstasy.

*extender [eksten'der] *v* extend; spread. **extenderse** *v* spread; range; enlarge. **extendido** *adj* extended; widespread; outstretched. **extensamente** *adv* at length. **extensible** *adj* extending. **extensión** *sf* extension; expanse; extent; area. **extensivo** *adj* extendible. **extenso** *adj* extensive; large; widespread; full.

extenuar [ekste'nwar] *v* weaken; exhaust. **extenuación** *sf* emaciation; extenuation.

exterior [ekste'rjor] *adj* exterior, external; foreign. **asuntos exteriores** *sm pl* foreign affairs. *sm* outside, exterior; appearance. **al exterior** outside. **del exterior** from abroad.

exterminar [ekstermi'nar] *v* exterminate. **exterminación** *sf* extermination. **exterminador, -a** *sm, sf* exterminator.

externo [eks'terno], **-a** *sm, sf* day pupil. *adj* external; outward. **externado** *sm* day school.

extinguir [ekstin'gir] *v* extinguish; wipe out; put down. **extinguirse** *v* die out. **extinción** *sf* extinction. **extinto** *adj* extinct. **extintor** *sm* fire extinguisher.

extirpar [ekstir'par] *v* uproot; remove. **extirpación** *sf* uprooting; extraction.

extra ['ekstra] *adj invar* extra; best-quality. *sm* (*cine, teatro*) extra.

*extraer [ekstra'er] *v* extract; release. **extracción** *sf* extraction; birth. **extracto** *sm* extract; excerpt; abstract.

extranjero [ekstran'xero], **-a** *sm, sf* foreigner; foreign countries *pl*. *adj* foreign.

extrañar [ekstra'nar] *v* be surprised; surprise; be shy; banish. **extrañarse** *v* go into exile. **extrañamiento** *sm* surprise; banishment. **extrañeza** *sf* strangeness; surprise. **extraño, -a** *sm, sf* stranger. **extraño** *adj* strange; peculiar; foreign.

extraordinario [ekstraorði'narjo] *adj* extraordinary. *sm* (*diario*) special edition.

extravagancia [ekstraβa'ganθja] *sf* extravagance; strangeness. **extravagante** *adj* extravagant; eccentric.

extraviar [ekstra'βjar] *v* lose; mislay; mislead. **extraviarse** *v* get lost; be missing; go astray.

extremar [ekstre'mar] *v* take to extremes. **extremarse** *v* do one's best.

extremo [ek'stremo] *adj* extreme, last. **en caso extremo** as a last resort. *sm* extreme; end; point. **al extremo de** to the point of. **de extremo a extremo** from end to end. **Extremo Oriente** Far East. **extremidad** *sf* extremity; end; limit.

exuberancia [eksuβe'ranθja] *sf* exuberance; abundance. **exuberante** *adj* exuberant.

exudar [eksu'ðar] *v* exude. **exudación** *sf* exudation.

exultar [eksul'tar] *v* exult. **exultación** *sf* exultation.

F

fábrica ['faβrika] *sf* factory; manufacture. **fabricación** *sf* manufacture. **de fabricación casera** home-made. **fabricación en serie** mass production. **fabricante** *s(m+f)* manufacturer. **fabricar** *v* manufacture; make; build.

fábula ['faβula] *sf* fable; story; gossip. **fabuloso** *adj* fabulous; incredible.

facción [fak'θjon] *sf* faction; gang. **facciones** *sf pl* features.

faceta [fa'θeta] *sf* facet.

facial [fa'θjal] *adj* facial.

fácil ['faθil] *adj* easy; simple; likely; well-behaved. **facilidad** *sf* facility; ease; fluency; gift. **facilitar** *v* facilitate; supply; provide; arrange. **fácilmente** *adv* easily.

facsímil [fak'simil] *sm, adj also* **facsímile** facsimile.

factible [fak'tiβle] *adj* feasible.

factor [fak'tor] *sm* factor; agent.

facturar [faktu'rar] *v* invoice; (*ferrocarril*) register luggage. **factura** *sf* invoice. **facturación** *sf* invoicing.

facultad [fakul'taθ] *sf* faculty; authority; school. **facultar** *v* commission; authorize. **facultativo** *adj* optional.

facha ['fatʃa] *sf* (*fam*) appearance; looks; (*fam*) mess.

fachada [fa'tʃaða] *sf* façade.

faena [fa'ena] *sf* task; (*fam*) dirty trick. **estar de faena** to be at work. **faenas domésticas** housework.

fagot [fa'got] *sm* bassoon.

faisán [fai'san] *sm* pheasant.

faja ['faxa] *sf* bandage; sash; belt; wrapper; strip of land. **fajar** *v* wrap; bandage.

falaz [fa'laθ] *adj* fallacious; deceitful.

falda ['falda] *sf* skirt; side of a hill; hat brim; lap.

falsear [false'ar] *v* falsify. **falseador, -a** *sm, sf* forger; counterfeiter. **falseamiento** *sm* misrepresentation. **falsedad** *sf* falsity. **falseo** *sm* bevelling. **falso** *adj* false; treacherous; sham.

falsificar [falsifi'kar] *v* falsify; forge; adulterate. **falsificación** *sf* falsification; adulteration.

falta ['falta] *sf* lack, want, need; shortage; failure; (*deporte*) foul. **faltar** *v* be lacking; fail; be absent; be untrue. **falto** *sm* shortage; deficiency; fault. **falto** *adj* short; deficient; incomplete.

fallar [fa'ʎar] *v* (*jur*) judge; sentence; fail; (*naipes*) trump. **no falla** it's always the same. **sin falla** without fail.

***fallecer** [faʎe'θer] *v* die. **fallecido** *adj* deceased. **fallecimiento** *sm* death.

fallido [fa'ʎiðo] *sm* bankrupt. *adj* bankrupt; unsuccessful. **fallo** *sm* (*jur*) sentence, judgment; failure; fault; (*naipes*) trump.

fama ['fama] *sf* fame; reputation. **es fama que** it is rumoured that. **famoso** *adj* famous.

familia [fa'milja] *sf* family; household. **familiar** *adj* family; familiar; simple. **familiar** *sm* friend; relative. **familiaridad** *sf* familiarity. **familiarizar** *v* familiarize.

fanático [fa'natiko] *adj, sm* fanatic(al). **fanatismo** *sm* fanaticism.

fanfarrón [fanfar'ron], **-ona** *sm, sf* bully; braggart. *adj* boastful. **fanfarronear** *v* brag.

fango ['fango] *sm* mire, mud. **fangal** *sm* quagmire. **fangoso** *adj* muddy.

fantasía [fanta'sia] *sf* fantasy; fancy; whim. **joyas de fantasía** imitation jewellery.

fantasma [fan'tasma] *sm* ghost. **fantasmal** *adj* ghostly.

fantástico [fan'tastiko] *adj* fantastic; wonderful; vain.

fantoche [fan'totʃe] *sm* puppet; foolish figure.

fardo ['farðo] *sm* bundle, pack; burden.

fariseo [fari'seo] *sm* Pharisee; (*fam*) hypocrite. **farisaico** *adj* (*fam*) hypocritical.

farmacia [far'maθja] *sf* chemist's shop. **farmacia de guardia** all-night chemist's. **farmacéutico** *adj* pharmaceutical.

faro [faro] *sm* lighthouse; beacon; (*auto*) headlamp.

farol [fa'rol] *sm* lantern; lamp; street lamp; (*fam*) swank.

farsa ['farsa] *sf* farce; humbug. **farsante** *sm* charlatan.

fas [fas] *adv* (*fam*) **por fas o por nefas** rightly or wrongly; by hook or by crook.

fascinar [fasθi'nar] *v* fascinate. **fascinación** *sf* fascination. **fascinador** *adj* fascinating.

fascismo [fas'θismo] *sm* fascism. **fascista** *s*, *adj* fascist.

fase ['fase] *sf* phase.

fastidiar [fasti'ðjar] *v* annoy; bore; upset. **¡no fastidies!** don't talk rot! **fastidio** *sm* annoyance; nuisance. **fastidioso** *adj* annoying; tedious.

fastuoso [fas'twoso] *adj* magnificent, grand, splendid.

fatal [fa'tal] *adj* fatal; inevitable; (*fam*) awful. **fatalidad** *sf* fatality; bad luck; destiny; disaster. **fatalista** *s*(*m + f*) fatalist. **fatalismo** *sm* fatalism.

fatigar [fati'gar] *v* weary; annoy. **fatigarse** *v* get tired. **fatiga** *sf* fatigue. **fatigas** *sf pl* troubles. **fatigoso** *adj* tiring; tiresome; laboured.

fatuidad [fatwi'ðað] *sf* fatuity; vanity. **fausto** ['fausto] *adj* lucky; happy. *sm* display; pomp.

favor [fa'βor] *sm* favour; gift; grace; help. **a favor de** in favour of. **de favor** complimentary. **hacer el favor de** be so kind as to. **por favor** please. **favorable** *adj* favourable. **favorecer** *v* favour; help. **favoritismo** *sm* favouritism. **favorito, -a** *s*, *adj* favourite.

faz [faθ] *sf* face; obverse.

fe [fe] *sf* faith; faithfulness; trust; witness; certificate. **a fe de** on the word of. **dar fe de** certify. **prestar fe a** believe in.

fealdad [feal'ðað] *sf* ugliness.

febrero [fe'βrero] *sm* February.

febril [fe'βril] *adj* feverish; (*fig*) anxious.

fecundar [fekun'dar] *v* fertilize. **fecundación** *sf* fertilization. **fecundidad** *sf* fertility; fruitfulness. **fecundizar** *v* fertilize. **fecundo** *adj* fertile; fruitful; prolific. **fecundo en** full of.

fecha ['fetʃa] *sf* date. **hasta la fecha** to date. **fechar** *v* date.

federación [feðera'θjon] *sf* federation.

federal *adj* federal. **federalismo** *sm* federalism. **federar** *v* federate. **federativo** *adj* federative.

fehaciente [fea'θjente] *adj* (*jur*) authentic; irrefutable; reliable.

felicidad [feliθi'ðað] *sf* happiness; success. **¡felicidades!** congratulations! **feliz** *adj* happy; fortunate.

felicitar [feliθi'tar] *v* congratulate. **felicitación** *sf* congratulation; compliment.

feligrés [feli'gres], **-esa** *sm*, *sf* parishioner. **feligresía** *sf* parish.

felino [fe'lino] *sm*, *adj* feline.

felpa ['felpa] *sf* plush; towelling; (*fam*) beating. **felpar** *v* cover with plush. **felpudo** *adj* plushy.

femenino [feme'nino] *adj* feminine; female. **feminismo** *sm* feminism. **feminista** *s*, *adj* feminist.

*****fenecer** [fene'θer] *v* die; end. **fenecimiento** *sm* death; end.

fenómeno [fe'nomeno] *sm* phenomenon; freak. *adj* fantastic.

feo ['feo] *adj* ugly.

féretro ['feretro] *sm* coffin; bier.

feria ['ferja] *sf* fair; show; festival; holiday. **feria de muestras** trade fair.

fermentar [fermen'tar] *v* ferment; agitate. **fermentación** *sf* fermentation.

ferocidad [feroθi'ðað] *sf* ferocity; fury. **feroz** *adj* savage; wild; fierce.

férreo ['ferreo] *adj* iron; ferrous; (*fig*) stern. **ferretería** *sf* ironmonger's shop; hardware shop. **ferretero** *sm* ironmonger.

ferrocarril [ferrokar'ril] *sm* railway. **ferroviario** *adj* railway.

fértil ['fertil] *adj* fertile; abundant. **fertilidad** *sf* fertility. **fertilizante** *sm* fertilizer. **fertilizar** *v* fertilize.

ferviente [fer'βjente] *adj* fervent. **fervor** *sm* fervour. **fervoroso** *adj* fervid, ardent.

festejar [feste'xar] *v* entertain; feast; celebrate; woo. **festejo** *sm* entertainment; celebration; courtship.

festival [festi'βal] *sm* festival. *adj* festive. **festividad** *sf* festivity. **festivo** *adj* festive.

fétido ['fetiðo] *adj* fetid; stinking.

feto ['feto] *sm* foetus. **fetal** *adj* foetal.

feudal [feu'ðal] *adj* feudal. **feudalismo** *sm* feudalism.

fiado ['fjaðo] *sm* trust. **comprar al fiado** buy on credit. **fiador, -a** *sm*, *sf* guarantor. **fiador** *sm* press stud; pin; bracket; tumbler; safety catch. **salir fiador de** go bail for. **fianza** *sf* deposit; guarantor; surety.

libertad bajo fianza release on bail. **fiar** v guarantee; go bail for; sell on credit; trust. **no se fía** no credit given.

fiambre ['fjambre] sm cold cooked meat; (coll) corpse.

fiasco [fi'asko] sm fiasco; flop.

fibra ['fiβra] sf fibre; (fig) vigour. **fibra de vidrio** fibreglass.

ficción [fik'θjon] sf fiction; invention. **ficticio** adj fictitious.

ficha ['fitʃa] sf counter, chip; (juegos) piece; filing card.

fidedigno [fiðe'ðigno] adj trustworthy. **fidelidad** sf loyalty, fidelity. **alta fidelidad** hi-fi.

fideos [fi'ðeos] sm pl noodles.

fiebre ['fjeβre] sf fever. **tener fiebre** be feverish.

fiel [fjel] adj faithful; true; accurate; reliable; honourable. sm good Christian; inspector; scale pointer.

fieltro ['fjeltro] sm (tejido) felt; felt hat.

fiera ['fjera] sf wild beast; (persona) brute. **casa de fieras** menagerie. **fiero** adj wild.

fiesta ['fjesta] sf feast day; holiday; party. **estar de fiesta** be in high spirits. **hacer fiestas a uno** make a fuss over someone.

figurar [figu'rar] v shape; adorn; figure; pretend. **figurarse** v imagine, seem. **figura** sf shape; figure; face; (música) note; (naipes) court card; (fig) personality. (fam) unpleasant person. **figurado** adj also **figurativo** figurative.

fijar [fi'xar] v fasten; fix; stick; secure; draw up. **fijarse** v settle; take notice; look. **¡fíjate!** just think! **¡fíjamos en esto!** that's settled! **fijación** sf setting; fixing; sticking. **fijador** sm fixative. **fijeza** sf fixity; certainty; firmness. **fijo** adj fixed; permanent; steady.

fila ['fila] sf row; line; file; column. **en fila india** in single file.

filantropía [filantro'pia] sf philanthropy. **filantrópico** adj philanthropic. **filántropo, -a** sm, sf philanthropist.

filete [fi'lete] sm sirloin; fillet; (ropa) edging; (tecn) screw thread.

filiación [filja'θjon] sf filiation; relationship; association; personal description. **filial** [fi'ljal] adj filial. sf subsidiary.

filigrana [fili'grana] sf filigree work; watermark; delicate object.

filo ['filo] sm cutting edge; dividing line. **dar un filo a** sharpen. **por filo** exactly.

filón [fi'lon] sm (mineral) vein, seam; (fam) cushy job.

filosofía [filoso'fia] sf philosophy. **filosofar** v philosophize. **filósofo, -a** sm, sf philosopher. **filosófico** adj philosophic(al).

filtrar [fil'trar] v filter; strain. **filtrarse** v seep through. **filtración** sf filtration; (fig) leak. **filtrador** sm filter. **filtro** sm filter; strainer; love potion.

fin [fin] sm end; death; aim. **a fin de** in order to. **a fines de** at the end of. **al fin y al cabo** when all is said and done. **por fin** at last.

final [fi'nal] adj final. sm end. **al final de** at the end of. **finalidad** sf aim; purpose; finality. **finalizar** v finalize.

financiar [finan'θjar] v finance. **financiero** sm financier. **financiero** adj financial. **finanzas** sf pl finances.

finca ['finka] sf property; estate; farm.

fineza [fi'neθa] sf refinement; kindness; gift.

fingir [fin'xir] v pretend; sham. **fingirse** v pretend to be. **fingimiento** sm pretence; deceit.

Finlandia [fin'landja] sf Finland. **finlandés, -esa** s, adj Finn(ish).

fino ['fino] adj fine; refined; delicate; sharp; shrewd; elegant; precious; select; pure.

firmar [fir'mar] v sign. **firma** sf signature; (negocio) firm.

firme ['firme] adj firm; steady; rigid; hard; settled. sm firm ground; foundation; roadbed. **de firme** steadily. **oferta en firme** firm offer. **¡firmes!** (mil) attention! **firmeza** sf firmness; steadfastness.

fiscal [fis'kal] adj fiscal; tax. sm treasury official; (jur) public prosecutor. **fiscalizar** v control; criticize; pry into. **fisco** sm exchequer.

física ['fisika] sf physics. **físico** sm physician; physique. **físico** adj physical. **físico, -a** sm, sf physicist.

fisiología [fisjolo'xia] sf physiology. **fisiológico** adj physiological. **fisiólogo, -a** sm, sf physiologist.

fisionomía [fisjono'mia] sf physiognomy.

fisioterapia [fisjote'rapja] sf physiotherapy. **fisioterapeuta** s(m+f) physiotherapist.

flaco ['flako] adj thin; weak; (memoria) short. sm weak point. **flaquear** v weaken; slacken; flag; fail. **flaqueza** sf thinness; frailty.

flagrante [fla'grante] *adj* flagrant, blatant. **en flagrante** in the act.

flamante [fla'mante] *adj* blazing; brand-new.

flamenco[1] [fla'menko] *adj* Flemish; gypsy; flamenco.

flamenco[2] *sm* flamingo.

flanco [flanko] *sm* flank. **coger por el flanco** catch unawares.

flauta ['flauta] *sf* flute. **flautista** *s(m+f)* flautist.

fleco ['fleko] *sm* fringe.

flecha ['fletʃa] *sf* arrow. **flecha de dirección** traffic indicator. **flecha de mar** squid. **subir en flecha** shoot up. **flechar** v shoot with an arrow; (*fam*) inspire love at first sight; (*fam*) rush. **flechero** *sm* archer.

fletar [fle'tar] v charter; hire. **fletamento** *also* **fletamiento** *sm* charter. **flete** *sm* freight.

flexible [flek'siβle] *adj* flexible. *sm* flex. **flexibilidad** *sf* flexibility. **flexión** *sf* flexing; (*gram*) inflexion.

flojo ['floxo] *adj* loose; weak; meagre; lazy. **flojear** v slacken; grow weak. **flojedad** *sf* slackness; weakness; carelessness.

flor [flor] *sf* flower. **a flor de tierra** at ground level. **echar flores** flatter. **en flor** in bloom. **flor de lis** lily. **floral** *adj* floral. **florar** v flower. **florecer** v flourish; flower. **florecerse** v mildew. **florería** *sf* florist's shop. **florero** *sm* vase. **florido** *adj* flowery; florid. **florista** *s(m+f)* florist.

flotar [flo'tar] v float; flutter; stream. **flota** *sf* fleet. **flotable** *adj* buoyant. **flotación** *sf* floatation; fluttering. **flotante** *adj* floating; flowing. **flote** *sm* floatation. **a flote** afloat.

fluctuar [fluk'twar] v fluctuate. **fluctuación** *sf* fluctuation.

*****fluir** [flu'ir] v flow. **fluente** *adj* fluid; flowing. **fluidez** *sf* fluidity; fluency. **fluido** *sm, adj* fluid. **flujo** *sm* stream; flow; rising tide. **flujo de vientre** diarrhoea.

fluorescencia [fluores'θenθja] *sf* fluorescence. **fluorescente** *adj* fluorescent.

fluoruro [flwo'ruro] *sm* fluoride.

fobia ['foβja] *sf* phobia.

foca ['foka] *sf* (*zool*) seal.

foco ['foko] *sm* focus; centre; source. **focal** *adj* focal.

fogata [fo'gata] *sf* blaze; bonfire.

fogón [fo'gon] *sm* fireplace; stove.

fogoso [fo'goso] *adj* fiery; impetuous.

follaje [fo'ʎaxe] *sm* foliage; excessive decoration.

folletín [foʎe'tin] *sm* serial story; newspaper article. **folleto** *sm* pamphlet. **folletista** *s(m+f)* pamphleteer.

follón [fo'ʎon] *adj* lazy; arrogant; blustering; cowardly. **follón, -ona** *sm, sf* good-for-nothing; coward; loafer.

fomentar [fomen'tar] v foment; warm; incubate; (*fig*) encourage.

fonda ['fonda] *sf* inn, boarding house.

fondear [fonde'ar] v anchor; sound; search.

fondo ['fondo] *sm* bottom; depth; essence; capital; fund; character; disposition. **a fondo** thoroughly. **artículo de fondo** leading article. **en el fondo** at heart. **estar en fondos** be well off.

fontanero [fonta'nero] *sm* plumber. **fontanar** *sm* spring. **fontanería** *sf* plumbing.

forajido [fora'xiðo], **-a** *sm, sf* outlaw; fugitive.

forastero [foras'tero], **-a** *sm, sf* stranger; alien. *adj* strange.

forcejear [forθexe'ar] v struggle, strive. **forcej(e)o** *sm* struggle.

forense [fo'rense] *adj* forensic; strange.

forjar [for'xar] v forge; beat into shape; invent. **forja** *sf* forge; forging.

formal [for'mal] *adj* formal; regular; methodical; serious; steady; reliable. **formalidad** *sf* formality; seriousness; orderliness; propriety. **formalismo** *sm* formalism. **formalizar** v formulate; legalize. **formalizarse** v take seriously.

formar [for'mar] v form; educate; train. **formarse** v be trained; develop. **forma** *sf* form; shape; manner; convention; mould. **de forma que** so that. **tener buenas formas** be polite.

formidable [formi'ðaβle] *adj* formidable; tremendous. **¡formidable!** great!

fórmula ['formula] *sf* formula; (*med*) prescription.

fornicar [forni'kar] v fornicate. **fornicación** *sf* fornication. **fornicador, -a** *sm, sf* fornicator.

fornido [for'niðo] *adj* robust, husky.

foro ['foro] *sm* forum; legal profession; leasehold; (*teatro*) back.

forraje [for'raxe] *sm* fodder; forage; (*fam*) hodgepodge. **forrajeador** *sm* forager. **forrajear** v forage.

forrar [for'rar] v line; pad; put a cover on. forrarse v line one's pockets. forro sm lining; cover.

*fortalecer [fortale'θer] v strengthen; encourage. fortalecimiento sm fortification; strengthening. fortaleza sf fortress; fortitude; vigour. fortificación sf fortification. fortificar v fortify; strengthen. fortificarse v gain strength.

fortuito [for'twito] adj fortuitous; accidental.

fortuna [for'tuna] sf fortune, wealth; good luck; happiness; fate. por fortuna luckily. probar fortuna try one's luck.

*forzar [for'θar] v force; rape. forzadamente adv forcibly. forzado adj forced; hard; far-fetched. forzosamente adv unavoidably. forzoso adj unavoidable; necessary.

fosa ['fosa] sf grave; (anat) cavity.

fosfato [fos'fato] sm phosphate. fosforescencia sf phosphorescence. fosforescente adj phosphorescent. fósforo sm phosphorus; match.

fósil ['fosil] sm fossil. fosilizarse v fossilize.

foso ['foso] sm hole; ditch; (teatro) pit; (mil) trench.

fotocopiar [fotoko'pjar] v photocopy. fotocopia sf photocopy. fotocopiadora sf copier.

fotografía [fotogra'fia] sf photography; photograph. fotografiar v photograph. fotográfico adj photographic. fotógrafo, -a sm, sf photographer.

frac [frak] sm dress coat, tails pl.

fracasar [fraka'sar] v fail. fracaso sm failure.

fracción [frak'θjon] sf (mat) fraction; portion; fragment. fraccionamiento sm breaking-up. fraccionar v break up; divide.

fractura [frak'tura] sf (med) fracture. robo con fractura sm burglary. fracturar v fracture.

fragancia [fra'ganθja] sf fragrance. fragante adj fragrant; flagrant.

fragata [fra'gata] sf frigate.

frágil ['fraxil] adj fragile; weak. fragilidad sf fragility; weakness.

fragmento [frag'mento] sm fragment. fragmentar v fragment. fragmentario adj fragmentary.

fragor [fra'gor] sm row, noise. fragoroso adj deafening.

fraguar [fra'gwar] v (hierro) forge; concoct; (cemento) harden. fragua sf forge. fraguador, -a sm, sf schemer, plotter.

fraile ['fraile] sm friar, monk.

frambuesa [fram'bwesa] sf raspberry. frambueso sm raspberry bush.

Francia ['franθja] sf France. francés, -esa sm, sf Frenchman/woman. francés sm, adj French.

francmasón [frankma'son] sm freemason. francmasonería sf freemasonry.

franco ['franko] adj frank, open; generous; free; (com) post or duty free.

franela [fra'nela] sf flannel.

franja ['franxa] sf fringe; border. franjar v fringe, trim.

franquear [franke'ar] v free; clear; exempt; grant. franquearse v open one's heart. franqueo sm franking, stamping; postage.

franqueza [fran'keθa] sf frankness; generosity; freedom.

frasco ['frasko] sm flask.

frase ['frase] sf (gram) sentence; phrase; expression. frase hecha cliché. fraseología sf phraseology.

fraternal [frater'nal] adj fraternal. fraternidad sf fraternity. fraternizar v fraternize. fraterno adj fraternal.

fraude ['frauðe] sm fraud; deception. fraudulencia sf dishonesty. fraudulento adj fraudulent.

fray [fraj] sm (rel) friar, brother.

frecuencia [fre'kwenθja] sf frequency. con frecuencia often. frecuentar v frequent. frecuente adj frequent.

*fregar [fre'gar] v rub; scrub; wash up. fregadero sm sink. fregado sm rubbing; scrubbing; washing; (fam) intrigue. fregador, -a sm, sf dishwasher; sm sink, dishcloth.

*freír [fre'ir] v fry; (fam) bother. freiduría sf frying. freiduría sf fish shop.

fréjol ['frexol] sm kidney bean.

frenar [fre'nar] v brake; check. freno sm brake; bridle. freno de mano handbrake. poner/soltar el freno apply/release the brake.

frenesí [frene'si] sm frenzy.

frente ['frente] sm front; face; façade. al frente at the head. de frente forward. en frente opposite. sf forehead; head. frente a frente face to face.

fresa ['fresa] *sf* strawberry.

fresco ['fresko] *adj* cool; fresh; new; calm. **frescura** *sf* coolness; freshness; fertility; calmness; indifference; *(fam)* insolence.

fresno ['fresno] *sm (bot)* ash.

fricción [frik'θjon] *sf* friction; *(med)* massage. **friccionar** *v* rub; massage.

frigidez [frixi'δeθ] *sf* frigidity. **frígido** *adj* frigid. **frigorífico** *sm* refrigerating; refrigerator.

frijón [fri'xon] *sm* bean.

frío ['frio] *adj* cold; cool; indifferent. *sm* cold. **coger frío** catch cold. **tener frío** be cold. **frialdad** *sf* coldness; indifference; impotence.

friolera [frjo'lera] *sf* triviality, trifle.

frisar [fri'sar] *v* frizz, curl. **frisar en** *(edad)* border on.

frito ['frito] *V* **freír**. *adj* fried. **estar frito** be fed up. **patatas fritas** chips. **quedarse frito** *(fam)* nod off.

frívolo ['friβolo] *adj* frivolous. **frivolidad** *sf* frivolity.

frondoso [fron'doso] *adj* leafy; lush. **frondosidad** *sf* leafiness; lushness.

frontera [fron'tera] *sf* frontier.

frotar [fro'tar] *v* rub; *(cerilla)* strike. **frotación** *sf* rubbing; friction. **frote** *sm* rub.

fructífero [fruk'tifero] *adj* fruit-bearing; fruitful.

frugal [fru'gal] *adj* frugal. **frugalidad** *sf* frugality.

fruncir [frun'θir] *v* wrinkle; gather; pleat. **fruncir el ceño** frown. **fruncido** *adj* gathered; wrinkled. **fruncimiento** *sm* gathering; wrinkling.

frustrar [frus'trar] *v* frustrate. **frustrarse** *v* fail.

fruta ['fruta] *sf* fruit. **fruta de sartén** fritter. **frutal** *adj* fruit. **frutería** *sf* fruiterer's. **frutero, -a** *sm, sf* fruiterer. **fruto** *sm* fruit; product; result; offspring; profit. **frutos civiles** *(jur)* unearned income.

fue¹ ['fue] *V* **ir**.

fue² ['fue] *V* **ser**.

fuego ['fwego] *sm* fire; light; burner; heat; rash; passion; zeal. **apagar el fuego** put out the fire. **arma de fuego** firearm. **cocer a fuego lento/vivo** cook slowly/quickly. **fuegos artificiales** fireworks. **prender fuego a** set fire to.

fuelle ['fweλe] *sm* bellows.

fuente ['fwente] *sf* fountain; spring; source; serving dish.

fuera ['fwera] *adv* outside; out; abroad. **aquí/allí fuera** out here/there. **estar fuera** be away. **¡fuera!** get out! **ir fuera** go outside. **por fuera** on the outside.

fuero ['fwero] *sm* law; code of laws; jurisdiction.

fuerte ['fwerte] *adj* strong; large; heavy; concentrated. **precio fuerte** full price. *sm (mil)* fort; stronghold. **fuerza** *sf* strength; loudness; power; effort; electric current. **fuerza pública** police force.

fugarse [fu'garse] *v* run away; escape. **fuga** *sf* escape; elopement; *(gas, etc.)* leak; *(música)* fugue. **ponerse en fuga** take flight. **fugaz** *adj* fleeting. **fugitivo, -a** *s, adj* fugitive.

fulano [fu'lano] *sm* so-and-so, what's-his-name. **fulana** *sf* whore.

fulcro ['fulkro] *sm* fulcrum.

fulgor [ful'gor] *sm* glow; sparkle; brilliance. **fulgente** also **fúlgido** *adj* brilliant. **fulgir** *v* shine. **fulgurante** *adj* shining; glowing. **fulgurar** *v* flash; shine; glow.

fulminante [fulmi'nante] *adj* explosive; thundering; *(med)* grave; *(med)* mortal. **fulminar** *v* strike (by lightning); thunder; explode.

fumar [fu'mar] *v* smoke. **prohibido fumar** no smoking. **fumarse** *v* squander. **fumada** *sf (de humo)* puff.

fumigar [fumi'gar] *v* fumigate. **fumigación** *sf* fumigation. **fumigador** *sm* fumigator.

funcionar [funθjo'nar] *v* function, work, go. **no funciona** out of order. **función** *sf* function; performance; party; duty. **funcional** *adj* functional. **funcionamiento** *sm* functioning; operation; performance. **funcionario, -a** *sm, sf* public official.

funda ['funda] *sf* case, cover. **funda de almohada** pillowcase.

fundar [fun'dar] *v* found; establish; base. **fundarse** *v* be based. **fundación** *sf* foundation. **fundado** *adj* founded; justified. **fundamental** *adj* fundamental. **fundamento** *sm* foundation; basis; reason; reliability.

fundir [fun'dir] *v* cast; smelt; melt; merge. **fundición** *sf* melting; smelting; foundry.

fúnebre ['funeβre] *adj* funeral; mournful. **coche fúnebre** hearse.

funesto [fu'nesto] *adj* ill-fated; disastrous; fatal.

furgón [fur'gon] *sm* wagon; truck; van. **furgón de cola** guard's van. **furgoneta** *sf* van. **furgoneta familiar** station wagon.

furia ['furja] *sf* fury; violence; frenzy. **furioso** *adj* furious; raging; enormous. **furor** *sm* fury; passion; fever. **con furor** furiously. **hacer furor** be all the rage.

furtivo [fur'tiβo] *adj* furtive; sly.

furúnculo [fu'runkulo] *sm* (*med*) boil.

fusible [fu'siβle] *adj* fusible. *sm* fuse.

fusil [fu'sil] *sm* rifle.

fusión [fu'sjon] *sf* fusion; melting; thawing. **fusionar** *v* fuse; merge. **fusionamiento** *sm* merger.

fuste ['fuste] *sm* wood; (*fig*) importance. **gente de fuste** people of consequence.

fútbol ['futβol] *sm* football. **futbolista** *sm* footballer.

fútil ['futil] *adj* futile, trivial. **futilidad** *sf* futility; triviality.

futuro [fu'turo] *sm*, *adj* future. **futurista** *adj* futuristic.

G

gabán [ga'βan] *sm* overcoat.

gabardina [gaβar'ðina] *sf* raincoat.

gabinete [gaβi'nete] *sm* (*pol*) cabinet; study; studio.

gacela [ga'θela] *sf* gazelle.

gaceta [ga'θeta] *sf* gazette; journal. **gacetero** *sm* journalist; **gacetilla** *sf* gossip column.

gachas ['gatʃas] *sf pl* porridge *sing*; slops *pl*.

gacho ['gatʃo] *adj* drooping.

gafas ['gafas] *sf pl* spectacles. **gafas de sol** sunglasses.

gajo ['gaxo] *sm* (*de horcas*) prong; (*de naranja*) segment; (*de frutas*) cluster.

gala ['gala] *sf* full dress; pomp; elegance. **de gala** in full dress. **hacer gala de** show off. **tener a gala** pride oneself in.

galán [ga'lan] *sm* gallant; suitor; handsome man; (*teatro*) leading man. **galante** *adj* gallant; flirtatious. **galantear** *v* woo; flirt; flatter. **galanteo** *sm* flirtation; courting; flattery. **galantería** *sf* gallantry; elegance.

galardón [galar'ðon] *sm* reward. **galardonar** *v* reward.

galeón [gale'on] *sm* galleon.

galera [ga'lera] *sf* (*mar*) galley; wagon.

galería [gale'ria] *sf* gallery.

Gales ['gales] *sm* Wales. **galés, -esa** *sm, sf* Welshman/woman. **galés** *sm* (*lengua*) Welsh.

galgo ['galgo] *sm* greyhound.

galón[1] [ga'lon] *sm* braid; (*mil*) stripe. **quitar los galones** demote.

galón[2] *sm* gallon.

galopar [galo'par] *v* gallop. **galope** *sm* gallop. **a medio galope** at a canter.

galvanizar [galβani'θar] *v* galvanize.

gallardo [ga'ʎarðo] *adj* elegant; gallant. **gallardía** *sf* elegance; charm. **gallardear** *v* behave gracefully.

galleta [ga'ʎeta] *sf* biscuit.

gallina [ga'ʎina] *sf* hen, chicken. **gallo** *sm* cock, rooster.

gamuza [ga'muθa] *sf* chamois; (*trapo*) duster.

gana ['gana] *sf* desire; wish; appetite. **de buena/mala gana** willingly/unwillingly. **tener ganas de** want to.

ganadería [ganaðe'ria] *sf* cattle-raising; cattle farm; cattle; breed. **ganadero, -a** *sm, sf* cattle-raiser; stockbreeder. **ganado** *sm* cattle; livestock.

ganar [ga'nar] *v* gain, get; earn; take; surpass. **ganar en peso** put on weight. **ganancia** *sf* profit. **ganancias** *sf pl* earnings; winnings.

gancho ['gantʃo] *sm* hook; (*fam*) decoy; (*fam*) pimp; (*fam*) sex appeal.

ganga ['ganga] *sf* (*fam*) bargain; (*fam*) cushy job.

gangrena [gan'grena] *sf* gangrene. **gangrenoso** *adj* gangrenous.

ganso ['ganso] *sm* goose, gander; (*fam*) boor. **gansada** *sf* (*fam*) stupid thing.

garabatear [garaβate'ar] *v* scribble; (*fam*) beat about the bush. **garabateo** *sm* scribbling. **garabato** *sm* scribble.

garaje [ga'raxe] *sm* garage.

garantizar [garanti'θar] *v* guarantee. **garantía** *sf* guarantee.

garbanzo [gar'βanθo] *sm* chickpea.

garbo [gar'βo] *sm* grace; generosity; jauntiness. **garboso** *adj* graceful; generous; jaunty.

garganta [gar'ganta] *sf* throat. **tener buena garganta** have a good voice. **gargantear** *v* warble.

gargarizar [gargari'θar] v gargle. **gárgara** sf gargle.

gárgola ['gargola] sf gargoyle.

garita [ga'rita] sf sentry box; lavatory; porter's lodge. **garita de señales** signal-box.

garra ['garra] sf claw.

garrafa [ga'rrafa] sf decanter.

garrapata [garra'pata] sf (zool) tick.

garrote [ga'rrote] sm stick, club; garotte; (med) tourniquet. **dar garrote a** execute.

garza ['garθa] sf heron.

gas [gas] sm gas. **a todo gas** flat out.

gasa ['gasa] sf gauze.

gaseosa [gase'osa] sf lemonade.

gasolina [gaso'lina] sf gasoline. **gasolinera** sf gasoline pump.

gastar [gas'tar] v spend; waste; wear out or away. **gasto** sm expense; outlay. **gastos** sm pl expenses; costs. **gastos generales** overheads.

gatillo [ga'tiλo] sm trigger; dentist's forceps; (tecn) jack.

gato ['gato] sm cat; (tecn) jack; (fam) hoard. **a gatas** on all fours. **gatear** v clamber; (fam) crawl. **gatearse** v scratch.

gavilán [gaβi'lan] sm hawk; (pluma) nib; (bot) thistle.

gavilla [ga'βiλa] sf sheaf; bundle; (fam) gang.

gaviota [ga'βjota] sf seagull.

gazapo [ga'θapo] sm young rabbit; slip of the tongue; blunder; misprint.

gazpacho [gaθ'patʃo] sm cold vegetable soup.

gelatina [xela'tina] sf gelatine.

gelignita [xelig'nita] sf gelignite.

gemelo [xe'melo] sm, adj twin. sm pl cufflinks; opera glasses.

*****gemir** [xe'mir] v groan. **gemido** sm groan; wail.

genealogía [xenealo'xia] sf genealogy. **genealógico** adj genealogical. **árbol genealógico** family tree.

generación [xenera'θjon] sf generation. **generador** sm (tecn) generator. **generar** v generate.

generalizar [xenerali'θar] v generalize. **general** adj general. **general** sm (mil) general. **generalidad** sf majority. **generalización** sf generalization.

genérico [xe'neriko] adj generic. **género** sm race; kind; style; material; article; gender. **géneros** sm pl goods, merchandise sing.

generoso [xene'roso] adj generous. **generosidad** sf generosity.

genética [xe'netika] sf genetics. **genético** adj genetic.

genial [xe'njal] adj brilliant; outstanding; pleasant. **genio** sm genius; character. **estar de mal genio** be in a bad temper.

genital [xeni'tal] adj genital. **genitales** sm pl genitals.

gente ['xente] sf people. **gente baja** lower classes. **gente menuda** children.

gentil [xen'til] adj charming; genteel; civil; gentile; heathen. sm gentile; heathen; pagan. **gentileza** sf grace; elegance; gentility; civility.

gentío [xen'tio] sm crowd.

genuino [xe'nwino] adj genuine.

geografía [xeogra'fia] sf geography. **geográfico** adj geographic(al). **geógrafo** sm geographer.

geología [xeolo'xia] sf geology. **geológico** adj geological. **geólogo** sm geologist.

geometría [xeome'tria] sf geometry. **geométrico** adj geometric.

geranio [xe'ranjo] sm geranium.

gerencia [xe'renθja] sf management. **gerente** sm manager.

germinar [xermi'nar] v germinate. **germen** sm germ.

gesticular [xestiku'lar] v gesticulate. **gesticulación** sf gesticulation; grimace.

gestión [xes'tjon] sf arrangement; measure; management. **gestionar** v negotiate; get hold of.

gesto ['xesto] sm expression; countenance; gesture.

geyser [xejser] sm geyser.

gigante [xi'gante] sm giant. adj gigantic.

gimnasia [xim'nasja] sf gymnastics. **gimnasio** sm gymnasium. **gimnasta** s(m + f) gymnast.

ginebra [xi'neβra] sf gin.

ginecología [xinekolo'xia] sf gynaecology. **ginecólogo, -a** sm, sf gynaecologist.

gira ['xira] sf tour; excursion; picnic.

giralda [xi'ralda] sf weathercock.

girar [xi'rar] v turn; swivel; send; (com) draw. **girar dinero** remit money. **giratorio** adj gyratory. **puerta giratoria** revolving door. **giro** sm turn; (com) draft. **giro postal** sm postal order; money order.

girasol [xira'sol] sm sunflower.

gitano [xi'tano], -a s, adj gypsy.

glacial [gla'θjal] *adj* freezing.

glaciar [gla'θjar] *sm* glacier.

gladio [gla'δjo] *sm* (*bot*) gladiolus.

glándula ['glandula] *sf* gland. **glandular** *adj* glandular.

glicerina [gliθe'rina] *sf* glycerine.

global [glo'βal] *adj* global; comprehensive; total. **globo** *sm* globe, sphere. **en globo** all in all. **globo ocular** eyeball. **globular** *adj* globular. **glóbulo** *sm* globule.

gloriarse [glo'rjarse] *v* boast; glory. **gloria** *sf* glory; (*culin*) custard tart. **glorificación** *sf* glorification. **glorificar** *v* glorify. **glorioso** *adj* glorious; conceited.

glosar [glo'sar] *v* annotate. **glosa** *sf* annotation. **glosario** *sm* glossary.

glotón [glo'ton], **-ona** *sm, sf* glutton. *adj* gluttonous.

glucosa [glu'kosa] *sf* glucose.

*gobernar [goβer'nar] *v* govern; control; manage. **gobernación** *sf* government. **gobernador** *sm* governor. **gobierno** *sm* (*pol*) government; guidance.

goce ['goθe] *sm* enjoyment.

gol [gol] *sm* (*deporte*) goal. **golear** *v* score a goal.

golfo ['golfo] *sm* gulf; (*geog*) bay; guttersnipe.

golondrina [golon'drina] *sf* (*zool*) swallow.

golosina [golo'sina] *sf* sweet; delicacy; (*fig*) desire; (*fig*) greed. **goloso** *adj* sweettoothed; appetizing; greedy.

golpear [golpe'ar] *v* strike, hit. **golpe** *sm* blow; coup; large amount; attack. **golpe de estado** coup d'état. **golpe de gracia** coup de grâce.

goma ['goma] *sf* rubber; gum; rubber band; elastic. **goma de borrar** eraser. **goma espuma** foam rubber.

gordo [gorδo] *sm, adj* fat. **gordura** *sf* fatness, obesity.

gorila [go'rila] *sf* gorilla.

gorjear [gorxe'ar] *v* chirp, trill; twitter. **gorjeo** *sm* chirping; trilling; twittering.

gorra ['gorra] *sf* peaked cap; bonnet; (*fam*) sponger. **de gorra** free. **vivir de gorra** sponge.

gorrión [gor'rjon] *sf* sparrow.

gorro ['gorro] *sm* cap.

gotear [gote'ar] *v* drip; trickle; leak. **gota** *sf* drop. **gotera** *sf* leak; gutter. **goteras** *sf pl* (*fig*) aches and pains.

gótico ['gotiko] *adj* Gothic.

gozar [go'θar] *v* enjoy; possess. **gozarse** *v* rejoice. **gozo** *sm* joy. **gozoso** *adj* joyful.

gozne ['goθne] *sm* hinge.

grabar [gra'βar] *v* engrave; carve; imprint; record. **grabado** *sm* engraving; picture; recording. **grabador de cinta** *sm* tape recorder.

gracia ['graθja] *sf* grace; favour; charm; joke. **me hace gracia** it amuses me. **tener gracia** be amusing.

gracias ['graθjas] *sf pl* thanks. **acción de gracias** thanksgiving. **dar gracias** thank. **muchas gracias** many thanks.

gracioso [gra'θjoso] *adj* graceful; amusing; gracious. *sm* (*teatro*) buffoon.

grada ['graδa] *sf* step; stair. **gradería** *sf* flight of steps; row of seats.

grado ['graδo] *sm* grade; degree; rank; pleasure. **de grado** willingly. **graduación** *sf* graduation. **gradual** *adj* gradual. **graduando, -a** *sm, sf* undergraduate. **graduar** *v* graduate; award a degree to. **graduarse** *v* gain a degree.

gráfico ['grafiko] *adj* graphic. *sm* graph; diagram.

grajo ['graxo] *sm* (*zool*) rook.

gramática [gra'matika] *sf* grammar. **gramático** *adj* grammatical.

gramo ['gramo] *sm* gramme.

gramófono [gra'mofono] *sm* gramophone.

gran [gran] *V* grande.

grana¹ ['grana] *sf* small seed; seeding time.

grana² *sf, adj* scarlet.

granada [gra'naδa] *sf* pomegranate.

grande ['grande] *adj also* **gran** large, big, great. **grandeza** *sf* greatness; size. **grandioso** *adj* grandiose; grand.

granel [gra'nel] *adv* **a granel** in bulk.

granero [gra'nero] *sm* granary.

granito [gra'nito] *sm* granite.

granizar [grani'θar] *v* hail. **granizo** *sm* hail.

granja ['granxa] *sf* farm. **granja avícola** poultry farm. **granjero, -a** *sm, sf* farmer.

grano ['grano] *sm* grain; bean; pimple. **ir al grano** come to the point. **granoso** *adj* granular.

grapa ['grapa] *sf* clamp; staple; dowel.

grasa ['grasa] *sf* grease; fat. **grasera** *sf* dripping pan. **grasiento** *adj* greasy; oily; filthy. **graso** *adj* fatty.

gratificar [gratifi'kar] *v* gratify; reward; tip. **gratificación** *sf* reward; gratuity; bonus; gratification.

gratis ['gratis] *adv* free.

gratitud [grati'tuð] *sf* gratitude.

grato ['grato] *adj* pleasing; pleasant; welcome. **me es grato** ... I am pleased ....

gratuito [gra'twito] *adj* free; gratuitous.

gravamen [gra'βamen] *sm* charge; obligation; burden; tax. **gravar** *v* burden; oppress. **gravar impuestos a** or **sobre** tax.

grave ['graβe] *adj* grave, serious; weighty. **ponerse grave** become gravely ill. **gravedad** *sf* gravity, seriousness.

gravitar [graβi'tar] *v* gravitate. **gravitación** *sf* gravitation, gravity.

graznar [graθ'nar] *v* croak; cackle. **graznido** *sm* croak; cackle.

Grecia ['greθja] *sf* Greece. **griego** *s*, *adj* Greek. **griego** *sm* (*idioma*) Greek; (*fam*) gibberish.

greda ['greða] *sf* clay. **gredoso** *adj* clayey.

gregario [gre'garjo] *adj* gregarious.

gremio ['gremjo] *sm* guild; fraternity; union. **gremio obrero** trade union.

greña ['grena] *sf* tangled hair. **andar a la greña** (*fam*) squabble.

grey [grej] *sf* congregation; flock, herd.

grieta ['grjeta] *sf* crack.

grifo ['grifo] *sm* tap. **al grifo** on draught.

grillo ['griʎo] *sm* (*zool*) cricket. **grillos** *sm pl* shackles, fetters.

gringo ['gringo], **-a** *sm*, *sf* (*fam*) foreigner.

gripe ['gripe] *sf* (*med*) influenza, flu.

gris [gris] *adj* grey.

gritar [gri'tar] *v* shout, scream, yell. **grito** *sm* shout, scream, yell. **el último grito** the latest fashion.

grosella [gro'seʎa] *sf* currant. **grosella espinosa/negra/roja** gooseberry/blackcurrant/redcurrant.

grosería [grose'ria] *sf* vulgarity. **grosero** *adj* vulgar.

grotesco [gro'tesko] *adj* grotesque; absurd.

grúa ['grua] *sf* (*tecn*) crane.

grueso [gru'eso] *adj* thick; large; heavy; dull; slow; coarse. *sm* thickness; heaviness. **gruesa** *sf* (*número*) gross.

grulla ['gruʎa] *sf* (*zool*) crane.

grumete [gru'mete] *sm* cabin boy.

*gruñir [gru'nir] *v* growl. **gruñido** *sm* growl.

grupo ['grupo] *sm* group. **grupo sanguíneo** blood group.

gruta ['gruta] *sf* grotto; cave.

guadaña [gwa'ðana] *sf* scythe.

guante ['gwante] *sm* glove. **guantear** *v* slap.

guapo ['gwapo] *adj* handsome; pretty; flashy. *sm* boaster; bully; (*fam*) lover.

guardar [gwar'ðar] *v* guard; keep; protect; respect. **guarda** *s(m+f)* guard; keeper. **guarda** *sf* custody; protection. **guardacostas** *sm invar* coastguard. **guardafuego** *sm* hearth fender. **guardapolvo** *sm* dust-cover. **guardarropa** *sm* wardrobe; cloakroom. **guardia** *sf* guard; police force. **guardia civil** Civil Guard.

guardián [gwar'ðjan], **-a** *sm*, *sf* guardian; keeper; caretaker.

guardilla [gwar'ðiʎa] *sf* attic.

guarida [gwa'riða] *sf* den, lair; haunt; shelter.

*guarnecer [gwarne'θer] *v* equip; provide; furnish; adorn; garnish; plaster. **guarnición** *sf* adornment; provision; (*mil*) garrison. **guarnicionar** *v* garrison.

guasa ['gwasa] *sf* joke. **sin guasa** seriously. **guasearse** *v* (*fam*) joke; tease. **guaseo** *sm* leg-pull.

gubernamental [guβernamen'tal] *adj* governmental.

guerra ['gerra] *sf* war. **guerra mundial** world war. **guerrear** *v* wage war. **guerrero, -a** *sm*, *sf* warrior. **guerrilla** *sf* guerrilla band; guerrilla warfare. **guerrillero** *sm* guerrilla fighter.

guiar [gi'ar] *v* guide; steer; drive. **guía** *sm* (*persona*) guide. **guía** *sf* (*libro*) guide, guidebook. **guía sonora** soundtrack.

guija ['gixa] *sf* pebble.

guillotina [giʎo'tina] *sf* guillotine. **guillotinar** *v* guillotine.

guiñar [gi'nar] *v* wink. **guiño** *sm* wink.

guión [gi'on] *sm* hyphen; film script; outline; subtitle.

guisa ['gisa] *sf* way, manner. **a guisa de** like. **de tal guisa** in such a manner.

guisado [gi'saðo] *sm* stew. **guisar** *v* cook; prepare. **guiso** *sm* cooked dish; stew.

guisante [gi'sante] *sm* pea. **guisante de olor** sweet pea.

guitarra [gi'tarra] *sf* guitar. **guitarrista** *s(m+f)* guitarist.

gula ['gula] *sf* greed.

gusano [gu'sano] *sm* worm; maggot; caterpillar. **gusano de seda** silkworm.

gustar [gus'tar] *v* please; like; taste; try. **gustar de** enjoy. **¡así me gusta!** that's what I like! **gusto** *sm* pleasure; fancy;

style; taste; flavour. **de buen/mal gusto** in good/bad taste. **con mucho gusto** with great pleasure. **¡mucho gusto!** how do you do? **gustoso** adj tasty; pleasant.

gutural [gutu'ral] adj guttural.

H

haba ['aβa] sf broad bean; swelling; bruise.

*****haber** [a'βer] v have. **haber de** have to. **hay que** one must. **no hay de que** don't mention it. **haberes** sm pl assets; property sing; income sing.

habichuela [aβi'tʃwela] sf bean. **habichuela verde** French bean.

hábil ['aβil] adj clever; able. **habilidad** sf cleverness; ability.

habilitar [aβili'tar] v qualify; enable. **habilitación** sf qualification.

habitar [aβi'tar] v inhabit. **habitable** adj habitable. **habitación** sf habitation; room; lodgings pl. **habitante** s(m+f) inhabitant.

hábito [a'βito] sm habit; attire. **habitual** adj habitual. **habituar** v accustom. **habituarse** v become accustomed to.

hablar [a'βlar] v speak, talk. **¿quién habla?** (al teléfono) who's speaking? **se habla español** Spanish spoken. **habla** sf language; speech. **hablador, -a** sm, sf chatterbox. **habilla** sf rumour; gossip.

hacedero [aθe'ðero] adj feasible. **hacedor, -a** sm, sf creator.

hacendado [aθen'daðo] sm landowner.

*****hacer** [a'θer] v do; make; perform; produce. **hacer calor/frío** be hot/cold. **hacer fiesta** take a holiday. **hace mucho tiempo que** it is a long time since. **hacer para** make an effort to. **hacerse** v become.

hacia [aθja] prep towards; about. **hacia atrás** backwards.

hacienda [a'θjenda] sf estate; ranch.

hacina [a'θina] sf stack, rick. **hacinar** v stack; amass.

hacha [atʃa] sf axe.

hada [aða] sf fairy. **hada madrina** fairy godmother. **cuento de hadas** sm fairy tale.

hado ['aðo] sm fate.

halagar [ala'gar] v flatter. **halago** sm flattery. **halagüeño** adj flattering.

halcón [al'kon] sm falcon. **halconería** sf falconry.

hálito ['alito] sm breath.

hallar [a'Aar] v find; find out. **hallarse** v be situated. **hallarse bien con** be pleased with. **hallazgo** sm discovery.

hamaca [a'maka] sf hammock.

hambre ['ambre] sf hunger; starvation. **pasar hambre** go hungry. **tener hambre** be hungry. **hambriento** adj hungry.

hamburguesa [ambur'gesa] sf hamburger.

haragán [ara'gan] adj lazy. **haraganear** v idle.

harapiento [ara'pjento] adj ragged. **harapo** sm rag.

harina [a'rina] sf flour. **harinero** adj also **harinoso** floury.

hartar [ar'tar] v stuff; gorge; weary; bore. **harto** adj satiated. **hartura** sf satiety.

hasta ['asta] prep until; up to; as much as; as far as. adv even. **hasta ahora** up to now. **hasta aquí** so far. **hasta luego** (interj) so long, good-bye. **hasta que** until.

hastío [as'tio] sm disgust; weariness. **hastiar** v disgust; bore.

hato ['ato] sm herd; flock; gang.

hay [aj] there is; there are. **hay que** one must.

haya ['aja] sf beech.

haz¹ [aθ] sm bunch; bundle; sheaf.

haz² sf face; surface. **a sobre haz** on the surface.

hazaña [a'θaɲa] sf deed; feat; exploit.

hazmerreír [aθmerre'ir] sm laughing-stock.

hebilla [e'βiAa] sf buckle; clasp.

hebra ['eβra] sf fibre; thread; (de madera) grain.

hebreo [e'βreo] s, adj Hebrew. sm (lengua) Hebrew.

hechicero [etʃi'θero] sm sorcerer; wizard. **hechicera** sf sorceress; witch. **hechicería** sf witchcraft; sorcery; enchantment. **hechizar** v bewitch. **hechizo** sm magic spell.

hecho ['etʃo] V hacer. adj mature; finished; cooked. **hecho y derecho** in every sense of the word. **muy/poco hecho** overdone/underdone. sm fact; deed; feat; matter; event. **de hecho** in fact. **hechura** sf making; making-up; shape; workmanship.

hediondo [e'ðjondo] *adj* stinking; repulsive. **heder** *v* stink; vex. **hedor** *sm* stink.

*****helar** [e'lar] *v* freeze. **helada** *sf* frost. **helado** *sm* ice cream.

helecho [e'letʃo] *sm* fern.

hélice [eliθe] *sf* helix; spiral; propeller.

helicóptero [eli'koptero] *sm* helicopter.

hembra ['embra] *sf* female; clasp; socket; (*de tornillo*) nut.

hemisferio [emis'ferjo] *sm* hemisphere. **hemisférico** *adj* hemispheric, hemispherical.

hemorragia [emor'raxja] *sf* haemorrhage. **hemorroides** [emor'rojðes] *sf pl* haemorrhoids.

*****henchirse** [en'tʃirse] *v* swell up; stuff oneself. **henchidura** *sf* filling.

*****hender** [en'der] *v* split. **hendidura** *sf* split; crack.

heno ['eno] *sm* hay.

heraldo [e'raldo] *sm* herald. **heráldica** *sf* heraldry. *adj* heraldic.

herbaje [er'βaxe] *sm* pasture. **herbario** *adj* herbal. **herbicida** *sm* weedkiller. **herbívoro, -a** *sm, sf* herbivore. **herbívoro** *adj* herbivorous. **herbolario** *sm* herbalist. **herboso** *adj* grassy.

heredar [ere'ðar] *v* inherit. **heredad** *sf* estate. **heredero, -a** *sm, sf* heir/heiress. **hereditario** *adj* hereditary.

hereje [e'rexe] *s(m+f)* heretic. **herejía** *sf* heresy. **herético** *adj* heretic.

herencia [e'renθja] *sf* inheritance; heredity.

*****herir** [e'rir] *v* wound. **herida** *sf* wound. **herido** *sm* casualty.

hermano [er'mano] *sm* brother. **hermana** *sf* sister. **hermandad** *sf* brotherhood. **hermanastro, -a** *sm, sf* stepbrother/stepsister.

hermético [er'metiko] *adj* hermetic.

hermoso [er'moso] *adj* beautiful; handsome. **hermosura** *sf* beauty; handsomeness.

héroe ['eroe] *sm* hero. **heroico** *adj* heroic. **heroína** *sf* heroine. **heroísmo** *sm* heroism. **heroína** [ero'ina] *sf* heroin.

herramienta [erra'mjenta] *sf* tool; implement.

*****herrar** [er'rar] *v* (*caballo*) shoe. **herradura** *sf* horseshoe. **camino de herradura** bridle path. **herrería** *sf* smithy, forge. **herrero** *sm* blacksmith.

herrumbre [er'rumbre] *sf* rust. **herrumbrar** *v* rust. **herrumbroso** *adj* rusty.

*****hervir** [er'βir] *v* boil. **hervidero** *sm* boiling; bubbling; (*fig*) swarm; crowd; hotbed. **hervidor** *sm* kettle. **hervor** *sm* boiling; fervour.

hesitar [esi'tar] *v* hesitate. **hesitación** *sf* hesitation.

hez [eθ] *sf, pl* **heces** dregs *pl*; scum.

hibernar [iβer'nar] *v* hibernate. **hibernación** *sf* hibernation.

híbrido ['iβriðo] *sm, adj* hybrid. **hibridación** *sf* hybridization. **hibridizar** *v* hybridize.

hidalgo [i'ðalgo] *sm* nobleman. *adj* noble. **hidalguía** *sf* nobility.

hidráulico [i'ðrauliko] *adj* hydraulic. **freno hidráulico** *sm* hydraulic brake.

hidroala [iðro'ala] *sf* hovercraft.

hidroavión [iðroa'βjon] *sm* seaplane.

hidroeléctrico [iðroe'lektriko] *adj* hydroelectric.

hidrofobia [iðro'foβja] *sf* hydrophobia.

hidrógeno [i'ðroxeno] *sm* hydrogen.

hidropesía [iðrope'sia] *sf* dropsy.

hiedra ['jeðra] *sf* ivy.

hielo ['jelo] *sm* ice.

hiena ['jena] *sf* hyena.

hierba ['jerβa] *sf* grass; herb. **mala hierba** weed.

hierbabuena [jerβa'βwena] *sf* mint.

hierro ['jerro] *sm* iron. **hierro colado** cast iron. **hierro forjado** wrought iron.

hígado [igaðo] *sm* liver.

higiene [i'xjene] *sf* hygiene. **higiénico** *adj* hygienic. **paños higiénicos** *sm pl* sanitary towels.

higo ['igo] *sm* fig. **higuera** *sf* fig-tree.

hijo ['ixo] *sm* son. **hijos** *sm pl* children. **hija** *sf* daughter. **hijo/hija político,** *sm* son/daughter-in-law.

hilar [i'lar] *v* spin; infer. **hiladora** *sf* spinning wheel. **hilandería** *sf* spinning. **hilandero, -a** *sm, sf* (*persona*) spinner.

hilarante [ila'rante] *adj* hilarious. **hilaridad** *sf* hilarity.

hilera [i'lera] *sf* row; rank; file.

hilo ['ilo] *sm* thread; yarn; wire. **hilo de coser** sewing thread. **hilo de perlas** string of pearls. **telegrafía sin hilos** *sf* wireless telegraphy.

himno ['imno] *sm* hymn; anthem. **himno nacional** national anthem. **himnario** *sm* hymn book.

hincapié [inka'pje] *sm* foothold; emphasis. **hacer hincapié en** insist on.

hincar [in'kar] v drive in; sink; plunge. **hincarse de rodillas** kneel down.

hinchar [in't∫ar] v inflate; swell. **hincharse v** puff up; (fam) become bigheaded. **hinchazón** sm (med) swelling; arrogance.

hinojo [i'noxo] sm fennel. **hinojos** sm pl knees.

hípico ['ipiko] adj equine. **hipismo** sm show-jumping. **hipódromo** sm race course.

hipnosis [ip'nosis] sm hypnosis. **hipnótico** adj hypnotic. **hipnotismo** sm hypnotism. **hipnotizador, -a** sm, sf hypnotist. **hipnotizar** v hypnotize.

hipo ['ipo] sm hiccup; longing; grudge. **tener hipo** have the hiccups.

hipocondría [ipokon'dria] sf hypochondria. **hipocondríaco, -a** sm, sf hypochondriac.

hipocresía [ipokre'sia] sf hypocrisy. **hipócrita** adj hypocritical. **hipócrita** s(m+f) hypocrite.

hipodérmico [ipo'ðermiko] adj hypodermic.

hipopótamo [ipo'potamo] sm hippopotamus.

hipotecar [ipote'kar] v mortgage. **hipoteca** sf mortgage.

hipótesis [i'potesis] sf hypothesis. **hipotético** adj hypothetical.

hirsuto [ir'suto] adj hairy.

hirviente [ir'βjente] adj boiling.

hispánico [is'paniko] adj Hispanic.

hispanoamericano [ispanoameri'kano] s, adj Spanish American.

histerectomía [isterekto'mia] sf hysterectomy.

histeria [i'sterja] sf hysteria. **histérico** adj hysterical.

historia [is'torja] sf history; story; fib; gossip; trouble. **armar historias** (fam) make trouble. **historiador, -a** sm, sf historian. **histórico** adj historical; historic.

hogar [o'gar] sm hearth; home.

hoguera [o'gera] sf bonfire.

hoja ['oxa] sf leaf; petal; sheet; layer; flake; blade; newspaper; (formulario) form. **hoja de afeitar** razor blade. **hoja de paga** payroll.

hojalata [oxa'lata] sf tinplate; tin.

hojear [oxe'ar] v leaf through.

Holanda [o'landa] sf Holland. **holandés** adj Dutch. **holandés** sm Dutchman; (lengua) Dutch. **holandesa** sf Dutchwoman.

*****holgar** [ol'gar] v rest; be idle; be unnecessary. **holgarse** v enjoy oneself. **holgazán** adj idle. **holgazanear** v idle. **holgura** sf roominess; comfort.

*****hollar** [o'ʎar] v tread; trample down.

hollín [o'ʎin] sm soot. **hollimiento** adj sooty.

hombre ['ombre] sm man. **hombre bueno** arbiter. **hombre de negocios** businessman. **¡hombre!** good heavens, man! **hombrear** v act the man.

hombro ['ombro] sm (anat) shoulder. **echarse al hombro** shoulder.

homenaje [ome'naxe] sm homage. **homenajear** v pay homage to.

homeópata [ome'opata] s(m+f) homeopath. adj homeopathic. **homeopatía** sf homeopathy.

homicida [omi'ðiða] s(m+f) murderer. adj homicidal. **homicidio** sm murder.

homogéneo [omo'xeneo] adj homogeneous. **homogeneidad** sf homogeneity, homogeneousness.

homólogo [o'mologo] adj corresponding; synonymous.

honda ['onda] sf catapult; sling.

hondo ['ondo] adj deep. sm bottom. **hondonada** sf depression; hollow. **hondura** sf depth.

honesto [o'nesto] adj honest; modest; chaste. **honestidad** sf honesty; modesty; chastity.

hongo ['ongo] sm mushroom; bowler hat.

honor [o'nor] sm honour. **honorable** adj honourable. **honorario** adj honorary. **honorario** sm honorarium. **honra** sf honour; reputation; dignity; respect. **tener a mucha honra** be very proud of. **honradez** sf honesty; uprightness. **honrado** adj honest; upright. **honrar** v honour; be a credit to. **honrarse** v be honoured. **honroso** adj honourable.

hora ['ora] sf hour. **pedir hora** make an appointment. **¿qué hora es?** what time is it? **horario** adj hour. **horario** sm hours of work; timetable.

horca ['orka] sf gallows pl; pitchfork. **horcado** adj forked.

horda ['orða] sf horde.

horizonte [ori'ðonte] sm horizon. **horizontal** adj horizontal.

hormiga [or'miga] sf ant; itch. **hormigoso** adj ant-eaten; itchy. **hormiguear** v swarm; creep; itch. **hormigueo** sm itching; swarming. **hormiguero** sm anthill; swarm.

hormigón [ormi'gon] sm concrete. **hormigón armado** reinforced concrete.

hormona [or'mona] sf hormone.

hornero [or'nero], -a sm, sf baker. **hornear** v bake. **hornería** sf baking.

horno ['orno] sm oven; furnace. **hornillo** sm stove, cooker; gas or electric ring.

horóscopo [o'roskopo] sm horoscope.

horquilla [or'kiʎa] sf pitchfork; hairpin; rowlock.

horrible [or'riβle] adj horrible.

horror [or'ror] sm horror. **horrendo** adj hideous; horrible. **horrífico** adj horrific, horrifying. **horrorizar** v horrify. **horroroso** adj horrid, horrible.

hortaliza [orta'liθa] sf green vegetable. **hortelano**, -a sm, sf gardener. **hortelano** adj market-gardening.

horticultura [ortikul'tura] sf horticulture. **hortícula** adj horticultural.

hosco ['osko] adj grim; surly; gloomy. **hoscoso** adj bristly.

hospedar [ospe'ðar] v lodge, put up. **hospedarse** v have lodgings. **hospedaje** sf lodging. **hospedería** sf inn, hostelry.

hospicio [os'piθjo] sm orphanage; poorhouse.

hospital [ospi'tal] sm hospital. **hospitalario** adj hospitable. **hospitalidad** sf hospitality. **hospitalización** sf hospitalization. **hospitalizar** v hospitalize.

hostelero [oste'lero], -a sm, sf innkeeper. **hostería** sf inn.

hostia ['ostja] sf (rel) wafer; (fam) bashing.

hostigar [osti'gar] v whip; harass; molest. **hostigamiento** sm harassing; molesting; lashing. **hostigo** sm lash.

hostil [os'til] adj hostile. **hostilidad** sf hostility.

hotel [o'tel] sm hotel; villa. **hotelería** sf hotel-keeping. **hotelero**, -a sm, sf hotelkeeper.

hoy [oj] adv today; now. **de hoy en adelante** from now on. **hoy en día** nowadays. **hoy por hoy** for the time being.

hoya ['oja] sf hole; valley.

hoyo ['ojo] sm pit; hole; dent; grave. **hoyuelo** sm small hole; dimple.

hoz [oθ] sf sickle; ravine.

hueco ['weko] adj hollow; empty; vain; resonant. sm hollow; gap; cavity; vacancy.

huelga ['welga] sf (de obreros) strike. **huelgista** s(m+f) striker.

huelgo ['welgo] sm breath; (tecn) play.

huella ['weʎa] sf footprint; tread; impression. **huella digital** fingerprint. **huella de sonido** soundtrack.

huérfano ['werfano], -a sm, sf orphan.

huerta ['werta] sf vegetable garden; orchard; irrigated land. **huerto** sm orchard; kitchen garden.

hueso ['weso] sm bone; stone; pip; (fam) drudgery. **dar con sus huesos** end up. **estar en los huesos** be very thin. **huesudo** adj bony.

huésped ['wespeð], -a sm, sf guest; lodger. **casa de huéspedes** boarding house.

hueva ['weβa] sf roe. **huevas** sf pl spawn.

huevo ['weβo] sm egg. **huevo de Pascua** Easter egg. **huevo duro** hard-boiled egg. **huevo escalfado** poached egg. **huevo frito** fried egg. **huevo pasado por agua** soft-boiled egg. **huevo revuelto** scrambled egg.

*¹**huir** [wir] v flee. **huida** sf flight; escape.

hule¹ ['ule] sm oilskin; rubber.

hule² sm (cornada) goring.

hulla ['uʎa] sf coal.

humano [u'mano] adj human; humane. sm human being. **humanar** v humanize. **humanidad** sf humanity. **humanismo** sm humanism. **humanista** s(m+f) humanist. **humanitario**, -a s, adj humanitarian.

húmedo ['umeðo] adj humid, damp, moist. **humedad** sf humidity, dampness. **humedecer** v dampen, moisten.

humillar [umi'ʎar] v humiliate; shame. **humildad** sf humility. **humilde** adj humble. **humillación** sf humiliation.

humo ['umo] sm smoke; fumes pl. **vender humos** boast. **humear** v smoke. **humoso** adj smoky.

humor [u'mor] sm humour; temper; mood. **buen/mal humor** good/bad temper. **humorada** sf witticism. **humorista** s(m+f) humorist. **humorístico** adj humorous.

hundir [un'dir] v sink; drive in; crush. **hundirse** v go under; collapse. **hundimiento** sm sinking; collapse.

Hungría [un'gria] sf Hungary. **húngaro** s, adj Hungarian.

huracán [ura'kan] sm hurricane.

hurgar [ur'gar] v poke; stir; pick. **hurgón** sm poker.

hurón [u'ron] *sm* ferret. **huronear** *v* hunt with a ferret; *(fam)* pry.

hurtadillas [urta'ðiʎas] *adv* **a hurtadillas** slyly, stealthily.

hurtar [ur'tar] *v* steal; remove; cheat. **hurtar el cuerpo** dodge. **hurtador, -a** *sm, sf* thief. **hurto** *sm* theft; thing stolen.

husmear [usme'ar] *v* scent; track; *(fam)* pry; *(fam: carne)* smell high. **husmeo** *sm* scenting; smelling; prying.

huso ['uso] *sm* spindle; *(avión)* fuselage.

I

íbice ['iβiθe] *sm* ibex.

ictericia [ikte'riθja] *sf* jaundice.

ida ['iða] *sf* departure; journey. **idas y venidas** coming and going.

idea [i'ðea] *sf* idea; intention. **tener idea de** intend to. **ideal** *adj* ideal; imaginary. **idealismo** *sm* idealism. **idealista** *s, adj* idealist. **idealizar** *v* idealize. **idear** *v* imagine; plan.

idéntico [i'ðentiko] *adj* identical. **identidad** *sf* identity. **identificación** *sf* identification. **identificar** *v* identify.

ideología [iðeolo'xia] *sf* ideology. **ideológico** *adj* ideological.

idilio [i'ðiljo] *sm* idyll. **idílico** *adj* idyllic.

idioma [i'ðjoma] *sm* language. **idiomático** *adj* idiomatic; linguistic.

idiosincrasia [iðjosin'krasja] *sf* idiosyncrasy. **idiosincrásico** *adj* idiosyncratic.

idiota [i'ðjota] *s(m+f)* idiot. *adj* idiotic. **idiotez** *sf* idiocy. **idiótico** *adj* idiotic.

ídolo ['iðolo] *sm* idol. **idólatra** *s(m+f)* idolater. **idólatra** *adj* idolatrous. **idolatrar** *v* idolize. **idolatría** *sf* idolatry.

idóneo [i'ðoneo] *adj* apt, fit. **idoneidad** *sf* aptness, fitness.

iglesia [i'glesja] *sf* church.

ignición [igni'θjon] *sf* ignition. **ignito** *adj* ignited.

ignominia [igno'minja] *sf* ignominy. **ignominioso** *adj* ignominious.

ignorar [igno'rar] *v* be unaware of; refuse to know. **ignorancia** *sf* ignorance. **ignorante** *adj* ignorant.

igual [i'gwal] *adj* same; equal; even. **por** igual evenly. **es igual** it makes no difference. **igualar** *v* equalize. **igualación** *sf* equalization. **igualdad** *sf* equality.

ijada [i'xaða] *sf* flank. **ijadear** *v* pant.

ilegal [ile'gal] *adj* illegal. **ilegalidad** *sf* illegality.

ilegible [ile'xiβle] *adj* illegible.

ilegítimo [ile'xitimo] *adj* illegitimate. **ilegitimidad** *sf* illegitimacy.

ileso [i'leso] *adj* unharmed.

ilícito [i'liθito] *adj* illicit.

ilógico [i'loxiko] *adj* illogical.

iluminar [ilumi'nar] *v* illuminate. **iluminación** *sf* illumination.

ilusión [ilu'sjon] *sf* illusion; delusion; expectation. **ilusionado** *adj* eager. **ilusionar** *v* fascinate. **ilusionarse** *v* delude oneself; build up hopes. **ilusionismo** *sm* conjuring trick. **ilusionista** *s(m+f)* conjurer. **iluso** *adj* deceived; deluded. **ilusorio** *adj* illusory.

ilustrar [ilu'strar] *v* illustrate. **ilustración** *sf* illustration; enlightenment. **ilustrador, -a** *sm, sf* illustrator.

imaginar [imaxi'nar] *v* imagine. **imagen** *sf* image. **imaginación** *sf* imagination. **imaginario** *adj* imaginary. **imaginativo** *adj* imaginative.

imán [i'man] *sm* magnet. **imanar** *v* also **imantar** magnetize. **imantación** *sf* magnetization.

imbécil [im'βeθil] *adj* imbecile. **imbecilidad** *sf* imbecility.

imborrable [imbor'raβle] *adj* unforgettable.

*imbuir [imbu'ir] *v* imbue.

imitar [imi'tar] *v* imitate, copy. **imitable** *adj* imitable. **imitación** *sf* imitation. **imitador, -a** *sm, sf* imitator. **imitativo** *adj* imitative.

impaciente [impa'θjente] *adj* impatient. **impaciencia** *sf* impatience. **impacientarse** *v* become impatient.

impacto [im'pakto] *sm* impact.

impar [im'par] *adj* *(mat)* odd. **número impar** odd number.

imparcial [impar'θjal] *adj* impartial. **imparcialidad** *sf* impartiality.

impartir [impar'tir] *v* impart.

impasible [impa'siβle] *adj* impassive. **impasibilidad** *sf* impassivity.

impávido [im'paβiðo] *adj* fearless, dauntless. **impavidez** *sf* fearlessness, dauntlessness.

impecable [impe'kaβle] *adj* impeccable. **impecabilidad** *sf* impeccability.

*impedir [impe'ðir] *v* impede; prevent. **impediente** *adj* obstructing. **impedimento** *sm* impediment.

impeler [impe'ler] *v* impel; drive; propel.

impenetrable [impene'traβle] *adj* impenetrable.

impenitente [impeni'tente] *adj* impenitent.

imperar [impe'rar] *v* rule; prevail. **imperativo** *adj* imperative; commanding.

imperceptible [imperθep'tiβle] *adj* imperceptible.

imperdible [imper'ðiβle] *sm* safety pin.

imperdonable [imperðo'naβle] *adj* unforgivable.

imperfecto [imper'fekto] *adj* imperfect. **imperfección** *sf* imperfection.

imperio [im'perjo] *sm* empire. **imperial** *adj* imperial. **imperialismo** *sm* imperialism. **imperialista** *s, adj* imperialist.

impermeable [imperme'aβle] *adj* waterproof. *sm* mackintosh.

impersonal [imperso'nal] *adj* impersonal.

impertinente [imperti'nente] *adj* impertinent. **impertinencia** *sf* impertinence.

imperturbable [impertur'βaβle] *adj* imperturbable. **imperturbabilidad** *sf* imperturbability.

ímpetu ['impetu] *sm* impetus. **impetuosidad** *sf* impetuosity.

impío [im'pio] *adj* godless, impious. **impiedad** *sf* impiety.

implacable [impla'kaβle] *adj* implacable. **implacabilidad** *sf* implacability.

implantar [implan'tar] *v* implant.

implicar [impli'kar] *v* imply; implicate; entail. **implicación** *sf* implication; contradiction. **implicatorio** *adj* contradictory.

implícito [im'pliθito] *adj* implicit.

implorar [implo'rar] *v* implore, beg. **imploración** *sf* entreaty.

*imponer [impo'ner] *v* impose; inflict; acquaint; inspire; deposit; impute falsely. **imponerse** *v* dominate. **imponente** *adj* imposing; striking; (*fam*) sensational, smashing.

impopular [impopu'lar] *adj* unpopular. **impopularidad** *sf* unpopularity.

importante [impor'tante] *adj* important. **importancia** *sf* importance. **importar** *v* matter, concern. **no importa** it doesn't matter.

importunar [importu'nar] *v* importune,

pester. **importunidad** *sf* importunity. **importuno** *adj* importunate, pestering.

imposible [impo'siβle] *adj* impossible. **imposibilidad** *sf* impossibility. **imposibilitar** *v* make impossible.

imposición [imposi'θjon] *sf* imposition; tax.

impostor [impos'tor], **-a** *sm, sf* impostor.

impotente [impo'tente] *adj* impotent; powerless. **impotencia** *sf* impotence.

impracticable [imprakti'kaβle] *adj* impracticable.

imprecar [impre'kar] *v* curse. **imprecación** *sf* curse. **imprecatorio** *adj* abusive.

impreciso [impre'θiso] *adj* imprecise. **imprecisión** *sf* imprecision.

impregnar [impreg'nar] *v* impregnate; saturate. **impregnable** *adj* absorbent. **impregnación** *sf* impregnation.

imprescindible [impresθin'diβle] *adj* indispensable.

impreso [im'preso] *adj* printed. **imprenta** *sf* press; printing. **impresión** *sf* impression; imprint; stamp; print; printing; edition. **impresionable** *adj* impressionable. **impresionar** *v* impress; shock. **impresionarse** *v* be deeply moved. **impresionismo** *sm* impressionism. **impresionista** *s(m+f)* impressionist. **impresor** *sm* printer.

imprevisto [impre'βisto] *adj* unexpected.

imprimir [impri'mir] *v* print; implant.

improbable [impro'βaβle] *adj* improbable. **improbabilidad** *sf* improbability.

ímprobo ['improβo] *adj* wicked; arduous. **improbidad** *sf* dishonesty.

improcedente [improθe'ðente] *adj* improper; inappropriate; (*jur*) inadmissible. **improcedencia** *sf* impropriety; inappropriateness; (*jur*) inadmissibility.

improductivo [improduk'tiβo] *adj* unproductive.

impropio [im'propjo] *adj* improper; unbecoming. **impropiedad** *sf* impropriety.

imprévido [im'proβiðo] *adj* improvident. **improvidencia** *sf* improvidence.

improvisar [improβi'sar] *v* improvise. **improvisación** *sf* improvisation.

improvisto [impro'βisto] *adj* unforeseen. **a la improvista** without warning.

imprudente [impru'ðente] *adj* imprudent. **imprudencia** *sf* imprudence.

impúdico [im'puðiko] *adj* shameless, immodest.

impuesto [im'pwesto] *sm* tax; duty.

impugnar [impug'nar] *v* impugn; oppose; refute.

impulsar [impul'sar] *v* impel; drive; move. **impulsión** *sf* impulse; impetus. **impulso** *sm* impulse; drive; momentum.

impune [im'pune] *adj* unpunished. **impunidad** *sf* impunity.

impuro [im'puro] *adj* impure; lewd. **impureza** *sf* impurity; lewdness. **impurificación** *sf* defilement. **impurificar** *v* defile.

imputar [impu'tar] *v* impute; ascribe. **imputable** *adj* chargeable. **imputación** *sf* imputation; accusation.

inacabable [inaka'βaβle] *adj* endless.

inaccesible [inakθe'siβle] *adj* inaccessible. **inaccesibilidad** *sf* inaccessibility.

inaceptable [inaθep'taβle] *adj* unacceptable.

inacostumbrado [inakostum'braðo] *adj* unaccustomed.

inactivo [inak'tiβo] *adj* inactive. **inactividad** *sf* inactivity.

inadecuado [inaðe'kwaðo] *adj* inadequate. **inadecuación** *sf* inadequacy.

inadmisible [inaðmi'siβle] *adj* inadmissible.

inadvertido [inaðβer'tiðo] *adj* inadvertent. **inadvertencia** *sf* inadvertence, carelessness.

inagotable [inago'taβle] *adj* inexhaustible.

inaguantable [inagwan'taβle] *adj* unbearable.

inajenable [inaxe'naβle] *adj* inalienable.

inalterable [inalte'raβle] *adj* unalterable; imperturbable. **inalterabilidad** *sf* immutability; imperturbability. **inalterado** *adj* unchanged.

inanición [inani'θjon] *sf* starvation; weakness; exhaustion.

inanimado [inani'maðo] *adj* inanimate, lifeless.

inapagable [inapa'gaβle] *adj* unquenchable.

inaplicable [inapli'kaβle] *adj* inapplicable. **inaplicado** *adj* indolent.

inapreciable [inapre'θjaβle] *adj* priceless; invaluable.

inapto [in'apto] *adj* unsuitable; incapable.

inasequible [inase'kiβle] *adj* unattainable.

inaudible [inau'ðiβle] *adj* inaudible.

inaudito [inau'ðito] *adj* unheard of; outrageous.

inaugurar [inaugu'rar] *v* inaugurate. **inauguración** *sf* inauguration.

incalculable [inkalku'laβle] *adj* incalculable.

incandescente [inkandes'θente] *adj* incandescent. **incandescencia** *sf* incandescence.

incansable [inkan'saβle] *adj* indefatigable, untiring.

incapacitar [inkapaθi'tar] *v* incapacitate; disable; disqualify. **incapacidad** *sf* incapacity; incompetence; disability. **incapaz** *adj* unfit; incompetent.

incautarse [inkau'tarse] *v* (*jur*) confiscate. **incautación** *sf* confiscation.

incauto [in'kauto] *adj* incautious; gullible.

incendiar [inθen'djar] *v* set on fire. **incendiarse** *v* catch fire. **incendiario, -a** *sm, sf* arsonist. **incendiario** *adj* incendiary. **incendio** *sm* fire. **incendio provocado** arson.

incentivo [inθen'tiβo] *sm* incentive. **incentivar** *v* incite.

incertidumbre [inθerti'ðumbre] *sf* uncertainty.

incesante [inθe'sante] *adj* incessant.

incesto [in'θesto] *sm* incest. **incestuoso** *adj* incestuous.

incidente [inθi'ðente] *sm* incident. *adj* incidental. **incidencia** *sf* incident; incidence. **incidental** *adj* incidental.

incienso [in'θjenso] *sm* incense.

incierto [in'θjerto] *adj* uncertain; untrue.

incinerar [inθine'rar] *v* incinerate; cremate. **incineración** *sf* incineration; cremation.

incipiente [inθi'pjente] *adj* incipient.

incisivo [inθi'siβo] *adj* incisive; cutting. *sm* (*diente*) incisor. **incisión** *sf* incision, cut. **inciso** *adj* cut.

incitar [inθi'tar] *v* incite; instigate. **incitación** *sf* incitement; enticement. **incitador, -a** *sm, sf* instigator.

incivil [inθi'βil] *adj* uncivil, impolite.

inclemente [inkle'mente] *adj* inclement; harsh. **inclemencia** *sf* inclemency; harshness.

inclinar [inkli'nar] *v* incline; lean; influence; induce; lower. **inclinarse** *v* feel disposed; bow; stoop. **inclinación** *sf* inclination; leaning; slope; dip. **inclinado** *adj* inclined; sloping.

***incluir** [inklu'ir] *v* include. **inclusión** *sf* inclusion. **inclusivo** *adj* inclusive. **incluso** *adj* included; enclosed. **incluso** *adv* even.

incógnito [in'kognito] *adj* unknown. **de incógnito** incognito.

incoherente [inkoe'rente] *adj* incoherent. **incoherencia** *sf* incoherence.

incoloro [inko'loro] *adj* colourless.

incombustible [inkombus'tiβle] *adj* incombustible, fireproof.

incomodar [inkomo'ðar] *v* disturb, annoy, molest. **incomodidad** *sf* inconvenience; discomfort. **incómodo** *adj* uncomfortable; annoying.

incomparable [inkompa'raβle] *adj* incomparable.

incompatible [inkompa'tiβle] *adj* incompatible. **incompatibilidad** *sf* incompatibility.

incompetente [inkompe'tente] *adj* incompetent. **incompetencia** *sf* incompetence.

incompleto [inkom'pleto] *adj* incomplete. **incompletamente** *adv* incompletely.

incomprensible [inkompren'siβle] *adj* incomprehensible. **incomprensibilidad** *sf* incomprehensibility. **incomprensión** *sf* lack of understanding.

incomunicado [inkomuni'kaðo] *adj* isolated. **incomunicable** *adj* incommunicable. **incomunicación** *sf* isolation. **incomunicar** *v* isolate.

inconcebible [inkonθe'βiβle] *adj* inconceivable.

inconcluso [inkon'kluso] *adj* unfinished; inconclusive.

incondicional [inkondiθjo'nal] *adj* unconditional. *s(m+f)* staunch supporter.

inconfundible [inkonfun'diβle] *adj* unmistakable.

incongruente [inkongru'ente] *adj* incongruous; incongruent. **incongruencia** *sf* incongruousness; incongruity.

inconmensurable [inkonmensu'raβle] *adj* immeasurable.

inconmovible [inkonmo'βiβle] *adj* unshakable; firm.

inconsciente [inkons'θjente] *adj* unconscious; unaware; thoughtless. **inconsciencia** *sf* unconsciousness; unawareness; thoughtlessness.

inconsecuente [inkonse'kwente] *adj* inconsequential; inconsistent. **inconsecuencia** *sf* inconsistency.

inconsiderado [inkonsiðe'raðo] *adj* ill-considered. **inconsideración** *sf* inconsiderateness.

inconstante [inkon'stante] *adj* inconstant, fickle. **inconstancia** *sf* inconstancy, fickleness.

incontable [inkon'taβle] *adj* innumerable.

incontestable [inkontes'taβle] *adj* incontestable, indisputable.

incontinente [inkonti'nente] *adj* incontinent. **incontinencia** *sf* incontinence.

inconveniente [inkonβe'njente] *adj* inconvenient, impolite. *sm* objection; trouble; obstacle. **inconveniencia** *sf* inconvenience; impropriety; unsuitability.

incorporar [inkorpo'rar] *v* incorporate. **incorporarse** *v* sit up; become a member. **incorporación** *sf* incorporation. **incorporado** *adj* incorporated.

incorrecto [inkor'rekto] *adj* incorrect. **incorrección** *sf* inaccuracy. **incorregibilidad** *sf* incorrigibility. **incorregible** *adj* incorrigible.

incorrupto [inkor'rupto] *adj* incorrupt, pure. **incorruptible** *adj* incorruptible.

incrédulo [in'kreðulo] *adj* incredulous, sceptical. **incredulidad** *sf* incredulity, scepticism. **increíble** *adj* incredible.

incremento [inkre'mento] *sm* increase.

increpar [inkre'par] *v* reproach; rebuke. **increpación** *sf* rebuke.

incriminar [inkrimi'nar] *v* incriminate; exaggerate. **incriminación** *sf* incrimination.

incrustar [inkrus'tar] *v* encrust. **incrustación** *sf* encrustation.

incubar [inku'βar] *v* incubate; *(med)* be sickening for. **incubación** *sf* incubation. **incubadora** *sf* incubator.

inculcar [inkul'kar] *v* inculcate. **inculcarse** *v* be obstinate. **inculcación** *sf* inculcation.

inculpable [inkul'paβle] *adj* blameless. **inculpabilidad** *sf* blamelessness.

inculto [in'kulto] *adj* uncouth; uneducated. **incultura** *sf* lack of culture.

incumbencia [inkum'benθja] *sf* responsibility, duty. **incumbir** *v* be incumbent upon.

incurable [inku'raβle] *adj* incurable.

incurrir [inkur'rir] *v* incur; fall; commit. **incursión** [inkur'sjon] *sf* incursion, raid.

indagar [inda'gar] *v* investigate. **indagación** *sf* investigation. **indagador, -a** *sm, sf* investigator.

indebido [inde'βiðo] *adj* unjust; improper.

indecente [inde'θente] *adj* indecent; foul; wretched. **indecencia** *sf* indecency; obscenity.

indecible [inde'θiβle] *adj* indescribable; unspeakable.

indecifrable [indeθi'fraβle] *adj* indecipherable.

indecisión [inde'θisjon] *sf* indecision. **indeciso** *adj* indecisive.

indecoroso [indeco'roso] *adj* indecorous. **indecoro** *sm* lack of propriety.

indefectible [indefek'tiβle] *adj* unfailing.

indefenso [inde'fenso] *adj* defenceless. **indefendible** *adj* indefensible.

indefinible [indefi'niβle] *adj* indefinable. **indefinido** *adj* indefinite.

indeleble [inde'leβle] *adj* indelible.

indelicado [indeli'kaðo] *adj* indelicate. **indelicadeza** *sf* indelicacy.

indemne [in'demne] *adj* unhurt. **indemnidad** *sf* indemnity. **indemnización** *sf* compensation. **indemnizar** *v* indemnify, compensate.

independencia [independen'θja] *sf* independence. **independiente** *adj* independent.

indescriptible [indescrip'tiβle] *adj* indescribable.

indeseable [indese'aβle] *adj* undesirable.

indestructible [indestruk'tiβle] *adj* indestructible. **indestructibilidad** *sf* indestructibility.

indeterminado [indetermi'naðo] *adj* indeterminate; undetermined.

India ['indja] *sf* India. **indio, -a** *s*, *adj* Indian.

indicar [indi'kar] *v* indicate; show; suggest. **indicación** *sf* indication. **indicado** *adj* suitable; recommended. **indicador** *sm* pointer; gauge. **indicativo** *adj* indicative. *sm* (gram) indicative.

índice ['indiθe] *sm* index.

indicio [in'diθjo] *sm* sign; trace. **indicios** *sm pl* (jur) evidence *sing*.

indiferencia [indife'renθja] *sf* indifference. **indiferente** *adj* indifferent.

indígena [in'dixena] *s(m+f)*, *adj* native.

indigestión [indixes'tjon] *sf* indigestion. **indigestible** *adj* indigestible.

indignar [indig'nar] *v* anger, annoy. **indignarse** *v* become indignant. **indignación** *sf* indignation. **indignidad** *sf* indignity. **indigno** *adj* unworthy; disgraceful.

indirecta [indi'rekta] *sf* innuendo. **indirecto** *adj* indirect.

indisciplina [indisθi'plina] *sf* indiscipline. **indisciplinado** *adj* undisciplined.

indiscreción [indiskre'θjon] *sf* indiscretion. **indiscreto** *adj* indiscreet.

indisculpable [indiskul'paβle] *adj* inexcusable.

indiscutible [indisku'tiβle] *adj* unquestionable.

indisoluble [indiso'luβle] *adj* indissoluble.

indispensable [indispen'saβle] *adj* indispensable.

***indisponer** [indispo'ner] *v* upset; render unfit. **indisponerse** *v* become ill. **indisposición** *sf* indisposition. **indispuesto** *adj* indisposed, poorly.

indisputable [indispu'taβle] *adj* indisputable.

indistinto [indis'tinto] *adj* indistinct; vague.

individual [indiβi'ðwal] *adj* individual. **individualidad** *sf* individuality. **individualismo** *sm* individualism. **individualista** *s(m+f)* individualist. **individualizar** *v* individualize. **individuo, -a** *sm*, *sf* individual.

indivisible [indiβi'siβle] *adj* indivisible. **indiviso** *adj* undivided.

índole ['indole] *sf* nature.

indolente [indo'lente] *adj* indolent; painless. **indolencia** *sf* indolence; painlessness.

indómito [in'domito] *adj* untamed; indomitable.

indubitable [induβi'taβle] *adj* indubitable.

***inducir** [indu'θir] *v* persuade; lead; infer. **inducción** *sf* induction. **inducimiento** *sm* inducement.

indudable [indu'ðaβle] *adj* unquestionable.

indulgente [indul'xente] *adj* indulgent. **indulgencia** *sf* indulgence.

indultar [indul'tar] *v* pardon; excuse. **indulto** *sm* mercy; reprieve; exemption. **indumento** [indu'mento] *sm* apparel.

industria [in'dustrja] *sf* industry; business; ingenuity. **de industria** on purpose. **industrial** *adj* industrial. **industrial** *sm* industrialist. **industrialismo** *sm* industrialism. **industrializar** *v* industrialize. **industrioso** *adj* industrious.

inédito [i'neðito] *adj* unpublished.

inefable [ine'faβle] *adj* ineffable.

ineficaz [inefi'kaθ] *adj* inefficient. **ineficacia** *sf* inefficiency.

ineludible [inelu'ðiβle] *adj* inevitable.

inepto [i'nepto] *adj* inept. **ineptitud** *sf* ineptitude.

inequívoco [ine'kiβoko] *adj* unmistakable.

inercia [i'nerθja] *sf* inertia; lifelessness.

inerme [i'nerme] *adj* unarmed.

inerte [i'nerte] *adj* inert.

inesperado [inespe'raðo] *adj* unexpected, unforeseen.

inestable [ines'taβle] *adj* unstable. **inestabilidad** *sf* instability.

inestimable [inesti'maβle] *adj* invaluable.

inevitable [ineβi'taβle] *adj* inevitable.

inexacto [inek'sakto] *adj* inaccurate. **inexactitud** *sf* inaccuracy.

inexcusable [ineksku'saβle] *adj* inexcusable; essential.

inexorable [inekso'raβle] *adj* inexorable.

inexperto [ineks'perto] *adj* inexperienced.

inexplicable [inekspli'kaβle] *adj* inexplicable.

infalible [infa'liβle] *adj* infallible. **infalibilidad** *sf* infallibility.

infamar [infa'mar] *v* dishonour. **infamación** *sf* defamation. **infame** *adj* infamous. **infamia** *sf* infamy.

infante [in'fante] *sm, adj* infant. *sm* prince. **infancia** *sf* infancy. **infantil** *adj* infantile.

infantería [infante'ria] *sf* infantry.

infatigable [infati'gaβle] *adj* indefatigable.

infausto [in'fausto] *adj* ill-omened; ill-famed.

infectar [infek'tar] *v* infect. **infección** *sf* infection. **infeccioso** *adj* infectious.

infeliz [infe'liθ] *adj* unhappy. *s(m+f)* luckless person.

inferior [infe'rjor] *adj* inferior; lower. *sm* inferior. **inferioridad** *sf* inferiority.

*inferir [infe'rir] *v* infer; inflict. **inferirse** *v* follow.

infernal [infer'nal] *adj* infernal.

infestar [infes'tar] *v* infest; overrun. **infestación** *sf* infestation.

infiel [in'fjel] *adj* unfaithful. *s(m+f)* infidel.

infierno [in'fjerno] *sm* hell.

ínfimo ['infimo] *adj* lowest; vilest.

infinito [infi'nito] *adj* infinite. **infinidad** *sf* infinity. **infinitivo** *sm* (*gram*) infinitive.

inflamar [infla'mar] *v* inflame. **inflamable** *adj* inflammable. **inflamación** *sf* inflammation.

inflar [in'flar] *v* inflate. **inflación** *sf* inflation; swelling.

inflexible [inflek'siβle] *adj* inflexible. **inflexibilidad** *sf* inflexibility.

infligir [infli'xir] *v* inflict.

*influir [influ'ir] *v* influence; affect. **influencia** *sf* influence; authority. **influente** *adj also* **influyente** influential. **influjo** *sm* influence; flood.

informal [infor'mal] *adj* informal; unreliable. **informalidad** *sf* informality; unreliability.

informar [infor'mar] *v* inform; notify. **informarse** *v* find out. **información** *sf* information; judicial inquiry. **informador, -a** *sm, sf* informant. **informe** *sm* report; testimonial. **informe** *adj* shapeless.

infortunio [infor'tunjo] *sm* misfortune. **infortunado** *adj* unfortunate.

infracción [infrak'θjon] *sf* breach; infringement. **infractor, -a** *sm, sf* transgressor.

infranqueable [infranke'aβle] *adj* impassable; insurmountable.

infringir [infrin'xir] *v* infringe; violate.

infructuoso [infruk'twoso] *adj* fruitless.

infundado [infun'daðo] *adj* unfounded.

infundir [infun'dir] *v* instil. **infusión** *sf* inspiration.

ingeniería [inxenje'ria] *sf* engineering. **ingeniero** *sm* engineer.

ingenio [in'xenjo] *sm* talent; wit; ingenuity; device. **ingeniosidad** *sf* ingenuity. **ingenioso** *adj* ingenious.

ingenuo [in'xenwo] *adj* naïve; frank; simple. **ingenuidad** *sf* frankness; credulity.

*ingerir [inxe'rir] *v* (*comida*) consume. **ingerirse** *v* meddle. **ingerencia** *sf* interference.

Inglaterra [ingla'terra] *sf* England. **inglés** *adj* English; *sm* Englishman; (*idioma*) English. **inglesa** *sf* Englishwoman.

ingrato [in'grato] *adj* ungrateful; unpleasant. **ingratitud** *sf* ingratitude.

ingrediente [ingre'ðjente] *sm* ingredient.

ingresar [ingre'sar] *v* enter; join; (*hospital*) be admitted; (*dinero*) deposit. **ingreso** *sm* entrance; (*com*) deposit; admission. **derecho de ingreso** *sm* entrance fee.

inhábil [i'naβil] *adj* incompetent; tactless. **día inhábil** non-working day. **inhabilidad** *sf* incompetence; inability. **inhabilitar** *v* disqualify; disable.

inhabitable [inaβi'taβle] *adj* uninhabitable. **inhabitado** *adj* uninhabited.

inhalar [ina'lar] *v* inhale. **inhalación** *sf* inhalation.

inherente [ine'rente] *adj* inherent. **inherencia** *sf* inherence.

inhibir [ini'βir] *v* inhibit. **inhibirse** *v* refrain. **inhibición** *sf* inhibition. **inhibitorio** *adj* inhibitive.

inhospitalario [inospita'larjo] *adj* inhospitable. **inhospitalidad** *sf* inhospitableness.

inhumano [inu'mano] *adj* inhuman. **inhumanidad** *sf* inhumanity.

inhumar [inu'mar] *v* bury.

inicial [ini'θjal] *adj, sf* initial. **iniciación** *sf* initiation. **iniciado, -a** *sm, sf* initiate. **iniciador, -a** *sm, sf* initiator. **iniciar** *v* initiate. **iniciativa** *sf* initiative.

inicuo [i'nikwo] *adj* wicked. **iniquidad** *sf* iniquity.

injertar [inxer'tar] *v* graft. **injerto** *sm* graft. grafting.

injuriar [inxuri'ar] *v* insult; damage; injure. **injuria** *sf* offence; harm. **injuriador** *adj* offensive. **injurioso** *adj* insulting.

injusticia [inxus'tiθja] *sf* injustice. **injusto** *adj* unjust.

inmediato [inme'δjato] *adj* immediate. **de inmediato** immediately.

inmejorable [inmexo'raβle] *adj* unsurpassable.

inmemorial [inmemo'rjal] *adj* immemorial.

inmenso [in'menso] *adj* immense.

inmerecido [inmere'θiδo] *adj* undeserved.

inmigrar [inmi'grar] *v* immigrate. **inmigración** *sf* immigration. **inmigrante** *s(m+f), adj* immigrant.

inminente [inmi'nente] *adj* imminent. **inminencia** *sf* imminence.

inmoderado [inmoδe'raδo] *adj* excessive. **inmoderación** *sf* excess.

inmodestia [inmoδes'tia] *sf* immodesty. **inmodesto** *adj* immodest.

inmolar [inmo'lar] *v* sacrifice. **inmolación** *sf* sacrifice.

inmoral [inmo'ral] *adj* immoral. **inmoralidad** *sf* immorality.

inmortal [inmor'tal] *adj, s(m+f)* immortal. **inmortalidad** *sf* immortality. **inmortalizar** *v* immortalize.

inmóvil [in'moβil] *adj* motionless. **inmovible** *adj* immovable. **inmovilidad** *sf* immobility. **inmovilizar** *v* immobilize.

inmueble [in'mweβle] *sm* property; real estate.

inmundo [in'mundo] *adj* filthy; impure. **inmundicia** *sf* filth; impurity.

inmune [in'mune] *adj* immune; exempt. **inmunidad** *sf* immunity; exemption. **inmunización** *sf* immunization. **inmunizar** *v* immunize.

inmutar [inmu'tar] *v* change. **inmutarse** *v* change one's expression. **inmutabilidad** *sf* immutability. **inmutable** *adj* immutable.

innato [in'nato] *adj* innate.

innecesario [inneθe'sarjo] *adj* unnecessary.

innegable [in'negaβle] *adj* undeniable.

innoble [in'noβle] *adj* ignoble.

innocuo [in'nokwo] *adj also* inocuo innocuous.

innovar [inno'βar] *v* innovate. **innovación** *sf* innovation. **innovador, -a** *sm, sf* innovator. **innovador** *adj* innovative. **innovamiento** *sm* innovation.

innumerable [innume'raβle] *adj* innumerable.

inobediente [inoβe'δjente] *adj* disobedient. **inobediencia** *sf* disobedience.

inocente [ino'θente] *adj* innocent. **inocencia** *sf* innocence.

inocular [inoku'lar] *v* inoculate; contaminate. **inoculación** *sf* inoculation.

inodoro [ino'δoro] *adj* odourless.

inofensivo [inofen'siβo] *adj* harmless.

inolvidable [inolβi'δaβle] *adj* unforgettable.

inoperable [inope'raβle] *adj* inoperable.

inopinado [inopi'naδo] *adj* unexpected.

inoportuno [inopor'tuno] *adj* inopportune.

inoxidable [inoksi'δaβle] *adj* rustless; stainless. **acero inoxidable** *sm* stainless steel.

inquebrantable [inkeβran'taβle] *adj* unbreakable; unyielding.

inquietar [inkje'tar] *v* disturb; disquiet. **inquietador** *adj* disquieting. **inquietante** *adj* disquieting. **inquieto** *adj* restless. **inquietud** *sf* restlessness.

inquilino [inki'lino], **-a** *sm, sf* tenant. **inquilinato** *sm* lease.

*****inquirir** [inki'rir] *v* investigate; examine. **inquiridor, -a** *sm, sf* inquirer. **inquisición** *sf* inquisition; inquiry. **inquisidor** *sm* inquisitor. **inquisitivo** *adj* inquisitive.

insaciable [insa'θjaβle] *adj* insatiable.

insalubre [insa'luβre] *adj* unhealthy. **insalubridad** *sf* unhealthiness.

insanable [insa'naβle] *adj* incurable.

insano [in'sano] *adj* insane; unhealthy. **insania** *sf* insanity.

inscribir [inskri'βir] *v* inscribe; register. **inscripción** *sf* inscription; registration.

insecto [in'sekto] *sm* insect. **insecticida** *sm* insecticide. **insectólogo, -a** *sm, sf* entomologist.

inseguro [inse'guro] *adj* insecure; unsafe; uncertain. **inseguridad** *sf* insecurity; uncertainty.

insensato [insen'sato] *adj* senseless; wild. **insensatez** *sf* folly.

insensible [insen'siβle] *adj* insensible; insensitive; imperceptible. **insensibilidad** *sf* insensibility; insensitiveness.

insertar [inser'tar] *v* insert. **inserto** *sm* insertion.

inservible [inser'βiβle] *adj* useless.

insidioso [insi'ðjoso] *adj* insidious.

insigne [in'signe] *adj* illustrious, distinguished.

insignia [in'signja] *sf* badge; banner. **insignias** *sf pl* insignia.

insignificante [insignifi'kante] *adj* insignificant. **insignificancia** *sf* insignificance.

insincero [insin'θero] *adj* insincere. **insinceridad** *sf* insincerity.

insinuar [insinu'ar] *v* insinuate, suggest. **insinuarse** *v* work one's way (into); make advances. **insinuación** *sf* insinuation; suggestiveness. **insinuante** *adj* insinuating; suggestive.

insípido [in'sipiðo] *adj* insipid, tasteless. **insipidez** *sf* tastelessness.

insistir [insis'tir] *v* insist; persist. **insistencia** *sf* insistence; persistence. **insistente** *adj* insistent; persistent.

insociable [inso'θjaβle] *adj* unsociable. **insociabilidad** *sf* unsociability, unsociableness.

insolación [insola'θjon] *sf* sunstroke. **insolar** *v* expose to the sun. **insolarse** *v* get sunstroke.

insolente [inso'lente] *adj* insolent. **insolencia** *sf* insolence.

insólito [in'solito] *adj* unusual.

insolvente [insol'βente] *adj* insolvent, penniless. **insoluble** *adj* insoluble. **insolvencia** *sf* insolvency.

insomne [in'somne] *s(m + f), adj* insomniac. **insomnio** *sm* insomnia.

insondable [inson'daβle] *adj* unfathomable.

insoportable [insopor'taβle] *adj* intolerable.

inspeccionar [inspekθjo'nar] *v* inspect. **inspección** *sf* inspection. **inspector, -a** *sm, sf* inspector.

inspirar [inspi'rar] *v* inhale; inspire. **inspiración** *sf* inhalation; inspiration. **inspirador** *adj* inspirational.

instable [in'staβle] *adj* unstable. **instabilidad** *sf* instability.

instalar [insta'lar] *v* install; establish. **instalación** *sf* installation; (*fábrica*) plant. **instalador** *sm* fitter.

instancia [instan'θja] *sf* petition; application form.

instante [in'stante] *sm* instant; moment. *adj* insistent. **instantánea** *sf* snapshot. **instantáneo** *adj* instantaneous. **instantemente** *adv* insistingly.

instaurar [instau'rar] *v* set up; restore. **instauración** *sf* restoration. **instaurativo** *adj* restorative.

instigar [insti'gar] *v* instigate; incite. **instigación** *sf* instigation. **instigador, -a** *sm, sf* instigator.

instintivo [instin'tiβo] *adj* instinctive. **instinto** *sm* instinct.

*****instituir** [institu'ir] *v* institute. **institución** *sf* institution. **instituto** *sm* institute; state secondary school.

*****instruir** [instru'ir] *v* instruct. **instrucción** *sf* instruction; education; knowledge. **instructivo** *adj* instructive. **instructor, -a** *sm, sf* instructor. **instruido** *adj* educated.

instrumento [instru'mento] *sm* instrument. **instrumentación** *sf* orchestration. **instrumental** *adj* instrumental. **instrumentar** *v* orchestrate. **instrumentista** *s(m + f)* instrumentalist; instrument-maker.

insubordinar [insuβorði'nar] *v* incite to rebellion. **insubordinarse** *v* rebel. **insubordinación** *sf* insubordination. **insubordinado** *adj* insubordinate.

insubstancial [insuβstan'θjal] *adj* insubstantial.

insuficiente [insufi'θjente] *adj* insufficient; inadequate. **insuficiencia** *sf* insufficiency; inadequacy.

insufrible [insu'friβle] *adj* insufferable.

insular [insu'lar] *adj* insular.

insulso [in'sulso] *adj* dull; tasteless. **insulsez** *sf* tastelessness.

insultar [insul'tar] *v* insult. **insultador** *adj* also **insultante** insulting. **insulto** *sm* insult.

insuperable [insupe'raβle] *adj* insuperable.

insurgente [insur'xente] *s(m+f)* rebel. *adj* rebellious. **insurrección** *sf* rebellion. **insurreccionarse** *v* rebel. **insurrecto, -a** *s*, *adj* insurgent.

intacto [in'takto] *adj* intact.

intachable [inta'tʃaβle] *adj* irreproachable.

intangible [intan'xiβle] *adj* intangible. **intangibilidad** *sf* intangibility.

integrar [inte'grar] *v* integrate; compose; complete; repay. **integración** *sf* integration. **integral** *adj* integral. **pan integral** *sm* wholemeal bread. **integrante** *adj* integral. **integridad** *sf* integrity. **integro** *adj* entire, whole.

intelecto [inte'lekto] *sm* intellect. **intelectual** *s(m+f)*, *adj* intellectual. **intelectualidad** *sf* intelligentsia. **intelectualismo** *sm* intellectualism.

inteligente [inteli'xente] *adj* intelligent. **inteligencia** *sf* intelligence; knowledge; comprehension. **inteligibilidad** *sf* intelligibility. **inteligible** *adj* intelligible.

intemperante [intempe'rante] *adj* intemperate. **intemperancia** *sf* intemperance. **intemperie** [intem'perje] *sf* bad weather. **estar a la intemperie** be out in the open.

intempestivo [intempes'tiβo] *adj* inopportune.

intención [inten'θjon] *sf* intention. **primera intención** frankness. **segunda intención** duplicity. **intencionadamente** *adv* deliberately. **intencionado** *adj* deliberate. **intencional** *adj* intentional.

intenso [in'tenso] *adj* intense. **intensidad** *sf* intensity. **intensificar** *v* intensify. **intensión** *sf* intensity. **intensivo** *adj* intensive.

intentar [inten'tar] *v* try. **intento** *sm* attempt.

intercalar [interka'lar] *v* insert.

intercambio [inter'kambjo] *sm* interchange. **intercambiar** *v* interchange, exchange. **intercambiable** *adj* interchangeable.

interceder [interθe'ðer] *v* intercede. **intercesión** *sf* intercession.

interceptar [interθep'tar] *v* intercept; block. **intercepción** *sf* interception.

interdecir [interðe'θir] *v* prohibit. **interdicción** *sf* also **interdicto** *sm* prohibition.

interesar [intere'sar] *v* interest. **interés** *sm* interest. **llevar interés** bear interest. **interesante** *adj* interesting.

*****interferir** [interfe'rir] *v* interfere. **interferencia** *sf* interference.

interin ['interin] *sm* interim. **interino** *adj* provisional; acting.

interior [inte'rjor] *adj* interior; internal; inner; home. *sm* interior; inside; inland.

interjección [interxek'θjon] *sf* interjection.

intermedio [inter'meðjo] *sm* interval; interlude. *adj* intermediate. **intermediar** *v* mediate. **intermediario, -a** *s*, *adj* intermediary.

interminable [intermi'naβle] *adj* interminable.

intermisión [intermi'sjon] *sf* intermission.

intermitente [intermi'tente] *adj* intermittent.

internacional [internaθjo'nal] *adj* international. **internacionalismo** *sm* internationalism. **internacionalista** *s(m+f)* internationalist.

internar [inter'nar] *v* intern; confine. **internarse** *v* penetrate; intrude. **internamiento** *sm* internment. **interno** *adj* internal; domestic. **escuela interna** *sf* boarding school.

interpelar [interpe'lar] *v* appeal to, implore. **interpelación** *sf* appeal.

*****interponer** [interpo'ner] *v* interpose. **interponerse** *v* intervene. **interposición** *sf* intervention; *(jur)* lodging of an appeal.

interpretar [interpre'tar] *v* interpret. **interpretación** *sf* interpretation. **intérprete** *s(m+f)* interpreter.

interrogar [interro'gar] *v* question. **interrogación** *sf* question; question mark. **interrogativo** *adj* interrogative. **interrogatorio** *sm* interrogation.

interrumpir [interrum'pir] *v* interrupt. **interrupción** *sf* interruption. **interruptor** *sm* electrical switch.

intervalo [inter'βalo] *sm* interval; gap.

*****intervenir** [interβe'nir] *v* intervene; interfere; participate; happen; control; *(med)* operate on; *(com)* audit. **intervención** *sf* intervention; control; operation; audit. **interventor** *sm* auditor; inspector; supervisor.

intestado [intes'taðo] *adj* intestate.

intestino [intes'tino] *adj* internal. *sm* intestine. **intestinal** *adj* intestinal.

intimar [inti'mar] *v* intimate; become close friends. **intimación** *sf* declaration.

intimidad [intimi'ðað] *sf* intimacy. **en la intimidad** privately. **íntimo** *adj* intimate.

intimidar [intimi'ðar] *v* intimidate. **intimidación** *sf* intimidation.

intolerable [intole'raβle] *adj* intolerable. **intolerancia** *sf* intolerance. **intolerante** *adj* intolerant.

intoxicar [intoksi'kar] *v* poison. **intoxicación** *sf* poisoning.

intraducible [intraðu'θiβle] *adj* untranslatable.

intranquilo [intran'kilo] *adj* restless. **intranquilidad** *sf* restlessness.

intransigente [intransi'xente] *adj* intransigent. **intransigencia** *sf* intransigence.

intransitable [intransi'taβle] *adj* impassable.

intransitivo [intransi'tiβo] *adj* (*gram*) intransitive.

intratable [intra'taβle] *adj* intractable; unsociable.

intrépido [in'trepiðo] *adj* brave. **intrepidez** *sf* valour.

intrigar [intri'gar] *v* intrigue. **intriga** *sf* intrigue. **intrigante** *adj* intriguing.

intrincado [intrin'kaðo] *adj* intricate; entangled.

intrínseco [in'trinseko] *adj* intrinsic.

****introducir** [introðu'θir] *v* introduce. **introducción** *sf* introduction. **introductor** *adj* introductory.

intruso [in'truso], **-a** *sm*, *sf* intruder. *adj* intrusive. **intrusarse** *v* intrude. **intrusión** *sf* intrusion.

intuición [intwi'θjon] *sf* intuition. **intuir** *v* feel; sense. **intuitivo** *adj* intuitive.

inundar [inun'dar] *v* flood. **inundación** *sf* flood. **inundante** *adj* flooding.

inusitado [inusi'taðo] *adj* unusual.

inútil [i'nutil] *adj* useless. **inutilidad** *sf* uselessness. **inutilizar** *v* render useless.

invadir [inβa'ðir] *v* invade. **invasión** *sf* invasion. **invasor**, **-a** *sm*, *sf* invader.

invalidar [inβali'ðar] *v* invalidate. **invalidación** *sf* invalidity. **inválido**, **-a** *sm*, *sf* invalid. *adj* invalid, void.

invariable [inva'rjaβle] *adj* invariable.

invencible [inβen'θiβle] *adj* invincible. **invencibilidad** *sf* invincibility.

inventar [inβen'tar] *v* invent. **invención** *sf* invention. **inventivo** *adj* inventive. **invento** *sm* invention. **inventor**, **-a** *sm*, *sf* inventor.

inventario [inβen'tarjo] *sm* inventory.

invernáculo [inβer'nakulo] *sm also* **invernadero** greenhouse, hothouse.

****invernar** [inβer'nar] *v* winter; hibernate. **invernada** *sf* winter; hibernation. **invernal** *adj* wintry.

inverosímil [inβero'simil] *adj* improbable. **inverosimilitud** *sf* improbability.

invertebrado [inβerte'βraðo] *sm*, *adj* invertebrate.

****invertir** [inβer'tir] *v* invert; (*com*) invest. **inversión** *sf* inversion; investment. **inverso** *adj* inverse, inverted. **por la inversa** the other way round.

investigar [inβesti'gar] *v* investigate. **investigación** *sf* investigation. **investigador**, **-a** *sm*, *sf* investigator; researcher.

****investir** [inβes'tir] *v* invest; confer upon. **investidura** *sf* investiture.

inveterado [inβete'raðo] *adj* inveterate, confirmed.

invicto [in'βikto] *adj* undefeated.

invierno [in'βjerno] *sm* winter.

inviolable [inβjo'laβle] *adj* inviolable. **inviolado** *adj* inviolate.

invisible [inβi'siβle] *adj* invisible. **invisibilidad** *sf* invisibility.

invitar [inβi'tar] *v* invite; call on. **invitar a una copa** stand a drink. **invitación** *sf* invitation. **invitado**, **-a** *sm*, *sf* guest.

invocar [inβo'kar] *v* invoke. **invocación** *sf* invocation.

involuntario [inβolun'tarjo] *adj* involuntary.

invulnerable [inβulne'raβle] *adj* invulnerable. **invulnerabilidad** *sf* invulnerability.

inyectar [injek'tar] *v* inject. **inyección** *sf* injection. **inyectado** *adj* congested.

****ir** [ir] *v* go; walk; come; suit. **irse** *v* go away. **ir a medias** go halves. **ir tirando** get by.

ira ['ira] *sf* anger. **iracundia** *sf* wrath. **iracundo** *adj* wrathful.

iris ['iris] *sm* (*anat*) iris. **arco iris** *sm* rainbow.

Irlanda [ir'landa] *sf* Ireland. **irlandés** *adj* Irish. *sm* Irishman; (*idioma*) Irish. **irlandesa** *sf* Irishwoman.

ironía [iro'nia] *sf* irony. **irónico** *adj* ironic(al).

irracional [irraθjo'nal] *adj* irrational. **irracionalidad** *sf* irrationality.

irradiar [irra'ðjar] *v* irradiate, radiate. **irradiación** *sf* irradiation.

irrazonable [irraðo'naβle] *adj* unreasonable.

irreal [irre'al] *adj* unreal. **irrealidad** *sf* unreality.

irreconciliable [irrekonθi'ljaβle] *adj* irreconcilable.

irrecuperable [irrekupe'raβle] *adj* irretrievable.

irreemplazable [irreempla'θaβle] *adj* irreplaceable.

irreflexión [irreflek'sjon] *sf* hastiness; thoughtlessness. **irreflexivo** hasty; thoughtless.

irrefrenable [irrefre'naβle] *adj* uncontrollable.

irrefutable [irrefu'taβle] *adj* irrefutable.

irregular [irregu'lar] *adj* irregular. **irregularidad** *sf* irregularity.

irreligioso [irreli'xjoso] *adj* irreligious.

irremediable [irreme'ðjaβle] *adj* incurable.

irreprimible [irrepri'miβle] *adj* irrepressible.

irresistible [irresis'tiβle] *adj* irresistible.

irresoluto [irreso'luto] *adj* irresolute. **irresoluble** *adj* unsolvable. **irresolución** *sf* irresolution, indecision.

irrespetuoso [irrespe'twoso] *adj* disrespectful.

irresponsable [irrespon'saβle] *adj* irresponsible. **irresponsabilidad** *sf* irresponsibility.

irrigar [irri'gar] *v* irrigate. **irrigación** *sf* irrigation. **irrigador** *sm* sprinkler.

irritable [irri'taβle] *adj* irritable. **irritabilidad** *sf* irritability. **irritación** *sf* irritation. **irritante** *sm, adj* irritant. **irritar** *v* irritate.

isla ['isla] *sf* island. **en isla** isolated. **isleño, -a** *sm, sf* islander.

Islandia [is'landja] *sf* Iceland. **islandés, -esa** *sm, sf* Icelander; *sm (idioma)* Icelandic. **islandés** *adj* Icelandic.

istmo ['istmo] *sm* isthmus.

Italia [i'talja] *sf* Italy. **italiano, -a** *s, adj* Italian.

itinerario [itine'rarjo] *sm* itinerary.

izar [i'θar] *v* hoist.

izquierda [iθ'kjerða] *sf* left; left hand; left wing. **mantenerse a la izquierda** keep left. **izquierdo** *adj* left; left-handed.

J

jabalí [xaβa'li] *sm* wild boar.

jabalina [xaβa'lina] *sf* javelin; (*zool*) wild sow.

jabón [xa'βon] *sm* soap. **jabón de tocador** toilet soap. **jabonar** *v* soap. **jabonera** *sf* soap-dish. **jabonoso** *adj* soapy.

jaca [xaka] *sf* pony.

jacinto [xa'θinto] *sm* hyacinth.

jactarse [xak'tarse] *v* boast. **jactancia** *sf* boasting. **jactancioso** *adj* boastful.

jadear [xaðe'ar] *v* pant. **jadeante** *adj* panting. **jadeo** *sm* pant; panting.

jalear [xale'ar] *v* urge on. **jaleo** *sm* row, din. **armar un jaleo** start a row.

jamás [xa'mas] *adv* never. **nunca jamás** never ever.

jamón [xa'mon] *sm* ham. **jamón serrano** cured ham.

Japón [xa'pon] *sm* Japan. **japonés** *s(m+f), adj* Japanese.

jaque [xake] *sm (ajedrez)* check.

jaqueca [xa'keka] *sf* migraine. **dar jaqueca a** *(fam)* pester.

jarabe [xa'raβe] *sm* syrup.

jarana [xa'rana] *sf* spree; rumpus; trick. **dar jarabe a uno** *(fam)* butter someone up.

jardín [xar'ðin] *sm* garden. **jardinería** *sf* gardening. **jardinero, -a** *sm, sf* gardener.

jarra [xarra] *sf* jug, pitcher. **jarro** *sm* jug; jar. **jarrón** *sm* vase.

jaula [xaula] *sf* cage; crate; playpen.

jazmín [xaθ'min] *sm* jasmine.

jefe ['xefe] *sm* chief; head; leader. **jefa** *sf* head; manageress. **jefatura** *sf* leadership; managership; chieftaincy. **jefatura de policía** police headquarters.

jengibre [xen'xiβre] *sm* ginger.

jeque ['xeke] *sm* sheikh.

jerarquía [xerar'kia] *sf* hierarchy. **jerárquico** *adj* hierarchical.

jerez [xe'reθ] *sm* sherry.

jerga [xerga] *sf also* **jerigonza** jargon.

jeringa [xe'ringa] *sf* syringe. **jeringar** *v* syringe; *(fam)* annoy.

jeroglífico [xero'glifiko] *s, adj* hieroglyphic.

jersey [xer'sei] *sm* jersey.

jesuita [xesu'ita] *sm, adj* Jesuit. **jesuítico** *adj* jesuitical.

jeta ['xeta] *sf* snout; thick lips; (*fam*) face, mug. **poner jeta** pull a face.

jilguero [xil'gero] *sm* goldfinch.

jinete [xi'nete] *sm* horseman; saddle horse; thoroughbred horse. **jinetear** *v* ride on horseback.

jirafa [xi'rafa] *sf* giraffe.

jocoso [xo'koso] *adj* amusing. **jocosidad** *sf* humour.

jofaina [xo'faina] *sf* washbowl.

jornada [xor'naða] *sf* journey; working day; session; expedition; (*teatro*) act. **al fin de la jornada** at the end of the day. **jornal** *sm* day's wage. **jornalero** *sm* day labourer.

joroba [xo'roβa] *sf* hump; (*fam*) pest. **jorobado, -a** *s, adj* hunchback.

jota ['xota] *sf* letter *j*; jot; Spanish dance.

joven [xoβen] *adj* young. **jovenes** *s(m+f) pl* youth.

joya ['xoja] *sf* jewel. **joyería** *sf* jewellery. **joyero** *sm* jeweller.

jubilar [xuβi'lar] *v* retire; pension off. **jubilarse** *v* retire; rejoice. **jubilación** *sf* pension; retirement; jubilation.

jubileo [xuβi'leo] *sm* jubilee; comings and goings *pl*.

júbilo ['xuβilo] *sm* jubilation, rejoicing. **jubiloso** *adj* jubilant.

judía [xu'ðia] *sf* bean. **judía blanca** haricot bean. **judía escarlata** runner bean. **judía verde** French bean.

judicial [xuði'θjal] *adj* judicial. **judicatura** *sf* judicature.

judío [xu'ðio], **-a** *sm, sf* Jew. *adj* Jewish. **judaico** *adj* Jewish. **judaísmo** *sm* Judaism.

juego ['xwego] *sm* game; sport; gambling; play; (*platos, tazas, etc.*) set; service.

juerga ['xwerga] *sf* (*fam*) spree, binge. **juergista** *s(m+f)* reveller.

jueves ['xweβes] *sm* Thursday.

juez [xweθ] *sm* judge, justice. **juez de hecho** juror.

*****jugar** [xu'gar] *v* play; bet; gamble. **jugarse** *v* bet; risk. **jugada** move; throw; stroke; shot; play. **mala jugada** dirty trick. **jugador, -a** *sm, sf* player; gambler.

juglar [xu'glar], **-a** *sm, sf* minstrel.

jugo ['xugo] *sm* juice; sap. **jugoso** *adj* juicy.

juguete [xu'gete] *sm* toy; plaything. **juguetear** *v* frolic. **jugueteo** *sm* frolicking. **juguetería** *sf* toyshop.

juicio [xwiθjo] *sm* (*jur*) trial; judgment;

opinion; sense. **a juicio de** in the opinion of. **perder el juicio** lose one's mind. **juicioso** *adj* judicious.

julio ['xuljo] *sm* July.

jumento [xu'mento] *sm* ass.

junco[1] ['xunko] *sm* (*bot*) reed.

junco[2] *sm* (*mar*) junk.

jungla ['xungla] *sf* jungle.

junio ['xunjo] *sm* June.

junquera [xun'kera] *sf* (*bot*) rush.

junquillo [xun'kiʎo] *sm* (*bot*) jonquil.

juntar [xun'tar] *v* join; assemble; unite; collect. **juntarse** *v* meet; join; gather; live together. **junta** *sf* meeting; session; board; council; junta. **junto, -a** *adj* joined, united, together. *adv* **junto a** near. **muy junto** very close.

juramentar [xuramen'tar] *v* swear in. **juramentarse** *v* take an oath. **jura** *sf* oath; swearing. **jurado** *adj* sworn; *sm* jury. **jurado de cuentas** chartered accountant. **juramento** *sm* oath; curse. **juramento falso** perjury. **jurar** *v* swear. **jurar al cargo** take the oath of office.

jurídico [xu'riðiko] *adj* juridical, legal. **jurisconsulto** [xuriskon'sulto] *sm* legal expert. **jurisdicción** *sf* jurisdiction. **jurisprudencia** *sf* jurisprudence. **jurista** *sm* jurist, lawyer.

justa ['xusta] *sf* joust; contest.

justificar [xustifi'kar] *v* justify. **justificarse** *v* clear oneself. **justamente** *adv* justly; exactly. **¡justamente!** precisely! **justicia** *sf* justice; execution. **justiciable** *adj* actionable. **justiciero** *adj* just. **justificable** *adj* justifiable. **justificación** *sf* justification. **justificado** *adj* justified.

justo ['xusto] *adj* just; lawful; precise. *adv* exactly; tightly.

juvenil [xuβe'nil] *adj* youthful. *s(m+f)* junior. **juventud** *sf* youth.

juzgar [xuθ'gar] *v* judge; consider. **juzgar mal** misjudge. **juzgado** *sm* court.

K

kaki ['kaki] *sm, adj* khaki.

kilo ['kilo] *sm* kilo.

kilogramo [kilo'gramo] *sm* kilogramme.

kilolitro [kilo'litro] *sm* kilolitre.

kilómetro [ki'lometro] *sm* kilometre.
kilométrico *adj* kilometric.
kilovatio [kilo'βatjo] *sm* kilowatt.
kiosco ['kjosko] *sm* kiosk.

L

la [la] *art f* the. *pron* her, it.
laberinto [laβe'rinto] *sm* labyrinth; maze.
labio ['laβjo] *sm* lip. **labial** *adj* labial.
labor [la'βor] *sf* work; labour. **laborador** *sm* worker; farmer. **laborar** *v* work; till. **laborear** *v* work; till; mine. **laboreo** *sm* working; tilling; mining. **laborioso** *adj* industrious; laborious. **laborismo** *sm* (*pol*) Labour party. **laborista** *s(m+f)* Labour-party member.
laboratorio [laβora'torjo] *sm* laboratory.
labrar [la'βrar] *v* fashion; carve; work; cultivate; build; bring about. **labrable** *adj* workable; arable. **labrador, -a** *sm, sf* peasant. **labranza** *sf* farming; farmland. **labriego** *sm* peasant; farmhand.
laburno [la'βurno] *sm* laburnum.
laca ['laka] *sf* lacquer, varnish.
lacayo [la'kajo] *sm* lackey.
lacerar [laθe'rar] *v* lacerate; harm; (*fruta*) damage. **laceración** *sf* laceration; damage.
lacio ['laθjo] *adj* limp; lank; withered.
lacónico [la'koniko] *adj* laconic.
lacrar [la'krar] *v* infect; damage. **lacra** *sf* blemish.
lacrar *v* seal. **lacre** *sm* sealing wax.
lacrimoso [lakri'moso] *adj* tearful.
lácteo ['lakteo] *adj* milky. **vía láctea** *sf* Milky Way. **productos lácteos** *sm pl* dairy products. **lactante** *adj* suckling; nursling. **lactar** *v* suckle.
ladear [lade'ar] *v* tip, tilt, overturn; deviate; skirt. **ladeo** *sm* tipping, tilting.
ladera [la'ðera] *sf* slope; hillside.
ladino [la'ðino] *adj* multilingual; crafty.
lado ['laðo] *sm* side; way; space; direction; protection. **al lado** close. **al lado de** beside. **por el lado de** in the direction of.
ladrar [la'ðrar] *v* bark. **ladrido** *sm* bark; barking.
ladrillo [la'ðriʎo] *sm* brick, tile.
ladrón [la'ðron]. **-a** *sm, sf* thief, robber. *sm* sluice gate; multiple socket.

lagarto [la'garto] *sm* lizard.
lago ['lago] *sm* lake.
lágrima ['lagrima] *sf* tear; drop. **verter lágrimas** shed tears. **lagrimoso** *adj* tearful.
laguna [la'guna] *sf* lagoon; pond; gap.
laico ['laiko] *adj* lay, secular.
lamentar [lamen'tar] *v* lament; regret; grieve. **lamentarse** *v* complain. **lamentable** *adj* deplorable. **lamentación** *sf* lamentation, lament. **lamento** *sm* lament; mourning. **lamentoso** *adj* lamentable, mournful.
lamer [la'mer] *v* lick.
lámina ['lamina] *sf* metal sheet; picture; engraving. **laminar** *v* laminate.
lámpara ['lampara] *sf* lamp; light; valve.
lana ['lana] *sf* wool; fleece. **lana de vidrio** fibreglass. **lanudo** *adj* woolly; shaggy.
lance ['lanθe] *sm* throw; event; move; stroke. **lance de fortuna** chance. **de lance** second-hand.
lanceta [lan'θeta] *sf* lancet.
lancha ['lantʃa] *sf* launch; flagstone. **lancha salvavidas** lifeboat. **lanchero** *sm* boatman.
langosta [lan'gosta] *sf* lobster; locust.
*****languidecer** [langiðe'θer] *v* languish. **languidez** *sf* languour. **lánguido** *adj* languid.
lanza ['lanθa] *sf* spear; lance; pike; nozzle.
lanzar [lan'θar] *v* throw; fling; evict. **lanzarse** *v* spring. **lanzamiento** *sm* launching.
lápida ['lapiða] *sf* stone slab; tablet.
lápiz ['lapiθ] *sm* pencil. **lapicero** *sm* pencil-holder.
lapso ['lapso] *sm* lapse.
lar [lar] *sm* hearth; home.
largar [lar'gar] *v* loosen; free. **largarse** *v* go away.
largo ['largo] *adj* long; (*fam*) generous. *sm* length. **a lo largo de** the length of. **dar largas** a delay. **largueza** *sf* length; generosity.
laringe [la'rinxe] *sf* larynx.
larva ['larβa] *sf* larva.
lascivo [las'θiβo] *adj* lascivious. **lascivia** *sf* lasciviousness.
laso ['laso] *adj* weary. **lasitud** *sf* lassitude.
lástima ['lastima] *sf* pity; complaint. **¡qué lástima!** what a pity! **lastimar** *v* hurt. **lastimarse** *v* pity; complain. **lastimoso** *adj* pitiable, pitiful.

lastre ['lastre] *sm* ballast.

lata ['lata] *sf* tin, can; (*fam*) nuisance. **dar la lata** (*fam*) pester.

latente [la'tente] *adj* latent.

lateral [late'ral] *adj* lateral, side.

látigo ['latigo] *sm* whip. **latigazo** *sm* whip-lash.

latín [la'tin] *sm* Latin. **latinoamericano, -a** *s, adj* Latin American.

latir [la'tir] *v* beat; throb. **latido** *sm* heart-beat; throb.

latitud [lati'tuð] *sf* latitude; breadth. **lato** *adj* broad.

latón [la'ton] *sm* brass.

latoso [la'toso] *adj* (*fam*) annoying; boring.

latrocinio [latro'θinjo] *sm* theft.

laúd [la'uð] *sm* lute.

laudable [lau'ðaβle] *adj* praiseworthy.

laurel [lau'rel] *sm* laurel; laurel wreath. **laureado** *adj* laureate. **laurear** *v* honour; reward. **lauro** *sm* (*fig*) glory.

lava ['laβa] *sf* lava.

lavar [la'βar] *v* wash. **lavable** *adj* washable. **lavabo** *sm* wash-basin. **lavación** *sf* lotion; wash. **lavadero** *sm* washing-place. **lavado** *sm* wash; washing. **lavadora** *sf* washing machine. **lavandería** *sf* laundry.

laxante [lak'sante] *sm* laxative. **laxidad** *sf* laxity.

lazo ['laθo] *sm* lasso; loop; bow; knot; snare; link.

leal [le'al] *adj* loyal. **lealdad** *sf* loyalty.

lebrel [le'βrel] *sm* greyhound.

lección [lek'θjon] *sf* lesson. **lector, -a** *sm, sf* reader; lecturer. **lectura** *sf* reading matter.

leche ['letʃe] *sf* milk. **lechería** *sf* dairy. **lechero** *sm* milkman.

lecho ['letʃo] *sm* bed; layer.

lechuga [le'tʃuga] *sf* lettuce.

lechuza [le'tʃuθa] *sf* owl.

***leer** [le'er] *v* read.

legación [lega'θjon] *sf* legation. **legado** *sm* legacy; ambassador.

legal [le'gal] *adj* legal; lawful. **legalidad** *sf* legality. **legalización** *sf* legalization. **legalizar** *v* legalize.

legar [le'gar] *v* bequeath; depute.

legendario [lexen'darjo] *adj* legendary.

legible [le'xiβle] *adj* legible.

legión [le'xjon] *sf* legion.

legislar [lexis'lar] *v* legislate. **legislación** *sf* legislation. **legislador, -a** *sm, sf* legislator.

legislativo *adj* legislative. **legislatura** *sf* legislature.

legitimar [lexiti'mar] *v* prove; justify. **legitimidad** *sf* legitimacy. **legítimo** *adj* legitimate.

lego ['lego] *adj* lay. *sm* layman.

legua ['legwa] *sf* league.

legumbre [le'gumbre] *sf* vegetable.

lejía [le'xia] *sf* bleach.

lejos ['lexos] *adv* far away. **a lo lejos** in the distance. *sm* perspective; background. **lejanía** *sf* distance. **lejano** *adj* far-away.

lema ['lema] *sf* motto.

lencería [lenθe'ria] *sf* linen goods; lingerie.

lengua ['lengwa] *sf* tongue; language. **trabarse la lengua** become tongue-tied. **lenguaje** *sm* language; speech; style. **lenguado** [len'gwaðo] *sm* (*zool*) sole. **lengüeta** [len'gweta] *sf* (*de zapato*) tongue. **lenidad** [leni'ðað] *sf* lenience; mildness.

lente ['lente] *s(m+f)* lens. **lente de aumento** magnifying glass. **lentes** *pl* glasses, spectacles. **lentes de contacto** contact lenses.

lenteja [len'texa] *sf* lentil.

lento ['lento] *adj* slow. **lentitud** *sf* slowness.

leña ['leɲa] *sf* firewood.

león [le'on] *sm* lion. **leona** *sf* lioness. **leonino** *adj* leonine.

lepra ['lepra] *sf* leprosy. **leproso** *adj* leprous.

lesión [le'sjon] *sf* injury. **lesionar** *v* injure. **lesivo** *adj* injurious.

letanía [leta'nia] *sf* litany; long list.

letargo [le'targo] *sm* lethargy. **letárgico** *adj* lethargic.

letra ['letra] *sf* letter; handwriting; lyric; (*com*) draft. **Letras** *sf pl* literature; Arts. **letra mayúscula** capital letter. **letra minúscula** lower-case letter. **letrado** *sm* lawyer. **letrero** *sm* label; sign.

leva ['leβa] *sf* (*tecn*) cam; lever. **árbol de levas** camshaft.

levadizo [leβa'ðiθo] *adj* that can be lifted. **puente levadizo** *sm* drawbridge.

levadura [leβa'ðura] *sf* leaven, yeast.

levantar [leβan'tar] *v* lift; raise; erect. **levantarse** *v* rise, get up. **levantamiento** *sm* raising; insurrection. **levantado** *adj* raised; lofty.

leve ['leβe] *adj* slight; trifling. **levedad** *sf* lightness; slightness.

léxico ['leksiko] *adj* lexical. *sm* dictionary; vocabulary.

ley [lej] *sf* law; loyalty; standard. **a toda ley** according to rule. **tener ley a** be very fond of.

leyenda [le'jenda] *sf* legend.

liar [ljar] *v* bind; tie up; *(fam)* involve. **liarlas** *v* *(fam)* clear off. **liarse** *v* *(fam)* join; start an affair; get involved.

libélula [li'βelula] *sf* dragonfly.

liberal [liβe'ral] *adj* generous. **liberalidad** *sf* generosity.

libertar [liβer'tar] *v also* **liberar** liberate, free. **libertad** *sf* freedom; independence. **libertador, -a** *sm, sf* liberator.

libertinaje [liβerti'naxe] *sm* licentiousness. **libertino, -a** *s, adj* libertine.

libra ['liβra] *sf* (*peso*) pound. **libra esterlina** pound sterling.

librar [li'βrar] *v* free; exempt; deliver; despatch; expedite; *(com)* draw; pass sentence. **librador, -a** *sm, sf* liberator. **libramiento** *sm* delivery; rescue; *(com)* draft. **libranza** *sf (com)* draft. **libre** *adj* free; vacant; isolated; loose.

librería [liβre'ria] *sf* bookshop; bookselling; bookcase. **librero, -a** *sm, sf* bookseller.

libreta [li'βreta] *sf* notebook; cashbook; one-pound loaf.

libro ['liβro] *sm* book. **libro diario** journal. **libro mayor** ledger.

licenciar [liβen'θjar] *v* license. **licenciarse** *v* graduate. **licencia** *sf* licence; degree; *(mil)* leave. **licenciado, -a** *sm, sf* graduate; *sm* lawyer; discharged soldier. **licenciatura** *sf* Bachelor's degree.

licencioso [liβen'θjoso] *adj* licentious.

liceo [li'θeo] *sm* lyceum; secondary school.

licitar [liθi'tar] *v* (*subasta*) bid. **licitación** *sf* bid. **licitador, -a** *sm, sf* bidder.

lícito [li'θito] *adj* authorized.

licor [li'kor] *sm* liquor; liqueur.

líder [li'ðer] *sm* leader.

lidiar [li'ðjar] *v* (*toros*) fight. **lidia** *sf* bullfight. **lidiador** *sm* bullfighter.

liebre ['ljeβre] *sf* hare. **coger una liebre** *(fam)* come a cropper.

lienzo [li'jenθo] *sm* canvas; linen.

liga ['liga] *sf* garter; league; alloy. **ligadura** *sf* ligature; bond. **ligamento** *sm* ligament; bond. **ligar** *v* bind; tie; unite; alloy. **ligarse** *v* join; band together.

ligero [li'xero] *adj* light; swift; frivolous.

ligereza *sf* lightness; swiftness; frivolousness.

lija ['lixa] *sf* sandpaper; (*zool*) dogfish. **lijar** *v* sandpaper.

lila ['lila] *sf (bot)* lilac. *sm (color)* lilac. *adj (fam)* foolish.

lima[1] ['lima] *sf* file; polish. **limar** *v* file; polish; undermine. **limadura** *sf* filing.

lima[2] *sf* lime; lime tree.

limaza [li'maθa] *sf* slug.

limitar [limi'tar] *v* limit. **limitación** *sf* limitation. **límite** *sm* limit; boundary.

limón [li'mon] *sm* lemon; lemon tree. **limonada** *sf* lemonade. **limonero** *sm* lemon tree.

limosna [li'mosna] *sf* alms *pl*.

limpiabotas [limpja'βotas] *sm invar* bootblack.

limpiadera [limpja'ðera] *sf* clothes brush. **limpiadientes** [limpja'ðjentes] *sm invar* toothpick.

limpiar [lim'pjar] *v* clean; wipe; prune; weed. **limpiador, -a** *sm, sf* cleaner. **limpiadura** *sf* cleaning. **limpieza** *sf* cleanness. **limpio** *adj* clean; clear; pure. **jugar limpio** play fair. **poner en limpio** copy out.

linaje [li'naxe] *sm* lineage. **linaje humano** mankind.

linaza [li'naθa] *sf* linseed.

lince [li'nθe] *sm* lynx.

linchar [lin'tʃar] *v* lynch. **linchamiento** *sm* lynching.

lindar [lin'dar] *v* **lindar con** border; adjoin. **linde** *sf* boundary. **lindero** *sm* limit.

lindo ['lindo] *adj* pretty; handsome; nice. **de lo lindo** a great deal. **lindeza** *sf* beauty; niceness. **lindura** *sf* prettiness.

línea ['linea] *sf* line; boundary; class. **línea aérea** airline. **lineal** *adj* linear.

lingüista [lin'gwista] *s(m+f)* linguist. **lingüística** *sf* linguistics. **lingüístico** *adj* linguistic.

linimento [lini'mento] *sm* liniment.

lino ['lino] *sm* linen.

linóleo [li'noleo] *sm* linoleum.

linterna [lin'terna] *sf* lantern; lamp; torch; lighthouse.

lío ['lio] *sm* parcel; trouble; mess. **armar un lío** raise a rumpus.

liquidar [liki'ðar] *v* liquefy; liquidate, settle up. **liquidez** *sf* fluidity. **líquido** *sm, adj* liquid; *(com)* net. **líquido imponible** net taxable amount.

lira ['lira] sf lyre; inspiration.

lírica ['lirika] sf lyric poetry. **lírico** adj lyric.

lirio ['lirjo] sm lily.

lirón [li'ron] sm dormouse. **dormir como un lirón** sleep like a log.

lisiar [li'sjar] v cripple. **lisiado** adj crippled.

liso ['liso] adj smooth.

lisonjear [lisonxe'ar] v flatter. **lisonja** sf flattery. **lisonjero** adj flattering.

lista ['lista] sf list; stripe; band. **a listas** striped. **lista de correos** poste restante. **lista de platos** menu.

listo ['listo] adj ready; finished; clever.

litera [li'tera] sf berth; bunk; (cama) litter.

literato [lite'rato], -a sm, sf literary person. adj literary. **literatura** sf literature.

litigar [liti'gar] v go to law, litigate. **litigación** sf litigation. **litigio** sm lawsuit. **litigioso** adj contentious.

litografía [lito'grafja] sf lithograph; lithography. **litográfico** adj lithographic.

litoral [lito'ral] adj coastal. sm shore.

litro ['litro] sm litre.

liturgia [litur'xja] sf liturgy. **litúrgico** adj liturgical.

liviano [li'βjano] adj light; trivial; lewd. **liviandad** sf lightness; triviality; lewdness.

lívido [li'βiðo] adj livid.

lo [lo] art m him, it; that, what.

loable [lo'aβle] adj praiseworthy. **loa** sf praise. **loador** adj praising. **loar** v praise.

lobo ['loβo] sm wolf. **lobo marino** seal. **lobero** adj wolfish.

lóbrego [lo'βrego] adj gloomy, murky. **lobreguecer** v darken; grow dark. **lobreguez** sf gloom; murk.

lóbulo [lo'βulo] sm lobe.

local [lo'kal] adj local. sm place. **localidad** sf locality; (teatro) seat. **sacar localidades** get tickets. **localizar** v localize.

loción [lo'θjon] sf lotion.

loco ['loko], -a adj mad; excessive. sm, sf mad person. **volverse loco** go mad. **locura** sf madness; folly. **hacer locuras** act madly.

locomoción [lokomo'θjon] sf locomotion. **locomotora** sf locomotive.

locuaz [lo'kwaθ] adj talkative. **locuacidad** sf talkativeness.

locutor [loku'tor], -a sm, sf radio announcer; commentator.

lodo ['loðo] sm mud. **lodoso** adj muddy.

lógica ['loxika] sf logic. **lógico** adj logical. **lógicamente** adv logically; naturally. **logística** sf logistics.

lograr [lo'grar] v get; achieve. **lograrse** v succeed. **logrería** sf profiteering. **logro** sm success; profit; usury.

loma ['loma] sf hill; slope.

lombriz [lom'briθ] sf worm; earthworm. **lombriz solitaria** tapeworm.

lomo ['lomo] sm (carne) loin; (animal) back; (libro) spine.

lona ['lona] sf canvas.

Londres ['londres] sm London.

longaniza [longa'niθa] sf pork sausage.

longevidad [lonxeβi'ðað] sf longevity.

longitud [lonxi'tuð] sf longitude. **longitudinal** adj longitudinal.

lonja ['lonxa] sf (de carne) slice; grocer's shop; strap; church porch.

loro ['loro] sm parrot.

losa ['losa] sf stone slab; tile.

lote ['lote] sm (com) lot; share; prize.

loza ['loθa] sf crockery; pottery.

lozano [lo'θano] adj luxuriant; lush; robust; sprightly. **lozanía** sf luxuriance.

lubrificar [luβrifi'kar] v also **lubricar** lubricate. **lubricación** sf also **lubrificación** lubrication. **lubricante** sm, adj also **lubrificante** lubricant.

lúcido [lu'θiðo] adj lucid; shining. **lucidez** sf lucidity; brilliance.

luciérnaga [lu'θjernaga] sf glow-worm.

*lucir [lu'θir] v shine; gleam; excel; show off. **lucirse** v be successful; dress up.

lucro ['lukro] sm profit, gain. **lucros y daños** profit and loss.

luchar [lu'tʃar] v fight, struggle. **lucha** sf fight, struggle. **lucha libre** all-in wrestling. **luchador, -a** sm, sf fighter.

luego ['lwego] adv then; next; later; presently. conj as; therefore. **luego que** as soon as. **desde luego** of course. **hasta luego** so long.

lugar [lu'gar] sm place; occasion; chance; opportunity. **en lugar de** instead of. **tener lugar** take place.

lugarteniente [lugarte'njente] sm lieutenant.

lúgubre ['luguβre] adj lugubrious.

lujo ['luxo] sm luxury. **de lujo** de luxe. **lujoso** adj luxurious.

lujuria [lu'xurja] sf lust; lechery. **lujuriar** v lust. **lujurioso** adj lustful; lecherous.

lumbago [lum'bago] *sm* lumbago.
lumbre ['lumbre] *sf* fire; brightness; light; skylight. **echar lumbres** spark. **lumbrera** *sf* luminary; skylight; air vent; *(fig)* leading light.
luminoso [lumi'noso] *adj* bright; luminous.
luna ['luna] *sf* moon. **luna de miel** honeymoon. **lunar** *adj* lunar. **lunático, -a** *s, adj* lunatic.
lunar [lu'nar] *sm* mole; beauty spot; blemish.
lunes ['lunes] *sm* Monday.
lupa ['lupa] *sf* magnifying glass.
lupanar [lupa'nar] *sm* brothel.
lustrar [lus'trar] *v* polish; purify. **lustre** *sm* lustre; gloss; splendour.
luto ['luto] *sm* mourning; bereavement. **ir de luto** be in mourning.
Luxemburgo [luksem'burgo] *sm* Luxembourg.
luz [luθ] *sf* light; daylight; window. **a todas luces** clearly. **dar la luz** put the light on.

LL

llaga ['ʎaga] *sf* ulcer; sore; wound. **llagar** *v* ulcerate; wound.
llama[1] ['ʎama] *sf (fuego)* flame. **estar en llamas** burst into flames. **llamear** *v* blaze.
llama[2] *sf (pantano)* swamp.
llama[3] *sf (zool)* llama.
llamar [ʎa'mar] *v* call; appeal to; name; attract. **llamarse** *v* be called. ¿**cómo se llama?** what is your name? **llamado** *adj* so-called. **llamada** *sf* call; summons. **llamador** -a *sm, sf* caller; messenger.
llana ['ʎana] *sf* trowel.
llano ['ʎano] *adj* flat; plain; straightforward. **número llano** Roman numeral. *sm* plain; flatness. **llanura** *sf* evenness; flat land.
llanta ['ʎanta] *sf* iron hoop; rim.
llanto ['ʎanto] *sm* lament; crying.
llave ['ʎaβe] *sf* key; spanner. **llave maestra** skeleton key. **llave inglesa** adjustable spanner.
llegar [ʎe'gar] *v* arrive; reach; suffice;

happen. **llegarse** *v* come or go round. **llegar a** end up at. **llegar a ser** become. **llegada** *sf* arrival. **a la llegada** on arrival.
llenar [ʎe'nar] *v* fill; be satisfied. **lleno** *adj* full; covered; complete. **de lleno** completely. **llenura** *sf* abundance.
llevar [ʎe'βar] *v* take; carry; wear; deal with; sever; charge; manage; *(tiempo)* spend. **llevar a cabo** carry out. **llevarse** *v* take away. **llevarse bien con** get on well with.
llorar [ʎo'rar] *v* weep, cry; mourn. **llorón, -ona** *adj* weepy. **lloroso** *adj* tearful.
llover [ʎo'βer] *v* rain. **llover a cántaros** pour down. **lloverse** *v (tejado)* leak. **llovizna** *v* drizzle. **llovizna** *sf* drizzle. **lluvia** *sf* rain. **lluvioso** *adj* rainy.

M

macabro [ma'kaβro] *adj* macabre.
macarrón [makar'ron] *sm* macaroon. **macarrones** *sm pl* macaroni *sing*.
macanudo [maka'nuðo] *adj (fam)* terrific.
maceta [ma'θeta] *sf* flowerpot.
macilento [maθi'lento] *adj* lean; wan.
macizo [ma'θiθo] *adj* solid. *sm* mass; flowerbed. **macizar** *v* fill up.
mácula ['makula] *sf* spot, stain. **macular** *v* spot, stain.
machacar [matʃa'kar] *v* pound; crush; bombard; *(fig)* harp on. **machacón, -ona** *sm, sf* bore; swot. **machaconería** *sf* tiresomeness. **machaqueo** *sm* pounding; crushing; harping.
machete [ma'tʃete] *sm* machete; hunting-knife.
macho ['matʃo] *adj* male; masculine; virile. *sm (fam)* he-man; sledgehammer; he-mule. **machismo** *sm* virility.
machucar [matʃu'kar] *v* beat; pound; bruise.
madeja [ma'ðexa] *sf* skein; mop of hair.
madera [ma'ðera] *sf* wood; timber; horn. **tener madera de** have the makings of. **maderería** *sf* timber yard. **madero** *sm* beam; log.
madrastra [ma'ðrastra] *sf* stepmother.
madre ['maðre] *sf* mother. **madre política** mother-in-law.

madreselva [maðre'selβa] *sf* honeysuckle.

madriguera [maðri'gera] *sf* den; warren.

madrina [ma'ðrina] *sf* godmother; patroness. **madrina de boda** bridesmaid.

madrugar [maðru'gar] *v* rise early. **madrugada** *sf* early morning. **madrugador, -a** *sm, sf* early riser.

madurar [maðu'rar] *v* mature, ripen. **madurez** *sf* maturity; wisdom. **maduro** *adj* ripe; middle-aged.

maestría [maes'tria] *sf* mastery. **maestrar** *v* direct; conduct; domineer. **maestra** *sf* mistress; schoolmistress. **maestro** *sm* master; teacher; *adj* master, main, chief. **magistral** *adj* masterly.

magia ['maxja] *sf* magic. **mágico** *adj* magic(al). **magico** *sm* magician.

magistrado [maxi'straðo] *sm* magistrate. **magistratura** *sf* judicature.

magnánimo [mag'nanimo] *adj* magnanimous. **magnanimidad** *sf* magnanimity.

magnético [mag'netiko] *adj* magnetic. **magnetismo** *sm* magnetism. **magnetizar** *v* magnetize.

magnetofón [magneto'fon] *sm also* **magnetófono** tape recorder. **cinta magnetofónica** recording tape.

magnífico [mag'nifiko] *adj* magnificent. **magnificencia** *sf* magnificence.

magnitud [magni'tuð] *sf* size, magnitude.

mago ['mago] *sm* magician, wizard.

magro ['magro] *adj* thin, lean. *sm* lean meat.

magullar [magu'ʎar] *v* bruise. **magulladura** *sf* bruise.

maíz [ma'iθ] *sm* maize. **harina de maíz** *sf* cornflour.

majadero [maxa'ðero] *adj* silly; boring. *sm* pestle. **majadería** *sf* nonsense. **majadura** *sf* crushing, pounding. **majar** *v* crush, pound.

majestad [maxes'tað] *sf* majesty; royalty; grandeur. **majestuoso** *adj* majestic; stately; solemn.

majo ['maxo], **-a** *sm, sf* dandy. *adj* sporty; swaggering; genial.

mal [mal] *adj V* **malo**. *adv* badly; poorly; wrongly. *sm* wrong; evil; illness; harm. **de mal en peor** from bad to worse. **echar a mal** despise; waste. **llevar a mal** take offence at. **mal que bien** somehow or other.

malaconsejado [malakonse'xaðo] *adj* ill-advised.

malacostumbrado [malakostum'braðo] *adj* spoiled.

malaventura [malaβen'tura] *sf* misfortune. **malaventurado** *adj* unlucky.

malbaratar [malβara'tar] *v* squander; undersell.

malcontento [malkon'tento], **-a** *sm, sf* malcontent. *adj* discontented.

malcriado [malkri'aðo] *adj* ill-bred. **malcriar** *v* spoil.

maldad [mal'ðað] *sf* wickedness.

***maldecir** [malðe'θir] *v* curse. **maldecir de** speak ill of. **maldición** *sf* curse. **maldito** *adj* accursed.

maleable [male'aβle] *adj* malleable. **maleabilidad** *sf* malleability.

malear [male'ar] *v* damage; spoil. **malearse** *v* go wrong.

maleficio [male'fiðjo] *sm* injury; witchcraft. **maleficiar** *v* hurt; bewitch.

malestar [males'tar] *sm* uneasiness.

maleta [ma'leta] *sf* suitcase; (*auto*) trunk. **hacer la maleta** pack up.

malévolo [ma'leβolo] *adj* malevolent. **malevolencia** *sf* malevolence.

maleza [ma'leθa] *sf* thicket; weeds *pl*.

malgastar [malgas'tar] *v* squander, waste. **malgastador, -a** *s, adj* spendthrift.

malhablado [mala'βlaðo] *adj* foulmouthed.

malhechor [male'tʃor], **-a** *sm, sf* wrongdoer. **malhecho** *sm* misdeed.

malhumorado [malumo'raðo] *adj* ill-tempered.

malicia [ma'liθja] *sf* malice; slyness; mischievousness. **maliciable** *adj* suspicious. **maliciarse** *v* go bad. **malicioso** *adj* malicious; shrewd; sly.

maligno [ma'ligno] *adj* malignant; malicious. **malignidad** *sf* malignity; malice.

malintencionado [malintenθjo'naðo] *adj* ill-disposed.

malo ['malo] *adj also* **mal** bad; evil; wrong; poor; difficult; sick. **estar malo** be ill. **mala fama** ill fame. **venir de malas** have bad intentions.

malograr [malo'grar] *v* waste; miss. **malograrse** *v* fail; fall through. **malogrado** *adj* abortive. **malogro** *sm* failure.

***malquerer** [malke'rer] *v* hate. **malquerencia** *sf* ill-will; hatred.

malsano [mal'sano] *adj* unhealthy; sick; insanitary.

malta ['malta] *sf* malt.

Malta ['malta] *sf* Malta. **maltés, -esa** *s, adj* Maltese; *sm (idioma)* Maltese.

maltratar [maltra'tar] *v* ill-treat. **maltraer** *v* hurt; abuse. **maltrato** *sm* ill-treatment.

malva ['malβa] *sf* mallow. **malva real** hollyhock.

malvado [mal'βaðo], **-a** *sm, sf* evildoer. *adj* wicked.

malla ['maʎa] *sf* mesh; network; (*de metal*) mail. **mallas** *sf pl* tights.

mallo ['maʎo] *smí* mallet.

mamá [ma'ma] *sf also* **mama** mum(my), mother.

mamar [ma'mar] *v* suck; acquire. **mamarse** *v* get drunk; fiddle, wangle. **mamoso** *adj* sucking.

mamífero [ma'mifero] *sm* mammal.

mampostería [mamposte'ria] *sf* masonry. **mampuesto** *sm* rubble.

manada [ma'naða] *sf* herd, flock; crowd. **manadero** *sm* herdsman; shepherd.

manantial [manan'tjal] *sm* spring; source, origin. **manar** *v* flow; issue.

mancebo [man'θeβo] *sm* youth; shop assistant; bachelor.

manco ['manko] *adj* one-handed; one-armed; crippled; faulty. **mancar** *v* cripple.

mancomunar [mankomu'nar] *v* join, unite. **mancomún** *adv* jointly. **mancomunarse** *v* merge. **mancomunidad** *sf* association, confederation.

manchar [man'tʃar] *v* stain; mark. **mancha** *sf* stain; mark; dishonour.

mandar [man'dar] *v* order; command; send; bequeath. **mandarse** *v* manage by oneself. **mandadero, -a** *sm, sf* messenger. **mandado** *sm* order; errand. **mandamiento** *sm* commandment, order.

mandatario [manda'tarjo] *sm* attorney; agent; mandatary. **mandato** *sm* commandment; mandate. **mandato judicial** writ.

mandíbula [man'diβula] *sf* jawbone.

mando ['mando] *sm* command; power; authority.

manejar [mane'xar] *v* operate; handle; manage. **manejable** *adj* manageable. **manejo** *sm* operation; handling; control; stratagem.

manera [ma'nera] *sf* manner; mode; way; fashion. **a manera de** by way of. **de ninguna manera** by no means. **de todas maneras** by all means. **manera de ver** outlook.

manga ['manga] *sf* sleeve; hosepipe; waterspout. **manga de agua** shower. **manga de viento** whirlwind. **manguera** *sf* garden hose.

mango[1] ['mango] *sm (bot)* mango.

mango[2] *sm* handle; stock.

manía [ma'nia] *sf* mania, craze. **maníaco** *adj, sm* maniac.

maniatar [manja'tar] *v* manacle.

manicomio [mani'komjo] *sm* lunatic asylum.

***manifestar** [manifes'tar] *v* show; declare; manifest. **manifestación** *sf* manifestation. **manifestante** *s(m+f)* demonstrator. **manifiesto** *adj* clear, evident. **manifiesto** *sm* manifesto.

maniobrar [manjo'βrar] *v* manoeuvre; operate; manipulate; plot. **maniobra** *sf* manoeuvre; stratagem; handling.

manipular [manipu'lar] *v* manipulate. **manipulación** *sf* manipulation. **manipulador, -a** *sm, sf* manipulator.

maniquí [mani'ki] *sm* tailor's dummy; puppet; *sf* mannequin; model.

manivela [mani'βela] *sf (auto)* crank.

mano ['mano] *sf* hand; paw; (*pintura*) coat; (*juego*) hand, round, turn. **a mano** by hand. **a mano salva** without risk. **de segunda mano** secondhand. **darse las manos** shake hands. **mano a mano** in a friendly way. **manojo** *sm* handful.

manosear [manose'ar] *v* handle; paw; fondle. **manoseado** *adj* hackneyed.

mansión [man'sjon] *sf* mansion.

manso ['manso] *adj* tame; gentle; meek. **mansedumbre** *sf* tameness; meekness.

manta ['manta] *sf* blanket; rug; (*fam*) thrashing.

manteca [man'teka] *sf* grease; lard; butter; cream. **mantecada** *sf* slice of bread and butter.

mantecado [mante'kaðo] *sm* ice-cream; bun.

mantel [man'tel] *sm* tablecloth.

***mantener** [mante'ner] *v* maintain; hold; defend; feed; sustain. **mantenimiento** *sm* maintenance.

mantequilla [mante'kiʎa] *sf* butter. **mantequera** *sf* churn; butter-dish. **mantequería** *sf* dairy.

mantilla [man'tiʎa] *sf* mantilla, shawl.

manto ['manto] *sm* cloak. **mantón** *sf* shawl.

manual [ma'nwal] *sm* handbook. *adj* manual.

manubrio [manu'βrio] *sm* handle; crank.

manufactura [manufak'tura] *sf* manufacture; factory. **manufacturado** *adj* manufactured. **manufacturar** *v* manufacture.

manuscrito [manu'skrito] *sm* manuscript.

manzana [man'θana] *sf* apple; block of flats. **manzano** *sm* apple tree.

maña ['maɲa] *sf* skill; bad habit; cunning. **mañoso** *adj* clever; crafty.

mañana [ma'ɲana] *sf* morning. *sm, adv* tomorrow. **de mañana** early. **hasta mañana** see you tomorrow. **pasado mañana** the day after tomorrow.

mapa ['mapa] *sm* map; chart.

máquina ['makina] *sf* machine; locomotive; engine; car; bicycle. **a toda máquina** at full speed. **máquina de coser** sewing machine. **máquina de escribir** typewriter. **máquina registradora** cash register.

maquinación [makina'θjon] *sf* machination; plotting. **maquinal** *adj* automatic; mechanical. **maquinar** *v* plot.

mar [mar] *s(m+f)* sea. **alta mar** high seas. **baja mar** low tide.

maraña [ma'raɲa] *sf* thicket; tangle; perplexity. **marañar** *v* tangle. **marañoso** *adj* entangling.

maravillar [maraβi'ʎar] *v* wonder; amaze. **maravilla** *sf* marvel; wonder. **maravilloso** *adj* wonderful.

marcar [mar'kar] *v* mark; brand; show; dial; score. **marca** *sf* mark; make; gauge; label. **marca registrada** registered trademark.

marcial [mar'θjal] *adj* martial; warlike.

marco ['marko] *sm* frame; setting; (*moneda*) mark.

marchar [mar'tʃar] *v* march; go; run; work; depart. **marcharse** *v* go away. **marcha** *sf* march; course; movement; departure. **poner en marcha** set in motion.

marchitar [martʃi'tar] *v* fade; wither; shrivel. **marchitable** *adj* perishable. **marchito** *adj* faded.

marea [ma'rea] *sf* tide; light breeze; dew. **marea creciente/menguante** flood/ebb tide.

marearse [mare'arse] *v* feel (sea) sick. **mareado** *adj* (sea) sick; dizzy. **mareo** *sm* sickness; (*fam*) nuisance.

marfil [mar'fil] *sm* ivory.

margarina [marga'rina] *sf* margarine.

margarita [marga'rita] *sf* daisy; pearl.

margen [mar'xen] *sm* border; margin; verge; shoulder; fringe. **al margen de** in addition to. *sf* river bank; seashore.

marica [ma'rika] *sf* magpie. *sm* (*fam*) sissy. **maricón** *sm* homosexual.

marido [ma'riðo] *sm* husband.

mariguana [mari'gwana] *sf* also **marihuana** marijuana.

marina [ma'rina] *sf* navy; shore; seamanship. **marinero** *sm* sailor. **marinero** *adj* seafaring; seaworthy. **marino** *sm* sailor. **marino** *adj* marine.

mariposa [mari'posa] *sf* butterfly.

mariquita [mari'kita] *sf* ladybird.

mariscal [maris'kal] *sm* marshal. **mariscal de campo** field marshal.

marisco [ma'risko] *sm* seafood; shellfish.

marítimo [ma'ritimo] *adj* maritime.

marmita [mar'mita] *sf* stewpot.

mármol [marmol] *sm* marble. **marmóreo** *adj* marble.

marqués [mar'kes] *sm* marquis. **marquesa** *sf* marchioness.

marrano [mar'rano] *sm* pig. *adj* filthy.

marrón [mar'ron] *adj* brown; maroon. *sm* (*color*) chestnut.

marsopa [mar'sopa] *sf* porpoise.

martes ['martes] *sm invar* Tuesday.

martillar [marti'ʎar] *v* hammer. **martillo** *sm* hammer.

martín pescador [mar'tin peska'ðor] *sm* kingfisher.

mártir ['martir] *s(m+f)* martyr. **martirio** *sm* martyrdom.

marxista [mark'sista] *s(m+f)* Marxist. **marxismo** *sm* Marxism.

marzo ['marθo] *sm* March.

mas [mas] *conj* but; yet. **mas que** although.

más [mas] *adv* more; most. **nada más** nothing else. **es más** moreover. **más bien** rather. **por más que** however much. *sm* plus.

masa ['masa] *sf* mass; volume; dough; mortar.

masaje [ma'saxe] *sm* massage. **masajista** *s(m+f)* masseur, masseuse.

mascar [mas'kar] *v* chew; (*fam*) mumble. **mascadura** *sf* chewing.

máscara ['maskara] *sf* mask. **mascarada** *sf* masquerade.

masculino [masku'lino] *adj* masculine, male. *sm* (*gram*) masculine. **masculinidad** *sf* masculinity.

masón [ma'son] *sm* freemason. **masonería** *sf* freemasonry.

masoquismo [maso'kismo] *sm* masochism. **masoquista** *s(m+f)* masochist. **masoquista** *adj* masochistic.

masticar [masti'kar] *v* chew. **masticación** *sf* mastication.

mástil ['mastil] *sm (mar)* mast; pole; post.

mastín [mas'tin] *sm* mastiff. **mastín danés** Great Dane.

masturbación [mastur'βa'θjon] *sf* masturbation. **masturbarse** *v* masturbate.

mata ['mata] *sf* bush; shrub; grove; mop of hair.

matafuego [mata'fwego] *sm* fire extinguisher.

matar [ma'tar] *v* kill, slaughter; tire out; put out. **matadero** *sm* slaughterhouse. **matador** *sm* bullfighter. **matanza** *sf* slaughter.

matamoscas [mata'moskas] *sm invar* flyswatter.

matarratas [matar'ratas] *sm invar* rat poison.

mate[1] ['mate] *sm* (check)mate.

mate[2] *adj* mat, dull.

matemáticas [mate'matikas] *sf* mathematics. **matemático, -a** *sm, sf* mathematician. **matemático** *adj* mathematical.

materia [ma'terja] *sf* matter; stuff; subject. **materia prima** raw material. **en materia de** as regards. **material** *adj* material. **material** *sm* stuff, material. **materiales de derribo** rubble *sing.* **materialismo** *sm* materialism. **materialista** *s(m+f)* materialist. **materialista** *adj* materialistic. **materializar** *v* materialize.

maternal [mater'nal] *adj* maternal. **maternidad** *sf* maternity. **casa de maternidad** maternity hospital. **materno** *adj* maternal.

matinal [mati'nal] *adj* morning.

matiz ['matiθ] *sm* tint; hue; shade; shade of meaning. **matizado** *adj* variegated. **matizar** *v* blend; shade.

matorral [mator'ral] *sm* bush; thicket; scrubland.

matricular [matriku'lar] *v* enrol; register; matriculate. **matricularse** *v* register; *(contienda)* enter. **matrícula** *sf* register; enrolment; matriculation; *(auto)* licence plate.

matrimonio [matri'monjo] *sm* matrimony, marriage; *(par)* married couple.

matriz [ma'triθ] *sf* matrix; womb. *adj* mother; chief. **casa matriz** headquarters.

matrona [ma'trona] *sf* matron; midwife.

matute [ma'tute] *sm* smuggling; contraband. **matutear** *v* smuggle. **matutero, -a** *sm, sf* smuggler.

matutino [matu'tino] *adj also* **matutinal** morning.

maullar [mau'ʎar] *v* mew. **maullido** *sm* mewing.

mausoleo [mauso'leo] *sm* mausoleum.

máxima ['maksima] *sf* maxim.

máxime ['maksime] *adv* especially; principally. **máximo** *adj, sm* maximum.

maya ['maja] *sf* daisy.

mayo ['majo] *sm* May; maypole.

mayonesa [majo'nesa] *sf* mayonnaise.

mayor [ma'jor] *sm* head, chief. *adj* older, elder; major, main; larger; adult. **calle mayor** high street. **al por mayor** wholesale. **mayoral** *sm* foreman; farm manager.

mayorazgo [majo'raθgo] *sm* primogeniture; first born son; entailed estate.

mayordomo [major'ðomo] *sm* butler; steward.

mayoría [majo'ria] *sf* majority; coming of age.

mayorista [majo'rista] *sm* wholesaler. *adj* wholesale.

mayúscula [ma'juskula] *sf* capital letter.

maza ['maθa] *sf* mace; club; butt. **mazada** *sf* blow with a club.

mazapán [maθa'pan] *sm* marzipan.

mazmorra [maθ'morra] *sf* dungeon.

me [me] *pron* me, myself.

mear [me'ar] *v (vulgar)* piss. **mearse** *v* wet oneself. **meadero** *sm* urinal.

mecánica [me'kanika] *sf* mechanics; machinery. **mecánico** *sm* mechanic; driver. **mecanismo** *sm* mechanism. **mecanizar** *v* mechanize.

mecanógrafo, -a [meka'nografo] *sm, sf* typist. **mecanografía** *sf* typewriting. **mecanografiar** *v* type.

mecer [me'θer] *v* rock; swing; shake; stir. **mecedor** *sm* swing. **mecedora** *sf* rocking-chair.

mecha ['metʃa] *sf* wick; fuse; match.

mechera [me'tʃera] *sf (fam)* shoplifter.

mechero [me'tʃero] *sm* cigarette lighter; gas burner.

medalla [me'ðaʎa] *sf* medal.

media ['meðja] *sf* stocking.

mediado [me'ðjaðo] *adj* half-full; halfway through; half-finished. **a mediados de** in *or* about the middle of.

mediano [me'ðjano] *adj* medium; average; mediocre. **medianero** *adj* intermediate; interceding.

medianoche [meðja'notʃe] *sf* midnight.

mediante [me'ðjante] *adj* intervening. *prep* by means of. **mediar** *v* intervene; mediate; elapse.

medicina [meði'θina] *sf* medicine. **medicación** *sf* medication. **medicamento** *sm* medicament. **medicar** *v* medicate. **medicinal** *adj* medicinal. **médico** *sm* doctor. *médico adj* medical.

medio [me'ðjo] *sm* middle; half; medium; way. **de medio a medio** completely. **medios** *pl* means; resources. *adv* half; partly. **medidas a medias** half-measures. *adj* half; middle; average; medium. **de medio cuerpo** half-length.

mediocre [me'ðjokre] *adj* mediocre. **mediocridad** *sf* mediocrity.

mediodía [meðjo'ðia] *sm* midday; noon; south.

medioeval [meðjoe'βal] *adj* medieval.

*medir [me'ðir] *v* measure; scan. **medirse** *v* act prudently. **medida** *sf* measure(ment); step; moderation. **a medida que** according as.

meditar [meði'tar] *v* meditate (on). **meditabundo** *adj* pensive. **meditación** *sf* meditation.

mediterráneo [meðiter'raneo] *adj* Mediterranean.

medrar [me'ðrar] *v* prosper, thrive; grow. **medra** *sf* prosperity; growth. **medro** *sm* progress; improvement.

medroso [me'ðroso] *adj* fearful; timid; frightening.

médula [me'ðula] *sf also* **medula** marrow; *(fig)* essence.

medusa [me'ðusa] *sf* jellyfish.

megáfono [me'gafono] *sm* megaphone.

megalómano [mega'lomano]. **-a** *sm, sf* megalomaniac. **megalomanía** *sf* megalomania.

mejilla [me'xiʎa] *sf* cheek.

mejor [me'xor] *adj* better; best. *adv* better; best; rather. **a lo mejor** probably. **mejor que mejor** better still. **tanto mejor** so much the better. **mejora** *sf* improvement. **mejorar** *v* improve; surpass. **mejorarse** *v* get better.

melancólico [melan'koliko] *adj* melancholy. **melancolía** *sf* melancholy.

melandro [me'landro] *sm* badger.

melaza [me'laθa] *sf* molasses; treacle.

melena [me'lena] *sf* mane; long hair.

melindroso [melin'droso] *adj* finicky; squeamish.

melocotón [meloko'ton] *sm* peach; peach tree.

melodía [melo'ðia] *sf* melody; tune. **melodioso** *adj* melodious.

melodrama [melo'ðrama] *sm* melodrama. **melodramático** *adj* melodramatic.

melón [me'lon] *sm* melon.

meloso [me'loso] *adj* honeyed; mild; sickly.

mella ['meʎa] *sf* notch; dent; impression. **hacer mella a** make a deep impression on.

mellizo [me'ʎiθo]. **-a** *s, adj* twin.

membrana [mem'brana] *sf* membrane.

membrillo [mem'briʎo] *sm* quince; quince tree.

memorable [memo'raβle] *adj* memorable. **memorar** *v* remember. **memoria** *sf* memory; record. **de memoria** by heart. **memorial** *sm* memorial; petition.

mencionar [menθjo'nar] *v* mention, name. **mención** *sf* mention.

mendigar [mendi'gar] *v* beg. **mendicación** *sf* begging. **mendicante** *adj* begging. **mendigante** *sm* beggar. **mendigo, -a** *sm, sf* beggar.

menear [mene'ar] *v* stir; shake; sway; manage; run. **meneo** *sm* wag; shake; rearranging.

menester [menes'ter] *sm* need; want; occupation. **ser menester** be necessary. **menesteroso** *adj* needy.

menguar [men'gwar] *v* lessen; decline. **mengua** *sf* lessening; decline. **menguado** *adj* impaired; diminished; wretched.

menopausia [meno'pausja] *sf* menopause.

menor [me'nor] *adj* minor; lesser; least; younger; youngest; smaller; smallest. **al por menor** retail.

menos ['menos] *adj* less, fewer. *adv* less; minus; except. **al, a lo** *or* **por lo menos** at least. **echar de menos** miss.

menoscabar [menoska'βar] *v* lessen; impair; discredit. **menoscabo** *sm* reduction; impairment.

menospreciar [menospre'θjar] *v* underrate; despise. **menospreciable** contemptible. **menosprecio** *sm* contempt; scorn; disrespect; undervaluation.

mensaje [men'saxe] *sm* message. **mensajero, -a** *sm, sf* messenger.

menstruar [menstru'ar] v menstruate. **menstruación** sf menstruation. **menstrual** adj menstrual.

mensual [men'swal] adj monthly. **mensualidad** sf monthly salary.

mensurar [mensu'rar] v measure. **mensura** sf measure. **mensural** adj measuring.

menta ['menta] sf mint; peppermint.

mental [men'tal] adj mental; intellectual. **mentalidad** sf mentality. **mente** sf mind. **irse de la mente** slip one's mind.

mentecato [mente'kato], **-a** sm, sf simpleton. adj foolish; half-witted.

*__mentir__ [men'tir] v lie. **mentir con disagree. mentira** sf lie; error. **parece mentira** it's hard to believe.

menudear [menuðe'ar] v repeat frequently; happen often. **menudencia** sf detail; minuteness; pettiness. **menudencias** sf pl or **menudas** sm pl offal sing. **menudo** adj small, tiny; petty. **a menudo** often.

meñique [me'ɲike] sm little finger. adj tiny.

meollo [me'oʎo] sm (anat) marrow; brains pl; (fig) essence.

meple ['meple] sm maple.

mercado [mer'kaðo] sm market. **Mercado Común** Common Market. **mercadear** v trade. **mercader** sm merchant. **mercadería** sf merchandise. **mercancía** sf goods pl. **mercante** adj merchant. **mercantil** adj mercantile.

merced [mer'θeð] sf mercy; favour. **merced a** thanks to.

mercenario [merθe'narjo], **-a** s, adj mercenary.

mercero [mer'θero], **-a** sm, sf haberdasher. **mercería** sf haberdashery.

mercurio [mer'kurjo] sm mercury. **mercurial** adj mercurial.

*__merecer__ [mere'θer] v deserve; be worthy of. **merecer la pena** be worthwhile. **merecimiento** sm merit.

*__merendar__ [meren'dar] v take afternoon tea; have an afternoon snack. **merendarse a** get the better of. **merendero** sm open-air café. **merienda** sf afternoon snack.

merengue [me'renge] sm meringue.

meridiano [meri'ðjano] sm adj meridian. **meridiana** sf couch. **meridional** adj southern.

mérito ['merito] sm merit; value. **hacer mérito de** mention. **meritorio** adj meritorious.

merla ['merla] sf blackbird.

merluza [mer'luθa] sf hake.

mermar [mer'mar] v decrease, reduce. **merma** sf reduction; wastage; loss.

mermelada [merme'laða] sf marmalade; jam.

mero ['mero] adj mere, pure.

merodear [meroðe'ar] v maraud. **merodeador. -a** sm, sf marauder.

mes [mes] sm month. **al mes** per month.

mesa ['mesa] sf table; desk. **mesa de cambios** bank. **alzar la mesa** clear the table.

meseta [me'seta] sf plateau; staircase landing.

mesón [me'son] sm inn, hostelry. **mesonero, -a** sm, sf innkeeper.

mestizo [mes'tiθo], **-a** s, adj half-caste.

mesura [me'sura] sf dignity; politeness; moderation.

meta ['meta] sf goal; aim; destination. **guardameta** sm goalkeeper.

metabolismo [metabo'lismo] sm metabolism.

metafísica [meta'fisika] sf metaphysics. **metafísico** adj metaphysical.

metáfora [me'tafora] sf metaphor. **metafórico** adj metaphorical.

metal [me'tal] sm metal; (música) brass; (voz) timbre. **metálico** adj metallic. **metalurgia** sf metallurgy.

meteoro [mete'oro] sm meteor. **meteórico** adj meteoric. **meteorito** sm meteorite. **meteorología** sf meteorology.

meter [me'ter] v insert, put in; smuggle; produce; reduce. **meterse** v interfere; intervene. **meterse a** turn to. **meterse con** quarrel with. **metido** adj compressed.

meticuloso [metiku'loso] adj meticulous.

metodista [meto'ðista] s(m+f), adj Methodist. **metodismo** sm Methodism.

método [metoðo] sm method, manner. **metódico** adj methodical.

métrico [metriko] adj metric(al). **metro** sm metre; underground railway.

metrónomo [me'tronomo] sm metronome.

metrópoli [me'tropoli] sf metropolis. **metropolitano** adj metropolitan.

mezclar [meθ'klar] v mix; blend. **mezclarse** v mingle; intermarry. **mezcla** sf mixture, medley. **mezcladora** sf mixer, blender. **mezcolanza** sf hotchpotch.

mezquino [meθ'kino] adj mean. **mezquindad** sf meanness.

mezquita [meθ'kita] sf mosque.

mi [mi] adj my. **mí** pron me.

miaja ['mjaxa] sf crumb; bit.

mico ['miko] sm monkey.

microbio [mi'kroβjo] sm microbe. **microbiología** sf microbiology.

micrófono [mi'krofono] sm microphone.

microscopio [mikro'skopjo] sm microscope. **microscópico** adj microscopic.

miedo [mi'eðo] sm fear. **dar miedo a** frighten. **tener miedo** be afraid. **miedoso** adj frightened.

miel [mi'el] sf honey. **miel de caña** molasses.

miembro ['mjembro] sm member; limb.

miente [mi'ente] sf mind; thought. **caer en mientes** come to mind. **¡ni por mientes!** not on your life! **parar mientes en** consider.

mientras ['mjentras] adv, conj while; meanwhile; so long as. **mientras tanto** meanwhile.

miércoles [mi'erkoles] sm Wednesday. **miércoles de ceniza** Ash Wednesday.

mierda ['mjerða] sf (fam) shit; muck. **¡váyase a la mierda!** go to hell!

mies [mjes] sf corn. **mieses** sf pl cornfield.

miga ['miga] sf crumb; substance. **hacer buenas migas con** get on well with.

migración [migra'θjon] sf migration. **migratorio** adj migratory.

migraña [mi'graŋa] sf migraine.

mil [mil] sm, adj thousand. **milésimo** adj thousandth. **miles de** masses of.

milagro [mi'lagro] sm miracle; wonder. **milagroso** adj miraculous.

milano [mi'lano] sm (ave) kite.

mildeu [mil'deu] sm mildew.

milicia [mi'liθja] sf militia; military service. **militar** adj military. sm soldier.

miligramo [mili'gramo] sm milligramme.

milla ['miʎa] sf mile.

millar [mi'ʎar] sm thousand. **a millares in** thousands.

millón [mi'ʎon] sm million. **millonésimo** adj millionth. **millonario, -a** sm, sf millionaire.

mimar [mi'mar] v spoil; pamper.

mimbre ['mimbre] s(m + f) wicker.

minar [mi'nar] y mine. **mina** sf mine; store; pencil lead. **minador** sm miner; (mar) minelayer. **minero** sm miner; mine-owner.

minarete [mina'rete] sm minaret.

mineral [mine'ral] sm, adj mineral. **mineralogía** sf mineralogy.

miniatura [minja'tura] sf miniature.

mínimo ['minimo] sm, adj minimum.

ministerio [mini'sterjo] sm ministry; office. **ministerial** adj ministerial. **ministrador** sm administrator. **ministrar** v minister; administer. **ministro** sm minister; judge. **primer ministro** prime minister.

minoría [mino'ria] sf minority. **minorar** v diminish.

minucioso [minu'θjoso] adj meticulous; minute.

minué [minu'e] sm minuet.

minúscula [mi'nuskula] sf small letter.

minuta [mi'nuta] sf memo; menu; list. **minutar** v make notes on.

minutía [minu'tia] sf carnation.

minuto [mi'nuto] sm minute.

mío ['mio] adj, pron pers mine.

miope [mi'ope] adj shortsighted. **miopía** sf myopia.

miosotis [mjo'sotis] sm forget-me-not.

mirar [mi'rar] v look; consider. **mira** sf sight. **estar a la mira de** be on the lookout. **con miras a** with a view to. **mirada** sf look; glance. **miradero** sm centre of attention; vantage point. **mirado** adj circumspect. **mirador** sm bay window. **miramiento** sm look; consideration; respect.

mirasol [mira'sol] sm sunflower.

mirlo ['mirlo] sm blackbird.

mirra ['mirra] sf myrrh.

mirto ['mirto] sf mass. **misal** sm missal.

miserable [mise'raβle] adj wretched, miserable. **miseria** sf misery; poverty. **misericordia** sf mercy; compassion. **misericordioso** adj merciful; compassionate. **mísero** adj wretched.

misión [misi'on] sf mission.

mismo [mi'smo] adj same; own; very; just; right. **aquí mismo** right here. **lo mismo con** the same goes for. **yo mismo** I myself.

misterio [mi'sterjo] sm mystery. **misterioso** adj mysterious. **misticismo** sm mysticism. **místico, -a** s, adj mystic. **mistificación** sf falsification; trick. **mistificar** v falsify; deceive.

mitad [mi'tað] sf half; middle.

mítico ['mitiko] adj mythical. **mito** m myth. **mitología** sf mythology. **mitológico** adj mythological.

mitigar [miti'gar] v mitigate; relieve. **mitigación** sf mitigation. **mitigante** adj mitigating.

mitin ['mitin] sm political rally.

mitón [mi'ton] sm mitten.

mitra ['mitra] sf mitre.

mixto ['miksto] adj mixed. sm compound. **mixtura** sf mixture. **mixturar** v mix.

mobiliario [moβili'arjo] sm furniture.

mocasín [moka'sin] sm moccasin.

mocero [mo'θero] adj sensual. **mocear** v act like a youngster. **mocedad** sf youth; youthful prank.

moción [mo'θjon] sf motion.

moco ['moko] sm mucus. **mocoso** adj mucous.

mochila [mo'tʃila] sf rucksack.

mocho ['motʃo] adj shorn; lopped; (sin cuernos) hornless.

moda ['moða] sf fashion. **de moda** in fashion. **pasado de moda** old-fashioned.

modales [mo'ðales] sm pl manners.

modelo [mo'ðelo] sm, adj model. **modela** sf fashion model. **modelar** v model.

moderar [moðe'rar] v moderate; restrain. **moderación** sf moderation. **moderado** adj moderate. **moderador, -a** sm, sf moderator. **moderativo** adj moderating.

moderno [mo'ðerno] adj modern. **modernidad** sf modernity. **modernizar** v modernize. **modernizarse** v get up-to-date.

modesto [mo'ðesto] adj modest. **modestia** sf modesty.

módico ['moðiko] adj moderate. **modicidad** sf moderateness.

modificar [moðifi'kar] v modify. **modificación** sf modification.

modismo [mo'ðismo] sm idiom.

modista [mo'ðista] sf dressmaker.

modo ['moðo] sm mode; manner; method. **de modo que** so that. **de todos modos** in any case.

modorra [mo'ðorra] sf drowsiness. **modorro** adj drowsy.

modular [moðu'lar] v modulate. **modulación** sf modulation.

mofar [mo'far] v scoff; mock. **mofarse de** jeer at. **mofa** sf mockery. **mofador** adj mocking.

mohín [mo'in] sm grimace. **mohíno** adj sulky.

moho ['moo] sm mould; rust. **mohoso** adj mouldy; rusty. **ponerse mohoso** go mouldy; rust.

mojar [mo'xar] v wet; moisten; soak. **mojado** adj wet; damp.

mojigato [moxi'gato], -a sm, sf hypocrite; prude. adj hypocritical; prudish.

mojón [mo'xon] sm landmark.

moldar [mol'ðar] v also **moldear** mould. **molde** sm mould. **moldura** sf moulding.

molécula [mo'lekula] sf molecule. **molecular** adj molecular.

***moler** [mo'ler] v grind; crush; (fig) bore, weary. **moledura** sf grinding; milling; exhaustion.

molestar [moles'tar] v annoy; bother; disturb. **molestarse** v worry. **no se moleste** don't bother. **molestia** sf trouble. **molesto** adj tiresome; embarrassing.

molinero [moli'nero] sm miller. **molino** sm mill.

molusco [mo'lusko] sm mollusc.

mollera [mo'ʎera] sf crown of the head; (fig) brains. **cerrado de mollera** dense; obstinate.

momentáneo [momen'taneo] adj momentary. **momento** sm moment; momentum. **al momento** immediately.

momia ['momja] sf (cadáver) mummy. **momificación** sf mummification. **momificar** v mummify.

monada [mo'naða] sf kindness; flattery; dirty trick. **¡qué monada!** how lovely!

monarca [mo'narka] sm monarch. **monarquía** sf monarchy. **monárquico** adj monarchic(al).

monasterio [monas'terjo] sm monastery. **monástico** adj monastic.

mondar [mon'dar] v clean; prune; strip; trim; peel. **monda** sf pruning; trimming; cleaning. **mondadientes** m invar toothpick. **mondador, -a** sm, sf pruner; peeler; cleaner. **mondo** adj pure; bare; clean.

moneda [mo'neða] sf money; coin. **monedero** sm purse. **monedero falso** counterfeiter.

monitor [moni'tor], -a sm, sf monitor.

monja ['monxa] sf nun. **monje** sm monk.

mono¹ ['mono] sm monkey; ape.

mono² adj lovely; cute.

monólogo [mo'nologo] sm monologue.

monopolizar [monopoli'θar] v monopolize. **monopolio** sm monopoly.

monosílabo [mono'silaβo] sm monosyllable.

monótono [mo'notono] adj monotonous. **monotonía** sf monotony.

monstruo ['monstruo] *sm* monster. **monstruosidad** *sf* monstrosity. **monstruoso** *adj* monstrous.

monta ['monta] *sf* mounting; amount. **montacargas** *sm invar* service lift. **montaje** *sm* mounting.

montaña [mon'taɲa] *sf* mountain. **montañés** *adj* of mountains. **montañismo** *sm* mountaineering. **montañoso** *adj* mountainous. **monte** *sm* mountain; mount.

montar [mon'tar] *v* mount; ride; assemble; establish. **montura** *sf* mount; saddle; frame; mounting.

montera [mon'tera] *sf* cloth cap; bull-fighter's hat; skylight. **montero** *sm* hunter.

montón [mon'ton] *sm* heap, pile. **a montones** lots of.

monumento [monu'mento] *sm* monument; memorial. **monumental** *adj* monumental.

moño ['moɲo] *sm* bun, topknot. **ponerse moños** put on airs.

mora[1] ['mora] *sf* blackberry; mulberry.

mora[2] *sf* delay.

morada [mo'raða] *sf* abode; sojourn. **morar** *v* dwell.

morado [mo'raðo] *adj* purple; violet. **ponerse morado** stuff oneself.

moral [mo'ral] *adj* moral. **morales** *sf pl* morals. **moraleja** *sf (de un cuento)* moral. **moralidad** *sf* morality. **moralista** *s(m+f)* moralist. **moralizar** *v* moralize.

mórbido ['morβiðo] *adj* morbid; delicate. **morbidez** *sf* tenderness. **morbilidad** *sf* morbidity. **morboso** *adj* morbid; diseased.

morcilla [mor'θiʎa] *sf* black pudding.

mordaz [mor'ðaθ] *adj* mordant; pungent. **mordaza** [mor'ðaθa] *sf (en la boca)* gag.

*morder [mor'ðer] *v* bite. **mordedura** *sf* bite. **mordiente** *adj* biting. **mordiscar** *v* nibble. **mordiscón** *sm* nibble; mouthful.

moreno [mo'reno] *adj* brown; tanned; dark.

morera [mo'rera] *sf* mulberry tree.

morfina [mor'fina] *sf* morphine.

moribundo [mori'βundo] *adj* moribund.

*morir [mo'rir] *v* die; end; fade. **morirse por** crave.

mormón [mor'mon], **-a** *sm, sf* Mormon. **mormonismo** *sm* Mormonism.

moro ['moro], **-a** *sm, sf* Moor. *adj* Moorish.

moroso [mo'roso] *adj* slow; sluggish; late. **morosidad** *sf* slowness; inactivity.

morralla [mor'raʎa] *sf* rubbish; *(fig)* rabble.

morriña [mor'riɲa] *sf* nostalgia; homesickness.

mortaja [mor'taxa] *sf* shroud.

mortal [mor'tal] *adj* mortal; lethal; awful. *s(m+f)* mortal. **mortalidad** *sf* mortality.

mortero [mor'tero] *sm* mortar.

mortífero [mor'tifero] *adj* deadly, fatal.

mortificar [mortifi'kar] *v* mortify. **mortificación** *sf* mortification.

mosca ['moska] *sf* fly. **papar moscas** gape. **moscarda** *sf* bluebottle. **moscardón** *sm* blowfly; hornet.

mosquete [mos'kete] *sm* musket. **mosquetero** *sm* musketeer.

mosquito [mos'kito] *sm* mosquito; gnat. **mosquitero** *sm* mosquito net.

mostaza [mos'taθa] *sf* mustard.

*mostrar [mos'trar] *v* show; exhibit; point out. **mostrable** *adj* demonstrable. **mostrador** *sm (reloj)* dial; *(tienda)* counter.

mote ['mote] *sm* nickname. **motejar** *v* label; name.

motín [mo'tin] *sm* uprising; mutiny.

motivar [moti'βar] *v* cause, give rise to; justify; explain. **motivación** *sf* motivation. **motivo** *sm* motive; grounds *pl*. **con motivo de** owing to.

motocicleta [motoθi'kleta] *sf* motor cycle. **motociclista** *s(m+f)* motor-cyclist.

motor ['motor] *sm* motor; engine. **motorista** *s(m+f)* motor-cyclist. **motorizar** *v* motorize.

motriz [mo'triθ] *adj* motive.

mover [mo'βer] *v* move; shake; stir; incite. **moverse** *v* get a move on. **movedizo** *adj* movable; inconstant. **movible** *adj* mobile. **móvil** *adj* mobile; fickle. **movilidad** *sf* mobility. **movilizar** *v* mobilize. **movilización** *sf* mobilization. **movimiento** *sm* movement; motion; activity.

mozo ['moθo] *sm* youth, lad; waiter. **moza** *sf* girl; servant.

mucoso [mu'koso] *adj* mucous. **mucosidad** *sf* mucus.

muchacho [mu'tʃatʃo] *sm* boy; chap. **muchacha** *sf* girl; servant.

muchedumbre [mutʃe'ðumbre] *sf* crowd; *(fig)* a lot.

mucho ['mutʃo] *adj* a lot of; much; great; many. *pron* many; a lot. *adv* much; a lot; a long time. **con mucho** by far. **por mucho que** however much.

mudar [mu'ðar] *v* change; remove; shed. **mudarse** *v* move house; change one's clothes. **muda** *sf* change; moulting. **mudable** *adj* changeable; variable. **mudanza** *sf* change; removal. **camión de mudanzas** *sm* removal van.

mudo ['muðo] *adj* dumb, mute. **mudez** *sf* dumbness.

mueble ['mweβle] *sm* piece of furniture. **muebles** *sm pl* furniture *sing*.

mueca ['mweka] *sf* grimace.

muela ['mwela] *sf* molar. **muela del juicio** wisdom tooth.

muelle ['mweʎe] *adj* soft; luxurious. *sm* wharf; embankment; spring.

muérdago [mu'erðago] *sm* mistletoe.

muerte ['mwerte] *sf* death; murder. **de mala muerte** (*fam*) rotten, lousy.

muerto ['mwerto] *V* **morir**. *adj* dead. *sm* corpse.

muestra ['mwestra] *sf* sample, example; specimen; sign.

mugir [mu'xir] *v* roar; bellow; low. **mugido** *sm* roar; bellow; lowing.

mujer [mu'xer] *sf* woman; wife.

muleta [mu'leta] *sf* crutch; bullfighter's cape.

mulo ['mulo] *sm* mule.

multar [mul'tar] *v* fine. **multa** *sf* fine.

múltiple ['multiple] *adj* multiple; many. **multiplicación** *sf* multiplication. **multiplicar** *v* multiply, increase.

multitud [multi'tuθ] *sf* multitude, crowd.

*mullir [mu'ʎir] *v* beat; break up; loosen. **mullido** *adj* soft; fluffy.

mundo ['mundo] *sm* world; (*fam*) crowd. **todo el mundo** everybody. **mundanal** *adj* worldly. **mundanería** *sf* worldliness. **mundial** *adj* world; worldwide. **mundovisión** *sm* broadcasting by satellite.

municipal [muniθi'pal] *adj* municipal. *sm* policeman. **municipalidad** *sf* municipality. **municipio** *sm* town council.

munífico [mu'nifiko] *adj* munificent; liberal. **munificencia** *sf* munificence; liberality.

muñeca [mu'neka] *sf* doll; dressmaker's dummy; wrist.

muralla [mu'raʎa] *sf* wall; rampart. **mural** *adj*, *sm* mural. **murar** *v* wall. **muro** *sm* wall.

murciélago [mur'θielago] *sm* (*zool*) bat.

murmullo [mur'muʎo] *sm* murmur; whisper; rustle.

murmurar [murmu'rar] *v* murmur; whisper; mutter; gossip. **murmuración** *sf* gossiping. **murmurio** *sm* murmuring.

músculo ['muskulo] *sm* muscle. **muscular** *adj* muscular.

muselina [muse'lina] *sf* muslin.

museo [mu'seo] *sm* museum; art gallery.

musgo ['musgo] *sm* moss.

música ['musika] *sf* music. **musical** *adj* musical. **músico, -a** *sm, sf* musician. **musicología** *sf* musicology.

muslo ['muslo] *sm* thigh.

mustio ['mustjo] *adj* withered; sad. **mustiarse** *v* wither.

mutación [muta'θjon] *sf* mutation; change. **mutabilidad** *sf* mutability. **mutante** *sm, adj* mutant.

mutilar [muti'lar] *v* mutilate; cripple. **mutilación** *sf* mutilation. **mutilado, -a** *sm, sf* cripple.

mutual ['mutwal] *adj* mutual. **mutuo** *adj* mutual; joint.

muy [mwi] *adv* very; quite; too; much. **muy señor mío** (*carta*) Dear Sir.

N

nabo ['naβo] *sm* turnip.

nácar ['nakar] *sm* mother-of-pearl.

*nacer [na'θer] *v* be born; originate. **nacido** *adj* born. **naciente** *adj* growing. **nacimiento** *sm* birth; origin.

nación [na'θjon] *sf* nation. **nacional** *adj* national. *s(m+f)* national; native. **nacionalidad** *sf* nationality. **nacionalismo** *sm* nationalism. **nacionalizar** *v* nationalize.

nada ['naða] *sf* nothing. *adv* by no means. **de nada** don't mention it. **nada más** only.

nadar [na'ðar] *v* swim. **nadador, -a** *sm, sf* swimmer.

nadie ['naðje] *pron* nobody, no one.

naipe ['naipe] *sm* playing-card.

nalga ['nalga] *sf* buttock.

naranja [na'ranxa] *sf* orange. **naranjada** *sf* orangeade. **naranjo** *sm* orange tree.

narciso [nar'θiso] *sm* narcissus. **narcisismo** *sm* narcissism.

narcótico [nar'kotiko] *sm, adj* narcotic.

nariz [na'riθ] *sf, pl* **narices** nose.

narrar [nar'rar] *v* narrate. **narración** *sf* narration. **narrador, -a** *sm, sf* narrator. **narrativa** *sf* narrative.

nasal [na'sal] *adj* nasal.

nata ['nata] *sf* cream; curd; (*fig*) the best. **natillas** *sf pl* custard *sing.*

natación [nata'θjon] *sf* swimming.

natal [na'tal] *adj* natal; native. *sm* birth; birthday. **natalidad** *sf* birthrate.

nativo [na'tiβo], **-a** *s, adj* native. **natividad** *sf* nativity. **nato** *adj* born.

natural [natu'ral] *s(m+f)* native; citizen. *sm* nature. *adj* natural. **naturaleza** *sf* nature; nationality. **naturalidad** *sf* naturalness; citizenship.

naufragar [naufra'gar] *v* sink; be shipwrecked. **naufragio** *sm* shipwreck. **náufrago** *adj* shipwrecked.

náusea ['nausea] *sf* nausea. **nauseabundo** *adj* nauseous; nauseating.

náutico ['nautiko] *adj* nautical. **náutica** *sf* navigation.

navaja [na'βaxa] *sf* penknife; razor. **navajada** *sf* stab; gash.

naval [na'βal] *adj* naval. **nave** *sf* or **navío** *sm* ship. **navegable** *adj* navigable. **navegación** *sf* navigation; sailing. **navegante** *sm* navigator.

neblina [ne'βlina] *sf* mist; fog. **nebulosidad** *sf* nebulosity; haziness. **nebuloso** *adj* nebulous.

necedad [neθe'ðað] *sf* foolishness; nonsense. **necio** *adj* foolish.

necesario [neθe'sarjo] *adj* necessary. **necesidad** *sf* necessity; poverty. **necesitado** *adj* needy. **necesitar** *v* need.

néctar ['nektar] *sm* nectar.

nefario [ne'farjo] *adj* nefarious.

nefasto [ne'fasto] *adj* ill-omened; unlucky.

*negar [ne'gar] *v* deny; refuse. **negarse** *v* decline; refuse. **negación** *sf* negation. **negativa** *sm* (*foto*) negative; *sf* refusal.

negligencia [negli'xenθja] *sf* negligence. **negligente** *adj* negligent.

negociar [nego'θjar] *v* trade; negotiate. **negociable** *adj* negotiable. **negociación** *sf* transaction; negotiation. **negociado** *sm* bureau; divison. **negociador, -a** *sm, sf*

negotiator; agent. **negociante** *sm* businessman; merchant. **negocio** *sm* business; trade; negotiation.

negro ['negro], **-a** *s, adj* black. **negrura** *sf* blackness.

nene ['nene], **-a** *sm, sf* baby.

nenúfar [ne'nufar] *sm* waterlily.

neón [ne'on] *sm* neon.

nepotismo [nepo'tismo] *sm* nepotism.

nervio ['nerβjo] *sm* nerve; (*de una hoja*) rib; sinew. **crisparle los nervios a uno** get on someone's nerves. **tener los nervios en punta** be on edge. **nerviosidad** *sf* nervousness. **nervioso** *adj* nervous. **crisis nerviosa** *sf* nervous breakdown.

neto ['neto] *adj* pure; clear; (*com*) net.

neumático [neu'matiko] *sm* tyre. *adj* pneumatic.

neumonía [neumo'nia] *sf* pneumonia.

neuralgia [neu'ralxja] *sf* neuralgia. **neurálgico** *adj* neuralgic.

neurótico [neu'rotiko] *adj* neurotic. **neurosis** *sf* neurosis.

neutro ['neutro] *adj* neutral; (*gram*) neuter. **neutral** *s(m+f), adj* neutral. **neutralidad** *sf* neutrality. **neutralizar** *v* neutralize.

*nevar [ne'βar] *v* snow. **nevada** *sf* snow storm. **nevasca** *sf* snowfall. **nevera** *sf* refrigerator. **nevisca** *sf* light snowfall. **neviscar** *v* snow lightly. **nevoso** *adj* snowy.

nexo ['nekso] *sm* link, tie.

ni [ni] *conj* neither; nor; or; not even. **ni uno ni otro** neither one nor the other.

nicotina [niko'tina] *sf* nicotine.

nicho ['nitʃo] *sm* niche.

nido [ni'ðo] *sm* nest. **cunas de nido** pull-out beds. **nidada** *sf* brood; clutch. **nidal** *sm* nest; nest egg.

niebla [ni'eβla] *sf* fog; mist; mildew.

nieto [ni'eto] *sm* grandson. **nieta** *sf* granddaughter.

nieve [ni'eβe] *sf* snow.

nilón [ni'lon] *sm* nylon.

ninfa ['ninfa] *sf* nymph.

ninguno [nin'guno] *adj also* **ningún** no; not one. **de ninguna manera** in no way. *pron* nobody.

niña ['nina] *sf* little girl; (*del ojo*) pupil. **niñada** *sf* childishness. **niñera** *sf* nanny. **niñez** *sf* childhood. **niño** *sm* little boy; child. **desde niño** from childhood.

níquel ['nikel] *sm* nickel. **niquelar** *v* nickel-plate.

níspero ['nispero] *sm* medlar tree. **níspola** *sf* medlar.

nítido [ni'tiðo] *adj* clear; bright. **nitidez** *sf* brightness; neatness.

nitrógeno [ni'troxeno] *sm* nitrogen. **nitrato** *sm* nitrate. **nítrico** *adj* nitric. **nitro** *sm* nitre; saltpetre. **nitroso** *adj* nitrous.

nivelar [niβe'lar] *v* level; balance. **nivelarse** *v* become level. **nivelarse con** get even with. **nivel** *sm* level; standard. **nivel de aire** spirit-level. **nivel de vida** standard of living. **paso a nivel** level-crossing. **nivelación** *sf* levelling.

no [no] *adv* no; not. **no bien** no sooner. **no más** only. **no obstante** in spite of. **que no** if only.

noble ['noβle] *adj* noble. *sm* nobleman. **nobleza** *sf* nobility.

noción [no'θjon] *sf* notion; idea. **nociones** *sf pl* smattering *sing*; rudiments.

nocivo [no'θiβo] *adj* noxious; harmful.

nocturno [nok'turno] *adj* nocturnal; night. **noctámbulo, -a** *sm, sf* sleepwalker.

noche ['notʃe] *sf* night; evening. **por la noche** at night. **Nochebuena** *sf* Christmas Eve.

nódulo ['noðulo] *sm* nodule.

nogal [no'gal] *sm also* **noguera** *sf* walnut tree.

nómada ['nomaða] *s(m+f)* nomad. *adj* nomadic.

nombrar [nom'brar] *v* name; nominate; mention. **nombradía** *sf* reputation. **nombramiento** *sm* naming; nomination. **nombre** *sm* name; title. **nombre de pila** Christian name. **nomenclatura** *sf* nomenclature; terminology; catalogue. **nómina** *sf* list; payroll. **nominación** *sf* nomination. **nominal** *adj* nominal. **nominativo** *sm* (*gram*) nominative.

non [non] *adj* (*mat*) odd. *sm* odd number.

nonagésimo [nona'xesimo] *adj* ninetieth. **nonagenario, -a** *s adj* nonagenarian.

norabuena [nora'βwena] *sf* congratulations *pl*. *adv* by good fortune. **noramala** *adv* unfortunately.

nordeste [nor'ðeste] *sm* north-east; (*viento*) northeaster. *adj* north-east.

noria [no'ria] *sf* waterwheel.

norma ['norma] *sf* norm; rule. **normal** *adj* normal. **normalidad** *sf* normality. **normalizar** *v* normalize.

noroeste [noro'este] *sm* north-west; (*viento*) northwesterly. *adj* north-west.

norte ['norte] *sm, adj* north. **perder el norte** lose one's bearings. **norteño** *adj* northern.

Noruega [nor'wega] *sf* Norway. **noruego, -a** *sm, sf* (*persona*) Norwegian; *sm* (*idioma*) Norwegian.

nos [nos] *pron* us, ourselves.

nosotros [no'sotros] *pron* we; us, ourselves.

nostalgia [nos'talxja] *sf* nostalgia. **nostálgico** *adj* nostalgic; homesick.

notar [no'tar] *v* note; notice; note down. **nota** *sf* (*música, etc.*) note; mark; report; repute. **notabilidad** *sf* notability. **notable** *adj* notable. **notación** *sf* notation.

notario [no'tarjo] *sm* notary. **notaría** *sf* notary's office.

noticiar [noti'θjar] *v* notify. **noticia(s)** *sf* (*pl*) news *sing*. **noticiario** *sm* news bulletin. **noticiero, -a** *sm, sf* reporter. **noticón** *sm* (*fam*) big news. **noticioso** *adj* well-informed. **notificación** *sf* notification.

notorio [no'torjo] *adj* notorious. **notoriedad** *sf* notoriety.

novato [no'βato], **-a** *s, adj* novice.

novecientos [noβe'θjentos] *adj, s* nine hundred.

novedad [noβe'ðað] *sf* novelty; change. **novedades** *sf pl* latest models.

novela [no'βela] *sf* novel. **novelista** *s(m+f)* novelist.

noveno [no'βeno] *adj* ninth. **noventa** *adj* ninety.

novia ['noβja] *sf* girlfriend; fiancée; bride. **traje de novia** wedding dress. **novio** *sm* boyfriend; fiancé; bridegroom.

novicio [no'βiθjo] *sm* beginner; apprentice. **noviciado** *sm* novitiate; apprenticeship.

noviembre [no'βjembre] *sm* November.

novilla [no'βiʎa] *sf* heifer. **novillada** *sf* bullfight with young bulls. **novillero** *sm* novice bullfighter. **novillo** *sm* young bull. **hacer novillos** play truant.

nube ['nuβe] *sf* cloud. **estar por las nubes** (*precios*) be sky-high. **poner por las nubes** praise to the skies. **nublado** *adj* overcast. **nublar** *v* cloud over. **nubloso** *adj* cloudy; ill-fated.

núcleo ['nukleo] *sm* nucleus; core; (*bot*) stone. **nuclear** *adj* nuclear.

nudillo [nu'ðiʎo] *sm* knuckle.

nudo[1] ['nuðo] *sm* knot; bond; tumour.

nudo[2] *adj* nude.

351

obvio

nuera ['nwera] *sf* daughter-in-law.
nuestro ['nwestro] *adj* our. *pron* ours.
nueva ['nweβa] *sf* news. **nuevo** *adj* new. **de nuevo** again. **nuevo flamante** brand new.
nueve ['nweβe] *adj*, *sm* nine.
nuez [nweθ] *sf* nut; walnut. **nuez de la garganta** Adam's apple.
nulo ['nulo] *adj* null; void; (*fig*) hopeless.
numerar [nume'rar] *v* number. **numeral** *sm*, *adj* numeral. **numérico** *adj* numerical. **número** *sm* number; size; quantity. **numeroso** *adj* numerous.
nunca ['nunka] *adv* never; ever. **casi nunca** hardly ever.
nuncio ['nunθjo] *sm* nuncio; (*fig*) omen.
nupcial [nup'θjal] *adj* nuptial. **nupcias** *sf pl* nuptials.
nutria [nu'tria] *sf also* **nutra** *sf* otter.
nutrir [nu'trir] *v* nourish. **nutrición** *sf* nutrition. **nutrimento** *sm* nutriment.

Ñ

ñaque ['nake] *sm* odds and ends.
ñoño ['nono] *adj* insipid; prudish; fussy. **ñoñería** *sf also* **ñoñez** *sf* insipidity; prudery; fussiness.
ñu [nu] *sm* gnu.

O

o [o] *conj* or. **o . . . o** either . . . or. **o sea** in other words.
obcecar [oβθe'kar] *v* blind; deceive. **obcecarse** *v* become blind; be dazzled. **obcecado** *adj* blind; obdurate.
obduración [oβðura'θjon] *sf* obduracy; obstinacy.
*****obedecer** [oβeðe'θer] *v* obey. **obediencia** *sf* obedience. **obediente** *adj* obedient.
obertura [oβer'tura] *sf* (*música*) overture.
obesidad [oβesi'ðað] *sf* obesity. **obeso** *adj* obese.
obispo [o'βispo] *sm* bishop. **obispado** *sm* bishopric.
obituario [oβi'twarjo] *sm* obituary.

objetar [oβxe'tar] *v* object (to). **objeción** *sf* objection. **objetivo** *sm* objective. **objeto** *sm* object.
oblicuo [o'βlikwo] *adj* oblique. **oblicuar** *v* slant.
obligar [oβli'gar] *v* oblige; force. **verse obligado a** be forced to. **obligación** *sf* obligation. **obligado** *adj* essential. **obligatorio** *adj* compulsory.
obliterar [oβlite'rar] *v* obliterate; obstruct.
oblongo [o'βlongo] *adj* oblong.
obrar [o'βrar] *v* work; operate; make; build; behave. **obra** *sf* work. **obra maestra** masterpiece. **obrero, -a** *sm, sf* worker.
obsceno [oβs'θeno] *adj* obscene. **obscenidad** *sf* obscenity.
*****obscurecer** [oβskure'θer] *v also* **oscurecer** obscure, darken. **obscuridad** *sf* obscurity. **obscuro** *adj* obscure.
obsequiar [oβseki'ar] *v* entertain; treat; present. **obsequio** *sm* courtesy; gift. **obsequioso** *adj* obsequious; attentive.
observar [oβser'var] *v* observe. **observación** *sf* observation. **observador, -a** *sm, sf* observer. **observancia** *sf* observance. **observante** *adj* observant. **observatorio** *sm* observatory.
obsesión [oβse'sjon] *sf* obsession. **obsesionante** *adj* obsessive. **obseso** *adj* obsessed.
obsoleto [oβso'leto] *adj* obsolete.
obstáculo [oβs'takulo] *sm* obstacle.
obstante [oβs'tante] *prep* in spite of. *adv* **no obstante** notwithstanding; nevertheless. **obstar** *v* hinder; oppose.
obstetricia [oβste'triθja] *sf* obstetrics. **obstétrico** *adj* obstetric.
obstinarse [oβsti'narse] *v* be obstinate; persist. **obstinación** *sf* obstinacy. **obstinado** *adj* obstinate.
*****obstruir** [oβstru'ir] *v* obstruct. **obstrucción** *sf* obstruction. **obstructivo** *adj* obstructive.
*****obtener** [oβte'ner] *v* obtain. **obtención** *sf* attainment.
obturar [oβtu'rar] *v* stop up, plug. **obturación** *sf* plugging; sealing. **velocidad de obturación** (*foto*) shutter speed. **obturador** *sm* plug; (*foto*) shutter.
obtuso [oβ'tuso] *adj* obtuse.
obús [o'βus] *sm* howitzer.
obvio ['oββjo] *adj* obvious. **obviar** *v* obviate.

oca ['oka] *sf* goose.

ocasión [oka'sjon] *sf* occasion; opportunity; reason. **ocasional** *adj* occasional; chance. **ocasionalmente** *adv* occasionally; accidentally. **ocasionar** *v* cause.

ocaso [o'kaso] *sm* sunset; decline; west.

occidental [okθiðen'tal] *adj* western, occidental. **occidente** *sm* west.

océano [o'θeano] *sm* ocean.

ocio ['oθjo] *sm* leisure; idleness. **ociosidad** *sf* idleness. **ocioso** *adj* idle.

ocre ['okre] *sm* ochre.

octágono [ok'tagono] *adj* octagonal. *sm* octagon.

octava [ok'taβa] *sf* octave. **octavo** *adj* eighth. **octogenario, -a** *sm*, *sf* octogenarian. **octogésimo** *adj* eightieth.

octubre [ok'tuβre] *sm* October.

ocular [oku'lar] *adj* ocular. **testigo ocular** eyewitness. *sm* eyepiece. **oculista** *s(m+f)* oculist.

ocultar [okul'tar] *v* hide. **ocultación** *sf* concealment; dissimulation. **oculto** *adj* secret; hidden; occult.

ocupar [oku'par] *v* occupy; employ; take over. **ocuparse (de)** look after; do; employ. **ocupación** *sf* occupation. **ocupado** *adj* occupied; taken; engaged. **ocupante** *s(m+f)* occupant.

ocurrir [okur'rir] *v* occur. **ocurrencia** *sf* occurrence; (*fig*) witticism; idea. **ocurrente** *adj* witty.

ochenta [o'tʃenta] *sm, adj* eighty. **ocho** *sm, adj* eight.

oda ['oða] *sf* ode.

odiar [o'ðjar] *v* hate. **odio** *sm* hate, hatred. **tener odio a uno** hate someone. **odiosidad** *sf* hatefulness; odiousness. **odioso** *adj* odious; hateful.

odorífero [oðo'rifero] *adj* odoriferous, fragrant.

oeste [o'este] *sm* west.

ofender [ofen'der] *v* offend; insult. **ofenderse** *v* resent. **ofensa** *sf* offence; insult. **ofensiva** *sf* attack. **ofensivo** *adj* offensive; insulting. **ofensor** *s m*, *sf* offender.

oferta [o'ferta] *sf* offer; bid; tender; gift. **ley de la oferta y la demanda** law of supply and demand.

oficial [ofi'θjal] *adj, sm* official. **oficialía** *sf* clerkship. **oficina** *sf* office; agency; laboratory. **oficio** *sm* job; appointment; calling. **oficioso** *adj* diligent; meddlesome.

ofrecer [ofre'θer] *v* offer. **ofrecerse** *v* volunteer. ¿qué se le ofrece a usted? may I help you? **ofrecimiento** *sm* offer. **ofrendar** *v* contribute. **ofrenda** *sf* offer.

ofuscar [ofus'kar] *v* bewilder; dazzle.

ogro ['ogro] *sm* ogre.

oigo [o'igo] *V* oír.

oír [o'ir] *v* hear; listen to. **oírse** *v* be heard. **oír decir que** hear 'that. **oída** *sf* hearing. **oíble** *adj* audible. **oído** *sm* hearing; ear. **dolor de oídos** earache.

ojal [o'xal] *sm* buttonhole.

ojalá [oxa'la] *interj* let's hope so! would to God! *conj* if only.

ojear [oxe'ar] *v* look at. **ojeada** *sf* glance.

ojear² *v* (*en la caza*) start game; (*espantar*) scare off.

ojo ['oxo] *sm* eye; opening; hole; keyhole; (*puente*) span. ¡ojo! look out!

ola ['ola] *sf* wave. **ola de calor** heatwave.

olé [o'le] *interj* bravo!

oleandro [ole'andro] *sm* oleander.

óleo ['oleo] *sm* oil. **pintura al óleo** *sf* oil painting. **oleoducto** *sm* pipeline. **oleosidad** *sf* oiliness. **oleoso** *adj* oily.

oler [o'ler] *v* smell. **oler bien/mal** smell good/bad. **olfatear** *v* smell; sniff; sniff out. **olfato** *sm* sense of smell. **olfatorio** *adj* olfactory. **oliente** *adj* smelling. **olor** *sm* smell. **oloroso** *adj* fragrant.

oligarquía [oligar'kia] *sf* oligarchy.

olímpico [o'limpiko] *adj* Olympic. **juegos olímpicos** Olympic games.

oliva [o'liβa] *sf* olive; olive tree. **olivar** *sm* olive grove. **olivo** *sm* olive tree.

olmo ['olmo] *sm* elm tree. **olmeda** *sf* elm grove.

olvidar [olβi'ðar] *v* forget. **olvidadizo** *adj* forgetful. **olvido** *sm* forgetfulness.

olla ['oʎa] *sf* pot; kettle; stew; (*remolino*) eddy. **olla exprés** pressure cooker. **olla podrida** hotpot.

ombligo [om'bligo] *sm* navel; (*fig*) core.

ominoso [omi'noso] *adj* ominous.

omitir [omi'tir] *v* omit; neglect. **omisión** *sf* omission. **omiso** *adj* careless. **hacer caso omiso de** ignore; overlook.

ómnibus ['omniβus] *sm* omnibus.

omnipotencia [omnipo'tenθja] *sf* omnipotence. **omnipotente** *adj* omnipotent.

omnisciencia [omnis'θjenθja] *sf* omniscience. **omniscio** *adj* omniscient.

omnívoro [om'niβoro] *adj* omnivorous.

once ['onθe] *sm, adj* eleven.

onda ['onda] *sf* wave; ripple. **onda corta/larga/media** short/long/medium wave. **onda luminosa** light wave. **onda sonora** sound wave. **ondear** *v* wave. **ondearse** *v* swing. **ondulación** *sf* undulation. **ondulado** *adj* wavy. **ondulante** *adj* undulating. **ondular** *v* undulate; wriggle.

oneroso [one'roso] *adj* onerous.

ónice ['oniθe] *sm also* **ónique**, **ónix** onyx.

onza ['onθa] *sf (peso y animal)* ounce.

opaco [o'pako] *adj* opaque; dull. **opacidad** *sf* opacity.

opción [op'θjon] *sf* option. **opcional** *adj* optional.

ópera ['opera] *sf* opera.

operar [ope'rar] *v* operate. **operación** *sf* operation. **operador, -a** *sm, sf* operator; surgeon; projectionist. **operante** *adj* operative. **operario, -a** *sm, sf* operative, worker. **operativo** *adj* operative.

opinar [opi'nar] *v* think; judge. **opinión** *sf* opinion.

opio ['opjo] *sm* opium.

***oponer** [opo'ner] *v* oppose; hinder; contradict. **oponerse a** compete for. **oposición** *sf* opposition. **opositor, -a** *sm, sf* opponent; competitor.

oportunidad [oportuni'ðað] *sf* opportunity. **oportunista** *adj* opportunist. **oportuno** *adj* opportune.

oprimir [opri'mir] *v* oppress; depress. **opresión** *sf* oppression. **opresivo** *adj* oppressive. **opresor, -a** *sm, sf* oppressor.

oprobio [o'proβjo] *sm* opprobrium, disgrace. **oprobioso** *adj* disgraceful.

optar [op'tar] *v* opt, choose.

óptico ['optiko] *adj* optic, optical. *sm* optician.

optimismo [opti'mismo] *sm* optimism. **optimista** *s(m+f)* optimist.

óptimo ['optimo] *adj* optimum, best.

opuesto [o'pwesto] *adj* opposed; against.

opulento [opu'lento] *adj* opulent. **opulencia** *sf* opulence.

oquedad [oke'ðað] *sf* hole; hollow.

ora ['ora] *conj* now.

oráculo [o'rakulo] *sm* oracle.

orangután [orangu'tan] *sm* orangutan.

orar [o'rar] *v* pray; plead; make a speech. **oración** *sf* oration; prayer. **partes de la oración** parts of speech. **orador, -a** *sm, sf* orator. **orador sagrado** preacher. **oral** *adj* oral.

orbe ['orβe] *sm* orb, globe.

órbita ['orβita] *sf* orbit. **orbitar** *v* orbit.

ordenar [orðe'nar] *v* order, command; tidy; direct; ordain. **ordenarse** *v* become ordained. **orden** *sm* order, sequence. **por su orden** successively. **ordenación** *sf* arrangement; ordination. **ordenanza** *sf* arrangement; ordinance.

ordeñar [orðe'nar] *v* milk.

ordinal [orði'nal] *adj* ordinal.

ordinario [orði'narjo] *adj* ordinary; common. **de ordinario** usually.

orear [ore'ar] *v* air, ventilate. **orearse** *v* get a breath of fresh air.

oreja [o'rexa] *sf* ear. **bajar las orejas** knuckle under.

orfebre [or'feβre] *sm* goldsmith; silversmith. **orfebrería** *sf* goldwork; silverwork.

orfeón [orfe'on] *sm* choral society.

orgánico [or'ganiko] *adj* organic. **organismo** *sm* organism. **organista** *s(m+f)* organist. **organización** *sf* organization. **organizador, -a** *sm, sf* organizer. **órgano** *sm* organ.

orgasmo [or'gasmo] *sm* orgasm.

orgía [or'xia] *sf* orgy.

orgulloso [orgu'loso] *adj* proud. *sm* pride.

orientarse [orjen'tarse] *v* find one's bearings. **orientación** *sf* orientation. **oriental** *adj* oriental, eastern. **oriente** *sm* orient, east. **Extremo Oriente** Far East. **Oriente Medio** Middle East.

orificio [ori'fiθjo] *sm* orifice, hole.

origen [o'rixen] *sm* origin; native country. **original** *adj* original. **originalidad** *sf* originality. **originar** *v* originate. **originarse** *v* arise.

orilla [o'riʎa] *sf* edge; bank; shore. **a orillas de** on the banks of.

orín [o'rin] *sm* rust.

orina [o'rina] *sf* urine. **orinal** *sm* chamber pot. **orinar** *v* urinate.

oriundo [o'rjundo] *adj* native of.

orlar [or'lar] *v* border, edge. **orla** *sf* border, trimming.

ornamentar [ornamen'tar] *v* adorn, decorate. **ornamentación** *sf* ornamentation. **ornamental** *adj* ornamental. **ornamento** *sm* ornament. **ornar** *v* adorn. **ornato** *sm* adornment.

ornitología [ornitolo'xia] *sf* ornithology. **ornitólogo** *sm* ornithologist.

oro ['oro] *sm* gold. **oro batido** gold leaf. **oro en bruto** bullion. **oropel** *sm* tinsel.

orquesta [or'kesta] *sf* orchestra. orquestación *sf* orchestration. orquestar *v* orchestrate.

orquídea [or'kiðea] *sf* orchid.

ortega [or'tega] *sf* grouse.

ortodoxo [orto'ðokso] *adj* orthodox. ortodoxia *sf* orthodoxy.

ortografía [ortogra'fia] *sf* orthography, spelling.

ortopédico [orto'peðiko], -a *sm, sf* orthopedist. ortopedia *sf* orthopedic.

oruga [o'ruga] *sf* caterpillar.

os [os] *pron pl* you.

osa ['osa] *sf* she-bear. oso bear. oso blanco polar bear.

osar [o'sar] *v* dare. osadía *sf* daring. osado *adj* daring.

oscilar [osθi'lar] *v* oscillate, swing. oscilación *sf* oscillation.

oscuro [os'kuro] *adj* dark, obscure. oscurecer *v* darken; confuse. oscuridad *sf* obscurity.

ostensible [osten'siβle] *adj* ostensible; apparent. ostentación *sf* ostentation. ostentar *v* show off. ostentativo *adj also* ostentoso ostentatious.

ostra ['ostra] *sf* oyster.

otear [ote'ar] *v* make out; watch; scan.

otoño [o'toɲo] *sm* autumn. otoñada *f* autumn season. otoñal *adj* autumnal. otoñarse *v* be seasoned.

otorgar [otor'gar] *v* grant; award; confer. otorgamiento *sm* granting; authorization.

otro ['otro] *adj* other; another. otra vez again. otro tanto the same (again). *pron* another. algún otro some other.

ovación [oβa'θjon] *sf* ovation. ovacionar *v* give an ovation to.

óvalo ['oβalo] *sm* oval; ellipse. oval *adj* oval.

ovario [o'βarjo] *sm* ovary.

oveja [o'βexa] *sf* ewe; sheep.

ovillo [o'βiʎa] *sm* (*de lana*) ball; heap.

oxidar [oksi'ðar] *v* oxidize. óxido *sm* oxide. oxígeno *sm* oxygen.

oye ['oje] *V* oír.

oyente [o'jente] *adj* hearing. *s(m+f)* listener.

ozono [o'θono] *sm* ozone.

P

pabellón [paβe'ʎon] *sm* pavilion; bell tent; summerhouse; hospital block; flag.

*pacer [pa'θer] *v* graze, pasture.

paciencia [pa'θjenθja] *sf* patience. paciente *s(m+f)*. *adj* patient. pacienzudo *adj* long-suffering.

pacificar [paθifi'kar] *v* pacify. pacificación *sf* pacification. pacificador *adj* pacifying. pacífico *adj* pacific, peaceful. Oceano Pacífico Pacific Ocean. pacifismo *sm* pacifism. pacifista *s(m+f)* pacifist.

pacotilla [pako'tiʎa] *sf* inferior goods *pl*. de pacotilla shoddy.

pactar [pak'tar] *v* make a pact, agree. pacto *sm* pact, agreement.

pachorra [pa'tʃorra] *sf* sluggishness; indolence.

*padecer [paðe'θer] *v* suffer; endure. padecer de suffer from. padecimiento *sm* suffering; ailment.

padre ['paðre] *sm* father. padres *sm pl* parents. padrastro *sm* stepfather. Padre Nuestro Lord's Prayer. padrino *sm* godfather; second; sponsor. padrino de boda best man.

padrón [pa'ðron] *sm* census; pattern; memorial; (*fam*) indulgent father.

pagano [pa'gano], -a *sm, sf, adj* pagan.

pagar [pa'gar] *v* pay. pagarse de take a liking to. paga *sf* payment; salary. pagadero *adj* payable. pagador, -a *sm, sf* payer. pagaduría *sf* pay office. pagaré *sm* IOU. pago *sm* payment; reward.

página ['paxina] *sf* page.

país [pa'is] *sm* country. paisaje *sm* landscape; countryside. paisanaje *sm* peasantry. paisano, -na *sm, sf* compatriot; peasant.

Países Bajos [pa'ises'βaxos] *sm pl* The Netherlands.

paja ['paxa] *sf* straw. echar pajas draw lots. pajita *sf* drinking straw.

pájaro ['paxaro] *sm* bird. pajarera *sf* birdcage.

paje ['paxe] *sm* (*niño*) page.

pala ['pala] *sf* shovel; spade; scoop; dustpan; bat. palazo *sm* blow with a stick.

palabra [pa'laβra] *sf* word. de palabra by word of mouth. faltar a la palabra break one's word. palabreo *sm* verbiage.

palabrista s(m+f) chatterbox. **palabrota** sf swear word at court.

palacio [pa'laθjo] sm palace; mansion. **en palacio** at court.

paladar [pala'ðar] sm palate. **paladear** v taste, relish.

palanca [pa'lanka] sf crowbar; lever; (fam) influence.

palangana [palaŋ'gana] sf washbasin.

palco ['palko] sm (teatro) box.

paleta [pa'leta] sf shovel; trowel; (de pintor) palette; (de hélice) blade; (anat) shoulder blade.

paliar [pal'jar] v alleviate. **paliativo** adj palliative.

*****palidecer** [paliðe'θer] v become pale. **palidez** paleness. **pálido** adj pale.

palillo [pa'liλo] sm toothpick; small stick.

paliza [pa'liθa] sf beating, hiding.

palma ['palma] sf palm tree; (anat) palm. **palmada** sf slap; applause. **palmar** adj clear, obvious. **palmatoria** sf candlestick; cane. **palmear** v clap hands. **palmera** sf palm tree.

palmo ['palmo] sm (medida) span, handbreadth. **palmotear** v applaud. **palmoteo** sm applause.

palo ['palo] sm stick; pole; handle; blow with a stick; mast. **dar de palos** thrash.

paloma [pa'loma] sf dove; pigeon. **palomar** sm dovecote. **palomino** sm young pigeon.

palpable [pal'paβle] adj palpable.

palpar [pal'par] v feel, touch. **palparse** v grope.

palpitar [palpi'tar] v palpitate, throb. **palpitación** sf palpitation. **palpitante** adj palpitating, throbbing.

paludismo [palu'ðismo] sm malaria.

palurdo [pa'lurðo] sm, adj rustic.

palustre[1] [pa'lustre] adj marshy.

palustre[2] sm trowel.

pan [pan] sm bread; loaf; dough. **pan ácimo** unleavened bread. **panadería** sf bread shop. **panadero, -a** sm, sf baker.

pana ['pana] sf corduroy. **pana lisa** velvet.

panal [pa'nal] sm honeycomb.

panamá [pana'ma] sm Panama hat.

panamericano [panameri'kano] adj pan-American.

pancarta [paŋ'karta] sf placard.

pandereta [pande'reta] sf tambourine.

pandilla [pan'diλa] sf gang; clique.

panfleto [pan'fleto] sm pamphlet. **panfletista** s(m+f) pamphleteer.

pánico ['paniko] sm, adj panic.

pantalón [panta'lon] sm also **pantalones** trousers.

pantalla [pan'taλa] sf lampshade; screen.

pantano [pan'tano] sm marsh; bog. **pantanal** sm marshland. **pantanoso** adj swampy.

panteísta [pante'ista] s(m+f) pantheist. **panteísmo** sm pantheism.

pantera [pan'tera] sf panther.

pantomima [panto'mima] sf pantomime.

pantorrilla [pantor'riλa] sf (anat) calf.

pantufla [pan'tufla] sf or **pantuflo** sm slipper.

panza ['panθa] sf belly. **panzada** sf bellyful.

pañal [pa'nal] sm nappy.

pañería [paɲe'ria] sf drapery. **pañero** sm draper. **paño** sm light cloth. **paño** sm cloth. **paños menores** underclothes. **pañuelo** sm handkerchief.

papa[1] ['papa] sm pope. **papado** sm papacy. **papal** adj papal.

papa[2] sf potato.

papá [pa'pa] sm daddy.

papada [pa'paða] sf double chin.

papagayo [papa'gajo] sm parrot.

papar [pa'par] v eat; gulp. **papamoscas** m invar flycatcher; (fig) simpleton. **papar moscas** gape.

papel [pa'pel] sm paper. **papel de forrar** brown paper. **papel de fumar** cigarette paper. **papeleo** sm paper work; (fam) red tape. **papelera** sf wastepaper basket. **papelería** sf stationer's.

papera [pa'pera] sf goitre. **paperas** sf pl mumps sing.

papiro [pa'piro] sm papyrus.

paquete [pa'kete] sm packet.

par [par] sm pair. adj equal. **sin par** matchless.

para ['para] prep for; towards. **para mañana** by tomorrow. ¿**para qué**? why?.

parábola [pa'raβola] sf parable; parabola.

parabrisas [para'βrisas] sm invar windshield.

paracaídas [paraka'iðas] sm invar parachute. **paracaidista** s(m+f) parachutist.

parachoques [para'ʃtokes] sm invar (auto) bumper.

parada [pa'raða] sf stop; stopping; (taxi) rank; pause; parade; dam. **paradero** sm whereabouts; destination; home. **parado** adj motionless; unemployed.

paradoja [para'ðoxa] *sf* paradox. **paradójico** *adj* paradoxical.

parador [para'ðor] *sm* tourist hotel.

parafina [para'fina] *sf* paraffin.

paráfrasis [pa'rafrasis] *sf invar* paraphrase. **parafrasear** *v* paraphrase.

paraguas [pa'raɣwas] *sm invar* umbrella.

paraíso [para'iso] *sm* paradise; (*teatro*) gallery.

paralela [para'lela] *sf* parallel. **paralelas** *sf pl* parallel bars. **paralelo** *sm, adj* parallel.

parálisis [pa'ralisis] *sf* paralysis. **paralítico** *sm, adj* paralytic. **paralizar** *v* paralyse.

páramo ['paramo] *sm* wilderness; bleak plateau. **paramera** *sf* desert.

parangón [paran'gon] *sm* comparison. **parangonar** *v* compare.

parapeto [para'peto] *sm* parapet; railing.

parar [pa'rar] *v* stop; check. **pararse** *v* stay; end up. **parar en mal** come to a bad end.

pararrayos [parar'rajos] *sm invar* lightning conductor.

parásito [pa'rasito] *sm* parasite. *adj* parasitic.

parasol [para'sol] *sm* parasol.

parcela [par'ðela] *sf* (*de tierra*) plot. **parcelar** *v* parcel out.

parcial [par'ðjal] *adj* partial. **parcialidad** *sf* partiality.

parco ['parko] *adj* frugal; mean; sparing.

parche ['partʃe] *sm* plaster; patch; drumhead.

pardo ['parðo] *adj* dark; brown.

parear [pare'ar] *v* match, pair.

****parecer** [pare'θer] *v* seem; appear. **parecerse** *v* resemble. **parecido** *adj* similar. **bien parecido** good-looking.

pared [pa'reð] *sf* wall. **paredón** *sm* large wall.

pareja [pa'rexa] *sf* pair; couple. **parejo** *adj* even; equal.

parentela [paren'tela] *sf* kindred. **parentesco** *sm* kinship.

paréntesis [pa'rentesis] *sm* parenthesis; bracket.

paridad [pari'ðað] *sf* comparison; parity.

pariente [pa'rjente] *sm* relation.

parir [pa'rir] *v* give birth to.

París [pa'ris] *s* Paris.

parla [parla] *sf* gossip; chatter. **parlador, -a** *sm, sf* talker. **parlanchín** *adj* talkative. **parlante** *adj* chattering. **parlar** *v* chatter. **parleta** *sf* small talk.

parlamento [parla'mento] *sm* parliament. **parlamentario** *adj* parliamentary.

paro ['paro] *sm* stoppage; unemployment.

parodiar [paro'ðjar] *v* parody. **parodia** *sf* parody.

paroxismo [parok'sismo] *sm* paroxysm.

parpadear [parpaðe'ar] *v* blink; wink. **parpadeo** *sm* blinking; winking. **párpado** *sm* eyelid.

parque ['parke] *sm* park.

parra ['parra] *sf* vine. **hoja de parra** figleaf. **parra virgen** Virginia creeper.

párrafo ['parrafo] *sm* paragraph.

parricida [parri'θiða] *s(m+f)* (*criminal*) parricide. **parricidio** *sm* (*crimen*) parricide.

parrilla [par'riʎa] *sf* grill; gridiron; grate; grillroom.

párroco ['parroko] *sm* parish priest. **parroquia** *sf* parish; parish church. **parroquial** *adj* parochial. **parroquiano, -a** *sm, sf* parishioner; regular customer.

parsimonia [parsi'monja] *sf* parsimony; frugality; calmness.

parte ['parte] *sf* part; share; point; side; way; party; role; actor. **en otra parte** elsewhere. **por todas partes** everywhere. **por una parte y por otra** on the one hand and on the other.

partera [par'tera] *sf* midwife.

partición [parti'θjon] *sf* partition; division. **partible** *adj* divisible.

participar [partiθi'par] *v* participate; partake; invest; inform; announce. **participación** *sf* participation; share; announcement. **participante** *s(m+f)* participant; informant; competitor. **partícipe** *s(m+f)* participant.

participio [parti'θipjo] *sm* (*gram*) participle.

partícula [par'tikula] *sf* particle.

particular [partiku'lar] *adj* particular; peculiar; individual; personal. **casa particular** private house. *sm* matter; individual; civilian. **particularidad** *sf* peculiarity. **particularizar** *v* specify; distinguish; prefer. **particularizarse** *v* stand out. **particularmente** *adv* in particular.

partida [par'tiða] *sf* departure; certificate; (*com*) entry; item; party; game. **partida de campo** picnic. **partida doble** double entry. **partidario, -a** *sm, sf* follower; partisan.

partido [par'tiðo] *sm* (*deporte*) match;

(*pol*) party. *adj* divided. **darse a partido** give in. **sacar partido** benefit from.

partir [par'tir] *v* leave, depart; divide; share. **a partir de hoy** from today on. **partirse** *v* differ in opinion; depart. **partidor** *sm* distributor.

partitura [parti'tura] *sf* (*música*) score.

parto ['parto] *sm* childbirth; delivery; (*fig*) brainchild.

parvo ['parβo] *adj* little. **párvulo** *adj* very small.

pasa ['pasa] *sf* raisin. **pasa de Corinto** currant.

pasada [pa'saða] *sf* passage; (*aves*) flight. **de pasada** in passing. **mala pasada** dirty trick. **pasadero** *adj* tolerable.

pasado [pa'saðo] *sm, adj* past. **lo pasado, pasado** let bygones be bygones. **pasado mañana** the day after tomorrow.

pasador [pasa'ðor], **-a** *sm, sf* smuggler. *sm* filter; colander; bolt; pin; fastener. **pasadores** *sm pl* cufflinks *pl*.

pasaje [pa'saxe] *sm* passage; fare; ticket; voyage; passengers *pl*. **pasajero, -a** *sm, sf* passenger.

pasamano [pasa'mano] *sm* bannister; handrail.

pasapasa [pasa'pasa] *sm* sleight-of-hand.

pasaporte [pasa'porte] *sm* passport.

pasar [pa'sar] *v* pass; give; spend; take; send; run; cross; penetrate. **pasar de moda** be out of fashion. **pasarlo bien/mal** have a good/bad time. **pasar por** be considered. **pasar por alto** overlook. **¿qué pasa?** what's up? **pasarse** pass off; be over; miss. **pasarse de be** too. **pasarse por** call in at.

pasarela [pasa'rela] *sf* footbridge; gangway.

pasatiempo [pasa'tjempo] *sm* pastime; amusement.

pascua ['paskwa] *sf* (*rel*) feast; Christmas; Easter; Epiphany; Passover. **¡felices pascuas y próspero año nuevo!** merry Christmas and a happy New Year!

pase ['pase] *sm* invitation; permission; (*autorización*) pass.

pasear [pase'ar] *v* go for a walk; take for a walk; go for a ride. **paseo** *sm* walk; drive; ride.

pasillo [pa'siʎo] *sm* corridor; passage.

pasión [pasi'on] *sf* passion. **pasional** *adj* passionate.

pasivo [pa'siβo] *adj* passive. *sm* (*com*) liabilities *pl*. **pasividad** *sf* passivity.

pasmar [pas'mar] *v* chill; stun; amaze. **pasmo** *sm* amazement; convulsion. **pasmoso** *adj* wonderful.

paso ['paso] *sm* step; pace; walk; passage; situation. **paso a nivel** level-crossing. **paso a paso** step by step. **salir del paso** get out of a difficulty.

pasta ['pasta] *sf* pasta; dough; paste. **pastas** *sf pl* noodles.

pastar [pas'tar] *v* graze, pasture.

pastel [pas'tel] *sm* cake, pastry; (*color*) pastel. **pastel de carne** meat pie. **pastelería** *sf* cake shop; cakes *pl*; confectionery. **pastelero, -a** *sm, sf* pastrycook.

pastilla [pas'tiʎa] *sf* bar; piece; tablet.

pastinaca [pasti'naka] *sf* (*bot*) turnip; (*zool*) stingray.

pasto ['pasto] *sm* grass; pasture. **a pasto** galore. **pastor** *sm* shepherd; pastor. **pastoral** *adj* pastoral. **pastorear** *v* pasture.

pastura [pas'tura] *sf* pasture; fodder.

pata ['pata] *sf* (*de animal*) foot; leg; paw. **meter la pata** (*fam*) put one's foot in it. **tener mala pata** (*fam*) be unlucky. **patada** *sf* kick; stamp. **patalear** *v* stamp; kick about. **pataleo** *sm* kicking.

patán [pa'tan] *sm* lout. *adj* churlish. **patanería** *sf* boorishness.

patata [pa'tata] *sf* potato. **patatas fritas** french fries.

patear [pate'ar] *v* kick; stamp.

patente [pa'tente] *sm* (*com*) patent. *adj* obvious.

paternal [pater'nal] *adj* paternal. **paternidad** *sf* paternity. **paterno** *adj* paternal.

patético [pa'tetiko] *adj* pathetic.

patíbulo [pa'tiβulo] *sm* gallows *pl*.

patillas [pa'tiʎas] *sf pl* whiskers *pl*; sideboards *pl*.

patín [pa'tin] *sm* skate. **patín de ruedas** roller skate. **patinadero** *sm* skating rink. **patinador, -a** *sm, sf* skater. **patinaje** *sm* skating. **patinar** *v* skate; skid. **patinazo** *sm* skid; (*fam*) blunder. **patinete** *sm* child's scooter.

patio [pa'tjo] *sm* patio; yard.

pato ['pato] *sm* duck. **pagar el pato** (*fam*) carry the can.

patochada [pato'tʃaða] *sf* blunder.

patología [patolo'xia] *sf* pathology. **patológico** *adj* pathological. **patólogo** *sm* pathologist.

patraña [pa'traɲa] *sf* cock-and-bull story; fib.

patria ['patrja] *sf* native land. **patriota** *s(m+f)* patriot. **patriótico** *adj* patriotic. **patriotismo** *sm* patriotism.

patriarca [pa'trjarka] *sm* patriarch. **patriarcal** *adj* patriarchal.

patricio [pa'triθjo], -a *sm, sf, adj* patrician.

patrimonio [patri'monjo] *sm* patrimony, birthright. **patrimonial** *adj* patrimonial.

patrocinar [patroθi'nar] *v* patronize; sponsor. **patrocinador**, -a *sm, sf* patron; sponsor. **patrocinio** *sm* patronage; sponsorship.

patrón [pa'tron] *sm* patron; owner; landlord; pattern. **patronato** *sm* patronage; board of trustees; society.

patrono [pa'trono] *sm* boss; patron saint; owner.

patrulla [pa'truʎa] *sf* patrol. **patrullar** *v* patrol.

paulatino [paula'tino] *adj* slow, gradual. **paulatinamente** *adj* gradually; little by little.

pausa ['pausa] *sf* pause; *(música)* rest. **pausado** *adj* slow; deliberate. **pausar** *v* pause; interrupt.

pauta ['pauta] *sf* rule; model; lines *pl.* **pautar** *v* rule; give instructions. **papel pautado** ruled paper.

pávido ['paβiðo] *adj* timid.

pavimentar [paβimen'tar] *v* pave; surface. **pavimento** *sm* pavement.

pavo ['paβo] *sm* turkey. **pavo real** peacock. **pavonear** *v* show off.

pavor [pa'βor] *sm* terror; dread. **pavorido** *adj* terror-stricken. **pavoroso** *adj* dreadful; awful. **pavura** *sf* fear; dread.

payaso [pa'jaso] *sm* clown. **payasada** *sf* clowning.

paz [paθ] *sf* peace. **hacer las paces** make it up. **¡paz!** hush!

peaje [pe'axe] *sm* toll. **peajero** *sm* toll-collector.

peatón [pea'ton] *sm* pedestrian.

peca ['peka] *sf* spot; freckle. **pecoso** *adj* freckled.

pecar [pe'kar] *v* sin. **pecado** *sm* sin. **pecador**, -a *sm, sf* sinner. **pecaminoso** *adj* sinful.

pécora ['pekora] *sf* sheep; *(fam)* slut.

peculiar [peku'ljar] *adj* peculiar; special. **peculiaridad** *sf* peculiarity. **peculiarmente** *adv* peculiarly.

pechera [pe'tʃera] *sf* bib; shirt-front.

pecho ['petʃo] *sm* chest; bosom; breast; courage; tax. **dar el pecho** suckle. **enfermo del pecho** consumptive. **pechuga** *sf (de ave)* breast.

pedagogía [peðaɣo'xia] *sf* pedagogy. **pedagógico** *adj* teaching. **pedagogo** *sm* teacher.

pedal [pe'ðal] *sm* pedal. **pedalear** *v* pedal.

pedante [pe'ðante] *s(m+f)* pedant. *adj* pedantic. **pedantería** *sf* pedantry.

pedazo [pe'ðaθo] *sm* piece. **hacerse pedazos** be smashed to bits.

pedernal [peðer'nal] *sm* flint.

pedestal [peðe'stal] *sm* pedestal.

pedestre [pe'ðestre] *adj* pedestrian.

pediatría [peðja'tria] *sf* paediatrics. **pediatra** or **pediatra** *sm* paediatrician.

pedicuro [peði'kuro], -a *sm, sf* chiropodist. *sf* chiropody.

***pedir** [pe'ðir] *v* ask; ask for; order. **pedir limosna** beg. **pedir prestado** borrow. **pedido** *sm* demand; *(com)* order. **pedimento** *sm* petition.

pedo ['peðo] *sm (vulgar)* fart.

pedregal [peðre'ɣal] *sm* stony ground. **pedrea** *sf* stoning; hailstorm. **pedregoso** *adj* stony. **pedrería** *sf* jewels *pl.* **pedrero** *sm* stone-cutter. **pedrisco** *sm* hailstorm.

pegar [pe'ɣar] *v* hit; glue; *(med)* infect; take effect; give; let out; fire; sew on. **pegar fuego a** set fire to. **pegar un tiro** fire a shot. **pega** *sf* difficulty; hoax; snag. **poner pegas a** find fault with. **pegajoso** *adj* sticky; infectious.

peinar [pei'nar] *v* comb. **peinado** *sm* coiffure. **peinador**, -a *sm, sf* hairdresser; *sm* bathrobe. **peine** *sm* comb.

pelar [pe'lar] *v* cut; peel; shear; skin; shell. **pelar la pava** woo. **pelado** *adj* shorn; peeled; bare. **pelaje** *sm* fur. **pelambre** *sm (de animales)* hair. **pelambrera** *sf* fleece.

peldaño [pel'ðaɲo] *sm* stair; step.

pelear [pele'ar] *v* fight. **pelearse con alguien** fight somebody. **pelea** *sf* fight. **peleador** *sm* fight.

pelele [pe'lele] *sm* puppet; dummy.

pelingudo [pelin'guðo] *adj (fig)* difficult, tough.

pelícano [pe'likano] *sm* pelican.

película [pe'likula] *sf* film.

peligro [pe'liɣro] *sm* danger. **peligrarse** *v* be in danger. **peligroso** *adj* dangerous.

pelmazo [pel'maθo] *sm also* **pelma** *sf* bore; crushed mass.

pelo ['pelo] *sm* hair; (*en madera*) grain; nap. **de medio pelo** low-class. **soltarse el pelo** show one's true colours. **pelón** *adj* bald.

pelota [pe'lota] *sf* ball. **echarse la pelota** pass the buck. **en pelota** naked.

pelotón [pelo'ton] *sm* platoon; squad.

peltre ['peltre] *sm* pewter.

peluca [pe'luka] *sf* wig.

peludo [pe'luðo] *adj* hairy.

peluquero [pelu'kero], **-a** *sm, sf* hairdresser. **peluquería** *sf* hairdresser's.

pelusa [pe'lusa] *sf* down; fuzz; (*fam*) jealousy.

pelleja [pe'ʎexa] *sf also* **pellejo** *sm* hide, skin. **jugarse el pellejo** risk one's neck.

pellizcar [peʎiθ'kar] *v* nip, pinch. **pellizco** *sm* nip, pinch.

pellizo [pe'ʎiθo] *sm* fur jacket.

pena ['pena] *sf* pain; grief; hardship; penalty; effort. **pena capital** capital punishment. **¡qué pena!** what a shame! **penable** *adj* punishable. **penado** *adj* painful. **penal** *adj* penal. **penalidad** *sf* penalty. **penar** *v* punish; suffer. **penarse** *v* grieve.

pender [pen'der] *v* hang; (*jur*) be pending. **pendiente** *adj* hanging; pending. **estar pendiente de** depend on.

péndulo ['pendulo] *sm* pendulum.

pene ['pene] *sm* penis.

penetrar [pene'trar] *v* penetrate; comprehend. **penetrarse** *v* become aware of; imbibe. **penetrable** *adj* penetrable. **penetración** *sf* penetration. **penetrante** *adj* penetrating.

penicilina [peniθi'lina] *sf* penicillin.

península [pe'ninsula] *sf* peninsula. **peninsular** *adj* peninsular.

penique [pe'nike] *sm* penny.

penitencia [peni'tenθja] *sf* penitence. **hacer penitencia** (*fam*) take pot-luck. **penitencial** *adj* penitential. **penitenciaria** *sf* penitentiary. **penitente** *adj* penitent.

penoso [pe'noso] *adj* painful; difficult.

*****pensar** [pen'sar] *v* think; think over; intend. **pensar en** think about. **pensado** *adj* deliberate. **de pensado** on purpose. **pensador**, **-a** *sm, sf* thinker. **pensamiento** *sm* thought. **pensativo** *adj* thoughtful.

pensión [pensi'on] *sf* pension; boarding house; hardship. **pensionado**, **-a** *sm, sf* pensioner. **pensionar** *v* pension. **pensionista** *s(m+f)* pensioner; boarder.

pentágono [pen'tagono] *sm* pentagon.

penúltimo [pe'nultimo] *adj* penultimate.

penumbra [pe'numβra] *sf* half-light.

penuria [pe'nurja] *sf* penury; shortage.

peña ['pena] *sf* crag; rock; cliff; group of friends. **peñasco** *sm* large rock. **peñascoso** *adj* rocky. **peñón** *sm* rocky mountain. **el Peñón de Gibraltar** the Rock of Gibraltar.

peón [pe'on] *sm* unskilled labourer; pedestrian; foot-soldier; (*ajedrez*) pawn.

peonía [peo'nia] *sf* peony.

peor [pe'or] *adj, adv* worse; worst. **peoría** *sf* worsening.

pepino [pe'pino] *sm* cucumber. **no valer un pepino** not be worth a damn. **pepinillo** *sm* gherkin.

pepita [pe'pita] *sf* seed, pip; (*oro*) nugget.

pequeño [pe'keno] *adj* small; humble. **pequeñez** *sf* smallness; pettiness.

pera ['pera] *sf* pear; light-switch; (*barba*) goatee; sinecure. **peral** *sm* pear tree.

perca ['perka] *sf* (*zool*) perch.

percance [per'kanθe] *sm* mishap; profit.

percatarse [perka'tarse] *v* notice.

percibir [perθi'βir] *v* perceive; collect. **percepción** *sf* perception; collection. **perceptible** *adj* perceptible. **perceptivo** *adj* perceptive. **perceptor**, **-a** *sm, sf* perceiver. **percibo** *sm* collecting.

percusión [perku'sjon] *sf* percussion.

percha ['pertʃa] *sf* perch; pole; hat-stand; coat-rack.

*****perder** [per'ðer] *v* lose; spoil; waste. **perderse por** be inordinately fond of. **perdición** *sf* loss; perdition. **pérdida** *sf* damage; waste. **perdido** *adj* lost; dissolute.

perdiz [per'ðiθ] *sf* partridge.

perdonar [perðo'nar] *v* pardon; excuse. **pardón** *sm* pardon; mercy. **con perdón** by your leave. **perdonable** *adj* pardonable. **perdonavidas** *m invar* (*fam*) bully.

perdurar [perðu'rar] *v* endure. **perdurable** *adj* everlasting.

*****perecer** [pere'θer] *v* perish. **perecerse por** crave. **perecedero** *adj* perishable.

peregrinar [peregri'nar] *v* travel; go on a pilgrimage. **peregrinación** *sf* pilgrimage. **peregrino**, **-a** *sm, sf* pilgrim.

perejil [pere'xil] *sm* parsley.

perenne [pe'renne] *adj* perennial.

perentorio [peren'torjo] *adj* peremptory; urgent.

perezoso 360

perezoso [pere'θoso] *adj* lazy. **pereza** *sf* laziness.
perfecto [per'fekto] *adj* perfect. **perfección** *sf* perfection. **perfeccionamiento** *sm* improvement; perfection. **perfeccionar** *v* perfect; improve.
pérfido ['perfiðo] *adj* perfidious. **perfidia** *sf* perfidy.
perfilar [perfi'lar] *v* outline. **perfil** *sm* profile; outline.
perforar [perfo'rar] *v* perforate; drill; puncture. **perforación** *sf* perforation. **perforadora** *sf* drill.
perfumar [perfu'mar] *v* perfume. **perfume** *sm* perfume. **perfumería** *sf* perfume shop.
perfunctorio [perfunk'torjo] *adj* perfunctory.
pericial [peri'θjal] *adj* expert. **pericia** *sf* skill.
perico [pe'riko] *sm* parakeet; toupee.
periferia [peri'ferja] *sf* periphery.
perímetro [pe'rimetro] *sm* perimeter.
periódico [peri'oðiko] *sm* periodical; newspaper. *adj* periodic. **periodicidad** *sf* recurrence. **periodismo** *sm* journalism. **periodista** *s(m+f)* journalist. **periodístico** *adj* journalistic. **periodo** *or* **período** *sm* period. **periodo de prácticas** probationary period.
peripecia [peri'peθja] *sf* vicissitude; incident; adventure.
periscopio [peris'kopjo] *sm* periscope.
perjudicar [perxuði'kar] *v* prejudice; harm. **perjudicial** *adj* harmful. **perjuicio** *sm* prejudice; damage.
perjurar [perxu'rar] *v* perjure oneself. **perjurio** *sm* perjury. **perjuro, -a** *sm, sf* perjurer.
perla ['perla] *sf* pearl. **de perlas** perfectly.
*****permanecer** [permane'θer] *v* stay, remain. **permanencia** *sf* stay; permanence. **permanente** *adj* permanent.
permitir [permi'tir] *v* permit. **¿me permite?** may I? **permisible** *adj* permissible. **permisivo** *adj* permissive. **permiso** *sm* permission; permit; leave; licence. **con permiso** if I may.
permutar [permu'tar] *v* permute; exchange. **permuta** *sf* exchange; permutation. **permutación** *sf* permutation.
perniabierto [pernia'βjerto] *adj* bandy-legged.
pernicioso [perni'θjoso] *adj* pernicious.
pernoctar [pernok'tar] *v* spend the night.

pero¹ ['pero] *conj* but; yet. **¡pero bueno!** why!
pero² *sm* pear tree.
perogrullada [perogru'λaða] *sf* platitude.
perorar [pero'rar] *v* make a speech. **peroración** *sf* peroration.
peróxido [pe'roksiðo] *sm* peroxide.
perpendicular [perpendiku'lar] *sf, adj* perpendicular.
perpetrar [perpe'trar] *v* perpetrate. **perpetración** *sf* perpetration.
perpetuar [perpe'twar] *v* perpetuate. **perpetuación** *sf* perpetuation. **perpetuidad** *sf* perpetuity. **perpetuo** *adj* perpetual.
perplejo [per'plexo] *adj* perplexed; perplexing. **perplejidad** *sf* perplexity.
perro ['perro] *sm* dog; (*fam*) penny. **perra** *sf* bitch. **perrera** *sf* kennel; dog pound; dogcatcher's wagon. **perrero** *sm* dogcatcher.
*****perseguir** [perse'gir] *v* pursue; persecute. **persecución** *sf* pursuit; persecution. **perseguidor, -a** *sm, sf* pursuer; persecutor.
perseverar [perseβe'rar] *v* persevere. **perseverancia** *sf* perseverance. **perseverante** *adj* persevering.
persiana [per'sjana] *sf* slatted shutter. **persiana veneciana** venetian blind.
persistir [persis'tir] *v* persist. **persistencia** *sf* persistence. **persistente** *adj* persistent.
persona [per'sona] *sf* person. **persona a persona** man to man. **personaje** *sm* personage; (*teatro*) character. **personal** *adj* personal. **personalidad** *sf* personality. **personalismo** *sm* partiality. **personalizar** *v* personalize. **personarse** *v* appear in person. **personificar** *v* personify.
perspectiva [perspek'tiβa] *sf* perspective; outlook.
perspicaz [perspi'kaθ] *adj* perspicacious. **perspicacia** *sf* perspicacity.
persuadir [perswa'ðir] *v* persuade. **persuasión** *sf* persuasion. **persuasivo** *adj* persuasive.
*****pertenecer** [pertene'θer] *v* belong. **perteneciente** *adj* belonging. **pertenencia** *sf* ownership; property; membership.
pértiga ['pertiga] *sf* pole. **salto de pértiga** pole vault.
pertiguero [perti'gero] *sm* verger.
pertinaz [perti'naθ] *adj* pertinacious. **pertinacia** *sf* pertinacity.
pertinente [perti'nente] *adj* pertinent. **pertinencia** *sf* pertinence.

pertrechar [pertre'tʃar] v supply; equip. **pertrechos** sm pl equipment sing; munitions pl.

perturbar [pertur'βar] v perturb. **perturbación** sf perturbation. **perturbador** adj perturbing.

***pervertir** [perβer'tir] v pervert. **perversidad** sf perversity. **perversión** sf perversion. **perverso** adj perverse.

pesa ['pesa] sf weight. **pesas y medidas** weights and measures. **pesadez** sf heaviness; drowsiness; hardship.

pesadilla [pesa'ðiʎa] sf nightmare.

pesado [pe'saðo] adj heavy; sluggish. sm bore. **pesadumbre** sf grief.

pésame ['pesame] sm condolence.

pesar [pe'sar] v weigh. **a pesar de** in spite of. **me pesa mucho** I'm very sorry.

pescar [pes'kar] v fish. **pesca** sf fishing. **pescada** sf hake. **pescadería** sf fish shop; fish market. **pescadero** sm fishmonger. **pescado** sm fish. **pescador** sm fisherman. **pescador de caña** angler.

pescuezo [pes'kweθo] sm neck.

pesebre [pe'seβre] sm crib; manger.

pesimista [pesi'mista] s(m+f) pessimist. adj pessimistic. **pesimismo** sm pessimism.

pésimo ['pesimo] adj worthless.

peso ['peso] sm weight; balance; scales pl; peso. **en peso** bodily. **peso específico** specific gravity.

pesquisa [pes'kisa] sf inquiry.

pestañear [pestaɲe'ar] v blink. **pestaña** sf eyelash; fringe; hem. **pestañeo** sm blink.

peste ['peste] sf plague; corruption; poison. **echar pestes** curse. **pesticida** sf pesticide. **pestilencia** sf pestilence. **pestilente** adj pestilent; stinking.

pestillo [pes'tiʎo] sm bolt; latch.

petaca [pe'taka] sf tobacco pouch; cigarette case.

pétalo ['petalo] sm petal.

petardo [pe'tarðo] sm firework; (fam) swindle.

petición [peti'θjon] sf petition; plea. **peticionario, -a** sm, sf petitioner.

petirrojo [petir'roxo] sm robin.

peto ['peto] sm bib; breastplate.

petrificar [petrifi'kar] v petrify. **pétreo** adj stony.

petróleo [pe'troleo] sm petroleum. **petrolero** sm oil-tanker.

petulante [petu'lante] adj petulant; insolent. **petulancia** sf petulance; insolence.

peyorativo [pejora'tiβo] adj pejorative.

pez [peθ] sm fish. sf pitch, tar.

pezón [pe'θon] sm (bot) stalk; (anat) nipple.

pezuña [pe'θuɲa] sf hoof.

piadoso [pja'ðoso] adj pious; merciful.

piano ['pjano] sm piano. **pianista** s(m+f) pianist.

piar [pjar] v chirp.

piara ['pjara] sf herd.

pica ['pika] sf lance, pike; goad; pick; magpie.

picadillo [peka'ðiʎo] sm minced meat.

picante [pi'kante] adj hot; spicy; pungent; biting.

picaporte [pika'porte] sm door handle; latch; knocker; latch-key.

picar [pi'kar] v prick, pierce; sting; burn; punch; bite, eat; chop up. **picado** adj bitten; stung; minced; sour; bad. **picadura** sf bite; sting; peck.

picardear [pikar'ðjar] v corrupt; get up to mischief. **picardía** sf dirty trick; craftiness; mischief. **picaresco** adj roguish. **pícaro, -a** sm, sf rogue.

pico ['piko] sm beak; peak; pickaxe. **darse el pico** kiss. **pico carpintero** woodpecker. **son las cuatro y pico** it is just after four.

picotear [pikote'ar] v peck; chatter. **picotearse** v wrangle. **picotada** sf also **picotazo** sm peck. **picotero, -a** sm, sf chatterbox.

pichón [pi'tʃon] sm pigeon. **pichona** sf (fam) darling.

pie [pje] sm foot; base; stem. **a cuatro pies** on all fours. **dar pie a** give cause for. **de pies a cabeza** from head to foot.

piedad [pje'ðað] sf piety; pity.

piedra ['pjeðra] sf stone.

piel [pjel] sf skin.

pienso ['pjenso] sm fodder. **ni por pienso** not likely.

pierna ['pjerna] sf leg.

pieza ['pjeθa] sf piece; part; room. **dejar de una pieza** leave speechless.

pífano ['pifano] sm fife.

pigmento [pig'mento] sm pigment.

pigmeo [pig'meo] -a s, adj pygmy.

pijama [pi'xama] sm pyjamas pl.

pila¹ ['pila] sf heap; battery.

pila² sf basin; trough; font. **nombre de pila** Christian name.

pilar [pi'lar] sm pillar; pier; milestone; basin.

píldora [pil'ðora] *sf* pill.

pilón [pi'lon] *sm* basin; trough; mortar; pylon.

piloto [pi'loto] *sm* pilot; *(auto)* rear light, parking light.

piltrafa [pil'trafa] *sf* gristly meat. **piltrafas** *sf pl* scraps *pl.*

pillar [pi'ʎar] *v* pillage; get; run over; *(fam)* catch. **pillaje** *sm* pillage.

pillo [pi'ʎo], **-a** *sm, sf* scoundrel. *adj* villainous. **pillastre** *sm or* **pillastron** *sm* rogue. **pillería** *sf* gang of villains; knavery.

pimienta [pi'mjenta] *sf* pepper. **pimiento** *sm (planta)* pepper. **pimentón** *sm* paprika.

pimpollo [pim'poʎo] *sm* sprout; sapling; *(fam)* handsome boy, pretty girl.

pináculo [pi'nakulo] *sm* pinnacle.

pinar [pi'nar] *sm* pine forest.

pincel [pin'θel] *sm* paintbrush. **pincelada** *sf* brush-stroke. **pincelar** *v* paint.

pinchar [pin'tʃar] *v* puncture. **pincharse** *v* have a puncture. **pinchazo** *sm* puncture. **pincho** *sm* point; prickle; spine.

pingo [pingo] *sm* rag; devil. **pingos** *sm pl (fam)* togs.

pingüe ['pingwe] *adj* fatty; abundant. **pingüino** [pin'gwino] *sm* penguin.

pino [pi'no] *sm* pine tree. **pinocha** *sf* pine needle.

pintar [pin'tar] *v* paint. **pintarse** *v* make oneself up. **pinta** *sf* spot. **tener buena/mala pinta** look good/bad. **pintor, -a** *sm, sf* painter. **pintoresco** *adj* picturesque. **pintorrear** *v (fam)* daub. **pintura** *sf* painting; picture.

pinzas ['pinθas] *sf pl* tweezers; pincers; forceps; tongs; clothes pegs.

pinzón [pin'θon] *sm* finch.

piña ['pina] *sf* pineapple; pine cone.

piñón [pi'non] *sm* pinion.

pío¹ ['pio] *sm* chirp.

pío² *adj* pious; merciful.

piojo ['pjoxo] *sm* louse. **piojoso** *adj* lousy.

pipa ['pipa] *sf* pipe; pip.

pique ['pike] *sm* pique; resentment. **echar a pique** sink; ruin.

piqueta [pi'keta] *sf* pickaxe.

piquete [pi'kete] *sm* picket; squad; sting; hole.

piragua [pi'ragwa] *sf* canoe.

pirámide [pi'ramiðe] *sf* pyramid. **piramidal** *adj* pyramidal.

pirata [pi'rata] *sm, adj* pirate.

Pirineos [piri'neos] *sm pl* Pyrenees *pl.*

piropear [pirope'ar] *v (fam)* compliment. **piropo** *sm* compliment.

pirotecnia [piro'teknja] *sf* fireworks *pl.*

pirueta [pi'rweta] *sf* pirouette. **piruetear** *v* pirouette.

pisar [pi'sar] *v* tread; trample. **pisada** *sf* footprint; step. **pisapapeles** *sm invar* paperweight.

piscina [pis'θina] *sf* swimming pool.

piscolabis [pisko'laβis] *sm invar (fam)* snack.

piso ['piso] *sm* floor; storey; flat. **piso bajo** ground floor.

pisotear [pisote'ar] *v* trample. **pisoteo** *sm* trampling.

pista ['pista] *sf* track; trail; runway; court; ring; rink. **pista de baile** dance floor.

pistola [pis'tola] *sf* pistol. **pistolera** *sf* holster. **pistolero** *sm* gunman.

pistón [pis'ton] *sm* piston.

pitar [pi'tar] *v* whistle at; blow a whistle; boo. hiss. **pitada** *sf* whistle.

pitón [pi'ton] *sm* python.

pizarra [pi'θarra] *sf* blackboard; slate.

pizca ['piθka] *sf (fam)* crumb; drop; pinch.

placa ['plaka] *sf* plate; badge; plaque. **placa de matrícula** *(auto)* number plate.

***placer** [pla'θer] *v* please. *sm* pleasure. **a placer** at one's leisure.

plácido [pla'θiðo] *adj* placid; pleasant.

plagar [pla'gar] *v* plague. **plaga** *sf* plague.

plagiar [pla'xjar] *v* plagiarize. **plagio** *sm* plagiarism.

plan [plan] *sm* plan; project.

plana ['plana] *sf (imprenta)* page; *(llanura)* plain.

planchar [plan'tʃar] *v* iron, press. **mesa de planchar** *sf* ironing board. **plancha** *sf* iron. **planchado** *sm* ironing.

planear [plane'ar] *v* plan; glide. **planeo** *sm* gliding.

planeta [pla'neta] *sm* planet. **planetario** *sm* planetarium.

planicie [pla'niθje] *sf* plain; plateau.

planificar [planifi'kar] *v* plan. **planificación** *sf* planning.

plano ['plano] *adj* flat; level; smooth. *sm* map; plan; plane. **de plano** directly. **plano acotado** contour map. **primer plano** close-up.

plantar [plan'tar] v plant; erect. **plantarse** v stop; settle; stand firm. **planta** sf plant; (pie) sole; plan; floor. **plantación** sf plantation. **plante** sm strike; mutiny. **plantío** sm field; vegetable plot. **plantón** sm seedling.

plantear [plante'ar] v expound; create; institute; introduce. **planteamiento** sm exposition; introduction; layout.

plantel [plan'tel] sm (bot) nursery.

plantilla [plan'tiʎa] sf model, pattern; sole (of shoe); (com) payroll.

plasma ['plasma] sm plasma.

plasmar [plas'mar] v mould. **plasmarse** v materialize.

plástico ['plastiko] sm, adj plastic. **plasticidad** sf plasticity.

plata ['plata] sf silver; (fig) money. **hablar en plata** speak frankly.

plataforma [plata'forma] sf platform; flatcar; oilrig. **plataforma de lanzamiento** launching pad.

plátano ['platano] sm banana; banana tree; plane tree.

platea [pla'tea] sf (teatro) stalls pl.

platear [plate'ar] v silverplate. **platero** sm silversmith.

plática [pla'tika] sf chat; sermon.

platija [pla'tixa] sf plaice.

platillo [pla'tiʎo] sm saucer. **platillo volante** flying saucer.

platino [pla'tino] sm platinum.

plato ['plato] sm plate; course; dish. **hacer plato** serve a meal.

platónico [pla'toniko] adj platonic.

plausible [plau'siβle] adj plausible; praiseworthy. **plausibilidad** sf plausibility; praiseworthiness.

playa ['plaja] sf beach; seaside.

plaza ['plaθa] sf town square; market; town; position. **¡plaza!** make way!

plazo ['plaθo] sm time limit; instalment. **comprar a plazos** buy on hire-purchase.

pleamar [plea'mar] sf high tide.

plebe ['pleβe] sf common people pl. **plebeye** adj plebeian.

plebiscito [pleβis'θito] sm plebiscite.

*****plegar** [ple'gar] v fold; bend; pleat. **plegable** adj folding; collapsible; pliable. **plegadera** sf paper-knife. **pliegue** sm crease; tuck; pleat.

pleitear [pleite'ar] v litigate; plead. **pleito** sm lawsuit.

pleno ['pleno] adj complete; full. **plenamente** adv fully. **plenitud** sf fullness; abundance.

pliego ['pljego] sm sheet of paper; sealed letter. **pliego de condiciones** specifications pl.

plomo ['plomo] sm lead; fuse. **a plomo** straight down. **plomada** sf lead pencil; plumb line. **plomería** sf plumbing. **plomero** sm plumber.

pluma ['pluma] sf feather; pen. **pluma estilográfica** fountain pen. **plumaje** sm plumage.

plural [plu'ral] sm, adj plural. **pluralidad** sf majority.

plus [plus] sm bonus. **plus de carestía de vida** cost-of-living bonus.

pluscuamperfecto [pluskwamper'fekto] sm pluperfect.

plusmarca [plus'marka] (deporte) sm record. **plusmarquista** s(m+f) record-holder.

*****poblar** [po'βlar] v populate; inhabit; stock; colonize; plant. **poblarse** v bud; leaf. **población** sf population; town. **poblado** sm town; village. **poblador, -a** sm, sf settler.

pobre ['poβre] adj poor. sm pauper. **¡pobre de ti!** you poor thing! **pobrete** adj wretched. **pobretón** adj very poor. **pobreza** sf poverty.

pocilga [po'θilga] sf pigsty.

poción [po'θjon] sf potion.

poco ['poko] adj (cantidad) little; small. adv little; not very; not long. sm poco a little. **pocos** adj pl few. **poco antes** shortly before. **poco a poco** little by little. **por poco** nearly.

podar [po'ðar] v prune. **poda** sf pruning. **podadera** sf pruning shears.

podenco [po'ðenko] sm hound.

*****poder¹** [po'ðer] v can, be able to; be possible. **hasta más no poder** as much as one can. **no poder más** be exhausted. **puede ser** perhaps.

poder² sm power; capacity; possession. **casarse por poderes** marry by proxy. **hacer un poder** make an effort. **poder disuasivo** deterrent. **poderío** sm authority; wealth. **poderoso** adj powerful.

poema [po'ema] sm poem. **poesía** sf poetry. **poeta** sm poet. **poético** adj poetic. **poetisa** sf poetess.

*****podrir** V **pudrir.**

polaco [po'lako] *adj* Polish. *sm* Pole; (*idioma*) Polish.

polar [po'lar] *adj* polar. **polaridad** *sf* polarity. **polarizar** *v* polarize.

polea [po'lea] *sf* pulley.

polémica [po'lemika] *sf* polemic; polemics *pl*. **polémico** *adj* polemical.

polen [po'leθon] *sm* pollen.

policía [poli'θia] *sf* police force. *sm* policeman. **policíaco** *adj* police. **novela policíaca** detective novel.

poligamia [poli'ɣamja] *sf* polygamy. **polígamo** *adj* polygamous.

polígono [po'liɣno] *sm* polygon. **polígono industrial** industrial estate. **poligonal** *adj* polygonal.

polilla [po'liʎa] *sf* moth.

pólipo [po'lipo] *sm* polyp.

política [po'litika] *sf* politics; policy. **político** *sm* politician. **padre político** father-in-law.

póliza ['poliθa] *sf* policy; contract; stamp. **poliza de seguros** insurance policy.

polizón [poli'θon] *sm* stowaway.

polo ['polo] *sm* (*geog*) pole; (*tecn*) terminal; (*deporte*) polo; ice lolly. **polo acuático** water polo. **Polo Norte/Sur** North/South Pole.

Polonia [po'lonja] *sf* Poland. **polonesa** *sf* polonaise.

poltrona [pol'trona] *sf* easy chair. **poltrón** *adj* lazy.

polvo ['polβo] *sm* powder; dust. **café en polvo** instant coffee. **polvos** *sm pl* powder *sing*. **polvos de talco** talcum powder. **polvareda** *sf* dust cloud; (*fig*) to-do. **polvera** *sf* powder compact. **pólvora** *sf* gunpowder.

polla ['poʎa] *sf* pullet. **pollo** *sm* chicken. **polluelo** *sm* chick.

pómez ['pomeθ] *sf* pumice.

pomo ['pomo] *sm* pommel; doorknob.

pompa ['pompa] *sf* pomp; bubble; display. **pomposidad** *sf* pomposity. **pomposo** *adj* pompous.

pómpulo ['pompulo] *sm* cheekbone.

ponche ['pontʃe] *sm* (*bebida*) punch.

poncho ['pontʃo] *sm* poncho. *adj* listless.

ponderar [ponde'rar] *v* weigh up; praise highly. **ponderable** *adj* praiseworthy. **ponderación** *sf* weighing up; exaggerated praise. **ponderado** *adj* measured; prudent. **ponderativo** *adj* excessive; deliberative.

ponente [po'nente] *sm* reporter. **ponencia** *sf* report.

***poner** [po'ner] *v* put; set. **poner al día** bring up to date. **poner casa** move (house). **poner de comer** feed. **ponerse** *v* turn oneself; dress; get down to; arrive. **ponerse bueno** recover. **ponerse guapo** smarten oneself up.

poniente [po'njente] *sm* west.

pontificado [pontifi'kaðo] *sm* papacy. **pontifical** *adj* pontifical. **pontífice** *sm* pope.

pontón [pon'ton] *sm* (*puente*) pontoon.

ponzoña [pon'θoɲa] *sf* poison. **ponzoñoso** *adj* poisonous.

popa ['popa] *sf* stern. **a popa** astern.

popelina [pope'lina] *sf* poplin.

populacho [popu'latʃo] *sm* rabble.

popular [popu'lar] *adj* popular. **popularidad** *sf* popularity. **popularizar** *v* popularize.

por [por] *prep* for; by; through; during; in exchange for. **por ciento** per cent. **por más que** however. **por si acaso** in case. **por supuesto** of course.

porcelana [porθe'lana] *sf* porcelain.

porcentaje [porθen'taxe] *sm* percentage.

porción [por'θjon] *sf* portion.

porche ['portʃe] *sm* porch.

pordiosero [porðjo'sero], **-a** *sm, sf* beggar.

porfiar [por'fjar] *v* insist; persist; argue. **porfía** *sf* insistence. **porfiado** *adj* stubborn.

pormenor [porme'nor] *sm* detail. **al pormenor** retail.

pornografía [pornoɣra'fia] *sf* pornography.

poro ['poro] *sm* pore. **poroso** *adj* porous.

porque ['porke] *conj* because.

porqué [por'ke] *sm* reason.

porquería [porke'ria] *sf* disgusting mess; muck.

porra ['porra] *sf* club; truncheon. **porrazo** *sm* blow.

porro ['porro] *sm* leek.

porrón [por'ron] *adj* dull, stupid. **a porrones** (*fam*) galore.

portador [porta'ðor] *sm* (*com*) bearer.

portar *v* bear, carry. **portarse** *v* behave oneself. **portátil** *adj* portable.

portal [por'tal] *sm* entrance hall, portal.

portamonedas [portamo'neðas] *sm invar* wallet.

portavoz [porta'βoθ] *sm* megaphone; spokesman.

365 **preconizar**

portazgo [por'taθgo] sm toll.
portazo [por'taθo] sm slam. **dar un portazo** slam the door.
porte ['porte] sm transport; carriage; conduct.
portento [por'tento] sm marvel. portentoso adj marvellous.
portería [porte'ria] sf porter's lodge. portero, -a sm, sf porter.
portezuela [porte'θwela] sf (auto) door.
pórtico [por'tiko] sm portico.
portilla [por'tiʎa] sf porthole.
Portugal [portu'gal] sm Portugal. portugués, -esa s, adj Portuguese; sm (idioma) Portuguese.
porvenir [porβe'nir] sm future. **sin porvenir** without prospects.
pos [pos] adj **en pos de** behind.
posada [po'saða] sf inn; lodging. posadero, -a sm, sf innkeeper.
posar [po'sar] v alight; pose; lodge; lay down. posarse v settle; land.
*poseer [pose'er] v possess; hold; master. posesión sf possession. posesiones sf pl property sing.
posible [po'siβle] adj possible. posibilidad sf possibility. posibilitar v facilitate.
posición [posi'θjon] sf position.
positivo [posi'tiβo] adj, sm positive.
*posponer [pospo'ner] v postpone; value less.
postal [pos'tal] adj postal. sf postcard. **giro postal** sm money order; postal order.
postdata [post'ðata] sf postscript.
poste ['poste] sm pole; pillar; post. **poste indicador** signpost.
postergar [poster'gar] v pass over; postpone; adjourn. postergación sf postponement; adjournment.
posteridad [posteri'ðað] sf posterity. posterior adj posterior; subsequent; later.
postizo [pos'tiθo] adj false; artificial; assumed. sm hairpiece. **pierna postiza** sf artificial leg.
postrar [pos'trar] v prostrate. postrarse v kneel down; weaken. postración sf prostration. postrado adj prostrate.
postre ['postre] sm dessert.
postremo [pos'tremo] adj last. postrimería sf end, death.
postular [postu'lar] v postulate; request; apply for; collect. postulación sf collection. postulado sm postulate. postulante, -a sm, sf collector; applicant.

póstumo ['postumo] adj posthumous.
postura [pos'tura] sf posture; attitude.
potable [po'taβle] adj drinkable.
potaje [po'taxe] sm stew; soup.
potasio [po'tasjo] sm potassium.
pote ['pote] sm jar; jug.
potencia [po'tenθja] sf power; ability; potential. potencial adj potential. potentado sm potentate. potente adj powerful.
potestad [potes'tað] sf authority; power.
potro ['potro] sm colt; instrument of torture.
pozo ['poθo] sm hole; well; shaft; bilge.
práctica ['praktika] sf practice; method. practicabilidad sf practicability. practicable adj practicable. practicante s(m+f) nurse; practitioner. practicar v practise; play; perform. práctico adj practical; experienced.
pradera [pra'ðera] sf meadow; prairie. prado sm field, meadow.
pragmático [prag'matiko] adj pragmatic. pragmatismo sm pragmatism.
preámbulo [pre'ambulo] sm preamble.
precario [pre'karjo] adj precarious. precariedad sf precariousness.
precaución [prekau'θjon] sf precaution. **con precaución** cautiously. precaver v forestall. precaverse v be on one's guard (against).
preceder [preθe'ðer] v precede. precedencia sf precedence; preference. precedente sm precedent.
precepto [pre'θepto] sm precept; regulation. preceptivo adj compulsory.
preciar [pre'θjar] v value. preciarse v boast. preciado adj prized; boastful. precio sm price; esteem. preciosidad sf excellence. precioso adj precious; witty.
precipicio [preθi'piθjo] sm precipice.
precipitar [preθipi'tar] v precipitate. precipitarse v rush. precipitación sf precipitation; haste. precipitado adj also precipitoso hasty, rash.
precisar [preθi'sar] v need; be necessary; define; fix. precisamente adv precisely; necessarily. precisión sf precision; necessity. preciso adj precise; necessary.
*preconcebir [prekonθe'βir] v preconceive. preconcebido adj preconceived.
preconizar [prekoni'θar] v praise; recommend; suggest. preconización sf recommendation; praise.

precoz [pre'koθ] *adj* precocious. **precocidad** *sf* precocity.

precursor [prekur'sor] *sm* forerunner.

predecesor [predeθe'sor], -a *sm, sf* predecessor.

*predecir [prede'θir] *v* predict. **predicción** *sf* prediction.

predestinar [predesti'nar] *v* predestine. **predestinación** *sf* predestination.

prédica ['preðika] *sf* sermon; preaching. **predicación** *sf* preaching. **predicaderas** *sf pl* (*fam*) eloquence *sing*. **predicador**, -a *sm, sf* preacher. **predicar** *v* preach.

predicado [preði'kaðo] *sm* (*gram*) predicate.

predicamento [preðika'mento] *sm* predicament; prestige.

predilección [preðilek'θjon] *sf* predilection.

*predisponer [predispo'ner] *v* predispose. **predisponer contra** prejudice against. **predisposición** *sf* predisposition.

predominar [preðomi'nar] *v* predominate. **predominancia** *sf* predominance. **predominante** *adj* predominant.

preeminente [preemi'nente] *adj* pre-eminent. **preeminencia** *sf* pre-eminence.

prefabricar [prefaβri'kar] *v* prefabricate. **prefabricación** *sf* prefabrication.

prefacio [pre'faθjo] *sm* preface.

prefecto [pre'fekto] *sm* prefect. **prefectura** *sf* prefecture.

*preferir [prefe'rir] *v* prefer. **preferencia** *sf* preference. **preferente** *adj* preferential; preferable. **preferible** *adj* preferable. **preferido** *adj* favourite.

prefigurar [prefigu'rar] *v* prefigure, foreshadow. **prefiguración** *sf* prefiguration.

prefijo [pre'fixo] *adj* prefixed. *sm* prefix. **prefijar** *v* prefix; prearrange.

pregonar [prego'nar] *v* proclaim, announce. **pregón** *sm* proclamation. **pregonero** *sm* town crier.

preguntar [pregun'tar] *v* ask; query; inquire. **preguntarse** *v* wonder. **pregunta** *sf* question. **preguntador**, -a *sm, sf* questioner.

prehistórico [preis'toriko] *adj* prehistoric.

prejuicio [pre'xwiθjo] *sm* prejudice. **prejuzgar** *v* prejudge.

prelado [pre'laðo] *sm* prelate.

preliminar [prelimi'nar] *adj, sm* preliminary. **preliminares** *sm pl* preliminaries *pl*.

preludio [pre'luðjo] *sm* prelude.

prematuro [prema'turo] *adj* premature.

premeditar [premeði'tar] *v* premeditate. **premeditación** *sf* premeditation.

premiar [pre'mjar] *v* reward. **premio** *sm* reward; prize; (*com*) premium. **premio gordo** first prize.

premisa [pre'misa] *sf* premise, assumption.

premonición [premoni'θjon] *sf* premonition.

premura [pre'mura] *sf* urgency; tightness.

prenda ['prenda] *sf* pledge; (*com*) security; garment; darling. **en prenda** as a token of. **prendar** *v* pledge; pawn; please. **prendarse de** fall in love with. **prendería** *sf* second-hand shop. **prendero**, -a *sm, sf* second-hand dealer; pawnbroker.

prensa ['prensa] *sf* press; printing press. **dar a la prensa** publish. **prensar** *v* press.

prensil [pren'sil] *adj* prehensile.

preñado [pre'naðo] *adj* pregnant; bulging; full. **preñar** *v* become pregnant; impregnate. **preñez** *sf* pregnancy.

preocupar [preoku'par] *v* preoccupy; worry; get worried. **¡no se preocupe!** don't worry! **preocupación** *sf* preoccupation; prejudice; worry. **preocupado** *adj* preoccupied; worried.

preparar [prepa'rar] *v* prepare. **preparación** *sf* preparation. **preparativo** *adj also* **preparatorio** preparatory.

preponderar [preponde'rar] *v* preponderate, prevail. **preponderancia** *sf* preponderance. **preponderante** *adj* preponderant.

preposición [preposi'θjon] *sf* (*gram*) preposition.

prerrogativa [prerroga'tiβa] *sf* prerogative.

presa¹ ['presa] *sf* capture; prey; victim; quarry; seizure. **presas** *sf pl* fangs *pl*; talons *pl*. **ave de presa** bird of prey.

presa² *sf* dam; weir. **presa de contención** reservoir.

presagiar [presa'xjar] *v* presage. **presagio** *sm* omen.

présbita ['presβita] *adj also* **présbite** long-sighted. **presbicia** *sf* longsightedness.

presbítero [pres'βitero] *sm* priest. **presbiterado** *sm* priesthood.

prescindir [presθin'dir] *v* do without. **prescindible** *adj* dispensable.

prescribir [preskri'βir] *v* prescribe; determine. **prescripción** *sf* prescription. **prescrito** *adj* prescribed.

presenciar [presen'θjar] *v* attend; witness. **presencia** *sf* presence; appearance. **presencia de ánimo** presence of mind.

presentar [presen'tar] *v* present; introduce; submit; propose; tender. **le presento a may I** introduce you to. **presentarse** *v* present oneself; arise; turn up; report; apply. **presentable** *adj* presentable. **presentación** *sf* presentation; introduction. **presente** *adj* present. **mejorando lo presente** present company excepted.

*presentir [presen'tir] *v* have forebodings of. **presentimiento** *sm* presentiment.

preservar [preser'βar] *v* preserve; protect. **preservación** *sf* preservation; protection. **preservador** *adj* preservative. **preservativo** *sm* condom.

presidencia [presi'ðenθja] *sf* presidency. **presidente** *sm* president.

presidiario [presi'ðjarjo] *sm* convict. **presidio** *sm* prison; penal servitude.

presidir [presi'ðir] *v* preside over; dominate.

presilla [pre'siλa] *sf* loop; fastener.

presión [pre'sjon] *sf* pressure.

preso ['preso] *sm* prisoner. *adj* captured.

prestar [pres'tar] *v* lend. **prestación** *sf* lending. **prestado** *adj* loaned. **dar/pedir prestado** lend/borrow. **prestador**, **-a** *sm*, *sf* lender. **prestamista** *s(m+f)* moneylender. **préstamo** *sm* loan. **prestario**, **-a** *sm*, *sf* borrower.

presteza [pres'teθa] *sf* promptness.

prestidigitador [prestiðixita'ðor] *sm* conjurer; magician. **prestidigitación** *sf* conjuring; magic.

prestigio [pres'tixjo] *sm* prestige; trick. **prestigiado** *adj also* **prestigioso** prestigious.

presto ['presto] *adj* prompt; ready. *adv* promptly.

presumir [presu'mir] *v* presume, assume. **según cabe presumir** presumably. **presumirse** *v* swank; be presumptuous. **presumible** *adj* presumable. **presunción** *sf* assumption; presumptuousness. **presunto** *adj* presumed. **presuntuosidad** *sf* conceit. **presuntuoso** *adj* conceited.

*presuponer [presupo'ner] *v* presuppose; budget. **presupuesto** *sm* budget; reason; supposition.

presura [pre'sura] *sf* promptness; persistence. **presuroso** *adj* prompt; hasty.

pretender [preten'der] *v* claim; aspire to; seek; want; apply for; allege; pretend. **pretendiente** *sm* pretender; claimant; suitor. **pretensión** *sf* pretension; claim.

pretérito [pre'terito] *sm* (*gram*) past.

pretexto [pre'teksto] *sm* pretext.

*prevalecer [preβale'θer] *v* prevail. **prevaleciente** *adj* prevailing.

prevaricar [preβari'kar] *v* prevaricate. **prevaricación** *sf* prevarication; breach of trust. **prevaricador**, **-a** *sm*, *sf* prevaricator.

*prevenir [preβe'nir] *v* prevent; warn; prepare; foresee. **prevención** *sf* prevention; warning; preparation; prejudice; police station. **prevenido** *adj* prepared; forewarned. **bien prevenido** full. **preventivo** *adj* preventive.

*prever [pre'βer] *v* foresee; anticipate. **previsión** *sf* foresight; forecast. **caja de previsión** *sf* social security.

previo ['preβjo] *adj* previous. **previo pago** after payment.

prieto ['prjeto] *adj* dark; mean.

prima ['prima] *sf* premium; bonus.

primado [pri'maðo] *sm* (*rel*) primate.

primario [pri'marjo] *adj* primary.

primavera [prima'βera] *sf* spring.

primer [pri'mer] *adj* first. **primeramente** *adv* first; mainly. **primero** *adj* first; best; principal. **de primera** first-class.

primitivo [primi'tiβo] *adj* primitive; original.

primo ['primo] *adj* prime. *sm* cousin.

primogénito [primo'xenito] *adj* first-born.

primor [pri'mor] *sm* beauty; delicacy; skill. **primoroso** *adj* exquisite; skilful.

princesa [prin'θesa] *sf* princess.

principal [prinθi'pal] *adj*, *sm* principal.

príncipe ['prinθipe] *sm* prince.

principiar [prinθi'pjar] *v* start. **principiante** *s(m+f)* novice. **principio** *sm* beginning.

pringar [prin'gar] *v* stain with grease; wound; involve; slander. **pringarse** *v* embezzle. **pringón** *adj* greasy. **pringoso** *adj* fatty, greasy. **pringue** *s(m+f)* grease stain; dripping.

prior [pri'or] *sm* (*rel*) prior. *adj* prior. **priora** *sf* prioress. **priorato** *sm* priory. **prioridad** *sf* priority.

prisa ['prisa] *sf* hurry. **darse prisa** hurry. **tener prisa** be in a hurry.

prisión [pri'sjon] *sf* prison; imprisonment. **prisionero**, **-a** *sm*, *sf* prisoner.

prisma 368

prisma ['prisma] *sm* prism. prismático *adj* prismatic.

privar[1] [pri'βar] *v* deprive; prohibit. privación *sf* deprivation. privado *adj* private.

privar[2] *v* be in favour; be popular.

privilegiar [priβile'xjar] *v* grant a favour to. privilegio *sm* privilege.

pro [pro] *sm* benefit, profit. en pro de on behalf of. hombre de pro *sm* honest man.

proa ['proa] *sf* (*mar*) prow, bow, bows *pl*. mascarón de proa *sm* figurehead.

probable [pro'βaβle] *adj* probable. probabilidad *sf* probability.

*probar [pro'βar] *v* test; try; taste; prove. probarse *v* try on. probador *sm* fitting-room. probanza *sf* proof. probeta *sf* test tube.

probidad [proβi'ðað] *sf* probity, integrity.

problema [pro'βlema] *sm* problem.

proceder [proθe'ðer] *v* proceed; behave; originate. procedencia *sf* origin; port of departure. procedente *adj* originating; reasonable; proper. procedimiento *sm* process.

procesar [proθe'sar] *v* prosecute. procesado, -a *sm*, *sf* accused. procesal *adj* procedural. procesamiento *sm* prosecution.

procesión [proθe'sjon] *sf* procession.

proclamar [prokla'mar] *v* proclaim. proclama *sf also* proclamación proclamation.

procrear [prokre'ar] *v* procreate. procreación *sf* procreation. procreador, -a *sm*, *sf* procreator.

procurar [proku'rar] *v* cause; attempt; obtain; succeed; give. procura *sf* power of attorney. procurador, -a *sm*, *sf* lawyer.

prodigar [proði'gar] *v* squander; lavish. prodigalidad *sf* prodigality.

prodigio [pro'ðixjo] *sm* prodigy. prodigioso *adj* prodigious.

pródigo ['proðigo] *adj* prodigal; wasteful.

*producir [proðu'θir] *v* produce. producirse *v* happen. producción *sf* production. productivo *adj* productive. producto *sm* product. productor, -a *sm*, *sf* producer.

proeza [pro'eθa] *sf* deed; feat.

profanar [profa'nar] *v* profane. profanación *sf* profanation. profano *adj* profane.

profecía [profe'θia] *sf* prophecy. profeta *sm* prophet. profético *adj* prophetic. profetisa *sf* prophetess. profetizar *v* prophesy.

*proferir [profe'rir] *v* utter.

profesar [profe'sar] *v* profess; manifest; practise a profession. profesión *sf* profession. profesional *adj* professional. profesor, -a *sm*, *sf* professor, teacher. profesorado *sm* professorship; teaching staff.

prófugo ['profugo], -a *s*, *adj* fugitive.

profundizar [profundi'θar] *v* deepen. profundidad *sf* depth. profundo *adj* deep.

profusión [profu'sjon] *sf* profusion. profuso *adj* profuse.

progenie [pro'xenje] *sf* progeny. progenitor *sm* progenitor. progenitores *sm pl* ancestors *pl*; parents *pl*. progenitura *sf* offspring.

programa [pro'grama] *sm* programme.

progresar [progre'sar] *v* progress. progresión *sf* progression. progresivo *adj* progressive. progreso *sm* progress.

prohibir [proi'βir] *v* prohibit. se prohibe fumar no smoking. prohibición *sf* prohibition. prohibitivo *adj* prohibitive.

prohijar [proi'xar] *v* adopt. prohijamiento *sm* adoption.

prójimo ['proximo] *sm* fellow man; neighbour; (*fam*) bloke.

prole ['prole] *sf* offspring.

prolapso [pro'lapso] *sm* prolapse.

proletario [prole'tarjo], -a *s*, *adj* proletarian.

prolífico [pro'lifiko] *adj* prolific.

prolijo [pro'lixo] *adj* tedious; long-winded. prolijidad *sf* long-windedness.

prólogo ['prologo] *sm* prologue.

prolongar [prolon'gar] *v* prolong. prolongación *sf* prolongation. prolongado *adj* prolonged.

promediar [prome'ðjar] *v* bisect; average out; mediate. promedio *sm* middle; average.

promesa [pro'mesa] *sf* promise. prometer *v* promise. prometerse *v* expect; become engaged. prometérselas felices have high hopes. prometida *sf* fiancée. prometido *sm* fiancé.

prominencia [promi'nenθja] *sf* prominence; projection; bulge. prominente *adj* prominent.

promiscuo [pro'miskwo] *adj* promiscuous; ambiguous.

promontorio [promon'torjo] *sm* promontory.

*promover [promo'βer] *v* promote. promoción *sf* promotion. promotor, -a *sm*, *sf* promoter.

promulgar [promul'gar] *v* promulgate. **promulgación** *sf* promulgation.

pronombre [pro'nombre] *sm* pronoun.

pronosticar [pronosti'kar] *v* prognosticate. **pronosticación** *sf* prognostication, forecast. **pronóstico** *sm* prediction.

prontitud [pronti'tuð] *sf* promptness. **pronto** *adv* quickly. at once. ¡hasta pronto! see you soon!

pronunciar [pronun'θjar] *v* pronounce. **pronunciarse** *v* rebel. **pronunciación** *sf* pronunciation. **pronunciamiento** *sm* rising; (*jur*) pronouncement.

propagar [propa'gar] *v* propagate. **propagación** *sf* propagation. **propaganda** *sf* propaganda.

propalar [propa'lar] *v* publish; divulge.

propenso [pro'penso] *adj* prone. **propender** *v* incline. **propensión** *sf* inclination.

propicio [pro'piθjo] *adj* propitious. **propiciación** *sf* propitiation. **propiciar** *v* propitiate.

propiedad [propje'ðað] *sf* property; ownership; propriety; resemblance. **propietario, -a** *sm, sf* landlord/lady.

propina [pro'pina] *sf* (*dinero*) tip.

propio ['propjo] *adj* proper; own; particular. **nombre propio** *sm* proper noun. **ser propio de** be typical of. **sus propias palabras** his very words. **propiamente** *adv* properly.

*proponer [propo'ner] *v* propose. **proponente** *s(m+f)* proposer. **proposición** *sf* proposition; proposal.

proporción [propor'θjon] *sf* proportion. **proporcionado** *adj* proportionate. **bien proporcionado** well proportioned. **proporcional** *adj* proportional. **proporcionar** *v* supply; cause; adapt.

propósito [pro'posito] *sm* purpose; intention. **a propósito** by the way. **a propósito de** with regard to. **de propósito** on purpose.

propuesta [pro'pwesta] *sf* proposal.

propulsar [propul'sar] *v* propel. **propulsión** *sf* propulsion. **propulsor** *sm* propeller.

prorrata [pro'rrata] *sf* quota. **a prorrata** pro rata.

prórroga [pro'rroɣa] *sf* prorogation, extension. **prorrogar** *v* prorogue, adjourn. **prorrumpir** [prorrum'pir] *v* break out.

prosa ['prosa] *sf* prose. **prosaico** *adj* prosaic.

proscribir [proskri'βir] *v* proscribe, ban. **proscripción** *sf* proscription, prohibition. **proscrito** *adj* outlawed, banished.

prosecución [proseku'θjon] *sf* pursuit; continuation. **proseguir** *v* pursue; continue.

prosélito [pro'selito] *sm* proselyte.

prospecto [pros'pekto] *sm* prospectus.

prosperar [prospe'rar] *v* prosper. **prosperidad** *sf* prosperity. **próspero** *adj* prosperous.

prosternarse [proster'narse] *v* prostrate oneself.

*prostituir [prostitu'ir] *v* prostitute. **prostíbulo** *sm* brothel. **prostitución** *sf* prostitution. **prostituta** *sf* prostitute.

protagonista [protago'nista] *s(m+f)* protagonist.

proteger [prote'xer] *v* protect. **protección** *sf* protection. **protector** *adj* protective. **protegido** *sm* protégé.

proteína [prote'ina] *sf* protein.

protestar [protes'tar] *v* protest. **protesta** *sf* protest. **protestación** *sf* protestation. **protestante** *s(m+f), adj* Protestant. **protestantismo** *sm* Protestantism.

protocolo [proto'kolo] *sm* protocol.

prototipo [proto'tipo] *sm* prototype.

protuberancia [protuβe'ranθja] *sf* protuberance. **protuberante** *adj* protuberant.

provecho [pro'βetʃo] *sm* advantage; profit. **de provecho** useful. **sacar provecho de** benefit from. **provechoso** *adj* profitable.

proveer [proβe'er] *v* provide; deal with; decide; fill. **proveedor, -a** *sm, sf* supplier.

*provenir [proβe'nir] *v* originate. **proveniente** *adj* originating.

proverbio [pro'βerβjo] *sm* proverb. **proverbial** *adj* proverbial.

providencia [proβi'ðenθja] *sf* providence; foresight. **providencial** *adj* providential. **proviviente** *adj* provident.

provincia [pro'βinθja] *sf* province. **provincial** *adj* provincial. **provincialismo** *sm* provincialism.

provisión [proβisi'on] *sf* provision. **provisional** *adj* provisional. **provisionalmente** *adv* provisionally. **provisor** *sm* purveyer. **provisto** *adj* supplied.

provocar [proβo'kar] *v* provoke; cause. **provocación** *sf* provocation. **provocador** *adj* provocative. **provocante** *adj* provoking.

próximo ['proksimo] *adj* next; neighbouring. **la semana próxima** next week. **proximamente** *adv* closely; soon. **proximidad** *sf* proximity.

proyectar [projek'tar] *v* project; plan; throw. **proyección** *sf* projection. **proyectil** *sm* projectile. **proyecto** *sm* project. **proyector** *sm* projector; searchlight; spotlight.

prudencia [pru'δenθja] *sf* prudence. **prudencial** *adj (fam)* moderate. **prudente** *adj* prudent.

prueba ['prweβa] *sf* test; proof; tasting; *(deporte)* event. **a prueba** on trial. **a prueba de** proof against.

prurito [pru'rito] *sm* itch; urge.

psicoanálisis [psikoa'nalisis] *sm invar* psychoanalysis. **psicoanalista** *s(m+f)* psychoanalyst. **psicoanalizar** *v* psychoanalyse.

psicología [psikolo'xia] *sf* psychology. **psicológico** *adj* psychological. **psicólogo, -a** *sm, sf* psychologist.

psiquiatría [psikja'tria] *sf* psychiatry. **psiquiatra** *s(m+f)* psychiatrist. **psiquiátrico** *adj* psychiatric.

púa ['pua] *sf* prong; barb; thorn; sharp point.

pubertad [puβer'taδ] *sf* puberty.

publicar [puβli'kar] *v* publish. **publicación** *sf* publication. **publicidad** *sf* publicity; advertising. **público** *sm, adj* public. **dar al público** publish.

puchero [pu'tʃero] *sm* stew; cooking-pot. **ganarse el puchero** earn one's daily bread.

pucho ['putʃo] *sm* cigarette *or* cigar end; fag-end.

púdico ['puδiko] *adj* chaste; modest. **pudicia** *sf* chastity; modesty.

pudiente [pu'δjente] *adj* rich.

pudín [pu'δin] *sm* pudding.

pudor [pu'δor] *sm* modesty; shame. **pudoroso** *adj* modest.

°pudrir [pu'δrir] *v* rot, decay. **pudrición** *sf* putrefaction. **pudrimiento** *sm* rotting.

pueblo ['pweβlo] *sm* people; town; village. **de pueblos** from the country.

puente ['pwente] *sm* bridge. **puente colgante** suspension bridge.

puerco ['pwerko] *sm* pig. *adj* filthy. **puerca** *sf* sow. **puerco espín** porcupine.

pueril [pue'ril] *adj* childish. **puerilidad** *sf* childishness.

puerro ['pwerro] *sm* leek.

puerta ['pwerta] *sf* door; entrance. **puerta principal** front door. **puerta trasera** back door.

puerto ['pwerto] *sm* port; harbour; mountain pass.

pues [pwes] *adv, conj* then; since; because; well; so; yes. **pues bien** OK. **¡pues claro!** of course! **¿pues qué?** so what?

puesta ['pwesta] *sf (del sol)* setting; bet; putting. **puesta en escena** staging.

puesto ['pwesto] *sm* small shop; place; stall; job. **puesto de periódicos** newspaper stand.

pugnar [pug'nar] *v* fight; struggle. **pugna** *sf* fight. **pugnaz** *adj* pugnacious.

pujar [pu'xar] *v* strain; strive; outbid. **pujante** *adj* strong. **pujanza** *sf* strength.

pulcritud [pulkri'tuδ] *sf* neatness; care. **pulcro** *adj* neat, tidy.

pulga ['pulga] *sf* flea. **pulgoso** *adj* flea-ridden.

pulgada [pul'gaδa] *sf* inch. **pulgar** *sm* thumb.

pulir [pu'lir] *v* polish; adorn. **pulidez** *sf* polish; neatness. **pulido** *adj* polished; smooth; neat. **pulidor** *sm* polisher. **pulimentar** *v* polish. **pulimento** *sm* polish, shine.

pulmón [pul'mon] *sm* lung. **pulmonía** *sf* pneumonia.

pulpa ['pulpa] *sf* pulp.

púlpito ['pulpito] *sm* pulpit.

pulpo ['pulpo] *sm* octopus.

pulsar [pul'sar] *v* pulsate. **pulso** *sm* pulse; wrist; steady hand.

pulsera [pul'sera] *sf* bracelet; watch strap. **reloj de pulsera** *sm* wristwatch.

pulverizar [pulβeri'θar] *v* pulverize; spray. **pulverización** *sf* pulverization. **pulverizador** *sm* spray; atomizer.

pulla ['puʎa] *sf* taunt; obscenity.

punción [pun'θjon] *sf (med)* puncture.

punición [puni'θjon] *sf* punishment. **punible** *adj* punishable. **punitivo** *adj* punitive.

punta ['punta] *sf* point; tip; head; end; nail. **horas punta** *sf pl* rush hours *pl*. **sacar punta a** sharpen. **velocidad punta** *sf* top speed.

puntada [pun'taδa] *sf* stitch.

puntapié [punta'p je] *sm* kick. **echar a puntapiés** kick out.

puntear [punte'ar] *v* stitch; tick off; perforate. **punteado** *sm* (*música*) plucking.

puntería [punte'ria] *sf* aim; marksmanship. **puntero** *adj* outstanding.

puntilla [pun'tiʎa] *sf* tack; nib; fine lace. **de puntillas** on tiptoe.

punto ['punto] *sm* point; full stop; stitch; mark; honour; matter; item. **al punto** at once. **dos puntos** colon. **en punto** on the dot. **¡punto en boca!** mum's the word!

puntual [puntu'al] *adj* punctual; reliable. **puntualidad** *sf* punctuality; reliability.

puntualizar [puntwali'θar] *v* arrange; determine; perfect; settle.

puntuar [pun'twar] *v* punctuate. **puntuación** *sf* punctuation. **signos de puntuación** *sm pl* punctuation marks *pl*.

punzar [pun'θar] *v* pierce. **punzada** *sf* prick; twinge. **punzante** *adj* sharp. **punzón** *sm* awl. punch.

puñado [pu'ɲaðo] *sm* handful. **puñada** *sf* also **puñetazo** *sm* blow. clout. **puño** *sm* fist; cuff. **de propio puño** in one's own handwriting.

puñal [pu'ɲal] *sm* dagger. **puñalada** *sf* stab.

pupila [pu'pila] *sf* (*anat*) pupil.

pupilaje [pupi'laxe] *sm* boarding-house; tutelage.

pupitre [pu'pitre] *sm* desk.

puré [pu're] *sm* purée. **puré de patatas** mashed potatoes *pl*.

pureza [pu'reθa] *sf* purity. **purificación** *sf* purification. **purificar** *v* purify. **purista** *s*(*m+f*) purist. **puro** *adj* pure; simple.

purgar [pur'gar] *v* purge; purify. **purgante** *sm* purgative. **purgativo** *adj* purgative. **purgatorio** *sm* purgatory.

puritano [puri'tano], **-a** *s, adj* puritan. **puritanismo** *sm* puritanism.

púrpura [pur'pura] *sf* purple.

pus [pus] *sm* pus. matter.

pusilánime [pusi'lanime] *adj* cowardly. **pusilanimidad** *sf* cowardliness.

pústula ['pustula] *sf* (*med*) pustule. pimple.

puta ['puta] *sf* (*fam*) whore. prostitute. **puto** *sm* (*fam*) bugger.

putrefacción [putrefak'θjon] *sf* putrefaction. **putrefacto** *adj* rotten. **pútrido** *adj* putrid.

puya ['puja] *sf* goad; (*fig*) gibe.

Q

que [ke] *pron* who; whom; that; which. *conj* that; because; than. **que sí** of course. **más que** more than.

qué [ke] *pron, adj* what. **¿qué pasa?** what's going on? **¡qué miedo!** what a fright! **¡qué raro!** how extraordinary!

*****quebrar** [ke'βrar] *v* break; go bankrupt. **quebrado** *adj* broken; bankrupt. **quebradura** *sf* crack; gap. **quebrantar** *v* shatter. **quebranto** *sm* exhaustion.

queda ['keða] *sf* curfew.

quedar [ke'ðar] *v* stay; remain; sojourn. **quedarse** *v* stay behind. **quedar en nada** come to nothing.

quedo ['keðo] *adj* quiet; still. *adv* quietly.

quehaceres [kea'θeres] *sm pl* chores; duties.

quejarse [ke'xarse] *v* complain; moan. **queja** *sf* complaint. **quejido** *sm* groan. **quejoso** *adj* plaintive; complaining.

quemar [ke'mar] *v* burn; scorch. **quema** *sf* burning; fire. **quemadura** *sf* burn; scald. **quemante** *adj* burning. **quemazón** *sf* burning; burn.

querella [ke'reʎa] *sf* quarrel; (*jur*) complaint. **querellarse** *v* lodge a complaint.

*****querer** [ke'rer] *v* love; want; try; determine. *sm* affection. **querido** *adj* dear.

queso ['keso] *sm* cheese. **queso rallado** grated cheese.

quiá [ki'a] *interj* never! surely not!

quicio ['kiθjo] *sm* hinge. **fuera de quicio** out of order.

quiebra [ki'eβra] *sf* bankruptcy; slump; fissure.

quien [ki'en] *pron* who; whom; whoever. **quién** *pron interrog* who. **¿quién sabe?** who knows? **quienquiera** *pron* whoever, whosoever.

quieto [ki'eto] *adj* still, quiet. **quietud** *sf* stillness.

quijote [ki'xote] *sm* quixotic person; idealist.

quilate [ki'late] *sm* carat.

quilla ['kiʎa] *sf* keel.

quimera [ki'mera] *sf* hallucination; quarrel. **quimérico** *adj* fantastic.

química [kimika] *sf* chemistry.

quincalla [kin'kaʎa] *sf* hardware; ironmongery. **quincallero, -a** *sm, sf* ironmonger.

quince ['kinθe] sm, adj fifteen. **quincena** sf fortnight. **quincuagésima** adj fiftieth. **quinientos** adj invar five hundred.

quinta ['kinta] sf country house; conscription; (música) fifth.

quintal [kin'tal] sm hundredweight.

quinto ['kinto] adj fifth.

quiosco [ki'osko] sm kiosk.

quirúrgico [ki'rurxiko] adj surgical.

quisquilla [kis'kiʎa] sf quibble; trifle; (zool) shrimp.

quiste ['kiste] sm (med) cyst.

quitamanchas [kita'mantʃas] sm invar stain-remover.

quitar [ki'tar] v remove; take off; take away. **quitarse** v get rid of; withdraw; abstain. **de quita y pon** easily detachable.

quitasol [kita'sol] sm parasol, sunshade.

quizá(s) [ki'θa(s)] adv perhaps, maybe.

R

rábano ['raβano] sm radish.

rabiar [ra'βjar] v rave, rage. **rabiar por** long for. **rabia** sf rage, fury; (med) rabies. **rabioso** adj rabid.

rabino [ra'βino] sm rabbi.

rabo ['raβo] sm tail; stalk. **hacer rabona** play truant.

racial [ra'θjal] adj racial.

racimo [ra'θimo] sm bunch; cluster.

raciocinar [raθoθi'nar] v also **racionar** ration. **ración** sf portion, ration.

racional [raθjo'nal] adj rational. **racionalidad** sf rationality. **racionalista** adj rationalist.

racista [ra'θista] s(m+f) racist.

racha ['ratʃa] sf gust of wind; streak of luck; split.

radiactivo [raðjak'tiβo] adj radioactive. **radioactividad** sf radioactivity.

radiar [ra'ðjar] v radiate; broadcast. **radiación** sf radiation; broadcasting. **radiador** sm radiator. **radiante** adj radiant.

radicar [raði'kar] v take root; settle. **radicación** sf taking root.

radical [raði'kal] adj radical, fundamental. **radicalismo** sm radicalism.

radio¹ ['raðjo] sm radius.

radio² sm radium.

radio³ sf radio. **radiodifusión** sf broadcasting. **radiomisora** sf radio station. **radioyente** s(m+f) listener.

*raer [ra'er] v scrape; erase.

raíz [ra'iθ] sf root. **bienes raíces** real estate sing.

rajar [ra'xar] v slit; crack; slice. **raja** sf crack; slice.

ralea [ra'lea] sf sort; breed.

rallar [ra'ʎar] v grate. **rallador** sm grater. **rallo** sm rasp.

rama ['rama] sf (bot) branch, bough.

rambla ['rambla] sf avenue; gully.

ramificarse [ramifi'karse] v branch out. **ramificación** sf ramification.

ramillete [rami'ʎete] sm bunch of flowers, posy; cluster.

ramo ['ramo] sm (bot) branch; cluster; bouquet.

rampa ['rampa] sf ramp.

rampión [ram'plon] adj coarse, vulgar.

rana ['rana] sf frog.

rancio ['ranθjo] adj rancid, rank, stale.

rancho ['rantʃo] sm (comida) mess; farm; ranch. **ranchero** sm rancher.

rango ['rango] sm class, rank.

ranura [ra'nura] sf groove.

rapaz [ra'paθ] adj rapacious. **rapacidad** sf rapacity.

rapé [ra'pe] sm snuff.

rápido [ra'piðo] adj rapid. **rapidez** sf speed.

rapiña [ra'pina] sf robbery with violence.

rapsodia [rap'soðja] sf rhapsody.

raptar [rap'tar] v carry off, abduct; kidnap. **rapto** sm abduction. **raptor, -a** sm, sf kidnapper.

raquero [ra'kero] sm beachcomber.

raqueta [ra'keta] sf racket.

raro ['raro] adj rare. **rareza** sf rarity.

ras [ras] sm level. **a ras de tierra** at ground level.

rascacielos [raska'θjelos] sm invar skyscraper.

rascar [ras'kar] v scratch; scrape. **rascadura** sf scratching.

rasgar [ras'gar] v tear; rip; slash.

rasgo ['rasgo] sm feature; feat; (de pluma) stroke.

raso ['raso] adj flat; level; smooth.

raspar [ras'par] v rasp. **raspa** sf rasp. **raspadura** sf rasping.

rastra ['rastra] sf trail; trace; sledge.

rastrear [rastre'ar] v trace; track; rake.
rastrillar ['rastri'ʎar] v rake. **rastrillo** sm rake.
rastro ['rastro] sm track; trail.
rastrojo [ras'troxo] sm stubble.
rasurar [rasu'rar] v shave. **rasura** sf shaving.
rata ['rata] sf rat.
ratería [rate'ria] sf larceny, petty thieving. **ratero, -a** sm, sf petty thief.
ratificar [ratifi'kar] v ratify. **ratificación** sf ratification.
rato ['rato] sm a little while, short period of time. **al poco rato** shortly after.
ratón [ra'ton] sm mouse. **ratonera** sf mousetrap.
rayar [ra'jar] v rule; draw lines on; underline. **raya** sf line; stripe; limit. **a raya** within bounds. **rayado** adj lined; striped.
rayo ['rajo] sm beam, ray of light; flash of lightning.
raza ['raθa] sf race; lineage; breed.
razón [ra'θon] sf reason; rationale. **tener razón** be right. **razonable** adj reasonable. **razonar** v reason; justify.
reacción [reak'θjon] sf reaction. **reaccionar** v react. **reaccionario** s(m+f) reactionary. **reactor** sm reactor.
reacio [re'aθjo] adj obstinate.
real[1] [re'al] adj real.
real[2] adj royal.
realce [re'alθe] sm (arte) relief; highlight; importance.
realizar [reali'θar] v realize; make; perform.
realzar [real'θar] v raise; emboss; dignify.
reanimar [reani'mar] v revive; encourage.
reanudar [reanu'ðar] v renew. **reanudarse** v start again.
*__recuperar__ [reapare'θer] v reappear. **reaparición** sf reappearance.
rebajar [reβa'xar] v lessen, reduce; lower; allow discount; (bebida) weaken. **rebaja** sf reduction.
rebanada [reβa'naða] sf slice. **rebanar** v slice.
rebaño [re'βaɲo] sm flock; herd.
rebasar [reβa'sar] v go beyond, exceed; overtake; overflow.
rebatir [reβa'tir] v rebut, refute; repel. **reboto** sm (mil) alarm, call to arms; surprise attack.
rebeca [re'βeka] sf cardigan.

rebelarse [reβe'larse] v rebel. **rebelde** adj rebellious. **rebeldía** sf rebelliousness. **rebelión** sf rebellion.
rebosar [reβo'sar] v overflow. **rebosadura** sf overflowing.
rebotar [reβo'tar] v bend back; rebound; bounce. **rebotación** sf bouncing. **rebote** sm bounce.
rebozar [reβo'θar] v muffle. **rebozo** sm muffler. **sin rebozo** openly.
rebuscar [reβus'kar] v search for. **rebusca** sf search. **rebuscado** adj elaborate.
rebuznar [reβuθ'nar] v bray. **rebuzno** sm bray.
recado [re'kaðo] sm errand; message. **recadista** s(m+f) messenger.
*__recaer__ [reka'er] v relapse. **recaída** sf relapse.
recalcar [rekal'kar] v cram; pack; stress. **recalcadura** sf pressing; packing.
recalcitrante [rekalθi'trante] adj recalcitrant.
*__recalentar__ [rekalen'tar] v reheat; rekindle. **recalentarse** v overheat.
recambio [re'kambjo] sm re-exchange. **piezas de recambio** sf pl spare parts.
recargar [rekar'gar] v reload; overload; increase; recharge. **recarga** sf refill. **recargable** adj refillable. **recargo** sm additional load; surcharge.
recatarse [reka'tarse] v be cautious. **recatar** v cover up. **recatado** adj prudent. **recato** sm prudence.
recaudar [rekau'ðar] v collect. **recaudación** sf collection. **recaudador** sm tax collector. **a buen recaudo** in safe keeping.
recelar [reθe'lar] v suspect; fear. **recelo** sm mistrust. **receloso** adj suspicious.
recepción [reθep'θjon] sf reception; receipt; admission.
receptáculo [reθep'takulo] sm receptacle.
receptor [reθep'tor] sm recipient, receiver.
recesión [reθe'sjon] sf recession.
receta [re'θeta] sf formula; recipe; prescription.
recibir [reθi'βir] v receive. **recibidor, -a** sm, sf receiver. **recibo** sm reception; (com) receipt. **acusar recibo** (com) acknowledge receipt.
recién [re'θjen] adv recently, lately, just. **recién llegado** sm newcomer. **reciente** adj recent, new.
recinto [re'θinto] sm enclosure; precinct; district.

recio ['reθjo] *adj* tough, strong. *adv* loud-ly.

recipiente [reθi'pjente] *sm* receptacle; recipient.

reciprocar [reθipro'kar] *v* reciprocate. **recíproco** *adj* reciprocal.

recitar [reθi'tar] *v* recite. *sm* recital. **recitación** *sf* recitation.

reclamar [rekla'mar] *v* claim; demand; appeal. **reclamación** *sf* claim; protest. **reclamo** *sm* call; advertisement.

reclinar [rekli'nar] *v* lean, recline. **reclinación** *sf* leaning.

reclusión [reklu'sjon] *sf* seclusion; imprisonment. **recluso, -a** *sm, sf* recluse; convict.

recluta [re'kluta] *sm* recruit; conscript. **reclutamiento** *sm* recruitment. **reclutar** *v* recruit; conscript.

recobrar [reko'βrar] *v* recover; recuperate; regain. **recobro** *sm* recovery.

recoger [reko'xer] *v* pick up; gather; collect; confiscate; take in; shrink. **recogerse** *v* withdraw within oneself. **recogida** *sf* collection; harvest; withdrawal. **recogido** *adj* short; small; secluded. **recogimiento** *sm* withdrawal.

recolección [rekolek'θjon] *sf* gathering; harvest; recollection; compilation. **recolectar** *v* harvest.

*recomendar [rekomen'dar] *v* recommend; commend. **recomendación** *sf* recommendation. **recomendado, -a** *sm, sf* protégé/protégée.

recompensar [rekompen'sar] *v* recompense, reward. **recompenso** *sf* compensation; recompense.

reconciliarse [rekonθi'ljarse] *v* reconcile oneself. **reconciliación** *sf* reconciliation.

recóndito [re'kondito] *adj* secret; obscure.

*reconocer [rekono'θer] *v* recognize; acknowledge; examine closely. **reconocible** *adj* recognizable. **reconocimiento** *sm* recognition; acknowledgement; examination.

reconquista [rekon'kista] *sf* reconquest. **reconquistar** *v* reconquer.

reconsiderar [rekonsiðe'rar] *v* reconsider.

*reconstituir [rekonstitu'ir] *v* reconstitute. **reconstitución** *sf* reconstitution.

*reconstruir [rekonstru'ir] *v* reconstruct.

*reconvenir [rekonβe'nir] *v* reproach; rebuke. **reconvención** *sf* reproach.

recopilar [rekopi'lar] *v* compile; summarize. **recopilación** *sf* compilation; summary. **recopilador** *sm* compiler.

*recordar [rekor'ðar] *v* remember; commemorate; remind. **recordarse** *v* wake up. **para recordar** in memory. **recordable** *adj* memorable. **recordativo** *adj* reminiscent.

recorrer [reko'rrer] *v* go over; traverse; examine; survey; repair. **recorrido** *sm* journey; run; revision.

recortar [rekor'tar] *v* cut out; cut down; clip; trim; stand out. **recorte** *sm* cutting; outline.

recoveco [reko'βeko] *sm* bend; nook; recess.

recrearse [rekre'arse] *v* amuse oneself. **recreación** *sf* recreation. **recreo** *sm* recreation; amusement.

recriminar [rekrimi'nar] *v* recriminate. **recriminación** *sf* recrimination.

*recrudecer [rekruðe'θer] *v* recur; break out again.

rectángulo [rek'tangulo] *sm* rectangle. **rectangular** *adj* rectangular.

rectificar [rektifi'kar] *v* rectify; correct. **rectificación** *sf* rectification.

rectitud [rekti'tuð] *sf* rectitude; rightness. **recto** *adj* right; just; straight.

rector [rek'tor] *sm* rector; principal; governor. **rectoría** *sf* rectory.

recua ['rekwa] *sf* drove, herd; *(fig)* gang. **recuento** [re'kwento] *sm* recount; calculation; inventory.

recuerdo [re'kwerðo] *sm* recollection; memory. **recuerdos** *sm pl* regards *pl*.

recular [reku'lar] *v* recoil. **reculada** *sf* recoil.

recuperar [rekupe'rar] *v* recuperate. **recuperación** *sf* recovery.

recurrir [rekur'rir] *v* revert; resort (to). **recurrir a** have recourse to. **recurso** *sm* recourse; appeal.

recusar [reku'sar] *v* refuse; reject. **recusación** *sf* refusal; rejection.

rechazar [retʃa'θar] *v* repel; deny. **rechazamiento** *sm* repulsion. **rechazo** *sm* rebound; rejection.

rechinar [retʃi'nar] *v* creak; squeak; *(los dientes)* gnash. **rechinamiento** *sm* creaking; squeaking.

rechoncho [re'tʃontʃo] *adj* squat; chubby.

red [reð] *sf* net; grid; grille; grating; snare. **caer en la red** fall into the trap. **red ferroviaria** railway system.

redactar [reðak'tar] v edit. **redacción** sf editing; journalism. **redactor. -a** sm. sf editor; writer.

redención [reðen'θjon] sf redemption; help; salvation. **redentor. -a** sm. sf redeemer.

redimir [reði'mir] v redeem; ransom. **redimible** adj redeemable.

rédito ['reðito] sm income. **rédito imponible** taxable income.

redoblar [reðo'βlar] v double; redouble; repeat. **redobladura** sf redoubling.

redondear [reðonde'ar] v round; round off. **redondo** adj round; spherical. **negocio redondo** sm square deal.

*__reducir__ [reðu'θir] v reduce; lessen; compress; scale down **reducción** sf reduction. **reducido** adj reduced; abridged.

redundar [reðun'dar] v redound; overflow.

reembolsar [reembol'sar] v reimburse; repay. **reembolso** sm reimbursement; refund. **contra reembolso** cash on delivery.

reemplazar [reempla'θar] v replace. **reemplazable** adj replaceable. **reemplazo** sm replacement.

referencia [refe'renθja] sf reference; account; allusion. **referente** adj referring. **referido** adj aforementioned; in question.

referéndum [refe'rendum] sm referendum.

*__referir__ [refe'rir] v refer; narrate; describe.

refinar [refi'nar] v refine; polish; perfect. **refinación** sf refinement. **refinado** adj refined; slick. **refinadura** sf refinement. **refinería** sf refinery.

reflectar [reflek'tar] v reflect. **reflector** sm reflector; searchlight.

reflejar [refle'xar] v reflect; show. **refleja** sf reflection. **reflejo** sm reflection; reflex; glare.

reflexión [reflek'sjon] sf reflection. **reflexionar** v reflect. **reflexivo** adj (gram) reflexive.

reflujo [re'fluxo] sm ebb.

reformar [refor'mar] v reform; amend; remake; improve; repair. **reforma** sf reform, reformation. **reformación** sf reformation. **reformador. -a** sm. sf reformer. **reformativo** adj reformative. **reformatorio** sm reformatory.

*__reforzar__ [refor'θar] v reinforce; strengthen; encourage; boost. **reforzado** adj reinforced.

refractario [refrak'tarjo] adj refractory. **refracción** sf refraction. **refractar** v refract.

refrán [re'fran] sm proverb, saying.

*__refregar__ [refre'gar] v rub; scour; scold. **refregadura** sf rubbing, friction.

refrenar [refre'nar] v curb, control. **refrenamiento** sm restraint.

refrescar [refres'kar] v refresh; cool; repeat; revise. **refrescadura** sf refreshing. **refrescante** adj refreshing; cooling. **refresco** sm refreshment; cold drink.

refuerzo [re'fwerθo] sm reinforcement; backing; help.

refugiarse [refu'xjarse] v shelter. **refugio** sm refuge. **refugio de peatones** traffic island. **refugiado. -a** sm. sf refugee.

refulgir [reful'xir] v shine, gleam. **refulgencia** sf brilliance. **refulgente** adj brilliant.

refundir [refun'dir] v recast; adapt; refurbish. **refundición** sf recasting; adaptation.

refunfuñar [refunfu'nar] v grumble, grouse. **refunfuñadura** sf also **refunfuño** sm grumbling.

refutar [refu'tar] v refute. **refutable** adj refutable. **refutación** sf refutation.

regadera [rega'ðera] sf watering-can; channel; irrigation ditch. **regadío** sm irrigated land. **regadizo** adj irrigable. **regadura** sf irrigation. **regar** v water; irrigate; sprinkle.

regalar [rega'lar] v give; treat; regale; entertain. **regalador. -a** sm. sf entertainer. **regalo** sm gift; pleasure; treat; entertainment.

regaliz [rega'liθ] sm liquorice.

regañar [rega'nar] v scold; quarrel; growl; grumble. **regaño** sm scolding; quarrel; growl; grumble.

regata [re'gata] sf regatta.

regatear [regate'ar] v haggle; bargain; retail; begrudge; dodge. **regate** sm dodge. **regateo** sm haggling. **regatería** sf retail. **regatero. -a** sm. sf retailer.

regazo [re'gaθo] sm lap.

regencia [re'xenθja] sf regency.

regenerar [rexene'rar] v regenerate. **regeneración** sf regeneration. **regenerativo** adj regenerative.

regentar [rexen'tar] *v* manage; govern; boss. **regente** *sm* regent; director; professor. **regentear** *v* domineer.

régimen ['reximen] *sm* regime; system; rate; diet; performance.

regimiento [rexi'mjento] *sm* regiment; administration; government; town council. **regimentación** *sf* regimentation. **regimental** *adj* regimental. **regimentar** *v* regiment.

región [re'xjon] *sf* region; territory; area; space. **regional** *adj* regional.

*regir [re'xir] *v* govern; manage; control; obtain; prevail; steer.

registrar [rexis'trar] *v* register; inspect; record; search; show. **registración** *sf* registration. **registrado** *adj* registered; examined. **registrador** *sm* registrar; inspector. **registradora** *sf* cash register. **registro** *sm* register; registry; inspection.

reglar [re'glar] *v* rule; regulate; control. **reglarse** *v* conform; reform. **regla** *sf* rule; method; discipline; menstruation. **a regla** by rule. **regla de cálculo** slide rule. **regladamente** *adv* regularly. **reglado** *adj* regular; regulated; temperate. **reglamentación** *sf* regulation. **reglamentar** *v* regulate. **reglamentario** *adj* statutory. **reglamento** *sm* statute; rules and regulations *pl*.

regocijar [regoθi'xar] *v* rejoice; gladden. **regocijarse** *v* rejoice; exult. **regocijador** *adj* cheering. **regocijo** *sm* joy, gladness.

regresar [regre'sar] *v* return.

regular [regu'lar] *adj* regular; average; ordinary. **por lo regular** as a rule. *v* regulate; control; adjust. **regulación** *adj* regulation; control. **regulación a distancia** remote control. **regulado** *adj* regulated; regular. **regulador** *sm* regulator; throttle. **regulador de volumen** volume control. **regularidad** *sf* regularity; ordinariness. **regularización** *sf* regularization. **regularizar** *v* regularize.

rehabilitar [reaβili'tar] *v* rehabilitate. **rehabilitación** *sf* rehabilitation.

*rehacer [rea'θer] *v* remake; recover; renovate; repair. **rehacerse** *v* recuperate. **rehecho** *adj* remade; squat.

rehén [re'en] *sm* hostage.

*rehuir [re'wir] *v* flee; shrink from; avoid; shirk. **rehuida** *sf* flight.

rehusar [reu'sar] *v* refuse; reject.

reimprimir [reimpri'mir] *v* reprint. **reimpresión** *sf* reprint. **reimpreso** *adj* reprinted.

reinar [rei'nar] *v* reign; prevail. **reina** *sf* queen. **reinante** *adj* reigning. **reinado** *sm* reign. **reino** *sm* kingdom, reign. **reino animal** animal kingdom.

reincidir [reinθi'ðir] *v* backslide; relapse into; reiterate. **reincidencia** *sf* backsliding; reiteration. **reincidente** *adj* backsliding; relapsing; reiterating.

reintegrar [reinte'grar] *v* reintegrate; reimburse; recover. **reintegrarse** *v* recoup oneself. **reintegrable** *adj* reimbursable. **reintegración** *sf* reintegration; restoration. **reintegro** *sm* recovery; reimbursement.

*reír [re'ir] *v* laugh. **reírse de** make fun of.

reiterar [reite'rar] *v* reiterate. **reiteración** *sf* reiteration.

reivindicar [reiβindi'kar] *v* reclaim; claim; rehabilitate. **reivindicación** *sf* claim; recovery.

reja ['rexa] *sf* grating; grille; ploughshare; lattice. **rejado** *sm* grating; railing. **rejería** *sf* ornamental ironwork. **rejilla** *sf* small grating; (*tren*) luggage rack.

*rejuvenecer [rexuβene'θer] *v* rejuvenate. **rejuvenecimiento** *sm* rejuvenation.

relación [rela'θjon] *sf* relation; connection; report; narrative; intercourse; relationship. **relaciones** *sf pl* courtship *sing*; engagement *sing*. **relacionado** *adj* related. **relacionar** *v* relate; report; connect. **relacionarse** *v* be related; be connected.

relajar [rela'xar] *v* relax; remit; loosen; debauch. **relajación** *sf* relaxation; loosening; laxity; rupture. **relajadamente** *adv* loosely, dissolutely. **relajado** *adj* lax; ruptured. **relajador** *adj* relaxing.

relámpago [re'lampago] *sm* lightning. **relámpago difuso** sheet lightning.

relatar [rela'tar] *v* report; relate; tell. **relatador, -a** *sm, sf* narrator.

relatividad [relatiβi'ðað] *sf* relativity.

relevar [rele'βar] *v* relieve; absolve; replace; free; emboss. **relevación** *sf* relief; liberation; remission. **relevante** *adj* outstanding. **relevo** *sm* relay race. **relieve** *sm* relief; prominence. **en relieve** embossed.

relicario [reli'karjo] *sm* reliquary, shrine; locket.

religión [reli'xjon] *sf* religion; faith; creed.

religioso [reli'xjoso] *sm* friar, monk; religious person. *adj* religious.

reliquia [re'likja] *sf* relic; memento; ailment. **reliquia de familia** heirloom.

reloj [re'lox] *sm* clock; watch. **reloj de caja** grandfather clock. **reloj de cuclillo** cuckoo clock. **reloj despertador** alarm clock. **reloj pulsera** wristwatch. **relojería** *sf* watchmaker's shop. **relojero** *sm* watchmaker.

*****relucir** [relu'θir] *v* shine; excel. **sacar a relucir** show off. **reluciente** *adj* gleaming.

reluctante [reluk'tante] *adj* reluctant.

relumbrar [relum'brar] *v* dazzle; glare. **relumbrante** *adj* dazzling. **relumbre** *sm* sparkle; flash. **relumbro** *sm* glare; tinsel. **relumbroso** *adj* dazzling.

rellenar [reʎe'nar] *v* refill; fill; stuff; cram. **rellenable** *adj* refillable. **relleno** *sm* filling; stuffing; packing.

remachar [rema'tʃar] *v* rivet; stress. **remachado** *adj* riveted; (*fam*) quiet. **remache** *sm* rivet.

remanente [rema'nente] *sm* remains *pl*.

remanso [re'manso] *sm* backwater; sluggishness.

remar [re'mar] *v* row; toil.

rematar [rema'tar] *v* finish; kill; knock down at auction. **rematado** *adj* completely ruined. **rematante** *sm* highest bidder. **remate** *sm* end; finishing touch; highest bid.

remediar [reme'ðjar] *v* remedy; help; prevent. **remediable** *adj* remediable. **remedio** *sm* remedy. **no hay remedio** it can't be helped.

*****remendar** [remen'dar] *v* repair; patch; darn. **remendado** *adj* spotty; patched. **remendón, -ona** *sm, sf* mender; repairer. **remiendo** *sm* repair; patch. **echar un remiendo a** put a patch on.

remero [re'mero] *sm* oarsman.

remesa [re'mesa] *sf* remittance; consignment; shipment. **remesar** *v* remit; ship.

remilgado [remil'gaðo] *adj* mincing; prim; squeamish. **remilgarse** *v* simper. **remilgo** *sm* smirk; primness.

reminiscencia [reminis'θenθja] *sf* reminiscence.

remirado [remi'raðo] *adj* considerate; cautious; discreet. **remirar** *v* review. **remirarse** *v* take great pains; enjoy looking over.

remisión [remi'sjon] *sf* remission; pardon; reference. **remisible** *adj* pardonable. **remiso** *adj* remiss.

remitir [remi'tir] *v* send; pardon; adjourn; abate. **remitirse a** quote from. **remitido** *sm* dispatch.

remo ['remo] *sm* oar; paddle; rowing. **remos** *sm pl* limbs *pl*.

remojar [remo'xar] *v* soak; steep. **remojo** *sm* soaking; steeping.

remolacha [remo'latʃa] *sf* beetroot.

remolcar [remol'kar] *v* tow; haul. **remolcador** *sm* tug.

remolino [remo'lino] *sm* whirlwind; whirlpool; (*fig*) throng. **remolinar** *v* eddy.

remontar [remon'tar] *v* remount; mend; go back in time; raise; frighten. **remonte** *sm* repair; remounting; rising.

remordimiento [remorði'mjento] *sm* remorse.

remoto [re'moto] *adj* remote; improbable.

*****remover** [remo'βer] *v* remove; move; stir; discharge. **removimiento** *sm* removal.

remunerar [remune'rar] *v* remunerate. **remuneración** *sf* remuneration. **remunerativo** *adj* remunerative.

*****renacer** [rena'θer] *v* be reborn; recover. **renacimiento** *sm* rebirth; renaissance.

renacuajo [rena'kwaxo] *sm* tadpole.

rencilla [ren'θiʎa] *sf* squabble; feud. **rencilloso** *adj* quarrelsome.

rencor [ren'kor] *sm* rancour. **rencoroso** *adj* rancorous.

*****rendir** [ren'dir] *v* conquer; yield; surrender. **rendirse** *v* wear oneself out. **rendición** *sf* surrender; (*com*) profit. **rendido** *adj* submissive. **rendimiento** *sm* humility; weariness; output.

*****renegar** [rene'gar] *v* disown; detest; curse. **renegado, -a** *sm, sf* renegade. **renegador, -a** *sm, sf* blasphemer.

renglón [ren'glon] *sm* written or printed line. **leer entre renglones** read between the lines.

reno ['reno] *sm* reindeer.

renombre [re'nombre] *sm* renown; surname. **renombrado** *adj* renowned.

*****renovar** [reno'βar] *v* renovate; renew. **renovable** *adj* renewable. **renovación** *sf* renovation; renewal. **renuevo** *sm* renewal; sprout.

rentar [ren'tar] *v* yield an income or profit. **renta** *sf* income; profit. **rentero, -a** *sm,* *sf* tenant farmer. **rentista** *s(m+f)* stockholder. **rentístico** *adj* financial.

renunciar [renun'θjar] *v* renounce; resign. **renuncia** *sf* renunciation; resignation.

***reñir** [re'ɲir] *v* scold; quarrel. **reñido** *adj* on bad terms. **reñidor** *adj* quarrelsome.

reo ['reo]. **-a** *sm*, *sf* defendant. *adj* guilty.

reojo [re'oxo] *sm* **mirar de reojo** look askance.

reorganizar [reorgani'θar] *v* reorganize. **reorganización** *sf* reorganization.

reparar [repa'rar] *v* repair; restore; correct; make amends for; observe; parry. **reparable** *adj* noteworthy. **reparador, -a** *sm*, *sf* repairer; faultfinder. **reparo** *sm* repair; remedy; observation; protection.

repartir [repar'tir] *v* share; distribute. **repartición** *sf* distribution. **repartidor, -a** *sm*, *sf* distributor. **reparto** *sm* distribution; (*teatro*) cast.

repasar [repa'sar] *v* revise; review; retrace. **repaso** *sm* review; (*fam*) reprimand.

repatriar [repa'trjar] *v* repatriate. **repatriación** *sf* repatriation. **repatriado, -a** *sm*, *sf* repatriate.

repeler [repe'ler] *v* repel. **repelente** *adj* repellent.

repente [re'pente] *sm* sudden impulse. **de repente** suddenly.

repercutir [reperku'tir] *v* re-echo; rebound. **repercusión** *sf* repercussion; reverberation.

repertorio [reper'torjo] *sm* repertory; repertoire.

***repetir** [repe'tir] *v* repeat; recite. **repetición** *sf* repetition; recital.

repisa [re'pisa] *sf* shelf; ledge; bracket. **repisa de chimenea** mantelpiece. **repisa de ventana** window sill.

***replegar** [reple'gar] *v* refold; (*mil*) retreat. **replegable** *adj* folding. **repliegue** *sm* fold, crease; retreat.

repleto [re'pleto] *adj* replete; plump.

réplica ['replika] *sf* answer; replica. **replicar** *v* argue; answer back. **replicato** *sm* argument; answer.

repoblación [repoβla'θjon] *sf* repopulation; restocking; reforestation. **repoblar** *v* repopulate; restock; reforest.

repollo [re'poʎo] *sm* cabbage.

***reponer** [repo'ner] *v* replace; restore. **reponerse** *v* recover.

reportar [repor'tar] *v* restrain; obtain; bring. **reportarse** *v* contain oneself. **reportamiento** *sm* restraint.

reposar [repo'sar] *v* rest; lie down; settle; lie buried. **reposo** *sm* repose.

repostería [reposte'ria] *sf* pastry shop; pantry. **repostero, -a** *sm*, *sf* pastrycook; confectioner.

reprender [repren'der] *v* reprimand. **reprensible** *adj* reprehensible. **reprensor** *adj* reproachful.

represalia [repre'salja] *sf* reprisal.

representar [represen'tar] *v* represent; signify; describe; express; perform; appear to have. **representarse** *v* imagine. **representable** *adj* representable; performable. **representación** *sf* representation; performance. **representante** *s(m+f)* representative; actor, actress. **representativo** *adj* representative.

represión [repre'sjon] *sm* repression; control. **represivo** *adj* repressive.

reprimenda [repri'menda] *sf* reprimand.

reprimir [repri'mir] *v* repress; suppress. **reprimible** *adj* repressible.

***reprobar** [repro'βar] *v* reprove; condemn; (*examen*) fail. **reprobable** *adj* reprehensible. **reprobación** *sf* reproof; failure. **reprobado, -a** *sm*, *sf* also **réprobo, -a.** *sf* reprobate.

reprochar [repro'tʃar] *v* reproach; challenge. **reprochable** *adj* reproachable; reproachful. **reprochador, -a** *sm*, *sf* reproacher.

***reproducir** [reproðu'θir] *v* reproduce. **reproducible** *adj* reproducible. **reproducción** *sf* reproduction. **reproductor, -a** *sm*, *sf* breeder.

reptil [rep'til] *sm* reptile.

república [re'puβlika] *sf* republic. **republicanismo** *sm* republicanism. **republicano, -a** *sm*, *sf* republican.

repudiar [repu'ðjar] *v* repudiate. **repudiación** *sf* repudiation.

repuesto [re'pwesto] *sm* supply; store; sideboard. **de repuesto** spare, extra. *adj* replaced; secluded; recovered.

repugnar [repug'nar] *v* contradict; object to; be repugnant. **repugnarse** *v* conflict. **repugnacia** *sf* repugnance; opposition. **repugnante** *adj* repugnant.

repulsivo [repul'siβo] *adj* repulsive. **repulsa** *sf* refusal; rebuke. **repulsar** *v* reject; refuse. **repulsión** *sf* rejection; refusal.

reputar [repu'tar] v repute; consider; esteem. **reputación** sf reputation. **reputado** adj reputed.

*****requebrar** [reke'βrar] v woo; flatter; flirt with. **requebrador, -a** sm, sf flirt.

requemar [reke'mar] v scorch; inflame; overcook. **requemarse** v smoulder; become tanned. **requemado** adj burnt; tanned. **requemamiento** sm bite; sting. **requemante** adj burning; stinging.

*****requerir** [reke'rir] v request; require; urge; notify; summon; examine. **requeriente** adj requiring. **requerimiento** sm requisition; summons; notification; request.

requesón [reke'son] sm curd; cottage cheese.

requisar [reki'sar] v requisition. **requisa** sf tour of inspection; requisition. **requisición** sf requisition. **requisito** adj requisite.

res [res] sf head of cattle; animal.

resabio [re'saβjo] sm bad habit; unpleasant aftertaste. **resabiado** adj crafty; wicked; spoiled. **resabiar** v pervert; become vicious. **resabiarse** v become annoyed.

resaca [re'saka] sf undertow; surf; surge.

resaltar [resal'tar] v rebound, stand out. **resalte** sm projection. **resalto** sm rebound.

resarcir [resar'θir] v compensate. **resarcirse de** make up for. **resarcimiento** sm compensation.

resbalar [resβa'lar] v slide; skid; slip. **resbaladero** also **resbaladizo, resbalante** adj slippery. **resbalador** adj sliding. **resbaldura** sf skid mark. **resbalón** sm slide; slip; skid.

rescatar [reska'tar] v rescue; recover; save; ransom; make up for. **rescate** sm redemption; rescue; ransom.

rescindir [resθin'dir] v rescind. **rescisión** sf annulment.

rescoldo [res'koldo] sm misgiving; embers pl.

resecar [rese'kar] v dry thoroughly. **reseco** adj desiccated.

*****resentirse** [resen'tirse] v feel the effects; be weakened.

reseñar [rese'nar] v review; outline. **reseña** sf review; outline.

reservar [reser'βar] v reserve; preserve; conceal. **reserva** sf reserve; reservation. **a reserva de** with the intention of. **reserva de asiento** reservation. **sin reserva** frankly. **reservado** adj reserved; discreet.

resfriar [resfri'ar] v cool; turn cold. **resfriarse** v catch cold. **resfriado** m (med) cold.

resguardar [resgwar'ðar] v defend; preserve. **resguardarse** v protect oneself. **resguardo** sm defence; protection; guarantee. **resguardo de correos** postal receipt.

residencia [resi'ðenθja] sf residence; boarding house. **residencial** adj residential. **residente** s(m+f) resident. **residir** v reside.

residuo [re'siðwo] sm residue. **residuos** sm pl refuse sing. **residual** adj residual.

resignar [resig'nar] v resign; renounce. **resignarse** v resign oneself. **resigna** sf renunciation. **resignación** sf resignation.

resina [re'sina] sf resin.

resistir [resis'tir] v resist; refuse. **resistencia** sf resistance; stamina. **resistente** adj resistant.

resolución [resolu'θjon] sf resolution; decision. **resoluto** adj resolute; skilled.

*****resolver** [resol'βer] v resolve; decide; analyse. **resolverse** v make up one's mind.

*****resollar** [reso'Aar] v pant; puff; snort.

*****resonar** [reso'nar] v resound. **resonancia** sf resonance. **resonante** adj resonant.

resoplar [reso'plar] v snort; puff. **resoplido** sm snort; puff.

resorte [re'sorte] sm resort; means; motive; (mec) spring; elasticity.

respaldar [respal'ðar] v back; support; endorse. **respaldarse** v lean. **respaldo** sm chair back; support.

respecto [res'pekto] sm respect. **con respecto a** with regard to.

respetar [respe'tar] v respect. **respetabilidad** sf respectability. **respetable** adj respectable. **respetador** adj respectful. **respeto** sm respect. **respetuoso** adj respectful.

respirar [respi'rar] v breathe. **respiración** sf respiration, breath. **respiro** sm breathing. **respiradero** sm ventilator.

*****resplandecer** [resplanðe'θer] v glitter. **resplandeciente** adj glittering. **resplandor** sm glitter.

responder [respon'der] v respond. **responder por** vouch for. **respondón** adj saucy. **responsivo** adj responsive. **respuesta** sf reply; refutation.

responsable [respon'saβle] adj responsible. **responsabilidad** sf responsibility.

resquebrajar [reske'βra'xar] v also resquebrar split; crack. **resquebra(ja)dura** sf crack.

resquemar [reske'mar] v sting the tongue. sm sting in the mouth; remorse; resentment.

resquicio [res'kiθjo] sm crack; chink; (fig) slight chance.

restablecer [restaβle'θer] v re-establish. **restablecerse** v recover from illness. **restablecimiento** sm re-establishment; recovery.

restallar [resta'ʎar] v crack; crackle.

restante [re'stante] adj remaining. sm remainder.

restar [res'tar] v subtract; remain.

restaurante [restau'rante] sm restaurant. **restauración** sf restoration. **restaurar** v restore; recover; repair.

restituir [restitu'ir] v restore; pay back. **restituirse** v return. **restitución** sf restitution.

resto [ˈresto] sm rest. remainder.

restregar [restre'gar] v rub; scrub; wipe. **restregón** sm rubbing; scrubbing; wiping.

restricción [restrik'θjon] sf restriction. **restrictivo** adj restrictive.

restringir [restrin'xir] v restrict.

resucitar [resuθi'tar] v resuscitate. **resucitación** sf resuscitation.

resuello [re'sweʎo] sm breathing.

resuelto [re'swelto] adj resolute; resolved; firm.

resultar [resul'tar] v result; happen; turn out; go. **resulta** sf result, effect. **resultado** sm result. **resultante** adj resultant.

resumir [resu'mir] v summarize; abbreviate. **resumen** sm summary. **en resumen** in brief. **resumido** adj summarized.

retablo [re'taβlo] sm altarpiece.

retaguardia [reta'gwarðja] sf rearguard.

retal [re'tal] sm remnant.

retama [re'tama] sf (bot) broom.

retardar [retar'ðar] v retard, delay; (reloj) put back. **retardación** sf delay. **retardo** sm delay.

retén [re'ten] sm spare, reserve.

retener [rete'ner] v retain; deduct; detain; arrest. **retención** sf retention; deduction; detention. **retentiva** sf memory. **retentivo** adj retentive.

retina [re'tina] sf retina.

retintín [retin'tin] sm jingle.

retirar [reti'rar] v withdraw. **retirarse** v go into seclusion. **retirada** sf retreat. **retirado** adj retired; remote. **retiro** sm retirement; retreat.

reto [ˈreto] sm challenge.

retocar [reto'kar] v retouch. **retoque** sm retouching.

retorcer [retor'θer] v twist; distort. **retorcerse** v writhe. **retorcimiento** sm contortion.

retórica [re'torika] sf rhetoric. **retórico** adj rhetorical.

retornar [retor'nar] v return. **retorno** sm return; remuneration.

retractar [retrak'tar] v retract. **retracción** sf retraction. **retractable** adj also **retráctil** retractable.

retraer [retra'er] v dissuade; bring again. **retraerse** v shelter; retreat. **retraído** adj retiring; unsociable. **retraimiento** sm retirement; retreat.

retrasar [retra'sar] v delay; put back; (reloj) be slow. **retrasarse** v be late. **retraso** sm delay; lateness.

retratar [retra'tar] v portray. **retratista** s(m+f) portrait painter. **retrato** sm portrait.

retrete [re'trete] sm lavatory.

retribuir [retriβu'ir] v recompense; repay. **retribución** sf retribution; recompense.

retroceder [retroθe'ðer] v recede; fall back. **retroceso** sm retreat; (com) slump. **retrogresión** sf retrogression.

retruécano [retru'ekano] sm pun.

retumbar [retum'bar] v resound. **retumbante** adj resounding. **retumbo** sm rumble.

reuma [ˈreuma] sm rheumatism. **reumático** adj rheumatic. **reumatismo** sm rheumatism.

reunir [reu'nir] v reunite; unite; gather; reconcile. **reunión** sf meeting.

revalidar [reβali'ðar] v ratify; confirm. **revalidación** sf ratification.

revancha [re'βantʃa] sf revenge.

revelar [reβe'lar] v reveal; (foto) develop. **revelación** sf revelation. **revelador** adj revealing.

revendedor [reβende'ðor], -a sm, sf retailer. **revender** v retail.

reventar [reβen'tar] v burst. **reventarse** v blow up. **reventón** sm burst; blowout.

reverberar [reβerβe'rar] v reverberate. **reverberación** sf reverberation. **reverbero** sm reverberation; reflector.

*reverdecer [reβerðe'θer] v grow green again; revive.

reverenciar [reβeren'θjar] v reverence, venerate. reverencia sf reverence. reverendo adj reverend. reverente adj reverent.

reversión [reβer'sjon] sf reversion. reversible adj revertible. reverso adj reverse.

revés [re'βes] sm reverse; back; setback. al revés upside down; inside out; back to front. revesado adj complicated; unruly.

revisar [reβi'sar] v revise; review. revisión sf revision; review; (com) audit. revista sf review; journal.

revivir [reβi'βir] v revive. revivicar v revive.

revocar [reβo'kar] v revoke; dissuade.

*revolcar [reβol'kar] v knock down; defeat; (fam) fail an exam. revolcarse v wallow.

revoltillo [reβol'tiλo] sm also revoltijo jumble; mess.

revoltoso [reβol'toso] adj mischievous; unruly.

revolución [reβolu'θjon] sf revolution. revolucionario, -a sm, -a revolutionary.

*revolver [reβol'βer] v revolve; stir; disturb. revolverse v turn round.

revólver [re'βolβer] sm revolver.

revoque [re'βoke] sm plaster; stucco; whitewash.

revuelta [re'βwelta] sf revolt; turn; bend; change. revuelto adj difficult; unruly; upside down; disturbed.

rey [rej] sm king.

reyerta [re'jerta] sf quarrel; brawl.

rezagar [reθa'gar] v defer; postpone; leave behind. rezagarse v straggle. rezagado sm (mil) straggler. rezago sm remainder.

rezar [re'θar] v pray, pray for. rezo sm prayer; prayers pl.

rezumarse [reθu'marse] v ooze, drip; leak out.

riachuelo [rja'tʃwelo] sm brook. ría sf estuary.

ribera [ri'βera] sf river bank; shore.

ribete [ri'βete] sm (de ropa) border, edging; trimmings pl. ribetear v border; edge.

ricino [ri'θino] sm castor-oil plant. aceite de ricino sm castor oil.

rico ['riko], -a sm, sf rich person. adj rich; handsome; tasty.

ridiculizar [riðikuli'θar] v ridicule. ridículo adj ridiculous.

riego ['rjego] sm irrigation.

riel [rjel] sm ingot; (ferro) rail.

rienda ['rjenda] sf rein. a rienda suelta at full speed. llevar las riendas be in control.

riesgo ['rjesgo] sm risk.

rifar [ri'far] v raffle. rifa sf raffle.

rifle ['rifle] sm rifle.

rígido ['rixiðo] adj rigid. rigidez sf rigidity.

rigor [ri'gor] sm severity; rigour. rigorismo sm austerity. riguroso adj rigorous.

rimar [ri'mar] v rhyme. rima sf rhyme.

rimbombante [rimbom'bante] adj grandiloquent; bombastic. rimbombancia sf grandiloquence.

rincón [rin'kon] sm corner. rinconada sf corner table.

rinoceronte [rinoθe'ronte] sm rhinoceros.

riña ['rina] sf brawl; fight; quarrel.

riñón [ri'non] sm kidney.

río ['rio] sm river. río arriba upstream.

ripio ['ripjo] sm rubble; refuse; residue. no perder ripio not to miss a trick.

riqueza [ri'keθa] sf wealth.

risa ['risa] sf laughter; laugh. risueño adj smiling; happy.

ristre ['ristre] sm en ristre at the ready.

ritmo ['ritmo] sm rhythm. rítmico adj rhythmic.

rito ['rito] sm rite. ritual sm ritual. ritualismo sm ritualism. ritualista adj ritualistic.

rival [ri'βal] s(m+f), adj rival. rivalidad sf rivalry. rivalizar v vie. rivalizar con rival.

rizar [ri'θar] v (pelo) curl. rizado sm curling. rizador sm curling-iron. rizo adj curly.

robar [ro'βar] v rob, steal; kidnap. robo sm robbery.

roble ['roβle] sm oak.

*robustecer [roβuste'θer] v strengthen. robustecerse v gain strength. robustecimiento sm strengthening. robustez sf robustness. robusto adj robust.

roca ['roka] sf rock.

roce ['roθe] sm friction; rubbing; chafing.

rociar [ro'θjar] v sprinkle; spray; strew; moisten. rociada sf sprinkling; spraying; dew. rociadera sf watering can. rociador sm sprinkler.

rocín [ro'θin] sm nag; hack.

rodapié [roða'pje] sm skirting-board.

***rodar** [ro'ðar] v roll; revolve; rotate. **rodado** adj (auto) run-in. **tránsito rodado** sm road traffic. **rodaja** sf small wheel. **rodaje** sm wheels pl.

rodear [roðe'ar] v encircle; enclose; go round. **rodearse** v surround oneself. **rodeo** sm detour; evasion; rodeo.

rodezno [ro'ðeθno] sm waterwheel; cogwheel.

rodilla [ro'ðiʎa] sf knee. **de rodillas** kneeling.

rodillo [ro'ðiʎo] sm rolling pin; roller; mangle.

***roer** [ro'er] v gnaw; nibble. **roerse** v bite. **roedor** adj gnawing.

***rogar** [ro'gar] v beg; pray. **rogación** sf petition. **rogativa** sf supplication.

rojo ['roxo] adj red. sm red; rouge. **rojear** v redden. **rojizo** adj reddish.

rollizo [ro'ʎiθo] adj chubby; plump.

rollo ['roʎo] sm roll; cylinder; (foto) film.

romance [ro'manθe] sm, adj romance. ballad. **romancero** sm ballad collection; ballad singer. **romántico** adj romantic.

romería [rome'ria] sf pilgrimage. **romero, -a** sm sf pilgrim; sm rosemary.

romo ['romo] adj snub-nosed; blunt; dull.

rompecabezas [rompeka'βeθas] sm invar puzzle; jigsaw; riddle.

rompeolas [rompe'olas] sm invar breakwater.

romper [rom'per] v break; fracture; break out. **rompimiento** sm break; breach.

ron [ron] sm rum.

roncar [ron'kar] v snore; roar; boast. **ronca** sf bellow; roar. **ronquido** sm snore.

ronco ['ronko] adj hoarse. **ronquedad** sf hoarseness.

rondar [ron'dar] v patrol; go round; pursue; haunt; serenade. **rondador** sm patrolman. **ronda** sf patrol; round of drinks.

ronronear [ronrone'ar] v purr.

ronzal [ron'θal] sm halter.

roña ['roɲa] sf filth; mange; rust; (fam) meanness. adj stingy. **roñoso** adj mangy; filthy; stingy.

ropa ['ropa] sf clothes pl. clothing. **ropa de cama** bed linen. **ropa interior** underclothes. **ropero** sm wardrobe.

roque ['roke] sm (ajedrez) rook.

rosa ['rosa] sf rose. **novela rosa** sf romantic novel. **rosado** adj rose-coloured. **rosal** sm rosebush.

rosario [ro'sarjo] sm rosary.

rosca ['roska] sf thread of a screw; doughnut; bread roll.

rostro ['rostro] sm countenance; face. **hacer rostro** a face.

rotación [rota'θjon] sf rotation. **rotativo** adj rotary.

roto ['roto] adj broken; torn. sm hole.

rotular [rotu'lar] v label. **rótula** sf label; placard.

rotundo [ro'tundo] adj round; (fig) emphatic. **rotundidad** sf roundness.

roturar [rotu'rar] v (tierra) break up. **rotura** sf breaking.

rozar [ro'θar] v graze; scrape. **rozarse** v be tongue-tied; trip over one's feet. **rozamiento** sm rubbing, friction.

rubí [ru'βi] sm, pl **rubíes** ruby.

rubio ['ruβjo] sm, adj blond. **rubia** sf blonde.

rubor [ru'βor] sm blush. **ruborizarse** v blush. **ruboroso** adj blushing.

rúbrica ['ruβrika] sf rubric; heading; flourish after a signature. **rubricar** v sign with a flourish.

rudeza [ru'ðeθa] sf roughness, rudeness. **rudo** adj rough; coarse; crude.

rudimento [ruði'mento] sm rudiment.

rueca [ru'eka] sf distaff.

rueda [ru'eða] sf wheel. **rueda de recambio** spare wheel.

ruedo [ru'eðo] sm edge; hem; round mat.

ruego [ru'ego] sm request; supplication.

rugir [ru'xir] v roar; bellow; howl. **rugido** sm roar; bellow; howl.

rugoso [ru'goso] adj wrinkled.

ruibarbo [rui'βarβo] sm rhubarb.

ruido [ru'iðo] sm noise; rumour. **meter ruido** make a noise. **ruidoso** adj noisy.

ruin [ru'in] adj mean; foul; puny. **ruindad** sf meanness; villainy.

ruina [ru'ina] sf ruin; ruins pl. **ruinoso** adj ruinous.

ruiseñor [ruise'ɲor] sm nightingale.

rumbo ['rumbo] sm course; direction; (fam) pomp. **hacer rumbo** set a course. **rumboso** adj splendid; lavish.

rumiar [ru'mjar] v ruminate; chew; grumble. **rumiante** sm ruminant.

rumor [ru'mor] sm rumour; noise; murmur. **rumorear** v rumour. **rumoroso** adj murmuring.

ruptura [rup'tura] *sf* rupture; break.

rural [ru'ral] *adj* rural.

Rusia ['rusja] *sf* Russia. **ruso, -a** *sm, sf* Russian.

rústico ['rustiko] *adj* rustic.

ruta ['ruta] *sf* route; road.

rutina [ru'tina] *sf* routine. **rutinario** *adj* routine; unimaginative.

S

sábado ['saβaðo] *sm* Saturday.

sabana [sa'βana] *sf* savannah.

sábana ['saβana] *sf* sheet.

sabanilla [saβa'niʎa] *sf* small cloth, napkin.

sabañón [saβa'ɲon] *sm* chilblain.

*****saber** [sa'βer] *v* know; know how to; be aware of. **a saber** namely. **sabedor** *adj* well-informed. **sabidillo, -a** *sm, sf* (*fam*) know-all. **sabido** *adj* known; learned. **sabiduría** *sf* knowledge; wisdom. **sabio** *adj* wise.

sabor [sa'βor] *sm* taste; flavour. **saborear** *v* taste; savour. **saborearse** *v* smack one's lips. **saboroso** *adj* tasty; savoury.

sabotear [saβote'ar] *v* sabotage. **saboteador, -a** *sm, sf* saboteur. **sabotaje** *sm* sabotage.

sabroso [sa'βroso] *adj* delicious; tasty; pleasant; racy.

sabueso [sa'βweso] *sm* bloodhound.

sacabocados [sakaβo'kaðos] *sm invar* (*tecn*) punch.

sacacorchos [saka'kortʃos] *sm invar* corkscrew.

sacamanchas [saka'mantʃas] *sm invar* stain-remover.

sacar [sa'kar] *v* get out; put out; draw; publish; take out; buy tickets; (*tenis*) serve. **saca** *sf* extraction; exportation.

sacarina [saka'rina] *sf* saccharine.

sacerdote [saker'ðote] *sm* priest. **sacerdocio** *sm* priesthood. **sacerdotal** *adj* priestly. **sacerdotisa** *sf* priestess.

saciar [sa'θjar] *v* satiate. **saciedad** *sf* satiety.

saco ['sako] *sm* sack; bag; plunder. **entrar a saco** plunder.

sacramento [sakra'mento] *sm* sacrament. **sacramental** *adj* sacramental.

sacrificar [sakrifi'kar] *v* sacrifice. **sacrificadero** *sm* slaughterhouse. **sacrificio** *sm* sacrifice; slaughter.

sacrilegio [sakri'lexjo] *sm* sacrilege. **sacrílego** *adj* sacrilegious.

sacro ['sakro] *adj* sacred. **sacrosanto** *adj* sacrosanct.

sacudir [saku'ðir] *v* shake, jolt. **sacudirse** *v* shake off; repel. **sacudida** *sf* shake, jolt.

sádico ['saðiko] *adj* sadistic. **sadismo** *sm* sadism. **sadista** *s(m+f)* sadist.

saeta [sa'eta] *sf* arrow; watch *or* clock hand. **saetada** *sf* arrow wound. **saetera** *sf* loophole. **saetero** *sm* bowman.

sagacidad [sagaθi'ðað] *sf* shrewdness. **sagaz** *adj* shrewd, wise.

sagrado [sa'graðo] *adj* sacred, holy. *sm* sanctuary.

sajón [sa'xon], **-ona** *s, adj* Saxon.

sal [sal] *sf* salt; wit; charm. **salero** *sm* salt cellar; wit; charm. **saleroso** *adj* (*fam*) witty; charming.

sala ['sala] *sf* hall; drawing-room; (*med*) ward; (*teatro*) house. **sala de conferencias** lecture hall. **sala de espera** waiting-room.

salacidad [salaθi'ðað] *sf* lechery.

salar [sa'lar] *v* salt. **salado** *adj* salty; witty.

salario [sa'larjo] *sm* salary, pay.

salchicha [sal'tʃitʃa] *sf* sausage. **salchichón** *sm* salami.

saldar [sal'ðar] *v* settle; liquidate; pay off. **saldo** *sm* payment; balance; bargain sale.

salida [sa'liða] *sf* departure; exit; start; outskirts *pl*; pretext; (*del sol*) rising; outcome; projection; witticism. **calle sin salida** *sf* cul-de-sac. **dar salida a** sell. **tener buenas salidas** be full of witty remarks. **saliente** *adj* projecting.

salina [sa'lina] *sm* salt mine. **salino** *adj* saline.

*****salir** [sa'lir] *v* leave; emerge; (*astron*) rise; happen. **salir para** leave for. **salir por alguien** vouch for someone. **salirse** *v* leak; overflow; escape.

saliva [sa'liβa] *sf* saliva. **salivar** *v* salivate.

salmo ['salmo] *sm* psalm. **salmista** *s(m+f)* psalmist. **salmodia** *sf* psalmody.

salmón [sal'mon] *sm* salmon.

salmuera [sal'mwera] *sf* brine.

salón [sa'lon] *sm* large hall; drawing-room.

salpicar [salpi'kar] *v* splash; sprinkle. **salpicadura** *sf* splash; spatter.

salpimentar [salpimen'tar] *v* season with salt and pepper.

salpullido [salpuˈʎiðo] *sm* (*med*) rash.

salsa [ˈsalsa] *sf* sauce, gravy.

saltamontes [saltaˈmontes] *sm invar* grasshopper.

saltar [salˈtar] *v* jump; skip; break; explode. **salto** *sm* jump; hop; chasm. **salto de agua** waterfall. **salto de altura** high jump. **salto con garrocha** pole vault. **salto mortal** somersault.

saltear [salteˈar] *v* rob; assault. **salteador** *sm* highwayman. **salteamiento** *sm* highway robbery.

salubre [saˈluβre] *adj* salubrious, healthy. **salubridad** *sf* wholesomeness. **salud** *sf* health. **¡salud!** cheers! **saludable** *adj* salutary. **saludador** *sm* quack doctor.

salvaguardar [salβaɣwarˈðar] *v* safeguard. **salvaguardia** *sf* safeguard.

saludar [saluˈðar] *v* salute; greet. **le saluda atentamente** yours faithfully. **saludo** *sm* greeting; salute. **saludos** *sm pl* regards *pl*, best wishes *pl*. **salutación** *sf* greeting.

salvaje [salˈβaxe] *adj* wild; uncultivated; savage. **salvajada** *sf* barbarity. **salvajería** *sf* savagery.

salvamanteles [salβamanˈteles] *sm invar* table mat.

salvar [salˈβar] *v* save; rescue; except; cross; overcome. **salvarse** *v* escape. **salvamento** *sm* salvation; salvage. **salvador** *adj* healing; saving.

salvavidas [salβaˈβiðas] *sm invar* lifebelt; life buoy; lifeboat.

salvedad [salβeˈðað] *sf* proviso; reservation; distinction.

salvia [ˈsalβja] *sf* sage.

salvo [ˈsalβo] *adv* except, saving. *adj* safe. **a salvo** safe. **poner a salvo** rescue. **salvo que** unless.

salvoconducto [salβokonˈdukto] *sm* safeconduct.

san [san] *adj* saint; holy. *V* santo.

sanar [saˈnar] *v* heal; cure; get better. **sanable** *adj* curable. **sanatorio** *sm* sanatorium.

sanción [sanˈθjon] *sf* sanction. **sancionar** *v* sanction.

sandalia [sanˈdalja] *sf* sandal.

sandía [sanˈdia] *sf* watermelon.

sanear [saneˈar] *v* guarantee; drain; repair. **saneado** *adj* unencumbered; nett. **saneamiento** *sm* surety; drainage.

sangrar [sanˈgrar] *v* bleed; drain off. **sangradera** *sf* lancet. **sangre** *sf* blood. **a sangre fría** in cold blood. **sangriento** *adj* bloody. **sanguinario** *adj* bloodthirsty. **sanguinolento** *adj* bloody.

sangría [sanˈgria] *sf* bleeding; drink made of fruit and red wine.

sanguijuela [sangiˈxwela] *sf* leech.

sanidad [saniˈðað] *sf* health; sanitation. **sanitario** *adj* sanitary. **sano** *adj* healthy; wholesome; sound; good.

santiamén [santjaˈmen] *sm* instant. **en un santiamén** in a jiffy.

santificar [santifiˈkar] *v* sanctify, consecrate. **santificación** *sf* sanctification.

santiguar [santiˈgwar] *v* bless. **santiguarse** *v* cross oneself.

santo [ˈsanto], **-a** *sm*, *sf* saint. *adj* sacred; saintly; holy. **santo y bueno** all well and good.

santuario [sanˈtwarjo] *sm* sanctuary, shrine.

saña [ˈsaɲa] *sf* rage; cruelty. **sañoso** *adj* furious; cruel.

sapo [ˈsapo] *sm* toad.

saquear [sakeˈar] *v* plunder. **saqueo** *sm* plunder. **saqueador, -a** *sm*, *sf* looter.

sarampión [saramˈpjon] *sm* measles.

sarcasmo [sarˈkasmo] *sm* sarcasm. **sarcástico** *adj* sarcastic.

sarcófago [sarˈkofago] *sm* sarcophagus.

sardina [sarˈðina] *sf* sardine.

sardónico [sarˈðoniko] *adj* sardonic.

sargento [sarˈxento] *sm* sergeant.

sarna [ˈsarna] *sf* scabies; itch. **sarnoso** *adj* mangy.

sartén [sarˈten] *sf* frying pan.

sastre [ˈsastre] *sm* tailor. **sastrería** *sf* tailoring; tailor's shop.

satélite [saˈtelite] *sm* satellite.

sátira [ˈsatira] *sf* satire. **satírico** *adj* satirical. **satirizar** *v* satirize.

***satisfacer** [satisfaˈθer] *v* satisfy; please. **satisfacerse** *v* satisfy oneself; take revenge. **satisfacción** *sf* satisfaction. **satisfactorio** *adj* satisfactory. **satisfecho** *adj* satisfied.

saturar [satuˈrar] *v* saturate. **saturación** *sf* saturation.

sauce [ˈsauθe] *sm* willow.

saúco [saˈuko] *sm* (*bot*) elder.

savia [ˈsaβja] *sf* sap.

saxófono [sakˈsofono] *sm* saxophone.

saya [ˈsaja] *sf* skirt, petticoat. **sayo** *sm* smock.

sazonar [saθoˈnar] *v* (*culin*) season; ripen.

sazón *sf* season; (*culin*) flavour; mellowness. **a la sazón** at the time. **sazonado** *adj* tasty; well seasoned.

se [se] *pron* himself; herself; yourself; oneself; itself; themselves; yourselves; one another; each other. se **dice** they say. se **habla inglés** English is spoken.

sebo ['seβo] *sm* grease. **seboso** *adj* greasy.

secar [se'kar] *v* dry. **secarse** *v* dry oneself; dry up. **seca** *sf* drought; sandbank. **secador** *sm* hair-dryer. **secadora** *sf* clothes-dryer. **secano** *sm* dry land. **secante** *sm* blotting paper. **seco** *adj* dry; lean; hoarse. **en seco** high and dry.

sección [sek'θjon] *sf* section.

secretario [sekre'tarjo], -a *sm, sf* secretary. **secretaría** *sf* secretariat.

secreto [se'kreto] *adj* secret; private; hidden. *sm* secrecy, secret knowledge. **secreto a voces** open secret. **secreteo** *sm* private conversation.

secta ['sekta] *sf* sect. **sectario**, -a *sm, sf* sectarian.

secuaz [se'kwaθ] *sm* follower, supporter.

secuestrar [sekwes'trar] *v* kidnap; hijack. **secuestrador**, -a *sm, sf* kidnapper; hijacker. **secuestro** *sm* kidnap; hijack.

secular [seku'lar] *adj* secular. **secularizar** *v* secularize.

secundar [sekun'dar] *v* second, support.

sed [seð] *sf* thirst. **tener sed** be thirsty. **sediento** *adj* thirsty.

seda ['seða] *sf* silk. **sedoso** *adj* silky.

sedante [se'ðante] *sm* sedative. *adj* calming.

sede ['seðe] *sf* (*rel*) see; (*de gobierno*) seat. **Santa Sede** Holy See.

sedentario [seðen'tarjo] *adj* sedentary.

sedería [seðe'ria] *sf* silk trade; drapery.

sedición [seði'θjon] *sf* sedition. **sedicioso** *adj* seditious.

sedimento [seði'mento] *sm* sediment. **sedimentar** *v* deposit.

*seducir [seðu'θir] *v* seduce; attract. **seducción** *sf* seduction. **seductivo** *adj* seductive. **seductor**, -a *sm, sf* seducer.

*segar [se'gar] *v* reap; mow. **segadora** *sf* mower; reaper.

seglar [se'glar] *sm* layman. *adj* secular.

segmento [seg'mento] *sm* segment.

segregar [segre'gar] *v* segregate. **segregación** *sf* segregation.

*seguir [se'gir] *v* follow; pursue; continue. **seguida** *sf* continuation. **en seguida** at once. **seguido** *adj* successive; straight;

cuatro días seguidos four days running. **seguimiento** *sm* pursuit; following.

según [se'gun] *prep* according to. *adv* it all depends. *conj* as.

segundo [se'gundo] *adj, sm* second. **segundón** [segun'don] *sm* second son.

seguro [se'guro] *adj* sure; safe. *sm* safety catch; insurance. **seguridad** *sf* safety; certainty.

seis ['seis] *sm, adj* six.

selección [selek'θjon] *sf* selection. **seleccionar** *v* select. **selectivo** *adj* selective. **selecto** *adj* select.

selva ['selβa] *sf* forest; jungle. **selvoso** *adj* wooded, forested.

sello ['seʎo] *sm* stamp; seal. **selladura** *sf* sealing. **sellar** *v* stamp; seal.

semáforo [se'maforo] *sm* semaphore; traffic lights *pl*.

semana [se'mana] *sf* week. **semanal** *adj* weekly. **semanario** *sm* weekly publication.

semblante [sem'blante] *sm* face; appearance.

*sembrar [sem'brar] *v* sow; scatter. **sembradera** *sf* seed-drill. **sembrador**, -a *sm, sf* sower.

semejar [seme'xar] *v* resemble. **semejante** *adj* similar. **semejanza** *sf* similarity.

semen ['semen] *sm* semen. **semental** *sm* sire. **sementera** *sf* sowing; seed-time.

semestre [se'mestre] *sm* semester. **semestral** *adj* half-yearly.

semicírculo [semi'θirkulo] *sm* semicircle. **semicircular** *adj* semicircular.

semilla [se'miʎa] *sf* seed. **semillero** *sm* seedbed.

seminario [semi'narjo] *sm* seminary; seminar; seedbed.

senado [se'naðo] *sm* senate. **senador** *sm* senator.

sencillo [sen'θiʎo] *adj* simple; easy. **sencillez** *sf* simplicity.

senda ['senda] *sf* path. **sendero** *sm* path.

sendos ['sendos] *adj pl* each.

senectud [senek'tuð] *sf* old age.

senil [se'nil] *adj* senile. **senilidad** *sf* senility.

seno ['seno] *sm* bosom, breast; haven, refuge.

sensación [sensa'θjon] *sf* sensation. **sensacional** *adj* sensational.

sensatez [sensa'teθ] *sf* good sense. **sensato** *adj* sensible.

sensibilidad [sensiβili'ðað] *sf* sensibility; sensitivity. **sensible** *adj* sensitive; sensible; considerable.

sensiblería [sensiβle'ria] *sf* sentimentality. **sensiblero** *adj* sentimental.

sensitivo [sensi'tiβo] *adj* relating to the senses; sensitive.

sensual [sen'swal] *adj* sensual. **sensualidad** *sf* sensuality.

*sentar [sen'tar] *v* seat; place; locate; establish; press; suit; fit. **sentarse** *v* sit down; settle. **sentada** *sf* sit-in. **sentado** *adj* seated; established.

sentencia [sen'tenθja] *sf* (jur) sentence. **sentenciar** *v* (jur) sentence. **sentencioso** *adj* sententious.

sentido [sen'tiðo] *sm* sense; meaning; direction; feeling. **sin sentido** meaningless. **tener sentido** make sense. *adj* heartfelt; moving; sincere.

sentimiento [senti'mjento] *sm* feeling; emotion; sentiment; grief. **sentimental** *adj* sentimental.

*sentir [sen'tir] *v* feel; hear; regret. **lo siento mucho** I am very sorry. **sentirse** *v* feel; suffer from. **sentirse enfermo** feel ill. **sentirse obligado** a feel obliged to.

seña ['seɲa] *sf* mark; sign; signal; password. **señas** *pl* address *sing*.

señal [se'ɲal] *sf* signal; sign; mark. **en señal de** in proof of. **señaladamente** *adv* signally. **señalado** *adj* famous. **señalar** *v* mark; signal; point out; denote. **señalarse** *v* distinguish oneself.

señor [se'ɲor] *sm* mister; gentleman; lord; master. **El Señor** the Lord. **señora** *sf* lady; wife; mistress; madam. **la señora de García** Mrs García. **señorear** *v* domineer. **señorearse** *v* take possession. **señoría** *sf* lordship. **señorío** *sm* dominion; stateliness. **señorita** *sf* miss; young lady.

separar [sepa'rar] *v* separate; divide; discharge. **separable** *adj* separable. **separación** *sf* separation; dismissal. **separado** *adj* separate. **por separado** separately.

septentrional [septentrjo'nal] *adj* northern.

séptico ['septiko] *adj* septic.

septiembre [sep'tjembre] *sm* September.

séptimo ['septimo] *adj* seventh.

septuagésimo [septwa'xesimo] *adj* seventieth.

sepulcro [se'pulkro] *sm* tomb, grave.

sepultar [sepul'tar] *v* bury. **sepultura** *sf* grave; burial. **sepulturero** *sm* gravedigger.

sequedad [seke'ðað] *sf* dryness; curtness. **sequía** *sf* drought.

séquito ['sekito] *sm* entourage, followers *pl*.

*ser [ser] *v* be; exist; occur. **a no ser por** but for. **sea lo que sea** come what may. **si no es que** unless.

seráfico [se'rafiko] *adj* seraphic. **serafín** *sm* seraph.

serenar [sere'nar] *v* calm; settle. **sereno** *adj* serene; calm. **serenidad** *sf* serenity; calmness.

serenata [sere'nata] *sf* serenade.

serie ['serje] *sf* series. **fabricación en serie** *sf* mass production.

serio ['serjo] *adj* serious. **tomar en serio** take seriously. **seriedad** *sf* seriousness; sincerity.

sermón [ser'mon] *sm* sermon.

serpiente [ser'pjente] *sf* serpent. **serpiente de cascabel** rattlesnake. **serpentear** *v* wriggle. **serpentino** *adj* serpentine.

serrano [ser'rano] *adj* of the mountains. *sm* highlander. **serranía** *sf* mountainous country.

*serrar [ser'rar] *v* saw. **serrado** *adj* serrated. **serrín** *sm* sawdust.

servicio [ser'βiθjo] *sm* service; attendance. **estar de servicio** be on duty. **servicios** *sm pl* toilet *sing*. **servible** *adj* serviceable. **servidor, -a** *sm, sf* servant. **su seguro servidor** yours faithfully. **servidumbre** *sf* household staff; servitude. **servil** *adj* servile. **servilismo** *sm* servility.

servilleta [serβi'ʎeta] *sf* napkin.

*servir [ser'βir] *v* serve. **para servir a usted** at your service. **servir de** act as. **servirse** *v* help oneself. **servirse de** make use of.

sesenta [se'senta] *sm, adj* sixty.

sesgar [ses'gar] *v* slant; twist. **sesgo** *sm* slant; twist.

sesión [se'sjon] *sf* session; conference.

seso ['seso] *sm* brain; sense, understanding, wisdom. **perder el seso** go mad.

seta ['seta] *sf* mushroom.

setenta [se'tenta] *sm, adj* seventy.

setiembre *V* septiembre.

seto ['seto] *sm* fence.

seudónimo [seu'ðonimo] *sm* pseudonym. **seudo** *adj* (fam) pseudo.

387

severo [se'βero] *adj* severe; harsh. **severidad** *sf* severity.

sexagésimo [seksa'xesimo] *adj* sixtieth. **sexagenario, -a** *sm, sf* sexagenarian.

sexo ['sekso] *sm* sex. **sexual** *adj* sexual. **sexualidad** *sf* sexuality.

sexto ['seksto] *adj* sixth. **sexteto** *sm* sextet.

si [si] *conj* if; whether. **si bien** although.

sí[1] [si] *adv* yes; indeed. **eso sí que es** yes, that's it. *sm* consent. **dar el sí** agree.

sí[2] *pron* himself; herself; itself; oneself; themselves; yourselves. **de por sí** in itself. **entre sí** among themselves. **metido en sí** pensive.

sibilante [siβi'lante] *adj* sibilant.

siderurgia [siðe'rurxja] *sf* iron and steel industry.

sidra ['siðra] *sf* cider.

siega ['sjeɣa] *sf* reaping, harvesting.

siembra ['sjembra] *sf* sowing.

siempre ['sjempre] *adv* always. **siempre jamás** for ever and ever. **siempre que** whenever; provided that.

sien [sjen] *sf* (*anat*) temple.

sierra ['sjerra] *sf* saw; mountain range.

siervo ['sjerβo] *sm* slave; servant.

siesta ['sjesta] *sf* siesta.

siete ['sjete] *adj, sm* seven.

sífilis ['sifilis] *sm* syphilis. **sifilítico, -a** *s, adj* syphilitic.

sifón [si'fon] *sm* soda water; syphon.

sigilar [sixi'lar] *v* conceal. **sigilo** *sm* secrecy. **sigiloso** *adj* secretive.

siglo ['siglo] *sm* century. **siglo de oro** golden age.

signar [sig'nar] *v* sign, seal. **signarse** *v* cross oneself. **signatura** *sf* signature.

significar [signifi'kar] *v* signify; notify. **significado** *sm* meaning; significance. **significativo** *adj* significant.

signo ['signo] *sm* sign; symbol.

siguiente [si'gjente] *adj* following, next.

sílaba ['silaβa] *sf* syllable.

silbar [sil'βar] *v* whistle; hiss. **silbido** *sm* whistle, hiss.

silencio [si'lenθjo] *sm* silence. **silenciador** *sm* (*de arma*) silencer. **silenciar** *v* silence. **silencioso** *adj* silent.

silueta [si'lweta] *sf* silhouette, outline.

silvestre [sil'βestre] *adj* wild. **silvicultura** *sf* forestry.

silla ['siλa] *sf* chair; seat; saddle. **silla de tijera** deck chair. **sillón** *sm* armchair.

sima ['sima] *sf* abyss.

símbolo ['simbolo] *sm* symbol. **simbólico** *adj* symbolic. **simbolismo** *sm* symbolism. **simbolizar** *v* symbolize.

simetría [sime'tria] *sf* symmetry. **simétrico** *adj* symmetrical.

simiente [si'mjente] *sf* seed.

símil ['simil] *adj* similar. *sm* comparison; simile. **similar** *adj* similar. **similitud** *sf* similarity.

simpatía [simpa'tia] *sf* affection; sympathy; friendliness; charm. **simpático** *adj* charming; friendly; nice. **simpatizar** *v* sympathize; get on.

simple ['simple] *adj* simple; pure; naïve. **simplemente** *adv* merely. **simpleza** *sf* simplicity; simpleness; silly thing. **simplicidad** *sf* simplicity. **simplificar** *v* simplify. **simplón, -ona** *sm, sf* simpleton.

simulacro [simu'lakro] *sm* image; semblance.

simular [simu'lar] *v* simulate. **simulación** *sf* pretence. **simulado** *adj* sham.

simultáneo [simul'taneo] *adj* simultaneous. **simultaneidad** *sf* simultaneousness.

sin [sin] *prep* without; but for; apart from. **sin embargo** nevertheless. **sin falta** without fail. **sin que** without.

sinagoga [sina'goga] *sf* synagogue.

sincero [sin'θero] *adj* sincere. **sinceridad** *sf* sincerity.

síncopa ['sinkopa] *sf* syncopation. **sincopar** *v* syncopate.

sindicato [sindi'kato] *sm* trade union; syndicate. **sindical** *adj* trade-union. **sindicalismo** *sm* trade-unionism. **síndico** *sm* trustee.

sinfín [sin'fin] *sm* endless number.

sinfonía [sinfo'nia] *sf* symphony. **sinfónico** *adj* symphonic.

singular [singu'lar] *adj* singular; exceptional; unique; excellent. **singularidad** *sf* singularity; excellence. **singularizar** *v* single out. **singularizarse** *v* distinguish oneself.

siniestro [si'njestro] *adj* (*dirección*) left; sinister. *sm* catastrophe. **siniestrado, -a** *sm, sf* victim of an accident.

sinnúmero [sin'numero] *sm* endless number.

sino[1] ['sino] *conj* but, except. **no sólo ... sino ...** not only ... but also ....

sino[2] *sm* fate.

sinónimo [si'nonimo] *sm* synonym. *adj* synonymous.

sinopsis [si'nopsis] *sf* synopsis (*pl* -ses).

sinrazón [sinra'θon] *sf* injustice.

sinsabor [sinsa'βor] *sm* trouble.

sintaxis [sin'taksis] *sf* syntax. **sintáctico** *adj* syntactic.

síntesis ['sintesis] *sf* synthesis (*pl* -ses). **sintético** *adj* synthetic.

síntoma ['sintoma] *sm* symptom. **sintomático** *adj* symptomatic.

sintonizar [sintoni'θar] *v* (*radio*) tune in. **sintonía** *sf* signature tune.

sinvergüenza [sinβer'gwenθa] *adj* shameless. *s(m+f)* cad.

siquiera [si'kjera] *adv* at least; even; just. **ni siquiera** not at all. *conj* even if; even though. **siquiera ... siquiera ...** whether ... or whether ... .

sirena [si'rena] *sf* (*ninfa*) siren, mermaid; (*tecn*) siren, fog-horn.

sirviente [sir'βjente] *sm* servant.

sisar [si'sar] *v* pilfer; cheat. **sisa** *sf* theft, pilfering.

sísmico ['sismiko] *adj* seismic. **sismógrafo** *sm* seismograph.

sistema [sis'tema] *sm* system, method. **sistemático** *adj* systematic.

sitiar [si'tjar] *sm* besiege; surround.

sitio ['sitjo] *sm* place; room, space; siege. **no hay sitio** there is no room.

situar [si'twar] *v* situate; put. **situación** *sf* situation.

so [so] *prep* under. **so pena de** under penalty of.

sobaco [so'βako] *sm* armpit.

sobado [so'βaðo] *adj* kneaded; (*fam*) shabby, well-worn. **sobar** *v* knead; thrash; crumple; fondle.

soberanía [soβera'nia] *sf* sovereignty. **soberano, -a** *s, adj* sovereign.

soberbia [so'βerβja] *sf* pride; magnificence, pomp. **soberbio** *adj* proud; superb.

sobornar [soβor'nar] *v* bribe. **soborno** *sm* bribe; bribery.

sobrar [so'βrar] *sf* surplus. **de sobra** in excess. **sobras** *sf pl* remains *pl*. **sobradamente** *adv* excessively. **sobrado** *adj* abundant; superfluous. **sobrancero** *adj* unemployed. **sobrante** *adj* spare.

sobre[1] ['soβre] *prep* on; upon; over; above; about. **sobre las diez** about ten o'clock. **sobre todo** above all.

sobre[2] *sm* envelope.

sobrecama [soβre'kama] *sm* bedspread.

sobrecargar [soβrekar'gar] *v* overload. **sobrecarga** *sf* extra burden. **sobrecargo** *sm* purser.

sobrecejo [soβre'θexo] *sm* frown.

sobrecoger [soβreko'xer] *v* surprise, take aback. **sobrecogerse** *v* be startled.

sobredicho [soβre'ðitʃo] *adj* aforesaid.

sobrehumano [soβreu'mano] *adj* superhuman.

sobremanera [soβrema'nera] *adv* exceedingly.

sobremesa [soβre'mesa] *sf* dessert; table cover; after-dinner chat.

sobrenatural [soβrenatu'ral] *adj* supernatural.

sobrepasar [soβrepa'sar] *v* surpass.

***sobreponer** [soβrepo'ner] *v* superimpose. **sobreponerse** *v* overcome. **sobrepuesto** *adj* superimposed.

sobreprecio [soβre'preθjo] *sm* surcharge.

***sobresalir** [soβresa'lir] *v* excel. **sobresaliente** *adj* outstanding.

sobresaltar [soβresal'tar] *v* attack; frighten. **sobresalto** *sm* sudden attack; shock. **de sobresalto** suddenly.

sobrescrito [soβres'krito] *sm* (*en un sobre*) address.

sobretodo [soβre'toðo] *sm* overcoat.

***sobrevenir** [soβreβe'nir] *v* happen suddenly.

sobrevivir [soβreβi'βir] *v* survive. **sobreviviente** *s(m+f)* survivor.

sobriedad [soβrie'ðað] *sf* sobriety. **sobrio** *adj* sober, moderate.

sobrino [so'βrino] *sm* nephew. **sobrina** *sf* niece.

socarrón [sokar'ron] *adj* sarcastic; sly. **socarronería** *sf* sarcasm; slyness.

socavar [soka'βar] *v* undermine. **socavón** *sm* excavation.

sociable [so'θjaβle] *adj* sociable. **sociabilidad** *sf* sociability.

social [so'θjal] *adj* social. **socializar** *v* socialize. **socialismo** *sm* socialism. **socialista** *s(m+f)* socialist.

sociedad [soθje'ðað] *sf* society. **socio, -a** *sm, sf* associate.

sociología [soθjolo'xia] *sf* sociology. **sociólogo, -a** *sm, sf* sociologist.

socorrer [sokor'rer] *v* help. **socorrido** *adj* helpful; handy. **socorro** *sm* succour; relief. **¡socorro!** help!

soda ['soða] *sf* soda-water.

soez [so'eθ] *adj* obscene; vulgar.

sofá [so'fa] *sf* sofa, settee.

sofocar [sofo'kar] *v* suffocate. **sofocación** *sf* suffocation. **sofocado** *adj* breathless. **sofoco** *sm* suffocation.

soga ['soga] *sf* rope, cord. **hacer soga** lag behind.

soja ['soxa] *sf* soya.

sojuzgar [soxuθ'gar] *v* subdue.

sol [sol] *sm* sun; sunlight. **hace sol** it's sunny. **tomar el sol** sunbathe.

solamente [sola'mente] *adv* only. **no solamente** not only.

solapa [so'lapa] *sf* flap; lapel; (*fig*) pretext. **solapado** *adj* sly. **solapar** *v* overlap; (*fig*) cover up, hide.

*solar [so'lar] *adj* solar. *sm* lot; plot; building site.

solaz [so'laθ] *sm* recreation; solace. **a solaz** with pleasure. **solazar** *v* distract; amuse; solace.

soldado [sol'ðaðo] *sm* soldier.

*soldar [sol'ðar] *v* solder; weld; (*huesos*) knit. **soldador** *sm* soldering iron. **soldadura** *sf* welding.

soledad [sole'ðað] *sf* loneliness, solitude.

solemne [so'lemne] *adj* solemn. **solemnidad** *sf* solemnity. **solemnizar** *v* solemnize.

*soler [so'ler] *v* be in the habit of; usually *be or do*. **suele comer mucho** he usually eats a lot.

solera [so'lera] *sf* prop; stone pavement; tradition; strong old wine.

solicitar [soliθi'tar] *v* request; pursue; canvass. **solicitación** *sf* solicitation; application. **solicitador, -a** *sm, sf or* **solicitante** *sm* petitioner; applicant. **solícito** *adj* solicitous. **solicitud** *sf* solicitude.

solidaridad [soliðari'ðað] *sf* solidarity. **solidar** *v* consolidate. **solidario** *adj* mutual. **solidez** *sf* solidity. **solidificar** *v* solidify. **sólido** *adj* solid.

solitario [soli'tarjo], **-a** *sm, sf* hermit, recluse. *adj* lonely; solitary; alone; single.

solo ['solo] *adj* alone; single; unique; only; (*música*) solo. *sm* (*música*) solo. **sólo** ['solo] *adv* only, merely.

*soltar [sol'tar] *v* release; free; loosen; break; shed. **soltarse** *v* break loose; become unscrewed; lose one's inhibitions.

soltero [sol'tero] *sm* bachelor. *adj* single. **soltera** *sf* spinster. **soltería** *sf* celibacy. **solterona** *sf* old maid.

soltura [sol'tura] *sf* looseness; agility; fluency. **con soltura** fluently.

soluble [so'luβle] *adj* soluble. **solubilidad** *sf* solubility. **solución** *sf* solution. **solucionar** *v* solve.

solvencia [sol'βenθja] *sf* solvency; settlement. **solvente** *adj* solvent.

sollo ['soʎo] *sm* sturgeon.

sollozar [soʎo'θar] *v* sob. **sollozo** *sm* sob.

sombra ['sombra] *sf* shadow; shade. **dar sombra** a shade.

sombrero [som'brero] *sm* hat.

sombrilla [som'briʎa] *sf* parasol.

sombrío [som'brio] *sm* shady spot. *adj* shady; gloomy. **sombroso** *adj* shady.

somero [so'mero] *adj* superficial.

someter [some'ter] *v* submit; subdue. **sometimiento** *sm* submission.

somnífero [som'nifero] *sm* sleeping pill.

somnolencia [somno'lenθja] *sf* sleepiness. **somnámbulo, -a** *sm, sf* sleepwalker. **somnolente** *adj* sleepy.

son [son] *sm* sound; rumour; manner. **por este son** by this means.

*sonar [so'nar] *v* sound; ring; chime. **sonarse** *v* blow one's nose. **sonante** *adj* sounding; ringing.

sondear [sonde'ar] *v* fathom; sound out. **soneto** [so'neto] *sm* sonnet.

sonido [so'niðo] *sm* sound.

sonoro [so'noro] *adj* sonorous; resonant. **sonoridad** *sf* sonority.

*sonreír [sonre'ir] *v* smile. **sonriente** *adj* smiling. **sonrisa** *sf* smile.

sonrojar [sonro'xar] *v* blush; flush. **sonrojo** *sm* blush.

*soñar [so'nar] *v* dream. **soñador, -a** *sm, sf* dreamer. **soñera** *sf* drowsiness. **soñoliento** *adj* drowsy.

sopa ['sopa] *sf* soup. **como una sopa** soaked to the skin. **sopero** *sm* soup plate.

sopapo [so'papo] *sm* (*fam*) blow, punch. **sopapear** *v* chuck under the chin; punch.

soplar [so'plar] *v* blow; blow out; blow away; prompt. **sopladura** *sf* blowing. **soplillo** *sm* fan; blower. **soplo** *sm* blowing; puff of wind. **soplón, -ona** *sm, sf* informer.

sopor [so'por] *sm* drowsiness.

soportar [sopor'tar] *v* support; tolerate; endure. **soporte** *sm* support; stand.

sor [sor] *sf* (*rel*) sister.

sorber [sor'βer] *v* sip; suck; soak up. **sorbete** *sm* sherbet; water ice. **sorbetón**

sm large draught. **sorbo** *sm* sip; swallow; gulp.

sordera [sor'ðera] *sf* deafness. **sordo** *adj* deaf; muffled.

sórdido ['sorðiðo] *adj* squalid. **sordidez** *sf* squalor.

sordomudo [sorðo'muðo], -a *sm, sf* deafmute. *adj* deaf and dumb.

sorprender [sorpren'der] *v* surprise. **sorprendente** *adj* surprising. **sorpresa** *sf* surprise.

sortear [sorte'ar] *v* cast lots for; avoid, get round. **sorteable** *adj* avoidable. **sorteo** *sm* raffle; casting of lots; dodging.

sortija [sor'tixa] *sf* ring; (*de pelo*) curl.

sortilegio [sorti'lexjo] *sm* sorcery; charm. **sortilega** *sf* sorceress. **sortilego** *sm* sorcerer.

*****sosegar** [sose'gar] *v* calm, quieten. **sosiego** *sm* calm, quiet.

soslayar [sosla'jar] *v* place obliquely; dodge; avoid. **soslayo** *adj* oblique.

soso ['soso] *adj* tasteless; dull.

sospechar [sospe'tʃar] *v* suspect. **sospecha** *sf* suspicion. **sospechoso** *adj* suspicious, suspect.

*****sostener** [soste'ner] *v* support; sustain. **sostén** *sm* support; brassière. **sostenedor**, -a *sm, sf* supporter. **sostenido** *adj* sustained; constant.

sota ['sota] *sf* (*deporte*) jack; (*fam*) hussy.

sotana [so'tana] *sf* cassock.

sótano ['sotano] *sm* basement, cellar.

soto ['soto] *sm* thicket, copse.

soviet [so'βjet] *sm* Soviet. **soviético** *adj* Soviet.

spaghettis [spa'getis] *sm pl* spaghetti *sing*.

su [su] *adj* his; her; its; your; their; one's.

suave ['swaβe] *adj* smooth; soft; mild. **suavidad** *sf* smoothness; softness. **suavizar** *v* soften; smooth; strop.

*****subarrendar** [suβarren'dar] *v* sublet, sublease. **subarriendo** *sm* subletting.

subasta [su'βasta] *sf* auction. **subastar** *v* auction.

subcampeón [subkam'pjon], -ona *sm, sf* runner-up.

subconsciencia [subkons'θjenθja] *sf* subconscious. **subconsciente** *adj* subconscious.

subdesarrollado [subðesarro'ʎaðo] *adj* underdeveloped. **subdesarrollo** *sm* underdevelopment.

súbdito ['suβðito] *sm* subject, citizen.

subdividir [suβðiβi'ðir] *v* subdivide. **subdivisión** *sf* subdivision.

subir [su'βir] *v* climb; go up; rise; lift; promote. **subir al coche** get into the car. **subirse** *v* rise; become conceited. **subida** *sf* ascent. **subido** *adj* (*color*) bright.

súbito ['suβito] *adj* sudden. *adv* suddenly.

subjuntivo [subxun'tiβo] *sm* (*gram*) subjunctive.

sublevar [suβle'βar] *v* incite to rebellion. **sublevarse** *v* rebel. **sublevación** *sf* rebellion.

sublime [su'βlime] *adj* sublime, lofty. **sublimación** *sf* sublimation. **sublimidad** *sf* sublimity.

submarino [subma'rino] *adj* underwater. *sm* submarine.

subordinado [suβorði'naðo] *adj* subordinate. **subordinar** *v* subordinate.

subproducto [suβpro'ðukto] *sm* by-product.

subrayar [suβra'jar] *v* underline, underscore; emphasize. **subrayado** *sm* underlining; emphasis.

subsanar [suβsa'nar] *v* excuse; redeem.

subscribir [subskri'βir] *v* subscribe; sign. **subscripción** *sf* subscription.

*****subseguir** [suβse'gir] *v* follow. **subsiguiente** *adj* subsequent.

subsidiario [suβsi'ðjarjo] *adj* subsidiary.

subsidio [suβ'siðjo] *sm* subsidy, grant, allowance.

subsistir [suβsis'tir] *v* subsist; exist. **subsistencia** *sf* permanence; subsistence. **subsistente** *adj* subsisting.

substancia [suβs'taɴja] *sf* substance. **en substancia** briefly, in substance. **substancial** *adj* substantial. **substanciar** *v* summarize; substantiate. **substancioso** *adj* substantial.

*****substituir** [suβstitu'ir] *v* substitute. **substitución** *sf* substitution. **substitutivo** *adj* substitute.

*****substraer** [suβstra'er] *v* subtract; remove; steal. **substraerse** *v* evade; withdraw. **substracción** *sf* subtraction; stealing.

subterfugio [suβter'fuxjo] *sm* subterfuge.

subterráneo [suβter'raneo] *adj* subterranean.

subtítulo [suβ'titulo] *sm* subtitle.

suburbio [su'βurβjo] *sm* outskirts *pl*; slum. **suburbano** *adj* suburban.

subvención [suββen'θjon] *sf* subsidy. **subvencionar** *v* subsidize.

subvertir [suββer'tir] v subvert. **subversión** sf subversion. **subversivo** adj subversive.

subyugar [suβju'gar] v subjugate. **subyugación** sf subjugation.

suceder [suθe'ðer] v succeed; follow; happen. **sucedido** sm event. **sucediente** adj following. **sucesión** sf succession; offspring. **sucesivamente** adv successively. **sucesivo** adj successive. **en lo sucesivo** hereafter. **suceso** sm event; outcome.

suciedad [suθje'ðað] sf dirt, dirtiness. **sucio** adj dirty; vile, mean.

sucinto [su'θinto] adj succinct, brief.

sucumbir [sukum'bir] v succumb.

sucursal [sukur'sal] sm branch.

sud [suð] adj, sm south.

sudamericano [suðameri'kano], **-a** s, adj South American.

sudar [su'ðar] v sweat. **sudar tinta** (fam) sweat blood. **sudor** sm sweat. **sudoroso** adj sweaty.

sudeste [su'ðeste] adj, sm. south-east.

sudoeste [suðo'este] sm. adj south-west.

Suecia [swe'θja] sf Sweden.

sueco ['sweko], **-a** sm, sf Swede. sm (idioma) Swedish. adj Swedish.

suegro ['swegro] sm father-in-law.

suela ['swela] sf (de zapato) sole. **suelas** sf pl sandals pl.

sueldo ['swelðo] sm salary; wage; pay. **a sueldo** paid.

suelo ['swelo] sm ground; soil; floor. **echar al suelo** demolish.

suelto ['swelto] adj free; loose; separate; agile.

sueño ['sweɲo] sm dream; sleep. **tener sueño** be sleepy.

suero ['swero] sm serum; whey.

suerte ['swerte] sf luck; fate; chance; kind; manner; quality. ¡**buena suerte**! good luck! **de otra suerte** otherwise. **de tal suerte que** in such a way that.

suéter ['sweter] sm sweater.

suficiencia [sufiθjenθja] sf sufficiency; ability; self-importance. **suficiente** adj sufficient; capable.

sufragar [sufra'gar] v help; finance. **sufragar por** vote for. **sufragio** sm suffrage.

sufrir [su'frir] v suffer; endure. **sufrido** adj long-suffering. **sufrimiento** sm suffering; patience.

*****sugerir** [suxe'rir] v suggest, hint. **sugerencia** sf suggestion. **sugerente** adj suggestive. **sugestión** sf suggestion. **sugestionable** adj suggestible. **sugestionar** v influence. **sugestivo** adj suggestive; stimulating.

suicidarse [swiθi'ðarse] v commit suicide. **suicida** s(m + f) (persona) suicide. **suicidio** sm suicide.

Suiza ['swiθa] sf Switzerland. **suizo**, **-a** s, adj Swiss.

sujetar [suxe'tar] v secure; hold; fasten; seize; tie; restrain; subordinate. **sujetarse** v hang on; hold up; subject oneself to; abide by. **sujeción** sf subjection; control. **sujetapapeles** sm invar paperclip. **sujeto** sm subject; individual.

sumar [su'mar] v add. add up. **sumarse** v join in. **suma** sf sum; summary; essence. **en suma** in short. **sumadora** sf adding machine. **sumamente** adv extremely. **sumaria** sf (jur) indictment. **sumario** sm summary.

sumergir [sumer'xir] v submerge, plunge. **sumersión** sf submersion.

suministrar [sumini'strar] v supply, provide. **suministro** sm supply. **suministros** sm pl supplies pl, provisions pl.

sumir [su'mir] v submerge; sink.

sumisión [sumi'sjon] sf submission. **sumiso** adj submissive.

sumo ['sumo] adj greatest; supreme. **tribunal supremo** sm supreme court.

suntuoso [sun'twoso] adj sumptuous. **suntuosidad** sf sumptuousness.

supeditar [supeði'tar] v subdue, subordinate. **supeditación** sf subjection.

superar [supe'rar] v surpass; overcome. **superable** adj surmountable. **superación** sf overcoming.

superávit [supe'raβit] sm surplus.

superchería [supertʃe'ria] sf fraud; swindle.

superficial [superfi'θjal] adj superficial. **superficie** sf surface; area.

superfluo [super'fluo] adj superfluous. **superfluidad** sf superfluity.

superior [supe'rjor] adj better; superior. sm superior.

superlativo [superla'tiβo] adj superlative.

supermercado [supermer'kaðo] sm supermarket.

supersecreto [superse'kreto] adj top secret.

superstición [supersti'θjon] *sf* superstition. **supersticioso** *adj* superstitious.

supervivencia [superβi'βenθja] *sf* survival. **superviviente** *s(m+f)* survivor.

supino [su'pino] *adj* supine.

suplantar [suplan'tar] *v* supplant; forge.

suplemento [suple'mento] *sm* supplement. **suplementario** *adj* supplementary; extra. **horas suplementarias** *sf pl* overtime *sing*.

suplente [su'plente] *s, adj* substitute.

súplica ['suplika] *sf* supplication; petition. **suplicación** *sf* supplication; wafer biscuit. **suplicante** *s(m+f)* supplicant. **suplicar** *v* implore; beseech.

suplicio [su'pliθjo] *sm* torture.

suplir [su'plir] *v* make up for; substitute.

*suponer [supo'ner] *v* suppose; believe; mean; guess. **suposición** *sf* supposition; slander.

supremo [su'premo] *adj* supreme. **supremacía** *sf* supremacy.

suprimir [supri'mir] *v* suppress; delete; omit; eliminate. **supresión** *sf* suppression; deletion.

supuesto [su'pwesto] *adj* supposed; so-called; hypothetical; feigned. **¡por supuesto!** of course! **supuesto que** since; if. *sm* hypothesis (*pl* -ses).

sur [sur] *adj* southern. *sm* south.

surcar [sur'kar] *v* plough; cleave.

surgir [sur'xir] *v* rise; spring forth; appear; anchor. **surgidero** *sm* anchorage.

surrealista [surrea'lista] *s(m+f)* surrealist. **surrealismo** *sm* surrealism.

surtido [sur'tiðo] *adj* assorted. **bien surtido** well stocked. *sm* stock; range; assortment. **surtidor** *sm* jet; fountain; petrol pump. **surtir** *v* supply. **surtir un pedido** fill an order.

susceptibilidad [susθeptiβili'ðað] *sf* susceptibility. **susceptible** *adj* susceptible.

suscitar [susθi'tar] *v* agitate, stir up. **suscitar interés** arouse interest.

suscribir *V* subscribir.

susodicho [suso'ðitʃo] *adj* aforementioned.

suspender [suspen'der] *v* suspend; adjourn; hang; fail; interrupt. **suspensión** *sf* suspension. **suspenso** *sm* (*examen*) failure.

suspicacia [suspi'kaθja] *sf* suspicion; misgiving. **suspicaz** *adj* suspicious.

suspirar [suspi'rar] *v* sigh. **suspirado** *adj* longed for, wished for. **suspiro** *sm* sigh.

sustancia *V* substancia.

sustentar [susten'tar] *v* sustain; maintain. **sustentamiento** *sm* sustenance; maintenance. **sustento** *sm* sustenance.

*sustituir *V* substituir.

susto ['susto] *sm* fright. **dar susto a** frighten.

susurrar [susur'rar] *v* whisper; murmur. **susurrarse** *v* be rumoured. **susurrante** *adj* whispering. **susurro** *sm* whisper; murmur.

sutil [su'til] *adj* subtle; sharp; slender; delicate. **sutileza** *sf* subtlety; thinness; sharpness. **sutilizar** *v* thin down; polish; sharpen.

sutura [su'tura] *sf* suture.

suyo ['sujo] *adj* of his; of hers; of yours; of theirs. *pron* his; hers; yours; its; theirs. **lo suyo** one's share. **muy suyo** typical of one.

T

tabaco [ta'βako] *sm* tobacco. **tabacalero, -a** *sm, sf* tobacconist.

tábano [ta'βano] *sm* horsefly.

taberna [ta'βerna] *sf* tavern; public house.

tabique [ta'βike] *sm* partition; dividing wall. **tabicar** *v* wall up.

tabla ['taβla] *sf* board, plank; tablet; slab; index; vegetable plot. **tablas** *sf pl* (*teatro*) stage *sing*. **pisar las tablas** go on the stage. **tablado** *sm* wooden platform; bedstead; gallows. **tablaje** *sm* boards *pl*. **tablajería** *sf* gambling. **tablear** *vb* saw into planks. **tablero** *sm* planking; blackboard; gambling den. **tableta** *sf* tablet. **tablilla** *sf* notice-board. **tablón** *sm* beam.

tabú [ta'βu] *sm* taboo.

tabular [tabu'lar] *adj* tabular. *v* tabulate.

taburete [tabu'rete] *sm* stool.

tacaño [ta'kaɲo] *adj* mean, stingy. **tacañería** *sf* meanness.

tácito ['taθito] *adj* tacit. **taciturnidad** *sf* taciturnity. **taciturno** *adj* taciturn.

taco ['tako] *sm* wad; plug; billiard cue; draught; oath. **soltar un taco** utter an oath.

tacón [ta'kon] *sm* heel. **taconazo** *sm* blow *or* tap with the heel.

tacto ['takto] *sm* touch; sense of touch; tact.

tachar [ta'tʃar] *v* accuse; erase. **tacha** *sf* fault; tack, small nail. **poner tacha** find fault. **tachón** *sm* (*carpintería*) stud. **tachonado** *adj* studded. **tachonar** *v* stud. **tachoso** *adj* defective. **tachuela** *sf* small tack.

tahona [ta'ona] *sf* bakery.

taimado [tai'maðo] *adj* sly, crafty; sullen.

tajar [ta'xar] *v* cut; hew; cleave. **taja** *sf* incision. **tajada** *sf* slice. **sacar tajada** profit. **tajadero** *sm* chopping-block. **tajador** *sm* chopper.

tal [tal] *adj* such; such a. **el tal** that fellow. **tal como** such as. **tal vez** perhaps. **como tal** as such. *adv* so; as though. **como tal as such.** *adv* so; as though. **pron** someone; such a person *or* thing.

taladrar [tala'ðrar] *v* bore, drill. **taladro** *sm* bore, drill.

talante [ta'lante] *sm* mood; look; grace. **de buen/mal talante** in a good/bad mood.

talar[1] [ta'lar] *v* cut down, fell.

talar[2] *adj* full-length.

talco ['talko] *sm* tinsel; talcum powder.

talega [ta'lega] *sf* money bag; nappy.

talento [ta'lento] *sm* talent. **talentoso** *adj* talented. **talentudo** *adj* over-talented.

talón [ta'lon] *sm* heel; counterfoil; voucher; coupon.

talud [ta'luð] *sm* slope.

tallar [ta'ʎar] *v* carve; appraise; deal cards.

tallarín [taʎa'rin] *sm* noodle.

talle ['taʎe] *sm* figure; waist.

taller [ta'ʎer] *sm* workshop; studio.

tallo ['taʎo] *sm* stem, stalk.

tamaño [ta'maɲo] *sm* size. **de tamaño natural** life-size.

tambalearse [tambale'arse] *v* stagger; wobble; sway.

también [tam'bjen] *adv* also, too.

tambor [tam'bor] *sm* drum. **tambor-mayor** drum major.

Támesis ['tamesis] *sm* Thames.

tamiz [ta'miθ] *sm* sieve. **pasar por tamiz** sift.

tampoco [tam'poko] *adv* neither.

tan [tan] *adv* so. **tan siquiera** even if only.

tanda ['tanda] *sf* turn; shift; relay; gang.

tangente [tan'xente] *sm*, *adj* tangent.

tangerina [tanxe'rina] *sf* tangerine.

tangible [tan'xiβle] *adj* tangible.

tanque ['tanke] *sm* tank.

tantear [tante'ar] *v* try; test; sound; keep score. **tantearse** *v* think carefully. **tanteo** *sm* calculation; score.

tanto ['tanto] *adj* as much; so much; as great; so great. *adv* so much; as much; so; thus. **tanto como** as much as. **por lo tanto** therefore. *sm* amount; sum. **otro tanto** as much again.

***tañer** [ta'ɲer] *v* (*música*) play. **tañido** *sm* tune; twanging.

tapacubo [tapa'kuβo] *sm* hub-cap.

tapar [ta'par] *v* cover up; plug; cap; cork. **tapa** *sf* lid; cover. **tapadero** *sm* stopper. **taparrabo** *sm* loincloth. **tapón** *sm* cork; stopper.

tapia ['tapja] *sf* garden wall. **tapiar** *v* wall up.

tapicería [tapiθe'ria] *sf* tapestry; upholstery. **tapicero, -a** *sm*, *sf* upholsterer. **tapiz** *sm* tapestry. **tapizar** *v* hang with tapestry; upholster.

taquigrafía [takigra'fia] *sf* shorthand. **taquígrafo, -a** *sm*, *sf* stenographer.

taquilla [ta'kiʎa] *sf* box office; till.

tararear [tarare'ar] *v* hum.

tardar [tar'ðar] *v* delay; take a long time. **tardanza** *sf* slowness.

tarde ['tarðe] *sf* afternoon; evening. *adv* late. **se hace tarde** it's getting late. **tardecer** *v* grow late.

tarea [ta'rea] *sf* task; homework.

tarifa [ta'rifa] *sf* tariff; price list; rate.

tarima [ta'rima] *sf* stand; platform.

tarjeta [tar'xeta] *sf* card. **tarjeta postal** postcard.

tarro ['tarro] *sm* jar.

tarta ['tarta] *sf* cake, tart.

tartamudear [tartamuðe'ar] *v* stammer, stutter. **tartamudeo** *sm* stammer, stutter. **tartamudo, -a** *sm*, *sf* stutterer.

tasar [ta'sar] *v* appraise; value. **tasa** *sf* rate; valuation. **sin tasa** without limit. **tasación** *sf* valuation.

tatarabuelo [tatara'βwelo] *sm* great-great-grandfather. **tatarabuela** *sf* great-great-grandmother.

tatuaje [ta'twaxe] *sm* tattoo. **tatuar** *v* tattoo.

tauromaquia [tauro'makja] *sf* bullfighting.

taxidermia [taksi'ðermja] *sf* taxidermy. **taxidermista** *s*(*m*+*f*) taxidermist.

taxi ['taksi] *sm* taxi. **taxímetro** *sm* taximeter. **taxista** *s(m+f)* taxi-driver.

taza ['taθa] *sf* cup.

te [te] *pron* you; to you; yourself; to yourself.

té [te] *sm* tea.

teatro [te'atro] *sm* theatre. **teátrico** *adj* theatrical. **teatrero**. **-a** *sm*, *sf* theatregoer.

tecla ['tekla] *sf* key. **teclado** *sm* keyboard. **teclear** *v* strum; try.

técnica ['teknika] *sf* technique. **técnico**, **-a** *sm*, *sf* technician. **tecnología** *sf* technology. **tecnólogo**, **-a** *sm*, *sf* technologist.

techado [te'tʃaðo] *sm* roof; ceiling. **bajo techado** under cover. **techar** *v* put a roof on. **techo** *sm* roof; ceiling.

tedio ['teðjo] *sm* tedium. **tedioso** *adj* tedious.

teja ['texa] *sf* tile. **tejado** *sm* tiled roof. **tejar** *v* tile. **tejaroz** *sm* eaves *pl*.

tejer [te'xer] *v* knit; weave. **tejedor**, **-a** *sm*, *sf* weaver. **tejedura** *sf* texture; weaving.

tejón [te'xon] *sm* (*zool*) badger.

tela ['tela] *sf* cloth; material. **tela de araña** spider's web. **telar** *sm* loom.

telaraña [tela'raɲa] *sf* cobweb.

telefonear [telefone'ar] *v* telephone. **teléfono** *sm* telephone.

telegrafiar [telegra'fjar] *v* telegraph. **telegrafía** *sf* telegraphy. **telégrafo** *sm* telegraph.

telegrama [tele'grama] *sm* telegram.

telemando [tele'mando] *sm* remote control.

telepatía [telepa'tia] *sf* telepathy. **telepático** *adj* telepathic.

telescopio [tele'skopjo] *sm* telescope. **telescópico** *adj* telescopic.

telestudio [tele'stuðjo] *sm* television studio.

televisión [teleβi'sjon] *sf* television. **televisar** *v* televise. **televisor** *sm* television set.

telina [te'lina] *sf* clam.

telón [te'lon] *sm* curtain. **telón de acero** Iron Curtain.

tema ['tema] *sm* theme. **temático** *adj* thematic.

*temblar [tem'blar] *v* tremble, shiver, shake. **temblor** *sm* shudder. **temblor de tierra** earthquake. **tembloroso** *adj* trembling, shuddering.

temer [te'mer] *v* fear, be afraid. **temeridad**

sf temerity. **temeroso** *adj* fearful. **temor** *sm* fear.

temperamento [tempera'mento] *sm* temperament, nature. **temperancia** *sf* temperance. **temperar** *v* temper.

temperatura [tempera'tura] *sf* temperature.

tempestad [tempes'taδ] *sf* storm. **tempestuoso** *adj* stormy.

templar [tem'plar] *v* temper; moderate. **templado** *adj* temperate.

temple ['temple] *sm* temperature; mood; distemper. **pintura al temple** *sf* painting in distemper.

templo ['templo] *sm* temple.

temporada [tempo'raδa] *sf* space of time, season, period.

temporal [tempo'ral] *adj also* **temporáneo** temporary; temporal, worldly, secular. *sm* bad weather.

temprano [tem'prano] *adj, adv* early.

tenaz [te'naθ] *adj* tenacious. **tenacidad** *sf* tenacity. **tenazas** *sf pl* pincers pl.

tendedero [tende'δero] *sm* clothes line; place for drying clothes.

tendencia [ten'denθja] *sf* tendency.

*tender [ten'der] *v* spread out; extend; hang up; lay; set.

tendero [ten'dero], **-a** *sm*, *sf* shopkeeper.

tendón [ten'don] *sm* (*anat*) tendon.

tenebroso [tene'βroso] *adj* dark, gloomy. **tenebrosidad** *sf* gloom.

tenedor [tene'δor] *sm* fork; holder. **tenedor de libros** bookkeeper. **teneduría** *sf* bookkeeping.

tenencia [te'nenθja] *sf* tenancy, occupancy; tenure.

*tener [te'ner] *v* have; possess; hold; spend. **tener en mucho** esteem. **tener para sí** think. **tener puesto** wear.

tenería [tene'ria] *sf* tannery.

tenia ['tenja] *sf* tapeworm.

teniente [te'njente] *sm* lieutenant. **teniente coronel** *sm* lieutenant-colonel.

tenis ['tenis] *sm* tennis.

tenor¹ ['tenor] *sm* tenor.

tenor² *sm* meaning, purport.

tenso ['tenso] *adj* tense, taut. **tensión** *sf* tension. **tensión arterial** blood pressure.

*tentar [ten'tar] *v* tempt; feel; attempt; examine. **tentación** *sf* temptation. **tentador** *sm* tempter. **tentadora** *sf* temptress. **tentativa** *sf* attempt. **tentativo** *adj* tentative.

tentáculo [ten'takulo] *sm* tentacle.

tentempié [tentempi'e] *sm* (*fam*) snack.

tenue ['tenwe] *adj* tenuous; faint; subdued. **tenuidad** *sf* slightness.

*teñir [te'ɲir] *v* dye, stain, colour. **teñidura** *sf* dyeing.

teología [teolo'xia] *sf* theology. **teólogo** *sm* theologian.

teorema [teo'rema] *sf* theorem.

teoría [teo'ria] *sf* theory. **teórico** *adj* theoretical. **teorizar** *v* theorize.

teosofía [teoso'fia] *sf* theosophy.

tercero [ter'θero] *adj*, *sm* third.

terapéutico [tera'peutiko] *adj* therapeutic. **terapéutica** *sf* therapeutics.

terciar [ter'θjar] *v* tilt sideways; divide into three; mediate. **tercio** *adj* third. **terciopelo** [terθjo'pelo] *sm* velvet. **terciopelado** *adj* velvety.

terco ['terko] *adj* stubborn.

tergiversar [terxiβer'sar] *v* misrepresent; distort. **tergiversación** *sf* distortion.

terminar [termi'nar] *v* finish, end; complete. **terminación** *sf* end. **terminal** *adj* terminal. **terminante** *adj* decisive. **terminología** *sf* terminology.

término ['termino] *sm* end. **dar término a** bring to an end. **término medio** average. **termita** [ter'mita] *sf* also **termite** *sm* termite.

termo ['termo] *sm* vacuum flask.

termodinámica [termoδi'namika] *sf* thermodynamics.

termómetro [ter'mometro] *sm* thermometer.

termonuclear [termonukle'ar] *adj* thermonuclear.

termostato [termo'stato] *sm* thermostat.

ternero [ter'nero] *sm* calf; veal.

terneza [ter'neθa] *sf* tenderness; endearment.

ternilla [ter'niʎa] *sf* gristle.

terquedad [terke'ðað] *sf* stubbornness, obstinacy.

terraplén [terra'plen] *sm* terrace; embankment.

terraza [ter'raβa] *sf* terrace.

terremoto [terre'moto] *sm* earthquake.

terreno [ter'reno] *sm* terrain; land. **ceder terreno** give ground.

terrestre [ter'restre] *adj* terrestrial.

terrible [ter'riβle] *adj* terrible. **terrífico** *adj* terrifying.

territorial [territo'rjal] *adj* territorial. **territorio** *sm* territory.

terrón [ter'ron] *sm* lump of sugar; clod of earth.

terror [ter'ror] *sm* terror. **terrorismo** *sm* terrorism. **terrorista** *s(m+f)* terrorist.

terso ['terso] *adj* smooth; glossy; polished. **tersar** *v* smooth. **tersura** *sf* smoothness.

tertulia [ter'tulja] *sf* social gathering; company.

tesis ['tesis] *sf invar* thesis.

tesón [te'son] *sm* tenacity; persistence; inflexibility. **tesonería** *sf* doggedness.

tesoro [te'soro] *sm* treasure. **tesorería** *sf* treasury. **tesorero, -a** *sm*, *sf* treasurer.

testa ['testa] *sf* head.

testar [tes'tar] *v* make a will. **testamento** *sm* will, testament.

testarudo [testa'ruðo] *adj* stubborn, obstinate. **testarudez** *sf* obstinacy.

testificar [testifi'kar] *v* testify; witness. **testigo** *sm* witness. **testimonial** *adj* bearing witness. **testimoniar** *v* bear witness to. **testimonio** *sm* witness; testimony.

testículo [tes'tikulo] *sm* testicle.

teta ['teta] *sf* teat, nipple; mammary gland; udder.

tetera [te'tera] *sf* teapot.

tétrico ['tetriko] *adj* gloomy; grave; sullen.

textil [teks'til] *sm*, *adj* textile.

texto ['teksto] *sm* text; textbook.

textura [teks'tura] *sf* texture.

tez [teθ] *sf* complexion, skin.

ti [ti] *pron* (*fam*) you. **de ti para mi** between you and me.

tía ['tia] *sf* aunt; old mother; (*fam*) tart. **no hay tu tía** nothing doing.

tibio ['tiβjo] *adj* lukewarm. **tibieza** *sf* tepidity.

tiburón [tiβu'ron] *sm* shark.

tiempo ['tjempo] *sm* time; weather; (*gram*) tense. **al poco tiempo** soon after. **tiempo atrás** some time ago. **tiempo de perros** filthy weather.

tienda ['tjenda] *sf* shop, store; tent. **tienda de modas** boutique.

tienta ['tjenta] *sf* probe. **andar a tientas** feel one's way.

tiento ['tjento] *sm* feel, tough; tact. **a tiento** by touch.

tierno ['tjerno] *adj* tender; fresh. **pan tierno** fresh bread.

tierra ['tjerra] *sf* earth; land; country; ground. **echar por tierra** wreck. **tierra vegetal** topsoil.

tieso ['tjeso] *adj* stiff; firm. **adv** strongly. **tiesura** *sf* stiffness.

tiesto ['tjesto] *sm* flower pot.

tifo ['tifo] *sm* typhus.

tifoideo [tifoi'ðeo] *adj* typhoid. **fiebre tifoidea** *sf* typhoid fever.

tifón [ti'fon] *sm* typhoon.

tigre ['tiɣre] *sm* tiger.

tijeras [ti'xeras] *sf pl* scissors; shears.

tilín [ti'lin] *sm* ting-a-ling. **en un tilín** in a flash.

tilo ['tilo] *sm* lime, linden tree.

timar [ti'mar] *v* cheat. **timador** *sm* swindler.

timbrar [tim'brar] *v* stamp; seal. **timbre** *sm* bell; postage stamp.

tímido ['timiðo] *adj* timid. **timidez** *sf* timidity.

timo ['timo] *sm* cheat; swindle.

timón [ti'mon] *sm* helm; rudder. **timonear** *v* (*mar*) steer. **timonero** *sm* helmsman.

tímpano ['timpano] *sm* (*anat*) eardrum; (*música*) kettledrum.

tina ['tina] *sf* tub. **tinaja** *sf* large earthen jar.

tinglado [tiŋ'glaðo] *sm* shed; platform.

tinieblas [ti'njeβlas] *sf pl* darkness *sing*; (*fig*) confusion *sing*.

tino ['tino] *sm* tact; moderation; skill. **sin tino** stupidly.

tinta ['tinta] *sf* ink; hue, colour. **tinte** *sm* dye; stain; shade. **tintero** *sm* inkstand, inkwell. **tintorería** *sf* dyeing; dry-cleaning. **tintorero**, -a *sm, sf* dyer; dry-cleaner. **tintura** dye; rouge.

tintín [tin'tin] *sm* tinkle. **tintinear** *v* tinkle.

tinto ['tinto] *adj* dyed. **vino tinto** *sm* red wine.

tiña ['tiɲa] *sf* ringworm.

tío ['tio] *sm* uncle.

tiovivo [tjo'βiβo] *sm* merry-go-round.

típico ['tipiko] *adj* typical; characteristic.

tiple ['tiple] *sm* (*música*) treble. *sf* soprano.

tipo ['tipo] *sm* type, pattern; model; standard; (*fam*) fellow. **tipo de cambio** rate of exchange.

tipografía [tipoɣra'fia] *sf* printing. **tipógrafo** *sm* printer.

tira ['tira] *sf* long strip, band.

tirada [ti'raða] *sf* throw; stretch; circulation. **tirador** *sm* marksman; handle.

tirado [ti'raðo] *adj* streamlined; (*fam*) dead easy; (*fam*) dirt cheap.

tiranía [tira'nia] *sf* tyranny. **tirano**, -a *sm, sf* tyrant. **tiranizar** *v* tyrannize.

tirante [ti'rante] *adj* taut. **tirantez** *sf* tautness.

tirar [ti'rar] *v* throw, fling; pull. **tirar por una calle** turn down a street.

tiritar [tiri'tar] *v* shiver. **tiritón** *sm* shiver.

tiro ['tiro] *sm* throw; shot; discharge; report; blow; practical joke. **tiro al blanco** target practice.

tiroides [ti'roiðes] *sm* thyroid.

tirón [ti'ron] *sm* haul, jerk; cramp; tyro, beginner. **de un tirón** straight off.

tiroteo [tiro'teo] *sm* firing, crossfire. **tirotear** *v* snipe at.

tisis ['tisis] *sf* tuberculosis.

títere ['titere] *sm* puppet; marionette.

titubear [tituβe'ar] *v* vacillate; totter, stagger; stammer. **titubeo** *sm* staggering; hesitation.

título ['titulo] *sm* title; license, diploma; degree. **titular** *adj* titular.

tiza ['tiθa] *sf* chalk.

tiznar [tiθ'nar] *v* stain, tarnish. **tiznado** *adj* stained, grimy. **tiznajo** *sm* smudge.

toalla [to'aʎa] *sf* towel. **toalla de baño** bathtowel. **toallero** *sm* towel-rail.

tobillo [to'βiʎo] *sm* ankle.

tobogán [toβa'gan] *sm* slide; chute.

tocadiscos [toka'ðiskos] *sm invar* record-player.

tocado [to'kaðo] *sm* coiffure.

tocador [toka'ðor] *sm* dressing-table.

tocar [to'kar] *v* touch; feel; (*música*) play; belong; concern; border on; be one's turn. **tocarse** *v* put on one's hat.

tocino [to'θino] *sm* bacon; salt pork.

todavía [toða'βia] *adv* yet, still; nevertheless. **todavía más** even more.

todo ['toðo] *adj* all; entire; every; each. **todo el mundo** everybody. **todo o nada** all or nothing.

toldo ['toldo] *sm* awning.

tolerar [tole'rar] *v* tolerate; bear. **tolerable** *adj* tolerable. **tolerancia** *sf* tolerance. **tolerante** *adj* tolerant.

tomar [to'mar] *v* take; hold; get; gather. **tomarse** *v* get rusty. **tomada** *sf* capture. **tomadura** *sf* taking.

tomate [to'mate] *sm* tomato. **tomatera** *sf* tomato plant.

tomillo [to'miʎo] *sm* thyme.

tomo ['tomo] *sm* tome, volume; bulk.

ton [ton] *sm* motive; occasion. **sin ton ni son** without rhyme or reason.

tonada [to'naða] *sf* song. **tonalidad** *sf* tonality.

tonel [to'nel] *sm* cask, barrel.

tonelada [tone'laða] *sf* ton. **tonelaje** *sm* tonnage.

tónico ['toniko] *sm, adj* (*música*) tonic. **tonificar** *v* (*med*) tone up.

tono ['tono] *sm* (*música*) pitch; tone; manner. **darse tono** put on airs.

tontería [tonte'ria] *sf* foolishness, nonsense. **tonto** *adj* foolish, silly; stupid; ignorant.

topacio [to'paθjo] *sm* topaz.

topar [to'par] *v* collide with; strike against; encounter; meet by chance.

tope ['tope] *sm* top, summit; end. **al tope** end to end.

tópico ['topiko] *sm* topic. *adj* topical.

topo ['topo] *sm* mole. **topera** *sf* molehill.

topografía [topoɣra'fia] *sf* topography. **topográfico** *adj* topographical.

toque ['toke] *sm* touch; peal of bells; test, trial.

tórax ['toraks] *sm* thorax.

torbellino [torβe'ʎino] *sm* whirlwind; whirlpool.

***torcer** [tor'θer] *v* twist; turn; wrench; bend. **torcedura** *sf* twisting; sprain. **torcido** *adj* twisted; bent. **torcimiento** *sm* distortion.

tordo [tor'ðo] *sm* thrush.

torear [tore'ar] *v* fight the bull. **torero** *sm* bullfighter.

tormenta [tor'menta] *sf* storm. **tormentoso** *adj* stormy.

tormentar [tormen'tar] *v* torment. **tormento** *sm* torment; affliction; pain.

tornar [tor'nar] *v* turn; return; do again. **torna** *sf* return. **tornarse** *v* become.

tornasol [torna'sol] *sm* (*bot*) sunflower; litmus.

torneo [tor'neo] *sm* tournament.

tornillo [tor'niʎo] *sm* screw.

torniquete [torni'kete] *sm* tourniquet; turnstile.

toro ['toro] *sm* bull. **toros** *sm pl* bullfight.

toronja [to'ronxa] *sf* grapefruit.

torpe ['torpe] *adj* clumsy; indecent. **torpeza** *sf* clumsiness; indecency.

torpedo [tor'peðo] *sm* torpedo. **torpedero** *sm* torpedo-boat.

tórpido [tor'piðo] *adj* torpid. **torpor** *sm* torpor.

torre ['torre] *sf* tower.

torrente [tor'rente] *sm* torrent. **torrencial** *adj* torrential.

tórrido ['torriðo] *adj* torrid.

torta ['torta] *sf* cake; pie. **tortada** *sf* meat pie. **tortera** *sf* pie dish.

tortilla [tor'tiʎa] *sf* omelette.

tortuga [tor'tuɣa] *sf* tortoise; turtle.

tortura [tor'tura] *sf* torture. **tortuoso** *adj* tortuous.

tos [tos] *sf* cough. **tos ferina** whooping-cough. **toser** *v* cough.

tosco ['tosko] *adj* coarse; crude; clumsy. **tosquedad** *sf* roughness; crudeness.

***tostar** [tos'tar] *v* toast; roast; tan. **tostada** *sf* piece of toast.

total [to'tal] *sm* total. **totalidad** *sf* totality. **totalitario** *adj* totalitarian. **totalizar** *v* total.

tóxico ['toksiko] *sm* poison. *adj* poisonous. **toxicar** *v* poison.

toxicómano [toksi'komano], **-a** *sm, sf* drug-addict. **toxicomanía** *sf* drug-addiction.

tozudo [to'θuðo] *adj* stubborn.

traba ['traβa] *sf* link; fetter; hindrance. **poner trabas** hinder. **trabadura** *sf* bond. **trabamiento** *sm* joining. **trabar** *v* join; fetter; strike up. **trabar amistad** become friends. **trabón** *sm* fetter.

trabajar [traβa'xar] *v* work; work on; elaborate; trouble; deal in. **trabajado** *adj* elaborate. **trabajador, -a** *sm, sf* worker. **trabajo** *sm* work; toil; exertion; hardship. **trabajoso** *adj* laborious.

trabalenguas [traβa'lengwas] *sm invar* tongue-twister.

tracción [trak'θjon] *sf* traction. **tractor** *sm* tractor.

tradición [traði'θjon] *sf* tradition. **tradicional** *adj* traditional.

***traducir** [traðu'θir] *v* translate; interpret. **traducción** *sf* translation. **traductor, -a** *sm, sf* translator.

***traer** [tra'er] *v* bring; carry; fetch; result in; wear. **traer a mal traer** treat roughly. **traer a cuento** mention. **traerse** *v* be dressed; behave.

traficar [trafi'kar] *v* trade; travel. **traficante** *s*(*m+f*) dealer. **tráfico** *sm* trade; traffic.

tragaluz [traɣa'luθ] *sf* skylight.

tragar [tra'gar] *v* swallow. **no puedo tragarle** I can't stand him. **tragadero** *sm* gullet. **trago** *sm* swallow; gulp.

tragedia [tra'xeðia] *sf* tragedy. **tragico** *adj* tragic.

traicionar [traiθjo'nar] *v* betray. **traición** *sf* treason; treachery. **traicionero** *adj* treacherous. **traidor, -a** *sm, sf* traitor.

traje ['traxe] *sm* dress; suit; costume. **traje de etiqueta** evening dress. **baile de trajes** fancy-dress ball.

trajín [tra'xin] *sm* haulage; coming and going. **trajinante** *sm (com)* carrier.

tramar [tra'mar] *v* weave; plan, plot. **trama** *sf* weft; plot.

tramitar [trami'tar] *v* negotiate, arrange. **tramitación** *sf* arrangements *pl.* **trámite** *sm* procedure; formality.

tramo ['tramo] *sm (puente)* span; *(escaleras)* flight; *(terreno)* stretch.

trampa ['trampa] *sf* trap; trapdoor; fraud. **tramposo** *adj* deceitful.

trampear [trampe'ar] *v* defraud; scrape by. **trampeador, -a** *sm, sf* swindler.

trampolín [trampo'lin] *sm* ski jump; springboard.

trancar [tran'kar] *v (puerta)* bar; stride. **tranca** *sf* stick; club; *(fam)* drunkenness. **tranco** *sm* stride.

trance ['tranθe] *sm* trance; critical situation. **a todo trance** at all costs.

tranquilizar [trankili'θar] *v* tranquillize. **tranquilidad** *sf* tranquillity. **tranquilo** *adj* tranquil.

transacción [transak'θjon] *sf* transaction.

transatlántico [transat'lantiko] *adj* transatlantic. *sm (mar)* liner.

transbordar [transβor'ðar] *v* transfer. **transbordo** *sm* transfer.

transcribir [transkri'βir] *v* transcribe. **transcripción** *sf* transcription.

transcurrir [transkur'rir] *v* elapse, pass. **transcurso** *sm* course or lapse of time.

transeúnte [transe'unte] *adj* transitory, transient. *s(m+f)* transient, passer-by.

*****transferir** [transfe'rir] *v* transfer. **transferible** *adj* transferable.

transfigurar [transfigu'rar] *v* transfigure. **transfiguración** *sf* transfiguration.

transformar [transfor'mar] *v* transform. **transformación** *sf* transformation.

tránsfuga ['transfuga] *sm* deserter.

*****transgredir** [transgre'ðir] *v* transgress, violate. **transgresión** *sf* transgression. **transgresor, -a** *sm, sf* transgressor.

transición [transi'θjon] *sf* transition.

transido [tran'siðo] *adj* overwhelmed; stricken.

transigir [transi'xir] *v* compromise. **transigencia** *sf* tolerance. **transigente** *adj* tolerant.

transistor [transis'tor] *sm* transistor.

transitar [transi'tar] *v* travel; pass. **transitivo** *adj (gram)* transitive. **tránsito** *sm* transit; passage; transition. **transitorio** *adj* transitory.

transmitir [transmi'tir] *v* transmit. **transmisión** *sf* transmission. **transmisor** *sm* transmitter.

transparencia [transpa'renθja] *sf* transparency. **transparente** *adj* transparent.

transpirar [transpi'rar] *v* perspire; transpire. **transpiración** *sf* perspiration.

*****transponer** [transpo'ner] *v* transpose; transplant. **transponerse** *v* get down; get sleepy.

transportar [transpor'tar] *v* transport; *(música)* transpose. **transportarse** get carried away. **transporte** *sm* transport. **transposición** *sf* transposition.

tranvía [tran'βia] *sm* tramway; tram.

trapaza [tra'paθa] *sf* swindle, fraud; trick. **trapacear** *v* defraud. **trapacista** *s(m+f)* swindler.

trapecio [tra'peθjo] *sm* trapeze.

trapo ['trapo] *sm* rag. *pl* old clothes.

traquetear [trakete'ar] *v* shake up; rattle. **traqueteo** *sm* rattling; jolting.

tras [tras] *prep* after; behind; beyond. **tras de** in addition to.

*****trascender** [trasθen'der] *v* transcend; leak out; spread. **trascendencia** *sf* transcendence. **trascendental** *adj* momentous. **trascendente** *adj* transcendent.

*****trasegar** [trase'gar] *v* decant; upset.

trasero [tra'sero] *adj* rear. *sm* behind. **trasera** *sf* back; rear.

trasladar [trasla'ðar] *v* transfer; translate; postpone. **trasladarse** *v* go; move. **traslación** *sf* transfer; translation. **traslado** *sm* copy; transfer.

*****traslucirse** [traslu'θirse] *v* shine; show through. **traslúcido** *adj* translucent.

traslumbrar [traslum'brar] *v* dazzle.

trasmutar [trasmu'tar] *v* transmute. **trasmutación** *sf* transmutation.

trasnochar [trasno'tʃar] *v* be up all or most of the night.

traspasar [traspa'sar] *v* transfer; transfix; transgress. **traspasador, -a** *sm, sf* transgressor. **traspaso** *sm* transfer; transgression.

traspié [tras'pje] *sm* stumble.

trasplantar [trasplan'tar] *v* transplant. **trasplantarse** *v* migrate. **trasplante** *sm* transplant.

trasquilar [traski'lar] *v* shear, snip, clip. **trasquilado** *adj* sheared; cropped.

traste ['traste] *sm* (*música*) fret. **ir al traste** fall through, fail.

trasto ['trasto] *sm* tool; weapon; equipment; piece of furniture.

trastornar [trastor'nar] *v* upset; turn upside down. **trastornado** *adj* unbalanced. **trastorno** *sm* upheaval; inconvenience.

trasunto [tra'sunto] *sm* copy, reproduction; likeness. **trasuntar** *v* copy.

tratar [tra'tar] *v* treat; deal with; handle. **tratable** *adj* manageable. **tratamiento** *sm* treatment. **trato** *sm* treatment; behaviour; bargain. **mal trato** ill-treatment.

través [tra'βes] *sm* slant; bias; reverse. **a través de** across.

travesero [traβe'sero] *adj* transverse. **travesía** *sf* crossroad.

travesura [traβe'sura] *sf* trick, prank.

traviesa [tra'βjesa] *sf* (*ferrocarril*) sleeper; (*arq*) rafter; bet.

travieso [tra'βjeso] *adj* transverse, cross; lively; mischievous. **a campo traviesa** cross-country.

trayecto [tra'jekto] *sm* route; fare stage; distance; way; itinerary. **trayectoria** *sf* trajectory.

trazar [tra'θar] *v* draw; plot; trace; design. **traza** *sf* sketch. **bien/mal trazado** good/bad looking. **trazador, -a** *sm*, *sf* designer.

trébol [tre'βol] *sm* clover.

trece ['treθe] *adj*, *sm* thirteen.

trecho ['tretʃo] *sm* space; distance; lapse; stretch.

tregua ['treγwa] *sf* truce; respite.

treinta ['treinta] *adj*, *sm* thirty.

tremendo [tre'mendo] *adj* tremendous.

trémulo ['tremulo] *adj* tremulous.

tren [tren] *sm* train. **tren botijo** excursion train.

trenzar [tren'θar] *v* braid. **trenza** *sf* plait, braid.

trementina [tremen'tina] *sf* turpentine.

trepar [tre'par] *v* climb. **trepa** *sf* climbing. **trepadoras** *sf pl* climbing plants.

trepidar [trepi'ðar] *v* shake, tremble. **trepidación** *sf* tremor.

tres [tres] *adj*, *sm* three.

triángulo [tri'aŋgulo] *sm* triangle. **triangular** *adj* triangular.

tribu ['triβu] *sf* tribe.

tribuna [tri'βuna] *sf* tribune; gallery; grandstand. **tribunal** *sm* tribunal.

tributar [triβu'tar] *v* pay. **tributable** *adj* tributary. **tributación** *sf* tax. **tributante** *s(m+f)* taxpayer. **tributo** *sm* tribute; tax.

triciclo [tri'θiklo] *sm* tricycle.

tricotar [triko'tar] *v* knit.

trigo ['triγo] *sm* wheat. **trigal** *sm* wheatfield.

trigésimo [tri'xesimo] *adj* thirtieth.

trigonometría [triγonome'tria] *sf* trigonometry.

trillar [tri'λar] *v* thresh; beat. **trilla** *sf* threshing. **trillador, -a** *sm*, *sf* threshing machine.

trimestre [tri'mestre] *sm* three-month term. **trimestral** *adj* quarterly.

trinar [tri'nar] *v* trill. **trinado** *sm* trill.

trincar [trin'kar] *v* break; bind; hold down.

trinchar [trin'tʃar] *v* carve. **trinchante** *sm* carving-knife. **trinchero** *adj* carving.

trinchera [trin'tʃera] *sf* trench.

trineo [tri'neo] *sm* sledge, sled, sleigh.

trinidad [trini'ðað] *sf* trinity.

trinitaria [trini'tarja] *sf* pansy.

tripa ['tripa] *sf* intestine. **tener malas tripas** be cruel.

triple ['triple] *adj* triple.

trípode ['tripoðe] *sm* tripod.

tripulación [tripula'θjon] *sf* crew. **tripulante** *sm* member of the crew.

triscar [tris'kar] *v* mingle; stamp; frisk. **trisca** *sf* crunch.

triste ['triste] *adj* sad, mournful, gloomy. **tristeza** *sf* sadness.

triturar [tritu'rar] *v* grind, crush. **trituración** *sf* grinding.

triunfar [triun'far] *v* triumph. **triunfador, -a** *sm*, *sf* victor. **triunfal** *adj* triumphal. **triunfante** *adj* triumphant. **triunfo** *sm* triumph.

trivial [tri'βjal] *adj* trivial. **trivialidad** *sf* triviality.

triza [tri'θa] *sf* shred; particle, fragment.

trocar [tro'kar] *v* exchange. **trocarse** *v* change into. **trocamiento** *sm* exchange.

trochemoche [trotʃe'motʃe] *adv* higgledy-piggledy.

trofeo [tro'feo] *sm* trophy.

trole ['trole] *sm* trolley.

tromba ['tromba] *sf* waterspout.

trombón [trom'bon] *sm* trombone.

trompa ['trompa] *sf* hunting horn; (*elefante*) trunk; proboscis.

trompada [trom'paða] *sf* bump; thump.

trompeta [trom'peta] *sf* trumpet. **trompetero** *sm* trumpeter.

*****tronar** [tro'nar] *v* thunder. **tronada** *sf* thunderstorm. **tronante** *adj* thunderous. **tronido** *sm* thunderclap.

tronco ['tronko] *sm* tree trunk; stalk; stern.

tronchar [tron'tʃar] *v* bring down; break up.

trono ['trono] *sm* throne.

tropa ['tropa] *sf* troop.

tropel [tro'pel] *sm* crowd. **en tropel** in a rush. **tropelía** *sf* rush, hurry.

*****tropezar** [trope'θar] *v* stumble; run into. **tropiezo** *sm* stumble.

trópico ['tropiko] *sm* tropic. **tropical** *adj* tropical.

trotar [tro'tar] *v* trot. **trote** *sm* trot.

trozo ['troθo] *sm* piece, fragment, bit.

truco ['truko] *sm* trick.

trucha ['trutʃa] *sf* trout; (*mec*) crane.

trueno ['trueno] *sm* thunder.

trueque [tru'eke] *sm* exchange, barter.

trufa ['trufa] *sf* truffle.

truncar [trun'kar] *v* truncate, abridge. **truncado** *adj* truncated.

tu [tu] *adj* (*fam*) your.

tú [tu] *pron* (*fam*) you.

tubérculo [tu'βerkulo] *sm* tubercle; tuber. **tuberculosis** *sf* tuberculosis. **tuberculoso** *adj* tubercular.

tubo ['tuβo] *sm* tube, pipe. **tubería** *sf* tubing. **tubular** *adj* tubular.

tuerca ['twerka] *sf* (*mec*) nut. **tuerca a mariposa** wing nut.

tuerto ['twerto], **-a** *sm, sf* one-eyed person. *adj* one-eyed.

tuétano [tu'etano] *sm* (*anat*) marrow.

tufo ['tufo] *sm* vapour; fume; stench. **tufarada** *sf* whiff.

tul [tul] *sm* tulle.

tulipán [tuli'pan] *sm* tulip.

tullido [tu'ʎiðo] *adj* cripple. **tullirse** *v* be crippled.

tumba¹ ['tumba] *sf* tomb.

tumba² *sf* tumble. **tumbar** *v* knock down; tumble.

tumor [tu'mor] *sm* tumour.

tumulto [tu'multo] *sm* tumult. **tumultuoso** *adj* tumultuous.

tunante [tu'nante] *s(m+f)* rascal, crook. *adj* rascally. **tunantería** *sf* crookedness.

túnel ['tunel] *sm* tunnel.

túnica ['tunika] *sf* tunic.

tuno ['tuno] *sm* rogue.

tupé [tu'pe] *sm* toupee.

tupido [tu'piðo] *adj* thick; dense.

turba ['turβa] *sf* crowd; heap; peat. **turbal** *sm* peat bog.

turbante [tur'βante] *sm* turban.

turbar [tur'βar] *v* disturb. **turbarse** *v* be embarrassed.

turbina [tur'βina] *sf* turbine.

turbulento [turβu'lento] *adj* turbulent, disorderly. **turbulencia** *sf* turbulence.

turismo [tu'rismo] *sm* tourism. **turista** *s(m+f)* tourist.

turnar [tur'nar] *v* alternate, take turns. **turno** *sm* turn, shift. **por turno** in turn.

turón [tu'ron] *sm* polecat.

turquesa [tur'kesa] *sf* turquoise.

turrón [tur'ron] *sm* nougat.

tutear [tute'ar] *v* address as *tú*.

tutela [tu'tela] *sf* protection; tutelage. **tutelar** *adj* guardian.

tutor [tu'tor] *sm* tutor; guardian. **tutoría** *sf* guardianship.

tuyo ['tujo] *pron* (*fam*) yours; of yours.

U

u [u] *conj* or (before words beginning with *o* or *ho*).

ubicar [uβi'kar] *v* be situated; (*auto*) park. **ubicarse** *v* place oneself. **ubicuidad** *sf* ubiquity. **ubicuo** *adj* ubiquitous.

ubre ['uβre] *sf* udder.

ufanarse [ufa'narse] *v* boast. **ufano** *adj* proud, conceited. **ufanía** *sf* pride, arrogance.

ujier [u'xjer] *sm* usher.

úlcera ['ulθera] *sf* ulcer. **ulcerado** *adj* ulcerated.

ulterior [ulte'rjor] *adj* further, farther; ulterior. **ulteriormente** *adv* later.

ultimar [ulti'mar] *v* conclude, finish. **ultimación** *sf* conclusion. **últimamente**

adv finally; recently. **ultimátum** *sm* ultimatum. **último** *adj* last; latest. **por último** finally.

ultrajar [ultra'xar] *v* outrage; insult. **ultraje** *sm* outrage. **ultrajoso** *adj* outrageous.

ultramarino [ultrama'rino] *adj* overseas. **ultramar** *sm* overseas countries *pl.* **ir a ultramar** go abroad.

ultranza [ul'tranθa] *adv* **a ultranza** to the death; at all costs.

umbral [um'bral] *sm* threshold. **pisar los umbrales** cross the threshold.

umbrío [um'brio] *adj* *also* **umbroso** shady.

un [un] *art* *also* **una** a; one. *adj* one.

unánime [u'nanime] *adj* unanimous. **unanimidad** *sf* unanimity.

unción [un'θjon] *sf* anointing, unction. **extremaunción** *sf* (*rel*) extreme unction.

uncir [un'θir] *v* yoke.

undécimo [un'deθimo], **-a** *s, adj* eleventh.

undoso [un'doso] *adj* wavy. **undulación** *sf* undulation. **undulante** *adj* undulating. **undular** *v* undulate.

ungir [un'xir] *v* anoint. **ungimiento** *sm* unction. **ungüento** *sm* ointment.

único ['uniko] *adj* only, sole, single; unique. **únicamente** *adv* only, solely.

unicornio [uni'kornjo] *sm* unicorn.

unidad [uni'ðað] *sf* unity; union; unit. **unido** *adj* united. **unificación** *sf* unification. **unificar** *v* unify.

uniformar [unifor'mar] *v* make uniform; standardize. **uniforme** *adj, sm* uniform. **uniformidad** *sf* uniformity.

unión [u'njon] *sf* union; unity; marriage. **unir** *v* join; mix. **unirse** *v* join; mingle.

Unión Soviética [u'njon so'βjetika] *sf* Soviet Union.

unísono [u'nisono] *adj* harmonious. **al unísono** in unison; unanimously.

universidad [uniβersi'ðað] *sf* university. **universitario** *adj* of a university.

universo [uni'βerso] *sm* universe. **universal** *adj* universal. **universalidad** *sf* universality.

uno ['uno] *adj* one; only. *pron* one; someone. **unos** *pron pl* some; a few. **unos y otros** all.

untar [un'tar] *v* grease; smear; stain; spread. **unto** *sm* grease; ointment.

uña ['uɲa] *sf* (*anat*) nail; talon, claw; hoof. **esconder las uñas** hide one's feelings. **uñero** *sm* ingrowing toenail.

uranio [u'ranjo] *sm* uranium.

urbano [ur'βano] *adj* urban; urbane. **urbanidad** *sf* urbanity. **urbanístico** *adj* urban. **urbanización** *sf* town planning. **urbe** *sf* large city.

urdir [ur'ðir] *v* warp; (*fig*) plot, scheme.

urgencia [ur'xenθja] *sf* urgency; emergency. **urgente** *adj* urgent. **urgir** *v* be urgent; urge. **me urge el tiempo** I am pressed for time.

urinario [uri'narjo] *sm* urinal.

urna ['urna] *sf* urn; ballot box.

urogallo [uro'gaʎo] *sm* (*zool*) grouse.

urraca [ur'raka] *sf* magpie.

usar [u'sar] *v* use; employ; be accustomed. **usado** *adj* used; worn. **usanza** *sf* custom; usage. **uso** *sm* use; wear; custom; enjoyment; fashion. **al uso de** in the style of.

usted [u'steð] *pron* *also* **Vd** you. **¡a usted!** thank you!

usual [u'swal] *adj* usual.

usufructo [u'sufrukto] *sm* use; enjoyment.

usura [u'sura] *sf* usury. **usurero, -a** *sm, sf* usurer.

usurpar [usur'par] *v* usurp. **usurpación** *sf* usurpation. **usurpador, -a** *sm, sf* usurper.

utensilio [uten'siljo] *sm* utensil; implement, tool.

útero ['utero] *sm* uterus. **uterino** *adj* uterine.

útil [u'til] *sm* tool. *adj* useful; fit. **utilidad** *sf* utility, usefulness. **utilitario** *adj* utilitarian. **utilizar** *v* utilize, use.

uva ['uβa] *sf* grape. **uva pasa** raisin.

V

vaca ['baka] *sf* cow; beef.

vacaciones [baka'θjones] *sf pl* vacation *sing;* holidays *pl.* **irse de vacaciones** go on holiday.

vacante [βa'kante] *adj* vacant. *sf* vacancy. **vacar** *v* fall vacant.

vacilar [baθi'lar] *v* hesitate. **vacilante** *adj* unstable, unsteady. **vacilación** *sf* vacillation.

vacío [βa'θio] *adj* empty. *sm* void; vacuum. **vaciar** *v* empty; pour out. **vacuo** *adj* empty; vacuous.

vacunar [βaku'nar] v vaccinate. **vacunación** sf vaccination.

vadear [βaðe'ar] v wade; surmount, overcome. **vadeable** adj fordable.

vagar [βa'gar] v wander, move about. sm leisure; ease. **vagabundo, -a** sm, sf vagabond. **vagante** adj vagrant.

vago ['βago] adj vague, indolent. sm tramp; loafer. **vaguedad** sf vagueness.

vagón [βa'gon] sm railway carriage; wagon. **vagón restaurante** dining-car. **vagoneta** sf small truck.

vahear [βae'ar] v steam. **vaho** sm vapour.

vahído [βa'iðo] sm vertigo, dizziness.

vaina ['βaina] sf sheath; scabbard; pod.

vainilla [βai'niʎa] sf vanilla.

vaivén [βai'βen] sm fluctuation; sway; swinging movement.

vajilla [βa'xiʎa] sf tableware, dishes pl.

vale ['βale] sm voucher; receipt; IOU.

valedero [βale'ðero] adj valid.

valentía [βalen'tia] sf valour, courage; brave or courageous act; bragging. **valentón, -ona** sm, sf braggart.

*****valer** [βa'ler] v be worth; cost; be equal to. **vale la pena** be worthwhile. **válgame la frase** if you don't mind my saying so. **valerse** v make use of. **valía** sf value, worth.

valeroso [βale'roso] adj brave; valuable.

validar [βali'ðar] v validate; make binding. **validación** sf validation; ratification. **válido** adj valid. **validez** sf validity.

valiente [βa'ljente] adj valiant, courageous; strong; first-rate.

valija [βa'lixa] sf valise; case; mail bag.

valimiento [βali'mjento] sm value; good will; protection; favour.

valor [βa'lor] sm value, worth; price; valour, courage. adj valuable. **valoración** sf valuation. **valorar** v value, appraise.

valsar [βal'sar] v waltz. **vals** sm waltz.

valuar [βalu'ar] v value, appraise, assess. **valuación** sf valuation.

válvula ['βalβula] sf valve.

vallar [βa'ʎar] v fence in, enclose. **valla** sf fence. **vallado** sm enclosure.

valle ['βaʎe] sm valley.

vampiro [βam'piro] sm vampire.

vanagloriarse [βanaglor'jarse] v boast. **vanagloria** sf boasting, vainglory.

vándalo ['βandalo] sm, adj vandal. **vandalismo** sm vandalism.

vanguardia [βan'gwarðja] sf vanguard; avant-garde.

vano ['βano] adj vain; idle. **en vano** in vain. **vanidad** sf vanity. **vanidoso** adj vain.

vapor [βa'por] sm vapour; steam; (mar) steamer. **vaporización** sf evaporation. **vaporizar** v evaporate.

vaquero [βa'kero] sm cowboy. **vaquería** sf herd of cows.

vaqueta [βa'keta] sf cowhide.

vara ['βara] sf rod, pole, staff; (medida) yard. **tener vara alta** have the upper hand.

varar [βa'rar] v launch; run aground.

variar [βa'rjar] v vary, change. **variable** adj variable. **variación** sf variation. **variado** adj varied. **variante** sf variant; version.

varice [βa'riθe], sf also **várice** varicose vein.

varilla [βa'riʎa] sf small stick; jawbone; curtain rail.

vario ['βarjo] adj varied, diverse. **varios** adj several.

varón [βa'ron] sm, adj male. **varonil** adj manly, virile.

vaselina ® [βase'lina] sf Vaseline ®.

vasija [βa'sixa] sf vessel; bowl; dish. **vaso** sm glass, tumbler.

vástago ['βastago] sm stem, shoot, sprout; scion, offspring.

vasto [βasto] adj vast. **vastedad** sf vastness.

vaticinar [βatiθi'nar] v predict, foretell. **vaticinador, -a** sm, sf prophet, seer. **vaticinio** sm divination, prophecy.

vatio [βatjo] sm (elec) watt.

vecino [βe'θino] sm, a, sf neighbour. **vecinal** adj local. **vecindad** sf neighbourhood.

vedar [βe'ðar] v veto; prohibit; hinder. **veda** sf prohibition. **vedado** sm game preserve.

vega ['βega] sf plain; tract of fertile ground.

vegetación [βexeta'θjon] sf vegetation. **vegetal** adj vegetable. **vegetar** v grow; (fig) vegetate. **vegetariano, -a** sm, sf vegetarian.

vehemencia [βee'menθja] sf vehemence. **vehemente** adj vehement.

vehículo [βe'ikulo] sm vehicle.

veinte ['βeinte] sm, adj twenty.

vejar [βe'xar] v vex, harass, annoy. **vejación** sf vexation. **vejatorio** adj vexatious.

vejez [βe'xeθ] sf old age.

vejiga [βe'xiɣa] sf blister; bladder.

vela ['βela] sf vigil, watch; candle; sail. **velar** v keep watch; stay awake.

veleidad [βelei'ðað] sf whim; fickleness. **veleidoso** adj fickle.

velero [βe'lero] sm sailing ship; glider.

velo ['βelo] sm veil.

velocidad [βeloθi'ðað] sf velocity. **velocímetro** sm speedometer. **veloz** adj fast, quick.

vello ['βeʎo] sm soft hair, down; fluff. **velloso** adj dowry.

vena ['βena] sf vein; scan. **trabajar por venas** work in fits and starts.

venablo [βe'naβlo] sm javelin.

venado [βe'naðo] sm deer; (culin) venison.

venal [βe'nal] adj venal.

vencer [βen'θer] v defeat; win; (com) fall due. **vencerse** v control oneself. **vencible** adj beatable. **los vencidos** the losers. **vencimiento** sm victory; (com) expiration, falling due.

vendar [βen'dar] v bandage. **venda** sf also **vendaje** sm bandage.

vendaval [βenda'βal] sm gale.

vender [βen'der] v sell. **vendedor** sm seller, vendor; salesperson. **vendible** adj saleable.

vendimia [βen'ðimja] sf grape harvest; vintage.

veneno [βe'neno] sm venom, poison. **venenoso** adj poisonous.

venerar [βene'rar] v venerate. **venerable** adj venerable. **veneración** sf veneration. **venéreo** [βe'nereo] adj venereal.

venero [βe'nero] sm spring of water; source, origin, root.

vengar [βen'gar] v avenge. **vengador, -a** sm, sf avenger. **venganza** sf vengeance. **vengativo** adj vindictive.

venia ['βenja] sf forgiveness, pardon; permission, leave.

*****venir** [βe'nir] v come. **venir bien** be suitable or convenient. **venirse** v come or go back. **venida** sf arrival, coming; return. **venidero** adj coming, future.

venta ['βenta] sf sale, market; inn. **venta a plazos** hire purchase. **ventero, -a** sm, sf innkeeper.

ventaja [βen'taxa] sf advantage. **ventajoso** adj advantageous.

ventana [βen'tana] sf window.

ventilar [βenti'lar] v ventilate. **ventilación** sf ventilation. **ventilador** sm ventilator; fan.

ventosa [βen'tosa] sf vent.

ventoso [βen'toso] sf vent.

ventoso [βen'toso] adj windy. **ventosidad** sf flatulence.

ventrílocuo [βen'trilokwo] sm ventriloquist. **ventriloquia** sf ventriloquism.

ventura [βen'tura] sf joy, happiness; good luck. **mala ventura** ill luck. **venturado, venturero** or **venturoso** adj lucky; happy.

*****ver** [βer] v see. sm view; aspect; opinion; looks pl. appearance. **echar de ver** notice. **estar viendo** have a feeling. **vamos a ver** let's see.

vera ['βera] sf border, edge.

verano [βe'rano] sm summer. **veranear** v spend the summer. **veraneo** sm summer holiday.

veras ['βeras] sf pl truth sing. **de veras** indeed, really. **veracidad** sf veracity. **veraz** adj truthful.

verbo ['βerβo] sm verb. **verbosidad** sf verbosity. **verboso** adj verbose.

verdad [βer'ðað] sf truth. **verdadero** adj true; real, authentic; sincere; truthful.

verde ['βerðe] adj green; immature; fresh; young; immodest, obscene. **darse un verde** amuse oneself.

verdugo [βer'ðugo] sm executioner; hangman; scourge. **verdugón** sm weal (from whiplash).

verdulero [βerðu'lero] sm greengrocer. **verdulería** sf greengrocer's. **verdura** sf greenness. **verduras** sf pl vegetables.

veredicto [βere'ðikto] sm verdict.

vergüenza [βer'gwenθa] sf shame; affront; disgrace; shyness, timidity. **sin vergüenza** shameless. **vergonzoso** adj shy; shameful.

verídico [βe'riðiko] adj truthful.

verificar [βerifi'kar] v verify; examine, inspect; check. **verificarse** v prove true; be verified. **verificación** sf verification. **verificativo** adj corroborative.

verosímil [βero'simil] adj likely, probable. **verosimilitud** sf probability.

verruga [βer'ruga] sf wart.

versado [βer'saðo] adj versed, experienced; skilful.

versar [βer'sar] v go round; spin. **versar sobre** to treat of, deal with.

versátil [βer'satil] adj versatile; variable; inconstant. **versatilidad** sf versatility; changeableness.

versículo [βer'sikulo] sm verse. **versificar** v versify. **verso** sm verse. **verso suelto** blank verse.

versión [βer'sjon] sf version.

vértebra ['βerteβra] sf vertebra. **vertebrado** sm, adj vertebrate.

*verter [βer'ter] v spill, empty; pour; interpret, translate. **vertedero** sm drain. **vertedor** sm sewer.

vertical [βerti'kal] adj vertical.

vértice ['βertiθe] sm apex.

vértigo ['βertigo] sm vertigo. **vertiginoso** adj giddy.

vesícula [βe'sikula] sf (anat) vesicle; blister.

vestíbulo [βes'tiβulo] sm vestibule, entrance hall; lobby.

vestigio [βes'tixjo] sm vestige; footstep; trace.

*vestir [βes'tir] v dress; clothe. **vestirse** get dressed. **vestido** sm dress.

veta ['βeta] sf vein of ore, etc.; grain in wood; streak.

veterano [βete'rano] sm, adj veteran.

veterinaria [βeteri'narja] sf veterinary science. **veterinario** sm vet.

veto ['βeto] sm veto.

vez [βeθ] sf turn; time; occasion. **a la vez** at once. **a veces** sometimes. **otra vez** once more. **tal vez** perhaps.

vía ['βia] sf road; way; track. **vía aérea** air mail. **en vías de** in the process of. **Vía Láctea** Milky Way.

viable ['βjaβle] adj viable.

viaducto [βja'ðukto] sm viaduct.

viajar [βja'xar] v travel. **viajante** s(m+f) traveller. **viaje** sm trip, journey. **viajero, -a** sm, sf traveller; passenger.

víbora ['βiβora] sf viper.

vibrar [βi'βrar] v vibrate, shake. **vibración** sf vibration. **vibrador** sm vibrator. **vibrante** adj vibrating; vibrant.

vicario [βi'karjo] sm vicar.

viciar [βi'θjar] v vitiate; corrupt. **vicio** sm vice; defect. **de vicio** for no reason at all. **vicioso** adj vicious.

vicisitud [βiθisi'tuð] sf vicissitude, mishap.

víctima ['βiktima] sf victim; sacrifice.

victoria [βik'torja] sf victory. **victorioso** adj victorious.

vid [βið] sf vine.

vida ['βiða] sf life. **en mi vida** never in my life. **nivel de vida** sm standard of living.

vidriar [βi'ðrjar] v glaze. **vidriera** sf stained glass. **vidrio** sm glass. **vidrioso** adj glassy.

viejo ['βjexo] adj old. sm old man. **vieja** sf old woman.

viento ['βjento] sm wind.

vientre ['βjentre] sm abdomen, belly; womb; bowels pl.

viernes ['βjernes] sm Friday. **Viernes Santo** Good Friday.

viga ['βiga] sf beam; timber.

vigente [βi'xente] adj (jur) in force, valid. **vigencia** sf validity. **en vigencia** in effect; in force.

vigésimo [βi'xesimo] adj twentieth.

vigilar [βixi'lar] v watch over. **vigilancia** sf vigilance. **vigilante** adj vigilant. **vigilia** sf watchfulness; vigil.

vigor [βi'gor] sm vigour. **vigoroso** adj vigorous.

vil [βil] adj vile. **vileza** sf vileness.

vilo ['βilo] adv **en vilo** aloft; suspended; (fig) on tenterhooks.

villa ['βiʎa] sf villa; town.

villancico [βiʎan'θiko] sm Christmas carol.

villanía [βiʎa'nia] sf villainy; coarse expression.

vinagre [βi'nagre] sm vinegar. **vinagroso** adj vinegary.

vínculo [βinkulo] sm link; chain; tie.

vindicar [βindi'kar] v vindicate. **vindicación** sf vindication.

vino¹ ['βino] sm wine. **vino tinto** red wine. **vino de solera** vintage wine. **vinícola** adj relating to wine or wine production. **viña** sf vineyard.

viñeta [βi'ɲeta] sf vignette.

violar [βjo'lar] v violate; rape. **violación** sf violation; rape. **violador** sm rapist.

violencia [βjo'lenθja] sf violence. **violentar** v force, open by force; violate; do violence to.

violeta [βjo'leta] adj, sf violet.

violín [βjo'lin] sm violin. **violinista** s(m+f) violinist. **violón** sm double-bass.

virar [βi'rar] v veer; change direction; (mar) tack.

virgen [βir'xen] adj, sf virgin. **virginidad** sf virginity.

viril [βi'ril] adj virile. **virilidad** sf virility.

virtual [βir'twal] adj virtual; potential.

virtud [βir'tuð] sf virtue. **virtuoso** adj virtuous. **virtuosidad** sf virtuosity.

viruela [βi'rwela] *sf* smallpox.

virulencia [βiru'lenθja] *sf* virulence. **virulento** *adj* virulent.

visado [βi'saðo] *sm* visa.

visaje [βi'saxe] *sm* smirk, grimace. **visajero** *adj* grimacing.

vísceras ['βisθeras] *sf pl* viscera *pl*.

viscoso [βis'koso] *adj* viscous. **viscosidad** *sf* viscosity.

visera [βi'sera] *sf* visor.

visible [βi'siβle] *adj* visible. **visibilidad** *sf* visibility.

visión [βi'sjon] *sf* vision, eyesight; dream, fantasy; view. **visionario, -a** *sm, sf* visionary.

visitar [βisi'tar] *v* visit; inspect. **visita** *sf* visit; visitor. **hacer una visita** pay a visit.

vislumbrar [βislum'brar] *v* catch a glimpse of. **vislumbre** *sf* glimpse; glimmer.

viso ['βiso] *sm* aspect, appearance; gleam.

víspera ['βispera] *sf* eve; (*fig*) approach. **en vísperas de** on the eve of.

vista ['βista] *sf* view; eyesight; appearance, look; gaze. **a primera vista** at first sight. **con vistas de** with a view to. **¡hasta la vista!** good-bye!

visto ['βisto] *adj* seen; obvious. **visto bueno** approved of. **visto bueno** authorized. **visto que** seeing that.

vistoso [βis'toso] *adj* showy; (*fam*) loud.

visual [βi'swal] *adj* visual.

vital [βi'tal] *adj* vital. **vitalidad** *sf* vitality.

vitamina [βita'mina] *sf* vitamin.

vitela [βi'tela] *sf* vellum.

vitorear [βitore'ar] *v* shout, cheer, acclaim. **¡vítor!** bravo!

vítreo [βi'treo] *adj* vitreous. **vitrina** *sf* showcase.

vitriólico [βi'trjoliko] *adj* vitriolic. **vitriolo** *sm* vitriol.

vituperar [βitupe'rar] *v* vituperate; abuse; insult. **vituperación** *sf* blame.

viuda ['βjuða] *sf* widow. **viudo** *sm* widower. **viudez** *sf* widowhood.

vivaz [βi'βaθ] *adj* vivacious. **vivacidad** *sf* vivacity.

víveres ['βiβeres] *sm pl* provisions *pl*.

vivero [βi'βero] *sm* fishpond.

viveza [βi'βeθa] *sf* gaiety, liveliness.

vivienda [βi'βjenda] *sf* housing; dwelling, lodgings *pl*. **vividero** *adj* habitable.

vivificar [βiβifi'kar] *v* animate, bring to life.

vivir [βi'βir] *v* live. **¿quién vive?** who goes there? *sm* way of life.

vivisección [βiβisek'θjon] *sf* vivisection.

vivo ['βiβo] *adj* living, alive; vivid. **al vivo** to the life.

vizconde [βiθ'konde] *sm* viscount. **vizcondesa** *sf* viscountess.

vocablo [βo'kaβlo] *sm* word. **vocabulario** *sm* vocabulary.

vocación [βoka'θjon] *sf* vocation.

vocal [βo'kal] *adj* vocal. *sm* voter. *sf* vowel.

vocear [βoθe'ar] *v* bawl. **vocerío** *sm* bawling. **vocero** *sm* spokesman.

vociferar [βoθife'rar] *v* bawl; shout.

vocinglero [βoθin'glero] *adj* vociferous; loud-mouthed; talkative. **vocinglería** *sf* clamour, uproar.

volante [βo'lante] *adj* flying. *sm* steering-wheel; shuttlecock.

*****volar** [βo'lar] *v* fly; blow up, explode. **volarse** *v* become furious.

volátil [βo'latil] *adj* volatile.

volcán [βol'kan] *sm* volcano. **volcánico** *adj* volcanic.

*****volcar** [βol'kar] *v* upset; capsize. **volcarse** *v* fall over; bend over backwards.

volear [βole'ar] *v* volley. **voleo** *sm* volley.

volición [βoli'θjon] *sf* volition.

voltaje [βol'taxe] *sm* voltage. **voltio** *sm* volt.

voltear [βolte'ar] *v* overturn; revolve; tumble. **volteador, -a** *sm, sf* tumbler. **volteo** *sm* somersault.

voluble [βo'luβle] *adj* changeable. **volubilidad** *sf* changeable.

volumen [βolu'men] *sm* volume. **voluminoso** *adj* voluminous.

voluntad [βolun'taθ] *sf* volition; affection. **a voluntad** at will. **buena voluntad** good-will.

voluntario [βolun'tarjo] *adj* voluntary. **voluntariedad** *sf* free will.

voluptuoso [βolup'twoso] *adj* voluptuous. **voluptuosidad** *sf* voluptuousness.

*****volver** [βol'βer] *v* return; turn; turn over. **volver sobre sí** pull oneself together. **volverse** *v* become; go back. **volverse loco** go mad.

vomitar [βomi'tar] *v* vomit. **vómito** *sm* vomit.

voraz [βo'raθ] *adj* voracious. **voracidad** *sf* voracity.

vórtice ['βortiθe] *sm* vortex.

vosotros [βo'sotros] *pron pl* (*fam*) you.

votar [βo'tar] *v* vote. **votante** *s*(*m*+*f*) voter. **voto** *sm* vote; vow.

voz [βoθ] *sf* voice; shout; report. **a media voz** in a whisper. **dar voces** call out.

vuelco ['βwelko] *sm* upset; overturning.

vuelo ['βwelo] *sm* flight; flying; wing. **al vuelo** in flight. **en un vuelo** in a jiffy.

vuelta ['βwelta] *sf* turn; return; bend; reverse; recompense. **dar una vuelta** take a stroll. **estar de vuelta** be back.

vuestro ['βwestro] *pron* yours. *adj* your.

vulcanizar [βulkani'θar] *v* vulcanize.

vulgar [βul'gar] *adj* common; ordinary; vulgar. **el hombre vulgar** the common man.

vulnerar [βulne'rar] *v* wound. **vulnerabilidad** *sf* vulnerability. **vulnerable** *adj* vulnerable.

X

xilófono [ksi'lofono] *sm* xylophone.

Y

y [i] *conj* and.

ya [ja] *adv* already; now; yet; later. **ya que** since. **ya voy** I'm just coming.

yacimiento [jaθi'mjento] *sm* (*minerales*) bed. **yacente** *adj* recumbent.

yanqui [jan'ki] *adj, sm* (*fam*) Yankee.

yarda [jarða] *sf* yard.

yate ['jate] *sm* yacht.

yedra [je'ðra] *sf* ivy.

yegua [jegwa] *sf* mare.

yelmo ['jelmo] *sm* helmet.

yema ['jema] *sf* yolk; bud; button. **yema del dedo** tip of the finger.

yerba [jer'βa] *sf* grass; herb.

yermo ['jermo] *sm* waste land. *adj* barren; desert.

yerno ['jerno] *sm* son-in-law.

yerro [je'rro] *sm* error; mistake.

yeso ['jeso] *sm* gypsum; plaster; plaster cast.

yo [jo] *pron* I; myself; me; ego.

yodo [joðo] *sm* iodine.

yogur [jo'gur] *sm* yoghurt.

yugo ['jugo] *sm* yoke.

yugular [jugu'lar] *adj* jugular.

yunque ['junke] *sm* anvil.

yunta ['junta] *sf* couple, pair; (*de bueys*) yoke.

yute ['jute] *sm* jute.

****yuxtaponer** [jukstapo'ner] *v* juxtapose. **yuxtaposición** *sf* juxtaposition. **yuxtapuesto** *adj* juxtaposed.

Z

zafar [θa'far] *v* loosen; free; clear; lighten. **zafarse** *v* run away.

zafio [θa'fjo] *adj* uncouth.

zafiro [θa'firo] *sm* sapphire.

zaga [θaga] *sf* rear; back.

zaguán [θa'gwan] *sm* entrance hall.

****zaherir** [θae'rir] *v* censure; mock; reproach.

zahurda [θa'urða] *sf* pigsty.

zalamería [θalame'ria] *sf* flattery. **zalamero, -a** *sm, sf* flatterer.

zamarra [θa'marra] *sf* sheepskin jacket.

zambo [θambo] *adj* knock-kneed. *sm* half-breed; monkey.

****zambullir** [θambu'ʎir] *v* dive. **zambullida** *sf* dive.

zampar [θam'par] *v* polish off; shove in; devour. **zamparse** *v* rush.

zanahoria [θana'orja] *sf* carrot.

zancada [θan'kaða] *sf* long stride. **en dos zancadas** in a trice. **zancadilla** *sf* trip; trap. **echar la zancadilla** trip up.

zanco [θanko] *sm* stilt.

zancudo [θan'kuðo] *adj* long-legged.

zángano [θangano] *sm* (*insecto*) drone; (*fig*) loafer; fool.

zangolotear [θangolote'ar] *v* shake; fidget; rattle. **zangoloteo** *sm* shaking; rattling.

zanja [θanxa] *sf* ditch; trench. **abrir las zanjas** lay the foundations.

zapa [θapa] *sf* spade; trench. **zapapico** *sm* pickaxe. **zapar** *v* undermine.

zapatear [θapate'ar] *v* kick; ill-treat; tap-dance. **zapateado** *sm* Andalusian dance. **zapatería** *sf* shoe shop; shoe factory.

zapatero, -a *sm, sf* shoemaker. **zapatilla** *sf* slipper. **zapato** *sm* shoe.

zar [θar] *sm* tsar.

zarandear [θarande'ar] *v* sift; winnow; shake. **zaranda** *sf* sieve.

zaraza [θa'raθa] *sf* chintz.

zarcillo [θar'θiλo] *sm* hoe; barrel hoop; vine tendril; ear-ring.

zarco ['θarko] *adj* (*ojos*) light blue.

zarpa ['θarpa] *v* claw; paw. **echar la zarpa** grab hold. **zarpar** *v* weigh anchor. **zarpazo** *sm* whack.

zarza ['θarθa] *sf* bramble, blackberry bush. **zarzamora** *sf* (*fruto*) blackberry.

zarzo ['θarθo] *sm* hurdle.

zarzuela [θar'θwela] *sf* light *or* comic opera.

zeta ['θeta] *sf* letter *z*.

zigzaguear [θigθage'ar] *v* zigzag. **zigzag** *sm* zigzag.

zinc [θink] *sm* zinc.

zócalo ['θokalo] *sm* plinth; skirting board.

zodiaco [θo'ðjako] *sm* zodiac.

zona ['θona] *sf* zone; area. **zona edificada** built-up area. **zonas verdes** green belt *sing*.

zoología [θoolo'xia] *sf* zoology. **zoológico** *adj* zoological. **parque zoológico** *sm* zoological gardens *pl*, zoo. **zoólogo, -a** *sm, sf* zoologist.

zoquete [θo'kete] *sm* chunk of wood; piece of stale bread; (*fam*) blockhead.

zorro ['θorro] *sm* fox. **zorra** *sf* vixen. **zorrera** *sf* foxhole.

zozobrar [θoθo'βrar] *v* wreck; capsize; founder; (*fig*) worry. **zozobra** *sf* foundering; worry.

zueco ['θweko] *sm* clog; galosh.

zumbar [θum'bar] *v* buzz; hum; strike; whack. **zumbarse de** make fun of. **zumbido** *sm* humming; buzzing.

zumbón [θum'bon], **-a** *sm, sf* jester; tease. *adj* waggish.

zumo ['θumo] *sm* juice. **zumoso** *adj* juicy.

zurcir [θur'θir] *v* darn. **zurcido** *sm* darn; stitch. **zurcidura** *sf* darning.

zurdo ['θurðo], **-a** *sm, sf* left-handed person. *adj* left-handed.

zurrar [θur'rar] *v* thrash; (*cuero*) dress; curry. **zurra** *sf* tanning; thrashing. **zurrador** *sm* tanner.

zurrón [θur'ron] *sm* leather bag; husk.

zutano, -a *sm, sf* so-and-so. **fulano, zutano y mengano** Tom, Dick, and Harry.